The Rights of the Child:
Annotated Materials

The Rights of the Child: Annotated Materials

Alistair MacDonald QC
St Philips Chambers, Birmingham

Family Law

Published by Family Law
A publishing imprint of Jordan Publishing Limited
21 St Thomas Street
Bristol BS1 6JS

© Jordan Publishing Limited 2014

British Library Cataloguing-in-Publication Data

A catalogue record for this book is available from the British Library.

ISBN 978 1 84661 792 8

Typeset by Letterpart Limited, Caterham on the Hill, Surrey CR3 5XL

Printed in Great Britain by CPI Antony Rowe, Chippenham and Eastbourne

DEDICATION

For my nephews and niece, William, Charles and Tatiana

CONTENTS

TABLE OF CASES

References are to page numbers.

TABLE OF STATUTES

References are to page numbers.

TABLE OF STATUTORY INSTRUMENTS

References are to page numbers.

TABLE OF INTERNATIONAL MATERIAL

References are to page numbers.

CHAPTER 1

INTRODUCTION

One of the aims of writing *The Rights of the Child – Law and Practice* was to reflect the increasing recognition in the domestic jurisprudence of the significance of the United Nations Convention on the Rights of the Child ('UNCRC') and other international instruments relevant to the protection and advancement of children's rights. In *R (Axon) v Secretary of State for Health and the Family Planning Association*[1] Silber J, having reviewed the rights of children enshrined in the UNRC had felt compelled to observe in 2006 that there had been a 'change in the landscape of family matters, in which the rights of children are becoming increasingly important.' Between 2006 and 2011, when *The Rights of the Child – Law and Practice* was published, the higher and appellate courts increasingly relied on the UNRC.

In 2006, in *Re D (A Child) (Abduction: Custody Rights)*[2] the court noted that the principle, enshrined in Art 11(2) of the Brussels II Revised Regulation, that a child is given the opportunity to be heard during proceedings unless it is inappropriate having regard to his or her age or maturity is 'of universal application and consistent with our international obligations under Art 12 of the United Nations Convention on the Rights of the Child'. In 2008 in *Re B (Children) (Sexual Abuse: Standard of Proof)*[3] Baroness Hale again referred to the Convention in recognising the special protection afforded to the family in a democratic society.[4] In *R (E) v Office of the Schools Adjudicator*[5] Lord Mance made specific reference to Art 3 of the CRC, noting that 'under Art 3 of the United Nations Convention on the Rights of the Child 1989 it is the best interests of the child which the United Kingdom is obliged to treat as a primary consideration'. In 2011 in *ZH v (Tanzania) (FC) v Secretary of State for the Home Department*,[6] the Supreme Court relied on the terms of Art 3(1) of the UNCRC when considering the question of what weight should be given to the best interests of children who are affected by the decision to remove or deport one or both of their parents from the United Kingdom, Baroness Hale holding that:

> 'For our purposes the most relevant national and international obligation of the United Kingdom is contained in article 3(1) of the UNCRC: "In all actions concerning children, whether undertaken by public or private social welfare institutions, courts of law, administrative authorities or legislative bodies, the best interests of the child shall be a primary consideration." This is a binding obligation in international law, and the spirit, if not the precise language, has also been translated into our national law. Section 11 of the Children Act 2004 places a duty upon a wide range of public bodies to carry out their functions having regard to the need to safeguard and promote the welfare of children. The immigration authorities were at first excused from this duty, because the United Kingdom

---

1   [2006] EWHC 37 (Admin), [2006] 2 FLR 206, paras 76–80.
2   [2006] UKHL 51, [2007] 1 AC 619, para 58.
3   [2008] UKHL 35, [2009] AC 11, para 20.
4   See also *Re M and another (Children) (Abduction)* [2007] UKHL 55, [2008] 1 All ER 1157, para 46 per Baroness Hale and *AL (Serbia) v Secretary of State for the Home Department; R (Rudi) v Secretary of State for the Home Department* [2008] UKHL 42, [2008] 4 All ER 1127 per Baroness Hale.
5   [2009] UKSC 15, [2010] 1 All ER 319.
6   [2011] UKSC 4, [2011] 2 AC 166.

had entered a general reservation to the UNCRC concerning immigration matters. But that reservation was lifted in 2008 and, as a result, section 55 of the Borders, Citizenship and Immigration Act 2009 now provides that, in relation among other things to immigration, asylum or nationality, the Secretary of State must make arrangements for ensuring that those functions "are discharged having regard to the need to safeguard and promote the welfare of children who are in the United Kingdom" ... Further, it is clear from the recent jurisprudence that the Strasbourg Court will expect national authorities to apply article 3(1) of UNCRC and treat the best interests of a child as "a primary consideration".'

Since the decision in *ZH v (Tanzania) (FC) v Secretary of State for the Home Department*[7] in 2011, the reliance by the higher and appellate courts on the UNCRC has been maintained.

In *S v L*[8] the Supreme Court relied on the UNRC for support for the proposition that, in relation to adoption, the child's best interest should be paramount. In *Re E (Children) (Abduction: Custody Appeal)*[9] the Supreme Court referred to Art 3(1) of the UNRC when interpreting the best interests provisions of the Hague Convention on the Civil Aspects of International Child Abduction 1980 and Council Regulation (EC) 2201/2003 (Brussels II Revised), Lord Wilson noting that the UNRC Art 3(1) *requires* that in all actions concerning children, their best interests shall be a primary consideration. In *Re B (Care Proceedings: Appeal)*[10] the Supreme Court relied heavily on the provisions of the UNRC in articulating the need for adoption orders to be orders of last resort where nothing else will do, Lord Neuberger PSC stating in terms that the Adoption and Children Act 2002 must be construed and applied bearing in mind the provisions of the UNRC.[11] In addition to these decisions of the Supreme Court, the UNRC has been cited, either in argument or in judgment, in many other cases since 2011.

In addition to these domestic developments, the General Assembly of the United Nations has now adopted a *Resolution on the Optional Protocol to the Convention on the Rights of the Child on a Communications Procedure*.[12] This third Optional Protocol to the UNRC provides a mechanism whereby communications may be submitted by or on behalf of an individual or group of individuals within the jurisdiction of a State party who claim to be victims of a violation by that State party of any of the rights set forth in the UNCRC or its first two Optional Protocols. It was opened for signature on 28 February 2012 and will come into force three months after the tenth State Party to deposit an instrument of ratification or accession does so. The United Kingdom has yet to sign or ratify the Optional Protocol. The third Optional Protocol for the first time permits children to take complaints directly to the United Nations Committee on the Rights of the Child and represents a significant step forward in children becoming moral actors in respect of their own rights.

This companion volume to *The Rights of the Child – Law and Practice* (indeed, in all but name the second volume of the original work) aims to make more familiar and more accessible the cardinal international, European and domestic instruments and materials relevant to the advancing of rights based arguments by and on behalf of children before the domestic courts and with respect to the decisions of domestic administrative bodies. Some of the material covered in this work will be well known to readers, including the

---

7   [2011] UKSC 4, [2011] 2 AC 166.
8   [2012] UKSC 30, 2012 SLT 961, 156 Sol Jo (28) 31.
9   [2012] 1 AC 144.
10 [2013] 1 WLR 1911.
11 [2013] 1 WLR 1911 at paras 73, 76 and 105.
12 A/66/457 and see chapter 6 below.

European Convention on Human Rights and Fundamental Freedoms and the Human Rights Act 1998. Some material will be less familiar, for example the Geneva Conventions and the Revised European Social Charter.

The Rights of the Child – Annotated Materials sets out each of the cardinal instruments which are the subject of extensive commentary in *The Rights of the Child – Law and Practice*. Each of the cardinal instruments set out in this work is annotated to allow the reader easily to indentify in respect of each provision of a given instrument the cardinal principles of interpretation and application of that provision. Further, the annotation in this volume is structured by reference to *The Rights of the Child – Law and Practice* to permit the reader to look in even greater depth at the provision in question.

The cross references to *The Rights of the Child – Law and Practice* are provided in bold as an integral part of the annotation. Thus, for example, the reference to [**RCLP para 11.53**] in the annotations to Art 10(1) of the European Convention on Human Rights and Fundamental Freedoms 1950 is a reference to paragraph 11.53 in *The Rights of the Child – Law and Practice*, that paragraph providing detailed commentary on the positive duty on the State under Art 10(1) of the ECHR to take steps to ensure that the right to freedom of expression is protected from interference by private individuals as well as by the State. Note that the annotations contained in this work constitute a summary of the basic principles of interpretation and application relevant to the provision in question. Reference should be made to the relevant paragraph in *The Rights of the Child – Law and Practice* for the full exposition of the provision or principle with which the reader is concerned.

As with *The Rights of the Child – Law and Practice*, within the annotations contained in this book international, regional and domestic statutes and case law are cited in the normal fashion by name, date and reference if appropriate. Additional source material which may be unfamiliar to some readers is also relied on. Treaties such as the Convention on the Rights of the Child and the Vienna Convention on the Law of Treaties are cited by their full name or appropriate acronym and reference number where appropriate. Declarations such as the Declaration on the Elimination of All Forms of Intolerance and Discrimination Based on Religion or Belief are likewise cited by the full name or appropriate acronym and reference number where appropriate. The General Comments of relevant human rights committees of the United Nations, including the Committee on the Rights of the Child are cited by committee, name and their United Nations documentation reference system number, for example: 'Committee on the Rights of the Child General Comment No 10 *Children's Rights in Juvenile Justice* CRC/C/GC/10'. References in the footnotes to particular countries followed by a UN documentation reference system citation are references to the concluding observations of the Committee on the Rights of the Child on the reports submitted to the Committee by that state, for example: 'United Kingdom of Great Britain and Northern Ireland (2002) CRC/C/15/Add188 or United Kingdom of Great Britain and Northern Ireland (2008) CRC/C/GBR/CO/4'. Session reports of the relevant UN Committees are cited by reference to their committee, date and UN documentation reference system number, for example: 'Committee on the Rights of the Child *Report on the Fifth Session* (1994) CRC/C/24'.

The cardinal instruments contained and annotated in this work underpin the rights of children, which rights in turn provide a comprehensive and consistent normative framework within which all children can grow through childhood as subjects entitled to the benefit of universally accepted legal norms to the point of being able to take full responsibility as free, rational agents for their own system of ends.[13] As with *The Rights of the Child – Law and Practice,* the aim of this work is to assist in facilitating the implementation of children's rights through the day to day practice of the law, as well as within the myriad instances of daily administrative decision making which touch and concern children.

The central message of *The Rights of the Child – Law and Practice* was that the UNRC, and associated international instruments can be relied on before the domestic courts, tribunals and decision making bodies of this jurisdiction notwithstanding that the Convention has not been formally incorporated into domestic law. The case law that has issued from our higher and appellate courts since 2011 suggests that this message is a valid one. In this regard, Fortin's observation in *Children's Rights and the Developing Law* that 'practitioners and the judiciary are now not only far more open to arguments based on children's rights, but also more willing to consider international instruments as an important source of guidance over standards to be reached by domestic law'[14] appears to be holding true. It is hoped that this book will make a modest contribution to keeping this trend alive.

---

13 M Freeman *The Rights and Wrongs of Children* (1983, Frances Pinter), p 57.
14 J Fortin *Children's Rights and the Developing Law* (2009, 3rd edn, Cambridge), p ix.

CHAPTER 2

UNIVERSAL DECLARATION OF HUMAN RIGHTS

Adopted and proclaimed by General Assembly resolution 217 A (III) of 10 December 1948

Status in domestic law—The Universal Declaration of Human Rights was ratified by the United Kingdom in 1950. It entered into force on 3 September 1953. The Universal Declaration of Human Rights does not constitute a binding legal instrument in domestic law. However, the European Court of Human Rights has employed the Universal Declaration of Human Rights as an aid to interpretation of the ECHR (*Golder Case* ILR 57, 201 and see *Fogarty v United Kingdom* (2002) 34 EHRR 302 [**RCLP para 3.48**]). The Universal Declaration of Human Rights should be taken into account as persuasive authority when interpreting and applying domestic legislation, including Sch 1 to the Human Rights Act 1998 [**RCLP para 3.94**].

PREAMBLE

Whereas recognition of the inherent dignity and of the equal and inalienable rights of all members of the human family is the foundation of freedom, justice and peace in the world,

Whereas disregard and contempt for human rights have resulted in barbarous acts which have outraged the conscience of mankind, and the advent of a world in which human beings shall enjoy freedom of speech and belief and freedom from fear and want has been proclaimed as the highest aspiration of the common people,

Whereas it is essential, if man is not to be compelled to have recourse, as a last resort, to rebellion against tyranny and oppression, that human rights should be protected by the rule of law,

Whereas it is essential to promote the development of friendly relations between nations,

Whereas the peoples of the United Nations have in the Charter reaffirmed their faith in fundamental human rights, in the dignity and worth of the human person and in the equal rights of men and women and have determined to promote social progress and better standards of life in larger freedom,

Whereas Member States have pledged themselves to achieve, in co-operation with the United Nations, the promotion of universal respect for and observance of human rights and fundamental freedoms,

Whereas a common understanding of these rights and freedoms is of the greatest importance for the full realization of this pledge,

Now, Therefore **THE GENERAL ASSEMBLY** proclaims **THIS UNIVERSAL DECLARATION OF HUMAN RIGHTS** as a common standard of achievement for all peoples and all nations, to the end that every individual and every organ of society, keeping this Declaration constantly in mind, shall strive by teaching and education to promote respect for these rights and freedoms and by progressive measures, national and international, to secure their universal and effective recognition and observance, both among the peoples of Member States themselves and among the peoples of territories under their jurisdiction.

'human rights should be protected by the rule of law'—The right to fair and equal treatment under the law is a right which itself enshrines the fundamental principle of the rule of law (*Salabiaku v France* (1988) 13 EHRR 379, para 28 [RCLP para 16.1]).

Article 1

All human beings are born free and equal in dignity and rights. They are endowed with reason and conscience and should act towards one another in a spirit of brotherhood.

'All human beings' (Art 1) [RCLP para 4.75]—The term 'all human beings' necessarily encompasses all children.

'endowed with reason and conscience' (Art 1)—Note that the stipulation in Art 1 that all human beings are 'endowed with reason and conscience' recognises the fact that children are endowed with the reason and conscience which forms the basis of the right to freedom of thought, conscience and religion ([RCLP para 10.2] and see Art 18 of the Universal Declaration of Human Rights below).

Article 2

Everyone is entitled to all the rights and freedoms set forth in this Declaration, without distinction of any kind, such as race, colour, sex, language, religion, political or other opinion, national or social origin, property, birth or other status. Furthermore, no distinction shall be made on the basis of the political, jurisdictional or international status of the country or territory to which a person belongs, whether it be independent, trust, non-self-governing or under any other limitation of sovereignty.

Discrimination—Art 2 does not contain a definition of discrimination. See however UN Committee on the Rights of the Child General Comment No 7 *Implementing Child Rights in Early Childhood* HRI/GEN/1/Rev 8, p 436, para 11. See further *South West Africa Cases (Second Phase)* ICJ Reports 1966 305-306 and 313-314 per Judge Tanaka; *R (Carson) v Secretary of State for Work and Pensions; R (Reynolds) v Secretary of State for Work and Pensions* [2005] UKHL 37, [2005] 4 All ER 545 at para 14; and *Carson v United Kingdom* [2008] All ER (D) 18 (Nov) paras 73 and 77. See also Definition of discrimination under Art 26 of the International Covenant on Civil and Political Rights below and Art 1 of the International Convention on the Elimination of All Forms of Racial Discrimination, Art 1 of the International Convention on the Elimination of All Forms of Discrimination against Women, Art 1 of the Convention against Discrimination in Education and Art 2(2) of the Declaration on the Elimination of all forms of Intolerance and Discrimination based on Religion or Belief.

Article 3

Everyone has the right to life, liberty and security of person.

Article 4

No one shall be held in slavery or servitude; slavery and the slave trade shall be prohibited in all their forms.

'slavery or servitude' (Art 4)—Art 4 of the Universal Declaration of Human Rights will be relevant when seeking to prevent the sexual exploitation of children [RCLP para 15.44]. The provisions of Art 4 are echoed in the provisions of UNCRC Art 32 [RCLP para 15.73].

Article 5

No one shall be subjected to torture or to cruel, inhuman or degrading treatment or punishment.

Right not to be subjected to torture or to cruel, inhuman or degrading treatment or punishment (Art 5)—The provisions of Art 5 of the Universal Declaration of Human Rights is reflected in Art 37(a) of the UNCRC [RCLP para 15.13].

Article 6

Everyone has the right to recognition everywhere as a person before the law.

Right to recognition everywhere as a person before the law (Art 6)—Note that the UNCRC contains no comparable provision. Art 41 of the UNCRC will mitigate the impact of this omission. In the circumstances, with the International Covenant on Civil and Political Rights Art 16, Art 6 forms the basis of the child's right to recognition everywhere as a person before the law **[RCLP para 3.18]**.

Article 7

All are equal before the law and are entitled without any discrimination to equal protection of the law. All are entitled to equal protection against any discrimination in violation of this Declaration and against any incitement to such discrimination.

'All are equal before the law' (Art 7)—Art 7 requires State Parties to ensure that children are equal before the law **[RCLP para 4.59]**. The guarantee of equality in Art 7 of the Universal Declaration of Human Rights has been described by the domestic courts as freestanding and comprehensive (*R (Pretty) v DPP (Secretary of State for the Home Department Intervening)* [2001] UKHL 61, [2002] 1 AC 800, para 56 **[RCLP para 2.73]**).

Article 8

Everyone has the right to an effective remedy by the competent national tribunals for acts violating the fundamental rights granted him by the constitution or by law.

Article 9

No one shall be subjected to arbitrary arrest, detention or exile.

Article 10

Everyone is entitled in full equality to a fair and public hearing by an independent and impartial tribunal, in the determination of his rights and obligations and of any criminal charge against him.

'determination of his rights and obligations and of any criminal charge' (Art 10)—Whilst Art 40 of the UNCRC omits expressly to confer on the child the right to fair and equal treatment under the law in determination of the child's civil rights and obligations, the right of everyone under Art 10 of the Universal Declaration of Human Rights in full equality to a fair and public hearing by an independent and impartial tribunal applies not only to criminal proceedings but to any proceedings determining rights and obligations (**[RCLP paras 16.7 and 16.19]** and see Art 14(1) of the International Covenant on Civil and Political Rights and the UN Standard Minimum Rules for the Administration of Juvenile Justice r 3(2)).

Article 11

(1) Everyone charged with a penal offence has the right to be presumed innocent until proved guilty according to law in a public trial at which he has had all the guarantees necessary for his defence.

(2) No one shall be held guilty of any penal offence on account of any act or omission which did not constitute a penal offence, under national or international law, at the time when it was committed. Nor shall a heavier penalty be imposed than the one that was applicable at the time the penal offence was committed.

'the right to be presumed innocent until proved guilty' (Art 11(1))—See also UNCRC Art 40(2)(b)(i) and the International Covenant on Civil and Political Rights Art 14(2) **[RCLP para 16.35]**.

No retrospective legislation (Art 11(2))—Whilst the UNCRC Art 40(2)(a) (which stipulates that no child shall be alleged as, or accused of, or recognised as having infringed the penal law by reason of acts or omissions that were not prohibited by national or international law the time they were committed) does not reflect entirely the provisions of Art 11(2) of the Universal Declaration of Human Rights in that it omits reference to sentencing, the UN Committee on the Rights of the Child makes clear that Art 40(2)(a) will, like Art 11(2), encompass sentencing (see the Committee on the Rights of the Child General Comment No 10 *Children's Rights in Juvenile Justice* CRC/C/GC/10, para 41 and **[RCLP paras 16.32–16.34]**).

Article 12

No one shall be subjected to arbitrary interference with his privacy, family, home or correspondence, nor to attacks upon his honour and reputation. Everyone has the right to the protection of the law against such interference or attacks.

'arbitrary interference' (Art 12)—Note that, in contrast to UNCRC Art 16 which uses the term 'arbitrary or unlawful', Art 12 of the Universal Declaration on Human Rights omits the word 'unlawful' in this context [RCLP para 8.69].

Housing—For an analysis of the role of Art 12 in relation to the issue of housing provision for children see *Hunter and others v Canary Wharf Ltd; Hunter and others v London Docklands Corporation* [1997] AC 655, [1997] 2 All ER 426, [1997] 2 FLR 342 per Lord Cooke of Thorndon dissenting.

Article 13

(1) Everyone has the right to freedom of movement and residence within the borders of each state.

(2) Everyone has the right to leave any country, including his own, and to return to his country.

Article 14

(1) Everyone has the right to seek and to enjoy in other countries asylum from persecution.

(2) This right may not be invoked in the case of prosecutions genuinely arising from non-political crimes or from acts contrary to the purposes and principles of the United Nations.

Article 15

(1) Everyone has the right to a nationality.

(2) No one shall be arbitrarily deprived of his nationality nor denied the right to change his nationality.

Article 16

(1) Men and women of full age, without any limitation due to race, nationality or religion, have the right to marry and to found a family. They are entitled to equal rights as to marriage, during marriage and at its dissolution.

(2) Marriage shall be entered into only with the free and full consent of the intending spouses.

(3) The family is the natural and fundamental group unit of society and is entitled to protection by society and the State.

The right to marry (Art 16)—The domestic courts have referred to Art 16 of the Universal Declaration of Human Rights in *R (Baiai and another) v Secretary of State for the Home Department (Nos 1 and 2); R (Bigoku and another) v Secretary of State for the Home Department; R (Tilki) v Secretary of State for the Home Department* [2008] UKHL 53, [2008] 3 All ER 1094.

'natural and fundamental group unit of society' (Art 16(3)) [RCLP para 2.31]—Art 16(3) emphasises the primacy of the family unit within the context of the international human rights framework.

'entitled to protection by society and the State' (Art 16(3)) [RCLP para 2.31]—The words 'entitled to protection by society and the State' articulate a duty to protect the family unit as a key element of the social context within which human rights subsist.

Article 17

(1) Everyone has the right to own property alone as well as in association with others.

(2) No one shall be arbitrarily deprived of his property.

Article 18

Everyone has the right to freedom of thought, conscience and religion; this right includes freedom to change his religion or belief, and freedom, either alone or in community with others and in public or private, to manifest his religion or belief in teaching, practice, worship and observance.

'Everyone has the right to freedom of thought, conscience and religion' (Art 18)—Note that the stipulation in Art 1 of the Universal Declaration of Human Rights that all human beings are 'endowed with reason and conscience' recognises the fact that children are endowed with the reason and conscience which forms the basis of the right to freedom of thought, conscience and religion ([RCLP para 10.2] and see Art 1 of the Universal Declaration of Human Rights above). Note that Art 18 of the Universal Declaration of Human Rights specifies a wider range of elements of the right than Art 14 of the UNCRC [RCLP para 3.18].

Article 19

Everyone has the right to freedom of opinion and expression; this right includes freedom to hold opinions without interference and to seek, receive and impart information and ideas through any media and regardless of frontiers.

Article 20

(1) Everyone has the right to freedom of peaceful assembly and association.

(2) No one may be compelled to belong to an association.

Right to freedom of peaceful assembly and association (Art 20(1))—Note that Art 15(1) of the UNCRC simply recognises the child's right to freedom of association and to freedom of peaceful assembly rather than granting the right itself. In circumstances where the UNCRC ensures only the recognition of the child's right to freedom of association and to freedom of peaceful assembly the right of 'everyone' to freedom of peaceful assembly and association under Art 20 of the Universal Declaration of Human Rights is one of the primary sources of the child's right in this regard [RCLP paras 12.1, 12.15].

'No one may be compelled to belong to an association' (Art 20(1))—Art 15(1) of the UNCRC does not repeat the terms of Art 20(2). However, the term 'no-one' in Art 20(2) will include children. Further the freedom of association enshrined in Art 15(1) of the UNCRC implies the right to join and leave associations (P Newell and R Hodgkin *Implementation Handbook for the Convention on the Rights of the Child* (2008, 3rd edn, UNICEF), p 198 and [RCLP para 12.14]).

Article 21

(1) Everyone has the right to take part in the government of his country, directly or through freely chosen representatives.

(2) Everyone has the right of equal access to public service in his country.

(3) The will of the people shall be the basis of the authority of government; this shall be expressed in periodic and genuine elections which shall be by universal and equal suffrage and shall be held by secret vote or by equivalent free voting procedures.

Article 22

Everyone, as a member of society, has the right to social security and is entitled to realization, through national effort and international co-operation and in accordance with the organization and resources of each State, of the economic, social and cultural rights indispensable for his dignity and the free development of his personality.

Article 23

(1) Everyone has the right to work, to free choice of employment, to just and favourable conditions of work and to protection against unemployment.

(2) Everyone, without any discrimination, has the right to equal pay for equal work.

(3) Everyone who works has the right to just and favourable remuneration ensuring for himself and his family an existence worthy of human dignity, and supplemented, if necessary, by other means of social protection.

(4) Everyone has the right to form and to join trade unions for the protection of his interests.

The right to work (Art 23)—The provisions of Art 23 of the Universal Declaration of Human Rights are echoed in the provisions of UNCRC Art 32 [RCLP para 15.73].

Article 24

Everyone has the right to rest and leisure, including reasonable limitation of working hours and periodic holidays with pay.

The right to rest and leisure (Art 24)—See also principle 7 of the Declaration of the Rights of the Child 1959 and Art 31 of the UNCRC [RCLP para 5.192].

Article 25

(1) Everyone has the right to a standard of living adequate for the health and well-being of himself and of his family, including food, clothing, housing and medical care and necessary social services, and the right to security in the event of unemployment, sickness, disability, widowhood, old age or other lack of livelihood in circumstances beyond his control.

(2) Motherhood and childhood are entitled to special care and assistance. All children, whether born in or out of wedlock, shall enjoy the same social protection.

'Motherhood and childhood' (Art 25(2)) [RCLP para 2.31]—The Universal Declaration of Human Rights recognises childhood as a state requiring 'special care and assistance'. The wording of Art 25 is reflected in the Preamble to the UNCRC in the words 'for the full and harmonious development or his or her own personality [the child] should grow up in a family environment, in an atmosphere of happiness, love and understanding' [RCLP para 5.80].

'whether born in or out of wedlock' (Art 25(2)) [RCLP para 2.31]—Art 25(2) makes clear that the principle of non-discrimination applies to the social protection of children, requiring such protection to be afforded equally to marital and non-marital children.

'shall enjoy the same social protection' (Art 25(2))—The equivalent provision in the American Convention on Human Rights Art 17(5) is worded far more tightly, providing that 'The law shall recognize the equal rights for children born out of wedlock and those born in wedlock' [RCLP para 4.60].

Article 26

(1) Everyone has the right to education. Education shall be free, at least in the elementary and fundamental stages. Elementary education shall be compulsory. Technical and professional education shall be made generally available and higher education shall be equally accessible to all on the basis of merit.

(2) Education shall be directed to the full development of the human personality and to the strengthening of respect for human rights and fundamental freedoms. It shall promote understanding, tolerance and friendship among all nations, racial or religious groups, and shall further the activities of the United Nations for the maintenance of peace.

(3) Parents have a prior right to choose the kind of education that shall be given to their children.

The right to education (Art 26(1))—The right to education has been classed as an economic, social, cultural, civil and political right (see the Committee on Economic, Social and Cultural Rights General Comment No 11 *Plans for Action for Primary Education (Art 14)* HRI/GEN/1/Rev 8, p 61, para 2).

Purpose of education (Art 26(2)—The objectives of education set out in Art 26(2) are couched in broad terms [RCLP para 13.8].

'Parents have a prior right' (Art 26(3))—By virtue of the UNCRC the parental right to choose the kind of education that shall be given to their children is made expressly subject to the child's best interests (UNCRC Art 3(1)), evolving capacity (UNCRC Art 5) and right to participate (UNCRC Art 12), to the wider canon of the child's rights under the UNCRC and to the nature of parental responsibility prescribed by Art 18 of the UNCRC (P Newell and R Hodgkin *Implementation Handbook for the Convention on the Rights of the Child* (2008, 3rd edn, UNICEF), p 411, [**RCLP para 13.29**] and see Human Rights Committee General Comment No 22 *Article 18 (Freedom of Thought, Conscience and Religion)* HRI/GEN/1/Rev 8, p 196, para 8). Note that neither Art 28 or Art 29 of the UNCRC contain a provision enshrining a right of parents to choose educational establishments for their children or to ensure their moral or religious education in accordance with their own convictions [RCLP **para 13.30**].

Article 27

(1) Everyone has the right freely to participate in the cultural life of the community, to enjoy the arts and to share in scientific advancement and its benefits.

(2) Everyone has the right to the protection of the moral and material interests resulting from any scientific, literary or artistic production of which he is the author.

Article 28

Everyone is entitled to a social and international order in which the rights and freedoms set forth in this Declaration can be fully realized.

Article 29

(1) Everyone has duties to the community in which alone the free and full development of his personality is possible.

(2) In the exercise of his rights and freedoms, everyone shall be subject only to such limitations as are determined by law solely for the purpose of securing due recognition and respect for the rights and freedoms of others and of meeting the just requirements of morality, public order and the general welfare in a democratic society.

(3) These rights and freedoms may in no case be exercised contrary to the purposes and principles of the United Nations.

Article 30

Nothing in this Declaration may be interpreted as implying for any State, group or person any right to engage in any activity or to perform any act aimed at the destruction of any of the rights and freedoms set forth herein.

(3) Parents have a prior right to choose the kind of education that shall be given to their children.

The right to education (Art 26(1))—The right to education has been described as [illegible] economic, social, cultural, civil and political rights: see the Committee on Economic, Social and Cultural Rights General Comment No 11 Plans of Action for Primary Education (Art 14) E/C.12/1999/4, para 2.

Purpose of education (Art 26(2))—The objectives of education set out in Art 26(2) are couched in broad terms (RCLP para 13.5).

Parents have a prior right (Art 26(3))—By virtue of the UNCRC, the parental right to choose the kind of education that shall be given to their children is made expressly subject to the child's best interests (UNCRC Art 3(1)), evolving capacities (UNCRC Art 5) and right to participate (UNCRC Art 12), to the wider canon of the child's rights under the UNCRC and to the limits of parental responsibility prescribed by Art 18 of the UNCRC (Hodgkin and Newell Implementation Handbook for the Convention on the Rights of the Child (2008, 3rd edn) UNICEF p 411; RCLP para 13.29) and see Human Rights Committee General Comment No 22 Article 18 (Freedom of Thought, Conscience and Religion) HRI/GEN/1/Rev.9, para 8). Note that neither Art 28 or Art 29 of the UNCRC contain a provision [illegible] a duty on parties to ensure educational establishments for their children or to ensure their moral or religious education in accordance with their own convictions (RCLP para 13.30).

Article 27

(1) Everyone has the right freely to participate in the cultural life of the community, to enjoy the arts and to share in scientific advancement and its benefits.

(2) Everyone has the right to the protection of the moral and material interests resulting from any scientific, literary or artistic production of which he is the author.

Article 28

Everyone is entitled to a social and international order in which the rights and freedoms set forth in this Declaration can be fully realized.

Article 29

(1) Everyone has duties to the community in which alone the free and full development of his personality is possible.

(2) In the exercise of his rights and freedoms, everyone shall be subject only to such limitations as are determined by law solely for the purpose of securing due recognition and respect for the rights and freedoms of others and of meeting the just requirements of morality, public order and the general welfare in a democratic society.

(3) These rights and freedoms may in no case be exercised contrary to the purposes and principles of the United Nations.

Article 30

Nothing in this Declaration may be interpreted as implying for any State, group or person any right to engage in any activity or to perform any act aimed at the destruction of any of the rights and freedoms set forth herein.

CHAPTER 3

UN CONVENTION ON THE RIGHTS OF THE CHILD

Adopted and opened for signature, ratification and accession by General Assembly resolution 44/25 of 20 November 1989 entry into force 2 September 1990, in accordance with article 49

Status in domestic law—The UN Convention on the Rights of the Child (UNCRC) was ratified by the United Kingdom on 16 December 1991. The UNCRC is a binding international convention **[RCLP paras 3.20–3.22]**. Art 41 of the UNCRC provides that nothing in the UNCRC shall affect any provision of the law of the States Parties or the international law in force for States Parties which are more conducive to the realisation of the rights of the child than the UNCRC itself ([**RCLP para 2.3**] and see Committee on the Rights of the Child, Report on the Second Session September/October 1992 CC/C/10, para 68).

Status in domestic law—statutory interpretation [RCLP paras 3.28–3.29, 3.33–3.38]—Whilst the UNCRC is not the subject of an enabling Act of Parliament the domestic courts will seek to interpret domestic legislation in accordance with the provisions of the UNCRC (see *R v Secretary of State for the Home Department, ex parte Venables and Thompson* [1997] 3 WLR 23 at 49F and H; *R (R) Durham Constabulary* [2005] UKHL 21, [2005] 2 All ER 369, [2005] 1 WLR 1184; *R (Williamson) v Secretary of State for Education* [2005] UKHL 15, [2005] 2 AC 246, [2005] 2 All ER 1; *Smith v Secretary of State for Work and Pensions* [2006] UKHL 35, [2006] 1 WLR 2024, [2006] 3 All ER 907 at [78]; *Re D (A Child) (Abduction: Custody Rights)* [2006] UKHL 51, [2007] 1 AC 619, para 58; *Re B (Children) (Sexual Abuse: Standard of Proof)* [2008] UKHL 35, [2009] AC 11, para 20; *R (E) v Office of the Schools Adjudicator* [2009] UKSC 15, [2010] 1 All ER 319; *ZH (Tanzania) v Secretary of State for the Home Department* [2011] UKSC 4, [2011] 2 All ER 783; *S v L* [2012] UKSC 30; *Re E (Children) (Abduction: Custody Appeal)* [2012] 1 AC 144; *Re B (Care Proceedings: Appeal)* [2013] 1 WLR 1911; *R (Children's Rights Alliance for England v Secretary of State for Justice* [2013] 1 WLR 3667. See also the decisions of the lower courts in *R v Accrington Youth Court exp Flood* [1998] 1 WLR 156; *Payne v Payne* [2001] EWCA Civ 166, [2001] Fam 473 at 487 (citing the United Nations Declaration on the Rights of the Child 1959); *R (P) v Secretary of State for the Home Department* [2001] EWCA Civ 1151, [2001] 1 WLR 2002 at 2028, para 85; *R (Howard League for Penal Reform) v Secretary of State for the Home Department* [2002] EWHC 2497 (Admin), [2002] All ER (D) 465 (Nov), paras 51–52; *R (Kenny) v Leeds Magistrates Court* [2004] 1 All ER 1333, para 41; *Haringey London Borough Council v C, E and Another Intervening* [2006] EWHC 1620 (Fam), [2007] 1 FLR 1035, para 15 and *Webster and others v Governors of the Ridgeway Foundation School* [2009] EWHC 1140 (QB), [2009] All ER (D) 196 (May)); *JR38's Application for Judicial Review* [2013] NIQB 44.

Status in domestic law—interpretation of common law [RCLP paras 3.30 and 3.39]—The domestic courts have demonstrated willingness to resolve issues arising at common law by reference to the UNCRC (*A v Secretary of State for the Home Department (No 2)* [2005] UKHL 71, [2006] 2 AC 221, para 27 and see for example *Hunter and others v Canary Wharf Ltd; Hunter and others v London Docklands Corporation* [1997] AC 655, [1997] 2 All ER 426, [1997] 2 FLR 342, paras 120 and 121; *Cheall v Association of Professional, Executive, Clerical and Computer Staff* [1983] 2 AC 180, HL; and *R (Axon) v Secretary of State for Health* [2006] EWHC 37 (Admin), [2006] 1 FCR 175 at para 64).

Status in domestic law—application to administrative discretion [RCLP paras 3.31 and 3.40–3.42]—Public authorities exercising discretionary administrative powers will have regard to the human rights context in determining whether the public authority has acted reasonably and with regard to all relevant considerations (*Ahmed and Patel v Secretary of State for the Home Department* [1999] Imm AR 22 approving the judgment of the High Court of Australia in *Minister for Immigration and Ethnic Affairs v Teoh* (1995) 183 CLR 273 and see for example *European Roma Rights Centre v Immigration Officer at Prague Airport (United Nations High Comr Intervening)* [2004] UKHL 55, [2005] 2 AC 1; *R v Ministry of Defence ex p Smith* [1996] QB 517 at 554E–554G and *R (Begum) v Headteacher and Governor of Denbigh High School* [2006] UKHL 15, [2007] 1 AC 100, para 68). Within this context the UNCRC applies to the exercise of administrative discretion (see *D v Home*

Office [2005] EWCA Civ 38, [2006] 1 All ER 183, para 111; *Re C (Children) (Abduction: Separate Representation of Children)* [2008] EWHC 517 (Fam), [2009] 1 FCR 194) at least to the extent of determining a public authoritiy's obligations under the ECHR (*R (Pounder) v HM Coroner for the North and South Districts of Darlington* [2009] 3 All ER 150, para 51 and see below at **Status in domestic law – interpretation of the ECHR and Human Rights Act 1998 Sch 1**).

Status in domestic law – interpretation of the ECHR and Human Rights Act 1998, Sch 1 [RCLP paras 3.43–3.46]—The European Court of Human Rights has held that it is appropriate to interpret the ECHR as far as possible in harmony with other rules of international law (*Al Adsani v United Kingdom* (2001) 12 BHRC 88 at 103). This principle will apply to the UNCRC, requiring the ECHR and, by extension, the Human Rights Act 1998 Sch 1, to be interpreted in so far as possible in accordance with the provisions of the UNCRC (*R (R) Durham Constabulary* [2005] UKHL 21, [2005] 2 All ER 369, [2005] 1 WLR 1184; *Smith v Secretary of State for Work and Pensions* [2006] UKHL 35, [2006] 1 WLR 2024, [2006] 3 All ER 907; *ZH (Tanzania) v Secretary of State for the Home Department* [2011] UKSC 4, [2011] 2 All ER 783; *Dyer (Procurator Fiscal, Linlithgow) v Watson; JK v HM Advocate* [2002] UKPC D1, [2004] 1 AC 379, [2002] 4 All ER 1; *R (MXL and others) v Secretary of State for the Home Department* [2010] EWHC 2397 (Admin)).

PREAMBLE

The States Parties to the present Convention,

Considering that, in accordance with the principles proclaimed in the Charter of the United Nations, recognition of the inherent dignity and of the equal and inalienable rights of all members of the human family is the foundation of freedom, justice and peace in the world,

Bearing in mind that the peoples of the United Nations have, in the Charter, reaffirmed their faith in fundamental human rights and in the dignity and worth of the human person, and have determined to promote social progress and better standards of life in larger freedom,

Recognizing that the United Nations has, in the Universal Declaration of Human Rights and in the International Covenants on Human Rights, proclaimed and agreed that everyone is entitled to all the rights and freedoms set forth therein, without distinction of any kind, such as race, colour, sex, language, religion, political or other opinion, national or social origin, property, birth or other status,

Recalling that, in the Universal Declaration of Human Rights, the United Nations has proclaimed that childhood is entitled to special care and assistance,

Convinced that the family, as the fundamental group of society and the natural environment for the growth and well-being of all its members and particularly children, should be afforded the necessary protection and assistance so that it can fully assume its responsibilities within the community,

Recognizing that the child, for the full and harmonious development of his or her personality, should grow up in a family environment, in an atmosphere of happiness, love and understanding,

Considering that the child should be fully prepared to live an individual life in society, and brought up in the spirit of the ideals proclaimed in the Charter of the United Nations, and in particular in the spirit of peace, dignity, tolerance, freedom, equality and solidarity,

Bearing in mind that the need to extend particular care to the child has been stated in the Geneva Declaration of the Rights of the Child of 1924 and in the Declaration of the Rights of the Child adopted by the General Assembly on 20 November 1959 and recognized in the Universal Declaration of Human Rights, in the International Covenant on Civil and Political Rights (in particular in articles 23 and 24), in the International

Covenant on Economic, Social and Cultural Rights (in particular in article 10) and in the statutes and relevant instruments of specialized agencies and international organizations concerned with the welfare of children,

Bearing in mind that, as indicated in the Declaration of the Rights of the Child, "the child, by reason of his physical and mental immaturity, needs special safeguards and care, including appropriate legal protection, before as well as after birth",

Recalling the provisions of the Declaration on Social and Legal Principles relating to the Protection and Welfare of Children, with Special Reference to Foster Placement and Adoption Nationally and Internationally; the United Nations Standard Minimum Rules for the Administration of Juvenile Justice (The Beijing Rules); and the Declaration on the Protection of Women and Children in Emergency and Armed Conflict,

Recognizing that, in all countries in the world, there are children living in exceptionally difficult conditions, and that such children need special consideration,

Taking due account of the importance of the traditions and cultural values of each people for the protection and harmonious development of the child, Recognizing the importance of international cooperation for improving the living conditions of children in every country, in particular in the developing countries,

Have agreed as follows:

Status of Preamble—The preamble does not itself prescribe binding principles but is a frame of reference by which the articles in the Convention are interpreted (Vienna Convention on the Law of Treaties 1969 Art 31) [RCLP **paras 2.8–2.10**].

Protection and assistance for the family—The Preamble's statement that 'the family, as the fundamental group of society and the natural environment for the growth and well-being of all its members and particularly children, should be afforded the necessary protection and assistance so that it can fully assume its responsibilities within the community' reflects Art 25 of the Universal Declaration of Human Rights which provides that 'Motherhood and childhood are entitled to special care and assistance. All children, whether born in or out of wedlock, shall enjoy the same social protection' [RCLP **para 2.8**].

'fully prepared to live an individual life in society'—These words appear to be a reference to the preparation constituted by a child's upbringing rather than requirement of the state of childhood itself. As such they do not conflict with the statement that childhood is a state requiring special care and assistance [RCLP **para 2.9**].

'before as well as after birth'—The UNCRC does not define the point at which it *begins* to apply and, in particular, does not make clear whether it applies to an unborn child. In relation to the words 'before as well as after birth' the *travaux preparatoires* to the UNCRC record that 'In adopting this preambular paragraph, the Working Group does not intend to prejudice the interpretation of article 1 or any provision of the Convention by State Parties' (E/CN 4/1989/48, pp 8–15). For a detailed discussion see **Definition of child** under Art 1 [RCLP **para 4.4**].

PART I

Article 1

For the purposes of the present Convention, a child means every human being below the age of eighteen years unless under the law applicable to the child, majority is attained earlier.

Definition of child—Art 1 defines the upper age of those to whom the UNCRC applies, being those below the age of eighteen years unless under the law applicable to the child majority is attained earlier [RCLP **para 4.15–4.17**]. The UNCRC does not define the point at which the UNCRC begins to apply and in particular does not make clear whether the UNCRC applies to the unborn child. In any event, Art 1 does not restrict a State's discretion to provide under its domestic law the point at which childhood begins. See also **'before as well as after birth'** above under Preamble [RCLP **para 4.4**].

United Kingdom reservation—Upon ratifying the UNCRC declared that it would interpret the Convention as applying only following a live birth (UN Doc CRC/C/2/Rev 8, p 42 1991).

'unless under the law applicable to the child, majority is attained earlier' (Art 1)—These words allow States parties which set a lower age than eighteen as the end of childhood to retain that lower age. The word 'majority' is not qualified in Art 1 by the word 'age', recognising that childhood may come to an end by reference to criteria other than age [RCLP para 4.15].

Minimum ages—The UN Committee on the Rights of the Child recognises that States parties may set minimum ages in relation to certain activities which touch and concern children. The Committee expects the *protective* minimum ages be set as high as possible and minimum ages designed to encourage autonomy be flexible and sensitive to the needs of the individual child. All minimum ages must be set having regard to the totality of the Convention. In relation to the age of sexual consent the Committee on the Rights of the Child has stated that 12 years old is manifestly too low (Indonesia CRC/C/15/Add 233, para 18) and 14 years old would give cause for concern (Iceland CRC/C/15/Add 217, para 38) [RCLP para 4.14].

Matters relating to criminal justice—The UN Human Rights Committee has stated that all persons under the age of 18 should be treated as juveniles, at least in relation to matters relating to criminal justice (Human Rights Committee General Comment No 21 *Article 10 (Humane Treatment of Persons Deprived of their Liberty* HRI/GEN/1/Rev 8, p 194, para 13). The UN Rules for the Protection of Children Deprived of their Liberty r 18 defines a 'juvenile' as a person under the age of eighteen. Every person under the age of eighteen at the time of the alleged commission of an offence must be treated in accordance with the rules of juvenile justice (Committee on the Rights of the Child General Comment No 10 *Children's Rights in Juvenile Justice* CRC/C/GC/10, para 37) [RCLP para 16.6].

Article 2

1. States Parties shall respect and ensure the rights set forth in the present Convention to each child within their jurisdiction without discrimination of any kind, irrespective of the child's or his or her parent's or legal guardian's race, colour, sex, language, religion, political or other opinion, national, ethnic or social origin, property, disability, birth or other status.

2. States Parties shall take all appropriate measures to ensure that the child is protected against all forms of discrimination or punishment on the basis of the status, activities, expressed opinions, or beliefs of the child's parents, legal guardians, or family members.

Discrimination—Art 2 does not contain a definition of discrimination and the UN Committee on the Rights of the Child has not to date published a General Comment with respect to Art 2. See however UN Committee on the Rights of the Child General Comment No 7 *Implementing Child Rights in Early Childhood* HRI/GEN/1/Rev 8, p 436, para 11. See further *South West Africa Cases (Second Phase)* ICJ Reports 1966 305-306 and 313-314 per Judge Tanaka, *R (Carson) v Secretary of State for Work and Pensions; R (Reynolds) v Secretary of State for Work and Pensions* [2005] UKHL 37, [2005] 4 All ER 545 at para 14; and *Carson v United Kingdom* [2008] All ER (D) 18 (Nov) paras 73 and 77. See also Definition of discrimination under Art 26 of the International Covenant on Civil and Political Rights below and Art 1 of the International Convention on the Elimination of All Forms of Racial Discrimination, Art 1 of the International Convention on the Elimination of All Forms of Discrimination against Women, Art 1 of the Convention against Discrimination in Education and Art 2(2) of the Declaration on the Elimination of all forms of Intolerance and Discrimination based on Religion or Belief [RCLP paras 4.90–4.91].

Scope of protection from discrimination—Each of the articles of the UNCRC must be read in light of the provisions of Art 2. The protection against discrimination on the grounds of the child's or his or her parents' or legal guardian's race, colour, sex, language, religion, political or other opinion, national, ethnic or social origin, property, disability, birth or other status provided by Art 2(1) is further extended by the non-discrimination provisions in Art 22(1) in respect of refugee children, Art 23(1) in respect of children with disabilities (see also the UN Convention on the Rights of Persons with Disabilities Art 7(1) and the UN Standard Rules on the Equalisation of Opportunities for Persons with Disabilities), Arts 28 and 29(1)(d) concerning the education of children (see also UN Convention against Discrimination in Education Art 1 and the Committee on the Rights of the Child General Comment No 1 *The Aims of Education* CRC/GC/2001/1, p 351, para 10), Art 30 in respect of children of minority or indigenous groups (see also Committee on the Rights of the Child General Comment No 11 *Indigenous Children and their Rights under the Convention* CRC/C/GC/11), Art 31 in respect of the provision of appropriate equal opportunities for cultural, artistic, recreational and leisure activity and Art 40(2)(b)(iv) in respect of conditions of equality when participating in and examining witnesses in criminal trials. In respect of discrimination on the grounds of religion reference should also be made to the UN Declaration on the Elimination of All Forms of Intolerance and of Discrimination based on Religion or Belief. Article 24 of the International Covenant on Civil and Political Rights applies the principle of non-discrimination to the right of the child to specific protection based on his or her status as a child. The non-discrimination provisions of Art 2 of the UNCRC must also be read within the context of Art 2 of the Universal Declaration of Human Rights, Art 26 of the International Covenant on Civil and Political Rights, Art 2 of the International Convention on the Elimination of All Forms of Racial Discrimination and Art 2 of the International Convention on the Elimination of All Forms of Discrimination against Women. The principal of non-discrimination applies to equally to the State, private institutions and individuals (Zimbabwe CRC/C/15/Add55, para 12) [**RCLP paras 4.87–4.89**].

'ensure' (Art 2(1))—The use of the word 'ensure' in Art 2(1) implies an affirmative obligation on the State to take measures necessary to enable children to enjoy and exercise their rights without discrimination (see Bolivia CRC/C/15/Add, para 14). Care however must be taken in the application of the principle of 'positive discrimination' (*Equal Opportunities Commissioner v Director of Education* [2001] HKLRD 690). See also '**shall take all appropriate measures**' below [RCLP para 4.88].

'the rights set forth in the present convention' (Art 2(1))—The provisions of Art 2(1) of the UNCRC do not appear to constitute a prohibition on discrimination against children *per se*, the prohibitions contained in Art 2(1) being always referable to the rights contained in the Convention. By contrast see Art 26 of the International Covenant on Civil and Political Rights. Likewise, Art 2 of the UNCRC does not embody the concept of equality of children before the law. However, the Committee on the Rights of the Child has made clear that differentiation between the legal status of children based on an improper distinction between the state of marital and non-marital children or otherwise will be a breach of Art 2(1) (see Bulgaria CRC/C/15/Add 66). Note also the wording of the Preamble which recognises 'the inherent dignity and of the equal and inalienable rights of all members of the human family' as the foundation of justice [**RCLP para 4.87**].

'to each child within their jurisdiction' (Art 2(1))—The non-discrimination principle enshrined in Art 2(1) applies to all children in the jurisdiction, including visitors, children of migrant workers, refugees and children within the jurisdiction illegally (see Committee on the Rights of the Child General Comment No 6 *Treatment of Unaccompanied and Separated Children Outside their Country of Origin* HRI/GEN/1/Rev 8, p 413, para 18).

'or his or her parent's or legal guardian's' (Art 2(2))—These words ensure that the rights of the child are not infringed by acts of discrimination which result from the status, activities, expressed opinions or beliefs of his or her parents, legal guardians or family members which may bring those adults into conflict with the state.

'shall take all appropriate measures' (Art 2(2))—States parties have a positive duty under Art 2(2) to protect the child from discrimination by reason of the statuses, activities and expressed opinion or beliefs stipulated in Art 2(1). See also '**ensure**' above [RCLP para 4.88].

Article 3

1. In all actions concerning children, whether undertaken by public or private social welfare institutions, courts of law, administrative authorities or legislative bodies, the best interests of the child shall be a primary consideration.

2. States Parties undertake to ensure the child such protection and care as is necessary for his or her well-being, taking into account the rights and duties of his or her parents, legal guardians, or other individuals legally responsible for him or her, and, to this end, shall take all appropriate legislative and administrative measures.

3. States Parties shall ensure that the institutions, services and facilities responsible for the care or protection of children shall conform with the standards established by competent authorities, particularly in the areas of safety, health, in the number and suitability of their staff, as well as competent supervision.

'Best Interests' (Art 3(1))—The UNCRC does not contain a definition of the concept of best interests. The UN Committee on the Rights of the Child has very recently published its General Comment No 14 entitled *The Right of the Child to have His or Her best Interests taken as a Primary Consideration* (see Chapter 28 below) which makes clear that the content of the concept of 'best interests' must be determined on a case by case basis and that the concept is thus flexible and adaptable. The elements of a child's best interests are multifarious and in reality incapable of exhaustive definition (*Ex parte Devine* (1981) 398 So. 2d 6868 Ala). The UN Committee on the Rights of the Child has suggested that it is for individual States to analyse and objectively implement Art 3(1) (see for example Canada CRC/C/15/Add 215, para 25 and Czech Republic CRC/C/15/Add 201, para 32). The principles of non-discrimination, maximum survival and development and respect for the child's views will all be relevant in determining the question of what is in the child's best interests (see P Newell and R Hodgkin

Implementation Handbook for the Convention on the Rights of the Child (2008, 3rd edn, UNICEF), p 37). States may not use their own interpretation of 'best interests' as to deny children their rights under the UNCRC (see P Newell and R Hodgkin *Implementation Handbook for the Convention on the Rights of the Child* (2008, 3rd edn, UNICEF), p 38). Thus the best interests principle may not be used to justify 'reasonable' or 'moderate' corporal punishment (Committee on the Rights of the Child General Comment No 8 *The Right of the Child to Protection from Corporal Punishment and Other Cruel or Degrading Forms of Punishment* CRC/C/GC/8, p 7, para 26). The best interests of the child are also referred to (without reference to the weight that is to be attached to those interests) in Arts 9(1), 9(3), 20, 37(c) and 40(2)(b)(iii) **[RCLP paras 4.135–4.136]**.

'all actions ... whether undertaken by public or private social welfare institutions, courts of law, administrative authorities or legislative bodies' (Art 3(1))—The term 'all actions' encompasses both acts and omissions. It requires active measures to be taken by State bodies to apply the best interests to all decisions and actions affecting children both directly and indirectly as individuals as well as a constituency (Committee on the Rights of the Child General Comment No 5 *General Measures of Implementation for the CRC* CRC/GC/2003/5, para 12 and General Comment 7 *Implementing Child Rights in Early Childhood* CRC/C/GC/7/Rev 1, para 13. See also Burundi CRC/C/15/Add 193 and Canada CRC/C/15/Add 215). It has been argued that the wording of Art 3(1) is wide enough to include also the actions of private bodies (see P Newell and R Hodgkin *Implementation Handbook for the Convention on the Rights of the Child* (2008, 3rd edn, UNICEF), p 36). Note however that the words 'The best interests of the child will be their basic concern' in Art 18(1) (see below) do not extend the application of the best interests principle in Art 3(1) to private individuals but rather address States which legislate in respect of parental responsibility so as to ensure that such legislation reflects the well established legal responsibility of parents to act in the best interest of their children (see P Newell and R Hodgkin *Implementation Handbook for the Convention on the Rights of the Child* (2008, 3rd edn, UNICEF), p 232). For further observations on the interpretation of the term 'all actions' see also the Australian cases of *Minister of State for Immigration and Ethnic Affairs v Teoh* (1995) 128 ALR 353; *Re Anais Moala Kailomani* (1996) IRT Ref No N94.01675; *Yad Ram v Deparment for Immigration and Ethnic Affairs* (1996) No Q95/646 and the New Zealand cases of *Schier v Removal Review Authority* [1998] NZAR 203; *Patel v Minister of Immigration* [1997] 1 LZLR 257; *Puli'uvea v Removal Review Authority* [1996] 3 NZLR 538; *Elika v Ministry of Immigration* [1996] 1 NZLR 741; and *Walsh v Department of Social Security* (1996) No 5795. The term 'all actions' in Art 3(1) of the UNCRC does not cover the repossession of a parent's car used to drive the child to after school lessons (*Issaac John MacKay Shields v Official Receive in Bankrupcy and Official Trustee in Bankruptcy* (1995) Fed. Ct NSW No 441/96) **[RCLP paras 4.139–4.140]**.

'a primary consideration' (Art 3(1))—By contrast to domestic legislation Art 3(1) provides that the child's best interests are 'a primary consideration'. This wording arose from concerns that there may be other interests that compete with those of the child and must be balance against them. Each of the rights conferred by the UNCRC must be interpreted and applied having regard to the primary status of the best interests of the child. Where consideration is being give to whether a particular right conferred by the UNCRC has been properly implemented it must be demonstrated that the child's best interests have been explored and taken into account as a primary consideration. The Supreme Court has endorsed the use of the best interests formulation in Art 3(1) when interpreting domestic legislation (see *ZH (Tanzania) v Secretary State for the Home Department* [2011] UKSC 4, [2011] 2 AC 166). The European Court of Human Rights has confirmed that the best interests principle enshrined in Art 3(1) will be relevant when considered whether there has been a violation of a child's rights under Art 8(1) of the ECHR (see *Mubilanzila Mayeka and Kaniki Mitunga v Belgium* [2007] 1 FLR 1726, para 83 and *R (MXL and others v Secretary of State for the Home Department* [2010] EWHC 2397 (Admin), [2010] All ER (D) 05 (Oct) 8 Oct 2010; *R and H v United Kingdom* [2011] 2 FLR 1236, para 73 and *YC v United Kingdom* (2012) 55 EHRR 967, para 134 and see also '**Art 8 and best interests**' under Art 8 of the European Convention on Human Rights in Chapter 20 below). Note that under Art 18(1) the child's best interests are stated to be the 'basic concern' of a person who has parental responsibility for the child. It has been suggested that the reference to best interests in Arts 9(1), 9(3), 20, 37(c) and 40(2)(b)(iii) extends the primary nature of those best interests articulated in Art 3(1) to those articles (see P Newell and R Hodgkin *Implementation Handbook for the Convention on the Rights of the Child* (2008, 3rd edn, UNICEF), p 39) **[RCLP paras 4.137–4.138]**.

Adoption—Under Art 21 the child's best interests are to be the 'paramount consideration' in respect of adoption. As such no other interests will take precedence over the best interests of the child (P Newell and R Hodgkin *Implementation Handbook for the Convention on the Rights of the Child* (2008, 3rd edn, UNICEF), p 295). The child best interests must be evaluated by reference to, *inter alia*, the child's need for affection and right to security and continuing care (Art 5 of the Declaration of Social and Legal Principles Relating to the Welfare of Children with Special Reference to Foster Care Placement and Adoption Nationally and Internationally A/RES/41/85 3 December 1986). It is arguable that in all matters relating to the placement of children outside the care of their own parents the best interests of the child should be the paramount consideration (see Art 5 of the Declaration of Social and Legal Principles Relating to the Welfare of Children with Special Reference to Foster Care Placement and Adoption Nationally and Internationally A/RES/41/85 3 December 1986, the UN Guidelines for the

Alternative Care of Children (2010) A/RES/64/142, para 7 and the Committee on the Rights of the Child General Comment No 7 *Implementing Child Rights in Early Childhood* HRI/GEN/1/Rev 8, p 448, para 36(b)) [RCLP **paras 8.146–8.147**].

'**the rights and duties of his or her parents, legal guardians, or other individuals legally responsible**' (Art 3(2))—Art 3(2) requires an acknowledgement of the rights and duties of parents, legal guardians and others legally responsible for children when States seek to ensure protection and care for the child necessary for his or her wellbeing [**RCLP para 8.34**].

'**standards established by competent authorities**' (Art 3(3))—The standards to be applied by the State in providing alternative care for children will be measured in part against the provisions of Art 3(3) [RCLP **paras 8.159–8.161**]. The effect of Art 3(3) is that legislation must stipulate, *inter alia*, that all agencies and facilities be registered and authorised and that authorisation should be the subject of regular review by competent authorities on the basis of standard criteria (see UN Guidelines for the Alternative Care of Children (2010) A/RES/64/142, para 105). Art 3(3) covers not only State care but extends to alternative care provided by all those responsible for the care and protection of children. Thus the oversight required by Art 3(3) will apply to foster carers and provision made by private and voluntary agencies (P Newell and R Hodgkin *Implementation Handbook for the Convention on the Rights of the Child* (2008, 3rd edn, UNICEF), pp 42 and 282. See also see Declaration of Social and Legal Principles Relating to the Welfare of Children with Special Reference to Foster Care Placement and Adoption Nationally and Internationally A/RES/41/85 3 December 1986, Arts 6, 10, 11 and 12 and the UN Guidelines for the Alternative Care of Children (2010) A/RES/64/142, paras 118–122). The applicable standards are not defined by the CRC. The Committee on the Rights of the Child has however stipulated that 'States parties must ensure that the institutions, services and facilities responsible for early childhood conform to quality standards, particularly in the areas of health and safety, and that staff possess the appropriate psychosocial qualities and are suitable, sufficiently numerous and well-trained. Provision of services appropriate to the circumstances, age and individuality of young children requires that all staff be trained to work with this age group. Work with young children should be socially valued and properly paid, in order to attract a highly qualified workforce, men as well as women. It is essential that they have sound, up-to-date theoretical and practical understanding about children's rights and development; that they adopt appropriate child-centred care practices, curricula and pedagogies; and that they have access to specialist professional resources and support, including a supervisory and monitoring system for public and private programmes, institutions and services.' A residential setting for the care of children should be as close as possible to a family or small group situation (UN Guidelines for the Alternative Care of Children (2010) A/RES/64/142, paras 123–127). The words '**in the areas of safety, health, in the number and suitability of their staff, as well as competent supervision**' in Art 3(3) do not constitute an exhaustive list. It is implicit in Art 3(3) that an adequate system of independent inspection and monitoring is required (P Newell and R Hodgkin *Implementation Handbook for the Convention on the Rights of the Child* (2008, 3rd edn, UNICEF), p 41 and see Art 25 below).

Article 4

States Parties shall undertake all appropriate legislative, administrative, and other measures for the implementation of the rights recognized in the present Convention. With regard to economic, social and cultural rights, States Parties shall undertake such measures to the maximum extent of their available resources and, where needed, within the framework of international co-operation.

'**States Parties shall undertake all appropriate legislative, administrative, and other measures for the implementation of the rights recognized in the present Convention**' (Art 4)—See also Art 26 of the Vienna Convention on the Law of Treaties 1969. The method by which the implementation of the UNCRC by individual States pursuant to Art 4 is monitored is through States parties reporting their efforts to the UN Committee on the Rights of the Child rather than by way of complaint by individuals or enforcement through court proceedings (see Art 44 below). Note that on 19 December 2011, the UN General Assembly approved a third optional protocol to the UNCRC on a Communications Procedure. That procedure will allow individual children to submit complaints to the Committee on the Rights of the Child regarding specific violations of their rights under the Convention and its first two optional protocols. The Protocol opens for signature in 2012 and will enter into force upon ratification by 10 UN Member States [**RCLP para 2.17 and 2.24**].

'**to the maximum extent of their available resources**' (Art 4)—These words recognise that the inclusion within the UNCRC of obligations designed to give practical effect to substantive rights exacts a necessary price in resources. This qualification applies only to economic, social and cultural rights and not to civil and political rights such as the child's right to participate under Art 12 (P Newell and R Hodgkin *Implementation Handbook for the Convention on the Rights of the Child* (2008, 3rd edn, UNICEF), p 160).

Article 5

States Parties shall respect the responsibilities, rights and duties of parents or, where applicable, the members of the extended family or community as provided for by local custom, legal guardians or other persons legally responsible for the child, to provide, in a manner consistent with the evolving capacities of the child, appropriate direction and guidance in the exercise by the child of the rights recognized in the present Convention.

Evolving capacity (Art 5)—The rights of children remain constant but the manner in which they are given effect is dependent on the age, development and understanding of the child. The principle of 'evolving capacity' refers to the process of maturation and learning whereby children progressively acquire knowledge, competencies and understanding, including acquiring understanding about their rights about how best they can be realised (Committee on the Rights of the Child General Comment No 7 *Implementing Child Rights in Early Childhood* HRI/GEN/1/Rev 8, p 436, para 17). Art 5 recognises that, as between children, parents and the State, the application and enforcement of children's rights moves from being an exercise of parental responsibility (or State intervention) to an exercise in participation and, finally, to an exercise in self determination. Each of the rights articulated by the UNCRC must be read subject to Art 5. For a domestic articulation of the concept of evolving capacity see *Gillick v West Norfolk and Wisbech AHA* [1985] 2 WLR 830 at 835 per Lord Scarman, 'The underlying principle of the law ... is that parental right yields to the child's right to make his own decision when he reaches a sufficient understanding and intelligence to be capable of making his own mind up on the matter in question.' [RCLP paras 4.28–4.30].

'shall respect the responsibilities, rights and duties of parents ...' (Art 5)—The use of the words 'parents or, where applicable, the members of the extended family or community as provided for by local custom, legal guardians or other persons legally responsible for the child' provides a flexible description of the 'family' unit that plays a crucial role in achieving the child's rights under Art 5 (P Newell and R Hodgkin *Implementation Handbook for the Convention on the Rights of the Child* (2008, 3rd edn, UNICEF), p 75 and Committee on the Rights of the Child General Comment No 7 *Implementing Child Rights in Early Childhood* HRI/GEN/1/Rev 8, p 440, para 15). For guidance on the interrelationship between the responsibilities, rights and duties of the parents and the evolving capacity of the child see the Committee on the Rights of the Child General Comment No 12 *The Right of the Child to be Heard* CRC/C/GC/12, pp 18–19. Note in the context of the responsibilities, rights and duties of the parents that Art 18 of the UNCRC provides that 'States Parties shall use their best efforts to ensure recognition of the principle that both parents have common responsibilities for the upbringing and development of the child. Parents or, as the case may be, legal guardians, have the primary responsibility for the upbringing and development of the child. The best interests of the child will be their basic concern.' See also UNCRC Art 27(2) which requires that the parent(s) or others responsible for the child have the primary responsibility to secure, within their abilities and financial capacities, the conditions of living necessary for the child's development [RCLP para 4.27].

'consistent with the evolving capacities of the child' (Art 5)—The concept of 'evolving capacity' must be considered by reference to the individual child acknowledging that there may not be an exponential link between increasing knowledge, experience and cognitive capacity and an evolving capacity to make rational 'mature' decisions (*R (Begum) v Headteacher and Governors of Denbigh High School* [2006] UKHL 15, [2006] 2 WLR 719) nor between chronological age and developmental age (Committee on the Rights of the Child General Comment No 12 *The Right of the Child to be Heard* CRC/C/GC/12, para 29). See also Art 3 of the UN Convention on the Rights of Persons with Disabilities which provides that a cardinal principle of that Convention is 'Respect for the evolving capacities of children with disabilities and respect for the right of children with disabilities to preserve their identities'. The European Court of Human Rights has historically taken an overtly paternalistic approach to the concept of 'evolving capacity', favouring an interpretation of Art 8 of the ECHR that emphasises the authority of the parent over the child (see *Nielsen v Denmark* (1988) 11 EHRR 175). However, more recent domestic case law has sought to decouple the link articulated in *Nielsen v Denmark* between Art 8 and parental authority at the point where the child reaches a level of development sufficient to understand the consequences of different choices and to make decisions relating to them (*R (Axon) v Secretary of State for Health and another* [2006] EWHC 37 (Admin), [2006] 1 FCR 175) [RCLP paras 4.32–4.34].

'appropriate direction and guidance' (Art 5)—Within the context of the child's right to freedom of thought, conscience and religion, the Committee on the Rights of the Child has stipulated that direction and guidance provided to the child should not go beyond that which is necessary to provide direction and guidance to the child (Committee on the Rights of the Child General Comment No 7 *Implementing Child Rights in Early Childhood* HRI/GEN/1/Rev 8, para 17). Within the context of the child's right to freedom of expression under UNCRC Art 13 an appropriate balance must be struck between parental guidance and the realisation of the child's right to freedom of expression (Committee on the Rights of the Child, *Report on the Fifth Session* (1994) CRC/C/24, Annex V, p 63). The term 'appropriate direction and guidance' in Art 5 does not leave room for justification of corporal punishment within the family setting (Committee on the Rights of the Child General Comment No 8 *The Right of the Child to Protection from Corporal Punishment and Other Cruel or Degrading Forms of Punishment* CRC/C/GC/8, p 8, para 28).

Right to participate (Art 12)—Art 12 of the UNCRC provides that the views of children should be 'given due weight in accordance with the age and maturity of the child'.

Freedom of thought, conscience and religion (Art 14(2))—Art 14(2) of the UNCRC also refers to the evolving capacity of the child in the context of the child's right to freedom of thought, conscience and religion. Children will move along a continuum from relying on the direction and guidance provided by their parents to ultimately having their own ideas and making their own choices about matters of religion and conscience (see *Christian Education South Africa v Minister of Education* (2009) 9 BHRC 53, Const Ct of South Africa) [RCLP paras 10.13–10.15].

Freedom of association and peaceful assembly (Art 15)—The *travaux préparatoires* of the UNCRC indicate that it was anticipated by those drafting the UNCRC that the child's freedom of association and peaceful assembly would be exercised commensurate with the child's age, maturity and development (UN Doc E/CN 4/1988/28, para 48).

Right to liberty and security of the person (Art 37)—Art 37(c) of the UNCRC provides that 'Every child deprived of liberty shall be treated with humanity and respect for the inherent dignity of the human person, and in a manner which takes into account the needs of persons of his or her age.' These words import the concept of 'evolving capacity' into Art 37. The principle of evolving capacity must be applied, observed and respected through the entire juvenile justice process (Committee on the Rights of the Child General Comment No 10 *Children's Rights in Juvenile Justice* CRC/C/GC/10, p 6, para 13).

Article 6

1. States Parties recognize that every child has the inherent right to life.

2. States Parties shall ensure to the maximum extent possible the survival and development of the child.

Right to life (Art 6(1))—The most basic human right is the right to life (Human Rights Committee General Comment No 6 *Article 6 (The Right to Life)* HRI/GEN/1/Rev 8, para 1, p 178). The right to life is a guiding principle of cardinal importance to the existence and efficacy of all other rights of the child (P Newell and R Hodgkin *Implementation Handbook for the Convention on the Rights of the Child* (2008, 3rd edn, UNICEF), p 83). The child's right to life applies to all children without exception. The right to life enshrined in Art 6(1) of the UNCRC is non-derogable and contains no exceptions to accommodated, for example, armed conflict or the death penalty. There is a cogent argument that the right to life, and thus the child's right to life, forms part of the rules of customary international law and may be a norm of *jus cogens* (Human Rights Committee General Comment No 6 *Article 6 (The Right to Life)* HRI/GEN/1/Rev 8, p 166, para 1) [RCLP paras 5.6–5.8].

Positive obligation (Art 6(1))—The child's right to life should not be interpreted narrowly and imposes upon States a positive obligation to adopt measures to protect the right (Human Rights Committee General Comment No 6 (1982) HRI/GEN/1/Rev 8, para 5, p 167; *Manual on Human Rights Reporting* (1997) HR/PUB/91/1 (Rev 1), p 424; Committee on the Rights of the Child General *Treatment of Unaccompanied and Separated Children outside their Country of Origin* CRC/GC/2005/6, p 9, para 23 and see UNCRC Arts 19 (protection from all forms of violence), Art 37 (protection from torture and cruel, inhuman or degrading treatment) and Art 38 (protection of children in armed conflict)). The right warrants special consideration in respect of disabled children (Committee on the Rights of the Child General Comment No 9 *The Rights of Children with Disabilities* CRC/C/GC/9, para 31) [RCLP para 5.7].

Procedural requirements (Art 6(1))—For the right to life to be effective States must have in place procedural requirements for the reporting and adequate investigation of child deaths (P Newell and R Hodgkin *Implementation Handbook for the Convention on the Rights of the Child* (2008, 3rd edn, UNICEF), p 92). See also UNCRC Art 9(4), which confers on the parents of a child killed as the result of action initiated by a State Party the right to be provided with essential information concerning the whereabouts of the deceased child, and the UN Rules for the Protection of Juveniles Deprived of their Liberty, r 57 [RCLP para 5.18].

The child's right to life and abortion—Art 1 of the UNCRC does not restrict a State's discretion to provide under its domestic law the point at which childhood begins (for a detailed discussion see '**Definition of child**' under Art 1). Within this context the Committee on the Rights of the Child has made clear that the UNCRC does not restrict the State's discretion to provide under its domestic law the point at which childhood commences and thus the extent to which the unborn child benefits from the right to life (UN Doc E/CN 4/1989/48, pp 8–15). Note that in relation to the words 'before as well as after birth' the *travaux preparatoires* to the UNCRC record that 'In adopting this preambular paragraph, the Working Group does not intend to prejudice the interpretation of article 1 or any provision of the Convention by State Parties' (E/CN 4/1989/48, pp 8–15). Whilst the Committee on the Rights of the Child has not sought to use Art 1 to define the extent to which the unborn child benefits from the right to life, the Committee has commented adversely on high rates of abortion, the use of a abortion as a method of family planning, clandestine abortions and abortions by gender (P Newell and R Hodgkin *Implementation Handbook for the Convention on the Rights of the Child* (2008, 3rd edn, UNICEF), p 85). The Committee has also commented negatively on the issue of selective abortion following pre-natal gender selection (see India CRC/C/15/Add 228, paras 33 and 34, China CRC/C/15/Add 56, paras 15 and 16 and China CRC/C/CHN/2, paras 28 and 29) **[RCLP paras 5.10–5.11]**.

The child's right to life and the death penalty—Art 6(1) of the UNCRC permits no derogation whatsoever. Within this context Art 37(a) of the UNCRC prohibits capital punishment 'for offences committed by persons below eighteen years of age'. The age *at the time of the commission of the offence* is the decisive criterion for the application of Art 37(a) (Committee on the Rights of the Child General Comment No 10 *Children's Rights in Juvenile Justice* CRC/C/GC/10, p 21, para 75). See also Art 6(5) of the International Covenant on Civil and Political Rights which provides that 'Sentence of death shall not be imposed for crimes committed by persons below 18 years of age and shall not be carried out on pregnant women'. The UN has recognised that the use of the death penalty against children is contrary to the rules of customary international law (Preamble to UN Resolution 2000/17 on *The Death Penalty in Relation to Juvenile Offences*). The Inter-American Commission on Human Rights considers that the prohibition on the execution of offenders under the age of 18 at the time of the commission of the crime is a norm of *jus cogens* (The Michael Domingues Case: Report of the Inter-American Commission on Human Rights, Report No 62/02, Merits Case 12.285 (2002)) **[RCLP para 5.17]**.

Right to survival and development (Art 6(2))—The right to life is of little practical value unless accompanied by rights securing the continuation and development of life and a life of right quality (Committee on the Rights of the Child General Comment No 3 *HIV/AIDS and the Rights of the Child* HRI/GEN/1/Rev 8, p 366, para 9). Art 6(2) adds a further dimension to the right to life under Art 6(1) not limited to the physical perspective but promoting life that is compatible with the dignity of the child (*Manual on Human Rights Reporting* (1997) HR/PUB/91/1 (Rev 1), p 425). The Committee on the Rights of the Child expects the implementation of all other articles of the UNCRC to be carried out with a view to achieving the maximum survival and development of the child (P Newell and R Hodgkin *Implementation Handbook for the Convention on the Rights of the Child* (2008, 3rd edn, UNICEF), p 93). See also the International Covenant on Economic, Social and Cultural Rights Art 12 **[RCLP paras 5.82–5.84]**.

'maximum extent possible' (Art 6(2))—The State is under a positive obligation to give effect to the child's right to survival and development, that positive obligation requiring that all necessary steps are taken within the concept of the dynamic concepts of survival and development **[RCLP para 5.85]**.

'development' (Art 6(2))—The UN Declaration of the Right to Development describes that right as 'an inalienable human right by virtue of which every human person and all peoples are entitled to participate in, contribute to, and enjoy economic, social, cultural and political development, in which all human rights and fundamental freedoms can be fully realised' (Resol. 41/128 Art 1(1)) **[RCLP paras 5.86–5.87]**. The individual is the central subject of development and should be the active participant and beneficiary of the right to development (UN Declaration of the Right to Development Resol. 41/128 Art 2(1)). The concept of development as applied to children is not simply about preparing the child for adulthood but requires the provision of optimal conditions in the child's life at all times (P Newell and R Hodgkin *Implementation Handbook for the Convention on the Rights of the Child* (2008, 3rd edn, UNICEF), p 83). Children with disabilities have an equal right to development to the maximum extent possible (UNCRC Art 23(3)) **[RCLP para 5.88]**. Having regard to the non-discrimination provisions of Art 2 of the CRC, refugee children likewise have an equal right to survival and development (UNCRC Art 22(1)) **[RCLP para 5.89]**.

The right to survival and development and available resources—The right of the child to survival and development under Art 6(2) of the UNCRC is not qualified by reference to the availability of resources.

Rights supportive of the right to survival and development (Arts 24, 26, 27 and 31)—Elements of the child's right to survival and development under Art 6(2) are further articulated in other provisions of the CRC. In particular, the right of the child to the highest attainable standard of health (Art 24), the right to adequate welfare provision (Art 26), the right to enjoy nutritious food, clean drinking water and an adequate standard of living (Art 27) and the right to play (Art 31).

Article 7

1. The child shall be registered immediately after birth and shall have the right from birth to a name, the right to acquire a nationality and as far as possible, the right to know and be cared for by his or her parents.

2. States Parties shall ensure the implementation of these rights in accordance with their national law and their obligations under the relevant international instruments in this field, in particular where the child would otherwise be stateless.

Right to cardinal elements of identity (Art 7(1))—Art 7(1) makes clear that the child's right to identity encompasses a number of further rights that are foundational aspects of the right to identity, namely the child's right to be registered immediately after birth, the right to a name, the right to acquire a nationality and the right to be cared for by his or her parents. The right to a name, registration of birth and nationality are articulated in other international human rights instruments. Arts 24(2) and (3) of the International Covenant on Civil and Political Rights provide that every child shall be registered immediately after birth and shall have a name and that every child has the right to acquire a nationality. The child's right to a name, and to registration and nationality are particularly important for child refugees and unaccompanied asylum seeking children. Art 7 should be read with Art 3 (best interests), Art 8 (preservation of identity), Art 9 (separation from parents), Art 10 (family reunification), Art 20 (continuity in upbringing of children deprived of their family environment) and Art 29 (aims of education) [RCLP para 7.16].

Right to identity applicable from birth (Art 7(1))—The wording of Art 7(1) makes clear that the child's right to identity is not something that evolves as the child develops but rather is a fully developed concept 'from birth', applicable immediately upon the birth of the child (see Declaration of the Rights of the Child 1959 Principle 3 and Committee on the Rights of the Child General Comment No 7 *Implementing Child Rights in Early Childhood* HRI/GEN/1/Rev 8, p 434). Art 24 of the International Covenant on Civil and Political Rights expressly links the child's right to registration, name and nationality with the concept of the protection required by the child by reason of his or her status as a minor [RCLP para 7.17 and 7.20].

'shall be registered immediately after birth' (Art 7(1))—Registration is 'a decisively important step to further ensure that children are recognised as persons' (*Manual on Human Rights Reporting* HR/PUB/91/1 (Rev 1), p 431). Registration will provide access to State health, education and social welfare provision, protect from abduction or abandonment and proof in respect of minimum age limits (*Handbook on Civil Registration and Vital Statistics Systems* (1998) ST/ESA/STAT/SER.F/ 70, paras 7–8, Human Rights Committee General Comment No 17 *Article 24 (Rights of the Child)* HRI/GEN/1/Rev 87, p 185 and P Newell and R Hodgkin *Implementation Handbook for the Convention on the Rights of the Child* (2008, 3rd edn, UNICEF), pp 98–99). The importance of the right is demonstrated by the fact that Art 7(1) requires registration to take place *immediately* after birth. The word 'immediately' should be interpreted as meaning 'as soon as possible' (*Manual of Human Rights Reporting* HR/PUB/91/1 (Rev 1), p 491) and implies a defined period of days rather than months (P Newell and R Hodgkin *Implementation Handbook for the Convention on the Rights of the Child* (2008, 3rd edn, UNICEF), p 100). The information registered should comprise the child's name at birth, the child's sex, the child's date of birth, the location of the child's birth, the parents' names and addresses and the parents' nationality status (P Newell and R Hodgkin *Implementation Handbook for the Convention on the Rights of the Child* (2008, 3rd edn, UNICEF), p 101). Art 16(2) of the UNCRC (protection from interference in the child's right to privacy) will require registration records to be kept in such a way as to protect against arbitrary or unlawful interference in the child's privacy (see *Handbook on Civil Registration and Vital Statistics Systems* (1998) ST/ESA/STAT/SER.F/ 70) [RCLP para 7.18].

'the right ... to a name' (Art 7(1))—Art 7(1) requires that a child has a name 'from birth'. The UNCRC does not seek to specify what type of name a child should have but domestic law should allow for mechanisms that prevent the registration of a name that might make the child the subject of ridicule or discrimination (P Newell and R Hodgkin *Implementation Handbook for the Convention on the Rights of the Child* (2008, 3rd edn, UNICEF), p 103 and see Malawi CRC/C/15/Add 174, paras 31–32). The child's right to a name is especially important for a child born out of wedlock (Human Rights Committee General Comment No 17 *Article 24 (Rights of the Child)* HRI/GEN/1/Rev 87, p 185). Any national law which seeks to prescribe names given to children should not conflict with the principle of non-discrimination under Art 2 of the UNCRC nor with the child's right under Art 30 to enjoy peacefully cultural practices. Children should have an opportunity to change their name at a later date in accordance with the provisions of Art 5 and Art 12 (P Newell and R Hodgkin *Implementation Handbook for the Convention on the Rights of the Child* (2008, 3rd edn, UNICEF), p 102). Once given, children should not be deprived of their name unless the child thereby acquires a new name (The Declaration of Social and Legal Principles relating to the Protection and Welfare of Children with Special Reference to Foster Placement and Adoption Nationally and Internationally A/RES/41/84) [RCLP paras 7.21–7.22].

'the right to acquire a nationality' (Art 7(1))—The Universal Declaration of Human Rights Art 15(1) provides that everyone has the right to a nationality. The Declaration of the Rights of the Child 1959 Principle 3 provides that a child is entitled to acquire a nationality from birth [RCLP para 7.23]. See also the International Covenant on Civil and Political Rights Art 24(3). The child should at all times have a nationality and should not be deprived of it unless the child thereby acquires a new one (The Declaration on Social and Legal Principles relating to the Protection and Welfare of Children with Special Reference to Foster Placement and Adoption Nationally and Internationally A/RES/41/84). Under the Hague Convention on Certain Questions Relating to the Conflict of Nationality Laws 1930 Art 14 an abandoned child will, unless the contrary is proved, be presumed to have been born on the territory of the State in which the child was found. Practices whereby a child automatically takes nationality from his or her father or can only inherit nationality from a married father are potentially discriminatory (P Newell and R Hodgkin *Implementation Handbook for the Convention on the Rights of the Child* (2008, 3rd edn, UNICEF), p 105) as will legislation which prevents a child inheriting nationality from his or her parents. There should be no discrimination with regard to the acquisition of nationality as between children born in wedlock and child born out of wedlock or in respect of stateless persons or on nationality status of one or both parents (Human Rights Committee General Comment No 17 *Article 24 (Rights of the Child)* HRI/GEN/1/Rev 87, p 185) [RCLP para 7.24]. The Convention on the Reduction of Statelessness 1961 Art 1 makes provision for the acquisition of nationality by children in order to prevent statelessness where they would otherwise be stateless (1961 Treaty Series Vol 989, p 175) [RCLP para 7.27]. Art 9(2) of the UN Convention on the Elimination of All Forms of Discrimination against Women provides that 'State Parties shall grant women equal rights with men with respect to the nationality of children'. Domestic provisions which seek to prevent the acquisition of nationality notwithstanding a significant period of residence will not be compliant with the UNCRC (P Newell and R Hodgkin *Implementation Handbook for the Convention on the Rights of the Child* (2008, 3rd edn, UNICEF), p 114). However, the right to nationality does not place an obligation on the State to confer its nationality on every child born in its territory (Human Rights Committee General Comment No 17 *Article 24 (Rights of the Child)* HRI/GEN/1/Rev 87, p 185) [RCLP para 7.25]. The right to acquire a nationality implies the right to all of the benefits which derive from nationality (P Newell and R Hodgkin *Implementation Handbook for the Convention on the Rights of the Child* (2008, 3rd edn, UNICEF), p 103).

'the right to know and be cared for by his or her parents' (Art 7(1))—The Committee on the Rights of the Child has made clear the role of the parents in the formulation of the child's developing identity at a young age (see the Committee on the Rights of the Child General Comment No 7 *Implementing Child Rights in Early Childhood* HRI/GEN/1/Rev 8, p 439) [RCLP para 7.29]. Art 7(1) provides for the child's right to know and be cared for by his or her parents not the parents' right to know and care for the child (see E/CN 4/1989/48, pp 18–22).

'as far as possible' (Art 7(1))—The words 'as far as possible' in Art 7(1) recognise that it might not be possible to locate the child's parents and that the child's right to know and be cared for by his or her parents is subject to the best interests principle in Art 3. Note also Art 9 which provides that a child shall not be separated from his or her parents against their will except when such separation is necessary for the best interests of the child. The phrase 'as far as possible' constitutes a stricter and less subjective test than the concept of best interests and, thus, the circumstances in which it will be in the child's best interests not to know and be cared for by his or her parents will be relatively narrow and strictly construed (P Newell and R Hodgkin *Implementation Handbook for the Convention on the Rights of the Child* (2008, 3rd edn, UNICEF), p 107) [RCLP paras 7.35–7.37]. The burden will be on the State to show that such circumstances exist (P Newell and R Hodgkin *Implementation Handbook for the Convention on the Rights of the Child* (2008, 3rd edn, UNICEF), p 109). There must be cogent reasons for denying the child knowledge of his or her parentage in light of the imperative contained in Art 7(1) (*Re H and A (Children)* [2002] EWCA Civ 383, [2002] 2 FCR 469 *sub nom Re H and A (Paternity: Blood Tests)* [2002] 1 FLR 1145). Art 5 and Art 12 mean that an appropriate point the child must be given the opportunity to reconsider the position with a view to re-establishing knowledge or and care by his or her parents.

'cared for' (Art 7(1))—The term 'cared for' implies a more active involvement on the part of the non-resident parent than simply paying child-maintenance (P Newell and R Hodgkin *Implementation Handbook for the Convention on the Rights of the Child* (2008, 3rd edn, UNICEF), p 108) [RCLP para 7.34].

'parent' (Art 7(1))—The word 'parent' as used in Art 7(1) is likely to be interpreted to mean genetic parents, birth parents and 'psychological' parents (P Newell and R Hodgkin *Implementation Handbook for the Convention on the Rights of the Child* (2008, 3rd edn, UNICEF), p 106) [RCLP paras 7.32–7.33]. Note that the United Kingdom has entered a reservation concerning the meaning of the word 'parents'. In ordinary circumstances it will be in the child's best interests to know and be cared for by his or her parents (P Newell and R Hodgkin *Implementation Handbook for the Convention on the Rights of the Child* (2008, 3rd edn, UNICEF), p 109).

Knowledge of origins—The child's right to know and be cared for by his or her parents has been interpreted as conferring upon the child a right to knowledge of origins (see Great Britain and Northern Ireland CRC/C/15/Add 188) [RCLP para 7.31]. Note that Art 8 of the UNCRC is much wider in it articulation of the child's right to know his or her family, using the term 'family relations' rather than 'parents' (Art 8(1)). In *Serrano-Cruz Sisters v El Salvador* IACHR 1 March 2005 Series C No 120, para 22 Judge Cançado Trindade observed in a dissenting judgment that 'The right to identity requires the right to know personal and family information, and to have access to this, to satisfy and existential need and safeguard individual rights'. Art 7 has been referred to in *Re O (A Child) (Blood Tests: Constraint); Re J (A Child) (Blood Tests: Constraint)* [2002] 2 All ER 29, *Re H (A Minor) (Blood Tests: Parental Rights)* [1996] 4 All ER 28 and *Re F (A Minor) (Blood Tests: Parental Rights)* [1993] 3 All ER 596 **[RCLP para 7.38]**.

Adoption—Art 9 non-binding Declaration of Social and Legal Principles relating to the Protection and Welfare of Children with Special Reference to Foster Placement and Adoption Nationally and Internationally provides that 'The need for a foster or adopted child to know about his or her background should be recognised by persons responsible for the child's care unless this is contrary to the child's best interests'. This will require the child to have information concerning his or her birth parents preserved and made available and to have access to information concerning his or her background and vital medical history, including that of his or her biological parents (P Newell and R Hodgkin *Implementation Handbook for the Convention on the Rights of the Child* (2008, 3rd edn, UNICEF), p 107, Armenia CRC/C/15/Add 225, para 38 and Russian Federation CRC/C/RUS/CO/3, para 40–41). Note that in situations where a parent does not wish to know or care for their child by reason of their having been placed for adoption, perhaps due to fear of social condemnation, ostracism of even risk of death, Art 7(1) does not require that the right of the child to know and be cared for by his or her parents be balanced against the parents' right to privacy. In such circumstances the State must make provision for the release of information to the child concerning his or her background and biological parents by way either of the parents' consent or at a time when the parent will not suffer any harm (P Newell and R Hodgkin *Implementation Handbook for the Convention on the Rights of the Child* (2008, 3rd edn, UNICEF), p 110). There is no obligation on an adopted child to trace his or her birth parents or be told information about them (P Newell and R Hodgkin *Implementation Handbook for the Convention on the Rights of the Child* (2008, 3rd edn, UNICEF), p 107) **[RCLP paras 7.39–7.41]**.

Human fertilisation and embryology—In circumstances where it is important for the child born by way of donor conception to know the medical history of his or her genetic parents it is difficult to anticipate a situation in which the child's right to know his or her parents under Art 7(1) would not be strictly construed to enable the child to ascertain his or her genetic parentage (Switzerland CRC/C/15/Add 182, paras 28–29 and United Kingdom CRC/C/15/Add 188).

Identity of children of minorities or indigenous peoples—Art 30 of the UNCRC stipulates that in those States in which ethnic, religious or linguistic minorities or persons of indigenous origin exist, a child belonging to such a minority or who is indigenous shall not be denied the right, in community with other members of his or her group, to enjoy his or her own culture, to profess and practice his or her own religion, or to use his or her own language. Art 30 seeks to ensure that children belonging to minorities or who are indigenous can develop and understanding of and sustain their cultural identity (Human Rights Committee General Comment No 23 *Article 27 (Rights of Minorities)* HRI/GEN/1/Rev 8, p 199). See also Part I of the ILO Convention Concerning Indigenous and Tribal Peoples in Independent Countries **[RCLP paras 7.42–7.44]**.

'States Parties shall ensure the implementation of these rights' (Art 7(2))—The wording of Art 7(2) makes clear that there is a positive duty on the State to assure to the child the rights enshrined in Art 7(1). Note that the International Covenant on Economic, Social and Cultural Rights Art 10(1) requires State Parties to 'reduce the constraints faced by men and women in reconciling professional and family responsibilities by promoting adequate polices for childcare and care of dependent family members' (see Committee on Economic, Social and Cultural Rights General Comment No 16 *The Equal Right of Men and Women to Enjoyment of all Economic, Social and Cultural Rights* HRI/GEN/1/Rev 8, p 127). State Parties to the UNCRC must make registration a compulsory duty of both parents and of the relevant administrative authorities (P Newell and R Hodgkin *Implementation Handbook for the Convention on the Rights of the Child* (2008, 3rd edn, UNICEF), p 100) but the imposition of civil or criminal sanctions for failure to register is counter-productive (see Albania CRC/C/1/Add 249, para 34 and Guinea Bissau CRC/C/15/Add 177, para 33). The registration requirements should encompass every child under the State's jurisdiction including non-nationals, asylum seekers, refugees and stateless children (*Manual of Human Rights Reporting* HR/PUB/91/1 (Rev 1), p 431). Where a child is not registered however this should not result in discrimination against that child in terms of access to health care, protection, education and other social services (Committee on the Rights of the Child General Comment No 7 *Implementing Child Rights in Early Childhood* HRI/GEN/1/Rev 8, para 25) **[RCLP para 7.28]**.

Article 8

1. States Parties undertake to respect the right of the child to preserve his or her identity, including nationality, name and family relations as recognized by law without unlawful interference.

2. Where a child is illegally deprived of some or all of the elements of his or her identity, States Parties shall provide appropriate assistance and protection, with a view to re-establishing speedily his or her identity.

Right to preserve identity (Art 8(1))—Art 8(1) enshrines the child's right to preserve his or her identity once the same has been established by name, nationality, family relations and all of the other factors which comprise the child's identity. The aim of Art 8 is to ensure the widest possible respect for and protection of the child's identity as established under Art 7(1) (*Manual of Human Rights Reporting* HR/PUB/91/1 (Rev 1), p 433) [RCLP paras 7.46–7.47].

'preserve' (Art 8(1))—The use of the word preserve in Art 8(2) implies not only a requirement not to interfere with the child's identity but also to take proactive steps to preserve the same (P Newell and R Hodgkin *Implementation Handbook for the Convention on the Rights of the Child* (2008, 3rd edn, UNICEF), p 115). This interpretation is emphasised by the words 'provide appropriate assistance and protection' in Art 8(2) [RCLP para 7.49].

'undertake to respect' (Art 8(1))—The term 'undertake to respect' is declaratory rather than obligatory. From the perspective of enforcement of the right this is unfortunate. Reference to Art 8(2) suggests that 'respect' on the part of the State will comprise appropriate assistance and protection for the child where there has been unlawful interference or illegal deprivation with the child's identity or elements thereof [RCLP para 7.49].

'identity' (Art 8(1))—Identity is not defined by the UNCRC. Whilst under the provisions of the UNCRC (and other international instruments) the child's right to identity is formulated by specific reference to registration, name, nationality and family, the use of the word 'including' in Art 8(1) indicates that the list is not exhaustive. The child's identity will be comprised of many other factors including personal history since birth, race, culture, religion, language, physical appearance, abilities, gender identity and sexual orientation (P Newell and R Hodgkin *Implementation Handbook for the Convention on the Rights of the Child* (2008, 3rd edn, UNICEF), p 115 and *Manual of Human Rights Reporting* HR/PUB/91/1 (Rev 1), p 491) and by reference to other rights such as freedom of thought, conscience and religion and freedom of expression (*Serrano-Cruz Sisters v El Salvador* IACHR 1 March 2005 Series C No 120, para 22 dissenting judgment of Judge Cançado Trindade). Age will be an important element in the child's identity for the purposes of Art 7 and Art 8 of the UNCRC (*R (NA) v London Borough of Croydon* [2009] EWHC 2357 (Admin)) [RCLP para 7.47].

'family relations recognised by law' (Art 8(1))—The use of the term 'recognised by law' is unfortunate as the child's family relations will clearly extend beyond the child's legal relationships with family members (P Newell and R Hodgkin *Implementation Handbook for the Convention on the Rights of the Child* (2008, 3rd edn, UNICEF), p 114). The phrase 'family relations' demonstrates clearly that the family element of the child's identity for the purposes of Art 8(1) extends beyond merely knowing the identity of his or her parents to relationships with those parents and with extended family, including siblings, grandparents and other relatives (see E/CN/1986/39, pp 8–10). Indeed, having regard to the interpretation of the word 'family' in the UNCRC more widely, the term 'family relations' is likely to be interpreted for the purposes of Art 8(1) to mean a variety of arrangements that can provide for a young child's care, nurturance and development, including the nuclear family, the extended family, and other traditional and community based arrangements, provided these are consistent with the child's rights and best interests (Committee on the Rights of the Child General Comment No 7 *Implementing Child Rights in Early Childhood* HRI/GEN/1/Rev 8, para 15. See also Human Rights Committee General Comment No 17 *Article 24 (Rights of the Child)* HRI/GEN/1/Rev 87, p 184, para 6 and the Human Rights Committee General Comment No 19 *Article 23 (The Family)* HRI/GEN/1/Rev 8, p 188, para 2) [RCLP para 7.50].

Adoption—It is unclear whether Art 8(1) confers a right to preserve relations with his or her birth family as an aspect of preserving his or her identity as most adoptions will not be considered to amount to 'unlawful influence' under Art 8(1) or 'illegal deprivation' under Art 8(2) [RCLP para 7.49].

'unlawful interference' (Art 8(1))—Precisely what constitutes unlawful interference with the right of the child to preserve his or her identity is unclear and awaits further developments in the jurisprudence [RCLP para 7.51].

Enforcement (Art 8(2))—Where the child is illegally deprived of some of all of the elements of his or her identity Art 8(2) requires the State to provide appropriate assistance and protection with a view to speedily re-establishing the child's identity. Other articles relevant to enforcement of a breach of the child's right to preserve his or her identity will be Art 2 (non-discrimination), Art 7 (right to a name, nationality and to know and be cared for by parents), Art 16 (protection from arbitrary interference in privacy and family home), Art 30 (right to enjoy culture, religion and language) and Art 20 (right to continuity of upbringing) (see also Principles 16 and 20 of the UN High Commissioner for Children's Rights *Guiding Principles on Internal Displacement* E/CN 4/1998/53/Add 2 and the International Convention for the Protection of All Persons from Enforced Disappearance, Art 25) [RCLP para 7.52].

'**illegally deprived**' (Art 8(2))—The phrase 'illegally deprived' will encompass illegal deprivation under both domestic and international law [**RCLP para 7.53**].

'**appropriate assistance and protection**' (Art 8(2))—Appropriate assistance for the purposes of Art 8(2) will comprise legislative measures, including civil and penal sanctions (*Manual of Human Rights Reporting* HR/PUB/91/1 (Rev 1), pp 432–433). Protection for the purpose of Art 8(2) will include making sure the child is safe whilst his or her identity is re-established and making sure the child understands his or her situation (P Newell and R Hodgkin *Implementation Handbook for the Convention on the Rights of the Child* (2008, 3rd edn, UNICEF), p 117) and will also encompass the protection of data relating to the child's identity (see UNCRC Art 16(2)) [**RCLP para 7.54–7.55**].

Article 9

1. States Parties shall ensure that a child shall not be separated from his or her parents against their will, except when competent authorities subject to judicial review determine, in accordance with applicable law and procedures, that such separation is necessary for the best interests of the child. Such determination may be necessary in a particular case such as one involving abuse or neglect of the child by the parents, or one where the parents are living separately and a decision must be made as to the child's place of residence.

2. In any proceedings pursuant to paragraph 1 of the present article, all interested parties shall be given an opportunity to participate in the proceedings and make their views known.

3. States Parties shall respect the right of the child who is separated from one or both parents to maintain personal relations and direct contact with both parents on a regular basis, except if it is contrary to the child's best interests.

4. Where such separation results from any action initiated by a State Party, such as the detention, imprisonment, exile, deportation or death (including death arising from any cause while the person is in the custody of the State) of one or both parents or of the child, that State Party shall, upon request, provide the parents, the child or, if appropriate, another member of the family with the essential information concerning the whereabouts of the absent member(s) of the family unless the provision of the information would be detrimental to the well-being of the child. States Parties shall further ensure that the submission of such a request shall of itself entail no adverse consequences for the person(s) concerned.

Right not to be separated from parents (Art 9)—Art 9(1) enshrines the principle that children should not be separated from their parents unless their best interests demand such separation. The Committee on the Rights of the Child has observed that the obligation under Art 9(1) not to separate children from their parents unless it is in the child's best interests forms part of the respect States Parties should accord the primary responsibility of parents for promoting the child's development and wellbeing (Committee on the Rights of the Child General Comment No 7 *Implementing Child Rights in Early Childhood* HRI/GEN/1/Rev 8, para 18). Whilst expressed as an obligation on the State not to separate a child from his or her parents, Art 9(1) plainly accords to the child a right not to be so separated against his or her will (see S Detrick *A Commentary on the United Nations Convention on the Rights of the Child* (1999, Martinus Nijhoff), p 171). Whilst the Committee on the Rights of the Child has commented on the particular adverse consequences of separating a young child from his or her parents (Committee on the Rights of the Child General Comment No 7 *Implementing Child Rights in Early Childhood* HRI/GEN/1/Rev 8, para 18) the right not to be separated applies to every child regardless of age [**RCLP para 8.79**].

Positive obligation (Art 9(1))—The child's right not to be separated from his or her parents accorded by Art 9(1) places a positive obligation on the State to promote parental care with a view to preventing the separation of the child from his or her family (UN Guidelines for the Alternative Care of Children (2010) A/RES/64/142). This positive obligation applies equally to children with disabilities (P Newell and R Hodgkin *Implementation Handbook for the Convention on the Rights of the Child* (2008, 3rd edn, UNICEF), p 286). Where separation has occurred it is incumbent upon the State to take positive steps to promote the reintegration of the child into the family unit subject to the child's best interests (UN Guidelines for the Alternative Care of Children (2010) A/RES/64/142, paras 49–52). See also Arts 10, 18(2) and (3) below [**RCLP para 8.79**].

'**against their will**' (Art 9(1))—The phrase 'against their will' refers to the will of both the parents and the child (P Newell and R Hodgkin *Implementation Handbook for the Convention on the Rights of the Child* (2008, 3rd edn, UNICEF), p 122). Note that in *Re T (Adoption)* [1996] 1 NZLR 368 the court held that once an adoption order has been made the word 'parent' in Art 9(1) ceased to mean biological parent [**RCLP para 8.86**].

'**competent authorities subject to judicial review**' (Art 9(1))—The term 'competent authorities' refers to the authorised position of the authority in question rather than the aptitude and ability of that authority (P Newell and R Hodgkin *Implementation Handbook for the Convention on the Rights of the Child* (2008, 3rd edn, UNICEF), p 127 and Slovenia CRC/C/15/Add 230, paras 30 and 31). The courts dealing with the judicial review of whether the separation of a child from his or her parents is necessary for the best interests of the child should be both specialised and properly funded (see Nicaragua CRC/C/15/Add 265, para 37). The need to avoid delay an implicit element of the application of Art 9(1) (E/1982/12/Add 1 C, pp 49–55). Reading Art 3(1) (best interests) with Art 16 (right to privacy) suggests that proceedings in respect of the separation of children from their parents governed by Art 9(1) should be held in private [**RCLP para 8.87–8.88**].

'**necessary for the best interest of the child**' (Art 9(1))—The child's best interests are the *only* ground for separating the child from his or her parents. Thus, for example, poverty is not a ground justifying the separation of children from their families (see Nepal CRC/C/15/Add 261, para 54, Azerbaijan CRC/C/AZE/CO/2, paras 37 and 38, Hungary CRC/C/HUN/CO/2, para 30 and UN Guidelines for the Alternative Care of Children (2010) A/RES/64/142, para 15) nor is disability (Convention on the Rights of Persons with Disabilities Art 23). The terms of Art 9(1) suggest strongly that immigration law and procedures which result in the separation of children from their parents for reasons other than the children's best interests will contravene Art 9(1). The Committee on the Rights of the Child has deprecated the accommodation of children with their imprisoned parents (see Nepal CRC/C/15/Add 261, paras 51 and 52) and non-custodial alternatives for parents should be the preference (P Newell and R Hodgkin *Implementation Handbook for the Convention on the Rights of the Child* (2008, 3rd edn, UNICEF), p 124). A child should not be punished for the activities of his or her parents (Art 2(2)). See also Art 3(1) above [**RCLP para 8.90**].

'**abuse or neglect of the child by the parents, or … where the parents are living separately**' (Art 9(1))—These examples are not meant to be exhaustive (see E/1982/12/Add 1C, pp 49–55). Before considering separating a child from his or her family on the basis that the child is at risk of abuse or neglect States should apply proper criteria based on sound professional principles for assessing the child and the family (UN Guidelines for the Alternative Care of Children (2010) A/RES/64/142, paras 39 and 57 and see the Committee on the Rights of the Child General Comment No 4 *Adolescent Health and Development in the Context of the Convention on the Rights of the Child* HRI/GEN/1/Rev 8, p 380). Separation effected pursuant to Art 9(1) in cases of neglect or abuse should be temporary (Committee on the Rights of the Child General Comment No 7 *Implementing Child Rights in Early Childhood* HRI/GEN/1/Rev 8, p 447, para 36(b) and UN Guidelines for the Alternative Care of Children (2010) A/RES/64/142, para 2). Where a child is separated from his or her parents due to neglect of abuse the parents do not thereby lose their rights nor are they absolved of their responsibilities towards the child (see Luxembourg CRC/C/15/Add 250, paras 34 and 35).

'**interested parties shall be given an opportunity to participate**' (Art 9(2))—The requirement that all interested parties shall be given the opportunity to participate in proceedings concerning the separation of children from their parents includes the child (CRC/C/58, p 17, para 69 and P Newell and R Hodgkin *Implementation Handbook for the Convention on the Rights of the Child* (2008, 3rd edn, UNICEF), p 129). The child's right to participate is also guaranteed by Art 12 (see Committee on the Rights of the Child General Comment No 12 *Right to be Heard* CRC/C/GC/12, p 13, para 53). The views expressed by the child concerning the separation from his or her parents must be considered by the judicial authority dealing with the proceedings in accordance with the child's age and maturity (Arts 9(1) and (2), P Newell and R Hodgkin *Implementation Handbook for the Convention on the Rights of the Child* (2008, 3rd edn, UNICEF), p 128 and Committee on the Rights of the Child General Comment No 12 *Right to be Heard* CRC/C/GC/12, p 13, para 53). Steps should be taken to avoid the process of participating in proceedings from becoming itself damaging to the child (Committee on the Rights of the Child, Report of the forty third session, September 2006, Day of General Discussion, Recommendations, para 48 and the UN Standard Minimum Rules for the Administration of Juvenile Justice (the 'Beijing Rules') as applied to care and welfare proceedings by r 5) [**RCLP para 8.83**].

'**right to maintain personal relations and direct contact**' (Art 9(3))—Art 9(3) enshrines the right of the child to maintain contact with his or her parents. It has been held expressly that the continuation of the relationship between parent and child does not depend on the subsistence of the marriage between the parents (*Hendriks v Netherlands* (1985) No 201/1985, D&R 5) [**RCLP para 8.115**]. In *Hendriks v Netherlands* the Human Rights Committee held that it was necessary to provide for the child to have contact with both parents save in 'exceptional circumstances' but that a child's best interests could result in the child having no contact with a parent. The fact that a child's best interests require his or her removal from the care of his parents by the State should not lead automatically to the conclusion that it is not in the child's best interests to continue to have contact with those parents [**RCLP para 8.117**]. The Committee on the Rights of the Child has not yet considered the extent to which Art 9(3) will act to compel the continuation of contact between an adopted child and his or her birth parents [**RCLP para 8.118**]. Children deprived of their liberty will be entitled to continuing contact with their parents pursuant to Art 9(3) (see also UNCRC Art 37(c), the Committee on the Rights of the Child General Comment No 10 *Children's Rights in Juvenile Justice* CRC/C/GC/10, p 23, para 87, the International Convention on Civil and Political Rights Art 10(3), the Human Rights Committee General Comment No 19 *Article 23 (The Family)* HRI/GEN/1/Rev 8, p 194, paras 12 and 13, the UN Standard Minimum Rules for the Administration of Juvenile Justice (the 'Beijing Rules') 40/33 r 1.1 and the UN Rules for the Protection of Juveniles Deprived of their Liberty r 61 A/RES/45/113) [**RCLP para 8.119**]. The rights enshrined in Art 9(3) will apply to children whose parents reside in different States (see Art 10(2) below) [**RCLP para 8.120**]. Whilst Art 9(3) does not assure to the child contact with other family members, including siblings, such contact will be protected by Art 16 in that denying a child contact with his or her siblings or extended family without justification will amount to an arbitrary and/or unlawful interference with his or her family (see Art 16 below). Read with Arts 7 and 18, Art 9(3) implies that the law should presume that, unless proved to the contrary, the continued involvement of both parents in the child's life is in his or her best interests (P Newell and R Hodgkin *Implementation Handbook for the Convention on the Rights of the Child* (2008, 3rd edn, UNICEF), p 237). Art 9(3) has been referred to in *Re L (A Child) (Contact: Domestic Violence)* [2000] All ER 609.

Provision of essential information (Art 9(4))—Art 9(4) enshrines the right of the child to receive information concerning the whereabouts of absent members of his or her family unless the provision of the information would be detrimental to the well-being of the child. Where a parent seeks to relinquish a child the State must ensure that this can take place in conditions of confidentiality and safety for the child, respecting the child's right to access information on his or her origins where appropriate and possible under the law of the State (UN Guidelines for the Alternative Care of Children (2010) A/RES/64/142, para 42) [**RCLP para 8.85**].

Article 10

1. In accordance with the obligation of States Parties under article 9, paragraph 1, applications by a child or his or her parents to enter or leave a State Party for the purpose of family reunification shall be dealt with by States Parties in a positive, humane and expeditious manner. States Parties shall further ensure that the submission of such a request shall entail no adverse consequences for the applicants and for the members of their family.

2. A child whose parents reside in different States shall have the right to maintain on a regular basis, save in exceptional circumstances personal relations and direct contacts with both parents. Towards that end and in accordance with the obligation of States Parties under article 9, paragraph 1, States Parties shall respect the right of the child and his or her parents to leave any country, including their own, and to enter their own country. The right to leave any country shall be subject only to such restrictions as are prescribed by law and which are necessary to protect the national security, public order (ordre public), public health or morals or the rights and freedoms of others and are consistent with the other rights recognized in the present Convention.

Facilitating family reunification (Art 10)—Art 10 deals with the process by which family reunification may be achieved where the child has been separated from his or her parents by reason of the parents and the child residing in different states [**RCLP para 8.102**]. Art 10 ensures procedural protection in relation to applications to enter or leave the State. See also Committee on the Rights of the Child General Comment No 6 *Treatment of Unaccompanied and Separated Children Outside their Country of Origin* CRC/GC/2005/6. Art 10 should be read with Art 9(1) which mandates that States Parties shall ensure that a child shall not be separated from his or her parents against their will, except when competent authorities subject to judicial review determine, in accordance with applicable law and procedures, that such separation is necessary for the best interests of the child [**RCLP para 8.103**]. The principles of Art 12 should be applied in respect of all immigration procedures including asylum applications (P Newell and R Hodgkin *Implementation Handbook for the Convention on the Rights of the Child* (2008, 3rd edn, UNICEF), p 169 and *Refugee Children – Guidelines on Protection and Care* (1994) Office of the UN High Commissioner for Refugees). Efforts should be made to ensure that siblings can be maintained together (Committee on the Rights of the Child General Comment No 6 *Treatment of Unaccompanied and Separated Children Outside their Country of Origin* CRC/GC/2005/6, p 419, para 40) and to reunify children separated from their parents by abandonment or conflict (Colombia CRC/C/15/Add 137, paras 40 and 42). Reference should also be made to Art 11 which provides that States Parties shall take measures to combat the illicit transfer and non-return of children abroad. Note however that, whilst Art 19(2) of the UNCRC recognises the right of children and parents to leave any country, including their own, and to enter their own country, Art 10 does not expressly enshrine a 'right to family reunion' for children and parents residing in differing countries nor an express right to remain to avoid separation.

State immigration laws (Art 10)—Art 10 is not intended to affect the general rights of States to establish and regulate their respective immigration laws in accordance with their international obligations (E/CN 4/1998/48, para 203). Art 10 will however apply to children who are under threat of deportation (P Newell and R Hodgkin *Implementation Handbook for the Convention on the Rights of the Child* (2008, 3rd edn, UNICEF), p 137). For children separated from their parents due to immigration issues see the decisions of the Human Rights Commission of Australia in its *Report on the Complaint of Mr and Mrs M Yilmas* (1985) Volume 22 Issue 7 and *Report on the Complaint of Mr and Mrs An Yeung* (1985) Volume 22 Issue 9 **[RCLP para 8.103].**

'positive, humane and expeditious manner' (Art 10(1))—The use of the word 'positive' ensures that a State can apply Art 10 without being compelled invariably to grant the application (E/CN 4/1989/48, pp 37–40). The word 'humane' requires that the procedure applied to the application must be humane in execution (P Newell and R Hodgkin *Implementation Handbook for the Convention on the Rights of the Child* (2008, 3rd edn, UNICEF), p 138 and see UNCRC Art 37 in cases where deprivation of liberty accompanies the decision making process). The use of the word 'expeditious' highlights the needs for State Parties to complete judicial or administrative processes concerning children as soon as possible so as to avoid decisions imposed solely as the result of the passage of time **[RCLP para 8.105].**

'no adverse consequences' (Art 10(1))—Any application made for permission to enter or leave the State must not persecution or discrimination. The words 'adverse consequences' in Art 10(1) extend beyond malice and will encompass, for example, breaching the family's confidentiality during the course of investigations in a manner hazardous to the family (P Newell and R Hodgkin *Implementation Handbook for the Convention on the Rights of the Child* (2008, 3rd edn, UNICEF), p 316 and see Art 22(2) and the Committee on the Rights of the Child General Comment No 6 *Treatment of Unaccompanied and Separated Children Outside their Country of Origin* CRC/GC/2005/6, paras 82 and 83 where the child has or may have refugee status) **[RCLP para 8.106].**

'right to leave any country, including their own, and enter their own country' (Art 10(2))—The words 'own country' in Art 10(2) are likely to be interpreted more widely than denoting simply the concept of nationality. The concept will embrace at the very least a child or parent who, by reason of his or her special ties to or claims in relation to a given country cannot be considered a mere alien (see Human Rights Committee General Comment No 27 *Freedom of Movement* (1999) HRI/GEN1/Rev 8, para 20 and see Communication No 538/1993, *Stewart v Canada* UN Doc CPR/C/58/D/538/1993) **[RCLP para 8.107].**

'restrictions as are prescribed by law and which are necessary' (Art 10(2))—Art 12(2) of the International Covenant on Civil and Politic Rights stipulates that 'Everyone shall be free to leave any country including his own'. The right to leave any country articulated by Art 10 of the UNCRC is not absolute as it is subject to such restrictions as are prescribed by law and which are necessary to protect the national security, public order (ordre public), public health or morals or the rights and freedoms of others and are consistent with the other rights recognized in the present Convention. The use of the words 'subject only' in Art 10(2) strongly suggests that this list of exceptions to the right to leave any country is exhaustive. The words 'consistent with the other rights recognized in the present Convention' means any restriction must be measured not only against national laws but also against the imperatives of the CRC. Art 10(2) places no qualification or restriction on the right of children and parents to enter their own country. The words 'prescribed by law' suggest that the restrictions contained in Art 10(2) must be embodied in statute or common law (see M Novak *UN Covenant on Civil and Political Rights: CCPR Commentary* (1993), p 208 and p 394) **[RCLP paras 8.108–8.109].**

Children of migrant workers—Art 44 of the International Convention on the Protection of the Rights of All Migrant Workers and Members of their Families provides that State Parties shall take measures that they deem appropriate and that fall within their competence to facilitate the reunification of migrant workers with dependent children.

Article 11

1. States Parties shall take measures to combat the illicit transfer and non-return of children abroad.

2. To this end, States Parties shall promote the conclusion of bilateral or multilateral agreements or accession to existing agreements.

Illicit transfer and non-return of children abroad (Art 11)—Art 11 is concerned primarily with parental abduction and retention of children (P Newell and R Hodgkin *Implementation Handbook for the Convention on the Rights of the Child* (2008, 3rd edn, UNICEF), p 143). The provisions concerning the abduction, sale and trafficking of children are contained in Art 35 and the Optional Protocol on the Sale of Children, Child Prostitution and Child Pornography. The domestic courts have referred to Arts 11 and 35 of the UNCRC in the context of illegal adoptions (see *Northumberland County Council v Z and others* [2009] EWHC 498 (Fam), [2010] 1 FCR 494 and see also *Re S (Care: Jurisdiction)* [2008] EWHC (Fam), [2009] 2 FLR 550) **[RCLP para 8.95]**.

Conclusion of bilateral or multilateral agreements (Art 11(2))—In the United Kingdom the measures taken pursuant to Art 11(2) are the ratification of the Hague Convention on the Civil Aspects of International Child Abduction (enacted by the United Kingdom in Sch 1 of the Child Abduction and Custody Act 1985) and Council Regulation (EC) No 2201/2003 of 27 November 2003 on Jurisdiction and the Recognition and Enforcement of Judgments in Matrimonial Matters of Parental Responsibility for Children of both Spouses ('Brussels II revised') concerning child abduction **[RCLP para 8.95]**.

Article 12

1. States Parties shall assure to the child who is capable of forming his or her own views the right to express those views freely in all matters affecting the child, the views of the child being given due weight in accordance with the age and maturity of the child.

2. For this purpose, the child shall in particular be provided the opportunity to be heard in any judicial and administrative proceedings affecting the child, either directly, or through a representative or an appropriate body, in a manner consistent with the procedural rules of national law.

Right to participate (Art 12)—The child's right to participate under Art 12 is one of the guiding principles of the UNCRC required for any and all of the other rights under the UNCRC to be realised (Committee on the Rights of the Child General Comment No 12 *The Right of the Child to be Heard* CRC/C/GC12, para 2). Art 12 facilitates the child's participation thorough the expression by the child of his or her views, wishes and feelings, coupled with an allied duty to give due weight to those expressed views. Art 12 highlights the role of the child as an active participant in the promotion, protection and monitoring of his or her own rights (Committee on the Rights of the Child General Comment No 5 *General Measures of Implementation of the Convention on the Rights of the Child* HRI/GEN/1/Rev, p 387). Art 12 applies both to individual children and to groups of children (Committee on the Rights of the Child General Comment No 12 *The Right of the Child to be Heard* CRC/C/GC12, para 10). The domestic courts have made clear that they will comply with the international obligations under Art 12 (see *Re C (Children) (Abduction: Separate Representation of Children)* [2008] EWHC 517 (Fam), [2009] 1 FCR 194 per Ryder J). Note that the corollary of the right to participate under Art 12 is the right of the child not to exercise his or her right to participate (Committee on the Rights of the Child General Comment No 12 *The Right of the Child to be Heard* CRC/C/GC12, para 16). Governments should develop direct relationships with children and children should be able to participate at local and national level in the implantation of the UNUNCRC (Committee on the Rights of the Child General Comment No 5 *General Measures of Implementation of the Convention on the Rights of the Child* CRC/GC/2003/5 **[RCLP paras 6.65–6.66]**). The domestic courts have explicitly recognised the child's right to participate under Art 12 (see *Mabon v Mabon* [2005] 2 FLR 1011 and *Re M and anor (Children) (Abduction)* [2008] 1 All ER 1157).

Relationship to other rights—The right to participate under Art 12 is closely allied to the child's right to freedom of expression under Art 13, the child's right to freedom of though, conscience and religion under Art 14 (see also *Christian Education South Africa v Minister of Education*) (2000) 9 BHRC 53 per Sachs J) and the child's right to freedom of association under Art 15. The right to information under Art 17 is a key element of effective participation. The UN Convention on the Rights of Persons with Disabilities Art 13 requires State Parties to ensure effective access to justice for children, including measures to facilitate their effective role both as direct and indirect participants. See also Art 31(2) which provides that State Parties shall respect and promote the right of the child to participate fully in cultural and artistic life and shall encourage the provision of appropriate and equal opportunities for cultural, artistic, recreational and leisure activity.

Relationship to right to freedom of expression—The right to participate under Art 12 and the right to freedom of expression under Art 13, whilst closely allied, do articulate different rights (see Committee on the Rights of the Child General Comment No 12 *The Right of the Child to be Heard* CRC/C/GC12, para 68). Art 12 relates to the right to express views specifically about matters which affect the child and the right to be involved in actions and decisions that impact on his or her life. Art 13 relates to the child's right to hold and express opinions and not to be restricted therein and to seek and receive information through any media (Committee on the Rights of the Child General Comment No 12 *The Right of the Child to be Heard* CRC/C/GC12, para 81). The right under Art 12 is that of the child to express his or her own views, it is not a right to express the views of others (Committee on the Rights of the Child General Comment No 12 *The Right of the Child to be Heard* CRC/C/GC12, para 22).

Implementation and resources—The qualification contained in Art 4 in relation to economic, social and cultural rights, that States Parties shall undertake implementation of those rights 'to the maximum extent of their available resources' does not apply to civil and political rights, including those enshrined in Art 12. Accordingly, implementation of Art 12 should not be dependent on the availability of resources.

Best interests—The child's participation is a cardinal element when considering the child's best interests. The UN Committee on the Rights of the Child sees no tension between the child's right to participate under Art 12 and the best interests principle under Art 3(1) (see Committee on the Rights of the Child General Comment No 12 *The Right of the Child to be Heard* CRC/C/GC12, para 74) but the domestic courts have taken a different view (see for example *Re W (A Minor) (Medical Treatment: Court's Jurisdiction)* [1993] Fam 64 and *Re L (Medical Treatment: Gillick Competence)* [1998] 2 FLR 810).

'shall assure to' (Art 12(1))—The term 'shall assure to' renders State Parties under a strict obligation to fully implement the right to participate for all children and leaves no discretion (Committee on the Rights of the Child General Comment No 12 *The Right of the Child to be Heard* CRC/C/GC12, para 19). The Committee on the Rights of the Child has made clear the steps required for proper implementation of the right to participate proceeding from the proper preparation of the child, through the assessment of the child's capacity, the hearing of the child, the feedback to be given to the child and concluding with arrangements for complaints, remedies and redress (Committee on the Rights of the Child General Comment No 12 *The Right of the Child to be Heard* CRC/C/GC12, para 40). The process must be transparent and informative, voluntary, respectful, relevant, child friendly, inclusive, supported by training, safe and sensitive to risk and accountable (Committee on the Rights of the Child General Comment No 12 *The Right of the Child to be Heard* CRC/C/GC12, para 134).

'capable of forming his or her own views' (Art 12(1))—The use of the word 'forming' makes clear that the right to participate is not conditional upon the child being capable of expressing his or her views. The right thus applies to pre-verbal children and children unable to express their views by reason of a disability (Committee on the Rights of the Child General Comment No 12 *The Right of the Child to be Heard* CRC/C/GC12, para 21 and Committee on the Rights of the Child General Comment No 7 *Implementing Child Rights in Early Childhood* HRI/GEN/1/Rev 8, p 432). The words 'capable of forming his or her own views' should not be viewed as a limiting criteria but rather as an obligation on States Parties to assess the capacity of the child to form an autonomous opinion to the greatest extent possible, starting from the presumption that the child is so capable (Committee on the Rights of the Child General Comment No 12 *The Right of the Child to be Heard* CRC/C/GC12, para 20). Within this context mandatory age limits on the right to participate are questionable legitimacy (P Newell and R Hodgkin *Implementation Handbook for the Convention on the Rights of the Child* (2008, 3rd edn, UNICEF), p 130 and the Committee on the Rights of the Child General Comment No 12 *The Right of the Child to be Heard* CRC/C/GC12, para 21). The concept of evolving capacity under Art 5 will be key in determining whether a child is capable of forming his or her own views. A child needs only a 'sufficient understanding' of the issue to be considered capable of forming his or her own views for the purposes of Art 12 (Committee on the Rights of the Child General Comment No 12 *The Right of the Child to be Heard* CRC/C/GC12, para 21).

'right to express those views freely' (Art 12(1))—The word 'freely' requires that the child be able to express his or her views without pressure, constraint, manipulation or undue influence (Manual on Human Rights Reporting (1997) HR/PUB/91/1 (Rev 1), p 426 and P Newell and R Hodgkin *Implementation Handbook for the Convention on the Rights of the Child* (2008, 3rd edn, UNICEF), p 130). States Parties should ensure that the child's social situation is considered and that an environment is provided in which the child feels respected and secure (Committee on the Rights of the Child General Comment No 12 *The Right of the Child to be Heard* CRC/C/GC12, paras 22–24). A pre-requisite to the child being able to express his or her views freely is the provision of information concerning the options and possible decisions to be taken and their consequences (Committee on the Rights of the Child General Comment No 12 *The Right of the Child to be Heard* CRC/C/GC12, para 25). The right to express views freely is not an unqualified right to express them directly – see the commentary on **'either directly, or through a representative or appropriate body'** below.

'in all matters affecting the child' (Art 12(1)) [RCLP paras 6.24–6.25]—The child's right to participate under Art 12 will include matters not specifically covered by the UNCRC (Manual on Human Rights Reporting (1997) HR/PUB/91/1 (Rev 1), pp 426–427). If the matter under discussion affects the child then the child must be heard in accordance with the provisions of Art 12 (Committee on the Rights of the Child General Comment No 12 *The Right of the Child to be Heard* CRC/C/GC12, para 26). There is thus no area of decision making concerning children into which adults have exclusive input.

Participation and family life [RCLP para 6.42]—The child's right to participate applies within the context of the child's family life (Committee on the Rights of the Child General Comment No 12 *The Right of the Child to be Heard* CRC/C/GC12, paras 84 and 90–92, Committee on the Rights of the Child General Comment No 7 *Implementing Child Rights in Early Childhood* HRI/GEN/Rev 8, p 440, para 17 and see *Polovchak v Meese* (1985) 774 F.2.d 731).

Participation and healthcare [RCLP paras 6.43–6.46]—Under Art 12 the child has a right to participate in both individual health care decisions concerning them and more widely in the development of healthcare policies and services (Committee on the Rights of the Child General Comment No 12 *The Right of the Child to be Heard* CRC/C/GC12, para 98 and see Committee on the Rights of the Child General Comment No 3 *HIV/AIDS and the Right of the Child* HRI/GE/Rev 8, p 364). Where a young child can demonstrate capacity to express an informed view on her or her medical treatment due weight should be given to his or her views (Committee on the Rights of the Child General Comment No 12 *The Right of the Child to be Heard* CRC/C/GC12, para 102). In respect of an older child they must be given a chance to express their views freely before parents given consent to medical treatment and their views should be give due weight (Committee on the Rights of the Child General Comment No 4 *Adolescent Health and Development in the Context of the Rights of the Child* HRI/GEN/1/Rev 8, pp 377–383). In order to participate effectively the child must be provided with information concerning proposed treatments, their effects and their outcomes together with access to confidential counselling (Committee on the Rights of the Child General Comment No 12 *The Right of the Child to be Heard* CRC/C/GC12, paras 100–101). See also Art 24(2)(e).

'due weight in accordance with the age and maturity of the child' (Art 12(1)) **[RCLP paras 6.30–6.32]**—The words 'due weight in accordance with the age and maturity of the child' make clear that the views of the child must not only be listened to but must be considered seriously and accorded weight where the child is capable of forming those views (Committee on the Rights of the Child General Comment No 12 *The Right of the Child to be Heard* CRC/C/GC12, para 28). These words incorporate into Art 12(1) the principle of 'evolving capacity' articulated in Art 5. The incorporation into Art 12 of the principle of evolving capacity ensures that the right under Art 12 is a right to participate and not a right to autonomy. The use of the words 'age and maturity' in Art 12 highlight the fact that the child's chronological age and developmental age may not necessarily coincide (Committee on the Rights of the Child General Comment No 12 *The Right of the Child to be Heard* CRC/C/GC12, paras 29–30). The views of the child and the weight to be accorded to them must therefore be examined on a cases by case basis (Committee on the Rights of the Child General Comment No 12 *The Right of the Child to be Heard* CRC/C/GC12, paras 29). For evolving capacity in the context of wishes and feelings concerning the provision of health services see the United Nations Committee on the Rights of the Child General Comment No 4 *Adolescent Health and Development in the Context of the Rights of the Child* HRI/GEN/1/Rev 8, p 383. In domestic legislation the link between the child's wishes and feelings and the concept of evolving capacity is made by the Children Act 1989 s 1(3)(a).

'For this purpose' (Art 12(2)) **[RCLP para 6.29]**—The opening words of Art 12(2) indicate that Art 12(2) must be read in conjunction with Art 12(1).

'judicial and administrative proceedings' (Art 12(2) **[RCLP paras 6.30–6.32]**—Art 12(2) covers all judicial and administrative proceedings concerning the child (Committee on the Rights of the Child General Comment No 12 *The Right of the Child to be Heard* CRC/C/GC12, paras 32). This will include religious courts such as Sharia courts (Lebanon CRC/C/LBN/CO/3, paras 35 and 36). It is likely also to encompass proceedings concerning the criminal prosecution of parents, the outcome of which can affect the child (P Newell and R Hodgkin *Implementation Handbook for the Convention on the Rights of the Child* (2008, 3rd edn, UNICEF), p 156). All children within the jurisdiction, including those present illegally, will benefit from the rights conferred by Art 12 **[RCLP para 6.47]**. The term 'administrative proceedings' is interpreted widely and will cover broad range of administrative decision making processes (see Committee on the Rights of the Child General Comment No 5 *General Measures of Implementation of the Convention on the Rights of the Child* HRI/GEN/1/Rev p 446, HRI/GEN/1/Rev 8, p 415, Committee on the Rights of the Child General Comment No 12 *The Right of the Child to be Heard* CRC/C/GC12, paras 67 and P Newell and R Hodgkin *Implementation Handbook for the Convention on the Rights of the Child* (2008, 3rd edn, UNICEF), p 149). The term 'administrative proceedings' will also encompass alternative dispute resolution mechanisms such as mediation and arbitration (Committee on the Rights of the Child General Comment No 12 *The Right of the Child to be Heard* CRC/C/GC12, paras 32) and complaints procedures (P Newell and R Hodgkin *Implementation Handbook for the Convention on the Rights of the Child* (2008, 3rd edn, UNICEF), p 149 and see Committee on the Rights of the Child General Comment No 9 *The Rights of Children with Disabilities* CRC/C/GC/9, paras 42–43). All children involved in judicial and administrative proceedings must be informed in a child friendly manner about their right to be heard and the available methods for doing so (Committee on the Rights of the Child *Report on the forty-third session*, September 2006, Day of General Discussion, Recommendations, para 40, **[RCLP para 6.48]**). As participation is dependent on reliable communication, where necessary interpreters should be made available at all stages of the procedure (Committee on the Rights of the Child General Comment No 6 *Treatment of Unaccompanied Children and Separated Children Outside their Country of Origin* HRI/GEN/1/Rev 8, p 407).

Proceedings concerning the separation of children from their parents—See also Art 9(2) concerning participation in proceedings concerning the separation of children from their parents **[RCLP paras 6.50 and 8.78]**. All legislation on divorce and separation must make provision for the child to be heard by decision makers and in mediation processes (Committee on the Rights of the Child General Comment No 12 *The Right of the Child to be Heard* CRC/C/GC12, para 52). In any decision making process which may result in the removal of the child from his or her family by reason of abuse or neglect must take account of the views of the child as being central to determining that child's best interests ([**RCLP paras 6.51–6.55**], Committee on the Rights of the Child General Comment No 12 *The Right of the Child to be Heard* CRC/C/GC12, para 53 and see the UN Guidelines for the Alternative Care of Children (2010) A/RES/64/142, para 57). This will include obtaining the child's views concerning the development of care plans and their review, placement in foster care and contact with parents and family ([**RCLP para 8.131**], Committee on the Rights of the Child General Comment No 12 *The Right of the Child to be Heard* CRC/C/GC12, para 54 and see the UN Guidelines for the Alternative Care of Children (2010) A/RES/64/142, para 6). Note that r 3(2) of the UN Standard Minimum Rules for the Administration of Juvenile Justice (the 'Beijing Rules') extends the scope of those rules to cover care and welfare proceedings [**RCLP para 6.54**]. In respect of children placed into care there must be mechanisms to ensure children are able to express their views and for those views to be given due weight and consideration ([**RCLP para 8.131**] and see Committee on the Rights of the Child General Comment No 12 *The Right of the Child to be Heard* CRC/C/GC12, para 97 and the UN Guidelines for the Alternative Care of Children (2010) A/RES/64/142, para 99). Children will have the right under Art 12 to participate fully in the period reviews required by Art 25 [**RCLP para 6.55**]. Note that where a child has been separated from his or her parents it is likely that Art 12 requires the same weight to be attached to the views of a child who wishes to return to his or her parent(s) as to the views of a child who objects to returning [**RCLP paras 6.67–6.70**] and see *S v S* [1999] 3 NZLR 513 at 521 and Art 13 of the Hague Convention on the Civil Aspects of International Child Abduction).

Proceedings relating to adoption—In proceedings for adoption the views of the child should be obtained in relation to both cases concerning adoptions placing the child outside the birth family and step-parent adoptions (Committee on the Rights of the Child General Comment No 12 *The Right of the Child to be Heard* CRC/C/GC12, para 55 [**RCLP para 6.56**]). Effective participation of the child in proceedings for adoption necessarily involves informing the child of the meaning and effect of adoption (Committee on the Rights of the Child General Comment No 12 *The Right of the Child to be Heard* CRC/C/GC12, para 56). Art 21(a) requiring informed consent to adoption by 'persons concerned' should be interpreted in accordance with Art 12 (P Newell and R Hodgkin *Implementation Handbook for the Convention on the Rights of the Child* (2008, 3rd edn, UNICEF), pp 296–297).

Criminal proceedings—Where a child is accused of or recognised as having infringed the penal law his or her effective participation will be predicated on being informed not only as to the charges but also as to the juvenile justice process (Committee on the Rights of the Child General Comment No 10 *Children's Rights in Juvenile Justice* CRC/C/GC/10, para 4, Committee on the Rights of the Child General Comment No 12 *The Right of the Child to be Heard* CRC/C/GC12, para 59 and [**RCLP para 6.57 and 6.59**]). See further Art 40 in respect of the participation in proceedings of children who are accused of or recognised as having infringed the penal law [**RCLP para 6.58**]. Rule 14(2) of the UN Standard Minimum Rules for the Administration of Juvenile Justice require a juvenile justice process that allows the child to participate and express him or herself freely. The right of the child to participate in criminal proceedings is the choice of the child and not an obligation. Accordingly, the child's right to participate under Art 12 does not conflict with the child's right under Art 40(2)(b)(iv) to stay silent (Committee on the Rights of the Child General Comment No 12 *The Right of the Child to be Heard* CRC/C/GC12, para 58 and see UN Standard Minimum Rules on the Administration of Juvenile Justice r 7). A child deprived of his or her liberty by the juvenile justice system must have access to complaints procedures in accordance with the principles of Art 12 (Committee on the Rights of the Child General Comment No 10 *Children's Rights in Juvenile Justice* CRC/C/GC/10, para 28c [**RCLP para 6.60**]). Children who are victims of or witnesses to crime must be given the opportunity to exercise fully their right to freely express their view. (The UN Economic and Social Council Resolution *Guidelines on Justice Involving Child Victims and Witnesses of Crime* UNODC/UNICEF 2005/20 of 22 July 2005 [**RCLP para 6.61**]).

Immigration proceedings [RCLP paras 6.62–6.63]—Art 12 should be applied in respect of all immigration procedures including asylum applications (Committee on the Rights of the Child General Comment No 6 *Treatment of Unaccompanied and Separated Children Outside their Country of Origin* HRI/GEN/1/Rev 8. p 215, para 25, Committee on the Rights of the Child General Comment No 12 *The Right of the Child to be Heard* CRC/C/GC12, para 124 and see *Refugee Children – Guidelines on Protection and Care* (1994) Office of the United Nations High Commissioner for Refugees (UNHCR)).

Participation in the context of education [RCLP para 6.64]—The child's right to participation under Art 12 is a central element of the child's education, including participation by the child in the development and evaluation of school curricula (Committee on the Rights of the Child General Comment No 1 *The Aims of Education* HRI/GEN/1/Rev 8, p 350–351 and see [**RCLP para 13.13**] and Committee on the Rights of the Child General Comment No 12 *The Child's Right to be Heard* CRC/GC/C/12, paras 106–110). Where it is sought to exclude a child from school the process of exclusion must conform with the rules of natural justice and the child's right to participate under Art 12 ([**RCLP paras 13.73–13.74**] and see Committee on the Rights of the Child General Comment No 12 *The Child's Right to be Heard* CRC/GC/C/12, para 113 and P Newell and R Hodgkin *Implementation Handbook for the Convention on the Rights of the Child* (2008, 3rd edn, UNICEF), p 430).

'either directly, or through a representative or appropriate body' (Art 12(2)) [RCLP paras 6.33–6.36]—Art 12 of the UNCRC does not confer upon the child an unqualified right to express views directly. The words 'either directly, or through a representative or appropriate body' recognise that the child's best interests under Art 3(1) may dictate that it is not in the child's interests to participate directly in a given decision. However, whilst Art 12(2) does not specify when the child should be heard directly and when through a representative in judicial and administrative proceedings, wherever possible the child should be given an opportunity to be heard directly in such proceedings (Committee on the Rights of the Child General Comment No 12 *The Right of the Child to be Heard* CRC/C/GC12, para 35). Proceedings involving children should ensure the availability of child-friendly information, advice, advocacy, with access to independent complaints procedures and to the courts with necessary other legal assistance (Committee on the Rights of the Child General Comment No 5 *General Measures of Implementation of the Convention on the Rights of the Child* CRC/GC/2003/5, para 24). For what is required to make proceedings 'child sensitive' reference should also be made to the UN Economic and Social Council Resolution *Guidelines on Justice Involving Child Victims and Witnesses of Crime* UNODC/UNICEF 2005/20 of 22 July 2005, para 9(d). The rules of natural justice are likely to demand that a representative or body charged with 'freely' expressing the child's views be able to demonstrate that there is no conflict of interest (Committee on the Rights of the Child General Comment No 12 *The Right of the Child to be Heard* CRC/C/GC12, paras 36–37).

'in a manner consistent with the procedural rules of national law' (Art 12(2)) [RCLP para 6.37]—This formulation permits States Parties to enact procedural rules to give effect to the child's right to participate but does not permit States Parties to circumscribe that right.

Article 13

1. The child shall have the right to freedom of expression; this right shall include freedom to seek, receive and impart information and ideas of all kinds, regardless of frontiers, either orally, in writing or in print, in the form of art, or through any other media of the child's choice.

2. The exercise of this right may be subject to certain restrictions, but these shall only be such as are provided by law and are necessary:

(a) For respect of the rights or reputations of others; or
(b) For the protection of national security or of public order (ordre public), or of public health or morals.

Right to freedom of expression (Art 13)—The freedom of expression is the freedom to outwardly manifest an opinion and had a broad scope that includes all aspects relating to the circulation of information in any form and through any media (UN Manual on Human Rights Reporting HR/PUB/91/1 (Rev 1), p 234). The child's right to freedom of expression on the Internet should not be unduly curtailed subject to the need for the child to be protected from inappropriate material (Republic of Korea CRC/C/Add 197, para 36 and [RCLP para 11.45]). Nor should the child's right to freedom of expression be unduly curtailed in school (see *Tucker v Des Moines Community School District* (1969) 393 US 503 and [RCLP para 11.46]). Aspects of freedom of expression not incompatible with the deprivation of liberty must be accorded to children deprived of their liberty (P Newell and R Hodgkin *Implementation Handbook for the Convention on the Rights of the Child* (2008, 3rd edn, UNICEF), p 180. See also the UN Rules for the Protection of Juveniles Deprived of their Liberty r 13 and [RCLP para 11.49]). Expression may be constituted by silence (*Brown v Louisiana* 383 US 131 (1966) US Sup Ct) and will encompass not only ideas capable of relative precise explication but also inexpressible emotions ([RCLP para 11.8] and *Cohen v California* 403 US 15 at 26, US Sup Ct but see *X v United Kingdom* (1977) 3 EHRR 63 where the European Commission held that expression for the purposes of Art 10 of the ECHR did not extent to the physical expression of feelings of love). The right to freedom of expression will encompass unpopular and offensive opinions ([RCLP para 11.9] and see for example *Redmond-Bate v DPP* (1999) 163 JP 789 per Sedley J). This will not however extend to the dissemination of ideas based on racial superiority or hatred (Committee for the Elimination of Racial Discrimination *General Recommendation XV on Article 4 of the Convention* HRI/GEN/1/Rev 8, p 248, para 4). The child's right to freedom of expression under Art 13(1) does not extend to the formal expression of political ideas through the medium of suffrage where national laws do not permit voting by children (see Human Rights Committee General Comment No 25 *Article 25 (Participation in Public Affairs and the Right to Vote)* HRI/GE/1/Rev 8, p 209, para 10 and [RCLP para 11.48]). The child's right to freedom of expression imposes on the State an obligation to refrain from interfering in the expression of the views the child holds or in access to information by the child, whilst protecting the rights of access to means of communication and public dialogue (Committee on the Rights of the Child General Comment No 12 *The Right of the Child to be Heard* CRC/C/GC12, para 81).

Positive obligation [RCLP para 11.14]—Art 13(1) imposes upon State Parties a duty to take positive steps to facilitate the child's right to freedom of expression (see the Human Rights Committee General Comment No 17 *Art 24 (The Rights of the Child)* HRI/GEN/1/Rev 8, p 184, para 3). This positive obligation will include a positive obligation on State Parties to ensure the right of children with disabilities to freedom of expression ([RCLP para 11.16], Art 21 of the UN Convention on the Rights of Persons with Disabilities and Committee on the Rights of the Child General Comment No 12 *The Right of the Child to be Heard* CRC/C/GC12, p 7).

Derogation [RCLP para 11.10]—Art 13 contains no provision for the derogation of the right of freedom of expression (contrast the position under the International Covenant on Civil and Political Rights Art 4 and the European Convention on Human Rights Art 15).

Relationship to other rights [RCLP para 11.4]—The right to freedom of expression under Art 13 is closely allied to the child's right to participate under Art 12 (Committee on the Rights of the Child General Comment No 12 *The Right of the Child to be Heard* CRC/C/GC/12, para 68). There is a close interplay between the child right to freedom of expression under Art 13 and the child's right to freedom of though, conscience and religion under Art 14 (see also *Christian Education South Africa v Minister of Education)* (2000) 9 BHRC 53 per Sachs J) and the child's cultural, religious and linguistic rights under Art 30. The child's right under Art 31 to engage in play and recreation and in cultural life and the arts under Art 31 is likewise closely linked to the child's right to freedom of expression under Art 13. There is a close relationship between the child's right to freedom of expression under Art 13 and the child's right to information under Art 17.

Relationship to right to participate—The right to freedom of expression under Art 13 and the right to participate under Art 12, whilst closely allied, do articulate different rights (see Committee on the Rights of the Child General Comment No 12 *The Right of the Child to be Heard* CRC/C/GC12, para 68). Art 13 relates to the child's right to hold and express opinions and not to be restricted therein and to seek and receive information through any media (Committee on the Rights of the Child General Comment No 12 *The Right of the Child to be Heard* CRC/C/GC12, para 81). Art 12 relates to the right to express views specifically about matters which affect the child and the right to be involved in actions and decisions that impact on his or her life.

'the right to freedom of expression' (Art 13(1)) [RCLP paras 11.12–11.18]—Whilst the freedom to hold opinions is a condition precedent of the right freedom of expression [RCLP para 11.6] Art (13)(1) omits the words contained in Art 19 of the International Covenant on Civil and Political Rights that state 'everyone shall have the right to hold opinions without interference'. It is suggestion however that the freedom to hold opinions must be implicit in Art 13 [RCLP para 11.12] and the UN Committee on the Rights of the Child considers the child's freedom to hold opinions in its Concluding Observations reports (see H Thorgeirdóttir *Article 13—The Right to Freedom of Expression* in A Alen, J Vande Lanotte, E Verhellen, E Berghams and M Verheyde (eds) *A Commentary on the United Nations Conventions on the Rights of the Child* (2006, Martinus Nijhoff), p 22).

'freedom to seek, receive and impart information and ideas' (Art 13(1)) [RCLP paras 11.19–11.20]—Access to information is an essential component of the child's right to freedom of expression, being the necessary ingredient for the formation of opinion. There will be categories of information it is not in the child's best interests to receive having regard to the restrictions on the child's freedom to seek and receive information set out in Art 13(2). UNCRC jurisprudence indicates that States Parties have a positive obligation to protect children from harmful material whilst the child is exercising his or her right to seek and receive information (see H Thorgeirdóttir *Article 13—The Right to Freedom of Expression* in A Alen, J Vande Lanotte, E Verhellen, E Berghams and M Verheyde (eds) *A Commentary on the United Nations Conventions on the Rights of the Child* (2006, Martinus Nijhoff), p 33). See also Arts 17, 24(2)(e), 9(4) and 42 below and [RCLP paras 11.21–11.33].

'regardless of frontiers' (Art 13(1)) [RCLP para 11.37]—The child's right to freedom of expression is not prescribed by the confines of any political or territorial entity (see also Art 19(2) of the International Covenant on Civil and Political Rights).

'the child's choice' (Art 13(1)) [RCLP para 11.38]—The child may choose the media through which he or she expresses themselves.

'The exercise of this right may subject to certain restrictions' (Art 13(2))—The rights enshrined in Art 13(1) are neither absolute nor non-derogable ([RCLP para 11.39–11.40]). The restrictions that can be legitimately placed on the child's right to freedom of expression under Art 13 are limited to those set out in Art 13(2) (see below under **'respect of the rights or reputations of others'** and **'protection of national security or of public order (ordre public), or of public health or morals'**). Art 13 contains no restrictions based on the authority, rights or responsibilities of parents or legal guardians (see UN Docs E/CN 4/1986/39, p 17; E/CN 4/1987/25, pp 26–27; E/CN 4/1988/28, pp 9–13). However, the child's right to freedom of expression must be read with Art 3 concerning the child's best interests, Art 5 concerning the child's evolving capacity and Art 12 concerning the child's right to participate and an appropriate balance must be struck between parental guidance and the exercise of the child's right to freedom of expression on his or her own behalf in accordance with his or her evolving capacity ([**RCLP paras 11.15** and **11.45**] and see Committee on the Rights of the Child, Report of the Fifth Session (1994) CRC/C/24, Annex V, p 63 and Committee on the Rights of the Child General Comment No 12 *The Right of the Child to be Heard* CRC/C/GC12, para 80). Note that the terms of Art 13(2) are narrower than the restrictions on the right to freedom of expression enshrined in Art 10(2) of the ECHR (see [**RCLP para 11.61**]). See also Art 19(3) of the International Covenant on Civil and Political Rights [**RCLP para 11.40**].

'**only be such as are provided by law and are necessary**' (Art 13(2)) [**RCLP para 11.41**]—Only those narrow restrictions stipulated by Art 13(2) may be placed on the child's right to freedom of expression. The phrase 'provided by law and are necessary' is conjunctive not disjunctive and accordingly a restriction must be both proscribed by law *and* necessary in order to come within the ambit of Art 13(2). Any restriction must be set out in legislation (P Newell and R Hodgkin *Implementation Handbook for the Convention on the Rights of the Child* (2008, 3rd edn, UNICEF), p 180). Any restriction must be applied only for the purpose for which it is prescribed and must be directed related to and proportionate to the specific need on which it is predicated (Human Rights Committee General Comment No 10 HRI/GEN/1/Rev 8, p 172, para 4). The interplay between the principle of freedom of expression and the restrictions permissible under Art 13(2) determine the scope of the child's right to freedom of expression (see Human Rights Committee General Comment No 10 HRI/GEN/1/Rev 8, p 171, para 3).

'**respect of the rights or reputations of others**' (Art 13(2)) [**RCLP para 11.43**]—it is likely that the term 'rights ... of others' will be interpreted to mean rights enshrined in the UNCRC, and possibly in other human rights instruments.

'**protection of national security or of public order (ordre public), or of public health or morals**' (Art 13(2)) [**RCLP para 11.44**]—The term public morals describes principles which the majority of citizens accept as guidelines for behaviour even though those principles may not constitute legally enforceable laws (see *Reno v American Civil Liberties Union* 521 US 844 (1997), US Sup Ct; *Ashcroft v ACLU* 535 US 564 (2002), US Sup Ct; *Curtis v Minister of Safety* (1996) BHRC 541, Const Ct of South Africa and *De Reuck v DPP* [2004] 4 LRC 72, Const Ct of South Africa). Restrictions on the child's right to freedom of expression must be based on moral principles not deriving from a single social, philosophical and religious tradition (see Human Rights Committee General Comment No 22 *Art 18 (Freedom of Thought, Conscience and Religion)* HRI/GEN/1/Rev 8, p 196, para 8 and *A, B and C v Ireland* (2010) Application No 25579/05, para 222).

Article 14

1. States Parties shall respect the right of the child to freedom of thought, conscience and religion.

2. States Parties shall respect the rights and duties of the parents and, when applicable, legal guardians, to provide direction to the child in the exercise of his or her right in a manner consistent with the evolving capacities of the child.

3. Freedom to manifest one's religion or beliefs may be subject only to such limitations as are prescribed by law and are necessary to protect public safety, order, health or morals, or the fundamental rights and freedoms of others.

Right to freedom of thought, conscience and religion (Art 14)—Whilst Art 14 requires States Parties to respect the child's right to freedom of thought, conscience and religion it omits many of the additional elements of the right enshrined in Art 18 of the Universal Declaration of Human Rights [**RCLP para 3.18**]. The right to freedom of religion should accommodate a wide range of beliefs, diversity of tastes and pursuits, customs and codes of conduct (*R v Big M Drug Mart* [1985] 1 SCR 295, [**RCLP para 10.1**]). Religious beliefs and convictions are part of the humanity of every individual (*R (Williamson) v Secretary of State for Education and Employment* [2005] UKHL 15, [2005] 2 AC 246 [**RCLP para 10.2**]). The child's right to participate under Art 12 closely allied with the child's right to freedom of thought, conscience and religion (see *Christian Education South Africa v Minister of Education* (2000) 9 BHRC 53 and *Kwazulu-Natal v Pillay* [2007] ZACC 21 (Const Ct South Africa), [**RCLP para 6.2**]). Art 2(1) of the UNCRC requires States parties to respect and ensure the rights set forth in the UNCRC without discrimination of any kind irrespective of, *inter alia*, the child's religion or the religion or beliefs of his or her parents [**RCLP paras 10.17 and 10.30**] (see also Art 5(3) of the Declaration on the Elimination of All Forms of Intolerance and Discrimination Based on Religion or Belief). A child should not be discriminated against on the grounds that he or she practices a religion that is not the 'State' religion or does not have a religious belief (Human Rights Committee General Comment No 22 *Article 18 (Freedom of Thought, Conscience and Religion)* HRI/GEN/1/Rev 8, p 196, para 9).

Best interests and freedom of thought, conscience and religion [**RCLP para 10.12**]—The child's right to freedom of thought, conscience and religion must be interpreted in accordance with the best interests of the child in accordance with Art 3(1) of the UNCRC (see *P v S* 108 DLR (4th) 287 at 317 and *Prince v Massachusetts* (1944) 321 US 158 in the context of the conflict between parental religious beliefs and the best interests of the child).

Evolving capacity and freedom of thought, conscience and religion [RCLP paras 10.13–10.15]—The concept of evolving capacity under Art 5 of the UNCRC is of central importance to the implementation of the child's right to freedom of thought, conscience and religion. As a child's capacity evolves over time the child's facility to understand, appreciate and engage rationally with competing ideas and beliefs will also evolve (see *Prince v Massachusetts* (1944) 321 US 158, *Christian Education South Africa v Minister of Education* (2000) 9 BHRC 53, *Kwazulu-Natal v Pillay* [2007] ZACC 21 (Const Ct South Africa) and the dissenting judgment of Justice Douglas in *Wisconsin v Yoder* (1972) 406 US 205). See also below **Parental direction and evolving capacity.**

'freedom' (Art 14(1)) [RCLP para 10.9]—The concept of freedom is central to the exercise of the right to freedom of thought, conscience and religion (see *Church of New Faith v Comr for Pay-Roll Tax* (1982) 154 CLR 120 (High Court of Australia) and *R v Big M Drug Mart* [1985] 1 SCR 295). The concept of 'freedom' necessarily implies the absence of coercion (*R v Big M Drug Mart* [1985] 1 SCR 295, **[RCLP para 10.10]**). Art 18(2) of the ICCPR provides that 'No one shall be subject to coercion which would impair his freedom to have or to adopt a religion or belief of his choice' (see also Art 1(2) of the Declaration on the Elimination of All Forms of Intolerance and Discrimination Based on Religion or Belief). The freedom of girls to practice religion should not be constrained by rules requiring permission from third parties or by interference from fathers, husbands, brothers or others (Committee on Economic, Social and Cultural Rights General Comment No 28 *Article 3 (The Equality of Rights between Men and Women)* HRI/GEN/Rev 8, p 222, para 21).

'thought, conscience and religion' (Art 14(1)) [RCLP paras 10.7–10.8]—The UNCRC does not attempt definitions of 'thought', 'conscience' or 'religion' (for judicial attempts to define 'religion' see *Malnak v Yogi* (1979) 592 F 2d 197 (US Court of Appeals, Third Circuit); *Church of New Faith v Comr for Pay-Roll Tax* (1982) 154 CLR 120 (High Court of Australia); and *Christian Education South Africa v Minister of Education* (2000) 9 BHRC 53). The Human Rights Committee has stated that religious beliefs may the theistic or non-theistic beliefs, whether or not traditional or institutional in character, with the concept of religion and belief being broadly construed (Human Rights Committee General Comment No 22 *Article 18 (Freedom of Thought, Conscience and Religion)* HRI/GEN/1/Rev 8, p 195, para 2). The child's freedom of thought is closely linked to the child's right to participate under Art 12, the child's freedom to seek, receive and impart information and ideas of all kinds under Art 13, the child's right to access to appropriate information under Art 17 and the child's right to education under Arts 28 and 29. The restrictions set out in Art 14(3) do not apply to the child's thoughts or conscience and, accordingly, no child can be compelled to reveal his or her thoughts or conscience (Human Rights Committee General Comment No 22 *Article 18 (Freedom of Thought, Conscience and Religion)* HRI/GEN/1/Rev 8, p 195, para 3) **[RCLP para 10.20–10.21]**.

Ambit of the child's right to freedom of religion [RCLP paras 10.23–10.24]—The child's right to freedom of religion is circumscribed only by the provisions of Art 14(2) concerning parental direction and Art 14(3) concerning manifestation of religious belief (see below). The child's right to freedom of religion will protect theistic, non-theistic and atheistic beliefs, whether or not traditional or institutional in character, as well as the child's right not to profess any religion or belief, whether in terms of religion or belief more broadly construed (Human Rights Committee General Comment No 22 *Article 18 (Freedom of Thought, Conscience and Religion)* HRI/GEN/1/Rev 8, p 195, para 2). Art 14 and Art 16 operate to ensure that no child can be compelled to reveal his or her adherence to a particular religion or belief. Art 14 omits the express right to choice of religion enshrined in the ICCPR Art 18(1). It is however arguable that the right of the child to choice of religion is implied in Art 14(1) **[RCLP paras 10.26–10.28]** as is the right to change religions or abandon religious belief **[RCLP para 10.29]**. The interpretation by the Human Rights Committee of Art 18 of the ICCPR as it relates to the concept of conscientious objection to military service suggests that it is implicit in Art 14(1) that an obligation to use lethal force will conflict with the child's freedom of conscience and the right to manifest his or her religious belief where the child objects to military service (**[RCLP para 10.59—10.60]** and see the Human Rights Committee General Comment No 22 *Article 18 (Freedom of Thought, Conscience and Religion)* HRI/GEN/1/Rev 8, p 198, para 11). Art 14(1) will apply to children deprived of their liberty (**[RCLP para 10.61]** and see the UN Rules for the Protection of Juveniles Deprived of their Liberty r 48).

Child's right to freedom of religion and education—The child's right to freedom of thought, conscience and religion will continue to apply within the context of the child's education and in particular the implantation of the child's right to the development of his or her personality, talents and mental and physical abilities under Art 29(1)(a) (**[RCLP para 10.53]** and see Committee on the Rights of the Child General Comment No 1 *The Aims of Education* CRC/GC/2001/1, para 8). A child may choose not to undergo religious education where sufficiently mature to make the choice (**[RCLP para 10.55]** and see Cyprus CRC/C/SR.1172 (A996), para 29). A child should not require the consent of his or her parents where he or she is of sufficient age and understanding to choose to participate or not to participate in religious education (**[RCLP para 10.55]** and see Poland CRC/C/15/Add 194 (2002) para 32). A child should not be marginalised if they choose to abstain from religious education (**[RCLP para 10.55]** and see Italy CRC/C/Add 198, paras 29 and 30) and must be able to obtain dispensation from compulsory religious education ([**RCLP para 10.55**] and see Ireland CRC/C/SR.1182 (2006) para 9) and must be able to choose an alternative subject ([**RCLP para 10.55**] and see Poland CRC/C/15/Add 194 (2002) para 32). The UN Human Rights Committee has expressed the view that provision should be made for non-discriminatory exemptions or alternatives which will accommodate the wishes and feelings of parents and guardians ([RCLP **para 10.56**] and see Human Rights Committee General Comment No 22 *Article 18 (Freedom of Thought, Conscience and Religion)* HRI/GEN/1/Rev 8, p 196, para 6. See also *Hartikainen v Finland* R 9/40 HRC 36, 147, *Lerwig v Norway* (2003) Communication 1155/2003 and see Art 13(3) of the CESCR and Committee on Economic, Social and Cultural Rights General Comment No 13 *The Right to Education* HRI/GEN/1/Rev 8, p 71). Any prohibition on the wearing of religious symbols is deprecated, including the wearing of headscarfs (see the Human Rights Committee General Comment No 28 *Article 3 (The Equality of Rights Between Men and Women)* HRI/GEN/1/Rev 8, para 13, *Hudoyberganova v Uzbekistan* Communication (2005) 931/2000 and *Multani v Commission Scolaire Marguerite-Bourgeoys* (2006) SCC 6 (CanLII)).

Freedom of religion for minority ethnic, religious or linguistic children and indigenous children [RCLP **paras 10.31–10.34**]—Art 30 of the UNCRC enshrines the right of a child who belongs to a minority ethnic, religious or linguistic community or indigenous population to profess and practice his or her own religion in community with other members of his or her group (see also Art 27 of the ICCPR, General Comment No 23 *Article 27 (Rights of Minorities)* HRI/GEN/Rev 8, p 197 at 198–199 and *Wisconsin v Yoder* (1972) 406 US 205).

Parental direction and evolving capacity (Art 14(2)) [**RCLP paras 10.35–10.38**]—Art 14(2) requires States parties to respect the rights of parents to provide 'direction' to the child in matters of religion subject to the evolving capacity of the child (see '**Evolving capacity and freedom of thought, conscience and religion**' above. See also Art 9(2) of the African Charter on the Rights and Welfare of the Child which, by contrast to Art 14(2) places a *duty* on parents to provide guidance and direction to the child in the exercise of his or her right to freedom of thought, conscience and religion [**RCLP para 10.105**]). The extent of this qualified parental direction will be dependent on the age, development and understanding of the child. Direction and guidance provided by parents should be 'child centred' and achieved through dialogue (Committee on the Rights of the Child General Comment No 7 *Implementing Child Rights in Early Childhood* CRC/C/GC/7, para 17) and should not go beyond that which is necessary to provide direction and guidance. It is the child and not the parent who exercises the right to freedom of thought, conscience and religion (see Norway CRC/C/SR.150 (1994) at 42, The Holy See CRC/C/SR.256 (1995) at 10 and Turkey CRC/C/SR.701 (2001) at 25). In principle, the child's right to freedom of thought, conscience and religion is non derogable (see Bangladesh CRC/C/SR.380 (1997) at 19). Note that the position of the child in relation to parental direction concerning matters of conscience and religion is significantly stronger than the position of the child concerning parental direction as to the provision of religious education [**RCLP paras 10.39–10.43**] (see Universal Declaration of Human Rights Art 26(3), Covenant on Civil and Political Rights Art 18(4), Covenant on Economic, Social and Cultural Rights Art 13(3), the Declaration of Elimination of All Forms of Intolerance and Discrimination Based on Religion or Belief Art 5(2) and Human Rights Committee General Comment No 22 *Article 18 (Freedom of Thought, Conscience and Religion)* HRI/GEN/1/Rev 8, p 196, para 6).

Restriction on manifestation of religion or beliefs (Art 14(3)) [**RCLP paras 10.45**]—Art 14(3) limits the child's right to manifest his or her religion or belief on the grounds of public safety, order, health or morals, or the fundamental rights and freedoms of others (see also Art 5(5) of the Declaration on the Elimination of Religious Intolerance and Discrimination based on Religious Belief). In contrast to Art 18(1) of the ICCPR Art 14(1) of the UNCRC does not contain an express right of the child to manifest his religion or belief in worship, observance, practice or teaching. However, Art 14(3) implies such a right in that Art 14(3) seeks to limit the same. Art 14(3) concerns only the freedom to manifest religion or belief and accordingly does not limit in anyway the child's thoughts or moral conscience (UN Doc A/4625, para 48 and see Human Rights Committee General Comment No 22 *Article 18 (Freedom of Thought, Conscience and Religion)* HRI/GEN/1/Rev 8). For the justification for restricting the manifestation of religion and belief see *Christian Education South Africa v Minister of Education* (2000) 9 BHRC 53. The word 'manifest' in Art 14(3) is not defined by the UNCRC [RCLP para 10.47] but see Human Rights Committee General Comment No 22 *Article 18 (Freedom of Thought, Conscience and Religion)* HRI/GEN/1/Rev 8, p 195, para 4 and the decisions of the Human Rights Committee in *Boodoo v Trinidad and Tobago* (2002) Communication 721/1997 and *Sister Immaculate Joseph and 80 Teaching Sisters of the Holy Cross of the Third Order of St Francis in Mensingen of Sri Lanka* (2005) Communication 1249/2004. The limitations prescribed by Art 14(3) are to be interpreted strictly, must be applied only for the purposes for which they are prescribed, must be directly related and proportionate to the specific need on which they are predicated and must not be applied in a discriminatory manner (Human Rights Committee General Comment No 22 *Article 18 (Freedom of Thought, Conscience and Religion)* HRI/GEN/1/Rev 8, p 196, paras 3 and 8).

Article 15

1. States Parties recognize the rights of the child to freedom of association and to freedom of peaceful assembly.

2. No restrictions may be placed on the exercise of these rights other than those imposed in conformity with the law and which are necessary in a democratic society in the interests of national security or public safety, public order (ordre public), the protection of public health or morals or the protection of the rights and freedoms of others.

Right to freedom of association and to freedom of peaceful assembly (Art 15)—Freedom of association is the freedom to combine together for the pursuit of common purposes of the advancement of a common cause (*Re Public Service Employee Relations Act* [1987] 1 SCR. 313 (Sup Ct of Canada) and see *The 'Street Children Case' (Villagrán Morales et al)* Judgment of November 19, 1999 Series C No 63). Freedom of association and freedom of peaceful assembly constitutes one of the foundations of a democratic society (*Rassemblement Jurrasien Unité v Switzerland* 17 DR 93 (1979) and *Ziliberberg v Moldova* (2004) Application No 61821/00 (unreported)) [RCLP para 12.1]. The child's Art 15 right to freedom of association and to freedom of peaceful assembly is closely allied to the child's right to freedom of expressed (*NAACP v Patterson* 357 US 449 (1958) and *Committee of the Commonwealth of Canada v Canada* (1991) 77 DLR (4th) 385 (Sup Ct of Canada)) [RCLP para 12.2], the child's right participate under Art 12 [RCLP para 6.2] and may also be engaged with Art 31(2) which enshrines the child's right to participate fully in cultural and artistic life [RCLP para 5.199]. See also Art 20 of the Universal Declaration of Human Rights, Art 21 and Art 22 of the ICCPR, Art 8 of the ICESCR and Art 29(b)(i) of the Convention on the Rights of Persons with Disabilities. In contrast to Art 21 and Art 22 of the ICCPR, Art 15 of the UNCRC contains no provision for the derogation of the right to freedom of association or the right to freedom of peaceful assembly [RCLP para 12.11].

Right to freedom of association and to freedom of peaceful assembly and evolving capacity—The right to freedom of association and freedom of peaceful assembly will be exercised in accordance with the child's best interest (Art 3(1)) [RCLP Para 12.9].

Right to freedom of association and to freedom of peaceful assembly and evolving capacity—The child's freedom of association and freedom of peaceful assembly will be exercised commensurate with the child's age, maturity and development (UN Doc E/CN 4/1988/28, para 48) [RCLP para 12.9]. Art 15(1) will not support limitations on the child's freedom of association based on parental consent (Japan CRC/C/15/Add 231, paras 29 and 30).

'recognise' (Art 15(1))—Art 15(1) of the UNCRC recognises the right of the child to freedom of association and to freedom of peaceful assembly rather than granting the right itself (see UN Doc A/2929 Chapter VI, para 140) [RCLP para 12.13]. The source of the child's right to freedom of association and freedom of peaceful assembly lies in Art 20 of the Universal Declaration of Human Rights, which stipulates that the right applies to 'everyone' [RCLP para 12.1].

'freedom of association' (Art 15(1))—Freedom of association has been held to mean the freedom to enter into consensual arrangements to promote the common-interest objectives of the associating group and that those objects may be any of many (*Collymore v Attorney-General* [1970] AC 538 Privy Council approving the decision of the Trinidad and Tobago Court of Appeal *Collymore v Attorney-General* (1967) 12 WIR 5) [RCLP para 12.6]. The UNCRC does not repeat the words of Art 20(2) of the Universal Declaration of Human Rights, namely that 'No one may be compelled to belong to an association'. It has however been argued that the terms of Art 15(1) imply the right to join *and* leave associations (P Newell and R Hodgkin *Implementation Handbook for the Convention on the Rights of the Child* (2008, 3rd edn, UNICEF), p 198) [RCLP para 12.14]. Restrictions on children joining or establishing political organisations may breach Art 15(1) (see Japan CRC/C/15/Add 231, paras 29 and 30 and Costa Rica CRC/C/15/Add 266, paras 23 and 24).

'peaceful assembly' (Art 15(1))—The word 'peaceful' relates to the nature of the assembly, not its object or purpose [RCLP para 12.8].

Restrictions on the child's right to freedom of association and freedom of peaceful assembly (Art 15(2)) [RCLP paras 12.15–12.22]—The only restrictions which may be placed on the child's rights under Art 15(1) are those in imposed in conformity with the law and which are necessary in a democratic society in the interests of national security or public safety, public order (ordre public), the protection of public health or morals or the protection of the rights and freedoms of others [RCLP para 12.15]. The interplay between the rights enshrined in Art 15(1) and the limitations imposed by Art 15(2) that will determine the scope of the child's right to freedom of association and to freedom of peaceful assembly (see the Human Rights Committee General Comment No 10 1983 HRI/GEN/1/Rev, p 171, para 3) [RCLP para 12.17]. The limitations prescribed by Art 15(2) are to be interpreted strictly, must be applied only for the purposes for which they are prescribed, must be directly related and proportionate to the specific need on which they are predicated (Human Rights Committee General Comment No 10 *Article 19 (Freedom of Opinion)* HRI/GEN/Rev 8, p 127, para 4). The words 'in conformity with the law' suggest that the restrictions on the child's right to freedom of association and freedom of peaceful assembly must be lawful by reference to existing laws but that the restrictions themselves need not be embodied in the substantive law [RCLP para 12.17].

Article 16

1. No child shall be subjected to arbitrary or unlawful interference with his or her privacy, family, home or correspondence, nor to unlawful attacks on his or her honour and reputation.

2. The child has the right to the protection of the law against such interference or attacks.

Child's right to respect for family (Art 16)—Whilst Art 16(1) uses the word 'family' in preference to 'family life' or 'family environment' Art 16(1) will encompass the child's family life and environment as well as the bare constitution of that family **[RCLP para 8.70]**. The protection provided by Art 16(1) will extend to siblings, grandparents and other's important to the child (P Newell and R Hodgkin *Implementation Handbook for the Convention on the Rights of the Child* (2008, 3rd edn, UNICEF), p 210).

Child's right to respect for privacy (Art 16)—For definitions of the concept of privacy see *The Right to Privacy,* Warren and Brandeis (1890) 4 Harv L Rev 193, *Bernstein v Bester* (1996) (4) BCLR 449, (1996) (2) SA 751 (CC) and *R (Countryside Alliance) v A-G* [2007] UKHL 52, [2008] 1 AC 719 **[RCLP paras 9.1–9.4]**. The child's right to privacy will be relevant to the right of the child to the preservation of his or her identity **[RCLP para 7.52]**. The child's right to respect of privacy must be protected in all situations ((P Newell and R Hodgkin *Implementation Handbook for the Convention on the Rights of the Child* (2008, 3rd edn, UNICEF), p 203) **[RCLP para 9.6]**. The child's right to privacy will encompass the child's religious beliefs (Manual on Human Rights Reporting HR/PUB/91/1 (Rev 1), p 436) **[RCLP para 10.23]**. Public authorities should only be able to call for information on an individual where the same is essential in the interests of society (Human Rights Committee General Comment No 16 *Article 17 (Right to Privacy)* HRI/GEN/1/Rev 8, p 181, para 7) **[RCLP para 9.17]**. Effective protection of the right to privacy under Art 16 will require that the child knows of the existence of the information stored about him or her, knows why such information is stored and by whom it is held, has access to such records and is able to challenge, if necessary, there content (P Newell and R Hodgkin *Implementation Handbook for the Convention on the Rights of the Child* (2008, 3rd edn, UNICEF), p 209 and see UN Rules for the Protection of Juveniles Deprived of their Liberty) **[RCLP para 9.18]**).

Privacy of correspondence (Art 16(1))—Art 16(1) protects a child's correspondence from arbitrary or unlawful interference **[RCLP para 9.19]**. Any arrangement permitting interference with a child's correspondence (which will encompass both letters and more modern forms of communication) must be set out in law and must not be arbitrary, must be compatible with the other provisions of the UNCRC and must be reasonable in the particular circumstances (see Human Rights Committee General Comment No 16 *Article 17 (Right to Privacy)* HRI/GEN/1/Rev 8, p 181, para 8 and P Newell and R Hodgkin *Implementation Handbook for the Convention on the Rights of the Child* (2008, 3rd edn, UNICEF), p 210). This will include correspondence received pursuant to Art 37(c) **[RCLP para 9.20]**.

'home' (Art 16(1))—The child's right not to be subject to arbitrary or unlawful interference with his or her home is an important element in defining the right to adequate housing under Art 27(3) of the UNCRC (see Committee on the Rights of the Child, Report of the Seventh Session, January 1996, CRC/C/50, para 9) **[RCLP para 5.160]**. Protection of the home under Art 16(1) will include prohibition of interference with the amenities provided by the home (see *Hunter and others v Canary Wharf Ltd; Hunter and others v London Docklands Corporation* [1997] AC 655, [1997] 2 All ER 426, [1997] 2 FLR 342).

'arbitrary' (Art 16(1))—The concept of arbitrariness in Art 16(1) ensures that even interference with the child's right to privacy that is provided for by law must accord with the provisions, aims and objectives of the UNCRC and should in any event be reasonable in the particular circumstances (see Human Rights Committee General Comment No 17 *Right to Privacy* HRI/GEN/1/Rev 8, p 181, para 4) **[RCLP para 9.7]**.

'unlawful' (Art 16(1))—By reference to the interpretation of Art 17 of the ICCPR the term 'unlawful in Art 16(1) is likely to mean that there can be no interference in the child's right to privacy save in accordance with the law, which law must itself comply with the provisions, aims and objectives of the UNCRC (see Human Rights Committee General Comment No 17 *Right to Privacy* HRI/GEN/1/Rev 8, p 181) **[RCLP para 9.8]**. Within the context of the protection of the family, in relation to Art 17 of the ICCPR the Human Rights Committee has interpreted the word 'unlawful' to imply that State interference or interference by legal or natural persons with the family and family life may only be justified on the basis of law, which should not be arbitrary in operation, and reasonable in the particular circumstances (*Shirin Aumeeruddy-Cziffa and 19 other Mauritanian Women v Mauritius Corporation* No R.9/35 (2 May 1978), UN Doc Supp No 40 (A/36/40) at 134 (1981)) **[RCLP para 8.71]**. There is a positive duty on the State to prevent arbitrary or unlawful interference (*Shirin Aumeeruddy-Cziffa and 19 other Mauritanian Women v Mauritius Corporation* No R.9/35 (2 May 1978), UN Doc Supp No 40 (A/36/40) at 134 (1981)) **[RCLP para 8.71]**. The interpretation of the word 'unlawful' is likely to be the same in respect of Art 16(1) as, save for the addition of the word 'child' the wording of Art 16(1) is identical to that of Art 17 of the ICCPR (P Newell and R Hodgkin *Implementation Handbook for the Convention on the Rights of the Child* (2008, 3rd edn, UNICEF), p 210) **[RCLP para 8.72]**.

'**interference**' (Art 16(1)—Within the context of Art 17 of the ICCPR the Human Rights Committee has interpreted the word 'interference' is considered to encompass both State interference and interference by legal or natural persons (see Human Rights Committee General Comment No 17 *Right to Privacy* HRI/GEN/1/Rev 8, p 181) **[RCLP para 9.9]**.

The child's right to privacy and court proceedings [RCLP paras 9.10–9.15]—Art 40(2)(b)(vii) of the UNCRC requires that a child accused of having infringed the penal law should have his or her privacy respected at all stages of the proceedings. The provisions of Art 16 will also apply with full effect in this context (Committee on the Rights of the Child General Comment No 10 *Children's Rights in Juvenile Justice* CRC/C/GC/10, para 64) **[RCLP para 9.11]**. See also r 8.1 of the UN Standard Minimum Rules for the Administration of Juvenile Justice **[RCLP para 9.12]** and Art 14(1) of the ICCPR **[RCLP para 9.13]**. Reading Art 16(1) with Art 3(1) of the UNCRC suggests a presumption that proceedings in respect of the separation of children governed by Art 9 of the UNCRC should be held in private (P Newell and R Hodgkin *Implementation Handbook for the Convention on the Rights of the Child* (2008, 3rd edn, UNICEF), p 236 and see Art 14(1) of the ICCPR and Art 3(2) of the UN Standard Minimum Rules of Juvenile Justice (the 'Beijing Rules')) **[RCLP para 8.92]**. Art 40(2)(b)(vii) should also apply to family proceedings and where children are the victims of violence (Committee on the Rights of the Child *Report of the Eleventh Session* (1996) CRC/C/50, Annex IX, p 80 and P Newell and R Hodgkin *Implementation Handbook for the Convention on the Rights of the Child* (2008, 3rd edn, UNICEF), p 203) **[RCLP para 9.14]**. However, they will not extend to children indirectly involved in the proceedings, for example as witnesses (see *Re S (A Child) (Identification: Restriction on Publication)* [2004] UKHL, [2004] 4 All ER 683, para 26) **[RCLP para 16.57]**. See also the UN Standard Minimum Rules for the Administration of Juvenile Justice r 3(2) which extends the scope of those rules to cover care and welfare proceedings concerning children **[RCLP para 9.14]**. Professionals concerned with the child in the context of proceedings will be under a duty to protect the privacy of the child (see Committee on the Rights of the Child General Comment No 10 *Children's Rights in Juvenile Justice* CRC/C/GC/10, para 66) **[RCLP para 9.15]**. Effective procedures for reporting physical or mental violence, injury or abuse, neglect or negligent treatment, maltreatment or exploitation should take account of the child's right to privacy under Art 16 **[RCLP para 15.39]**. Exceptions to the principle that hearings in relation to children who in conflict with the law should be conducted in private should be very limited and clearly stated in law (Committee on the Rights of the Child General Comment No 10 *Children's Rights in Juvenile Justice* CRC/C/GC/10, para 66) **[RCLP para 9.13]**.

Confidentiality of advice and counselling—The effective counselling of a child in respect of health matters and the obtaining of informed consent requires privacy and confidentiality (see the Committee on the Rights of the Child General Comment No 4 *Adolescent Health and Development in the Context of the Convention on the Rights of the Child* CRC/GC/2003/4, para 7) **[RCLP para 9.16]**.

Article 17

States Parties recognize the important function performed by the mass media and shall ensure that the child has access to information and material from a diversity of national and international sources, especially those aimed at the promotion of his or her social, spiritual and moral well-being and physical and mental health. To this end, States Parties shall:

(a)   Encourage the mass media to disseminate information and material of social and cultural benefit to the child and in accordance with the spirit of article 29;

(b)   Encourage international co-operation in the production, exchange and dissemination of such information and material from a diversity of cultural, national and international sources;

(c)   Encourage the production and dissemination of children's books;

(d)   Encourage the mass media to have particular regard to the linguistic needs of the child who belongs to a minority group or who is indigenous;

(e)   Encourage the development of appropriate guidelines for the protection of the child from information and material injurious to his or her well-being, bearing in mind the provisions of articles 13 and 18.

Right to access to information (Art 17)—Art 17 is particularly focused on the role of the mass media in relation to children's rights (see the recommendations arising out of the General Day of Discussion 1996, Committee on the Rights of the Child *Report of the Thirteenth Session* CRC/C/57, paras 242 et seq, the Committee on the Rights of the Child *Report of the Eleventh Session* January 1996 CRC/C/50, Annex IX, pp 80–83 and the Committee on the Rights of the Child General Comment No 7 CRC/C/GC/7/Rev 1, para 35) [RCLP paras 11.22, 11.23–24]. See also the UN Guidelines for the Prevention of Juvenile Delinquency paras 40–44 [RCLP para 11.25]. The media should respect and promote the participatory rights of children (P Newell and R Hodgkin *Implementation Handbook for the Convention on the Rights of the Child* (2008, 3rd edn, UNICEF), p 217) [RCLP par 11.24]. Art 17 also contains a general obligation on States parties to ensure that the child has access to information and material from diverse sources (P Newell and R Hodgkin *Implementation Handbook for the Convention on the Rights of the Child* (2008, 3rd edn, UNICEF), p 217 and see the UN Rules for the Protection of Juveniles Deprived of their Liberty r 62).

Right to access to information and best interests—The European Court of Justice has referred to Art 17 in the context of considering the relationship between the mass media and the welfare of the child (*Dynamic Medien Ventriebs GmBH v Avides Media AG* (Case C-244/06) [2008] All ER (D) 198 (Feb)) [RCLP para 11.79].

Right to access to information and the child's right to freedom of thought, conscience and religion—The practical implementation of the right to freedom of thought, conscience and religion is related to the child's right to access appropriate information under Art 17 [RCLP para 10.20].

'promotion of his or her social, spiritual and moral well-being and physical and mental health' (Art 17)—The promotion of these aspects of the child's life is the overall aim of the strategies enumerated at Art 17(a) to 17(e) (P Newell and R Hodgkin *Implementation Handbook for the Convention on the Rights of the Child* (2008, 3rd edn, UNICEF), p 220) [RCLP para 11.25].

'in accordance with the spirit of article 29' (Art 17(a))—The activities of the media should not undermine the requirements of Art 29 of the UNCRC (Committee on the Rights of the Child General Comment No 1 *The Aims of Education* CRC/GC/2001/1, para 21) [RCLP para 11.26].

'international co-operation' (Art 17(b))—Art 17(b) emphasises the diversity of information that should be available to the child (P Newell and R Hodgkin *Implementation Handbook for the Convention on the Rights of the Child* (2008, 3rd edn, UNICEF), p 223) [RCLP para 11.27].

'linguistic needs of children of minority and indigenous groups' (Art 17(d))—Art 17(d) should be read with Arts 29(d) and 30 of the UNCRC [RCLP para 11.29]. For the position in respect of children with disabilities see Committee on the Rights of the Child General Comment No 9 *The Rights of Children with Disabilities* CRC/C/GC/9, para 37, Art 8(2)(c) of the Convention on the Rights of Persons with Disabilities and the UN Standard Rules on the Equalisation of Opportunity for Persons with Disabilities r 9(3) [RCLP paras 11.29–11.31].

'appropriate guidelines' (Art 17(e))—Art 17(e) seeks to ensure that children are protected from the negative aspects of mass media (Committee on the Rights of the Child *Report of the 11th Session* January 1996, CRC/C/50, Annex IX, pp 80–81 and Committee on the Rights of the Child General Comment No 7 *Implementing Child Rights in Early Childhood* CRC/C/GC/7/Rev 1, para 35) [RCLP para 11.32]. The guidelines formulated must not interfere with the child's right to access information or with parental discretion within the ambit of Art 5 and Art 18 of the UNCRC (P Newell and R Hodgkin *Implementation Handbook for the Convention on the Rights of the Child* (2008, 3rd edn, UNICEF), p 225) [RCLP para 11.33].

Article 18

1. States Parties shall use their best efforts to ensure recognition of the principle that both parents have common responsibilities for the upbringing and development of the child. Parents or, as the case may be, legal guardians, have the primary responsibility for the upbringing and development of the child. The best interests of the child will be their basic concern.

2. For the purpose of guaranteeing and promoting the rights set forth in the present Convention, States Parties shall render appropriate assistance to parents and legal guardians in the performance of their child-rearing responsibilities and shall ensure the development of institutions, facilities and services for the care of children.

3. States Parties shall take all appropriate measures to ensure that children of working parents have the right to benefit from child-care services and facilities for which they are eligible.

Parental responsibility (Art 18)—Art 18(1), with Art 5, constitute statements in support of the primacy of parental responsibility over the responsibility of the State [**RCLP para 8.28**]. The wider provisions of the UNCRC must be read in light of the requirement in Art 18(1) that both parents have common responsibility for the upbringing and development of the child [**RCLP para 8.59**]. The legal relationship of parents to their child derives from their responsibility to act in the child's best interests rather than from an unimpeachable right over them (P Newell and R Hodgkin *Implementation Handbook for the Convention on the Rights of the Child* (2008, 3rd edn, UNICEF), p 76 and see Committee on the Rights of the Child General Comment No 7 *Implementing Child Rights in Early Childhood* HRI/GEN/1/Rev 8, para 18) [**RCLP para 8.28**]. Realising the rights of the child is in large measure dependent on the wellbeing and resources available to those with responsibility for the child's care (Committee on the Rights of the Child General Comment No 7 *Implementing Child Rights in Early Childhood* HRI/GEN/1/Rev 8, para 20) [**RCLP para 5.84**]. See also Art 27(2) of the UNCRC which requires that the parent(s) or others responsible for the child have the primary responsibility to secure, within their abilities and financial capacities, the conditions of living necessary for the child's development [**RCLP para 5.143**].

Parental responsibility and evolving capacity—The parental responsibility articulated in Art 18 must be viewed through the prism of evolving capacity as articulated by Art 5 (see *Polovchak v Meese* (1985) 774 F.2.d 731, the Committee on the Rights of the Child General Comment No 12 *Right to be Heard* CRC/C/GC/12, pp 18–19 and the Committee on the Rights of the Child General Comment No 4 *Adolescent Health and Development in the Context of the Convention on the Rights of the Child* HRI/GEN/1/Rev 8, p 377) [**RCLP paras 8.28–8.29**].

'The best interests of the child will be their basic concern'—Art 18(1) does not extend the application of the best interests principle in Art 3(1) to private individuals but rather is intended to address States which legislate in respect of parental responsibility so as to ensure that such legislation reflects the well established legal responsibility of parents to act in the best interest of their children (see P Newell and R Hodgkin *Implementation Handbook for the Convention on the Rights of the Child* (2008, 3rd edn, UNICEF), p 232) [**RCLP para 4.140**]. Art 18(1) must be read in light of the best interests principle in Art 3(1) [**RCLP para 8.60**].

'States Parties shall render appropriate assistance to parents and legal guardians' (Art 18(2))—The terms 'appropriate assistance' should be taken to mean assistance at a level which enables to the family to assume its responsibilities fully within the community (see the Declaration of Social Progress and Development 1969 A/RES/24/2542 Art 4) [**RCLP para 8.43**]. State intervention as distinct from State assistance should be a measure of last resort [**RCLP para 8.34**]. The assistance provided should cover all children and not just the very young (Committee on the Rights of the Child General Comment No 4 *Adolescent Health and Development in the Context of the Convention on the Rights of the Child* (2003) CRC/GC/2003/4, para 16) [**RCLP para 8.42**]. For a non-exhaustive list of measures see Committee on the Rights of the Child General Comment No 7 *Implementing Child Rights in Early Childhood* CRC/C/GC/7/Rev 1, para 20(c) and (d) and 29(a) and (b). See also Arts 3(2), 19(1), 23 and 27(3) [**RCLP para 8.41**].

'the right to benefit from child-care services and facilities' (Art 18(3))—The emphasis of Art 18(3) is on the provision of day care services for children (see the Committee on the Rights of the Child General Comment No 7 *Implementing Child Rights in Early Childhood* CRC/C/GC/7/Rev 1, para 31, the Maternity Protection Convention Revised 1951 (C103), the ILO Recommendation *Supplementing the Maternity Protection Convention* 2000 (No 191) and the ICESCR Art 7(a)) [**RCLP para 8.43**].

Article 19

1. States Parties shall take all appropriate legislative, administrative, social and educational measures to protect the child from all forms of physical or mental violence, injury or abuse, neglect or negligent treatment, maltreatment or exploitation, including sexual abuse, while in the care of parent(s), legal guardian(s) or any other person who has the care of the child.

2. Such protective measures should, as appropriate, include effective procedures for the establishment of social programmes to provide necessary support for the child and for those who have the care of the child, as well as for other forms of prevention and for identification, reporting, referral, investigation, treatment and follow-up of instances of child maltreatment described heretofore, and, as appropriate, for judicial involvement.

Protection from physical or mental violence, injury or abuse, neglect or negligent treatment, maltreatment or exploitation, including sexual abuse (Art 19)—Art 19 must be read in light of the positive obligations created by Art 6(1) of the UNCRC [**RCLP para 5.8**]. The ambit of Art 19 is much wider than that of the Art 37 protection from cruel, inhuman or degrading treatment (see P Newell and R Hodgkin *Implementation Handbook for the Convention on the Rights of the Child* (2008, 3rd edn, UNICEF), p 249) [**RCLP para 15.27**]. Reference should also be made to the Committee on the Rights of the Child General Comment No 13 *The Right of the Child to Freedom from All Forms of Violence* (see Chapter 28 below).

'physical ... violence, injury or abuse' (Art 19(1))—The meaning of physical violence, injury or abuse is largely self evident (see *World Report on Violence and Health* (2002) World Health Organisation, p 5) [**RCLP para 15.28**]. Art 19(1) leaves no room for legalised violence against children in the form of corporal punishment (Committee on the Rights of the Child General Comment No 8 *The Right of the Child to Protection from Corporal Punishment and Other Cruel or Degrading Forms of Punishment* CRC/C/GC/8, p 6, para 18). The Art 19(1) prohibition on physical violence, injury or abuse includes a positive obligation to protect children from self-harm, including suicide and attempted suicide (see P Newell and R Hodgkin *Implementation Handbook for the Convention on the Rights of the Child* (2008, 3rd edn, UNICEF), p 265) [**RCLP para 15.28**].

'violence, injury or abuse' (Art 19(1))—The term will include humiliation, harassment, verbal abuse, the effects of isolation and will include the witnessing of violence or ill treatment of another (see P Newell and R Hodgkin *Implementation Handbook for the Convention on the Rights of the Child* (2008, 3rd edn, UNICEF), p 256) [**RCLP para 15.29**].

'neglect or negligent treatment' (Art 19(1))—Neglect may be deliberate or the result of omission consequent upon family or community incapacity (see P Newell and R Hodgkin *Implementation Handbook for the Convention on the Rights of the Child* (2008, 3rd edn, UNICEF), p 257) [**RCLP para 15.30**].

'maltreatment or exploitation including sexual abuse' (Art 19(1))—Maltreatment is a catch all term that covers any other adverse treatment by parents, legal guardians or others with care of the child See P Newell and R Hodgkin *Implementation Handbook for the Convention on the Rights of the Child* (2008, 3rd edn, UNICEF), p 257) [**RCLP para 15.31**]. The child's right to protection from sexual abuse is enshrined in both Art 19(1) and in Art 34. The words 'while in the care of parent(s), legal guardian(s) or any other person who has the care of the child' indicate that Art 19(1) contemplates familial and institutional sexual abuse with sexual abuse by strangers and more widely being dealt with under Art 34 and the Optional Protocol to the Convention on the Rights of the Child on the Sale of Children, Child Prostitution and Child Pornography [**RCLP para 15.32**].

Article 20

1. A child temporarily or permanently deprived of his or her family environment, or in whose own best interests cannot be allowed to remain in that environment, shall be entitled to special protection and assistance provided by the State.

2. States Parties shall in accordance with their national laws ensure alternative care for such a child.

3. Such care could include, inter alia, foster placement, kafalah of Islamic law, adoption or if necessary placement in suitable institutions for the care of children. When considering solutions, due regard shall be paid to the desirability of continuity in a child's upbringing and to the child's ethnic, religious, cultural and linguistic background.

Right to alternative care upon removal from family environment (Art 20)—Art 20 should be read in conjunction with Principle 6 of the Declaration of the Rights of the Child (G.A. Res. 1386 (XIV), 14 UN. GAOR Supp (No 16) at 19, UN Doc a/4354), the Declaration of Social and Legal Principles Relating to the Protection and Welfare of Children with Special Reference to Foster Care Placement and Adoption Nationally and Internationally (A/RES/41/85 3 December 1986) and the UN Guidelines for the Alternative Care of Children (2010) A/RES/64/142 [**RCLP paras 8.121–8.123**]. In considering alternative care arrangements State parties must systematically bear in mind all the relevant rights of the child and obligations under the UNCRC (Committee on the Rights of the Child General Comment No 7 *Implementing Child Rights in Early Childhood* HRI/GEN/1/Rev 8, p 448) [**RCLP paras 8.127; 8.161**]. This will include having regard to the views of the child (UNCRC Art 12 and see Committee on the Rights of the Child General Comment No 12 *Right to be Heard* CRC/C/GC/12, p 13, para 54 and UN Guidelines for the Alternative Care of Children (2010) A/RES/64/142, para 6) [**RCLP para 8.131**]. The key principles of good practice in relation to alternative care of children are contained in Part B of UN Guidelines for the Alternative Care of Children (2010) A/RES/64/142 [**RCLP para 8.134**]. The proper review of alternative placements for children is vital to ensuring the protection and promotion of the rights of children placed outside their family (UN Guidelines for the Alternative Care of Children (2010) A/RES/64/142, para 67 and see Art 25) [**RCLP paras 8.162–8.163**].

'temporarily or permanently deprived' (Art 20(1))—This phrase will encompass all children not in the overnight care of at least one of their parents for whatever reason and under whatever circumstances (UN Guidelines for the Alternative Care of Children (2010) A/RES/64/142, para 29(a)) [**RCLP para 8.123**].

'family environment' (Art 20(1))—The words 'family environment' make clear that alternative care outside the family will not be triggered by removal of the child from his or her parents. Where the child's best interests demand removal from his or her parents the State should give consideration to placing the child within his or her family before considering alternative care outside the family save where the family are unsuitable or notifying the family would place the child at risk (Committee on the Rights of the Child General Comment No 7 *Implementing Child Rights in Early Childhood* HRI/GEN/1/Rev 8, para 15 and Declaration of Social and Legal Principles Relating to the Protection and Welfare of Children with Special Reference to Foster Care Placement and Adoption Nationally and Internationally (A/RES/41/85 3 December 1986)) **[RCLP para 8.135]**.

'best interests' (Art 20(1))—Art 20 contains no guidance as to the meaning of best interests in this context **[RCLP para 1.141]**. The words 'best interests' in Art 20(1) should be interpreted in accordance with Art 3(1). Note that in relation to adoption the child's best interests will be paramount (Art 21) **[RCLP para 8.127]**. It is arguable that the child's best interests will be paramount in all matters relating to the placement of children outside the care of their own parents (Declaration of Social and Legal Principles Relating to the Protection and Welfare of Children with Special Reference to Foster Care Placement and Adoption Nationally and Internationally Art 5 (A/RES/41/85 3 December 1986)) **[RCLP para 8.127]**. The standards of care being provided to children in alternative care will be measured by reference to Art 3(3) (and see UN Guidelines for the Alternative Care of Children (2010) A/RES/64/142, para 105) **[RCLP paras 8.133; 8.159–8.161]**.

'shall be entitled' (Art 20(1))—The use of the word stresses the obligation on State parties owed to children who cannot be cared for by their own families (P Newell and R Hodgkin *Implementation Handbook for the Convention on the Rights of the Child* (2008, 3rd edn, UNICEF), p 279) **[RCLP para 8.136]**.

Forms of alternative care (Art 20(3))—The use of the words 'could include' in Art 20(3) indicate that the forms of alternative care listed in the article are not exhaustive **[RCLP para 8.137]**. The use of the words 'if necessary' before the option of institutional care indicates that this is an option of last resort (*Manual on Human Rights Reporting* HR/PUB/91/1 (Rev 1), p 450 and UN Guidelines for the Alternative Care of Children (2010) A/RES/64/142, para 23) **[RCLP para 8.137]**. Residential care should only be used where such care is professionally indicated and in the best interests of the child (Lithuania CRC/C/LTU/CO/2, para 42 and see UN Guidelines for the Alternative Care of Children (2010) A/RES/64/142, para 21) **[RCLP para 8.158]**. This principle will apply to children with disabilities (Convention on the Rights of Persons with Disabilities Art 23 and see Committee on the Rights of the Child General Comment No 9 *The Rights of Children with Disabilities* CRC/C/GC/9, paras 47–49) **[RCLP para 8.158]**. UN Guidelines for the Alternative Care of Children differentiate between informal forms of alternative care and formal forms of alternative care (UN Guidelines for the Alternative Care of Children (2010) A/RES/64/142, paras 29(b)(i) and 29(b)(ii)) **[RCLP para 8.124]**. The formal forms of alternative care include kinship care, foster care, other forms of family based or family-like placements, residential care and supervised independent living arrangements but not arrangements depriving a child of his or her liberty, care by adoptive parents or informal arrangements whereby the child voluntarily stays with relatives or friends for reasons unconnected with his or her parents inability or unwillingness to provide adequate care (UN Guidelines for the Alternative Care of Children (2010) A/RES/64/142, para 30) **[RCLP para 8.124]**. Note that in relation to adoption the UN Guidelines for the Alternative Care of Children appear to contradict the terms of Art 20(3). The Committee on the Rights of the Child emphasises the importance of 'family like' solutions when considering alternative care for children (Committee on the Rights of the Child General Comment No 7 *Implementing Child Rights in Early Childhood* HRI/GEN/1/Rev 8, p 448, para 36(b) and UN Guidelines for the Alternative Care of Children (2010) A/RES/64/142, para 22) **[RCLP para 8.126]**. It is vital that legal responsibility for the child within the context of the alternative placement is clearly defined (UN Guidelines for the Alternative Care of Children (2010) A/RES/64/142, para 101–104) **[RCLP para 8.132]**.

'continuity in a child's upbringing' (Art 20(3))—States parties should prioritise alternative placements which ensure security, continuity of care an affection and which provide children with the opportunity to form long term attachments (Committee on the Rights of the Child General Comment No 7 *Implementing Child Rights in Early Childhood* HRI/GEN/1/Rev 8, p 448 and UN Guidelines for the Alternative Care of Children (2010) A/RES/64/142, para 60) **[RCLP para 8.128]**. The phrase 'continuity in a child's upbringing implies continuity of contact with parents, family and the wider community (P Newell and R Hodgkin *Implementation Handbook for the Convention on the Rights of the Child* (2008, 3rd edn, UNICEF), p 289) **[RCLP para 8.129]**. Delay should be avoided in securing alternative care (UN Guidelines for the Alternative Care of Children (2010) A/RES/64/142, paras 60–61) **[RCLP para 8.130]**.

Article 21

States Parties that recognize and/or permit the system of adoption shall ensure that the best interests of the child shall be the paramount consideration and they shall:

(a) Ensure that the adoption of a child is authorized only by competent authorities who determine, in accordance with applicable law and procedures and on the basis of all pertinent and reliable information, that the adoption is permissible in view of the child's status concerning parents, relatives and legal guardians and that, if required, the persons concerned have given their informed consent to the adoption on the basis of such counselling as may be necessary;

(b)   Recognize that inter-country adoption may be considered as an alternative means of child's care, if the child cannot be placed in a foster or an adoptive family or cannot in any suitable manner be cared for in the child's country of origin;

(c)   Ensure that the child concerned by inter-country adoption enjoys safeguards and standards equivalent to those existing in the case of national adoption;

(d)   Take all appropriate measures to ensure that, in inter-country adoption, the placement does not result in improper financial gain for those involved in it;

(e)   Promote, where appropriate, the objectives of the present article by concluding bilateral or multilateral arrangements or agreements, and endeavour, within this framework, to ensure that the placement of the child in another country is carried out by competent authorities or organs.

Children's rights and adoption (Art 21)—Art 21 encompasses specific rights of the child in relation to adoption [**RCLP para 8.143**]. See also Declaration of Social and Legal Principles Relating to the Protection and Welfare of Children with Special Reference to Foster Care Placement and Adoption Nationally and Internationally Art 5(A/RES/41/85 3 December 1986 [**RCLP para 8.144**]. Delay in determining a decision as to adoption will be inimical to the child's best interests (Switzerland CRC/C/15/Add 182, para 36 and Philippines CRC/C/15/Add 259, para 48) [**RCLP para 8.145**].

'best interests of the child shall be paramount' (Art 21)—By contrast with Art 3(1) in systems of adoption the child best interests shall be paramount rather than a primary consideration [**RCLP para 8.146**]. The child's best interests in relation to adoption can only be determined and defined after consideration of the child's views in accordance with Art 12 (Committee on the Rights of the Child General Comment No 12 *Right to be Heard* CRC/C/GC/12, p 13, paras 55–56 and see Mexico CRC/C/15/Add 13 and Germany CRC/C/GC/15/Add 43, para 29) [**RCLP paras 6.56 and 8.147**].

'informed consent' (Art 21(a))—Those giving consent should be provided with such counselling as may be necessary to assist with the decision whether to consent or not (P Newell and R Hodgkin *Implementation Handbook for the Convention on the Rights of the Child* (2008, 3rd edn, UNICEF), p 296) [**RCLP para 8.151**].

'cannot in any suitable manner be cared for' (Art 21(b))—Prolonged residential care is unlikely to constitute a suitable care in the child's country of origin for the purposes of Art 21(b) (P Newell and R Hodgkin *Implementation Handbook for the Convention on the Rights of the Child* (2008, 3rd edn, UNICEF), p 297 and 298) [**RCLP para 8.153**].

'intercountry adoption' (Art 21(c))—For intercountry adoption and unaccompanied or refugee children see Committee on the Rights of the Child General Comment No 6 *Treatment of Unaccompanied and Separated Children Outside their Country of Origin* CRC/GC/2005/6, para 91 and [**RCLP paras 8.156–8.157**].

Article 22

1. States Parties shall take appropriate measures to ensure that a child who is seeking refugee status or who is considered a refugee in accordance with applicable international or domestic law and procedures shall, whether unaccompanied or accompanied by his or her parents or by any other person, receive appropriate protection and humanitarian assistance in the enjoyment of applicable rights set forth in the present Convention and in other international human rights or humanitarian instruments to which the said States are Parties.

2. For this purpose, States Parties shall provide, as they consider appropriate, co-operation in any efforts by the United Nations and other competent intergovernmental organizations or nongovernmental organizations co-operating with the United Nations to protect and assist such a child and to trace the parents or other members of the family of any refugee child in order to obtain information necessary for

reunification with his or her family. In cases where no parents or other members of the family can be found, the child shall be accorded the same protection as any other child permanently or temporarily deprived of his or her family environment for any reason, as set forth in the present Convention.

The rights of refugee children (Art 22)—Pursuant to Art 22(1) a child who seeks refugee status or is considered a refugee receive appropriate protection and humanitarian assistance in the enjoyment of applicable rights set forth in the present Convention and in other international human rights or humanitarian instruments [RCLP paras 5.89, 5.153, 6.62]. See also Committee on the Rights of the Child General Comment No 6 *Treatment of Unaccompanied and Separated Children Outside their Country of Origin* CRC/GC/2005/6. The United Kingdom has now removed its reservation in respect of Art 22 [RCLP para 14.134]. Art 22(2) should be read in conjunction with Art 9(1) and Art 10 [RCLP para 8.111].

Article 23

1. States Parties recognize that a mentally or physically disabled child should enjoy a full and decent life, in conditions which ensure dignity, promote self-reliance and facilitate the child's active participation in the community.

2. States Parties recognize the right of the disabled child to special care and shall encourage and ensure the extension, subject to available resources, to the eligible child and those responsible for his or her care, of assistance for which application is made and which is appropriate to the child's condition and to the circumstances of the parents or others caring for the child.

3. Recognizing the special needs of a disabled child, assistance extended in accordance with paragraph 2 of the present article shall be provided free of charge, whenever possible, taking into account the financial resources of the parents or others caring for the child, and shall be designed to ensure that the disabled child has effective access to and receives education, training, health care services, rehabilitation services, preparation for employment and recreation opportunities in a manner conducive to the child's achieving the fullest possible social integration and individual development, including his or her cultural and spiritual development.

4. States Parties shall promote, in the spirit of international cooperation, the exchange of appropriate information in the field of preventive health care and of medical, psychological and functional treatment of disabled children, including dissemination of and access to information concerning methods of rehabilitation, education and vocational services, with the aim of enabling States Parties to improve their capabilities and skills and to widen their experience in these areas. In this regard, particular account shall be taken of the needs of developing countries.

The rights of children with disabilities (Art 23)—Art 23 provides that all children with disabilities should enjoy a full and decent life, in conditions which ensure dignity, promote self-reliance and facilitate the child's active participation in the community [RCLP para 4.2]. In respect of children with disabilities reference should also be made to the UN Convention on the Rights of Persons with Disabilities and the UN Standard Rules on the Equalisation of Opportunities for Persons with Disabilities [RCLP para 2.14]. See also the recently published Committee on the Rights of the Child General Comment No 16 *State Obligations Regarding the Impact of the Business Sector on Children's Rights* (see Chapter 28 below).

'effective access to and receives education ... in a manner conducive to the child's achieving the fullest possible social integration' (Art 23(3))—There is an important distinction between 'integration' and 'inclusion', the latter being preferable (UN General Discussion Day on Children with Disabilities UN Doc CRC/C/66, para 335) [RCLP para 13.94]. See also Convention on the Rights of Persons with Disabilities Arts 24(2) and 24(3) [RCLP para 13.93–13.94] and the Committee on the Rights of the Child General Comment No 9 *The Rights of Children with Disabilities* CRC/C/GC/9, para 67 [RCLP para 13.95].

Article 24

1. States Parties recognize the right of the child to the enjoyment of the highest attainable standard of health and to facilities for the treatment of illness and rehabilitation of health. States Parties shall strive to ensure that no child is deprived of his or her right of access to such health care services.

2. States Parties shall pursue full implementation of this right and, in particular, shall take appropriate measures:

(a)   To diminish infant and child mortality;

(b)   To ensure the provision of necessary medical assistance and health care to all children with emphasis on the development of primary health care;

(c)   To combat disease and malnutrition, including within the framework of primary health care, through, inter alia, the application of readily available technology and through the provision of adequate nutritious foods and clean drinking-water, taking into consideration the dangers and risks of environmental pollution;

(d)   To ensure appropriate pre-natal and post-natal health care for mothers;

(e)   To ensure that all segments of society, in particular parents and children, are informed, have access to education and are supported in the use of basic knowledge of child health and nutrition, the advantages of breastfeeding, hygiene and environmental sanitation and the prevention of accidents;

(f)   To develop preventive health care, guidance for parents and family planning education and services.

3. States Parties shall take all effective and appropriate measures with a view to abolishing traditional practices prejudicial to the health of children.

4. States Parties undertake to promote and encourage international co-operation with a view to achieving progressively the full realization of the right recognized in the present article. In this regard, particular account shall be taken of the needs of developing countries.

Right to the enjoyment of the highest attainable standard of health (Art 24)—The principles of the UNCRC concerning the health of children were developed from provisions contained in the Universal Declaration of Human Rights, the Covenant on Civil and Political Rights, the Covenant on Economic, Social and Cultural Rights and from definitions and principles formulated by UNICEF and the World Health Organisation (WHO). See also The World Declaration on the Survival, Protection and Development of Children 1990 for both general and specific commitments to child health related to the standards set by the CRC. The UN Millennium Declaration (UN General Assembly Resolution 55/2) builds on the 1990 World Declaration in prescribing basic goals for child development, which were in turn reaffirmed in 2005 (see General Assembly Sixteenth Session, October 2005 A/RES/60/1) [**RCLP para 5.99**]. See also the Covenant on Economic, Social and Cultural Rights Art 12(1) [**RCLP para 5.100**]. Art 24 places a heavy emphasis on primary health care for children (see also the Declaration of Alma-Ata (1978) principle VI and VII) [**RCLP para 5.104**]. The obligations in respect of the health of children cannot be abandoned or derogated in time of emergency (including economic emergency) having regard to the non-derogable nature of the right to live under Art 6 of the UNCRC and Art 4 of the Covenant on Civil and Political Rights [**RCLP para 5.105**]. In relation to the participation of the child in healthcare decisions Art 12 requires the provision of information concerning proposed treatments, their effects and their outcomes and access to confidential counselling without parental consent irrespective the child's age where this is needed for the child's safety or wellbeing (Committee on the Rights of the Child General Comment No 12 *The Right to be Heard* CRC/C/GC/12, paras 100–101) [**RCLP para 6.44**]. Reference should also be made to the recently published Committee on the Rights of the Child General Comment No 15 *The Right of the Child to the Enjoyment of the Highest Attainable Standard of Health* (see Chapter 28 below).

'**the highest attainable standard of health**' (Art 24(1))—Cultural Rights makes it clear that the right to the highest attainable standard of health comprises the essential elements of availability, accessibility, acceptability and quality (Committee on Economic, Social and Cultural Rights General Comment No 14 *The Right to the Highest Attainable Standard of Health (Art 12)* HRI/GEN/1/Rev 8, para 12) [**RCLP para 5.101**]. When read with Art 2, Art 24(1) requires State parties to eradicate any differentials in the standard of health and availability of facilities as between different children (Committee on Economic, Social and Cultural Rights General Comment No 14 *The Right to the Highest Attainable Standard of Health (Art 12)* HRI/GEN/1/Rev 8, para 12) **[RCLP para 5.102]**.

Health of children with disabilities—When considering the right of children with disabilities to the highest attainable standard of health Art 24(1) should be read with Art 23 and the Committee on the Rights of the Child General Comment No 9 *The Rights of Children with Disabilities* CRC/C/GC/9, paras 44 and 45 **[RCLP para 5.102]**. See also Art 25 of the Convention on the Rights of Persons with Disabilities **[RCLP para 5.103]**.

'shall pursue full implementation of this right' (Art 24(2))—The list of specific elements of child health set out in Art 24(2) is a non-exhaustive list of measures (P Newell and R Hodgkin *Implementation Handbook for the Convention on the Rights of the Child* (2008, 3rd edn, UNICEF), p 344 and 355 and see also Committee on the Rights of the Child General Comment No 7 *Implementing Child Rights in Early Childhood* HRI/GEN/1/Rev 8, p 443, para 27) **[RCLP para 5.105]**.

'diminish infant and child mortality' (Art 24(2)(a))—The use of the word 'child' in Art 24(2)(a) indicates that the duty to diminish child mortality applies up to the age of 18 (P Newell and R Hodgkin *Implementation Handbook for the Convention on the Rights of the Child* (2008, 3rd edn, UNICEF), p 356) **[RCLP para 5.106]**. State parties are under a positive duty to take measures to reduce infant and child mortality (Human Rights Committee General Comment No 6 *Article 6 (The Right to Life)* HRI/GEN/1/Rev 8, para 5 and see Committee on Economic, Social and Cultural Rights General Comment No 14 *The Right to the Highest Attainable Standard of Health* HRI/GEN/1/Rev 8, para 14) **[RCLP para 5.106]**.

'provision of necessary medical assistance and health care' (Art 24(2)(b))—See also Arts 12(1) and 15(1)(b) of the Covenant on Economic, Social and Cultural Rights and Committee on Economic, Social and Cultural Rights General Comment No 14 *The Right to the Highest Attainable Standard of Health* HRI/GEN/1/Rev 8, para 17 **[RCLP para 5.108]**.

'combat disease and malnutrition' (Art 24(2)(c))—See also Art 12(1)(c) of the Covenant for Economic, Social and Cultural Rights and the Committee on Economic, Social and Cultural Rights General Comment No 14 *The Right to the Highest Attainable Standard of Health General* HRI/GEN/1/Rev 8, para 16 **[RCLP para 5.109]**. See also the Committee on the Rights of the Child General Comment No 3 *HIV/AIDS and the Rights of the Child* HRI/GEN/1/Rev 8, p 363 **[RCLP para 5.110]**. Children should not serve as test subjects in medical research into disease until the intervention under investigation has been thoroughly tested on adults (Committee on the Rights of the Child General Comment No 3 *HIV/AIDS and the Rights of the Child* HRI/GEN/1/Rev 8, para 26) **[RCLP para 5.111]**.

'adequate nutritious foods and clean drinking-water' (Art 24(2)(c))—Art 24(2)(c) does not create a new right to food for children but refines and focuses the existing right to food under Art 11(2) of the Covenant on Economic, Social and Cultural Rights **[RCLP para 5.112]**. The right to adequate food should be interpreted broadly (see UN Doc E/CN 4/1989/SR.20 and Committee on Economic, Social and Cultural Rights General Comment No 12 *The Right to Adequate Food (Art 11)* HRI/GEN/1/Rev 8, para 1, 6 and 8) **[RCLP para 5.113]**. Note that Art 24(2)(e) makes specific reference to 'the advantages of breast feeding' (see Report on the WHO Collaborative Study on Breast Feeding (1981) World Health Organisation, Geneva. See also the International Code of Marketing of Breast Milk Substitutes (1981) Resolution WHA 34.22, the Global Strategy for Infant and Young Child Feeding (WHA55/2002/REC/1, Annex 2 and the Innocenti Declaration on Infant and Young Child Feeding 2005) **[RCLP para 5.114]**. See also Art 27(3) and Art 25 of the Universal Declaration of Human Rights and Art 10(b) of the Declaration on Social Progress and Development 1969 **[RCLP para 5.114]**. In respect of the right to clean drinking water the right entitles everyone to sufficient, safe, acceptable, physically accessible and affordable water for personal and domestic use (see Committee on Economic, Social and Cultural Rights General Comment No 15 *The Right to Water* HRI/GEN/1/Rev 8, paras 10–11) **[RCLP para 5.114]**. See also see Art 14(2)(c) of the African Charter on the Rights and Welfare of the Child which guarantees to the child the right to 'adequate nutrition and safe drinking water' **[RCLP para 5.115]**.

Enforcement of the right to food and water—The Committee on Economic, Social and Cultural Rights has commented that any person or group who is a victim of a violation of the right to adequate food should have access to effective judicial or other appropriate remedies at both national and international levels (see Committee on Economic, Social and Cultural Rights General Comment No 12 *The Right to Adequate Food (Art 11)* HRI/GEN/1/Rev 8, para 32) **[RCLP para 5.115]**. For examples of the enforcement of the right to food and water see *Peoples Union for Civil Liberties v Union of India & Ors* Writ Petition (Civil) 196 of 2001; *S Jaganath v Union of India* (1997) 2 SCC 87; *Samatha v State of Andhra Pradesh* (1997) 8SCC 191, AIR 1997 SC 3297 (in relation to food); and *State of Karnataka v Appa Balu Ingale* (1995) Supp (4) SCC 469, AIR 1993 1126 (SC) (in relation to water). See also *Union Inter africaine de Droits de l'Homme v Zaire* Communication 100/93, Ninth Activity Report 1995–1996, Annex VIII **[RCLP para 5.115]**. Note that the African Committee of Experts on the Rights and Welfare of the Child will have jurisdiction to receive individual communications under Art 44 in respect of complaints under Art 14(2)(c) of the African Charter on the Rights and Welfare of the Child guaranteeing to the child the right to 'adequate nutrition and safe drinking water' **[RCLP para 5.115]**.

'dangers and risks of environmental pollution' (Art 24(2)(c))—Art 24(2)(c) highlights the dangers of environmental pollution to the provision of adequate nutrition and clean drinking water (see for example Philippines CRC/C/15/Add 259, paras 60–61 and Ecuador CRC/C/15/Add 93, para 24 and CRC/C/15/Add 262, para 54). Note also that Article 24(2)(e) points up the need to educate children and parents in respect of, and support the use of their basic knowledge of, environmental sanitation **[RCLP para 5.116]**. See also the Covenant on Economic, Social and Cultural Rights and the General Comment No 14 *The Right to the Highest Attainable Standard of Health* HRI/GEN/1/Rev 8, para 15. See also Principle 1 of the Stockholm Declaration of 1972, the General Assembly Resolution 45/94 on the need to ensure a healthy environment for the well-being of individuals, Principle 1 of the Rio Declaration and regional human rights instruments such as Art 10 of the San Salvador Protocol to the American Convention on Human Rights **[RCLP para 5.116]**.

'appropriate pre-natal and post-natal health care' (Art 24(2)(d))—See also Art 10(2) of the Covenant on Economic, Social and Cultural Rights **[RCLP para 5.107]**.

Access to education and support in relation to health (Art 24(2)(e))—There is a self evident link between education and primary and preventative health care (World Health Organisation Global Strategy for Health for All by the Year 2000: 'Health for All' No 3 (1981), p 21and the Declaration of Alma-Ata and the Tehran Proclamation on Human Rights 1968, the UN Declaration on Social Progress and Development 1969 and the Plan of Action of the World Population Conference 1974) **[RCLP para 5.117]**. See also Art 28 (right to education) and Art 18 (requiring States to render assistance to the parents in the performance of their child-rearing duties) **[RCLP para 5.117]**. Note the right of the child to access information embodied in Art 24(2)(e) (see the Committee on the Rights of the Child General Comment No 4 *Adolescent Health an Development in the Context of the Convention on the Rights of the Child* HRI/GEN/1/Rev 8, p 382, para 26 and Committee on the Rights of the Child General Comment No 3 *HIV/AIS and the Rights of the Child* CRC/GC/2003/3, para 17) **[RCLP para 11.34]**. The child's right to access to information promoting his or her physical and mental health under Art 17 will also be relevant to health education (Committee on the Rights of the Child General Comment No 4 *Adolescent Health an Development in the Context of the Convention on the Rights of the Child* HRI/GEN/1/Rev 8, p 382, para 22) **[RCLP para 5.117]**.

'preventive health care' (Art 24(2)(f))—Preventative health care will include immunisation and family planning. Whilst family planning is a controversial topic in many jurisdictions (see for example the reservation of the Holy See to Art 24(2)(f) which provides that it 'interprets the phrase "family planning education and services" in Art 24(2) to mean only those methods of family planning which it considers morally acceptable, that is natural methods of family planning'), the Committee on the Rights of the Child emphasises the need for uncensored information on sexuality and access to appropriate services (Committee on the Rights of the Child General Comment No 3 *HIV/AIDS and the Rights of the Child* HRI/GEN/1/Rev 8, p 363 and Committee on the Rights of the Child General Comment No 4 *Adolescent Health and Development in the Context of the Convention on the Rights of the Child* HRI/GEN/1/Rev 8, p 376. See also the Report of the International Conference on Population Development 1994 and A/RES/S-23/3, para 79(f)) **[RCLP para 5.118]**.

'abolishing traditional practices prejudicial to the health of children' (Art 24(3))—The term 'traditional practices prejudicial to the health of children will encompass all forms of genital mutilation, including female circumcision and male circumcision, traditional birth practices, binding, scarring, burning, branding, coin rubbing, tattooing, piercing, initiation ceremonies involving harmful practices, deliberate discriminatory treatment including the preferential feeding of male infants, witchcraft, violent forms of discipline and disciplinary techniques prejudicial to health (see P Newell and R Hodgkin *Implementation Handbook for the Convention on the Rights of the Child* (2008, 3rd edn, UNICEF), pp 344 and 373. See also UN Doc E/CN 4/Sub.2/1989/42 and the Report of the Working Group on Traditional Practices Affecting the Health of Women and Children (1986) UNDocE/CN 4/1986/42 and United Nations General Assembly Resolution A/RES/56/128 19 December 2001. In relation to female circumcision see also Committee on the Elimination of Discrimination against Women General Recommendation No 14 *Female Circumcision* HRI/GEN/1/Rev 8, p 298. In relation to preferential treatment of male children see also the Committee on the Rights of the Child Report of the Eighth Session January 1995 CRC/C/38, p 49 and the Committee on the Elimination of Discrimination Against Women General Recommendation No 24 *Article 12 of the Convention (Women and Health)* HRI/GEN/1/Rev 8, pp 331 et seq) **[RCLP paras 5.119–5.120]**.

Article 25

States Parties recognize the right of a child who has been placed by the competent authorities for the purposes of care, protection or treatment of his or her physical or mental health, to a periodic review of the treatment provided to the child and all other circumstances relevant to his or her placement.

'placed by the competent authorities for the purposes of care, protection or treatment' (Art 25)—Placements for the purpose of Art 25 of the UNCRC include foster and adoptive families, children's homes and institutions, immigration and refugee centres, hospitals, health units and wards, therapeutic centres, boarding schools, detention centres, prisons and residential schools (P Newell and R Hodgkin *Implementation Handbook for the Convention on the Rights of the Child* (2008, 3rd edn, UNICEF), p 380) [RCLP para 6.55]. Private placements arranged by parents will not fall within the ambit of Art 25 (see E/CN 4/1986/39, pp 11–13 and Detrick, p 360 but see also Guinea CRC/C/15/Add 100, para 21 and Chad CRC/C/15/Add 107, para 22) [RCLP para 8.165].

'all other circumstances relevant to his or her placement' (Art 25)—This term will necessarily encompass the reasons for that placement and whether such reasons persist schools (P Newell and R Hodgkin *Implementation Handbook for the Convention on the Rights of the Child* (2008, 3rd edn, UNICEF), pp 379 and 380) [RCLP para 8.165].

Standards of review—The Declaration of Social and Legal Principles Relating to the Protection and Welfare of Children with Special Reference to Foster Care Placement and Adoption Nationally and Internationally (A/RES/41/85 3 December 1986) requires that a competent authority or agency should be responsible for supervision of foster placements to ensure the welfare of the child [RCLP para 8.165]. See further Art 3(3) and Committee on the Rights of the Child General Comment No 7 *Implementing Child Rights in Early Childhood* CRC/C/GC/7/Rev 1, para 23 [RCLP paras 8.159–8.161]. See also the Declaration of Social and Legal Principles Relating to the Protection and Welfare of Children with Special Reference to Foster Placement and Adoption Nationally and Internationally (A/RES/41/85 3 December 1986), Arts 6, 10, 11 and 12 and the UN Guidelines for the Alternative Care of Children (2010) A/RES/64/142, paras 188–122 [RCLP para 8.141].

Placement in care and the child's right to be heard—Children must be able to express their views in matters of placement, the regulation of care in foster families or homes and their daily lives (Committee on the Rights of the Child General Comment No 12 (2009) The Right of the Child to Be Heard (CRC/C/GC/12, para 97) and must be able to report in confidence and safety (Committee on the Rights of the Child General Comment No 12 (2009) The Right of the Child to Be Heard (CRC/C/GC/12, para 121) [RCLP para 6.55].

Article 26

1. States Parties shall recognize for every child the right to benefit from social security, including social insurance, and shall take the necessary measures to achieve the full realization of this right in accordance with their national law.

2. The benefits should, where appropriate, be granted, taking into account the resources and the circumstances of the child and persons having responsibility for the maintenance of the child, as well as any other consideration relevant to an application for benefits made by or on behalf of the child.

Right to benefit from social security (Art 26(1))—The child has a right to 'benefit from' social security rather than an independent right to welfare provision [RCLP para 5.181]. See however 'application for benefits made by or on behalf of the child' below and Art 9 of the Covenant on Economic, Social and Cultural Rights. States parties must take active steps to ensure there is full uptake of social security entitlements where appropriate by or on behalf of children (P Newell and R Hodgkin *Implementation Handbook for the Convention on the Rights of the Child* (2008, 3rd edn, UNICEF), p 388) [RCLP para 5.181]. National provisions which limit the payment of social security to children by reference to a lower age limit will contravene the provisions of Art 26 (see for example Iceland CRC/C/15/Add 203, para 20 and Georgia CRC/C15/Add 222, para 52) [RCLP para 5.182].

'social security, including social insurance' (Art 26(1))—Minimum standards of 'social security' are provided by the International Labour Organisation Social Security (Minimum Standards) Convention (No 102) ILO C102 [RCLP para 183]. However, note that the words 'in accordance with their national law' in Art 26(1) mean that the standard against which the adequacy of social security is measured is that of the State and not more widely against some minimum international standard [RCLP para 5.185].

'resources' (Art 26(2))—Art 26 must be read in light of the proviso provided by Art 4 that 'With regard to economic, social and cultural rights, States Parties shall undertake such measures to the maximum extent of their available resources and, where needed, within the framework of international cooperation'. Within this context means testing is desirable to ensure limited resources can be targeted at those most in need (P Newell and R Hodgkin *Implementation Handbook for the Convention on the Rights of the Child* (2008, 3rd edn, UNICEF), p 389) [RCLP para 5.184].

'**application for benefits made by or on behalf of the child**' (Art 26(2))—Children must be directly eligible and entitled to apply for welfare provision where necessary (P Newell and R Hodgkin *Implementation Handbook for the Convention on the Rights of the Child* (2008, 3rd edn, UNICEF), p 389) [**RCLP para 5.182**].

Article 27

1. States Parties recognize the right of every child to a standard of living adequate for the child's physical, mental, spiritual, moral and social development.

2. The parent(s) or others responsible for the child have the primary responsibility to secure, within their abilities and financial capacities, the conditions of living necessary for the child's development.

3. States Parties, in accordance with national conditions and within their means, shall take appropriate measures to assist parents and others responsible for the child to implement this right and shall in case of need provide material assistance and support programmes, particularly with regard to nutrition, clothing and housing.

4. States Parties shall take all appropriate measures to secure the recovery of maintenance for the child from the parents or other persons having financial responsibility for the child, both within the State Party and from abroad. In particular, where the person having financial responsibility for the child lives in a State different from that of the child, States Parties shall promote the accession to international agreements or the conclusion of such agreements, as well as the making of other appropriate arrangements.

Right to an adequate standard of living (Art 27)—The Covenant on Economic, Social and Cultural Rights Art 11 also enshrines the right to an adequate standard of living [**RCLP para 5.139**].

'**adequate standard of living**' (Art 27(1))—Art 27 recognises that the child's development cannot be divorced from, and is intrinsically linked to his or her standard of living (P Newell and R Hodgkin *Implementation Handbook for the Convention on the Rights of the Child* (2008, 3rd edn, UNICEF), p 394) [**RCLP para 5.141**]. Whilst the term 'adequate' is subjective, having regard to the requirement in Art 6(2) to ensure 'to the maximum extent possible' the survival and development of the child and the requirement in Art 24(1) to ensure 'the highest attainable standard of health', an 'adequate' standard of living equates to the minimum standard required to promote the child's maximum development and achieve for him or her the highest attainable standard of health (M Candappa 'Human Rights and Refugee Children in the UK' in B Franklin (ed) *The New Handbook of Children's Rights* (2002, Routlege), p 226) [**RCLP para 5.142**]. Art 23(1) of the UNCRC is relevant to achieving an adequate standard of living for children with disabilities (see also the Convention on the Rights of Persons with Disabilities Art 28 and the Committee on the Economic, Social and Cultural Rights General Comment No 5 *Persons with Disabilities* HRI/GEN/1/Rev 8, p 32, para 33) [**RCLP paras 5.150–5.151**]. Art 27 also applies to children who are refugees (M Candappa 'Human Rights and Refugee Children in the UK' in B Franklin (ed) *The New Handbook of Children's Rights* (2002, Routlege), p 226). See also United Nations High Commissioner for Refugees Refugee Children: Guidelines on Protection and Care (1994) Geneva: UNHCR and the UN Convention Relating to the Status of Refugees Art 21) [**RCLP para 5.153**].

'**parent(s) or others responsible for the child have the primary responsibility**' (Art 27(2))—Art 27(2) links the child's right to development with the parents' responsibility to secure that development (see also Art 3(2), Art 5 ('States Parties shall respect the responsibilities, rights and duties of parents ... to provide ... appropriate direction and guidance in the exercise by the child of the rights recognised in the ... Convention'), Art 7 ('The child...shall have the right ... as far as possible ... to know and be cared for by his or her parents') and Art 18 ('States Parties shall use their best efforts to ensure recognition of the principle that both parents have common responsibilities for the upbringing and development of the child. Parents or, as the case may be, legal guardians, have the primary responsibility for the upbringing and development of the child. The best interests of the child will be their basic concern') [**RCLP paras 5.143–5.144**].

'**shall take appropriate measures**' (Art 27(3))—The right to an adequate standard of living under Art 27 imposes on States parties a positive obligation to give effect to the right (Committee on the Rights of the Child General Comment No 7 *Implementing Child Rights in Early Childhood* HRI/GEN/1/Rev 8, p 443, para 26) [**RCLP para 5.140**]. See also Art 4 [**RCLP para 5.140**]. The primary State responsibility under Art 27(3) is to secure the living conditions of children as a group rather than to assist individual children [**RCLP para 5.149**]. The obligation to provide material assistance is one that requires more than doing the bare minimum as the assistance must be sufficient to foster the child's physical, mental, spiritual, moral and social development (see R Kimbrough

'Entitlement to "Adequacy": Application of Article 27 to US Law' in AB Andrews and NH Kaufman (eds) *Implementing the UN Convention on the Rights of the Child: A Standard of Living Adequate for Development* (1999, Praeger), p 169–170) [**RCLP para 5.149**].

'**nutrition**' (Art 27(3))—See '**adequate nutritious foods and clean drinking-water**' under Art 24 [**RCLP para 5.155**].

'**clothing**' (Art 27(3))—See for example the recommendation of the Committee on the Rights of the Child that street children in Bosnia-Herzegovina be provided with clothing, in addition to nutrition, housing, health-care and education opportunities (Bosnia-Herzegovina CRC/C/15/Add 260, para 66) [**RCLP para 5.156**].

'**housing**' (Art 27(3))—See also Art 11 of the Covenant on Economic, Social and Cultural Rights and Committee on Economic, Social and Cultural Rights General Comment No 4 *The Right to Adequate Housing (Art 11(1) of the Covenant)* HRI/GEN/1/Rev 8, p 19 which has been endorsed by the Committee on the Rights of the Child (Committee on the Rights of the Child, Report on the eleventh session, January 1996, CRC/C/50, pp 77 and 79) [**RCLP paras 5.157–5.159**]. The right not to be subjected to arbitrary or unlawful interference with a person's privacy, family, home or correspondence is a very important dimension of the right to adequate housing (see Committee on the Rights of the Child, Report on the eleventh session, January 1996, CRC/C/50, para 9 and Art 16(1)) [**RCLP para 5.160**]. The child's views will be crucial in respect of the whole built environment (P Newell and R Hodgkin *Implementation Handbook for the Convention on the Rights of the Child* (2008, 3rd edn, UNICEF), p 400 and see *Children's Rights and Habitat: Working Towards Child Friendly Cities* (1997) UNICEF Appendix 1, pp 27–28) [**RCLP para 5.161**]. For an example of enforcement of the right to housing see *Government of South Africa v Grootboom* 2000 (11) BCLE 1169 [**RCLP para 5.162**]. See also *Hunter and Others v Canary Wharf Ltd; Hunter and Others v London Docklands Corporation* [1997] AC 655, [1997] 2 All ER 426, [1997] 2 FLR 342 [**RCLP para 5.178**].

'**all appropriate measures to secure the recovery of maintenance for the child**' (Art 27(4))—State parties must ensure dissemination of knowledge of law regarding maintenance for children is widespread (see Côte d'Ivoire CRC/C/15/Add 155, para 33 and Zambia CRC/C/15/Add 206, paras 40 and 41) [**RCLP para 5.145**]. Delays in recovering maintenance should be avoided (see Ukraine CRC/C/15/Add 191, para 42) [**RCLP para 5.145**]. The term 'maintenance' must be read broadly having regard to the terms of Art 18(1) (P Newell and R Hodgkin *Implementation Handbook for the Convention on the Rights of the Child* (2008, 3rd edn, UNICEF), p 235) [**RCLP para 5.145**]. Art 27(4) requires States parties to revoke maintenance from parents and persons responsible for the child who are abroad (see also E/CN 4/1988/28, p 17) [**RCLP para 5.146**]. For the impact of Art 27(4) on domestic maintenance provisions see [**RCLP paras 5.175–5.177**].

Article 28

1. States Parties recognize the right of the child to education, and with a view to achieving this right progressively and on the basis of equal opportunity, they shall, in particular:

    (a)   Make primary education compulsory and available free to all;

    (b)   Encourage the development of different forms of secondary education, including general and vocational education, make them available and accessible to every child, and take appropriate measures such as the introduction of free education and offering financial assistance in case of need;

    (c)   Make higher education accessible to all on the basis of capacity by every appropriate means;

    (d)   Make educational and vocational information and guidance available and accessible to all children;

    (e)   Take measures to encourage regular attendance at schools and the reduction of drop-out rates.

2. States Parties shall take all appropriate measures to ensure that school discipline is administered in a manner consistent with the child's human dignity and in conformity with the present Convention.

3. States Parties shall promote and encourage international cooperation in matters relating to education, in particular with a view to contributing to the elimination of ignorance and illiteracy throughout the world and facilitating access to scientific and

technical knowledge and modern teaching methods. In this regard, particular account shall be taken of the needs of developing countries.

Right of the child to education (Art 28)—Art 28 does not create a right to education but rather recognises a pre-existing right [**RCLP para 13.39**]. Art 28 deals with the child's right to education in terms of provision, access and equality of opportunity and Art 29 deals with the aims of education. Arts 28 and 29 should be read together (Committee on the Rights of the Child General Comment No 1 *The Aims of Education* HRI/GEN/1/Rev 8, p 349, para 1 and 2) [**RCLP paras 13.10 and 13.37**]. The child's right to education must be recognised on the basis of equal opportunity (Committee on the Rights of the Child, General Comment No 1 *The Aims of Education* CRC/GC/2001/1, p 351, paras 10 and 11 and see Art 2) [**RCLP para 13.27**]. The key aims of the child's right to education are the right to access education, the right to quality education and the right to respect in the learning environment (*A Human Rights-based Approach to Education for All: A Framework for the Realization of Children's Right to Education and Rights within Education* UNICEF/UNESCO (2007), p 28) [**RCLP para 13.41**]. The core minimum provision to satisfy the right to education is the provision of free, compulsory primary education and the provision of different forms of secondary education and vocational guidance (P Newell and R Hodgkin *Implementation Handbook for the Convention on the Rights of the Child* (2008, 3rd edn, UNICEF), p 408) [**RCLP para 13.42**]. The right to quality education requires a minimum cognitive development to be the primary objective (see *A Human Rights-based Approach to Education for All: A Framework for the Realization of Children's Right to Education and Rights within Education* UNICEF/UNESCO (2007) p 17 and p 32, Art 29 UNCRC and the Plan of Action agreed in 2000 at the World Education Forum at Dakar, p 67 as endorsed by the UN General Assembly's special session on childhood in 2002 'A World Fit for Children', Report of the Ad Hoc Committee of the Whole of the twenty-seventh special session of the General Assembly, 2002, A/S-27/19/Rev 1, paras 39 and 40) [**RCLP para 13.45**]. A quality education must encompass basic skills of literacy and numeracy (Brazil CRC/C/15/Add 241, para 58) [**RCLP para 13.45**]. The right to respect in the learning environment incorporates respect for the child's identity, the child's right to express his or her views in all matters concerning him or her and the child's physical and personal integrity (*A Human Rights-based Approach to Education for All: A Framework for the Realization of Children's Right to Education and Rights within Education* UNICEF/UNESCO (2007), p 35) [**RCLP para 13.46**]. For education of children suffering from HIV or AIDS see [**RCLP para 13.97**]. For education of children deprived of their liberty see [**RCLP paras 13.98–13.101**]. For education of children in care see [**RCLP para 13.102**].

Parental choice and the child's right to education (Art 28(1))—The parental 'right' to choose their child's education is expressly subject to the child's best interests, evolving capacity and right to participate, to the wider canon of children's rights under the UNCRC and to the nature of parental responsibility as prescribed in Art 18 (P Newell and R Hodgkin *Implementation Handbook for the Convention on the Rights of the Child* (2008, 3rd edn, UNICEF), p 411). Note however that Art 29(2) does safeguard the rights of parents and others to establish schools outside the state system (see also the Committee on Economic, Social and Cultural Rights, General Comment No 13 *The Right to Education* HRI/GEN/1/Rev 8, p 77, para 30) [**RCLP para 13.30**].

'education' (Art 28(1))—The word 'education' in Art 28 is noted limited to formal instruction delivered in schools but also recognises information education (P Newell and R Hodgkin *Implementation Handbook for the Convention on the Rights of the Child* (2008, 3rd edn, UNICEF), p 411–412 and see also I Szabo *Cultural Rights* (1974, Leiden) [**RCLP para 13.40**].

'achieving this right progressively' (Art 28(1))—The word 'progressively recognises the provision of education is expensive and applies not only to financial expenditure but also the administrative burden (P Newell and R Hodgkin *Implementation Handbook for the Convention on the Rights of the Child* (2008, 3rd edn, UNICEF), p 407). See also Art 4 and Committee on Economic, Social and Cultural Rights, General Comment No 3 *The Nature of the State Parties' Obligations* HRI/GEN/1/Rev 8, para 11, pp 17 and 18 with which the Committee on the Rights of the Child has concurred in its General Comment No 5 *General measures of implementation of the Convention on the Rights of the Child* CRC/GC/2003/5, para 8) [**RCLP para 13.47**].

'primary education compulsory and available free to all' (Art 28(1)(a))—See also Committee on Economic, Social and Cultural Rights General Comment No 11 *Plans for Action for Primary Education (Art 14)* HRI/GEN/1/Rev 8, p 60) [**RCLP para 13.48**]. Art 28(1)(a) should be read in light of Art 2 and Art 14 of the ICESCR [**RCLP para 13.48**]. The word 'compulsory' means that neither parents, not guardians nor the State are entitled to treat as optional the decision as to whether the child should have access to primary education (Committee on Economic, Social and Cultural Rights General Comment No 11 *Plans for Action for Primary Education (Art 14)* HRI/GEN/1/Rev 8, p 61, para 6) [**RCLP paras 13.51–13.52**]. The term 'free to all' in Art 28(1)(a) requires that education at the primary stage should be secured for all children regardless of family means (P Newell and R Hodgkin *Implementation Handbook for the Convention on the Rights of the Child* (2008, 3rd edn, UNICEF), p 421). See also Art 26(1) of the Universal Declaration of Human Rights and Art 13(2)(a) of the ICESCR. The Declaration of Human Rights Art 26(1) suggests that States should be moving in the direction of free education at secondary and higher levels as well [**RCLP para 13.53**]. Note that the Soviet delegation proposed an amendment to the Declaration of the Rights of the Child which would have resulted in the extension of the principle of free education to secondary education (see UN Doc E/CN 4/L 539 Rev 1). See also Art XII of the American Declaration of the Rights and Duties of Man and Principle 7 of the Declaration of the Rights of the Child 1959 **[RCLP para 13.53]**.

Pre-primary or 'early years' education—Whilst Art 21(1)(a) does not mention pre-primary or 'early years' education the Committee on the Rights of the Child has recognised the importance of that form of education and expects that it will be included in States Parties general framework of education provision (Committee on the Rights of the Child, General Comment No 7 *Implementing child Rights in Early Childhood* CRC/C/GC/7/Rev 1, paras 28, 30 and 33 and see India CRC/C/15/Add 228, para 65) **[RCLP para 13.50]**. The provision of pre-primary or early years education will be closely linked to the right to play under Art 31(1) (Committee on the Rights of the Child, General Comment No 7 *Implementing Child Rights in Early Childhood* CRC/C/GC/7/Rev 1, para 34). See also the International Charter of Physical Education and Sport (UNESCO 21 November 1978), Art 1 which provides in relation to the practice of physical education **[RCLP para 13.50]**.

'development of different forms of secondary education' (Art 28(1)(b))—See Committee on Economic, Social and Cultural Rights, General Comment No 13 *The Right to Education* HRI/GEN/1/Rev 8, p 74, para 12. The ILO Minimum Age Convention 1973 (No 138) Art 2 would suggest that the minimum age for the end of secondary education is 15 years of age **[RCLP para 13.55]**.

'general and vocational education' (Art 28(1)(b))—Note the inclusion of vocational training in Art 28(1)(b) (P Newell and R Hodgkin *Implementation Handbook for the Convention on the Rights of the Child* (2008, 3rd edn, UNICEF), p 423 and see Committee on Economic, Social and Cultural Rights, General Comment No 13, 1999, HRI/GEN/1/Rev 8, p 74, para 12) **[RCLP para 13.56]**. Vocational training is also incorporated in Art 13(2)(b) of the Covenant on Economic, Social and Cultural Rights. See also Committee on Economic, Social and Cultural Rights, General Comment No 13 *The Right to Education* HRI/GEN/1/Rev 8, p 74, paras 15 and 16. See also Art 6(a)(i) of the Revised Recommendation Concerning Technical and Vocational Education (adopted by the General Conference of UNESCO in 1974) and the ILO Convention (No 142) Human Resources and Development Convention concerning Vocational Guidance Art 2 **[RCLP para 13.60]**.

'available and accessible to every child' (Art 28(1)(b))—For an interpretation of the phrase 'available and accessible' in relation to secondary education see Committee on Economic, Social and Cultural Rights, General Comment No 13 *The Right to Education* HRI/GEN/1/Rev 8, p 74, para 13. Accessibility has three overlapping dimensions, namely non-discrimination, physical accessibility and economic accessibility (Committee on Economic, Social and Cultural Rights General Comment No 13 *The Right to Education* HRI/GEN/1/Rev 8, p 73, para 6) **[RCLP paras 13.58–13.59]**.

'higher education accessible to all' (Art 28(1)(c))—The inclusion of higher Education is logical given its place in the continuum of the child's education and the fact that there will be circumstances where children younger than 18 will qualify for higher education based on their capacity **[RCLP para 13.61]**. Higher education must be available in different forms (Committee on Economic, Social and Cultural Rights, General Comment No 13 *The Right to Education* HRI/GEN/1/Rev 8, p 75, para 18) **[RCLP para 13.63]**.

'on the basis of capacity' (Art 28(1)(c))—The term ' on the basis of capacity' in Art 28(1)(c) refers to the capacity of the student rather than the capacity of the State to make provision for higher education (Committee on Economic, Social and Cultural Rights, General Comment No 13 *The Right to Education* HRI/GEN/1/Rev 8, p 75, para 18 and P Newell and R Hodgkin *Implementation Handbook for the Convention on the Rights of the Child* (2008, 3rd edn, UNICEF), p 425) **[RCLP para 13.64]**.

'educational and vocational information and guidance' (Art 28(1)(d))—Art 28(1)(d) recognises that child can only develop their potential if a range of opportunities are available and they know about those opportunities (see also the ILO Human Resources Development Convention (No 142) Art 2 and P Newell and R Hodgkin *Implementation Handbook for the Convention on the Rights of the Child* (2008, 3rd edn, UNICEF), p 426) **[RCLP para 13.65]**.

'measures to encourage regular attendance at schools' (Art 28(1)(e))—Art 28(1(e))(e) constitutes a positive duty on States parties to take steps to ensure that children remain in school **[RCLP para 13.66]**. Particular attention should be given to children who drop out of school or otherwise do not complete their education (Committee on the Rights of the Child General Comment No 10 *Children's Rights in Juvenile Justice* CRC/C/GC/10, p 7, para 18) **[RCLP para 13.66]**.

Administration of school discipline (Art 28(2))—The key principle articulated by Art 28(2) is that school discipline should conform with the child's dignity and rights under the UNCRC as a whole (CRC/C/15/Add 46, para 12) **[RCLP para 13.68]**. Whilst Art 28(2) does not refer specifically to a prohibition on corporal punishment such practices directly conflict with the equal and inalienable right of children to respect for their human dignity and physical integrity (Committee on the Rights of the Child General Comment No 8 *The Right of the Child to Protection from Corporal Punishment and other Cruel or Degrading forms of Punishment* CRC/C/GC/8, paras 20 and 21 and Committee on the Rights of the Child, General Comment No 1 *The Aims of Education*, CRC/GC/2001/1, para 8) [**RCLP para 13.69**]. All forms of corporal punishment are unacceptable (P Newell and R Hodgkin *Implementation Handbook for the Convention on the Rights of the Child* (2008, 3rd edn, UNICEF), p 431 and Committee on the Rights of the Child, General Comment No 1, 2001, CRC/GC/2001/1, pp 353–354, para 19). See also Sweden CRC/C/15/Add 248, paras 35 and 36 and Committee on Economic, Social and Cultural Rights, General Comment No 13 *The Right to Education* HRI/GEN/1/Rev 8, p 79, para 41 [**RCLP para 13.70**]. Art 28(2) prohibits all forms of punishment that are inconsistent with the child's human dignity and rights (Committee on Economic, Social and Cultural Rights, General Comment No 11 *Plans for Action for Primary Education (Art 14)* HRI/GEN/1/Rev 8, p 79, para 41) [**RCLP para 13.75**]. The prohibition on corporal punishment does not exclude a positive concept of discipline (see Committee on the Rights of the Child General Comment No 8 *The Right of the Child to Protection from Corporal Punishment and other Cruel or Degrading forms of Punishment (arts. 19; 28, para 2; and 37, inter alia)* CRC/C/GC/8, paras 13 to 15 and 29) [**RCLP paras 13.71–13.72**].

Exclusion from school—Where it is necessary to exclude a child from school the process of exclusion should accord with the rules of natural justice and with the child's right to participate under Art 12 (P Newell and R Hodgkin *Implementation Handbook for the Convention on the Rights of the Child* (2008, 3rd edn, UNICEF), p 430 and Committee on the Rights of the Child General Comment No 12 (2009) *The Right of the Child to be Heard* CRC/C/GC/12, p 22, para 113) [**RCLP para 13.73**]. In relation to the requirement of due process in this context see *Goss v Lopez* 419 US 565 (1975) [**RCLP para 13.74**].

Article 29

1. States Parties agree that the education of the child shall be directed to:

(a)   The development of the child's personality, talents and mental and physical abilities to their fullest potential;

(b)   The development of respect for human rights and fundamental freedoms, and for the principles enshrined in the Charter of the United Nations;

(c)   The development of respect for the child's parents, his or her own cultural identity, language and values, for the national values of the country in which the child is living, the country from which he or she may originate, and for civilizations different from his or her own;

(d)   The preparation of the child for responsible life in a free society, in the spirit of understanding, peace, tolerance, equality of sexes, and friendship among all peoples, ethnic, national and religious groups and persons of indigenous origin;

(e)   The development of respect for the natural environment.

2. No part of the present article or article 28 shall be construed so as to interfere with the liberty of individuals and bodies to establish and direct educational institutions, subject always to the observance of the principle set forth in paragraph 1 of the present article and to the requirements that the education given in such institutions shall conform to such minimum standards as may be laid down by the State.

The aims of education (Art 29)—Art 29 represents a consensus of world opinion on the fundamental purposes of educating children (Committee on the Rights of the Child General Comment No 1 *The Aims of Education* HRI/GEN/1/Rev 8, p 349, para 1 and 2) [**RCLP paras 13.10–13.11**]. Art 28 articulates the child's right to education and Art 29 stipulates the purposes and objectives of that education [**RCLP para 13.36**]. Arts 28 and 29 should be read together [**RCLP para 13.37**]. The aims of education are articulated in *A Human Rights-based Approach to Education for All: A Framework for the Realization of Children's Right to Education and Rights within Education* UNICEF/UNESCO (2007), p 1 [**RCLP para 13.12**]. Art 29 must be read with the other rights in the UNCRC and in particular the child's right to participate under Art 12 (Committee on the Rights of the Child General Comment No 12 (2009) *The Right of the Child to be Heard* CRC/C/GC/12, pp 21–22, paras 106–110) [**RCLP para 13.13**]. The activities of the media should not undermine the aims of Art 29 (Committee on the Rights of the Child General Comment No 1 *The Aims of Education* CRC/GC/2001/1, para 21) [**RCLP para 11.26**].

'personality, talents and mental and physical abilities' (Art 29(1)(a))—See Committee on the Rights of the Child, General Comment No 1 *The Aims of Education* CRC/GC/2001/1, p 351, para 9 [**RCLP para 13.14**]. The use of the word 'talents' highlights the extremely wide ambit of Art 29 (Committee on the Rights of Child General

Comment No 4 *Adolescent Health and Development in the Context of the Rights of the Child* HRI/GEN/1/Rev 8, p 380, para 13 and see also Art 21 of the Riyadh Guidelines on the Prevention of Juvenile Delinquency) [RCLP **para 13.15**].

'respect for human rights and fundamental freedoms, and for ... the Charter of the United Nations' (Art 29(1)(b))—Art 29(1)(b) seeks promote respect for human rights and fundamental freedoms as a tool for social change (P Newell and R Hodgkin *Implementation Handbook for the Convention on the Rights of the Child* (2008, 3rd edn, UNICEF), p 442 and see also the UNESCO Convention against Discrimination in Education, Art 5(1)(a), the Committee on the Rights of the Child General Comment No 1 *The Aims of Education* CRC/GC/2001/1, pp 353–354, para 19 and Armenia CRC/C/15/Add 225, para 53) [RCLP **para 13.16**]. In this context the entire approach to education should reflect the contents of the UNCRC (P Newell and R Hodgkin *Implementation Handbook for the Convention on the Rights of the Child* (2008, 3rd edn, UNICEF), p 442 and see the Committee on the Rights of the Child, General Comment No 1 *The Aims of Education* CRC/GC/2001/1, para 8 and the Committee on the Rights of the Child General Comment No 5 *General Measures of Implementation of the Convention on the Rights of the Child* (Arts 4, 42 and 44(6) HRI/GEN/1/Rev 8, p 402) [RCLP **para 13.16**]. This will include the education of children deprived of their liberty (Committee on the Rights of the Child General Comment No 10 *Children's Rights in Juvenile Justice* CRC/C/GC/10, p 6, paras 7, 13 and 77) [RCLP **para 13.101**].

'respect' (Art 29(1)(c))—Art 29 requires States Parties to direct education to the development of respect for the child's parents, his or her own cultural identity, language and values, for the national values of the country in which the child is living, the country from which he or she may originate, and for civilizations different from his or her own [RCLP **para 13.17**]. The word 'respect' in this context means acknowledging the equal worth of peoples of all cultures without condescension (P Newell and R Hodgkin *Implementation Handbook for the Convention on the Rights of the Child* (2008, 3rd edn, UNICEF), p 445, Committee on the Rights of the Child, General Comment No 1 *The Aims of Education* CRC/GC/2001/1, paras 4 and 10 and Committee on the Rights of the Child, Report on the twenty-ninth session, January/February 2002, CRC/C/114, p 191) [RCLP **paras 13.18–13.19**].

'preparation of the child for responsible life in a free society' (Art 29(1)(d))—Art 29(1)(d) further reflects the broader aims of education propounded by Art 29 (see also the UNESCO Convention against Discrimination in Education, Art 5(1)(a)) [RCLP **para 13.20**].

'development of respect for the natural environment' (Art 29(1)(e))—See also the Rio Declaration on Environment and Development (1992) Principles 10 and 21 and Committee on the Rights of the Child, General Comment No 1 *The Aims of Education* CRC/GC/2001/1, para 13 [RCLP **para 13.24**].

Article 30

In those States in which ethnic, religious or linguistic minorities or persons of indigenous origin exist, a child belonging to such a minority or who is indigenous shall not be denied the right, in community with other members of his or her group, to enjoy his or her own culture, to profess and practise his or her own religion, or to use his or her own language.

Child belonging to ethnic, religious or linguistic minorities or of indigenous origin (Art 30)—Art 30 seeks to ensure that children belonging to minority or indigenous groups can develop an understanding of, and sustain their cultural identity (see the Human Rights Committee General Comment No 23 *Article 27 (Rights of Minorities)*, HRI/GEN/1/Rev 8, p 199, para 6.2, the Report of the ad hoc Committee of the Whole of the twenty-seventh special session of the General Assembly (2002) A/S-27/19/Rev 1, p 17 and the General Recommendation XXIII on the Rights of Indigenous Peoples HRI/GEN/1/Rev 8, paras 3 and 4) [RCLP **para 7.45**]. The wording of Art 30 reflects that in Art 27 of the Covenant on Civil and Political Rights (see also see the Human Rights Committee General Comment No 23 *Article 27 (Rights of Minorities)* HRI/GEN/1/Rev 8, pp 198–199) [RCLP **para 10.31**].

Article 31

1. States Parties recognize the right of the child to rest and leisure, to engage in play and recreational activities appropriate to the age of the child and to participate freely in cultural life and the arts.

2. States Parties shall respect and promote the right of the child to participate fully in cultural and artistic life and shall encourage the provision of appropriate and equal opportunities for cultural, artistic, recreational and leisure activity.

The right to play (Art 31)—Art 31 is the first legally binding international human rights provision to expressly recognise the right of the child to engage in play and recreational activities (S Detrick A *Commentary on the United Nations Convention on the Rights of the Child* (1999, Martinus Nijhoff), p 279 and E/CN 4/L.1575, p 551) **[RCLP para 5.194]**. Art 31 confers a positive obligation on States Parties to promote children's play (see Guinea Bissau CRC/C/15/Add 177, paras 46 and 47, Rwanda CRC/C/15/Add 234, para 59, Albania CRC/C/15/Add 249, paras 62 and 63 and Mexico CRC/C/MEX/CO/3, paras 58 and 59 and see Committee on the Rights of the Child General Comment No 7 *Implementing Child Rights in Early Childhood* HRI/GEN/1/Rev 8, p 446, para 34) **[RCLP para 5.194]**. The provision of opportunities for rest, leisure, recreational activities and play should be achieved in accordance with the principles of non-discrimination in Art 2 and Art 23 (see the UN Rules for the Protection of Juveniles Deprived of their Liberty rr 18(c) and 47, the Guidelines for the Alternative Care of Children (2010) A/RES/64/142, paras 37, 86 and the Committee on the Rights of the Child General Comment No 6 *Treatment of Unaccompanied and Separated Children Outside their Country of Origin* HRI/GEN/1/Rev 8, p 424, para 63 and see also the Convention on the Rights of Persons with Disabilities, Art 30, the General Comment No 9 *The Rights of Children with Disabilities* CRC/C/GC/9, paras 44–46 and the Standard Rules on the Equalisation of Opportunities for Persons with Disabilities, rr 4(7) and 11 (A/RES/48/96) **[RCLP para 5.195]**. Reference should also be made to the recently published Committee on the Rights of the Child General Comment No 17 *The Right of the Child to Rest, Leisure, Play, Recreational Activities, Cultural Life and Art* (see Chapter 28 below).

Rest, leisure, recreational activities and play (Art 31(1))—'Rest' includes the basic necessities of physical or mental relaxation, 'leisure' is a wider term implying the time and freedom to do as one pleases, 'recreational activities' embrace the whole range of activities undertaken by choice for pleasure and 'play' includes children's activities which are not controlled by adults and which do not necessarily conform to any rules (P Newell and R Hodgkin *Implementation Handbook for the Convention on the Rights of the Child* (2008, 3rd edn, UNICEF), p 469 and see also the ILO Night Work of Young Persons (Non-Industrial Occupations) Convention 1946 (No 79), Art 2 and the ILO Night Work of Young Persons (Industry) Convention (Revised) 1948 (No 90), Art 2). Note that 'play' may nonetheless be facilitated and overseen by adults **[RCLP para 5.196]**. Reasonable limitations should be placed on school and working hours in order to ensure rights under Art 31 are effective (P Newell and R Hodgkin *Implementation Handbook for the Convention on the Rights of the Child* (2008, 3rd edn, UNICEF), p 469 and see E/CN 4/1983/ 62 Annex II and S Detrick (ed) *The United Convention on the Rights of the Child: A Guide to the Travaux Préparatoires* (1992), p 415) **[RCLP para 5.196]**.

'appropriate to the age of the child' (Art 31(1))—The term 'appropriate to the age of the child' requires activities not to be excessive, entail any inappropriate risk or in anyway be harmful to the development, health or education of the child (UN Manual on Human Rights Reporting HR/PUB/91/1 (Rev 1), p 469. See also Art 24 of the Universal Declaration of Human Rights) **[RCLP para 5.197]**.

'cultural and artistic life' (Art 31(2))—The right of the child to participate fully in cultural and artistic life includes both the right to joint with adults in their cultural and artistic pursuits and the right to child-centred culture and arts (P Newell and R Hodgkin *Implementation Handbook for the Convention on the Rights of the Child* (2008, 3rd edn, UNICEF), pp 43 and 469) **[RCLP paras 5.198–5.199]**.

Article 32

1. States Parties recognize the right of the child to be protected from economic exploitation and from performing any work that is likely to be hazardous or to interfere with the child's education, or to be harmful to the child's health or physical, mental, spiritual, moral or social development.

2. States Parties shall take legislative, administrative, social and educational measures to ensure the implementation of the present article. To this end, and having regard to the relevant provisions of other international instruments, States Parties shall in particular:

(a)   Provide for a minimum age or minimum ages for admission to employment;

(b)   Provide for appropriate regulation of the hours and conditions of employment;

(c)   Provide for appropriate penalties or other sanctions to ensure the effective enforcement of the present article.

Right to protection from economic exploitation and hazardous work (Art 32)—Art 32 reflects the provisions of Arts 4 and 23 of the Universal Declaration of Human Rights and Art 8 of the Convention on Civil and Political Rights **[RCLP para 15.73]**. Art 32 does not prohibit all work by children but rather prevents children from working in certain specified circumstances (Child General Comment No 4 *Adolescent health and development in the context of the Convention on the Rights of the Child* CRC/GC/2003/4, paras 18 and para 36(e) [RCLP

paras 15.74–15.75]. Where economic exploitation reaches the threshold of cruel and degrading treatment for the purposes of Art 37(a) State Parties have a responsibility of immediate abolition **[RCLP para 15.77]**.

'economic exploitation' (Art 32(1))—Activities that will be considered economically exploitative under Art 32(1) will include activities involving cruel, inhuman or degrading treatment, the sale of children or situations of servitude; activities that are dangerous or harmful to the child's harmonious physical, mental and spiritual development or are liable to jeopardise the future education and training of the child; activities involving discrimination, particularly with regard to vulnerable and marginalised social groups; all activities under the minimum ages referred to in Art 32(2) of the UNCRC and in particular those recommended by ILO and all activities using the child for legally punishable criminal acts, such as trafficking in drugs or prohibited goods (The Committee on the Rights of the Child *Report on the Fifth Session* (1994) CRC/C/24, p 42 and see the ILO Minimum Age Convention 1973 (No 138) and ILO Recommendation (No 146)) **[RCLP para 15.76]**. Working for less than the minimum wage prescribed by statute can constitute a form of forced service (*People's Union for Democratic Rights v Union* (1982) 1 SCR 546 Supreme Court of India) **[RCLP para 15.76]**.

Slavery—Slavery is defined by Art 1 of Slavery Convention 1926 as 'the status or condition of a person over whom any or all of the powers attaching to the right of ownership are exercised' and the slave trade as including 'all acts involved in the capture, acquisition or disposal of a person with intent to reduce him to slavery; all acts involved in the acquisition of a slave with a view to selling or exchanging him; all acts of disposal by sale or exchange of a slave acquired with a view to being sold or exchanged, and, in general, every act of trade or transport in slaves' (see also Art 1 of the Supplementary Convention on the Abolition of Slavery, the Slave Trade and Institutions and Practices Similar to Slavery and the ILO Convention (No 29) on Forced or Compulsory Labour) **[RCLP paras 15.78–15.79]**. Slavery is outlawed by Art 4 of the Universal Declaration of Human Rights and Art 8 of the Convention on Civil and Political Rights and is a norm of *jus cogens* (see the *Barcelona Traction Case (Second Phase)* ICJ Reports 3 at 32 and the Restatement of the Law, 3rd Restatement of the Foreign Relations Law of the United States 702(b)) **[RCLP para 15.78]**.

'work' (Art 32(1))—Other international instruments dealing with the issue of work by children tend to use the term 'child labour' **[RCLP para 15.80]**. The term 'child labour' encompasses work which violates international standards as labour performed by a child who is under a minimum age specified in national legislation in line with international standards for that kind of work, labour that jeopardises the physical, mental and moral wellbeing of the child (known as hazardous work) and the unconditional worst forms of child labour (see *A Future without Child Labour – Global Report under the Follow-up to the ILO Declaration on Fundamental Principles and Rights at Work* International Labour Conference, Ninetieth Session (2002) Report I(B) Executive Summary, p X, P Newell and R Hodgkin *Implementation Handbook for the Convention on the Rights of the Child* (2008, 3rd edn, UNICEF), p 481 and Supplementary Convention on the Abolition of Slavery, the Slave Trade and Institutions and Practices Similar to Slavery 1956, Art 1(d)) **[RCLP para 15.81]**.

Hazardous work—See Child Labour: Targeting the Intolerable International Labour Conference, Eighty-sixth Session (1998) ILO, p 9 **[RCLP para 15.82]**.

'relevant provisions of other international instruments' (Art 32(2))—This phrase encompasses the International Labour Organisation (ILO) Conventions and Recommendations and in particular the ILO Minimum Age Convention 1973 (No 138) read with ILO Recommendation (No 146) and the Worst Forms of Child Labour Convention 1999 (No 182) read with the Worst Forms of Child Labour Recommendation (No 190) **[RCLP para 15.84]**. See also the Minimum Age (Industry) Convention 1919 (No 5) and the Minimum Age (Industry) Convention (Revised) 1937 (No 59), the Night Work of Young Persons (Industry) Convention 1919 (No 6) and the Night Work of Young Persons (Industry) Convention (Revised) 1948 (No 90), the Minimum Age (Sea) Convention 1920 (No 7) and the Minimum Age (Sea) Convention (Revised) 1936 (No 58), the Minimum Age (Agriculture) Convention 1921 (No 10), the Minimum Age (Trimmers and Stokers) Convention 1921 (No 15), the Forced Labour Convention 1930 (No 29), the Minimum Age (Non-Industrial Employment) Convention 1923 (No 33) and the Minimum Age (Non-Industrial Employment Convention (Revised) 1937 (No 60), the Medical Examination of Young Persons (Industry) Convention 1946 (No 77), the Medical Examination of Young Persons (Non-Industrial Occupations) Convention 1946 (No 78), the Night Work of Young Persons (Non-Industrial Occupations) Convention 1946 (No 79), the Minimum Age (Fisherman) Convention 1959 (No 112), the Minimum Age (Underground Work) Convention 1965 (No132) and the Medical Examination of Young Persons (Underground Work) Convention 1965 (No 124) **[RCLP para 15.84]**. Regard must also be had to the provisions of the Convention Economic, Social and Cultural Rights, the Convention on Civil and Political Rights, the Supplementary Convention on the Abolition of Slavery, the Slave Trade, and Institutions and Practices Similar to Slavery, the Convention for the Suppression of the Traffic in Persons and of the Exploitation of the Prostitution of Others and both Optional Protocols to the UNCRC **[RCLP para 15.84]**.

'minimum age or minimum ages' (Art 32(2)(a))—Art 32(2)(a) does not define minimum ages, which will be set by reference to ILO Minimum Age Convention 1973 (No 138) and the ILO Recommendation (No 146) **[RCLP para 15.85]**.

'**appropriate regulation of the hours and conditions**' (Art 32(2)(b))—International law does not define a minimum number of hours it is permissible for a child who meets the age requirements of international law to work. Reference should be made to ILO Recommendation No 146 and the Night Work of Young Persons (Industry) Convention 1919 (No 6), Art 1, the Night Work of Young Persons (Industry) Convention (Revised) 1948 (No 90) and the Night Work of Young Persons (Non-Industrial Occupations) Convention 1946 (No 79) [**RCLP para 15.87**]. Art 12(1) and 12(2) of the ILO Recommendation No 146 regulate the conditions of work for children (see also the Night Work of Young Persons (Industry) Convention 1919 (No 6), Art 1, the Night Work of Young Persons (Industry) Convention (Revised) 1948 (No 90) and the Night Work of Young Persons (Non-Industrial Occupations) Convention 1946 (No 79), the Medical Examination of Young Persons (Industry) Convention 1946 (No 77), the Medical Examination of Young Persons (Non-Industrial Occupations) Convention 1946 (No 78) and the Examination of Young Persons (Underground Work) Convention 1965 (No 124), the Minimum Age (Industry) Convention (Revised) 1937 (No 59), the Minimum Age (Sea) Convention (Revised) 1936 (No 58), the Forced Labour Convention 1930 (No 29), the Minimum Age (Non-Industrial Employment) Convention 1923 (No 33) and the Minimum Age (Non-Industrial Employment Convention (Revised) 1937 (No 60), the Minimum Age (Fisherman) Convention 1959 (No 112), the Minimum Age (Underground Work) Convention 1965 (No 132) and Committee on the Rights of the Child General Comment No 8 *The Right of the Child to Protection from Corporal Punishment and Other Cruel or Degrading Forms of Punishment* CRC/C/GC/8, p 9, para 36. [**RCLP para 15.88**]. These provisions will apply to children deprived of their liberty (see the UN Rules for the Protection of Children Deprived of their Liberty rr 18(b) and 46) [**RCLP para 15.89**].

'**appropriate penalties or other sanctions**' (Art 32(2)(c))—See the ILO Minimum Age Convention 1973 (No 138) Art 9 and the ILO Worst Forms of Child Labour Convention 1999 (No 182) Art 7 [**RCLP para 15.90**].

Article 33

States Parties shall take all appropriate measures, including legislative, administrative, social and educational measures, to protect children from the illicit use of narcotic drugs and psychotropic substances as defined in the relevant international treaties, and to prevent the use of children in the illicit production and trafficking of such substances.

Protection of children from harm caused by drugs (Art 33)—Art 33 seeks to protect children from the illicit use of narcotic drugs and psychotropic substances [**RCLP para 15.67**].

'**all appropriate measures**' (Art 33)—Art 33 contains a non-exhaustive list of measures which States Parties should take (see also the UN Guidelines for the Prevention of Juvenile Delinquency (the 'Riyadh Guidelines'), para 44) [**RCLP para 15.71**]. Measures taken in respect of children should be 'protective' rather than punitive (P Newell and R Hodgkin *Implementation Handbook for the Convention on the Rights of the Child* (2008, 3rd edn, UNICEF), p 508. See also UN Rules for the Protection of Juveniles Deprived of their Liberty, r 5) [**RCLP para 15.71**]. See also P Newell and R Hodgkin *Implementation Handbook for the Convention on the Rights of the Child* (2008, 3rd edn, UNICEF), p 506 and Committee on the Rights of the Child General Comment No 7 *Implementing Child Rights in Early Childhood* HRI/GEN/1/Rev 8, p 448, para 36(f).

'**narcotic drugs and psychotropic substances**' (Art 33)—The narcotic drugs and psychotropic substances covered by Art 33 will be those specified in the Single Convention on Narcotic Drugs (1961) as amended by the 1972 Protocol and the Convention on Psychotropic Substances (1971) [**RCLP para 15.68**]. Whilst alcohol, tobacco and chemical solvents are not the subject of the Single Convention on Narcotic Drugs other articles of the UNCRC will be relevant in relation to the use of these substances (Committee on the Rights of the Child General Comment No 4 *Adolescent Health and Development in the Context of the Convention on the Rights of the Child* CRC/GC/2003/4, para 22) [**RCLP para 15.69**].

'**use of children in the illicit production and trafficking**' (Art 33)—See also the ILO Worst Forms of Child Labour Convention 1999 (No 182) Art 3(c) [**RCLP para 15.70**].

Article 34

States Parties undertake to protect the child from all forms of sexual exploitation and sexual abuse. For these purposes, States Parties shall in particular take all appropriate national, bilateral and multilateral measures to prevent:

(a)   The inducement or coercion of a child to engage in any unlawful sexual activity;

(b)   The exploitative use of children in prostitution or other unlawful sexual practices;

(c)   The exploitative use of children in pornographic performances and materials.

Protection of children from sexual exploitation and abuse (Art 34)—Art 34 deals widely with sexual exploitation by strangers. See also Art 37(a), Art 19(1), which contemplates familial and institutional sexual abuse, and the Optional Protocol to the Convention on the Rights of the Child on the Sale of Children, Child Prostitution and Child Pornography [RCLP paras 15.32 and 15.45] and Art 4 of the Universal Declaration of Human Rights, the similar provisions of Art 8 of the Convention on Civil and Political Rights and Art 1(d) of the UN Supplementary Convention on the Abolition of Slavery, the Slave Trade and Institutions and Practices Similar to Slavery [RCLP para 15.44]. Art 24 of the Convention on Civil and Political Rights encompasses a duty on States parties to prevent children from being exploited by means of prostitution or by any other means (Human Rights Committee General Comment No 17 *Article 24 (Rights of the Child)* HRI/GEN/1/Rev 8, p 184, para 3). See also the Convention on the Elimination of All Forms of Discrimination against Women Art 6 provides, Art 2 of the ILO Forced Labour Convention 1930 (No 29) 107, Art 3(b) of the ILO Worst Forms of Child Labour Convention 1999 (No 182), Art 16 of the UN Convention on the Rights of Persons with Disabilities, the UN Standard Rules on the Equalisation of Opportunities for Persons with Disabilities, r 9(4), the UN Convention for the Suppression of the Traffic of Persons and of the Exploitation of the Prostitution of Others (GA Res 317(IV) 1949), Art 1 and the UN Convention against Transnational Organised Crime and the associated Protocol to Prevent, Suppress and Punish Trafficking in Persons, Especially Women and Children [RCLP para 15.46].

'sexual exploitation' (Art 34)—For a definition of 'sexual exploitation' beyond the provisions of Art 34(a) to (c) see the 1997 Declaration and Agenda for Action of the World Congress against Commercial Sexual Exploitation of Children A/51/385, para 5 [RCLP para 15.47]. See also Arts 2 and 3 of the Optional Protocol to the Convention on the Rights of the Child on the Sale of Children, Child Prostitution and Child Pornography [RCLP para 15.48].

'sexual abuse' (Art 34)—The term 'sexual abuse' will include not only violent sexual assaults but other sexual activity, whether consensual or not, with children who are below the defined age of sexual consent (P Newell and R Hodgkin *Implementation Handbook for the Convention on the Rights of the Child* (2008, 3rd edn, UNICEF), p 257) [RCLP para 15.49].

'all appropriate national, bilateral and multilateral measures' (Art 34)—For the measures contemplated see the Declaration from the First World Congress against Commercial Sexual Exploitation of Children Agenda for Action against Commercial Exploitation of Children (1996), paras 1–6 [RCLP para 15.50]. A key measure will be establishing an appropriate age of consent. The Committee on the Rights of the Child is not prescriptive about the age of sexual consent but see Indonesia CRC/C/15/Add 233, para 81 and Iceland CRC/C/15/Add 217, para 38 [RCLP para 15.50]. Appropriate measures will also include the criminalisation of the use of child prostitutes and the possession of child pornography (see Finland CRC/C/15/Add 53, para 19 and 29 and the UN Convention for the Suppression of the Traffic in Persons and of the Exploitation of the Prostitution of Others 1949, Arts 1 and 2) [RCLP para 15.50]. See also *Sexual Violence against Refugees: Guidelines on Prevention and Response*, UNHCR,1995, preface and, para 1.2, the Committee on the Rights of the Child General Comment No 6 *Treatment of Unaccompanied and Separated Children Outside their County of Origin* CRC/GC/2005/6, para 50 and 51 and General Comment No 11 *Indigenous Children and their Rights under the Convention* CRC/C/GC/11, paras 72–73 [RCLP para 15.51].

'inducement or coercion of a child to engage in any unlawful sexual activity' (Art 34(a))—Note that the use of the word 'unlawful' in Art 34(a) would appear to be otiose and unhelpful as the main body of Art 34 has the effect of prohibiting the use of children in all sexual practices which are exploitative, whether they are lawful or unlawful [RCLP para 15.53].

'exploitative use of children in prostitution or other unlawful sexual practices' (Art 34(b))—Art 2 of the Optional Protocol to the Convention on the Rights of the Child on the Sale of Children, Child Prostitution and Child Pornography defines child prostitution as 'the use of a child in sexual activities for remuneration or any other form of consideration'. Once again, the use of the word 'other unlawful sexual practices' in Art 34(b) would appear to be otiose and unhelpful as the main body of Art 34 has the effect of prohibiting the use of children in all sexual practices which are exploitative, whether they are lawful or unlawful [RCLP para 15.54].

'exploitative use of children in pornographic performances and materials' (Art 34(c))—Art 2 of the Optional Protocol to the Convention on the Rights of the Child on the Sale of Children, Child Prostitution and Child Pornography defines child pornography as 'any representation, by whatever means, of a child engaged in real or simulated explicit sexual activities or any representation of the sexual parts of a child for primarily sexual purposes'. The word 'exploitative' in Art 34(c) would appear otiose and unhelpful, implying as it does that provided the use of the child in pornographic performances or materials is not exploitative it does not come within the ambit of Art 34(c) [RCLP para 15.55].

Article 35

States Parties shall take all appropriate national, bilateral and multilateral measures to prevent the abduction of, the sale of or traffic in children for any purpose or in any form.

Protection of children from abduction, sale and trafficking (Art 35)—See also the Optional Protocol to the Convention on the Rights of the Child on the Sale of Children, Child Prostitution and Child Pornography and also Art 35 of the UNCRC to the UN Convention for the Suppression of the Traffic of Persons and of the Exploitation of the Prostitution of Others and the UN Convention against Transnational Organised Crime and its associated Protocol to Prevent, Suppress and Punish Trafficking in Persons, Especially Women and Children [**RCLP para 15.57**].

Article 36

States Parties shall protect the child against all other forms of exploitation prejudicial to any aspects of the child's welfare.

Protection of children from all other forms of exploitation (Art 36)—Art 36 is a 'catch all' provision (P Newell and R Hodgkin *Implementation Handbook for the Convention on the Rights of the Child* (2008, 3rd edn, UNICEF), p 543 and see the Committee on the Rights of the Child Report on the 11th Session CRC/C/50, p 80 and Human Rights Committee General Comment No 20 HRI/GEN/1/Rev 8, p 191, para 7) [**RCLP para 15.107**].

Use of children for scientific or medical experimentation—Art 36 will cover the consensual and non-consensual medical or scientific experimentation on children (see Committee on the Rights of the Child General Comment No 3 *HIV/AIDS and the Rights of the Child* CRC/GC/2003/3, para 29 and also the International Ethical Guidelines for Biomedical Research Involving Human Subjects (2002) Council for International Organisations of Medical Sciences and WHO Guideline 13) [**RCLP paras 15.15 and 15.107**].

Article 37

States Parties shall ensure that:

(a) No child shall be subjected to torture or other cruel, inhuman or degrading treatment or punishment. Neither capital punishment nor life imprisonment without possibility of release shall be imposed for offences committed by persons below eighteen years of age;

(b) No child shall be deprived of his or her liberty unlawfully or arbitrarily. The arrest, detention or imprisonment of a child shall be in conformity with the law and shall be used only as a measure of last resort and for the shortest appropriate period of time;

(c) Every child deprived of liberty shall be treated with humanity and respect for the inherent dignity of the human person, and in a manner which takes into account the needs of persons of his or her age. In particular, every child deprived of liberty shall be separated from adults unless it is considered in the child's best interest not to do so and shall have the right to maintain contact with his or her family through correspondence and visits, save in exceptional circumstances;

(d) Every child deprived of his or her liberty shall have the right to prompt access to legal and other appropriate assistance, as well as the right to challenge the legality of the deprivation of his or her liberty before a court or other competent, independent and impartial authority, and to a prompt decision on any such action.

Related provisions—Art 37 should be read in the context of the related provisions of the UN Guidelines on the Prevention of Juvenile Delinquency (the 'Riyadh Guidelines') (see Committee on the Rights of the Child General Comment No 10 Children's Rights in Juvenile Justice CRC/C/GC/10, p 7, para 18) [**RCLP para 14.8**].

'child' (Art 37(a))—in relation to the definition of 'child' in Art 37 of the CRC, Art 1 of the UNCRC will apply, namely 'a child means every human being below the age of eighteen years unless under the law applicable to the child, majority is attained earlier.' Note also the view of the Human Rights Committee that 'all persons under the age of 18 should be treated as juveniles, at least in matters relating to criminal justice' (Human Rights Committee General Comment No 21 *Article 10 (Humane Treatment of Persons Deprived of their Liberty* HRI/GEN/1/Rev 8, p 194, para 13) [RCLP para 14.6].

'torture or other cruel, inhuman or degrading treatment or punishment' (Art 37(a))—Art 37(a) reflects the provisions of Art 5 of the Universal Declaration of Human Rights and Art 7 of the Convention on Civil and Political Rights [RCLP para 15.13]. See also the UN Convention against Torture and other Cruel, Inhuman or Degrading Treatment or Punishment Art 2 [RCLP para 15.14]. The prohibition in Art 37(a) is absolute (P Newell and R Hodgkin *Implementation Handbook for the Convention on the Rights of the Child* (2008, 3rd edn, UNICEF), p 548 and the UN Committee against Torture and Other Cruel, Inhuman or Degrading Treatment or Punishment General Comment No 2 *Implementation of Article 2 by State Parties* CAT/C/GC/2, para 5) [RCLP para 15.16]. The Committee on the Rights of the Child has stipulated that any statement made as the result of torture or other cruel, inhuman or degrading treatment cannot be accepted as evidence (see General Comment No 10 *Children's Rights in Juvenile Justice* CRC/C/GC/10, para 56) and Art 15 of the Convention against Torture and Other Cruel, Inhuman or Degrading Treatment or Punishment) [RCLP para 15.16]. The general prohibition on the exploitation of children contained in Art 36 of the UNCRC will cover non-consensual medical or scientific experimentation on children (see Human Rights Committee General Comment No 20: *Article 7 (Prohibition of Torture or Other Cruel, Inhuman or Degrading Treatment or Punishment* HRI/GEN/1/Rev 8, p 190, para 7 and the Committee on the Rights of the Child General Comment No 3 *HIV/AIDS and the Rights of the Child* CRC/GC/2003/3, para 29) [RCLP para 15.15].

'torture' (Art 37(a))—'Torture' is defined as 'any act by which severe pain or suffering, whether physical or mental, is intentionally inflicted on a person for such purposes as obtaining from him or a third person information or a confession, punishing him for an act he or a third person has committed or is suspected of having committed, or intimidating or coercing him or a third person, or for any reason based on discrimination of any kind, when such pain or suffering is inflicted by or at the instigation of or with the consent or acquiescence of a public official or other person acting in an official capacity. It does not include pain or suffering arising only from, inherent in or incidental to lawful sanctions' (UN Convention against Torture and Other Cruel, Inhuman or Degrading Treatment or Punishment Art 1(1) and see also *Quinteros v Uruguay* (1983) Human Rights Committee A/38/40) [RCLP para 15.19]. Note that the forms of harmful treatment comprising torture or other cruel, inhuman or degrading treatment or punishment are indivisible, interdependent and interrelated (Committee Against Torture and Other Cruel, Inhuman or Degrading Treatment or Punishment General Comment No 2 *Implementation of Article 2 by State Parties* CAT/C/GC/2, para 3) [RCLP paras 15.17–15.18].

'cruel' (Art 37(a))—Whether conduct amounts to cruel treatment for the purposes of Art 37(a) depends on the circumstance of each case (see *Pratt and Morgan v Jamaica Human Rights Committee* Communications Nos 210/1986 and 225/1987 (1989)) [RCLP para 15.20].

'inhuman or degrading' (Art 37(a))—See Human Rights Committee *Antti Vuolanne v Finland* (265/1987) A/44/40, Annex X [RCLP para 15.21].

Corporal punishment—Any form of corporal punishment of children, however light, is incompatible with the prohibition on torture or cruel, inhuman or degrading treatment or punishment contained in Art 37(a) (P Newell and R Hodgkin *Implementation Handbook for the Convention on the Rights of the Child* (2008, 3rd edn, UNICEF), p 249 and the Committee on the Rights of the Child General Comment No 8 *The Right of the Child to Protection from Corporal Punishment and Other Cruel or Degrading Forms of Punishment* CRC/C/GC/8, p 6, para 18) [RCLP para 15.22]. The term 'corporal punishment' is defined as 'The Committee defines "corporal" or "physical" punishment as any punishment in which physical force is used and intended to cause some degree of pain or discomfort, however light. Most involves hitting ("smacking", "slapping", "spanking") children, with the hand or with an implement–a whip, stick, belt, shoe, wooden spoon, etc. But it can also involve, for example, kicking, shaking or throwing children, scratching, pinching, biting, pulling hair or boxing ears, forcing children to stay in uncomfortable positions, burning, scalding or forced ingestion (for example, washing children's mouths out with soap or forcing them to swallow hot spices). In the view of the Committee, corporal punishment is invariably degrading. In addition, there are other non-physical forms of punishment that are also cruel and degrading and thus incompatible with the Convention. These include, for example, punishment which belittles, humiliates, denigrates, scapegoats, threatens, scares or ridicules the child' (Committee on the Rights of the Child General Comment No 8 *The Right of the Child to Protection from Corporal Punishment and Other Cruel or Degrading Forms of Punishment* CRC/C/GC/8, p 4, para 11) [RCLP para 15.22]. The best interests principle under Art 3 of the UNCRC cannot be used to justify 'reasonable' or 'moderate' corporal punishment at home, which punishment conflicts with the child's human dignity and right to physical integrity (Committee on the Rights of the Child General Comment No 8 *The Right of the Child to Protection from Corporal Punishment and Other Cruel or Degrading Forms of Punishment* CRC/C/GC/8, p 7, para 26) [RCLP paras 15.23–15.24]. The UN Standard Minimum Rules for the Administration of Juvenile Justice r 17(3) prohibits the use of corporal punishment in detention as to the UN Rules for the Protection of Children Deprived of their Liberty r 67 (see also

UN Rules for the Protection of Children Deprived of their Liberty r 66 and the Committee on the Rights of the Child General Comment No 8 *The Right of the Child to Protection from Corporal Punishment and Other Cruel or Degrading forms of Punishment* CRC/C/GC/8, para 39) **[RCLP para 15.25]**.

Prohibition on capital punishment below the age of 18 (Art 37(a))—The prohibition on capital punishment in Art 37(a) is reinforced by the non-derogable nature of the Art 6(1) right to life (Committee on the Rights of the Child General Comment No 10 *Children's Rights in Juvenile Justice* CRC/C/GC/10, p 21, para 75. See also *The Michael Domingues Case: Report on the Inter-American Commission on Human Rights*, Report No 62/02, Merits, Case 12.285 (2002), para 84) **[RCLP para 5.17]**. The prohibition on executions of those under 18 must be confirmed in legislation (see Burkina Faso CRC/C/15/Add 193, para 60 and Saudi Arabia CRC/C/SAU/CO/, paras 32 and 33) **[RCLP para 5.17]**.

Customary international law—For the child's right not to be subjected to torture or other cruel, inhuman or degrading treatment or punishment including capital punishment as a rule of customary international law see *Roach and Pinkerton v United States* Case 9647, Res 3/87, 22 September 1987, Annual Report of the IACHR 1986-87 and *The Michael Domingues Case: Report on the Inter American Commission on Human Rights*, Report No 62/02, Merits Case 12.285 (2002) **[RCLP paras 2.64-2.67]**.

***Jus cogens* norms**—For the child's right not to be subjected to capital punishment as a *jus cogens* norm see *The Michael Domingues Case: Report on the Inter American Commission on Human Rights*, Report No 62/02, Merits Case 12.285 (2002) and *Roper v Simmons* 543 US 551 (2005)). See also *Gary Graham v United States* Report No 97/03, Case No 11 December 29 2003; *Napoleon Beazley v United States* Report No 101/103, Merits Case 12.412, December 29 2003 and *Douglas Christopher Thomas v United States* Report No 100/03 Case No 12.240 December 29 2003 **[RCLP para 2.68]**.

'deprived of his or her liberty' (Art 37(b))—The term 'deprivation of his or her liberty' means any form of detention or imprisonment or the placement of a person in another public or private setting from which this person is not permitted to leave at will, by order of any judicial, administrative or other public authority (see UN Rules for the Protection of Juveniles Deprived of their Liberty r 11(b), the Committee on the Rights of the Child Guidelines for Periodic Reports, paras 138–146 (CRC/C/58) and P Newell and R Hodgkin *Implementation Handbook for the Convention on the Rights of the Child* (2008, 3rd edn, UNICEF), p 557) **[RCLP para 14.15]**. The term 'deprivation of his or her liberty' relates not only to the deprivation of liberty of children in conflict with the law but also to restrictions to liberty on the grounds of welfare, mental health and in relation to asylum and immigration issues (P Newell and R Hodgkin *Implementation Handbook for the Convention on the Rights of the Child* (2008, 3rd edn, UNICEF), pp 548 and 560, Committee on the Rights of the Child General Comment No 10 *Children's Rights in Juvenile Justice* CRC/C/GC/10, p 5, n 1, the Human Rights Committee General Comment No 8 *The Right of the Child to Protection from Corporal Punishment and other Cruel or Degrading Forms of Punishment* HRI/GEN/1/Rev 8, p 169, para 1 and the Committee on the Rights of the Child General Comment No 11 *Indigenous Children and their Rights under the Convention* CRC/C/GC/11, paras 74–77) **[RCLP para 14.13]**. For an example of the domestic courts having regard to Art 37(b) see *R (B) v Brent Youth Court* [2010] All ER (D) 76 (Jul); *Re CK (A Minor)* [2009] NICA 17, [2010] NI 15) **[RCLP para 14.14]**; *R (R) v Durham Constabulary* [2005] UKHL 21, [2005] 1 WLR 1184 **[RCLP para 16.156]**; and *R (Howard League for Penal Reform) v Secretary of State for the Home Department* [2002] EWHC 2497 (Admin), [2003] 1 FLR 484 **[RCLP para 14.132]**.

'unlawfully or arbitrarily' (Art 37(b))—See Art 40(3)(a) which provides that States Parties shall seek the establishment of a minimum age below which States Parties are prohibited from depriving the child of his or her liberty set by reference to the UN Standard Minimum Rules for the Administration of Juvenile Justice (the 'Beijing Rules') (see also the UN Guidelines for the Alternative Care of Children (2010) A/RES/64/142, para 92) **[RCLP para 14.16]**. A child's status as an asylum seeker or a refugee cannot of itself justify as lawful a restriction on that child's liberty even where the child has breached the law governing access to and remaining in a territory (Committee on the Rights of the Child General Comment No 6 *Treatment of Unaccompanied and Separated Children Outside their Country of Origin* CRC/GC/2005/6, paras 61–63, the UN Guidelines for the Alternative Care of Children (2010) A/RES/64/142, para 43 and the UNHCR Executive Conclusion Detention of Refugees and Asylum Seekers No 44 (XXXVII) 1986 UNHCR) **[RCLP paras 14.19–14.20]**.

'in conformity with the law' (Art 37(b))—the term 'conformity with the law' in Art 37(b) of the UNCRC suggests that the restrictions on the child's liberty must be lawful by reference to existing laws but that the restrictions themselves need not be embodied in the substantive law **[RCLP para 14.17]**.

Deprivation of liberty and best interests—All decision taken in relation to the deprivation of the child's liberty under Art 37 the child's best interests must be a primary consideration (Committee on the Rights of the Child General Comment No 10 *Children's Rights in Juvenile Justice* CRC/C/GC/10, p 5, para 10) **[RCLP para 14.7]**. The Committee on the Rights of the Child deprecates the deprivation of a child's liberty on the grounds of welfare (see P Newell and R Hodgkin *Implementation Handbook for the Convention on the Rights of the Child* (2008,

3rd edn, UNICEF), p 562, the Committee on the Rights of the Child Report on the Tenth Session October/November 1995 CRC/C/46, para 228 and Nepal CRC/C/15/Add 57, para 38 and note that r 3.2 of the UN Standard Minimum Rules for the Administration of Juvenile Justice (the 'Beijing Rules') extends the ambit of those rules to welfare and care proceedings) **[RCLP para 14.18]**.

'**used only as a measure of last resort**' (Art 37(b))—The term 'measure of last resort' emphasises that the deprivation of a child's liberty should be exceptional and unlawful unless so (P Newell and R Hodgkin *Implementation Handbook for the Convention on the Rights of the Child* (2008, 3rd edn, UNICEF), p 556 and the UN Rules for the Protection of Juveniles Deprived of their Liberty rr 1, 2 and 17) **[RCLP para 14.21]**. See also Art 37(b) and the UN Standard Minimum Rules for the Administration of Juvenile Justice **[RCLP para 14.22]**. The principle of 'last resort' will apply to pre-trial detention (UN Standard Minimum Rules for the Administration of Juvenile Justice (the 'Beijing Rules'), r 13.1 and the UN Rules for the Protection of Juveniles Deprived of their Liberty r 17) **[RCLP para 14.24]**. Juveniles who are detained pending trial are entitled to the guarantees enshrined in the UN Standard Minimum Rules for the Treatment of Prisoners (Committee on the Rights of the Child General Comment No 10 CRC/C/GC/10, p 21, para 80) **[RCLP para 14.24]**.

Preventative measures—See the UN Guidelines on the Prevention of Juvenile Delinquency (the 'Riyadh Guidelines') (see Committee on the Rights of the Child General Comment No 10 *Children's Rights in Juvenile Justice* CRC/C/GC/1, p 7, para 18) in relation to preventative measures **[RCLP paras 14.8–14.9]**.

Alternatives to the deprivation of liberty—See Arts 40(4) and 40(3)(b), the Committee on the Rights of the Child General Comment No 9 *The Rights of Children with Disabilities* CRC/C/GC/9, paras 73 and 74 and the Committee on the Rights of the Child General Comment No 10 *Children's Rights in Juvenile Justice* CRC/C/GC/10, p 9, para 26 in relation to alternatives to deprivation of liberty **[RCLP paras 14.10 and 14.23]**. The UN Standard Minimum Rules for Non-custodial Measures (the 'Tokyo Rules') and r 18 of the UN Standard Minimum Rules for the Administration of Juvenile Justice provide a framework of rules governing non-custodial measures and are applicable to children (see also P Newell and R Hodgkin *Implementation Handbook for the Convention on the Rights of the Child* (2008, 3rd edn, UNICEF), p 557 and Canada CRC/C/15/Add 215, para 57(d) and Latvia CRC/C/LVA/CO/2, para 62(d)) **[RCLP para 14.23]**.

'**shortest appropriate period of time**' (Art 37(b))—The requirement that deprivation of liberty should be for the shortest period of time will apply to both pre and post trial detention (see also *Re CK (A Minor)* [2009] NICA 17, [2010] NI 15) **[RCLP para 14.15]**. The UN Standard Minimum Rules for the Administration of Juvenile Justice r 19.1 reinforces this provision as do the UN Rules for the Protection of Juveniles Deprived of their Liberty **[RCLP para 14.15]**.

Treatment of children deprived of their liberty (Art 37(c))—Art 37(c) ensures that children do not lose their fundamental rights during the course of the deprivation of their liberty (P Newell and R Hodgkin *Implementation Handbook for the Convention on the Rights of the Child* (2008, 3rd edn, UNICEF), p 563 and Human Rights Committee General Comment No 29 *Article 4: Derogations during a State of Emergency* HRI/GEN/1/Rev 8, p 228, para 13(a)) **[RCLP para 14.29]**. See also Art 10(1) of the Convention on Civil and Political Rights, Art 40(1), the Committee on the Rights of the Child General Comment No 10 *Children's Rights in Juvenile Justice* CRC/C/GC/10, p 7, paras 13 and 89 and the UN Rules for the Protection of Juveniles Deprived of their Liberty r 36 in relation to the proper treatment of children deprived of their liberty **[RCLP paras 14.11–14.12 and 14.27–14.28]**. The UN Standard Minimum Rules for the Administration of Juvenile Justice rr 13.3 and 13.5 also prescribe the manner in which children who are detained should be treated (see also Committee on the Rights of the Child General Comment No 10 *Children's Rights in Juvenile Justice* CRC/C/GC/10, p 23, para 89) **[RCLP paras 14.32–14.33]**. Children who are asylum seekers or refugees deprived of their liberty must be treated in accordance with the principles of international law, Art 37 of the UNCRC and Art 31(1) of the Refugee Convention 1951 (see also the Human Rights Committee General Comment No 15 *The Position of Aliens under the Covenant* HRI/GEN/1/Rev 8, p 180, para 7) **[RCLP para 14.19]**.

'**in a manner which takes into account the needs of persons of his or her age**' (Art 37(c))—This phrase applies the concept of evolving capacity articulated in Art 5 to the treatment of children deprived of their liberty (Committee on the Rights of the Child General Comment No 10 *Children's Rights in Juvenile Justice* CRC/C/GC/10, p 6, para 13) **[RCLP para 14.31]**.

'**shall be separated from adults**' (Art 37(c))—See also Convention on Civil and Political Rights Art 10(2)(b) and Art 10(3) which provisions will apply to children (see Jordan CRC/C/15/Add 21, para 16, Paraguay CRC/C/15/Add 75, para 28 and Costa Rica CRC/C/15/Add 266, para 56) **[RCLP para 14.34]**. The protection provided by Art 37(c) is broader than that provided by the Convention on Civil and Political Rights **[RCLP para 14.35]**. The United Kingdom has entered a reservation in respect of Arts 10(2)(b) and 10(3) of the Convention on Civil and Political Rights but not in respect of Art 37(c) **[RCLP para 14.35]**.

'unless it is considered in the child's best interest not to do so' (Art 37(c))—The best interests exception in Art 37(c) regarding the separation of children from adults should however be interpreted narrowly and never for the convenience of the State parties [**RCLP para 36**]. See also Human Rights Committee General Comment No 9 *Article 10 (Humane Treatment of Persons Deprived of their Liberty)* HRI/GEN/1/Rev 8, para 2, pp 170–171. For an example of when it is in a child's best interests *not* to be separated from adults see UN Rules for the Protection of Children Deprived of their Liberty r 29 [**RCLP para 14.36**].

'right to maintain contact with his or her family' (Art 37(c))—Art 37(c) should be read with Art 9(4) (Committee on the Rights of the Child General Comment No 10 *Children's Rights in Juvenile Justice* CRC/C/GC/10, p 23, para 87) [**RCLP para 14.37 and 8.119**].

'save in exceptional circumstances' (Art 37(c))—The exception to maintaining contact with family members should be exercised in accordance with the child's best interests and never as a disciplinary measure (Committee on the Rights of the Child General Comment No 10 *Children's Rights in Juvenile Justice* CRC/C/GC/10, p 23, para 87) [**RCLP para 14.38**].

Children of detained or imprisoned mothers—The UN Standard Minimum Rules for the Treatment of Prisoners and the UN Guidelines for the Alternative Care of Children set out the principles governing children of detained or imprisoned mothers (UN Standard Minimum Rules for the Treatment of Prisoners r 23 and UN Guidelines for the Alternative Care of Children (2010) A/RES/64/142, para 48). See also the Human Rights Committee General Comment No 28 *Article 3 (The Equality of Rights between Men and Women)* HRI/GEN/1/Rev 8, p 221, para 15 [**RCLP para 14.39**].

'the right to prompt access to legal and other appropriate assistance' (Art 37(d))—See Art 8 of the Universal Declaration of Human Rights and Art 9(4) of the Convention on Civil and Political Rights (see also the Body of Principles for the Protection of All Persons under Any Form of Detention or Imprisonment Principle 32 GA Res 43/173 1988 and the decision of the Human Rights Committee *Antti Vuolanne v Finland* (265/1987) A/44/40, Annex X) [**RCLP para 14.41**].

'right to challenge the legality of the deprivation' (Art 37(d))—See General Comment No 10 *Children's Rights in Juvenile Justice* CRC/C/GC/10, p 22, paras 83–84 [**RCLP paras 14.42–14.43**]. All procedures which are put in place to satisfy Art 37(d) must also satisfy the provisions of Art 12 (see UN Rules for the Protection of Juveniles Deprived of their Liberty, rr 24 and 75–78) [**RCLP para 14.44**].

'prompt decision' (Art 37(d))—The term 'prompt decision' requires that a decision is rendered as soon as possible and in any event no later than 2 weeks after the challenge is made (see Committee on the Rights of the Child General Comment No 10 *Children's Rights in Juvenile Justice* CRC/C/GC/10, p 22, para 51, Art 40(2)(b)(iii) and Art 14(3)(c) of the Convention on Civil and Political Rights, Human Rights Committee General Comment No 8 *Article 9 (Right to Liberty and Security of the Person)* HRI/GEN/1/Rev 8, p 169, paras 2 and 3 and r 10(2) of the 'Beijing Rules') [**RCLP para 14.45**].

Article 38

1. States Parties undertake to respect and to ensure respect for rules of international humanitarian law applicable to them in armed conflicts which are relevant to the child.

2. States Parties shall take all feasible measures to ensure that persons who have not attained the age of fifteen years do not take a direct part in hostilities.

3. States Parties shall refrain from recruiting any person who has not attained the age of fifteen years into their armed forces. In recruiting among those persons who have attained the age of fifteen years but who have not attained the age of eighteen years, States Parties shall endeavour to give priority to those who are oldest.

4. In accordance with their obligations under international humanitarian law to protect the civilian population in armed conflicts, States Parties shall take all feasible measures to ensure protection and care of children who are affected by an armed conflict.

Protection from involvement in armed conflict (Art 38)—Note that the drafting and agreement of Art 38 of the UNCRC was considered by some to be the result of an entirely unsatisfactory process (see E/CN 4/1989/48, pp 110–116 and E/CN 4/1989/48, pp 50–58 and S Detrick *The United Nations Convention on the Rights of the Child: A Guide to the Travaux Préparatoires* (Martinus Nijhoff, 1992), pp 512 and 630 [**RCLP para 15.91**]. Art 38(1) of the UNCRC is supplemented by the Optional Protocol to the Convention on the Rights of the Child on the Involvement of Children in Armed Conflict which has the effect of amending Art 38 in relation to the minimum age for the involvement in armed conflict and for the recruitment into armed forces and armed groups [RCLP paras 15.92 and 15.96].

'respect for rules of international humanitarian law' (Art 38(1))—Armed conflict takes place in accordance with rules of international humanitarian law (HCJ 1730/96 *Sabih v The Commander of IDF Forces in the Judea and Samaria Area* 50(1) PD 353, 369 (Israeli Supreme Court) [RCLP para 15.92]. The term 'rules of international humanitarian law' for the purposes of Art 38 of the UNCRC includes the four Geneva Conventions and additional protocols thereto, the Declaration on the Protection of Women and Children in Emergency and Armed Conflict, the Declaration on the Rights of the Child and the UNCRC generally Committee on the Rights of the Child Report of the Second Session: September/October 1992 CRC/C/10, para 65) [RCLP para 15.92]. The International Committee of the Red Cross, the International Federation of Red Cross and Red Crescent Societies and the National Red Cross and Red Crescent Societies have adopted the following definition of international humanitarian law, namely the 'international rules, established by treaties or custom, which are specifically intended to solve humanitarian problems directly arising from international or non-international armed conflicts and which, for humanitarian reasons, limit the right of parties to a conflict to use the methods and means of warfare of their choice or protect persons and property that are, or may be, affected by conflict' (see G Machal *Impact of Armed Conflict on Children* (1996) A/51/306, para 211, n 40) [RCLP para 15.92]. Regard must be had to the United Nations Children's Fund (UNICEF) Paris Commitments to Protect Children from Unlawful Recruitment or use by Armed Forces or Armed Groups and the UNICEF Principles and Guidelines on Children Associated with Armed Forces or Armed Groups (the 'Paris Principles') [RCLP para 15.92]. The Rome Statute of the International Criminal Court 1998, the ILO Convention on the Worst Forms of Child Labour (No 182) Art 32, the Red Cross Resolution on Protection of Children in Armed Conflicts (1986), the Red Cross Resolution on Assistance to Children in Emergency Situations (1986) and Security Council Resolutions 1261 (1999), 1314 (2001), 1379 (2001), 1460 (2003), 1539 (2004) and 1612 (2006) will also be relevant and the 'traditional norms' of war adopted by belligerents as 'time honoured taboos' (see Report of the Special Representative of the Secretary General on Children and Armed Conflict to the Commission on Human Rights (2005) E/CN 4/2005.77, para 18) [RCLP para 15.92].

Minimum age for participation in hostilities—Art 32(2) must be read with Arts 1 and 4 of the Optional Protocol to the Convention on the Rights of the Child on the Involvement of Children in Armed Conflict (see also Protocol I to the Geneva Conventions Art 77) [RCLP para 15.93]. The effect of these provisions is that no child under the age of 15 years may take direct part in hostilities and where a child over the age of 15 is a member of the armed forces or an armed group, that child should not take a direct part in hostilities where they have not attained the age of 18. Whilst there is a lacuna in respect of children who are aged between 15 and 18 and not a member of any armed forces or armed group, the Committee on the Rights of the Child has expressed the view that no child under the age of 18 should be allowed to be involved in hostilities, either directly or indirectly (Committee on the Rights of the Child *General Discussion on Children in Armed Conflict* Report on the Second Session, September/October (1992) CRC/C/10, para 67 and see P Newell and R Hodgkin *Implementation Handbook for the Convention on the Rights of the Child* (2008, 3rd edn, UNICEF), pp 573 and 583) [RCLP para 15.93].

'shall refrain from recruiting any person who has not attained the age of fifteen years' (Art 38(3))—Art 38(3) must be read with Arts 2, 3 and 4 of the Optional Protocol to the Convention on the Rights of the Child on the Involvement of Children in Armed Conflict [RCLP para 15.96]. The term 'recruitment' covers both voluntary and compulsory recruitment. Within this context the Paris Principles: Principles and Guidelines on Children Associated with Armed Forces or Armed Groups (2007) UNICEF, para 2.4 defines 'recruitment' as 'compulsory, forced and voluntary conscription or enlistment of children into any kind of armed force or armed group' [RCLP para 15.97]. Read with the Optional Protocol to the Convention on the Rights of the Child on the Involvement of Children in Armed Conflict the minimum age for compulsory recruitment into the armed forces or armed groups under Art 38(3) of the UNCRC is 18 years of age. The minimum age for the voluntary recruitment under Art 38(3) of the UNCRC into the armed forces is 15 years of age although States parties to the Optional Protocol are under an obligation to raise this minimum age and, where they seek to recruit children under the age of 18 [RCLP para 15.98]. Note that in any event the Committee on the Rights of the Child has expressed the view that no child under the age of 18 should be recruited into the armed forces, either through conscription or voluntary enlistment (Committee on the Rights of the Child *General Discussion on Children in Armed Conflict* Report on the Second Session, September/October (1992) CRC/C/10, para 67 and see P Newell and R Hodgkin *Implementation Handbook for the Convention on the Rights of the Child* (2008, 3rd edn, UNICEF), pp 573 and 583) [RCLP para 15.98].

'all feasible measures' (Art 38(4))—Art 38(4) requires States parties to fulfil their obligations under international humanitarian law and in particular under the Geneva Convention IV Relative to the Protection of Civilian Persons in Time of War [RCLP para 15.101]. Note that later instruments adopt the stronger formulation of 'all necessary measures' in respect of the protection of civilians during situations of armed conflict (see Art 11 of the Convention on the Rights of Persons with Disabilities) [RCLP para 15.101]. Having regard to the provisions of Art 41 in those States where the Geneva Convention IV Relative to the Protection of Civilian Persons in Time of

War has been ratified, the higher standards of protection afforded to children affected by armed conflict by that Convention will apply in preference to the weaker provisions of Art 38(4) of the UNCRC (Committee on the Rights of the Child General Comment No 6 *Treatment of Unaccompanied and Separated Children Outside their Country of Origin* CRC/GC/2005/6, para 56 and 57) [RCLP para 15.102].

Unexploded ordnance—See the UN Convention on the Use, Stockpiling, Production and Transfer of Anti-personnel Mines and on their Destruction Art 1(1), the Committee on the Rights of the Child General Comment No 9 *The Rights of Children with Disabilities* CRC/C/GC/9, para 23 and Cambodia CRC/C/15/Add 128 and Nicaragua CRC/C/OPAC/ NIC/1, p 5) [RCLP para 15.104].

Children accused of war crimes—Children should not be prosecuted for war crimes (P Newell and R Hodgkin *Implementation Handbook for the Convention on the Rights of the Child* (2008, 3rd edn, UNICEF), p 584, Paris Principles: Principles and Guidelines on Children Associated with Armed Forces or Armed Groups (2007) UNICEF, para 3.6. and Rawanda CRC/C/15/Add 234, paras 70 and 71) [RCLP para 15.105]. The International Criminal Court has specifically excluded children under the age of 18 from its jurisdiction (Rome Statute of the International Criminal Court, Art 26) [RCLP para 15.105].

Article 39

States Parties shall take all appropriate measures to promote physical and psychological recovery and social reintegration of a child victim of: any form of neglect, exploitation, or abuse; torture or any other form of cruel, inhuman or degrading treatment or punishment; or armed conflicts. Such recovery and reintegration shall take place in an environment which fosters the health, self-respect and dignity of the child.

Promotion of physical and psychological recovery and social reintegration of child victims (Art 39)—Art 39 should be read with Arts 19(1), 20(1), 25 and 40(1) (see also Art 14(4) of the Convention on Civil and Political Rights) [RCLP para 15.109]. The provisions of Art 39 of the UNCRC are supplemented by the Optional Protocol to the Convention on the Rights of the Child on the Sale of Children, Child Prostitution and Child Pornography Art 8 [RCLP para 15.110]. The provisions of Art 39 of the UNCRC are further supplemented by the provisions of the Optional Protocol to the Convention on the Rights of the Child on the Involvement of Children in Armed Conflict Art 6(3) [RCLP para 15.111] and Arts 6(3) and (4) of the Protocol to Prevent, Suppress and Punish Trafficking in Persons, Especially Women and Children [RCLP para 15.112]. See also Art 16(4) of the UN Convention on the Rights of Persons with Disabilities [RCLP para 15.113] and Art 14(1) of the Convention against Torture and Other Cruel, Inhuman or Degrading Treatment or Punishment [RCLP para 15.114]. The juvenile justice system has a central role to play in the recovery and reintegration of child victims (Committee on the Rights of the Child *Report on 25th Session September/October 2000* CRC/C/100, para 688.9 and the Committee on the Rights of the Child General Comment No 10 *Children's Rights in Juvenile Justice* CRC/C/GC/10, para 13. See also, paras 23, 29 and 40) [RCLP para 15.117]. Art 39 will be engaged in respect of victims of corporal punishment (Committee on the Rights of the Child General Comment No 8 *The Right of the Child to Protection from Corporal Punishment and Other Cruel or Degrading Forms of Punishment* CRC/C/GC/8, p 10, para 37) [RCLP para 15.119] and victims of economic harm (Committee on the Rights of the Child *Report on the 5th Session January 1994* CRC/C/24, p 39 and *Child Labour: Targeting the Intolerable* International Labour Conference Eighty-sixth Session (1998) ILO, p 54) [RCLP para 15.120].

'child victim' (Art 39)—The phrase child victim will be interpreted widely (see Committee on the Rights of the Child General Comment No 6 *Treatment of Unaccompanied and Separated Children Outside their Country of Origin* CRC/GC/2005/6, paras 47 and 56 and P Newell and R Hodgkin *Implementation Handbook for the Convention on the Rights of the Child* (2008, 3rd edn, UNICEF), p 590) [RCLP para 15.115].

'appropriate measures to promote physical and psychological recovery and social reintegration' (Art 39)—Appropriate measures will include social, medical and psychological counselling, the prevention of the social stigmatisation of the child and his or her family, programmes to facilitate recovery and reintegration in the community and the promotion of alternative means of livelihood for child victims (Agenda for Action adopted by the First World Congress against Sexual Exploitation of Children(A/51/385, para 5 and see also *Gaurav Jain v Union of India* (1997) 8 SCC 114, AIR 1997 SC 3021) [RCLP para 15.116]. It is important that children who are in need of protection by reason of their association with activities that are considered criminal are not treated as offenders but rather are dealt with under child protection mechanisms in order to promote psychological recovery and social reintegration (Committee on the Rights of the Child *Report on 25th Session September/October 2000* CRC/C/100, para 688.9 and see also Brunei CRC/C/15/Add 219, para 53 and Bangladesh CRC/C/15/Add 221, para 49) [RCLP para 15.116].

Article 40

1. States Parties recognize the right of every child alleged as, accused of, or recognized as having infringed the penal law to be treated in a manner consistent with the promotion of the child's sense of dignity and worth, which reinforces the child's respect for the human rights and fundamental freedoms of others and which takes into account the child's age and the desirability of promoting the child's reintegration and the child's assuming a constructive role in society.

2. To this end, and having regard to the relevant provisions of international instruments, States Parties shall, in particular, ensure that:

(a)   No child shall be alleged as, be accused of, or recognized as having infringed the penal law by reason of acts or omissions that were not prohibited by national or international law at the time they were committed;

(b)   Every child alleged as or accused of having infringed the penal law has at least the following guarantees:

(i)   To be presumed innocent until proven guilty according to law;

(ii)   To be informed promptly and directly of the charges against him or her, and, if appropriate, through his or her parents or legal guardians, and to have legal or other appropriate assistance in the preparation and presentation of his or her defence;

(iii)   To have the matter determined without delay by a competent, independent and impartial authority or judicial body in a fair hearing according to law, in the presence of legal or other appropriate assistance and, unless it is considered not to be in the best interest of the child, in particular, taking into account his or her age or situation, his or her parents or legal guardians;

(iv)   Not to be compelled to give testimony or to confess guilt; to examine or have examined adverse witnesses and to obtain the participation and examination of witnesses on his or her behalf under conditions of equality;

(v)   If considered to have infringed the penal law, to have this decision and any measures imposed in consequence thereof reviewed by a higher competent, independent and impartial authority or judicial body according to law;

(vi)   To have the free assistance of an interpreter if the child cannot understand or speak the language used;

(vii)   To have his or her privacy fully respected at all stages of the proceedings.

3. States Parties shall seek to promote the establishment of laws, procedures, authorities and institutions specifically applicable to children alleged as, accused of, or recognized as having infringed the penal law, and, in particular:

(a)   The establishment of a minimum age below which children shall be presumed not to have the capacity to infringe the penal law;

(b)   Whenever appropriate and desirable, measures for dealing with such children without resorting to judicial proceedings, providing that human rights and legal safeguards are fully respected.

4. A variety of dispositions, such as care, guidance and supervision orders; counselling; probation; foster care; education and vocational training programmes and other alternatives to institutional care shall be available to ensure that children are dealt with in a manner appropriate to their well-being and proportionate both to their circumstances and the offence.

Child's right to fair and equal treatment under the law (Art 40)—Art 40 enshrines the cardinal rights of all children alleged as, accused of or recognised as having infringed the penal law (P Newell and R Hodgkin *Implementation Handbook for the Convention on the Rights of the Child* (2008, 3rd edn, UNICEF), p 602 and Committee on the Rights of the Child General Comment No 10 *Children's Rights in Juvenile Justice* CRC/C/GC/10, para 15) [**RCLP para 16.18 and 16.27–16.28**]. Whilst the UNCRC, Art 40 omits to expressly confer on the child the right to fair and equal treatment under the law in determination of the child's civil rights and obligations, Art 10 of the Universal Declaration of Human Rights makes clear that the right of everyone to fair and equal treatment before the law applies in determination of 'rights and obligations' as well as in respect of any criminal charge (see also Art 14(1) of the Convention on Civil and Political Rights and the UN Standard Minimum Rules on the Administration of Juvenile Justice r 3(2)) [**RCLP para 16.19**]. Art 40 must be read with the UN Guidelines on the Prevention of Juvenile Delinquency (the 'Riyadh Guidelines'), the UN Standard Minimum Rules for the Administration of Juvenile Justice (the 'Beijing Rules'), the UN Standard Minimum Standards for Non-Custodial Measures (the 'Tokyo Rules'), the UN Rules for the Protection of Juveniles Deprived of their Liberty and the Committee on the Rights of the Child General Comment No 10 *Children's Rights in Juvenile Justice* [**RCLP para 16.20**]. The provisions of Art 40(2) of the UNCRC must be read in the context of Art 40(1) and represent the minimum guarantees that must be available to children [**RCLP para 16.30**].

Preventative measures—See the UN Guidelines on the Prevention of Juvenile Delinquency (the 'Riyadh Guidelines') and the Committee on the Rights of the Child General Comment No 10 *Children's Rights in Juvenile Justice* CRC/C/GC/10, p 7, para 18) in relation to preventative measures [**RCLP para 16.21**].

Diversions—Art 40(3)(b) and the UN Standard Minimum Rules on the Administration of Juvenile Justice Art 40 (the 'Beijing Rules') require that where possible there must be a diversion of children away from the formal aspects of juvenile justice (see also ESC Resolution 1997/30, para 15, the Committee on the Rights of the Child General Comment No 10 *Children's Rights in Juvenile Justice* CRC/C/GC/10, paras 24 and 27, the UN Standard Minimum Standards for Non-Custodial Measures (the 'Tokyo Rules') and the Economic and Social Council Resolution 2002/12 Basic Principles for the Use of Restorative Justice Programmes in Criminal Matters) [**RCLP paras 16.22–16.25**].

No retrospective legislation (Art 40(2)(a))—The principle requiring the penal law not to be retrospective in nature is enshrined in Art 11(2) of the Universal Declaration of Human Rights which prohibits, unlike Art 40(2)(a) of the CRC, retrospectivity in relation to both offences and any sentence passed in relation to an offence (but see the Committee on the Rights of the Child General Comment No 10 *Children's Rights in Juvenile Justice* CRC/C/GC/10, para 41 in respect of retrospective sentencing) [**RCLP paras 16.33–16.34**].

Presumption of innocence (Art 40(2)(b)(i))—All children are presumed innocent until proven guilty according to law (Committee on the Rights of the Child General Comment No 10 *Children's Rights in Juvenile Justice* CRC/C/GC/10, para 42) [**RCLP paras 16.35–36**].

Proper information on charge and legal assistance (Art 40(2)(b)(ii))—See also Art 14(3)(a) of the Convention on Civil and Political Rights [**RCLP para 16.37**]. The right of the child to be informed promptly and directly of the charges against him or her under CRC, Art 40(2)(b)(ii) is an unqualified right (Committee on the Rights of the Child General Comment No 10 *Children's Rights in Juvenile Justice* CRC/C/GC/10, paras 47 and 48 and P Newell and R Hodgkin *Implementation Handbook for the Convention on the Rights of the Child* (2008, 3rd edn, UNICEF), p 614) [**RCLP para 16.38**]. Parental involvement is encouraged (Committee on the Rights of the Child General Comment No 10 *Children's Rights in Juvenile Justice* CRC/C/GC/10, para 54 and see the UN Standard Minimum Rules on the Administration of Juvenile Justice r 10(1)) [**RCLP paras 16.39–16.40**]. The child's right under Art 40(2)(b)(ii) to have legal or other appropriate assistance in the preparation and presentation of his or her defence is unqualified (Committee on the Rights of the Child General Comment No 10 *Children's Rights in Juvenile Justice* CRC/C/GC/10, para 49 and UN Standard Minimum Rules on the Administration of Juvenile Justice r 15(1) and see also Nigeria CRC/C/15/Add 257, para 81(b) in relation to the particular importance of the right in a criminal context) [**RCLP para 16.41**]. Provision must be made for the child to communicate confidentially with his or her legal advised (Committee on the Rights of the Child General Comment No 10 *Children's Rights in Juvenile Justice* CRC/C/GC/10, para 50) [**RCLP para 16.41**].

Determination without delay (Art 40(2)(b)(iii))—By comparison with Art 14(3)(c) of the Convention on Civil and Political Rights the removal of the word 'undue' from the terminology used in Art 40(2)(b)(iii) connotes an even greater need to avoid delay in relation to children in conflict with the law and in proceedings concerning children generally (Committee on the Rights of the Child General Comment No 10 *Children's Rights in Juvenile Justice* CRC/C/GC/10, para 51) [**RCLP paras 16.43–16.44**].

Presence of legal or other appropriate assistance (Art 40(2)(b)(iii))—The words 'legal or other appropriate assistance' indicate that the assistance provided need not necessarily be legal assistance provided that the assistance made available is a 'appropriate' (Committee on the Rights of the Child General Comment No 10

Children's Rights in Juvenile Justice CRC/C/GC/10, para 49 and see Nigeria CRC/C/15/Add 257, para 81(b) in relation to the particular importance of legal assistance in a criminal context) **[RCLP para 16.45]**.

Presence of parents or guardians (Art 40(2)(b)(iii))—The words 'unless it is considered not to be in the best interests of the child' indicate that it is acceptable to exclude the attendance of parents or legal guardians in certain cases (but see Committee on the Rights of the Child General Comment No 10 *Children's Rights in Juvenile Justice* CRC/C/GC/10, para 54 on the desirability of the maximum possible involvement of parents or legal guardians) **[RCLP para 16.47]**.

Presence of child at the hearing—Having regard to Arts 3, 5 and 12 of the CRC, it must be implicit in Art 40(2)(b)(iii) that the child has the right, subject to his or her best interests and capacity, to be present at any hearing which determines a criminal charge against the child and, having regard in particular to CRC, Art 12(2), where any right or obligation of the child is determined **[RCLP para 16.46]**.

Competent, independent and impartial authority or judicial body (Art 40(2)(b)(iii))—The word 'authority' will encompass all bodies of a judicatory nature which have responsibility for juvenile justice **[RCLP para 16.48]**.

Fair hearing (Art 40(2)(b)(iii))—Fairness will include taking into account all the circumstances of the case prior to final determination, including all those aspects which mitigate the final disposition (see UN Standard Minimum Rules for the Administration of Juvenile Justice, r 16) **[RCLP para 16.49]**.

Protection against self incrimination and the right to call and challenge evidence (Art 40(2)(b)(iv))— The term 'compelled' in Art 40(2)(b)(iv) should be interpreted in a broad manner and is not limited to physical force or other clear violations of human rights (Committee on the Rights of the Child General Comment No 10 *Children's Rights in Juvenile Justice* CRC/C/GC/10, para 50) **[RCLP para 16.51]**. The UN Standard Minimum Rules on the Administration of Juvenile Justice make clear that the child's right to silence applies at all stages of the proceedings (see UN Standard Minimum Rules on the Administration of Juvenile Justice, r 7 and Committee on the Rights of the Child General Comment No 10 *Children's Rights in Juvenile Justice* CRC/C/GC/10, para 50) **[RCLP para 16.51]**. Art 40(2)(b)(iv) enshrines the right of the child to 'equality of arms' within the context of the administration of juvenile justice (Committee on the Rights of the Child General Comment No 10 *Children's Rights in Juvenile Justice* CRC/C/GC/10, para 59 and see also Art 14(3)(e) of the Convention on Civil and Political Rights) **[RCLP para 16.52]** and the child's right of appeal Committee on the Rights of the Child General Comment No 10 *Children's Rights in Juvenile Justice* CRC/C/GC/10, para 60) **[RCLP para 16.53]**.

Assistance of an interpreter (Art 40(2)(b)(vi))—The assistance of an interpreter should not be limited to the final determination of the matter but should be available at all stages of the (Committee on the Rights of the Child General Comment No 10 *Children's Rights in Juvenile Justice* CRC/C/GC/10, para 62 and see also Committee on the Rights of the Child General Comment No 9 *The Rights of Children with Disabilities* CRC/C/GC/9, p 9, para 32 and the Committee on the Rights of the Child General Comment No 11 *Indigenous Children and their Rights under the Convention* CRC/C/GC/11, para 76) **[RCLP para 16.54]**.

Full respect for privacy in proceedings (Art 40(2)(b)(vii))—'All stage of the proceedings' in Art 40(2)(b)(vii) means from the point of initial contact with law enforcement agencies to the point of final determination by a competent authority (Committee on the Rights of the Child General Comment No 10 *Children's Rights in Juvenile Justice* CRC/C/GC/10, para 64) **[RCLP para 16.57]**. See also r 8.1 of the UN Standard Minimum Rules for the Administration of Juvenile Justice (the 'Beijing Rules') **[RCLP para 16.58]**. Any exceptions to these rules must be very limited and clearly stated in law (Committee on the Rights of the Child General Comment No 10 *Children's Rights in Juvenile Justice* CRC/C/GC/10, para 66) **[RCLP para 16.59]**. Whilst there is no specific provision contained in the various international human rights instruments requiring family proceeding to be held in private, it is clearly established that those instruments support this proposition **[RCLP para 16.60]**.

Minimum age of criminal responsibility (Art 40(3))—The appropriate age under Art 40(3)(a) should be set by reference to the UN Standard Minimum Rules for the Administration of Juvenile Justice r 4. The Committee on the Rights of the Child has made clear that 10 years is too low as a minimum age of criminal responsibility and recommends that State parties should regard 12 as the absolute minimum age of criminal responsibility 146 and stipulates an ideal of between 14 and 16 years. The Committee has however welcomed proposals to set the age at 18 years (see United Kingdom CRC/C/15/Add 188, paras 59 and 62(a) and Committee on the Rights of the Child General Comment No 10 *Children's Rights in Juvenile Justice* CRC/C/GC/10, paras 32, 33 and 39) **[RCLP para 16.63]**.

Alternative methods of disposal (Art 40(3)(b) and 40(4))—See also the UN Standard Minimum Rules for the Administration of Juvenile Justice r 17 and Committee on the Rights of the Child, General Comment No 10 *Children's Rights in Juvenile Justice* CRC/C/GC/10, para 71 **[RCLP paras 16.65–16.67 and 14.23]**.

Article 41

Nothing in the present Convention shall affect any provisions which are more conducive to the realization of the rights of the child and which may be contained in:

(a)   The law of a State party; or
(b)   International law in force for that State.

PART II

Article 42

States Parties undertake to make the principles and provisions of the Convention widely known, by appropriate and active means, to adults and children alike.

Publicity of the principles and provision of the CRC—See [RCLP para 2.22].

Article 43

1. For the purpose of examining the progress made by States Parties in achieving the realization of the obligations undertaken in the present Convention, there shall be established a Committee on the Rights of the Child, which shall carry out the functions hereinafter provided.

2. The Committee shall consist of ten experts of high moral standing and recognized competence in the field covered by this Convention. The members of the Committee shall be elected by States Parties from among their nationals and shall serve in their personal capacity, consideration being given to equitable geographical distribution, as well as to the principal legal systems.

3. The members of the Committee shall be elected by secret ballot from a list of persons nominated by States Parties. Each State Party may nominate one person from among its own nationals.

4. The initial election to the Committee shall be held no later than six months after the date of the entry into force of the present Convention and thereafter every second year. At least four months before the date of each election, the Secretary-General of the United Nations shall address a letter to States Parties inviting them to submit their nominations within two months. The Secretary-General shall subsequently prepare a list in alphabetical order of all persons thus nominated, indicating States Parties which have nominated them, and shall submit it to the States Parties to the present Convention.

5. The elections shall be held at meetings of States Parties convened by the Secretary-General at United Nations Headquarters. At those meetings, for which two thirds of States Parties shall constitute a quorum, the persons elected to the Committee shall be those who obtain the largest number of votes and an absolute majority of the votes of the representatives of States Parties present and voting.

6. The members of the Committee shall be elected for a term of four years. They shall be eligible for re-election if renominated. The term of five of the members elected at the first election shall expire at the end of two years; immediately after the first election, the names of these five members shall be chosen by lot by the Chairman of the meeting.

7. If a member of the Committee dies or resigns or declares that for any other cause he or she can no longer perform the duties of the Committee, the State Party which nominated the member shall appoint another expert from among its nationals to serve for the remainder of the term, subject to the approval of the Committee.

8. The Committee shall establish its own rules of procedure.

9. The Committee shall elect its officers for a period of two years.

10. The meetings of the Committee shall normally be held at United Nations Headquarters or at any other convenient place as determined by the Committee. The Committee shall normally meet annually.

The duration of the meetings of the Committee shall be determined, and reviewed, if necessary, by a meeting of the States Parties to the present Convention, subject to the approval of the General Assembly.

11. The Secretary-General of the United Nations shall provide the necessary staff and facilities for the effective performance of the functions of the Committee under the present Convention.

12. With the approval of the General Assembly, the members of the Committee established under the present Convention shall receive emoluments from United Nations resources on such terms and conditions as the Assembly may decide.

UN Committee on the Rights of the Child—For the status and procedures of the UN Committee on the Rights of the Child see [RCLP para 2.23].

Article 44

1. States Parties undertake to submit to the Committee, through the Secretary-General of the United Nations, reports on the measures they have adopted which give effect to the rights recognized herein and on the progress made on the enjoyment of those rights

   (a)   Within two years of the entry into force of the Convention for the State Party concerned;
   (b)   Thereafter every five years.

2. Reports made under the present article shall indicate factors and difficulties, if any, affecting the degree of fulfilment of the obligations under the present Convention. Reports shall also contain sufficient information to provide the Committee with a comprehensive understanding of the implementation of the Convention in the country concerned.

3. A State Party which has submitted a comprehensive initial report to the Committee need not, in its subsequent reports submitted in accordance with paragraph 1 (b) of the present article, repeat basic information previously provided.

4. The Committee may request from States Parties further information relevant to the implementation of the Convention.

5. The Committee shall submit to the General Assembly, through the Economic and Social Council, every two years, reports on its activities.

6. States Parties shall make their reports widely available to the public in their own countries.

Reporting procedures—For the mechanism and status of the reporting procedures under the UNCRC see [RCLP paras 2.24–2.25]

Article 45

In order to foster the effective implementation of the Convention and to encourage international cooperation in the field covered by the Convention:

   (a)   The specialized agencies, the United Nations Children's Fund, and other United Nations organs shall be entitled to be represented at the consideration of the implementation of such provisions of the present Convention as fall within the scope of their mandate. The Committee may invite the specialized agencies, the United Nations Children's Fund and other competent bodies as it may consider appropriate to provide expert advice on the implementation of the Convention in areas falling within the scope of their respective mandates. The Committee may invite the specialized agencies, the United Nations Children's Fund, and other United Nations organs to submit reports on the implementation of the Convention in areas falling within the scope of their activities;

(b) The Committee shall transmit, as it may consider appropriate, to the specialized agencies, the United Nations Children's Fund and other competent bodies, any reports from States Parties that contain a request, or indicate a need, for technical advice or assistance, along with the Committee's observations and suggestions, if any, on these requests or indications;

(c) The Committee may recommend to the General Assembly to request the Secretary-General to undertake on its behalf studies on specific issues relating to the rights of the child;

(d) The Committee may make suggestions and general recommendations based on information received pursuant to articles 44 and 45 of the present Convention. Such suggestions and general recommendations shall be transmitted to any State Party concerned and reported to the General Assembly, together with comments, if any, from States Parties.

PART III

Article 46

The present Convention shall be open for signature by all States.

Article 47

The present Convention is subject to ratification. Instruments of ratification shall be deposited with the Secretary-General of the United Nations.

Article 48

The present Convention shall remain open for accession by any State. The instruments of accession shall be deposited with the Secretary-General of the United Nations.

Article 49

1. The present Convention shall enter into force on the thirtieth day following the date of deposit with the Secretary-General of the United Nations of the twentieth instrument of ratification or accession.

2. For each State ratifying or acceding to the Convention after the deposit of the twentieth instrument of ratification or accession, the Convention shall enter into force on the thirtieth day after the deposit by such State of its instrument of ratification or accession.

Article 50

1. Any State Party may propose an amendment and file it with the Secretary-General of the United Nations. The Secretary-General shall thereupon communicate the proposed amendment to States Parties, with a request that they indicate whether they favour a conference of States Parties for the purpose of considering and voting upon the proposals. In the event that, within four months from the date of such communication, at least one third of the States Parties favour such a conference, the Secretary-General shall convene the conference under the auspices of the United Nations. Any amendment

adopted by a majority of States Parties present and voting at the conference shall be submitted to the General Assembly for approval.

2. An amendment adopted in accordance with paragraph 1 of the present article shall enter into force when it has been approved by the General Assembly of the United Nations and accepted by a two thirds majority of States Parties.

3. When an amendment enters into force, it shall be binding on those States Parties which have accepted it, other States Parties still being bound by the provisions of the present Convention and any earlier amendments which they have accepted.

Article 51

1. The Secretary-General of the United Nations shall receive and circulate to all States the text of reservations made by States at the time of ratification or accession.

2. A reservation incompatible with the object and purpose of the present Convention shall not be permitted.

3. Reservations may be withdrawn at any time by notification to that effect addressed to the Secretary-General of the United Nations, who shall then inform all States. Such notification shall take effect on the date on which it is received by the Secretary-General.

Article 52

A State Party may denounce the present Convention by written notification to the Secretary-General of the United Nations. Denunciation becomes effective one year after the date of receipt of the notification by the Secretary-General.

Article 53

The Secretary-General of the United Nations is designated as the depositary of the present Convention.

Article 54

The original of the present Convention, of which the Arabic, Chinese, English, French, Russian and Spanish texts are equally authentic, shall be deposited with the Secretary-General of the United Nations.

IN WITNESS THEREOF the undersigned plenipotentiaries, being duly authorized thereto by their respective governments, have signed the present Convention.

CHAPTER 4

OPTIONAL PROTOCOL TO THE UN CONVENTION ON THE RIGHTS OF THE CHILD ON THE SALE OF CHILDREN, CHILD PROSTITUTION AND CHILD PORNOGRAPHY

PREAMBLE

The States Parties to the present Protocol,

Considering that, in order further to achieve the purposes of the Convention on the Rights of the Child and the implementation of its provisions, especially articles 1, 11, 21, 32, 33, 34, 35 and 36, it would be appropriate to extend the measures that States Parties should undertake in order to guarantee the protection of the child from the sale of children, child prostitution and child pornography,

Considering also that the Convention on the Rights of the Child recognizes the right of the child to be protected from economic exploitation and from performing any work that is likely to be hazardous or to interfere with the child's education, or to be harmful to the child's health or physical, mental, spiritual, moral or social development,

Gravely concerned at the significant and increasing international traffic of children for the purpose of the sale of children, child prostitution and child pornography,

Deeply concerned at the widespread and continuing practice of sex tourism, to which children are especially vulnerable, as it directly promotes the sale of children, child prostitution and child pornography,

Recognizing that a number of particularly vulnerable groups, including girl children, are at greater risk of sexual exploitation, and that girl children are disproportionately represented among the sexually exploited,

Concerned about the growing availability of child pornography on the Internet and other evolving technologies, and recalling the International Conference on Combating Child Pornography on the Internet (Vienna, 1999) and, in particular, its conclusion calling for the worldwide criminalization of the production, distribution, exportation, transmission, importation, intentional possession and advertising of child pornography, and stressing the importance of closer cooperation and partnership between Governments and the Internet industry,

Believing that the elimination of the sale of children, child prostitution and child pornography will be facilitated by adopting a holistic approach, addressing the contributing factors, including underdevelopment, poverty, economic disparities, inequitable socio-economic structure, dysfunctioning families, lack of education, urban-rural migration, gender discrimination, irresponsible adult sexual behaviour, harmful traditional practices, armed conflicts and trafficking of children,

Believing that efforts to raise public awareness are needed to reduce consumer demand for the sale of children, child prostitution and child pornography, and also believing in the importance of strengthening global partnership among all actors and of improving law enforcement at the national level,

Noting the provisions of international legal instruments relevant to the protection of children, including the Hague Convention on the Protection of Children and Cooperation with Respect to Inter-Country Adoption, the Hague Convention on the Civil Aspects of International Child Abduction, the Hague Convention on Jurisdiction, Applicable Law, Recognition, Enforcement and Cooperation in Respect of Parental Responsibility and Measures for the Protection of Children, and International Labour Organization Convention No. 182 on the Prohibition and Immediate Action for the Elimination of the Worst Forms of Child Labour,

Encouraged by the overwhelming support for the Convention on the Rights of the Child, demonstrating the widespread commitment that exists for the promotion and protection of the rights of the child,

Recognizing the importance of the implementation of the provisions of the Programme of Action for the Prevention of the Sale of Children, Child Prostitution and Child Pornography and the Declaration and Agenda for Action adopted at the World Congress against Commercial Sexual Exploitation of Children, held at Stockholm from 27 to 31 August 1996, and the other relevant decisions and recommendations of pertinent international bodies,

Taking due account of the importance of the traditions and cultural values of each people for the protection and harmonious development of the child,

Have agreed as follows:

Status—The Optional Protocol to the UN Convention on the Rights of the Child on the Sale of Children, Child Prostitution and Child Pornography was adopted by the UN General Assembly in 2000 and entered into force on 18 January 2002. The Optional Protocol expands the right of the child beyond those prescribed by the original terms of the UNCRC. The United Kingdom ratified the Optional Protocol on 3 July 2003 [RCLP para 2.5]. The Optional Protocol is closely linked with, and will overlap with, Arts 19(1) and 34 of the UNCRC [RCLP **para 15.32**]. The Optional Protocol has been referred to by the domestic courts (see *R (E and others v Director of Public Prosecutions* [2011] EWHC 1465 (Admin), [2011] All ER (D) 56 (Jun)). See also *R v L and other cases* [2013] EWCA Crim 991.

Article 1

States Parties shall prohibit the sale of children, child prostitution and child pornography as provided for by the present Protocol.

'sale' (Art 1)—Note that Art 3 of the Optional Protocol provides further guidance as to the meaning of the word 'sale' within the context of the Optional Protocol [RCLP para 15.61].

Article 2

For the purpose of the present Protocol:

(a) Sale of children means any act or transaction whereby a child is transferred by any person or group of persons to another for remuneration or any other consideration;

(b) Child prostitution means the use of a child in sexual activities for remuneration or any other form of consideration;

(c)   Child pornography means any representation, by whatever means, of a child engaged in real or simulated explicit sexual activities or any representation of the sexual parts of a child for primarily sexual purposes.

Article 3

1. Each State Party shall ensure that, as a minimum, the following acts and activities are fully covered under its criminal or penal law, whether these offences are committed domestically or transnationally or on an individual or organized basis:

(a)   In the context of sale of children as defined in Article 2:
    (i)   The offering, delivering or accepting, by whatever means, a child for the purpose of:
        a.   Sexual exploitation of the child;
        b.   Transfer of organs of the child for profit;
        c.   Engagement of the child in forced labour;
    (ii)   Improperly inducing consent, as an intermediary, for the adoption of a child in violation of applicable international legal instruments on adoption;
(b)   Offering, obtaining, procuring or providing a child for child prostitution, as defined in Article 2;
(c)   Producing, distributing, disseminating, importing, exporting, offering, selling or possessing for the above purposes child pornography as defined in Article 2.

2. Subject to the provisions of a State Party's national law, the same shall apply to an attempt to commit any of these acts and to complicity or participation in any of these acts.

3. Each State Party shall make these offences punishable by appropriate penalties that take into account their grave nature.

4. Subject to the provisions of its national law, each State Party shall take measures, where appropriate, to establish the liability of legal persons for offences established in paragraph I of the present Article. Subject to the legal principles of the State Party, this liability of legal persons may be criminal, civil or administrative.

5. States Parties shall take all appropriate legal and administrative measures to ensure that all persons involved in the adoption of a child act in conformity with applicable international legal instruments.

'Transfer of organs of the child for profit' (Art 3(1)(a)(i)(b)—See also the Guiding Principles on Human Organ Transplantation (WHO) Principles 4 and 5 [RCLP paras 15.61–15.62].

'Improperly inducing consent, as an intermediary, for the adoption of a child' (Art 3(1)(a)(ii)—See also Art 3(5) [RCLP para 15.61] and Art 32 of the Hague Convention on Protection of Children and Co-operation in respect of Intercountry Adoption [RCLP para 8.154].

Article 4

1. Each State Party shall take such measures as may be necessary to establish its jurisdiction over the offences referred to in Article 3, paragraph 1, when the offences are committed in its territory or on board a ship or aircraft registered in that State.

2. Each State Party may take such measures as may be necessary to establish its jurisdiction over the offences referred to in Article 3, paragraph 1, in the following cases:

(a)   When the alleged offender is a national of that State or a person who has his habitual residence in its territory;
(b)   When the victim is a national of that State.

3. Each State Party shall also take such measures as may be necessary to establish its jurisdiction over the above-mentioned offences when the alleged offender is present in its territory and it does not extradite him or her to another State Party on the ground that the offence has been committed by one of its nationals.

4. This Protocol does not exclude any criminal jurisdiction exercised in accordance with internal law.

Jurisdiction (Art 4)—Art 4 of the Optional Protocol deals with jurisdictional issues concerning the criminal actions which are stipulated in Arts 3, 5 and 6 [**RCLP para 15.61**].

Article 5

1. The offences referred to in Article 3, paragraph 1, shall be deemed to be included as extraditable offences in any extradition treaty existing between States Parties and shall be included as extraditable offences in every extradition treaty subsequently concluded between them, in accordance with the conditions set forth in those treaties.

2. If a State Party that makes extradition conditional on the existence of a treaty receives a request for extradition from another State Party with which it has no extradition treaty, it may consider this Protocol as a legal basis for extradition in respect of such offences. Extradition shall be subject to the conditions provided by the law of the requested State.

3. States Parties that do not make extradition conditional on the existence of a treaty shall recognize such offences as extraditable offences between themselves subject to the conditions provided by the law of the requested State.

4. Such offences shall be treated, for the purpose of extradition between States Parties, as if they had been committed not only in the place in which they occurred but also in the territories of the States required to establish their jurisdiction in accordance with Article 4.

5. If an extradition request is made with respect to an offence described in Article 3, paragraph 1, and if the requested State Party does not or will not extradite on the basis of the nationality of the offender, that State shall take suitable measures to submit the case to its competent authorities for the purpose of prosecution.

Article 6

1. States Parties shall afford one another the greatest measure of assistance in connection with investigations or criminal or extradition proceedings brought in respect of the offences set forth in Article 3, paragraph 1, including assistance in obtaining evidence at their disposal necessary for the proceedings.

2. States Parties shall carry out their obligations under paragraph 1 of the present Article in conformity with any treaties or other arrangements on mutual legal assistance that may exist between them. In the absence of such treaties or arrangements, States Parties shall afford one another assistance in accordance with their domestic law.

Article 7

States Parties shall, subject to the provisions of their national law:

(a)   Take measures to provide for the seizure and confiscation, as appropriate, of:
  (i)   Goods such as materials, assets and other instrumentalities used to commit or facilitate offences under the present Protocol;
  (ii)   Proceeds derived from such offences;

(b)   Execute requests from another State Party for seizure or confiscation of goods or proceeds referred to in subparagraph (a) (i);

(c)   Take measures aimed at closing, on a temporary or definitive basis, premises used to commit such offences.

Article 8

1. States Parties shall adopt appropriate measures to protect the rights and interests of child victims of the practices prohibited under the present Protocol at all stages of the criminal justice process, in particular by:

(a)   Recognizing the vulnerability of child victims and adapting procedures to recognize their special needs, including their special needs as witnesses;

(b)   Informing child victims of their rights, their role and the scope, timing and progress of the proceedings and of the disposition of their cases;

(c)   Allowing the views, needs and concerns of child victims to be presented and considered in proceedings where their personal interests are affected, in a mariner consistent with the procedural rules of national law;

(d)   Providing appropriate support services to child victims throughout the legal process;

(e)   Protecting, as appropriate, the privacy and identity of child victims and taking measures in accordance with national law to avoid the inappropriate dissemination of information that could lead to the identification of child victims;

(f)   Providing, in appropriate cases, for the safety of child victims, as well as that of their families and witnesses on their behalf, from intimidation and retaliation;

(g)   Avoiding unnecessary delay in the disposition of cases and the execution of orders or decrees granting compensation to child victims.

2. States Parties shall ensure that uncertainty as to the actual age of the victim shall not prevent the initiation of criminal investigations, including investigations aimed at establishing the age of the victim.

3. States Parties shall ensure that, in the treatment by the criminal justice system of children who are victims of the offences described in the present Protocol, the best interest of the child shall be a primary consideration.

4. States Parties shall take measures to ensure appropriate training, in particular legal and psychological training, for the persons who work with victims of the offences prohibited under the present Protocol.

5. States Parties shall, in appropriate cases, adopt measures in order to protect the safety and integrity of those persons and/or organizations involved in the prevention and/or protection and rehabilitation of victims of such offences.

6. Nothing in the present Article shall be construed as prejudicial to or inconsistent with the rights of the accused to a fair and impartial trial.

'**shall adopt appropriate measures**' (Art 8(1))—Art 8 of the Optional Protocol places a positive duty on State Parties to protect the rights and interests of child victims of the practices prohibited by the Optional Protocol at all stages of the criminal process [**RCLP para 2.28**].

Article 9

1. States Parties shall adopt or strengthen, implement and disseminate laws, administrative measures, social policies and programmes to prevent the offences referred to in the present Protocol. Particular attention shall be given to protect children who are especially vulnerable to these practices.

2. States Parties shall promote awareness in the public at large, including children, through information by all appropriate means, education and training, about the preventive measures and harmful effects of the offences referred to in the present Protocol. In fulfilling their obligations under this Article, States Parties shall encourage the participation of the community and, in particular, children and child victims, in such information and education and training programmes, including at the international level.

3. States Parties shall take all feasible measures with the aim of ensuring all appropriate assistance to victims of such offences, including their full social reintegration and their full physical and psychological recovery.

4. States Parties shall ensure that all child victims of the offences described in the present Protocol have access to adequate procedures to seek, without discrimination, compensation for damages from those legally responsible.

5. States Parties shall take appropriate measures aimed at effectively prohibiting the production and dissemination of material advertising the offences described in the present Protocol.

'States Parties shall adopt or strengthen' (Art 9(1))—Art 9 imposes a positive obligation on State Parties to take proactive steps to prevent the activities prohibited by the Optional Protocol [RCLP para 2.28].

Article 10

1. States Parties shall take all necessary steps to strengthen international cooperation by multilateral, regional and bilateral arrangements for the prevention, detection, investigation, prosecution and punishment of those responsible for acts involving the sale of children, child prostitution, child pornography and child sex tourism. States Parties shall also promote international cooperation and coordination between their authorities, national and international non-governmental organizations and international organizations.

2. States Parties shall promote international cooperation to assist child victims in their physical and psychological recovery, social reintegration and repatriation.

3. States Parties shall promote the strengthening of international cooperation in order to address the root causes, such as poverty and underdevelopment, contributing to the vulnerability of children to the sale of children, child prostitution, child pornography and child sex tourism.

4. States Parties in a position to do so shall provide financial, technical or other assistance through existing multilateral, regional, bilateral or other programmes.

Article 11

Nothing in the present Protocol shall affect any provisions that are more conducive to the realization of the rights of the child and that may be contained in:

(a)   The law of a State Party;
(b)   International law in force for that State.

Article 12

1. Each State Party shall submit, within two years following the entry into force of the Protocol for that State Party, a report to the Committee on the Rights of the Child providing comprehensive information on the measures it has taken to implement the provisions of the Protocol.

2. Following the submission of the comprehensive report, each State Party shall include in the reports they submit to the Committee on the Rights of the Child, in accordance with Article 44 of the Convention, any further information with respect to the implementation of the Protocol. Other States Parties to the Protocol shall submit a report every five years.

3. The Committee on the Rights of the Child may request from States Parties further information relevant to the implementation of this Protocol.

Article 13

1. The present Protocol is open for signature by any State that is a party to the Convention or has signed it.

2. The present Protocol is subject to ratification and is open to accession by any State that is a party to the Convention or has signed it. Instruments of ratification or accession shall be deposited with the Secretary-General of the United Nations.

'subject to ratification' (Art 13(2))—Note that the Optional Protocol is not automatically binding on States Parties who have ratified the UNCRC and the Protocol contains its own ratification mechanism independent of Part III of the UNCRC [RCLP **para 2.27**].

Article 14

1. The present Protocol shall enter into force three months after the deposit of the tenth instrument of ratification or accession.

2. For each State ratifying the present Protocol or acceding to it after its entry into force, the present Protocol shall enter into force one month after the date of the deposit of its own instrument of ratification or accession.

Article 15

1. Any State Party may denounce the present Protocol at any time by written notification to the Secretary-General of the United Nations, who shall thereafter inform the other States Parties to the Convention and all States that have signed the Convention. The denunciation shall I take effect one year after the date of receipt of the notification by the Secretary- General of the United Nations.

2. Such a denunciation shall not have the effect of releasing the State Party from its obligations under this Protocol in regard to any offence that occurs prior to the date on which the denunciation becomes effective. Nor shall such a denunciation prejudice in any way the continued consideration of any matter that is already under consideration by the Committee prior to the date on which the denunciation becomes effective.

Article 16

1. Any State Party may propose an amendment and file it with the Secretary-General of the United Nations. The Secretary-General shall thereupon communicate the proposed amendment to States Parties, with a request that they indicate whether they favour a conference of States Parties for the purpose of considering and voting upon the proposals. In the event that, within four months from the date of such communication, at least one third of the States Parties favour such a conference, the Secretary-General shall convene the conference under the auspices of the United Nations. Any amendment adopted by a majority of States Parties present and voting at the conference shall be submitted to the General Assembly for approval.

2. An amendment adopted in accordance with paragraph I of the present Article shall enter into force when it has been approved by the General Assembly of the United Nations and accepted by a two-thirds majority of States Parties.

3. When an amendment enters into force, it shall be binding on those States Parties that have accepted it, other States Parties still being bound by the provisions of the present Protocol and any earlier amendments that they have accepted.

Article 17

1. The present Protocol, of which the Arabic, Chinese, English, French, Russian and Spanish texts are equally authentic, shall be deposited in the archives of the United Nations.

2. The Secretary-General of the United Nations shall transmit certified copies of the present Protocol to all States Parties to the Convention and all States that have signed the Convention.

CHAPTER 5

OPTIONAL PROTOCOL TO THE UN CONVENTION ON THE RIGHTS OF THE CHILD ON THE INVOLVEMENT OF CHILDREN IN ARMED CONFLICT

PREAMBLE

The States Parties to the present Protocol,

Encouraged by the overwhelming support for the Convention on the Rights of the Child, demonstrating the widespread commitment that exists to strive for the promotion and protection of the rights of the child,

Reaffirming that the rights of children require special protection, and calling for continuous improvement of the situation of children without distinction, as well as for their development and education in conditions of peace and security,

Disturbed by the harmful and widespread impact of armed conflict on children and the long-term consequences this has for durable peace, security and development,

Condemning the targeting of children in situations of armed conflict and direct attacks on objects protected under international law, including places generally having a significant presence of children, such as schools and hospitals,

Noting the adoption of the Statute of the International Criminal Court and, in particular, its inclusion as a war crime of conscripting or enlisting children under the age of 15 years or using them to participate actively in hostilities in both international and non-international armed conflicts,

Considering, therefore, that to strengthen further the implementation of rights recognized in the Convention on the Rights of the Child there is a need to increase the protection of children from involvement in armed conflict,

Noting that article 1 of the Convention on the Rights of the Child specifies that, for the purposes of that Convention, a child means every human being below the age of 18 years unless, under the law applicable to the child, majority is attained earlier,

Convinced that an optional protocol to the Convention raising the age of possible recruitment of persons into armed forces and their participation in hostilities will contribute effectively to the implementation of the principle that the best interests of the child are to be a primary consideration in all actions concerning children,

Noting that the twenty-sixth international Conference of the Red Cross and Red Crescent in December 1995 recommended, inter alia, that parties to conflict take every feasible step to ensure that children under the age of 18 years do not take part in hostilities,

Welcoming the unanimous adoption, in June 1999, of International Labour Organization Convention No. 182 on the Prohibition and Immediate Action for the Elimination of the Worst Forms of Child Labour, which prohibits, inter alia, forced or compulsory recruitment of children for use in armed conflict,

Condemning with the gravest concern the recruitment, training and use within and across national borders of children in hostilities by armed groups distinct from the armed forces of a State, and recognizing the responsibility of those who recruit, train and use children in this regard,

Recalling the obligation of each party to an armed conflict to abide by the provisions of international humanitarian law,

Stressing that this Protocol is without prejudice to the purposes and principles contained in the Charter of the United Nations, including Article 51, and relevant norms of humanitarian law,

Bearing in mind that conditions of peace and security based on full respect of the purposes and principles contained in the Charter and observance of applicable human rights instruments are indispensable for the full protection of children, in particular during armed conflicts and foreign occupation,

Recognizing the special needs of those children who are particularly vulnerable to recruitment or use in hostilities contrary to this Protocol owing to their economic or social status or gender,

Mindful of the necessity of taking into consideration the economic, social and political root causes of the involvement of children in armed conflicts,

Convinced of the need to strengthen international cooperation in the implementation of this Protocol, as well as the physical and psychosocial rehabilitation and social reintegration of children who are victims of armed conflict,

Encouraging the participation of the community and, in particular, children and child victims in the dissemination of informational and educational programmes concerning the implementation of the Protocol,

Have agreed as follows:

Status—The Optional Protocol to the UN Convention on the Rights of the Child on the Involvement of Children in Armed Conflict was adopted by the UN General Assembly in 2000 and entered into force on 12 February 2002. The Optional Protocol expands the rights of the child beyond those prescribed by the original terms of the UNCRC. The United Kingdom ratified the Optional Protocol on 24 June 2003 **[RCLP para 2.5]**. The Optional Protocol has the effect of extending the protection provided by Arts 38(2) and 38(3) of the UNCRC following concern that Art 38 of the UNCRC was not consistent with the level of protection afforded to children by the rest of the UNCRC (see P Newell and R Hodgkin *Implementation Handbook for the Convention on the Rights of the Child* (2008, 3rd edn, UNICEF), p 600) **[RCLP para 2.29]**. The Optional Protocol has been referred to by the domestic courts (see *AA v Secretary of State for the Home Department and another* [2012] UKUT 00016 (IAC)).

Article 1

States Parties shall take all feasible measures to ensure that members of their armed forces who have not attained the age of 18 years do not take a direct part in hostilities.

Article 2

States Parties shall ensure that persons who have not attained the age of 18 years are not compulsorily recruited into their armed forces.

'not compulsorily recruited' (Art 2)—See also the ILO Convention on the Worst Forms of Child Labour (No 182) Art 3(a) and the Rome Statute of the International Criminal Court Art 8(2)(b)(xxvi) **[RCLP para 15.97]**. For the meaning of the word 'recruited' see the *Paris Principles: Principles and Guidelines on Children Associated with Armed Forces or Armed Groups* (2007) UNICEF para 2.4 [**RCLP para 15.97**]. The term 'recruitment' does not necessarily mean recruitment as front line soldiers (P Newell and R Hodgkin *Implementation Handbook for the Convention on the Rights of the Child* (2008, 3rd edn, UNICEF), p 583).

Article 3

1. States Parties shall raise the minimum age for the voluntary recruitment of persons into their national armed forces from that set out in article 38, paragraph 3, of the Convention on the Rights of the Child, taking account of the principles contained in that article and recognizing that under the Convention persons under 18 are entitled to special protection.

2. Each State Party shall deposit a binding declaration upon ratification of or accession to this Protocol that sets forth the minimum age at which it will permit voluntary recruitment into its national armed forces and a description of the safeguards that it has adopted to ensure that such recruitment is not forced or coerced.

3. States Parties that permit voluntary recruitment into their national armed forces under the age of 18 shall maintain safeguards to ensure, as a minimum, that:

    (a)   Such recruitment is genuinely voluntary;
    (b)   Such recruitment is done with the informed consent of the person's parents or legal guardians;
    (c)   Such persons are fully informed of the duties involved in such military service;
    (d)   Such persons provide reliable proof of age prior to acceptance into national military service.

4. Each State Party may strengthen its declaration at any time by notification to that effect addressed to the Secretary-General of the United Nations, who shall inform all States Parties. Such notification shall take effect on the date on which it is received by the Secretary-General.

5. The requirement to raise the age in paragraph 1 of the present article does not apply to schools operated by or under the control of the armed forces of the States Parties, in keeping with articles 28 and 29 of the Convention on the Rights of the Child.

'**shall raise the minimum age for the voluntary recruitment**' (Art 3(1))—Note that the United Kingdom made a declaration upon signing the Optional Protocol that it would take all feasible measures to ensure that members of its armed forces who have not attained the age of 18 years do not take a direct part in hostilities but that Art 1 of the Optional Protocol would not exclude the deployment of soldiers under the age of 18 in hostilities where (a) there is a genuine military need to deploy and (b) by reason of the urgency of the situation (i) it is not practicable to withdraw such persons before deployment; or (ii) to do so would undermine operational effectiveness and thereby put at risk the successful completion of the mission and/or the safety of other personnel [**RCLP para 2.29**].

Conditions for voluntary recruitment (Art 3(3))—See also Art 38(3) and Protocol I to the Geneva Conventions Art 77 [**RCLP para 15.98**].

Article 4

1. Armed groups that are distinct from the armed forces of a State should not, under any circumstances, recruit or use in hostilities persons under the age of 18 years.

2. States Parties shall take all feasible measures to prevent such recruitment and use, including the adoption of legal measures necessary to prohibit and criminalize such practices.

3. The application of the present article under this Protocol shall not affect the legal status of any party to an armed conflict.

'**Armed groups that are distinct from armed forces ...**' (Art 4(1))—Art 4 is designed to criminalise the use of child soldiers by militia, guerrilla and other military groups (P Newell and R Hodgkin *Implementation Handbook for the Convention on the Rights of the Child* (2008, 3rd edn, UNICEF), p 600) [**RCLP para 2.29**].

Article 5

Nothing in the present Protocol shall be construed as precluding provisions in the law of a State Party or in international instruments and international humanitarian law that are more conducive to the realization of the rights of the child.

Article 6

1. Each State Party shall take all necessary legal, administrative and other measures to ensure the effective implementation and enforcement of the provisions of this Protocol within its jurisdiction.

2. States Parties undertake to make the principles and provisions of the present Protocol widely known and promoted by appropriate means, to adults and children alike.

3. States Parties shall take all feasible measures to ensure that persons within their jurisdiction recruited or used in hostilities contrary to this Protocol are demobilized or otherwise released from service. States Parties shall, when necessary, accord to these persons all appropriate assistance for their physical and psychological recovery and their social reintegration.

Positive obligation—Art 6 places upon State Parties a positive obligation to effectively implement the provisions of the Optional Protocol [**RCLP para 2.29**].

'**demobilized or otherwise released from service**' (Art 6(3))—See also Art 39 of the UNCRC [**RCLP para 15.111**] and the Committee on the Rights of the Child General Comment No 6 *Treatment of Unaccompanied and Separated Children Outside their Country of Origin* CRC/GC/2005/6, para 56 [**RCLP para 15.118**].

Article 7

1. States Parties shall cooperate in the implementation of the present Protocol, including in the prevention of any activity contrary to the Protocol and in the rehabilitation and social reintegration of persons who are victims of acts contrary to this Protocol, including through technical cooperation and financial assistance. Such assistance and cooperation will be undertaken in consultation with concerned States Parties and relevant international organizations.

2. States Parties in a position to do so shall provide such assistance through existing multilateral, bilateral or other programmes, or, inter alia, through a voluntary fund established in accordance with the rules of the General Assembly.

Positive obligation—Art 7 places upon State Parties a positive obligation to effectively implement the provisions of the Optional Protocol [**RCLP para 2.29**].

'**rehabilitation and social reintegration of persons who are victims**' (Art 7(1))—See also Art 39 of the UNCRC [**RCLP para 15.111**] and the Committee on the Rights of the Child General Comment No 6 *Treatment of Unaccompanied and Separated Children Outside their Country of Origin* CRC/GC/2005/6, para 56 [**RCLP para 15.118**].

Article 8

1. Each State Party shall submit, within two years following the entry into force of the Protocol for that State Party, a report to the Committee on the Rights of the Child providing comprehensive information on the measures it has taken to implement the provisions of the Protocol, including the measures taken to implement the provisions on participation and recruitment.

2. Following the submission of the comprehensive report, each State Party shall include in the reports they submit to the Committee on the Rights of the Child, in accordance with article 44 of the Convention, any further information with respect to the implementation of the Protocol. Other States Parties to the Protocol shall submit a report every five years.

3. The Committee on the Rights of the Child may request from States Parties further information relevant to the implementation of this Protocol.

Article 9

1. The present Protocol is open for signature by any State that is a party to the Convention or has signed it.

2. The present Protocol is subject to ratification and is open to accession by any State.

Instruments of ratification or accession shall be deposited with the Secretary-General of the United Nations.

3. The Secretary-General, in his capacity as depositary of the Convention and the Protocol, shall inform all States Parties to the Convention and all States that have signed the Convention of each instrument of declaration pursuant to article 13.

'subject to ratification' (Art 19(2))—Note that the Optional Protocol is not automatically binding on States Parties who have ratified the UNCRC and the Protocol contains its own ratification mechanism independent of Part III of the UNCRC [RCLP para 2.27].

Article 10

1. The present Protocol shall enter into force three months after the deposit of the tenth instrument of ratification or accession.

2. For each State ratifying the present Protocol or acceding to it after its entry into force, the present Protocol shall enter into force one month after the date of the deposit of its own instrument of ratification or accession.

Article 11

1. Any State Party may denounce the present Protocol at any time by written notification to the Secretary-General of the United Nations, who shall thereafter inform the other States Parties to the Convention and all States that have signed the Convention. The denunciation shall take effect one year after the date of receipt of the notification by the Secretary- General. If, however, on the expiry of that year the denouncing State Party is engaged in armed conflict, the denunciation shall not take effect before the end of the armed conflict.

2. Such a denunciation shall not have the effect of releasing the State Party from its obligations under the present Protocol in regard to any act that occurs prior to the date on which the denunciation becomes effective. Nor shall such a denunciation prejudice in any way the continued consideration of any matter that is already under consideration by the Committee prior to the date on which the denunciation becomes effective.

Article 12

1. Any State Party may propose an amendment and file it with the Secretary-General of the United Nations. The Secretary-General shall thereupon communicate the proposed amendment to States Parties, with a request that they indicate whether they favour a conference of States Parties for the purpose of considering and voting upon the proposals. In the event that, within four months from the date of such communication, at least one third of the States Parties favour such a conference, the Secretary-General

shall convene the conference under the auspices of the United Nations. Any amendment adopted by a majority of States Parties present and voting at the conference shall be submitted to the General Assembly for approval.

2. An amendment adopted in accordance with paragraph 1 of the present article shall enter into force when it has been approved by the General Assembly of the United Nations and accepted by a two-thirds majority of States Parties.

3. When an amendment enters into force, it shall be binding on those States Parties that have accepted it, other States Parties still being bound by the provisions of the present Protocol and any earlier amendments that they have accepted.

Article 13

1. The present Protocol, of which the Arabic, Chinese, English, French, Russian and Spanish texts are equally authentic, shall be deposited in the archives of the United Nations.

2. The Secretary-General of the United Nations shall transmit certified copies of the present Protocol to all States Parties to the Convention and all States that have signed the Convention.

CHAPTER 6

OPTIONAL PROTOCOL TO THE CONVENTION ON THE RIGHTS OF THE CHILD ON A COMMUNICATIONS PROCEDURE

Resolution adopted by the General Assembly

[on the report of the Third Committee (A/66/457)]

The General Assembly,

Taking note with appreciation of the adoption by the Human Rights Council, through its resolution 17/18 of 17 June 2011, of the Optional Protocol to the Convention on the Rights of the Child on a communications procedure,

1 *Adopts* the Optional Protocol to the Convention on the Rights of the Child on a communications procedure as contained in the annex to the present resolution;

2 *Recommends* that the Optional Protocol be opened for signature at a signing ceremony to be held in 2012, and requests the Secretary-General and the United Nations High Commissioner for Human Rights to provide the necessary assistance.

89th plenary meeting

19 December 2011

Scope—The Optional Protocol on the Convention on the Rights of the Child on a Communications Procedure provides a mechanism whereby communications may be submitted by or on behalf of an individual or group of individuals within the jurisdiction of a State party who claim to be victims of a violation by that State party of any of the rights set forth in the UNCRC or its first two Optional Protocols.

Status in domestic law—The Optional Protocol on a Communications Procedure was adopted on 19 December 2011 (UN Resolution 66/138). The Optional Protocol was opened for signature on 28 February 2012 and will come into force three months after the tenth State Party to deposit a instrument of ratification or accession does so. The United Kingdom has yet to sign or ratify the Optional Protocol.

ANNEX
OPTIONAL PROTOCOL TO THE CONVENTION ON THE RIGHTS OF THE CHILD ON A COMMUNICATIONS PROCEDURE

The States parties to the present Protocol,

Considering that, in accordance with the principles proclaimed in the Charter of the United Nations, the recognition of the inherent dignity and the equal and inalienable rights of all members of the human family is the foundation of freedom, justice and peace in the world,

Noting that the States parties to the Convention on the Rights of the Child (hereinafter referred to as 'the Convention') recognize the rights set forth in it to each child within their jurisdiction without discrimination of any kind, irrespective of the child's or his or her parent's or legal guardian's race, colour, sex, language, religion, political or other opinion, national, ethnic or social origin, property, disability, birth or other status,

Reaffirming the universality, indivisibility, interdependence and interrelatedness of all human rights and fundamental freedoms,

Reaffirming also the status of the child as a subject of rights and as a human being with dignity and with evolving capacities,

Recognizing that children's special and dependent status may create real difficulties for them in pursuing remedies for violations of their rights,

Considering that the present Protocol will reinforce and complement national and regional mechanisms allowing children to submit complaints for violations of their rights,

Recognizing that the best interests of the child should be a primary consideration to be respected in pursuing remedies for violations of the rights of the child, and that such remedies should take into account the need for child-sensitive procedures at all levels,

Encouraging States parties to develop appropriate national mechanisms to enable a child whose rights have been violated to have access to effective remedies at the domestic level,

Recalling the important role that national human rights institutions and other relevant specialized institutions, mandated to promote and protect the rights of the child, can play in this regard,

Considering that, in order to reinforce and complement such national mechanisms and to further enhance the implementation of the Convention and, where applicable, the Optional Protocols thereto on the sale of children, child prostitution and child pornography and on the involvement of children in armed conflict, it would be appropriate to enable the Committee on the Rights of the Child (hereinafter referred to as 'the Committee') to carry out the functions provided for in the present Protocol,

Have agreed as follows:

PART I
GENERAL PROVISIONS

Article 1
Competence of the Committee on the Rights of the Child

1 A State party to the present Protocol recognizes the competence of the Committee as provided for by the present Protocol.

2 The Committee shall not exercise its competence regarding a State party to the present Protocol on matters concerning violations of rights set forth in an instrument to which that State is not a party.

3 No communication shall be received by the Committee if it concerns a State that is not a party to the present Protocol.

Article 2
General principles guiding the functions of the Committee

In fulfilling the functions conferred on it by the present Protocol, the Committee shall be guided by the principle of the best interests of the child. It shall also have regard for the rights and views of the child, the views of the child being given due weight in accordance with the age and maturity of the child.

Article 3
Rules of procedure

1 The Committee shall adopt rules of procedure to be followed when exercising the functions conferred on it by the present Protocol. In doing so, it shall have regard, in particular, for article 2 of the present Protocol in order to guarantee child-sensitive procedures.

2 The Committee shall include in its rules of procedure safeguards to prevent the manipulation of the child by those acting on his or her behalf and may decline to examine any communication that it considers not to be in the child's best interests.

Article 4
Protection measures

1 A State party shall take all appropriate steps to ensure that individuals under its jurisdiction are not subjected to any human rights violation, ill-treatment or intimidation as a consequence of communications or cooperation with the Committee pursuant to the present Protocol.

2 The identity of any individual or group of individuals concerned shall not be revealed publicly without their express consent.

PART II
COMMUNICATIONS PROCEDURE

Article 5
Individual communications

1 Communications may be submitted by or on behalf of an individual or group of individuals, within the jurisdiction of a State party, claiming to be victims of a violation by that State party of any of the rights set forth in any of the following instruments to which that State is a party:

(a) The Convention;
(b) The Optional Protocol to the Convention on the sale of children, child prostitution and child pornography;
(c) The Optional Protocol to the Convention on the involvement of children in armed conflict.

2 Where a communication is submitted on behalf of an individual or group of individuals, this shall be with their consent unless the author can justify acting on their behalf without such consent.

Article 6
Interim measures

1 At any time after the receipt of a communication and before a determination on the merits has been reached, the Committee may transmit to the State party concerned for

its urgent consideration a request that the State party take such interim measures as may be necessary in exceptional circumstances to avoid possible irreparable damage to the victim or victims of the alleged violations.

2 Where the Committee exercises its discretion under paragraph 1 of the present article, this does not imply a determination on admissibility or on the merits of the communication.

Article 7
Admissibility

The Committee shall consider a communication inadmissible when:

(a)   The communication is anonymous;

(b)   The communication is not in writing;

(c)   The communication constitutes an abuse of the right of submission of such communications or is incompatible with the provisions of the Convention and/or the Optional Protocols thereto;

(d)   The same matter has already been examined by the Committee or has been or is being examined under another procedure of international investigation or settlement;

(e)   All available domestic remedies have not been exhausted. This shall not be the rule where the application of the remedies is unreasonably prolonged or unlikely to bring effective relief;

(f)   The communication is manifestly ill-founded or not sufficiently substantiated;

(g)   The facts that are the subject of the communication occurred prior to the entry into force of the present Protocol for the State party concerned, unless those facts continued after that date;

(h)   The communication is not submitted within one year after the exhaustion of domestic remedies, except in cases where the author can demonstrate that it had not been possible to submit the communication within that time limit.

Article 8
Transmission of the communication

1 Unless the Committee considers a communication inadmissible without reference to the State party concerned, the Committee shall bring any communication submitted to it under the present Protocol confidentially to the attention of the State party concerned as soon as possible.

2 The State party shall submit to the Committee written explanations or statements clarifying the matter and the remedy, if any, that it may have provided. The State party shall submit its response as soon as possible and within six months.

Article 9
Friendly settlement

1 The Committee shall make available its good offices to the parties concerned with a view to reaching a friendly settlement of the matter on the basis of respect for the obligations set forth in the Convention and/or the Optional Protocols thereto.

2 An agreement on a friendly settlement reached under the auspices of the Committee closes consideration of the communication under the present Protocol.

Article 10
Consideration of communications

1 The Committee shall consider communications received under the present Protocol as quickly as possible, in the light of all documentation submitted to it, provided that this documentation is transmitted to the parties concerned.

2 The Committee shall hold closed meetings when examining communications received under the present Protocol.

3 Where the Committee has requested interim measures, it shall expedite the consideration of the communication.

4 When examining communications alleging violations of economic, social or cultural rights, the Committee shall consider the reasonableness of the steps taken by the State party in accordance with article 4 of the Convention. In doing so, the Committee shall bear in mind that the State party may adopt a range of possible policy measures for the implementation of the economic, social and cultural rights in the Convention.

5 After examining a communication, the Committee shall, without delay, transmit its views on the communication, together with its recommendations, if any, to the parties concerned.

Article 11
Follow-up

1 The State party shall give due consideration to the views of the Committee, together with its recommendations, if any, and shall submit to the Committee a written response, including information on any action taken and envisaged in the light of the views and recommendations of the Committee. The State party shall submit its response as soon as possible and within six months.

2 The Committee may invite the State party to submit further information about any measures the State party has taken in response to its views or recommendations or implementation of a friendly settlement agreement, if any, including as deemed appropriate by the Committee, in the State party's subsequent reports under article 44 of the Convention, article 12 of the Optional Protocol to the Convention on the sale of children, child prostitution and child pornography or article 8 of the Optional Protocol to the Convention on the involvement of children in armed conflict, where applicable.

Article 12
Inter-State communications

1 A State party to the present Protocol may, at any time, declare that it recognizes the competence of the Committee to receive and consider communications in which a State party claims that another State party is not fulfilling its obligations under any of the following instruments to which the State is a party:

(a)   The Convention;
(b)   The Optional Protocol to the Convention on the sale of children, child prostitution and child pornography;
(c)   The Optional Protocol to the Convention on the involvement of children in armed conflict.

2 The Committee shall not receive communications concerning a State party that has not made such a declaration or communications from a State party that has not made such a declaration.

3 The Committee shall make available its good offices to the States parties concerned with a view to a friendly solution of the matter on the basis of the respect for the obligations set forth in the Convention and the Optional Protocols thereto.

4 A declaration under paragraph 1 of the present article shall be deposited by the States parties with the Secretary-General of the United Nations, who shall transmit copies thereof to the other States parties. A declaration may be withdrawn at any time by notification to the Secretary-General. Such a withdrawal shall not prejudice the consideration of any matter that is the subject of a communication already transmitted under the present article; no further communications by any State party shall be received under the present article after the notification of withdrawal of the declaration has been received by the Secretary-General, unless the State party concerned has made a new declaration.

PART III
INQUIRY PROCEDURE

Article 13
Inquiry procedure for grave or systematic violations

1 If the Committee receives reliable information indicating grave or systematic violations by a State party of rights set forth in the Convention or in the Optional Protocols thereto on the sale of children, child prostitution and child pornography or on the involvement of children in armed conflict, the Committee shall invite the State party to cooperate in the examination of the information and, to this end, to submit observations without delay with regard to the information concerned.

2 Taking into account any observations that may have been submitted by the State party concerned, as well as any other reliable information available to it, the Committee may designate one or more of its members to conduct an inquiry and to report urgently to the Committee. Where warranted and with the consent of the State party, the inquiry may include a visit to its territory.

3 Such an inquiry shall be conducted confidentially, and the cooperation of the State party shall be sought at all stages of the proceedings.

4 After examining the findings of such an inquiry, the Committee shall transmit without delay these findings to the State party concerned, together with any comments and recommendations.

5 The State party concerned shall, as soon as possible and within six months of receiving the findings, comments and recommendations transmitted by the Committee, submit its observations to the Committee.

6 After such proceedings have been completed with regard to an inquiry made in accordance with paragraph 2 of the present article, the Committee may, after consultation with the State party concerned, decide to include a summary account of the results of the proceedings in its report provided for in article 16 of the present Protocol.

7 Each State party may, at the time of signature or ratification of the present Protocol or accession thereto, declare that it does not recognize the competence of the Committee provided for in the present article in respect of the rights set forth in some or all of the instruments listed in paragraph 1.

8 Any State party having made a declaration in accordance with paragraph 7 of the present article may, at any time, withdraw this declaration by notification to the Secretary-General of the United Nations.

Article 14
Follow-up to the inquiry procedure

1 The Committee may, if necessary, after the end of the period of six months referred to in article 13, paragraph 5, invite the State party concerned to inform it of the measures taken and envisaged in response to an inquiry conducted under article 13 of the present Protocol.

2 The Committee may invite the State party to submit further information about any measures that the State party has taken in response to an inquiry conducted under article 13, including as deemed appropriate by the Committee, in the State party's subsequent reports under article 44 of the Convention, article 12 of the Optional Protocol to the Convention on the sale of children, child prostitution and child pornography or article 8 of the Optional Protocol to the Convention on the involvement of children in armed conflict, where applicable.

PART IV
FINAL PROVISIONS

Article 15
International assistance and cooperation

1 The Committee may transmit, with the consent of the State party concerned, to United Nations specialized agencies, funds and programmes and other competent bodies its views or recommendations concerning communications and inquiries that indicate a need for technical advice or assistance, together with the State party's observations and suggestions, if any, on these views or recommendations.

2 The Committee may also bring to the attention of such bodies, with the consent of the State party concerned, any matter arising out of communications considered under the present Protocol that may assist them in deciding, each within its field of competence, on the advisability of international measures likely to contribute to assisting States parties in achieving progress in the implementation of the rights recognized in the Convention and/or the Optional Protocols thereto.

Article 16
Report to the General Assembly

The Committee shall include in its report submitted every two years to the General Assembly in accordance with article 44, paragraph 5, of the Convention a summary of its activities under the present Protocol.

Article 17
Dissemination of and information on the Optional Protocol

Each State party undertakes to make widely known and to disseminate the present Protocol and to facilitate access to information about the views and recommendations of the Committee, in particular with regard to matters involving the State party, by appropriate and active means and in accessible formats to adults and children alike, including those with disabilities.

Article 18
Signature, ratification and accession

1 The present Protocol is open for signature to any State that has signed, ratified or acceded to the Convention or either of the first two Optional Protocols thereto.

2 The present Protocol is subject to ratification by any State that has ratified or acceded to the Convention or either of the first two Optional Protocols thereto. Instruments of ratification shall be deposited with the Secretary-General of the United Nations.

3 The present Protocol shall be open to accession by any State that has ratified or acceded to the Convention or either of the first two Optional Protocols thereto.

4 Accession shall be effected by the deposit of an instrument of accession with the Secretary-General.

Article 19
Entry into force

1 The present Protocol shall enter into force three months after the deposit of the tenth instrument of ratification or accession.

2 For each State ratifying the present Protocol or acceding to it after the deposit of the tenth instrument of ratification or instrument of accession, the present Protocol shall enter into force three months after the date of the deposit of its own instrument of ratification or accession.

Article 20
Violations occurring after the entry into force

1 The Committee shall have competence solely in respect of violations by the State party of any of the rights set forth in the Convention and/or the first two Optional Protocols thereto occurring after the entry into force of the present Protocol.

2 If a State becomes a party to the present Protocol after its entry into force, the obligations of that State vis-à-vis the Committee shall relate only to violations of the rights set forth in the Convention and/or the first two Optional Protocols thereto occurring after the entry into force of the present Protocol for the State concerned.

Article 21
Amendments

1 Any State party may propose an amendment to the present Protocol and submit it to the Secretary-General of the United Nations. The Secretary-General shall communicate any proposed amendments to States parties with a request to be notified whether they favour a meeting of States parties for the purpose of considering and deciding upon the proposals. In the event that, within four months of the date of such communication, at least one third of the States parties favour such a meeting, the Secretary-General shall convene the meeting under the auspices of the United Nations. Any amendment adopted by a majority of two thirds of the States parties present and voting shall be submitted by the Secretary-General to the General Assembly for approval and, thereafter, to all States parties for acceptance.

2 An amendment adopted and approved in accordance with paragraph 1 of the present article shall enter into force on the thirtieth day after the number of instruments of acceptance deposited reaches two thirds of the number of States parties at the date of adoption of the amendment. Thereafter, the amendment shall enter into force for any State party on the thirtieth day following the deposit of its own instrument of acceptance. An amendment shall be binding only on those States parties that have accepted it.

Article 22
Denunciation

1 Any State party may denounce the present Protocol at any time by written notification to the Secretary-General of the United Nations. The denunciation shall take effect one year after the date of receipt of the notification by the Secretary-General.

2 Denunciation shall be without prejudice to the continued application of the provisions of the present Protocol to any communication submitted under articles 5 or 12 or any inquiry initiated under article 13 before the effective date of denunciation.

Article 23
Depositary and notification by the Secretary-General

1 The Secretary-General of the United Nations shall be the depositary of the present Protocol.

2 The Secretary-General shall inform all States of:

(a)   Signatures, ratifications and accessions under the present Protocol;
(b)   The date of entry into force of the present Protocol and of any amendment thereto under article 21;
(c)   Any denunciation under article 22 of the present Protocol.

Article 24
Languages

1 The present Protocol, of which the Arabic, Chinese, English, French, Russian and Spanish texts are equally authentic, shall be deposited in the archives of the United Nations.

2 The Secretary-General of the United Nations shall transmit certified copies of the present Protocol to all States.

CHAPTER 7

THE INTERNATIONAL COVENANT ON CIVIL AND POLITICAL RIGHTS

PREAMBLE

The States Parties to the present Covenant,

Considering that, in accordance with the principles proclaimed in the Charter of the United Nations, recognition of the inherent dignity and of the equal and inalienable rights of all members of the human family is the foundation of freedom, justice and peace in the world,

Recognizing that these rights derive from the inherent dignity of the human person,

Recognizing that, in accordance with the Universal Declaration of Human Rights, the ideal of free human beings enjoying civil and political freedom and freedom from fear and want can only be achieved if conditions are created whereby everyone may enjoy his civil and political rights, as well as his economic, social and cultural rights,

Considering the obligation of States under the Charter of the United Nations to promote universal respect for, and observance of, human rights and freedoms,

Realizing that the individual, having duties to other individuals and to the community to which he belongs, is under a responsibility to strive for the promotion and observance of the rights recognized in the present Covenant,

Agree upon the following articles:

Status—The International Covenant on Civil and Political Rights was ratified by the United Kingdom on 20 May 1976 [RCLP para 2.32]. The status of the International Covenant on Civil and Political Rights is that of a binding international Convention not incorporated into domestic law [RCLP para 3.94] but see also *Young v Young* [2012] EWHC 138 (Fam), [2012] 2 FLR 470. The International Covenant on Civil and Political Rights is recognised as a source of the fundamental principles of European Community law (see *Mendoza v Ghaidan* [2002] EWCA Civ 1533, [2003] 1 FLR 468, para 29, *Grant v South West Trains Ltd (Case C-249/96)* [1998] 1 FLR 839, *Orkem v Commission (Case 374/87)* [1989] ECR 3283, para 31, and *Dzodzi v Belgian State (Cases C-297/88 and C-197/89)* [1990] ECR I-3763, para 68). In *European Roma Rights Centre v Immigration Officer at Prague Airport (United Nations High Comr intervening)* [2004] UKHL 55, [2005] 2 AC 1 the House of Lords relied, *inter alia*, on the International Covenant on Civil and Political Rights [RCLP para 3.31]. The International Covenant on Civil and Political Rights establishes the UN Human Rights Committee which receives and adjudicates upon complaints. The UN Committee on Human Rights has been called a judicial body of high standing (see *Tavista v Ministry of Immigration* [1994] 2 NZLR 257) [RCLP para 2.32]. Note that the International Covenant on Civil and Political Rights has two Optional Protocols (not included in this work). The first Optional Protocol provides a mechanism for private individuals to pursue complaints concerning alleged violations of the Convention (see *Laureano Atachahua v Peru (Communication 540/1993)* (1996) 1 BHRC 338). The United Kingdom has declined to ratify the first Optional Protocol [RCLP para 2.32]. The second Optional Protocol to the Convention seeks by Art 1 to abolish the death penalty (see *Thompson v Marksman* [2000] 5 LRC 402). The second Optional Protocol was ratified by the United Kingdom on 10 December 1999 [RCLP para 2.32]. The Convention and its Optional Protocols to the International Convention on Civil and Political Rights have been referred to in a number of domestic and Commonwealth decisions (see *R (Saadi and others) v Secretary of State for the Home Department* [2001] 4 All ER 961, *Dunkley and another v R* [1995] 1 All ER 279, *R (Nadarajah) v Secretary of State for the Home Department and another; R (Amirthanathan) v Secretary of State for the Home Department* [2003] EWCA Civ 1768, [2003] All ER (D) 129 (Dec), *AG v Chapman* [2011] NZSC 110, 32 BHRC 561, *Kennedy v Trinidad and Tobago* (1999) 8 BHRC 230, *Thompson v Marksman* [2000] 5 LRC 402 and *Tavita v Minister of Immigration* [1994] 1 LRC 421).

PART I

Article 1

1. All peoples have the right of self-determination. By virtue of that right they freely determine their political status and freely pursue their economic, social and cultural development.

2. All peoples may, for their own ends, freely dispose of their natural wealth and resources without prejudice to any obligations arising out of international economic co-operation, based upon the principle of mutual benefit, and international law. In no case may a people be deprived of its own means of subsistence.

3. The States Parties to the present Covenant, including those having responsibility for the administration of Non-Self-Governing and Trust Territories, shall promote the realization of the right of self-determination, and shall respect that right, in conformity with the provisions of the Charter of the United Nations.

PART II

Article 2

1. Each State Party to the present Covenant undertakes to respect and to ensure to all individuals within its territory and subject to its jurisdiction the rights recognized in the present Covenant, without distinction of any kind, such as race, colour, sex, language, religion, political or other opinion, national or social origin, property, birth or other status.

2. Where not already provided for by existing legislative or other measures, each State Party to the present Covenant undertakes to take the necessary steps, in accordance with its constitutional processes and with the provisions of the present Covenant, to adopt such laws or other measures as may be necessary to give effect to the rights recognized in the present Covenant.

3. Each State Party to the present Covenant undertakes:

(a)   To ensure that any person whose rights or freedoms as herein recognized are violated shall have an effective remedy, notwithstanding that the violation has been committed by persons acting in an official capacity;

(b)   To ensure that any person claiming such a remedy shall have his right thereto determined by competent judicial, administrative or legislative authorities, or by any other competent authority provided for by the legal system of the State, and to develop the possibilities of judicial remedy;

(c)   To ensure that the competent authorities shall enforce such remedies when granted.

Principle of equality (Art 2)—For a definition of discrimination see UN Human Rights Committee General Observations No 18 of 10 November 1989 CCPR/C/21/Rev 1/Add 1 **[RCLP paras 4.77 and 4.90]**.

Article 3

The States Parties to the present Covenant undertake to ensure the equal right of men and women to the enjoyment of all civil and political rights set forth in the present Covenant.

Article 4

1. In time of public emergency which threatens the life of the nation and the existence of which is officially proclaimed, the States Parties to the present Covenant may take measures derogating from their obligations under the present Covenant to the extent strictly required by the exigencies of the situation, provided that such measures are not inconsistent with their other obligations under international law and do not involve discrimination solely on the ground of race, colour, sex, language, religion or social origin.

2. No derogation from articles 6, 7, 8 (paragraphs 1 and 2), 11, 15, 16 and 18 may be made under this provision.

3. Any State Party to the present Covenant availing itself of the right of derogation shall immediately inform the other States Parties to the present Covenant, through the intermediary of the Secretary-General of the United Nations, of the provisions from which it has derogated and of the reasons by which it was actuated. A further communication shall be made, through the same intermediary, on the date on which it terminates such derogation.

Article 5

1. Nothing in the present Covenant may be interpreted as implying for any State, group or person any right to engage in any activity or perform any act aimed at the destruction of any of the rights and freedoms recognized herein or at their limitation to a greater extent than is provided for in the present Covenant.

2. There shall be no restriction upon or derogation from any of the fundamental human rights recognized or existing in any State Party to the present Covenant pursuant to law, conventions, regulations or custom on the pretext that the present Covenant does not recognize such rights or that it recognizes them to a lesser extent.

PART III

Article 6

1. Every human being has the inherent right to life. This right shall be protected by law. No one shall be arbitrarily deprived of his life.

2. In countries which have not abolished the death penalty, sentence of death may be imposed only for the most serious crimes in accordance with the law in force at the time of the commission of the crime and not contrary to the provisions of the present Covenant and to the Convention on the Prevention and Punishment of the Crime of Genocide. This penalty can only be carried out pursuant to a final judgement rendered by a competent court.

3. When deprivation of life constitutes the crime of genocide, it is understood that nothing in this article shall authorize any State Party to the present Covenant to derogate in any way from any obligation assumed under the provisions of the Convention on the Prevention and Punishment of the Crime of Genocide.

4. Anyone sentenced to death shall have the right to seek pardon or commutation of the sentence. Amnesty, pardon or commutation of the sentence of death may be granted in all cases.

5. Sentence of death shall not be imposed for crimes committed by persons below eighteen years of age and shall not be carried out on pregnant women.

6. Nothing in this article shall be invoked to delay or to prevent the abolition of capital punishment by any State Party to the present Covenant.

Abolition of death penalty—Note that Art 1 of the second Optional Protocol to the International Covenant on Civil and Political Rights (not included in this work) aims to abolish the death penalty [RCLP para 5.19].

'persons below eighteen years of age' (Art 18(5))—The Committee on the Rights of the Child has described the principle enshrined in Art 6(5) that the death penalty shall not be imposed for a crime committed by a person who at the time was under the age of 18 years old as an 'internationally accepted standard' (see Committee on the Rights of the Child General Comment No 10 *Children's Rights in Juvenile Justice* CRC/C/GC/10, p 21, para 75) [RCLP para 5.17]. See also *The Queen on the application of Smeaton on behalf of the Society for the Protection of Unborn Children v Secretary of State for Health (Schering Health Care Ltd and Family Planning Association as Interested Parties)* [2002] EWHC (Admin) and [2002] EWHC 886 (Admin), [2002] 2 FLR 146, para 286.

Article 7

No one shall be subjected to torture or to cruel, inhuman or degrading treatment or punishment. In particular, no one shall be subjected without his free consent to medical or scientific experimentation.

'medical or scientific experimentation' (Art 7)—In the context of children the UN Human Rights Committee has noted that special protection is necessary in cases of persons not capable of giving valid consent (see UN Human Rights Committee General Comment No 20 *Article 7 (Prohibition of Torture or Other Cruel, Inhuman or Degrading Treatment or Punishment)* HRI/GEN/Rev 8, p 190, para 7). See also Art 15(1) of the Convention on the Rights of Persons with Disabilities [RCLP para 15.15]. See also the Committee on the Rights of the Child General Comment No 3 *HIV/AIDS and the Rights of the Child* CRC/GC/2003/3, para 29 [RCLP para 15.107].

Corporal Punishment—The prohibition in Art 7 against torture or cruel, inhuman or degrading treatment of punishment extends to corporal punishment (see UN Human Rights Committee General Comment No 20 *Article 7 (Prohibition of Torture or Other Cruel, Inhuman or Degrading Treatment or Punishment)* HRI/GEN/Rev 8 and *R (Williamson) v Secretary of State for Education and Employment* [2002] EWCA Civ 1820, [2003] 1 FLR 726, para 310).

Article 8

1. No one shall be held in slavery; slavery and the slave-trade in all their forms shall be prohibited.

2. No one shall be held in servitude.

3.

(a)   No one shall be required to perform forced or compulsory labour;

(b)   Paragraph 3 (a) shall not be held to preclude, in countries where imprisonment with hard labour may be imposed as a punishment for a crime, the performance of hard labour in pursuance of a sentence to such punishment by a competent court;

(c)   For the purpose of this paragraph the term "forced or compulsory labour" shall not include:

    (i)   Any work or service, not referred to in subparagraph (b), normally required of a person who is under detention in consequence of a lawful order of a court, or of a person during conditional release from such detention;

    (ii)   Any service of a military character and, in countries where conscientious objection is recognized, any national service required by law of conscientious objectors;

    (iii)   Any service exacted in cases of emergency or calamity threatening the life or well-being of the community;

    (iv)   Any work or service which forms part of normal civil obligations.

Article 9

1. Everyone has the right to liberty and security of person. No one shall be subjected to arbitrary arrest or detention. No one shall be deprived of his liberty except on such grounds and in accordance with such procedure as are established by law.

2. Anyone who is arrested shall be informed, at the time of arrest, of the reasons for his arrest and shall be promptly informed of any charges against him.

3. Anyone arrested or detained on a criminal charge shall be brought promptly before a judge or other officer authorized by law to exercise judicial power and shall be entitled to trial within a reasonable time or to release. It shall not be the general rule that persons awaiting trial shall be detained in custody, but release may be subject to guarantees to appear for trial, at any other stage of the judicial proceedings, and, should occasion arise, for execution of the judgement.

4. Anyone who is deprived of his liberty by arrest or detention shall be entitled to take proceedings before a court, in order that that court may decide without delay on the lawfulness of his detention and order his release if the detention is not lawful.

5. Anyone who has been the victim of unlawful arrest or detention shall have an enforceable right to compensation.

'liberty and security of person' (Art 9(1))—The UN Human Rights Committee considers that the concepts of 'liberty' and 'security of person' are separate, with security of person denoting the physical security of all individuals (*Páez v Colombia* UN Human Rights Committee Communication No 195/1985 (1990)) [RCLP para 14.4]. For the contrary view see the decision of the European Court of Human Rights in *East African Asians v United Kingdom* (1973) Application No 4626/70 [RCLP para 14.4].

'trial within a reasonable time' (Art 9(3))—Contrast the provisions of Art 37(b) of the UNCRC and see also *Re CK (A Minor)* [2009] NICA 17, [2010] NI 15 [RCLP para 14.25].

'entitled to take proceedings before a court' (Art 9(4))—See also the Body of Principles for the Protection of All Persons under Any Form of Detention or Imprisonment, Principle 32 GA Res 43/173 1988. The provisions of Art 9(4) extend to deprivations of liberty effected by administrative bodies (see *Antti Vuolanne v Finland* (265/1987) A/44/40, Annex X) [RCLP para 14.41].

Article 10

1. All persons deprived of their liberty shall be treated with humanity and with respect for the inherent dignity of the human person.

2.

    (a)   Accused persons shall, save in exceptional circumstances, be segregated from convicted persons and shall be subject to separate treatment appropriate to their status as unconvicted persons;

    (b)   Accused juvenile persons shall be separated from adults and brought as speedily as possible for adjudication.

3. The penitentiary system shall comprise treatment of prisoners the essential aim of which shall be their reformation and social rehabilitation. Juvenile offenders shall be segregated from adults and be accorded treatment appropriate to their age and legal status.

'treated with humanity and respect for the inherent dignity of the human person' (Art 10(1))—See the UN Human Rights Committee General Comment No 9 *Article 10 (Humane Treatment of Persons Deprived of their Liberty)* HRI/GEN/1/Rev 8, p 193, para 4) [RCLP para 14.27]. See also *Dickson v United Kingdom (Application No 44362/04)* [2008] 1 FLR 1315, para 29.

Separation of juveniles from adults (Arts 10(2)(b) and 10(3))—See also the UN Standard Minimum Rules for Prisoners r 8(b) which applies to children (Jordan CRC/C/15/Add 21, para 16, Paraguay CRC/C/15/Add 75, para 28 and Costa Rica CRC/C/15/Add 266, para 56) **[RCLP para 14.34]**. The requirements of Art 10(2)(b) are unconditional in nature (see UN Human Rights Committee General Comment No 9 *Article 10 (Humane Treatment of Persons Deprived of their Liberty)* HRI/GE/1/Rev 8, pp 170–171, para 2). However, see also Art 37(c) of the UNCRC **[RCLP para 14.36]**. The UN Rules for the Protection of Juveniles Deprived of their Liberty r 29 provides examples of when it may be in a child's best interests not to be separated from adults. Note that the United Kingdom has entered a reservation in respect of Arts 10(2)(b) and 10(3) but not in respect of the similar provisions of Art 37(c) of the UNCRC **[RCLP para 14.35]**.

Article 11

No one shall be imprisoned merely on the ground of inability to fulfil a contractual obligation.

Article 12

1. Everyone lawfully within the territory of a State shall, within that territory, have the right to liberty of movement and freedom to choose his residence.

2. Everyone shall be free to leave any country, including his own.

3. The above-mentioned rights shall not be subject to any restrictions except those which are provided by law, are necessary to protect national security, public order (ordre public), public health or morals or the rights and freedoms of others, and are consistent with the other rights recognized in the present Covenant.

4. No one shall be arbitrarily deprived of the right to enter his own country.

Article 13

An alien lawfully in the territory of a State Party to the present Covenant may be expelled therefrom only in pursuance of a decision reached in accordance with law and shall, except where compelling reasons of national security otherwise require, be allowed to submit the reasons against his expulsion and to have his case reviewed by, and be represented for the purpose before, the competent authority or a person or persons especially designated by the competent authority.

Article 14

1. All persons shall be equal before the courts and tribunals. In the determination of any criminal charge against him, or of his rights and obligations in a suit at law, everyone shall be entitled to a fair and public hearing by a competent, independent and impartial tribunal established by law. The press and the public may be excluded from all or part of a trial for reasons of morals, public order (ordre public) or national security in a democratic society, or when the interest of the private lives of the parties so requires, or to the extent strictly necessary in the opinion of the court in special circumstances where publicity would prejudice the interests of justice; but any judgement rendered in a criminal case or in a suit at law shall be made public except where the interest of juvenile persons otherwise requires or the proceedings concern matrimonial disputes or the guardianship of children.

2. Everyone charged with a criminal offence shall have the right to be presumed innocent until proved guilty according to law.

3. In the determination of any criminal charge against him, everyone shall be entitled to the following minimum guarantees, in full equality:

    (a)   To be informed promptly and in detail in a language which he understands of the nature and cause of the charge against him;

    (b)   To have adequate time and facilities for the preparation of his defence and to communicate with counsel of his own choosing;

(c)   To be tried without undue delay;

(d)   To be tried in his presence, and to defend himself in person or through legal assistance of his own choosing; to be informed, if he does not have legal assistance, of this right; and to have legal assistance assigned to him, in any case where the interests of justice so require, and without payment by him in any such case if he does not have sufficient means to pay for it;

(e)   To examine, or have examined, the witnesses against him and to obtain the attendance and examination of witnesses on his behalf under the same conditions as witnesses against him;

(f)   To have the free assistance of an interpreter if he cannot understand or speak the language used in court;

(g)   Not to be compelled to testify against himself or to confess guilt.

4. In the case of juvenile persons, the procedure shall be such as will take account of their age and the desirability of promoting their rehabilitation.

5. Everyone convicted of a crime shall have the right to his conviction and sentence being reviewed by a higher tribunal according to law.

6. When a person has by a final decision been convicted of a criminal offence and when subsequently his conviction has been reversed or he has been pardoned on the ground that a new or newly discovered fact shows conclusively that there has been a miscarriage of justice, the person who has suffered punishment as a result of such conviction shall be compensated according to law, unless it is proved that the non-disclosure of the unknown fact in time is wholly or partly attributable to him.

7. No one shall be liable to be tried or punished again for an offence for which he has already been finally convicted or acquitted in accordance with the law and penal procedure of each country.

'All persons shall be equal before the courts and tribunals' (Art 14(1))—Children enjoy at least the same guarantees and protection accorded to adults under Art 14 (see UN Human Rights Committee General Comment No 13 *Article 14 (Administration of Justice)* HRI/GEN/1/Rev 8, p 177 and *Haly v Ohio* 332 US 596 (1948) US Supreme Court and *Re Gault* 387 US 1 (1967) US Supreme Court) **[RCLP para 16.2]**.

Privacy of proceedings concerning children (Art 14(1))—In respect of the words 'except where the interest of juvenile persons otherwise requires or the proceedings concern matrimonial disputes or the guardianship of children' in Art 14(1) see also Committee on the Rights of the Child General Comment No 10 *Children's Rights in Juvenile Justice* CRC/C/GC/10, para 66 **[RCLP para 9.13]**. See also *W v M (TOLATA Proceedings: Anonymity)* [2012] EWHC 1679 (Fam), [2013] 1 FLR 1513 and *B v United Kingdom; P v United Kingdom (Cases 36337/97 and 35974/97)* [2001] 2 FLR 261, p 275.

'undue delay' (Art 14(3)(c))—Note that Art 37(d) of the UNCRC requiring a 'prompt' decision is stronger than the term 'without undue delay' used in Art 14(3)(c) (see Committee on the Rights of the Child General Comment No 10 *Children's Rights in Juvenile Justice* CRC/C/GC/10, p 22, para 84) **[RCLP para 14.45]**.

'To be tried in his presence' (Art 14(3)(d))—In relation to children see Committee on the Rights of the Child General Comment No 10 *Children's Rights in Juvenile Justice* CRC/C/GC/10, para 46 **[RCLP para 16.46]**.

'rehabilitation' (Art 14(4))—Note that the UNCRC Arts 39 and 40(1) and the 'Beijing Rules' r 80 use the term 'reintegration' in preference to rehabilitation **[RCLP para 16.10]**.

Reversal of conviction or pardon (Art 14(6))—Art 14(6) of the International Covenant on Civil and Political Rights is given effect in domestic law by s 133 of the Criminal Justice Act 1988 (see *R (Mullen) v Secretary of State for the Home Department* [2002] EWCA Civ 1882, [2003] QB 993) **[RCLP para 16.129]**.

Article 15

1. No one shall be held guilty of any criminal offence on account of any act or omission which did not constitute a criminal offence, under national or international law, at the time when it was committed. Nor shall a heavier penalty be imposed than the one that

was applicable at the time when the criminal offence was committed. If, subsequent to the commission of the offence, provision is made by law for the imposition of the lighter penalty, the offender shall benefit thereby.

2. Nothing in this article shall prejudice the trial and punishment of any person for any act or omission which, at the time when it was committed, was criminal according to the general principles of law recognized by the community of nations.

No retrospective legislation (Art 15(1))—Contrast the provisions of UNCRC Art 40(2)(a) [RCLP para 16.34].

Article 16

Everyone shall have the right to recognition everywhere as a person before the law.

Article 17

1. No one shall be subjected to arbitrary or unlawful interference with his privacy, family, or correspondence, nor to unlawful attacks on his honour and reputation.

2. Everyone has the right to the protection of the law against such interference or attacks.

'arbitrary or unlawful' (Art 17(1))—The term 'arbitrary or unlawful' means that even where interference in family life is lawful it must also be reasonable in the particular circumstances (see *Shirin Aumeeruddy-Cziffra and Nineteen other Mauritanian Women v Mauritius* Communication No 35/178) [RCLP para 8.71]. The word 'unlawful' means that no interference can take place except in cases envisaged by law, which law itself must comply with the provisions, aims and objectives of the Covenant (see UN Human Rights Committee General Comment No 16 *Article 17 (Right to Privacy)* HRI/GEN/1/Rev 8, p 181, para 3) [RCLP para 9.8].

'interference' (Art 17(1))—No distinction is made between interference by State authorities and interference from natural or legal persons (see UN Human Rights Committee General Comment No 16 *Article 17 (Right to Privacy)* HRI/GEN/1/Rev 8, p 181) [RCLP para 9.9].

'privacy' (Art 17(1))—The concept of privacy is necessarily a relative one (see UN Human Rights Committee General Comment No 16 *Article 17 (Right to Privacy)* HRI/GEN/1/Rev 8, p 181, para 7) [RCLP para 9.9].

'correspondence' (Art 17(1))—See UN Human Rights Committee General Comment No 16 *Article 17 (Right to Privacy)* HRI/GEN/1/Rev 8, p 181, para 8 [RCLP para 9.19].

'family' (Art 17(1))—The UN Committee on Human Rights has made clear that the term 'family' should be understood in the wide sense (see the UN Human Rights Committee General Comment No 4 *The Right to Adequate Housing (Art 11(1) of the Covenant)* HRI/GEN/1/Rev 8, p 20, para 6, the UN Human Rights Committee General Comment No 16 *Article 17 (Right to Privacy)* HRI/GEN/1/Rev 8, p 182, para 5 and the *Manual on Human Rights Reporting* HR/PUB/91/1/(Rev 1), p 117) [RCLP para 8.8]. See also Art 23 below and *Shirin Aumeeruddy-Cziffra and Nineteen other Mauritanian Women v Mauritius* Communication No 35/178 and *Hendriks v Netherlands* (1985) No 201/1985 [RCLP para 8.9].

Derogation—Note that whilst Art 4 permits derogation from Art 17 when proclaiming a state of emergency the UNCRC permits no such derogation in respect of the right to respect for family life [RCLP para 8.70].

Scope—Art 17 will apply to aliens (see UN Human Rights Committee General Comment No 15 *The Position of Aliens under the Covenant* HRI/GEN/1/Rev 8, p 180, para 7) [RCLP para 8.71].

Article 18

1. Everyone shall have the right to freedom of thought, conscience and religion. This right shall include freedom to have or to adopt a religion or belief of his choice, and freedom, either individually or in community with others and in public or private, to manifest his religion or belief in worship, observance, practice and teaching.

2. No one shall be subject to coercion which would impair his freedom to have or to adopt a religion or belief of his choice.

3. Freedom to manifest one's religion or beliefs may be subject only to such limitations as are prescribed by law and are necessary to protect public safety, order, health, or morals or the fundamental rights and freedoms of others.

4. The States Parties to the present Covenant undertake to have respect for the liberty of parents and, when applicable, legal guardians to ensure the religious and moral education of their children in conformity with their own convictions.

'religion or belief' (Art 18(1))—The words 'religion or belief' will be broadly construed (see UN Human Rights Committee General Comment No 22 *Article 18 (Freedom of Thought, Conscience and Religion)* HRI/GEN/1/Rev 8, p 195, para 2) [RCLP para 10.23].

'coercion' (Art 18(2))—See also the Declaration on the Elimination or All Forms of Intolerance and Discrimination Based on Religion or Belief Art 1(2) and the UN Committee on Economic, Social and Cultural Rights General Comment No 28 *Article 3 (The Equality of Rights Between Men and Women)* HRI/GEN/1/Rev 8, p 222, para 21) [RCLP para 10.10].

'freedom to have or to adopt a religion or belief' (Art 18(2))—See UN Human Rights Committee General Comment No 22 *Article 18 (Freedom of Thought, Conscience and Religion)* HRI/GEN/1/Rev 8, p 195, para 5 and UN Doc A/37/40 (1982), p 40, para 180) [RCLP para 10.27]. The freedom to have or adopt a religion necessarily entails the freedom to choose a religion or belief, including the right to replace one's current religion or belief with another or to adopt atheistic views, as well as the right to retain one's religion or belief (see UN Human Rights Committee General Comment No 22 *Article 18 (Freedom of Thought, Conscience and Religion)* HRI/GEN/1/Rev 8, p 195, para 5) [RCLP para 10.27]. The Human Rights Committee has accepted that, in principle, a child has the right to adopt a religion or his or her choice (see UN Doc A/36/40/1981) [RCLP para 10.27].

'Freedom to manifest one's religion or beliefs' (Art 18(3))—For the interpretation of the term 'manifest' see UN Human Rights Committee General Comment No 22 *Article 18 (Freedom of Thought, Conscience and Religion)* HRI/GEN/1/Rev 8, p 195, para 4 and the decisions of the Human Rights Committee in *Boodoo v Trinidad and Tobago* (2002) Communication 721/1997 and *Sister Immaculate Joseph and 80 Teaching Sisters of the Holy Cross of the Third Order of St Francis in Mensingen of Sri Lanka v Sri Lanka* (2005) Communication 1249/2004 [RCLP para 10.47]. In relation to the wearing of religious symbols and clothing see the decision of the UN Human Rights Committee in *Hudoyberganova v Uzbekistan* Communication 931/2000 (2005) [RCLP para 10.57]. See also the decision of the Supreme Court of Canada in *Multani v Commission Scolaire Marguerite-Bourgeoys* 2006 SCC 6 (CanLII) [RCLP para 10.57].

'respect for the liberty of parents and ... legal guardians' (Art 18(4))—See UN Human Rights Committee General Comment No 22 *Article 18 (Freedom of Thought, Conscience and Religion)* HRI/GEN/1/Rev 8, p 196, para 6 [RCLP para 10.56].

Conscientious objection—Whilst Art 18 does not refer explicitly to conscientious objection to military service the UN Human Rights Committee has stated that a right to such objection can be derived from Art 18 (see UN Human Rights Committee General Comment No 22 *Article 18 (Freedom of Thought, Conscience and Religion)* HRI/GEN/1/Rev 8, p 198, para 11) [RCLP para 10.59].

Article 19

1. Everyone shall have the right to hold opinions without interference.

2. Everyone shall have the right to freedom of expression; this right shall include freedom to seek, receive and impart information and ideas of all kinds, regardless of frontiers, either orally, in writing or in print, in the form of art, or through any other media of his choice.

3. The exercise of the rights provided for in paragraph 2 of this article carries with it special duties and responsibilities. It may therefore be subject to certain restrictions, but these shall only be such as are provided by law and are necessary:

(a)   For respect of the rights or reputations of others;
(b)   For the protection of national security or of public order (ordre public), or of public health or morals.

'special duties and responsibilities' (Art 19(3))—The provisions of Art 19(3) will operate with protective effect in respect of children in so far as they act to regulate the freedom of expression exercised by the media [RCLP para 11.40].

Freedom of expression and teaching—In *Páez v Colombia* Communication No 195/1985 the UN Human Rights Committee held that Art 19(1) will usually cover the freedom of teachers to teach their subjects in accordance with their own views, without interference [RCLP para 11.47].

Prohibition on dissemination of ideas based on racial superiority or hatred—See Committee on the Elimination of Racial Discrimination *General Recommendation XV on Article 4 of the Convention* HRI/GEN/1/Rev 8, p 248, para 4 [RCLP para 11.9].

Article 20

1. Any propaganda for war shall be prohibited by law.

2. Any advocacy of national, racial or religious hatred that constitutes incitement to discrimination, hostility or violence shall be prohibited by law.

Article 21

The right of peaceful assembly shall be recognized. No restrictions may be placed on the exercise of this right other than those imposed in conformity with the law and which are necessary in a democratic society in the interests of national security or public safety, public order (ordre public), the protection of public health or morals or the protection of the rights and freedoms of others.

Article 22

1. Everyone shall have the right to freedom of association with others, including the right to form and join trade unions for the protection of his interests.

2. No restrictions may be placed on the exercise of this right other than those which are prescribed by law and which are necessary in a democratic society in the interests of national security or public safety, public order (ordre public), the protection of public health or morals or the protection of the rights and freedoms of others. This article shall not prevent the imposition of lawful restrictions on members of the armed forces and of the police in their exercise of this right.

3. Nothing in this article shall authorize States Parties to the International Labour Organisation Convention of 1948 concerning Freedom of Association and Protection of the Right to Organize to take legislative measures which would prejudice, or to apply the law in such a manner as to prejudice, the guarantees provided for in that Convention.

Article 23

1. The family is the natural and fundamental group unit of society and is entitled to protection by society and the State.

2. The right of men and women of marriageable age to marry and to found a family shall be recognized.

3. No marriage shall be entered into without the free and full consent of the intending spouses.

4. States Parties to the present Covenant shall take appropriate steps to ensure equality of rights and responsibilities of spouses as to marriage, during marriage and at its dissolution. In the case of dissolution, provision shall be made for the necessary protection of any children.

'**family**' (Art 23(1))—The UN Committee on Human Rights has made clear that the term 'family' should be understood in the wide sense (see the UN Human Rights Committee General Comment No 4 *The Right to Adequate Housing (Art 11(1) of the Covenant)* HRI/GEN/1/Rev 8, p 20, para 6, the UN Human Rights Committee General Comment No 16 *Article 17 (Right to Privacy)* HRI/GEN/1/Rev 8, p 182, para 5 and the *Manual on Human Rights Reporting* HR/PUB/91/1/(Rev 1), p 117) **[RCLP para 8.8]**. See also Art 23 below and *Shirin Aumeeruddy-Cziffra and Nineteen other Mauritanian Women v Mauritius* Communication No 35/178 and *Hendriks v Netherlands* (1985) No 201/1985 **[RCLP para 8.9]**. The concept of family may differ from State to State (*Shirin Aumeeruddy-Cziffra and Nineteen other Mauritanian Women v Mauritius* Communication No 35/178) and will survive separation and divorce (*Hendriks v Netherlands* (1985) No 201/1985) **[RCLP para 8.9]**. See also *Re B (Care Proceedings: Standard of Proof)* [2008] UKHL 35, [2009] 1 AC 11, [2008] 2 FLR 141, para 20.

Right to marry (Art 23(2))—See *R (Baiai and Others) v Secretary of State for the Home Department* [2008] 2 FLR 1462, paras 13 and 44.

'**free and full consent**' (Art 23(3))—See *R (Quila); R (Bibi) v Secretary of State for the Home Department* [2011] UKSC 45, [2012] 1 FLR 788).

'**provision shall be made for the necessary protection of any children**' (Art 23(4))—Such provision will include the provision of contact with his or her parents (*Hendriks v Netherlands* (1985) No 201/1985) **[RCLP para 8.115]**.

Article 24

1. Every child shall have, without any discrimination as to race, colour, sex, language, religion, national or social origin, property or birth, the right to such measures of protection as are required by his status as a minor, on the part of his family, society and the State.

2. Every child shall be registered immediately after birth and shall have a name.

3. Every child has the right to acquire a nationality.

Children's rights (Art 24)—Note that, as individuals, children will benefit from *all* of the civil rights enunciated by the International Covenant on Civil and Political Rights and not just those articulated in Art 24 (UN Committee on Human Rights General Comment No 17 *Article 24 (Rights of the Child)* HRI/GEN/Rev 8, p 183, para 2). A State party to the International Covenant on Civil and Political Rights cannot absolve itself from its obligations under the Covenant in respect of persons under the age of 18 even though they have reached the age of majority under domestic law (UN Committee on Human Rights General Comment No 17 *Article 24 (Rights of the Child)* HRI/GEN/Rev 8, p 184, para 4).

Non-discrimination (Art 24(1))—The UN Human Rights Committee has made clear that whilst children will benefit from the non-discrimination provisions of Arts 2 and 26 the provisions of Art 24(1) pertain specifically to the measures of protection provided by Art 24 (UN Human Rights Committee General Comment No 17 *Article 24 (Rights of the Child)* HRI/GEN/1/Rev 8, para 5) **[RCLP para 4.77]**. Art 24 encompasses a duty on States parties to prevent children from being exploited by means of prostitution or any other means (UN Human Rights Committee General Comment No 17 *Article 24 (Rights of the Child)* HRI/GEN/1/Rev 8, p 184, para 3) **[RCLP para 15.46]**.

Right to registration and a name (Art 24(2))—Art 24 expressly links the child's right to protection with the child's right to registration and a name (see UN Human Rights Committee General Comment No 17 *Article 24 (Rights of the Child)* HRI/GEN/1/Rev 8, p 185) **[RCLP paras 7.9–7.10]**.

'**right to acquire a nationality**' (Art 24(3))—Art 24(3) requires State parties to adopt every appropriate measure, both internally and in cooperation with other States, to ensure that every child has a nationality when he or she is born (UN Human Rights Committee General Comment No 17 *Article 24 (Rights of the Child)* HRI/GEN/1/Rev 8, p 185) **[RCLP para 7.26]**. Note however that Art 24(3) does not necessarily require a State to give its nationality to *every* child born in its territory (UN Human Rights Committee General Comment No 17 *Article 24 (Rights of the Child)* HRI/GEN/1/Rev 8, p 432) **[RCLP para 7.25]**.

Best interests—The International Covenant on Civil and Political Rights does not incorporate the best interests principle. However, the UN Committee on Human Rights has stated that the child's interests are 'paramount in cases involving parental separation and divorce' (see UN Human Rights Committee General Comment No 16 *Article 17 (Right to Privacy)* HRI/GEN/Rev 8, p 185 and UN Human Rights Committee General Comment No 18 *Art 2 (Non-discrimination)* HRI/GEN/Rev 8, p 189 and see also Communication No 201/1985 in Report of Human Rights Committee A/43/40 (1988) Annex VII para 1) **[RCLP para 4.125]**. See also *ZH (Tanzania) v*

Secretary of State for the Home Department [2011] UKSC 4, [2011] 1 FLR 2170, para 22; *Neulinger and Shuruk v Switzerland* [2011] 1 FLR 122, para 55; *R and H v United Kingdom* [2011] 2 FLR 1236, para 73 and *YC v United Kingdom* (2012) 55 EHRR 967, para 134.

Article 25

Every citizen shall have the right and the opportunity, without any of the distinctions mentioned in article 2 and without unreasonable restrictions:

  (a)   To take part in the conduct of public affairs, directly or through freely chosen representatives;

  (b)   To vote and to be elected at genuine periodic elections which shall be by universal and equal suffrage and shall be held by secret ballot, guaranteeing the free expression of the will of the electors;

  (c)   To have access, on general terms of equality, to public service in his country.

'Every citizen' (Art 25)—See Committee on the Rights of the Child General Comment No 5 *General Measures of Implementation for the Convention on the Rights of the Child* CRC/GC/2003/5, para 12) [RCLP para 6.65]. Setting a minimum age limit for voting will not contravene Art 25 (see UN Human Rights Committee General Comment No 25 *Article 25 (Participation in Public Affairs and the Right to Vote)* HRI/GEN/1/Rev 8, p 209, para 10) [RCLP para 11.48].

Article 26

All persons are equal before the law and are entitled without any discrimination to the equal protection of the law. In this respect, the law shall prohibit any discrimination and guarantee to all persons equal and effective protection against discrimination on any ground such as race, colour, sex, language, religion, political or other opinion, national or social origin, property, birth or other status.

'discrimination' (Art 26)—Discrimination for the purposes of Art 26 of the Covenant will include discrimination based on sexual orientation (see *Tooner v Australia*, Communication [1994] 1-3 IHRR 97 of the UN Human Rights Committee).

Article 27

In those States in which ethnic, religious or linguistic minorities exist, persons belonging to such minorities shall not be denied the right, in community with the other members of their group, to enjoy their own culture, to profess and practise their own religion, or to use their own language.

'ethnic, religious or linguistic minorities' (Art 27)—See UN Human Rights Committee General Comment No 23 *Article 27 (Rights of Minorities)* HRI/GEN/1/Rev 8, p 197 at 198-199 [RCLP para 10.31].

PART IV

Article 28

1. There shall be established a Human Rights Committee (hereafter referred to in the present Covenant as the Committee). It shall consist of eighteen members and shall carry out the functions hereinafter provided.

2. The Committee shall be composed of nationals of the States Parties to the present Covenant who shall be persons of high moral character and recognized competence in the field of human rights, consideration being given to the usefulness of the participation of some persons having legal experience.

3. The members of the Committee shall be elected and shall serve in their personal capacity.

Article 29

1. The members of the Committee shall be elected by secret ballot from a list of persons possessing the qualifications prescribed in article 28 and nominated for the purpose by the States Parties to the present Covenant.

2. Each State Party to the present Covenant may nominate not more than two persons. These persons shall be nationals of the nominating State.

3. A person shall be eligible for renomination.

Article 30

1. The initial election shall be held no later than six months after the date of the entry into force of the present Covenant.

2. At least four months before the date of each election to the Committee, other than an election to fill a vacancy declared in accordance with article 34, the Secretary-General of the United Nations shall address a written invitation to the States Parties to the present Covenant to submit their nominations for membership of the Committee within three months.

3. The Secretary-General of the United Nations shall prepare a list in alphabetical order of all the persons thus nominated, with an indication of the States Parties which have nominated them, and shall submit it to the States Parties to the present Covenant no later than one month before the date of each election.

4. Elections of the members of the Committee shall be held at a meeting of the States Parties to the present Covenant convened by the Secretary General of the United Nations at the Headquarters of the United Nations. At that meeting, for which two thirds of the States Parties to the present Covenant shall constitute a quorum, the persons elected to the Committee shall be those nominees who obtain the largest number of votes and an absolute majority of the votes of the representatives of States Parties present and voting.

Article 31

1. The Committee may not include more than one national of the same State.

2. In the election of the Committee, consideration shall be given to equitable geographical distribution of membership and to the representation of the different forms of civilization and of the principal legal systems.

Article 32

1. The members of the Committee shall be elected for a term of four years. They shall be eligible for re-election if renominated. However, the terms of nine of the members elected at the first election shall expire at the end of two years; immediately after the first election, the names of these nine members shall be chosen by lot by the Chairman of the meeting referred to in article 30, paragraph 4.

2. Elections at the expiry of office shall be held in accordance with the preceding articles of this part of the present Covenant.

Article 33

1. If, in the unanimous opinion of the other members, a member of the Committee has ceased to carry out his functions for any cause other than absence of a temporary character, the Chairman of the Committee shall notify the Secretary-General of the United Nations, who shall then declare the seat of that member to be vacant.

2. In the event of the death or the resignation of a member of the Committee, the Chairman shall immediately notify the Secretary-General of the United Nations, who shall declare the seat vacant from the date of death or the date on which the resignation takes effect.

Article 34

1. When a vacancy is declared in accordance with article 33 and if the term of office of the member to be replaced does not expire within six months of the declaration of the vacancy, the Secretary-General of the United Nations shall notify each of the States Parties to the present Covenant, which may within two months submit nominations in accordance with article 29 for the purpose of filling the vacancy.

2. The Secretary-General of the United Nations shall prepare a list in alphabetical order of the persons thus nominated and shall submit it to the States Parties to the present Covenant. The election to fill the vacancy shall then take place in accordance with the relevant provisions of this part of the present Covenant.

3. A member of the Committee elected to fill a vacancy declared in accordance with article 33 shall hold office for the remainder of the term of the member who vacated the seat on the Committee under the provisions of that article.

Article 35

The members of the Committee shall, with the approval of the General Assembly of the United Nations, receive emoluments from United Nations resources on such terms and conditions as the General Assembly may decide, having regard to the importance of the Committee's responsibilities.

Article 36

The Secretary-General of the United Nations shall provide the necessary staff and facilities for the effective performance of the functions of the Committee under the present Covenant.

Article 37

1. The Secretary-General of the United Nations shall convene the initial meeting of the Committee at the Headquarters of the United Nations.

2. After its initial meeting, the Committee shall meet at such times as shall be provided in its rules of procedure.

3. The Committee shall normally meet at the Headquarters of the United Nations or at the United Nations Office at Geneva.

Article 38

Every member of the Committee shall, before taking up his duties, make a solemn declaration in open committee that he will perform his functions impartially and conscientiously.

Article 39

1. The Committee shall elect its officers for a term of two years. They may be re-elected.

2. The Committee shall establish its own rules of procedure, but these rules shall provide, inter alia, that:

    (a)   Twelve members shall constitute a quorum;

(b)   Decisions of the Committee shall be made by a majority vote of the members present.

Article 40

1. The States Parties to the present Covenant undertake to submit reports on the measures they have adopted which give effect to the rights recognized herein and on the progress made in the enjoyment of those rights:

(a)   Within one year of the entry into force of the present Covenant for the States Parties concerned;

(b)   Thereafter whenever the Committee so requests.

2. All reports shall be submitted to the Secretary-General of the United Nations, who shall transmit them to the Committee for consideration. Reports shall indicate the factors and difficulties, if any, affecting the implementation of the present Covenant.

3. The Secretary-General of the United Nations may, after consultation with the Committee, transmit to the specialized agencies concerned copies of such parts of the reports as may fall within their field of competence.

4. The Committee shall study the reports submitted by the States Parties to the present Covenant. It shall transmit its reports, and such general comments as it may consider appropriate, to the States Parties. The Committee may also transmit to the Economic and Social Council these comments along with the copies of the reports it has received from States Parties to the present Covenant.

5. The States Parties to the present Covenant may submit to the Committee observations on any comments that may be made in accordance with paragraph 4 of this article.

Article 41

1. A State Party to the present Covenant may at any time declare under this article that it recognizes the competence of the Committee to receive and consider communications to the effect that a State Party claims that another State Party is not fulfilling its obligations under the present Covenant. Communications under this article may be received and considered only if submitted by a State Party which has made a declaration recognizing in regard to itself the competence of the Committee. No communication shall be received by the Committee if it concerns a State Party which has not made such a declaration. Communications received under this article shall be dealt with in accordance with the following procedure:

(a)   If a State Party to the present Covenant considers that another State Party is not giving effect to the provisions of the present Covenant, it may, by written communication, bring the matter to the attention of that State Party. Within three months after the receipt of the communication the receiving State shall afford the State which sent the communication an explanation, or any other statement in writing clarifying the matter which should include, to the extent possible and pertinent, reference to domestic procedures and remedies taken, pending, or available in the matter;

(b)   If the matter is not adjusted to the satisfaction of both States Parties concerned within six months after the receipt by the receiving State of the initial communication, either State shall have the right to refer the matter to the Committee, by notice given to the Committee and to the other State;

(c)   The Committee shall deal with a matter referred to it only after it has ascertained that all available domestic remedies have been invoked and exhausted in the matter, in conformity with the generally recognized principles of international law. This shall not be the rule where the application of the remedies is unreasonably prolonged;

(d)   The Committee shall hold closed meetings when examining communications under this article;

(e)   Subject to the provisions of subparagraph (c), the Committee shall make available its good offices to the States Parties concerned with a view to a friendly solution of the matter on the basis of respect for human rights and fundamental freedoms as recognized in the present Covenant;

(f)   In any matter referred to it, the Committee may call upon the States Parties concerned, referred to in subparagraph (b), to supply any relevant information;

(g)   The States Parties concerned, referred to in subparagraph (b), shall have the right to be represented when the matter is being considered in the Committee and to make submissions orally and/or in writing;

(h)   The Committee shall, within twelve months after the date of receipt of notice under subparagraph (b), submit a report:

(i)   If a solution within the terms of subparagraph (e) is reached, the Committee shall confine its report to a brief statement of the facts and of the solution reached;

(ii)   If a solution within the terms of subparagraph (e) is not reached, the Committee shall confine its report to a brief statement of the facts; the written submissions and record of the oral submissions made by the States Parties concerned shall be attached to the report. In every matter, the report shall be communicated to the States Parties concerned.

2. The provisions of this article shall come into force when ten States Parties to the present Covenant have made declarations under paragraph I of this article. Such declarations shall be deposited by the States Parties with the Secretary-General of the United Nations, who shall transmit copies thereof to the other States Parties. A declaration may be withdrawn at any time by notification to the Secretary-General. Such a withdrawal shall not prejudice the consideration of any matter which is the subject of a communication already transmitted under this article; no further communication by any State Party shall be received after the notification of withdrawal of the declaration has been received by the Secretary-General, unless the State Party concerned has made a new declaration.

Article 42

1.

(a)   If a matter referred to the Committee in accordance with article 41 is not resolved to the satisfaction of the States Parties concerned, the Committee may, with the prior consent of the States Parties concerned, appoint an ad hoc Conciliation Commission (hereinafter referred to as the Commission). The good offices of the Commission shall be made available to the States Parties concerned with a view to an amicable solution of the matter on the basis of respect for the present Covenant;

(b)   The Commission shall consist of five persons acceptable to the States Parties concerned. If the States Parties concerned fail to reach agreement within three months on all or part of the composition of the Commission, the members of the Commission concerning whom no agreement has been reached shall be elected by secret ballot by a two-thirds majority vote of the Committee from among its members.

2. The members of the Commission shall serve in their personal capacity. They shall not be nationals of the States Parties concerned, or of a State not Party to the present Covenant, or of a State Party which has not made a declaration under article 41.

3. The Commission shall elect its own Chairman and adopt its own rules of procedure.

4. The meetings of the Commission shall normally be held at the Headquarters of the United Nations or at the United Nations Office at Geneva. However, they may be held at such other convenient places as the Commission may determine in consultation with the Secretary-General of the United Nations and the States Parties concerned.

5. The secretariat provided in accordance with article 36 shall also service the commissions appointed under this article.

6. The information received and collated by the Committee shall be made available to the Commission and the Commission may call upon the States Parties concerned to supply any other relevant information.

7. When the Commission has fully considered the matter, but in any event not later than twelve months after having been seized of the matter, it shall submit to the Chairman of the Committee a report for communication to the States Parties concerned:

   (a)   If the Commission is unable to complete its consideration of the matter within twelve months, it shall confine its report to a brief statement of the status of its consideration of the matter;
   (b)   If an amicable solution to the matter on tie basis of respect for human rights as recognized in the present Covenant is reached, the Commission shall confine its report to a brief statement of the facts and of the solution reached;
   (c)   If a solution within the terms of subparagraph (b) is not reached, the Commission's report shall embody its findings on all questions of fact relevant to the issues between the States Parties concerned, and its views on the possibilities of an amicable solution of the matter. This report shall also contain the written submissions and a record of the oral submissions made by the States Parties concerned;
   (d)   If the Commission's report is submitted under subparagraph (c), the States Parties concerned shall, within three months of the receipt of the report, notify the Chairman of the Committee whether or not they accept the contents of the report of the Commission.

8. The provisions of this article are without prejudice to the responsibilities of the Committee under article 41.

9. The States Parties concerned shall share equally all the expenses of the members of the Commission in accordance with estimates to be provided by the Secretary-General of the United Nations.

10. The Secretary-General of the United Nations shall be empowered to pay the expenses of the members of the Commission, if necessary, before reimbursement by the States Parties concerned, in accordance with paragraph 9 of this article.

Article 43

The members of the Committee, and of the ad hoc conciliation commissions which may be appointed under article 42, shall be entitled to the facilities, privileges and immunities of experts on mission for the United Nations as laid down in the relevant sections of the Convention on the Privileges and Immunities of the United Nations.

Article 44

The provisions for the implementation of the present Covenant shall apply without prejudice to the procedures prescribed in the field of human rights by or under the constituent instruments and the conventions of the United Nations and of the specialized agencies and shall not prevent the States Parties to the present Covenant from having recourse to other procedures for settling a dispute in accordance with general or special international agreements in force between them.

Article 45

The Committee shall submit to the General Assembly of the United Nations, through the Economic and Social Council, an annual report on its activities.

PART V

Article 46

Nothing in the present Covenant shall be interpreted as impairing the provisions of the Charter of the United Nations and of the constitutions of the specialized agencies which define the respective responsibilities of the various organs of the United Nations and of the specialized agencies in regard to the matters dealt with in the present Covenant.

Article 47

Nothing in the present Covenant shall be interpreted as impairing the inherent right of all peoples to enjoy and utilize fully and freely their natural wealth and resources.

PART VI

Article 48

1. The present Covenant is open for signature by any State Member of the United Nations or member of any of its specialized agencies, by any State Party to the Statute of the International Court of Justice, and by any other State which has been invited by the General Assembly of the United Nations to become a Party to the present Covenant.

2. The present Covenant is subject to ratification. Instruments of ratification shall be deposited with the Secretary-General of the United Nations.

3. The present Covenant shall be open to accession by any State referred to in paragraph 1 of this article.

4. Accession shall be effected by the deposit of an instrument of accession with the Secretary-General of the United Nations.

5. The Secretary-General of the United Nations shall inform all States which have signed this Covenant or acceded to it of the deposit of each instrument of ratification or accession.

Article 49

1. The present Covenant shall enter into force three months after the date of the deposit with the Secretary-General of the United Nations of the thirty-fifth instrument of ratification or instrument of accession.

2. For each State ratifying the present Covenant or acceding to it after the deposit of the thirtyfifth instrument of ratification or instrument of accession, the present Covenant shall enter into force three months after the date of the deposit of its own instrument of ratification or instrument of accession.

Article 50

The provisions of the present Covenant shall extend to all parts of federal States without any limitations or exceptions.

Article 51

1. Any State Party to the present Covenant may propose an amendment and file it with the Secretary-General of the United Nations. The Secretary-General of the United Nations shall thereupon communicate any proposed amendments to the States Parties to the present Covenant with a request that they notify him whether they favour a conference of States Parties for the purpose of considering and voting upon the proposals. In the event that at least one third of the States Parties favours such a conference, the Secretary-General shall convene the conference under the auspices of the United Nations. Any amendment adopted by a majority of the States Parties present and voting at the conference shall be submitted to the General Assembly of the United Nations for approval.

2. Amendments shall come into force when they have been approved by the General Assembly of the United Nations and accepted by a two-thirds majority of the States Parties to the present Covenant in accordance with their respective constitutional processes.

3. When amendments come into force, they shall be binding on those States Parties which have accepted them, other States Parties still being bound by the provisions of the present Covenant and any earlier amendment which they have accepted.

Article 52

1. Irrespective of the notifications made under article 48, paragraph 5, the Secretary-General of the United Nations shall inform all States referred to in paragraph I of the same article of the following particulars:

(a) Signatures, ratifications and accessions under article 48;
(b) The date of the entry into force of the present Covenant under article 49 and the date of the entry into force of any amendments under article 51.

Article 53

1. The present Covenant, of which the Chinese, English, French, Russian and Spanish texts are equally authentic, shall be deposited in the archives of the United Nations.

2. The Secretary-General of the United Nations shall transmit certified copies of the present Covenant to all States referred to in article 48.

CHAPTER 8

INTERNATIONAL COVENANT ON ECONOMIC, SOCIAL AND CULTURAL RIGHTS

Adopted and opened for signature, ratification and accession by General Assembly resolution 2200A (XXI) of 16 December 1966 entry into force 3 January 1976, in accordance with article 27

PREAMBLE

The States Parties to the present Covenant,

Considering that, in accordance with the principles proclaimed in the Charter of the United Nations, recognition of the inherent dignity and of the equal and inalienable rights of all members of the human family is the foundation of freedom, justice and peace in the world,

Recognizing that these rights derive from the inherent dignity of the human person,

Recognizing that, in accordance with the Universal Declaration of Human Rights, the ideal of free human beings enjoying freedom from fear and want can only be achieved if conditions are created whereby everyone may enjoy his economic, social and cultural rights, as well as his civil and political rights,

Considering the obligation of States under the Charter of the United Nations to promote universal respect for, and observance of, human rights and freedoms,

Realizing that the individual, having duties to other individuals and to the community to which he belongs, is under a responsibility to strive for the promotion and observance of the rights recognized in the present Covenant,

Agree upon the following articles:

Status—The International Covenant on Economic, Social and Cultural Rights was ratified by the United Kingdom on 20 May 1976 [**RCLP para 2.32**]. The status of the International Covenant on Civil and Political Rights is that of a binding international Convention not incorporated into domestic law [**RCLP para 3.94**] and see *R (TS) v Secretary of State for the Home Department* [2010] EWHC 2614 (Admin), [2010] All ER (D) 275 (Oct) para 30, *R (Omedwar) v Secretary of State for the Home Department* [2011] EWHC 110 (Admin), [2011] All ER (D) 222 (Jan) and *AAM (a child acting by his litigation friend FJ) v Secretary of State for the Home Department* [2012] EWHC 2567 (QB) para 123). The International Covenant on Civil and Political Rights establishes the UN Committee on Economic, Social and Cultural Rights which receives and adjudicates upon complaints. Note that the International Covenant on Economic, Social and Cultural Rights has an Optional Protocol (not included in this work) that provides a mechanism for private individuals to pursue complaints concerning alleged violations of the Convention [**RCLP para 2.33**]. The rights enshrined in the International Covenant on Economic, Social and Cultural rights can present problems of justiciability [**RCLP para 3.11**]. Within this context, the concept of 'progressive realisation' will be important [**RCLP paras 3.12 and 13.47**] and see Committee on Economic, Social and Cultural Rights General Comment No 3 *The Nature of State Parties' Obligations* HRI/GEN/1/Rev 8, pp 17-18, para 11.

PART I

Article 1

1. All peoples have the right of self-determination. By virtue of that right they freely determine their political status and freely pursue their economic, social and cultural development.

2. All peoples may, for their own ends, freely dispose of their natural wealth and resources without prejudice to any obligations arising out of international economic co-operation, based upon the principle of mutual benefit, and international law. In no case may a people be deprived of its own means of subsistence.

3. The States Parties to the present Covenant, including those having responsibility for the administration of Non-Self-Governing and Trust Territories, shall promote the realization of the right of self-determination, and shall respect that right, in conformity with the provisions of the Charter of the United Nations.

PART II

Article 2

1. Each State Party to the present Covenant undertakes to take steps, individually and through international assistance and co-operation, especially economic and technical, to the maximum of its available resources, with a view to achieving progressively the full realization of the rights recognized in the present Covenant by all appropriate means, including particularly the adoption of legislative measures.

2. The States Parties to the present Covenant undertake to guarantee that the rights enunciated in the present Covenant will be exercised without discrimination of any kind as to race, colour, sex, language, religion, political or other opinion, national or social origin, property, birth or other status.

3. Developing countries, with due regard to human rights and their national economy, may determine to what extent they would guarantee the economic rights recognized in the present Covenant to nonnationals.

Article 3

The States Parties to the present Covenant undertake to ensure the equal right of men and women to the enjoyment of all economic, social and cultural rights set forth in the present Covenant.

Article 4

The States Parties to the present Covenant recognize that, in the enjoyment of those rights provided by the State in conformity with the present Covenant, the State may subject such rights only to such limitations as are determined by law only in so far as this may be compatible with the nature of these rights and solely for the purpose of promoting the general welfare in a democratic society.

Article 5

1. Nothing in the present Covenant may be interpreted as implying for any State, group or person any right to engage in any activity or to perform any act aimed at the destruction of any of the rights or freedoms recognized herein, or at their limitation to a greater extent than is provided for in the present Covenant.

2. No restriction upon or derogation from any of the fundamental human rights recognized or existing in any country in virtue of law, conventions, regulations or custom shall be admitted on the pretext that the present Covenant does not recognize such rights or that it recognizes them to a lesser extent.

PART III

Article 6

1. The States Parties to the present Covenant recognize the right to work, which includes the right of everyone to the opportunity to gain his living by work which he freely chooses or accepts, and will take appropriate steps to safeguard this right.

2. The steps to be taken by a State Party to the present Covenant to achieve the full realization of this right shall include technical and vocational guidance and training programmes, policies and techniques to achieve steady economic, social and cultural development and full and productive employment under conditions safeguarding fundamental political and economic freedoms to the individual.

Article 7

The States Parties to the present Covenant recognize the right of everyone to the enjoyment of just and favourable conditions of work which ensure, in particular:

    (a)   Remuneration which provides all workers, as a minimum, with:
        (i)   Fair wages and equal remuneration for work of equal value without distinction of any kind, in particular women being guaranteed conditions of work not inferior to those enjoyed by men, with equal pay for equal work;
        (ii)   A decent living for themselves and their families in accordance with the provisions of the present Covenant;
    (b)   Safe and healthy working conditions;
    (c)   Equal opportunity for everyone to be promoted in his employment to an appropriate higher level, subject to no considerations other than those of seniority and competence;
    (d)   Rest, leisure and reasonable limitation of working hours and periodic holidays with pay, as well as remuneration for public holidays

'**just and favourable work conditions**' (Art 7)—In relation to children and dependents see the Committee on Economic, Social and Cultural Rights General Comment No 16 *The Equal Right of Men and Women to Enjoyment of All Economic, Social and Cultural Rights* HRI/GEN/1/Rev 8, p 127, para 24 [**RCLP para 8.43**].

Article 8

1. The States Parties to the present Covenant undertake to ensure:

    (a)   The right of everyone to form trade unions and join the trade union of his choice, subject only to the rules of the organization concerned, for the promotion and protection of his economic and social interests. No restrictions may be placed on the exercise of this right other than those prescribed by law and which are necessary in a democratic society in the interests of national security or public order or for the protection of the rights and freedoms of others;
    (b)   The right of trade unions to establish national federations or confederations and the right of the latter to form or join international trade-union organizations;

(c)   The right of trade unions to function freely subject to no limitations other than those prescribed by law and which are necessary in a democratic society in the interests of national security or public order or for the protection of the rights and freedoms of others;

(d)   The right to strike, provided that it is exercised in conformity with the laws of the particular country.

2. This article shall not prevent the imposition of lawful restrictions on the exercise of these rights by members of the armed forces or of the police or of the administration of the State.

3. Nothing in this article shall authorize States Parties to the International Labour Organisation Convention of 1948 concerning Freedom of Association and Protection of the Right to Organize to take legislative measures which would prejudice, or apply the law in such a manner as would prejudice, the guarantees provided for in that Convention.

Article 9

The States Parties to the present Covenant recognize the right of everyone to social security, including social insurance.

Article 10

The States Parties to the present Covenant recognize that:

1. The widest possible protection and assistance should be accorded to the family, which is the natural and fundamental group unit of society, particularly for its establishment and while it is responsible for the care and education of dependent children. Marriage must be entered into with the free consent of the intending spouses.

2. Special protection should be accorded to mothers during a reasonable period before and after childbirth. During such period working mothers should be accorded paid leave or leave with adequate social security benefits.

3. Special measures of protection and assistance should be taken on behalf of all children and young persons without any discrimination for reasons of parentage or other conditions. Children and young persons should be protected from economic and social exploitation. Their employment in work harmful to their morals or health or dangerous to life or likely to hamper their normal development should be punishable by law. States should also set age limits below which the paid employment of child labour should be prohibited and punishable by law.

'widest possible protection and assistance' (Art 10(1))—See Committee on Economic, Social and Cultural Rights General Comment No 16 *The Equal Right of Men and Women to Enjoyment of All Economic, Social and Cultural Rights* HRI/GEN/1/Rev 8, p 127, para 27 and Committee on Economic, Social and Cultural Rights General Comment No 5 *Persons with Disabilities* HRI/GEN/1/Rev 8, p 31, para 30 [RCLP para 8.46].

'free consent' (Art 10(1))—See *R (Quila); R (Bibi) v Secretary of State for the Home Department* [2011] UKSC 45, [2012] 1 FLR 788, para 66.

Article 11

1. The States Parties to the present Covenant recognize the right of everyone to an adequate standard of living for himself and his family, including adequate food, clothing and housing, and to the continuous improvement of living conditions. The States Parties will take appropriate steps to ensure the realization of this right, recognizing to this effect the essential importance of international cooperation based on free consent.

2. The States Parties to the present Covenant, recognizing the fundamental right of everyone to be free from hunger, shall take, individually and through international co-operation, the measures, including specific programmes, which are needed:

(a) To improve methods of production, conservation and distribution of food by making full use of technical and scientific knowledge, by disseminating knowledge of the principles of nutrition and by developing or reforming agrarian systems in such a way as to achieve the most efficient development and utilization of natural resources;

(b) Taking into account the problems of both food-importing and food-exporting countries, to ensure an equitable distribution of world food supplies in relation to need.

'adequate food' (Art 11(1))—The right to adequate food comprises physical and economic access at all times to adequate food or means for its procurement and the right should not be interpreted in the narrow sense of calories, proteins and other specific nutrients (see Committee on Economic, Social and Cultural Rights General Comment No 12 *The Right to Adequate Food (Art 11)* HRI/GEN/1/Rev 8, para 1) [**RCLP para 5.113**].

'adequate housing' (Art 11(1))—See the Committee on Economic, Social and Cultural Rights General Comment No 4 *The Right to Adequate Housing (Art 11(1) of the Covenant)* HRI/GEN/1/Rev 8, p 19, paras 6-11 [**RCLP para 5.158**].

Persons with disabilities—See the Committee on Economic, Social and Cultural Rights General Comment No 5 *Persons with Disabilities* HRI/GEN/1/Rev 8, p 32, para 33 [**RCLP para 5.152**].

Article 12

1. The States Parties to the present Covenant recognize the right of everyone to the enjoyment of the highest attainable standard of physical and mental health.

2. The steps to be taken by the States Parties to the present Covenant to achieve the full realization of this right shall include those necessary for:

(a) The provision for the reduction of the stillbirth-rate and of infant mortality and for the healthy development of the child;

(b) The improvement of all aspects of environmental and industrial hygiene;

(c) The prevention, treatment and control of epidemic, endemic, occupational and other diseases;

(d) The creation of conditions which would assure to all medical service and medical attention in the event of sickness.

'improvement of all aspects of environmental and industrial hygiene' (Art 12(2)(b))—See the Committee on Economic, Social and Cultural Rights General Comment No 14 *Right to the Highest Attainable Standard of Health* HRI/GEN/1/Rev 8, para 15 and see Principle 1 of the Stockholm Declaration of 1972 [**RCLP para 5.116**].

'prevention, treatment and control of epidemic, endemic, occupational and other diseases' (Art 12(2)(c))—See Committee on Economic, Social and Cultural Rights General Comment No 14 *Right to the Highest Attainable Standard of Health* HRI/GEN/1/Rev 8, para 16 [**RCLP para 5.109**].

'all medical service and medical attention in the event of sickness' (Art 12(2)(d))—See Committee on Economic, Social and Cultural Rights General Comment No 14 *Right to the Highest Attainable Standard of Health* HRI/GEN/1/Rev 8, para 17 [**RCLP para 5.108**].

Article 13

1. The States Parties to the present Covenant recognize the right of everyone to education. They agree that education shall be directed to the full development of the human personality and the sense of its dignity, and shall strengthen the respect for human rights and fundamental freedoms. They further agree that education shall enable all persons to participate effectively in a free society, promote understanding, tolerance

and friendship among all nations and all racial, ethnic or religious groups, and further the activities of the United Nations for the maintenance of peace.

2. The States Parties to the present Covenant recognize that, with a view to achieving the full realization of this right:

(a) Primary education shall be compulsory and available free to all;

(b) Secondary education in its different forms, including technical and vocational secondary education, shall be made generally available and accessible to all by every appropriate means, and in particular by the progressive introduction of free education;

(c) Higher education shall be made equally accessible to all, on the basis of capacity, by every appropriate means, and in particular by the progressive introduction of free education;

(d) Fundamental education shall be encouraged or intensified as far as possible for those persons who have not received or completed the whole period of their primary education;

(e) The development of a system of schools at all levels shall be actively pursued, an adequate fellowship system shall be established, and the material conditions of teaching staff shall be continuously improved.

3. The States Parties to the present Covenant undertake to have respect for the liberty of parents and, when applicable, legal guardians to choose for their children schools, other than those established by the public authorities, which conform to such minimum educational standards as may be laid down or approved by the State and to ensure the religious and moral education of their children in conformity with their own convictions.

4. No part of this article shall be construed so as to interfere with the liberty of individuals and bodies to establish and direct educational institutions, subject always to the observance of the principles set forth in paragraph I of this article and to the requirement that the education given in such institutions shall conform to such minimum standards as may be laid down by the State.

Aims of education (Art 13(1))—States parties are required to ensure that the curricula for all levels of the education system are directed to the objectives identified in Art 13(1) (see Committee on Economic, Social and Cultural Rights General Comment No 13 *The Right to Education (Art 13)* HRI/GEN/1/Rev 8, p 81, para 49) [RCLP para 13.33].

'Primary education ... available free to all' (Art 13(2)(a))—The nature of this requirement is unequivocal (see Committee on Economic, Social and Cultural Rights General Comment No 11 *Plans for Action for Primary Education (Art 14)* HRI/GEN/1/Rev 8, p 62, para 7) [RCLP para 13.53].

'including technical and vocational secondary education' (Art 13(2)(b))—Technical and vocational education should be included at all levels of the curriculum (see Committee on Economic, Social and Cultural Rights General Comment No 13 *The Right to Education (Art 13)* HRI/GEN/1/Rev 8, p 74, para 15) [RCLP para 13.60].

'Fundamental education' (Art 13(2)(d))—The term 'fundamental education' corresponds to the concept of 'basic education' (see World Declaration on Education for All A/S-27/19/Rev 1, paras 39 and 40 and Committee on Economic, Social and Cultural Rights General Comment No 13 *The Right to Education (Art 13)* HRI/GEN/1/Rev 8, p 76, para 23 [RCLP para 13.34].

'have respect for the liberty of parents and ... legal guardians' (Art 13(3))—Respect for the religious and moral liberty of parents and guardians should not be allowed to lead to extreme disparities of educational opportunity between different groups in society (see Committee on Economic, Social and Cultural Rights General Comment No 13 *The Right to Education (Art 13)* HRI/GEN/1/Rev 8, paras 28-30) [RCLP para 13.86].

Article 14

Each State Party to the present Covenant which, at the time of becoming a Party, has not been able to secure in its metropolitan territory or other territories under its jurisdiction compulsory primary education, free of charge, undertakes, within two years, to work out and adopt a detailed plan of action for the progressive implementation, within a reasonable number of years, to be fixed in the plan, of the principle of compulsory education free of charge for all.

Article 15

1. The States Parties to the present Covenant recognize the right of everyone:

(a)   To take part in cultural life;
(b)   To enjoy the benefits of scientific progress and its applications;
(c)   To benefit from the protection of the moral and material interests resulting from any scientific, literary or artistic production of which he is the author.

2. The steps to be taken by the States Parties to the present Covenant to achieve the full realization of this right shall include those necessary for the conservation, the development and the diffusion of science and culture.

3. The States Parties to the present Covenant undertake to respect the freedom indispensable for scientific research and creative activity.

4. The States Parties to the present Covenant recognize the benefits to be derived from the encouragement and development of international contacts and co-operation in the scientific and cultural fields.

PART IV

Article 16

1. The States Parties to the present Covenant undertake to submit in conformity with this part of the Covenant reports on the measures which they have adopted and the progress made in achieving the observance of the rights recognized herein.

2.

(a)   All reports shall be submitted to the Secretary-General of the United Nations, who shall transmit copies to the Economic and Social Council for consideration in accordance with the provisions of the present Covenant;
(b)   The Secretary-General of the United Nations shall also transmit to the specialized agencies copies of the reports, or any relevant parts therefrom, from States Parties to the present Covenant which are also members of these specialized agencies in so far as these reports, or parts therefrom, relate to any matters which fall within the responsibilities of the said agencies in accordance with their constitutional instruments.

Article 17

1. The States Parties to the present Covenant shall furnish their reports in stages, in accordance with a programme to be established by the Economic and Social Council within one year of the entry into force of the present Covenant after consultation with the States Parties and the specialized agencies concerned.

2. Reports may indicate factors and difficulties affecting the degree of fulfilment of obligations under the present Covenant.

3. Where relevant information has previously been furnished to the United Nations or to any specialized agency by any State Party to the present Covenant, it will not be necessary to reproduce that information, but a precise reference to the information so furnished will suffice.

Article 18

Pursuant to its responsibilities under the Charter of the United Nations in the field of human rights and fundamental freedoms, the Economic and Social Council may make arrangements with the specialized agencies in respect of their reporting to it on the progress made in achieving the observance of the provisions of the present Covenant falling within the scope of their activities. These reports may include particulars of decisions and recommendations on such implementation adopted by their competent organs.

Article 19

The Economic and Social Council may transmit to the Commission on Human Rights for study and general recommendation or, as appropriate, for information the reports concerning human rights submitted by States in accordance with articles 16 and 17, and those concerning human rights submitted by the specialized agencies in accordance with article 18.

Article 20

The States Parties to the present Covenant and the specialized agencies concerned may submit comments to the Economic and Social Council on any general recommendation under article 19 or reference to such general recommendation in any report of the Commission on Human Rights or any documentation referred to therein.

Article 21

The Economic and Social Council may submit from time to time to the General Assembly reports with recommendations of a general nature and a summary of the information received from the States Parties to the present Covenant and the specialized agencies on the measures taken and the progress made in achieving general observance of the rights recognized in the present Covenant.

Article 22

The Economic and Social Council may bring to the attention of other organs of the United Nations, their subsidiary organs and specialized agencies concerned with furnishing technical assistance any matters arising out of the reports referred to in this part of the present Covenant which may assist such bodies in deciding, each within its field of competence, on the advisability of international measures likely to contribute to the effective progressive implementation of the present Covenant.

Article 23

The States Parties to the present Covenant agree that international action for the achievement of the rights recognized in the present Covenant includes such methods as the conclusion of conventions, the adoption of recommendations, the furnishing of technical assistance and the holding of regional meetings and technical meetings for the purpose of consultation and study organized in conjunction with the Governments concerned.

Article 24

Nothing in the present Covenant shall be interpreted as impairing the provisions of the Charter of the United Nations and of the constitutions of the specialized agencies which define the respective responsibilities of the various organs of the United Nations and of the specialized agencies in regard to the matters dealt with in the present Covenant.

Article 25

Nothing in the present Covenant shall be interpreted as impairing the inherent right of all peoples to enjoy and utilize fully and freely their natural wealth and resources.

PART V

Article 26

1. The present Covenant is open for signature by any State Member of the United Nations or member of any of its specialized agencies, by any State Party to the Statute of the International Court of Justice, and by any other State which has been invited by the General Assembly of the United Nations to become a party to the present Covenant.

2. The present Covenant is subject to ratification. Instruments of ratification shall be deposited with the Secretary-General of the United Nations.

3. The present Covenant shall be open to accession by any State referred to in paragraph 1 of this article.

4. Accession shall be effected by the deposit of an instrument of accession with the Secretary-General of the United Nations.

5. The Secretary-General of the United Nations shall inform all States which have signed the present Covenant or acceded to it of the deposit of each instrument of ratification or accession.

Article 27

1. The present Covenant shall enter into force three months after the date of the deposit with the Secretary-General of the United Nations of the thirty-fifth instrument of ratification or instrument of accession.

2. For each State ratifying the present Covenant or acceding to it after the deposit of the thirty-fifth instrument of ratification or instrument of accession, the present Covenant shall enter into force three months after the date of the deposit of its own instrument of ratification or instrument of accession.

Article 28

The provisions of the present Covenant shall extend to all parts of federal States without any limitations or exceptions.

Article 29

1. Any State Party to the present Covenant may propose an amendment and file it with the Secretary- General of the United Nations. The Secretary-General shall thereupon communicate any proposed amendments to the States Parties to the present Covenant with a request that they notify him whether they favour a conference of States Parties for the purpose of considering and voting upon the proposals. In the event that at least one third of the States Parties favours such a conference, the Secretary-General shall convene the conference under the auspices of the United Nations. Any amendment adopted by a

majority of the States Parties present and voting at the conference shall be submitted to the General Assembly of the United Nations for approval.

2. Amendments shall come into force when they have been approved by the General Assembly of the United Nations and accepted by a two-thirds majority of the States Parties to the present Covenant in accordance with their respective constitutional processes.

3. When amendments come into force they shall be binding on those States Parties which have accepted them, other States Parties still being bound by the provisions of the present Covenant and any earlier amendment which they have accepted.

Article 30

Irrespective of the notifications made under article 26, paragraph 5, the Secretary-General of the United Nations shall inform all States referred to in paragraph I of the same article of the following particulars:

(a) Signatures, ratifications and accessions under article 26;
(b) The date of the entry into force of the present Covenant under article 27 and the date of the entry into force of any amendments under article 29.

Article 31

1. The present Covenant, of which the Chinese, English, French, Russian and Spanish texts are equally authentic, shall be deposited in the archives of the United Nations.

2. The Secretary-General of the United Nations shall transmit certified copies of the present Covenant to all States referred to in article 26.

CHAPTER 9

CONVENTION AGAINST TORTURE AND OTHER CRUEL, INHUMAN OR DEGRADING TREATMENT OR PUNISHMENT

Adopted and opened for signature, ratification and accession by General Assembly resolution 39/46 of 10 December 1984 entry into force 26 June 1987, in accordance with article 27 (1)

PREAMBLE

The States Parties to this Convention,

Considering that, in accordance with the principles proclaimed in the Charter of the United Nations, recognition of the equal and inalienable rights of all members of the human family is the foundation of freedom, justice and peace in the world,

Recognizing that those rights derive from the inherent dignity of the human person,

Considering the obligation of States under the Charter, in particular Article 55, to promote universal respect for, and observance of, human rights and fundamental freedoms,

Having regard to article 5 of the Universal Declaration of Human Rights and article 7 of the International Covenant on Civil and Political Rights, both of which provide that no one shall be subjected to torture or to cruel, inhuman or degrading treatment or punishment,

Having regard also to the Declaration on the Protection of All Persons from Being Subjected to Torture and Other Cruel, Inhuman or Degrading Treatment or Punishment, adopted by the General Assembly on 9 December 1975,

Desiring to make more effective the struggle against torture and other cruel, inhuman or degrading treatment or punishment throughout the world,

Have agreed as follows:

Status—The Convention against Torture and Other Cruel, Inhuman or Degrading Treatment or Punishment was ratified by the United Kingdom on 8 December 1988 [RCLP para 2.35]. The status of the Convention against Torture and Other Cruel, Inhuman or Degrading Treatment or Punishment is that of a binding international Convention not incorporated into domestic law [RCLP para 3.94]. Note that the Convention against Torture and Other Cruel, Inhuman or Degrading Treatment or Punishment has an Optional Protocol (not included in this work) which was ratified by the United Kingdom on 10 December 2003 (see *GJ and others (post civil war: returnees)* [2013] UKUT 00319 (IAC) para 78). Art 1 of the Optional Protocol establishes a system of regular visits by independent international and national bodies to places where people are deprived of their liberty in order to prevent torture or other cruel, inhuman or degrading treatment or punishment [RCLP para 2.35].

PART I

Article 1

1. For the purposes of this Convention, the term "torture" means any act by which severe pain or suffering, whether physical or mental, is intentionally inflicted on a person for such purposes as obtaining from him or a third person information or a confession, punishing him for an act he or a third person has committed or is suspected of having committed, or intimidating or coercing him or a third person, or for any reason based on discrimination of any kind, when such pain or suffering is inflicted by or at the instigation of or with the consent or acquiescence of a public official or other person acting in an official capacity. It does not include pain or suffering arising only from, inherent in or incidental to lawful sanctions.

2. This article is without prejudice to any international instrument or national legislation which does or may contain provisions of wider application.

'person' (Art 1(1))—The word 'person' will necessarily include child.

Jus cogens nature of torture—The prohibition against torture has become a norm of *jus cogens* in international law (see *Prosecutor v Anto Furundzija* (1998) ILR 121, para 153) [RCLP para 15.140]. The *jus cogens* nature of the prohibition against torture has been recognised by the domestic courts (see *R v Bow Street Metropolitan Stipendiary Magistrate ex p Pinochet Ugarte (No 3)* [2000] 1 AC 147 HL) and has been recognised as encompassing the harmful treatment of children (see *Re E (A Child) (Northern Ireland)* [2008] UKHL 66, [2008] 3 WLR 1208, para 7 and see also *Van Eden v Minister for Safety and Security* (2003)(1) SA 389 Supreme Court of Appeal of South Africa) [RCLP para 15.204].

Article 2

1. Each State Party shall take effective legislative, administrative, judicial or other measures to prevent acts of torture in any territory under its jurisdiction.

2. No exceptional circumstances whatsoever, whether a state of war or a threat of war, internal political in stability or any other public emergency, may be invoked as a justification of torture.

3. An order from a superior officer or a public authority may not be invoked as a justification of torture.

'State Party' (Art 2(1))—Note that the Convention imposes obligations on State Parties and not on individuals. However, States bear international responsibility for the acts and omissions of their officials and others, including agents, private contractors and others acting in official capacity or acting on behalf of the State, in conjunction with the State, under its direction or control, or otherwise under colour of law (UN Committee Against Torture and Other Cruel, Inhuman or Degrading Treatment or Punishment General Comment No 2 *Implementation of Article 2 by State Parties* CAT/C/GC/2, para 15) [RCLP para 15.14].

'effective legislative, administrative, judicial or other measures' (Art 2(1))—These words specifically require State parties to ensure that all acts of torture are offences under its criminal law and are punishable by appropriate penalties [RCLP para 15.14].

'any territory under its jurisdiction' (Art 2(1))—For the meaning of this term see UN Committee Against Torture and Other Cruel, Inhuman or Degrading Treatment or Punishment General Comment No 2 *Implementation of Article 2 by State Parties* CAT/C/GC/2, para 7 [RCLP para 15.14].

'No exceptional circumstances whatsoever' (Art 2(2))—The prohibition against torture is absolute and non-derogable (see UN Committee Against Torture and Other Cruel, Inhuman or Degrading Treatment or Punishment General Comment No 2 *Implementation of Article 2 by State Parties* CAT/C/GC/2, para 5) [RCLP para 15.16].

'order from a superior officer or a public authority' (Art 2(3))—See UN Committee Against Torture and Other Cruel, Inhuman or Degrading Treatment or Punishment General Comment No 2 *Implementation of Article 2 by State Parties* CAT/C/GC/2, para 26 and also Principle IV of the Nuremberg Principles which stipulates that 'The fact that a person acted pursuant to an order of his Government or of a superior does not relieve him of his responsibility under international law, provided a moral choice was in fact possible to him' [**RCLP paras 15.10 and 15.14**].

Article 3

1. No State Party shall expel, return ("refouler") or extradite a person to another State where there are substantial grounds for believing that he would be in danger of being subjected to torture.

2. For the purpose of determining whether there are such grounds, the competent authorities shall take into account all relevant considerations including, where applicable, the existence in the State concerned of a consistent pattern of gross, flagrant or mass violations of human rights.

Article 4

1. Each State Party shall ensure that all acts of torture are offences under its criminal law. The same shall apply to an attempt to commit torture and to an act by any person which constitutes complicity or participation in torture.

2. Each State Party shall make these offences punishable by appropriate penalties which take into account their grave nature.

Article 5

1. Each State Party shall take such measures as may be necessary to establish its jurisdiction over the offences referred to in article 4 in the following cases:

   (a)   When the offences are committed in any territory under its jurisdiction or on board a ship or aircraft registered in that State;
   (b)   When the alleged offender is a national of that State;
   (c)   When the victim is a national of that State if that State considers it appropriate.

2. Each State Party shall likewise take such measures as may be necessary to establish its jurisdiction over such offences in cases where the alleged offender is present in any territory under its jurisdiction and it does not extradite him pursuant to article 8 to any of the States mentioned in paragraph I of this article.

3. This Convention does not exclude any criminal jurisdiction exercised in accordance with internal law.

Article 6

1. Upon being satisfied, after an examination of information available to it, that the circumstances so warrant, any State Party in whose territory a person alleged to have committed any offence referred to in article 4 is present shall take him into custody or take other legal measures to ensure his presence. The custody and other legal measures shall be as provided in the law of that State but may be continued only for such time as is necessary to enable any criminal or extradition proceedings to be instituted.

2. Such State shall immediately make a preliminary inquiry into the facts.

3. Any person in custody pursuant to paragraph I of this article shall be assisted in communicating immediately with the nearest appropriate representative of the State of which he is a national, or, if he is a stateless person, with the representative of the State where he usually resides.

4. When a State, pursuant to this article, has taken a person into custody, it shall immediately notify the States referred to in article 5, paragraph 1, of the fact that such

person is in custody and of the circumstances which warrant his detention. The State which makes the preliminary inquiry contemplated in paragraph 2 of this article shall promptly report its findings to the said States and shall indicate whether it intends to exercise jurisdiction.

Article 7

1. The State Party in the territory under whose jurisdiction a person alleged to have committed any offence referred to in article 4 is found shall in the cases contemplated in article 5, if it does not extradite him, submit the case to its competent authorities for the purpose of prosecution.

2. These authorities shall take their decision in the same manner as in the case of any ordinary offence of a serious nature under the law of that State. In the cases referred to in article 5, paragraph 2, the standards of evidence required for prosecution and conviction shall in no way be less stringent than those which apply in the cases referred to in article 5, paragraph 1.

3. Any person regarding whom proceedings are brought in connection with any of the offences referred to in article 4 shall be guaranteed fair treatment at all stages of the proceedings.

Article 8

1. The offences referred to in article 4 shall be deemed to be included as extraditable offences in any extradition treaty existing between States Parties. States Parties undertake to include such offences as extraditable offences in every extradition treaty to be concluded between them.

2. If a State Party which makes extradition conditional on the existence of a treaty receives a request for extradition from another State Party with which it has no extradition treaty, it may consider this Convention as the legal basis for extradition in respect of such offences. Extradition shall be subject to the other conditions provided by the law of the requested State.

3. States Parties which do not make extradition conditional on the existence of a treaty shall recognize such offences as extraditable offences between themselves subject to the conditions provided by the law of the requested State.

4. Such offences shall be treated, for the purpose of extradition between States Parties, as if they had been committed not only in the place in which they occurred but also in the territories of the States required to establish their jurisdiction in accordance with article 5, paragraph 1.

Article 9

1. States Parties shall afford one another the greatest measure of assistance in connection with criminal proceedings brought in respect of any of the offences referred to in article 4, including the supply of all evidence at their disposal necessary for the proceedings.

2. States Parties shall carry out their obligations under paragraph I of this article in conformity with any treaties on mutual judicial assistance that may exist between them.

Article 10

1. Each State Party shall ensure that education and information regarding the prohibition against torture are fully included in the training of law enforcement personnel, civil or military, medical personnel, public officials and other persons who

may be involved in the custody, interrogation or treatment of any individual subjected to any form of arrest, detention or imprisonment.

2. Each State Party shall include this prohibition in the rules or instructions issued in regard to the duties and functions of any such person.

Article 11

Each State Party shall keep under systematic review interrogation rules, instructions, methods and practices as well as arrangements for the custody and treatment of persons subjected to any form of arrest, detention or imprisonment in any territory under its jurisdiction, with a view to preventing any cases of torture.

Article 12

Each State Party shall ensure that its competent authorities proceed to a prompt and impartial investigation, wherever there is reasonable ground to believe that an act of torture has been committed in any territory under its jurisdiction.

Article 13

Each State Party shall ensure that any individual who alleges he has been subjected to torture in any territory under its jurisdiction has the right to complain to, and to have his case promptly and impartially examined by, its competent authorities. Steps shall be taken to ensure that the complainant and witnesses are protected against all ill-treatment or intimidation as a consequence of his complaint or any evidence given.

Article 14

1. Each State Party shall ensure in its legal system that the victim of an act of torture obtains redress and has an enforceable right to fair and adequate compensation, including the means for as full rehabilitation as possible. In the event of the death of the victim as a result of an act of torture, his dependants shall be entitled to compensation.

2. Nothing in this article shall affect any right of the victim or other persons to compensation which may exist under national law.

Right to redress (Art 14(1)—See also Art 15 of the International Convention for the Protection of All Persons from Enforced Disappearance [**RCLP para 15.114**].

Article 15

Each State Party shall ensure that any statement which is established to have been made as a result of torture shall not be invoked as evidence in any proceedings, except against a person accused of torture as evidence that the statement was made.

Article 16

1. Each State Party shall undertake to prevent in any territory under its jurisdiction other acts of cruel, inhuman or degrading treatment or punishment which do not amount to torture as defined in article I, when such acts are committed by or at the instigation of or with the consent or acquiescence of a public official or other person acting in an official capacity. In particular, the obligations contained in articles 10, 11, 12 and 13 shall apply with the substitution for references to torture of references to other forms of cruel, inhuman or degrading treatment or punishment.

2. The provisions of this Convention are without prejudice to the provisions of any other international instrument or national law which prohibits cruel, inhuman or degrading treatment or punishment or which relates to extradition or expulsion.

Relationship between torture and other acts of cruel, inhuman or degrading treatment or punishment (Art 16(1))—Torture and other acts of cruel, inhuman or degrading treatment of punishment are considered to be indivisible, interdependent and interrelated (see UN Committee Against Torture and Other Cruel, Inhuman or Degrading Treatment or Punishment General Comment No 2 *Implementation of Article 2 by State Parties* CAT/C/GC/2, para 3) [RCLP para 15.17]. But note that in respect of children distinctions between torture and other acts of cruel, inhuman or degrading treatment or punishment may serve a purpose [RCLP para 15.18].

'cruel' (Art 16(1))—Whether conduct amounts to 'cruel' treatment or punishment will depending on the circumstances of each case (see *Pratt and Morgan v Jamaica* Human Rights Committee Communications Nos 2010/1986 and 225/1987 (1989)) [RCLP para 15.20].

'inhuman or degrading' (Art 16(1))—For what constitutes 'inhuman or degrading' treatment or punishment see *Antti Vuolanne v Finland* Human Rights Committee Communication No 265/1987 (1989) [RCLP para 15.21].

PART II

Article 17

1. There shall be established a Committee against Torture (hereinafter referred to as the Committee) which shall carry out the functions hereinafter provided. The Committee shall consist of ten experts of high moral standing and recognized competence in the field of human rights, who shall serve in their personal capacity. The experts shall be elected by the States Parties, consideration being given to equitable geographical distribution and to the usefulness of the participation of some persons having legal experience.

2. The members of the Committee shall be elected by secret ballot from a list of persons nominated by States Parties. Each State Party may nominate one person from among its own nationals. States Parties shall bear in mind the usefulness of nominating persons who are also members of the Human Rights Committee established under the International Covenant on Civil and Political Rights and who are willing to serve on the Committee against Torture.

3. Elections of the members of the Committee shall be held at biennial meetings of States Parties convened by the Secretary-General of the United Nations. At those meetings, for which two thirds of the States Parties shall constitute a quorum, the persons elected to the Committee shall be those who obtain the largest number of votes and an absolute majority of the votes of the representatives of States Parties present and voting.

4. The initial election shall be held no later than six months after the date of the entry into force of this Convention. At least four months before the date of each election, the Secretary-General of the United Nations shall address a letter to the States Parties inviting them to submit their nominations within three months. The Secretary-General shall prepare a list in alphabetical order of all persons thus nominated, indicating the States Parties which have nominated them, and shall submit it to the States Parties.

5. The members of the Committee shall be elected for a term of four years. They shall be eligible for re-election if renominated. However, the term of five of the members elected at the first election shall expire at the end of two years; immediately after the first election the names of these five members shall be chosen by lot by the chairman of the meeting referred to in paragraph 3 of this article.

6. If a member of the Committee dies or resigns or for any other cause can no longer perform his Committee duties, the State Party which nominated him shall appoint another expert from among its nationals to serve for the remainder of his term, subject to the approval of the majority of the States Parties. The approval shall be considered

given unless half or more of the States Parties respond negatively within six weeks after having been informed by the Secretary-General of the United Nations of the proposed appointment.

7. States Parties shall be responsible for the expenses of the members of the Committee while they are in performance of Committee duties.

Article 18

1. The Committee shall elect its officers for a term of two years. They may be re-elected.

2. The Committee shall establish its own rules of procedure, but these rules shall provide, inter alia, that:

(a) Six members shall constitute a quorum;
(b) Decisions of the Committee shall be made by a majority vote of the members present.

3. The Secretary-General of the United Nations shall provide the necessary staff and facilities for the effective performance of the functions of the Committee under this Convention.

4. The Secretary-General of the United Nations shall convene the initial meeting of the Committee. After its initial meeting, the Committee shall meet at such times as shall be provided in its rules of procedure.

5. The States Parties shall be responsible for expenses incurred in connection with the holding of meetings of the States Parties and of the Committee, including reimbursement to the United Nations for any expenses, such as the cost of staff and facilities, incurred by the United Nations pursuant to paragraph 3 of this article.

Article 19

1. The States Parties shall submit to the Committee, through the Secretary-General of the United Nations, reports on the measures they have taken to give effect to their undertakings under this Convention, within one year after the entry into force of the Convention for the State Party concerned. Thereafter the States Parties shall submit supplementary reports every four years on any new measures taken and such other reports as the Committee may request.

2. The Secretary-General of the United Nations shall transmit the reports to all States Parties.

3. Each report shall be considered by the Committee which may make such general comments on the report as it may consider appropriate and shall forward these to the State Party concerned. That State Party may respond with any observations it chooses to the Committee.

4. The Committee may, at its discretion, decide to include any comments made by it in accordance with paragraph 3 of this article, together with the observations thereon received from the State Party concerned, in its annual report made in accordance with article 24. If so requested by the State Party concerned, the Committee may also include a copy of the report submitted under paragraph I of this article.

Article 20

1. If the Committee receives reliable information which appears to it to contain well-founded indications that torture is being systematically practised in the territory of

a State Party, the Committee shall invite that State Party to co-operate in the examination of the information and to this end to submit observations with regard to the information concerned.

2. Taking into account any observations which may have been submitted by the State Party concerned, as well as any other relevant information available to it, the Committee may, if it decides that this is warranted, designate one or more of its members to make a confidential inquiry and to report to the Committee urgently.

3. If an inquiry is made in accordance with paragraph 2 of this article, the Committee shall seek the co-operation of the State Party concerned. In agreement with that State Party, such an inquiry may include a visit to its territory.

4. After examining the findings of its member or members submitted in accordance with paragraph 2 of this article, the Commission shall transmit these findings to the State Party concerned together with any comments or suggestions which seem appropriate in view of the situation.

5. All the proceedings of the Committee referred to in paragraphs I to 4 of this article shall be confidential , and at all stages of the proceedings the co-operation of the State Party shall be sought. After such proceedings have been completed with regard to an inquiry made in accordance with paragraph 2, the Committee may, after consultations with the State Party concerned, decide to include a summary account of the results of the proceedings in its annual report made in accordance with article 24.

'systemically practiced' (Art 20(1))—The UN Committee against Torture is empowered by the Convention to investigate allegations of systemic torture [RCLP para 2.35].

Article 21

1. A State Party to this Convention may at any time declare under this article that it recognizes the competence of the Committee to receive and consider communications to the effect that a State Party claims that another State Party is not fulfilling its obligations under this Convention. Such communications may be received and considered according to the procedures laid down in this article only if submitted by a State Party which has made a declaration recognizing in regard to itself the competence of the Committee. No communication shall be dealt with by the Committee under this article if it concerns a State Party which has not made such a declaration. Communications received under this article shall be dealt with in accordance with the following procedure;

    (a)   If a State Party considers that another State Party is not giving effect to the provisions of this Convention, it may, by written communication, bring the matter to the attention of that State Party. Within three months after the receipt of the communication the receiving State shall afford the State which sent the communication an explanation or any other statement in writing clarifying the matter, which should include, to the extent possible and pertinent, reference to domestic procedures and remedies taken, pending or available in the matter;

    (b)   If the matter is not adjusted to the satisfaction of both States Parties concerned within six months after the receipt by the receiving State of the initial communication, either State shall have the right to refer the matter to the Committee, by notice given to the Committee and to the other State;

    (c)   The Committee shall deal with a matter referred to it under this article only after it has ascertained that all domestic remedies have been invoked and exhausted in the matter, in conformity with the generally recognized principles of international law. This shall not be the rule where the application of the remedies is unreasonably prolonged or is unlikely to bring effective relief to the person who is the victim of the violation of this Convention;

(d)   The Committee shall hold closed meetings when examining communications under this article;

(e)   Subject to the provisions of subparagraph (c), the Committee shall make available its good offices to the States Parties concerned with a view to a friendly solution of the matter on the basis of respect for the obligations provided for in this Convention. For this purpose, the Committee may, when appropriate, set up an ad hoc conciliation commission;

(f)   In any matter referred to it under this article, the Committee may call upon the States Parties concerned, referred to in subparagraph (b), to supply any relevant information;

(g)   The States Parties concerned, referred to in subparagraph (b), shall have the right to be represented when the matter is being considered by the Committee and to make submissions orally and/or in writing;

(h)   The Committee shall, within twelve months after the date of receipt of notice under subparagraph (b), submit a report:

    (i)   If a solution within the terms of subparagraph (e) is reached, the Committee shall confine its report to a brief statement of the facts and of the solution reached;

    (ii)   If a solution within the terms of subparagraph (e) is not reached, the Committee shall confine its report to a brief statement of the facts; the written submissions and record of the oral submissions made by the States Parties concerned shall be attached to the report. In every matter, the report shall be communicated to the States Parties concerned.

2. The provisions of this article shall come into force when five States Parties to this Convention have made declarations under paragraph 1 of this article. Such declarations shall be deposited by the States Parties with the Secretary-General of the United Nations, who shall transmit copies thereof to the other States Parties. A declaration may be withdrawn at any time by notification to the Secretary-General.

Such a withdrawal shall not prejudice the consideration of any matter which is the subject of a communication already transmitted under this article; no further communication by any State Party shall be received under this article after the notification of withdrawal of the declaration has been received by the Secretary-General, unless the State Party concerned has made a new declaration.

Interstate complaints (Art 21(1))—Whilst the United Kingdom recognises the jurisdiction of the UN Committee Against Torture to receive interstate complaints note that the United Kingdom does not recognise the jurisdiction to receive complaints from individuals under Art 22(1) **[RCLP para 2.35]**.

Article 22

1. A State Party to this Convention may at any time declare under this article that it recognizes the competence of the Committee to receive and consider communications from or on behalf of individuals subject to its jurisdiction who claim to be victims of a violation by a State Party of the provisions of the Convention. No communication shall be received by the Committee if it concerns a State Party which has not made such a declaration.

2. The Committee shall consider inadmissible any communication under this article which is anonymous or which it considers to be an abuse of the right of submission of such communications or to be incompatible with the provisions of this Convention.

3. Subject to the provisions of paragraph 2, the Committee shall bring any communications submitted to it under this article to the attention of the State Party to this Convention which has made a declaration under paragraph I and is alleged to be violating any provisions of the Convention. Within six months, the receiving State shall submit to the Committee written explanations or statements clarifying the matter and the remedy, if any, that may have been taken by that State.

4. The Committee shall consider communications received under this article in the light of all information made available to it by or on behalf of the individual and by the State Party concerned.

5. The Committee shall not consider any communications from an individual under this article unless it has ascertained that:

(a)   The same matter has not been, and is not being, examined under another procedure of international investigation or settlement;

(b)   The individual has exhausted all available domestic remedies; this shall not be the rule where the application of the remedies is unreasonably prolonged or is unlikely to bring effective relief to the person who is the victim of the violation of this Convention.

6. The Committee shall hold closed meetings when examining communications under this article.

7. The Committee shall forward its views to the State Party concerned and to the individual.

8. The provisions of this article shall come into force when five States Parties to this Convention have made declarations under paragraph 1 of this article. Such declarations shall be deposited by the States Parties with the Secretary-General of the United Nations, who shall transmit copies thereof to the other States Parties. A declaration may be withdrawn at any time by notification to the Secretary-General.

Such a withdrawal shall not prejudice the consideration of any matter which is the subject of a communication already transmitted under this article; no further communication by or on behalf of an individual shall be received under this article after the notification of withdrawal of the declaration has been received by the Secretary-General, unless the State Party has made a new declaration.

'communications from or on behalf of individuals' (Art 22(1))—Note that the United Kingdom does not recognise the jurisdiction of the UN Committee Against Torture to receive complaints from individuals under Art 22 [RCLP para 2.35].

Article 23

The members of the Committee and of the ad hoc conciliation commissions which may be appointed under article 21, paragraph I (e), shall be entitled to the facilities, privileges and immunities of experts on mission for the United Nations as laid down in the relevant sections of the Convention on the Privileges and Immunities of the United Nations.

Article 24

The Committee shall submit an annual report on its activities under this Convention to the States Parties and to the General Assembly of the United Nations.

PART III

Article 25

1. This Convention is open for signature by all States.

2. This Convention is subject to ratification. Instruments of ratification shall be deposited with the Secretary-General of the United Nations.

Article 26

This Convention is open to accession by all States. Accession shall be effected by the deposit of an instrument of accession with the Secretary General of the United Nations.

Article 27

1. This Convention shall enter into force on the thirtieth day after the date of the deposit with the Secretary-General of the United Nations of the twentieth instrument of ratification or accession.

2. For each State ratifying this Convention or acceding to it after the deposit of the twentieth instrument of ratification or accession, the Convention shall enter into force on the thirtieth day after the date of the deposit of its own instrument of ratification or accession.

Article 28

1. Each State may, at the time of signature or ratification of this Convention or accession thereto, declare that it does not recognize the competence of the Committee provided for in article 20.

2. Any State Party having made a reservation in accordance with paragraph I of this article may, at any time, withdraw this reservation by notification to the Secretary-General of the United Nations.

Article 29

1. Any State Party to this Convention may propose an amendment and file it with the Secretary-General of the United Nations. The Secretary General shall thereupon communicate the proposed amendment to the States Parties with a request that they notify him whether they favour a conference of States Parties for the purpose of considering and voting upon the proposal. In the event that within four months from the date of such communication at least one third of the States Parties favours such a conference, the Secretary General shall convene the conference under the auspices of the United Nations. Any amendment adopted by a majority of the States Parties present and voting at the conference shall be submitted by the Secretary-General to all the States Parties for acceptance.

2. An amendment adopted in accordance with paragraph I of this article shall enter into force when two thirds of the States Parties to this Convention have notified the Secretary-General of the United Nations that they have accepted it in accordance with their respective constitutional processes.

3. When amendments enter into force, they shall be binding on those States Parties which have accepted them, other States Parties still being bound by the provisions of this Convention and any earlier amendments which they have accepted.

Article 30

1. Any dispute between two or more States Parties concerning the interpretation or application of this Convention which cannot be settled through negotiation shall, at the request of one of them, be submitted to arbitration. If within six months from the date of the request for arbitration the Parties are unable to agree on the organization of the arbitration, any one of those Parties may refer the dispute to the International Court of Justice by request in conformity with the Statute of the Court.

2. Each State may, at the time of signature or ratification of this Convention or accession thereto, declare that it does not consider itself bound by paragraph I of this article. The other States Parties shall not be bound by paragraph I of this article with respect to any State Party having made such a reservation.

3. Any State Party having made a reservation in accordance with paragraph 2 of this article may at any time withdraw this reservation by notification to the Secretary-General of the United Nations.

Article 31

1. A State Party may denounce this Convention by written notification to the Secretary-General of the United Nations. Denunciation becomes effective one year after the date of receipt of the notification by the Secretary-General .

2. Such a denunciation shall not have the effect of releasing the State Party from its obligations under this Convention in regard to any act or omission which occurs prior to the date at which the denunciation becomes effective, nor shall denunciation prejudice in any way the continued consideration of any matter which is already under consideration by the Committee prior to the date at which the denunciation becomes effective.

3. Following the date at which the denunciation of a State Party becomes effective, the Committee shall not commence consideration of any new matter regarding that State.

Article 32

The Secretary-General of the United Nations shall inform all States Members of the United Nations and all States which have signed this Convention or acceded to it of the following:

   (a)   Signatures, ratifications and accessions under articles 25 and 26;
   (b)   The date of entry into force of this Convention under article 27 and the date of the entry into force of any amendments under article 29;
   (c)   Denunciations under article 31.

Article 33

1. This Convention, of which the Arabic, Chinese, English, French, Russian and Spanish texts are equally authentic, shall be deposited with the Secretary-General of the United Nations.

2. The Secretary-General of the United Nations shall transmit certified copies of this Convention to all States.

CHAPTER 10

INTERNATIONAL CONVENTION ON THE ELIMINATION OF ALL FORMS OF RACIAL DISCRIMINATION

Adopted and opened for signature and ratification by General Assembly resolution 2106 (XX) of 21 December 1965 entry into force 4 January 1969, in accordance with Article 19

PREAMBLE

The States Parties to this Convention,

Considering that the Charter of the United Nations is based on the principles of the dignity and equality inherent in all human beings, and that all Member States have pledged themselves to take joint and separate action, in co-operation with the Organization, for the achievement of one of the purposes of the United Nations which is to promote and encourage universal respect for and observance of human rights and fundamental freedoms for all, without distinction as to race, sex, language or religion,

Considering that the Universal Declaration of Human Rights proclaims that all human beings are born free and equal in dignity and rights and that everyone is entitled to all the rights and freedoms set out therein, without distinction of any kind, in particular as to race, colour or national origin,

Considering that all human beings are equal before the law and are entitled to equal protection of the law against any discrimination and against any incitement to discrimination,

Considering that the United Nations has condemned colonialism and all practices of segregation and discrimination associated therewith, in whatever form and wherever they exist, and that the

Declaration on the Granting of Independence to Colonial Countries and Peoples of 14 December 1960 (General Assembly resolution 1514 (XV)) has affirmed and solemnly proclaimed the necessity of bringing them to a speedy and unconditional end,

Considering that the United Nations Declaration on the Elimination of All Forms of Racial Discrimination of 20 November 1963 (General Assembly resolution 1904 (XVIII)) solemnly affirms the necessity of speedily eliminating racial discrimination throughout the world in all its forms and manifestations and of securing understanding of and respect for the dignity of the human person,

Convinced that any doctrine of superiority based on racial differentiation is scientifically false, morally condemnable, socially unjust and dangerous, and that there is no justification for racial discrimination, in theory or in practice, anywhere,

Reaffirming that discrimination between human beings on the grounds of race, colour or ethnic origin is an obstacle to friendly and peaceful relations among nations and is capable of disturbing peace and security among peoples and the harmony of persons living side by side even within one and the same State,

Convinced that the existence of racial barriers is repugnant to the ideals of any human society,

Alarmed by manifestations of racial discrimination still in evidence in some areas of the world and by governmental policies based on racial superiority or hatred, such as policies of apartheid, segregation or separation,

Resolved to adopt all necessary measures for speedily eliminating racial discrimination in all its forms and manifestations, and to prevent and combat racist doctrines and practices in order to promote understanding between races and to build an international community free from all forms of racial segregation and racial discrimination,

Bearing in mind the Convention concerning Discrimination in respect of Employment and Occupation adopted by the International Labour Organisation in 1958, and the Convention against Discrimination in Education adopted by the United Nations Educational, Scientific and Cultural Organization in 1960,

Desiring to implement the principles embodied in the United Nations Declaration on the Elimination of All Forms of Racial Discrimination and to secure the earliest adoption of practical measures to that end,

Have agreed as follows:

Status—The status of the International Convention on the Elimination of All Forms of Racial Discrimination is that of a binding international Convention not incorporated into domestic law [**RCLP para 3.94**] but see *A and others v Secretary of State for the Home Department; X v another v Secretary of State for the Home Department* [2004] UKHL 56, [2005] 3 All ER 169, paras 62 and 63 and *Mandla and another v Dowell Lee and another* [1983] 1 All ER 1062 at p 1068. The House of Lords relied on the International Convention on the Elimination of All Forms of Racial Discrimination in *European Roma Rights Centre v Immigration Officer at Prague Airport (United Nations High Comr intervening)* [2004] UKHL 55, [2005] 2 AC 1 [**RCLP para 3.31**] and the Convention has been referred to in other domestic authorities (see *R (E) v Office of the Schools Adjudicator (Governing Body of JFS and others, interested parties) (British Humanist Association and another intervening)* [2009] UKSC 15, [2010] 1 All ER 319, para 81, *A and others v Secretary of State for the Home Department; X v another v Secretary of State for the Home Department* [2004] UKHL 56, [2005] 3 All ER 169, paras 62 and 63, *R (Watkins-Singh) v Governing Body of Abedare Girls' High School* [2008] EWHC 1865 (Admin), [2008] All ER (D) 376 (Jul) at para 33 and *R v White* [2001] All ER (D) 158 (Feb) para 3).

PART I

Article 1

1. In this Convention, the term "racial discrimination" shall mean any distinction, exclusion, restriction or preference based on race, colour, descent, or national or ethnic origin which has the purpose or effect of nullifying or impairing the recognition, enjoyment or exercise, on an equal footing, of human rights and fundamental freedoms in the political, economic, social, cultural or any other field of public life.

2. This Convention shall not apply to distinctions, exclusions, restrictions or preferences made by a State Party to this Convention between citizens and non-citizens.

3. Nothing in this Convention may be interpreted as affecting in any way the legal provisions of States Parties concerning nationality, citizenship or naturalization, provided that such provisions do not discriminate against any particular nationality.

4. Special measures taken for the sole purpose of securing adequate advancement of certain racial or ethnic groups or individuals requiring such protection as may be necessary in order to ensure such groups or individuals equal enjoyment or exercise of human rights and fundamental freedoms shall not be deemed racial discrimination, provided, however, that such measures do not, as a consequence, lead to the maintenance of separate rights for different racial groups and that they shall not be continued after the objectives for which they were taken have been achieved.

'distinction' (Art 1(1))—for the meaning of the term 'distinction' see Committee on the Elimination of Racial Discrimination General Recommendation No 14 *Article 1 Paragraph 1 of the Convention* HRI/GEN/1/Rev 8, p 247, para 1 [RCLP para 4.78].

Article 2

1. States Parties condemn racial discrimination and undertake to pursue by all appropriate means and without delay a policy of eliminating racial discrimination in all its forms and promoting understanding among all races, and, to this end:

(a)   Each State Party undertakes to engage in no act or practice of racial discrimination against persons, groups of persons or institutions and to ensure that all public authorities and public institutions, national and local, shall act in conformity with this obligation;

(b)   Each State Party undertakes not to sponsor, defend or support racial discrimination by any persons or organizations;

(c)   Each State Party shall take effective measures to review governmental, national and local policies, and to amend, rescind or nullify any laws and regulations which have the effect of creating or perpetuating racial discrimination wherever it exists;

(d)   Each State Party shall prohibit and bring to an end, by all appropriate means, including legislation as required by circumstances, racial discrimination by any persons, group or organization;

(e)   Each State Party undertakes to encourage, where appropriate, integrationist multiracial organizations and movements and other means of eliminating barriers between races, and to discourage anything which tends to strengthen racial division.

2. States Parties shall, when the circumstances so warrant, take, in the social, economic, cultural and other fields, special and concrete measures to ensure the adequate development and protection of certain racial groups or individuals belonging to them, for the purpose of guaranteeing them the full and equal enjoyment of human rights and fundamental freedoms. These measures shall in no case en tail as a con sequence the maintenance of unequal or separate rights for different racial groups after the objectives for which they were taken have been achieved.

Article 3

States Parties particularly condemn racial segregation and apartheid and undertake to prevent, prohibit and eradicate all practices of this nature in territories under their jurisdiction.

Article 4

States Parties condemn all propaganda and all organizations which are based on ideas or theories of superiority of one race or group of persons of one colour or ethnic origin, or which attempt to justify or promote racial hatred and discrimination in any form, and undertake to adopt immediate and positive measures designed to eradicate all incitement to, or acts of, such discrimination and, to this end, with due regard to the principles embodied in the Universal Declaration of Human Rights and the rights expressly set forth in article 5 of this Convention, inter alia:

(a) Shall declare an offence punishable by law all dissemination of ideas based on racial superiority or hatred, incitement to racial discrimination, as well as all acts of violence or incitement to such acts against any race or group of persons of another colour or ethnic origin, and also the provision of any assistance to racist activities, including the financing thereof;

(b) Shall declare illegal and prohibit organizations, and also organized and all other propaganda activities, which promote and incite racial discrimination, and shall recognize participation in such organizations or activities as an offence punishable by law;

(c) Shall not permit public authorities or public institutions, national or local, to promote or incite racial discrimination.

Article 5

In compliance with the fundamental obligations laid down in article 2 of this Convention, States Parties undertake to prohibit and to eliminate racial discrimination in all its forms and to guarantee the right of everyone, without distinction as to race, colour, or national or ethnic origin, to equality before the law, notably in the enjoyment of the following rights:

(a) The right to equal treatment before the tribunals and all other organs administering justice;

(b) The right to security of person and protection by the State against violence or bodily harm, whether inflicted by government officials or by any individual group or institution;

(c) Political rights, in particular the right to participate in elections-to vote and to stand for election-on the basis of universal and equal suffrage, to take part in the Government as well as in the conduct of public affairs at any level and to have equal access to public service;

(d) Other civil rights, in particular:
  (i) The right to freedom of movement and residence within the border of the State;
  (ii) The right to leave any country, including one's own, and to return to one's country;
  (iii) The right to nationality;
  (iv) The right to marriage and choice of spouse;
  (v) The right to own property alone as well as in association with others;
  (vi) The right to inherit;
  (vii) The right to freedom of thought, conscience and religion;
  (viii) The right to freedom of opinion and expression;
  (ix) The right to freedom of peaceful assembly and association;

(e) Economic, social and cultural rights, in particular:
  (i) The rights to work, to free choice of employment, to just and favourable conditions of work, to protection against unemployment, to equal pay for equal work, to just and favourable remuneration;
  (ii) The right to form and join trade unions;
  (iii) The right to housing;
  (iv) The right to public health, medical care, social security and social services;
  (v) The right to education and training;
  (vi) The right to equal participation in cultural activities;

(f)   The right of access to any place or service intended for use by the general public, such as transport hotels, restaurants, cafes, theatres and parks.

Article 6

States Parties shall assure to everyone within their jurisdiction effective protection and remedies, through the competent national tribunals and other State institutions, against any acts of racial discrimination which violate his human rights and fundamental freedoms contrary to this Convention, as well as the right to seek from such tribunals just and adequate reparation or satisfaction for any damage suffered as a result of such discrimination.

Article 7

States Parties undertake to adopt immediate and effective measures, particularly in the fields of teaching, education, culture and information, with a view to combating prejudices which lead to racial discrimination and to promoting understanding, tolerance and friendship among nations and racial or ethnical groups, as well as to propagating the purposes and principles of the Charter of the United Nations, the Universal Declaration of Human Rights, the United Nations Declaration on the Elimination of All Forms of Racial Discrimination, and this Convention.

PART II

Article 8

1. There shall be established a Committee on the Elimination of Racial Discrimination (hereinafter referred to as the Committee) consisting of eighteen experts of high moral standing and acknowledged impartiality elected by States Parties from among their nationals, who shall serve in their personal capacity, consideration being given to equitable geographical distribution and to the representation of the different forms of civilization as well as of the principal legal systems.

2. The members of the Committee shall be elected by secret ballot from a list of persons nominated by the States Parties. Each State Party may nominate one person from among its own nationals.

3. The initial election shall be held six months after the date of the entry into force of this Convention. At least three months before the date of each election the Secretary-General of the United Nations shall address a letter to the States Parties inviting them to submit their nominations within two months. The Secretary-General shall prepare a list in alphabetical order of all persons thus nominated, indicating the States Parties which have nominated them, and shall submit it to the States Parties.

4. Elections of the members of the Committee shall be held at a meeting of States Parties convened by the Secretary-General at United Nations Headquarters. At that meeting, for which two thirds of the States Parties shall constitute a quorum, the persons elected to the Committee shall be nominees who obtain the largest number of votes and an absolute majority of the votes of the representatives of States Parties present and voting.

5.

(a)   The members of the Committee shall be elected for a term of four years. However, the terms of nine of the members elected at the first election shall expire at the end of two years; immediately after the first election the names of these nine members shall be chosen by lot by the Chairman of the Committee;

(b)   For the filling of casual vacancies, the State Party whose expert has ceased to function as a member of the Committee shall appoint another expert from among its nationals, subject to the approval of the Committee.

6. States Parties shall be responsible for the expenses of the members of the Committee while they are in performance of Committee duties.

Article 9

1. States Parties undertake to submit to the Secretary-General of the United Nations, for consideration by the Committee, a report on the legislative, judicial, administrative or other measures which they have adopted and which give effect to the provisions of this Convention:

(a)   within one year after the entry into force of the Convention for the State concerned; and

(b)   thereafter every two years and whenever the Committee so requests. The Committee may request further information from the States Parties.

2. The Committee shall report annually, through the Secretary General, to the General Assembly of the United Nations on its activities and may make suggestions and general recommendations based on the examination of the reports and information received from the States Parties. Such suggestions and general recommendations shall be reported to the General Assembly together with comments, if any, from States Parties.

Article 10

1. The Committee shall adopt its own rules of procedure.

2. The Committee shall elect its officers for a term of two years.

3. The secretariat of the Committee shall be provided by the Secretary General of the United Nations.

4. The meetings of the Committee shall normally be held at United Nations Headquarters.

Article 11

1. If a State Party considers that another State Party is not giving effect to the provisions of this Convention, it may bring the matter to the attention of the Committee. The Committee shall then transmit the communication to the State Party concerned. Within three months, the receiving State shall submit to the Committee written explanations or statements clarifying the matter and the remedy, if any, that may have been taken by that State.

2. If the matter is not adjusted to the satisfaction of both parties, either by bilateral negotiations or by any other procedure open to them, within six months after the receipt by the receiving State of the initial communication, either State shall have the right to refer the matter again to the Committee by notifying the Committee and also the other State.

3. The Committee shall deal with a matter referred to it in accordance with paragraph 2 of this article after it has ascertained that all available domestic remedies have been invoked and exhausted in the case, in conformity with the generally recognized principles of international law. This shall not be the rule where the application of the remedies is unreasonably prolonged.

4. In any matter referred to it, the Committee may call upon the States Parties concerned to supply any other relevant information.

5. When any matter arising out of this article is being considered by the Committee, the States Parties concerned shall be entitled to send a representative to take part in the proceedings of the Committee, without voting rights, while the matter is under consideration.

Article 12

1.

    (a)   After the Committee has obtained and collated all the information it deems necessary, the Chairman shall appoint an ad hoc Conciliation Commission (hereinafter referred to as the Commission) comprising five persons who may or may not be members of the Committee. The members of the Commission shall be appointed with the unanimous consent of the parties to the dispute, and its good offices shall be made available to the States concerned with a view to an amicable solution of the matter on the basis of respect for this Convention;

    (b)   If the States parties to the dispute fail to reach agreement within three months on all or part of the composition of the Commission, the members of the Commission not agreed upon by the States parties to the dispute shall be elected by secret ballot by a two-thirds majority vote of the Committee from among its own members.

2. The members of the Commission shall serve in their personal capacity. They shall not be nationals of the States parties to the dispute or of a State not Party to this Convention.

3. The Commission shall elect its own Chairman and adopt its own rules of procedure.

4. The meetings of the Commission shall normally be held at United Nations Headquarters or at any other convenient place as determined by the Commission.

5. The secretariat provided in accordance with article 10, paragraph 3, of this Convention shall also service the Commission whenever a dispute among States Parties brings the Commission into being.

6. The States parties to the dispute shall share equally all the expenses of the members of the Commission in accordance with estimates to be provided by the Secretary-General of the United Nations.

7. The Secretary-General shall be empowered to pay the expenses of the members of the Commission, if necessary, before reimbursement by the States parties to the dispute in accordance with paragraph 6 of this article.

8. The information obtained and collated by the Committee shall be made available to the Commission, and the Commission may call upon the States concerned to supply any other relevant information.

Article 13

1. When the Commission has fully considered the matter, it shall prepare and submit to the Chairman of the Committee a report embodying its findings on all questions of fact relevant to the issue between the parties and containing such recommendations as it may think proper for the amicable solution of the dispute.

2. The Chairman of the Committee shall communicate the report of the Commission to each of the States parties to the dispute. These States shall, within three months, inform the Chairman of the Committee whether or not they accept the recommendations contained in the report of the Commission.

3. After the period provided for in paragraph 2 of this article, the Chairman of the Committee shall communicate the report of the Commission and the declarations of the States Parties concerned to the other States Parties to this Convention.

Article 14

1. A State Party may at any time declare that it recognizes the competence of the Committee to receive and consider communications from individuals or groups of individuals within its jurisdiction claiming to be victims of a violation by that State Party of any of the rights set forth in this Convention. No communication shall be received by the Committee if it concerns a State Party which has not made such a declaration.

2. Any State Party which makes a declaration as provided for in paragraph I of this article may establish or indicate a body within its national legal order which shall be competent to receive and consider petitions from individuals and groups of individuals within its jurisdiction who claim to be victims of a violation of any of the rights set forth in this Convention and who have exhausted other available local remedies.

3. A declaration made in accordance with paragraph 1 of this article and the name of any body established or indicated in accordance with paragraph 2 of this article shall be deposited by the State Party concerned with the Secretary-General of the United Nations, who shall transmit copies thereof to the other States Parties. A declaration may be withdrawn at any time by notification to the Secretary-General, but such a withdrawal shall not affect communications pending before the Committee.

4. A register of petitions shall be kept by the body established or indicated in accordance with paragraph 2 of this article, and certified copies of the register shall be filed annually through appropriate channels with the Secretary-General on the understanding that the contents shall not be publicly disclosed.

5. In the event of failure to obtain satisfaction from the body established or indicated in accordance with paragraph 2 of this article, the petitioner shall have the right to communicate the matter to the Committee within six months.

6.

   (a)   The Committee shall confidentially bring any communication referred to it to the attention of the State Party alleged to be violating any provision of this Convention, but the identity of the individual or groups of individuals concerned shall not be revealed without his or their express consent. The Committee shall not receive anonymous communications;

   (b)   Within three months, the receiving State shall submit to the Committee written explanations or statements clarifying the matter and the remedy, if any, that may have been taken by that State.

7.

   (a)   The Committee shall consider communications in the light of all information made available to it by the State Party concerned and by the petitioner. The Committee shall not consider any communication from a petitioner unless it has ascertained that the petitioner has exhausted all available domestic remedies. However, this shall not be the rule where the application of the remedies is unreasonably prolonged;

(b)   The Committee shall forward its suggestions and recommendations, if any, to the State Party concerned and to the petitioner.

8. The Committee shall include in its annual report a summary of such communications and, where appropriate, a summary of the explanations and statements of the States Parties concerned and of its own suggestions and recommendations. 9. The Committee shall be competent to exercise the functions provided for in this article only when at least ten States Parties to this Convention are bound by declarations in accordance with paragraph I of this article.

Article 15

1. Pending the achievement of the objectives of the Declaration on the Granting of Independence to Colonial Countries and Peoples, contained in General Assembly resolution 1514 (XV) of 14 December 1960, the provisions of this Convention shall in no way limit the right of petition granted to these peoples by other international instruments or by the United Nations and its specialized agencies.

2.

(a)   The Committee established under article 8, paragraph 1, of this Convention shall receive copies of the petitions from, and submit expressions of opinion and recommendations on these petitions to, the bodies of the United Nations which deal with matters directly related to the principles and objectives of this Convention in their consideration of petitions from the inhabitants of Trust and Non-Self-Governing Territories and all other territories to which General Assembly resolution 1514 (XV) applies, relating to matters covered by this Convention which are before these bodies;

(b)   The Committee shall receive from the competent bodies of the United Nations copies of the reports concerning the legislative, judicial, administrative or other measures directly related to the principles and objectives of this Convention applied by the administering Powers within the Territories mentioned in subparagraph (a) of this paragraph, and shall express opinions and make recommendations to these bodies.

3. The Committee shall include in its report to the General Assembly a summary of the petitions and reports it has received from United Nations bodies, and the expressions of opinion and recommendations of the Committee relating to the said petitions and reports.

4. The Committee shall request from the Secretary-General of the United Nations all information relevant to the objectives of this Convention and available to him regarding the Territories mentioned in paragraph 2 (a) of this article.

Article 16

The provisions of this Convention concerning the settlement of disputes or complaints shall be applied without prejudice to other procedures for settling disputes or complaints in the field of discrimination laid down in the constituent instruments of, or conventions adopted by, the United Nations and its specialized agencies, and shall not prevent the States Parties from having recourse to other procedures for settling a dispute in accordance with general or special international agreements in force between them.

PART III

Article 17

1. This Convention is open for signature by any State Member of the United Nations or member of any of its specialized agencies, by any State Party to the Statute of the International Court of Justice, and by any other State which has been invited by the General Assembly of the United Nations to become a Party to this Convention.

2. This Convention is subject to ratification. Instruments of ratification shall be deposited with the Secretary-General of the United Nations.

Article 18

1. This Convention shall be open to accession by any State referred to in article 17, paragraph 1, of the Convention.

2. Accession shall be effected by the deposit of an instrument of accession with the Secretary-General of the United Nations.

Article 19

1. This Convention shall enter into force on the thirtieth day after the date of the deposit with the Secretary-General of the United Nations of the twenty-seventh instrument of ratification or instrument of accession.

2. For each State ratifying this Convention or acceding to it after the deposit of the twenty-seventh instrument of ratification or instrument of accession, the Convention shall enter into force on the thirtieth day after the date of the deposit of its own instrument of ratification or instrument of accession.

Article 20

1. The Secretary-General of the United Nations shall receive and circulate to all States which are or may become Parties to this Convention reservations made by States at the time of ratification or accession. Any State which objects to the reservation shall, within a period of ninety days from the date of the said communication, notify the Secretary-General that it does not accept it.

2. A reservation incompatible with the object and purpose of this Convention shall not be permitted, nor shall a reservation the effect of which would inhibit the operation of any of the bodies established by this Convention be allowed. A reservation shall be considered incompatible or inhibitive if at least two thirds of the States Parties to this Convention object to it.

3. Reservations may be withdrawn at any time by notification to this effect addressed to the Secretary-General. Such notification shall take effect on the date on which it is received.

Article 21

A State Party may denounce this Convention by written notification to the Secretary-General of the United Nations. Denunciation shall take effect one year after the date of receipt of the notification by the Secretary-General.

Article 22

Any dispute between two or more States Parties with respect to the interpretation or application of this Convention, which is not settled by negotiation or by the procedures expressly provided for in this Convention, shall, at the request of any of the parties to the dispute, be referred to the International Court of Justice for decision, unless the disputants agree to another mode of settlement.

Article 23

1. A request for the revision of this Convention may be made at any time by any State Party by means of a notification in writing addressed to the Secretary-General of the United Nations.

2. The General Assembly of the United Nations shall decide upon the steps, if any, to be taken in respect of such a request.

Article 24

The Secretary-General of the United Nations shall inform all States referred to in article 17, paragraph1, of this Convention of the following particulars:

    (a)   Signatures, ratifications and accessions under articles 17 and 18;
    (b)   The date of entry into force of this Convention under article 19;
    (c)   Communications and declarations received under articles 14, 20 and 23;
    (d)   Denunciations under article 21.

Article 25

1. This Convention, of which the Chinese, English, French, Russian and Spanish texts are equally authentic, shall be deposited in the archives of the United Nations.

2. The Secretary-General of the United Nations shall transmit certified copies of this Convention to all States belonging to any of the categories mentioned in article 17, paragraph 1, of the Convention.

CHAPTER 11

UN CONVENTION ON THE ELIMINATION OF ALL FORMS OF DISCRIMINATION AGAINST WOMEN

PREAMBLE

The States Parties to the present Convention,

Noting that the Charter of the United Nations reaffirms faith in fundamental human rights, in the dignity and worth of the human person and in the equal rights of men and women,

Noting that the Universal Declaration of Human Rights affirms the principle of the inadmissibility of discrimination and proclaims that all human beings are born free and equal in dignity and rights and that everyone is entitled to all the rights and freedoms set forth therein, without distinction of any kind, including distinction based on sex,

Noting that the States parties to the International Covenants on Human Rights have the obligation to ensure the equal right of men and women to enjoy all economic, social, cultural, civil and political rights,

Considering the international conventions concluded under the auspices of the United Nations and the specialized agencies promoting equality of rights of men and women,

Noting also the resolutions, declarations and recommendations adopted by the United Nations and the specialized agencies promoting equality of rights of men and women,

Concerned, however, that despite these various instruments extensive discrimination against women continues to exist,

Recalling that discrimination against women violates the principles of equality of rights and respect for human dignity, is an obstacle to the participation of women, on equal terms with men, in the political, social, economic and cultural life of their countries, hampers the growth of the prosperity of society and the family and makes more difficult the full development of the potentialities of women in the service of their countries and of humanity,

Concerned that in situations of poverty women have the least access to food, health, education, training and opportunities for employment and other needs,

Convinced that the establishment of the new international economic order based on equity and justice will contribute significantly towards the promotion of equality between men and women,

Emphasizing that the eradication of apartheid, all forms of racism, racial discrimination, colonialism, neocolonialism, aggression, foreign occupation and domination and interference in the internal affairs of States is essential to the full enjoyment of the rights of men and women that the strengthening of international peace and security, the relaxation of international tension, mutual cooperation among all States irrespective of their social and economic systems, general and complete disarmament, in particular nuclear disarmament under strict and effective international control, the affirmation of the principles of justice, equality and mutual benefit in relations among countries and the realization of the right of peoples under alien and colonial domination and foreign occupation to self- determination and independence, as well as respect for national sovereignty and territorial integrity, will promote social progress and development and as a consequence will contribute to the attainment of full equality between men and women,

Convinced that the full and complete development of a country, the welfare of the world and the cause of peace require the maximum participation of women on equal terms with men in all fields,

Bearing in mind the great contribution of women to the welfare of the family and to the development of society, so far not fully recognized, the social significance of maternity and the role of both parents in the family and in the upbringing of children, and aware that the role of women in procreation should not be a basis for discrimination but that the upbringing of children requires a sharing of responsibility between men and women and society as a whole,

Aware that a change in the traditional role of men as well as the role of women in society and in the family is needed to achieve full equality between men and women,

Determined to implement the principles set forth in the Declaration on the Elimination of Discrimination against Women and, for that purpose, to adopt the measures required for the elimination of such discrimination in all its forms and manifestations,

Have agreed on the following:

Status—The status of the International Convention on the Elimination of All Forms of Discrimination Against Women is that of a binding international Convention not incorporated into domestic law [**RCLP para 3.94**]. The Convention was ratified by the United Kingdom on 7 April 2006 although the United Kingdom has entered a series of reservations in respect of the Convention (see http://www.un.org/womenwatch/daw/cedaw/reservations-country.htm) [**RCLP para 4.79**]. Note that the Convention has an Optional Protocol (not included in this work) Arts 1, 2 and 8 of which provide a complaints mechanism by which individuals and groups of individuals may submit complaints to the Committee on the Elimination of Discrimination Against Women [**RCLP para 2.37**]. The United Kingdom ratified the Optional Protocol on 17 December 2004. For cases brought under the provisions of the Optional Protocol see Ms. *Constance Ragan Salgado v United Kingdom of Great Britain and Northern Ireland* CEDAW Communication 11/2006, UN Doc CEDAW/C/37/D/11/2003 (22 January 2007) and *N.S.F. v United Kingdom of Great Britain and Northern Ireland* CEDAW Communication 10/2005, UN Doc CEDAW/C/38/D/10/2005 (12 June 2007)). The Convention has been referred to in domestic authorities (see *EM (Lebanon) v Secretary of State for the Home Department* [2006] EWCA Civ 1531, [2007] 1 FLR 991, para 31 and *R (Quila); R (Bibi) v Secretary of State for the Home Department* [2011] UKSC 45, [2012] 1 FLR 788, para 66).

PART I

Article 1

For the purposes of the present Convention, the term "discrimination against women" shall mean any distinction, exclusion or restriction made on the basis of sex which has the effect or purpose of impairing or nullifying the recognition, enjoyment or exercise by women, irrespective of their marital status, on a basis of equality of men and women, of human rights and fundamental freedoms in the political, economic, social, cultural, civil or any other field.

Article 2

States Parties condemn discrimination against women in all its forms, agree to pursue by all appropriate means and without delay a policy of eliminating discrimination against women and, to this end, undertake:

(a)   To embody the principle of the equality of men and women in their national constitutions or other appropriate legislation if not yet incorporated therein and to ensure, through law and other appropriate means, the practical realization of this principle;

(b)   To adopt appropriate legislative and other measures, including sanctions where appropriate, prohibiting all discrimination against women;

(c)   To establish legal protection of the rights of women on an equal basis with men and to ensure through competent national tribunals and other public institutions the effective protection of women against any act of discrimination;

(d)   To refrain from engaging in any act or practice of discrimination against women and to ensure that public authorities and institutions shall act in conformity with this obligation;

(e)   To take all appropriate measures to eliminate discrimination against women by any person, organization or enterprise;

(f)   To take all appropriate measures, including legislation, to modify or abolish existing laws, regulations, customs and practices which constitute discrimination against women;

(g)   To repeal all national penal provisions which constitute discrimination against women.

Article 3

States Parties shall take in all fields, in particular in the political, social, economic and cultural fields, all appropriate measures, including legislation, to ensure the full development and advancement of women, for the purpose of guaranteeing them the exercise and enjoyment of human rights and fundamental freedoms on a basis of equality with men.

Article 4

1. Adoption by States Parties of temporary special measures aimed at accelerating de facto equality between men and women shall not be considered discrimination as defined in the present Convention, but shall in no way entail as a consequence the maintenance of unequal or separate standards, these measures shall be discontinued when the objectives of equality of opportunity and treatment have been achieved.

2. Adoption by States Parties of special measures, including those measures contained in the present Convention, aimed at protecting maternity shall not be considered discriminatory.

Article 5

States Parties shall take all appropriate measures:

(a)   To modify the social and cultural patterns of conduct of men and women, with a view to achieving the elimination of prejudices and customary and all other practices which are based on the idea of the inferiority or the superiority of either of the sexes or on stereotyped roles for men and women;

(b)   To ensure that family education includes a proper understanding of maternity as a social function and the recognition of the common responsibility of men and women in the upbringing and development of their children, it being understood that the interest of the children is the primordial consideration in all cases.

'primordial consideration' (Art 5(b))—Art 5(b) seeks to express the application of the best interests principle within the context of the responsibility of men and women in the upbringing and development of their children. Note that Art 16(1)(d) of the Convention provides that the child's best interests are paramount in matters relating to marriage. The use of the word primordial presents difficulties in determining precisely what weight is to be attached to the best interests of the child under Art 5(b) **[RCLP paras 4.124–4.125]**. See also Art 3(1) of the United Nations Convention on the Rights of the Child.

Article 6

States Parties shall take all appropriate measures, including legislation, to suppress all forms of traffic in women and exploitation of prostitution of women.

Suppression of trafficking, exploitation and prostitution (Art 6)—See also the Committee on the Elimination of Discrimination Against Women, General Recommendation No 19, 1991, HRI/GEN/1/Rev 8, para 15.

PART II

Article 7

States Parties shall take all appropriate measures to eliminate discrimination against women in the political and public life of the country and, in particular, shall ensure to women, on equal terms with men, the right:

(a) To vote in all elections and public referenda and to be eligible for election to all publicly elected bodies;

(b) To participate in the formulation of government policy and the implementation thereof and to hold public office and perform all public functions at all levels of government;

(c) To participate in non-governmental organizations and associations concerned with the public and political life of the country.

Article 8

States Parties shall take all appropriate measures to ensure to women, on equal terms with men and without any discrimination, the opportunity to represent their Governments at the international level and to participate in the work of international organizations.

Article 9

1. States Parties shall grant women equal rights with men to acquire, change or retain their nationality. They shall ensure in particular that neither marriage to an alien nor change of nationality by the husband during marriage shall automatically change the nationality of the wife, render her stateless or force upon her the nationality of the husband.

2. States Parties shall grant women equal rights with men with respect to the nationality of their children.

PART III

Article 10

States Parties shall take all appropriate measures to eliminate discrimination against women in order to ensure to them equal rights with men in the field of education and in particular to ensure, on a basis of equality of men and women:

(a)   The same conditions for career and vocational guidance, for access to studies and for the achievement of diplomas in educational establishments of all categories in rural as well as in urban areas; this equality shall be ensured in pre-school, general, technical, professional and higher technical education, as well as in all types of vocational training;

(b)   Access to the same curricula, the same examinations, teaching staff with qualifications of the same standard and school premises and equipment of the same quality;

(c)   The elimination of any stereotyped concept of the roles of men and women at all levels and in all forms of education by encouraging coeducation and other types of education which will help to achieve this aim and, in particular, by the revision of textbooks and school programs and the adaptation of teaching methods;

(d)   The same opportunities to benefit from scholarships and other study grants;

(e)   The same opportunities for access to programs of continuing education, including adult and functional literacy programs, particularly those aimed at reducing, at the earliest possible time, any gap in education existing between men and women;

(f)   The reduction of female student drop-out rates and the organization of programs for girls and women who have left school prematurely;

(g)   The same opportunities to participate actively in sports and physical education;

(h)   Access to specific educational information to help to ensure the health and well-being of families, including information and advice on family planning.

Article 11

1. States Parties shall take all appropriate measures to eliminate discrimination against women in the field of employment in order to ensure, on a basis of equality of men and women, the same rights, in particular:

(a)   The right to work as an inalienable right of all human beings;

(b)   The right to the same employment opportunities, including the application of the same criteria for selection in matters of employment;

(c)   The right to free choice of profession and employment, the right to promotion, job security and all benefits and conditions of service and the right to receive vocational training and retraining, including apprenticeships, advanced vocational training and recurrent training;

(d)   The right to equal remuneration, including benefits, and to equal treatment in respect of work of equal value, as well as equality of treatment in the evaluation of the quality of work;

(e)   The right to social security, particularly in cases of retirement, unemployment, sickness, invalidity and old age and other incapacity to work, as well as the right to paid leave;

(f)   The right to protection of health and to safety in working conditions, including the safeguarding of the function of reproduction.

2. In order to prevent discrimination against women on the grounds of marriage or maternity and to ensure their effective right to work, States Parties shall take appropriate measures;

(a)   To prohibit, subject to the imposition of sanctions, dismissal on the grounds of pregnancy or of maternity leave and discrimination in dismissals on the basis of marital status;

(b)   To introduce maternity leave with pay or with comparable social benefits without loss of former employment, seniority or social allowances;

(c)   To encourage the provision of the necessary supporting social services to enable parents to combine family obligations with work responsibilities and participation in public life, in particular through promoting the establishment and development of a network of child care facilities;

(d)   To provide special protection to women during pregnancy in types of work proved to be harmful to them.

3. Protective legislation relating to matters covered in this article shall be reviewed periodically in the light of scientific and technological knowledge and shall be revised, repealed or extended as necessary.

Article 12

1. States Parties shall take all appropriate measures to eliminate discrimination against women in the field of health care in order to ensure, on a basis of equality of men and women, access to health care services, including those related to family planning.

2. Notwithstanding the provisions of paragraph 1 of this article, States Parties shall ensure to women appropriate services in connection with pregnancy, confinement and the post-natal period, granting free services where necessary, as well as adequate nutrition during pregnancy and lactation.

Article 13

States Parties shall take all appropriate measures to eliminate discrimination against women in other areas of economic and social life in order to ensure, on a basis of equality of men and women, the same rights, in particular:

(a)   The right to family benefits;

(b)   The right to bank loans, mortgages and other forms of financial credit

(c)   The right to participate in recreational activities, sports and all aspects of cultural life.

Article 14

1. States Parties shall take into account the particular problems faced by rural women and the significant roles which rural women play in the economic survival of their families, including their work in the non-monetized sectors of the economy, and shall take all appropriate measures to ensure the application of the provisions of the present Convention to women in rural areas.

2. States Parties shall take all appropriate measures to eliminate discrimination against women in rural areas in order to ensure, on a basis of equality of men and women, that they participate in and benefit from rural development and, in particular, shall ensure to such women the right:

(a)   To participate in the elaboration and implementation of development planning at all levels;

(b)   To have access to adequate health care facilities, including information, counseling and services in family planning;

(c)   To benefit directly from social security programs;

(d)   To obtain all types of training and education, formal and non-formal, including that relating to functional literacy, as well as, inter alia, the benefit of all community and extension services, in order to increase their technical proficiency;

(e)   To organize self-help groups and co-operatives in order to obtain equal access to economic opportunities through employment or self-employment;

(f)   To participate in all community activities;

(g)   To have access to agricultural credit and loans, marketing facilities, appropriate technology and equal treatment in land and agrarian reform as well as in land resettlement schemes;

(h)   To enjoy adequate living conditions, particularly in relation to housing, sanitation, electricity and water supply, transport and communications.

PART IV

Article 15

1. States Parties shall accord to women equality with men before the law.

2. State Parties shall accord to women, in civil matters, a legal capacity identical to that of men and the same opportunities to exercise that capacity. In particular, they shall give women equal rights to conclude contracts and to administer property and shall treat them equally in all stages of procedure in courts and tribunals.

3. States Parties agree that all contracts and all other private instruments of any kind with a legal effect which is directed at restricting the legal capacity of women shall be deemed null and void.

4. States Parties shall accord to men and women the same rights with regard to the law relating to the movement of persons and the freedom to choose their residence and domicile.

Article 16

1. States Parties shall take all appropriate measures to eliminate discrimination against women in all matters relating to marriage and family relations and in particular shall ensure, on a basis of equality of men and women:

(a)   The same right to enter into marriage;

(b)   The same right freely to choose a spouse and to enter into marriage only with their free and full consent;

(c)   The same rights and responsibilities during marriage and at its dissolution;

(d)   The same rights and responsibilities as parents, irrespective of their marital status, in matters relating to their children; in all cases the interests of the children shall be paramount;

(e)   The same rights to decide freely and responsibly on the number and spacing of their children and to have access to the information, education and means to enable them to exercise these rights;

(f)   The same rights and responsibilities with regard to guardianship, wardship, trusteeship and adoption of children, or similar institutions where these concepts exist in national legislation; in all cases the interests of the children shall be paramount;

(g)   The same personal rights as husband and wife, including the right to choose a family name, a profession and an occupation;

(h)   The same rights for both spouses in respect of the ownership, acquisition, management, administration, enjoyment and disposition of property, whether free of charge or for a valuable consideration.

2. The betrothal and the marriage of a child shall have no legal effect, and all necessary action, including legislation, shall be taken to specify a minimum age for marriage and to make the registration of marriages in an official registry compulsory.

'**marriage and family relations**' (Art 16(1))—See UN General Assembly Resolution 843(IX) Status of Women in Private Law and Art 16(1) of the Convention on the Elimination of All Forms of Discrimination Against Women and General Recommendation No 21 Equality in Marriage and Family Relations HRI/GEN/1/Rev 8, p 308). See also *R (Quila); R (Bibi) v Secretary of State for the Home Department* [2011] UKSC 45, [2012] 1 FLR 788, para 66.

'same rights and responsibilities ... in matters relating to children' (Art 16(d))—See *Neulinger and another v Switzerland* (Application No 41615/07) [2011] 2 FCR 110, paras 53–55.

'paramount' (Art 16(d))—Pursuant to Art 16(1)(d) the child's best interests shall be paramount within the context of the rights and responsibilities of parents in matters relating to their children [RCLP paras 4.124–4.125]. Note that Art 5(b) seeks to express the application of the best interests principle within the context of the responsibility of men and women in the upbringing and development of their children.

PART V

Article 17

1. For the purpose of considering the progress made in the implementation of the present Convention, there shall be established a Committee on the Elimination of Discrimination against Women (hereinafter referred to as the Committee) consisting, at the time of entry into force of the Convention, of eighteen and, after ratification of or accession to the Convention by the thirty-fifth State Party, of twenty-three experts of high moral standing and competence in the field covered by the Convention. The experts shall be elected by States Parties from among their nationals and shall serve in their personal capacity, consideration being given to equitable geographical distribution and to the representation of the different forms of civilization as well as the principal legal systems.

2. The members of the Committee shall be elected by secret ballot from a list of persons nominated by States Parties. Each State Party may nominate one person from among its own nationals.

3. The initial election shall be held six months after the date of the entry into force of the present Convention. At least three months before the date of each election the Secretary-General of the United Nations shall address a letter to the States Parties inviting them to submit their nominations within two months. The Secretary-General shall prepare a list in alphabetical order of all persons thus nominated, indicating the States Parties which have nominated them, and shall submit it to the States Parties.

4. Elections of the members of the Committee shall be held at a meeting of States Parties convened by the Secretary-General at United Nations Headquarters. At that meeting, for which two thirds of the States Parties shall constitute a quorum, the persons elected to the Committee shall be those nominees who obtain the largest number of votes and an absolute majority of the votes of the representatives of States Parties present and voting.

5. The members of the Committee shall be elected for a term of four years. However, the terms of nine of the members elected at the first election shall expire at the end of two years; immediately after the first election the names of these nine members shall be chosen by lot by the Chairman of the Committee.

6. The election of the five additional members of the Committee shall be held in accordance with the provisions of paragraphs 2, 3 and 4 of this article, following the thirty-fifth ratification or accession. The terms of two of the additional members elected on this occasion shall expire at the end of two years, the names of these two members having been chosen by lot by the Chairman of the Committee.

7. For the filling of casual vacancies, the State Party whose expert has ceased to function as a member of the Committee shall appoint another expert from among its nationals, subject to the approval of the Committee.

8. The members of the Committee shall, with the approval of the General Assembly, receive emoluments from United Nations resources on such terms and conditions as the Assembly may decide, having regard to the importance of the Committee's responsibilities.

9. The Secretary-General of the United Nations shall provide the necessary staff and facilities for the effective performance of the functions of the Committee under the present Convention.

Article 18

1. States Parties undertake to submit to the Secretary-General of the United Nations, for consideration by the Committee, a report on the legislative, judicial, administrative or other measures which they have adopted to give effect to the provisions of the present Convention and on the progress made in this respect:

    (a)   Within one year after the entry into force for the State concerned.

    (b)   Thereafter at least every four years and further whenever the Committee so requests.

2. Reports may indicate factors and difficulties affecting the degree of fulfillment of obligations under the present Convention.

Article 19

1. The Committee shall adopt its own rules of procedure.

2. The Committee shall elect its officers for a term of two years.

Article 20

1. The Committee shall normally meet for a period of not more than two weeks annually in order to consider the reports submitted in accordance with article 18 of the present Convention.

2. The meetings of the Committee shall normally be held at United Nations Headquarters or at any other convenient place as determined by the Committee.

Article 21

1. The Committee shall, through the Economic and Social Council, report annually to the General Assembly of the United Nations on its activities and may make suggestions and general recommendations based on the examination of reports and information received from the States Parties. Such suggestions and general recommendations shall be included in the report of the Committee together with comments, if any, from States Parties.

2. The Secretary-General of the United Nations shall transmit the reports of the Committee to the Commission on the Status of Women for its information.

Article 22

The specialized agencies shall be entitled to be represented at the consideration of the implementation of such provisions of the present Convention as fall within the scope of their activities. The Committee may invite the specialized agencies to submit reports on the implementation of the Convention in areas falling within the scope of their activities.

PART VI

Article 23

Nothing in the present Convention shall affect any provisions that are more conducive to the achievement of equality between men and women which may be contained:

(a)   In the legislation of a State Party; or

(b)   In any other international convention, treaty or agreement in force for that State.

Article 24

States Parties undertake to adopt all necessary measures at the national level aimed at achieving the full realization of the rights recognized in the present Convention.

Article 25

1. The present Convention shall be open for signature by all States.

2. The Secretary-General of the United Nations is designated as the depository of the present Convention.

3. The present Convention is subject to ratification. Instruments of ratification shall be deposited with the Secretary-General of the United Nations.

4. The present Convention shall be open to accession by all States. Accession shall be effected by the deposit of an instrument of accession with the Secretary-General of the United Nations.

Article 26

1. A request for the revision of the present Convention may be made at any time by any State Party by means of a notification in writing addressed to the Secretary-General of the United Nations.

2. The General Assembly of the United Nations shall decide upon the steps, if any, to be taken in respect of such a request.

Article 27

1. The present Convention shall enter into force on the thirtieth day after the date of deposit with the Secretary-General of the United Nations of the twentieth instrument of ratification or accession.

2. For each State ratifying the present Convention or acceding to it after the deposit of the twentieth instrument of ratification or accession, the Convention shall enter into force on the thirtieth day after the date of the deposit of its own instrument of ratification or accession.

Article 28

1. The Secretary-General of the United Nations shall receive and circulate to all States the text of reservations made by States at the time of ratification or accession .

2. A reservation incompatible with the object and purpose of the present Convention shall not be permitted.

3. Reservations may be withdrawn at any time by notification to this effect addressed to the Secretary-General of the United Nations, who shall then inform all States thereof. Such notification shall take effect on the date on which it is received.

Article 29

1. Any dispute between two or more States Parties concerning the interpretation or application of the present Convention which is not settled by negotiation shall, at the request of one of them, be submitted to arbitration. If within six months from the date of the request for arbitration the parties are unable to agree on the organization of the arbitration, any one of those parties may refer the dispute to the International Court of Justice by request in conformity with the Statute of the Court.

2. Each State Party may at the time of signature or ratification of the present Convention or accession thereto declare that it does not consider itself bound by paragraph 1 of this article. The other States Parties shall not be bound by that paragraph with respect to any State Party which has made such a reservation.

3. Any State Party which has made a reservation in accordance with paragraph 2 of this article may at any time withdraw that reservation by notification to the Secretary General of the United Nations.

Article 30

The present Convention, the Arabic, Chinese, English, French, Russian and Spanish texts of which are equally authentic, shall be deposited with the Secretary General of the United Nations.

In witness whereof the undersigned, duly authorized, have signed the present Convention.

CHAPTER 12

CONVENTION ON THE RIGHTS OF PERSONS WITH DISABILITIES

PREAMBLE

The States Parties to the present Convention,

(a) *Recalling* the principles proclaimed in the Charter of the United Nations which recognize the inherent dignity and worth and the equal and inalienable rights of all members of the human family as the foundation of freedom, justice and peace in the world,

(b) *Recognizing* that the United Nations, in the Universal Declaration of Human Rights and in the International Covenants on Human Rights, has proclaimed and agreed that everyone is entitled to all the rights and freedoms set forth therein, without distinction of any kind,

(c) *Reaffirming* the universality, indivisibility, interdependence and interrelatedness of all human rights and fundamental freedoms and the need for persons with disabilities to be guaranteed their full enjoyment without discrimination,

(d) *Recalling* the International Covenant on Economic, Social and Cultural Rights, the International Covenant on Civil and Political Rights, the International Convention on the Elimination of All Forms of Racial Discrimination, the Convention on the Elimination of All Forms of Discrimination against Women, the Convention against Torture and Other Cruel, Inhuman or Degrading Treatment or Punishment, the Convention on the Rights of the Child, and the International Convention on the Protection of the Rights of All Migrant Workers and Members of Their Families,

(e) *Recognizing* that disability is an evolving concept and that disability results from the interaction between persons with impairments and attitudinal and environmental barriers that hinders their full and effective participation in society on an equal basis with others,

(f) *Recognizing* the importance of the principles and policy guidelines contained in the World Programme of Action concerning Disabled Persons and in the Standard Rules on the Equalization of Opportunities for Persons with Disabilities in influencing the promotion, formulation and evaluation of the policies, plans, programmes and actions at the national, regional and international levels to further equalize opportunities for persons with disabilities,

(g) *Emphasizing* the importance of mainstreaming disability issues as an integral part of relevant strategies of sustainable development,

(h) *Recognizing also* that discrimination against any person on the basis of disability is a violation of the inherent dignity and worth of the human person,

(i) *Recognizing further* the diversity of persons with disabilities, (*j*) *Recognizing* the need to promote and protect the human rights of all persons with disabilities, including those who require more intensive support,

(*k*) *Concerned* that, despite these various instruments and undertakings, persons with disabilities continue to face barriers in their participation as equal members of society and violations of their human rights in all parts of the world,

(*l*) *Recognizing* the importance of international cooperation for improving the living conditions of persons with disabilities in every country, particularly in developing countries,

(*m*) *Recognizing* the valued existing and potential contributions made by persons with disabilities to the overall well-being and diversity of their communities, and that the promotion of the full enjoyment by persons with disabilities of their human rights and fundamental freedoms and of full participation by persons with disabilities will result in their enhanced sense of belonging and in significant advances in the human, social and economic development of society and the eradication of poverty,

(*n*) *Recognizing* the importance for persons with disabilities of their individual autonomy and independence, including the freedom to make their own choices,

(*o*) *Considering* that persons with disabilities should have the opportunity to be actively involved in decision-making processes about policies and programmes, including those directly concerning them,

(*p*) *Concerned* about the difficult conditions faced by persons with disabilities who are subject to multiple or aggravated forms of discrimination on the basis of race, colour, sex, language, religion, political or other opinion, national, ethnic, indigenous or social origin, property, birth, age or other status,

(*q*) *Recognizing* that women and girls with disabilities are often at greater risk, both within and outside the home, of violence, injury or abuse, neglect or negligent treatment, maltreatment or exploitation,

(*r*) *Recognizing* that children with disabilities should have full enjoyment of all human rights and fundamental freedoms on an equal basis with other children, and recalling obligations to that end undertaken by States Parties to the Convention on the Rights of the Child,

(*s*) *Emphasizing* the need to incorporate a gender perspective in all efforts to promote the full enjoyment of human rights and fundamental freedoms by persons with disabilities,

(*t*) *Highlighting* the fact that the majority of persons with disabilities live in conditions of poverty, and in this regard recognizing the critical need to address the negative impact of poverty on persons with disabilities,

(*u*) *Bearing in mind* that conditions of peace and security based on full respect for the purposes and principles contained in the Charter of the United Nations and observance of applicable human rights instruments are indispensable for the full protection of persons with disabilities, in particular during armed conflicts and foreign occupation,

(*v*) *Recognizing* the importance of accessibility to the physical, social, economic and cultural environment, to health and education and to information and communication, in enabling persons with disabilities to fully enjoy all human rights and fundamental freedoms, (*w*) *Realizing* that the individual, having duties to other individuals and to the community to which he or she belongs, is under a responsibility to strive for the promotion and observance of the rights recognized in the International Bill of Human Rights,

(*x*) *Convinced* that the family is the natural and fundamental group unit of society and is entitled to protection by society and the State, and that persons with disabilities and their family members should receive the necessary protection and assistance to enable families to contribute towards the full and equal enjoyment of the rights of persons with disabilities,

(*y*) *Convinced* that a comprehensive and integral international convention to promote and protect the rights and dignity of persons with disabilities will make a significant contribution to redressing the profound social disadvantage of persons with disabilities and promote their participation in the civil, political, economic, social and cultural spheres with equal opportunities, in both developing and developed countries,

Have agreed as follows:

Status—The status of the Convention on the Rights of Persons with Disabilities is that of a binding international Convention not incorporated into domestic law **[RCLP para 3.94]** but see *R (D) v Worcestershire County Council* [2013] EWHC 2490 (Admin) para 16. Further, by the European Communities (Definition of Treaties) (United Nations Convention on the Rights of Persons with Disabilities) Order 2009, SI 2009/1181 the Convention is regarded in domestic law as one of the EU Treaties as defined by the European Communities Act 1972 s 1(2). The Convention was ratified by the United Kingdom on 8 June 2009. There is an Optional Protocol to the Convention (not included in this work) which allows States Parties to recognise the competence of the Committee on the Rights of Persons with Disabilities to consider complaints from individuals and provides a system to consider grave or systemic violations **[RCLP para 2.42]**. The United Kingdom ratified the Optional Protocol on 7 August 2010. See also Art 23(1) of the UNCRC and the UN Standard Rules on the Equalisation of Opportunities for Persons with Disabilities. The domestic courts have referred to the Convention (see for example *R (NM) v Secretary of State for Justice* [2012] EWCA Civ 1182, para 42 and *Burnip v Birmingham City Council and another; Trengove v Walsall Metropolitan Council and another; Gory v Wiltshire Council and another* [2012] EWCA Civ 629, para 19).

Children with disabilities—Note that Paragraph (r) of the Preamble expressly recognises that 'children with disabilities should have full enjoyment of all human rights and fundamental freedoms on an equal basis with other children, and recalling obligations to that end undertaken by States Parties to the Convention on the Rights of the Child' **[RCLP paras 2.41 and 4.82]**.

Article 1
Purpose

The purpose of the present Convention is to promote, protect and ensure the full and equal enjoyment of all human rights and fundamental freedoms by all persons with disabilities, and to promote respect for their inherent dignity. Persons with disabilities include those who have long-term physical, mental, intellectual or sensory impairments which in interaction with various barriers may hinder their full and effective participation in society on an equal basis with others.

'all persons' (Art 1)—The term 'all persons' ensures that children are included within the ambit of the Convention and the protection it provides **[RCLP para 13.94]**.

Article 2
Definitions

For the purposes of the present Convention:

"Communication" includes languages, display of text, Braille, tactile communication, large print, accessible multimedia as well as written, audio, plain-language, human-reader and augmentative and alternative modes, means and formats of communication, including accessible information and communication technology;

"Language" includes spoken and signed languages and other forms of non spoken languages;

"Discrimination on the basis of disability" means any distinction, exclusion or restriction on the basis of disability which has the purpose or effect of impairing or nullifying the recognition, enjoyment or exercise, on an equal basis with others, of all human rights and fundamental freedoms in the political, economic, social, cultural, civil or any other field. It includes all forms of discrimination, including denial of reasonable accommodation;

"Reasonable accommodation" means necessary and appropriate modification and adjustments not imposing a disproportionate or undue burden, where needed in a particular case, to ensure to persons with disabilities the enjoyment or exercise on an equal basis with others of all human rights and fundamental freedoms;

"Universal design" means the design of products, environments, programmes and services to be usable by all people, to the greatest extent possible, without the need for adaptation or specialized design. "Universal design" shall not exclude assistive devices for particular groups of persons with disabilities where this is needed.

Article 3
General principles

The principles of the present Convention shall be:

(a) Respect for inherent dignity, individual autonomy including the freedom to make one's own choices, and independence of persons;

(b) Non-discrimination;

(c) Full and effective participation and inclusion in society;

(d) Respect for difference and acceptance of persons with disabilities as part of human diversity and humanity;

(e) Equality of opportunity;

(f) Accessibility;

(g) Equality between men and women;

(h) Respect for the evolving capacities of children with disabilities and respect for the right of children with disabilities to preserve their identities.

Article 4
General obligations

1. States Parties undertake to ensure and promote the full realization of all human rights and fundamental freedoms for all persons with disabilities without discrimination of any kind on the basis of disability. To this end, States Parties undertake:

(a) To adopt all appropriate legislative, administrative and other measures for the implementation of the rights recognized in the present Convention;

(b) To take all appropriate measures, including legislation, to modify or abolish existing laws, regulations, customs and practices that constitute discrimination against persons with disabilities;

(c) To take into account the protection and promotion of the human rights of persons with disabilities in all policies and programmes;

(d) To refrain from engaging in any act or practice that is inconsistent with the present Convention and to ensure that public authorities and institutions act in conformity with the present Convention;

(e) To take all appropriate measures to eliminate discrimination on the basis of disability by any person, organization or private enterprise;

(f) To undertake or promote research and development of universally designed goods, services, equipment and facilities, as defined in article 2 of the present Convention, which should require the minimum possible adaptation and the least cost to meet the specific needs of a person with disabilities, to promote their availability and use, and to promote universal design in the development of standards and guidelines;

(g) To undertake or promote research and development of, and to promote the availability and use of new technologies, including information and communications technologies, mobility aids, devices and assistive technologies, suitable for persons with disabilities, giving priority to technologies at an affordable cost;

(h) To provide accessible information to persons with disabilities about mobility aids, devices and assistive technologies, including new technologies, as well as other forms of assistance, support services and facilities;

(i) To promote the training of professionals and staff working with persons with disabilities in the rights recognized in the present Convention so as to better provide the assistance and services guaranteed by those rights.

2. With regard to economic, social and cultural rights, each State Party undertakes to take measures to the maximum of its available resources and, where needed, within the framework of international cooperation, with a view to achieving progressively the full realization of these rights, without prejudice to those obligations contained in the present Convention that are immediately applicable according to international law.

3. In the development and implementation of legislation and policies to implement the present Convention, and in other decision-making processes concerning issues relating to persons with disabilities, States Parties shall closely consult with and actively involve persons with disabilities, including children with disabilities, through their representative organizations.

4. Nothing in the present Convention shall affect any provisions which are more conducive to the realization of the rights of persons with disabilities and which may be contained in the law of a State Party or international law in force for that State. There shall be no restriction upon or derogation from any of the human rights and fundamental freedoms recognized or existing in any State Party to the present Convention pursuant to law, conventions, regulation or custom on the pretext that the present Convention does not recognize such rights or freedoms or that it recognizes them to a lesser extent.

5. The provisions of the present Convention shall extend to all parts of federal States without any limitations or exceptions.

Article 5
Equality and non-discrimination

1. States Parties recognize that all persons are equal before and under the law and are entitled without any discrimination to the equal protection and equal benefit of the law.

2. States Parties shall prohibit all discrimination on the basis of disability and guarantee to persons with disabilities equal and effective legal protection against discrimination on all grounds.

3. In order to promote equality and eliminate discrimination, States Parties shall take all appropriate steps to ensure that reasonable accommodation is provided.

4. Specific measures which are necessary to accelerate or achieve de facto equality of persons with disabilities shall not be considered discrimination under the terms of the present Convention.

Article 6
Women with disabilities

1. States Parties recognize that women and girls with disabilities are subject to multiple discrimination, and in this regard shall take measures to ensure the full and equal enjoyment by them of all human rights and fundamental freedoms.

2. States Parties shall take all appropriate measures to ensure the full development, advancement and empowerment of women, for the purpose of guaranteeing them the exercise and enjoyment of the human rights and fundamental freedoms set out in the present Convention.

Article 7
Children with disabilities

1. States Parties shall take all necessary measures to ensure the full enjoyment by children with disabilities of all human rights and fundamental freedoms on an equal basis with other children.

2. In all actions concerning children with disabilities, the best interests of the child shall be a primary consideration.

3. States Parties shall ensure that children with disabilities have the right to express their views freely on all matters affecting them, their views being given due weight in accordance with their age and maturity, on an equal basis with other children, and to be provided with disability and age-appropriate assistance to realize that right.

Article 8
Awareness-raising

1. States Parties undertake to adopt immediate, effective and appropriate measures:

 (a) To raise awareness throughout society, including at the family level, regarding persons with disabilities, and to foster respect for the rights and dignity of persons with disabilities;

 (b) To combat stereotypes, prejudices and harmful practices relating to persons with disabilities, including those based on sex and age, in all areas of life;

 (c) To promote awareness of the capabilities and contributions of persons with disabilities.

2. Measures to this end include:

 (a) Initiating and maintaining effective public awareness campaigns designed:
  (i) To nurture receptiveness to the rights of persons with disabilities;
  (ii) To promote positive perceptions and greater social awareness towards persons with disabilities;
  (iii) To promote recognition of the skills, merits and abilities of persons with disabilities, and of their contributions to the workplace and the labour market;

 (b) Fostering at all levels of the education system, including in all children from an early age, an attitude of respect for the rights of persons with disabilities;

 (c) Encouraging all organs of the media to portray persons with disabilities in a manner consistent with the purpose of the present Convention;

(d)   Promoting awareness-training programmes regarding persons with disabilities and the rights of persons with disabilities.

'all organs of the media to portray persons with disabilities in a manner consistent with the purpose of the present Convention' (Art 8(2)(c))—See also the UN Standard Rules on the Equalisation of Opportunities for Persons with Disabilities r 1(3) and r 9(3) [RCLP para 11.31].

Article 9
Accessibility

1. To enable persons with disabilities to live independently and participate fully in all aspects of life, States Parties shall take appropriate measures to ensure to persons with disabilities access, on an equal basis with others, to the physical environment, to transportation, to information and communications, including information and communications technologies and systems, and to other facilities and services open or provided to the public, both in urban and in rural areas. These measures, which shall include the identification and elimination of obstacles and barriers to accessibility, shall apply to, inter alia:

(a)   Buildings, roads, transportation and other indoor and outdoor facilities, including schools, housing, medical facilities and workplaces;

(b)   Information, communications and other services, including electronic services and emergency services.

2. States Parties shall also take appropriate measures:

(a)   To develop, promulgate and monitor the implementation of minimum standards and guidelines for the accessibility of facilities and services open or provided to the public;

(b)   To ensure that private entities that offer facilities and services which are open or provided to the public take into account all aspects of accessibility for persons with disabilities;

(c)   To provide training for stakeholders on accessibility issues facing persons with disabilities;

(d)   To provide in buildings and other facilities open to the public signage in Braille and in easy to read and understand forms;

(e)   To provide forms of live assistance and intermediaries, including guides, readers and professional sign language interpreters, to facilitate accessibility to buildings and other facilities open to the public;

(f)   To promote other appropriate forms of assistance and support to persons with disabilities to ensure their access to information;

(g)   To promote access for persons with disabilities to new information and communications technologies and systems, including the Internet;

(h)   To promote the design, development, production and distribution of accessible information and communications technologies and systems at an early stage, so that these technologies and systems become accessible at minimum cost.

Article 10
Right to life

States Parties reaffirm that every human being has the inherent right to life and shall take all necessary measures to ensure its effective enjoyment by persons with disabilities on an equal basis with others.

Right to life (Art 10)—See also the Standard Rules on the Equalisation of Opportunities for Persons with Disabilities rr 2.3, 15.1 and 15.2 [RCLP para 5.2].

Article 11
Situations of risk and humanitarian emergencies

States Parties shall take, in accordance with their obligations under international law, including international humanitarian law and international human rights law, all necessary measures to ensure the protection and safety of persons with disabilities in situations of risk, including situations of armed conflict, humanitarian emergencies and the occurrence of natural disasters.

'situations of armed conflict' (Art 11)—See also Committee on the Rights of the Child General Comment No 9 *The Rights of Children with Disabilities* CCRC/C/GC/9, para 55 and the Standard Rules on the Equalisation of Opportunities for Persons with Disabilities r 22 [**RCLP para 15.101**].

Article 12
Equal recognition before the law

1. States Parties reaffirm that persons with disabilities have the right to recognition everywhere as persons before the law.

2. States Parties shall recognize that persons with disabilities enjoy legal capacity on an equal basis with others in all aspects of life.

3. States Parties shall take appropriate measures to provide access by persons with disabilities to the support they may require in exercising their legal capacity.

4. States Parties shall ensure that all measures that relate to the exercise of legal capacity provide for appropriate and effective safeguards to prevent abuse in accordance with international human rights law. Such safeguards shall ensure that measures relating to the exercise of legal capacity respect the rights, will and preferences of the person, are free of conflict of interest and undue influence, are proportional and tailored to the person's circumstances, apply for the shortest time possible and are subject to regular review by a competent, independent and impartial authority or judicial body. The safeguards shall be proportional to the degree to which such measures affect the person's rights and interests.

5. Subject to the provisions of this article, States Parties shall take all appropriate and effective measures to ensure the equal right of persons with disabilities to own or inherit property, to control their own financial affairs and to have equal access to bank loans, mortgages and other forms of financial credit, and shall ensure that persons with disabilities are not arbitrarily deprived of their property.

Article 13
Access to justice

1. States Parties shall ensure effective access to justice for persons with disabilities on an equal basis with others, including through the provision of procedural and age-appropriate accommodations, in order to facilitate their effective role as direct and indirect participants, including as witnesses, in all legal proceedings, including at investigative and other preliminary stages.

2. In order to help to ensure effective access to justice for persons with disabilities, States Parties shall promote appropriate training for those working in the field of administration of justice, including police and prison staff.

'effective access to justice' (Art 13(1))—See *RP and others v United Kingdom (Application No 38245/08)* [2013] 1 FLR 744.

Article 14
Liberty and security of person

1. States Parties shall ensure that persons with disabilities, on an equal basis with others:

(a) Enjoy the right to liberty and security of person;
(b) Are not deprived of their liberty unlawfully or arbitrarily, and that any deprivation of liberty is in conformity with the law, and that the existence of a disability shall in no case justify a deprivation of liberty.

2. States Parties shall ensure that if persons with disabilities are deprived of their liberty through any process, they are, on an equal basis with others, entitled to guarantees in accordance with international human rights law and shall be treated in compliance with the objectives and principles of the present Convention, including by provision of reasonable accommodation.

Article 15
Freedom from torture or cruel, inhuman or degrading treatment or punishment

1. No one shall be subjected to torture or to cruel, inhuman or degrading treatment or punishment. In particular, no one shall be subjected without his or her free consent to medical or scientific experimentation.

2. States Parties shall take all effective legislative, administrative, judicial or other measures to prevent persons with disabilities, on an equal basis with others, from being subjected to torture or cruel, inhuman or degrading treatment or punishment.

Article 16
Freedom from exploitation, violence and abuse

1. States Parties shall take all appropriate legislative, administrative, social, educational and other measures to protect persons with disabilities, both within and outside the home, from all forms of exploitation, violence and abuse, including their gender-based aspects.

2. States Parties shall also take all appropriate measures to prevent all forms of exploitation, violence and abuse by ensuring, inter alia, appropriate forms of gender- and age-sensitive assistance and support for persons with disabilities and their families and caregivers, including through the provision of information and education on how to avoid, recognize and report instances of exploitation, violence and abuse. States Parties shall ensure that protection services are age-, gender- and disability-sensitive.

3. In order to prevent the occurrence of all forms of exploitation, violence and abuse, States Parties shall ensure that all facilities and programmes designed to serve persons with disabilities are effectively monitored by independent authorities.

4. States Parties shall take all appropriate measures to promote the physical, cognitive and psychological recovery, rehabilitation and social reintegration of persons with disabilities who become victims of any form of exploitation, violence or abuse, including through the provision of protection services. Such recovery and reintegration shall take place in an environment that fosters the health, welfare, self-respect, dignity and autonomy of the person and takes into account gender- and age-specific needs.

5. States Parties shall put in place effective legislation and policies, including women- and child-focused legislation and policies, to ensure that instances of exploitation, violence and abuse against persons with disabilities are identified, investigated and, where appropriate, prosecuted.

Protection from abuse (Art 16(1))—See also the UN Standard Rules on the Equalisation of Opportunities for Persons with Disabilities r 9(4) **[RCLP para 15.46]** and the Committee on the Rights of the Child General Comment No 9 *The Rights of Children with Disabilities* CRC/C/GC/9, paras 43 and 44 **[RCLP para 15.35]**.

Article 17
Protecting the integrity of the person

Every person with disabilities has a right to respect for his or her physical and mental integrity on an equal basis with others.

Article 18
Liberty of movement and nationality

1. States Parties shall recognize the rights of persons with disabilities to liberty of movement, to freedom to choose their residence and to a nationality, on an equal basis with others, including by ensuring that persons with disabilities:

  (a)　Have the right to acquire and change a nationality and are not deprived of their nationality arbitrarily or on the basis of disability;

  (b)　Are not deprived, on the basis of disability, of their ability to obtain, possess and utilize documentation of their nationality or other documentation of identification, or to utilize relevant processes such as immigration proceedings, that may be needed to facilitate exercise of the right to liberty of movement;

  (c)　Are free to leave any country, including their own;

  (d)　Are not deprived, arbitrarily or on the basis of disability, of the right to enter their own country.

2. Children with disabilities shall be registered immediately after birth and shall have the right from birth to a name, the right to acquire a nationality and, as far as possible, the right to know and be cared for by their parents.

Article 19
Living independently and being included in the community

States Parties to the present Convention recognize the equal right of all persons with disabilities to live in the community, with choices equal to others, and shall take effective and appropriate measures to facilitate full enjoyment by persons with disabilities of this right and their full inclusion and participation in the community, including by ensuring that:

  (a)　Persons with disabilities have the opportunity to choose their place of residence and where and with whom they live on an equal basis with others and are not obliged to live in a particular living arrangement;

  (b)　Persons with disabilities have access to a range of in-home, residential and other community support services, including personal assistance necessary to support living and inclusion in the community, and to prevent isolation or segregation from the community;

  (c)　Community services and facilities for the general population are available on an equal basis to persons with disabilities and are responsive to their needs.

Article 20
Personal mobility

States Parties shall take effective measures to ensure personal mobility with the greatest possible independence for persons with disabilities, including by:

  (a)　Facilitating the personal mobility of persons with disabilities in the manner and at the time of their choice, and at affordable cost;

(b) Facilitating access by persons with disabilities to quality mobility aids, devices, assistive technologies and forms of live assistance and intermediaries, including by making them available at affordable cost;

(c) Providing training in mobility skills to persons with disabilities and to specialist staff working with persons with disabilities;

(d) Encouraging entities that produce mobility aids, devices and assistive technologies to take into account all aspects of mobility for persons with disabilities.

Article 21
Freedom of expression and opinion, and access to information

States Parties shall take all appropriate measures to ensure that persons with disabilities can exercise the right to freedom of expression and opinion, including the freedom to seek, receive and impart information and ideas on an equal basis with others and through all forms of communication of their choice, as defined in article 2 of the present Convention, including by:

(a) Providing information intended for the general public to persons with disabilities in accessible formats and technologies appropriate to different kinds of disabilities in a timely manner and without additional cost;

(b) Accepting and facilitating the use of sign languages, Braille, augmentative and alternative communication, and all other accessible means, modes and formats of communication of their choice by persons with disabilities in official interactions;

(c) Urging private entities that provide services to the general public, including through the Internet, to provide information and services in accessible and usable formats for persons with disabilities;

(d) Encouraging the mass media, including providers of information through the Internet, to make their services accessible to persons with disabilities;

(e) Recognizing and promoting the use of sign languages.

Article 22
Respect for privacy

1. No person with disabilities, regardless of place of residence or living arrangements, shall be subjected to arbitrary or unlawful interference with his or her privacy, family, home or correspondence or other types of communication or to unlawful attacks on his or her honour and reputation. Persons with disabilities have the right to the protection of the law against such interference or attacks.

2. States Parties shall protect the privacy of personal, health and rehabilitation information of persons with disabilities on an equal basis with others.

Article 23
Respect for home and the family

1. States Parties shall take effective and appropriate measures to eliminate discrimination against persons with disabilities in all matters relating to marriage, family, parenthood and relationships, on an equal basis with others, so as to ensure that:

(a) The right of all persons with disabilities who are of marriageable age to marry and to found a family on the basis of free and full consent of the intending spouses is recognized;

(b) The rights of persons with disabilities to decide freely and responsibly on the number and spacing of their children and to have access to age-appropriate

information, reproductive and family planning education are recognized, and
the means necessary to enable them to exercise these rights are provided;
(c) Persons with disabilities, including children, retain their fertility on an equal
basis with others.

2. States Parties shall ensure the rights and responsibilities of persons with disabilities,
with regard to guardianship, wardship, trusteeship, adoption of children or similar
institutions, where these concepts exist in national legislation; in all cases the best
interests of the child shall be paramount. States Parties shall render appropriate
assistance to persons with disabilities in the performance of their child-rearing
responsibilities.

3. States Parties shall ensure that children with disabilities have equal rights with respect
to family life. With a view to realizing these rights, and to prevent concealment,
abandonment, neglect and segregation of children with disabilities, States Parties shall
undertake to provide early and comprehensive information, services and support to
children with disabilities and their families.

4. States Parties shall ensure that a child shall not be separated from his or her parents
against their will, except when competent authorities subject to judicial review
determine, in accordance with applicable law and procedures, that such separation is
necessary for the best interests of the child. In no case shall a child be separated from
parents on the basis of a disability of either the child or one or both of the parents.

5. States Parties shall, where the immediate family is unable to care for a child with
disabilities, undertake every effort to provide alternative care within the wider family,
and failing that, within the community in a family setting.

'except when competent authorities subject to judicial review determine, in accordance with applicable law and
procedures' (Art 23(4)—It is likely that this phrase will be interpreted as holding the child's best interests as a
primary consideration (see Art 3(1) of the UNCRC) [RCLP para 8.90].

Article 24
Education

1. States Parties recognize the right of persons with disabilities to education. With a view
to realizing this right without discrimination and on the basis of equal opportunity,
States Parties shall ensure an inclusive education system at all levels and lifelong learning
directed to:

(a) The full development of human potential and sense of dignity and self-worth,
and the strengthening of respect for human rights, fundamental freedoms and
human diversity;
(b) The development by persons with disabilities of their personality, talents and
creativity, as well as their mental and physical abilities, to their fullest potential;
(c) Enabling persons with disabilities to participate effectively in a free society.

2. In realizing this right, States Parties shall ensure that:

(a) Persons with disabilities are not excluded from the general education system on
the basis of disability, and that children with disabilities are not excluded from
free and compulsory primary education, or from secondary education, on the
basis of disability;
(b) Persons with disabilities can access an inclusive, quality and free primary
education and secondary education on an equal basis with others in the
communities in which they live;
(c) Reasonable accommodation of the individual's requirements is provided;

(d)   Persons with disabilities receive the support required, within the general education system, to facilitate their effective education;

(e)   Effective individualized support measures are provided in environments that maximize academic and social development, consistent with the goal of full inclusion.

3. States Parties shall enable persons with disabilities to learn life and social development skills to facilitate their full and equal participation in education and as members of the community. To this end, States Parties shall take appropriate measures, including:

(a)   Facilitating the learning of Braille, alternative script, augmentative and alternative modes, means and formats of communication and orientation and mobility skills, and facilitating peer support and mentoring;

(b)   Facilitating the learning of sign language and the promotion of the linguistic identity of the deaf community;

(c)   Ensuring that the education of persons, and in particular children, who are blind, deaf or deafblind, is delivered in the most appropriate languages and modes and means of communication for the individual, and in environments which maximize academic and social development.

4. In order to help ensure the realization of this right, States Parties shall take appropriate measures to employ teachers, including teachers with disabilities, who are qualified in sign language and/or Braille, and to train professionals and staff who work at all levels of education. Such training shall incorporate disability awareness and the use of appropriate augmentative and alternative modes, means and formats of communication, educational techniques and materials to support persons with disabilities.

5. States Parties shall ensure that persons with disabilities are able to access general tertiary education, vocational training, adult education and lifelong learning without discrimination and on an equal basis with others. To this end, States Parties shall ensure that reasonable accommodation is provided to persons with disabilities.

Education (Art 24)—See also UNESCO Revised Recommendation Concerning Technical and Vocational Education (2001) paras 7(g), 29 and 52 [**RCLP para 13.92**] and the Committee on the Rights of the Child General Comment No 9 *The Rights of Children with Disabilities* CRC/C/GC/9, para 67 [**RCLP para 13.94**].

Article 25

Health

States Parties recognize that persons with disabilities have the right to the enjoyment of the highest attainable standard of health without discrimination on the basis of disability. States Parties shall take all appropriate measures to ensure access for persons with disabilities to health services that are gender-sensitive, including health-related rehabilitation. In particular, States Parties shall:

(a)   Provide persons with disabilities with the same range, quality and standard of free or affordable health care and programmes as provided to other persons, including in the area of sexual and reproductive health and population-based public health programmes;

(b)   Provide those health services needed by persons with disabilities specifically because of their disabilities, including early identification and intervention as appropriate, and services designed to minimize and prevent further disabilities, including among children and older persons;

(c)   Provide these health services as close as possible to people's own communities, including in rural areas;

(d)   Require health professionals to provide care of the same quality to persons with disabilities as to others, including on the basis of free and informed consent by, inter alia, raising awareness of the human rights, dignity, autonomy and needs of persons with disabilities through training and the promulgation of ethical standards for public and private health care;

(e)   Prohibit discrimination against persons with disabilities in the provision of health insurance, and life insurance where such insurance is permitted by national law, which shall be provided in a fair and reasonable manner;

(f)   Prevent discriminatory denial of health care or health services or food and fluids on the basis of disability.

Article 26
Habilitation and rehabilitation

1. States Parties shall take effective and appropriate measures, including through peer support, to enable persons with disabilities to attain and maintain maximum independence, full physical, mental, social and vocational ability, and full inclusion and participation in all aspects of life. To that end, States Parties shall organize, strengthen and extend comprehensive habilitation and rehabilitation services and programmes, particularly in the areas of health, employment, education and social services, in such a way that these services and programmes:

(a)   Begin at the earliest possible stage, and are based on the multidisciplinary assessment of individual needs and strengths;

(b)   Support participation and inclusion in the community and all aspects of society, are voluntary, and are available to persons with disabilities as close as possible to their own communities, including in rural areas.

2. States Parties shall promote the development of initial and continuing training for professionals and staff working in habilitation and rehabilitation services.

3. States Parties shall promote the availability, knowledge and use of assistive devices and technologies, designed for persons with disabilities, as they relate to habilitation and rehabilitation.

Article 27
Work and employment

1. States Parties recognize the right of persons with disabilities to work, on an equal basis with others; this includes the right to the opportunity to gain a living by work freely chosen or accepted in a labour market and work environment that is open, inclusive and accessible to persons with disabilities. States Parties shall safeguard and promote the realization of the right to work, including for those who acquire a disability during the course of employment, by taking appropriate steps, including through legislation, to, inter alia:

(a)   Prohibit discrimination on the basis of disability with regard to all matters concerning all forms of employment, including conditions of recruitment, hiring and employment, continuance of employment, career advancement and safe and healthy working conditions;

(b)   Protect the rights of persons with disabilities, on an equal basis with others, to just and favourable conditions of work, including equal opportunities and equal remuneration for work of equal value, safe and healthy working conditions, including protection from harassment, and the redress of grievances;

(c)   Ensure that persons with disabilities are able to exercise their labour and trade union rights on an equal basis with others;

(d)   Enable persons with disabilities to have effective access to general technical and vocational guidance programmes, placement services and vocational and continuing training;

(e)   Promote employment opportunities and career advancement for persons with disabilities in the labour market, as well as assistance in finding, obtaining, maintaining and returning to employment;

(f)   Promote opportunities for self-employment, entrepreneurship, the development of cooperatives and starting one's own business;

(g)   Employ persons with disabilities in the public sector;

(h)   Promote the employment of persons with disabilities in the private sector through appropriate policies and measures, which may include affirmative action programmes, incentives and other measures;

(i)   Ensure that reasonable accommodation is provided to persons with disabilities in the workplace;

(j)   Promote the acquisition by persons with disabilities of work experience in the open labour market;

(k)   Promote vocational and professional rehabilitation, job retention and return-to-work programmes for persons with disabilities.

2. States Parties shall ensure that persons with disabilities are not held in slavery or in servitude, and are protected, on an equal basis with others, from forced or compulsory labour.

Article 28
Adequate standard of living and social protection

1. States Parties recognize the right of persons with disabilities to an adequate standard of living for themselves and their families, including adequate food, clothing and housing, and to the continuous improvement of living conditions, and shall take appropriate steps to safeguard and promote the realization of this right without discrimination on the basis of disability.

2. States Parties recognize the right of persons with disabilities to social protection and to the enjoyment of that right without discrimination on the basis of disability, and shall take appropriate steps to safeguard and promote the realization of this right, including measures:

(a)   To ensure equal access by persons with disabilities to clean water services, and to ensure access to appropriate and affordable services, devices and other assistance for disability-related needs;

(b)   To ensure access by persons with disabilities, in particular women and girls with disabilities and older persons with disabilities, to social protection programmes and poverty reduction programmes;

(c)   To ensure access by persons with disabilities and their families living in situations of poverty to assistance from the State with disability related expenses, including adequate training, counselling, financial assistance and respite care;

(d)   To ensure access by persons with disabilities to public housing programmes;

(e)   To ensure equal access by persons with disabilities to retirement benefits and programmes.

Article 29
Participation in political and public life

States Parties shall guarantee to persons with disabilities political rights and the opportunity to enjoy them on an equal basis with others, and shall undertake:

(a)   To ensure that persons with disabilities can effectively and fully participate in political and public life on an equal basis with others, directly or through freely chosen representatives, including the right and opportunity for persons with disabilities to vote and be elected, inter alia, by:

   (i)   Ensuring that voting procedures, facilities and materials are appropriate, accessible and easy to understand and use;

   (ii)   Protecting the right of persons with disabilities to vote by secret ballot in elections and public referendums without intimidation, and to stand for elections, to effectively hold office and perform all public functions at all levels of government, facilitating the use of assistive and new technologies where appropriate;

   (iii) Guaranteeing the free expression of the will of persons with disabilities as electors and to this end, where necessary, at their request, allowing assistance in voting by a person of their own choice;

(b)   To promote actively an environment in which persons with disabilities can effectively and fully participate in the conduct of public affairs, without discrimination and on an equal basis with others, and encourage their participation in public affairs, including:

   (i)   Participation in non-governmental organizations and associations concerned with the public and political life of the country, and in the activities and administration of political parties;

   (ii)   Forming and joining organizations of persons with disabilities to represent persons with disabilities at international, national, regional and local levels.

'**Participation in non-governmental organizations and associations**' (Art 29(b)(i))—See also the Committee on Economic, Social and Cultural Rights General Comment No 5 *Persons with Disabilities* HRI/GEN/1/Rev 8, p 30, para 26 [RCLP para 12.10].

Article 30
Participation in cultural life, recreation, leisure and sport

1. States Parties recognize the right of persons with disabilities to take part on an equal basis with others in cultural life, and shall take all appropriate measures to ensure that persons with disabilities:

(a)   Enjoy access to cultural materials in accessible formats;

(b)   Enjoy access to television programmes, films, theatre and other cultural activities, in accessible formats;

(c)   Enjoy access to places for cultural performances or services, such as theatres, museums, cinemas, libraries and tourism services, and, as far as possible, enjoy access to monuments and sites of national cultural importance.

2. States Parties shall take appropriate measures to enable persons with disabilities to have the opportunity to develop and utilize their creative, artistic and intellectual potential, not only for their own benefit, but also for the enrichment of society.

3. States Parties shall take all appropriate steps, in accordance with international law, to ensure that laws protecting intellectual property rights do not constitute an unreasonable or discriminatory barrier to access by persons with disabilities to cultural materials.

4. Persons with disabilities shall be entitled, on an equal basis with others, to recognition and support of their specific cultural and linguistic identity, including sign languages and deaf culture.

5. With a view to enabling persons with disabilities to participate on an equal basis with others in recreational, leisure and sporting activities, States Parties shall take appropriate measures:

(a)   To encourage and promote the participation, to the fullest extent possible, of persons with disabilities in mainstream sporting activities at all levels;

(b)   To ensure that persons with disabilities have an opportunity to organize, develop and participate in disability-specific sporting and recreational activities and, to this end, encourage the provision, on an equal basis with others, of appropriate instruction, training and resources;

(c)   To ensure that persons with disabilities have access to sporting, recreational and tourism venues;

(d)   To ensure that children with disabilities have equal access with other children to participation in play, recreation and leisure and sporting activities, including those activities in the school system;

(e)   To ensure that persons with disabilities have access to services from those involved in the organization of recreational, tourism, leisure and sporting activities.

'recreational, leisure and sporting activities' (Art 30(5))—See also the Committee on the Rights of the Child General Comment No 9 *The Rights of Children with Disabilities* paras 44 to 46 and the UN Standard Rules on the Equalisation of Opportunities for Persons with Disabilities rr 4(7) and 11 [**RCLP para 5.195**].

Article 31
Statistics and data collection

1. States Parties undertake to collect appropriate information, including statistical and research data, to enable them to formulate and implement policies to give effect to the present Convention. The process of collecting and maintaining this information shall:

(a)   Comply with legally established safeguards, including legislation on data protection, to ensure confidentiality and respect for the privacy of persons with disabilities;

(b)   Comply with internationally accepted norms to protect human rights and fundamental freedoms and ethical principles in the collection and use of statistics.

2. The information collected in accordance with this article shall be disaggregated, as appropriate, and used to help assess the implementation of States Parties' obligations under the present Convention and to identify and address the barriers faced by persons with disabilities in exercising their rights.

3. States Parties shall assume responsibility for the dissemination of these statistics and ensure their accessibility to persons with disabilities and others.

Article 32
International cooperation

1. States Parties recognize the importance of international cooperation and its promotion, in support of national efforts for the realization of the purpose and objectives of the present Convention, and will undertake appropriate and effective measures in this regard, between and among States and, as appropriate, in partnership

with relevant international and regional organizations and civil society, in particular organizations of persons with disabilities. Such measures could include, inter alia:

(a)   Ensuring that international cooperation, including international development programmes, is inclusive of and accessible to persons with disabilities;

(b)   Facilitating and supporting capacity-building, including through the exchange and sharing of information, experiences, training programmes and best practices;

(c)   Facilitating cooperation in research and access to scientific and technical knowledge;

(d)   Providing, as appropriate, technical and economic assistance, including by facilitating access to and sharing of accessible and assistive technologies, and through the transfer of technologies.

2. The provisions of this article are without prejudice to the obligations of each State Party to fulfil its obligations under the present Convention.

Article 33
National implementation and monitoring

1. States Parties, in accordance with their system of organization, shall designate one or more focal points within government for matters relating to the implementation of the present Convention, and shall give due consideration to the establishment or designation of a coordination mechanism within government to facilitate related action in different sectors and at different levels.

2. States Parties shall, in accordance with their legal and administrative systems, maintain, strengthen, designate or establish within the State Party, a framework, including one or more independent mechanisms, as appropriate, to promote, protect and monitor implementation of the present Convention. When designating or establishing such a mechanism, States Parties shall take into account the principles relating to the status and functioning of national institutions for protection and promotion of human rights.

3. Civil society, in particular persons with disabilities and their representative organizations, shall be involved and participate fully in the monitoring process.

Article 34
Committee on the Rights of Persons with Disabilities

1. There shall be established a Committee on the Rights of Persons with Disabilities (hereafter referred to as "the Committee"), which shall carry out the functions hereinafter provided.

2. The Committee shall consist, at the time of entry into force of the present Convention, of twelve experts. After an additional sixty ratifications or accessions to the Convention, the membership of the Committee shall increase by six members, attaining a maximum number of eighteen members.

3. The members of the Committee shall serve in their personal capacity and shall be of high moral standing and recognized competence and experience in the field covered by the present Convention. When nominating their candidates, States Parties are invited to give due consideration to the provision set out in article 4, paragraph 3, of the present Convention.

4. The members of the Committee shall be elected by States Parties, consideration being given to equitable geographical distribution, representation of the different forms of civilization and of the principal legal systems, balanced gender representation and participation of experts with disabilities.

5. The members of the Committee shall be elected by secret ballot from a list of persons nominated by the States Parties from among their nationals at meetings of the Conference of States Parties. At those meetings, for which two thirds of States Parties shall constitute a quorum, the persons elected to the Committee shall be those who obtain the largest number of votes and an absolute majority of the votes of the representatives of States Parties present and voting.

6. The initial election shall be held no later than six months after the date of entry into force of the present Convention. At least four months before the date of each election, the Secretary-General of the United Nations shall address a letter to the States Parties inviting them to submit the nominations within two months. The Secretary-General shall subsequently prepare a list in alphabetical order of all persons thus nominated, indicating the State Parties which have nominated them, and shall submit it to the States Parties to the present Convention.

7. The members of the Committee shall be elected for a term of four years. They shall be eligible for re-election once. However, the term of six of the members elected at the first election shall expire at the end of two years; immediately after the first election, the names of these six members shall be chosen by lot by the chairperson of the meeting referred to in paragraph 5 of this article.

8. The election of the six additional members of the Committee shall be held on the occasion of regular elections, in accordance with the relevant provisions of this article.

9. If a member of the Committee dies or resigns or declares that for any other cause she or he can no longer perform her or his duties, the State Party which nominated the member shall appoint another expert possessing the qualifications and meeting the requirements set out in the relevant provisions of this article, to serve for the remainder of the term.

10. The Committee shall establish its own rules of procedure.

11. The Secretary-General of the United Nations shall provide the necessary staff and facilities for the effective performance of the functions of the Committee under the present Convention, and shall convene its initial meeting.

12. With the approval of the General Assembly of the United Nations, the members of the Committee established under the present Convention shall receive emoluments from United Nations resources on such terms and conditions as the Assembly may decide, having regard to the importance of the Committee's responsibilities.

13. The members of the Committee shall be entitled to the facilities, privileges and immunities of experts on mission for the United Nations as laid down in the relevant sections of the Convention on the Privileges and Immunities of the United Nations.

Article 35
Reports by States Parties

1. Each State Party shall submit to the Committee, through the Secretary- General of the United Nations, a comprehensive report on measures taken to give effect to its obligations under the present Convention and on the progress made in that regard, within two years after the entry into force of the present Convention for the State Party concerned.

2. Thereafter, States Parties shall submit subsequent reports at least every four years and further whenever the Committee so requests.

3. The Committee shall decide any guidelines applicable to the content of the reports.

4. A State Party which has submitted a comprehensive initial report to the Committee need not, in its subsequent reports, repeat information previously provided. When preparing reports to the Committee, States Parties are invited to consider doing so in an open and transparent process and to give due consideration to the provision set out in article 4, paragraph 3, of the present Convention.

5. Reports may indicate factors and difficulties affecting the degree of fulfilment of obligations under the present Convention.

Article 36
Consideration of reports

1. Each report shall be considered by the Committee, which shall make such suggestions and general recommendations on the report as it may consider appropriate and shall forward these to the State Party concerned. The State Party may respond with any information it chooses to the Committee. The Committee may request further information from States Parties relevant to the implementation of the present Convention.

2. If a State Party is significantly overdue in the submission of a report, the Committee may notify the State Party concerned of the need to examine the implementation of the present Convention in that State Party, on the basis of reliable information available to the Committee, if the relevant report is not submitted within three months following the notification. The Committee shall invite the State Party concerned to participate in such examination. Should the State Party respond by submitting the relevant report, the provisions of paragraph 1 of this article will apply.

3. The Secretary-General of the United Nations shall make available the reports to all States Parties.

4. States Parties shall make their reports widely available to the public in their own countries and facilitate access to the suggestions and general recommendations relating to these reports.

5. The Committee shall transmit, as it may consider appropriate, to the specialized agencies, funds and programmes of the United Nations, and other competent bodies, reports from States Parties in order to address a request or indication of a need for technical advice or assistance contained therein, along with the Committee's observations and recommendations, if any, on these requests or indications.

Article 37
Cooperation between States Parties and the Committee

1. Each State Party shall cooperate with the Committee and assist its members in the fulfilment of their mandate.

2. In its relationship with States Parties, the Committee shall give due consideration to ways and means of enhancing national capacities for the implementation of the present Convention, including through international cooperation.

Article 38
Relationship of the Committee with other bodies

In order to foster the effective implementation of the present Convention and to encourage international cooperation in the field covered by the present Convention:

(a)   The specialized agencies and other United Nations organs shall be entitled to be represented at the consideration of the implementation of such provisions of the present Convention as fall within the scope of their mandate. The Committee may invite the specialized agencies and other competent bodies as it may consider appropriate to provide expert advice on the implementation of the Convention in areas falling within the scope of their respective mandates. The Committee may invite specialized agencies and other United Nations organs to submit reports on the implementation of the Convention in areas falling within the scope of their activities;

(b)   The Committee, as it discharges its mandate, shall consult, as appropriate, other relevant bodies instituted by international human rights treaties, with a view to ensuring the consistency of their respective reporting guidelines, suggestions and general recommendations, and avoiding duplication and overlap in the performance of their functions.

Article 39
Report of the Committee

The Committee shall report every two years to the General Assembly and to the Economic and Social Council on its activities, and may make suggestions and general recommendations based on the examination of reports and information received from the States Parties. Such suggestions and general recommendations shall be included in the report of the Committee together with comments, if any, from States Parties.

Article 40
Conference of States Parties

1. The States Parties shall meet regularly in a Conference of States Parties in order to consider any matter with regard to the implementation of the present Convention.

2. No later than six months after the entry into force of the present Convention, the Conference of States Parties shall be convened by the Secretary-General of the United Nations. The subsequent meetings shall be convened by the Secretary-General biennially or upon the decision of the Conference of States Parties.

Article 41
Depositary

The Secretary-General of the United Nations shall be the depositary of the present Convention.

Article 42
Signature

The present Convention shall be open for signature by all States and by regional integration organizations at United Nations Headquarters in New York as of 30 March 2007.

Article 43
Consent to be bound

The present Convention shall be subject to ratification by signatory States and to formal confirmation by signatory regional integration organizations. It shall be open for accession by any State or regional integration organization which has not signed the Convention.

Article 44
Regional integration organizations

1. "Regional integration organization" shall mean an organization constituted by sovereign States of a given region, to which its member States have transferred competence in respect of matters governed by the present Convention. Such organizations shall declare, in their instruments of formal confirmation or accession, the extent of their competence with respect to matters governed by the present Convention. Subsequently, they shall inform the depositary of any substantial modification in the extent of their competence.

2. References to "States Parties" in the present Convention shall apply to such organizations within the limits of their competence.

3. For the purposes of article 45, paragraph 1, and article 47, paragraphs 2 and 3, of the present Convention, any instrument deposited by a regional integration organization shall not be counted.

4. Regional integration organizations, in matters within their competence, may exercise their right to vote in the Conference of States Parties, with a number of votes equal to the number of their member States that are Parties to the present Convention. Such an organization shall not exercise its right to vote if any of its member States exercises its right, and vice versa.

Article 45
Entry into force

1. The present Convention shall enter into force on the thirtieth day after the deposit of the twentieth instrument of ratification or accession.

2. For each State or regional integration organization ratifying, formally confirming or acceding to the present Convention after the deposit of the twentieth such instrument, the Convention shall enter into force on the thirtieth day after the deposit of its own such instrument.

Article 46
Reservations

1. Reservations incompatible with the object and purpose of the present Convention shall not be permitted.

2. Reservations may be withdrawn at any time.

Article 47
Amendments

1. Any State Party may propose an amendment to the present Convention and submit it to the Secretary-General of the United Nations. The Secretary- General shall communicate any proposed amendments to States Parties, with a request to be notified whether they favour a conference of States Parties for the purpose of considering and deciding upon the proposals. In the event that, within four months from the date of such

communication, at least one third of the States Parties favour such a conference, the Secretary-General shall convene the conference under the auspices of the United Nations. Any amendment adopted by a majority of two thirds of the States Parties present and voting shall be submitted by the Secretary-General to the General Assembly of the United Nations for approval and thereafter to all States Parties for acceptance.

2. An amendment adopted and approved in accordance with paragraph 1 of this article shall enter into force on the thirtieth day after the number of instruments of acceptance deposited reaches two thirds of the number of States Parties at the date of adoption of the amendment. Thereafter, the amendment shall enter into force for any State Party on the thirtieth day following the deposit of its own instrument of acceptance. An amendment shall be binding only on those States Parties which have accepted it.

3. If so decided by the Conference of States Parties by consensus, an amendment adopted and approved in accordance with paragraph 1 of this article which relates exclusively to articles 34, 38, 39 and 40 shall enter into force for all States Parties on the thirtieth day after the number of instruments of acceptance deposited reaches two thirds of the number of States Parties at the date of adoption of the amendment.

Article 48
Denunciation

A State Party may denounce the present Convention by written notification to the Secretary-General of the United Nations. The denunciation shall become effective one year after the date of receipt of the notification by the Secretary-General.

Article 49
Accessible format

The text of the present Convention shall be made available in accessible formats.

Article 50
Authentic texts

The Arabic, Chinese, English, French, Russian and Spanish texts of the present Convention shall be equally authentic.

IN WITNESS THEREOF the undersigned plenipotentiaries, being duly authorized thereto by their respective Governments, have signed the present Convention.

CHAPTER 13

CONVENTION AGAINST DISCRIMINATION IN EDUCATION

Adopted by the General Conference at its eleventh session, Paris, 14 December 1960
The General Conference of the United Nations Educational, Scientific and Cultural Organization, meeting in Paris from 14 November to 15 December 1960, at its eleventh session,

Recalling that the Universal Declaration of Human Rights asserts the principle of non-discrimination and proclaims that every person has the right to education,

Considering that discrimination in education is a violation of rights enunciated in that Declaration,

Considering that, under the terms of its Constitution, the United Nations Educational,

Scientific and Cultural Organization has the purpose of instituting collaboration among the nations with a view to furthering for all universal respect for human rights and equality of educational opportunity,

Recognizing that, consequently, the United Nations Educational, Scientific and Cultural Organization, while respecting the diversity of national educational systems, has the duty not only to proscribe any form of discrimination in education but also to promote equality of opportunity and treatment for all in education,

Having before it proposals concerning the different aspects of discrimination in education, constituting item 17.1.4 of the agenda of the session,

Having decided at its tenth session that this question should be made the subject of an international convention as well as of recommendations to Member States,

Adopts this Convention on the fourteenth day of December 1960.

Status—The Convention against Discrimination in Education was adopted by UNESCO on 14 December 1960 [RCLP para 13.26]. The United Kingdom accepted the Convention against Discrimination in Education on 14 March 1962 but has not ratified the Convention [RCLP para 2.45]. The status of the Convention against Discrimination in Education is that of a binding international Convention not incorporated into domestic law [RCLP para 3.94]. The Convention against Discrimination in Education has an Optional Protocol (not included in this work) establishes a Commission to seek amicable settlement of disputes under the Convention between State Parties [RCLP para 2.45].

Article 1

1. For the purposes of this Convention, the term 'discrimination' includes any distinction, exclusion, limitation or preference which, being based on race, colour, sex, language, religion, political or other opinion, national or social origin, economic condition or birth, has the purpose or effect of nullifying or impairing equality of treatment in education and in particular:

(a)   Of depriving any person or group of persons of access to education of any type or at any level;

(b)   Of limiting any person or group of persons to education of an inferior standard;

(c)   Subject to the provisions of Article 2 of this Convention, of establishing or maintaining separate educational systems or institutions for persons or groups of persons; or

(d)   Of inflicting on any person or group of persons conditions which are incompatible with the dignity of man.

2. For the purposes of this Convention, the term 'education' refers to all types and levels of education, and includes access to education, the standard and quality of education, and the conditions under which it is given.

Article 2

When permitted in a State, the following situations shall not be deemed to constitute discrimination, within the meaning of Article I of this Convention:

(a)   The establishment or maintenance of separate educational systems or institutions for pupils of the two sexes, if these systems or institutions offer equivalent access to education, provide a teaching staff with qualifications of the same standard as well as school premises and equipment of the same quality, and afford the opportunity to take the same or equivalent courses of study;

(b)   The establishment or maintenance, for religious or linguistic reasons, of separate educational systems or institutions offering an education which is in keeping with the wishes of the pupil's parents or legal guardians, if participation in such systems or attendance at such institutions is optional and if the education provided conforms to such standards as may be laid down or approved by the competent authorities, in particular for education of the same level;

(c)   The establishment or maintenance of private educational institutions, if the object of the institutions is not to secure the exclusion of any group but to provide educational facilities in addition to those provided by the public authorities, if the institutions are conducted in accordance with that object, and if the education provided conforms with such standards as may be laid down or approved by the competent authorities, in particular for education of the same level.

Article 3

In order to eliminate and prevent discrimination within the meaning of this Convention, the States Parties thereto undertake:

(a)   To abrogate any statutory provisions and any administrative instructions and to discontinue any administrative practices which involve discrimination in education;

(b)   To ensure, by legislation where necessary, that there is no discrimination in the admission of pupils to educational institutions;

(c)   Not to allow any differences of treatment by the public authorities between nationals, except on the basis of merit or need, in the matter of school fees and the grant of scholarships or other forms of assistance to pupils and necessary permits and facilities for the pursuit of studies in foreign countries;

(d)   Not to allow, in any form of assistance granted by the public authorities to educational institutions, any restrictions or preference based solely on the ground that pupils belong to a particular group;

(e)   To give foreign nationals resident within their territory the same access to education as that given to their own nationals.

Article 4

The States Parties to this Convention undertake furthermore to formulate, develop and apply a national policy which, by methods appropriate to the circumstances and to national usage, will tend to promote equality of opportunity and of treatment in the matter of education and in particular:

(a)   To make primary education free and compulsory; make secondary education in its different forms generally available and accessible to all; make higher education equally accessible to all on the basis of individual capacity; assure compliance by all with the obligation to attend school prescribed by law;

(b)   To ensure that the standards of education are equivalent in all public educational institutions of the same level, and that the conditions relating to the quality of the education provided are also equivalent;

(c)   To encourage and intensify by appropriate methods the education of persons who have not received any primary education or who have not completed the entire primary education course and the continuation of their education on the basis of individual capacity;

(d)   To provide training for the teaching profession without discrimination.

Article 5

1. The States Parties to this Convention agree that:

(a)   Education shall be directed to the full development of the human personality and to the strengthening of respect for human rights and fundamental freedoms; it shall promote understanding, tolerance and friendship among all nations, racial or religious groups, and shall further the activities of the United Nations for the maintenance of peace;

(b)   It is essential to respect the liberty of parents and, where applicable, of legal guardians, firstly to choose for their children institutions other than those maintained by the public authorities but conforming to such minimum educational standards as may be laid down or approved by the competent authorities and, secondly, to ensure in a manner consistent with the procedures followed in the State for the application of its legislation, the religious and moral education of the children in conformity with their own convictions; and no person or group of persons should be compelled to receive religious instruction inconsistent with his or their convictions;

(c)   It is essential to recognize the right of members of national minorities to carry on their own educational activities, including the maintenance of schools and, depending on the educational policy of each State, the use or the teaching of their own language, provided however:

(i)   That this right is not exercised in a manner which prevents the members of these minorities from understanding the culture and language of the community as a whole and from participating in its activities, or which prejudices national sovereignty;

(ii)   That the standard of education is not lower than the general standard laid down or approved by the competent authorities; and

(iii)   That attendance at such schools is optional.

2. The States Parties to this Convention undertake to take all necessary measures to ensure the application of the principles enunciated in paragraph 1 of this Article.

'**attendance at such schools is optional**' (Art 5(c)(iii))—Note that by reason of the fact that the attendance at schools arising out of the exercise of the right of members of national minorities to carry on their own educational activities, including the maintenance of school, is optional, the entitlements under Art 5 are not unconditional. See also the Committee on the Elimination of Racial Discrimination General Recommendation XXIX (2002) HRI/GEN/1/Rev 8, p 272 and *Jean Claude Mahe v Alberta* [1980] 1 SCR 342 (Sup Ct Canada), *Wisconsin v Yoder* 406 US 205 (1972) (US Sup Ct) and *Prince v Massachusetts* 321 US 158 (1944) (US Sup Ct) and Committee on Economic, Social and Cultural Rights General Comment No 13 *The Right to Education (Article 13)* E/C.12/1999/10, paras 28–30.

Article 6

In the application of this Convention, the States Parties to it undertake to pay the greatest attention to any recommendations hereafter adopted by the General Conference of the United Nations Educational, Scientific and Cultural Organization defining the measures to be taken against the different forms of discrimination in education and for the purpose of ensuring equality of opportunity and treatment in education.

Article 7

The States Parties to this Convention shall in their periodic reports submitted to the General Conference of the United Nations Educational, Scientific and Cultural Organization on dates and in a manner to be determined by it, give information on the legislative and administrative provisions which they have adopted and other action which they have taken for the application of this Convention, including that taken for the formulation and the development of the national policy defined in Article 4 as well as the results achieved and the obstacles encountered in the application of that policy.

Article 8

Any dispute which may arise between any two or more States Parties to this Convention concerning the interpretation or application of this Convention, which is not settled by negotiation shall at the request of the parties to the dispute be referred, failing other means of settling the dispute, to the International Court of Justice for decision.

Article 9

Reservations to this Convention shall not be permitted.

Article 10

This Convention shall not have the effect of diminishing the rights which individuals or groups may enjoy by virtue of agreements concluded between two or more States, where such rights are not contrary to the letter or spirit of this Convention.

Article 11

This Convention is drawn up in English, French, Russian and Spanish, the four texts being equally authoritative.

Article 12

1. This Convention shall be subject to ratification or acceptance by States Members of the United Nations Educational, Scientific and Cultural Organization in accordance with their respective constitutional procedures.

2. The instruments of ratification or acceptance shall be deposited with the Director-General of the United Nations Educational, Scientific and Cultural Organization.

Article 13

1. This Convention shall be open to accession by all States not Members of the United Nations Educational, Scientific and Cultural Organization which are invited to do so by the Executive Board of the Organization.

2. Accession shall be effected by the deposit of an instrument of accession with the Director-General of the United Nations Educational, Scientific and Cultural Organization.

Article 14

This Convention shall enter into force three months after the date of the deposit of the third instrument of ratification, acceptance or accession, but only with respect to those States which have deposited their respective instruments on or before that date. It shall enter into force with respect to any other State three months after the deposit of its instrument of ratification, acceptance or accession.

Article 15

The States Parties to this Convention recognize that the Convention is applicable not only to their metropolitan territory but also to all non-self-governing, trust, colonial and other territories for the international relations of which they are responsible; they undertake to consult, if necessary, the governments or other competent authorities of these territories on or before ratification, acceptance or accession with a view to securing the application of the Convention to those territories, and to notify the Director-General of the United Nations Educational, Scientific and Cultural Organization of the territories to which it is accordingly applied, the notification to take effect three months after the date of its receipt.

Article 16

1. Each State Party to this Convention may denounce the Convention on its own behalf or on behalf of any territory for whose international relations it is responsible.

2. The denunciation shall be notified by an instrument in writing, deposited with the Director-General of the United Nations Educational, Scientific and Cultural Organization.

3. The denunciation shall take effect twelve months after the receipt of the instrument of denunciation.

Article 17

The Director-General of the United Nations Educational, Scientific and Cultural Organization shall inform the States Members of the Organization, the States not members of the Organization which are referred to in Article 13, as well as the United Nations, of the deposit of all the instruments of ratification, acceptance and accession provided for in Articles 12 and 13, and of the notifications and denunciations provided for in Articles 15 and 16 respectively.

Article 18

1. This Convention may be revised by the General Conference of the United Nations Educational, Scientific and Cultural Organization. Any such revision shall, however, bind only the States which shall become Parties to the revising convention.

2. If the General Conference should adopt a new convention revising this Convention in whole or in part, then, unless the new convention otherwise provides, this Convention

shall cease to be open to ratification, acceptance or accession as from the date on which the new revising convention enters into force.

Article 19

In conformity with Article 102 of the Charter of the United Nations, this Convention shall be registered with the Secretariat of the United Nations at the request of the Director-General of the United Nations Educational, Scientific and Cultural Organization.

Done in Paris, this fifteenth day of December 1960, in two authentic copies bearing the signatures of the President of the eleventh session of the General Conference and of the Director-General of the United Nations Educational, Scientific and Cultural Organization, which shall be deposited in the archives of the United Nations Educational, Scientific and Cultural Organization, and certified true copies of which shall be delivered to all the States referred to in Articles 12 and 13 as well as to the United Nations. The foregoing is the authentic text of the Convention duly adopted by the General Conference of the United Nations Educational, Scientific and Cultural Organization during its eleventh session, which was held in Paris and declared closed the fifteenth day of December 1960.

IN FAITH WHEREOF we have appended our signatures this fifteenth day of December 1960.

The President of the General Conference
The Director-General

CHAPTER 14

CONVENTION CONCERNING MINIMUM AGE FOR ADMISSION TO EMPLOYMENT – CONVENTION C138

PREAMBLE

The General Conference of the International Labour Organisation,

Having been convened at Geneva by the Governing Body of the International Labour Office, and having met in its Fifty-eighth Session on 6 June 1973, and

Having decided upon the adoption of certain proposals with regard to minimum age for admission to employment, which is the fourth item on the agenda of the session, and

Noting the terms of the Minimum Age (Industry) Convention, 1919, the Minimum Age (Sea) Convention, 1920, the Minimum Age (Agriculture) Convention, 1921, the Minimum Age (Trimmers and Stokers) Convention, 1921, the Minimum Age (Non-Industrial Employment) Convention, 1932, the Minimum Age (Sea) Convention (Revised), 1936, the Minimum Age (Industry) Convention (Revised), 1937, the Minimum Age (Non-Industrial Employment) Convention (Revised), 1937, the Minimum Age (Fishermen) Convention, 1959, and the Minimum Age (Underground Work) Convention, 1965, and

Considering that the time has come to establish a general instrument on the subject, which would gradually replace the existing ones applicable to limited economic sectors, with a view to achieving the total abolition of child labour, and

Having determined that these proposals shall take the form of an international Convention, adopts this twenty-sixth day of June of the year one thousand nine hundred and seventy-three the following Convention, which may be cited as the Minimum Age Convention, 1973.

Status—The International Labour Organisation is a specialised agency of the United Nations which seeks to improve living and working conditions [**RCLP para 2.43**]. The ILO Convention Concerning Minimum Age for Admission into Employment consolidates principles established in earlier instruments, namely those set out in the Preamble and Art 10 below [**RCLP para 15.84**]. The ILO Convention Concerning Minimum Age for Admission into Employment must be read with the ILO Recommendation (No 146) [**RCLP para 15.84**]. The Convention applies to all sectors of economic activity in which children are involved.

Article 1

Each Member for which this Convention is in force undertakes to pursue a national policy designed to ensure the effective abolition of child labour and to raise progressively the minimum age for admission to employment or work to a level consistent with the fullest physical and mental development of young persons.

Article 2

1. Each Member which ratifies this Convention shall specify, in a declaration appended to its ratification, a minimum age for admission to employment or work within its territory and on means of transport registered in its territory; subject to Articles 4 to 8 of this Convention, no one under that age shall be admitted to employment or work in any occupation.

2. Each Member which has ratified this Convention may subsequently notify the Director-General of the International Labour Office, by further declarations, that it specifies a minimum age higher than that previously specified.

3. The minimum age specified in pursuance of paragraph 1 of this Article shall not be less than the age of completion of compulsory schooling and, in any case, shall not be less than 15 years.

4. Notwithstanding the provisions of paragraph 3 of this Article, a Member whose economy and educational facilities are insufficiently developed may, after consultation with the organisations of employers and workers concerned, where such exist, initially specify a minimum age of 14 years.

5. Each Member which has specified a minimum age of 14 years in pursuance of the provisions of the preceding paragraph shall include in its reports on the application of this Convention submitted under article 22 of the Constitution of the International Labour Organisation a statement–

   (a)   that its reason for doing so subsists; or
   (b)   that it renounces its right to avail itself of the provisions in question as from a
          stated date.

'**minimum age**' (Art 2(3))—Note that the provisions of Art 2(3) must be read with the general duty stipulated by Art 1 'to raise progressively the minimum age for admission to employment or work to a level consistent with the fullest physical and mental development of young persons' and Art 7(1) of the ILO Recommendation No 146 which recommends that States parties take as their objective the progressive raising to 16 years of the minimum age for admission to employment or work [**RCLP para 15.85**].

Article 3

1. The minimum age for admission to any type of employment or work which by its nature or the circumstances in which it is carried out is likely to jeopardise the health, safety or morals of young persons shall not be less than 18 years.

2. The types of employment or work to which paragraph 1 of this Article applies shall be determined by national laws or regulations or by the competent authority, after consultation with the organisations of employers and workers concerned, where such exist.

3. Notwithstanding the provisions of paragraph 1 of this Article, national laws or regulations or the competent authority may, after consultation with the organisations of employers and workers concerned, where such exist, authorise employment or work as from the age of 16 years on condition that the health, safety and morals of the young persons concerned are fully protected and that the young persons have received adequate specific instruction or vocational training in the relevant branch of activity.

Article 4

1. In so far as necessary, the competent authority, after consultation with the organisations of employers and workers concerned, where such exist, may exclude from

the application of this Convention limited categories of employment or work in respect of which special and substantial problems of application arise.

2. Each Member which ratifies this Convention shall list in its first report on the application of the Convention submitted under article 22 of the Constitution of the International Labour Organisation any categories which may have been excluded in pursuance of paragraph 1 of this Article, giving the reasons for such exclusion, and shall state in subsequent reports the position of its law and practice in respect of the categories excluded and the extent to which effect has been given or is proposed to be given to the Convention in respect of such categories.

3. Employment or work covered by Article 3 of this Convention shall not be excluded from the application of the Convention in pursuance of this Article.

Article 5

1. A Member whose economy and administrative facilities are insufficiently developed may, after consultation with the organisations of employers and workers concerned, where such exist, initially limit the scope of application of this Convention.

2. Each Member which avails itself of the provisions of paragraph 1 of this Article shall specify, in a declaration appended to its ratification, the branches of economic activity or types of undertakings to which it will apply the provisions of the Convention.

3. The provisions of the Convention shall be applicable as a minimum to the following: mining and quarrying; manufacturing; construction; electricity, gas and water; sanitary services; transport, storage and communication; and plantations and other agricultural undertakings mainly producing for commercial purposes, but excluding family and small-scale holdings producing for local consumption and not regularly employing hired workers.

4. Any Member which has limited the scope of application of this Convention in pursuance of this Article–

(a) shall indicate in its reports under Article 22 of the Constitution of the International Labour Organisation the general position as regards the employment or work of young persons and children in the branches of activity which are excluded from the scope of application of this Convention and any progress which may have been made towards wider application of the provisions of the Convention;

(b) may at any time formally extend the scope of application by a declaration addressed to the Director-General of the International Labour Office.

Article 6

This Convention does not apply to work done by children and young persons in schools for general, vocational or technical education or in other training institutions, or to work done by persons at least 14 years of age in undertakings, where such work is carried out in accordance with conditions prescribed by the competent authority, after consultation with the organisations of employers and workers concerned, where such exist, and is an integral part of–

(a) a course of education or training for which a school or training institution is primarily responsible;

(b) a programme of training mainly or entirely in an undertaking, which programme has been approved by the competent authority; or

(c) a programme of guidance or orientation designed to facilitate the choice of an occupation or of a line of training.

Article 7

1. National laws or regulations may permit the employment or work of persons 13 to 15 years of age on light work which is–

   (a)   not likely to be harmful to their health or development; and
   (b)   not such as to prejudice their attendance at school, their participation in vocational orientation or training programmes approved by the competent authority or their capacity to benefit from the instruction received.

2. National laws or regulations may also permit the employment or work of persons who are at least 15 years of age but have not yet completed their compulsory schooling on work which meets the requirements set forth in sub-paragraphs (a) and (b) of paragraph 1 of this Article.

3. The competent authority shall determine the activities in which employment or work may be permitted under paragraphs 1 and 2 of this Article and shall prescribe the number of hours during which and the conditions in which such employment or work may be undertaken.

4. Notwithstanding the provisions of paragraphs 1 and 2 of this Article, a Member which has availed itself of the provisions of paragraph 4 of Article 2 may, for as long as it continues to do so, substitute the ages 12 and 14 for the ages 13 and 15 in paragraph 1 and the age 14 for the age 15 in paragraph 2 of this Article.

Article 8

1. After consultation with the organisations of employers and workers concerned, where such exist, the competent authority may, by permits granted in individual cases, allow exceptions to the prohibition of employment or work provided for in Article 2 of this Convention, for such purposes as participation in artistic performances.

2. Permits so granted shall limit the number of hours during which and prescribe the conditions in which employment or work is allowed.

Article 9

1. All necessary measures, including the provision of appropriate penalties, shall be taken by the competent authority to ensure the effective enforcement of the provisions of this Convention.

2. National laws or regulations or the competent authority shall define the persons responsible for compliance with the provisions giving effect to the Convention.

3. National laws or regulations or the competent authority shall prescribe the registers or other documents which shall be kept and made available by the employer; such registers or documents shall contain the names and ages or dates of birth, duly certified wherever possible, of persons whom he employs or who work for him and who are less than 18 years of age.

'**All necessary measures**' (Art 9(1))—Taking all necessary measures will include stipulating the registers or other documents which shall be kept and made available by the employer containing the names and ages or dates or birth, duly certified wherever possible, of the persons employed or working who are less than 18 years of age (see ILO Recommendation No 146 Art 14 and *Child Labour: Targeting the Intolerable* International Labour Conference, Eighty-sixth Session (1998) ILO, pp 40–49) [RCLP para 15.90].

Article 10

1. This Convention revises, on the terms set forth in this Article, the Minimum Age (Industry) Convention, 1919, the Minimum Age (Sea) Convention, 1920, the Minimum

Age (Agriculture) Convention, 1921, the Minimum Age (Trimmers and Stokers) Convention, 1921, the Minimum Age (Non-Industrial Employment) Convention, 1932, the Minimum Age (Sea) Convention (Revised), 1936, the Minimum Age (Industry) Convention (Revised), 1937, the Minimum Age (Non-Industrial Employment) Convention (Revised), 1937, the Minimum Age (Fishermen) Convention, 1959, and the Minimum Age (Underground Work) Convention, 1965.

2. The coming into force of this Convention shall not close the Minimum Age (Sea) Convention (Revised), 1936, the Minimum Age (Industry) Convention (Revised), 1937, the Minimum Age (Non-Industrial Employment) Convention (Revised), 1937, the Minimum Age (Fishermen) Convention, 1959, or the Minimum Age (Underground Work) Convention, 1965, to further ratification.

3. The Minimum Age (Industry) Convention, 1919, the Minimum Age (Sea) Convention, 1920, the Minimum Age (Agriculture) Convention, 1921, and the Minimum Age (Trimmers and Stokers) Convention, 1921, shall be closed to further ratification when all the parties thereto have consented to such closing by ratification of this Convention or by a declaration communicated to the Director-General of the International Labour Office.

4. When the obligations of this Convention are accepted–

(a)   by a Member which is a party to the Minimum Age (Industry) Convention (Revised), 1937, and a minimum age of not less than 15 years is specified in pursuance of Article 2 of this Convention, this shall ipso jure involve the immediate denunciation of that Convention,

(b)   in respect of non-industrial employment as defined in the Minimum Age (Non-Industrial Employment) Convention, 1932, by a Member which is a party to that Convention, this shall ipso jure involve the immediate denunciation of that Convention,

(c)   in respect of non-industrial employment as defined in the Minimum Age (Non-Industrial Employment) Convention (Revised), 1937, by a Member which is a party to that Convention, and a minimum age of not less than 15 years is specified in pursuance of Article 2 of this Convention, this shall ipso jure involve the immediate denunciation of that Convention,

(d)   in respect of maritime employment, by a Member which is a party to the Minimum Age (Sea) Convention (Revised), 1936, and a minimum age of not less than 15 years is specified in pursuance of Article 2 of this Convention or the Member specifies that Article 3 of this Convention applies to maritime employment, this shall ipso jure involve the immediate denunciation of that Convention,

(e)   in respect of employment in maritime fishing, by a Member which is a party to the Minimum Age (Fishermen) Convention, 1959, and a minimum age of not less than 15 years is specified in pursuance of Article 2 of this Convention or the Member specifies that Article 3 of this Convention applies to employment in maritime fishing, this shall ipso jure involve the immediate denunciation of that Convention,

(f)   by a Member which is a party to the Minimum Age (Underground Work) Convention, 1965, and a minimum age of not less than the age specified in pursuance of that Convention is specified in pursuance of Article 2 of this Convention or the Member specifies that such an age applies to employment underground in mines in virtue of Article 3 of this Convention, this shall ipso jure involve the immediate denunciation of that Convention,

if and when this Convention shall have come into force.

5. Acceptance of the obligations of this Convention–

(a)   shall involve the denunciation of the Minimum Age (Industry) Convention, 1919, in accordance with Article 12 thereof,

(b)   in respect of agriculture shall involve the denunciation of the Minimum Age (Agriculture) Convention, 1921, in accordance with Article 9 thereof,

(c)   in respect of maritime employment shall involve the denunciation of the Minimum Age (Sea) Convention, 1920, in accordance with Article 10 thereof, and of the Minimum Age (Trimmers and Stokers) Convention, 1921, in accordance with Article 12 thereof, if and when this Convention shall have come into force.

Article 11

The formal ratifications of this Convention shall be communicated to the Director-General of the International Labour Office for registration.

Article 12

1. This Convention shall be binding only upon those Members of the International Labour Organisation whose ratifications have been registered with the Director-General.

2. It shall come into force twelve months after the date on which the ratifications of two Members have been registered with the Director-General.

3. Thereafter, this Convention shall come into force for any Member twelve months after the date on which its ratifications has been registered.

Article 13

1. A Member which has ratified this Convention may denounce it after the expiration of ten years from the date on which the Convention first comes into force, by an act communicated to the Director-General of the International Labour Office for registration. Such denunciation shall not take effect until one year after the date on which it is registered.

2. Each Member which has ratified this Convention and which does not, within the year following the expiration of the period of ten years mentioned in the preceding paragraph, exercise the right of denunciation provided for in this Article, will be bound for another period of ten years and, thereafter, may denounce this Convention at the expiration of each period of ten years under the terms provided for in this Article.

Article 14

1. The Director-General of the International Labour Office shall notify all Members of the International Labour Organisation of the registration of all ratifications and denunciations communicated to him by the Members of the Organisation.

2. When notifying the Members of the Organisation of the registration of the second ratification communicated to him, the Director-General shall draw the attention of the Members of the Organisation to the date upon which the Convention will come into force.

Article 15

The Director-General of the International Labour Office shall communicate to the Secretary-General of the United Nations for registration in accordance with Article 102 of the Charter of the United Nations full particulars of all ratifications and acts of denunciation registered by him in accordance with the provisions of the preceding Articles.

Article 16

At such times as it may consider necessary the Governing Body of the International Labour Office shall present to the General Conference a report on the working of this Convention and shall examine the desirability of placing on the agenda of the Conference the question of its revision in whole or in part.

Article 17

1. Should the Conference adopt a new Convention revising this Convention in whole or in part, then, unless the new Convention otherwise provides:

   (a)   the ratification by a Member of the new revising Convention shall ipso jure involve the immediate denunciation of this Convention, notwithstanding the provisions of Article 13 above, if and when the new revising Convention shall have come into force;
   (b)   as from the date when the new revising Convention comes into force this Convention shall cease to be open to ratification by the Members.

2. This Convention shall in any case remain in force in its actual form and content for those Members which have ratified it but have not ratified the revising Convention.

Article 18

The English and French versions of the text of this Convention are equally authoritative.

CHAPTER 15

CONVENTION CONCERNING THE PROHIBITION AND IMMEDIATE ACTION FOR THE ELIMINATION OF THE WORST FORMS OF CHILD LABOUR – CONVENTION C182

PREAMBLE

The General Conference of the International Labour Organization,

Having been convened at Geneva by the Governing Body of the International Labour Office, and having met in its 87th Session on 1 June 1999, and

Considering the need to adopt new instruments for the prohibition and elimination of the worst forms of child labour, as the main priority for national and international action, including international cooperation and assistance, to complement the Convention and the Recommendation concerning Minimum Age for Admission to Employment, 1973, which remain fundamental instruments on child labour, and

Considering that the effective elimination of the worst forms of child labour requires immediate and comprehensive action, taking into account the importance of free basic education and the need to remove the children concerned from all such work and to provide for their rehabilitation and social integration while addressing the needs of their families, and

Recalling the resolution concerning the elimination of child labour adopted by the International Labour Conference at its 83rd Session in 1996, and

Recognizing that child labour is to a great extent caused by poverty and that the long-term solution lies in sustained economic growth leading to social progress, in particular poverty alleviation and universal education, and

Recalling the Convention on the Rights of the Child adopted by the United Nations General Assembly on 20 November 1989, and

Recalling the ILO Declaration on Fundamental Principles and Rights at Work and its Follow-up, adopted by the International Labour Conference at its 86th Session in 1998, and

Recalling that some of the worst forms of child labour are covered by other international instruments, in particular the Forced Labour Convention, 1930, and the United Nations Supplementary Convention on the Abolition of Slavery, the Slave Trade, and Institutions and Practices Similar to Slavery, 1956, and

Having decided upon the adoption of certain proposals with regard to child labour, which is the fourth item on the agenda of the session, and

Having determined that these proposals shall take the form of an international Convention; adopts this seventeenth day of June of the year one thousand nine hundred and ninety-nine the following Convention, which may be cited as the Worst Forms of Child Labour Convention, 1999.

Status—The International Labour Organisation is a specialised agency of the United Nations which seeks to improve living and working conditions [**RCLP para 2.43**]. The ILO Convention concerning the Prohibition and Immediate Action for the Elimination of the Worst Forms of Child Labour requires State parties to take immediate and effective measures to prohibit the worst forms of child labour [**RCLP para 2.44**]. The Convention must be read with the ILO Worst Forms of Child Labour Recommendation (No 190) [**RCLP para 15.84**]. The status of the ILO Convention concerning the Prohibition and Immediate Action for the Elimination of the Worst Forms of Child Labour is that of a binding international Convention not incorporated into domestic law [**RCLP para 3.94**]. The United Kingdom ratified the Convention on 22 March 2000 [**RCLP para 2.44**]. The Convention should be read with Art 32 of the UNCRC [**RCLP para 15.80**]. See also *R v L and other cases* [2013] EWCA Crim 991 and *AA v Secretary of State for the Home Department and another* [2012] UKUT 00016 (IAC), para 85.

Article 1

Each Member which ratifies this Convention shall take immediate and effective measures to secure the prohibition and elimination of the worst forms of child labour as a matter of urgency.

Article 2

For the purposes of this Convention, the term *child* shall apply to all persons under the age of 18.

Article 3

For the purposes of this Convention, the term *the worst forms of child labour* comprises:

(a) all forms of slavery or practices similar to slavery, such as the sale and trafficking of children, debt bondage and serfdom and forced or compulsory labour, including forced or compulsory recruitment of children for use in armed conflict;

(b) the use, procuring or offering of a child for prostitution, for the production of pornography or for pornographic performances;

(c) the use, procuring or offering of a child for illicit activities, in particular for the production and trafficking of drugs as defined in the relevant international treaties;

(d) work which, by its nature or the circumstances in which it is carried out, is likely to harm the health, safety or morals of children.

Article 4

1. The types of work referred to under Article 3(d) shall be determined by national laws or regulations or by the competent authority, after consultation with the organizations of employers and workers concerned, taking into consideration relevant international standards, in particular Paragraphs 3 and 4 of the Worst Forms of Child Labour Recommendation, 1999.

2. The competent authority, after consultation with the organizations of employers and workers concerned, shall identify where the types of work so determined exist.

3. The list of the types of work determined under paragraph 1 of this Article shall be periodically examined and revised as necessary, in consultation with the organizations of employers and workers concerned.

Article 5

Each Member shall, after consultation with employers' and workers' organizations, establish or designate appropriate mechanisms to monitor the implementation of the provisions giving effect to this Convention.

Article 6

1. Each Member shall design and implement programmes of action to eliminate as a priority the worst forms of child labour.

2. Such programmes of action shall be designed and implemented in consultation with relevant government institutions and employers' and workers' organizations, taking into consideration the views of other concerned groups as appropriate.

Article 7

1. Each Member shall take all necessary measures to ensure the effective implementation and enforcement of the provisions giving effect to this Convention including the provision and application of penal sanctions or, as appropriate, other sanctions.

2. Each Member shall, taking into account the importance of education in eliminating child labour, take effective and time-bound measures to:

(a)   prevent the engagement of children in the worst forms of child labour;
(b)   provide the necessary and appropriate direct assistance for the removal of children from the worst forms of child labour and for their rehabilitation and social integration;
(c)   ensure access to free basic education, and, wherever possible and appropriate, vocational training, for all children removed from the worst forms of child labour;
(d)   identify and reach out to children at special risk; and
(e)   take account of the special situation of girls.

3. Each Member shall designate the competent authority responsible for the implementation of the provisions giving effect to this Convention.

Article 8

Members shall take appropriate steps to assist one another in giving effect to the provisions of this Convention through enhanced international cooperation and/or assistance including support for social and economic development, poverty eradication programmes and universal education.

Article 9

The formal ratifications of this Convention shall be communicated to the Director-General of the International Labour Office for registration.

Article 10

1. This Convention shall be binding only upon those Members of the International Labour Organization whose ratifications have been registered with the Director-General of the International Labour Office.

2. It shall come into force 12 months after the date on which the ratifications of two Members have been registered with the Director-General.

3. Thereafter, this Convention shall come into force for any Member 12 months after the date on which its ratification has been registered.

Article 11

1. A Member which has ratified this Convention may denounce it after the expiration of ten years from the date on which the Convention first comes into force, by an act communicated to the Director-General of the International Labour Office for registration. Such denunciation shall not take effect until one year after the date on which it is registered.

2. Each Member which has ratified this Convention and which does not, within the year following the expiration of the period of ten years mentioned in the preceding paragraph, exercise the right of denunciation provided for in this Article, will be bound for another period of ten years and, thereafter, may denounce this Convention at the expiration of each period of ten years under the terms provided for in this Article.

Article 12

1. The Director-General of the International Labour Office shall notify all Members of the International Labour Organization of the registration of all ratifications and acts of denunciation communicated by the Members of the Organization.

2. When notifying the Members of the Organization of the registration of the second ratification, the Director-General shall draw the attention of the Members of the Organization to the date upon which the Convention shall come into force.

Article 13

The Director-General of the International Labour Office shall communicate to the Secretary-General of the United Nations, for registration in accordance with article 102 of the Charter of the United Nations, full particulars of all ratifications and acts of denunciation registered by the Director-General in accordance with the provisions of the preceding Articles.

Article 14

At such times as it may consider necessary, the Governing Body of the International Labour Office shall present to the General Conference a report on the working of this Convention and shall examine the desirability of placing on the agenda of the Conference the question of its revision in whole or in part.

Article 15

1. Should the Conference adopt a new Convention revising this Convention in whole or in part, then, unless the new Convention otherwise provides –

(a) the ratification by a Member of the new revising Convention shall ipso jure involve the immediate denunciation of this Convention, notwithstanding the provisions of Article 11 above, if and when the new revising Convention shall have come into force;

(b) as from the date when the new revising Convention comes into force, this Convention shall cease to be open to ratification by the Members.

2. This Convention shall in any case remain in force in its actual form and content for those Members which have ratified it but have not ratified the revising Convention.

Article 16

The English and French versions of the text of this Convention are equally authoritative.

CHAPTER 16

CONVENTION (III) RELATIVE TO THE TREATMENT OF PRISONERS OF WAR GENEVA, 12 AUGUST 1949

PREAMBLE

The undersigned Plenipotentiaries of the Governments represented at the Diplomatic Conference held at Geneva from April 21 to August 12, 1949, for the purpose of revising the Convention concluded at Geneva on July 27, 1929, relative to the Treatment of Prisoners of War, have agreed as follows:

Status—The status of the four Geneva Conventions is that of binding international Conventions not incorporated into domestic law [RCLP para 3.94]. The four Geneva Conventions are Convention I for the Amelioration of the Condition of the Wounded and Sick in Armed Forces in the Field, Convention II for the Amelioration of the Condition of Wounded, Sick and Shipwrecked Members of the Armed Forces, Convention III Relative to the Treatment of Prisoners of War and Convention IV Relative to the Protection of Civilian Persons in Time of War [RCLP para 15.121]. Only Conventions III and IV are included in this work. Two additional protocols were added to the Geneva Conventions in 1977. Protocols I and II are included in this work. The United Kingdom ratified Protocols I and II on 28 January 1998 and registered reservations in respect of Protocol I [RCLP para 15.121]. Protocol III (which is not included in this work) provides for the addition of a non-religious and politically neutral emblem of the 'red crystal' to the Red Cross and Red Crescent emblems. The Geneva Conventions should be read with the Protocol to the UNCRC on the Protection of Children from Involvement in Armed Conflict and the Paris Commitments and Principles concerning the protection of children from unlawful recruitment or used by armed forces or armed groups [RCLP para 2.59].

PART I
GENERAL PROVISIONS

Article 1

The High Contracting Parties undertake to respect and to ensure respect for the present Convention in all circumstances.

Article 2

In addition to the provisions which shall be implemented in peace time, the present Convention shall apply to all cases of declared war or of any other armed conflict which may arise between two or more of the High Contracting Parties, even if the state of war is not recognized by one of them.

The Convention shall also apply to all cases of partial or total occupation of the territory of a High Contracting Party, even if the said occupation meets with no armed resistance.

Although one of the Powers in conflict may not be a party to the present Convention, the Powers who are parties thereto shall remain bound by it in their mutual relations. They shall furthermore be bound by the Convention in relation to the said Power, if the latter accepts and applies the provisions thereof.

Article 3

In the case of armed conflict not of an international character occurring in the territory of one of the High Contracting Parties, each Party to the conflict shall be bound to apply, as a minimum, the following provisions:

(1) Persons taking no active part in the hostilities, including members of armed forces who have laid down their arms and those placed hors de combat by sickness, wounds, detention, or any other cause, shall in all circumstances be treated humanely, without any adverse distinction founded on race, colour, religion or faith, sex, birth or wealth, or any other similar criteria. To this end the following acts are and shall remain prohibited at any time and in any place whatsoever with respect to the above-mentioned persons:

   (a)   violence to life and person, in particular murder of all kinds, mutilation, cruel treatment and torture;
   (b)   taking of hostages;
   (c)   outrages upon personal dignity, in particular, humiliating and degrading treatment;
   (d)   the passing of sentences and the carrying out of executions without previous judgment pronounced by a regularly constituted court affording all the judicial guarantees which are recognized as indispensable by civilized peoples.

(2) The wounded and sick shall be collected and cared for.

An impartial humanitarian body, such as the International Committee of the Red Cross, may offer its services to the Parties to the conflict.

The Parties to the conflict should further endeavour to bring into force, by means of special agreements, all or part of the other provisions of the present Convention.

The application of the preceding provisions shall not affect the legal status of the Parties to the conflict.

Article 4

A. Prisoners of war, in the sense of the present Convention, are persons belonging to one of the following categories, who have fallen into the power of the enemy:

(1) Members of the armed forces of a Party to the conflict, as well as members of militias or volunteer corps forming part of such armed forces.

(2) Members of other militias and members of other volunteer corps, including those of organized resistance movements, belonging to a Party to the conflict and operating in or outside their own territory, even if this territory is occupied, provided that such militias or volunteer corps, including such organized resistance movements, fulfil the following conditions:

   (a)   that of being commanded by a person responsible for his subordinates;
   (b)   that of having a fixed distinctive sign recognizable at a distance;
   (c)   that of carrying arms openly;
   (d)   that of conducting their operations in accordance with the laws and customs of war.

(3) Members of regular armed forces who profess allegiance to a government or an authority not recognized by the Detaining Power.

(4) Persons who accompany the armed forces without actually being members thereof, such as civilian members of military aircraft crews, war correspondents, supply contractors, members of labour units or of services responsible for the welfare of the

armed forces, provided that they have received authorization, from the armed forces which they accompany, who shall provide them for that purpose with an identity card similar to the annexed model.

(5) Members of crews, including masters, pilots and apprentices, of the merchant marine and the crews of civil aircraft of the Parties to the conflict, who do not benefit by more favourable treatment under any other provisions of international law.

(6) Inhabitants of a non-occupied territory, who on the approach of the enemy spontaneously take up arms to resist the invading forces, without having had time to form themselves into regular armed units, provided they carry arms openly and respect the laws and customs of war.

B. The following shall likewise be treated as prisoners of war under the present Convention:

(1) Persons belonging, or having belonged, to the armed forces of the occupied country, if the occupying Power considers it necessary by reason of such allegiance to intern them, even though it has originally liberated them while hostilities were going on outside the territory it occupies, in particular where such persons have made an unsuccessful attempt to rejoin the armed forces to which they belong and which are engaged in combat, or where they fail to comply with a summons made to them with a view to internment.

(2) The persons belonging to one of the categories enumerated in the present Article, who have been received by neutral or non-belligerent Powers on their territory and whom these Powers are required to intern under international law, without prejudice to any more favourable treatment which these Powers may choose to give and with the exception of Articles 8, 10, 15, 30, fifth paragraph, 58-67, 92, 126 and, where diplomatic relations exist between the Parties to the conflict and the neutral or non-belligerent Power concerned, those Articles concerning the Protecting Power. Where such diplomatic relations exist, the Parties to a conflict on whom these persons depend shall be allowed to perform towards them the functions of a Protecting Power as provided in the present Convention, without prejudice to the functions which these Parties normally exercise in conformity with diplomatic and consular usage and treaties.

C. This Article shall in no way affect the status of medical personnel and chaplains as provided for in Article 33 of the present Convention.

'persons belonging to one of the following categories' (Art 4)—The definition of prisoners of war is not age dependent and accordingly the protection provided by Geneva Convention III will extend to children even though the participation of children under the age of 15 is prohibited by under Art 77(2) of Protocol I and Art 4(3)(c) of Protocol II to the Geneva Conventions [RCLP para 14.46]. Note however that the requirements of Art 4A(2)(d) mean that children under the age of 15 years will be excluded from protection where taken by militias or volunteer corps [RCLP para 14.46].

Article 5

The present Convention shall apply to the persons referred to in Article 4 from the time they fall into the power of the enemy and until their final release and repatriation.

Should any doubt arise as to whether persons, having committed a belligerent act and having fallen into the hands of the enemy, belong to any of the categories enumerated in Article 4, such persons shall enjoy the protection of the present Convention until such time as their status has been determined by a competent tribunal.

Article 6

In addition to the agreements expressly provided for in Articles 10, 23, 28, 33, 60, 65, 66, 67, 72, 73, 75, 109, 110, 118, 119, 122 and 132, the High Contracting Parties may conclude other special agreements for all matters concerning which they may deem it suitable to make separate provision. No special agreement shall adversely affect the situation of prisoners of war, as defined by the present Convention, nor restrict the rights which it confers upon them.

Prisoners of war shall continue to have the benefit of such agreements as long as the Convention is applicable to them, except where express provisions to the contrary are contained in the aforesaid or in subsequent agreements, or where more favourable measures have been taken with regard to them by one or other of the Parties to the conflict.

Article 7

Prisoners of war may in no circumstances renounce in part or in entirety the rights secured to them by the present Convention, and by the special agreements referred to in the foregoing Article, if such there be.

Article 8

The present Convention shall be applied with the cooperation and under the scrutiny of the Protecting Powers whose duty it is to safeguard the interests of the Parties to the conflict. For this purpose, the Protecting Powers may appoint, apart from their diplomatic or consular staff, delegates from amongst their own nationals or the nationals of other neutral Powers. The said delegates shall be subject to the approval of the Power with which they are to carry out their duties.

The Parties to the conflict shall facilitate to the greatest extent possible the task of the representatives or delegates of the Protecting Powers.

The representatives or delegates of the Protecting Powers shall not in any case exceed their mission under the present Convention. They shall, in particular, take account of the imperative necessities of security of the State wherein they carry out their duties.

Article 9

The provisions of the present Convention constitute no obstacle to the humanitarian activities which the International Committee of the Red Cross or any other impartial humanitarian organization may, subject to the consent of the Parties to the conflict concerned, undertake for the protection of prisoners of war and for their relief.

Article 10

The High Contracting Parties may at any time agree to entrust to an organization which offers all guarantees of impartiality and efficacy the duties incumbent on the Protecting Powers by virtue of the present Convention.

When prisoners of war do not benefit or cease to benefit, no matter for what reason, by the activities of a Protecting Power or of an organization provided for in the first paragraph above, the Detaining Power shall request a neutral State, or such an organization, to undertake the functions performed under the present Convention by a Protecting Power designated by the Parties to a conflict.

If protection cannot be arranged accordingly, the Detaining Power shall request or shall accept, subject to the provisions of this Article, the offer of the services of a humanitarian organization, such as the International Committee of the Red Cross to assume the humanitarian functions performed by Protecting Powers under the present Convention.

Any neutral Power or any organization invited by the Power concerned or offering itself for these purposes, shall be required to act with a sense of responsibility towards the Party to the conflict on which persons protected by the present Convention depend, and shall be required to furnish sufficient assurances that it is in a position to undertake the appropriate functions and to discharge them impartially.

No derogation from the preceding provisions shall be made by special agreements between Powers one of which is restricted, even temporarily, in its freedom to negotiate with the other Power or its allies by reason of military events, more particularly where the whole, or a substantial part, of the territory of the said Power is occupied.

Whenever in the present Convention mention is made of a Protecting Power, such mention applies to substitute organizations in the sense of the present Article.

Article 11

In cases where they deem it advisable in the interest of protected persons, particularly in cases of disagreement between the Parties to the conflict as to the application or interpretation of the provisions of the present Convention, the Protecting Powers shall lend their good offices with a view to settling the disagreement.

For this purpose, each of the Protecting Powers may, either at the invitation of one Party or on its own initiative, propose to the Parties to the conflict a meeting of their representatives, and in particular of the authorities responsible for prisoners of war, possibly on neutral territory suitably chosen. The Parties to the conflict shall be bound to give effect to the proposals made to them for this purpose. The Protecting Powers may, if necessary, propose for approval by the Parties to the conflict a person belonging to a neutral Power, or delegated by the International Committee of the Red Cross, who shall be invited to take part in such a meeting.

PART II
GENERAL PROTECTION OF PRISONERS OF WAR

Article 12

Prisoners of war are in the hands of the enemy Power, but not of the individuals or military units who have captured them. Irrespective of the individual responsibilities that may exist, the Detaining Power is responsible for the treatment given them.

Prisoners of war may only be transferred by the Detaining Power to a Power which is a party to the Convention and after the Detaining Power has satisfied itself of the willingness and ability of such transferee Power to apply the Convention. When prisoners of war are transferred under such circumstances, responsibility for the application of the Convention rests on the Power accepting them while they are in its custody.

Nevertheless, if that Power fails to carry out the provisions of the Convention in any important respect, the Power by whom the prisoners of war were transferred shall, upon being notified by the Protecting Power, take effective measures to correct the situation or shall request the return of the prisoners of war. Such requests must be complied with.

Article 13

Prisoners of war must at all times be humanely treated. Any unlawful act or omission by the Detaining Power causing death or seriously endangering the health of a prisoner of war in its custody is prohibited, and will be regarded as a serious breach of the present Convention. In particular, no prisoner of war may be subjected to physical mutilation or to medical or scientific experiments of any kind which are not justified by the medical, dental or hospital treatment of the prisoner concerned and carried out in his interest.

Likewise, prisoners of war must at all times be protected, particularly against acts of violence or intimidation and against insults and public curiosity.

Measures of reprisal against prisoners of war are prohibited.

Article 14

Prisoners of war are entitled in all circumstances to respect for their persons and their honour.

Women shall be treated with all the regard due to their sex and shall in all cases benefit by treatment as favourable as that granted to men.

Prisoners of war shall retain the full civil capacity which they enjoyed at the time of their capture. The Detaining Power may not restrict the exercise, either within or without its own territory, of the rights such capacity confers except in so far as the captivity requires.

Article 15

The Power detaining prisoners of war shall be bound to provide free of charge for their maintenance and for the medical attention required by their state of health.

Article 16

Taking into consideration the provisions of the present Convention relating to rank and sex, and subject to any privileged treatment which may be accorded to them by reason of their state of health, age or professional qualifications, all prisoners of war shall be treated alike by the Detaining Power, without any adverse distinction based on race, nationality, religious belief or political opinions, or any other distinction founded on similar criteria.

PART III
CAPTIVITY

Section 1
Beginning of Captivity

Article 17

Every prisoner of war, when questioned on the subject, is bound to give only his surname, first names and rank, date of birth, and army, regimental, personal or serial number, or failing this, equivalent information.

If he wilfully infringes this rule, he may render himself liable to a restriction of the privileges accorded to his rank or status.

Each Party to a conflict is required to furnish the persons under its jurisdiction who are liable to become prisoners of war, with an identity card showing the owner's surname, first names, rank, army, regimental, personal or serial number or equivalent information, and date of birth. The identity card may, furthermore, bear the signature or the fingerprints, or both, of the owner, and may bear, as well, any other information the Party to the conflict may wish to add concerning persons belonging to its armed forces. As far as possible the card shall measure 6.5 x 10 cm. and shall be issued in duplicate. The identity card shall be shown by the prisoner of war upon demand, but may in no case be taken away from him.

No physical or mental torture, nor any other form of coercion, may be inflicted on prisoners of war to secure from them information of any kind whatever. Prisoners of war who refuse to answer may not be threatened, insulted, or exposed to unpleasant or disadvantageous treatment of any kind.

Prisoners of war who, owing to their physical or mental condition, are unable to state their identity, shall be handed over to the medical service. The identity of such prisoners shall be established by all possible means, subject to the provisions of the preceding paragraph.

The questioning of prisoners of war shall be carried out in a language which they understand.

Article 18

All effects and articles of personal use, except arms, horses, military equipment and military documents, shall remain in the possession of prisoners of war, likewise their metal helmets and gas masks and like articles issued for personal protection. Effects and articles used for their clothing or feeding shall likewise remain in their possession, even if such effects and articles belong to their regulation military equipment.

At no time should prisoners of war be without identity documents. The Detaining Power shall supply such documents to prisoners of war who possess none.

Badges of rank and nationality, decorations and articles having above all a personal or sentimental value may not be taken from prisoners of war.

Sums of money carried by prisoners of war may not be taken away from them except by order of an officer, and after the amount and particulars of the owner have been recorded in a special register and an itemized receipt has been given, legibly inscribed with the name, rank and unit of the person issuing the said receipt. Sums in the currency of the Detaining Power, or which are changed into such currency at the prisoner's request, shall be placed to the credit of the prisoner's account as provided in Article 64.

The Detaining Power may withdraw articles of value from prisoners of war only for reasons of security; when such articles are withdrawn, the procedure laid down for sums of money impounded shall apply.

Such objects, likewise sums taken away in any currency other than that of the Detaining Power and the conversion of which has not been asked for by the owners, shall be kept in the custody of the Detaining Power and shall be returned in their initial shape to prisoners of war at the end of their captivity.

Article 19

Prisoners of war shall be evacuated, as soon as possible after their capture, to camps situated in an area far enough from the combat zone for them to be out of danger.

Only those prisoners of war who, owing to wounds or sickness, would run greater risks by being evacuated than by remaining where they are, may be temporarily kept back in a danger zone.

Prisoners of war shall not be unnecessarily exposed to danger while awaiting evacuation from a fighting zone.

Article 20

The evacuation of prisoners of war shall always be effected humanely and in conditions similar to those for the forces of the Detaining Power in their changes of station.

The Detaining Power shall supply prisoners of war who are being evacuated with sufficient food and potable water, and with the necessary clothing and medical attention. The Detaining Power shall take all suitable precautions to ensure their safety during evacuation, and shall establish as soon as possible a list of the prisoners of war who are evacuated.

If prisoners of war must, during evacuation, pass through transit camps, their stay in such camps shall be as brief as possible.

Section II
Internment of Prisoners of War

Chapter I
General Observations

Article 21

The Detaining Power may subject prisoners of war to internment. It may impose on them the obligation of not leaving, beyond certain limits, the camp where they are interned, or if the said camp is fenced in, of not going outside its perimeter. Subject to the provisions of the present Convention relative to penal and disciplinary sanctions, prisoners of war may not be held in close confinement except where necessary to safeguard their health and then only during the continuation of the circumstances which make such confinement necessary.

Prisoners of war may be partially or wholly released on parole or promise, in so far as is allowed by the laws of the Power on which they depend. Such measures shall be taken particularly in cases where this may contribute to the improvement of their state of health. No prisoner of war shall be compelled to accept liberty on parole or promise.

Upon the outbreak of hostilities, each Party to the conflict shall notify the adverse Party of the laws and regulations allowing or forbidding its own nationals to accept liberty on parole or promise. Prisoners of war who are paroled or who have given their promise in conformity with the laws and regulations so notified, are bound on their personal honour scrupulously to fulfil, both towards the Power on which they depend and towards the Power which has captured them, the engagements of their paroles or promises. In such cases, the Power on which they depend is bound neither to require nor to accept from them any service incompatible with the parole or promise given.

Article 22

Prisoners of war may be interned only in premises located on land and affording every guarantee of hygiene and healthfulness. Except in particular cases which are justified by the interest of the prisoners themselves, they shall not be interned in penitentiaries.

Prisoners of war interned in unhealthy areas, or where the climate is injurious for them, shall be removed as soon as possible to a more favourable climate.

The Detaining Power shall assemble prisoners of war in camps or camp compounds according to their nationality, language and customs, provided that such prisoners shall not be separated from prisoners of war belonging to the armed forces with which they were serving at the time of their capture, except with their consent.

Article 23

No prisoner of war may at any time be sent to, or detained in areas where he may be exposed to the fire of the combat zone, nor may his presence be used to render certain points or areas immune from military operations.

Prisoners of war shall have shelters against air bombardment and other hazards of war, to the same extent as the local civilian population. With the exception of those engaged in the protection of their quarters against the aforesaid hazards, they may enter such shelters as soon as possible after the giving of the alarm. Any other protective measure taken in favour of the population shall also apply to them.

Detaining Powers shall give the Powers concerned, through the intermediary of the Protecting Powers, all useful information regarding the geographical location of prisoner of war camps.

Whenever military considerations permit, prisoner of war camps shall be indicated in the day-time by the letters PW or PG, placed so as to be clearly visible from the air. The Powers concerned may, however, agree upon any other system of marking. Only prisoner of war camps shall be marked as such.

Article 24

Transit or screening camps of a permanent kind shall be fitted out under conditions similar to those described in the present Section, and the prisoners therein shall have the same treatment as in other camps.

Chapter II
Quarters, Food and Clothing of Prisoners of War

Article 25

Prisoners of war shall be quartered under conditions as favourable as those for the forces of the Detaining Power who are billeted in the same area. The said conditions shall make allowance for the habits and customs of the prisoners and shall in no case be prejudicial to their health.

The foregoing provisions shall apply in particular to the dormitories of prisoners of war as regards both total surface and minimum cubic space, and the general installations, bedding and blankets.

The premises provided for the use of prisoners of war individually or collectively, shall be entirely protected from dampness and adequately heated and lighted, in particular between dusk and lights out. All precautions must be taken against the danger of fire.

In any camps in which women prisoners of war, as well as men, are accommodated, separate dormitories shall be provided for them.

Article 26

The basic daily food rations shall be sufficient in quantity, quality and variety to keep prisoners of war in good health and to prevent loss of weight or the development of nutritional deficiencies. Account shall also be taken of the habitual diet of the prisoners.

The Detaining Power shall supply prisoners of war who work with such additional rations as are necessary for the labour on which they are employed.

Sufficient drinking water shall be supplied to prisoners of war. The use of tobacco shall be permitted.

Prisoners of war shall, as far as possible, be associated with the preparation of their meals; they may be employed for that purpose in the kitchens. Furthermore, they shall be given the means of preparing, themselves, the additional food in their possession.

Adequate premises shall be provided for messing.

Collective disciplinary measures affecting food are prohibited.

Article 27

Clothing, underwear and footwear shall be supplied to prisoners of war in sufficient quantities by the Detaining Power, which shall make allowance for the climate of the region where the prisoners are detained. Uniforms of enemy armed forces captured by the Detaining Power should, if suitable for the climate, be made available to clothe prisoners of war.

The regular replacement and repair of the above articles shall be assured by the Detaining Power. In addition, prisoners of war who work shall receive appropriate clothing, wherever the nature of the work demands.

Article 28

Canteens shall be installed in all camps, where prisoners of war may procure foodstuffs, soap and tobacco and ordinary articles in daily use. The tariff shall never be in excess of local market prices.

The profits made by camp canteens shall be used for the benefit of the prisoners; a special fund shall be created for this purpose. The prisoners' representative shall have the right to collaborate in the management of the canteen and of this fund.

When a camp is closed down, the credit balance of the special fund shall be handed to an international welfare organization, to be employed for the benefit of prisoners of war of the same nationality as those who have contributed to the fund. In case of a general repatriation, such profits shall be kept by the Detaining Power, subject to any agreement to the contrary between the Powers concerned.

Chapter III
Hygiene and Medical Attention

Article 29

The Detaining Power shall be bound to take all sanitary measures necessary to ensure the cleanliness and healthfulness of camps and to prevent epidemics.

Prisoners of war shall have for their use, day and night, conveniences which conform to the rules of hygiene and are maintained in a constant state of cleanliness. In any camps in which women prisoners of war are accommodated, separate conveniences shall be provided for them.

Also, apart from the baths and showers with which the camps shall be furnished prisoners of war shall be provided with sufficient water and soap for their personal toilet and for washing their personal laundry; the necessary installations, facilities and time shall be granted them for that purpose.

Article 30

Every camp shall have an adequate infirmary where prisoners of war may have the attention they require, as well as appropriate diet. Isolation wards shall, if necessary, be set aside for cases of contagious or mental disease.

Prisoners of war suffering from serious disease, or whose condition necessitates special treatment, a surgical operation or hospital care, must be admitted to any military or civilian medical unit where such treatment can be given, even if their repatriation is contemplated in the near future. Special facilities shall be afforded for the care to be given to the disabled, in particular to the blind, and for their. rehabilitation, pending repatriation.

Prisoners of war shall have the attention, preferably, of medical personnel of the Power on which they depend and, if possible, of their nationality.

Prisoners of war may not be prevented from presenting themselves to the medical authorities for examination. The detaining authorities shall, upon request, issue to every prisoner who has undergone treatment, an official certificate indicating the nature of his illness or injury, and the duration and kind of treatment received. A duplicate of this certificate shall be forwarded to the Central Prisoners of War Agency.

The costs of treatment, including those of any apparatus necessary for the maintenance of prisoners of war in good health, particularly dentures and other artificial appliances, and spectacles, shall be borne by the Detaining Power.

Article 31

Medical inspections of prisoners of war shall be held at least once a month. They shall include the checking and the recording of the weight of each prisoner of war.

Their purpose shall be, in particular, to supervise the general state of health, nutrition and cleanliness of prisoners and to detect contagious diseases, especially tuberculosis, malaria and venereal disease. For this purpose the most efficient methods available shall be employed, e.g. periodic mass miniature radiography for the early detection of tuberculosis.

Article 32

Prisoners of war who, though not attached to the medical service of their armed forces, are physicians, surgeons, dentists, nurses or medical orderlies, may be required by the Detaining Power to exercise their medical functions in the interests of prisoners of war dependent on the same Power. In that case they shall continue to be prisoners of war, but shall receive the same treatment as corresponding medical personnel retained by the Detaining Power. They shall be exempted from any other work under Article 49.

Chapter IV
Medical Personnel and Chaplains Retained to Assist Prisoners of War

Article 33

Members of the medical personnel and chaplains while retained by the Detaining Power with a view to assisting prisoners of war, shall not be considered as prisoners of war. They shall, however, receive as a minimum the benefits and protection of the present Convention, and shall also be granted all facilities necessary to provide for the medical care of, and religious ministration to prisoners of war.

They shall continue to exercise their medical and spiritual functions for the benefit of prisoners of war, preferably those belonging to the armed forces upon which they depend, within the scope of the military laws and regulations of the Detaining Power and under the control of its competent services, in accordance with their professional etiquette. They shall also benefit by the following facilities in the exercise of their medical or spiritual functions:

(a)   They shall be authorized to visit periodically prisoners of war situated in working detachments or in hospitals outside the camp. For this purpose, the Detaining Power shall place at their disposal the necessary means of transport.

(b)   The senior medical officer in each camp shall be responsible to the camp military authorities for everything connected with the activities of retained medical personnel. For this purpose, Parties to the conflict shall agree at the outbreak of hostilities on the subject of the corresponding ranks of the medical personnel, including that of societies mentioned in Article 26 of the Geneva Convention for the Amelioration of the Condition of the Wounded and Sick in Armed Forces in the Field of August 12, 1949. This senior medical officer, as well as chaplains, shall have the right to deal with the competent authorities of the camp on all questions relating to their duties. Such authorities shall afford them all necessary facilities for correspondence relating to these questions.

(c)   Although they shall be subject to the internal discipline of the camp in which they are retained, such personnel may not be compelled to carry out any work other than that concerned with their medical or religious duties.

During hostilities, the Parties to the conflict shall agree concerning the possible relief of retained personnel and shall settle the procedure to be followed.

None of the preceding provisions shall relieve the Detaining Power of its obligations with regard to prisoners of war from the medical or spiritual point of view.

Chapter V
Religious, Intellectual and Physical Activities

Article 34

Prisoners of war shall enjoy complete latitude in the exercise of their religious duties, including attendance at the service of their faith, on condition that they comply with the disciplinary routine prescribed by the military authorities.

Adequate premises shall be provided where religious services may be held.

Article 35

Chaplains who fall into the hands of the enemy Power and who remain or are retained with a view to assisting prisoners of war, shall be allowed to minister to them and to exercise freely their ministry amongst prisoners of war of the same religion, in accordance with their religious conscience. They shall be allocated among the various camps and labour detachments containing prisoners of war belonging to the same forces, speaking the same language or practising the same religion. They shall enjoy the necessary facilities, including the means of transport provided for in Article 33, for visiting the prisoners of war outside their camp. They shall be free to correspond, subject to censorship, on matters concerning their religious duties with the ecclesiastical authorities in the country of detention and with international religious organizations. Letters and cards which they may send for this purpose shall be in addition to the quota provided for in Article 71.

Article 36

Prisoners of war who are ministers of religion, without having officiated as chaplains to their own forces, shall be at liberty, whatever their denomination, to minister freely to the members of their community. For this purpose, they shall receive the same treatment as the chaplains retained by the Detaining Power. They shall not be obliged to do any other work.

Article 37

When prisoners of war have not the assistance of a retained chaplain or of a prisoner of war minister of their faith, a minister belonging to the prisoners' or a similar denomination, or in his absence a qualified layman, if such a course is feasible from a confessional point of view, shall be appointed, at the request of the prisoners concerned, to fill this office. This appointment, subject to the approval of the Detaining Power, shall take place with the agreement of the community of prisoners concerned and, wherever necessary, with the approval of the local religious authorities of the same faith. The person thus appointed shall comply with all regulations established by the Detaining Power in the interests of discipline and military security.

Article 38

While respecting the individual preferences of every prisoner, the Detaining Power shall encourage the practice of intellectual, educational, and recreational pursuits, sports and games amongst prisoners, and shall take the measures necessary to ensure the exercise thereof by providing them with adequate premises and necessary equipment.

Prisoners shall have opportunities for taking physical exercise, including sports and games, and for being out of doors. Sufficient open spaces shall be provided for this purpose in all camps.

Chapter VI
Discipline

Article 39

Every prisoner of war camp shall be put under the immediate authority of a responsible commissioned officer belonging to the regular armed forces of the Detaining Power. Such officer shall have in his possession a copy of the present Convention; he shall ensure that its provisions are known to the camp staff and the guard and shall be responsible, under the direction of his government, for its application.

Prisoners of war, with the exception of officers, must salute and show to all officers of the Detaining Power the external marks of respect provided for by the regulations applying in their own forces.

Officer prisoners of war are bound to salute only officers of a higher rank of the Detaining Power; they must, however, salute the camp commander regardless of his rank.

Article 40

The wearing of badges of rank and nationality, as well as of decorations, shall be permitted.

Article 41

In every camp the text of the present Convention and its Annexes and the contents of any special agreement provided for in Article 6, shall be posted, in the prisoners' own language, in places where all may read them. Copies shall be supplied, on request, to the prisoners who cannot have access to the copy which has been posted.

Regulations, orders, notices and publications of every kind relating to the conduct of prisoners of war shall be issued to them in a language which they understand. Such regulations, orders and publications shall be posted in the manner described above and copies shall be handed to the prisoners' representative. Every order and command addressed to prisoners of war individually must likewise be given in a language which they understand.

Article 42

The use of weapons against prisoners of war, especially against those who are escaping or attempting to escape, shall constitute an extreme measure, which shall always be preceded by warnings appropriate to the circumstances.

Chapter VII
Rank of Prisoners of War

Article 43

Upon the outbreak of hostilities, the Parties to the conflict shall communicate to one another the titles and ranks of all the persons mentioned in Article 4 of the present Convention, in order to ensure equality of treatment between prisoners of equivalent rank. Titles and ranks which are subsequently created shall form the subject of similar communications.

The Detaining Power shall recognize promotions in rank which have been accorded to prisoners of war and which have been duly notified by the Power on which these prisoners depend.

Article 44

Officers and prisoners of equivalent status shall be treated with the regard due to their rank and age.

In order to ensure service in officers' camps, other ranks of the same armed forces who, as far as possible, speak the same language, shall be assigned in sufficient numbers, account being taken of the rank of officers and prisoners of equivalent status. Such orderlies shall not be required to perform any other work.

Supervision of the mess by the officers themselves shall be facilitated in every way.

Article 45

Prisoners of war other than officers and prisoners of equivalent status shall be treated with the regard due to their rank and age.

Supervision of the mess by the prisoners themselves shall be facilitated in every way.

Chapter VIII
Transfer of Prisoners of War after their Arrival in Camp

Article 46

The Detaining Power, when deciding upon the transfer of prisoners of war, shall take into account the interests of the prisoners themselves, more especially so as not to increase the difficulty of their repatriation.

The transfer of prisoners of war shall always be effected humanely and in conditions not less favourable than those under which the forces of the Detaining Power are transferred. Account shall always be taken of the climatic conditions to which the prisoners of war are accustomed and the conditions of transfer shall in no case be prejudicial to their health.

The Detaining Power shall supply prisoners of war during transfer with sufficient food and drinking water to keep them in good health, likewise with the necessary clothing, shelter and medical attention. The Detaining Power shall take adequate precautions especially in case of transport by sea or by air, to ensure their safety during transfer, and shall draw up a complete list of all transferred prisoners before their departure.

Article 47

Sick or wounded prisoners of war shall not be transferred as long as their recovery may be endangered by the journey, unless their safety imperatively demands it.

If the combat zone draws closer to a camp, the prisoners of war in the said camp shall not be transferred unless their transfer can be carried out in adequate conditions of safety, or unless they are exposed to greater risks by remaining on the spot than by being transferred.

Article 48

In the event of transfer, prisoners of war shall be officially advised of their departure and of their new postal address. Such notifications shall be given in time for them to pack their luggage and inform their next of kin.

They shall be allowed to take with them their personal effects, and the correspondence and parcels which have arrived for them. The weight of such baggage may be limited, if the conditions of transfer so require, to what each prisoner can reasonably carry, which shall in no case be more than twenty-five kilograms per head.

Mail and parcels addressed to their former camp shall be forwarded to them without delay. The camp commander shall take, in agreement with the prisoners' representative, any measures needed to ensure the transport of the prisoners' community property and of the luggage they are unable to take with them in consequence of restrictions imposed by virtue of the second paragraph of this Article.

The costs of transfers shall be borne by the Detaining Power.

Section III
Labour of Prisoners of War

Article 49

The Detaining Power may utilize the labour of prisoners of war who are physically fit, taking into account their age, sex, rank and physical aptitude, and with a view particularly to maintaining them in a good state of physical and mental health.

Non-commissioned officers who are prisoners of war shall only be required to do supervisory work. Those not so required may ask for other suitable work which shall, so far as possible, be found for them.

If officers or persons of equivalent status ask for suitable work, it shall be found for them, so far as possible, but they may in no circumstances be compelled to work.

Article 50

Besides work connected with camp administration, installation or maintenance, prisoners of war may be compelled to do only such work as is included in the following classes:

(a) agriculture;
(b) industries connected with the production or the extraction of raw materials, and manufacturing industries, with the exception of metallurgical, machinery and chemical industries; public works and building operations which have no military character or purpose;
(c) transport and handling of stores which are not military in character or purpose;
(d) commercial business, and arts and crafts;

(e)   domestic service;

(f)   public utility services having no military character or purpose.

Should the above provisions be infringed, prisoners of war shall be allowed to exercise their right of complaint, in conformity with Article 78.

Article 51

Prisoners of war must be granted suitable working conditions, especially as regards accommodation, food, clothing and equipment; such conditions shall not be inferior to those enjoyed by nationals of the Detaining Power employed in similar work; account shall also be taken of climatic conditions.

The Detaining Power, in utilizing the labour of prisoners of war, shall ensure that in areas in which such prisoners are employed, the national legislation concerning the protection of labour, and, more particularly, the regulations for the safety of workers, are duly applied.

Prisoners of war shall receive training and be provided with the means of protection suitable to the work they will have to do and similar to those accorded to the nationals of the Detaining Power. Subject to the provisions of Article 52, prisoners may be submitted to the normal risks run by these civilian workers.

Conditions of labour shall in no case be rendered more arduous by disciplinary measures.

Article 52

Unless he be a volunteer, no prisoner of war may be employed on labour which is of an unhealthy or dangerous nature.

No prisoner of war shall be assigned to labour which would be looked upon as humiliating for a member of the Detaining Power's own forces.

The removal of mines or similar devices shall be considered as dangerous labour.

Article 53

The duration of the daily labour of prisoners of war, including the time of the journey to and fro, shall not be excessive, and must in no case exceed that permitted for civilian workers in the district, who are nationals of the Detaining Power and employed on the same work.

Prisoners of war must be allowed, in the middle of the day's work, a rest of not less than one hour. This rest will be the same as that to which workers of the Detaining Power are entitled, if the latter is of longer duration. They shall be allowed in addition a rest of twenty-four consecutive hours every week, preferably on Sunday or the day of rest in their country of origin. Furthermore, every prisoner who has worked for one year shall be granted a rest of eight consecutive days, during which his working pay shall be paid him.

If methods of labour such as piece work are employed, the length of the working period shall not be rendered excessive thereby.

Article 54

The working pay due to prisoners of war shall be fixed in accordance with the provisions of Article 62 of the present Convention.

Prisoners of war who sustain accidents in connection with work, or who contract a disease in the course, or in consequence of their work, shall receive all the care their condition may require. The Detaining Power shall furthermore deliver to such prisoners of war a medical certificate enabling them to submit their claims to the Power on which they depend, and shall send a duplicate to the Central Prisoners of War Agency provided for in Article 123.

Article 55

The fitness of prisoners of war for work shall be periodically verified by medical examinations at least once a month. The examinations shall have particular regard to the nature of the work which prisoners of war are required to do.

If any prisoner of war considers himself incapable of working, he shall be permitted to appear before the medical authorities of his camp. Physicians or surgeons may recommend that the prisoners who are, in their opinion, unfit for work, be exempted therefrom.

Article 56

The organization and administration of labour detachments shall be similar to those of prisoner of war camps.

Every labour detachment shall remain under the control of and administratively part of a prisoner of war camp. The military authorities and the commander of the said camp shall be responsible, under the direction of their government, for the observance of the provisions of the present Convention in labour detachments.

The camp commander shall keep an up-to-date record of the labour detachments dependent on his camp, and shall communicate it to the delegates of the Protecting Power, of the International Committee of the Red Cross, or of other agencies giving relief to prisoners of war, who may visit the camp.

Article 57

The treatment of prisoners of war who work for private persons, even if the latter are responsible for guarding and protecting them, shall not be inferior to that which is provided for by the present Convention. The Detaining Power, the military authorities and the commander of the camp to which such prisoners belong shall be entirely responsible for the maintenance, care, treatment, and payment of the working pay of such prisoners of war.

Such prisoners of war shall have the right to remain in communication with the prisoners' representatives in the camps on which they depend.

Section IV
Financial Resources of Prisoners of War

Article 58

Upon the outbreak of hostilities, and pending an arrangement on this matter with the Protecting Power, the Detaining Power may determine the maximum amount of money in cash or in any similar form, that prisoners may have in their possession. Any amount in excess, which was properly in their possession and which has been taken or withheld from them, shall be placed to their account, together with any monies deposited by them, and shall not be converted into any other currency without their consent.

If prisoners of war are permitted to purchase services or commodities outside the camp against payment in cash, such payments shall be made by the prisoner himself or by the camp administration who will charge them to the accounts of the prisoners concerned. The Detaining Power will establish the necessary rules in this respect.

Article 59

Cash which was taken from prisoners of war, in accordance with Article 18, at the time of their capture, and which is in the currency of the Detaining Power, shall be placed to their separate accounts, in accordance with the provisions of Article 64 of the present Section.

The amounts, in the currency of the Detaining Power, due to the conversion of sums in other currencies that are taken from the prisoners of war at the same time, shall also be credited to their separate accounts.

Article 60

The Detaining Power shall grant all prisoners of war a monthly advance of pay, the amount of which shall be fixed by conversion, into the currency
of the said Power, of the following amounts:

Category I: Prisoners ranking below sergeants: eight Swiss francs.

Category II: Sergeants and other non-commissioned officers, or prisoners of equivalent rank: twelve Swiss francs.

Category III: Warrant officers and commissioned officers below the rank of major or prisoners of equivalent rank: fifty Swiss francs.

Category IV: Majors, lieutenant-colonels, colonels or prisoners of equivalent rank: sixty Swiss francs.

Category V: General officers or prisoners of war of equivalent rank: seventy-five Swiss francs.

However, the Parties to the conflict concerned may by special agreement modify the amount of advances of pay due to prisoners of the preceding categories.

Furthermore, if the amounts indicated in the first paragraph above would be unduly high compared with the pay of the Detaining Power's armed forces or would, for any reason, seriously embarrass the Detaining Power, then, pending the conclusion of a special agreement with the Power on which the prisoners depend to vary the amounts indicated above, the Detaining Power:

  (a)   shall continue to credit the accounts of the prisoners with the amounts indicated in the first paragraph above;
  (b)   may temporarily limit the amount made available from these advances of pay to prisoners of war for their own use, to sums which are reasonable, but which, for Category I, shall never be inferior to the amount that the Detaining Power gives to the members of its own armed forces.

The reasons for any limitations will be given without delay to the Protecting Power.

Article 61

The Detaining Power shall accept for distribution as supplementary pay to prisoners of war sums which the Power on which the prisoners depend may forward to them, on condition that the sums to be paid shall be the same for each prisoner of the same category, shall be payable to all prisoners of that category depending on that Power, and shall be placed in their separate accounts, at the earliest opportunity, in accordance with the provisions of Article 64. Such supplementary pay shall not relieve the Detaining Power of any obligation under this Convention.

Article 62

Prisoners of war shall be paid a fair working rate of pay by the detaining authorities direct. The rate shall be fixed by the said authorities, but shall at no time be less than one-fourth of one Swiss franc for a full working day. The Detaining Power shall inform prisoners of war, as well as the Power on which they depend, through the intermediary of the Protecting Power, of the rate of daily working pay that it has fixed.

Working pay shall likewise be paid by the detaining authorities to prisoners of war permanently detailed to duties or to a skilled or semi-skilled occupation in connection with the administration, installation or maintenance of camps, and to the prisoners who are required to carry out spiritual or medical duties on behalf of their comrades.

The working pay of the prisoners' representative, of his advisers, if any, and of his assistants, shall be paid out of the fund maintained by canteen profits. The scale of this working pay shall be fixed by the prisoners' representative and approved by the camp commander. If there is no such fund, the detaining authorities shall pay these prisoners a fair working rate of pay.

Article 63

Prisoners of war shall be permitted to receive remittances of money addressed to them individually or collectively.

Every prisoner of war shall have at his disposal the credit balance of his account as provided for in the following Article, within the limits fixed by the Detaining Power, which shall make such payments as are requested. Subject to financial or monetary restrictions which the Detaining Power regards as essential, prisoners of war may also have payments made abroad. In this case payments addressed by prisoners of war to dependents shall be given priority.

In any event, and subject to the consent of the Power on which they depend, prisoners may have payments made in their own country, as follows: the Detaining Power shall send to the aforesaid Power through the Protecting Power, a notification giving all the necessary particulars concerning the prisoners of war, the beneficiaries of the payments, and the amount of the sums to be paid, expressed in the Detaining Power's currency. The said notification shall be signed by the prisoners and countersigned by the camp commander. The Detaining Power shall debit the prisoners' account by a corresponding amount; the sums thus debited shall be placed by it to the credit of the Power on which the prisoners depend.

To apply the foregoing provisions, the Detaining Power may usefully consult the Model Regulations in Annex V of the present Convention.

Article 64

The Detaining Power shall hold an account for each prisoner of war, showing at least the following:

(1) The amounts due to the prisoner or received by him as advances of pay, as working pay or derived from any other source; the sums in the currency of the Detaining Power which were taken from him; the sums taken from him and converted at his request into the currency of the said Power.

(2) The payments made to the prisoner in cash, or in any other similar form; the payments made on his behalf and at his request; the sums transferred under Article 63, third paragraph.

Article 65

Every item entered in the account of a prisoner of war shall be countersigned or initialled by him, or by the prisoners' representative acting on his behalf.

Prisoners of war shall at all times be afforded reasonable facilities for consulting and obtaining copies of their accounts, which may likewise be inspected by the representatives of the Protecting Powers at the time of visits to the camp.

When prisoners of war are transferred from one camp to another, their personal accounts will follow them. In case of transfer from one Detaining Power to another, the monies which are their property and are not in the currency of the Detaining Power will follow them. They shall be given certificates for any other monies standing to the credit of their accounts.

The Parties to the conflict concerned may agree to notify to each other at specific intervals through the Protecting Power, the amount of the accounts of the prisoners of war.

Article 66

On the termination of captivity, through the release of a prisoner of war or his repatriation, the Detaining Power shall give him a statement, signed by an authorized officer of that Power, showing the credit balance then due to him. The Detaining Power shall also send through the Protecting Power to the government upon which the prisoner of war depends, lists giving all appropriate particulars of all prisoners of war whose captivity has been terminated by repatriation, release, escape, death or any other means, and showing the amount of their credit balances. Such lists shall be certified on each sheet by an authorized representative of the Detaining Power.

Any of the above provisions of this Article may be varied by mutual agreement between any two Parties to the conflict.

The Power on which the prisoner of war depends shall be responsible for settling with him any credit balance due to him from the Detaining Power on the termination of his captivity.

Article 67

Advances of pay, issued to prisoners of war in conformity with Article 60, shall be considered as made on behalf of the Power on which they depend. Such advances of pay, as well as all payments made by the said Power under Article 63, third paragraph, and Article 68, shall form the subject of arrangements between the Powers concerned, at the close of hostilities.

Article 68

Any claim by a prisoner of war for compensation in respect of any injury or other disability arising out of work shall be referred to the Power on which he depends, through the Protecting Power. In accordance with Article 54, the Detaining Power will, in all cases, provide the prisoner of war concerned with a statement showing the nature of the injury or disability, the circumstances in which it arose and particulars of medical or hospital treatment given for it. This statement will be signed by a responsible officer of the Detaining Power and the medical particulars certified by a medical officer.

Any claim by a prisoner of war for compensation in respect of personal effects monies or valuables impounded by the Detaining Power under Article 18 and not forthcoming on his repatriation, or in respect of loss alleged to be due to the fault of the Detaining Power or any of its servants, shall likewise be referred to the Power on which he depends. Nevertheless, any such personal effects required for use by the prisoners of war whilst in captivity shall be replaced at the expense of the Detaining Power. The Detaining Power will, in all cases, provide the prisoner of war with a statement, signed by a responsible officer, showing all available information regarding the reasons why such effects, monies or valuables have not been restored to him. A copy of this statement will be forwarded to the Power on which he depends through the Central Prisoners of War Agency provided for in Article 123.

Section V
Relations of Prisoners of War With the Exterior

Article 69

Immediately upon prisoners of war falling into its power, the Detaining Power shall inform them and the Powers on which they depend, through the Protecting Power, of the measures taken to carry out the provisions of the present Section. They shall likewise inform the parties concerned of any subsequent modifications of such measures.

Article 70

Immediately upon capture, or not more than one week after arrival at a camp, even if it is a transit camp, likewise in case of sickness or transfer to hospital or to another camp, every prisoner of war shall be enabled to write direct to his family, on the one hand, and to the Central Prisoners of War Agency provided for in Article 123, on the other hand, a card similar, if possible, to the model annexed to the present Convention, informing his relatives of his capture, address and state of health. The said cards shall be forwarded as rapidly as possible and may not be delayed in any manner.

Article 71

Prisoners of war shall be allowed to send and receive letters and cards. If the Detaining Power deems it necessary to limit the number of letters and cards sent by each prisoner of war, the said number shall not be less than two letters and four cards monthly, exclusive of the capture cards provided for in Article 70, and conforming as closely as possible to the models annexed to the present Convention. Further limitations may be imposed only if the Protecting Power is satisfied that it would be in the interests of the prisoners of war concerned to do so owing to difficulties of translation caused by the Detaining Power's inability to find sufficient qualified linguists to carry out the necessary censorship. If limitations must be placed on the correspondence addressed to prisoners of war, they may be ordered only by the Power on which the prisoners depend, possibly at the request of the Detaining Power. Such letters and cards must be conveyed by the most rapid method at the disposal of the Detaining Power; they may not be delayed or retained for isciplinary reasons.

Prisoners of war who have been without news for a long period, or who are unable to receive news from their next of kin or to give them news by the ordinary postal route, as well as those who are at a great distance from their homes, shall be permitted to send telegrams, the fees being charged against the prisoners of war's accounts with the Detaining Power or paid in the currency at their disposal. They shall likewise benefit by this measure in cases of urgency.

As a general rule, the correspondence of prisoners of war shall be written in their native language. The Parties to the conflict may allow correspondence in other languages.

Sacks containing prisoner of war mail must be securely sealed and labelled so as clearly to indicate their contents, and must be addressed to offices of destination.

Article 72

Prisoners of war shall be allowed to receive by post or by any other means individual parcels or collective shipments containing, in particular, foodstuffs, clothing, medical supplies and articles of a religious, educational or recreational character which may meet their needs, including books, devotional articles, scientific equipment, examination papers, musical instruments, sports outfits and materials allowing prisoners of war to pursue their studies or their cultural activities.

Such shipments shall in no way free the Detaining Power from the obligations imposed upon it by virtue of the present Convention.

The only limits which may be placed on these shipments shall be those proposed by the Protecting Power in the interest of the prisoners themselves, or by the International Committee of the Red Cross or any other organization giving assistance to the prisoners, in respect of their own shipments only, on account of exceptional strain on transport or communications.

The conditions for the sending of individual parcels and collective relief shall, if necessary, be the subject of special agreements between the Powers concerned, which may in no case delay the receipt by the prisoners of relief supplies. Books may not be included in parcels of clothing and foodstuffs. Medical supplies shall, as a rule, be sent in collective parcels.

Article 73

In the absence of special agreements between the Powers concerned on the conditions for the receipt and distribution of collective relief shipments, the rules and regulations concerning collective shipments, which are annexed to the present Convention, shall be applied.

The special agreements referred to above shall in no case restrict the right of prisoners' representatives to take possession of collective relief shipments intended for prisoners of war, to proceed to their distribution or to dispose of them in the interest of the prisoners.

Nor shall such agreements restrict the right of representatives of the Protecting Power, the International Committee of the Red Cross or any other organization giving assistance to prisoners of war and responsible for the forwarding of collective shipments, to supervise their distribution to the recipients.

Article 74

All relief shipments for prisoners of war shall be exempt from import, customs and other dues.

Correspondence, relief shipments and authorized remittances of money addressed to prisoners of war or despatched by them through the post office, either direct or through the Information Bureaux provided for in Article 122 and the Central Prisoners of War Agency provided for in Article 123, shall be exempt from any postal dues, both in the countries of origin and destination, and in intermediate countries.

If relief shipments intended for prisoners of war cannot be sent through the post office by reason of weight or for any other cause, the cost of transportation shall be borne by the Detaining Power in all the territories under its control. The other Powers party to the Convention shall bear the cost of transport in their respective territories. In the absence of special agreements between the Parties concerned, the costs connected with transport of such shipments, other than costs covered by the above exemption, shall be charged to the senders.

The High Contracting Parties shall endeavour to reduce, so far as possible, the rates charged for telegrams sent by prisoners of war, or addressed to them.

Article 75

Should military operations prevent the Powers concerned from fulfilling their obligation to assure the transport of the shipments referred to in Articles 70, 71, 72 and 77, the Protecting Powers concerned, the International Committee of the Red Cross or any other organization duly approved by the Parties to the conflict may undertake to ensure the conveyance of such shipments by suitable means (railway wagons, motor vehicles, vessels or aircraft, etc.). For this purpose, the High Contracting Parties shall endeavour to supply them with such transport and to allow its circulation, especially by granting the necessary safe-conducts.

Such transport may also be used to convey:

(a)   correspondence, lists and reports exchanged between the Central Information Agency referred to in Article 123 and the National Bureaux referred to in Article 122;

(b)   correspondence and reports relating to prisoners of war which the Protecting Powers, the International Committee of the Red Cross or any other body assisting the prisoners, exchange either with their own delegates or with the Parties to the conflict.

These provisions in no way detract from the right of any Party to the conflict to arrange other means of transport, if it should so prefer, nor preclude the granting of safe-conducts, under mutually agreed conditions, to such means of transport.

In the absence of special agreements, the costs occasioned by the use of such means of transport shall be borne proportionally by the Parties to the conflict whose nationals are benefited thereby.

Article 76

The censoring of correspondence addressed to prisoners of war or despatched by them shall be done as quickly as possible. Mail shall be censored only by the despatching State and the receiving State, and once only by each.

The examination of consignments intended for prisoners of war shall not be carried out under conditions that will expose the goods contained in them to deterioration; except in the case of written or printed matter, it shall be done in the presence of the addressee, or of a fellow-prisoner duly delegated by him. The delivery to prisoners of individual or collective consignments shall not be delayed under the pretext of difficulties of censorship.

Any prohibition of correspondence ordered by Parties to the conflict, either for military or political reasons, shall be only temporary and its duration shall be as short as possible.

Article 77

The Detaining Powers shall provide all facilities for the transmission, through the Protecting Power or the Central Prisoners of War Agency provided for in Article 123 of instruments, papers or documents intended for prisoners of war or despatched by them, especially powers of attorney and wills.

In all cases they shall facilitate the preparation and execution of such documents on behalf of prisoners of war; in particular, they shall allow them to consult a lawyer and shall take what measures are necessary for the authentication of their signatures.

Section VI
Relations Between Prisoners of War and the Authorities

Chapter I
Complaints of Prisoners of War Respecting the Conditions of Captivity

Article 78

Prisoners of war shall have the right to make known to the military authorities in whose power they are, their requests regarding the conditions of captivity to which they are subjected.

They shall also have the unrestricted right to apply to the representatives of the Protecting Powers either through their prisoners' representative or, if they consider it necessary, direct, in order to draw their attention to any points on which they may have complaints to make regarding their conditions of captivity.

These requests and complaints shall not be limited nor considered to be a part of the correspondence quota referred to in Article 71. They must be transmitted immediately. Even if they are recognized to be unfounded, they may not give rise to any punishment.

Prisoners' representatives may send periodic reports on the situation in the camps and the needs of the prisoners of war to the representatives of the Protecting Powers.

Chapter II
Prisoner of War Representatives

Article 79

In all places where there are prisoners of war, except in those where there are officers, the prisoners shall freely elect by secret ballot, every six months, and also in case of vacancies, prisoners' representatives entrusted with representing them before the military authorities, the Protecting Powers, the International Committee of the Red Cross and any other organization which may assist them. These prisoners' representatives shall be eligible for re-election.

In camps for officers and persons of equivalent status or in mixed camps, the senior officer among the prisoners of war shall be recognized as the camp prisoners' representative. In camps for officers, he shall be assisted by one or more advisers chosen by the officers; in mixed camps, his assistants shall be chosen from among the prisoners of war who are not officers and shall be elected by them.

Officer prisoners of war of the same nationality shall be stationed in labour camps for prisoners of war, for the purpose of carrying out the camp administration duties for which the prisoners of war are responsible. These officers may be elected as prisoners' representatives under the first paragraph of this Article. In such a case the assistants to the prisoners' representatives shall be chosen from among those prisoners of war who are not officers.

Every representative elected must be approved by the Detaining Power before he has the right to commence his duties. Where the Detaining Power refuses to approve a prisoner of war elected by his fellow prisoners of war, it must inform the Protecting Power of the reason for such refusal.

In all cases the prisoners' representative must have the same nationality, language and customs as the prisoners of war whom he represents. Thus, prisoners of war distributed in different sections of a camp, according to their nationality, language or customs, shall have for each section their own prisoners' representative, in accordance with the foregoing paragraphs.

Article 80

Prisoners' representatives shall further the physical, spiritual and intellectual well-being of prisoners of war.

In particular, where the prisoners decide to organize amongst themselves a system of mutual assistance, this organization will be within the province of the prisoners' representative, in addition to the special duties entrusted to him by other provisions of the present Convention.

Prisoners' representatives shall not be held responsible, simply by reason of their duties, for any offences committed by prisoners of war.

Article 81

Prisoners' representatives shall not be required to perform any other work, if the accomplishment of their duties is thereby made more difficult.

Prisoners' representatives may appoint from amongst the prisoners such assistants as they may require. All material facilities shall be granted them, particularly a certain freedom of movement necessary for the accomplishment of their duties (inspection of labour detachments, receipt of supplies, etc.).

Prisoners' representatives shall be permitted to visit premises where prisoners of war are detained, and every prisoner of war shall have the right to consult freely his prisoners' representative.

All facilities shall likewise be accorded to the prisoners' representatives for communication by post and telegraph with the detaining authorities, the Protecting Powers, the International Committee of the Red Cross and their delegates, the Mixed Medical Commissions and the bodies which give assistance to prisoners of war. Prisoners' representatives of labour detachments shall enjoy the same facilities for communication with the prisoners' representatives of the principal camp. Such communications shall not be restricted, nor considered as forming a part of the quota mentioned in Article 71.

Prisoners' representatives who are transferred shall be allowed a reasonable time to acquaint their successors with current affairs.

In case of dismissal, the reasons therefor shall be communicated to the Protecting Power.

Chapter III
Penal and Disciplinary Sanctions

I. General Provisions

Article 82

A prisoner of war shall be subject to the laws, regulations and orders in force in the armed forces of the Detaining Power; the Detaining Power shall be justified in taking judicial or disciplinary measures in respect of any offence committed by a prisoner of war against such laws, regulations or orders. However, no proceedings or punishments contrary to the provisions of this Chapter shall be allowed.

If any law, regulation or order of the Detaining Power shall declare acts committed by a prisoner of war to be punishable, whereas the same acts would not be punishable if committed by a member of the forces of the Detaining Power, such acts shall entail disciplinary punishments only.

Article 83

In deciding whether proceedings in respect of an offence alleged to have been committed by a prisoner of war shall be judicial or disciplinary, the Detaining Power shall ensure that the competent authorities exercise the greatest leniency and adopt, wherever possible, disciplinary rather than judicial measures.

Article 84

A prisoner of war shall be tried only by a military court, unless the existing laws of the Detaining Power expressly permit the civil courts to try a member of the armed forces of the Detaining Power in respect of the particular offence alleged to have been committed by the prisoner of war.

In no circumstances whatever shall a prisoner of war be tried by a court of any kind which does not offer the essential guarantees of independence and impartiality as generally recognized, and, in particular, the procedure of which does not afford the accused the rights and means of defence provided for in Article 105.

Article 85

Prisoners of war prosecuted under the laws of the Detaining Power for acts committed prior to capture shall retain, even if convicted, the benefits of the present Convention.

Article 86

No prisoner of war may be punished more than once for the same act or on the same charge.

Article 87

Prisoners of war may not be sentenced by the military authorities and courts of the Detaining Power to any penalties except those provided for in respect of members of the armed forces of the said Power who have committed the same acts.

When fixing the penalty, the courts or authorities of the Detaining Power shall take into consideration, to the widest extent possible, the fact that the accused, not being a national of the Detaining Power, is not bound to it by any duty of allegiance, and that he is in its power as the result of circumstances independent of his own will. The said courts or authorities shall be at liberty to reduce the penalty provided for the violation of which the prisoner of war is accused, and shall therefore not be bound to apply the minimum penalty prescribed.

Collective punishment for individual acts, corporal punishment, imprisonment in premises without daylight and, in general, any form of torture or cruelty, are forbidden.

No prisoner of war may be deprived of his rank by the Detaining Power, or prevented from wearing his badges.

Article 88

Officers, non-commissioned officers and men who are prisoners of war undergoing a disciplinary or judicial punishment, shall not be subjected to more severe treatment than that applied in respect of the same punishment to members of the armed forces of the Detaining Power of equivalent rank.

A woman prisoner of war shall not be awarded or sentenced to a punishment more severe, or treated whilst undergoing punishment more severely, than a woman member of the armed forces of the Detaining Power dealt with for a similar offence.

In no case may a woman prisoner of war be awarded or sentenced to a punishment more severe, or treated whilst undergoing punishment more severely, than a male member of the armed forces of the Detaining Power dealt with for a similar offence.

Prisoners of war who have served disciplinary or judicial sentences may not be treated differently from other prisoners of war.

II. Disciplinary Sanctions

Article 89

The disciplinary punishments applicable to prisoners of war are the following:

(1) A fine which shall not exceed 50 per cent of the advances of pay and working pay which the prisoner of war would otherwise receive under the provisions of Articles 60 and 62 during a period of not more than thirty days.

(2) Discontinuance of privileges granted over and above the treatment provided for by the present Convention.

(3) Fatigue duties not exceeding two hours daily.

(4) Confinement.

The punishment referred to under (3) shall not be applied to officers.

In no case shall disciplinary punishments be inhuman, brutal or dangerous to the health of prisoners of war.

Article 90

The duration of any single punishment shall in no case exceed thirty days. Any period of confinement awaiting the hearing of a disciplinary offence or the award of disciplinary punishment shall be deducted from an award pronounced against a prisoner of war.

The maximum of thirty days provided above may not be exceeded, even if the prisoner of war is answerable for several acts at the same time when he is awarded punishment, whether such acts are related or not.

The period between the pronouncing of an award of disciplinary punishment and its execution shall not exceed one month.

When a prisoner of war is awarded a further disciplinary punishment, a period of at least three days shall elapse between the execution of any two of the punishments, if the duration of one of these is ten days or more.

Article 91

The escape of a prisoner of war shall be deemed to have succeeded when:

(1) he has joined the armed forces of the Power on which he depends, or those of an allied Power;

(2) he has left the territory under the control of the Detaining Power, or of an ally of the said Power;

(3) he has joined a ship flying the flag of the Power on which he depends, or of an allied Power, in the territorial waters of the Detaining Power, the said ship not being under the control of the last named Power.

Prisoners of war who have made good their escape in the sense of this Article and who are recaptured, shall not be liable to any punishment in respect of their previous escape.

Article 92

A prisoner of war who attempts to escape and is recaptured before having made good his escape in the sense of Article 91 shall be liable only to a disciplinary punishment in respect of this act, even if it is a repeated offence.

A prisoner of war who is recaptured shall be handed over without delay to the competent military authority.

Article 88, fourth paragraph, notwithstanding, prisoners of war punished as a result of an unsuccessful escape may be subjected to special surveillance. Such surveillance must not affect the state of their health, must be undergone in a prisoner of war camp, and must not entail the suppression of any of the safeguards granted them by the present Convention.

Article 93

Escape or attempt to escape, even if it is a repeated offence, shall not be deemed an aggravating circumstance if the prisoner of war is subjected to trial by judicial proceedings in respect of an offence committed during his escape or attempt to escape.

In conformity with the principle stated in Article 83, offences committed by prisoners of war with the sole intention of facilitating their escape and which do not entail any violence against life or limb, such as offences against public property, theft without intention of self-enrichment, the drawing up or use of false papers, or the wearing of civilian clothing, shall occasion disciplinary punishment only.

Prisoners of war who aid or abet an escape or an attempt to escape shall be liable on this count to disciplinary punishment only.

Article 94

If an escaped prisoner of war is recaptured, the Power on which he depends shall be notified thereof in the manner defined in Article 122, provided notification of his escape has been made.

Article 95

A prisoner of war accused of an offence against discipline shall not be kept in confinement pending the hearing unless a member of the armed forces of the Detaining Power would be so kept if he were accused of a similar offence, or if it is essential in the interests of camp order and discipline.

Any period spent by a prisoner of war in confinement awaiting the disposal of an offence against discipline shall be reduced to an absolute minimum and shall not exceed fourteen days.

The provisions of Articles 97 and 98 of this Chapter shall apply to prisoners of war who are in confinement awaiting the disposal of offences against discipline.

Article 96

Acts which constitute offences against discipline shall be investigated immediately.

Without prejudice to the competence of courts and superior military authorities, disciplinary punishment may be ordered only by an officer having disciplinary powers in his capacity as camp commander, or by a responsible officer who replaces him or to whom he has delegated his disciplinary powers.

In no case may such powers be delegated to a prisoner of war or be exercised by a prisoner of war.

Before any disciplinary award is pronounced, the accused shall be given precise information regarding the offences of which he is accused, and given an opportunity of explaining his conduct and of defending himself. He shall be permitted, in particular, to call witnesses and to have recourse, if necessary, to the services of a qualified interpreter. The decision shall be announced to the accused prisoner of war and to the prisoners' representative.

A record of disciplinary punishments shall be maintained by the camp commander and shall be open to inspection by representatives of the Protecting Power.

Article 97

Prisoners of war shall not in any case be transferred to penitentiary establishments (prisons, penitentiaries, convict prisons, etc.) to undergo disciplinary punishment therein.

All premises in which disciplinary punishments are undergone shall conform to the sanitary requirements set forth in Article 25. A prisoner of war undergoing punishment shall be enabled to keep himself in a state of cleanliness, in conformity with Article 29.

Officers and persons of equivalent status shall not be lodged in the same quarters as non-commissioned officers or men.

Women prisoners of war undergoing disciplinary punishment shall be confined in separate quarters from male prisoners of war and shall be under the immediate supervision of women.

Article 98

A prisoner of war undergoing confinement as a disciplinary punishment, shall continue to enjoy the benefits of the provisions of this Convention except in so far as these are necessarily rendered inapplicable by the mere fact that he is confined. In no case may he be deprived of the benefits of the provisions of Articles 78 and 126.

A prisoner of war awarded disciplinary punishment may not be deprived of the prerogatives attached to his rank.

Prisoners of war awarded disciplinary punishment shall be allowed to exercise and to stay in the open air at least two hours daily.

They shall be allowed, on their request, to be present at the daily medical inspections. They shall receive the attention which their state of health requires and, if necessary, shall be removed to the camp infirmary or to a hospital.

They shall have permission to read and write, likewise to send and receive letters. Parcels and remittances of money however, may be withheld from them until the completion of the punishment; they shall meanwhile be entrusted to the prisoners' representative, who-will hand over to the infirmary the perishable goods contained in such parcels.

III. Juridicial Proceedings

Article 99

No prisoner of war may be tried or sentenced for an act which is not forbidden by the law of the Detaining Power or by international law, in force at the time the said act was committed.

No moral or physical coercion may be exerted on a prisoner of war in order to induce him to admit himself guilty of the act of which he is accused.

No prisoner of war may be convicted without having had an opportunity to present his defence and the assistance of a qualified advocate or counsel.

Article 100

Prisoners of war and the Protecting Powers shall be informed as soon as possible of the offences which are punishable by the death sentence under the laws of the Detaining Power.

Other offences shall not thereafter be made punishable by the death penalty without the concurrence of the Power on which the prisoners of war depend.

The death sentence cannot be pronounced on a prisoner of war unless the attention of the court has, in accordance with Article 87, second paragraph, been particularly called to the fact that since the accused is not a national of the Detaining Power, he is not bound to it by any duty of allegiance, and that he is in its power as the result of circumstances independent of his own will.

Article 101

If the death penalty is pronounced on a prisoner of war, the sentence shall not be executed before the expiration of a period of at least six months from the date when the Protecting Power receives, at an indicated address, the detailed communication provided for in Article 107.

Article 102

A prisoner of war can be validly sentenced only if the sentence has been pronounced by the same courts according to the same procedure as in the case of members of the armed forces of the Detaining Power, and if, furthermore, the provisions of the present Chapter have been observed.

Article 103

Judicial investigations relating to a prisoner of war shall be conducted as rapidly as circumstances permit and so that his trial shall take place as soon as possible. A prisoner of war shall not be confined while awaiting trial unless a member of the armed forces of the Detaining Power would be so confined if he were accused of a similar offence, or if it is essential to do so in the interests of national security. In no circumstances shall this confinement exceed three months.

Any period spent by a prisoner of war in confinement awaiting trial shall be deducted from any sentence of imprisonment passed upon him and taken into account in fixing any penalty.

The provisions of Articles 97 and 98 of this Chapter shall apply to a prisoner of war whilst in confinement awaiting trial.

Article 104

In any case in which the Detaining Power has decided to institute judicial proceedings against a prisoner of war, it shall notify the Protecting Power as soon as possible and at least three weeks before the opening of the trial. This period of three weeks shall run as from the day on which such notification reaches the Protecting Power at the address previously indicated by the latter to the Detaining Power.

The said notification shall contain the following information:

(1) Surname and first names of the prisoner of war, his rank, his army, regimental, personal or serial number, his date of birth, and his profession or trade, if any;

(2) Place of internment or confinement;

(3) Specification of the charge or charges on which the prisoner of war is to be arraigned, giving the legal provisions applicable;

(4) Designation of the court which will try the case, likewise the date and place fixed for the opening of the trial.

The same communication shall be made by the Detaining Power to the prisoners' representative.

If no evidence is submitted, at the opening of a trial, that the notification referred to above was received by the Protecting Power, by the prisoner of war and by the prisoners' representative concerned, at least three weeks before the opening of the trial, then the latter cannot take place and must be adjourned.

Article 105

The prisoner of war shall be entitled to assistance by one of his prisoner comrades, to defence by a qualified advocate or counsel of his own choice, to the calling of witnesses and, if he deems necessary, to the services of a competent interpreter. He shall be advised of these rights by the Detaining Power in due time before the trial.

Failing a choice by the prisoner of war, the Protecting Power shall find him an advocate or counsel, and shall have at least one week at its disposal for the purpose. The Detaining Power shall deliver to the said Power, on request, a list of persons qualified to present the defence. Failing a choice of an advocate or counsel by the prisoner of war or the Protecting Power, the Detaining Power shall appoint a competent advocate or counsel to conduct the defence.

The advocate or counsel conducting the defence on behalf of the prisoner of war shall have at his disposal a period of two weeks at least before the opening of the trial, as well as the necessary facilities to prepare the defence of the accused. He may, in particular, freely visit the accused and interview him in private. He may also confer with any witnesses for the defence, including prisoners of war. He shall have the benefit of these facilities until the term of appeal or petition has expired.

Particulars of the charge or charges on which the prisoner of war is to be arraigned, as well as the documents which are generally communicated to the accused by virtue of the laws in force in the armed forces of the Detaining Power, shall be communicated to the accused prisoner of war in a language which he understands, and in good time before the opening of the trial. The same communication in the same circumstances shall be made to the advocate or counsel conducting the defence on behalf of the prisoner of war.

The representatives of the Protecting Power shall be entitled to attend the trial of the case, unless, exceptionally, this is held in camera in the interest of State security. In such a case the Detaining Power shall advise the Protecting Power accordingly.

Article 106

Every prisoner of war shall have, in the same manner as the members of the armed forces of the Detaining Power, the right of appeal or petition from any sentence pronounced upon him, with a view to the quashing or revising of the sentence or the reopening of the trial. He shall be fully informed of his right to appeal or petition and of the time limit within which he may do so.

Article 107

Any judgment and sentence pronounced upon a prisoner of war shall be immediately reported to the Protecting Power in the form of a summary communication, which shall also indicate whether he has the right of appeal with a view to the quashing of the sentence or the reopening of the trial. This communication shall likewise be sent to the prisoners' representative concerned. It shall also be sent to the accused prisoner of war in a language he understands, if the sentence was not pronounced in his presence. The Detaining Power shall also immediately communicate to the Protecting Power the decision of the prisoner of war to use or to waive his right of appeal.

Furthermore, if a prisoner of war is finally convicted or if a sentence pronounced on a prisoner of war in the first instance is a death sentence, the Detaining Power shall as soon as possible address to the Protecting Power a detailed communication containing:

(1) the precise wording of the finding and sentence;

(2) a summarized report of any preliminary investigation and of the trial, emphasizing in particular the elements of the prosecution and the defence;

(3) notification, where applicable, of the establishment where the sentence will be served.

The communications provided for in the foregoing sub-paragraphs shall be sent to the Protecting Power at the address previously made known to the Detaining Power.

Article 108

Sentences pronounced on prisoners of war after a conviction has become duly enforceable, shall be served in the same establishments and under the same conditions as in the case of members of the armed forces of the Detaining Power. These conditions shall in all cases conform to the requirements of health and humanity.

A woman prisoner of war on whom such a sentence has been pronounced shall be confined in separate quarters and shall be under the supervision of women.

In any case, prisoners of war sentenced to a penalty depriving them of their liberty shall retain the benefit of the provisions of Articles 78 and 126 of the present Convention. Furthermore, they shall be entitled to receive and despatch correspondence, to receive at least one relief parcel monthly, to take regular exercise in the open air, to have the medical care required by their state of health, and the spiritual assistance they may desire. Penalties to which they may be subjected shall be in accordance with the provisions of Article 87, third paragraph.

PART IV
TERMINATION OF CAPTIVITY

Section I
Direct Repatriation and Accommodation in Neutral Countries

Article 109

Subject to the provisions of the third paragraph of this Article, Parties to the conflict are bound to send back to their own country, regardless of number or rank, seriously wounded and seriously sick prisoners of war, after having cared for them until they are fit to travel, in accordance with the first paragraph of the following Article.

Throughout the duration of hostilities, Parties to the conflict shall endeavour, with the cooperation of the neutral Powers concerned, to make arrangements for the accommodation in neutral countries of the sick and wounded prisoners of war referred to in the second paragraph of the following Article. They may, in addition, conclude agreements with a view to the direct repatriation or internment in a neutral country of able-bodied prisoners of war who have undergone a long period of captivity.

No sick or injured prisoner of war who is eligible for repatriation under the first paragraph of this Article, may be repatriated against his will during hostilities.

Article 110

The following shall be repatriated direct:

(1) Incurably wounded and sick whose mental or physical fitness seems to have been gravely diminished.

(2) Wounded and sick who, according to medical opinion, are not likely to recover within one year, whose condition requires treatment and whose mental or physical fitness seems to have been gravely diminished.

(3) Wounded and sick who have recovered, but whose mental or physical fitness seems to have been gravely and permanently diminished.

The following may be accommodated in a neutral country:

(1) Wounded and sick whose recovery may be expected within one year of the date of the wound or the beginning of the illness, if treatment in a neutral country might increase the prospects of a more certain and speedy recovery.

(2) Prisoners of war whose mental or physical health, according to medical opinion, is seriously threatened by continued captivity, but whose accommodation in a neutral country might remove such a threat.

The conditions which prisoners of war accommodated in a neutral country must fulfil in order to permit their repatriation shall be fixed, as shall likewise their status, by agreement between the Powers concerned. In general, prisoners of war who have been accommodated in a neutral country, and who belong to the following categories, should be repatriated:

(1) Those whose state of health has deteriorated so as to fulfil the condition laid down for direct repatriation;

(2) Those whose mental or physical powers remain, even after treatment, considerably impaired.

If no special agreements are concluded between the Parties to the conflict concerned, to determine the cases of disablement or sickness entailing direct repatriation or accommodation in a neutral country, such cases shall be settled in accordance with the principles laid down in the Model Agreement concerning direct repatriation and accommodation in neutral countries of wounded and sick prisoners of war and in the Regulations concerning Mixed Medical Commissions annexed to the present Convention.

Article 111

The Detaining Power, the Power on which the prisoners of war depend, and a neutral Power agreed upon by these two Powers, shall endeavour to conclude agreements which will enable prisoners of war to be interned in the territory of the said neutral Power until the close of hostilities.

Article 112

Upon the outbreak of hostilities, Mixed Medical Commissions shall be appointed to examine sick and wounded prisoners of war, and to make all appropriate decisions regarding them. The appointment, duties and functioning of these Commissions shall be in conformity with the provisions of the Regulations annexed to the present Convention.

However, prisoners of war who, in the opinion of the medical authorities of the Detaining Power, are manifestly seriously injured or seriously sick, may be repatriated without having to be examined by a Mixed Medical Commission.

Article 113

Besides those who are designated by the medical authorities of the Detaining Power, wounded or sick prisoners of war belonging to the categories listed below shall be entitled to present themselves for examination by the Mixed Medical Commissions provided for in the foregoing Article:

(1) Wounded and sick proposed by a physician or surgeon who is of the same nationality, or a national of a Party to the conflict allied with the Power on which the said prisoners depend, and who exercises his functions in the camp.

(2) Wounded and sick proposed by their prisoners' representative.

(3) Wounded and sick proposed by the Power on which they depend, or by an organization duly recognized by the said Power and giving assistance to the prisoners.

Prisoners of war who do not belong to one of the three foregoing categories may nevertheless present themselves for examination by Mixed Medical Commissions, but shall be examined only after those belonging to the said categories.

The physician or surgeon of the same nationality as the prisoners who present themselves for examination by the Mixed Medical Commission, likewise the prisoners' representative of the said prisoners, shall have permission to be present at the examination.

Article 114

Prisoners of war who meet with accidents shall, unless the injury is self-inflicted, have the benefit of the provisions of this Convention as regards repatriation or accommodation in a neutral country.

Article 115

No prisoner of war on whom a disciplinary punishment has been imposed and who is eligible for repatriation or for accommodation in a neutral country, may be kept back on the plea that he has not undergone his punishment.

Prisoners of war detained in connection with a judicial prosecution or conviction, and who are designated for repatriation or accommodation in a neutral country, may benefit by such measures before the end of the proceedings or the completion of the punishment, if the Detaining Power consents.

Parties to the conflict shall communicate to each other the names of those who will be detained until the end of the proceedings or the completion of the punishment.

Article 116

The cost of repatriating prisoners of war or of transporting them to a neutral country shall be borne, from the frontiers of the Detaining Power, by the Power on which the said prisoners depend.

Article 117

No repatriated person may be employed on active military service.

Section II
Release and Repatriation of Prisoners of War at the Close of Hostilities

Article 118

Prisoners of war shall be released and repatriated without delay after the cessation of active hostilities.

In the absence of stipulations to the above effect in any agreement concluded between the Parties to the conflict with a view to the cessation of hostilities, or failing any such agreement, each of the Detaining Powers shall itself establish and execute without delay a plan of repatriation in conformity with the principle laid down in the foregoing paragraph.

In either case, the measures adopted shall be brought to the knowledge of the prisoners of war.

The costs of repatriation of prisoners of war shall in all cases be equitably apportioned between the Detaining Power and the Power on which the prisoners depend. This apportionment shall be carried out on the following basis:

(a) If the two Powers are contiguous, the Power on which the prisoners of war depend shall bear the costs of repatriation from the frontiers of the Detaining Power.

(b) If the two Powers are not contiguous, the Detaining Power shall bear the costs of transport of prisoners of war over its own territory as far as its frontier or its port of embarkation nearest to the territory of the Power on which the prisoners of war depend. The Parties concerned shall agree between themselves as to the equitable apportionment of the remaining costs of the repatriation. The conclusion of this agreement shall in no circumstances justify any delay in the repatriation of the prisoners of war.

Article 119

Repatriation shall be effected in conditions similar to those laid down in Articles 46 to 48 inclusive of the present Convention for the transfer of prisoners of war, having regard to the provisions of Article 118 and to those of the following paragraphs.

On repatriation, any articles of value impounded from prisoners of war under Article 18, and any foreign currency which has not been converted into the currency of the Detaining Power, shall be restored to them. Articles of value and foreign currency which, for any reason whatever, are not restored to prisoners of war on repatriation, shall be despatched to the Information Bureau set up under Article 122.

Prisoners of war shall be allowed to take with them their personal effects, and any correspondence and parcels which have arrived for them. The weight of such baggage may be limited, if the conditions of repatriation so require, to what each prisoner can reasonably carry. Each prisoner shall in all cases be authorized to carry at least twenty-five kilograms.

The other personal effects of the repatriated prisoner shall be left in the charge of the Detaining Power which shall have them forwarded to him as soon as it has concluded an agreement to this effect, regulating the conditions of transport and the payment of the costs involved, with the Power on which the prisoner depends.

Prisoners of war against whom criminal proceedings for an indictable offence are pending may be detained until the end of such proceedings, and, if necessary, until the completion of the punishment. The same shall apply to prisoners of war already convicted for an indictable offence.

Parties to the conflict shall communicate to each other the names of any prisoners of war who are detained until the end of the proceedings or until punishment has been completed.

By agreement between the Parties to the conflict, commissions shall be established for the purpose of searching for dispersed prisoners of war and of assuring their repatriation with the least possible delay.

Section III
Death of Prisoners of War

Article 120

Wills of prisoners of war shall be drawn up so as to satisfy the conditions of validity required by the legislation of their country of origin, which will take steps to inform the Detaining Power of its requirements in this respect. At the request of the prisoner of war and, in all cases, after death, the will shall be transmitted without delay to the Protecting Power; a certified copy shall be sent to the Central Agency.

Death certificates, in the form annexed to the present Convention, or lists certified by a responsible officer, of all persons who die as prisoners of war shall be forwarded as rapidly as possible to the Prisoner of War Information Bureau established in accordance with Article 122. The death certificates or certified lists shall show particulars of identity as set out in the third paragraph of Article 17, and also the date and place of death, the cause of death, the date and place of burial and all particulars necessary to identify the graves.

The burial or cremation of a prisoner of war shall be preceded by a medical examination of the body with a view to confirming death and enabling a report to be made and, where necessary, establishing identity.

The detaining authorities shall ensure that prisoners of war who have died in captivity are honourably buried, if possible according to the rites of the religion to which they belonged, and that their graves are respected, suitably maintained and marked so as to be found at any time. Wherever possible, deceased prisoners of war who depended on the same Power shall be interred in the same place.

Deceased prisoners of war shall be buried in individual graves unless unavoidable circumstances require the use of collective graves. Bodies may be cremated only for imperative reasons of hygiene, on account of the religion of the deceased or in accordance with his express wish to this effect. In case of cremation, the fact shall be stated and the reasons given in the death certificate of the deceased.

In order that graves may always be found, all particulars of burials and graves shall be recorded with a Graves Registration Service established by the Detaining Power. Lists of graves and particulars of the prisoners of war interred in cemeteries and elsewhere shall be transmitted to the Power on which such prisoners of war depended. Responsibility for the care of these graves and for records of any subsequent moves of the bodies shall rest on the Power controlling the territory, if a Party to the present Convention. These provisions shall also apply to the ashes, which shall be kept by the Graves Registration Service until proper disposal thereof in accordance with the wishes of the home country.

Article 121

Every death or serious injury of a prisoner of war caused or suspected to have been caused by a sentry, another prisoner of war, or any other person, as well as any death the cause of which is unknown, shall be immediately followed by an official enquiry by the Detaining Power.

A communication on this subject shall be sent immediately to the Protecting Power. Statements shall be taken from witnesses, especially from those who are prisoners of war, and a report including such statements shall be forwarded to the Protecting Power.

If the enquiry indicates the guilt of one or more persons, the Detaining Power shall take all measures for the prosecution of the person or persons responsible.

PART V
INFORMATION BUREAUX AND RELIEF SOCIETIES FOR PRISONERS OF WAR

Article 122

Upon the outbreak of a conflict and in all cases of occupation, each of the Parties to the conflict shall institute an official Information Bureau for prisoners of war who are in its power. Neutral or non-belligerent Powers who may have received within their territory persons belonging to one of the categories referred to in Article 4, shall take the same action with respect to such persons. The Power concerned shall ensure that the Prisoners of War Information Bureau is provided with the necessary accommodation, equipment and staff to ensure its efficient working. It shall be at liberty to employ prisoners of war in such a Bureau under the conditions laid down in the Section of the present Convention dealing with work by prisoners of war.

Within the shortest possible period, each of the Parties to the conflict shall give its Bureau the information referred to in the fourth, fifth and sixth paragraphs of this Article regarding any enemy person belonging to one of the categories referred to in Article 4, who has fallen into its power. Neutral or non-belligerent Powers shall take the same action with regard to persons belonging to such categories whom they have received within their territory.

The Bureau shall immediately forward such information by the most rapid means to the Powers concerned, through the intermediary of the Protecting Powers and likewise of the Central Agency provided for in Article 123.

This information shall make it possible quickly to advise the next of kin concerned. Subject to the provisions of Article 17, the information shall include, in so far as available to the Information Bureau, in respect of each prisoner of war, his surname, first names, rank, army, regimental, personal or serial number, place and full date of birth, indication of the Power on which he depends, first name of the father and maiden name of the mother, name and address of the person to be informed and the address to which correspondence for the prisoner may be sent.

The Information Bureau shall receive from the various departments concerned information regarding transfers, releases, repatriations, escapes, admissions to hospital, and deaths, and shall transmit such information in the manner described in the third paragraph above.

Likewise, information regarding the state of health of prisoners of war who are seriously ill or seriously wounded shall be supplied regularly, every week if possible.

The Information Bureau shall also be responsible for replying to all enquiries sent to it concerning prisoners of war, including those who have died in captivity; it will make any enquiries necessary to obtain the information which is asked for if this is not in its possession.

All written communications made by the Bureau shall be authenticated by a signature or a seal.

The Information Bureau shall furthermore be charged with collecting all personal valuables, including sums in currencies other than that of the Detaining Power and documents of importance to the next of kin, left by prisoners of war who have been repatriated or released, or who have escaped or died, and shall forward the said valuables to the Powers concerned. Such articles shall be sent by the Bureau in sealed packets which shall be accompanied by statements giving clear and full particulars of the identity of the person to whom the articles belonged, and by a complete list of the contents of the parcel. Other personal effects of such prisoners of war shall be transmitted under arrangements agreed upon between the Parties to the conflict concerned.

Article 123

A Central Prisoners of War Information Agency shall be created in a neutral country. The International Committee of the Red Cross shall, if it deems necessary, propose to the Powers concerned the organization of such an Agency.

The function of the Agency shall be to collect all the information it may obtain through official or private channels respecting prisoners of war, and to transmit it as rapidly as possible to the country of origin of the prisoners of war or to the Power on which they depend. It shall receive from the Parties to the conflict all facilities for effecting such transmissions.

The High Contracting Parties, and in particular those whose nationals benefit by the services of the Central Agency, are requested to give the said Agency the financial aid it may require.

The foregoing provisions shall in no way be interpreted as restricting the humanitarian activities of the International Committee of the Red Cross, or of the relief societies provided for in Article 125.

Article 124

The national Information Bureaux and the Central Information Agency shall enjoy free postage for mail, likewise all the exemptions provided for in Article 74, and further, so far as possible, exemption from telegraphic charges or, at least, greatly reduced rates.

Article 125

Subject to the measures which the Detaining Powers may consider essential to ensure their security or to meet any other reasonable need, the representatives of religious organizations, relief societies, or any other organization assisting prisoners of war, shall receive from the said Powers, for themselves and their duly accredited agents, all necessary facilities for visiting the prisoners, for distributing relief supplies and material, from any source, intended for religious, educational or recreative purposes, and for assisting them in organizing their leisure time within the camps.

Such societies or organizations may be constituted in the territory of the Detaining Power or in any other country, or they may have an international character.

The Detaining Power may limit the number of societies and organizations whose delegates are allowed to carry out their activities in its territory and under its supervision, on condition, however, that such limitation shall not hinder the effective operation of adequate relief to all prisoners of war.

The special position of the International Committee of the Red Cross in this field shall be recognized and respected at all times.

As soon as relief supplies or material intended for the above-mentioned purposes are handed over to prisoners of war, or very shortly afterwards, receipts for each consignment, signed by the prisoners' representative, shall be forwarded to the relief society or organization making the shipment. At the same time, receipts for these consignments shall be supplied by the administrative authorities responsible for guarding the prisoners.

PART VI
EXECUTION OF THE CONVENTION

Section I
General Provisions

Article 126

Representatives or delegates of the Protecting Powers shall have permission to go to all places where prisoners of war may be, particularly to places of internment, imprisonment and labour, and shall have access to all premises occupied by prisoners of war; they shall also be allowed to go to the places of departure, passage and arrival of prisoners who are being transferred. They shall be able to interview the prisoners, and in particular the prisoners' representatives, without witnesses, either personally or through an interpreter.

Representatives and delegates of the Protecting Powers shall have full liberty to select the places they wish to visit. The duration and frequency of these visits shall not be restricted. Visits may not be prohibited except for reasons of imperative military necessity, and then only as an exceptional and temporary measure.

The Detaining Power and the Power on which the said prisoners of war depend may agree, if necessary, that compatriots of these prisoners of war be permitted to participate in the visits

The delegates of the International Committee of the Red Cross shall enjoy the same prerogatives. The appointment of such delegates shall be submitted to the approval of the Power detaining the prisoners of war to be visited.

Article 127

The High Contracting Parties undertake, in time of peace as in time of war, to disseminate the text of the present Convention as widely as possible in their respective countries, and, in particular, to include the study thereof in their programmes of military and, if possible, civil instruction, so that the principles thereof may become known to all their armed forces and to the entire population.

Any military or other authorities, who in time of war assume responsibilities in respect of prisoners of war, must possess the text of the Convention and be specially instructed as to its provisions.

Article 128

The High Contracting Parties shall communicate to one another through the Swiss Federal Council and, during hostilities, through the Protecting Powers, the official translations of the present Convention, as well as the laws and regulations which they may adopt to ensure the application thereof.

Article 129

The High Contracting Parties undertake to enact any legislation necessary to provide effective penal sanctions for persons committing, or ordering to be committed, any of the grave breaches of the present Convention defined in the following Article.

Each High Contracting Party shall be under the obligation to search for persons alleged to have committed. or to have ordered to be committed, such grave breaches, and shall bring such persons, regardless of their nationality, before its own courts. It may also, if it prefers, and in accordance with the provisions of its own legislation, hand such persons over for trial to another High Contracting Party concerned, provided such High Contracting Party has made out a prima facie case.

Each High Contracting Party shall take measures necessary for the suppression of all acts contrary to the provisions of the present Convention other than the grave breaches defined in the following Article.

In all circumstances, the accused persons shall benefit by safeguards of proper trial and defence, which shall not be less favourable than those provided by Article 105 and those following of the present Convention.

Article 130

Grave breaches to which the preceding Article relates shall be those involving any of the following acts, if committed against persons or property protected by the Convention: wilful killing, torture or inhuman treatment, including biological experiments, wilfully causing great suffering or serious injury to body or health, compelling a prisoner of war to serve in the forces of the hostile Power, or wilfully depriving a prisoner of war of the rights of fair and regular trial prescribed in this Convention.

Article 131

No High Contracting Party shall be allowed to absolve itself or any other High Contracting Party of any liability incurred by itself or by another High Contracting Party in respect of breaches referred to in the preceding Article.

Article 132

At the request of a Party to the conflict, an enquiry shall be instituted, in a manner to be decided between the interested Parties, concerning any alleged violation of the Convention.

If agreement has not been reached concerning the procedure for the enquiry, the Parties should agree on the choice of an umpire who will decide upon the procedure to be followed.

Once the violation has been established, the Parties to the conflict shall put an end to it and shall repress it with the least possible delay.

Section II
Final Provisions

Article 133

The present Convention is established in English and in French. Both texts are equally authentic.

The Swiss Federal Council shall arrange for official translations of the Convention to be made in the Russian and Spanish languages.

Article 134

The present Convention replaces the Convention of July 27, 1929, in relations between the High Contracting Parties.

Article 135

In the relations between the Powers which are bound by the Hague Convention respecting the Laws and Customs of War on Land, whether that of July 29, 1899, or that of October 18, 1907, and which are parties to the present Convention, this last Convention shall be complementary to Chapter II of the Regulations annexed to the above-mentioned Conventions of the Hague.

Article 136

The present Convention, which bears the date of this day, is open to signature until February 12, 1950, in the name of the Powers represented at the Conference which opened at Geneva on April 21, 1949; furthermore, by Powers not represented at that Conference, but which are parties to the Convention of July 27, 1929.

Article 137

The present Convention shall be ratified as soon as possible and the ratifications shall be deposited at Berne.

A record shall be drawn up of the deposit of each instrument of ratification and certified copies of this record shall be transmitted by the Swiss Federal Council to all the Powers in whose name the Convention has been signed, or whose accession has been notified.

Article 138

The present Convention shall come into force six months after not less than two instruments of ratification have been deposited.

Thereafter, it shall come into force for each High Contracting Party six months after the deposit of the instrument of ratification.

Article 139

From the date of its coming into force, it shall be open to any Power in whose name the present Convention has not been signed, to accede to this Convention.

Article 140

Accessions shall be notified in writing to the Swiss Federal Council, and shall take effect six months after the date on which they are received.

The Swiss Federal Council shall communicate the accessions to all the Powers in whose name the Convention has been signed, or whose accession has been notified.

Article 141

The situations provided for in Articles 2 and 3 shall give immediate effect to ratifications deposited and accessions notified by the Parties to the conflict before or after the beginning of hostilities or occupation. The Swiss Federal Council shall communicate by the quickest method any ratifications or accessions received from Parties to the conflict.

Article 142

Each of the High Contracting Parties shall be at liberty to denounce the present Convention.

The denunciation shall be notified in writing to the Swiss Federal Council, which shall transmit it to the Governments of all the High Contracting Parties.

The denunciation shall take effect one year after the notification thereof has been made to the Swiss Federal Council. However, a denunciation of which notification has been made at a time when the denouncing Power is involved in a conflict shall not take effect until peace has been concluded, and until after operations connected with release and repatriation of the persons protected by the present Convention have been terminated.

The denunciation shall have effect only in respect of the denouncing Power. It shall in no way impair the obligations which the Parties to the conflict shall remain bound to fulfil by virtue of the principles of the law of nations, as they result from the usages established among civilized peoples, from the laws of humanity and the dictates of the public conscience.

Article 143

The Swiss Federal Council shall register the present Convention with the Secretariat of the United Nations. The Swiss Federal Council shall also inform the Secretariat of the United Nations of all ratifications, accessions and denunciations received by it with respect to the present Convention.

IN WITNESS WHEREOF the undersigned, having deposited their respective full powers, have signed the present Convention.

DONE at Geneva this twelfth day of August 1949, in the English and French languages. The original shall be deposited in the Archives of the Swiss Confederation. The Swiss Federal Council shall transmit certified copies thereof to each of the signatory and acceding States.

ANNEX I
MODEL AGREEMENT CONCERNING DIRECT REPATRIATION AND ACCOMMODATION IN NEUTRAL COUNTRIES OF WOUNDED AND SICK PRISONERS OF WAR (SEE ART 110.)

I. Principles for Direct Repatriation and Accommodation in Neutral Countries

A. DIRECT REPATRIATION

The following shall be repatriated direct:

(1) All prisoners of war suffering from the following disabilities as the result of trauma: loss of a limb, paralysis, articular or other disabilities, when this disability is at least the loss of a hand or a foot, or the equivalent of the loss of a hand or a foot.

Without prejudice to a more generous interpretation, the following shall be considered as equivalent to the loss of a hand or a foot:

(a)   Loss of a hand or of all the fingers, or of the thumb and forefinger of one hand; loss of a foot, or of all the toes and metatarsals of one foot.

(b)   Ankylosis, loss of osseous tissue, cicatricial contracture preventing the functioning of one of the large articulations or of all the digital joints of one hand.

(c)   Pseudarthrosis of the long bones.

(d)   Deformities due to fracture or other injury which seriously interfere with function and weight-bearing power.

(2) All wounded prisoners of war whose condition has become chronic, to the extent that prognosis appears to exclude recovery–in spite of treatment–within one year from the date of the injury, as, for example, in case of:

(a)   Projectile in the heart, even if the Mixed Medical Commission should fail, at the time of their examination, to detect any serious disorders.

(b)   Metallic splinter in the brain or the lungs, even if the Mixed Medical Commission cannot, at the time of examination, detect any local or general reaction.

(c)   Osteomyelitis, when recovery cannot be foreseen in the course of the year following the injury, and which seems likely to result in ankylosis of a joint, or other impairments equivalent to the loss of a hand or a foot.

(d)   Perforating and suppurating injury to the large joints.

(e)   Injury to the skull, with loss or shifting of bony tissue.

(f)   Injury or burning of the face with loss of tissue and functional lesions.

(g)   Injury to the spinal cord.

(h)   Lesion of the peripheral nerves, the sequelae of which are equivalent to the loss of a hand or foot, and the cure of which requires more than a year from the date of injury, for example: injury to the brachial or lumbosacral plexus median or sciatic nerves, likewise combined injury to the radial and cubital nerves or to the lateral popliteal nerve (N. peroneous communis) and medial popliteal nerve (N. tibialis); etc. The separate injury of the radial (musculo-spiral), cubital, lateral or medial popliteal nerves shall not, however, warrant repatriation except in case of contractures or of serious neurotrophic disturbance.

(i)   Injury to the urinary system, with incapacitating results.

(3) All sick prisoners of war whose condition has become chronic to the extent that prognosis seems to exclude recovery–in, spite of treatment– within one year from the inception of the disease, as, for example, in case of:

(a)   Progressive tuberculosis of any organ which, according to medical prognosis, cannot be cured or at least considerably improved by treatment in a neutral country.

(b)   Exudate pleurisy.

(c)   Serious diseases of the respiratory organs of non-tubercular etiology, presumed incurable, for example: serious pulmonary emphysema, with or without bronchitis; chronic asthma *; chronic bronchitis * lasting more than one year in captivity; bronchiectasis *; etc.

(d)   Serious chronic affections of the circulatory system, for example: valvular lesions and myocarditis *, which have shown signs of circulatory failure during captivity, even though the Mixed Medical Commission cannot detect any such signs at the time of examination; affections of the pericardium and the vessels (Buerger's disease, aneurisms of the large vessels); etc.

(e)   Serious chronic affections of the digestive organs, for example: gastric or duodenal ulcer; sequelae of gastric operations performed in captivity; chronic gastritis, enteritis or colitis, having lasted more than one year and seriously affecting the general condition; cirrhosis of the liver; chronic cholecystopathy *; etc.

(f)   Serious chronic affections of the genito-urinary organs, for example: chronic diseases of the kidney with consequent disorders; nephrectomy because of a tubercular kidney; chronic pyelitis or chronic cystitis; hydronephrosis or pyonephrosis; chronic grave gynaecological conditions; normal pregnancy and obstetrical disorder, where it is impossible to accommodate in a neutral country; etc.

(g)   Serious chronic diseases of the central and peripheral nervous system, for example: all obvious psychoses and psychoneuroses, such as serious hysteria, serious captivity psychoneurosis, etc., duly verified by a specialist *; any epilepsy duly verified by the camp physician *; cerebral arteriosclerosis; chronic neuritis lasting more than one year; etc.

(h)   Serious chronic diseases of the neuro-vegetative system, with considerable diminution of mental or physical fitness, noticeable loss of weight and general asthenia.

(i)   Blindness of both eyes, or of one eye when the vision of the other is less than 1 in spite of the use of corrective glasses; diminution of visual acuity in cases where it is impossible to restore it by correction to an acuity of 1/2 in at least one eye *; other grave ocular affections, for example: glaucoma, iritis, choroiditis; trachoma; etc.

(k)   Auditive disorders, such as total unilateral deafness, if the other ear does not discern the ordinary spoken word at a distance of one metre *; etc.
        (l) Serious affections of metabolism, for example: diabetes mellitus requiring insulin treatment; etc.

(m)   Serious disorders of the endocrine glands, for example: thyrotoxicosis; hypothyrosis; Addison's disease; Simmonds' cachexia; tetany; etc.

(n)   Grave and chronic disorders of the blood-forming organs.

(o)   Serious cases of chronic intoxication, for example: lead poisoning, mercury poisoning, morphinism, cocainism, alcoholism; gas or radiation poisoning; etc.

(p)   Chronic affections of locomotion, with obvious functional disorders, for example: arthritis deformans; primary and secondary progressive chronic polyarthritis; rheumatism with serious clinical symptoms; etc.

(q)   Serious chronic skin diseases, not amenable to treatment.

(r)   Any malignant growth.

(s)   Serious chronic infectious diseases, persisting for one year after their inception, for example: malaria with decided organic impairment, amoebic or bacillary dysentery with grave disorders; tertiary visceral syphilis resistant to treatment; leprosy; etc.

(t)   Serious avitaminosis or serious inanition.

[NOTE] * The decision of the Mixed Medical Commission shall be based to a great extent on the records kept by camp physicians and surgeons of the same nationality as the prisoners of war, or on an examination by medical specialists of the Detaining Power.

B. ACCOMMODATION IN NEUTRAL COUNTRIES

The following shall be eligible for accommodation in a neutral country:

(1) All wounded prisoners of war who are not likely to recover in captivity, but who might be cured or whose condition might be considerably improved by accommodation in a neutral country.

(2) Prisoners of war suffering from any form of tuberculosis, of whatever organ, and whose treatment in a neutral country would be likely to lead to recovery or at least to considerable improvement, with the exception of primary tuberculosis cured before captivity.

(3) Prisoners of war suffering from affections requiring treatment of the respiratory, circulatory, digestive, nervous, sensory, genito-urinary, cutaneous, locomotive organs, etc., if such treatment would clearly have better results in a neutral country than in captivity.

(4) Prisoners of war who have undergone a nephrectomy in captivity for a non-tubercular renal affection; cases of osteomyelitis, on the way to recovery or latent; diabetes mellitus not requiring insulin treatment; etc.

(5) Prisoners of war suffering from war or captivity neuroses. Cases of captivity neurosis which are not cured after three months of accommodation in a neutral country, or which after that length of time are not clearly on the way to complete cure, shall be repatriated.

(6) All prisoners of war suffering from chronic intoxication (gases, metals, alkaloids, etc.), for whom the prospects of cure in a neutral country are especially favourable.

(7) All women prisoners of war who are pregnant or mothers with infants and small children.

The following cases shall not be eligible for accommodation in a neutral country:
(1) All duly verified chronic psychoses.

(2) All organic or functional nervous affections considered to be incurable.

(3) All contagious diseases during the period in which they are transmissible, with the exception of tuberculosis.

II. General Observations

(1) The conditions given shall, in a general way, be interpreted and applied in as broad a spirit as possible. Neuropathic and psychopathic conditions caused by war or captivity, as well as cases of tuberculosis in all stages, shall above all benefit by such liberal interpretation. Prisoners of war who have sustained several wounds, none of which, considered by itself, justifies repatriation, shall be examined in the same spirit, with due regard for the psychic traumatism due to the number of their wounds.

(2) All unquestionable cases giving the right to direct repatriation (amputation, total blindness or deafness, open pulmonary tuberculosis, mental disorder, malignant growth, etc.) shall be examined and repatriated as soon as possible by the camp physicians or by military medical commissions appointed by the Detaining Power.

(3) Injuries and diseases which existed before the war and which have not become worse, as well as war injuries which have not prevented subsequent military service, shall not entitle to direct repatriation.

(4) The provisions of this Annex shall be interpreted and applied in a similar manner in all countries party to the conflict. The Powers and authorities concerned shall grant to Mixed Medical Commissions all the facilities necessary for the accomplishment of their task.

(5) The examples quoted under (1) above represent only typical cases. Cases which do not correspond exactly to these provisions shall be judged in the spirit of the provisions of Article 110 of the present Convention, and of the principles embodied in the present Agreement.

ANNEX II
REGULATIONS CONCERNING MIXED MEDICAL COMMISSIONS (SEE ART 112.)

Article 1

The Mixed Medical Commissions provided for in Article 112 of the Convention shall be composed of three members, two of whom shall belong to a neutral country, the third being appointed by the Detaining Power. One of the neutral members shall take the chair.

Article 2

The two neutral members shall be appointed by the International Committee of the Red Cross, acting in agreement with the Protecting Power, at the request of the Detaining Power. They may be domiciled either in their country of origin, in any other neutral country, or in the territory of the Detaining Power.

Article 3

The neutral members shall be approved by the Parties to the conflict concerned, who shall notify their approval to the International Committee of the Red Cross and to the Protecting Power. Upon such notification, the neutral members shall be considered as effectively appointed.

Article 4

Deputy members shall also be appointed in sufficient number to replace the regular members in case of need. They shall be appointed at the same time as the regular members or, at least, as soon as possible.

Article 5

If for any reason the International Committee of the Red Cross cannot arrange for the appointment of the neutral members, this shall be done by the Power protecting the interests of the prisoners of war to be examined.

Article 6

So far as possible, one of the two neutral members shall be a surgeon and the other a physician.

Article 7

The neutral members shall be entirely independent of the Parties to the conflict, which shall grant them all facilities in the accomplishment of their duties.

Article 8

By agreement with the Detaining Power, the International Committee of the Red Cross, when making the appointments provided for in Articles 2 and 4 of the present Regulations, shall settle the terms of service of the nominees.

Article 9

The Mixed Medical Commissions shall begin their work as soon as possible after the neutral members have been approved, and in any case within a period of three months from the date of such approval.

Article 10

The Mixed Medical Commissions shall examine all the prisoners designated in Article 113 of the Convention. They shall propose repatriation, rejection, or reference to a later examination. Their decisions shall be made by a majority vote.

Article 11

The decisions made by the Mixed Medical Commissions in each specific case shall be communicated, during the month following their visit, to the Detaining Power, the Protecting Power and the International Committee of the Red Cross. The Mixed Medical Commissions shall also inform each prisoner of war examined of the decision made, and shall issue to those whose repatriation has been proposed, certificates similar to the model appended to the present Convention.

Article 12

The Detaining Power shall be required to carry out the decisions of the Mixed Medical Commissions within three months of the time when it receives due notification of such decisions.

Article 13

If there is no neutral physician in a country where the services of a Mixed Medical Commission seem to be required, and if it is for any reason impossible to appoint neutral doctors who are resident in another country, the Detaining Power, acting in agreement with the Protecting Power, shall set up a Medical Commission which shall undertake the same duties as a Mixed Medical Commission, subject to the provisions of Articles 1, 2, 3, 4, 5 and 8 of the present Regulations.

Article 14

Mixed Medical Commissions shall function permanently and shall visit each camp at intervals of not more than six months.

ANNEX III
REGULATIONS CONCERNING COLLECTIVE RELIEF (SEE ART 73.)

Article 1

Prisoners' representatives shall be allowed to distribute collective relief shipments for which they are responsible, to all prisoners of war administered by their camp, including those who are in hospitals, or in prisons or other penal establishments.

Article 2

The distribution of collective relief shipments shall be effected in accordance with the instructions of the donors and with a plan drawn up by the prisoners' representatives. The issue of medical stores shall, however, be made for preference in agreement with the senior medical officers, and the latter may, in hospitals and infirmaries, waive the said instructions, if the needs of their patients so demand. Within the limits thus defined, the distribution shall always be carried out equitably.

Article 3

The said prisoners' representatives or their assistants shall be allowed to go to the points of arrival of relief supplies near their camps, so as to enable the prisoners' representatives or their assistants to verify the quality as well as the quantity of the goods received, and to make out detailed reports thereon for the donors.

Article 4

Prisoners' representatives shall be given the facilities necessary for verifying whether the distribution of collective relief in all subdivisions and annexes of their camps has been carried out in accordance with their instructions.

Article 5

Prisoners' representatives shall be allowed to fill up, and cause to be filled up by the prisoners' representatives of labour detachments or by the senior medical officers of infirmaries and hospitals, forms or questionnaires intended for the donors, relating to collective relief supplies (distribution, requirements, quantities, etc.). Such forms and questionnaires, duly completed, shall be forwarded to the donors without delay.

Article 6

In order to secure the regular issue of collective relief to the prisoners of war in their camp, and to meet any needs that may arise from the arrival of new contingents of prisoners, prisoners' representatives shall be allowed to build up and maintain adequate reserve stocks of collective relief. For this purpose, they shall have suitable warehouses at their disposal; each warehouse shall be provided with two locks, the prisoners' representative holding the keys of one lock and the camp commander the keys of the other.

Article 7

When collective consignments of clothing are available, each prisoner of war shall retain in his possession at least one complete set of clothes. If a prisoner has more than one set of clothes, the prisoners' representative shall be permitted to withdraw excess clothing from those with the largest number of sets, or particular articles in excess of one, if this is necessary in order to supply prisoners who are less well provided. He shall not, however, withdraw second sets of underclothing, socks or footwear, unless this is the only means of providing for prisoners of war with none.

Article 8

The High Contracting Parties, and the Detaining Powers in particular, shall authorize, as far as possible and subject to the regulations governing the supply of the population, all purchases of goods made in their territories for the distribution of collective relief to prisoners of war. They shall similarly facilitate the transfer of funds and other financial measures of a technical or administrative nature taken for the purpose of making such purchases.

Article 9

The foregoing provisions shall not constitute an obstacle to the right of prisoners of war to receive collective relief before their arrival in a camp or in the course of transfer, nor to the possibility of representatives of the Protecting Power, the International Committee of the Red Cross, or any other body giving assistance to prisoners which may be responsible for the forwarding of such supplies, ensuring the distribution thereof to the addressees by any other means that they may deem useful.

ANNEX IV
(A) IDENTITY CARD (SEE ART 4.)

[Not reproduced]

CHAPTER 17

CONVENTION (IV) RELATIVE TO THE PROTECTION OF CIVILIAN PERSONS IN TIME OF WAR GENEVA, 12 AUGUST 1949

Preamble

The undersigned Plenipotentiaries of the Governments represented at the Diplomatic Conference held at Geneva from April 21 to August 12, 1949, for the purpose of establishing a Convention for the Protection of Civilian Persons in Time of War, have agreed as follows:

Status—The status of the four Geneva Conventions is that of binding international Conventions not incorporated into domestic law [**RCLP para 3.94**]. The four Geneva Conventions are Convention I for the Amelioration of the Condition of the Wounded and Sick in Armed Forces in the Field, Convention II for the Amelioration of the Condition of Wounded, Sick and Shipwrecked Members of the Armed Forces, Convention III Relative to the Treatment of Prisoners of War and Convention IV Relative to the Protection of Civilian Persons in Time of War [**RCLP para 15.121–15.122**]. Only Conventions III and IV are included in this work. Two additional protocols were added to the Geneva Conventions in 1977. Protocols I and II are included in this work. The United Kingdom ratified Protocols I and II on 28 January 1998 and registered reservations in respect of Protocol I [**RCLP para 15.121**]. Protocol III (which is not included in this work) provides for the addition of a non-religious and politically neutral emblem of the 'red crystal' to the Red Cross and Red Crescent emblems. The Geneva Conventions should be read with the Protocol to the UNCRC on the Protection of Children from Involvement in Armed Conflict and the Paris Commitments and Principles concerning the protection of children from unlawful recruitment or used by armed forces or armed groups [**RCLP para 2.59**]. Note that, in respect of Geneva Convention IV Relative to the Protection of Civilian Persons in Time of War Art 38(4) of the UNCRC requires States parties to fulfil their obligations under international humanitarian law to protect the civilian population in armed conflicts and to take all feasible measures to ensure the protection and care of children who are affected by armed conflict [**RCLP para 15.101**].

PART I
GENERAL PROVISIONS

Article 1

The High Contracting Parties undertake to respect and to ensure respect for the present Convention in all circumstances.

Article 2

In addition to the provisions which shall be implemented in peace-time, the present Convention shall apply to all cases of declared war or of any other armed conflict which may arise between two or more of the High Contracting Parties, even if the state of war is not recognized by one of them.

The Convention shall also apply to all cases of partial or total occupation of the territory of a High Contracting Party, even if the said occupation meets with no armed resistance.

Although one of the Powers in conflict may not be a party to the present Convention, the Powers who are parties thereto shall remain bound by it in their mutual relations. They shall furthermore be bound by the Convention in relation to the said Power, if the latter accepts and applies the provisions thereof.

Article 3

In the case of armed conflict not of an international character occurring in the territory of one of the High Contracting Parties, each Party to the conflict shall be bound to apply, as a minimum, the following provisions:

(1) Persons taking no active part in the hostilities, including members of armed forces who have laid down their arms and those placed hors de combat by sickness, wounds, detention, or any other cause, shall in all circumstances be treated humanely, without any adverse distinction founded on race, colour, religion or faith, sex, birth or wealth, or any other similar criteria.

To this end the following acts are and shall remain prohibited at any time and in any place whatsoever with respect to the above-mentioned persons:

(a)   violence to life and person, in particular murder of all kinds, mutilation, cruel treatment and torture;
(b)   taking of hostages;
(c)   outrages upon personal dignity, in particular humiliating and degrading treatment;
(d)   the passing of sentences and the carrying out of executions without previous judgment pronounced by a regularly constituted court, affording all the judicial guarantees which are recognized as indispensable by civilized peoples.

(2) The wounded and sick shall be collected and cared for.

An impartial humanitarian body, such as the International Committee of the Red Cross, may offer its services to the Parties to the conflict.

The Parties to the conflict should further endeavour to bring into force, by means of special agreements, all or part of the other provisions of the present Convention.

The application of the preceding provisions shall not affect the legal status of the Parties to the conflict.

Article 4

Persons protected by the Convention are those who, at a given moment and in any manner whatsoever, find themselves, in case of a conflict or occupation, in the hands of a Party to the conflict or Occupying Power of which they are not nationals.

Nationals of a State which is not bound by the Convention are not protected by it. Nationals of a neutral State who find themselves in the territory of a belligerent State, and nationals of a co-belligerent State, shall not be regarded as protected persons while the State of which they are nationals has normal diplomatic representation in the State in whose hands they are.

The provisions of Part II are, however, wider in application, as defined in Article 13.

Persons protected by the Geneva Convention for the Amelioration of the Condition of the Wounded and Sick in Armed Forces in the Field of 12 August 1949, or by the Geneva Convention for the Amelioration of the Condition of Wounded, Sick and Shipwrecked Members of Armed Forces at Sea of 12 August 1949, or by the Geneva

Convention relative to the Treatment of Prisoners of War of 12 August 1949, shall not be considered as protected persons within the meaning of the present Convention.

Article 5

Where in the territory of a Party to the conflict, the latter is satisfied that an individual protected person is definitely suspected of or engaged in activities hostile to the security of the State, such individual person shall not be entitled to claim such rights and privileges under the present Convention as would, if exercised in the favour of such individual person, be prejudicial to the security of such State.

Where in occupied territory an individual protected person is detained as a spy or saboteur, or as a person under definite suspicion of activity hostile to the security of the Occupying Power, such person shall, in those cases where absolute military security so requires, be regarded as having forfeited rights of communication under the present Convention.

In each case, such persons shall nevertheless be treated with humanity and, in case of trial, shall not be deprived of the rights of fair and regular trial prescribed by the present Convention. They shall also be granted the full rights and privileges of a protected person under the present Convention at the earliest date consistent with the security of the State or Occupying Power, as the case may be.

'**shall not be deprived of the rights of fair and regular trial**' (Art 5)—See also Arts 45(3) and 85(4)(e) of the Protocol I to the Geneva Conventions.

Article 6

The present Convention shall apply from the outset of any conflict or occupation mentioned in Article 2.

In the territory of Parties to the conflict, the application of the present Convention shall cease on the general close of military operations.

In the case of occupied territory, the application of the present Convention shall cease one year after the general close of military operations; however, the Occupying Power shall be bound, for the duration of the occupation, to the extent that such Power exercises the functions of government in such territory, by the provisions of the following Articles of the present Convention: 1 to 12, 27, 29 to 34, 47, 49, 51, 52, 53, 59, 61 to 77, 143.

Protected persons whose release, repatriation or re-establishment may take place after such dates shall meanwhile continue to benefit by the present Convention.

Article 7

In addition to the agreements expressly provided for in Articles 11, 14, 15, 17, 36, 108, 109, 132, 133 and 149, the High Contracting Parties may conclude other special agreements for all matters concerning which they may deem it suitable to make separate provision. No special agreement shall adversely affect the situation of protected persons, as defined by the present Convention, not restrict the rights which it confers upon them.

Protected persons shall continue to have the benefit of such agreements as long as the Convention is applicable to them, except where express provisions to the contrary are contained in the aforesaid or in subsequent agreements, or where more favourable measures have been taken with regard to them by one or other of the Parties to the conflict.

Article 8

Protected persons may in no circumstances renounce in part or in entirety the rights secured to them by the present Convention, and by the special agreements referred to in the foregoing Article, if such there be.

Article 9

The present Convention shall be applied with the cooperation and under the scrutiny of the Protecting Powers whose duty it is to safeguard the interests of the Parties to the conflict. For this purpose, the Protecting Powers may appoint, apart from their diplomatic or consular staff, delegates from amongst their own nationals or the nationals of other neutral Powers. The said delegates shall be subject to the approval of the Power with which they are to carry out their duties.

The Parties to the conflict shall facilitate to the greatest extent possible the task of the representatives or delegates of the Protecting Powers.

The representatives or delegates of the Protecting Powers shall not in any case exceed their mission under the present Convention. They shall, in particular, take account of the imperative necessities of security of the State wherein they carry out their duties.

Article 10

The provisions of the present Convention constitute no obstacle to the humanitarian activities which the International Committee of the Red Cross or any other impartial humanitarian organization may, subject to the consent of the Parties to the conflict concerned, undertake for the protection of civilian persons and for their relief.

Article 11

The High Contracting Parties may at any time agree to entrust to an international organization which offers all guarantees of impartiality and efficacy the duties incumbent on the Protecting Powers by virtue of the present Convention.

When persons protected by the present Convention do not benefit or cease to benefit, no matter for what reason, by the activities of a Protecting Power or of an organization provided for in the first paragraph above, the Detaining Power shall request a neutral State, or such an organization, to undertake the functions performed under the present Convention by a Protecting Power designated by the Parties to a conflict.

If protection cannot be arranged accordingly, the Detaining Power shall request or shall accept, subject to the provisions of this Article, the offer of the services of a humanitarian organization, such as the International Committee of the Red Cross, to assume the humanitarian functions performed by Protecting Powers under the present Convention.

Any neutral Power or any organization invited by the Power concerned or offering itself for these purposes, shall be required to act with a sense of responsibility towards the Party to the conflict on which persons protected by the present Convention depend, and shall be required to furnish sufficient assurances that it is in a position to undertake the appropriate functions and to discharge them impartially.

No derogation from the preceding provisions shall be made by special agreements between Powers one of which is restricted, even temporarily, in its freedom to negotiate with the other Power or its allies by reason of military events, more particularly where the whole, or a substantial part, of the territory of the said Power is occupied.

Whenever in the present Convention mention is made of a Protecting Power, such mention applies to substitute organizations in the sense of the present Article.

The provisions of this Article shall extend and be adapted to cases of nationals of a neutral State who are in occupied territory or who find themselves in the territory of a belligerent State in which the State of which they are nationals has not normal diplomatic representation.

Article 12

In cases where they deem it advisable in the interest of protected persons, particularly in cases of disagreement between the Parties to the conflict as to the application or interpretation of the provisions of the present Convention, the Protecting Powers shall lend their good offices with a view to settling the disagreement.

For this purpose, each of the Protecting Powers may, either at the invitation of one Party or on its own initiative, propose to the Parties to the conflict a meeting of their representatives, and in particular of the authorities responsible for protected persons, possibly on neutral territory suitably chosen. The Parties to the conflict shall be bound to give effect to the proposals made to them for this purpose. The Protecting Powers may, if necessary, propose for approval by the Parties to the conflict a person belonging to a neutral Power, or delegated by the International Committee of the Red Cross, who shall be invited to take part in such a meeting.

PART II
GENERAL PROTECTION OF POPULATIONS AGAINST CERTAIN CONSEQUENCES OF WAR

Article 13

The provisions of Part II cover the whole of the populations of the countries in conflict, without any adverse distinction based, in particular, on race, nationality, religion or political opinion, and are intended to alleviate the sufferings caused by war.

Article 14

In time of peace, the High Contracting Parties and, after the outbreak of hostilities, the Parties thereto, may establish in their own territory and, if the need arises, in occupied areas, hospital and safety zones and localities so organized as to protect from the effects of war, wounded, sick and aged persons, children under fifteen, expectant mothers and mothers of children under seven.

Upon the outbreak and during the course of hostilities, the Parties concerned may conclude agreements on mutual recognition of the zones and localities they have created. They may for this purpose implement the provisions of the Draft Agreement annexed to the present Convention, with such amendments as they may consider necessary.

The Protecting Powers and the International Committee of the Red Cross are invited to lend their good offices in order to facilitate the institution and recognition of these hospital and safety zones and localities.

Article 15

Any Party to the conflict may, either direct or through a neutral State or some humanitarian organization, propose to the adverse Party to establish, in the regions where fighting is taking place, neutralized zones intended to shelter from the effects of war the following persons, without distinction:

(a) wounded and sick combatants or non-combatants;
(b) civilian persons who take no part in hostilities, and who, while they reside in the zones, perform no work of a military character.

When the Parties concerned have agreed upon the geographical position, administration, food supply and supervision of the proposed neutralized zone, a written agreement shall be concluded and signed by the representatives of the Parties to the conflict. The agreement shall fix the beginning and the duration of the neutralization of the zone.

Article 16

The wounded and sick, as well as the infirm, and expectant mothers, shall be the object of particular protection and respect.

As far as military considerations allow, each Party to the conflict shall facilitate the steps taken to search for the killed and wounded, to assist the shipwrecked and other persons exposed to grave danger, and to protect them against pillage and ill-treatment.

Article 17

The Parties to the conflict shall endeavour to conclude local agreements for the removal from besieged or encircled areas, of wounded, sick, infirm, and aged persons, children and maternity cases, and for the passage of ministers of all religions, medical personnel and medical equipment on their way to such areas.

Article 18

Civilian hospitals organized to give care to the wounded and sick, the infirm and maternity cases, may in no circumstances be the object of attack but shall at all times be respected and protected by the Parties to the conflict.

States which are Parties to a conflict shall provide all civilian hospitals with certificates showing that they are civilian hospitals and that the buildings which they occupy are not used for any purpose which would deprive these hospitals of protection in accordance with Article 19.

Civilian hospitals shall be marked by means of the emblem provided for in Article 38 of the Geneva Convention for the Amelioration of the Condition of the Wounded and Sick in Armed Forces in the Field of 12 August 1949, but only if so authorized by the State.

The Parties to the conflict shall, in so far as military considerations permit, take the necessary steps to make the distinctive emblems indicating civilian hospitals clearly visible to the enemy land, air and naval forces in order to obviate the possibility of any hostile action.

In view of the dangers to which hospitals may be exposed by being close to military objectives, it is recommended that such hospitals be situated as far as possible from such objectives.

Article 19

The protection to which civilian hospitals are entitled shall not cease unless they are used to commit, outside their humanitarian duties, acts harmful to the enemy. Protection may, however, cease only after due warning has been given, naming, in all appropriate cases, a reasonable time limit and after such warning has remained unheeded.

The fact that sick or wounded members of the armed forces are nursed in these hospitals, or the presence of small arms and ammunition taken from such combatants and not yet been handed to the proper service, shall not be considered to be acts harmful to the enemy.

Article 20

Persons regularly and solely engaged in the operation and administration of civilian hospitals, including the personnel engaged in the search for, removal and transporting of and caring for wounded and sick civilians, the infirm and maternity cases shall be respected and protected.

In occupied territory and in zones of military operations, the above personnel shall be recognizable by means of an identity card certifying their status, bearing the photograph of the holder and embossed with the stamp of the responsible authority, and also by means of a stamped, water-resistant armlet which they shall wear on the left arm while carrying out their duties. This armlet shall be issued by the State and shall bear the emblem provided for in Article 38 of the Geneva Convention for the Amelioration of the Condition of the Wounded and Sick in Armed Forces in the Field of 12 August 1949.

Other personnel who are engaged in the operation and administration of civilian hospitals shall be entitled to respect and protection and to wear the armlet, as provided in and under the conditions prescribed in this Article, while they are employed on such duties. The identity card shall state the duties on which they are employed.

The management of each hospital shall at all times hold at the disposal of the competent national or occupying authorities an up-to-date list of such personnel.

Article 21

Convoys of vehicles or hospital trains on land or specially provided vessels on sea, conveying wounded and sick civilians, the infirm and maternity cases, shall be respected and protected in the same manner as the hospitals provided for in Article 18, and shall be marked, with the consent of the State, by the display of the distinctive emblem provided for in Article 38 of the Geneva Convention for the Amelioration of the Condition of the Wounded and Sick in Armed Forces in the Field of 12 August 1949.

Article 22

Aircraft exclusively employed for the removal of wounded and sick civilians, the infirm and maternity cases or for the transport of medical personnel and equipment, shall not be attacked, but shall be respected while flying at heights, times and on routes specifically agreed upon between all the Parties to the conflict concerned.

They may be marked with the distinctive emblem provided for in Article 38 of the Geneva Convention for the Amelioration of the Condition of the Wounded and Sick in Armed Forces in the Field of 12 August 1949.

Unless agreed otherwise, flights over enemy or enemy occupied territory are prohibited.

Such aircraft shall obey every summons to land. In the event of a landing thus imposed, the aircraft with its occupants may continue its flight after examination, if any.

Article 23

Each High Contracting Party shall allow the free passage of all consignments of medical and hospital stores and objects necessary for religious worship intended only for civilians of another High Contracting Party, even if the latter is its adversary. It shall likewise permit the free passage of all consignments of essential foodstuffs, clothing and tonics intended for children under fifteen, expectant mothers and maternity cases.

The obligation of a High Contracting Party to allow the free passage of the consignments indicated in the preceding paragraph is subject to the condition that this Party is satisfied that there are no serious reasons for fearing:

- (a) that the consignments may be diverted from their destination,
- (b) that the control may not be effective, or
- (c) that a definite advantage may accrue to the military efforts or economy of the enemy through the substitution of the above-mentioned consignments for goods which would otherwise be provided or produced by the enemy or through the release of such material, services or facilities as would otherwise be required for the production of such goods.

The Power which allows the passage of the consignments indicated in the first paragraph of this Article may make such permission conditional on the distribution to the persons benefited thereby being made under the local supervision of the Protecting Powers.

Such consignments shall be forwarded as rapidly as possible, and the Power which permits their free passage shall have the right to prescribe the technical arrangements under which such passage is allowed.

Article24

The Parties to the conflict shall take the necessary measures to ensure that children under fifteen, who are orphaned or are separated from their families as a result of the war, are not left to their own resources, and that their maintenance, the exercise of their religion and their education are facilitated in all circumstances. Their education shall, as far as possible, be entrusted to persons of a similar cultural tradition.

The Parties to the conflict shall facilitate the reception of such children in a neutral country for the duration of the conflict with the consent of the Protecting Power, if any, and under due safeguards for the observance of the principles stated in the first paragraph.

They shall, furthermore, endeavour to arrange for all children under twelve to be identified by the wearing of identity discs, or by some other means.

'identity discs, or by some other means' (Art 24)—See also Protocol I to the Geneva Conventions Art 78(3) [RCLP para 15.127].

Reception in a neutral country (Art 24)—Note that, in relation to non-international conflicts, Art 4(3)(e) of Protocol II to the Geneva Conventions will govern evacuation of children from an area in which hostilities are taking place [RCLP para 15.128].

Article 25

All persons in the territory of a Party to the conflict, or in a territory occupied by it, shall be enabled to give news of a strictly personal nature to members of their families, wherever they may be, and to receive news from them. This correspondence shall be forwarded speedily and without undue delay.

If, as a result of circumstances, it becomes difficult or impossible to exchange family correspondence by the ordinary post, the Parties to the conflict concerned shall apply to a neutral intermediary, such as the Central Agency provided for in Article 140, and shall decide in consultation with it how to ensure the fulfilment of their obligations under the best possible conditions, in particular with the cooperation of the National Red Cross (Red Crescent, Red Lion and Sun) Societies.

If the Parties to the conflict deem it necessary to restrict family correspondence, such restrictions shall be confined to the compulsory use of standard forms containing twenty-five freely chosen words, and to the limitation of the number of these forms despatched to one each month.

Article 26

Each Party to the conflict shall facilitate enquiries made by members of families dispersed owing to the war, with the object of renewing contact with one another and of meeting, if possible. It shall encourage, in particular, the work of organizations engaged on this task provided they are acceptable to it and conform to its security regulations.

PART III
STATUS AND TREATMENT OF PROTECTED PERSONS

Section I
Provisions common to the territories of the parties to the conflict and to occupied territories

Article 27

Protected persons are entitled, in all circumstances, to respect for their persons, their honour, their family rights, their religious convictions and practices, and their manners and customs. They shall at all times be humanely treated, and shall be protected especially against all acts of violence or threats thereof and against insults and public curiosity.

Women shall be especially protected against any attack on their honour, in particular against rape, enforced prostitution, or any form of indecent assault.

Without prejudice to the provisions relating to their state of health, age and sex, all protected persons shall be treated with the same consideration by the Party to the conflict in whose power they are, without any adverse distinction based, in particular, on race, religion or political opinion.

However, the Parties to the conflict may take such measures of control and security in regard to protected persons as may be necessary as a result of the war.

Article 28

The presence of a protected person may not be used to render certain points or areas immune from military operations.

Article 29

The Party to the conflict in whose hands protected persons may be, is responsible for the treatment accorded to them by its agents, irrespective of any individual responsibility which may be incurred.

Article 30

Protected persons shall have every facility for making application to the Protecting Powers, the International Committee of the Red Cross, the National Red Cross (Red Crescent, Red Lion and Sun) Society of the country where they may be, as well as to any organization that might assist them.

These several organizations shall be granted all facilities for that purpose by the authorities, within the bounds set by military or security considerations.

Apart from the visits of the delegates of the Protecting Powers and of the International Committee of the Red Cross, provided for by Article 143, the Detaining or Occupying Powers shall facilitate, as much as possible, visits to protected persons by the representatives of other organizations whose object is to give spiritual aid or material relief to such persons.

Article 31

No physical or moral coercion shall be exercised against protected persons, in particular to obtain information from them or from third parties.

Article 32

The High Contracting Parties specifically agree that each of them is prohibited from taking any measure of such a character as to cause the physical suffering or extermination of protected persons in their hands. This prohibition applies not only to murder, torture, corporal punishments, mutilation and medical or scientific experiments not necessitated by the medical treatment of a protected person, but also to any other measures of brutality whether applied by civilian or military agents.

Article 33

No protected person may be punished for an offence he or she has not personally committed. Collective penalties and likewise all measures of intimidation or of terrorism are prohibited.

Pillage is prohibited.

Reprisals against protected persons and their property are prohibited.

Article 34

The taking of hostages is prohibited.

Section II
Aliens in the territory of a party to the conflict

Article 35

All protected persons who may desire to leave the territory at the outset of, or during a conflict, shall be entitled to do so, unless their departure is contrary to the national interests of the State. The applications of such persons to leave shall be decided in accordance with regularly established procedures and the decision shall be taken as rapidly as possible. Those persons permitted to leave may provide themselves with the necessary funds for their journey and take with them a reasonable amount of their effects and articles of personal use.

If any such person is refused permission to leave the territory, he shall be entitled to have refusal reconsidered, as soon as possible by an appropriate court or administrative board designated by the Detaining Power for that purpose.

Upon request, representatives of the Protecting Power shall, unless reasons of security prevent it, or the persons concerned object, be furnished with the reasons for refusal of any request for permission to leave the territory and be given, as expeditiously as possible, the names of all persons who have been denied permission to leave.

Article 36

Departures permitted under the foregoing Article shall be carried out in satisfactory conditions as regards safety, hygiene, sanitation and food. All costs in connection therewith, from the point of exit in the territory of the Detaining Power, shall be borne by the country of destination, or, in the case of accommodation in a neutral country, by the Power whose nationals are benefited. The practical details of such movements may, if necessary, be settled by special agreements between the Powers concerned.

The foregoing shall not prejudice such special agreements as may be concluded between Parties to the conflict concerning the exchange and repatriation of their nationals in enemy hands.

Article 37

Protected persons who are confined pending proceedings or serving a sentence involving loss of liberty, shall during their confinement be humanely treated.

As soon as they are released, they may ask to leave the territory in conformity with the foregoing Articles.

Article 38

With the exception of special measures authorized by the present Convention, in particularly by Article 27 and 41 thereof, the situation of protected persons shall continue to be regulated, in principle, by the provisions concerning aliens in time of peace. In any case, the following rights shall be granted to them:

(1) they shall be enabled to receive the individual or collective relief that may be sent to them.

(2) they shall, if their state of health so requires, receive medical attention and hospital treatment to the same extent as the nationals of the State concerned.

(3) they shall be allowed to practise their religion and to receive spiritual assistance from ministers of their faith.

(4) if they reside in an area particularly exposed to the dangers of war, they shall be authorized to move from that area to the same extent as the nationals of the State concerned.

(5) children under fifteen years, pregnant women and mothers of children under seven years shall benefit by any preferential treatment to the same extent as the nationals of the State concerned.

Article 39

Protected persons who, as a result of the war, have lost their gainful employment, shall be granted the opportunity to find paid employment. That opportunity shall, subject to security considerations and to the provisions of Article 40, be equal to that enjoyed by the nationals of the Power in whose territory they are.

Where a Party to the conflict applies to a protected person methods of control which result in his being unable to support himself, and especially if such a person is prevented for reasons of security from finding paid employment on reasonable conditions, the said Party shall ensure his support and that of his dependents.

Protected persons may in any case receive allowances from their home country, the Protecting Power, or the relief societies referred to in Article 30.

Article 40

Protected persons may be compelled to work only to the same extent as nationals of the Party to the conflict in whose territory they are.

If protected persons are of enemy nationality, they may only be compelled to do work which is normally necessary to ensure the feeding, sheltering, clothing, transport and health of human beings and which is not directly related to the conduct of military operations.

In the cases mentioned in the two preceding paragraphs, protected persons compelled to work shall have the benefit of the same working conditions and of the same safeguards as national workers in particular as regards wages, hours of labour, clothing and equipment, previous training and compensation for occupational accidents and diseases.

If the above provisions are infringed, protected persons shall be allowed to exercise their right of complaint in accordance with Article 30.

Article 41

Should the Power, in whose hands protected persons may be, consider the measures of control mentioned in the present Convention to be inadequate, it may not have recourse to any other measure of control more severe than that of assigned residence or internment, in accordance with the provisions of Articles 42 and 43.

In applying the provisions of Article 39, second paragraph, to the cases of persons required to leave their usual places of residence by virtue of a decision placing them in assigned residence elsewhere, the Detaining Power shall be guided as closely as possible by the standards of welfare set forth in Part III, Section IV of this Convention.

Article 42

The internment or placing in assigned residence of protected persons may be ordered only if the security of the Detaining Power makes it absolutely necessary.

If any person, acting through the representatives of the Protecting Power, voluntarily demands internment, and if his situation renders this step necessary, he shall be interned by the Power in whose hands he may be.

Article 43

Any protected person who has been interned or placed in assigned residence shall be entitled to have such action reconsidered as soon as possible by an appropriate court or administrative board designated by the Detaining Power for that purpose. If the internment or placing in assigned residence is maintained, the court or administrative board shall periodically, and at least twice yearly, give consideration to his or her case, with a view to the favourable amendment of the initial decision, if circumstances permit.

Unless the protected persons concerned object, the Detaining Power shall, as rapidly as possible, give the Protecting Power the names of any protected persons who have been interned or subjected to assigned residence, or who have been released from internment or assigned residence. The decisions of the courts or boards mentioned in the first paragraph of the present Article shall also, subject to the same conditions, be notified as rapidly as possible to the Protecting Power.

Article 44

In applying the measures of control mentioned in the present Convention, the Detaining Power shall not treat as enemy aliens exclusively on the basis of their nationality de jure of an enemy State, refugees who do not, in fact, enjoy the protection of any government.

Article 45

Protected persons shall not be transferred to a Power which is not a party to the Convention.

This provision shall in no way constitute an obstacle to the repatriation of protected persons, or to their return to their country of residence after the cessation of hostilities.

Protected persons may be transferred by the Detaining Power only to a Power which is a party to the present Convention and after the Detaining Power has satisfied itself of the willingness and ability of such transferee Power to apply the present Convention. If protected persons are transferred under such circumstances, responsibility for the application of the present Convention rests on the Power accepting them, while they are in its custody. Nevertheless, if that Power fails to carry out the provisions of the present Convention in any important respect, the Power by which the protected persons were transferred shall, upon being so notified by the Protecting Power, take effective measures to correct the situation or shall request the return of the protected persons. Such request must be complied with.

In no circumstances shall a protected person be transferred to a country where he or she may have reason to fear persecution for his or her political opinions or religious beliefs. The provisions of this Article do not constitute an obstacle to the extradition, in pursuance of extradition treaties concluded before the outbreak of hostilities, of protected persons accused of offences against ordinary criminal law.

Article 46

In so far as they have not been previously withdrawn, restrictive measures taken regarding protected persons shall be cancelled as soon as possible after the close of hostilities.

Restrictive measures affecting their property shall be cancelled, in accordance with the law of the Detaining Power, as soon as possible after the close of hostilities.

Section III
Occupied territories

Article 47

Protected persons who are in occupied territory shall not be deprived, in any case or in any manner whatsoever, of the benefits of the present Convention by any change introduced, as the result of the occupation of a territory, into the institutions or government of the said territory, nor by any agreement concluded between the authorities of the occupied territories and the Occupying Power, nor by any annexation by the latter of the whole or part of the occupied territory.

Article 48

Protected persons who are not nationals of the Power whose territory is occupied, may avail themselves of the right to leave the territory subject to the provisions of Article 35, and decisions thereon shall be taken according to the procedure which the Occupying Power shall establish in accordance with the said Article.

Article 49

Individual or mass forcible transfers, as well as deportations of protected persons from occupied territory to the territory of the Occupying Power or to that of any other country, occupied or not, are prohibited, regardless of their motive.

Nevertheless, the Occupying Power may undertake total or partial evacuation of a given area if the security of the population or imperative military reasons so demand. Such evacuations may not involve the displacement of protected persons outside the bounds of the occupied territory except when for material reasons it is impossible to avoid such displacement. Persons thus evacuated shall be transferred back to their homes as soon as hostilities in the area in question have ceased.

The Occupying Power undertaking such transfers or evacuations shall ensure, to the greatest practicable extent, that proper accommodation is provided to receive the protected persons, that the removals are effected in satisfactory conditions of hygiene, health, safety and nutrition, and that members of the same family are not separated.

The Protecting Power shall be informed of any transfers and evacuations as soon as they have taken place.

The Occupying Power shall not detain protected persons in an area particularly exposed to the dangers of war unless the security of the population or imperative military reasons so demand.

The Occupying Power shall not deport or transfer parts of its own civilian population into the territory it occupies.

Article 50

The Occupying Power shall, with the cooperation of the national and local authorities, facilitate the proper working of all institutions devoted to the care and education of children.

The Occupying Power shall take all necessary steps to facilitate the identification of children and the registration of their parentage. It may not, in any case, change their personal status, nor enlist them in formations or organizations subordinate to it.

Should the local institutions be inadequate for the purpose, the Occupying Power shall make arrangements for the maintenance and education, if possible by persons of their own nationality, language and religion, of children who are orphaned or separated from their parents as a result of the war and who cannot be adequately cared for by a near relative or friend.

A special section of the Bureau set up in accordance with Article 136 shall be responsible for taking all necessary steps to identify children whose identity is in doubt. Particulars of their parents or other near relatives should always be recorded if available.

The Occupying Power shall not hinder the application of any preferential measures in regard to food, medical care and protection against the effects of war which may have been adopted prior to the occupation in favour of children under fifteen years, expectant mothers, and mothers of children under seven years.

Article 51

The Occupying Power may not compel protected persons to serve in its armed or auxiliary forces. No pressure or propaganda which aims at securing voluntary enlistment is permitted.

The Occupying Power may not compel protected persons to work unless they are over eighteen years of age, and then only on work which is necessary either for the needs of the army of occupation, or for the public utility services, or for the feeding, sheltering, clothing, transportation or health of the population of the occupied country. Protected persons may not be compelled to undertake any work which would involve them in the obligation of taking part in military operations. The Occupying Power may not compel protected persons to employ forcible means to ensure the security of the installations where they are performing compulsory labour.

The work shall be carried out only in the occupied territory where the persons whose services have been requisitioned are. Every such person shall, so far as possible, be kept in his usual place of employment. Workers shall be paid a fair wage and the work shall be proportionate to their physical and intellectual capacities. The legislation in force in the occupied country concerning working conditions, and safeguards as regards, in particular, such matters as wages, hours of work, equipment, preliminary training and compensation for occupational accidents and diseases, shall be applicable to the protected persons assigned to the work referred to in this Article.

In no case shall requisition of labour lead to a mobilization of workers in an organization of a military or semi-military character.

Article 52

No contract, agreement or regulation shall impair the right of any worker, whether voluntary or not and wherever he may be, to apply to the representatives of the Protecting Power in order to request the said Power's intervention.

All measures aiming at creating unemployment or at restricting the opportunities offered to workers in an occupied territory, in order to induce them to work for the Occupying Power, are prohibited.

Article 53

Any destruction by the Occupying Power of real or personal property belonging individually or collectively to private persons, or to the State, or to other public authorities, or to social or cooperative organizations, is prohibited, except where such destruction is rendered absolutely necessary by military operations.

Article 54

The Occupying Power may not alter the status of public officials or judges in the occupied territories, or in any way apply sanctions to or take any measures of coercion or discrimination against them, should they abstain from fulfilling their functions for reasons of conscience.

This prohibition does not prejudice the application of the second paragraph of Article 51. It does not affect the right of the Occupying Power to remove public officials from their posts.

Article 55

To the fullest extent of the means available to it, the Occupying Power has the duty of ensuring the food and medical supplies of the population; it should, in particular, bring in the necessary foodstuffs, medical stores and other articles if the resources of the occupied territory are inadequate.

The Occupying Power may not requisition foodstuffs, articles or medical supplies available in the occupied territory, except for use by the occupation forces and administration personnel, and then only if the requirements of the civilian population have been taken into account. Subject to the provisions of other international Conventions, the Occupying Power shall make arrangements to ensure that fair value is paid for any requisitioned goods.

The Protecting Power shall, at any time, be at liberty to verify the state of the food and medical supplies in occupied territories, except where temporary restrictions are made necessary by imperative military requirements.

Article 56

To the fullest extent of the means available to it, the Occupying Power has the duty of ensuring and maintaining, with the cooperation of national and local authorities, the medical and hospital establishments and services, public health and hygiene in the occupied territory, with particular reference to the adoption and application of the prophylactic and preventive measures necessary to combat the spread of contagious diseases and epidemics. Medical personnel of all categories shall be allowed to carry out their duties.

If new hospitals are set up in occupied territory and if the competent organs of the occupied State are not operating there, the occupying authorities shall, if necessary, grant them the recognition provided for in Article 18. In similar circumstances, the occupying authorities shall also grant recognition to hospital personnel and transport vehicles under the provisions of Articles 20 and 21.

In adopting measures of health and hygiene and in their implementation, the Occupying Power shall take into consideration the moral and ethical susceptibilities of the population of the occupied territory.

Article 57

The Occupying Power may requisition civilian hospitals only temporarily and only in cases of urgent necessity for the care of military wounded and sick, and then on condition that suitable arrangements are made in due time for the care and treatment of the patients and for the needs of the civilian population for hospital accommodation.

The material and stores of civilian hospitals cannot be requisitioned so long as they are necessary for the needs of the civilian population.

Article 58

The Occupying Power shall permit ministers of religion to give spiritual assistance to the members of their religious communities.

The Occupying Power shall also accept consignments of books and articles required for religious needs and shall facilitate their distribution in occupied territory.

Article 59

If the whole or part of the population of an occupied territory is inadequately supplied, the Occupying Power shall agree to relief schemes on behalf of the said population, and shall facilitate them by all the means at its disposal.

Such schemes, which may be undertaken either by States or by impartial humanitarian organizations such as the International Committee of the Red Cross, shall consist, in particular, of the provision of consignments of foodstuffs, medical supplies and clothing.

All Contracting Parties shall permit the free passage of these consignments and shall guarantee their protection.

A Power granting free passage to consignments on their way to territory occupied by an adverse Party to the conflict shall, however, have the right to search the consignments, to regulate their passage according to prescribed times and routes, and to be reasonably satisfied through the Protecting Power that these consignments are to be used for the relief of the needy population and are not to be used for the benefit of the Occupying Power.

Article 60

Relief consignments shall in no way relieve the Occupying Power of any of its responsibilities under Articles 55, 56 and 59. The Occupying Power shall in no way whatsoever divert relief consignments from the purpose for which they are intended, except in cases of urgent necessity, in the interests of the population of the occupied territory and with the consent of the Protecting Power.

Article 61

The distribution of the relief consignments referred to in the foregoing Articles shall be carried out with the cooperation and under the supervision of the Protecting Power. This duty may also be delegated, by agreement between the Occupying Power and the Protecting Power, to a neutral Power, to the International Committee of the Red Cross or to any other impartial humanitarian body.

Such consignments shall be exempt in occupied territory from all charges, taxes or customs duties unless these are necessary in the interests of the economy of the territory. The Occupying Power shall facilitate the rapid distribution of these consignments.

All Contracting Parties shall endeavour to permit the transit and transport, free of charge, of such relief consignments on their way to occupied territories.

Article 62

Subject to imperative reasons of security, protected persons in occupied territories shall be permitted to receive the individual relief consignments sent to them.

Article 63

Subject to temporary and exceptional measures imposed for urgent reasons of security by the Occupying Power:

    (a)   recognized National Red Cross (Red Crescent, Red Lion and Sun) Societies shall be able to pursue their activities in accordance with Red Cross principles, as defined by the International Red Cross Conferences. Other relief societies shall be permitted to continue their humanitarian activities under similar conditions;

    (b)   the Occupying Power may not require any changes in the personnel or structure of these societies, which would prejudice the aforesaid activities.

The same principles shall apply to the activities and personnel of special organizations of a non-military character, which already exist or which may be established, for the purpose of ensuring the living conditions of the civilian population by the maintenance of the essential public utility services, by the distribution of relief and by the organization of rescues.

Article 64

The penal laws of the occupied territory shall remain in force, with the exception that they may be repealed or suspended by the Occupying Power in cases where they constitute a threat to its security or an obstacle to the application of the present Convention.

Subject to the latter consideration and to the necessity for ensuring the effective administration of justice, the tribunals of the occupied territory shall continue to function in respect of all offences covered by the said laws.

The Occupying Power may, however, subject the population of the occupied territory to provisions which are essential to enable the Occupying Power to fulfil its obligations under the present Convention, to maintain the orderly government of the territory, and to ensure the security of the Occupying Power, of the members and property of the occupying forces or administration, and likewise of the establishments and lines of communication used by them.

Article 65

The penal provisions enacted by the Occupying Power shall not come into force before they have been published and brought to the knowledge of the inhabitants in their own language. The effect of these penal provisions shall not be retroactive.

Article 66

In case of a breach of the penal provisions promulgated by it by virtue of the second paragraph of Article 64 the Occupying Power may hand over the accused to its properly constituted, non-political military courts, on condition that the said courts sit in the occupied country. Courts of appeal shall preferably sit in the occupied country.

Article 67

The courts shall apply only those provisions of law which were applicable prior to the offence, and which are in accordance with general principles of law, in particular the principle that the penalty shall be proportionate to the offence. They shall take into consideration the fact the accused is not a national of the Occupying Power.

Article 68

Protected persons who commit an offence which is solely intended to harm the Occupying Power, but which does not constitute an attempt on the life or limb of members of the occupying forces or administration, nor a grave collective danger, nor seriously damage the property of the occupying forces or administration or the installations used by them, shall be liable to internment or simple imprisonment, provided the duration of such internment or imprisonment is proportionate to the offence committed. Furthermore, internment or imprisonment shall, for such offences, be the only measure adopted for depriving protected persons of liberty. The courts provided for under Article 66 of the present Convention may at their discretion convert a sentence of imprisonment to one of internment for the same period.

The penal provisions promulgated by the Occupying Power in accordance with Articles 64 and 65 may impose the death penalty against a protected person only in cases where the person is guilty of espionage, of serious acts of sabotage against the military installations of the Occupying Power or of intentional offences which have caused the death of one or more persons, provided that such offences were punishable by death under the law of the occupied territory in force before the occupation began.

The death penalty may not be pronounced against a protected person unless the attention of the court has been particularly called to the fact that since the accused is not a national of the Occupying Power, he is not bound to it by any duty of allegiance.

In any case, the death penalty may not be pronounced on a protected person who was under eighteen years of age at the time of the offence.

Article 69

In all cases the duration of the period during which a protected person accused of an offence is under arrest awaiting trial or punishment shall be deducted from any period of imprisonment of awarded.

Article 70

Protected persons shall not be arrested, prosecuted or convicted by the Occupying Power for acts committed or for opinions expressed before the occupation, or during a temporary interruption thereof, with the exception of breaches of the laws and customs of war.

Nationals of the occupying Power who, before the outbreak of hostilities, have sought refuge in the territory of the occupied State, shall not be arrested, prosecuted, convicted or deported from the occupied territory, except for offences committed after the outbreak of hostilities, or for offences under common law committed before the outbreak of hostilities which, according to the law of the occupied State, would have justified extradition in time of peace.

Article 71

No sentence shall be pronounced by the competent courts of the Occupying Power except after a regular trial.

Accused persons who are prosecuted by the Occupying Power shall be promptly informed, in writing, in a language which they understand, of the particulars of the charges preferred against them, and shall be brought to trial as rapidly as possible. The Protecting Power shall be informed of all proceedings instituted by the Occupying Power against protected persons in respect of charges involving the death penalty or imprisonment for two years or more; it shall be enabled, at any time, to obtain information regarding the state of such proceedings. Furthermore, the Protecting Power shall be entitled, on request, to be furnished with all particulars of these and of any other proceedings instituted by the Occupying Power against protected persons.

The notification to the Protecting Power, as provided for in the second paragraph above, shall be sent immediately, and shall in any case reach the Protecting Power three weeks before the date of the first hearing. Unless, at the opening of the trial, evidence is submitted that the provisions of this Article are fully complied with, the trial shall not proceed. The notification shall include the following particulars:

(a) description of the accused;
(b) place of residence or detention;
(c) specification of the charge or charges (with mention of the penal provisions under which it is brought);
(d) designation of the court which will hear the case;
(e) place and date of the first hearing.

Article 72

Accused persons shall have the right to present evidence necessary to their defence and may, in particular, call witnesses. They shall have the right to be assisted by a qualified advocate or counsel of their own choice, who shall be able to visit them freely and shall enjoy the necessary facilities for preparing the defence.

Failing a choice by the accused, the Protecting Power may provide him with an advocate or counsel. When an accused person has to meet a serious charge and the Protecting Power is not functioning, the Occupying Power, subject to the consent of the accused, shall provide an advocate or counsel.

Accused persons shall, unless they freely waive such assistance, be aided by an interpreter, both during preliminary investigation and during the hearing in court. They shall have the right at any time to object to the interpreter and to ask for his replacement.

Article73

A convicted person shall have the right of appeal provided for by the laws applied by the court. He shall be fully informed of his right to appeal or petition and of the time limit within which he may do so.

The penal procedure provided in the present Section shall apply, as far as it is applicable, to appeals. Where the laws applied by the Court make no provision for appeals, the convicted person shall have the right to petition against the finding and sentence to the competent authority of the Occupying Power.

Article 74

Representatives of the Protecting Power shall have the right to attend the trial of any protected person, unless the hearing has, as an exceptional measure, to be held in camera in the interests of the security of the Occupying Power, which shall then notify the Protecting Power. A notification in respect of the date and place of trial shall be sent to the Protecting Power.

Any judgement involving a sentence of death, or imprisonment for two years or more, shall be communicated, with the relevant grounds, as rapidly as possible to the Protecting Power. The notification shall contain a reference to the notification made under Article 71 and, in the case of sentences of imprisonment, the name of the place where the sentence is to be served. A record of judgements other than those referred to above shall be kept by the court and shall be open to inspection by representatives of the Protecting Power. Any period allowed for appeal in the case of sentences involving the death penalty, or imprisonment of two years or more, shall not run until notification of judgement has been received by the Protecting Power.

Article 75

In no case shall persons condemned to death be deprived of the right of petition for pardon or reprieve.

No death sentence shall be carried out before the expiration of a period of a least six months from the date of receipt by the Protecting Power of the notification of the final judgment confirming such death sentence, or of an order denying pardon or reprieve.

The six months period of suspension of the death sentence herein prescribed may be reduced in individual cases in circumstances of grave emergency involving an organized threat to the security of the Occupying Power or its forces, provided always that the Protecting Power is notified of such reduction and is given reasonable time and opportunity to make representations to the competent occupying authorities in respect of such death sentences.

Article 76

Protected persons accused of offences shall be detained in the occupied country, and if convicted they shall serve their sentences therein. They shall, if possible, be separated from other detainees and shall enjoy conditions of food and hygiene which will be sufficient to keep them in good health, and which will be at least equal to those obtaining in prisons in the occupied country.

They shall receive the medical attention required by their state of health.

They shall also have the right to receive any spiritual assistance which they may require.

Women shall be confined in separate quarters and shall be under the direct supervision of women.

Proper regard shall be paid to the special treatment due to minors.

Protected persons who are detained shall have the right to be visited by delegates of the Protecting Power and of the International Committee of the Red Cross, in accordance with the provisions of Article 143.

Such persons shall have the right to receive at least one relief parcel monthly.

Article 77

Protected persons who have been accused of offences or convicted by the courts in occupied territory, shall be handed over at the close of occupation, with the relevant records, to the authorities of the liberated territory.

Article 78

If the Occupying Power considers it necessary, for imperative reasons of security, to take safety measures concerning protected persons, it may, at the most, subject them to assigned residence or to internment.

Decisions regarding such assigned residence or internment shall be made according to a regular procedure to be prescribed by the Occupying Power in accordance with the provisions of the present Convention. This procedure shall include the right of appeal for the parties concerned. Appeals shall be decided with the least possible delay. In the event of the decision being upheld, it shall be subject to periodical review, if possible every six months, by a competent body set up by the said Power.

Protected persons made subject to assigned residence and thus required to leave their homes shall enjoy the full benefit of Article 39 of the present Convention.

Section IV
Regulations for the treatment of internees

Chapter I
General provisions

Article 79

The Parties to the conflict shall not intern protected persons, except in accordance with the provisions of Articles 41, 42, 43, 68 and 78.

Article 80

Internees shall retain their full civil capacity and shall exercise such attendant rights as may be compatible with their status.

Article 81

Parties to the conflict who intern protected persons shall be bound to provide free of charge for their maintenance, and to grant them also the medical attention required by their state of health.

No deduction from the allowances, salaries or credits due to the internees shall be made for the repayment of these costs.

The Detaining Power shall provide for the support of those dependent on the internees, if such dependents are without adequate means of support or are unable to earn a living.

Article 82

The Detaining Power shall, as far as possible, accommodate the internees according to their nationality, language and customs. Internees who are nationals of the same country shall not be separated merely because they have different languages.

Throughout the duration of their internment, members of the same family, and in particular parents and children, shall be lodged together in the same place of internment, except when separation of a temporary nature is necessitated for reasons of employment or health or for the purposes of enforcement of the provisions of Chapter IX of the present Section. Internees may request that their children who are left at liberty without parental care shall be interned with them.

Wherever possible, interned members of the same family shall be housed in the same premises and given separate accommodation from other internees, together with facilities for leading a proper family life.

Chapter II
Places of Internment

Article 83

The Detaining Power shall not set up places of internment in areas particularly exposed to the dangers of war.

The Detaining Power shall give the enemy Powers, through the intermediary of the Protecting Powers, all useful information regarding the geographical location of places of internment.

Whenever military considerations permit, internment camps shall be indicated by the letters IC, placed so as to be clearly visible in the daytime from the air. The Powers concerned may, however, agree upon any other system of marking. No place other than an internment camp shall be marked as such.

Article 84

Internees shall be accommodated and administered separately from prisoners of war and from persons deprived of liberty for any other reason.

Article 85

The Detaining Power is bound to take all necessary and possible measures to ensure that protected persons shall, from the outset of their internment, be accommodated in buildings or quarters which afford every possible safeguard as regards hygiene and health, and provide efficient protection against the rigours of the climate and the effects of the war. In no case shall permanent places of internment be situated in unhealthy areas or in districts, the climate of which is injurious to the internees. In all cases where the district, in which a protected person is temporarily interned, is in an unhealthy area or has a climate which is harmful to his health, he shall be removed to a more suitable place of internment as rapidly as circumstances permit.

The premises shall be fully protected from dampness, adequately heated and lighted, in particular between dusk and lights out. The sleeping quarters shall be sufficiently spacious and well ventilated, and the internees shall have suitable bedding and sufficient blankets, account being taken of the climate, and the age, sex, and state of health of the internees.

Internees shall have for their use, day and night, sanitary conveniences which conform to the rules of hygiene, and are constantly maintained in a state of cleanliness. They shall be provided with sufficient water and soap for their daily personal toilet and for washing their personal laundry; installations and facilities necessary for this purpose shall be granted to them. Showers or baths shall also be available. The necessary time shall be set aside for washing and for cleaning.

Whenever it is necessary, as an exceptional and temporary measure, to accommodate women internees who are not members of a family unit in the same place of internment as men, the provision of separate sleeping quarters and sanitary conveniences for the use of such women internees shall be obligatory.

Article 86

The Detaining Power shall place at the disposal of interned persons, of whatever denomination, premises suitable for the holding of their religious services.

Article 87

Canteens shall be installed in every place of internment, except where other suitable facilities are available. Their purpose shall be to enable internees to make purchases, at prices not higher than local market prices, of foodstuffs and articles of everyday use, including soap and tobacco, such as would increase their personal well-being and comfort.

Profits made by canteens shall be credited to a welfare fund to be set up for each place of internment, and administered for the benefit of the internees attached to such place of internment. The Internee Committee provided for in Article 102 shall have the right to check the management of the canteen and of the said fund.

When a place of internment is closed down, the balance of the welfare fund shall be transferred to the welfare fund of a place of internment for internees of the same nationality, or, if such a place does not exist, to a central welfare fund which shall be administered for the benefit of all internees remaining in the custody of the Detaining Power. In case of a general release, the said profits shall be kept by the Detaining Power, subject to any agreement to the contrary between the Powers concerned.

Article 88

In all places of internment exposed to air raids and other hazards of war, shelters adequate in number and structure to ensure the necessary protection shall be installed. In case of alarms, the measures internees shall be free to enter such shelters as quickly as possible, excepting those who remain for the protection of their quarters against the aforesaid hazards. Any protective measures taken in favour of the population shall also apply to them.

All due precautions must be taken in places of internment against the danger of fire.

Chapter III
Food and Clothing

Article 89

Daily food rations for internees shall be sufficient in quantity, quality and variety to keep internees in a good state of health and prevent the development of nutritional deficiencies. Account shall also be taken of the customary diet of the internees.

Internees shall also be given the means by which they can prepare for themselves any additional food in their possession.

Sufficient drinking water shall be supplied to internees. The use of tobacco shall be permitted.

Internees who work shall receive additional rations in proportion to the kind of labour which they perform.

Expectant and nursing mothers and children under fifteen years of age, shall be given additional food, in proportion to their physiological needs.

Article 90

When taken into custody, internees shall be given all facilities to provide themselves with the necessary clothing, footwear and change of underwear, and later on, to procure further supplies if required. Should any internees not have sufficient clothing, account being taken of the climate, and be unable to procure any, it shall be provided free of charge to them by the Detaining Power.

The clothing supplied by the Detaining Power to internees and the outward markings placed on their own clothes shall not be ignominious nor expose them to ridicule.

Workers shall receive suitable working outfits, including protective clothing, whenever the nature of their work so requires.

Chapter IV
Hygiene and Medical Attention

Article 91

Every place of internment shall have an adequate infirmary, under the direction of a qualified doctor, where internees may have the attention they require, as well as an appropriate diet. Isolation wards shall be set aside for cases of contagious or mental diseases.

Maternity cases and internees suffering from serious diseases, or whose condition requires special treatment, a surgical operation or hospital care, must be admitted to any institution where adequate treatment can be given and shall receive care not inferior to that provided for the general population.

Internees shall, for preference, have the attention of medical personnel of their own nationality.

Internees may not be prevented from presenting themselves to the medical authorities for examination. The medical authorities of the Detaining Power shall, upon request, issue to every internee who has undergone treatment an official certificate showing the nature of his illness or injury, and the duration and nature of the treatment given. A duplicate of this certificate shall be forwarded to the Central Agency provided for in Article 140.

Treatment, including the provision of any apparatus necessary for the maintenance of internees in good health, particularly dentures and other artificial appliances and spectacles, shall be free of charge to the internee.

Article 92

Medical inspections of internees shall be made at least once a month. Their purpose shall be, in particular, to supervise the general state of health, nutrition and cleanliness of internees, and to detect contagious diseases, especially tuberculosis, malaria, and venereal diseases. Such inspections shall include, in particular, the checking of weight of each internee and, at least once a year, radioscopic examination.

Chapter V
Religious, Intellectual and Physical Activities

Article 93

Internees shall enjoy complete latitude in the exercise of their religious duties, including attendance at the services of their faith, on condition that they comply with the disciplinary routine prescribed by the detaining authorities.

Ministers of religion who are interned shall be allowed to minister freely to the members of their community. For this purpose the Detaining Power shall ensure their equitable allocation amongst the various places of internment in which there are internees speaking the same language and belonging to the same religion. Should such ministers be too few in number, the Detaining Power shall provide them with the necessary facilities, including means of transport, for moving from one place to another, and they shall be authorized to visit any internees who are in hospital. Ministers of religion shall be at liberty to correspond on matters concerning their ministry with the religious authorities in the country of detention and, as far as possible, with the international religious organizations of their faith. Such correspondence shall not be considered as forming a part of the quota mentioned in Article 107. It shall, however, be subject to the provisions of Article 112.

When internees do not have at their disposal the assistance of ministers of their faith, or should these latter be too few in number, the local religious authorities of the same faith may appoint, in agreement with the Detaining Power, a minister of the internees' faith or, if such a course is feasible from a denominational point of view, a minister of similar religion or a qualified layman. The latter shall enjoy the facilities granted to the ministry he has assumed. Persons so appointed shall comply with all regulations laid down by the Detaining Power in the interests of discipline and security.

Article 94

The Detaining Power shall encourage intellectual, educational and recreational pursuits, sports and games amongst internees, whilst leaving them free to take part in them or not. It shall take all practicable measures to ensure the exercise thereof, in particular by providing suitable premises.

All possible facilities shall be granted to internees to continue their studies or to take up new subjects. The education of children and young people shall be ensured; they shall be allowed to attend schools either within the place of internment or outside.

Internees shall be given opportunities for physical exercise, sports and outdoor games. For this purpose, sufficient open spaces shall be set aside in all places of internment. Special playgrounds shall be reserved for children and young people.

Article 95

The Detaining Power shall not employ internees as workers, unless they so desire. Employment which, if undertaken under compulsion by a protected person not in internment, would involve a breach of Articles 40 or 51 of the present Convention, and employment on work which is of a degrading or humiliating character are in any case prohibited.

After a working period of six weeks, internees shall be free to give up work at any moment, subject to eight days' notice.

These provisions constitute no obstacle to the right of the Detaining Power to employ interned doctors, dentists and other medical personnel in their professional capacity on behalf of their fellow internees, or to employ internees for administrative and maintenance work in places of internment and to detail such persons for work in the kitchens or for other domestic tasks, or to require such persons to undertake duties connected with the protection of internees against aerial bombardment or other war risks. No internee may, however, be required to perform tasks for which he is, in the opinion of a medical officer, physically unsuited.

The Detaining Power shall take entire responsibility for all working conditions, for medical attention, for the payment of wages, and for ensuring that all employed internees receive compensation for occupational accidents and diseases. The standards prescribed for the said working conditions and for compensation shall be in accordance with the national laws and regulations, and with the existing practice; they shall in no case be inferior to those obtaining for work of the same nature in the same district. Wages for work done shall be determined on an equitable basis by special agreements between the internees, the Detaining Power, and, if the case arises, employers other than the Detaining Power to provide for free maintenance of internees and for the medical attention which their state of health may require. Internees permanently detailed for categories of work mentioned in the third paragraph of this Article, shall be paid fair wages by the Detaining Power. The working conditions and the scale of compensation for occupational accidents and diseases to internees, thus detailed, shall not be inferior to those applicable to work of the same nature in the same district.

Article 96

All labour detachments shall remain part of and dependent upon a place of internment. The competent authorities of the Detaining Power and the commandant of a place of internment shall be responsible for the observance in a labour detachment of the provisions of the present Convention. The commandant shall keep an up-to-date list of the labour detachments subordinate to him and shall communicate it to the delegates of the Protecting Power, of the International Committee of the Red Cross and of other humanitarian organizations who may visit the places of internment.

Chapter VI
Personal Property and Financial Resources

Article 97

Internees shall be permitted to retain articles of personal use. Monies, cheques, bonds, etc., and valuables in their possession may not be taken from them except in accordance with established procedure. Detailed receipts shall be given therefore.

The amounts shall be paid into the account of every internee as provided for in Article 98. Such amounts may not be converted into any other currency unless legislation in force in the territory in which the owner is interned so requires or the internee gives his consent.

Articles which have above all a personal or sentimental value may not be taken away.

A woman internee shall not be searched except by a woman.

On release or repatriation, internees shall be given all articles, monies or other valuables taken from them during internment and shall receive in currency the balance of any credit to their accounts kept in accordance with Article 98, with the exception of any articles or amounts withheld by the Detaining Power by virtue of its legislation in force. If the property of an internee is so withheld, the owner shall receive a detailed receipt.

Family or identity documents in the possession of internees may not be taken away without a receipt being given. At no time shall internees be left without identity documents. If they have none, they shall be issued with special documents drawn up by the detaining authorities, which will serve as their identity papers until the end of their internment.

Internees may keep on their persons a certain amount of money, in cash or in the shape of purchase coupons, to enable them to make purchases.

Article 98

All internees shall receive regular allowances, sufficient to enable them to purchase goods and articles, such as tobacco, toilet requisites, etc. Such allowances may take the form of credits or purchase coupons.

Furthermore, internees may receive allowances from the Power to which they owe allegiance, the Protecting Powers, the organizations which may assist them, or their families, as well as the income on their property in accordance with the law of the Detaining Power. The amount of allowances granted by the Power to which they owe allegiance shall be the same for each category of internees (infirm, sick, pregnant women, etc.) but may not be allocated by that Power or distributed by the Detaining Power on the basis of discriminations between internees which are prohibited by Article 27 of the present Convention.

The Detaining Power shall open a regular account for every internee, to which shall be credited the allowances named in the present Article, the wages earned and the remittances received, together with such sums taken from him as may be available under the legislation in force in the territory in which he is interned. Internees shall be granted all facilities consistent with the legislation in force in such territory to make remittances to their families and to other dependants. They may draw from their accounts the amounts necessary for their personal expenses, within the limits fixed by the Detaining Power. They shall at all times be afforded reasonable facilities for consulting and obtaining copies of their accounts. A statement of accounts shall be furnished to the Protecting Power, on request, and shall accompany the internee in case of transfer.

Chapter VII
Administration and Discipline

Article 99

Every place of internment shall be put under the authority of a responsible officer, chosen from the regular military forces or the regular civil administration of the Detaining Power. The officer in charge of the place of internment must have in his possession a copy of the present Convention in the official language, or one of the official languages, of his country and shall be responsible for its application. The staff in control of internees shall be instructed in the provisions of the present Convention and of the administrative measures adopted to ensure its application.

The text of the present Convention and the texts of special agreements concluded under the said Convention shall be posted inside the place of internment, in a language which the internees understand, or shall be in the possession of the Internee Committee.

Regulations, orders, notices and publications of every kind shall be communicated to the internees and posted inside the places of internment, in a language which they understand.

Every order and command addressed to internees individually must, likewise, be given in a language which they understand.

Article 100

The disciplinary regime in places of internment shall be consistent with humanitarian principles, and shall in no circumstances include regulations imposing on internees any physical exertion dangerous to their health or involving physical or moral victimization. Identification by tattooing or imprinting signs or markings on the body, is prohibited.

In particular, prolonged standing and roll-calls, punishment drill, military drill and manoeuvres, or the reduction of food rations, are prohibited.

Article 101

Internees shall have the right to present to the authorities in whose power they are, any petition with regard to the conditions of internment to which they are subjected.

They shall also have the right to apply without restriction through the Internee Committee or, if they consider it necessary, direct to the representatives of the Protecting Power, in order to indicate to them any points on which they may have complaints to make with regard to the conditions of internment.

Such petitions and complaints shall be transmitted forthwith and without alteration, and even if the latter are recognized to be unfounded, they may not occasion any punishment.

Periodic reports on the situation in places of internment and as to the needs of the internees may be sent by the Internee Committees to the representatives of the Protecting Powers.

Article 102

In every place of internment, the internees shall freely elect by secret ballot every six months, the members of a Committee empowered to represent them before the Detaining and the Protecting Powers, the International Committee of the Red Cross and any other organization which may assist them. The members of the Committee shall be eligible for re-election.

Internees so elected shall enter upon their duties after their election has been approved by the detaining authorities. The reasons for any refusals or dismissals shall be communicated to the Protecting Powers concerned.

Article 103

The Internee Committees shall further the physical, spiritual and intellectual well-being of the internees.

In case the internees decide, in particular, to organize a system of mutual assistance amongst themselves, this organization would be within the competence of the Committees in addition to the special duties entrusted to them under other provisions of the present Convention.

Article 104

Members of Internee Committees shall not be required to perform any other work, if the accomplishment of their duties is rendered more difficult thereby.

Members of Internee Committees may appoint from amongst the internees such assistants as they may require. All material facilities shall be granted to them, particularly a certain freedom of movement necessary for the accomplishment of their duties (visits to labour detachments, receipt of supplies, etc.).

All facilities shall likewise be accorded to members of Internee Committees for communication by post and telegraph with the detaining authorities, the Protecting Powers, the International Committee of the Red Cross and their delegates, and with the organizations which give assistance to internees. Committee members in labour detachments shall enjoy similar facilities for communication with their Internee Committee in the principal place of internment. Such communications shall not be limited, nor considered as forming a part of the quota mentioned in Article 107.

Members of Internee Committees who are transferred shall be allowed a reasonable time to acquaint their successors with current affairs.

Chapter VIII
Relations with the Exterior

Article 105

Immediately upon interning protected persons, the Detaining Powers shall inform them, the Power to which they owe allegiance and their Protecting Power of the measures taken for executing the provisions of the present Chapter. The Detaining Powers shall likewise inform the Parties concerned of any subsequent modifications of such measures.

Article 106

As soon as he is interned, or at the latest not more than one week after his arrival in a place of internment, and likewise in cases of sickness or transfer to another place of internment or to a hospital, every internee shall be enabled to send direct to his family, on the one hand, and to the Central Agency provided for by Article 140, on the other, an internment card similar, if possible, to the model annexed to the present Convention, informing his relatives of his detention, address and state of health. The said cards shall be forwarded as rapidly as possible and may not be delayed in any way.

Article 107

Internees shall be allowed to send and receive letters and cards. If the Detaining Power deems it necessary to limit the number of letters and cards sent by each internee, the said number shall not be less than two letters and four cards monthly; these shall be drawn up so as to conform as closely as possible to the models annexed to the present Convention. If limitations must be placed on the correspondence addressed to internees, they may be ordered only by the Power to which such internees owe allegiance, possibly at the request of the Detaining Power. Such letters and cards must be conveyed with reasonable despatch; they may not be delayed or retained for disciplinary reasons.

Internees who have been a long time without news, or who find it impossible to receive news from their relatives, or to give them news by the ordinary postal route, as well as those who are at a considerable distance from their homes, shall be allowed to send telegrams, the charges being paid by them in the currency at their disposal. They shall likewise benefit by this provision in cases which are recognized to be urgent.

As a rule, internees' mail shall be written in their own language. The Parties to the conflict may authorize correspondence in other languages.

Article 108

Internees shall be allowed to receive, by post or by any other means, individual parcels or collective shipments containing in particular foodstuffs, clothing, medical supplies, as well as books and objects of a devotional, educational or recreational character which may meet their needs. Such shipments shall in no way free the Detaining Power from the obligations imposed upon it by virtue of the present Convention.

Should military necessity require the quantity of such shipments to be limited, due notice thereof shall be given to the Protecting Power and to the International Committee of the Red Cross, or to any other organization giving assistance to the internees and responsible for the forwarding of such shipments.

The conditions for the sending of individual parcels and collective shipments shall, if necessary, be the subject of special agreements between the Powers concerned, which may in no case delay the receipt by the internees of relief supplies. Parcels of clothing and foodstuffs may not include books. Medical relief supplies shall, as a rule, be sent in collective parcels.

Article 109

In the absence of special agreements between Parties to the conflict regarding the conditions for the receipt and distribution of collective relief shipments, the regulations concerning collective relief which are annexed to the present Convention shall be applied.

The special agreements provided for above shall in no case restrict the right of Internee Committees to take possession of collective relief shipments intended for internees, to undertake their distribution and to dispose of them in the interests of the recipients. Nor shall such agreements restrict the right of representatives of the Protecting Powers, the International Committee of the Red Cross, or any other organization giving assistance to internees and responsible for the forwarding of collective shipments, to supervise their distribution to the recipients.

Article 110

An relief shipments for internees shall be exempt from import, customs and other dues.

All matter sent by mail, including relief parcels sent by parcel post and remittances of money, addressed from other countries to internees or despatched by them through the post office, either direct or through the Information Bureaux provided for in Article 136 and the Central Information Agency provided for in Article 140, shall be exempt from all postal dues both in the countries of origin and destination and in intermediate countries. To this end, in particular, the exemption provided by the Universal Postal Convention of 1947 and by the agreements of the Universal Postal Union in favour of civilians of enemy nationality detained in camps or civilian prisons, shall be extended to the other interned persons protected by the present Convention. The countries not signatory to the above-mentioned agreements shall be bound to grant freedom from charges in the same circumstances.

The cost of transporting relief shipments which are intended for internees and which, by reason of their weight or any other cause, cannot be sent through the post office, shall be borne by the Detaining Power in all the territories under its control. Other Powers which are Parties to the present Convention shall bear the cost of transport in their respective territories.

Costs connected with the transport of such shipments, which are not covered by the above paragraphs, shall be charged to the senders.

The High Contracting Parties shall endeavour to reduce, so far as possible, the charges for telegrams sent by internees, or addressed to them.

Article 111

Should military operations prevent the Powers concerned from fulfilling their obligation to ensure the conveyance of the mail and relief shipments provided for in Articles 106, 107, 108 and 113, the Protecting Powers concerned, the International Committee of the Red Cross or any other organization duly approved by the Parties to the conflict may undertake the conveyance of such shipments by suitable means (rail, motor vehicles, vessels or aircraft, etc.). For this purpose, the High Contracting Parties shall endeavour to supply them with such transport, and to allow its circulation, especially by granting the necessary safe-conducts.

Such transport may also be used to convey:

(a) correspondence, lists and reports exchanged between the Central Information Agency referred to in Article 140 and the National Bureaux referred to in Article 136;

(b) correspondence and reports relating to internees which the Protecting Powers, the International Committee of the Red Cross or any other organization assisting the internees exchange either with their own delegates or with the Parties to the conflict.

These provisions in no way detract from the right of any Party to the conflict to arrange other means of transport if it should so prefer, nor preclude the granting of safe-conducts, under mutually agreed conditions, to such means of transport.

The costs occasioned by the use of such means of transport shall be borne, in proportion to the importance of the shipments, by the Parties to the conflict whose nationals are benefited thereby.

Article 112

The censoring of correspondence addressed to internees or despatched by them shall be done as quickly as possible.

The examination of consignments intended for internees shall not be carried out under conditions that will expose the goods contained in them to deterioration. It shall be done in the presence of the addressee, or of a fellow-internee duly delegated by him. The delivery to internees of individual or collective consignments shall not be delayed under the pretext of difficulties of censorship.

Any prohibition of correspondence ordered by the Parties to the conflict either for military or political reasons, shall be only temporary and its duration shall be as short as possible.

Article 113

The Detaining Powers shall provide all reasonable execution facilities for the transmission, through the Protecting Power or the Central Agency provided for in Article 140, or as otherwise required, of wills, powers of attorney, letters of authority, or any other documents intended for internees or despatched by them.

In all cases the Detaining Powers shall facilitate the execution and authentication in due legal form of such documents on behalf of internees, in particular by allowing them to consult a lawyer.

Article 114

The Detaining Power shall afford internees all facilities to enable them to manage their property, provided this is not incompatible with the conditions of internment and the law which is applicable. For this purpose, the said Power may give them permission to leave the place of internment in urgent cases and if circumstances allow.

Article 115

In all cases where an internee is a party to proceedings in any court, the Detaining Power shall, if he so requests, cause the court to be informed of his detention and shall, within legal limits, ensure that all necessary steps are taken to prevent him from being in any way prejudiced, by reason of his internment, as regards the preparation and conduct of his case or as regards the execution of any judgment of the court.

Article116

Every internee shall be allowed to receive visitors, especially near relatives, at regular intervals and as frequently as possible.

As far as is possible, internees shall be permitted to visit their homes in urgent cases, particularly in cases of death or serious illness of relatives.

Chapter IX
Penal and Disciplinary Sanctions

Article 117

Subject to the provisions of the present Chapter, the laws in force in the territory in which they are detained will continue to apply to internees who commit offences during internment.

If general laws, regulations or orders declare acts committed by internees to be punishable, whereas the same acts are not punishable when committed by persons who are not internees, such acts shall entail disciplinary punishments only.

No internee may be punished more than once for the same act, or on the same count.

Article 118

The courts or authorities shall in passing sentence take as far as possible into account the fact that the defendant is not a national of the Detaining Power. They shall be free to reduce the penalty prescribed for the offence with which the internee is charged and shall not be obliged, to this end, to apply the minimum sentence prescribed.

Imprisonment in premises without daylight, and, in general, all forms of cruelty without exception are forbidden.

Internees who have served disciplinary or judicial sentences shall not be treated differently from other internees.

The duration of preventive detention undergone by an internee shall be deducted from any disciplinary or judicial penalty involving confinement to which he may be sentenced.

Internee Committees shall be informed of all judicial proceedings instituted against internees whom they represent, and of their result.

Article 119

The disciplinary punishments applicable to internees shall be the following:

(1) a fine which shall not exceed 50 per cent of the wages which the internee would otherwise receive under the provisions of Article 95 during a period of not more than thirty days.

(2) discontinuance of privileges granted over and above the treatment provided for by the present Convention

(3) fatigue duties, not exceeding two hours daily, in connection with the maintenance of the place of internment.

(4) confinement.

In no case shall disciplinary penalties be inhuman, brutal or dangerous for the health of internees. Account shall be taken of the internee's age, sex and state of health.

The duration of any single punishment shall in no case exceed a maximum of thirty consecutive days, even if the internee is answerable for several breaches of discipline when his case is dealt with, whether such breaches are connected or not.

Article 120

Internees who are recaptured after having escaped or when attempting to escape, shall be liable only to disciplinary punishment in respect of this act, even if it is a repeated offence.

Article 118, paragraph 3, notwithstanding, internees punished as a result of escape or attempt to escape, may be subjected to special surveillance, on condition that such surveillance does not affect the state of their health, that it is exercised in a place of internment and that it does not entail the abolition of any of the safeguards granted by the present Convention.

Internees who aid and abet an escape or attempt to escape, shall be liable on this count to disciplinary punishment only.

Article 121

Escape, or attempt to escape, even if it is a repeated offence, shall not be deemed an aggravating circumstance in cases where an internee is prosecuted for offences committed during his escape.

The Parties to the conflict shall ensure that the competent authorities exercise leniency in deciding whether punishment inflicted for an offence shall be of a disciplinary or judicial nature, especially in respect of acts committed in connection with an escape, whether successful or not.

Article 122

Acts which constitute offences against discipline shall be investigated immediately. This rule shall be applied, in particular, in cases of escape or attempt to escape. Recaptured internees shall be handed over to the competent authorities as soon as possible.

In cases of offences against discipline, confinement awaiting trial shall be reduced to an absolute minimum for all internees, and shall not exceed fourteen days. Its duration shall in any case be deducted from any sentence of confinement.

The provisions of Articles 124 and 125 shall apply to internees who are in confinement awaiting trial for offences against discipline.

Article 123

Without prejudice to the competence of courts and higher authorities, disciplinary punishment may be ordered only by the commandant of the place of internment, or by a responsible officer or official who replaces him, or to whom he has delegated his disciplinary powers.

Before any disciplinary punishment is awarded, the accused internee shall be given precise information regarding the offences of which he is accused, and given an opportunity of explaining his conduct and of defending himself. He shall be permitted, in particular, to call witnesses and to have recourse, if necessary, to the services of a qualified interpreter. The decision shall be announced in the presence of the accused and of a member of the Internee Committee.

The period elapsing between the time of award of a disciplinary punishment and its execution shall not exceed one month.

When an internee is awarded a further disciplinary punishment, a period of at least three days shall elapse between the execution of any two of the punishments, if the duration of one of these is ten days or more.

A record of disciplinary punishments shall be maintained by the commandant of the place of internment and shall be open to inspection by representatives of the Protecting Power.

Article 124

Internees shall not in any case be transferred to penitentiary establishments (prisons, penitentiaries, convict prisons, etc.) to undergo disciplinary punishment therein.

The premises in which disciplinary punishments are undergone shall conform to sanitary requirements: they shall in particular be provided with adequate bedding. Internees undergoing punishment shall be enabled to keep themselves in a state of cleanliness.

Women internees undergoing disciplinary punishment shall be confined in separate quarters from male internees and shall be under the immediate supervision of women.

Article 125

Internees awarded disciplinary punishment shall be allowed to exercise and to stay in the open air at least two hours daily.

They shall be allowed, if they so request, to be present at the daily medical inspections. They shall receive the attention which their state of health requires and, if necessary, shall be removed to the infirmary of the place of internment or to a hospital.

They shall have permission to read and write, likewise to send and receive letters. Parcels and remittances of money, however, may be withheld from them until the completion of their punishment; such consignments shall meanwhile be entrusted to the Internee Committee, who will hand over to the infirmary the perishable goods contained in the parcels.

No internee given a disciplinary punishment may be deprived of the benefit of the provisions of Articles 107 and 143 of the present Convention.

Article 126

The provisions of Articles 71 to 76 inclusive shall apply, by analogy, to proceedings against internees who are in the national territory of the Detaining Power.

Chapter X
Transfers of Internees

Article 127

The transfer of internees shall always be effected humanely. As a general rule, it shall be carried out by rail or other means of transport, and under conditions at least equal to those obtaining for the forces of the Detaining Power in their changes of station. If, as an exceptional measure, such removals have to be effected on foot, they may not take place unless the internees are in a fit state of health, and may not in any case expose them to excessive fatigue.

The Detaining Power shall supply internees during transfer with drinking water and food sufficient in quantity, quality and variety to maintain them in good health, and also with the necessary clothing, adequate shelter and the necessary medical attention. The Detaining Power shall take all suitable precautions to ensure their safety during transfer, and shall establish before their departure a complete list of all internees transferred.

Sick, wounded or infirm internees and maternity cases shall not be transferred if the journey would be seriously detrimental to them, unless their safety imperatively so demands.

If the combat zone draws close to a place of internment, the internees in the said place shall not be transferred unless their removal can be carried out in adequate conditions of safety, or unless they are exposed to greater risks by remaining on the spot than by being transferred.

When making decisions regarding the transfer of internees, the Detaining Power shall take their interests into account and, in particular, shall not do anything to increase the difficulties of repatriating them or returning them to their own homes.

Article 128

In the event of transfer, internees shall be officially advised of their departure and of their new postal address. Such notification shall be given in time for them to pack their luggage and inform their next of kin.

They shall be allowed to take with them their personal effects, and the correspondence and parcels which have arrived for them. The weight of such baggage may be limited if the conditions of transfer so require, but in no case to less than twenty-five kilograms per internee.

Mail and parcels addressed to their former place of internment shall be forwarded to them without delay.

The commandant of the place of internment shall take, in agreement with the Internee Committee, any measures needed to ensure the transport of the internees' community property and of the luggage the internees are unable to take with them in consequence of restrictions imposed by virtue of the second paragraph.

Chapter XI
Deaths

Article 129

The wills of internees shall be received for safe-keeping by the responsible authorities; and if the event of the death of an internee his will shall be transmitted without delay to a person whom he has previously designated.

Deaths of internees shall be certified in every case by a doctor, and a death certificate shall be made out, showing the causes of death and the conditions under which it occurred.

An official record of the death, duly registered, shall be drawn up in accordance with the procedure relating thereto in force in the territory where the place of internment is situated, and a duly certified copy of such record shall be transmitted without delay to the Protecting Power as well as to the Central Agency referred to in Article 140.

Article 130

The detaining authorities shall ensure that internees who die while interned are honourably buried, if possible according to the rites of the religion to which they belonged and that their graves are respected, properly maintained, and marked in such a way that they can always be recognized.

Deceased internees shall be buried in individual graves unless unavoidable circumstances require the use of collective graves. Bodies may be cremated only for imperative reasons of hygiene, on account of the religion of the deceased or in accordance with his expressed wish to this effect. In case of cremation, the fact shall be stated and the reasons given in the death certificate of the deceased. The ashes shall be retained for safe-keeping by the detaining authorities and shall be transferred as soon as possible to the next of kin on their request.

As soon as circumstances permit, and not later than the close of hostilities, the Detaining Power shall forward lists of graves of deceased internees to the Powers on whom deceased internees depended, through the Information Bureaux provided for in Article 136. Such lists shall include all particulars necessary for the identification of the deceased internees, as well as the exact location of their graves.

Article 131

Every death or serious injury of an internee, caused or suspected to have been caused by a sentry, another internee or any other person, as well as any death the cause of which is unknown, shall be immediately followed by an official enquiry by the Detaining Power.

A communication on this subject shall be sent immediately to the Protecting Power. The evidence of any witnesses shall be taken, and a report including such evidence shall be prepared and forwarded to the said Protecting Power.

If the enquiry indicates the guilt of one or more persons, the Detaining Power shall take all necessary steps to ensure the prosecution of the person or persons responsible.

Chapter XIII
Release, Repatriation and Accommodation in Neutral Countries

Article 132

Each interned person shall be released by the Detaining Power as soon as the reasons which necessitated his internment no longer exist.

The Parties to the conflict shall, moreover, endeavour during the course of hostilities, to conclude agreements for the release, the repatriation, the return to places of residence or the accommodation in a neutral country of certain classes of internees, in particular children, pregnant women and mothers with infants and young children, wounded and sick, and internees who have been detained for a long time.

Article 133

Internment shall cease as soon as possible after the close of hostilities.

Internees in the territory of a Party to the conflict against whom penal proceedings are pending for offences not exclusively subject to disciplinary penalties, may be detained until the close of such proceedings and, if circumstances require, until the completion of the penalty. The same shall apply to internees who have been previously sentenced to a punishment depriving them of liberty.

By agreement between the Detaining Power and the Powers concerned, committees may be set up after the close of hostilities, or of the occupation of territories, to search for dispersed internees.

Article 134

The High Contracting Parties shall endeavour, upon the close of hostilities or occupation, to ensure the return of all internees to their last place of residence, or to facilitate their repatriation.

Article 135

The Detaining Power shall bear the expense of returning released internees to the places where they were residing when interned, or, if it took them into custody while they were in transit or on the high seas, the cost of completing their journey or of their return to their point of departure.

Where a Detaining Power refuses permission to reside in its territory to a released internee who previously had his permanent domicile therein, such Detaining Power shall pay the cost of the said internee's repatriation. If, however, the internee elects to return to his country on his own responsibility or in obedience to the Government of the Power to which he owes allegiance, the Detaining Power need not pay the expenses of his journey beyond the point of his departure from its territory. The Detaining Power need not pay the cost of repatriation of an internee who was interned at his own request.

If internees are transferred in accordance with Article 45, the transferring and receiving Powers shall agree on the portion of the above costs to be borne by each.

The foregoing shall not prejudice such special agreements as may be concluded between Parties to the conflict concerning the exchange and repatriation of their nationals in enemy hands.

Section V
Information Bureaux and Central Agency

Article 136

Upon the outbreak of a conflict and in all cases of occupation, each of the Parties to the conflict shall establish an official Information Bureau responsible for receiving and transmitting information in respect of the protected persons who are in its power.

Each of the Parties to the conflict shall, within the shortest possible period, give its Bureau information of any measure taken by it concerning any protected persons who are kept in custody for more than two weeks, who are subjected to assigned residence or who are interned. It shall, furthermore, require its various departments concerned with such matters to provide the aforesaid Bureau promptly with information concerning all changes pertaining to these protected persons, as, for example, transfers, releases, repatriations, escapes, admittances to hospitals, births and deaths.

Article 137

Each national Bureau shall immediately forward information concerning protected persons by the most rapid means to the Powers in whose territory they resided, through the intermediary of the Protecting Powers and likewise through the Central Agency provided for in Article 140. The Bureaux shall also reply to all enquiries which may be received regarding protected persons.

Information Bureaux shall transmit information concerning a protected person unless its transmission might be detrimental to the person concerned or to his or her relatives. Even in such a case, the information may not be withheld from the Central Agency which, upon being notified of the circumstances, will take the necessary precautions indicated in Article 140.

All communications in writing made by any Bureau shall be authenticated by a signature or a seal.

Article 138

The information received by the national Bureau and transmitted by it shall be of such a character as to make it possible to identify the protected person exactly and to advise his next of kin quickly. The information in respect of each person shall include at least his surname, first names, place and date of birth, nationality last residence and distinguishing characteristics, the first name of the father and the maiden name of the mother, the date, place and nature of the action taken with regard to the individual, the address at which correspondence may be sent to him and the name and address of the person to be informed.

Likewise, information regarding the state of health of internees who are seriously ill or seriously wounded shall be supplied regularly and if possible every week.

Article 139

Each national Information Bureau shall, furthermore, be responsible for collecting all personal valuables left by protected persons mentioned in Article 136, in particular those who have been repatriated or released, or who have escaped or died; it shall forward the said valuables to those concerned, either direct, or, if necessary, through the Central Agency. Such articles shall be sent by the Bureau in sealed packets which shall be accompanied by statements giving clear and full identity particulars of the person to whom the articles belonged, and by a complete list of the contents of the parcel. Detailed records shall be maintained of the receipt and despatch of all such valuables.

Article 140

A Central Information Agency for protected persons, in particular for internees, shall be created in a neutral country. The International Committee of the Red Cross shall, if it deems necessary, propose to the Powers concerned the organization of such an Agency, which may be the same as that provided for in Article 123 of the Geneva Convention relative to the Treatment of Prisoners of War of 12 August 1949.

The function of the Agency shall be to collect all information of the type set forth in Article 136 which it may obtain through official or private channels and to transmit it as rapidly as possible to the countries of origin or of residence of the persons concerned, except in cases where such transmissions might be detrimental to the persons whom the said information concerns, or to their relatives. It shall receive from the Parties to the conflict all reasonable facilities for effecting such transmissions.

The High Contracting Parties, and in particular those whose nationals benefit by the services of the Central Agency, are requested to give the said Agency the financial aid it may require.

The foregoing provisions shall in no way be interpreted as restricting the humanitarian activities of the International Committee of the Red Cross and of the relief Societies described in Article 142.

Article 141

The national Information Bureaux and the Central Information Agency shall enjoy free postage for all mail, likewise the exemptions provided for in Article 110, and further, so far as possible, exemption from telegraphic charges or, at least, greatly reduced rates.

PART IV
EXECUTION OF THE CONVENTION

Section I
General Provisions

Article 142

Subject to the measures which the Detaining Powers may consider essential to ensure their security or to meet any other reasonable need, the representatives of religious organizations, relief societies, or any other organizations assisting the protected persons, shall receive from these Powers, for themselves or their duly accredited agents, all facilities for visiting the protected persons, for distributing relief supplies and material from any source, intended for educational, recreational or religious purposes, or for assisting them in organizing their leisure time within the places of internment. Such societies or organizations may be constituted in the territory of the Detaining Power, or in any other country, or they may have an international character.

The Detaining Power may limit the number of societies and organizations whose delegates are allowed to carry out their activities in its territory and under its supervision, on condition, however, that such limitation shall not hinder the supply of effective and adequate relief to all protected persons.

The special position of the International Committee of the Red Cross in this field shall be recognized and respected at all times.

Article 143

Representatives or delegates of the Protecting Powers shall have permission to go to all places where protected persons are, particularly to places of internment, detention and work.

They shall have access to all premises occupied by protected persons and shall be able to interview the latter without witnesses, personally or through an interpreter.

Such visits may not be prohibited except for reasons of imperative military necessity, and then only as an exceptional and temporary measure. Their duration and frequency shall not be restricted.

Such representatives and delegates shall have full liberty to select the places they wish to visit. The Detaining or Occupying Power, the Protecting Power and when occasion arises the Power of origin of the persons to be visited, may agree that compatriots of the internees shall be permitted to participate in the visits.

The delegates of the International Committee of the Red Cross shall also enjoy the above prerogatives. The appointment of such delegates shall be submitted to the approval of the Power governing the territories where they will carry out their duties.

Article 144

The High Contracting Parties undertake, in time of peace as in time of war, to disseminate the text of the present Convention as widely as possible in their respective countries, and, in particular, to include the study thereof in their programmes of military and, if possible, civil instruction, so that the principles thereof may become known to the entire population.

Any civilian, military, police or other authorities, who in time of war assume responsibilities in respect of protected persons, must possess the text of the Convention and be specially instructed as to its provisions.

Article 145

The High Contracting Parties shall communicate to one another through the Swiss Federal Council and, during hostilities, through the Protecting Powers, the official translations of the present Convention, as well as the laws and regulations which they may adopt to ensure the application thereof.

Article 146

The High Contracting Parties undertake to enact any legislation necessary to provide effective penal sanctions for persons committing, or ordering to be committed, any of the grave breaches of the present Convention defined in the following Article.

Each High Contracting Party shall be under the obligation to search for persons alleged to have committed, or to have ordered to be committed, such grave breaches, and shall bring such persons, regardless of their nationality, before its own courts. It may also, if it prefers, and in accordance with the provisions of its own legislation, hand such persons over for trial to another High Contracting Party concerned, provided such High Contracting Party has made out a prima facie case.

Each High Contracting Party shall take measures necessary for the suppression of all acts contrary to the provisions of the present Convention other than the grave breaches defined in the following Article.

In all circumstances, the accused persons shall benefit by safeguards of proper trial and defence, which shall not be less favourable than those provided by Article 105 and those following of the Geneva Convention relative to the Treatment of Prisoners of War of 12 August 1949.

Article 147

Grave breaches to which the preceding Article relates shall be those involving any of the following acts, if committed against persons or property protected by the present Convention: wilful killing, torture or inhuman treatment, including biological experiments, wilfully causing great suffering or serious injury to body or health, unlawful deportation or transfer or unlawful confinement of a protected person, compelling a protected person to serve in the forces of a hostile Power, or wilfully depriving a protected person of the rights of fair and regular trial prescribed in the present Convention, taking of hostages and extensive destruction and appropriation of property, not justified by military necessity and carried out unlawfully and wantonly.

Article 148

No High Contracting Party shall be allowed to absolve itself or any other High Contracting Party of any liability incurred by itself or by another High Contracting Party in respect of breaches referred to in the preceding Article.

Article 149

At the request of a Party to the conflict, an enquiry shall be instituted, in a manner to be decided between the interested Parties, concerning any alleged violation of the Convention.

If agreement has not been reached concerning the procedure for the enquiry, the Parties should agree on the choice of an umpire who will decide upon the procedure to be followed.

Once the violation has been established, the Parties to the conflict shall put an end to it and shall repress it with the least possible delay.

Section II
Final Provisions

Article 150

The present Convention is established in English and in French. Both texts are equally authentic.

The Swiss Federal Council shall arrange for official translations of the Convention to be made in the Russian and Spanish languages.

Article 151

The present Convention, which bears the date of this day, is open to signature until 12 February 1950, in the name of the Powers represented at the Conference which opened at Geneva on 21 April 1949.

Article 152

The present Convention shall be ratified as soon as possible and the ratifications shall be deposited at Berne.

A record shall be drawn up of the deposit of each instrument of ratification and certified copies of this record shall be transmitted by the Swiss Federal Council to all the Powers in whose name the Convention has been signed, or whose accession has been notified.

Article 153

The present Convention shall come into force six months after not less than two instruments of ratification have been deposited.

Thereafter, it shall come into force for each High Contracting Party six months after the deposit of the instrument of ratification.

Article 154

In the relations between the Powers who are bound by the Hague Conventions respecting the Laws and Customs of War on Land, whether that of 29 July 1899, or that of 18 October 1907, and who are parties to the present Convention, this last

Convention shall be supplementary to Sections II and III of the Regulations annexed to the above-mentioned Conventions of The Hague.

Article 155

From the date of its coming into force, it shall be open to any Power in whose name the present Convention has not been signed, to accede to this Convention.

Article 156

Accessions shall be notified in writing to the Swiss Federal Council, and shall take effect six months after the date on which they are received.

The Swiss Federal Council shall communicate the accessions to all the Powers in whose name the Convention has been signed, or whose accession has been notified.

Article 157

The situations provided for in Articles 2 and 3 shall effective immediate effect to ratifications deposited and accessions notified by the Parties to the conflict before or after the beginning of hostilities or occupation. The Swiss Federal Council shall communicate by the quickest method any ratifications or accessions received from Parties to the conflict.

Article 158

Each of the High Contracting Parties shall be at liberty to denounce the present Convention.

The denunciation shall be notified in writing to the Swiss Federal Council, which shall transmit it to the Governments of all the High Contracting Parties.

The denunciation shall take effect one year after the notification thereof has been made to the Swiss Federal Council. However, a denunciation of which notification has been made at a time when the denouncing Power is involved in a conflict shall not take effect until peace has been concluded, and until after operations connected with the release, repatriation and re-establishment of the persons protected by the present Convention have been terminated.

The denunciation shall have effect only in respect of the denouncing Power. It shall in no way impair the obligations which the Parties to the conflict shall remain bound to fulfil by virtue of the principles of the law of nations, as they result from the usages established among civilized peoples, from the laws of humanity and the dictates of the public conscience.

Article 159

The Swiss Federal Council shall register the present Convention with the Secretariat of the United Nations. The Swiss Federal Council shall also inform the Secretariat of the United Nations of all ratifications, accessions and denunciations received by it with respect to the present Convention.

In witness whereof the undersigned, having deposited their respective full powers, have signed the present Convention.

Done at Geneva this twelfth day of August 1949, in the English and French languages. The original shall be deposited in the Archives of the Swiss Confederation. The Swiss Federal Council shall transmit certified copies thereof to each of the signatory and acceding States.

ANNEX I
DRAFT AGREEMENT RELATING TO HOSPITAL AND SAFETY ZONES AND LOCALITIES

Article 1

Hospital and safety zones shall be strictly reserved for the persons mentioned in Article 23 of the Geneva Convention for the Amelioration of the Condition of the Wounded and Sick in Armed Forces in the Field of 12 August 1949, and in Article 14 of the Geneva Convention relative to the Protection of Civilian Persons in Time of War of 12 August 1949, and for the personnel entrusted with the organization and administration of these zones and localities, and with the care of the persons therein assembled.

Nevertheless, persons whose permanent residence is within such zones shall have the right to stay there.

Article 2

No persons residing, in whatever capacity, in a hospital and safety zone shall perform any work, either within or without the zone, directly connected with military operations or the production of war material.

Article 3

The Power establishing a hospital and safety zone shall take all necessary measures to prohibit access to all persons who have no right of residence or entry therein.

Article 4

Hospital and safety zones shall fulfil the following conditions:

(a)   they shall comprise only a small part of the territory governed by the Power which has established them

(b)   they shall be thinly populated in relation to the possibilities of accommodation

(c)   they shall be far removed and free from all military objectives, or large industrial or administrative establishments

(d)   they shall not be situated in areas which, according to every probability, may become important for the conduct of the war.

Article 5

Hospital and safety zones shall be subject to the following obligations:

(a)   the lines of communication and means of transport which they possess shall not be used for the transport of military personnel or material, even in transit

(b)   they shall in no case be defended by military means.

Article 6

Hospital and safety zones shall be marked by means of oblique red bands on a white ground, placed on the buildings and outer precincts.

Zones reserved exclusively for the wounded and sick may be marked by means of the Red Cross (Red Crescent, Red Lion and Sun) emblem on a white ground.

They may be similarly marked at night by means of appropriate illumination.

Article 7

The Powers shall communicate to all the High Contracting Parties in peacetime or on the outbreak of hostilities, a list of the hospital and safety zones in the territories governed by them. They shall also give notice of any new zones set up during hostilities.

As soon as the adverse party has received the above-mentioned notification, the zone shall be regularly established.

If, however, the adverse party considers that the conditions of the present agreement have not been fulfilled, it may refuse to recognize the zone by giving immediate notice thereof to the Party responsible for the said zone, or may make its recognition of such zone dependent upon the institution of the control provided for in Article 8.

Article 8

Any Power having recognized one or several hospital and safety zones instituted by the adverse Party shall be entitled to demand control by one or more Special Commissions, for the purpose of ascertaining if the zones fulfil the conditions and obligations stipulated in the present agreement.

For this purpose, members of the Special Commissions shall at all times have free access to the various zones and may even reside there permanently. They shall be given all facilities for their duties of inspection.

Article 9

Should the Special Commissions note any facts which they consider contrary to the stipulations of the present agreement, they shall at once draw the attention of the Power governing the said zone to these facts, and shall fix a time limit of five days within which the matter should be rectified. They shall duly notify the Power which has recognized the zone.

If, when the time limit has expired, the Power governing the zone has not complied with the warning, the adverse Party may declare that it is no longer bound by the present agreement in respect of the said zone.

Article 10

Any Power setting up one or more hospital and safety zones, and the adverse Parties to whom their existence has been notified, shall nominate or have nominated by the Protecting Powers or by other neutral Powers, persons eligible to be members of the Special Commissions mentioned in Articles 8 and 9.

Article 11

In no circumstances may hospital and safety zones be the object of attack. They shall be protected and respected at all times by the Parties to the conflict.

Article 12

In the case of occupation of a territory, the hospital and safety zones therein shall continue to be respected and utilized as such.

Their purpose may, however, be modified by the Occupying Power, on condition that all measures are taken to ensure the safety of the persons accommodated.

Article 13

The present agreement shall also apply to localities which the Powers may utilize for the same purposes as hospital and safety zones.

ANNEX II
DRAFT REGULATIONS CONCERNING COLLECTIVE RELIEF

Article 1

The Internee Committees shall be allowed to distribute collective relief shipments for which they are responsible to all internees who are dependent for administration on the said Committee's place of internment, including those internees who are in hospitals, or in prison or other penitentiary establishments.

Article 2

The distribution of collective relief shipments shall be effected in accordance with the instructions of the donors and with a plan drawn up by the Internee Committees. The issue of medical stores shall, however, be made for preference in agreement with the senior medical officers, and the latter may, in hospitals and infirmaries, waive the said instructions, if the needs of their patients so demand. Within the limits thus defined, the distribution shall always be carried out equitably.

Article 3

Members of Internee Committees shall be allowed to go to the railway stations or other points of arrival of relief supplies near their places of internment so as to enable them to verify the quantity as well as the quality of the goods received and to make out detailed reports thereon for the donors.

Article 4

Internee Committees shall be given the facilities necessary for verifying whether the distribution of collective relief in all subdivisions and annexes of their places of internment has been carried out in accordance with their instructions.

Article 5

Internee Committees shall be allowed to complete, and to cause to be completed by members of the Internee Committees in labour detachments or by the senior medical officers of infirmaries and hospitals, forms or questionnaires intended for the donors, relating to collective relief supplies (distribution, requirements, quantities, etc.). Such forms and questionnaires, duly completed, shall be forwarded to the donors without delay.

Article 6

In order to secure the regular distribution of collective relief supplies to the internees in their place of internment, and to meet any needs that may arise through the arrival of fresh parties of internees, the Internee Committees shall be allowed to create and maintain sufficient reserve stocks of collective relief. For this purpose, they shall have suitable warehouses at their disposal; each warehouse shall be provided with two locks, the Internee Committee holding the keys of one lock, and the commandant of the place of internment the keys of the other.

Article 7

The High Contracting Parties, and the Detaining Powers in particular, shall, so far as is in any way possible and subject to the regulations governing the food supply of the population, authorize purchases of goods to be made in their territories for the distribution of collective relief to the internees. They shall likewise facilitate the transfer of funds and other financial measures of a technical or administrative nature taken for the purpose of making such purchases.

Article 8

The foregoing provisions shall not constitute an obstacle to the right of internees to receive collective relief before their arrival in a place of internment or in the course of their transfer, nor to the possibility of representatives of the Protecting Power, or of the International Committee of the Red Cross or any other humanitarian organization giving assistance to internees and responsible for forwarding such supplies, ensuring the distribution thereof to the recipients by any other means they may deem suitable.

ANNEX III
I. INTERNMENT CARD

[Not reproduced here]

CHAPTER 18

PROTOCOL ADDITIONAL TO THE GENEVA CONVENTIONS OF 12 AUGUST 1949, AND RELATING TO THE PROTECTION OF VICTIMS OF INTERNATIONAL ARMED CONFLICTS (PROTOCOL I), 8 JUNE 1977

PREAMBLE

The High Contracting Parties,

Proclaiming their earnest wish to see peace prevail among peoples,

Recalling that every State has the duty, in conformity with the Charter of the United Nations, to refrain in its international relations from the threat or use of force against the sovereignty, territorial integrity or political independence of any State, or in any other manner inconsistent with the purposes of the United Nations,

Believing it necessary nevertheless to reaffirm and develop the provisions protecting the victims of armed conflicts and to supplement measures intended to reinforce their application,

Expressing their conviction that nothing in this Protocol or in the Geneva Conventions of 12 August 1949 can be construed as legitimizing or authorizing any act of aggression or any other use of force inconsistent with the Charter of the United Nations,

Reaffirming further that the provisions of the Geneva Conventions of 12 August 1949 and of this Protocol must be fully applied in all circumstances to all persons who are protected by those instruments, without any adverse distinction based on the nature or origin of the armed conflict or on the causes espoused by or attributed to the Parties to the conflict,

Have agreed on the following:

PART I
GENERAL PROVISIONS

Article 1
General principles and scope of application

1 The High Contracting Parties undertake to respect and to ensure respect for this Protocol in all circumstances.

2 In cases not covered by this Protocol or by other international agreements, civilians and combatants remain under the protection and authority of the principles of international law derived from established custom, from the principles of humanity and from dictates of public conscience.

3 This Protocol, which supplements the Geneva Conventions of 12 August 1949 for the protection of war victims, shall apply in the situations referred to in Article 2 common to those Conventions.

4 The situations referred to in the preceding paragraph include armed conflicts in which peoples are fighting against colonial domination and alien occupation and against racist regimes in the exercise of their right of self-determination, as enshrined in the Charter of the United Nations and the Declaration on Principles of International Law concerning Friendly Relations and Co-operation among States in accordance with the Charter of the United Nations.

Article 2
Definitions

For the purposes of this Protocol

(a) 'First Convention', 'Second Convention', 'Third Convention' and 'Fourth Convention' mean, respectively, the Geneva Convention for the Amelioration of the Condition of the Wounded and Sick in Armed Forces in the Field of 12 August 1949; the Geneva Convention for the Amelioration of the Condition of Wounded, Sick and Ship-wrecked Members of Armed Forces at Sea of 12 August 1949; the Geneva Convention relative to the Treatment of Prisoners of War of 12 August 1949; the Geneva Convention relative to the Protection of Civilian Persons in Time of War of 12 August 1949; 'the Conventions' means the four Geneva Conventions of 12 August 1949 for the protection of war victims;

(b) 'Rules of international law applicable in armed conflict' means the rules applicable in armed conflict set forth in international agreements to which the Parties to the conflict are Parties and the generally recognized principles and rules of international law which are applicable to armed conflict;

(c) 'Protecting Power' means a neutral or other State not a Party to the conflict which has been designated by a Party to the conflict and accepted by the adverse Party and has agreed to carry out the functions assigned to a Protecting Power under the Conventions and this Protocol;

(d) 'Substitute' means an organisation acting in place of a Protecting Power in accordance with Article 5.

Article 3
Beginning and end of application

Without prejudice to the provisions which are applicable at all times:

(a) the Conventions and this Protocol shall apply from the beginning of any situation referred to in Article 1 of this Protocol.

(b) the application of the Conventions and of this Protocol shall cease, in the territory of Parties to the conflict, on the general close of military operations and, in the case of occupied territories, on the termination of the occupation, except, in either circumstance, for those persons whose final release, repatriation or re-establishment takes place thereafter. These persons shall continue to benefit from the relevant provisions of the Conventions and of this Protocol until their final release repatriation or re-establishment.

Article 4
Legal status of the Parties to the conflict

The application of the Conventions and of this Protocol, as well as the conclusion of the agreements provided for therein, shall not affect the legal status of the Parties to the conflict. Neither the occupation of a territory nor the application of the Conventions and this Protocol shall affect the legal status of the territory in question.

Article 5
Appointment of Protecting Powers and of their substitute

1 It is the duty of the Parties to a conflict from the beginning of that conflict to secure the supervision and implementation of the Conventions and of this Protocol by the application of the system of Protecting Powers, including inter alia the designation and acceptance of those Powers, in accordance with the following paragraphs. Protecting Powers shall have the duty of safeguarding the interests of the Parties to the conflict.

2 From the beginning of a situation referred to in Article 1, each Party to the conflict shall without delay designate a Protecting Power for the purpose of applying the Conventions and this Protocol and shall, likewise without delay and for the same purpose, permit the activities or a Protecting Power which has been accepted by it as such after designation by the adverse Party.

3 If a Protecting Power has not been designated or accepted from the beginning of a situation referred to in Article 1, the International Committee of the Red Cross, without prejudice to the right of any other impartial humanitarian organization to do likewise, shall offer its good offices to the Parties to the conflict with a view to the designation without delay of a Protecting Power to which the Parties to the conflict consent. For that purpose it may inter alia ask each Party to provide it with a list of at least five States which that Party considers acceptable to act as Protecting Power on its behalf in relation to an adverse Party and ask each adverse Party to provide a list or at least five States which it would accept as the Protecting Power of the first Party; these lists shall be communicated to the Committee within two weeks after the receipt or the request; it shall compare them and seek the agreement of any proposed State named on both lists.

4 If, despite the foregoing, there is no Protecting Power, the Parties to the conflict shall accept without delay an offer which may be made by the International Committee of the Red Cross or by any other organization which offers all guarantees of impartiality and efficacy, after due consultations with the said Parties and taking into account the result of these consultations, to act as a substitute. The functioning of such a substitute is subject to the consent of the Parties to the conflict; every effort shall be made by the Parties to the conflict to facilitate the operations of the substitute in the performance of its tasks under the Conventions and this Protocol.

5 In accordance with Article 4, the designation and acceptance of Protecting Powers for the purpose of applying the Conventions and this Protocol shall not affect the legal status of the Parties to the conflict or of any territory, including occupied territory.

6 The maintenance of diplomatic relations between Parties to the conflict or the entrusting of the protection of a Party's interests and those of its nationals to a third State in accordance with the rules of international law relating to diplomatic relations is no obstacle to the designation of Protecting Powers for the purpose of applying the Conventions and this Protocol.

7 Any subsequent mention in this Protocol of a Protecting Power includes also a substitute.

Article 6
Qualified persons

1 The High Contracting Parties shall, also in peacetime, endeavour, with the assistance of the national Red Cross (Red Crescent, Red Lion and Sun) Societies, to train qualified personnel to facilitate the application of the Conventions and of this Protocol, and in particular the activities of the Protecting Powers.

2 The recruitment and training of such personnel are within domestic jurisdiction.

3 The International Committee of the Red Cross shall hold at the disposal of the High Contracting Parties the lists of persons so trained which the High Contracting Parties may have established and may have transmitted to it for that purpose.

4 The conditions governing the employment of such personnel outside the national territory shall, in each case, be the subject of special agreements between the Parties concerned.

Article 7
Meetings

The depositary of this Protocol shall convene a meeting of the High Contracting Parties, at the request of one or more of the said Parties and upon, the approval of the majority of the said Parties, to consider general problems concerning the application of the Conventions and of the Protocol.

PART II
WOUNDED, SICK AND SHIPWRECKED

Section I
General Protection

Article 8
Terminology

For the purposes of this Protocol:

(a)   'Wounded' and 'sick' mean persons, whether military or civilian, who, because of trauma, disease or other physical or mental disorder or disability, are in need of medical assistance or care and who refrain from any act of hostility. These terms also cover maternity cases, new-born babies and other persons who may be in need of immediate medical assistance or care, such as the infirm or expectant mothers, and who refrain from any act of hostility;

(b)   'Shipwrecked' means persons, whether military or civilian, who are in peril at sea or in other waters as a result of misfortune affecting them or the vessel or aircraft carrying them and who refrain from any act of hostility. These persons, provided that they continue to refrain from any act of hostility, shall continue to be considered shipwrecked during their rescue until they acquire another status under the Conventions or this Protocol;

(c)   'Medical personnel' means those persons assigned, by a Party to the conflict, exclusively to the medical purposes enumerated under e) or to the administration of medical units or to the operation or administration of medical transports. Such assignments may be either permanent or temporary. The term includes:

   (i)   medical personnel of a Party to the conflict, whether military or civilian, including those described in the First and Second Conventions, and those assigned to civil defence organizations;

    (ii)   medical personnel of national Red Cross (Red Crescent, Red Lion and Sun) Societies and other national voluntary aid societies duly recognized and authorized by a Party to the conflict;

    (iii) medical personnel or medical units or medical transports described in Article 9, paragraph 2.

(d) 'Religious personnel' means military or civilian persons, such as chaplains, who are exclusively engaged in the work of their ministry and attached:

    (i)   to the armed forces of a Party to the conflict;

    (ii)   to medical units or medical transports of a Party to the conflict;

    (iii) to medical units or medical transports described in Article 9, Paragraph 2; or

    (iv) to civil defence organizations of a Party to the conflict.

The attachment of religious personnel may be either permanent or temporary, and the relevant provisions mentioned under (k) apply to them;

(e) 'Medical units' means establishments and other units, whether military or civilian, organized for medical purposes, namely the search for, collection, transportation, diagnosis or treatment – including first-aid treatment – of the wounded, sick and shipwrecked, or for the prevention of disease. The term includes for example, hospitals and other similar units, blood transfusion centres, preventive medicine centres and institutes, medical depots and the medical and pharmaceutical stores of such units. Medical units may be fixed or mobile, permanent or temporary;

(f) 'Medical transportation' means the conveyance by land, water or air of the wounded, sick, shipwrecked, medical personnel, religious personnel, medical equipment or medical supplies protected by the Conventions and by this Protocol;

(g) 'Medical transports' means any means of transportation, whether military or civilian, permanent or temporary, assigned exclusively to medical transportation and under the control of a competent authority of a Party to the conflict;

(h) 'Medical vehicles' means any medical transports by land;

(i) 'Medical ships and craft' means any medical transports by water;

(j) 'Medical aircraft' means any medical transports by air;

(k) 'Permanent medical personnel', 'permanent medical units' and 'permanent medical transports' mean those assigned exclusively to medical purposes for an indeterminate period. 'Temporary medical personnel' 'temporary medical-units' and 'temporary medical transports' mean those devoted exclusively to medical purposes for limited periods during the whole of such periods. Unless otherwise specified, the terms 'medical personnel', 'medical units' and 'medical transports' cover both permanent and temporary categories;

(l) 'Distinctive emblem' means the distinctive emblem of the red cross, red crescent or red lion and sun on a white ground when used for the protection of medical units and transports, or medical and religious personnel, equipment or supplies;

(m) 'Distinctive signal' means any signal or message specified for the identification exclusively of medical units or transports in Chapter III of Annex I to this Protocol.

Article 9
Field of application

1 This Part, the provisions of which are intended to ameliorate the condition of the wounded, sick and shipwrecked, shall apply to all those affected by a situation referred

to in Article 1, without any adverse distinction founded on race, colour, sex, language, religion or belief political or other opinion, national or social origin, wealth, birth or other status, or on any other similar criteria.

2 The relevant provisions of Articles 27 and 32 of the First Convention shall apply to permanent medical units and transports (other than hospital ships, to which Article 25 of the Second Convention applies) and their personnel made available to a Party to the conflict for humanitarian purposes:

(a)   by a neutral or other State which is not a Party to that conflict;
(b)   by a recognized and authorized aid society of such a State;
(c)   by an impartial international humanitarian organization.

Article 10
Protection and care

1 All the wounded, sick and shipwrecked, to whichever Party they belong, shall be respected and protected.

2 In all circumstances they shall be treated humanely and shall receive, to the fullest extent practicable and with the least possible delay, the medical care and attention required by their condition. There shall be no distinction among them founded on any grounds other than medical ones.

Article 11
Protection of persons

1 The physical or mental health and integrity of persons who are in the power of the adverse Party or who are interned, detained or otherwise deprived of liberty as a result of a situation referred to in Article 1 shall not be endangered by any unjustified act or omission. Accordingly, it is prohibited to subject the persons described in this Article to any medical procedure which is not indicated by the state of health of the person concerned and which is not consistent with generally accepted medical standards which would be applied under similar medical circumstances to persons who are nationals of the Party conducting the procedure and who are in no way deprived of liberty.

2 It is, in particular, prohibited to carry out on such persons, even with their consent:

(a)   physical mutilations;
(b)   medical or scientific experiments;
(c)   removal of tissue or organs for transplantation, except where these acts are justified in conformity with the conditions provided for in paragraph 1.

3 Exceptions to the prohibition in paragraph 2 (c) may be made only in the case of donations of blood for transfusion or of skin for grafting, provided that they are given voluntarily and without any coercion or inducement, and then only for therapeutic purposes, under conditions consistent with generally accepted medical standards and controls designed for the benefit of both the donor and the recipient.

4 Any wilful act or omission which seriously endangers the physical or mental health or integrity of any person who is in the power of a Party other than the one on which he depends and which either violates any of the prohibitions in paragraphs 1 and 2 or fails to comply with the requirements of paragraph 3 shall be a grave breach of this Protocol.

5 The persons described in paragraph 1 have the right to refuse any surgical operation. In case of refusal, medical personnel shall endeavour to obtain a written statement to that effect, signed or acknowledged by the patient.

6 Each Party to the conflict shall keep a medical record for every donation of blood for transfusion or skin for grafting by persons referred to in paragraph 1, if that donation is made under the responsibility of that Party. In addition, each Party to the conflict shall endeavour to keep a record of all medical procedures undertaken with respect to any person who is interned, detained or otherwise deprived of liberty as a result of a situation referred to in Article 1. These records shall be available at all times for inspection by the Protecting Power.

Article 12
Protection of medical units

1 Medical units shall be respected and protected at all times and shall not be the object of attack.

2 Paragraph 1 shall apply to civilian medical units, provided that they:

(a) belong to one of the Parties to the conflict;
(b) are recognized and authorized by the competent authority of one of the Parties to the conflict; or
(c) are authorized in conformity with Article 9, paragraph 2, of this Protocol or Article 27 of the First Convention.

3 The Parties to the conflict are invited to notify each other of the location of their fixed medical units. The absence of such notification shall not exempt any of the Parties from the obligation to comply with the provisions of paragraph 1.

4 Under no circumstances shall medical units be used in an attempt to shield military objectives from attack. Whenever possible, the Parties to the conflict shall ensure that medical units are so sited that attacks against military objectives do not imperil their safety.

Article 13
Discontinuance of protection of civilian medical units

1 The protection to which civilian medical units are entitled shall not cease unless they are used to commit, outside their humanitarian function, acts harmful to the enemy. Protection may, however, cease only after a warning has been given setting, whenever appropriate, a reasonable time-limit, and after such warning has remained unheeded.

2 The following shall not be considered as acts harmful to the enemy:

(a) that the personnel of the unit are equipped with light individual weapons for their own defence or for that of the wounded and sick in their charge;
(b) that the unit is guarded by a picket or by sentries or by an escort;
(c) that small arms and ammunition taken from the wounded and sick, and not yet handed to the proper service, are found in the units;
(d) that members of the armed forces or other combatants are in the unit for medical reasons.

Article 14
Limitations on requisition of civilian medical units

1 The Occupying Power has the duty to ensure that the medical needs of the civilian population in occupied territory continue to be satisfied.

2 The Occupying Power shall not, therefore, requisition civilian medical units, their equipment, their materiel or the services of their personnel, so long as these resources are

necessary for the provision of adequate medical services for the civilian population and for the continuing medical care of any wounded and sick already under treatment.

3 Provided that the general rule in paragraph 2 continues to be observed, the Occupying Power may requisition the said resources, subject to the following particular conditions:

(a) that the resources are necessary for the adequate and immediate medical treatment of the wounded and sick members of the armed forces of the Occupying Power or of prisoners of war;

(b) that the requisition continues only while such necessity exists; and

(c) that immediate arrangements are made to ensure that the medical needs of the civilian population, as well as those of any wounded and sick under treatment who are affected by the requisition, continue to be satisfied.

Article 15
Protection of civilian medical and religious personnel

1 Civilian medical personnel shall be respected and protected.

2 If needed, all available help shall be afforded to civilian medical personnel in an area where civilian medical services are disrupted by reason of combat activity.

3 The Occupying Power shall afford civilian medical personnel in occupied territories every assistance to enable them to perform, to the best of their ability, their humanitarian functions. The Occupying Power may not require that, in the performance of those functions, such personnel shall give priority to the treatment of any person except on medical grounds. They shall not be compelled to carry out tasks which are not compatible with their humanitarian mission.

4 Civilian medical personnel shall have access to any place where their services are essential, subject to such supervisory and safety measures as the relevant Party to the conflict may deem necessary.

5 Civilian religious personnel shall be respected and protected. The provisions of the Conventions and of this Protocol concerning the protection and identification of medical personnel shall apply equally to such persons.

Article 16
General protection of medical duties

1 Under no circumstances shall any person be punished for carrying out medical activities compatible with medical ethics, regardless of the person benefiting therefrom.

2 Persons engaged in medical activities shall not be compelled to perform acts or to carry out work contrary to the rules of medical ethics or to other medical rules designed for the benefit of the wounded and sick or to the provisions of the Conventions or of this Protocol, or to refrain from performing acts or from carrying out work required by those rules and provisions.

3 No person engaged in medical activities shall be compelled to give to anyone belonging either to an adverse Party, or to his own Party except as required by the law of the latter Party, any information concerning the wounded and sick who are, or who have been, under his care, if such information would, in his opinion, prove harmful to the patients concerned or to their families. Regulations for the compulsory notification of communicable diseases shall, however, be respected.

Article 17
Role of the civilian population and of aid societies

1 The civilian population shall respect the wounded, sick and shipwrecked, even if they belong to the adverse Party, and shall commit no act of violence against them. The civilian population and aid societies, such as national Red Cross (Red Crescent, Red Lion and Sun) Societies, shall be permitted, even on their own initiative, to collect and care for the wounded, sick and shipwrecked, even in invaded or occupied areas. No one shall be harmed, prosecuted, convicted or punished for such humanitarian acts.

2 The Parties to the conflict may appeal to the civilian population and the aid societies referred to in paragraph 1 to collect and care for the wounded, sick and shipwrecked, and to search for the dead and report their location; they shall grant both protection and the necessary facilities to those who respond to this appeal. If the adverse Party gains or regains control of the area, that Party also shall afford the same protection and facilities for as long as they are needed.

Article 18
Identification

1 Each Party to the conflict shall endeavour to ensure that medical and religious personnel and medical units and transports are identifiable.

2 Each Party to the conflict shall also endeavour to adopt and to implement methods and procedures which will make it possible to recognize medical units and transports which use the distinctive emblem and distinctive signals.

3 In occupied territory and in areas where fighting is taking place or is likely to take place, civilian medical personnel and civilian religious personnel should be recognizable by the distinctive emblem and an identity card certifying their status.

4 With the consent of the competent authority, medical units and transports shall be marked by the distinctive emblem. The ships and craft referred to in Article 22 of this Protocol shall be marked in accordance with the provisions of the Second Convention.

5 In addition to the distinctive emblem, a Party to the conflict may, as provided in Chapter III of Annex I to this Protocol, authorize the use of distinctive signals to identify medical units and transports. Exceptionally, in the special cases covered in that Chapter, medical transports may use distinctive signals without displaying the distinctive emblem.

6 The application of the provisions of paragraphs 1 to 5 of this article is governed by Chapters I to III of Annex I to this Protocol. Signals designated in Chapter III of the Annex for the exclusive use of medical units and transports shall not, except as provided therein, be used for any purpose other than to identify the medical units and transports specified in that Chapter.

7 This article does not authorize any wider use of the distinctive emblem in peacetime than is prescribed in Article 44 of the First Convention.

8 The provisions of the Conventions and of this Protocol relating to supervision of the use of the distinctive emblem and to the prevention and repression of any misuse thereof shall be applicable to distinctive signals.

Article 19
Neutral and other States not Parties to the conflict

Neutral and other States not Parties to the conflict shall apply the relevant provisions of this Protocol to persons protected by this Part who may be received or interned within their territory, and to any dead of the Parties to that conflict whom they may find.

Article 20
Prohibition of reprisals

Reprisals against the persons and objects protected by this Part are prohibited.

Section II
Medical transportation

Article 21
Medical vehicles

Medical vehicles shall be respected and protected in the same way as mobile medical units under the Conventions and this Protocol.

Article 22
Hospital ships and coastal rescue craft

1 The provisions of the Conventions relating to:

    (a)   vessels described in Articles 22, 24, 25 and 27 of the Second Convention,
    (b)   their lifeboats and small craft,
    (c)   their personnel and crews, and
    (d)   the wounded; sick and shipwrecked on board.

shall also apply where these vessels carry civilian wounded, sick and shipwrecked who do not belong to any of the categories mentioned in Article 13 of the Second Convention. Such civilians shall not, however, be subject to surrender to any Party which is not their own, or to capture at sea. If they find themselves in the power of a Party to the conflict other than their own they shall be covered by the Fourth Convention and by this Protocol.

2 The protection provided by the Conventions to vessels described in Article 25 of the Second Convention shall extend to hospital ships made available for humanitarian purposes to a Party to the conflict:

    (a)   by a neutral or other State which is not a Party to that conflict; or
    (b)   by an impartial international humanitarian organization,

provided that, in either case, the requirements set out in that Article are complied with.

3 Small craft described in Article 27 of the Second Convention shall be protected, even if the notification envisaged by that Article has not been made. The Parties to the conflict are, nevertheless, invited to inform each other of any details of such craft which will facilitate their identification and recognition.

Article 23
Other medical ships and craft

1 Medical ships and craft other than those referred to in Article 22 of this Protocol and Article 38 of the Second Convention shall, whether at sea or in other waters, be respected and protected in the same way as mobile medical units under the Conventions and this Protocol. Since this protection can only be effective if they can be identified and

recognized as medical ships or craft, such vessels should be marked with the distinctive emblem and as far as possible comply with the second paragraph of Article 43 of the Second Convention.

2 The ships and craft referred to in paragraph 1 shall remain subject to the laws of war. Any warship on the surface able immediately to enforce its command may order them to stop, order them off, or make them take a certain course, and they shall obey every such command. Such ships and craft may not in any other way be diverted from their medical mission so long as they are needed for the wounded, sick and shipwrecked on board.

3 The protection provided in paragraph 1 shall cease only under the conditions set out in Articles 34 and 35 of the Second Convention. A clear refusal to obey a command given in accordance with paragraph 2 shall be an act harmful to the enemy under Article 34 of the Second Convention.

4 A Party to the conflict may notify any adverse Party as far in advance of sailing as possible of the name, description, expected time of sailing, course and estimated speed of the medical ship or craft, particularly in the case of ships of over 2,000 gross tons, and may provide any other information which would facilitate identification and recognition. The adverse Party shall acknowledge receipt of such information.

5 The provisions of Article 37 of the Second Convention shall apply to medical and religious personnel in such ships and craft.

6 The provisions of the Second Convention shall apply to the wounded, sick and shipwrecked belonging to the categories referred to in Article 13 of the Second Convention and in Article 44 of this Protocol who may be on board such medical ships and craft. Wounded, sick and shipwrecked civilians who do not belong to any or the categories mentioned in Article 13 of the Second Convention shall not be subject, at sea, either to surrender to any Party which is not their own, or to removal from such ships or craft; if they find themselves in the power of a Party to the conflict other than their own, they shall be covered by the Fourth Convention and by this Protocol.

Article 24
Protection of medical Aircraft

Medical aircraft shall be respected and protected, subject to the provisions of this Part.

Article 25
Medical aircraft in areas not controlled by an adverse Party

In and over land areas physically controlled by friendly forces, or in and over sea areas not physically controlled by an adverse Party, the respect and protection of medical aircraft of a Party to the conflict is not dependent on any agreement with an adverse Party. For greater safety, however, a Party to the conflict operating its medical aircraft in these areas may notify the adverse Party, as provided in Article 29, in particular when such aircraft are making flights bringing them within range of surface-to-air weapons systems of the adverse Party.

Article 26
Medical aircraft in contact or similar zones

1 In and over those parts of the contact zone which are physically controlled by friendly forces and in and over those areas the physical control of which is not clearly established, protection for medical aircraft can be fully effective only by prior agreement between the competent military authorities of the Parties to the conflict, as provided for

in Article 29. Although, in the absence of such an agreement, medical aircraft operate at their own risk, they shall nevertheless be respected after they have been recognized as such.

2 'Contact zone' means any area on land where the forward elements of opposing forces are in contact with each other, especially where they are exposed to direct fire from the ground.

Article 27
Medical aircraft in areas controlled by an adverse Party

1 The medical aircraft of a Party to the conflict shall continue to be protected while flying over land or sea areas physically controlled by an adverse Party, provided that prior agreement to such flights has been obtained from the competent authority of that adverse Party.

2 A medical aircraft which flies over an area physically controlled by an adverse Party without, or in deviation from the terms of, an agreement provided for in paragraph 1, either through navigational error or because of an emergency affecting the safety of the flight, shall make every effort to identify itself and to inform the adverse Party of the circumstances. As soon as such medical aircraft has been recognized by the adverse Party, that Party shall make all reasonable efforts to give the order to land or to alight on water, referred to in Article 30, paragraph 1, or to take other measures to safeguard its own interests, and, in either case, to allow the aircraft time for compliance, before resorting to an attack against the aircraft.

Article 28
Restrictions on operations of medical aircraft

1 The Parties to the conflict are prohibited from using their medical aircraft to attempt to acquire any military advantage over an adverse Party. The presence of medical aircraft shall not be used in an attempt to render military objectives immune from attack.

2 Medical aircraft shall not be used to collect or transmit intelligence data and shall not carry any equipment intended for such purposes. They are prohibited from carrying any persons or cargo not included within the definition in Article 8(f). The carrying on board of the personal effects of the occupants or of equipment intended solely to facilitate navigation, communication or identification shall not be considered as prohibited,

3 Medical aircraft shall not carry any armament except small arms and ammunition taken from the wounded, sick and shipwrecked on board and not yet handed to the proper service, and such light individual weapons as may be necessary to enable the medical personnel on board to defend themselves and the wounded, sick and shipwrecked in their charge.

4 While carrying out the flights referred to in Articles 26 and 27, medical aircraft shall not, except by prior agreement with the adverse Party, be used to search for the wounded, sick and shipwrecked.

Article 29
Notifications and agreements concerning medical aircraft

1 Notifications under Article 25, or requests for prior agreement under Articles 26, 27, 28, paragraph 4, or 31 shall state the proposed number of medical aircraft, their flight plans and means of identification, and shall be understood to mean that every flight will be carried out in compliance with Article 28.

2 A Party which receives a notification given under Article 25 shall at once acknowledge receipt of such notification.

3 A Party which receives a request for prior agreement under Articles 25, 27, 28, paragraph 4, or 31 shall, as rapidly as possible, notify the requesting Party:

(a)   that the request is agreed to;

(b)   that the request is denied; or

(c)   of reasonable alternative proposals to the request. It may also propose prohibition or restriction of other flights in the area during the time involved. If the Party which submitted the request accepts the alternative proposals, it shall notify the other Party of such acceptance.

4 The Parties shall take the necessary measures to ensure that notifications and agreements can be made rapidly.

5 The Parties shall also take the necessary measures to disseminate rapidly the substance of any such notifications and agreements to the military units concerned and shall instruct those units regarding the means of identification that will be used by the medical aircraft in question.

Article 30
Landing and inspection of medical aircraft

1 Medical aircraft flying over areas which are physically controlled by an adverse Party, or over areas the physical control of which is not clearly established, may be ordered to land or to alight on water, as appropriate, to permit inspection in accordance with the following paragraphs. Medical aircraft shall obey any such order.

2 If such an aircraft lands or alights on water, whether ordered to do so or for other reasons, it may be subjected to inspection solely to determine the matters referred to in paragraphs 3 and 4. Any such inspection shall be commenced without delay and shall be conducted expeditiously. The inspecting Party shall not require the wounded and sick to be removed from the aircraft unless their removal is essential for the inspection. That Party shall in any event ensure that the condition of the wounded and sick is not adversely affected by the inspection or by the removal.

3 If the inspection discloses that the aircraft:

(a)   is a medical aircraft within the meaning of Article 8, sub-paragraph j),

(b)   is not in violation of the conditions prescribed in Article 28, and

(c)   has not flown without or in breach of a prior agreement where such agreement is required, the aircraft and those of its occupants who belong to the adverse Party or to a neutral or other State not a Party to the conflict shall be authorized to continue the flight without delay.

4 If the inspection discloses that the aircraft:

(a)   is not a medical aircraft within the meaning of Article 8, sub-paragraph j),

(b)   is in violation or the conditions prescribed in Article 28, or

(c)   has flown without or in breach of a prior agreement where such agreement is required, the aircraft may be seized. Its occupants shall be treated in conformity with the relevant provisions of the Conventions and of this Protocol. Any aircraft seized which had been assigned as a permanent medical aircraft may be used thereafter only as a medical aircraft.

Article 31
Neutral or other States not Parties to the conflict

1 Except by prior agreement, medical aircraft shall not fly over or land in the territory of a neutral or other State not a Party to the conflict. However, with such an agreement, they shall be respected throughout their flight and also for the duration of any calls in the territory. Nevertheless they shall obey any summons to land or to alight on water, as appropriate.

2 Should a medical aircraft, in the absence of an agreement or in deviation from the terms of an agreement, fly over the territory of a neutral or other State not a Party to the conflict, either through navigational error or because of an emergency affecting the safety of the flight, it shall make every effort to give notice of the flight and to identify itself. As soon as such medical aircraft is recognized, that State shall make all reasonable efforts to give the order to land or to alight on water referred to in Article 30, paragraph 1, or to take other measures to safeguard its own interests, and, in either case, to allow the aircraft time for compliance, before resorting to an attack against the aircraft.

3 If a medical aircraft, either by agreement or in the circumstances mentioned in paragraph 2, lands or alights on water in the territory of a neutral or other State not Party to the conflict, whether ordered to do so or for other reasons, the aircraft shall be subject to inspection for the purposes of determining whether it is in fact a medical aircraft. The inspection shall be commenced without delay and shall be conducted expeditiously. The inspecting Party shall not require the wounded and sick of the Party operating the aircraft to be removed from it unless their removal is essential for the inspection. The inspecting Party shall in any event ensure that the condition of the wounded and sick is not adversely affected by the inspection or the removal. If the inspection discloses that the aircraft is in fact a medical aircraft, the aircraft with its occupants, other than those who must be detained in accordance with the rules of international law applicable in armed conflict, shall be allowed to resume its flight, and reasonable facilities shall be given for the continuation of the flight. If the inspection discloses that the aircraft is not a medical aircraft, it shall be seized and the occupants treated in accordance with paragraph 4.

4 The wounded, sick and shipwrecked disembarked, otherwise than temporarily, from a medical aircraft with the consent of the local authorities in the territory of a neutral or other State not a Party to the conflict shall, unless agreed otherwise between that State and the Parties to the conflict, be detained by that State where so required by the rules of international law applicable in armed conflict, in such a manner that they cannot again take part in the hostilities. The cost of hospital treatment and internment shall be borne by the State to which those persons belong.

5 Neutral or other States not Parties to the conflict shall apply any conditions and restrictions on the passage of medical aircraft over, or on the landing of medical aircraft in, their territory equally to all Parties to the conflict.

Section III
Missing and Dead Persons

Article 32
General principle

In the implementation of this Section, the activities of the High Contracting Parties, of the Parties to the conflict and of the international humanitarian organizations mentioned in the Conventions and in this Protocol shall be prompted mainly by the right of families to know the fate of their relatives.

Article 33
Missing persons

1 As soon as circumstances permit, and at the latest from the end of active hostilities, each Party to the conflict shall search for the persons who have been reported missing by an adverse Party. Such adverse Party shall transmit all relevant information concerning such persons in order to facilitate such searches.

2 In order to facilitate the gathering of information pursuant to the preceding paragraph, each Party to the conflict shall, with respect to persons who would not receive more favourable consideration under the Conventions and this Protocol:

(a) record the information specified in Article 138 of the Fourth Convention in respect of such persons who have been detained, imprisoned or otherwise held in captivity for more than two weeks as a result of hostilities or occupation, or who have died during any period of detention;

(b) to the fullest extent possible, facilitate and, if need be, carry out the search for and the recording of information concerning such persons if they have died in other circumstances as a result of hostilities or occupation.

3 Information concerning persons reported missing pursuant to paragraph 1 and requests for such information shall be transmitted either directly or through the Protecting Power or the Central Tracing Agency of the International Committee of the Red Cross or national Red Cross (Red Crescent, Red Lion and Sun) Societies. Where the information is not transmitted through the International Committee of the Red Cross and its Central Tracing Agency, each Party to the conflict shall ensure that such information is also supplied to the Central Tracing Agency.

4 The Parties to the conflict shall endeavour to agree on arrangements for teams to search for, identify and recover the dead from battlefield areas, including arrangements, if appropriate, for such teams to be accompanied by personnel of the adverse Party while carrying out these missions in areas controlled by the adverse Party. Personnel of such teams shall be respected and protected while exclusively carrying out these duties.

Article 34
Remains of deceased

1 The remains of persons who have died for reasons related to occupation or in detention resulting from occupation or hostilities and those or persons not nationals of the country in which they have died as a result of hostilities shall be respected, and the gravesites of all such persons shall be respected, maintained and marked as provided for in Article 130 of the Fourth Convention, where their remains or gravesites would not receive more favourable consideration under the Conventions and this Protocol.

2 As soon as circumstances and the relations between the adverse Parties permit, the High Contracting Parties in whose territories graves and, as the case may be, other

locations of the remains of persons who have died as a result of hostilities or during occupation or in detention are situated, shall conclude agreements in order:

(a) to facilitate access to the gravesites by relatives of the deceased and by representatives of official graves registration services and to regulate the practical arrangements for such access;

(b) to protect and maintain such gravesites permanently;

(c) to facilitate the return of the remains of the deceased and of personal effects to the home country upon its request or, unless that country objects, upon the request of the next of kin.

3 In the absence of the agreements provided for in paragraph 2 (b) or (c) and if the home country or such deceased is not willing to arrange at its expense for the maintenance of such gravesites, the High Contracting Party in whose territory the gravesites are situated may offer to facilitate the return of the remains of the deceased to the home country. Where such an offer has not been accepted the High Contracting Party may, after the expiry of five years from the date of the offer and upon due notice to the home country, adopt the arrangements laid down in its own laws relating to cemeteries and graves.

4 A High Contracting Party in whose territory the grave sites referred to in this Article are situated shall be permitted to exhume the remains only:

(a) in accordance with paragraphs 2 (c) and 3, or

(b) where exhumation is a matter or overriding public necessity, including cases of medical and investigative necessity, in which case the High Contracting Party shall at all times respect the remains, and shall give notice to the home country or its intention to exhume the remains together with details of the intended place of reinterment.

PART III
METHODS AND MEANS OF WARFARE COMBATANT AND PRISONERS-OF-WAR

Section I
Methods and Means of Warfare

Article 35
Basic rules

1 In any armed conflict, the right of the Parties to the conflict to choose methods or means of warfare is not unlimited.

2 It is prohibited to employ weapons, projectiles and material and methods of warfare of a nature to cause superfluous injury or unnecessary suffering.

3 It is prohibited to employ methods or means of warfare which are intended, or may be expected, to cause widespread, long-term and severe damage to the natural environment.

Article 36
New weapons

In the study, development, acquisition or adoption of a new weapon, means or method of warfare, a High Contracting Party is under an obligation to determine whether its employment would, in some or all circumstances, be prohibited by this Protocol or by any other rule of international law applicable to the High Contracting Party.

Article 37
Prohibition of Perfidy

1 It is prohibited to kill, injure or capture an adversary by resort to perfidy. Acts inviting the confidence of an adversary to lead him to believe that he is entitled to, or is obliged to accord, protection under the rules of international law applicable in armed conflict, with intent to betray that confidence, shall constitute perfidy. The following acts are examples of perfidy:

(a) the feigning of an intent to negotiate under a flag of truce or of a surrender;
(b) the feigning of an incapacitation by wounds or sickness;
(c) the feigning of civilian, non-combatant status; and
(d) the feigning of protected status by the use of signs, emblems or uniforms of the United Nations or of neutral or other States not Parties to the conflict.

2 Ruses of war are not prohibited. Such ruses are acts which are intended to mislead an adversary or to induce him to act recklessly but which infringe no rule of international law applicable in armed conflict and which are not perfidious because they do not invite the confidence of an adversary with respect to protection under that law. The following are examples of such ruses: the use of camouflage, decoys, mock operations and misinformation.

Article 38
Recognized emblems

1 It is prohibited to make improper use of the distinctive emblem of the red cross, red crescent or red lion and sun or of other emblems, signs or signals provided for by the Conventions or by this Protocol. It is also prohibited to misuse deliberately in an armed conflict other internationally recognized protective emblems, signs or signals, including the flag of truce, and the protective emblem of cultural property.

2 It is prohibited to make use of the distinctive emblem of the United Nations, except as authorized by that Organization.

Article 39
Emblems of nationality

1 It is prohibited to make use in an armed conflict of the flags or military emblems, insignia or uniforms of neutral or other States not Parties to the conflict.

2 It is prohibited to make use of the flags or military emblems, insignia or uniforms of adverse Parties while engaging in attacks or in order to shield, favour, protect or impede military operations.

3 Nothing in this Article or in Article 37, paragraph 1 (d), shall affect the existing generally recognized rules of international law applicable to espionage or to the use of flags in the conduct of armed conflict at sea.

Article 40
Quarter

It is prohibited to order that there shall be no survivors, to threaten an adversary therewith or to conduct hostilities on this basis.

Article 41
Safeguard of an enemy hors de combat

1 A person who is recognized or who, in the circumstances, should be recognized to be hors de combat shall not be made the object of attack.

2 A person is hors de combat if:

(a)   he is in the power of an adverse Party;

(b)   he clearly expresses an intention to surrender; or

(c)   he has been rendered unconscious or is otherwise incapacitated by wounds or sickness, and therefore s incapable of defending himself;

provided that in any of these cases he abstains from any hostile act and does not attempt to escape.

3 When persons entitled to protection as prisoners of war have fallen into the power of an adverse Party under unusual conditions of combat which prevent their evacuation as provided for in Part III, Section I, of the Third Convention, they shall be released and all feasible precautions shall be taken to ensure their safety.

Article 42
Occupants of aircraft

1 No person parachuting from an aircraft in distress shall be made the object of attack during his descent.

2 Upon reaching the ground in territory controlled by an adverse Party, a person who has parachuted from an aircraft in distress shall be given an opportunity to surrender before being made the object of attack, unless it is apparent that he is engaging in a hostile act.

3 Airborne troops are not protected by this Article.

Section II
Combatants and Prisoners of War

Article 43
Armed forces

1 The armed forces of a Party to a conflict consist of all organized armed forces, groups and units which are under a command responsible to that Party for the conduct of its subordinates, even if that Party is represented by a government or an authority not recognized by an adverse Party. Such armed forces shall be subject to an internal disciplinary system which, inter alia, shall enforce compliance with the rules of international law applicable in armed conflict.

2 Members of the armed forces of a Party to a conflict (other than medical personnel and chaplains covered by Article 33 of the Third Convention) are combatants, that is to say, they have the right to participate directly in hostilities.

3 Whenever a Party to a conflict incorporates a paramilitary or armed law enforcement agency into its armed forces it shall so notify the other Parties to the conflict.

Article 44
Combatants and prisoners of war

1 Any combatant, as defined in Article 43, who falls into the power of an adverse Party shall be a prisoner of war.

2 While all combatants are obliged to comply with the rules of international law applicable in armed conflict, violations of these rules shall not deprive a combatant of his right to be a combatant or, if he falls into the power of an adverse Party, of his right to be a prisoner of war, except as provided in paragraphs 3 and 4.

3 In order to promote the protection of the civilian population from the effects of hostilities, combatants are obliged to distinguish themselves from the civilian population while they are engaged in an attack or in a military operation preparatory to an attack. Recognizing, however, that there are situations in armed conflicts where, owing to the nature of the hostilities an armed combatant cannot so distinguish himself, he shall retain his status as a combatant, provided that, in such situations, he carries his arms openly:

(a) during each military engagement, and

(b) during such time as he is visible to the adversary while he is engaged in a military deployment preceding the launching of an attack in which he is to participate.

Acts which comply with the requirements of this paragraph shall not be considered as perfidious within the meaning of Article 37, paragraph 1 (c).

4 A combatant who falls into the power of an adverse Party while failing to meet the requirements set forth in the second sentence of paragraph 3 shall forfeit his right to be a prisoner of war, but he shall, nevertheless, be given protections equivalent in all respects to those accorded to prisoners of war by the Third Convention and by this Protocol. This protection includes protections equivalent to those accorded to prisoners of war by the Third Convention in the case where such a person is tried and punished for any offences he has committed.

5 Any combatant who falls into the power of an adverse Party while not engaged in an attack or in a military operation preparatory to an attack shall not forfeit his rights to be a combatant and a prisoner of war by virtue of his prior activities.

6 This Article is without prejudice to the right of any person to be a prisoner of war pursuant to Article 4 of the Third Convention.

7 This Article is not intended to change the generally accepted practice of States with respect to the wearing of the uniform by combatants assigned to the regular, uniformed armed units of a Party to the conflict.

8 In addition to the categories of persons mentioned in Article 13 of the First and Second Conventions, all members of the armed forces of a Party to the conflict, as defined in Article 43 of this Protocol, shall be entitled to protection under those Conventions if they are wounded or sick or, in the case of the Second Convention, shipwrecked at sea or in other waters.

Article 45
Protection of persons who have taken part in hostilities

1 A person who takes part in hostilities and falls into the power of an adverse Party shall be presumed to be a prisoner of war, and therefore shall be protected by the Third Convention, if he claims the status of prisoner of war, or if he appears to be entitled to such status, or if the Party on which he depends claims such status on his behalf by notification to the detaining Power or to the Protecting Power. Should any doubt arise as to whether any such person is entitled to the status of prisoner of war, he shall continue to have such status and, therefore, to be protected by the Third Convention and this Protocol until such time as his status has been determined by a competent tribunal.

2 If a person who has fallen into the power of an adverse Party is not held as a prisoner of war and is to be tried by that Party for an offence arising out of the hostilities, he shall have the right to assert his entitlement to prisoner-of-war status before a judicial tribunal and to have that question adjudicated. Whenever possible under the applicable

procedure, this adjudication shall occur before the trial for the offence. The representatives of the Protecting Power shall be entitled to attend the proceedings in which that question is adjudicated, unless, exceptionally, the proceedings are held in camera in the interest of State security. In such a case the detaining Power shall advise the Protecting Power accordingly.

3 Any person who has taken part in hostilities, who is not entitled to prisoner-of-war status and who does not benefit from more favourable treatment in accordance with the Fourth Convention shall have the right at all times to the protection of Article 75 of this Protocol. In occupied territory, any such person, unless he is held as a spy, shall also be entitled, notwithstanding Article 5 of the Fourth Convention, to his rights of communication under that Convention.

Article 46
Spies

1 Notwithstanding any other provision of the Conventions or of this Protocol, any member of the armed forces of a Party to the conflict who falls into the power of an adverse Party while engaging in espionage shall not have the right to the status of prisoner of war and may be treated as a spy.

2 A member of the armed forces of a Party to the conflict who, on behalf of that Party and in territory controlled by an adverse Party, gathers or attempts to gather information shall not be considered as engaging in espionage if, while so acting, he is in the uniform of his armed forces.

3 A member of the armed forces of a Party to the conflict who is a resident of territory occupied by an adverse Party and who, on behalf of the Party on which he depends, gathers or attempts to gather information of military value within that territory shall not be considered as engaging in espionage unless he does so through an act of false pretences or deliberately in a clandestine manner. Moreover, such a resident shall not lose his right to the status of prisoner of war and may not be treated as a spy unless he is captured while engaging in espionage.

4 A member of the armed forces of a Party to the conflict who is not a resident of territory occupied by an adverse Party and who has engaged in espionage in that territory shall not lose his right to the status of prisoner of war and may not be treated as a spy unless he is captured before he has rejoined the armed forces to which he belongs.

Article 47
Mercenaries

1 A mercenary shall not have the right to be a combatant or a prisoner of war.

2 A mercenary is any person who:

    (a)   is specially recruited locally or abroad in order to fight in an armed conflict;

    (b)   does, in fact, take a direct part in the hostilities;

    (c)   is motivated to take part in the hostilities essentially by the desire for private gain and, in fact, is promised, by or on behalf of a Party to the conflict, material compensation substantially in excess of that promised or paid to combatants of similar ranks and functions in the armed forces of that Party;

    (d)   is neither a national of a Party to the conflict nor a resident of territory controlled by a Party to the conflict;

    (e)   is not a member of the armed forces of a Party to the conflict; and

(f)   has not been sent by a State which is not a Party to the conflict on official duty as a member of its armed forces.

PART IV
CIVILIAN POPULATION

Section I
General Protection Against Effects of Hostilities

Chapter I
Basic rule and field of application

Article 48
Basic rule

In order to ensure respect for and protection of the civilian population and civilian objects, the Parties to the conflict shall at all times distinguish between the civilian population and combatants and between civilian objects and military objectives and accordingly shall direct their operations only against military objectives.

Article 49
Definition of attacks and scope of application

1 "Attacks" means acts of violence against the adversary, whether in offence or in defence.

2 The provisions of this Protocol with respect to attacks apply to all attacks in whatever territory conducted, including the national territory belonging to a Party to the conflict but under the control of an adverse Party.

3 The provisions of this section apply to any land, air or sea warfare which may affect the civilian population, individual civilians or civilian objects on land. They further apply to all attacks from the sea or from the air against objectives on land but do not otherwise affect the rules of international law applicable in armed conflict at sea or in the air.

4 The provisions of this section are additional to the rules concerning humanitarian protection contained in the Fourth Convention, particularly in Part II thereof, and in other international agreements binding upon the High Contracting Parties, as well as to other rules of international law relating to the protection of civilians and civilian objects on land, at sea or in the air against the effects of hostilities.

Chapter II
Civilians and civilian population

Article 50
Definition of civilians and civilian population

1 A civilian is any person who does not belong to one of the categories of persons referred to in Article 4 (A) (1), (2), (3) and (6) of the Third Convention and in Article 43 of this Protocol. In case of doubt whether a person is a civilian, that person shall be considered to be a civilian.

2 The civilian population comprises all persons who are civilians.

3 The presence within the civilian population of individuals who do not come within the definition of civilians does not deprive the population of its civilian character.

Article 51
Protection of the civilian population

1 The civilian population and individual civilians shall enjoy general protection against dangers arising from military operations. To give effect to this protection, the following rules, which are additional to other applicable rules of international law, shall be observed in all circumstances.

2 The civilian population as such, as well as individual civilians, shall not be the object of attack. Acts or threats of violence the primary purpose of which is to spread terror among the civilian population are prohibited.

3 Civilians shall enjoy the protection afforded by this section, unless and for such time as they take a direct part in hostilities.

4 Indiscriminate attacks are prohibited. Indiscriminate attacks are:

(a) those which are not directed at a specific military objective;
(b) those which employ a method or means of combat which cannot be directed at a specific military objective; or
(c) those which employ a method or means of combat the effects of which cannot be limited as required by this Protocol;

and consequently, in each such case, are of a nature to strike military objectives and civilians or civilian objects without distinction.

5 Among others, the following types of attacks are to be considered as indiscriminate:

(a) an attack by bombardment by any methods or means which treats as a single military objective a number of clearly separated and distinct military objectives located in a city, town, village or other area containing a similar concentration of civilians or civilian objects;

and

(b) an attack which may be expected to cause incidental loss of civilian life, injury to civilians, damage to civilian objects, or a combination thereof, which would be excessive in relation to the concrete and direct military advantage anticipated.

6 Attacks against the civilian population or civilians by way of reprisals are prohibited.

7 The presence or movements of the civilian population or individual civilians shall not be used to render certain points or areas immune from military operations, in particular in attempts to shield military objectives from attacks or to shield, favour or impede military operations. The Parties to the conflict shall not direct the movement of the civilian population or individual civilians in order to attempt to shield military objectives from attacks or to shield military operations.

8 Any violation of these prohibitions shall not release the Parties to the conflict from their legal obligations with respect to the civilian population and civilians, including the obligation to take the precautionary measures provided for in Article 57.

Chapter III
Civilian objects

Article 52
General Protection of civilian objects

1 Civilian objects shall not be the object of attack or of reprisals. Civilian objects are all objects which are not military objectives as defined in paragraph 2.

2 Attacks shall be limited strictly to military objectives. In so far as objects are concerned, military objectives are limited to those objects which by their nature, location, purpose or use make an effective contribution to military action and whose total or partial destruction, capture or neutralization, in the circumstances ruling at the time, offers a definite military advantage.

3 In case of doubt whether an object which is normally dedicated to civilian purposes, such as a place of worship, a house or other dwelling or a school, is being used to make an effective contribution to military action, it shall be presumed not to be so used.

Article 53
Protection of cultural objects and of places of worship

Without prejudice to the provisions of the Hague Convention for the Protection of Cultural Property in the Event of Armed Conflict of 14 May 1954, and of other relevant international instruments, it is prohibited:

(a) to commit any acts of hostility directed against the historic monuments, works of art or places of worship which constitute the cultural or spiritual heritage of peoples;
(b) to use such objects in support of the military effort;
(c) to make such objects the object of reprisals.

Article 54
Protection of objects indispensable to the survival of the civilian population

1 Starvation of civilians as a method of warfare is prohibited.

2 It is prohibited to attack, destroy, remove or render useless objects indispensable to the survival of the civilian population, such as food-stuffs, agricultural areas for the production of food-stuffs, crops, livestock, drinking water installations and supplies and irrigation works, for the specific purpose of denying them for their sustenance value to the civilian population or to the adverse Party, whatever the motive, whether in order to starve out civilians, to cause them to move away, or for any other motive.

3 The prohibitions in paragraph 2 shall not apply to such of the objects covered by it as are used by an adverse Party:

(a) as sustenance solely for the members of its armed forces; or
(b) if not as sustenance, then in direct support of military action, provided, however, that in no event shall actions against these objects be taken which may be expected to leave the civilian population with such inadequate food or water as to cause its starvation or force its movement.

4 These objects shall not be made the object of reprisals.

5 In recognition of the vital requirements of any Party to the conflict in the defence of its national territory against invasion, derogation from the prohibitions contained in paragraph 2 may be made by a Party to the conflict within such territory under its own control where required by imperative military necessity.

Article 55
Protection of the natural environment

1 Care shall be taken in warfare to protect the natural environment against widespread, long-term and severe damage. This protection includes a prohibition of the use of methods or means of warfare which are intended or may be expected to cause such damage to the natural environment and thereby to prejudice the health or survival of the population.

2 Attacks against the natural environment by way of reprisals are prohibited.

Article 56
Protection of works and installations containing dangerous forces

1 Works or installations containing dangerous forces, namely dams, dykes and nuclear electrical generating stations, shall not be made the object of attack, even where these objects are military objectives, if such attack may cause the release of dangerous forces and consequent severe losses among the civilian population. Other military objectives located at or in the vicinity of these works or installations shall not be made the object of attack if such attack may cause the release of dangerous forces from the works or installations and consequent severe losses among the civilian population.

2 The special protection against attack provided by paragraph 1 shall cease:

(a)   for a dam or a dyke only if it is used for other than its normal function and in regular, significant and direct support of military operations and if such attack is the only feasible way to terminate such support;

(b)   for a nuclear electrical generating station only if it provides electric power in regular, significant and direct support of military operations and if such attack is the only feasible way to terminate such support;

(c)   for other military objectives located at or in the vicinity of these works or installations only if they are used in regular, significant and direct support of military operations and if such attack is the only feasible way to terminate such support.

3 In all cases, the civilian population and individual civilians shall remain entitled to all the protection accorded them by international law, including the protection of the precautionary measures provided for in Article 57. If the protection Ceases and any of the works, installations or military objectives mentioned in paragraph 1 is attacked, all practical precautions shall be taken to avoid the release of the dangerous forces.

4 It is prohibited to make any of the works, installations or military objectives mentioned in paragraph 1 the object of reprisals.

5 The Parties to the conflict shall endeavour to avoid locating any military objectives in the vicinity of the works or installations mentioned in paragraph 1. Nevertheless, installations erected for the sole purpose of defending the protected works or installations from attack are permissible and shall not themselves be made the object of attack, provided that they are not used in hostilities except for defensive actions necessary to respond to attacks against the protected works or installations and that their armament is limited to weapons capable only of repelling hostile action against the protected works or installations.

6 The High Contracting Parties and the Parties to the conflict are urged to conclude further agreements among themselves to provide additional protection for objects containing dangerous forces.

7 In order to facilitate the identification of the objects protected by this article, the Parties to the conflict may mark them with a special sign consisting of a group of three bright orange circles placed on the same axis, as specified in Article 16 of Annex I to this Protocol [Article 17 of Amended Annex]. The absence of such marking in no way relieves any Party to the conflict of its obligations under this Article.

Chapter IV
Precautionary measures

Article 57
Precautions in attack

1 In the conduct of military operations, constant care shall be taken to spare the civilian population, civilians and civilian objects.

2 With respect to attacks, the following precautions shall be taken:

(a) those who plan or decide upon an attack shall:

(i) do everything feasible to verify that the objectives to be attacked are neither civilians nor civilian objects and are not subject to special protection but are military objectives within the meaning of paragraph 2 of Article 52 and that it is not prohibited by the provisions of this Protocol to attack them;

(ii) take all feasible precautions in the choice of means and methods of attack with a view to avoiding, and in any event to minimizing, incidental loss or civilian life, injury to civilians and damage to civilian objects;

(iii) refrain from deciding to launch any attack which may be expected to cause incidental loss of civilian life, injury to civilians, damage to civilian objects, or a combination thereof, which would be excessive in relation to the concrete and direct military advantage anticipated;

(b) an attack shall be cancelled or suspended if it becomes apparent that the objective is not a military one or is subject to special protection or that the attack may be expected to cause incidental loss of civilian life, injury to civilians, damage to civilian objects, or a combination thereof, which would be excessive in relation to the concrete and direct military advantage anticipated;

(c) effective advance warning shall be given of attacks which may affect the civilian population, unless circumstances do not permit.

3 When a choice is possible between several military objectives for obtaining a similar military advantage, the objective to be selected shall be that the attack on which may be expected to cause the least danger to civilian lives and to civilian objects.

4 In the conduct of military operations at sea or in the air, each Party to the conflict shall, in conformity with its rights and duties under the rules of international law applicable in armed conflict, take all reasonable precautions to avoid losses of civilian lives and damage to civilian objects.

5 No provision of this article may be construed as authorizing any attacks against the civilian population, civilians or civilian objects.

Article 58
Precautions against the effects of attacks

The Parties to the conflict shall, to the maximum extent feasible:

(a)   without prejudice to Article 49 of the Fourth Convention, endeavour to remove the civilian population, individual civilians and civilian objects under their control from the vicinity of military objectives;

(b)   avoid locating military objectives within or near densely populated areas;

(c)   take the other necessary precautions to protect the civilian population, individual civilians and civilian objects under their control against the dangers resulting from military operations.

Chapter V
Localities and zones under special protection

Article 59
Non-defended localities

1 It is prohibited for the Parties to the conflict to attack, by any means whatsoever, non-defended localities.

2 The appropriate authorities of a Party to the conflict may declare as a non-defended locality any inhabited place near or in a zone where armed forces are in contact which is open for occupation by an adverse Party.

Such a locality shall fulfil the following conditions:

(a)   all combatants, as well as mobile weapons and mobile military equipment must have been evacuated;

(b)   no hostile use shall be made of fixed military installations or establishments;

(c)   no acts of hostility shall be committed by the authorities or by the population; and

(d)   no activities in support of military operations shall be undertaken.

3 The presence, in this locality, of persons specially protected under the Conventions and this Protocol, and of police forces retained for the sole purpose of maintaining law and order, is not contrary to the conditions laid down in paragraph 2.

4 The declaration made under paragraph 2 shall be addressed to the adverse Party and shall define and describe, as precisely as possible, the limits of the non-defended locality. The Party to the conflict to which the declaration is addressed shall acknowledge its receipt and shall treat the locality as a non-defended locality unless the conditions laid down in paragraph 2 are not in fact fulfilled, in which event it shall immediately so inform the Party making the declaration. Even if the conditions laid down in paragraph 2 are not fulfilled, the locality shall continue to enjoy the protection provided by the other provisions of this Protocol and the other rules of international law applicable in armed conflict.

5 The Parties to the conflict may agree on the establishment of non-defended localities even if such localities do not fulfil the conditions laid down in paragraph 2. The agreement should define and describe, as precisely as possible, the limits of the non-defended locality; if necessary, it may lay down the methods of supervision.

6 The Party which is in control of a locality governed by such an agreement shall mark it, so far as possible, by such signs as may be agreed upon with the other Party, which shall be displayed where they are clearly visible, especially on its perimeter and limits and on highways.

7 A locality loses its status as a non-defended locality when its ceases to fulfil the conditions laid down in paragraph 2 or in the agreement referred to in paragraph 5. In

such an eventuality, the locality shall continue to enjoy the protection provided by the other provisions of this Protocol and the other rules of international law applicable in armed conflict.

Article 60
Demilitarized zones

1 It is prohibited for the Parties to the conflict to extend their military operations to zones on which they have conferred by agreement the status of demilitarized zone, if such extension is contrary to the terms of this agreement.

2 The agreement shall be an express agreement, may be concluded verbally or in writing, either directly or through a Protecting Power or any impartial humanitarian organization, and may consist of reciprocal and concordant declarations. The agreement may be concluded in peacetime, as well as after the outbreak of hostilities, and should define and describe, as precisely as possible, the limits of the demilitarized zone and, if necessary, lay down the methods of supervision.

3 The subject of such an agreement shall normally be any zone which fulfils the following conditions:

(a) all combatants, as well as mobile weapons and mobile military equipment, must have been evacuated;
(b) no hostile use shall be made of fixed military installations or establishments;
(c) no acts of hostility shall be committed by the authorities or by the population; and
(d) any activity linked to the military effort must have ceased.

The Parties to the conflict shall agree upon the interpretation to be given to the condition laid down in subparagraph (d) and upon persons to be admitted to the demilitarized zone other than those mentioned in paragraph 4.

4 The presence, in this zone, of persons specially protected under the Conventions and this Protocol, and of police forces retained for the sole purpose of maintaining law and order, is not contrary to the conditions laid down in paragraph 3.

5 The Party which is in control of such a zone shall mark it, so far as possible, by such signs as may be agreed upon with the other Party, which shall be displayed where they are clearly visible, especially on its perimeter and limits and on highways.

6 If the fighting draws near to a demilitarized zone, and if the Parties to the conflict have so agreed, none of them may use the zone for purposes related to the conduct of military operations or unilaterally revoke its status.

7 If one of the Parties to the conflict commits a material breach of the provisions of paragraphs 3 or 6, the other Party shall be released from its obligations under the agreement conferring upon the zone the status of demilitarized zone. In such an eventuality, the zone loses its status but shall continue to enjoy the protection provided by the other provisions of this Protocol and the other rules of international law applicable in armed conflict.

Chapter VI
Civil defence

Article 61
Definitions and scope

For the purpose of this Protocol:

(a)   'civil defence' means the performance of some or all of the undermentioned humanitarian tasks intended to protect the civilian population against the dangers, and to help it to recover from the immediate effects, of hostilities or disasters and also to provide the conditions necessary for its survival. These tasks are:

(i)   warning;

(ii)   evacuation;

(iii)   management of shelters;

(iv)   management of blackout measures;

(v)   rescue;

(vi)   medical services, including first aid, and religious assistance;

(vii) fire-fighting;

(viii) detection and marking of danger areas;

(ix)   decontamination and similar protective measures;

(x)   provision of emergency accommodation and supplies;

(xi)   emergency assistance in the restoration and maintenance of order in distressed areas;

(xii) emergency repair of indispensable public utilities;

(xiii) emergency disposal of the dead;

(xiv) assistance in the preservation of objects essential for survival;

(xv)   complementary activities necessary to carry out any of the tasks mentioned above, including, but not limited to, planning and organization;

(b)   'civil defence organizations' means those establishments and other units which are organized or authorized by the competent authorities of a Party to the conflict to perform any of the tasks mentioned under sub-paragraph (a), and which are assigned and devoted exclusively to such tasks;

(c)   'personnel' of civil defence organizations means those persons assigned by a Party to the conflict exclusively to the performance of the tasks mentioned under sub-paragraph (a), including personnel assigned by the competent authority of that Party exclusively to the administration of these organizations;

(d)   'matériel' of civil defence organizations means equipment, supplies and transports used by these organizations for the performance of the tasks mentioned under sub-paragraph (a).

Article 62
General protection

1 Civilian civil defence organizations and their personnel shall be respected and protected, subject to the provisions of this Protocol, particularly the provisions of this section. They shall be entitled to perform their civil defence tasks except in case of imperative military necessity.

2 The provisions of paragraph 1 shall also apply to civilians who, although not members of civilian civil defence organizations, respond to an appeal from the competent authorities and perform civil defence tasks under their control.

3 Buildings and matériel used for civil defence purposes and shelters provided for the civilian population are covered by Article 52. Objects used for civil defence purposes may not be destroyed or diverted from their proper use except by the Party to which they belong.

Article 63
Civil defence in occupied territories

1 In occupied territories, civilian civil defence organizations shall receive from the authorities the facilities necessary for the performance of their tasks. In no Circumstances shall their personnel be compelled to perform activities which would interfere with the proper performance of these tasks. The Occupying Power shall not change the structure or personnel of such organizations in any way which might jeopardize the efficient performance of their mission. These organizations shall not be required to give priority to the nationals or interests of that Power.

2 The Occupying Power shall not compel, coerce or induce civilian civil defence organizations to perform their tasks in any manner prejudicial to the interests of the civilian population.

3 The Occupying Power may disarm civil defence personnel for reasons of security.

4 The Occupying Power shall neither divert from their proper use nor requisition buildings or matériel belonging to or used by civil defence organizations if such diversion or requisition would be harmful to the civilian population.

5 Provided that the general rule in paragraph 4 continues to be observed, the Occupying Power may requisition or divert these resources, subject to the following particular conditions:

    (a)   that the buildings or matériel are necessary for other needs of the civilian population; and
    (b)   that the requisition or diversion continues only while such necessity exists.

6 The Occupying Power shall neither divert nor requisition shelters provided for the use of the civilian population or needed by such population.

Article 64
Civilian civil defence organizations of neutral or other States not Parties to the conflict and international co-ordinating organizations

1 Articles 62, 63, 65 and 66 shall also apply to the personnel and matériel of civilian civil defence organizations of neutral or other States not Parties to the conflict which perform civil defence tasks mentioned in Article 61 in the territory of a Party to the conflict, with the consent and under the control of that Party. Notification of such assistance shall be given as soon as possible to any adverse Party concerned. In no circumstances shall this activity be deemed to be an interference in the conflict. This activity should, however, be performed with due regard to the security interests of the Parties to the conflict concerned.

2 The Parties to the conflict receiving the assistance referred to in paragraph 1 and the High Contracting Parties granting it should facilitate international co-ordination of such civil defence actions when appropriate. In such cases the relevant international organizations are covered by the provisions of this Chapter.

3 In occupied territories, the Occupying Power may only exclude or restrict the activities of civilian civil defence organizations of neutral or other States not Parties to the conflict and of international co-ordinating organizations if it can ensure the adequate performance of civil defence tasks from its own resources or those of the occupied territory.

Article 65
Cessation of protection

1 The protection to which civilian civil defence organizations, their personnel, buildings, shelters and matériel are entitled shall not cease unless they commit or are used to commit, outside their proper tasks, acts harmful to the enemy. Protection may, however, cease only after a warning has been given setting, whenever appropriate, a reasonable time-limit, and after such warning has remained unheeded.

2 The following shall not be considered as acts harmful to the enemy:

    (a)   that civil defence tasks are carried out under the direction or control of military authorities;

    (b)   that civilian civil defence personnel co-operate with military personnel in the performance of civil defence tasks, or that some military personnel are attached to civilian civil defence organizations;

    (c)   that the performance of civil defence tasks may incidentally benefit military victims, particularly those who are hors de combat.

3 It shall also not be considered as an act harmful to the enemy that civilian civil defence personnel bear light individual weapons for the purpose of maintaining order or for self-defence. However, in areas where land fighting is taking place or is likely to take place, the Parties to the conflict shall undertake the appropriate measures to limit these weapons to handguns, such as pistols or revolvers, in order to assist in distinguishing between civil defence personnel and combatants. Although civil defence personnel bear other light individual weapons in such areas, they shall nevertheless be respected and protected as soon as they have been recognized as such.

4 The formation of civilian civil defence organizations along military lines, and compulsory service in them, shall also not deprive them of the protection conferred by this Chapter.

Article 66
Identification

1 Each Party to the conflict shall endeavour to ensure that its civil defence organizations, their personnel, buildings and matériel are identifiable while they are exclusively devoted to the performance of civil defence tasks. Shelters provided for the civilian population should be similarly identifiable.

2 Each Party to the conflict shall also endeavour to adopt and implement methods and procedures which will make it possible to recognize civilian shelters as well as civil defence personnel, buildings and matériel on which the international distinctive sign of civil defence is displayed.

3 In occupied territories and in areas where fighting is taking place or is likely to take place, civilian civil defence personnel should be recognizable by the international distinctive sign of civil defence and by an identity card certifying their status.

4 The international distinctive sign of civil defence is an equilateral blue triangle on an orange ground when used for the protection of civil defence organizations, their personnel, buildings and matériel and for civilian shelters.

5 In addition to the distinctive sign, Parties to the conflict may agree upon the use of distinctive signals for civil defence identification purposes.

6 The application of the provisions of paragraphs 1 to 4 is governed by Chapter V of Annex I to this Protocol.

7 In time of peace, the sign described in paragraph 4 may, with the consent of the competent national authorities, be used for civil defence identification purposes.

8 The High Contracting Parties and the Parties to the conflict shall take the measures necessary to supervise the display of the international distinctive sign of civil defence and to prevent and repress any misuse thereof.

9 The identification of civil defence medical and religious personnel, medical units and medical transports is also governed by Article 18.

Article 67
Members of the armed forces and military units assigned to civil defence organizations

1 Members of the armed forces and military units assigned to civil defence organizations shall be respected and protected, provided that:

(a) such personnel and such units are permanently assigned and exclusively devoted to the performance of any of the tasks mentioned in Article 61;

(b) if so assigned, such personnel do not perform any other military duties during the conflict;

(c) such personnel are clearly distinguishable from the other members of the armed forces by prominently displaying the international distinctive sign of civil defence, which shall be as large as appropriate, and such personnel are provided with the identity card referred to in Chapter V of Annex I to this Protocol certifying their status;

(d) such personnel and such units are equipped only with light individual weapons for the purpose of maintaining order or for self-defence. The provisions of Article 65, paragraph 3 shall also apply in this case;

(e) such personnel do not participate directly in hostilities, and do not commit, or are not used to commit, outside their civil defence tasks, acts harmful to the adverse Party;

(f) such personnel and such units perform their civil defence tasks only within the national territory of their Party.

The non-observance of the conditions stated in (e) above by any member of the armed forces who is bound by the conditions prescribed in (a) and (b) above is prohibited.

2 Military personnel serving within civil defence organizations shall, if they fall into the power of an adverse Party, be prisoners of war. In occupied territory they may, but only in the interest of the civilian population of that territory, be employed on civil defence tasks in so far as the need arises, provided however that, if such work is dangerous, they volunteer for such tasks.

3 The buildings and major items of equipment and transports of military units assigned to civil defence organizations shall be clearly marked with the international distinctive sign of civil defence. This distinctive sign shall be as large as appropriate.

4 The matériel and buildings of military units permanently assigned to civil defence organizations and exclusively devoted to the performance of civil defence tasks shall, if they fall into the hands of an adverse Party, remain subject to the laws of war. They may not be diverted from their civil defence purpose so long as they are required for the performance of civil defence tasks, except in case of imperative military necessity, unless previous arrangements have been made for adequate provision for the needs of the civilian population.

Section II
Relief in Favour of the Civilian Population

Article 68
Field of application

The provisions of this Section apply to the civilian population as defined in this Protocol and are supplementary to Articles 23, 55, 59, 60, 61 and 62 and other relevant provisions of the Fourth Convention.

Article 69
Basic needs in occupied territories

1 In addition to the duties specified in Article 55 of the Fourth Convention concerning food and medical supplies, the Occupying Power shall, to the fullest extent of the means available to it and without any adverse distinction, also ensure the provision of clothing, bedding, means of shelter, other supplies essential to the survival of the civilian population of the occupied territory and objects necessary for religious worship.

2 Relief actions for the benefit of the civilian population of occupied territories are governed by Articles 59, 60, 61, 62, 108, 109, 110 and 111 of the Fourth Convention, and by Article 71 of this Protocol, and shall be implemented without delay.

Article 70
Relief actions

1 If the civilian population of any territory under the control of a Party to the conflict, other than occupied territory, is not adequately provided with the supplies mentioned in Article 69, relief actions which are humanitarian and impartial in character and conducted without any adverse distinction shall be undertaken, subject to the agreement of the Parties concerned in such relief actions. Offers of such relief shall not be regarded as interference in the armed conflict or as unfriendly acts. In the distribution of relief consignments, priority shall be given to those persons, such as children, expectant mothers, maternity cases and nursing mothers, who, under the Fourth Convention or under this Protocol, are to be accorded privileged treatment or special protection.

2 The Parties to the conflict and each High Contracting Party shall allow and facilitate rapid and unimpeded passage of all relief consignments, equipment and personnel provided in accordance with this Section, even if such assistance is destined for the civilian population of the adverse Party.

3 The Parties to the conflict and each High Contracting Party which allow the passage of relief consignments, equipment and personnel in accordance with paragraph 2:

   (a)   shall have the right to prescribe the technical arrangements, including search, under which such passage is permitted;
   (b)   may make such permission conditional on the distribution of this assistance being made under the local supervision of a Protecting Power;
   (c)   shall, in no way whatsoever, divert relief consignments from the purpose for which they are intended nor delay their forwarding, except in cases of urgent necessity in the interest of the civilian population concerned.

4 The Parties to the conflict shall protect relief consignments and facilitate their rapid distribution.

5 The Parties to the conflict and each High Contracting Party concerned shall encourage and facilitate effective international co-ordination of the relief actions referred to in paragraph 1.

Article 71
Personnel participating in relief actions

1 Where necessary, relief personnel may form part of the assistance provided in any relief action, in particular for the transportation and distribution of relief consignments; the participation of such personnel shall be subject to the approval of the Party in whose territory they will carry out their duties.

2 Such personnel shall be respected and protected.

3 Each Party in receipt of relief consignments shall, to the fullest extent practicable, assist the relief personnel referred to in paragraph 1 in carrying out their relief mission. Only in case of imperative military necessity may the activities of the relief personnel be limited or their movements temporarily restricted.

4 Under no circumstances may relief personnel exceed the terms of their mission under this Protocol. In particular they shall take account of the security requirements of the Party in whose territory they are carrying out their duties. The mission of any of the personnel who do not respect these conditions may be terminated.

Section III
Treatment of Persons in the Power of a Party to the Conflict

Chapter I
Field of application and protection of persons and objects

Article 72
Field of application

The provisions of this Section are additional to the rules concerning humanitarian protection of civilians and civilian objects in the power of a Party to the conflict contained in the Fourth Convention, particularly Parts I and III thereof, as well as to other applicable rules of international law relating to the protection of fundamental human rights during international armed conflict.

Article 73
Refugees and stateless persons

Persons who, before the beginning of hostilities, were considered as stateless persons or refugees under the relevant international instruments accepted by the Parties concerned or under the national legislation of the State of refuge or State of residence shall be protected persons within the meaning of Parts I and III of the Fourth Convention, in all circumstances and without any adverse distinction.

Article 74
Reunion of dispersed families

The High Contracting Parties and the Parties to the conflict shall facilitate in every possible way the reunion of families dispersed as a result of armed conflicts and shall encourage in particular the work of the humanitarian organizations engaged in this task in accordance with the provisions of the Conventions and of this Protocol and in conformity with their respective security regulations.

Article 75
Fundamental guarantees

1 In so far as they are affected by a situation referred to in Article 1 of this Protocol, persons who are in the power of a Party to the conflict and who do not benefit from more favourable treatment under the Conventions or under this Protocol shall be treated

humanely in all circumstances and shall enjoy, as a minimum, the protection provided by this Article without any adverse distinction based upon race, colour, sex, language, religion or belief, political or other opinion, national or social origin, wealth, birth or other status, or on any other similar criteria. Each Party shall respect the person, honour, convictions and religious practices of all such persons.

2 The following acts are and shall remain prohibited at any time and in any place whatsoever, whether committed by civilian or by military agents:

(a)   violence to the life, health, or physical or mental well-being of persons, in particular:
    (i)   murder;
    (ii)   torture of all kinds, whether physical or mental;
    (iii)   corporal punishment; and
    (iv)   mutilation;

(b)   outrages upon personal dignity, in particular humiliating and degrading treatment, enforced prostitution and any form of indecent assault;

(c)   the taking of hostages;

(d)   collective punishments; and

(e)   threats to commit any of the foregoing acts.

3 Any person arrested, detained or interned for actions related to the armed conflict shall be informed promptly, in a language he understands, of the reasons why these measures have been taken. Except in cases of arrest or detention for penal offences, such persons shall be released with the minimum delay possible and in any event as soon as the circumstances justifying the arrest, detention or internment have ceased to exist.

4 No sentence may be passed and no penalty may be executed on a person found guilty of a penal offence related to the armed conflict except pursuant to a conviction pronounced by an impartial and regularly constituted court respecting the generally recognized principles of regular judicial procedure, which include the following:

(a)   the procedure shall provide for an accused to be informed without delay of the particulars of the offence alleged against him and shall afford the accused before and during his trial all necessary rights and means of defence;

(b)   no one shall be convicted of an offence except on the basis of individual penal responsibility;

(c)   no one shall be accused or convicted of a criminal offence on account or any act or omission which did not constitute a criminal offence under the national or international law to which he was subject at the time when it was committed; nor shall a heavier penalty be imposed than that which was applicable at the time when the criminal offence was committed; if, after the commission of the offence, provision is made by law for the imposition of a lighter penalty, the offender shall benefit thereby;

(d)   anyone charged with an offence is presumed innocent until proved guilty according to law;

(e)   anyone charged with an offence shall have the right to be tried in his presence;

(f)   no one shall be compelled to testify against himself or to confess guilt;

(g)   anyone charged with an offence shall have the right to examine, or have examined, the witnesses against him and to obtain the attendance and examination of witnesses on his behalf under the same conditions as witnesses against him;

(h)   no one shall be prosecuted or punished by the same Party for an offence in respect of which a final judgement acquitting or convicting that person has been previously pronounced under the same law and judicial procedure;

(i)   anyone prosecuted for an offence shall have the right to have the judgement pronounced publicly; and

(j)   a convicted person shall be advised on conviction of his judicial and other remedies and of the time-limits within which they may be exercised.

5 Women whose liberty has been restricted for reasons related to the armed conflict shall be held in quarters separated from men's quarters. They shall be under the immediate supervision of women. Nevertheless, in cases where families are detained or interned, they shall, whenever possible, be held in the same place and accommodated as family units.

6 Persons who are arrested, detained or interned for reasons related to the armed conflict shall enjoy the protection provided by this Article until their final release, repatriation or re-establishment, even after the end of the armed conflict.

7 In order to avoid any doubt concerning the prosecution and trial of persons accused of war crimes or crimes against humanity, the following principles shall apply:

(a)   persons who are accused of such crimes should be submitted for the purpose of prosecution and trial in accordance with the applicable rules of international law; and

(b)   any such persons who do not benefit from more favourable treatment under the Conventions or this Protocol shall be accorded the treatment provided by this Article, whether or not the crimes of which they are accused constitute grave breaches of the Conventions or of this Protocol.

8 No provision of this Article may be construed as limiting or infringing any other more favourable provision granting greater protection, under any applicable rules of international law, to persons covered by paragraph 1

Chapter II
Measures in favour of women and children

Article 76
Protection of women

1 Women shall be the object of special respect and shall be protected in particular against rape, forced prostitution and any other form of indecent assault.

2 Pregnant women and mothers having dependent infants who are arrested, detained or interned for reasons related to the armed conflict, shall have their cases considered with the utmost priority.

3 To the maximum extent feasible, the Parties to the conflict shall endeavour to avoid the pronouncement of the death penalty on pregnant women or mothers having dependent infants, for an offence related to the armed conflict. The death penalty for such offences shall not be executed on such women.

Article 77
Protection of children

1 Children shall be the object of special respect and shall be protected against any form of indecent assault. The Parties to the conflict shall provide them with the care and aid they require, whether because of their age or for any other reason.

2 The Parties to the conflict shall take all feasible measures in order that children who have not attained the age of fifteen years do not take a direct part in hostilities and, in particular, they shall refrain from recruiting them into their armed forces. In recruiting

among those persons who have attained the age of fifteen years but who have not attained the age of eighteen years the Parties to the conflict shall endeavour to give priority to those who are oldest.

3 If, in exceptional cases, despite the provisions of paragraph 2, children who have not attained the age of fifteen years take a direct part in hostilities and fall into the power of an adverse Party, they shall continue to benefit from the special protection accorded by this Article, whether or not they are prisoners of war.

4 If arrested, detained or interned for reasons related to the armed conflict, children shall be held in quarters separate from the quarters of adults, except where families are accommodated as family units as provided in Article 75, paragraph 5.

5 The death penalty for an offence related to the armed conflict shall not be executed on persons who had not attained the age of eighteen years at the time the offence was committed.

Article 78
Evacuation of children

1 No Party to the conflict shall arrange for the evacuation of children, other than its own nationals, to a foreign country except for a temporary evacuation where compelling reasons of the health or medical treatment of the children or, except in occupied territory, their safety, so require. Where the parents or legal guardians can be found, their written consent to such evacuation is required. If these persons cannot be found, the written consent to such evacuation of the persons who by law or custom are primarily responsible for the care of the children is required. Any such evacuation shall be supervised by the Protecting Power in agreement with the Parties concerned, namely, the Party arranging for the evacuation, the Party receiving the children and any Parties whose nationals are being evacuated. In each case, all Parties to the conflict shall take all feasible precautions to avoid endangering the evacuation.

2 Whenever an evacuation occurs pursuant to paragraph 1, each child's education, including his religious and moral education as his parents desire, shall be provided while he is away with the greatest possible continuity.

3 With a view to facilitating the return to their families and country of children evacuated pursuant to this Article, the authorities of the Party arranging for the evacuation and, as appropriate, the authorities of the receiving country shall establish for each child a card with photographs, which they shall send to the Central Tracing Agency of the International Committee of the Red Cross. Each card shall bear, whenever possible, and whenever it involves no risk of harm to the child, the following information:

   (a)   surname(s) of the child;
   (b)   the child's first name(s);
   (c)   the child's sex;
   (d)   the place and date of birth (or, if that date is not known, the approximate age);
   (e)   the father's full name;
   (f)   the mother's full name and her maiden name;
   (g)   the child's next-of-kin;
   (h)   the child's nationality;
   (i)   the child's native language, and any other languages he speaks;
   (j)   the address of the child's family;
   (k)   any identification number for the child;
   (l)   the child's state of health;

(m)   the child's blood group;
(n)   any distinguishing features;
(o)   the date on which and the place where the child was found;
(p)   the date on which and the place from which the child left the country;
(q)   the child's religion, if any;
(r)   the child's present address in the receiving country;
(s)   should the child die before his return, the date, place and circumstances of death and place of interment.

Chapter III
Journalists

Article 79
Measures or protection for journalists

1 Journalists engaged in dangerous professional missions in areas of armed conflict shall be considered as civilians within the meaning of Article 50, paragraph 1.

2 They shall be protected as such under the Conventions and this Protocol, provided that they take no action adversely affecting their status as civilians, and without prejudice to the right of war correspondents accredited to the armed forces to the status provided for in Article 4 (A) (4) of the Third Convention.

3 They may obtain an identity card similar to the model in Annex II of this Protocol. This card, which shall be issued by the government of the State of which the Journalist is a national or in whose territory he resides or in which the news medium employing him is located, shall attest to his status as a journalist.

PART V
EXECUTION OF THE CONVENTIONS AND OF ITS PROTOCOLS

Section I
General Provisions

Article 80
Measures for execution

1 The High Contracting Parties and the Parties to the conflict shall without delay take all necessary measures for the execution of their obligations under the Conventions and this Protocol.

2 The High Contracting Parties and the Parties to the conflict shall give orders and instructions to ensure observance of the Conventions and this Protocol, and shall supervise their execution.

Article 81
Activities of the Red Cross and other humanitarian organizations

1 The Parties to the conflict shall grant to the International Committee of the Red Cross all facilities, within their power so as to enable it to carry out the humanitarian functions assigned to it by the Conventions and this Protocol in order to ensure protection and assistance to the victims of conflicts; the International Committee of the Red Cross may also carry out any other humanitarian activities in favour of these victims, subject to the consent of the Parties to the conflict concerned.

2 The Parties to the conflict shall grant to their respective Red Cross (Red Crescent, Red Lion and Sun) organizations the facilities necessary for carrying out their humanitarian activities in favour of the victims of the conflict, in accordance with the provisions of the

Conventions and this Protocol and the fundamental principles of the Red Cross as formulated by the International Conferences of the Red Cross.

3 The High Contracting Parties and the Parties to the conflict shall facilitate in every possible way the assistance which Red Cross (Red Crescent, Red Lion and Sun) organizations and the League of Red Cross Societies extend to the victims of conflicts in accordance with the provisions of the Conventions and this Protocol and with the fundamental principles of the red Cross as formulated by the International Conferences of the Red Cross.

4 The High Contracting Parties and the Parties to the conflict shall, as far as possible, make facilities similar to those mentioned in paragraphs 2 and 3 available to the other humanitarian organizations referred to in the Conventions and this Protocol which are duly authorized by the respective Parties to the conflict and which perform their humanitarian activities in accordance with the provisions of the Conventions and this Protocol.

Article 82
Legal advisers in armed forces

The High Contracting Parties at all times, and the Parties to the conflict in time of armed conflict, shall ensure that legal advisers are available, when necessary, to advise military commanders at the appropriate level on the application of the Conventions and this Protocol and on the appropriate instruction to be given to the armed forces on this subject.

Article 83
Dissemination

1 The High Contracting Parties undertake, in time of peace as in time of armed conflict, to disseminate the Conventions and this Protocol as widely as possible in their respective countries and, in particular, to include the study thereof in their programmes of military instruction and to encourage the study thereof by the civilian population, so that those instruments may become known to the armed forces and to the civilian population.

2 Any military or civilian authorities who, in time of armed conflict, assume responsibilities in respect of the application of the Conventions and this Protocol shall be fully acquainted with the text thereof.

Article 84
Rules of application

The High Contracting Parties shall communicate to one another, as soon as possible, through the depositary and, as appropriate, through the Protecting Powers, their official translations of this Protocol, as well as the laws and regulations which they may adopt to ensure its application.

Section II
Repression of Breaches of the Conventions and of this Protocol

Article 85
Repression of breaches of this Protocol

1 The provisions of the Conventions relating to the repression of breaches and grave breaches, supplemented by this Section, shall apply to the repression of breaches and grave breaches of this Protocol.

2 Acts described as grave breaches in the Conventions are grave breaches of this Protocol if committed against persons in the power of an adverse Party protected by Articles 44, 45 and 73 of this Protocol, or against the wounded, sick and shipwrecked of the adverse Party who are protected by this Protocol, or against those medical or religious personnel, medical units or medical transports which are under the control of the adverse Party and are protected by this Protocol.

3 In addition to the grave breaches defined in Article 11, the following acts shall be regarded as grave breaches of this Protocol, when committed wilfully, in violation of the relevant provisions of this Protocol, and causing death or serious injury to body or health:

(a) making the civilian population or individual civilians the object of attack;

(b) launching an indiscriminate attack affecting the civilian population or civilian objects in the knowledge that such attack will cause excessive loss of life, injury to civilians or damage to civilian objects, as defined in Article 57, paragraph 2 (a)(iii);

(c) launching an attack against works or installations containing dangerous forces in the knowledge that such attack will cause excessive loss of life, injury to civilians or damage to civilian objects, as defined in Article 57, paragraph 2 (a)(iii);

(d) making non-defended localities and demilitarized zones the object of attack;

(e) making a person the object of attack in the knowledge that he is hors de combat;

(f) the perfidious use, in violation of Article 37, of the distinctive emblem of the red cross, red crescent or red lion and sun or of other protective signs recognized by the Conventions or this Protocol.

4 In addition to the grave breaches defined in the preceding paragraphs and in the Conventions, the following shall be regarded as grave breaches of this Protocol, when committed wilfully and in violation of the Conventions or the Protocol:

(a) the transfer by the occupying Power of parts of its own civilian population into the territory it occupies, or the deportation or transfer of all or parts of the population of the occupied territory within or outside this territory, in violation of Article 49 of the Fourth Convention;

(b) unjustifiable delay in the repatriation of prisoners of war or civilians;

(c) practices of apartheid and other inhuman and degrading practices involving outrages upon personal dignity, based on racial discrimination;

(d) making the clearly-recognized historic monuments, works of art or places of worship which constitute the cultural or spiritual heritage of peoples and to which special protection has been given by special arrangement, for example, within the framework of a competent international organization, the object of attack, causing as a result extensive destruction thereof, where there is no evidence of the violation by the adverse Party of Article 53, subparagraph (b), and when such historic monuments, works of art and places of worship are not located in the immediate proximity of military objectives;

(e) depriving a person protected by the Conventions or referred to in paragraph 2 of this Article of the rights of fair and regular trial.

5 Without prejudice to the application of the Conventions and of this Protocol, grave breaches of these instruments shall be regarded as war crimes.

Article 86
Failure to act

1 The High Contracting Parties and the Parties to the conflict shall repress grave breaches, and take measures necessary to suppress all other breaches, of the Conventions or of this Protocol which result from a failure to act when under a duty to do so.2 The fact that a breach of the Conventions or of this Protocol was committed by a subordinate does not absolve his superiors from penal or disciplinary responsibility, as the case may be, if they knew, or had information which should have enabled them to conclude in the circumstances at the time, that he was committing or was going to commit such a breach and if they did not take all feasible measures within their power to prevent or repress the breach.

Article 87
Duty of commanders

1 The High Contracting Parties and the Parties to the conflict shall require military commanders, with respect to members of the armed forces under their command and other persons under their control, to prevent and, where necessary, to suppress and to report to competent authorities breaches of the Conventions and of this Protocol.

2 In order to prevent and suppress breaches, High Contracting Parties and Parties to the conflict shall require that, commensurate with their level of responsibility, commanders ensure that members of the armed forces under their command are aware of their obligations under the Conventions and this Protocol.

3 The High Contracting Parties and Parties to the conflict shall require any commander who is aware that subordinates or other persons under his control are going to commit or have committed a breach of the Conventions or of this Protocol, to initiate such steps as are necessary to prevent such violations of the Conventions or this Protocol, and, where appropriate, to initiate disciplinary or penal action against violators thereof.

Article 88
Mutual assistance in criminal matters

1 The High Contracting Parties shall afford one another the greatest measure of assistance in connexion with criminal proceedings brought in respect of grave breaches of the Conventions or of this Protocol.

2 Subject to the rights and obligations established in the Conventions and in Article 85, paragraph 1 of this Protocol, and when circumstances permit, the High Contracting Parties shall co-operate in the matter of extradition. They shall give due consideration to the request of the State in whose territory the alleged offence has occurred.

3 The law of the High Contracting Party requested shall apply in all cases. The provisions of the preceding paragraphs shall not, however, affect the obligations arising from the provisions of any other treaty of a bilateral or multilateral nature which governs or will govern the whole or part of the subject of mutual assistance in criminal matters.

Article 89
Co-operation

In situations of serious violations of the Conventions or of this Protocol, the High Contracting Parties undertake to act jointly or individually, in co-operation with the United Nations and in conformity with the United Nations Charter.

Article 90
International Fact-Finding Commission

1

    (a)   An International Fact-Finding Commission (hereinafter referred to as 'the Commission') consisting of 15 members of high moral standing and acknowledged impartiality shall be established;

    (b)   When not less than 20 High Contracting Parties have agreed to accept the competence of the Commission pursuant to paragraph 2, the depositary shall then, and at intervals of five years thereafter, convene a meeting of representatives of those High Contracting Parties for the purpose of electing the members of the Commission. At the meeting, the representatives shall elect the members of the Commission by secret ballot from a list of persons to which each of those High Contracting Parties may nominate one person;

    (c)   The members of the Commission shall serve in their personal capacity and shall hold office until the election of new members at the ensuing meeting;

    (d)   At the election, the High Contracting Parties shall ensure that the persons to be elected to the Commission individually possess the qualifications required and that, in the Commission as a whole, equitable geographical representation is assured;

    (e)   In the case of a casual vacancy, the Commission itself shall fill the vacancy, having due regard to the provisions of the preceding subparagraphs;

    (f)   The depositary shall make available to the Commission the necessary administrative facilities for the performance of its functions.

2

    (a)   The High Contracting Parties may at the time of signing, ratifying or acceding to the Protocol, or at any other subsequent time, declare that they recognize ipso facto and without special agreement, in relation to any other High Contracting Party accepting the same obligation, the competence of the Commission to inquire into allegations by such other Party, as authorized by this Article;

    (b)   The declarations referred to above shall be deposited with the depositary, which shall transmit copies thereof to the High Contracting Parties;

    (c)   The Commission shall be competent to:

        (i)   inquire into any facts alleged to be a grave breach as defined in the Conventions and this Protocol or other serious violation of the Conventions or of this Protocol;

        (ii)   facilitate, through its good offices, the restoration of an attitude of respect for the Conventions and this Protocol;

    (d)   In other situations, the Commission shall institute an inquiry at the request of a Party to the conflict only with the consent of the other Party or Parties concerned;

    (e)   Subject to the foregoing provisions or this paragraph, the provisions of Article 52 of the First Convention, Article 53 of the Second Convention, Article 132 or the Third Convention and Article 149 of the Fourth Convention shall continue to apply to any alleged violation of the Conventions and shall extend to any alleged violation of this Protocol.

3

    (a)   Unless otherwise agreed by the Parties concerned, all inquiries shall be undertaken by a Chamber consisting of seven members appointed as follows:

    (i)   five members of the Commission, not nationals of any Party to the conflict, appointed by the President of the Commission on the basis of equitable representation of the geographical areas, after consultation with the Parties to the conflict;

    (ii)   two ad hoc members, not nationals of any Party to the conflict, one to be appointed by each side;

(b)   Upon receipt of the request for an inquiry, the President of the Commission shall specify an appropriate time-limit for setting up a Chamber. If any ad hoc member has not been appointed within the time-limit, the President shall immediately appoint such additional member or members of the Commission as may be necessary to complete the membership of the Chamber.

4.

(a)   The Chamber set up under paragraph 3 to undertake an inquiry shall invite the Parties to the conflict to assist it and to present evidence. The Chamber may also seek such other evidence as it deems appropriate and may carry out an investigation of the situation in loco;

(b)   All evidence shall be fully disclosed to the Parties, which shall have the right to comment on it to the Commission;

(c)   Each Party shall have the right to challenge such evidence.

5

(a)   The Commission shall submit to the Parties a report on the findings of fact of the Chamber, with such recommendations as it may deem appropriate;

(b)   If the Chamber is unable to secure sufficient evidence for factual and impartial findings, the Commission shall state the reasons for that inability;

(c)   The Commission shall not report its findings publicly, unless all the Parties to the conflict have requested the Commission to do so.

6 The Commission shall establish its own rules, including rules for the presidency or the Commission and the presidency of the Chamber. Those rules shall ensure that the functions of the President of the Commission are exercised at all times and that, in the case of an inquiry, they are exercised by a person who is not a national of a Party to the conflict.

7 The administrative expenses of the Commission shall be met by contributions from the High Contracting Parties which made declarations under paragraph 2, and by voluntary contributions. The Party or Parties to the conflict requesting an inquiry shall advance the necessary funds for expenses incurred by a Chamber and shall be reimbursed by the Party or Parties against which the allegations are made to the extent of 50 per cent of the costs of the Chamber. Where there are counter-allegations before the Chamber each side shall advance 50 per cent of the necessary funds.

Article 91
Responsibility

A Party to the conflict which violates the provisions of the Conventions or of this Protocol shall, if the case demands, be liable to pay compensation. It shall be responsible for all acts committed by persons forming part of its armed forces.

PART IV
FINAL RESOLUTIONS

Article 92
Signature

This Protocol shall be open for signature by the Parties to the Conventions six months after the signing of the Final Act and will remain open for a period or twelve months.

Article 93
Ratification

This Protocol shall be ratified as soon as possible. The instruments of ratification shall be deposited with the Swiss Federal Council, depositary of the Conventions.

Article 94
Accession

This Protocol shall be open for accession by any Party to the Conventions which has not signed it. The instruments of accession shall be deposited with the depositary.

Article 95
Entry into force

1 This Protocol shall enter into force six months after two instruments of ratification or accession have been deposited.

2 For each Party to the Conventions thereafter ratifying or acceding to this Protocol, it shall enter into force six months after the deposit by such Party of its instrument of ratification or accession.

Article 96
Treaty relations upon entry into force or this Protocol

1 When the Parties to the Conventions are also Parties to this Protocol, the Conventions shall apply as supplemented by this Protocol.

2 When one of the Parties to the conflict is not bound by this Protocol, the Parties to the Protocol shall remain bound by it in their mutual relations. They shall furthermore be bound by this Protocol in relation to each of the Parties which are not bound by it, if the latter accepts and applies the provisions thereof.

3 The authority representing a people engaged against a High Contracting Party in an armed conflict of the type referred to in Article 1, paragraph 4, may undertake to apply the Conventions and this Protocol in relation to that conflict by means of a unilateral declaration addressed to the depositary. Such declaration shall, upon its receipt by the depositary, have in relation to that conflict the following effects:

(a) the Conventions and this Protocol are brought into force for the said authority as a Party to the conflict with immediate effect;

(b) the said authority assumes the same rights and obligations as those which have been assumed by a High Contracting Party to the Conventions and this Protocol; and

(c) the Conventions and this Protocol are equally binding upon all Parties to the conflict.

Article 97
Amendment

1 Any High Contracting Party may propose amendments to this Protocol. The text of any proposed amendment shall be communicated to the depositary, which shall decide, after consultation with all the High Contracting Parties and the International Committee of the Red Cross, whether a conference should be convened to consider the proposed amendment.

2 The depositary shall invite to that conference all the High Contracting Parties as well as the Parties to the Conventions, whether or not they are signatories or this Protocol.

Article 98
Revision of Annex I

1 Not later than four years after the entry into force of this Protocol and thereafter at intervals of not less than four years, the International Committee of the Red Cross shall consult the High Contracting Parties concerning Annex I to this Protocol and, if it considers it necessary, may propose a meeting of technical experts to review Annex I and to propose such amendments to it as may appear to be desirable. Unless, within six months of the communication of a proposal for such a meeting to the High Contracting Parties, one third of them object, the International Committee of the Red Cross shall convene the meeting, inviting also observers of appropriate international organizations. Such a meeting shall also be convened by the International Committee of the Red Cross at any time at the request of one third of the High Contracting Parties.

2 The depositary shall convene a conference of the High Contracting Parties and the Parties to the Conventions to consider amendments proposed by the meeting of technical experts if, after that meeting, the International Committee of the Red Cross or one third of the High Contracting Parties so request.

3 Amendments to Annex I may be adopted at such a conference by a two-thirds majority of the High Contracting Parties present and voting.

4 The depositary shall communicate any amendment so adopted to the High Contracting Parties and to the Parties to the Conventions. The amendment shall be considered to have been accepted at the end of a period of one year after it has been so communicated, unless within that period a declaration of non-acceptance of the amendment has been communicated to the depositary by not less than one third of the High Contracting Parties.

5 An amendment considered to have been accepted in accordance with paragraph 4 shall enter into force three months after its acceptance for all High Contracting Parties other than those which have made a declaration of non-acceptance in accordance with that paragraph. Any Party making such a declaration may at any time withdraw it and the amendment shall then enter into force for that Party three months thereafter.

6 The depositary shall notify the High Contracting Parties and the Parties to the Conventions of the entry into force of any amendment, of the Parties bound thereby, of the date of its entry into force in relation to each Party, of declarations of non-acceptance made in accordance with paragraph 4, and of withdrawals of such declarations.

Article 99
Denunciation

1 In case a High Contracting Party should denounce this Protocol, the denunciation shall only take effect one year after receipt of the instrument of denunciation. If,

however, on the expiry of that year the denouncing Party is engaged in one of the situations referred to in Article I, the denunciation shall not take effect before the end of the armed conflict or occupation and not, in any case, before operations connected with the final release, repatriation or re-establishment of the persons protected by the Convention or this Protocol have been terminated.

2 The denunciation shall be notified in writing to the depositary, which shall transmit it to all the High Contracting Parties.

3 The denunciation shall have effect only in respect of the denouncing Party.

4 Any denunciation under paragraph 1 shall not affect the obligations already incurred, by reason of the armed conflict, under this Protocol by such denouncing Party in respect of any act committed before this denunciation becomes effective.

Article 100
Notifications

The depositary shall inform the High Contracting Parties as well as the Parties to the Conventions, whether or not they are signatories of this Protocol, of:

(a) signatures affixed to this Protocol and the deposit of instruments of ratification and accession under Articles 93 and 94;
(b) the date of entry into force of this Protocol under Article 95;
(c) communications and declarations received under Articles 84, 90 and 97;
(d) declarations received under Article 96, paragraph 3, which shall be communicated by the quickest methods; and
(e) denunciations under Article 99.

Article 101
Registration

1 After its entry into force, this Protocol shall be transmitted by the depositary to the Secretariat of the United Nations for registration and publication, in accordance with Article 102 of the Charter of the United Nations.

2 The depositary shall also inform the Secretariat of the United Nations of all ratifications, accessions and denunciations received by it with respect to this Protocol.

Article 102
Authentic texts

The original of this Protocol, of which the Arabic, Chinese, English, French, Russian and Spanish texts are equally authentic, shall be deposited with the depositary, which shall transmit certified true copies thereof to all the Parties to the Conventions.

CHAPTER 19

PROTOCOL ADDITIONAL TO THE GENEVA CONVENTIONS OF 12 AUGUST 1949, AND RELATING TO THE PROTECTION OF VICTIMS OF NON-INTERNATIONAL ARMED CONFLICTS (PROTOCOL II), 8 JUNE 1977

Preamble

The High Contracting Parties, Recalling that the humanitarian principles enshrined in Article 3 common to the Geneva Conventions of 12 August 1949, constitute the foundation of respect for the human person in cases of armed conflict not of an international character,

Recalling furthermore that international instruments relating to human rights offer a basic protection to the human person,

Emphasizing the need to ensure a better protection for the victims of those armed conflicts,

Recalling that, in cases not covered by the law in force, the human person remains under the protection of the principles of humanity and the dictates of the public conscience,

Have agreed on the following:

PART I

SCOPE OF THIS PROTOCOL

Article 1
Material field of application

1 This Protocol, which develops and supplements Article 3 common to the Geneva Conventions of 12 August 1949 without modifying its existing conditions of application, shall apply to all armed conflicts which are not covered by Article 1 of the Protocol Additional to the Geneva Conventions of 12 August 1949, and relating to the Protection of Victims of International Armed Conflicts (Protocol I) and which take place in the territory of a High Contracting Party between its armed forces and dissident armed forces or other organized armed groups which, under responsible command, exercise such control over a part of its territory as to enable them to carry out sustained and concerted military operations and to implement this Protocol.

2 This Protocol shall not apply to situations of internal disturbances and tensions, such as riots, isolated and sporadic acts of violence and other acts of a similar nature, as not being armed conflicts.

Article 2
Personal field of application

1 This Protocol shall be applied without any adverse distinction founded on race, colour, sex, language, religion or belief, political or other opinion, national or social origin, wealth, birth or other status, or on any other similar criteria (hereinafter referred to as "adverse distinction") to all persons affected by an armed conflict as defined in Article 1.

2 At the end of the armed conflict, all the persons who have been deprived of their liberty or whose liberty has been restricted for reasons related to such conflict, as well as those deprived of their liberty or whose liberty is restricted after the conflict for the same reasons, shall enjoy the protection of Articles 5 and 6 until the end of such deprivation or restriction of liberty.

Article 3
Non-intervention

1 Nothing in this Protocol shall be invoked for the purpose of affecting the sovereignty of a State or the responsibility of the government, by all legitimate means, to maintain or re-establish law and order in the State or to defend the national unity and territorial integrity of the State.

2 Nothing in this Protocol shall be invoked as a justification for intervening, directly or indirectly, for any reason whatever, in the armed conflict or in the internal or external affairs of the High Contracting Party in the territory of which that conflict occurs.

PART II
HUMANE TREATMENT

Article 4
Fundamental guarantees

1 All persons who do not take a direct part or who have ceased to take part in hostilities, whether or not their liberty has been restricted, are entitled to respect for their person, honour and convictions and religious practices. They shall in all circumstances be treated humanely, without any adverse distinction. It is prohibited to order that there shall be no survivors.

2 Without prejudice to the generality of the foregoing, the following acts against the persons referred to in paragraph I are and shall remain prohibited at any time and in any place whatsoever:

(a) violence to the life, health and physical or mental well-being of persons, in particular murder as well as cruel treatment such as torture, mutilation or any form of corporal punishment;
(b) collective punishments;
(c) taking of hostages;
(d) acts of terrorism;
(e) outrages upon personal dignity, in particular humiliating and degrading treatment, rape, enforced prostitution and any form or indecent assault;
(f) slavery and the slave trade in all their forms;
(g) pillage;
(h) threats to commit any or the foregoing acts.

3 Children shall be provided with the care and aid they require, and in particular:

(a) they shall receive an education, including religious and moral education, in keeping with the wishes of their parents, or in the absence of parents, of those responsible for their care;

(b) all appropriate steps shall be taken to facilitate the reunion of families temporarily separated;

(c) children who have not attained the age of fifteen years shall neither be recruited in the armed forces or groups nor allowed to take part in hostilities;

(d) the special protection provided by this Article to children who have not attained the age of fifteen years shall remain applicable to them if they take a direct part in hostilities despite the provisions of subparagraph (c) and are captured;

(e) measures shall be taken, if necessary, and whenever possible with the consent of their parents or persons who by law or custom are primarily responsible for their care, to remove children temporarily from the area in which hostilities are taking place to a safer area within the country and ensure that they are accompanied by persons responsible for their safety and well-being.

Article 5
Persons whose liberty has been restricted

1 In addition to the provisions of Article 4 the following provisions shall be respected as a minimum with regard to persons deprived of their liberty for reasons related to the armed conflict, whether they are interned or detained;

(a) the wounded and the sick shall be treated in accordance with Article 7;

(b) the persons referred to in this paragraph shall, to the same extent as the local civilian population, be provided with food and drinking water and be afforded safeguards as regards health and hygiene and protection against the rigours of the climate and the dangers of the armed conflict;

(c) they shall be allowed to receive individual or collective relief;

(d) they shall be allowed to practise their religion and, if requested and appropriate, to receive spiritual assistance from persons, such as chaplains, performing religious functions;

(e) they shall, if made to work, have the benefit of working conditions and safeguards similar to those enjoyed by the local civilian population.

2 Those who are responsible for the internment or detention of the persons referred to in paragraph 1 shall also, within the limits of their capabilities, respect the following provisions relating to such persons:

(a) except when men and women of a family are accommodated together, women shall be held in quarters separated from those of men and shall be under the immediate supervision of women;

(b) they shall be allowed to send and receive letters and cards, the number of which may be limited by competent authority if it deems necessary;

(c) places of internment and detention shall not be located close to the combat zone. The persons referred to in paragraph 1 shall be evacuated when the places where they are interned or detained become particularly exposed to danger arising out of the armed conflict, if their evacuation can be carried out under adequate conditions of safety;

(d) they shall have the benefit of medical examinations;

(e) their physical or mental health and integrity shall not be endangered by any unjustified act or omission. Accordingly, it is prohibited to subject the persons described in this Article to any medical procedure which is not indicated by the state of health of the person concerned, and which is not consistent with the generally accepted medical standards applied to free persons under similar medical circumstances.

3 Persons who are not covered by paragraph 1 but whose liberty has been restricted in any way whatsoever for reasons related to the armed conflict shall be treated humanely in accordance with Article 4 and with paragraphs 1 (a), (c) and (d), and 2 (b) of this Article.

4 If it is decided to release persons deprived of their liberty, necessary measures to ensure their safety shall be taken by those so deciding.

Article 6
Penal prosecutions

1 This Article applies to the prosecution and punishment of criminal offences related to the armed conflict.

2 No sentence shall be passed and no penalty shall be executed on a person found guilty of an offence except pursuant to a conviction pronounced by a court offering the essential guarantees of independence and impartiality.

In particular:

(a) the procedure shall provide for an accused to be informed without delay of the particulars of the offence alleged against him and shall afford the accused before and during his trial all necessary rights and means of defence;

(b) no one shall be convicted of an offence except on the basis of individual penal responsibility;

(c) no one shall be held guilty of any criminal offence on account of any act or omission which did not constitute a criminal offence, under the law, at the time when it was committed; nor shall a heavier penalty be imposed than that which was applicable at the time when the criminal offence was committed; if, after the commission of the offence, provision is made by law for the imposition of a lighter penalty, the offender shall benefit thereby;

(d) anyone charged with an offence is presumed innocent until proved guilty according to law;

(e) anyone charged with an offence shall have the right to be tried in his presence;

(f) no one shall be compelled to testify against himself or to confess guilt.

3 A convicted person shall be advised on conviction of his judicial and other remedies and of the time-limits within which they may be exercised.

4 The death penalty shall not be pronounced on persons who were under the age of eighteen years at the time of the offence and shall not be carried out on pregnant women or mothers of young children.

5 At the end of hostilities, the authorities in power shall endeavour to grant the broadest possible amnesty to persons who have participated in the armed conflict, or those deprived of their liberty for reasons related to the armed conflict, whether they are interned or detained.

PART III
WOUNDED, SICK AND SHIPWRECKED

Article 7
Protection and care

1 All the wounded, sick and shipwrecked, whether or not they have taken part in the armed conflict, shall be respected and protected.

2 In all circumstances they shall be treated humanely and shall receive to the fullest extent practicable and with the least possible delay, the medical care and attention required by their condition. There shall be no distinction among them founded on any grounds other than medical ones.

Article 8
Search

Whenever circumstances permit and particularly after an engagement, all possible measures shall be taken, without delay, to search for and collect the wounded, sick and shipwrecked, to protect them against pillage and ill-treatment, to ensure their adequate care, and to search for the dead, prevent their being despoiled, and decently dispose of them.

Article 9
Protection of medical and religious personnel

1 Medical and religious personnel shall be respected and protected and shall be granted all available help for the performance of their duties. They shall not be compelled to carry out tasks which are not compatible with their humanitarian mission.

2 In the performance of their duties medical personnel may not be required to give priority to any person except on medical grounds.

Article 10
General protection of medical duties

1 Under no circumstances shall any person be punished for having carried out medical activities compatible with medical ethics, regardless of the person benefiting therefrom.

2 Persons engaged in medical activities shall neither be compelled to perform acts or to carry out work contrary to, nor be compelled to refrain from acts required by, the rules of medical ethics or other rules designed for the benefit of the wounded and sick, or this Protocol.

3 The professional obligations of persons engaged in medical activities regarding information which they may acquire concerning the wounded and sick under their care shall, subject to national law, be respected.

4 Subject to national law, no person engaged in medical activities may be penalized in any way for refusing or failing to give information concerning the wounded and sick who are, or who have been, under his care.

Article 11
Protection of medical units and transports

1 Medical units and transports shall be respected and protected at all times and shall not be the object of attack.

2 The protection to which medical units and transports are entitled shall not cease unless they are used to commit hostile acts, outside their humanitarian function.

Protection may, however, cease only after a warning has been given, setting, whenever appropriate, a reasonable time-limit, and after such warning has remained unheeded.

Article 12
The distinctive emblem

Under the direction of the competent authority concerned, the distinctive emblem of the red cross, red crescent or red lion and sun on a white ground shall be displayed by medical and religious personnel and medical units, and on medical transports. It shall be respected in all circumstances. It shall not be used improperly.

PART IV
CIVILIAN POPULATION

Article 13
Protection of the civilian population

1 The civilian population and individual civilians shall enjoy general protection against the dangers arising from military operations. To give effect to this protection, the following rules shall be observed in all circumstances.

2 The civilian population as such, as well as individual civilians, shall not be the object of attack. Acts or threats of violence the primary purpose of which is to spread terror among the civilian population are prohibited.

3 Civilians shall enjoy the protection afforded by this part, unless and for such time as they take a direct part in hostilities.

Article 14
Protection of objects indispensable to the survival of the civilian population

Starvation of civilians as a method of combat is prohibited. It is therefore prohibited to attack, destroy, remove or render useless for that purpose, objects indispensable to the survival of the civilian population such as food-stuffs, agricultural areas for the production of food-stuffs, crops, livestock, drinking water installations and supplies and irrigation works.

Article 15
Protection of works and installations containing dangerous forces

Works or installations containing dangerous forces, namely dams, dykes and nuclear electrical generating stations, shall not be made the object of attack, even where these objects are military objectives, if such attack may cause the release of dangerous forces and consequent severe losses among the civilian population.

Article 16
Protection of cultural objects and of places of worship

Without prejudice to the provisions of the Hague Convention for the Protection of Cultural Property in the Event of Armed Conflict of 14 May 1954, it is prohibited to commit any acts of hostility directed against historic monuments, works of art or places of worship which constitute the cultural or spiritual heritage of peoples, and to use them in support of the military effort.

Article 17
Prohibition of forced movement of civilians

1 The displacement of the civilian population shall not be ordered for reasons related to the conflict unless the security of the civilians involved or imperative military reasons so

demand. Should such displacements have to be carried out, all possible measures shall be taken in order that the civilian population may be received under satisfactory conditions of shelter, hygiene, health, safety and nutrition.

2 Civilians shall not be compelled to leave their own territory for reasons connected with the conflict.

Article 18
Relief societies and relief actions

1 Relief societies located in the territory of the High Contracting Party, such as Red Cross (Red Crescent, Red Lion and Sun) organizations may offer their services for the performance of their traditional functions in relation to the victims of the armed conflict. The civilian population may, even on its own initiative, offer to collect and care for the wounded, sick and shipwrecked.

2 If the civilian population is suffering undue hardship owing to a lack of the supplies essential for its survival, such as food-stuffs and medical supplies, relief actions for the civilian population which are of an exclusively humanitarian and impartial nature and which are conducted without any adverse distinction shall be undertaken subject to the consent of the High Contracting Party concerned.

PART V
FINAL PROVISIONS

Article 19
Dissemination

This Protocol shall be disseminated as widely as possible.

Article 20
Signature

This Protocol shall be open for signature by the Parties to the Conventions six months after the signing of the Final Act and will remain open for a period of twelve months.

Article 21
Ratification

This Protocol shall be ratified as soon as possible. The instruments of ratification shall be deposited with the Swiss Federal Council, depositary of the Conventions.

Article 22
Accession

This Protocol shall be open for accession by any Party to the Conventions which has not signed it. The instruments of accession shall be deposited with the depositary.

Article 23
Entry into force

1 This Protocol shall enter into force six months after two instruments of ratification or accession have been deposited.

2 For each Party to the Conventions thereafter ratifying or acceding to this Protocol, it shall enter into force six months after the deposit by such Party of its instrument of ratification or accession.

Article 24
Amendment

1 Any High Contracting Party may propose amendments to this Protocol. The text of any proposed amendment shall be communicated to the depositary which shall decide, after consultation with all the High Contracting Parties and the International Committee of the Red Cross, whether a conference should be convened to consider the proposed amendment.

2 The depositary shall invite to that conference all the High Contracting Parties as well as the Parties to the Conventions, whether or not they are signatories of this Protocol.

Article 25
Denunciation

1 In case a High Contracting Party should denounce this Protocol, the denunciation shall only take effect six months after receipt of the instrument of denunciation. If, however, on the expiry of six months, the denouncing Party is engaged in the situation referred to in Article 1, the denunciation shall not take effect before the end of the armed conflict. Persons who have been deprived of liberty, or whose liberty has been restricted, for reasons related to the conflict shall nevertheless continue to benefit from the provisions of this Protocol until their final release.

2 The denunciation shall be notified in writing to the depositary, which shall transmit it to all the High Contracting Parties.

Article 26
Notifications

The depositary shall inform the High Contracting Parties as well as the Parties to the Conventions, whether or not they are signatories of this Protocol, of:

   (a)   signatures affixed to this Protocol and the deposit of instruments of ratification and accession under Articles 21 and 22;
   (b)   the date of entry into force of this Protocol under Article 23; and
   (c)   communications and declarations received under Article 24.

Article 27
Registration

1 After its entry into force, this Protocol shall be transmitted by the depositary to the Secretariat of the United Nations for registration and publication, in accordance with Article 102 of the Charter of the United Nations.

2 The depositary shall also inform the Secretariat of the United Nations of all ratifications, accessions and denunciations received by it with respect to this Protocol.

Article 28
Authentic texts

The original of this Protocol, of which the Arabic, Chinese, English, French, Russian and Spanish texts are equally authentic, shall be deposited with the depositary, which shall transmit certified true copies thereof to all the Parties to the Conventions.

CHAPTER 20

EUROPEAN CONVENTION FOR THE PROTECTION OF HUMAN RIGHTS AND FUNDAMENTAL FREEDOMS

Amended by Protocols No 11 and 14, Rome, 4.XI.1950

Text amended by the provisions of Protocol No 14 (CETS No 194) as from the date of its entry into force on 1 June 2010.

The text of the Convention had been previously amended according to the provisions of Protocol No 3 (ETS No 45), which entered into force on 21 September 1970, of Protocol No 5 (ETS No 55), which entered into force on 20 December 1971 and of Protocol No 8 (ETS No 118), which entered into force on 1 January 1990, and comprised also the text of Protocol No 2 (ETS No 44) which, in accordance with Article 5, paragraph 3 thereof, had been an integral part of the Convention since its entry into force on 21 September 1970. All provisions which had been amended or added by these Protocols were replaced by Protocol No 11 (ETS No 155), as from the date of its entry into force on 1 November 1998. As from that date, Protocol No 9 (ETS No 140), which entered into force on 1 October 1994, was repealed and Protocol No 10 (ETS No 146) had lost its purpose.

Preamble

The governments signatory hereto, being members of the Council of Europe,

Considering the Universal Declaration of Human Rights proclaimed by the General Assembly of the United Nations on 10 December 1948;

Considering that this Declaration aims at securing the universal and effective recognition and observance of the Rights therein declared;

Considering that the aim of the Council of Europe is the achievement of greater unity between its members and that one of the methods by which that aim is to be pursued is the maintenance and further realisation of human rights and fundamental freedoms;

Reaffirming their profound belief in those fundamental freedoms which are the foundation of justice and peace in the world and are best maintained on the one hand by an effective political democracy and on the other by a common understanding and observance of the human rights upon which they depend;

Being resolved, as the governments of European countries which are likeminded and have a common heritage of political traditions, ideals, freedom and the rule of law, to take the first steps for the collective enforcement of certain of the rights stated in the Universal Declaration,

Have agreed as follows:

Article 1
Obligation to respect human rights

The High Contracting Parties shall secure to everyone within their jurisdiction the rights and freedoms defined in Section I of this Convention.

'everyone' (Art 1)—The word 'everyone' in Art 1 clearly includes children [**RCLP para 2.78**]. Note however the absence of the best interests principle within the ECHR [**RCLP para 2.79**]. This is partly compensated for by repeated references in case authority to the applicability of the best interests principle to the ECHR (see for example *Johansen v Norway* (1996) 23 EHRR 33; *K and T v Finland* [2000] 3 FCR 248, [2000] 2 FLR 79; *Yousef v The Netherlands* [2002] 3 FCR 577, [2003] 1 FLR 210; *Kearns v France* Application No 35991/04 [2008] 2 FCR 19, [2008] 1 FLR 888; *R and H v United Kingdom* [2011] 2 FLR 1236; and *YC v United Kingdom* (2012) 55 EHRR 967) [RCLP para 2.79].

Unborn children—The European Commission on Human Rights rejected the proposition that an unborn child has an absolute right to life under Art 2 and hence, by implication, that childhood commences prior to birth (*Paton v United Kingdom* (1980) 3 EHRR 408) [RCLP para 4.5]. The ECtHR has since held that the question of when the right to life commenced falls within the margin of appreciation and that, accordingly, it was neither desirable nor possible to answer the question of whether an unborn child is a person for the purposes of Art 2 of the ECHR (*Vo v France* [2004] 2 FCR 577 and see also *A, B and C v Ireland* (2010) Application No 25579/05 and *Evans v United Kingdom* (2007) 43 EHRR 21) [RCLP para 4.5].

Positive obligations—Art 1 has resulted in a number of the Arts of the ECHR being interpreted as placing positive obligations on State Parties [RCLP para 2.84]. See for example *McCann v United Kingdom* (1995) 21 EHRR 97, *Jordan v United Kingdom* (2003) 37 EHRR 52; *McKerr v United Kingdom* (2002) 34 EHRR 553; and *Tyamuskhanovy v Russia* (2010) Application No 11528/07 [RCLP para 5.44]. See also *Z v United Kingdom* (2001) 34 EHRR 97, [2001] 2 FLR 612 [RCLP para 2.83].

Section I
Rights and freedoms

Article 2
Right to life

1. Everyone's right to life shall be protected by law. No one shall be deprived of his life intentionally save in the execution of a sentence of a court following his conviction of a crime for which this penalty is provided by law.

2. Deprivation of life shall not be regarded as inflicted in contravention of this Article when it results from the use of force which is no more than absolutely necessary:

(a)   in defence of any person from unlawful violence;
(b)   in order to effect a lawful arrest or to prevent the escape of a person lawfully detained;
(c)   in action lawfully taken for the purpose of quelling a riot or insurrection.

The right to life (Art 2)—The right to life under Art 2 is one of the absolute rights under the ECHR [RCLP para 3.66]. It is a fundament right that enshrines one of the basic values of the democratic societies making up the Council of Europe [RCLP para 5.24]. The right to life under Art 2 is an element of the positive obligation on State Parties to protect children from abusive treatment (*Z v United Kingdom* (2001) 34 EHRR 97, [2001] 2 FLR 612, paras 73–75) [RCLP para 2.83]. The ECtHR has made reference to the African Charter on Human and Peoples' Rights when considering the proper interpretation of Art 2 (*Vo v France* Application No 539/24 [2004] 2 FCR 577, para 63) [RCLP para 3.93]. The circumstances in which deprivation of life may be justified must be strictly construed (*Mikayil Mammadov v Azerbaijan* (2010) Application No 4762/05) [RCLP para 5.25]. The right to life must be given practical effect (*McCann v United Kingdom* (1995) 21 EHRR 97, para 146 and *Loizidou v Turkey* (1995) 20 EHRR 99, para 72) [RCLP para 5.25]. Art 2 does not confer upon the individual the diametrically opposed right to die nor does it create a right to self-determination in the sense of conferring on an individual the entitlement to choose death rather than life (*Pretty v United Kingdom* (2002) 35 EHRR 1, para 39) [RCLP paras 5.35–5.39].

Procedural safeguards—Implicit in Art 2 are procedural safeguards necessary to give effect to the right to life under Art 2 (*Savage v South Essex Partnership NHS Foundation Trust* [2008] UKHL 74, [2009] 1 AC 681, [2009] 2 WLR 115, [2009] 1 All ER 1053 and see *Rantsev v Cyprus and Russia* (2010) Application No 25965/04, para 232; *McCann v United Kingdom* (1995) 21 EHRR 97, para 161; *Jordan v United Kingdom* (2003) 37 EHRR 52, *R (JL) v Secretary of State for the Home Department* [2008] UKHL 68, [2009] 1 AC 588, 3 WLR 1325; *Menson v United Kingdom* (2003) 37 EHRR CE 220; and *Nachova v Bulgaria* [2005] ECHR 43577/98, para 160 citing *Menson v United Kingdom* (2003) 37 EHRR CE 220.) [RCLP paras 5.43–5.44]. See also *Nencheva and Others v Bulgaria* (2013) Application No 48609/06).

Victim—Under Art 2 the 'victim' for the purposes of the Human Rights Act 1998 s 7(7) my be the child of a close relation who has been murdered (*Yasa v Turkey* (1998) 28 EHRR, para 66; *Çakici v Turkey* (1999) 31 EHRR

133; and *Kilic v Turkey* (2000) 33 EHRR 1357. But see *Savage v South Essex Partnership NHS Foundation Trust* [2008] UKHL 74, [2009] 1 AC 681, [2009] 2 WLR 115, [2009] 1 All ER 1053, paras 2–5) [**RCLP para 5.30**].

Positive and negative obligations—Art 2(1) constitutes a negative obligation to refrain from the unlawful taking of life (*LCB v United Kingdom* (1998) 27 EHRR 212, para 36) and a positive obligation to safeguard life (*McCann v United Kingdom* (1995) 21 EHRR 97, para 184 and *W v United Kingdom* 32 DR 190 (1983) at 200) [**RCLP para 5.26**]. The Art 2(1) right to life includes a duty on State Parties to take appropriate steps to safeguard the lives of those within its jurisdiction (*Osman v United Kingdom* (1998) 29 EHRR 245, [1999] 1 FLR 193, para 115 and see *Tomašic v Croatia* (2009) Application No 56598/06 and *Rantsev v Cyprus and Russia* (2010) Application No 25965/04, para 232) [**RCLP para 5.26**] and see *Kayak v Turkey* (2012) Application No 6044/08, *Kemaloglu v Turkey* (2012) Application No 19986/06 and *Paşa and Erkan Erol v Turkey* (2006) Application No 51358/99. Appropriate steps will include effective criminal laws, enforcement and sanctions (*Kilic v Turkey* (2001) 33 EHRR 1357, para 62 and *Mahmut Kaya v Turkey* (unreported) 28 March 2000, para 85 citing *Osman v United Kingdom* (1998) 29 EHRR 245, para 115 and see also *Rantsev v Cyprus and Russia* (2010) Application No 25965/04, para 218), preventative operational measures to protect individuals from other individuals or themselves (*Mikayil Mammadov v Azerbaijan* (2010) Application No 4762/05) and protective provisions for persons in custody (*Salman v Turkey* (2002) 34 EHRR 425, *Edwards v United Kingdom* (2002) 35 EHRR 487, para 56 and see also *Ognyanova v Bulgaria* (2007) 44 EHRR 7, *Selmouni v France* (1999) 29 EHRR 403, para 87 and *Jordan v United Kingdom* (2003) 37 EHRR 52) including children in so called 'administrative custody (*Slimani v France* (2004) 43 EHRR 1068) [**RCLP para 5.27**].

The positive obligation to safeguard life will include the prevention of suicide in custody (*Savage v South Essex Partnership NHS Foundation Trust* [2008] UKHL 74, [2009] 1 AC 681, [2009] 2 WLR 115, para 9) and in respect of military conscripts (*Kilinc v Turkey* (2005) Application 48083/99 (unreported) and *Ataman v Turkey* (2006) Application 46252/99 (unreported) cited by Baroness Hale in *Savage v South Essex Partnership NHS Foundation Trust* [2008] UKHL 74, [2009] 1 AC 681, [2009] 2 WLR 115, [2009] 1 All ER 1053, para 61) [**RCLP para 5.27**]. See also *De Ponder and De Clippel v Belgium* (2011) Application No 8595/06 and *Coşelav v Turkey* (2012) Application No 1413/07. Whilst the positive obligation to safeguard life will extend to hospitals (*Calvelli v Italy* (2002) Application 32967/96 2002 (unreported), para 49; *Dodov v Bulgaria* (2008) Application 59548/00 (unreported), para 80 and *Vo v France* (2005) 40 EHRR 259, para 89 and see *Savage v South Essex Partnership NHS Foundation Trust* [2008] UKHL 74, [2009] 1 AC 681, [2009] 2 WLR 115, [2009] 1 All ER 1053, para 9) this is not an unqualified obligation (*R v Cambridgeshire District Health Authority, ex p B* [1995] 2 All ER 129, [1995] 1 WLR 898 and see also *Association X v United Kingdom* (1978) 14 DR 31 at 32, *Taylor Family and Others v United Kingdom* (1994) 79-A DR 127 and the decision of the Constitutional Court of South Africa in *Soobramoney v Minister of Health* (1997) 4 BHRC 308) [**RCLP para 5.27**]. It is highly unlikely that there is a general right to a particular standard of healthcare under Art 2 (*LCB v United Kingdom* (1998) 4 BHRC 447, (1998) 27 EHRR 212, *Buckley v United Kingdom* (1997) 23 EHRR 101, para 75 and *Hatton v United Kingdom* (2003) 27 EHRR 611, paras 97–103 but see *Wockel v Germany* (1997) 25 EHRR CD 156 and *Barratt v United Kingdom* (1997) 23 EHRR CD 185) [**RCLP para 5.122**].

It is an open question whether there is a positive duty under Art 2(1) to rescue a person from a life threatening situation (*Hughes v United Kingdom* (1986) 48 DR 258) [**RCLP para 5.27**]. There is a two stage test for whether a State has fulfilled its positive obligation under Art 2, namely (a) what was or should have been the state of the State's knowledge and (b) were the steps taken by the State reasonable in light of its knowledge (*Osman v United Kingdom* (1998) 29 EHRR 245; *Mastromatteo v Italy* (2002) Application 37703/97 (unreported), *Kontrová v Slovakia* (2007) Application 7510/04 (unreported) and *Keenan v United Kingdom* (2001) 33 EHRR 913, para 89) [**RCLP paras 5.28–5.29**].

The unborn child: abortion—The ECtHR has rejected the proposition that the unborn child has an absolute right to life under Art 2 (*Paton v United Kingdom* (1980) 3 EHRR 408, paras 18–20) [**RCLP para 4.5**]. Note however that the Commission was not prepared to entirely exclude the possibility of Art 2 being applicable to the unborn child in rare cases ((1980) 3 EHRR 408, para 7). See also *Brüggeman and Scheuten v Federal Republic of Germany* (1978) Application No 6959/75 (unreported) (which expressly left open the issue of whether an unborn child is covered by Art 2 of the ECHR), *H v Norway* (1992) Application No 17004/90 (unreported) (where the Commission did 'not exclude that in certain circumstances' a foetus would be protected under Art 2 of the ECHR) and *Open Door Counselling and Dublin Well Women v Ireland* (1992) 15 EHRR 244 (where the European Court of Human Rights acknowledged the possibility that Art 2 of the ECHR might in certain circumstances offer protection to an unborn child). See also *A, B and C v Ireland* (2010) Application No 25579/05, para 214. Recently, the ECtHR has determined that it is neither possible nor desirable to determine whether an unborn child was a person within the meaning of Art 2 given the margin of appreciation (*Vo v France* Application No 539/24 [2004] 2 FCR 577) [**RCLP para 4.5**]. In the circumstances, a Member State is permitted to have in place domestic laws which permit abortion to protect the physical and mental health of the mother (*X v United Kingdom* (1980) 19 DR 244) and from social hardship (*H v Norway* (1992) 73 DR 155) [**RCLP para 5.34**].

The unborn child: IVF—An embryo created by IVF and existing outside the womb is not a person for the purposes of Art 2 (*Evans v United Kingdom* (2007) 43 EHRR 21) [**RCLP para 4.5**]. See also the Convention for the Protection of Human Rights and Dignity of the Human Being with regard to the Application of Biology and Medicine (ETS No 64), Art 3 of the Charter of Fundamental Rights of the European Union and Directive 2004/23/EC of the European Parliament [RCLP paras 5.31–5.32]. See also *RR v Poland* (2011) Application No 27617/04.

Life threatening traditional practices—The killing of a child for reasons of so called 'honour' is a breach of the right to life under Art 2(1) (see *Opuz v Turkey* (2009) Application No 33401/02 (unreported)) [RCLP para 5.40].

The death penalty—Whilst Art 2(1) does not expressly prohibit the use of the death penalty against children, when read with Art 6(1) of the UNCRC and the principles of international law it is likely that Art 2 would be central to preventing the execution of a child [RCLP para 5.41]. See also the Sixth Protocol to the ECHR and the Thirteenth Protocol to the ECHR [RCLP para 5.41]. These Protocols, taken with Art 2 are likely to prevent the deportation of a child from the United Kingdom where it can be shown that there is an actual risk of the death penalty being imposed on the child (*Ocalan v Turkey* (2005) 41 EHRR 985; *Aylor v France* (1994) 100 ILR 665 and the decision of the Netherlands Supreme Court in *Short v Netherlands* (1990) Rechtspraak van de Week 358 reprinted in (1990) 29 ILM 1378 and see also the position taken by the Human Rights Committee in *Kindler v Canada* (Communication No 470/1991) (1994) 1 IHRR 98 and *NG v Canada* (Communication No 469/1991) (1992) 1 IHRR 161). Where it can be shown that the child is at risk of extra-judicial killing this is likely to be dealt with under Art 3 rather than Art 2 (*Aspichi Dehwari v Netherlands* (2000) Application No 37014/97 (unreported) and *Abdurrahim Incedursum v Netherlands* (1999) Application No 33124/96 (unreported) but see also *MAR v United Kingdom* (1996) 23 EHRR CD 120 and *Bahddar v Netherlands* (1998) 26 EHRR 278) [RCLP para 5.42].

Derogation—Save in respect of deaths resulting from lawful acts of war, derogation in respect of Art 2 is not permitted (Art 15(2)) [RCLP para 2.81]. Contrast Art 6(1) of the UNCRC [RCLP para 5.19]. Art 2(1) contains the circumstances in which the deprivation of life may be justified. Those circumstances must be construed strictly having regard to the fundamental nature of the right to life and the fact that no derogation is permitted in peacetime (*Soering v United Kingdom* (1989) 11 EHRR 439, para 89 and *McCann v United Kingdom* (1995) 21 EHRR 97, para 146) [RCLP para 5.45]. The use of the word 'absolutely' in Art 2(2) requires a more compelling test of necessity than that required by the term 'necessary in a democratic society' (*McCann v United Kingdom* (1995) 21 EHRR 97, para 149 and *Andronicou and Constantinou v Cyprus* (1997) 25 EHRR 491, para 171) [RCLP para 5.46].

Article 3
Prohibition of torture

No one shall be subjected to torture or to inhuman or degrading treatment or punishment.

Right not to be subjected to torture or to inhuman or degrading treatment or punishment (Art 3)—The right not to be subjected to torture or to inhuman or degrading treatment of punishment is an absolute right [RCLP para 3.66]. It is a fundamental right that enshrines one of the basic values of the democratic societies making up the Council of Europe (*Soering v United Kingdom* (1989) 11 EHRR 439) [RCLP para 5.24]. Discrimination can also amount to degrading treatment under Art 3 (*East African Asians Cases* (1973) 3 EHRR 76, *Cyprus v Turkey* (2002) 35 EHRR 731 and *Moldovan v Romania* (2007) 44 EHRR 302, paras 110–114. See also *Avsar v Turkey* (2003) 37 EHRR 1014, paras 418–420) [RCLP paras 4.102; 15.157] as may the conditions of detention facilities (*B v United Kingdom* (1981) 32 DR 5 and also The Greek Case 12 YB1 (1969) Com Rep and *Guzzardi v Italy* (1980) 3 EHRR 333) [RCLP para 5.165]. However, discrimination against non-marital children does not amount to degrading treatment for the purposes of Art 3 (*Abdulaziz, Cabales and Balkandali v United Kingdom* (1985) 7 EHRR 471, para 91 and *Marckx v Belgium* (1979) 2 EHRR 330 and see also *Smith and Grady v United Kingdom* (1999) 29 EHRR 493, paras 120–122) [RCLP para 15.157]. The withdrawal of welfare provision from a person unable to meet their own essential living needs by reason of destitution and inability to work may amount to a breach of Art 3 (*R (Limbuela) v Secretary of State for the Home Department* [2005] UKHL 66, [2006] 1 AC 396; *R (Husain) v Asylum Support Adjudicator* [2001] EWHC (Admin) 852, [2001] All ER (D) 107 (Oct) and *R (Chavda) v London Borough of Harrow* [2007] EWHC 3064 (Admin) but see also *R (Q) v Secretary of State for the Home Department* [2003] EWCA Civ 364, [2004] QB 36) [RCLP para 5.186]. A purposive interpretation of Art 3 is required (*Aksoy v Turkey* (1997) 23 EHRR 553, paras 98–99 relying on Art 12 of the UN Convention against Torture and Other Cruel, Inhuman or Degrading Treatment or Punishment) [RCLP para 15.144]. A delay in investigating and prosecuting the rape of a child can amount to a violation of the procedural element of Art 3 (*PM v Bulgaria* (2012) Application No 49669/07, *CAS and CS v Romania* (2012) Application No 49669/07, *RIP and DLP v Romania* (2012) Application No 27782/10, *P and S v Poland* (2012) Application No 57375/08).

Positive obligation—There is a positive duty under Art 3 to protect a child against inhuman and degrading treatment or punishment (*Z v United Kingdom* (2001) 34 EHRR 97, [2001] 2 FLR 612, paras 73–75 and see also

Marckx v Belgium (1979) 2 EHRR 330, *Hockkanen v Finland* (1994) 19 EHRR 139; *Hansen v Turkey* [2004] 1 FLR 142; *Kosmopoulou v Greece* Application (No 60457/00) [2004] 1 FLR 800 and *Maire v Portugal* [2004] 2 FLR 653 but see also *Glaser v United Kingdom* [2001] 1 FLR 153) [**RCLP para 2.84**]. This positive obligation includes a duty to take proactive steps to prevent treatment that falls within the ambit of Art 3 (*A v United Kingdom* (1999) 27 EHRR 611) [**RCLP para 15.144**] and see *O'Keefe v Ireland* (2014) Application No 35810/09. The positive obligation encompasses both State Parties and the agents of the State (*Ireland v United Kingdom* (1980) 2 EHRR 25, para 159) including the actions of unofficial groups such as private schools (*Costello-Roberts v United Kingdom* (1993) 19 EHRR 112, para 26–28) [**RCLP para 15.143**]. Children in particular are entitled to State protection in the form of effective deterrence against serious breaches of personal integrity (*Opuz v Turkey* (2009) Application No 33401/02, para 102 and see *A v United Kingdom* (1999) 27 EHRR 611, *Z v United Kingdom* (2001) 34 EHRR 97, para73 and *DP and JC v United Kingdom* (2003) 36 EHRR and *E v United Kingdom* (2003) 36 EHRR 519, para 99) [**RCLP para 15.145**]. The special vulnerability of children will be relevant to the scope of the positive obligation under Art 3 (*Re E (A Child) (Northern Ireland)* [2008] UKHL 66, [2008] 3 WLR 1208, para 9 per Baroness Hale citing *Mayeka v Belgium* (2008) 46 EHRR 23 at 53) [**RCLP para 15.145**]. The positive obligation under Art 3 includes an obligation to investigate violations of the Article (*Yükshel v Turkey* (2005), 41 EHRR 316, para 29, *Assenov v Bulgaria* (1998) 28 EHRR 652, para 102, *Veznedaroglu v Turkey* (2001) 33 EHRR 1412, para 32, *Indelicato v Italy* (2002) 35 EHRR 1330, *Gldani Congregation of Jehova's Witnesses v Georgia* (2008) 46 EHRR 613, para 97 and *Krastanov v Bulgaria* (2005) 41 EHRR 1137, paras 57–58) [**RCLP para 15.146**].

Relevant treatment—Treatment must attain a minimum level of severity to fall within the ambit of Art 3 (*Ireland v United Kingdom* (1980) 2 EHRR 25, para 162 and see *Costello-Roberts v United Kingdom* (1993) 19 EHRR 112, para 32 and *A v United Kingdom* (1999) 27 EHRR 611, para 21. See further *Kurt v Turkey* (1998) 27 EHRR 373 and *Çakici v Turkey* (1999) 31 EHRR 133, para 98, *Cyprus v Turkey* (2002) 35 EHRR 731, para 157 and *Osmanoglu v Turkey* (2008) Application 48804/99 (unreported)) [**RCLP para 15.147**]. The test for whether particular treatment engages Art 3 of the ECHR is a relative one and is dependent on all the circumstances of the case including the duration of that treatment, the physical and mental effects of that treatment and, in some cases, the age, sex, state of health (*Mouisel v France* (2004) 38 EHRR 735, paras 38 and 40) and the vulnerability of the victim of the treatment (*Ireland v United Kingdom* (1980) 2 EHRR 25, para 162 and see *Price v United Kingdom* (2002) 34 EHRR 1285, para 30) [**RCLP para 15.147**]. The victims own conduct is irrelevant for these purposes (*Ireland v United Kingdom* (1980) 2 EHRR 25, para 163 and *Lorsé v The Netherlands* (2003) 37 EHRR 105, para 58. See also *Abuki v A-G of Uganda* (1997) 3 BHRC 199 Constitutional Court of Uganda. But see *Tomasi v France* (1992) 15 EHRR, para 113 and *Veznedaroglu v Turkey* (2001) 33 EHRR 1412, para 29) [**RCLP para 15.148**]. The burden of proving the treatment complained of falls upon the applicant and the standard of proof is beyond reasonable doubt (*Ireland v United Kingdom* (1978) 2 EHRR 25, para 161) [**RCLP para 15.149**].

'**torture**' (Art 3)—Torture has been defined for the purpose of Art 3 as deliberate inhuman treatment causing very serious and cruel suffering (*Ireland v United Kingdom* (1978) 2 EHRR 25, para 167. See also *Denmark v Greece (The Greek Case)* 12 YB 186 (1972), *Selmouni v France* (2000) 29 EHRR 403, para 96 and *Menesheva v Russia* (2007) 44 EHRR 1162, paras 57–59) [**RCLP para 15.150**].

'**inhuman or degrading treatment or punishment**' (Art 3)—For the meaning of the phrase 'inhuman or degrading treatment or punishment' see *Kalashnikov v Russia* (2002) 36 EHRR 34, para 95, *R (Limbuela) and others v Secretary of State for the Home Department* [2005] UKHL 66, [2006] 1 AC 396, para 7, *Lorsé v Netherlands* (2003) 37 EHRR 105, para 58, *Campbell and Cosans v United Kingdom* (1980) 3 EHRR 531 and *Raninen v Finland* (1997) 26 EHRR 563, para 55 [**RCLP paras 15.51 and 15.154–15.155**]. Note the omission of the word 'cruel' from the Art 3 formulation [**RCLP para 15.152**]. Failure to provide medical assistance may be considering degrading (*Sarban v Moldova* (2005) Application No 3456/05 (unreported), para 90) as may be mutilation of the body of a murdered relative (*Akpinar v Turkey* (2007) Application No 56760/00 (unreported), paras 84–87) [**RCLP para 15.156**]. A punishment which involves a degree of humiliation and debasement which attains a particular level and which is other than that usual element of humiliation almost invariably involved in punishment will be considered degrading (*Kudla v Poland* (2002) 35 EHRR 11, paras 92–94) and see *Tyrer v United Kingdom* (1978) 2 EHRR 1, para 30 [**RCLP para 15.158**].

Corporal punishment—See *Tyrer v United Kingdom* (1978) 2 EHRR 1 and *Y v United Kingdom* (1992) 17 EHRR 238, para 42. The domestic defence of 'reasonable chastisement' does not provide adequate protection to the child against treatment contrary, or punishment contrary to Art 3 of the ECHR (*A v United Kingdom* (1999) 27 EHRR 611) [**RCLP paras 15.161 and 15.214**]. See also the Revised European Social Charter, Art 17(1)(b) (not yet ratified by the United Kingdom) [**RCLP paras 15.162–15.164**].

Detention—Acts of violence and physical force against detainees will amount to a violation of Art 3 unless the violence was not gratuitous and was at the minimum possible level and made strictly necessary by the conduct of the person complaining of a breach (*Tomasi v France* (1992) 15 EHRR, para 113 and *Veznedaroglu v Turkey*

(2001) 33 EHRR 1412, para 29) [**15.165**]. The detention of children on the grounds of their immigration status can give rise to breaches of Art 3 of the ECHR (*Mayeka v Belgium* (2008) 46 EHRR 23) [**RCLP para 15.166**].

Deportation—A Contracting State which deports or extradites a person is liable for any action the 'direct consequence' of which is the exposure of that deported individual to ill-treatment proscribed by Art 3 of the ECHR (*Mamatkulov v Turkey* (2003) 14 BHRC 149, para 66 and (2005) 41 EHRR 494 (Grand Chamber) and see also *Soering v United Kingdom* (1989) 11 EHRR 439, para 88) [**RCLP paras 15.167–15.168**]. Where it can be shown that the child is at risk of extra-judicial killing if deported this is likely to be dealt with under Art 3 rather than the Art 2 right to life (*Aspichi Dehwari v Netherlands* (2000) Application No 37014/97 (unreported) and *Abdurrahim Incedursum v Netherlands* (1999) Application No 33124/96 (unreported) but see also *MAR v United Kingdom* (1996) 23 EHRR CD 120 and *Bahddar v Netherlands* (1998) 26 EHRR 278) [**RCLP para 5.42**].

Derogation—Save in respect of deaths resulting from lawful acts of war, derogation in respect of Art 3 is not permitted (Art 15(2) and see *Saadi v Italy* (2008) BHRC 123, para 127) [**RCLP para 2.81**].

Article 4
Prohibition of slavery and forced labour

1. No one shall be held in slavery or servitude.

2. No one shall be required to perform forced or compulsory labour.

3. For the purpose of this Article the term "forced or compulsory labour" shall not include:

(a)   any work required to be done in the ordinary course of detention imposed according to the provisions of Article 5 of this Convention or during conditional release from such detention;

(b)   any service of a military character or, in case of conscientious objectors in countries where they are recognised, service exacted instead of compulsory military service;

(c)   any service exacted in case of an emergency or calamity threatening the life or well-being of the community;

(d)   any work or service which forms part of normal civic obligations.

Prohibition of slavery and forced labour—The right not to be held in slavery or servitude is an absolute right admitting of no exceptions (*Siliadin v France* (2005) 20 BHRC 654, paras 90 and 112). The same may be said of protection against forced or compulsory labour subject the narrowly construed exceptions in Art 4(1) (*Siliadin v France* (2005) 20 BHRC 654, paras 90 and 112) [**RCLP para 15.171**]. See also the ILO Forced Labour Convention (No 29) 1930, and the Supplementary Convention on the Abolition of Slavery, the Slave Trade, and Institutions and Practices Similar to Slavery [**RCLP para 15.172**].

'**slavery**' (Art 4(1))—The ECtHR adopts the definition of slavery contained in the Slavery Convention 1926, Art 1(1), namely 'the status or condition of a person over whom any or all of the powers attaching to the right of ownership are exercised' (*Siliadin v France* (2005) 20 BHRC 654, para 89) [**RCLP para 15.173**].

'**servitude**' (Art 4(1))—For the purposes of Art 4(1) 'servitude' means an obligation to provide one's services that is imposed by the use of coercion, and is to be linked with the concept of 'slavery' described above (*Siliadin v France* (2005) 20 BHRC 654, para 124 and see *Van Droogenbroeck v Belgium* B 44 (1980) Com Rep) [**RCLP para 15.175**]. See also *CN and V v France* (2012) Application No 67724/09 and *CN v United Kingdom* (2012) Application No 4239/08.

'**forced compulsory labour**' (Art 4(2))—The ILO Forced Labour Convention (No 29) is the starting point for interpreting the meaning of 'forced compulsory labour' (*Van der Mussele v Belgium* (1983) 6 EHRR 163, para 32). The term indicates physical or mental constraint and has been defined as work extracted from a person under threat of penalty for which he or she has not voluntary offered him or herself (*Van der Mussele v Belgium* (1983) 6 EHRR 163, para 33, *Siliadin v France* (2005) 20 BHRC 654, para 117 and *Reitmayr v Austria* (1995) 20 EHRR CD 89) [**RCLP para 15.176**].

Exceptions (Art 4(3))—Art 4(3) sets out exceptions to the prohibition on forced compulsory labour articulated by Art 4(2) [**RCLP para 15.177**]. It is not intended to limit the rights in Art 4(2) but rather to delimit them (*Schmidt v Germany* (1994) 18 EHRR 513, para 22 and see *Van der Mussele v Belgium* (1983) 6 EHRR 163, para 38) [**RCLP para 15.178**].

Article 5
Right to liberty and security

1. Everyone has the right to liberty and security of person. No one shall be deprived of his liberty save in the following cases and in accordance with a procedure prescribed by law:

(a) the lawful detention of a person after conviction by a competent court;

(b) the lawful arrest or detention of a person for non-compliance with the lawful order of a court or in order to secure the fulfilment of any obligation prescribed by law;

(c) the lawful arrest or detention of a person effected for the purpose of bringing him before the competent legal authority on reasonable suspicion of having committed an offence or when it is reasonably considered necessary to prevent his committing an offence or fleeing after having done so;

(d) the detention of a minor by lawful order for the purpose of educational supervision or his lawful detention for the purpose of bringing him before the competent legal authority;

(e) the lawful detention of persons for the prevention of the spreading of infectious diseases, of persons of unsound mind, alcoholics or drug addicts or vagrants;

(f) the lawful arrest or detention of a person to prevent his effecting an unauthorised entry into the country or of a person against whom action is being taken with a view to deportation or extradition.

2. Everyone who is arrested shall be informed promptly, in a language which he understands, of the reasons for his arrest and of any charge against him.

3. Everyone arrested or detained in accordance with the provisions of paragraph 1(c) of this Article shall be brought promptly before a judge or other officer authorised by law to exercise judicial power and shall be entitled to trial within a reasonable time or to release pending trial. Release may be conditioned by guarantees to appear for trial.

4. Everyone who is deprived of his liberty by arrest or detention shall be entitled to take proceedings by which the lawfulness of his detention shall be decided speedily by a court and his release ordered if the detention is not lawful.

5. Everyone who has been the victim of arrest or detention in contravention of the provisions of this Article shall have an enforceable right to compensation.

Right to liberty and security of person (Art 5(1))—The Council of Europe has expressly recognized the importance of have property preventative strategies in place with a view to avoiding the deprivation of children's liberty (Council of Europe Committee of Ministers Recommendation No R(87)20 on Social Reactions to Juvenile Delinquency (1987)) **[RCLP para 14.55]**.

Derogation—By contrast to Art 37 of the UNCRC States parties to the ECHR may derogate from Art 5 in times of war or other public emergency threatening the life of the nation (ECHR Art 15) **[RCLP para 14.55]**.

'liberty and security of person' (Art 5(1))—Art 5(1) of the ECHR contemplates physical liberty of the person (*Engel v Netherlands* (1976) 1 EHRR 647, para 58) **[RCLP para 14.56]**. The word 'security' serves simply to emphasise that the requirement that a person's liberty may not be deprived in an arbitrary fashion (*East African Asians v United Kingdom* (1973) Application No 4626/70 and *Bozano v France* (1986) 9 EHRR, para 54) **[RCLP para 14.56]**. Thus, the definitive object and purpose of Art 5 has been held to be that of ensuring that no one should be disposed of his or her liberty in an arbitrary manner (*Winterwerp v Netherlands* (1979) 2 EHRR 387, para 37; *Bozano v France* (1986) 9 EHRR 297, para 54 and *Engel v Netherlands* (1976) 1 EHRR 647, para 58) **[RCLP para 14.56]**. A deprivation of liberty will be considered arbitrary where it is not in keeping with the restrictions permissible under Art 5(1) or with the provisions of the ECHR generally (*Winterwerp v Netherlands* (1979) 2 EHRR 387, paras 37–39 and see *Van Droogenbroeck v Belgium* (1982) 4 EHRR 443, para 48; *Weeks v United Kingdom* (1987) 10 EHRR 293, para 49; *Bozano v France* (1986) 9 EHRR 297, para 54 and *Ashingdane v United Kingdom* (1985) 7 EHRR 528, para 44) **[RCLP para 14.57]**. No detention that is arbitrary can ever be regarded as lawful (*Winterwerp v Netherlands* (1979) 2 EHRR 387, paras 37–39) and any detention must be proportionate to the attainment of its purpose (*Winterwerp v Netherlands* (1979) 2 EHRR 387, paras 37–39, *Van Droogenbroeck v Belgium* (1982) 4 EHRR 443 and *Bouamar v Belgium* (1988) 11 EHRR 1, para 53. [RCLP para 14.57].

'deprived' (Art 5(1))—The word 'deprived' does not concern mere restrictions upon liberty of movement (for which see Art 2 of the Fourth Protocol (Art 2 4P) to which the United Kingdom is not party) (*Engel v Netherlands* (1976) 1 EHRR 647, para 58 and see also *Guzzardi v Italy* (1980) 3 EHRR 333, para 92 and *Raimondo v Italy* (1994) 18 EHRR 237, para 39) [RCLP para 14.58]. Art 5(1) is solely concerned with deprivation of liberty (*Guzzardi v Italy* (1980) 3 EHRR 333, para 93) [RCLP para 14.59]. In order to determine whether someone has been 'deprived of his liberty' within the meaning of Article 5, the starting point must be his concrete situation and account must be taken of a whole range of criteria such as the type, duration, effects and manner of implementation of the measure in question (*Guzzardi v Italy* (1980) 3 EHRR 333, para 92) [RCLP para 14.62]. The intention of the authorities in respect of the alleged deprivation will be a relevant factor (*X v Germany* 24 DR 158 (1981) at 161) [RCLP para 14.64]. In respect of the deprivation of a child's liberty the consent of the parents may be a relevant factor. However note that the decision of the ECtHR in *Nielsen v Denmark* (1988) 11 EHRR 175 concerning parental consent to the deprivation of liberty has been heavily criticised, the European Commission having recognised the seemingly obvious point missed by the majority of the Court that the case concerned 'detention in a psychiatric ward of a 12-year-old boy who was not mentally ill' (see *Nielsen v Denmark* DR 46 155 (1986)) [RCLP para 14.66]. It is suggested that, having regard to the decision of the European Commission, the force of the dissenting judgments in the European Court of Human Rights and the principles underpinning the application of Art 5 of the ECHR considered in the context of the Convention as a whole, that the decision of the court in *Nielsen v Denmark* cannot be considered safe and should not be relied upon [RCLP para 14.67]. The status of the individual will be relevant to whether a deprivation engages Art 5(1) (*Engel v Netherlands* (1976) 1 EHRR 647, para 59) [RCLP para 14.68]. Note that having the freedom to leave an area will only prevent a breach of Art 5(1) where that freedom is an effective one (*Amuur v France* (1996) 22 EHRR 533, para 48 and *SM and MT v Austria* (1993) 74 DR 179) [RCLP para 14.69]. The period of time for which a person is detained or imprisoned is a relevant but not an overriding factor in determining whether that detention or imprisonment is lawful (*X and Y v Sweden* 7 DR 123 (1976) and *X v Austria* 18 DR 154 (1979) and also *Bouamar v Belgium* (1987) 11 EHRR 1) [RCLP para 14.70].

Positive obligations—Art 5(1) imports positive obligations on States parties to protect the liberty of its citizens (*Storck v Germany* (2006) 43 EHRR 6, para 102) [RCLP para 14.60]. This will include the taking of effective measures to safeguard an individual's liberty and security of the person ensuring procedural measures for the prompt investigation of claims that a person has been deprived of their liberty (*Çakici v Turkey* (1999) 31 EHRR 133, para 104 and see also *Cicek v Turkey* (2003) 37 EHRR 20, para 164 and *Imakayeva v Russia* (2008) 27 EHRR 4, para 171) [RCLP para 14.61].

Permissible grounds for deprivation of liberty (Art 15(1)(a)-(f))—The list of permissible grounds for the deprivation of liberty contained in Art 5(1) is exhaustive (*Ireland v United Kingdom* (1978) 2 EHRR, para 194 and *Winterwerp v Netherlands* (1979) 2 EHRR 387, para 37) [RCLP para 14.71]. Further, the permissible grounds must be interpreted narrowly (*Winterwerp v Netherlands* (1979) 2 EHRR 387, para 37) and they are not mutually exclusive (*McVeigh, O'Neill and Evans v United Kingdom* 25 DR 15 (1981) and *Koniarska v United Kingdom* (2000) Application No 33670/96) [RCLP para 14.71]. For the proper test for determining whether a deprivation of liberty falls within one of the permissible lawful grounds see *R v Governor of Brockhill Prison ex p Evans (No 2)* [2001] 2 AC 19 at 38B–38E [RCLP para 14.72]. A detention must not only be lawful *per se* but must be carried out in accordance with a procedure prescribed by law (*Winterwerp v Netherlands* (1979) 2 EHRR 387, para 39; *Herczegfalvy v Austria* (1992) 15 EHRR 437, *Bozano v France* (1986) 9 EHRR 297, para 54, *Weeks v United Kingdom* (1987) 10 EHRR 293, para 42 and see also *E v Norway* (1990) 17 EHRR 30, para 49, *Caprino v United Kingdom* 12 DR 14 (1978) and *Öcalam v Turkey* (2003) 37 EHRR 288) [RCLP para 14.73].

Lawful detention after conviction (Art 15(1)(a))—The term 'conviction' means a finding of guilt in respect of an offence and the imposition of a penalty (*X v United Kingdom* (1981) 4 EHRR 188, para 39 and also *B v Austria* (1991) 13 EHRR 20, para 38). The word 'after' in Art 5(1)(a) denotes the need for a causal connection between the conviction and the deprivation of liberty (*Weeks v United Kingdom* (1987) 10 EHRR 293, para 42 and see also *Waite v United Kingdom* (2003) 36 EHRR 54). The term 'competent court' for the purposes of Art 5(1) means a body which gives to the individuals concerned guarantees appropriate to the kind of deprivation of liberty in question (*De Wilde, Ooms and Versyp v Belgium* (1971) 1 EHRR 373, para 76 and see *X v United Kingdom* (1981) 4 EHRR 188 and *Weeks v United Kingdom* (1987) 10 EHRR 293) [RCLP para 14.75].

Non-compliance with the law (Art 5(1)(b))—The order not complied with must be made by a court of competent jurisdiction, be capable of enforcement and denote clearly the nature of the conduct that is prohibited or the obligation that is required to be met (*Steel v United Kingdom* (1998) 28 EHRR 603 and *Hashman and Harrap v United Kingdom* (1999) 30 EHRR 241). The words 'to secure the fulfilment of any obligation prescribed by law' concern only those cases where the law permits the detention of a person to compel him to fulfil a 'specific and concrete' obligation which he has failed to satisfy (*Guzzardi v Italy* (1980) 3 EHRR 333, para 101) [**RCLP para 14.77**]. The fact that an order is *later* found to have been wrong in law will not necessarily retrospectively render the period of detention consequent upon the order unlawful for the purposes of Art 5(1) (*Douiyed v Netherlands* (2000) 30 EHRR 790, paras 44–45) [**RCLP para 14.78**].

Arrest on reasonable suspicion (Art 5(1)(c))—Art 5(1)(c) must be read in conjunction with Art 5(3) [**RCLP para 14.80**]. Art 5(1)(c) permits deprivation of liberty on the basis of reasonable suspicion only in connection with criminal proceedings (*Ciulla v Italy* (1989) 13 EHRR 346, para 38; *De Jong, Baljet and Van Den Brink v Netherlands* (1984) 8 EHRR 20 and *Guzzardi v Italy* (1980) 3 EHRR 333, para 102) and only for the purpose of bringing a person before the competent legal authority (*Ječius v Lithuania* (2002) 35 EHRR 400, paras 50–51) [**RCLP para 14.81**]. For the meaning of the term 'competent legal authority' see *Schiesser v Switzerland* (1979) 2 EHRR 417, para 29 [**RCLP para 14.81**]. Having a 'reasonable suspicion' presupposes the existence of facts or information which would satisfy an objective observer that the person concerned may have committed the offence (*Fox, Campbell and Hartley v United Kingdom* (1990) 13 EHRR 157, para 32 and see *X v Austria* (1989) 11 EHRR 112; *Murray v United Kingdom* (1994) 19 EHRR 193, para 55) [**RCLP para 14.82**].

Deprivation of the liberty of children (Art 5(1)(d))—Deprivation of liberty for the purposes of educational supervision as provided for by Art 5(1)(d) is not recognised in the UNCRC or any other international human rights instrument [**RCLP para 14.84**]. For the application of Art 5(1)(d) to the Children Act 1989, s 25 see *Koniarska v United Kingdom* (2000) Application No 33670/96 (unreported) and contrast the outcome in the case of *Bouamar v Belgium* (1988) 11 EHRR 1.

Medical and social reasons (Art 5(1)(e)—For deprivation of liberty due to infectious disease see *Enhorn v Sweden* (2005) 41 EHRR 633, para 43 [**RCLP para 14.88**]. Permitting the deprivation of liberty of persons of unsound mind Art 5(1)(e) of the ECHR does not permit the restriction of a person's liberty simply on the basis that their conduct differs from the norms which prevail within a particular society but rather only where (i) the behaviour of the person is of a nature to justify an 'emergency' confinement, (ii) other, less severe measures, have been considered and found to be insufficient to safeguard the individual or public interest which might require that the person concerned be detained such that the deprivation of liberty is necessary in the circumstances and (iii) he has he or she has been reliably shown to be of 'unsound mind' by reason a mental disorder of a kind or degree warranting compulsory confinement established on the basis of objective medical expertise (*Winterwerp v Netherlands* (1979) 2 EHRR 387, para 37) [**RCLP para 14.90**].

Vagrants and alcoholics—In respect of the deprivation of liberty of vagrants and alcoholics see *Guzzardi v Italy* (1980) 3 EHRR 333, para 98 [**RCLP para 14.91**].

Immigration, deportation and extradition—The word 'lawful' in Art 5(1)(f) of the ECHR means both lawful under domestic law and not arbitrary (*De Jong, Baljet and Van Den Brink v Netherlands* (1984) 8 EHRR 20 and *Bozano v France* (1986) 9 EHRR 297, para 54). The deprivation of liberty, insofar as it is justified under Art 5(1)(f) will only remain justified whilst the deportation or extradition proceedings subsist, there being a requirement to prosecute those proceedings with due diligence (*Lynas v Switzerland* 6 DR 141 (1976) and *Chahal v United Kingdom* (1997) 23 EHRR 413, paras 113–117) [**RCLP para 15.93**].

Prompt information on arrest and charge (Art 5(2))—The language used must be language that the detained person will understand (*Lamy v Belgium* (1989) 11 EHRR 529, para 31 and *Van der Leer v Netherlands* (1990) 12 EHRR 567, paras 27–29) [**RCLP para 14.95**]. The language used to indicate the reason for arrest and the nature of any charge will be particularly important in relation to providing information to children (*Fox, Campbell and Hartley v United Kingdom* (1990) 13 EHRR 157, para 40) [**RCLP para 14.96**].

'promptly' (Art 5(3))—The French text of Art 5(3) the ECHR uses the word 'aussitôt' which denotes more urgency than the English word 'promptly' (*Brogan v United Kingdom* (1988) 11 EHRR 117, paras 58 and 59) [**RCLP para 14.99**]. Whilst promptness must be assessed according to the features of each case (*De Jong, Baljet and Van Den Brink v Netherlands* (1984) 8 EHRR 20, para 52) those features must never be permitted to impair the essence of the right guaranteed by Art 5(3) of the ECHR (*Koster v Netherlands* (1991) 14 EHRR 396, para 24 and *TW v Malta* (2000) 29 EHRR 185, para 41) [**RCLP para 14.99**].

'judge or other officer authorised by law' (Art 5(3))—See *Schiesser v Switzerland* (1979) 2 EHRR 417, para 29. The 'judge' or judicial 'officer' must actually hear the detained person before taking the appropriate decision (*De Jong, Baljet and Van Den Brink v Netherlands* (1984) 8 EHRR 20, para 51; *Assenov v Bulgaria* (1998) 28 EHRR 652, para 146 and *TW v Malta* (2000) 29 EHRR 185, para 44 and see also *McGoff v Sweden* 31 DR 72 (1982)) [**RCLP para 14.100**].

'trial within a reasonable time or to release pending trial' (Art 5(3))—Note that the use of the word 'or' in the phrase 'trial within a reasonable time or to release pending trial' does not mean that a prompt trial is an alternative to release pending trial (*Nuemeister v Austria* (1968) 1 EHRR 91) [**RCLP para 14.101**]. The criteria for continued detention are strict (*Kudla v Poland* (2002) 35 EHRR 11, paras 110–111 and see also *Grisez v Belgium* (2003) 36 EHRR 854, para 49) [**RCLP para 14.101**]. The need for trial within a reasonable time is particularly acute in relation to children (*Assenov v Bulgaria* (1998) 28 EHRR 652) [**RCLP para 14.102**]. The burden of demonstrating that the criteria for continued pre-trial detention are satisfied remains on the authorities (*Letellier v France* (1991) 14 EHRR 83, para 35, *Ilijkov v Bulgaria* (2001) Application 33977/96 (unreported), paras 84–85 and *R (O) v Harrow Crown Court and another* [2006] UKHL 42, [2007] 1 AC 249, paras 27–28) [**RCLP para 14.102**].

'**Release may be conditioned by guarantees to appear for trial**' (Art 5(3))—Bail may only be refused on relatively narrow grounds, namely (i) a risk that the accused will fail to appear for trial (*Nuemeister v Austria* (1968) 1 EHRR 91) (ii) a risk that there will be interference with the course of justice (*Wemhoff v Germany* (1968) 1 EHRR 5) (iii) the need to prevent further offences (*Clooth v Belgium* (1991) 14 EHRR 717, para 40) and (iv) the need to preserve of public order (*Letellier v France* (1991) 14 EHRR 83, para 51) [**RCLP para 14.103**].

Habeas Corpus (Art 5(4))—The claim of *habeas corpus* is the fundamental instrument for safeguarding individual freedom against arbitrary or unlawful state action (*Harris v Nelson* 394 US 286, 290–91 (1969) and *R v Bournewood Community and Mental Health NHS Trust ex p L (Secretary of State for Health and others intervening)* [1998] 2 FCR 501). Art 5(4) guarantees the right to *habeas corpus* [**RCLP para 14.105**]. The minimum requirements constituting 'a court' for the purposes of Art 5(4) are the same as for Art 5(1)(a) [**RCLP para 14.107**]. Within the process determining whether the deprivation of liberty is lawful there should be equality of arms (*Toth v Austria* (1991) 14 EHRR 551, para 84 and *Megyeri v Germany* (1992) 15 EHRR 584, para 22) [**RCLP para 14.107**].

Article 6
Right to a fair trial

1. In the determination of his civil rights and obligations or of any criminal charge against him, everyone is entitled to a fair and public hearing within a reasonable time by an independent and impartial tribunal established by law. Judgment shall be pronounced publicly but the press and public may be excluded from all or part of the trial in the interests of morals, public order or national security in a democratic society, where the interests of juveniles or the protection of the private life of the parties so require, or to the extent strictly necessary in the opinion of the court in special circumstances where publicity would prejudice the interests of justice.

2. Everyone charged with a criminal offence shall be presumed innocent until proved guilty according to law.

3. Everyone charged with a criminal offence has the following minimum rights:

   (a) to be informed promptly, in a language which he understands and in detail, of the nature and cause of the accusation against him;
   (b) to have adequate time and facilities for the preparation of his defence;
   (c) to defend himself in person or through legal assistance of his own choosing or, if he has not sufficient means to pay for legal assistance, to be given it free when the interests of justice so require;
   (d) to examine or have examined witnesses against him and to obtain the attendance and examination of witnesses on his behalf under the same conditions as witnesses against him;
   (e) to have the free assistance of an interpreter if he cannot understand or speak the language used in court.

Right to a fair trial (Art 6(1))—The object and purpose of Art 6 of the ECHR has been stated to be to 'enshrine the fundamental principle of the rule of law' by protecting the right to a fair trial and in particular the right to be presumed innocent (*Salabiaku v France* (1988) 13 EHRR 379, para 28 and see also *Golder v United Kingdom* (1975) 1 EHRR 524, para 35) [**RCLP para 16.73**]. Art 6 applies to both criminal and civil proceedings, although State parties have a wider margin of appreciation in respect of the latter (*Dombo Beheer v Netherlands* (1993) 18 EHRR 213, para 32 and see *Albert and Le Compte v Belgium* (1983) 5 EHRR 533, para 30) [**RCLP para 16.74**]. Whilst the right to a fair trial under Art 6(1) is absolute several of the ancillary rights under Art 6 are not, including the right to disclosure of relevant evidence (*R v H* [2004] UKHL 3, [2004] 2 AC 134) [**RCLP para 9.85**]. The rights enshrined in Art 6 of the ECHR as a whole must be given a broad and purposive interpretation (*Delcourt v Belgium* (1970) 1 EHRR 355, para 25) [RCLP para 16.73]. For examples of civil disputes involving children in which Art 6(1) has been held to be engaged see [RCLP para 16.76].

Art 6 and children—Whilst applying to children, Art 6 does not enshrine child specific rights and must be interpreted in accordance with Art 40 of the UNCRC and the UN Standard Minimum Rules for the Administration of Juvenile Justice (the 'Beijing Rules') (see G Van Bueren *Child Rights in Europe* (2007, Council of Europe Publishing), p 111) [RCLP para 16.75]. See also *Blokhin v Russia* (2013) Application No 47152/06.

Need for a dispute—Art 6 is engaged in relation to the determination of a criminal charge and in relation to civil rights and obligations in respect of which there is an actionable domestic claim as a matter of substantive law (*H v Belgium* (1987) 10 EHRR 339, para 40). Art 6 will also apply to disputes of a 'genuine and serious nature' concerning the actual existence of the right as well as to the scope or manner in which it is exercised (*Markovic v Italy* 44 EHRR 1045, para 93 and see also *TP and KM v United Kingdom* (2001) 34 EHRR 42, para 94) [RCLP para 16.77].

'determination of his civil rights and obligations' (Art 6(1))—To engage Art 6 the civil rights and obligations in question must be the object, or one of the objects, of the dispute, whether as between individuals or as between individuals and the State, and the result of the proceedings must be directly decisive of such a right or obligation (*Süßmann v Germany* (1996) 25 EHRR 64, paras 39 and 41 and *Ringeisen v Austria* (1971) 1 EHRR 455, para 94) [RCLP para 16.79]. In determining whether the right or obligation at issue is a 'civil right or obligation' for the purposes of Art 6(1) the character of that right rather than the identity or nature of the parties is key (*Stran Greek Refineries and Stratis Andreadis v Greece* (1994) EHRR 293, para 39) [RCLP para 16.80]. The classification of a civil right in domestic law is not decisive (*Feldbrugge v Netherlands* (1986) 8 EHRR 425, para 29) and the rights and obligations between private individuals are always civil rights and obligations for the purposes of Art 6 (*Airey v Ireland* (1979) 2 EHRR 305) [RCLP para 16.80].

'determination of … any criminal charge' (Art 6(1))—Whether proceedings are 'criminal' for the purposes of Art 6(1) falls be determined by consideration of the classification of proceedings in domestic law, the nature of the offence and the severity of the penalty which may be imposed (which will often be the determinative factor), which factors will be alternative and not cumulative (*Engel v Netherlands* (1976) 1 EHRR 647 and para 82 and *Lutz v Germany* (1998) 10 EHRR 182, para 55 and see also *Brown v United Kingdom* (1998) 28 EHRR CD 233 and *R (McCann) v Manchester Crown Court* [2002] UKHL 39, [2003] 1 AC 787, para 30) [RCLP para 16.81]. A person will be the subject of a 'charge' for the purposes of Art 6(1) where that person is 'substantially affected' by the proceedings (*X v United Kingdom* 14 DR 26 (1978) [RCLP para 16.82].

Right of access to the court—The right of access to the court is inherent in Art 6(1) (*Golder v United Kingdom* (1975) 1 EHRR 524) [RCLP para 16.83]. The right of access is not however absolute and States may regulate access according to the needs and resources of the community and of individuals within the margin of appreciation (*Golder v United Kingdom* (1975) 1 EHRR 524, para 38) but the regulation of access must not impair the very essence of the right, must pursue a legitimate aim and must comply with the principle of proportionality (*Ashingdane v United Kingdom* (1985) 7 EHRR 528, para 57, *Stubbings v United Kingdom* (1996) 23 EHRR 213, para 48 and see also *Golder v United Kingdom* (1975) 1 EHRR 524, para 39) [RCLP para 16.84]. Any limitation must also be legally certain (*Société Levage Prestations v France* (1996) 24 EHRR 351) [RCLP para 16.84]. The right of access to the court requires that access be effective (*Airey v Ireland* (1979) 2 EHRR 305, para 26 and *Steel and Morris v United Kingdom* (2005) 41 EHRR 403) [RCLP para 16.85]. Effective access is particularly important for children in the context of cases concerning the child's relationship with his or her parents (*MLB v SLJ* 516 US 102 (1996), US Supreme Court) [RCLP para 16.85]. The right of effective access to the Court under Art 6(1) does not guarantee a right of appeal but where the national law provides a right of appeal Art 6 will apply to those appeal proceedings (*Delcourt v Belgium* (1970) 1 EHRR 35) [RCLP para 16.85]. For legal aid and the right to effective access see [RCLP para 16.86]. The right of access to the court pursuant to Art 6(1) of the ECHR requires that States make available a process by which administrative decisions can be challenged before a judicial body with full jurisdiction providing the guarantees enshrined in Art 6(1) (*Albert and Le Compte v Belgium* (1983) 5 EHRR 533, para 29). For the meaning of 'full jurisdiction' see the opinion of Judge Bratza in *Bryan v United Kingdom* (1995) 21 EHRR 342. See also *W v United Kingdom* (1987) 10 EHRR 29, para 82 and *Re S (Minors) (Care Order: Implementation of Care Plan)* [2002] UKHL 10, [2002] 2 AC 291, para 79 [RCLP para 16.87]. The right to effective access to the court implies a right to reasonable notice of administrative decisions in order that a challenge may be mounted in court if necessary (*De La Pradelle v France* (1992) A 253-B, para 34) [RCLP para 16.87]. For the right to effective access to the court as it relates to limitation periods see [RCLP para 16.88].

Right to a fair hearing (Art 6(1))—To establish whether a hearing has been fair the court will look at the proceedings as a whole (*Barberá, Messegué and Jabardo v Spain* (1988) 11 EHRR 360, para 68 and see also *Delcourt v Belgium* (1970) 1 EHRR 355, para 31 and *Borgers v Belgium* (1991) 15 EHRR 93, para 24) including whether any decision of appeal is capable of remedying unfairness which occurs at first instance (*Edwards v United Kingdom* (1993) 15 EHRR 417, paras 36–37 and *Rowe and Davis v United Kingdom* (2000) 30 EHRR 1, para 65) and the implementation of judicial decisions (*Hornsby v Greece* (1997) 24 EHRR 250, paras 40–41 and *Ryabykh v Russian* (2005) 40 EHRR 615, para 51) [RCLP para 16.89]. The right to a fair hearing is itself comprised of a number of cardinal rights, namely the right to a hearing in ones presence, equality of arms, access to evidence, the right to freedom from self incrimination and the right to a reasoned judgment.

Right to a hearing on ones presence—The presence of the accused at a criminal trial is an essential requirement of fairness (*Ekbatani v Sweden* (1988) 13 EHRR 504, para 25 and see also *Raja v Van Hoogstraten* [2004] EWCA Civ 968, [2004] 4 All ER 793, para 94) and a procedure which determines civil rights without hearing the parties cannot comply with Art 6(1) (*Karakasis v Greece* (2003) 36 EHRR 507, para 26 and *Góç v Turkey* (2002) 35 EHRR 134, para 47) [RCLP para 16.90]. For the application of the right to a hearing in ones presence in relation to criminal trials involving children see *V and T v United Kingdom* (1999) 30 EHRR 121, paras 85–91 [RCLP para 16.91].

Equality of arms—The principle of equality of arms provides that a party to proceedings must have a reasonable opportunity of presenting his or her case in a manner which does not place him or her at a substantial disadvantage compared to his or her opponent [RCLP para 16.93]. For children accused of serious criminal offences, this will require a specially adapted procedure which promotes the child's welfare, respects his or her privacy and enables him or her to understand and participate fully in the proceedings on an equal footing (*T and V v United Kingdom* (2000) 30 EHRR 121 and *SC v United Kingdom* (2005) 40 EHRR 226, para 27) [RCLP para 16.93]. This principle will apply equally in proceedings concerning state intervention in the child's family (*Buchberger v Austria* (2003) 37 EHRR 356, para 50 and *S v Principal Reporter and the Lord Advocate* [2001] UKHRR 514) [RCLP para 16.93]. In relation to administrative decisions, the principle of equality of arms will require that a party be informed of the detailed reasons for the decision to enable the applicant to mount a reasoned challenge to it (*Hentrich v France* (1994) 18 EHRR 440, para 56) [RCLP para 16.94]. The principle of 'equality of arms' also requires that each party must be given the opportunity to have knowledge of and comment on the evidence adduced by the other party [RCLP para 16.95]. This will include those where, by reason of them being concerned with the welfare of children, a less 'adversarial' approach is adopted (*McMichael v United Kingdom* (1995) 20 EHRR 205, para 80 and see also *McGinley and Egan v United Kingdom* (1998) 27 EHRR 1, para 86) [RCLP para 16.96].

Freedom from self incrimination—The right to silence and the right to freedom from self incrimination have been held to be generally recognised international standards which lie at the heart of the notion of a fair procedure under Art 6(1) (*Weh v Austria* (2005) 40 EHRR 37, para 39) [RCLP para 16.97]. In order to determine whether the essence of the applicant's right to remain silent and his or her privilege against self-incrimination has been infringed, the Court will focus on the nature and degree of compulsion used to obtain the evidence, the existence of any relevant safeguards in the procedure, and the use to which any material so obtained was put (*O'Halloran and Francis v United Kingdom* (2008) 46 EHRR 397, paras 55–57) [RCLP para 16.97]. The right to silence is not absolute (*O'Halloran and Francis v United Kingdom* (2008) 46 EHRR 397, paras 55–57) [RCLP para 16.98].

Right to a reasoned judgment—The ambit of the right to a reasoned judgment is dependent on the circumstances of the case (*Ruiz Torrija v Spain* (1994) 19 EHRR 553, para 29 and see also *Karakasis v Greece* (2003) 36 EHRR 507, para 27 and *Hirvisaari v Finland* (2004) 38 EHRR 139, para 30) [RCLP para 16.99].

Right to a public hearing (Art 6(1))—Art 6(1) enshrines the right to a public hearing save where the press and the public may be excluded from all or part of the hearing in the interests of morals, public order or national security in a democratic society, where the interests of juveniles or the protection of the private life of the parties require a private hearing or to the extent strictly necessary in the opinion of the court in special circumstances where publicity would prejudice the interests of justice [RCLP para 16.100]. Any waiver of this right must be made in an unequivocal manner and must not run counter to any important public interest (*Schuler-Zgraggen v Switzerland* (1993) 16 EHRR 405, para 58. See also *Zumtobel v Austria* (1993) 17 EHRR 116, para 34) [RCLP para 16.100]. The words 'in the interests of juveniles' in Art 6(1) appear to be a lower test than the best interests criterion, but the ECHR must be interpreted by reference to Art 3(1) of the UNCRC which will necessarily import the customary international law status of best interests into consideration of the application of Art 6(1) [RCLP para 16.101]. For the exclusion of the right to a public hearing in cases concerning children see *V v United Kingdom* (2000) 30 EHRR 121, para 87 and *B and P v United Kingdom* (2002) 34 EHRR 529 [RCLP paras 16.102 and 16.103].

Right to public pronouncement of judgment (Art 6(1))—The right to the public pronouncement of judgment is not subject to the limitations in Art 6(1) governing the exclusion of the press and the public (*Campbell and Fell v United Kingdom* (1984) 7 EHRR 165, para 90 and see also *Pretto v Italy* (1983) 6 EHRR 182, para 26) [RCLP para 16.104].

Right to a hearing within a reasonable time (Art 6(1))—In calculating whether the period of time in issue is 'reasonable' for the purposes of Art 6(1) in both criminal and civil cases the length of proceedings must be assessed in the light of the circumstances of the case and particularly the complexity of the case and the conduct of the applicant (*Fedorov v Russia* (2006) 43 EHRR 943, para 28 and see *König v Germany* (1978) 2 EHRR 170, paras 104–105 and *H v United Kingdom* (1987) 10 EHRR 95, paras 83–86) and the authorities (*Vilho Eskelinen v Finland* (2007) 45 EHRR 43, paras 67–71 and see *McFarlane v Ireland* (2010) Application No 31333/06, para 140) [**RCLP para 16.105**]. See also *Cengiz Kiliç v Turkey* (2011) Application No 16192/06. Note that the existence of any possibility or right on the part of the applicant to take steps to expedite does not dispense the State from ensuring that the proceedings progressed reasonably quickly (see *McFarlane v Ireland* (2010) Application No 31333/06, para 152) [**RCLP para 16.105**]. The threshold for proving that the period in question is unreasonable for the purposes of Art 6(1) of the ECHR is a high one (*Dyer (Procurator Fiscal), Linlithgow v Watson and another; K v Lord Advocate* [2002] UKPC D1, [2002] 3 WLR 1488, para 52 and see also *A-G's Reference (No 2 of 2001)* [2003] UKHL 68, [2004] 2 AC 72) [**RCLP para 16.105**]. The period of time to be considered runs, in civil cases, from the initiation of proceedings (*Guincho v Portugal* (1984) 7 EHRR 233, para 29) although time may in certain cases begin to run prior to the issue of proceedings (*Golder v United Kingdom* (1975) 1 EHRR 524, para 32 and *König v Germany* (1978) 2 EHRR 170, para 98) and in criminal cases the time will run from charge (*Schaal v Luxembourg* (2005) 41 EHRR 1071, para 35 and see *McFarlane v Ireland* (2010) Application No 31333/06, para 143) and will continue to run until the definitive determination of the proceedings, including any appeal (*König v Germany* (1978) 2 EHRR 170, para 98) [**RCLP para 16.106**]. It is essential that cases involving children are dealt with speedily (*Hokkanen v Finland* (1994) 19 EHRR 139, para 72) and in proceedings in which the separation of children from their parents is being contemplated, 'exceptional diligence' is required in respect of ensuring proceedings are determined within a reasonable time (*Johansen v Norway* (1996) 23 EHRR 33, para 88 and see also *H v United Kingdom* (1987) 10 EHRR 95, para 85) [**RCLP para 16.107**].

Right to an independent tribunal established by law (Art 6(1))—The word 'tribunal' in Art 6(1) means a body which has the jurisdiction to examine all questions of fact and law relevant to the dispute before it (*Terra Woningen v Netherlands* (1996) 24 EHRR 456, para 52) [**RCLP para 16.108**]. To establish whether a tribunal is independent for the purposes of Art 6(1) regard must be had to, amongst other factors, the manner of appointment of the members of the tribunal, to their term of office, to the existence of guarantees against outside pressure being exerted on the tribunal and to whether the tribunal body presents an appearance of independence (*Bryan v United Kingdom* (1995) 21 EHRR 342, para 37) and the appearance of independence is an objective test bearing in mind the importance of justice not only being done but being seen to be done (*Campbell and Fell v United Kingdom* (1984) 7 EHRR 165, para 81) [**RCLP para 16.109**]. Impartial for the purpose of Art 6(1) of the ECHR equals an absence of prejudice or bias (*Piersack v Belgium* (1982) 5 EHRR 169, para 30 and *Fey v Austria* (1993) 16 EHRR 387, para 30 and see also *Porter v Magill* [2001] UKHL 67, [2002] 2 AC 357) [**RCLP para 16.110**].

Right to be informed promptly of accusation (Art 6(3)(a))—Positive steps must be take by the authorities to ensure that the accused has been informed of the accusation (*Brozicek v Italy* (1989) 12 EHRR 371, paras 38–42) [**RCLP para 16.115**].

Adequate time and facilities to prepare a defence (Art 6(3)(b))—In determining the adequacy of the time allowed the court will take into account the complexity of the case (*Albert and Le Compte v Belgium* (1983) 5 EHRR 533, para 41) and there is a positive duty on the State to ensure the application of Art 6(3)(b) in each case (*Jespers v Belgium* 27 DR 61 (1981)) [**RCLP para 16.116**].

The right to defend in person (Art 6(3)(c))—The right to defend in person under does not extend a right to be represented by a lay-person (*Mayzit v Russia* (2005) Application No 63378/00 (unreported), para 70) [**RCLP para 16.118**].

The right to legal representation (Art 6(3)(c))—The legal representation secured for the purposes of Art 6(3)(c) must be effective legal representation (*Artico v Italy* (1980) 3 EHRR 1, para 36) [**RCLP para 16.118**]. For legal aid in criminal proceedings see [**RCLP para 16.119**]. See also *Nechiporuk and Yonkalo v Ukraine* (2011) Application No 42310/04 and *Husevn and Others v Azerbaijan* (2011) Application No 35485/05, 45553/05, 35680/05 and 36085/05.

Right to call and examine witnesses (Art 6(3)(d))—The term 'witness' has an 'autonomous' meaning in the Convention system (*Lucà v Italy* (2003) 36 EHRR 46, para 41) and the right to call and examine witnesses pursuant to Art 6(3)(d) of the ECHR implies a right to have the information necessary to do so (*Sadak v Turkey* (2003) 36 EHRR 431, para 65) [**RCLP para 16.120**]. All the evidence must normally be produced at a public hearing, in the presence of the accused, with a view to adversarial argument (*Kostovski v Netherlands* (1989) 12 EHRR 434, paras 40–41). For the exceptions to this principle see [**RCLP para 16.121**]. The fact that the relevant witness is a child will not relieve a State party from its obligations under Art 6(3)(d) of the ECHR although modifications to procedures are permitted to ensure the welfare of the child witness (*Bocos-Cuesta v Netherlands* (2005) Application No 54789/00, para 71 and *AS v Finland* (2010) Application No 40156/07, paras 55–56) [**RCLP para 16.122**].

Right to the free assistance of an interpreter (Art 6(3)(e))—The right to the free assistance from an interpreter is absolute (*Luedicke, Belkacem and Koç v Germany* (1978) 2 EHRR 149, para 40) **[RCLP para 16.123]**. The right applies not only to oral statements made at the trial hearing but also to documentary material and the pre-trial proceedings (*Hermi v Italy* (2008) 46 EHRR 1115, paras 69–70) **[RCLP para 16.124]**.

Art 6 and the child's right to participate—Art 6 requires the appearance of the fair administration of justice which in turn demands that a party must be able to participate effectively by being able to put forward the matters in support of his or her claims (*P, C and S v United Kingdom* [2002] 2 FLR 631). Thus, for example despite secure accommodation proceedings not qualifying as criminal proceedings for the purposes of Art 6 of the ECHR, the rights accorded by Art 6(3) should be accorded to children who are the subject of such proceedings as a matter of procedural fairness under English common law (*Re C (Secure Accommodation Order: Representation)* [2001] EWCA Civ 458, [2001] 2 FLR 169) **[RCLP para 6.76]**. The fair trial guaranteed by Art 6 is not confined to the 'purely judicial' part of proceedings concerning children and also encompasses 'administrative' proceedings concerning children, providing support for the child's right to participate within the context of administrative proceedings and decision making processes (*Re L (Care: Assessment Fair Trial)* [2002] EWHC 1379 (Fam), [2002] 2 FLR 730 and *Mantovanelli v France* Application No 21497/93 (1997) 24 EHRR 370) **[RCLP para 6.77]**.

Article 7
No punishment without law

1. No one shall be held guilty of any criminal offence on account of any act or omission which did not constitute a criminal offence under national or international law at the time when it was committed. Nor shall a heavier penalty be imposed than the one that was applicable at the time the criminal offence was committed.

2. This Article shall not prejudice the trial and punishment of any person for any act or omission which, at the time when it was committed, was criminal according to the general principles of law recognised by civilised nations.

No retrospective application of the penal law (Art 7(1))—Art 7 prohibits the retrospective application of the penal law and sentencing law (see *Waddington v Miah* [1974] 1 WLR 683 at 694 for consideration of Art 7 in a domestic context) **[RCLP para 16.126]**. Art 7 embodies more generally the principle that only the law can define a crime and prescribe a penalty (*Kokkinakis v Greece* (1993) 17 EHRR 397 at, para 52) **[RCLP para 16.126]**. Art 7(1) should be construed and applied, as follows from its object and purpose, so as to provide effective safeguards against arbitrary prosecution, conviction and punishment (*Kononov v Latvia* (2010) Application No 36376/04, para 185) **[RCLP para 16.126]**. Note however that, notwithstanding the plain words of Art 7 that 'Nor shall a heavier penalty be imposed than the one that was applicable at the time the criminal offence was committed' both the European Court of Human Rights and the domestic courts have held that there is no violation of Art 7 where a child is sentenced on the basis of the sentencing tariff applicable at the date of sentence as opposed to that applicable at the date of the commission of the offence (*Taylor v United Kingdom* (1999) Application No 48864/99 (unreported) and see *R v Bowker* (2008) 1 Cr App R (s) 72) **[RCLP para 16.127]**. *Taylor v United Kingdom* and *R v Bowker* are however hard to square with the plain wording of Art 7 of the ECHR and must be doubted **[RCLP para 16.128]**.

Article 8
Right to respect for private and family life

1. Everyone has the right to respect for his private and family life, his home and his correspondence.

2. There shall be no interference by a public authority with the exercise of this right except such as is in accordance with the law and is necessary in a democratic society in the interests of national security, public safety or the economic well-being of the country, for the prevention of disorder or crime, for the protection of health or morals, or for the protection of the rights and freedoms of others.

Right to respect for private and family life—The scope of Art 8 is clearly very wide (*R (Wright) v Secretary of State for Health* [2006] EWHC 2886 (Admin), [2007] 1 All ER 825 and [2009] UKHL 3, [2009] AC 739, para 30) **[RCLP para 8.171]**. Art 8 must be interpreted in light of the provisions of the UNCRC (*Sahin v Germany; Sommerfield v Germany* [2003] 2 FLR 671, p 680, para 39, *Juppala v Finland* [2009] 1 FLR 617, paras 23 and 41, *Pini v Bertani; Manera and Atripaldi v Romania* Application Nos 78028/01 and 78030/01 [2005] 2 FLR 596, para 139, *S and another v The United Kingdom* [2008] All ER (D) 56 (Dec), para 124, *Keegan* *v Ireland* [1994] 3 FCR 165, para 50 and *Mubilanzila Mayeka and Kaniki Mitunga v Belgium* [2007] 1 FLR 1726, para 83) **[RCLP paras 3.78–3.79]**. Interference with the family life of the child will be considered arbitrary unless it can be said to fall within the justifications set out in Art 8(2) (*Kroon v Netherlands* (1994) 19 EHRR 263) **[RCLP para 8.172]**. Art 8 must be considered a cardinal principle in domestic law (*Re MA (Care Threshold)* [2010] 1 FLR 431) and the domestic courts will apply with rigor the jurisprudence in respect of Art 8 that seeks to draw the appropriate boundary between the family and the State, both in judicial proceedings (*Re B (Care: Interference with Family Life)* [2003] EWCA Civ 786, [2003] 2 FLR 813, *R (P) v Secretary of State for the Home Department; R (Q) v Secretary of State for the Home Department* [2001] EWCA Civ 1151, [2001] 2 FLR 1122, *Re C (Care Proceeding: Disclosure of the Local Authority's Decision Making Process)* [2002] EWHC 1379 (Fam), [2002] 2 FCR 673 and *CF v Secretary of State for the Home Department* [2004] EWHC 111 (Fam), [2004] 2 FLR 517) and more widely (*Ghaidan v Mendoza* [2004] UKHL 30, [2004] 2 AC 557 and the dissenting judgment of Baroness Hale in *M v Secretary of State for Work and Pensions* [2006] UKHL 11, [2006] 2 AC 91) **[RCLP para 235]**. For the application of Art 8 to specific situations see **[RCLP paras 8.181–8.216]** and *Pontes v Portugal* (2012) Application No 19554/09 (contact with children in care), *Santos Nunes v Portugal* (2012) Application No 61173/08 (enforcement of custody (residence) orders), *A, K and L v Croatia* (2013) Application No 37956/11 (consent to placement for adoption), *Ilker Ensa Uyanik v Turkey* (2012) Application No 60328/09 and *Raw and Others v France* (2013) Application No 10131/11 (child abduction) and *B (No 2) v Romania* (2013) Application No 1285/03 and *RMS v Spain* (2013) Application No 28775/12 (taking children into care).

Art 8 and best interests—The recent decisions of the European Court of Human Rights have held that in all decisions concerning children the child's best interests will be paramount (*R and H v United Kingdom* [2011] 2 FLR 1236, para 73 and *YC v United Kingdom* (2012) 55 EHRR 967, para 134). It however remains unclear how the decisions in *R and H v United Kingdom* [2011] 2 FLR 1236 and *YC v United Kingdom* (2012) 55 EHRR 967 accord with the long line of authority, beginning with *Johansen v Norway* (1996) 23 EHRR 33, which stipulates that the correct approach to the child's best interests under Art 8 is to strike a 'fair balance' between the interests of the child and those of the parent, attaching particular importance to the best interest of the child, which interests, depending on their nature and seriousness, *may* override those of the parent: *Johansen v Norway* (1996) 23 EHRR 33, para 78. Prior to its decisions in *R and H v United Kingdom* [2011] 2 FLR 1236 and *YC v United Kingdom* (2012) 55 EHRR 967 the European Court of Human Rights has repeatedly cited the 'fair balance' test articulated in *Johansen v Norway* rather than relying on the 'paramount interests' formulation, by which latter formulation the child's best interests will always take priority over the rights of the child's parents rather than being placed in a fair balance with them (see for example *Frette v France* [2003] 2 FLR 9, para 42, *Hasse v Germany* [2004] 2 FLR 39, para 93; *Pini and Bertani; Manera v Antripaldi v Romania* [2005] 2 FLR 596, para 155; *HK v Finland* [2007] 1 FLR 633, para 109 and *Dolhamre v Sweden* [2010] 2 FLR 912, para 111) **[RCLP paras 4.143–4.150 and 4.169–4.175]**.

Art 8 and non-discrimination—It is a breach of Art 8 read with Art 14 to treat an unmarried father less favourably than a married father in respect of contact to his children (*Sommerfield v Germany* (2003) 36 EHRR 565, paras 51 and 55 and (2003) 38 EHRR 756, paras 93–94 and see also *PM v United Kingdom* (2005) 18 BHRC 668) or to treat parents differently in respect of contact based on their sexual orientation (*Salguiero Da Silva Mouta v Portugal* (1999) Application No 33290/96 (unreported)) or religious convictions (*Hoffman v Austria* (1993) 17 EHRR 293 and see also *Palau-Martinez v France* (2003) 41 EHRR 136, [2004] 2 FLR 810, *Ismailova v Russia* [2008] 1 FLR 533 and *Vojnity v Hungary* (2013) Application No 29617) **[RCLP para 8.63]**. It is a breach of Art 8 read with Art 14 to prevent the adoption of a child by an unmarried couple (*Re P (Adoption: Unmarried Couple)* [2008] UKHL 38, [2008] 2 FLR 1084) or on the basis of a person's sexual orientation (*EB v France* [2008] 1 FLR 850, *Gas and Dubois v France* (2012) Application No 25951/07 and *X and Others v Austria* (2013) Application No 19010/07) **[RCLP para 8.63]**. For differences in treatment that may be justified see *AL (Serbia) v Secretary of State for the Home Department* [2008] UKHL 42, [2008] 4 All ER 1127 and *Stec v United Kingdom* (2006) 20 BHRC 348 and **[RCLP para 8.64]**.

Positive obligations and Art 8—Positive obligations to secure respect for family and private life will arise where there is a direct and immediate link established between the measures sought by the applicant and the applicant's family life (*Botta v Italy* (1998) 26 EHRR 241, para 34 and see *Kroon v Netherlands* (1994) 19 EHRR 263 and *X & Y v The Netherlands*(1985) 8 EHRR 235) **[RCLP paras 8.174-8.175]**. The positive duties under Art 8 will also lead to 'horizontality' of effect such that Art 8 rights will operate not only to protect individuals from the actions of the State, but also to protect individuals through the agency of the State from the actions of other individuals (*Hokkanen v Finland* (1994) 19 EHRR 139, [1996] 1 FLR 289 and see also *X and Y v The Netherlands* (1985) 8 EHRR 235, para 23, *Hokkanen v Finland* (1994) 19 EHRR 139, [1996] 1 FLR 289 and *Evans v United Kingdom* (2008) 46 EHRR 728) **[RCLP para 8.176]**. In determining whether a positive obligation exists the court will have regard to the 'fair balance' that must be struck between the general interest of the community and the interests of the individual (*Gaskin v United Kingdom* (1989) 12 EHRR 36, para 42) **[RCLP paras 8.178–8.179]**. States are under a positive obligation arising out of Art 8 to take steps to ensure effective protection from domestic violence (*Kalucza v Hungary* (2012) Application No 57693/10) in addition to being under a positive obligation in this regard under Art 3 (*Valiuliené v Lithuania* (2013) Application No 33234/07 and *Eremia and Others v Moldova* (2013) Application No 3564/11).

'respect' (Art 8(1))—The notion of 'respect' as understood in Art 8 is not clear cut, especially as far as the positive obligations inherent in that concept are concerned. The notion's requirements will vary considerably from case to case and the margin of appreciation to be accorded to the authorities may be wider than that applied in other areas under the Convention (*Goodwin v United Kingdom* (2002) 35 EHRR 447, para 72) [RCLP para 8.173].

'private life' (Art 8(1))—A child has his or her own right to respect for his or her private life under Art 8, as distinct from his or her parents' right to respect for private life by reason of the child having a reasonable expectation of privacy in certain circumstances (*Murray v Express Newspapers Plc* [2008] EWCA Civ 446, [2008] 2 FLR 599) [RCLP para 9.25]. The child's Art 8 right to private life under Art 8 will extend to areas of communal activity (*Niemietz v German* (1993) 16 EHRR 97) [RCLP para 9.26]. A child's reasonable expectation of privacy will be relevant, although not conclusive, in determining whether a particular activity of the child falls within the scope of 'private life' for the purposes of Art 8 (*Pay v United Kingdom* (2009) 48 EHRR 15) [RCLP para 9.30].

The child's right to a private life under Art 8 will encompass the child's psychological integrity, mental health and also his or her physical integrity (*Bensaid v United Kingdom* (2001) 33 EHRR 205, *YF v Turkey* (2004) 39 EHRR 34 and see also *X and Y v Netherlands* (1985) 8 EHRR 235; *Costello-Roberts v United Kingdom* (1993) 19 EHRR 112 and *Stubbings v United Kingdom* (1996) 23 EHRR 213) [RCLP para 9.33]. Physical integrity will include the child's right not to be subjected to corporal punishment falling outside the ambit of Art 3 (*Costello-Roberts v United Kingdom* (1993) 19 EHRR 112 and see also *A v United Kingdom* (1999) 27 EHRR 611) [RCLP para 9.34]. The right of the child to respect for physical and psychological integrity will carry with it an element of positive duty which may involve the adoption of measures designed to secure respect for the child's physical and psychological integrity as an element of private life (*Stubbings v United Kingdom* (1996) 23 EHRR 213 cited with approval in *Deep Vein Thrombosis and Air Travel Group Litigation* [2002] EWHC 2825 (QB), [2002] All ER 935, para 176) and see also *X and Y v Netherlands* (1985) 8 EHRR 235, para 23 (applied in *R v G* [2008] UKHL 37, [2009] 1 AC 92); *August v United Kingdom* (2003) 36 EHRR CD 15, *Ivison v United Kingdom* (2002) 35 EHRR CD 20 and *R v G* [2008] UKHL 37, [2008] 1 WLR 1379, [2009] 1 AC 92, [2008] 3 All ER 1071, para 54) [RCLP paras 9.35–9.36].

Art 8 guarantees the right of a person to shape who they are through personal choice as a constituent of the right to a private life [RCLP para 9.37] which may give rise to tensions with respect to the operation of the best interests principle in relation to children [RCLP para 9.38]. A child's reputation and honour will also form a constituent element of the child's right to a private life (*Pfeifer v Austria* (2009) 48 EHRR 175, para 35) [RCLP para 9.40]. In respect to the child's image and the right to respect for private life under Art 8 see *Reklos and Davourlis v Greece* (2009) Application No 1234/05 and [RCLP para 9.41]. In respect of personal privacy and the right to respect for private life under Art 8 see [RCLP paras 9.42–9.44].

The protection of personal data is of fundamental importance to a person's enjoyment of his or her right to respect for private and family life, as guaranteed by Art 8 (*S & Marper v United Kingdom* (2008) Application No 30562/04 (unreported)) [RCLP para 9.45]. Data on individuals which is systematically stored, processed and disseminated by the State or by other individuals will also be encompassed by Art 8 (*S & Marper v United Kingdom* (2008) Application No 30562/04 (unreported) and Art 1 of the Convention for the Protection of Individuals with regard to Automatic Processing of Personal Data (Council of Europe ETS No 108) and see also EC Directives 95/46/EC and 97/66/EC) [RCLP para 9.46]. The individual has no automatic right to know what information is stored about him or her (*Leander v Sweden* (1987) 9 EHRR 433 and see also *Hewitt and Harman v United Kingdom* (1992) 14 EHRR 657; *Amann v Switzerland* (2000) 30 EHRR 843 and *Rotaru v Romania* (2000) 8 BHRC 449, para 43) [RCLP para 9.46]. For the child's right to respect for private life in the context of surveillance see [RCLP para 9.48] and see *Söderman v Sweden* (2013) Application No 5786/08.

The State has a positive obligation to ensure respect for private life under Art 8 (*Botta v Italy* (1998) 26 EHRR 241, *Von Hanover v Germany* (2005) 40 EHRR 1 and *Pretty v United Kingdom*(2002) 35 EHRR 1, [2002] 2 FLR 45 and see *X v Iceland* (1976) 5 DR 86; *McFeeley v United Kingdom* (1980) 20 DR 44; *Beljoudi v France* (1992) 14 EHRR 801) [RCLP paras 9.27–9.28]. See also [RCLP paras 9.63–9.66] and *Godelli v Italy* (2012) Application No 33783/09).

The right to identity—The child's right to understand and determine his or her identity is a fundament element of the Art 8 right to respect for private life and is closely linked with family life (*Gaskin v United Kingdom* (1989) 12 EHRR 36) [RCLP paras 7.2 and 7.59]. Note that where a particularly important facet of an individual's existence or identity is at stake, the margin allowed to the State will normally be restricted (see *A, B and C v Ireland* (2010) Application No 25579/05, para 232). Art 8 supports the child's right to identity as an element of the child's private life, encompassing both the cardinal elements of name, nationality and family relations, as well as wider aspects of the child's physical and social identity (*Niemietz v Germany* (1993) 16 EHRR 97, para 29) [RCLP para 7.59]. In relation to the right to identity as it relates to family, see *Schneider v Germany* (2011) Application No 17080/07, in which the ECtHR decided that the fact the applicant had no family life with the child in circumstances where it had not yet been proved that he was the child's father could not be raise against him as the question of whether he had a right of access to, or of information in respect of the child involved a significant part of his identity and therefore his private life. Art 8 has also been held to protect a person's right to decide on their personal identity as an element of his or her private life in relation to mode of dress and personal appearance (*McFeeley v United Kingdom* (1980) 20 DR 44; *Sutter v Switzerland* (1979) 16 DR 166; *Kara v*

United Kingdom (1998) 27 EHRR CD 272 and *R (E) v Ashworth Hospital Authority* [2001] EWHC (Admin) 1089, (2002) *The Times* 17 January) [**RCLP para 7.81**]. As it relates to identity Art 8 has negative dimension mandating a prohibition on State interference with the right of an individual to live and exist under an identity of their choice (*Burghartz v Switzerland* (1994) 18 EHRR 101, *B v France* (1993) 16 EHRR 1 and *Daroczy v Hungary* (2008) Application No 44378/05 (unreported)) and a positive dimension grounding a duty on the State to recognise a person's identity and, where elements of a person's identity are unclear or not established, to provide information and assistance to enable a person to establish clearly those elements (*Gaskin v United Kingdom* (1989) 12 EHRR 36) [**RCLP para 7.60**]. The boundaries between the State's positive and negative obligations under Art 8 do not lend themselves to precise definition and regard must be had to the fair balance which has to be struck between the competing interests; and in both contexts the State enjoys a certain margin of appreciation (*Hiedecker-Tiemann v Germany* (2008) 47 EHRR SE9) [**RCLP para 7.61**]. There is no express duty under Art 8 to register the child but failure to do so may amount to an unlawful interference in the child's right to respect for family life (*Kalderas' Gypsies v Federal Republic of Germany and Netherlands* Application No 7823 DR 11, 221) [**RCLP para 7.62**].

Names and the right to identity—Names will constitute central elements of self-identification and self-definition (*Daroczy v Hungary* Application 44378/05 (unreported) 1 July 2008, para 32). This principle will also encompass titles (see *Ardgowan (Baron) v Lord Lyon King of Arms* [2008] CSOH 36) [**RCLP paras 7.2 and 7.63**]. The issue of a child's name will fall within the ambit of Art 8 (*Johannson v Finland* (2008) 42 EHRR 369) from the moment of birth (*Znamenskaya v Russia* (2007) 44 EHRR 293) [**RCLP para 7.63**]. This will include both surnames and forenames (*Guillot v France* (1996) V No 19 1593) [**RCLP para 7.65**]. Unless the name chosen is ridiculous, whimsical or likely to prejudice the child, it will be an unjustified interference with the rights under Art 8 for the State to forbid a chosen name (*Johannson v Finland* (2008) 42 EHRR 369) [**RCLP paras 7.64–7.65**].

Nationality and the right to identity—The Convention does not enshrine a right to nationality (but see European Convention on Adoption, Art 11 in relation to adopted children) [**RCLP para 7.66**].

Family relationships and the right to identity—The need for the child to know and have a relationship with his or her parents as an essential component of the child's identity engages the rights under Art 8 (*Mikulic v Croatia* [2002] 1 FCR 720 and see *Rasmussen v Denmark* (1985) 7 EHRR 371) [**RCLP para 7.67**]. The State must act in a manner calculated to enable the tie between child and family to be developed, from the moment of birth or as soon as practicable thereafter and legal safeguards must be established to render that possible (*Marckx v Belgium* (1979) 2 EHRR 330, *Johnston v Ireland* (1987) 9 EHRR 203 and *Keegan v Ireland* 18 EHRR 342) [**RCLP para 7.67**]. The right to knowledge of parentage is an integral part of the notion of private life (*Jäggi v Switzerland* (2006) Application No 58757/00 (unreported), para 37 and *Phinikaridou v Cyprus* (2008) Application No 23890/02, para 45 and see *Re L (Family Proceedings Court) (Appeal: Jurisdiction)* [2003] EWHC 1682 (Fam), [2005] 1 FLR 210, para 23) [**RCLP para 7.68**]. Pursuant to Art 8 the child has the right to discover his or her genetic history and paternity through paternity testing (*Mikulic v Croatia* [2002] 1 FCR 720 and *Rassmussen v Denmark* (1984) 7 EHRR 371 and see also *AMM v Romania* (2012) Application No 2151/10, *Ahrens v Germany* (2012) Application No 45071/09 and *Kautzor v Germany* (2012) Application No 233308/09). It should be noted that a person's right to establish their parentage does not disappear with age (see *Jäggi v Switzerland* (2006) Application No 58757/00 (unreported)) [**RCLP para 7.68**]. For the right to identity in the context of adoption see *Gaskin v United Kingdom* [1990] 1 FLR 167 and [**RCLP paras 7.70–7.75**]. For the right to identity in the context of human fertilisation and embryology see *R (Rose) v Secretary of State for Health* [2002] EWHC 1593 (Admin), [2002] 3 FCR 731 sub nom *Rose v Secretary of State for Health and Human Fertilisation and Embryology Authority* [2002] 2 FLR 962 and [**RCLP paras 7.76–7.78**].

'correspondence' (Art 8(1))—The right to respect for correspondence under Art 8 will be engaged in relation to the opening or censoring of correspondence (*Puzinas v Lithuania* (2002) Application No 44800/98 (unreported)) the protection of correspondence after it has been received (*Warner v Verfides* [2008] EWHC 2609 (Ch), (2008) *The Times*, 6 November) and a refusal to send or deliver correspondence (*Faulkner v United Kingdom* (2002) 35 EHRR 686 and also *R (Nilson) v Governor of Whitmore Prison* [2002] EWHC 668 (Admin), [2002] All ER (D) 275 (Mar) or the dictation of the mode of correspondence (*R (Hirst) v Secretary of State for the Home Department* [2002] EWHC 602 (Admin), [2002] 1 WLR 2929 (a case determined by reference to Art 10 ECHR)) [**RCLP para 9.47**].

'family life' (Art 8(1))—The existence or non-existence under Art 8 of 'family life' for children will be a question of fact depending on the real existence in practice of close personal ties between those children and others (*K v United Kingdom* (1986) 50 DR 199 and see *Serife Yiğit v Turkey* (2010) Application No 3976/05 and *EM (Lebanon) v Secretary of State for the Home Department ALF intervening* [2008] UKHL 64, [2009] 1 All ER 559, para 37) [**RCLP para 8.11**]. In most circumstances family life will exist for the purposes of Art 8 between a child and his or her biological parents (*Sommerfeld v Germany* (2003) 36 EHRR) and may arise whether or not that child is a marital or non-marital child (*Sommerfeld v Germany* (2003) 36 EHRR, para 32, *Berrehab v Netherlands* (1988) 11 HERR 322, para 21, *Gül v Switzerland* (1996) 22 EHRR 93 and *Söderbeck v Sweden* (1998) 29 EHRR 95 and *Brauer v Germany* (2009) Application No 3545/04, para 40) [**RCLP para 8.12**] and see also *Genovese v Malta* (2011) Application No 53124/09. Family life will exist between an unmarried father and his child (*Kroon v Netherlands* (1994) 19 EHRR 263) provided a sufficient nexus is maintained between the child and his or her father (*X v United Kingdom* (1980) 19 DR244, pp 253–254; *MB v United Kingdom* (1994) 77–A DR 108; *Nylund v Finland* (1999) Application No 27110/95 (unreported) and *Lebbink v Netherlands* [2004] 2 FLR 463 and see also *Keegan v Ireland* (1994) 18 EHRR 342) [RCLP para 8.12]. A father who has never had any contact with his child will have no right to respect for family life with that child (*Lebbink v Netherlands* [2004] 2 FLR 463) [RCLP para 8.12]. Potential family life may come within the ambit of Art 8 (*Marckx v Belgium* (1979) 2 EHRR 330, *Abdulaziz, Cabales and Balkandali v UK* (1985) 7 EHRR 471 and *Nylund v Finland* (1999) Application No 27110/95 (unreported)) [RCLP para 8.12]. Cohabitation is not a necessary pre-condition of the existence of family life between parents and children (*Berrehab v Netherlands* (1988) 11 HERR 322 and *Boughanemi v France* (1996) 22 EHRR 227) [RCLP para 8.13]. The placing of the child in public care will not bring family life to an end for the purposes of Art 8 (*Andersson v Sweden* (1992) 14 EHRR 615) [RCLP para 8.13]. The Art 8 rights of the child may be engaged even after the death of a parent where the child's identity is in issue (*Mikulic v Croatia* [2002] 1 FCR 720, paras 64–66 but see also *Hass v Netherlands* (2004) Application No 36983/97 (unreported) [RCLP para 8.13]. Note that the dead do not have Art 8 rights (see *The Estate of Kresten Filtenborg Mortensen v Denmark* (2006) Application No 1338/03 (unreported)). A right of succession between children and parents comes within the sphere of Art 8 (*Brauer v Germany* (2009) Application No 3545/04, para 30) [RCLP para 8.13] and see *Fabris v France* (2013) Application No 16574/08). The existence of family life between a child and his or her siblings is consonant with the use of the word 'everyone' in Art 8 including family life as between half siblings (*Marckx v Belgium* (1979) 2 EHRR 330, para 31, *Keegan v Ireland* (1994) 18 EHRR 342, para 44 and *Kroon v Netherlands* (1994) 19 EHRR 263, para 30 and see also *Moustaquim v Belgium* (1991) 13 EHRR 802 and *Burden v United Kingdom* [2008] 2 FLR 787) [RCLP para 8.14]. Subject to the existence of close personal ties 'family life' for the purposes of Art 8 will include grandparents (*Price v United Kingdom* (1988) 55 DR 1988; *GHB v United Kingdom* Application 42455/98 (unreported) 4 May 2000 and *Bronda v Italy* Application No 22430/93 (unreported) 1998) and uncles and aunts (*Boyle v United Kingdom* (1994) 19 EHRR 179 but contrast the case of *R (Banks) v Governor of Wakefield Prison* [2001] EWHC 917 (Admin), [2002] 1 FCR 445) [RCLP para 8.14]. It has been argued that normally there will be, as a matter of fact, family life between foster carers and the children they care for (dissenting opinion of Schermers J in *Eriksson v Sweden* (1989) 12 EHRR 183 and Recommendation No R (87)6 of the Committee of Ministers in Respect of Foster Families and see also *Gaskin v United Kingdom* (1989) 12 EHRR 36; *X v Switzerland* (1978) 13 DR 248; *Rieme v Sweden* (1993) 16 EHRR 155 and *R (R) v Manchester City Council* [2002] 1 FLR 43) [RCLP para 8.15] and see *Kopf and Liberda v Austria* (2012) Application No 1598/06. The relationship between an adopted child and adoptive parents will be of the same nature as those relationships which fall within the ambit of Art 8 (*X v France* Application No 9993/82, *X v Belgium and the Netherlands* Application No 6482/74 and *Kurochkin v Ukraine* (2010) Application No 42276/08, para 37 and see *Pini and Others v Romania* [2005] 2 FLR 596) [RCLP para 8.15]. The donation of sperm does not, by virtue of the biologic link alone, establish for the donor a right to family life under Art 8 with any subsequent child (*M v Netherlands* (1993) 74 DR 120, *Re R (A Child) (IVF Child: Paternity Rights)* [2003] EWCA Civ 182, [2003] Fam 129 and *G v Netherlands* (1993) 16 EHRR CD 38) [RCLP para 8.16]. Family life does not exist between a non-biological parent and a child born to a lesbian relationship by means of artificial insemination (*Kerkhoven v Netherlands* (1992) Application No15666/89 (unreported) but see *Y and Z v United Kingdom* (1997) 24 EHRR 143) [RCLP para 8.16]. For other relationships see [RCLP paras 8.17–8.18].

'right to respect ... for his home' (Art 8(1))—The term 'home' denotes a physically defined area in which private and family life develops (*Giacomelli v Italy* (2007) 45 EHRR 38, para 76) and is the place where a person 'lives and to which he returns and which forms the centre of his existence' (*Uratemp Ventures Ltd v Collins* [2001] UKHL 43, [2002] 1 AC 301, para 31 and see *Buckley v United Kingdom* (1997) 23 EHRR 101, para 63) [RCLP para 5.163]. It cannot however be extended to mean 'homeland' (*Loizidou v Turkey* (1996) 23 EHRR 513, para 66) [RCLP para 5.163]. Art 8 does not guarantee the right to a home (*X v Federal Republic of Germany* (1956) No 159/56 1 YB 202; *Chapman v United Kingdom* (2001) 33 EHRR 399, para 99; *Marzari v Italy* (1999) 28 EHRR CD 175, p 179; *O'Rourke v United Kingdom* (2001) Application No 39022/97 (unreported); *London Borough of Harrow v Qazi* [2003] UKHL 43, [2004] 1 AC 983 and *Kay v Lambeth London Borough Council* [2006] UKHL 10, [2006] 2 AC 465, para 90) and the scope of the positive obligation to house the homeless is limited (*O'Rourke v United Kingdom* (2001) Application No 39022/97 (unreported), *Moldovan v Romania (No 2)* (2007) 44 EHRR 16, *Marzari v Italy* (1999) 28 EHRR CD 175 and *R (Bernard) v Enfield London Borough Council* [2002] EWHC 2282 (Admin), [2003] LGR 423) [RCLP para 5.164]. Homeless children are not guaranteed housing provision simply by virtue of the provisions of Art 8 (*R (W) v Lambeth London Borough Council* [2002] EWCA Civ 613, [2002] 2 All ER 901) [RCLP para 5.164]. Protection under Art 8 that may exist in circumstances where the environment has a substantial harmful effect on a person's private or family life (*Lough v First Secretary of State* [2004] EWCA Civ 905, [2004] 1 WLR 2557, para 43 and *Kyrtatos v Greece* (2005) 40 EHRR 16, para 52) [RCLP para 5.164]. Art 8 may protect against noise pollution (*Hatton v United Kingdom* (2003) 27 EHRR 611, *Baggs v United Kingdom* (1987) 9 EHRR CD, *Powell and Rayner v United Kingdom* (1990) 12 EHRR 355 and *Dennis v Ministry of Defence* [2003] EWHC 793 (QB), [2003] NLJR 634, para 60) emissions (*Guerra and Others v Italy* (1998) 26 ECHR 357 and *López Ostra v Spain* (1995) 20 EHRR

277) and pollution (*Fadeyeva v Russia* (2007) 45 EHRR 10 and *Taşkin v Turkey* (2006) 42 EHRR 50) [RCLP **para 5.165**]. See also The Children's Environment and Health Action Plan for Europe (EUR/04/5046267/7 25 June 2004) [RCLP **paras 5.124 and 5.165**]. Respect for the home pursuant to Art 8 of the ECHR includes protection for occupation of and access to the home (*Wiggins v United Kingdom* (1978) 13 DR 40 and *Cyprus v Turkey* (1976) 4 EHRR 482) [RCLP **para 5.166**]. Parents and those with responsibility for children may also obtain further protection from Art 1 of the First Protocol to the ECHR [RCLP **para 5.166**]. See also *Hunter and Others v Canary Wharf Ltd; Hunter and Others v London Docklands Corporation* [1997] AC 655, [1997] 2 All ER 426, [1997] 2 FLR 342 [RCLP **para 5.178**].

Art 8 and the unborn child—Art 8 cannot be interpreted as conferring a right of abortion (*A, B and C v Ireland* (2010) Application No 25579/05, para 214). However, the ECtHR has expressly declined to decide whether the term 'others' in Art 8(2) extends to the unborn child (*A, B and C v Ireland* (2010) Application No 25579/05, para 228) [RCLP **para 4.5**]. The domestic courts have held that for the purposes of granting *anticipatory* declaratory relief under the inherent jurisdiction for the purposes of protecting the child upon birth, it made no difference that the child whose future welfare was in issue had not yet been born (*Bury Metropolitan Borough Council v D; Re D (unborn baby) (birth plan: future harm)* [2009] EWHC 446 (Fam), [2009] 2 FCR 93) [RCLP **para 4.10**].

Adoption and Art 8—The obligations imposed by Art 8 in respect of adoption and the effect of adoption on relationships between adopters and adopted children must be interpreted in accordance with the Hague Convention on Protection of Children and Co-operation in Respect of Intercountry Adoption 1993, the United Nations Convention on the Rights of the Child 1989 and the European Convention on the Adoption of Children 1967 (*Pini v Bertani; Manera and Atripaldi v Romania* Application Nos 78028/01 and 78030/01 [2005] 2 FLR 596, para 139) [RCLP **para 3.78**]. See also *Zambotto Perrin v France* (2013) 4962/11, *Negrepontis-Giannis v Greece* (2011) Application No 56759/08. The domestic courts have recently reiterated in the strongest terms the need in each case where adoption is proposed for the proportionality of adoption in the circumstances of the case to be the subject of rigorous consideration (*Re B* [2013] 1 WLR 1911 and see *Re V (Children)* [2013] EWCA Civ 913, *K v London Borough of Brent and others* [2013] EWCA Civ 926; *Re B-S (Children)* [2013] EWCA Civ 1146; *Re Y (A Child)* [2013] EWCA Civ 1337; *Re W (A Child)* [2013] EWCA Civ 1227; *Re C (A Child)* [2013] EWCA Civ 1257; *Re P (A Child)* [2013] EWCA Civ 963 and *Re G (A Child)* [2013] EWCA Civ 695).

Child's right to participate and Art 8—Art 8 encompasses procedural safeguards against inappropriate interference with the substantive rights protected by Art 8 (*R (P) v Secretary of State for the Home Department; R (Q) v Secretary of State for the Home Department* [2001] EWCA Civ 1151; [2001] 2 FLR 1122, *CF v Secretary of State for the Home Department* [2004] EWHC 111 (Fam), [2004] 2 FLR 517 and see *P, C and S v United Kingdom* [2002] 2 FLR 631) [RCLP **para 6.73**]. This procedural protection will apply to any process which may interfere with the substantive rights conferred by Art 8 (*W v United Kingdom* (1987) 10 EHRR 29; *McMichael v United Kingdom* (1995) 20 EHRR 205; *Buchberger v Austria* (unreported) 20 December 2001; *Venema v Netherlands* (unreported) 17 December 2002; *R (P) v Secretary of State for the Home Department* and *R (Q) v Secretary of State for the Home Department* [2001] EWCA Civ 1151, [2001] 2 FLR 1122 and see also Munby, J *Making Sure the Child is Heard: Part 2 – Representation* (2004) Family Law, p 428) [RCLP **para 6.79**]. These procedural safeguards apply as much to children as they do to adults (*Dolhamre v Sweden* (2010) Application No 67/04, para 116 and *CF v Secretary of State for the Home Department* [2004] EWHC 111 (Fam), [2004] 2 FLR 517) [RCLP **paras 6.79 and 8.180**]. For examples of the procedural protections afforded by Art 8 protecting the child's right to participate see [RCLP **para 6.80**]. For the test for determining whether the procedural protection afforded under Art 8 may be invoked see *W v United Kingdom* (1988) 10 EHRR 29, paras 62 and 64 [RCLP **para 6.81**].

Interference in family life (Art 8(2))—Interference with the right to respect for private and family life will be justified only where that interference is in accordance with the law and is necessary in a democratic society in the interests of national security, public safety or the economic well-being of the country, for the prevention of disorder or crime, for the protection of health or morals, or for the protection of the rights and freedoms of others. See also [RCLP **paras 8.35–8.36 and 8.177**]. See also [RCLP **paras 4.172–4.174**].

Article 9
Freedom of thought, conscience and religion

1. Everyone has the right to freedom of thought, conscience and religion; this right includes freedom to change his religion or belief and freedom, either alone or in community with others and in public or private, to manifest his religion or belief, in worship, teaching, practice and observance.

2. Freedom to manifest one's religion or beliefs shall be subject only to such limitations as are prescribed by law and are necessary in a democratic society in the interests of public safety, for the protection of public order, health or morals, or for the protection of the rights and freedoms of others.

Freedom of thought, conscience and religion—The right to freedom of thought, conscience and religion is one of the foundations of a democratic society (*Grzelak v Poland* (2010) Application No 7710/02, para 85) [RCLP para 10.63]. For examples of the application of Art (1) see [RCLP paras 10.78–10.85]. In the context of the ECHR, most of the decisions which touch and concern the child's right to freedom of thought, conscience and religion have been decided by reference to the parental rights concerning the provision of education under Art 2 of the First Protocol to the ECHR rather than by specific reference to the child's right to freedom of thought, conscience and religion under Art 9(1) of the ECHR [RCLP para 10.64]. Thus see also Art 2 of the First Protocol to the ECHR for freedom of thought, conscience and religion in the context of education [RCLP paras 10.87–10.99].

'thought, conscience and religion' (Art 9(1))—Art 9 in its religious dimensions protects the elements that comprise the identity of believers and of their conception of life (*Kokkinakis v Greece* (1993) 17 EHRR 397) [RCLP para 10.65]. Art 9(1) will cover religious as well as non-religious beliefs based on thought and conscience (*Arrowsmith v United Kingdom* (1980) 19 DR 5) [RCLP para 10.66]. In order to come within the ambit of Art 9(1), a non-religious belief must relate to an aspect of human life or behaviour of comparable importance to that normally found with religious belief (*Campbell & Cosans v United Kingdom* (1982) 4 EHRR 293 cited with approval in *R (Williamson) v Secretary of State for Education and Employment* [2005] UKHL 15, [2005] 2 AC 246. See also *Refah Partisi (Welfare Party) v Turkey (No 2)* (2003) 37 EHRR 1, para 93 and *Whaley v Lord Advocate* [2007] UKHL 53, (2008) SC (HL) 107, (2008) HRLR 11) [RCLP para 10.67]. There is a limit on the extent to which the State may assess the legitimacy of religious views or as to the legitimacy of the manner in which those views are expressed (*Hasan and Chaush v Bulgaria* (2002) 34 EHRR 55, para 78 and *Metropolitan Church of Bessarabia v Moldova* (2002) 35 EHRR 306) [RCLP para 10.78]. As such, in determining cases brought under Art 9(1) of the ECHR, the European Court of Human Rights will often start from the assumption that the religion or belief in issue comes within the ambit of Art 9(1) of the ECHR (See for example *Chappell v United Kingdom* (1987) 53 DR 241) [RCLP paras 10.69–10.71].

'belief' (Art 9(1))—The word 'belief' in Art 9(1) denotes views which attain a certain level of cogency, seriousness, cohesion or importance and requires more than firmness (*Campbell and Cosans v United Kingdom* (1982) 4 EHRR 293 but see *R (Williamson) v Secretary of State for Education and Employment* [2005] UKHL 15, [2005] 2 AC 246, citing Arden LJ in *R (Williamson) v Secretary of State for Education and Employment* [2002] EWCA Civ 1926, [2003] QB 1300, in which the House of Lords held that to fall within Art 9(1) a belief must be consistent with the ideals of a democratic society and must be compatible with human dignity, serious and important, cogent and coherent.) [RCLP para 10.66].

Freedom to change religion—Article 9(1) expressly incorporates the freedom to change religion or belief [RCLP para 10.72]. The individual should be able to make a considered and unrestrained choice in matters of religious belief and affiliation (T Stahnke *Proselytism and the Freedom to Change Religion in International Human Rights Law* [1999] BYU L. rev. 251 at 330) [RCLP para 10.72]. Any form of compulsion to express thoughts or convictions or treatment intended to change the process of thinking may infringe Art 9(1) (in relation to children see *Riera Blume v Spain* (2000) 30 EHRR 632) [RCLP para 10.72]. The freedom to change religion does not prohibit acts of proselytisation in an attempt to convert a person from one belief to another (*Kokkinakis v Greece* (1993) 17 EHRR 397 and *Pedro Carrasco Carrasco* Boletín Official del Estado 156 30 June 200 40–46) [RCLP para 10.73].

Restrictions on manifesting religion or belief (Art 9(2))—The right to freedom of thought, conscience and religion *per se* is an absolute right which may not be the subject to any form of limitation or restriction and the limitations set out in Art 9(2) apply only to the right to *manifest* religion and belief (*Kokkinakis v Greece* (1993) 17 EHRR 397, para 33, *R (Williamson) v Secretary of State for Education and Employment* [2002] EWCA Civ 1926, [2003] QB 1300 and *R (Williamson) v Secretary of State for Education and Employment* [2005] UKHL 15, [2005] 2 AC 246 [RCLP paras 10.74–10.75]. The act constituting manifestation must be intimately linked to the belief it is said to manifest (*X v United Kingdom* (1983) 6 EHRR 558 and see also *R (Playfoot) v Governing Body of Millais School* [2007] EWHC 1698 (Admin), [2007] LGR 851, [2007] 3 FCR 754) [RCLP para 10.76].

Grounds for restriction (Art 9(2))—The manifestation of religion or beliefs by an individual may be interfered with provided such interference is prescribed by law and necessary in a democratic society in pursuit of a legitimate aim, namely public safety, the protection of public order, health or morals, or the protection of the rights and freedoms of others [RCLP para 10.77]. Whether a particular act constitutes interference in the rights enshrined in Art 9(1) will depend on all the circumstances of the case in question, including the extent to which in the circumstances an individual can reasonably be expected to be at liberty to manifest his or her beliefs in practice (*Kalac v Turkey* (1997) 27 EHRR 552 cited in *R (Williamson) v Secretary of State for Education and Employment* [2005] UKHL 15, [2005] 2 AC 246, para 38 and see also *Sahin v Turkey* (2007) 44 EHRR 5 and *R (Shabina Begum) v Denbigh High School Governors* [2006] UKHL 15, [2006] 2 WLR 719 **[RCLP para 10.77]**. See also *Lautsi and Others v Italy* (2011) Application No 30814/06.

Article 10
Freedom of expression

1. Everyone has the right to freedom of expression. This right shall include freedom to hold opinions and to receive and impart information and ideas without interference by public authority and regardless of frontiers. This Article shall not prevent States from requiring the licensing of broadcasting, television or cinema enterprises.

2. The exercise of these freedoms, since it carries with it duties and responsibilities, may be subject to such formalities, conditions, restrictions or penalties as are prescribed by law and are necessary in a democratic society, in the interests of national security, territorial integrity or public safety, for the prevention of disorder or crime, for the protection of health or morals, for the protection of the reputation or rights of others, for preventing the disclosure of information received in confidence, or for maintaining the authority and impartiality of the judiciary.

Right to freedom of expression (Art 10(1))—There is a positive duty on the State to take steps to ensure that the right to freedom of expression is protected from interference by private individuals as well as by the State (*Özgür Gundem v Turkey* (2001) 31 EHRR 1082, para 43 and see *Artze für das Leben v Austria* (1988) 13 EHRR 204) **[RCLP para 11.53]**. Freedom of expression will also protect the manner in which the expression is made (*Jersild v Denmark* (1994) 19 EHRR 1 and *Da Silva v Portugal* (2002) 34 EHRR 56) **[RCLP para 11.53]**. For communicative activity which breaches the values of the ECHR see **[RCLP paras 11.54–55]**. See also the Human Rights Act 1998 s 12 **[RCLP paras 11.91–11.92]**.

Right to freedom of expression and children—The word 'everyone' in Art 10(1) plainly encompasses all children **[RCLP para 11.52]**.

Ambit of Freedom of Expression—Any form of communication in principle falls without the scope of Art 10(1) (*Belfast City Council v Miss Behavin' Ltd* [2007] UKHL 19, [2007] 1 WLR 1420) **[RCLP para 11.53]**. The precise extent to which communicative activity is protected by Art 10 in a particular case will be evaluated by reference to the character of what is communicated when assessing the proportionality of any restriction and the margin of appreciation to be accorded to the State (*R v Secretary of State for the Home Department, ex p Simms* [2000] 2 AC 115) **[RCLP para 11.56]**. The right to freedom of expression does not extend to the physical expression of feelings of love (see *Cohen v California* 403 US 15 at 26 (1971), US Sup Ct) **[RCLP para 11.8]**.

Right to receive information—The right to receive information is a key aspect of Art 10 (*London Regional Transport v Mayor of London* [2001] EWCA Civ 1491, [2003] EMLR 88, para 55 and also *Observer and Guardian v United Kingdom* (1991) 14 EHRR 153, para 59) **[RCLP para 11.57]**. However, the right to receive information enshrined in Art 10 does not impart a positive obligation on the State to provide a person with information (*Leander v Sweden* (1987) 9 EHRR 433 and *Gaskin v United Kingdom* (1989) 12 EHRR 36 but see also European Convention on the Protection of Individuals with regard to Automatic Processing of Personal Data (ETS No 108) and *Open Door and Dublin Well Women v Ireland* (1992) 15 EHRR 244) **[RCLP para 11.58]**.

Right to impart information—The role of the media in imparting information has been emphasised by the ECtHR (*Observer and Guardian v United Kingdom* (1991) 14 EHRR 153, para 59) **[RCLP para 11.59]**. For the concept of 'responsible journalism' in the context of Art 10(1) see **[RCLP para 11.60]**.

Restrictions on the right to freedom of expression (Art 10(2))—The right to freedom of expression in Art 10(1) may be breached in the circumstances set out in Art 10(2) and as such is a qualified right (*R v Shayler* [2002] UKHL 11, [2003] 1 AC 247, para 23) **[RCLP paras 2.81 and 11.61–11.62]**. See also the Human Rights Act 1998 s 12(4) **[RCLP para 3.67]**. The restrictions under Art 10(2) must thus be narrowly interpreted and the necessity for any restriction must be convincingly established on the basis of cogent evidence (*Thorgierson v Iceland* 14 EHRR 843, para 63 and *Kelly v BBC* [2001] Fam 59). The burden of proving necessity is on the defendant **[RCLP para 11.63]**. Rights held by the child under the ECHR have been held to justify the interference with the right to freedom of expression under Art 10 (*T v United Kingdom* [2000] 30 EHRR 121 and see *Venables v News Group Newspapers* [2001] Fam 430 and *X (A Women formerly known as Mary Bell) v O'Brien* [2003] EWHC 1101 (QB), [2003] 2 FCR 686) **[RCLP para 11.63]**.

'duties and responsibilities' (Art 10(2))—The precise scope of the term 'duties and responsibilities' will depend on the situation of the person exercising the rights under Art 10(1) and the means employed to do so (*Müller v Switzerland* (1988) 13 EHRR 212 and see *Otto Preminger Institut v Austria* (1994) 19 EHRR 34) [RCLP para 11.64]. The term encompasses the duty to avoid expressions that are gratuitously offensive to others and which to not contribute to legitimate public debate (*Giniewski v France* (2007) 45 EHRR 589 and see *Handyside v UK* (1979) 1 EHRR 737) [RCLP para 11.64].

'prescribed by law' (Art 10(2))—See *Lindon, Otchakovsky-Laurens and July v France* (2008) 46 EHRR 761, *Sunday Times v United Kingdom* (1979) 2 EHRR 245 and *Gaweda v Poland* (2002) 12 BHRC 486, para 39 [RCLP para 11.65].

'necessary in a democratic society' (Art 10(2))—The adjective 'necessary', within the meaning of Art 10(2) is not synonymous with 'indispensable', neither has it the flexibility of such expressions as 'admissible', 'ordinary', 'reasonable' or 'desirable' [RCLP para 11.66]. For the definition of the term 'democratic society' see *Christian Democratic People's Party v Moldova (No 2)* (No 2) (2010) Application 25196/04 (unreported) [RCLP para 11.66].

'protection of health and morals' (Art 10(2))—States parties enjoy a wide margin of appreciation when imposing restrictions on freedom of expression based on the need to protect health and morals [RCLP para 11.68]. It is primarily for the State to assess the content of morals having regard to the importance of the Art 10(1) right to freedom of expression in a democracy, mediation between different groups in society, respect for legislation based on considered balancing of interests, recognition of 'holistic' policy areas which are not readily justiciable and respect for legislation representing the democratic will on moral and ethical questions *R (Pro Life Alliance) v BBC* [2003] UKHL 23, [2004] 1 AC 185 [RCLP para 11.68]. However, the measures taken for the protection of health and morals must nonetheless be necessary in a democratic society (*Open Door Counselling and Dublin Well Women v Ireland* (1992) 15 EHRR 244) [RCLP para 11.68]. For specific examples of measures taken to protect the health and morals of children see [RCLP paras 11.69–11.71]. See also *ECHR Art 10 – Media and the Courts* at [RCLP para 11.75].

'protection of the reputation or rights of others' (Art 10(2))—The limits of acceptable criticism of an individual will vary depending on the status of the individual in question (*Lingens v Austria* (1986) 8 EHRR 407 [RCLP para 11.72].

'preventing the disclosure of information received in confidence' (Art 10(2))—Information disclosed in confidence by children to counsellors and experts within family proceedings will fall to be protected under Art 10(1) of the ECHR (MacDonald, A *Bringing Rights Home for Children: Transparency and the Child's Right to Respect for Private Life* [2010] Fam Law 190) [RCLP para 11.74].

Voting—The European Commission on Human Rights has held that establishing a minimum age for those wishing to stand for election could not be considered an unreasonable or arbitrary restriction or interference with the right to freedom of expression (*W, X, Y, Z v Belgium* 6745 6/74 DR2, 110) [RCLP para 11.78].

Article 11
Freedom of assembly and association

1. Everyone has the right to freedom of peaceful assembly and to freedom of association with others, including the right to form and to join trade unions for the protection of his interests.

2. No restrictions shall be placed on the exercise of these rights other than such as are prescribed by law and are necessary in a democratic society in the interests of national security or public safety, for the prevention of disorder or crime, for the protection of health or morals or for the protection of the rights and freedoms of others. This Article shall not prevent the imposition of lawful restrictions on the exercise of these rights by members of the armed forces, of the police or of the administration of the State.

Freedom of assembly and association (Art 11)—The right to freedom of peaceful assembly and freedom of association have as one of their objectives the protection of personal opinions including political beliefs (*Vogt v Germany* (1995) 21 EHRR 205 and *Refah Partisi v Turkey* (2002) 35 EHRR 56) [RCLP para 12.24].

Positive obligation—Art 11(1) places a positive obligation on the State to ensure freedom of association and freedom of peaceful assembly even as between individuals (*Plattform Arzte für das Leben v Austria* 44 DR 65 (1985)) [RCLP para 12.25].

'everyone' (Art 11(1))—The word 'everyone' in Art 11(1) demonstrates that the freedom of peaceful assembly applies also to children (*Christian Democratic People's Party v Moldova* (2006) 45 EHRR 13) [RCLP para 12.27]. See *Anderson v United Kingdom* [1998] EHRR CD 172 as an example of an unsuccessful claim under Art 11(1) by a group of young people [RCLP paras 12.28–12.29].

Right to freedom of peaceful assembly (Art 11(1))—The right to freedom of peaceful assembly under Art 11(1) of the ECHR encompasses fixed meetings and assemblies as well as processions and marches both in private and in public (*Christians Against Racism and Fascism v United Kingdom* 21 DR 148 (1980) and *Rassemblement Jurrasien Unité v Switzerland* 17 DR 93 (1979)) [RCLP para 12.26]. The right does not concern the right of individuals to share the company of others (*McFeeley v United Kingdom* 20 DR 44 (1980) and see also *Anderson v United Kingdom* [1998] EHRR CD 172) [RCLP para 12.32].

Right to freedom of association (Art 11(1))—Under Art 11(1) the word 'association' encompasses the concept of a voluntary grouping of people for a common goal (*Association X v Sweden* 9 DR 1 (1978) and *Christian Democratic People's Party v Moldova* (2006) 45 EHRR 13 and see *United Communist Party of Turkey v Turkey* (1998) 26 EHRR 121 and *Refah Partisi v Turkey* (2002) 35 EHRR 56) [RCLP para 12.30]. There is implied in Art 11(1) a negative right not to associate (*Sigurour A Sigurjonnson v Iceland* (1993) 16 EHRR 462, para 35 and *Sørensen v Denmark; Rassmussen v Denmark* (2008) 46 EHRR 29 and see also *Le Compte, Van Leuven and De Meyere v Belgium* (1981) 4 EHRR 1; *A v Spain* 66 DR 1988 (1990) and see *Sigurour A Sigurjonnson v Iceland* (1993) 16 EHRR 462, *Cheall v United Kingdom* 42 DR 178 (1985) at 185, *ASLEF v United Kingdom* (2007) 45 EHRR 34 and *Damyanti v Union* [1971] 3 SCR 840 (Sup Ct of India) [RCLP para 12.31]. The right does not concern the right of individuals to share the company of others (*McFeeley v United Kingdom* 20 DR 44 (1980) and see also *Anderson v United Kingdom* [1998] EHRR CD 172) [RCLP para 12.32].

Restrictions (Art 11(2))—The right to freedom of peaceful assembly and peaceful association under Art 11(1) may only be restricted on the grounds set out in Art 11(2) [RCLP para 12.33]. See *Christian Democratic People's Party v Moldova (No 2)* (2010) Application 25196/04 (unreported) and see *United Communist Party of Turkey and Others v Turkey* (1998) 26 EHRR 121, para 47 [RCLP para 12.34]. See further [RCLP paras 12.39–12.41].

'prescribed by law' (Art 11(2))—A lack of foreseeability of all the legal consequences of assembling or associating may in itself be a sufficient basis for the conclusion that the impugned measures are not prescribed by law for the purposes of Art11(2) (*Christian Democratic People's Party v Moldova* (2006) 45 EHRR 13, para 53) [RCLP para 12.36].

'necessary in a democratic society' (Art 11(2))—The adjective 'necessary' is not synonymous with 'indispensable', neither has it the flexibility of such expressions as 'admissible', 'ordinary', 'reasonable'or 'desirable' [RCLP para 12.36]. It is for the national authorities to make the initial assessment of the reality of the pressing social need implied by the notion of 'necessity' (*Handyside v UK* (1979) 1 EHRR 737) [RCLP para 12.36].

'morals' (Art 11(2))—The term 'morals' describes 'principles which are not always legally enforceable but which are accepted by a great majority of the citizens as general guidelines for their individual and collective behaviour' (A Kiss 'Permissible Limitations on Rights' in L Henkin (ed) *The International Bill of Rights: The Covenant on Civil and Political Rights* (1981), pp 290–310, p 304. See also *Reno v American Civil Liberties Union* 521 US 844 (1997) US Sup Ct; *Ashcroft v ACLU* 535 US 564 (2002) US Sup Ct; *Curtis v Minister of Safety* (1996) BHRC 541, Const Ct of South Africa and *De Reuck v DPP* [2004] 4 LRC 72, Const Ct of South Africa) [RCLP para 12.38].

Article 12
Right to marry

Men and women of marriageable age have the right to marry and to found a family, according to the national laws governing the exercise of this right.

Right to marry and found a family (Art 12)—Art 12 is concerned with the protection of marriage as the basis of the family (*Rees v United Kingdom* (1986) 9 EHRR 56 and see *Pretty v DPP* [2001] UKHL 61, [2002] 1 AC 800 and *Marckx v Belgium* (1979) 2 EHRR 330, para 67) [RCLP para 8.218]. Art 12 does not confer a right to divorce (*Johnston v Ireland* (1987) 9 EHRR 203) [RCLP para 8.218].

'marriageable age' (Art 12)—The term marriage age is not further defined in the ECHR. See also the Council of Europe Resolution 1468 on Forced Marriages and Child Marriages and the Convention on the Elimination of All Forms of Discrimination Against Women Art 16(2) [RCLP paras 8.220–8.222].

'according to the national laws' (Art 12)—This phrase permits Member States to impose proportionate restrictions on marriage in accordance with national laws provided such laws do not impair the very essence of the right to marry (*Rees v United Kingdom* (1986) 9 EHRR 56 and *F v Switzerland* (1987) 10 EHRR 411) [RCLP para 8.219].

Article 13
Right to an effective remedy

Everyone whose rights and freedoms as set forth in this Convention are violated shall have an effective remedy before a national authority notwithstanding that the violation has been committed by persons acting in an official capacity.

Right to an effective remedy (Art 13)—Note that Sch 1 of the Human Rights Act 1998 omits Art 13 of the ECHR [RCLP para 3.57]. The domestic courts have however continued to have regard to Art 13 (*Re S (Minors) (Care Order: Implementation of Care Plan); Re W (Minors) (Care Order: Adequacy of Care Plan)* [2002] UKHL 10, [2002] 2 AC 291, paras 60 and 61) [RCLP para 16.131].

Effect of Art 13—The effect of Art 13 is to require the provision of a domestic remedy allowing the competent national authority both to deal with the substance of the relevant Convention complaint and to grant appropriate relief (see *DP and JC v United Kingdom*, para 134) [RCLP para 16.132]. For the principles of application of Art 13 see *Silver v United Kingdom* (1983) 5 EHRR 347, para 113 [RCLP para 16.133].

Article 14
Prohibition of discrimination

The enjoyment of the rights and freedoms set forth in this Convention shall be secured without discrimination on any ground such as sex, race, colour, language, religion, political or other opinion, national or social origin, association with a national minority, property, birth or other status.

Prohibition on discrimination (Art 14)—Any restriction imposed on a right conferred by the ECHR must not be discriminatory (see *The Belgian Linguistic Case (No 2)* 1 EHRR 252, para 10) [RCLP para 3.77]. Art 14 guarantees equality without discrimination by reference solely to the rights conferred by the ECHR (but see *Wilson v United Kingdom* (2002) 35 EHRR 20, [2002] IRLR 568, 13 BHRC 39, [2002] All ER (D) 35(Jul)) [RCLP paras 4.95 and 7.66]. This principle does not act to limit the importance of Art 14 (*Ghaidan v Mendoza* [2004] UKHL30, [2004] 2 AC 557, paras 131–132 and see also *A v Secretary of State for the Home Department* [2002] EWCA Civ 1502, [2004] QB 335, para 8 per Lord Woolf; *Belgian Linguistic Case (No 2)* (1968) 1 EHRR 252, para 9; *National Union of Belgian Police v Belgium* (1975) 1 EHRR 578, para 44 and *Marckx v Belgium* (1979) 2 EHRR, para 32) [RCLP para 4.95]. However, a complaint in relation to Art 14 must be linked to one of the other articles of the ECHR (*Beldjoudi v France* (1992) 14 EHRR 801). Note that Art 14 extends to both the elements of the substantive right that the State is required to guarantee and aspects of the right the State chooses to guarantee (*Belgian Linguistic Case (No 2)* (1968) 1 EHRR 252, para 9 and see for example *EB v France* (2008) 47 EHRR 21 (Grand Chamber), para 49) [RCLP para 4.96]. An action which satisfies the relevant article of the ECHR may nonetheless be discriminatory under Art 14 (*Belgian Linguistic Case (No 2)* (1968) 1 EHRR 252, para 9; *Airey v Ireland* (1979) 2 EHRR 305, para 30; *Marckx v Belgium* (1979) 2 EHRR 330, para 32) and thus it is 'necessary but it is also sufficient for the facts of the case to fall 'within the ambit' of one or more of the Convention Articles (*Burden and another v United Kingdom* Application No 13378/05, [2008] All ER (D) 391 (Apr), [2008] 2 FLR 787, para 58 and see also *Belgian Linguistics Case (No 2)* (1968) 1 EHRR 252, 277; *Rasmussen v Denmark* (1985) 7 EHRR 371, para 35; *Schmidt v Germany* [1994] ECHR 13580/88, para 22; *Van Raalte v Netherlands* (1997) 24 EHRR 503, para 33 and *Stec v United Kingdom* (2006) 20 BHRC 348) [RCLP para 4.96]. Thus, in order to successfully establish discrimination in contravention of Art 14 a child must demonstrate (i) that the facts fall within the ambit of one or more of the ECHR rights, (ii) that he or she has been treated differently on a prohibited ground (iii) to others in an analogous position and (iv) the difference in treatment cannot be objectively and reasonably justified having regard to the doctrine of proportionality and the margin of appreciation [RCLP para 4.97]. See also ECHR Protocol No 12 Art 1 [RCLP paras 4.99–4.101].

Domestic jurisdiction—In respect of its domestic application Art 14 of the ECHR applies only to those who are within the domestic jurisdiction (*Re J (Child Returned Abroad: Human Rights)* [2004] 2 FLR 85, para 34) [RCLP para 3.57].

'discrimination' (Art 14)—In *Carson v United Kingdom* [2008] All ER (D) 18 (Nov), paras 73 and 77 the ECtHR defined discrimination as follows 'The Court has established in its case-law that only differences in treatment based on an identifiable characteristic, or "status", are capable of amounting to discrimination within the meaning of Article 14. Moreover, in order for an issue to arise under Article 14 there must be a difference in the treatment of persons in analogous, or relevantly similar, situations ... Discrimination means a failure to treat like cases alike; there is no discrimination when the cases are relevantly different' [**RCLP paras 4.72 and 4.102**]. See also *DH v Czech Republic* (2008) 47 EHRR 3 and *Oršuš and Others v Croatia* (2010) Application No 15766/03 [**RCLP para 4.97**]. There has been a reluctance to limit or define restrictively the grounds on which discrimination is prohibited under Art 14 [**RCLP para 4.102**]. Art 14 will prohibit indirect discrimination (*DH and Others v Czech Republic* (2008) 47 EHRR 3, [2008] ELR 17, 23 BHRC 526 Grand Chamber but see *Esfandiari v Secretary of State for Work and Pensions* [2006] EWCA Civ 282, *The Times* 29 May 2006 (considered in *R (Primrose) v Secretary of State for Justice* [2008] EWHC 1625 (Admin), [2008] All ER (D) 156 (Jul)), *Gallagher (Valuation Officer) v Church of Jesus Christ of the Latter Day Saints* [2008] UKHL56, [2008] 1 WLR 1852)) [**RCLP para 4.103**]. Positive discrimination will not violate Art 14 if such difference in treatment can be said to have an objective and reasonable justification (*Belgian Linguistic Case (No 2)* (1968) 1 EHRR 252, para 10. See for example *Lindsay v United Kingdom* (1987) 9 EHRR 555, para 1(a) and see also the judgment of Powell J in *Regents of University of California v Bakke* 438 US 265 (1978)) [**RCLP para 4.104**].

Analogous situations—Article 14 has been interpreted, in line with the general principle of treating equal situations equally, as safeguarding against discriminatory differences of treatment individuals who are 'placed in analogous situations' (*Rasmussen v Denmark* (1985) 7 EHRR 371, para 35) [**RCLP para 4.106**]. Examples of family relationships which have been adjudged not to be analogous include comparisons between a married couple and an unmarried couple (see *Lindsay v United Kingdom* Application No 11089/84 (Dec), 11 November 1986 49 DR 181), a natural father and a natural mother (see *MB v United Kingdom* (6 April 1994) 77–A DR 108 and *Rasmussen v Denmark* (1985) 7 EHRR 371), a natural father and a married father concerning the rights of children (see *McMichael v United Kingdom* [1995] 2 FCR 718, (1995) 20 EHRR 205) and a stable lesbian relationship with family life (see *S v United Kingdom* Application No 11716/85, (1986) 47 DR 274). See also *Paulik v Slovakia* Application No 10699/05 [2006] 3 FCR 333 and *Ismailova v Russia* Application No 37614/02 [2008] 2 FCR 72 [**RCLP para 4.106**]. The European Court of Human Rights does not necessarily seek direct comparators but rather has often subsumed the issue of analogous situation with the issue of justification by asking itself whether differences in otherwise similar situations justify different treatment (see *Burden v UK* (2008) 47 EHRR 38, paras 60–66, *Andrejeva v Latvia* (2009) Application No 55707/00 (unreported) and *R (Carson) v Secretary of State for Work and Pensions* [2005] UKHL 37, [2005] 4 All ER 545, para 3, [2006] 1 AC 173) [**RCLP para 4.106**]. Whether a child is being discriminated against will depend in part on whether an analogy may be validly drawn between the situation of that child and the situation of the adult or child said to be enjoying more favourable treatment by comparison (*AL (Serbia) v Secretary of State for the Home Department; R (Rudi) v Secretary of State for the Home Department* [2008] UKHL 43, [2008] 1 WLR 1434, para 27) [**RCLP paras 4.107 and 8.64**].

Reasonable and objective justification—Art 14 affords protection against different treatment of persons in similar situations which is without an objective and reasonable justification (*Belgian Linguistic Case (No 2)* (1968) 1 EHRR 252, para 10 and see also *Fredin v Sweden* (1991) 13 EHRR 784, para 60 and *McMichael v United Kingdom* [1995] 2 FCR 718, (1995) 20 EHRR 205) [**RCLP para 4.108**]. States enjoy a margin of appreciation in assessing whether and to what extent differences in otherwise similar situations justify a different treatment in law (*Rasmussen v Denmark* (1985) 7 EHRR 371, para 40) [**RCLP para 4.109**].

Positive obligation—Art 14 places a positive obligation on Member States to secure equal treatment in the enjoyment of the rights enshrined in the Convention (*Belgian Linguistic Case (No 2)* (1968) 1 EHRR 252 at 278 and see also *Ghaidan v Mendoza* [2002] EWCA Civ 1533, [2003] Ch 380, para 5 per Buxton LJ (not considered by the House of Lords)) [**RCLP para 4.98**]. Other articles of the ECHR will create indirect positive obligations which themselves must be applied in a non-discriminatory fashion (see for example *Nachova v Bulgaria* (2006) 42 EHRR 43, para 161; *Bekos and Koutropoulos v Greece* (2006) 43 EHRR 2, para 70; *Angelova and Iliev v Bulgaria* (2008) 47 EHRR, paras 115 and 117 and *Cobzaru v Romania* (2008) 47 EHRR 10) [**RCLP para 4.98**].

Legal status of children—Distinguishing between the legal status of children or groups of children can be a violation of Art 8 when read with Art 14 prohibiting discrimination on the grounds of 'birth or other status' (*Marckx v Belgium* (1979) 2 EHRR 330 and also *Brauer v Germany* (2009) Application No 3545/04, para 40 and Lithuania: LTU-1995-2-005 01-06-1995/e 4/95 Restoration of the rights of ownership (g) Valstybes Zinios (Official Gazette) 47–1154, 7 June 2009) [**RCLP para 4.61**]. See also the European Convention on the Legal Status of Children Born out of Wedlock 1875 and *Inze v Austria* (1987) 10 EHRR 394 and *Johnston v Ireland* (1987) 9 EHRR 203 [**RCLP para 4.63**].

Examples of discrimination—For further examples of discrimination in respect of the right to family life under Art 8 read with Art 14 see [**RCLP paras 8.63 and 8.213**]. For examples of discrimination in respect of the right to freedom of thought, conscience and religion under Art 9 read with Art 14 see [**RCLP paras 10.79 and 10.86**]. For examples of discrimination in respect of education under Art 14 read with Art 2 of the First Protocol see [**RCLP paras 13.119-13.122**] and *Sampani and Others v Greece* (2012) Application No 59608/09, *Horvárth and Kiss v Hungary* (2013) Application No 11146/11 and *Lavida and Others v Greece* (2013) Application No 7973/10.

Article 15
Derogation in time of emergency

1. In time of war or other public emergency threatening the life of the nation any High Contracting Party may take measures derogating from its obligations under this Convention to the extent strictly required by the exigencies of the situation, provided that such measures are not inconsistent with its other obligations under international law.

2. No derogation from Article 2, except in respect of deaths resulting from lawful acts of war, or from Articles 3, 4 (paragraph 1) and 7 shall be made under this provision.

3. Any High Contracting Party availing itself of this right of derogation shall keep the Secretary General of the Council of Europe fully informed of the measures which it has taken and the reasons therefor. It shall also inform the Secretary General of the Council of Europe when such measures have ceased to operate and the provisions of the Convention are again being fully executed.

Derogation—Derogations in respect of Arts 2 (save in respect of death resulting in lawful acts of war), 3, 4(1) and 7 are prohibited by Art 15(2) **[RCLP para 2.81]**. See for example *Lawless v Ireland* (1961) 1 EHRR 1; *Vogt v Germany* (1995) 21 EHRR 205; *Brogan and Others v UK* (1988)11 EHRR 117 and *Brannigan and McBride v UK* (1993) 17 EHRR 557 **[RCLP para 2.81]**.

Article 16
Restrictions on political activity of aliens

Nothing in Articles 10, 11 and 14 shall be regarded as preventing the High Contracting Parties from imposing restrictions on the political activity of aliens.

Political activity of aliens—See for example *Piermont v France* (1995) Series A No 314, 20 EHRR 301 **[RCLP para 2.81]**.

Article 17
Prohibition of abuse of rights

Nothing in this Convention may be interpreted as implying for any State, group or person any right to engage in any activity or perform any act aimed at the destruction of any of the rights and freedoms set forth herein or at their limitation to a greater extent than is provided for in the Convention.

Prohibition of abuse of rights—See for example *Campbell and Cosans v United Kingdom* (1982) Series A No 48, 4 EHRR 293 and *WP and others v Poland* (2005) 40 EHRR SE1 **[RCLP paras 2.81, 11.55 and 12.41]**.

Article 18
Limitation on use of restrictions on rights

The restrictions permitted under this Convention to the said rights and freedoms shall not be applied for any purpose other than those for which they have been prescribed.

Restriction on rights—See *Quinn v France* (1995) 21 EHRR 529, para 57 **[RCLP paras 2.81 and 3.74]**.

Section II
European Court of Human Rights

Article 19
Establishment of the Court

To ensure the observance of the engagements undertaken by the High Contracting Parties in the Convention and the Protocols thereto, there shall be set up a European Court of Human Rights, hereinafter referred to as "the Court". It shall function on a permanent basis.

Article 20
Number of judges

The Court shall consist of a number of judges equal to that of the High Contracting Parties.

Article 21
Criteria for office

1. The judges shall be of high moral character and must either possess the qualifications required for appointment to high judicial office or be jurisconsults of recognised competence.

2. The judges shall sit on the Court in their individual capacity.

3. During their term of office the judges shall not engage in any activity which is incompatible with their independence, impartiality or with the demands of a full-time office; all questions arising from the application of this paragraph shall be decided by the Court.

Article 22
Election of judges

The judges shall be elected by the Parliamentary Assembly with respect to each High Contracting Party by a majority of votes cast from a list of three candidates nominated by the High Contracting Party.

Article 23
Terms of office and dismissal

1. The judges shall be elected for a period of nine years. They may not be re-elected.

2. The terms of office of judges shall expire when they reach the age of 70.

3. The judges shall hold office until replaced. They shall, however, continue to deal with such cases as they already have under consideration.

4. No judge may be dismissed from office unless the other judges decide by a majority of two-thirds that that judge has ceased to fulfil the required conditions.

Article 24
Registry and rapporteurs

1. The Court shall have a Registry, the functions and organisation of which shall be laid down in the rules of the Court.

2. When sitting in a single-judge formation, the Court shall be assisted by rapporteurs who shall function under the authority of the President of the Court. They shall form part of the Court's Registry.

Article 25
Plenary Court

The plenary Court shall

(a) elect its President and one or two Vice-Presidents for a period of three years; they may be re-elected;
(b) set up Chambers, constituted for a fixed period of time;
(c) elect the Presidents of the Chambers of the Court; they may be re-elected;
(d) adopt the rules of the Court;
(e) elect the Registrar and one or more Deputy Registrars;

(f)   make any request under Article 26 , paragraph 2.

Article 26
Single-judge formation, Committees, Chambers and Grand Chamber

1. To consider cases brought before it, the Court shall sit in a single-judge formation, in Committees of three judges, in Chambers of seven judges and in a Grand Chamber of seventeen judges. The Court's Chambers shall set up Committees for a fixed period of time.

2. At the request of the plenary Court, the Committee of Ministers may, by a unanimous decision and for a fixed period, reduce to five the number of judges of the Chambers.

3. When sitting as a single judge, a judge shall not examine any application against the High Contracting Party in respect of which that judge has been elected.

4. There shall sit as an *ex officio* member of the Chamber and the Grand Chamber the judge elected in respect of the High Contracting Party concerned. If there is none or if that judge is unable to sit, a person chosen by the President of the Court from a list submitted in advance by that Party shall sit in the capacity of judge.

5. The Grand Chamber shall also include the President of the Court, the Vice-Presidents, the Presidents of the Chambers and other judges chosen in accordance with the rules of the Court. When a case is referred to the Grand Chamber under Article 43, no judge from the Chamber which rendered the judgment shall sit in the Grand Chamber, with the exception of the President of the Chamber and the judge who sat in respect of the High Contracting Party concerned.

Article 27
Competence of single judges

1. A single judge may declare inadmissible or strike out of the Court's list of cases an application submitted under Article 34, where such a decision can be taken without further examination.

2. The decision shall be final.

3. If the single judge does not declare an application inadmissible or strike it out, that judge shall forward it to a Committee or to a Chamber for further examination.

Article 28
Competence of Committees

1. In respect of an application submitted under Article 34, a Committee may, by a unanimous vote,

(a)   declare it inadmissible or strike it out of its list of cases, where such decision can be taken without further examination; or

(b)   declare it admissible and render at the same time a judgment on the merits, if the underlying question in the case, concerning the interpretation or the application of the Convention or the Protocols thereto, is already the subject of well-established case-law of the Court.

2. Decisions and judgments under paragraph 1 shall be final.

3. If the judge elected in respect of the High Contracting Party concerned is not a member of the Committee, the Committee may at any stage of the proceedings invite

that judge to take the place of one of the members of the Committee, having regard to all relevant factors, including whether that Party has contested the application of the procedure under paragraph 1(b).

Article 29
Decisions by Chambers on admissibility and merits

1. If no decision is taken under Article 27 or 28, or no judgment rendered under Article 28, a Chamber shall decide on the admissibility and merits of individual applications submitted under Article 34. The decision on admissibility may be taken separately.

2. A Chamber shall decide on the admissibility and merits of inter-State applications submitted under Article 33. The decision on admissibility shall be taken separately unless the Court, in exceptional cases, decides otherwise.

Article 30
Relinquishment of jurisdiction to the Grand Chamber

Where a case pending before a Chamber raises a serious question affecting the interpretation of the Convention or the Protocols thereto, or where the resolution of a question before the Chamber might have a result inconsistent with a judgment previously delivered by the Court, the Chamber may, at any time before it has rendered its judgment, relinquish jurisdiction in favour of the Grand Chamber, unless one of the parties to the case objects.

Article 31
Powers of the Grand Chamber

The Grand Chamber shall

(a)   determine applications submitted either under Article 33 or Article 34 when a Chamber has relinquished jurisdiction under Article 30 or when the case has been referred to it under Article 43;
(b)   decide on issues referred to the Court by the Committee of Ministers in accordance with Article 46, paragraph 4; and
(c)   consider requests for advisory opinions submitted under Article 47.

Article 32
Jurisdiction of the Court

1. The jurisdiction of the Court shall extend to all matters concerning the interpretation and application of the Convention and the Protocols thereto which are referred to it as provided in Articles 33, 34, 46 and 47.

2. In the event of dispute as to whether the Court has jurisdiction, the Court shall decide.

Article 33
Inter-State cases

Any High Contracting Party may refer to the Court any alleged breach of the provisions of the Convention and the Protocols thereto by another High Contracting Party.

Article 34
Individual applications

The Court may receive applications from any person, non-governmental organisation or group of individuals claiming to be the victim of a violation by one of the High

Contracting Parties of the rights set forth in the Convention or the Protocols thereto. The High Contracting Parties undertake not to hinder in any way the effective exercise of this right.

'victim' (Art 34)—See [RCLP para 5.30].

Article 35
Admissibility criteria

1. The Court may only deal with the matter after all domestic remedies have been exhausted, according to the generally recognised rules of international law, and within a period of six months from the date on which the final decision was taken.

2. The Court shall not deal with any application submitted under Article 34 that

    (a)   is anonymous; or

    (b)   is substantially the same as a matter that has already been examined by the Court or has already been submitted to another procedure of international investigation or settlement and contains no relevant new information.

3. The Court shall declare inadmissible any individual application submitted under Article 34 if it considers that:

    (a)   the application is incompatible with the provisions of the Convention or the Protocols thereto, manifestly ill-founded, or an abuse of the right of individual application; or

    (b)   the applicant has not suffered a significant disadvantage, unless respect for human rights as defined in the Convention and the Protocols thereto requires an examination of the application on the merits and provided that no case may be rejected on this ground which has not been duly considered by a domestic tribunal.

4. The Court shall reject any application which it considers inadmissible under this Article. It may do so at any stage of the proceedings.

'all domestic remedies have been exhausted' (Art 35(1))—This requirement does not need to be met where the breach complained of concerns the administrative practice of the State complained against (*Ireland v United Kingdom* ILR 58, 190, paras 156–159) [RCLP para 2.87].

Article 36
Third party intervention

1. In all cases before a Chamber or the Grand Chamber, a High Contracting Party one of whose nationals is an applicant shall have the right to submit written comments and to take part in hearings.

2. The President of the Court may, in the interest of the proper administration of justice, invite any High Contracting Party which is not a party to the proceedings or any person concerned who is not the applicant to submit written comments or take part in hearings.

3. In all cases before a Chamber or the Grand Chamber, the Council of Europe Commissioner for Human Rights may submit written comments and take part in hearings.

Article 37
Striking out applications

1. The Court may at any stage of the proceedings decide to strike an application out of its list of cases where the circumstances lead to the conclusion that

(a)   the applicant does not intend to pursue his application; or

(b)   the matter has been resolved; or

(c)   for any other reason established by the Court, it is no longer justified to continue the examination of the application.

However, the Court shall continue the examination of the application if respect for human rights as defined in the Convention and the Protocols thereto so requires.

2. The Court may decide to restore an application to its list of cases if it considers that the circumstances justify such a course.

Article 38
Examination of the case

The Court shall examine the case together with the representatives of the parties and, if need be, undertake an investigation, for the effective conduct of which the High Contracting Parties concerned shall furnish all necessary facilities.

Article 39
Friendly settlements

1. At any stage of the proceedings, the Court may place itself at the disposal of the parties concerned with a view to securing a friendly settlement of the matter on the basis of respect for human rights as defined in the Convention and the Protocols thereto.

2. Proceedings conducted under paragraph 1 shall be confidential.

3. If a friendly settlement is effected, the Court shall strike the case out of its list by means of a decision which shall be confined to a brief statement of the facts and of the solution reached.

4. This decision shall be transmitted to the Committee of Ministers, which shall supervise the execution of the terms of the friendly settlement as set out in the decision.

Article 40
Public hearings and access to documents

1. Hearings shall be in public unless the Court in exceptional circumstances decides otherwise.

2. Documents deposited with the Registrar shall be accessible to the public unless the President of the Court decides otherwise.

Article 41
Just satisfaction

If the Court finds that there has been a violation of the Convention or the Protocols thereto, and if the internal law of the High Contracting Party concerned allows only partial reparation to be made, the Court shall, if necessary, afford just satisfaction to the injured party.

Article 42
Judgments of Chambers

Judgments of Chambers shall become final in accordance with the provisions of Article 44, paragraph 2.

Article 43
Referral to the Grand Chamber

1. Within a period of three months from the date of the judgment of the Chamber, any party to the case may, in exceptional cases, request that the case be referred to the Grand Chamber.

2. A panel of five judges of the Grand Chamber shall accept the request if the case raises a serious question affecting the interpretation or application of the Convention or the Protocols thereto, or a serious issue of general importance.

3. If the panel accepts the request, the Grand Chamber shall decide the case by means of a judgment.

Article 44
Final judgments

1. The judgment of the Grand Chamber shall be final.

2. The judgment of a Chamber shall become final

(a) when the parties declare that they will not request that the case be referred to the Grand Chamber; or

(b) three months after the date of the judgment, if reference of the case to the Grand Chamber has not been requested; or

(c) when the panel of the Grand Chamber rejects the request to refer under Article 43.

3. The final judgment shall be published.

Article 45
Reasons for judgments and decisions

1. Reasons shall be given for judgments as well as for decisions declaring applications admissible or inadmissible.

2. If a judgment does not represent, in whole or in part, the unanimous opinion of the judges, any judge shall be entitled to deliver a separate opinion.

Article 46
Binding force and execution of judgments

1. The High Contracting Parties undertake to abide by the final judgment of the Court in any case to which they are parties.

2. The final judgment of the Court shall be transmitted to the Committee of Ministers, which shall supervise its execution.

3. If the Committee of Ministers considers that the supervision of the execution of a final judgment is hindered by a problem of interpretation of the judgment, it may refer the matter to the Court for a ruling on the question of interpretation. A referral decision shall require a majority vote of two thirds of the representatives entitled to sit on the Committee.

4. If the Committee of Ministers considers that a High Contracting Party refuses to abide by a final judgment in a case to which it is a party, it may, after serving formal notice on that Party and by decision adopted by a majority vote of two-thirds of the representatives entitled to sit on the Committee, refer to the Court the question whether that Party has failed to fulfil its obligation under paragraph 1.

5. If the Court finds a violation of paragraph 1, it shall refer the case to the Committee of Ministers for consideration of the measures to be taken. If the Court finds no violation of paragraph 1, it shall refer the case to the Committee of Ministers, which shall close its examination of the case.

Article 47
Advisory opinions

1. The Court may, at the request of the Committee of Ministers, give advisory opinions on legal questions concerning the interpretation of the Convention and the Protocols thereto.

2. Such opinions shall not deal with any question relating to the content or scope of the rights or freedoms defined in Section I of the Convention and the Protocols thereto, or with any other question which the Court or the Committee of Ministers might have to consider in consequence of any such proceedings as could be instituted in accordance with the Convention.

3. Decisions of the Committee of Ministers to request an advisory opinion of the Court shall require a majority vote of the representatives entitled to sit on the Committee.

Article 48
Advisory jurisdiction of the Court

The Court shall decide whether a request for an advisory opinion submitted by the Committee of Ministers is within its competence as defined in Article 47.

Article 49
Reasons for advisory opinions

1. Reasons shall be given for advisory opinions of the Court.

2. If the advisory opinion does not represent, in whole or in part, the unanimous opinion of the judges, any judge shall be entitled to deliver a separate opinion.

3. Advisory opinions of the Court shall be communicated to the Committee of Ministers.

Article 50
Expenditure on the Court

The expenditure on the Court shall be borne by the Council of Europe.

Article 51
Privileges and immunities of judges

The judges shall be entitled, during the exercise of their functions, to the privileges and immunities provided for in Article 40 of the Statute of the Council of Europe and in the agreements made thereunder.

Section III
Miscellaneous provisions

Article 52

Inquiries by the Secretary General

On receipt of a request from the Secretary General of the Council of Europe any High Contracting Party shall furnish an explanation of the manner in which its internal law ensures the effective implementation of any of the provisions of the Convention.

Article 53
Safeguard for existing human rights

Nothing in this Convention shall be construed as limiting or derogating from any of the human rights and fundamental freedoms which may be ensured under the laws of any High Contracting Party or under any other agreement to which it is a party.

Article 54
Powers of the Committee of Ministers

Nothing in this Convention shall prejudice the powers conferred on the Committee of Ministers by the Statute of the Council of Europe.

Article 55
Exclusion of other means of dispute settlement

The High Contracting Parties agree that, except by special agreement, they will not avail themselves of treaties, conventions or declarations in force between them for the purpose of submitting, by way of petition, a dispute arising out of the interpretation or application of this Convention to a means of settlement other than those provided for in this Convention.

Article 56
Territorial application

1. Any State may at the time of its ratification or at any time thereafter declare by notification addressed to the Secretary General of the Council of Europe that the present Convention shall, subject to paragraph 4 of this Article, extend to all or any of the territories for whose international relations it is responsible.

2. The Convention shall extend to the territory or territories named in the notification as from the thirtieth day after the receipt of this notification by the Secretary General of the Council of Europe.

3. The provisions of this Convention shall be applied in such territories with due regard, however, to local requirements.

4. Any State which has made a declaration in accordance with paragraph 1 of this Article may at any time thereafter declare on behalf of one or more of the territories to which the declaration relates that it accepts the competence of the Court to receive applications from individuals, non-governmental organisations or groups of individuals as provided by Article 34 of the Convention.

Article 57
Reservations

1. Any State may, when signing this Convention or when depositing its instrument of ratification, make a reservation in respect of any particular provision of the Convention to the extent that any law then in force in its territory is not in conformity with the provision. Reservations of a general character shall not be permitted under this Article.

2. Any reservation made under this Article shall contain a brief statement of the law concerned.

Article 58
Denunciation

1. A High Contracting Party may denounce the present Convention only after the expiry of five years from the date on which it became a party to it and after six months'

notice contained in a notification addressed to the Secretary General of the Council of Europe, who shall inform the other High Contracting Parties.

2. Such a denunciation shall not have the effect of releasing the High Contracting Party concerned from its obligations under this Convention in respect of any act which, being capable of constituting a violation of such obligations, may have been performed by it before the date at which the denunciation became effective.

3. Any High Contracting Party which shall cease to be a member of the Council of Europe shall cease to be a party to this Convention under the same conditions.

4. The Convention may be denounced in accordance with the provisions of the preceding paragraphs in respect of any territory to which it has been declared to extend under the terms of Article 56.

Article 59
Signature and ratification

1. This Convention shall be open to the signature of the members of the Council of Europe. It shall be ratified. Ratifications shall be deposited with the Secretary General of the Council of Europe.

2. The European Union may accede to this Convention.

3. The present Convention shall come into force after the deposit of ten instruments of ratification.

4. As regards any signatory ratifying subsequently, the Convention shall come into force at the date of the deposit of its instrument of ratification.

5. The Secretary General of the Council of Europe shall notify all the members of the Council of Europe of the entry into force of the Convention, the names of the High Contracting Parties who have ratified it, and the deposit of all instruments of ratification which may be effected subsequently.

Done at Rome this 4th day of November 1950, in English and French, both texts being equally authentic, in a single copy which shall remain deposited in the archives of the Council of Europe. The Secretary General shall transmit certified copies to each of the signatories.

PROTOCOL TO THE CONVENTION FOR THE PROTECTION OF HUMAN RIGHTS AND FUNDAMENTAL FREEDOMS

Paris, 20.III.1952

The governments signatory hereto, being members of the Council of Europe,

Being resolved to take steps to ensure the collective enforcement of certain rights and freedoms other than those already included in Section I of the Convention for the Protection of Human Rights and Fundamental Freedoms signed at Rome on 4 November 1950 (hereinafter referred to as "the Convention"),

Have agreed as follows:

Article 1
Protection of property

Every natural or legal person is entitled to the peaceful enjoyment of his possessions. No one shall be deprived of his possessions except in the public interest and subject to the conditions provided for by law and by the general principles of international law.

The preceding provisions shall not, however, in any way impair the right of a State to enforce such laws as it deems necessary to control the use of property in accordance with the general interest or to secure the payment of taxes or other contributions or penalties.

Article 2
Right to education

No person shall be denied the right to education. In the exercise of any functions which it assumes in relation to education and to teaching, the State shall respect the right of parents to ensure such education and teaching in conformity with their own religious and philosophical convictions.

Article 3
Right to free elections

The High Contracting Parties undertake to hold free elections at reasonable intervals by secret ballot, under conditions which will ensure the free expression of the opinion of the people in the choice of the legislature.

Article 4
Territorial application

Any High Contracting Party may at the time of signature or ratification or at any time thereafter communicate to the Secretary General of the Council of Europe a declaration stating the extent to which it undertakes that the provisions of the present Protocol shall apply to such of the territories for the international relations of which it is responsible as are named therein.

Any High Contracting Party which has communicated a declaration in virtue of the preceding paragraph may from time to time communicate a further declaration modifying the terms of any former declaration or terminating the application of the provisions of this Protocol in respect of any territory.

A declaration made in accordance with this Article shall be deemed to have been made in accordance with paragraph 1 of Article 56 of the Convention.

Article 5
Relationship to the Convention

As between the High Contracting Parties the provisions of Articles 1, 2, 3 and 4 of this Protocol shall be regarded as additional Articles to the Convention and all the provisions of the Convention shall apply accordingly.

Article 6
Signature and ratification

This Protocol shall be open for signature by the members of the Council of Europe, who are the signatories of the Convention; it shall be ratified at the same time as or after the ratification of the Convention. It shall enter into force after the deposit of ten instruments of ratification. As regards any signatory ratifying subsequently, the Protocol shall enter into force at the date of the deposit of its instrument of ratification.

The instruments of ratification shall be deposited with the Secretary General of the Council of Europe, who will notify all members of the names of those who have ratified.

Done at Paris on the 20th day of March 1952, in English and French, both texts being equally authentic, in a single copy which shall remain deposited in the archives of the Council of Europe. The Secretary General shall transmit certified copies to each of the signatory governments.

PROTOCOL NO 4 TO THE CONVENTION FOR THE PROTECTION OF HUMAN RIGHTS AND FUNDAMENTAL FREEDOMS SECURING CERTAIN RIGHTS AND FREEDOMS OTHER THAN THOSE ALREADY INCLUDED IN THE CONVENTION AND IN THE FIRST PROTOCOL THERETO

Strasbourg, 16.IX.1963

The governments signatory hereto, being members of the Council of Europe,

Being resolved to take steps to ensure the collective enforcement of certain rights and freedoms other than those already included in Section I of the Convention for the Protection of Human Rights and Fundamental Freedoms signed at Rome on 4 November 1950 (hereinafter referred to as the "Convention") and in Articles 1 to 3 of the First Protocol to the Convention, signed at Paris on 20 March 1952,

Have agreed as follows:

Article 1
Prohibition of imprisonment for debt

No one shall be deprived of his liberty merely on the ground of inability to fulfil a contractual obligation.

Article 2
Freedom of movement

1. Everyone lawfully within the territory of a State shall, within that territory, have the right to liberty of movement and freedom to choose his residence.

2. Everyone shall be free to leave any country, including his own.

3. No restrictions shall be placed on the exercise of these rights other than such as are in accordance with law and are necessary in a democratic society in the interests of national security or public safety, for the maintenance of ordre public, for the prevention of crime, for the protection of health or morals, or for the protection of the rights and freedoms of others.

4. The rights set forth in paragraph 1 may also be subject, in particular areas, to restrictions imposed in accordance with law and justified by the public interest in a democratic society.

Article 3
Prohibition of expulsion of nationals

1. No one shall be expelled, by means either of an individual or of a collective measure, from the territory of the State of which he is a national.

2. No one shall be deprived of the right to enter the territory of the State of which he is a national.

Article 4
Prohibition of collective expulsion of aliens

Collective expulsion of aliens is prohibited.

Article 5
Territorial application

1. Any High Contracting Party may, at the time of signature or ratification of this Protocol, or at any time thereafter, communicate to the Secretary General of the Council

of Europe a declaration stating the extent to which it undertakes that the provisions of this Protocol shall apply to such of the territories for the international relations of which it is responsible as are named therein.

2. Any High Contracting Party which has communicated a declaration in virtue of the preceding paragraph may, from time to time, communicate a further declaration modifying the terms of any former declaration or terminating the application of the provisions of this Protocol in respect of any territory.

3. A declaration made in accordance with this Article shall be deemed to have been made in accordance with paragraph 1 of Article 56 of the Convention.

4. The territory of any State to which this Protocol applies by virtue of ratification or acceptance by that State, and each territory to which this Protocol is applied by virtue of a declaration by that State under this Article, shall be treated as separate territories for the purpose of the references in Articles 2 and 3 to the territory of a State.

5. Any State which has made a declaration in accordance with paragraph 1 or 2 of this Article may at any time thereafter declare on behalf of one or more of the territories to which the declaration relates that it accepts the competence of the Court to receive applications from individuals, non-governmental organisations or groups of individuals as provided in Article 34 of the Convention in respect of all or any of Articles 1 to 4 of this Protocol.

Article 6
Relationship to the Convention

As between the High Contracting Parties the provisions of Articles 1 to 5 of this Protocol shall be regarded as additional Articles to the Convention, and all the provisions of the Convention shall apply accordingly.

Article 7
Signature and ratification

1. This Protocol shall be open for signature by the members of the Council of Europe who are the signatories of the Convention; it shall be ratified at the same time as or after the ratification of the Convention. It shall enter into force after the deposit of five instruments of ratification. As regards any signatory ratifying subsequently, the Protocol shall enter into force at the date of the deposit of its instrument of ratification.

2. The instruments of ratification shall be deposited with the Secretary General of the Council of Europe, who will notify all members of the names of those who have ratified.

In witness whereof the undersigned, being duly authorised thereto, have signed this Protocol.

Done at Strasbourg, this 16th day of September 1963, in English and in French, both texts being equally authoritative, in a single copy which shall remain deposited in the archives of the Council of Europe. The Secretary General shall transmit certified copies to each of the signatory States.

PROTOCOL NO 6 TO THE CONVENTION FOR THE PROTECTION OF HUMAN RIGHTS AND FUNDAMENTAL FREEDOMS CONCERNING THE ABOLITION OF THE DEATH PENALTY

Strasbourg, 28.IV.1983

The member States of the Council of Europe, signatory to this Protocol to the Convention for the Protection of Human Rights and Fundamental Freedoms, signed at Rome on 4 November 1950 (hereinafter referred to as "the Convention"),

Considering that the evolution that has occurred in several member States of the Council of Europe expresses a general tendency in favour of abolition of the death penalty;

Have agreed as follows:

Article 1

Abolition of the death penalty

The death penalty shall be abolished. No one shall be condemned to such penalty or executed.

Article 2
Death penalty in time of war

A State may make provision in its law for the death penalty in respect of acts committed in time of war or of imminent threat of war; such penalty shall be applied only in the instances laid down in the law and in accordance with its provisions. The State shall communicate to the Secretary General of the Council of Europe the relevant provisions of that law.

Article 3
Prohibition of derogations

No derogation from the provisions of this Protocol shall be made under Article 15 of the Convention.

Article 4
Prohibition of reservations

No reservation may be made under Article 57 of the Convention in respect of the provisions of this Protocol.

Article 5
Territorial application

1. Any State may at the time of signature or when depositing its instrument of ratification, acceptance or approval, specify the territory or territories to which this Protocol shall apply.

2. Any State may at any later date, by a declaration addressed to the Secretary General of the Council of Europe, extend the application of this Protocol to any other territory specified in the declaration. In respect of such territory the Protocol shall enter into force on the first day of the month following the date of receipt of such declaration by the Secretary General.

3. Any declaration made under the two preceding paragraphs may, in respect of any territory specified in such declaration, be withdrawn by a notification addressed to the Secretary General. The withdrawal shall become effective on the first day of the month following the date of receipt of such notification by the Secretary General.

Article 6
Relationship to the Convention

As between the States Parties the provisions of Articles 1 and 5 of this Protocol shall be regarded as additional Articles to the Convention and all the provisions of the Convention shall apply accordingly.

Article 7
Signature and ratification

The Protocol shall be open for signature by the member States of the Council of Europe, signatories to the Convention. It shall be subject to ratification, acceptance or approval. A member State of the Council of Europe may not ratify, accept or approve this Protocol unless it has, simultaneously or previously, ratified the Convention. Instruments of ratification, acceptance or approval shall be deposited with the Secretary General of the Council of Europe.

Article 8
Entry into force

1. This Protocol shall enter into force on the first day of the month following the date on which five member States of the Council of Europe have expressed their consent to be bound by the Protocol in accordance with the provisions of Article 7.

2. In respect of any member State which subsequently expresses its consent to be bound by it, the Protocol shall enter into force on the first day of the month following the date of the deposit of the instrument of ratification, acceptance or approval.

Article 9
Depositary functions

The Secretary General of the Council of Europe shall notify the member States of the Council of:

(a)   any signature;
(b)   the deposit of any instrument of ratification, acceptance or approval;
(c)   any date of entry into force of this Protocol in accordance with Articles 5 and 8;
(d)   any other act, notification or communication relating to this Protocol.

In witness whereof the undersigned, being duly authorised thereto, have signed this Protocol.

Done at Strasbourg, this 28th day of April 1983, in English and in French, both texts being equally authentic, in a single copy which shall be deposited in the archives of the Council of Europe. The Secretary General of the Council of Europe shall transmit certified copies to each member State of the Council of Europe.

PROTOCOL NO 7 TO THE CONVENTION FOR THE PROTECTION OF HUMAN RIGHTS AND FUNDAMENTAL FREEDOMS

Strasbourg, 22.XI.1984

The member States of the Council of Europe signatory hereto,

Being resolved to take further steps to ensure the collective enforcement of certain rights and freedoms by means of the Convention for the Protection of Human Rights and Fundamental Freedoms signed at Rome on 4 November 1950 (hereinafter referred to as "the Convention"),

Have agreed as follows:

Article 1
Procedural safeguards relating to expulsion of aliens

1. An alien lawfully resident in the territory of a State shall not be expelled therefrom except in pursuance of a decision reached in accordance with law and shall be allowed:

   (a)   to submit reasons against his expulsion,
   (b)   to have his case reviewed, and
   (c)   to be represented for these purposes before the competent authority or a person or persons designated by that authority.

2. An alien may be expelled before the exercise of his rights under paragraph 1(a), (b) and (c) of this Article, when such expulsion is necessary in the interests of public order or is grounded on reasons of national security.

Article 2
Right of appeal in criminal matters

1. Everyone convicted of a criminal offence by a tribunal shall have the right to have his conviction or sentence reviewed by a higher tribunal. The exercise of this right, including the grounds on which it may be exercised, shall be governed by law.

2. This right may be subject to exceptions in regard to offences of a minor character, as prescribed by law, or in cases in which the person concerned was tried in the first instance by the highest tribunal or was convicted following an appeal against acquittal.

Article 3
Compensation for wrongful conviction

When a person has by a final decision been convicted of a criminal offence and when subsequently his conviction has been reversed, or he has been pardoned, on the ground that a new or newly discovered fact shows conclusively that there has been a miscarriage of justice, the person who has suffered punishment as a result of such conviction shall be compensated according to the law or the practice of the State concerned, unless it is proved that the non-disclosure of the unknown fact in time is wholly or partly attributable to him.

Article 4
Right not to be tried or punished twice

1. No one shall be liable to be tried or punished again in criminal proceedings under the jurisdiction of the same State for an offence for which he has already been finally acquitted or convicted in accordance with the law and penal procedure of that State.

2. The provisions of the preceding paragraph shall not prevent the reopening of the case in accordance with the law and penal procedure of the State concerned, if there is evidence of new or newly discovered facts, or if there has been a fundamental defect in the previous proceedings, which could affect the outcome of the case.

3. No derogation from this Article shall be made under Article 15 of the Convention.

Article 5
Equality between spouses

Spouses shall enjoy equality of rights and responsibilities of a private law character between them, and in their relations with their children, as to marriage, during marriage and in the event of its dissolution. This Article shall not prevent States from taking such measures as are necessary in the interests of the children.

Article 6
Territorial application

1. Any State may at the time of signature or when depositing its instrument of ratification, acceptance or approval, specify the territory or territories to which the Protocol shall apply and state the extent to which it undertakes that the provisions of this Protocol shall apply to such territory or territories.

2. Any State may at any later date, by a declaration addressed to the Secretary General of the Council of Europe, extend the application of this Protocol to any other territory specified in the declaration. In respect of such territory the Protocol shall enter into force on the first day of the month following the expiration of a period of two months after the date of receipt by the Secretary General of such declaration.

3. Any declaration made under the two preceding paragraphs may, in respect of any territory specified in such declaration, be withdrawn or modified by a notification addressed to the Secretary General. The withdrawal or modification shall become effective on the first day of the month following the expiration of a period of two months after the date of receipt of such notification by the Secretary General.

4. A declaration made in accordance with this Article shall be deemed to have been made in accordance with paragraph 1 of Article 56 of the Convention.

5. The territory of any State to which this Protocol applies by virtue of ratification, acceptance or approval by that State, and each territory to which this Protocol is applied by virtue of a declaration by that State under this Article, may be treated as separate territories for the purpose of the reference in Article 1 to the territory of a State.

6. Any State which has made a declaration in accordance with paragraph 1 or 2 of this Article may at any time thereafter declare on behalf of one or more of the territories to which the declaration relates that it accepts the competence of the Court to receive applications from individuals, non-governmental organisations or groups of individuals as provided in Article 34 of the Convention in respect of Articles 1 to 5 of this Protocol.

Article 7
Relationship to the Convention

As between the States Parties, the provisions of Article 1 to 6 of this Protocol shall be regarded as additional Articles to the Convention, and all the provisions of the Convention shall apply accordingly.

Article 8
Signature and ratification

This Protocol shall be open for signature by member States of the Council of Europe which have signed the Convention. It is subject to ratification, acceptance or approval. A member State of the Council of Europe may not ratify, accept or approve this Protocol without previously or simultaneously ratifying the Convention. Instruments of ratification, acceptance or approval shall be deposited with the Secretary General of the Council of Europe.

Article 9
Entry into force

1. This Protocol shall enter into force on the first day of the month following the expiration of a period of two months after the date on which seven member States of the Council of Europe have expressed their consent to be bound by the Protocol in accordance with the provisions of Article 8.

2. In respect of any member State which subsequently expresses its consent to be bound by it, the Protocol shall enter into force on the first day of the month following the expiration of a period of two months after the date of the deposit of the instrument of ratification, acceptance or approval.

Article 10
Depositary functions

The Secretary General of the Council of Europe shall notify all the member States of the Council of Europe of:

(a) any signature;
(b) the deposit of any instrument of ratification, acceptance or approval;
(c) any date of entry into force of this Protocol in accordance with Articles 6 and 9;
(d) any other act, notification or declaration relating to this Protocol.

In witness whereof the undersigned, being duly authorised thereto, have signed this Protocol.

Done at Strasbourg, this 22nd day of November 1984, in English and French, both texts being equally authentic, in a single copy which shall be deposited in the archives of the Council of Europe. The Secretary General of the Council of Europe shall transmit certified copies to each member State of the Council of Europe.

PROTOCOL NO 12 TO THE CONVENTION FOR THE PROTECTION OF HUMAN RIGHTS AND FUNDAMENTAL FREEDOMS

Rome, 4.XI.2000

The member States of the Council of Europe signatory hereto,

Having regard to the fundamental principle according to which all persons are equal before the law and are entitled to the equal protection of the law;

Being resolved to take further steps to promote the equality of all persons through the collective enforcement of a general prohibition of discrimination by means of the Convention for the Protection of Human Rights and Fundamental Freedoms signed at Rome on 4 November 1950 (hereinafter referred to as "the Convention");

Reaffirming that the principle of non-discrimination does not prevent States Parties from taking measures in order to promote full and effective equality, provided that there is an objective and reasonable justification for those measures,

Have agreed as follows:

Article 1
General prohibition of discrimination

1. The enjoyment of any right set forth by law shall be secured without discrimination on any ground such as sex, race, colour, language, religion, political or other opinion, national or social origin, association with a national minority, property, birth or other status.

2. No one shall be discriminated against by any public authority on any ground such as those mentioned in paragraph 1.

Article 2
Territorial application

1. Any State may, at the time of signature or when depositing its instrument of ratification, acceptance or approval, specify the territory or territories to which this Protocol shall apply.

2. Any State may at any later date, by a declaration addressed to the Secretary General of the Council of Europe, extend the application of this Protocol to any other territory specified in the declaration. In respect of such territory the Protocol shall enter into force on the first day of the month following the expiration of a period of three months after the date of receipt by the Secretary General of such declaration.

3. Any declaration made under the two preceding paragraphs may, in respect of any territory specified in such declaration, be withdrawn or modified by a notification addressed to the Secretary General of the Council of Europe. The withdrawal or modification shall become effective on the first day of the month following the expiration of a period of three months after the date of receipt of such notification by the Secretary General.

4. A declaration made in accordance with this Article shall be deemed to have been made in accordance with paragraph 1 of Article 56 of the Convention.

5. Any State which has made a declaration in accordance with paragraph 1 or 2 of this Article may at any time thereafter declare on behalf of one or more of the territories to which the declaration relates that it accepts the competence of the Court to receive applications from individuals, non-governmental organisations or groups of individuals as provided by Article 34 of the Convention in respect of Article 1 of this Protocol.

Article 3
Relationship to the Convention

As between the States Parties, the provisions of Articles 1 and 2 of this Protocol shall be regarded as additional Articles to the Convention, and all the provisions of the Convention shall apply accordingly.

Article 4
Signature and ratification

This Protocol shall be open for signature by member States of the Council of Europe which have signed the Convention. It is subject to ratification, acceptance or approval. A member State of the Council of Europe may not ratify, accept or approve this Protocol without previously or simultaneously ratifying the Convention. Instruments of ratification, acceptance or approval shall be deposited with the Secretary General of the Council of Europe.

Article 5
Entry into force

1. This Protocol shall enter into force on the first day of the month following the expiration of a period of three months after the date on which ten member States of the Council of Europe have expressed their consent to be bound by the Protocol in accordance with the provisions of Article 4.

2. In respect of any member State which subsequently expresses its consent to be bound by it, the Protocol shall enter into force on the first day of the month following the expiration of a period of three months after the date of the deposit of the instrument of ratification, acceptance or approval.

Article 6
Depositary functions

The Secretary General of the Council of Europe shall notify all the member States of the Council of Europe of:

    (a)   any signature;
    (b)   the deposit of any instrument of ratification, acceptance or approval;
    (c)   any date of entry into force of this Protocol in accordance with Articles 2 and 5;
    (d)   any other act, notification or communication relating to this Protocol.

In witness whereof the undersigned, being duly authorised thereto, have signed this Protocol.

Done at Rome, this 4th day of November 2000, in English and in French, both texts being equally authentic, in a single copy which shall be deposited in the archives of the Council of Europe. The Secretary General of the Council of Europe shall transmit certified copies to each member State of the Council of Europe.

PROTOCOL NO 13 TO THE CONVENTION FOR THE PROTECTION OF HUMAN RIGHTS AND FUNDAMENTAL FREEDOMS CONCERNING THE ABOLITION OF THE DEATH PENALTY IN ALL CIRCUMSTANCES

Vilnius, 3.V.2002

The member States of the Council of Europe signatory hereto,

Convinced that everyone's right to life is a basic value in a democratic society and that the abolition of the death penalty is essential for the protection of this right and for the full recognition of the inherent dignity of all human beings;

Wishing to strengthen the protection of the right to life guaranteed by the Convention for the Protection of Human Rights and Fundamental Freedoms signed at Rome on 4 November 1950 (hereinafter referred to as "the Convention");

Noting that Protocol No 6 to the Convention concerning the abolition of the death penalty, signed at Strasbourg on 28 April 1983, does not exclude the death penalty in respect of acts committed in time of war or of imminent threat of war;

Being resolved to take the final step in order to abolish the death penalty in all circumstances,

Have agreed as follows:

Article 1
Abolition of the death penalty

The death penalty shall be abolished. No one shall be condemned to such penalty or executed.

Article 2
Prohibitions of derogations

No derogation from the provisions of this Protocol shall be made under Article 15 of the Convention.

Article 3
Prohibitions of reservations

No reservation may be made under Article 57 of the Convention in respect of the provisions of this Protocol.

Article 4
Territorial application

1. Any State may, at the time of signature or when depositing its instrument of ratification, acceptance or approval, specify the territory or territories to which this Protocol shall apply.

2. Any State may at any later date, by a declaration addressed to the Secretary General of the Council of Europe, extend the application of this Protocol to any other territory specified in the declaration. In respect of such territory the Protocol shall enter into force on the first day of the month following the expiration of a period of three months after the date of receipt by the Secretary General of such declaration.

3. Any declaration made under the two preceding paragraphs may, in respect of any territory specified in such declaration, be withdrawn or modified by a notification addressed to the Secretary General. The withdrawal or modification shall become effective on the first day of the month following the expiration of a period of three months after the date of receipt of such notification by the Secretary General.

Article 5
Relationship to the Convention

As between the States Parties the provisions of Articles 1 to 4 of this Protocol shall be regarded as additional Articles to the Convention, and all the provisions of the Convention shall apply accordingly.

Article 6
Signature and ratification

This Protocol shall be open for signature by member States of the Council of Europe which have signed the Convention. It is subject to ratification, acceptance or approval. A member State of the Council of Europe may not ratify, accept or approve this Protocol without previously or simultaneously ratifying the Convention. Instruments of ratification, acceptance or approval shall be deposited with the Secretary General of the Council of Europe.

Article 7
Entry into force

1. This Protocol shall enter into force on the first day of the month following the expiration of a period of three months after the date on which ten member States of the

Council of Europe have expressed their consent to be bound by the Protocol in accordance with the provisions of Article 6.

2. In respect of any member State which subsequently expresses its consent to be bound by it, the Protocol shall enter into force on the first day of the month following the expiration of a period of three months after the date of the deposit of the instrument of ratification, acceptance or approval.

Article 8
Depositary functions

The Secretary General of the Council of Europe shall notify all the member States of the Council of Europe of:

(a)   any signature;
(b)   the deposit of any instrument of ratification, acceptance or approval;
(c)   any date of entry into force of this Protocol in accordance with Articles 4 and 7;
(d)   any other act, notification or communication relating to this Protocol;

In witness whereof the undersigned, being duly authorised thereto, have signed this Protocol.

Done at Vilnius, this 3rd day of May 2002, in English and in French, both texts being equally authentic, in a single copy which shall be deposited in the archives of the Council of Europe. The Secretary General of the Council of Europe shall transmit certified copies to each member State of the Council of Europe

CHAPTER 21

HUMAN RIGHTS ACT 1998

An Act to give further effect to rights and freedoms guaranteed under the European Convention on Human Rights; to make provision with respect to holders of certain judicial offices who become judges of the European Court of Human Rights; and for connected purposes.

9th November 1998

Be it enacted by the Queen's most Excellent Majesty, by and with the advice and consent of the Lords Spiritual and Temporal, and Commons, in this present Parliament assembled, and by the authority of the same, as follows:

Introduction

1 The Convention Rights

(1) In this Act "the Convention rights" means the rights and fundamental freedoms set out in –

- (a)   Articles 2 to 12 and 14 of the Convention,
- (b)   Articles 1 to 3 of the First Protocol, and
- (c)   Article 1 of the Thirteenth Protocol],

as read with Articles 16 to 18 of the Convention.

(2) Those Articles are to have effect for the purposes of this Act subject to any designated derogation or reservation (as to which see sections 14 and 15).

(3) The Articles are set out in Schedule 1.

(4) The Secretary of State may by order make such amendments to this Act as he considers appropriate to reflect the effect, in relation to the United Kingdom, of a protocol.

(5) In subsection (4) "protocol" means a protocol to the Convention –

- (a)   which the United Kingdom has ratified; or
- (b)   which the United Kingdom has signed with a view to ratification.

(6) No amendment may be made by an order under subsection (4) so as to come into force before the protocol concerned is in force in relation to the United Kingdom.

Amendments— SI 2003/1887; SI 2004/1574.

Commencement—The Human Rights Act 1998 came into force on 2 October 2000 (Human Rights Act (Commencement No 2) Order 2000, SI 2000/1851). By s 1(2) of the Human Rights Act 1998, Arts 2–12 and Art 14, together with Arts 1–3 of the First Protocol and Arts 1 and 2 of the Second Protocol, as read with Arts 16–18 are given effect in domestic law [**RCLP para 2.76**]. It should be noted that Sch 1 to the Act omits Art 1 of the ECHR (obligation to respect human rights), Art 13 (right to an effective remedy), Arts 15–50 (operational provisions of the European Court of Human Rights) and the remaining protocols of the ECHR [**RCLP para 3.57**].

Notwithstanding the Art 13 is not included in Sch 1 of the Act, the domestic courts have continued to have regard to it (*Re S (Minors) (Care Order: Implementation of Care Plan); Re W (Minors) (Care Order: Adequacy of Care Plan)* [2002] UKHL 10, [2002] 2 WLR 720, [2002] 1 FLR 815, paras 60 and 61) **[RCLP para 16.131]**.

'to have effect' (**s 1(2)**)—The Human Rights Act 1998 does not strictly incorporate the ECHR into domestic law but rather duplicates certain provisions of the ECHR in an Act of Parliament (see *R (Al-Jedda) v Secretary of State for Defence* [2007] UKHL 58, [2008] 1 AC 332 and *Re McKerr* [2004] UKHL 12, [2004] 1 WLR 807 at para 25) **[RCLP para 3.57]**. The principles of extraterritoriality developed by the European Court of Human Rights are applicable to claims made under the Human Rights Act 1998 (*R (Mazim Jumaa Gatteh Al Skeina & Others) v Secretary of State for Defence* [2008] 1 AC 153 and *Ghaidan v Godin-Mendoza* [2004] 2 FLR 600). But see *R (Al-Saadoon & Anther) v Secretary of State for Defence* [2010] QB 486. It has been held that, in respect of the domestic application of Arts 6, 8 and 14, they apply only those within the domestic jurisdiction (see *Re J (Child Returned Abroad: Human Rights)* [2004] 2 FLR 85, para 34) **[RCLP para 3.57]**. For jurisdictional position in relation to the exercise of executive authority see *R (Smith) v Secretary of State for Defence* [2011] 1 AC 1.

2 Interpretation of Convention rights

(1) A court or tribunal determining a question which has arisen in connection with a Convention right must take into account any –

(a) judgment, decision, declaration or advisory opinion of the European Court of Human Rights,

(b) opinion of the Commission given in a report adopted under Article 31 of the Convention,

(c) decision of the Commission in connection with Article 26 or 27(2) of the Convention, or

(d) decision of the Committee of Ministers taken under Article 46 of the Convention,

whenever made or given, so far as, in the opinion of the court or tribunal, it is relevant to the proceedings in which that question has arisen.

(2) Evidence of any judgment, decision, declaration or opinion of which account may have to be taken under this section is to be given in proceedings before any court or tribunal in such manner as may be provided by rules.

(3) In this section "rules" means rules of court or, in the case of proceedings before a tribunal, rules made for the purposes of this section –

(a) by the Lord Chancellor or the Secretary of State, in relation to any proceedings outside Scotland;

(b) by the Secretary of State, in relation to proceedings in Scotland; or

(c) by a Northern Ireland department, in relation to proceedings before a tribunal in Northern Ireland –

(i) which deals with transferred matters; and

(ii) for which no rules made under paragraph (a) are in force.

Amendments—SI 2003/1887; SI 2005/3429.

Jurisprudence of the ECtHR (**s 2(1)**)—Whilst the jurisprudence of the European Court of Human Rights, the opinions and decisions of the European Commission and the decisions of the Committee of Ministers are not binding on domestic courts in the strict sense (*Fitzpatrick v Sterling Housing Association Ltd* [2001] 1 AC 27, [1999] 3 WLR 113, [1999] 4 All ER 705, HL and *Ghaidan v Godin-Mendoza* [2004] UKHL 30, [2004] 2 AC 557, [2004] 2 FCR 481, [2004] 2 FLR 600) absent special circumstances the court should follow clear and constant jurisprudence from the ECtHR (*R (Alconbury Developments Ltd) v Secretary of State for the Environment, Transport and the Regions* [2001] UKHL 23, [2003] 2 AC 295, para 26 (cited with approval by Lord Bingham *in R (Ullah) v Special Adjudicator* [2004] UKHL 26, [2004] 2 AC 323, para 20 and *R (Anderson) v Secretary of State for the Home Department* [2002] UKHL 46, [2003] 1 AC 837, para 18) **[RCLP para 3.84]**. See however *R v Horncastle* [2010] 2 AC 373 and *Manchester City Council v Pinnock* [2011] 2 AC 104. The domestic court must adhere to the English rules of precedent (*Kay and Ors v London Borough of Lambeth and ors; Leeds City Council v Price and ors* [2006] 2 AC 465).

Legislation

3 Interpretation of legislation

(1) So far as it is possible to do so, primary legislation and subordinate legislation must be read and given effect in a way which is compatible with the Convention rights.

(2) This section –

(a) applies to primary legislation and subordinate legislation whenever enacted;

(b) does not affect the validity, continuing operation or enforcement of any incompatible primary legislation; and

(c) does not affect the validity, continuing operation or enforcement of any incompatible subordinate legislation if (disregarding any possibility of revocation) primary legislation prevents removal of the incompatibility.

'so far as it is possible to do so' (s 3(1))—The phrase 'so far as it is possible to do so' has been held to mean that it must be read and given effect in a way that is compatible with the ECHR unless it is plainly impossible to do so (*R v A* [2002] 1 AC 45 and see *Re S (Minors) (Care Order: Implementation of Care Plan)* [2002] 1 FLR 815 and *Hounslow LBC v Powell* [2011] 2 AC 186).

'read and given effect' (s 3(1))—The wording of s 3(1) is wide enough to encompass everyone concerned with interpreting legislation (*Ghaidan v Godin-Mendoza* [2004] UKHL 30, [2004] 2 AC 557, [2004] 2 FCR 481, [2004] 2 FLR 600) [**RCLP para 3.58**]. The application of s 3(1) is obligatory (*Re S (Minors) (Care Order: Implementation of Care Plan); Re W (Minors) (Care Order: Adequacy of Care Plan)* [2002] UKHL 10, [2002] 2 WLR 720, [2002] 1 FLR 815, paras 37–40) [**RCLP para 3.58**]. In order to achieve compatibility words may be read into a statutory provision or individual words removed (*Pickstone v Freemans PLC* [1989] 1 AC 66 *O'Brien v Sim-Chem Ltd* [1980] ICR 573 at 580F, *McMonagle v Westminster City Council* [1990] 2 AC 716, HL 726E. See also *De Freitas v Permanent Secretary for the Ministry of Agriculture, Fisheries, Lands and Housing* [1998] 3 WLR 675) [**RCLP para 3.58**]. The Act is designed to promote the search for compatibility (*Re S (Minors) (Care Order: Implementation of Care Plan); Re W (Minors) (Care Order: Adequacy of Care Plan)* [2002] UKHL 10, [2002] 2 WLR 720, [2002] 1 FLR 815, para 50) [**RCLP para 3.59**].

4 Declaration of incompatibility

(1) Subsection (2) applies in any proceedings in which a court determines whether a provision of primary legislation is compatible with a Convention right.

(2) If the court is satisfied that the provision is incompatible with a Convention right, it may make a declaration of that incompatibility.

(3) Subsection (4) applies in any proceedings in which a court determines whether a provision of subordinate legislation, made in the exercise of a power conferred by primary legislation, is compatible with a Convention right.

(4) If the court is satisfied –

(a) that the provision is incompatible with a Convention right, and

(b) that (disregarding any possibility of revocation) the primary legislation concerned prevents removal of the incompatibility,

it may make a declaration of that incompatibility.

(5) In this section "court" means –

(a) the Supreme Court;

(b) the Judicial Committee of the Privy Council;

(c) the Court Martial Appeal Court;

(d) in Scotland, the High Court of Justiciary sitting otherwise than as a trial court or the Court of Session;

(e) in England and Wales or Northern Ireland, the High Court or the Court of Appeal.

(f) the Court of Protection, in any matter being dealt with by the President of the Family Division, the Vice-Chancellor or a puisne judge of the High Court.

(6) A declaration under this section ("a declaration of incompatibility") –

(a) does not affect the validity, continuing operation or enforcement of the provision in respect of which it is given; and

(b) is not binding on the parties to the proceedings in which it is made.

Amendments— Mental Capacity Act 2005, s 67(1), Sch 6, para 43; Constitutional Reform Act 2005, s 40(4), Sch 9, Pt 1, para 66(1), (2); Armed Forces Act 2006, s 378(1), Sch 16, para 156; Crime and Courts Act 2013, s 21(4), Sch 14, Pt 3, para 5(5); SI 2013/2200.

'declaration of incompatibility' (s 4(2))—See *Wilson v First County Trust Ltd* (No 2) [2003] UKHL 40, [2004] 2 AC 816, [2003] 3 WLR 568, [2003] 4 All ER 97. Whether the incompatibility has to be established by reference to a Convention right under the ECHR binding on the UK in international law or by reference to a right given effect by the HRA 1998 and interpreted by the domestic courts is unclear (see *R v Animal Defenders International*) v *Secretary of State for Culture, Media and Sport* [2008] UKHL 15, [2008] 1 AC 1312, [2008] 2 WLR 781) [**RCLP para 3.59**]. A lacuna in legislation cannot be the subject of a declaration of incompatibility (*Re S (Minors) (Care Order: Implementation of Care Plan* [2002] 1 FLR 815).

5 Right of Crown to intervene

(1) Where a court is considering whether to make a declaration of incompatibility, the Crown is entitled to notice in accordance with rules of court.

(2) In any case to which subsection (1) applies –

(a) a Minister of the Crown (or a person nominated by him),

(b) a member of the Scottish Executive,

(c) a Northern Ireland Minister,

(d) a Northern Ireland department,

is entitled, on giving notice in accordance with rules of court, to be joined as a party to the proceedings.

(3) Notice under subsection (2) may be given at any time during the proceedings.

(4) A person who has been made a party to criminal proceedings (other than in Scotland) as the result of a notice under subsection (2) may, with leave, appeal to the Supreme Court against any declaration of incompatibility made in the proceedings.

(5) In subsection (4) –

"criminal proceedings" includes all proceedings before the Court Martial Appeal Court; and "leave" means leave granted by the court making the declaration of incompatibility or by the Supreme Court.

Amendments—Constitutional Reform Act 2005, s 40(4), Sch 9, Pt 1, para 66(1), (3); Armed Forces Act 2006, s 378(1), Sch 16, para 157.

Right of the Crown to intervene (s 5(1))—See *Poplar Housing and Regeneration Community Association Ltd v Donoghue* [2001] EWCA Civ 595, [2002] QB 48, paras 15–20 and CPR 1998 r 19.4A and associated Practice Direction) [**RCLP para 3.59**].

Public authorities

6 Acts of public authorities

(1) It is unlawful for a public authority to act in a way which is incompatible with a Convention right.

(2) Subsection (1) does not apply to an act if –

(a) as the result of one or more provisions of primary legislation, the authority could not have acted differently; or

(b) in the case of one or more provisions of, or made under, primary legislation which cannot be read or given effect in a way which is compatible with the Convention rights, the authority was acting so as to give effect to or enforce those provisions.

(3) In this section "public authority" includes –

(a) a court or tribunal, and

(b) any person certain of whose functions are functions of a public nature,

but does not include either House of Parliament or a person exercising functions in connection with proceedings in Parliament.

(4) ...

(5) In relation to a particular act, a person is not a public authority by virtue only of subsection (3)(b) if the nature of the act is private.

(6) "An act" includes a failure to act but does not include a failure to –

(a) introduce in, or lay before, Parliament a proposal for legislation; or

(b) make any primary legislation or remedial order.

Amendments—Constitutional Reform Act 2005, ss 40(4), 146, Sch 9, Pt 1, para 66(1), (4), Sch 18, Pt 5.

'public authority' (s 6(1), s 6(3))—The term 'public authority' is not definitively defined by the Act by s 6(3) (see *Aston Cantlow and Wilmcote with Billesly Parochial Church Council v Wallbank* [2003] UKHL 37, [2004] 1 AC 546, para 6). There is accordingly scope for argument as to what constitutes a 'public authority' for the purposes of the Act (see *R (Johnson) v London Borough of Havering and Others* [2006] EWHC 1714, (Admin) , [2006] All ER (D) 133 (July), *R (Johnson) v London Borough of Havering and Others*; *YL v Birmingham City Council and Others* [2007] EWCA Civ 26, [2007] All ER (D) 271 (Jan) and *YL v Birmingham City Council and Others* [2007] UKHL 27, [2007] All ER (D) 207 (Jun)). The term 'public authority' will include a United Kingdom public authority acting within its jurisdiction outside the United Kingdom (*R (Al-Skeini) v Secretary of State for Defence* [2007] UKHL 26, [2008] 1 AC 153, pars 54–59) **[RCLP para 3.60]**.

'act' (s 6(1))—It will generally be necessary to examine the compatibility of the act rather than the legislation under which the act is done (*Miss Behavin' Ltd v Belfast City Council* [2007] UKHL 19, [2007] 3 All ER 1007, [2007] 1 WLR 1420, paras 84–87) **[RCLP para 3.60]**.

'incompatible' (s 6(1))—The word 'incompatible' bears its ordinary meaning of 'inconsistent' (*A-G's Reference (No 2 of 2001)* [2003] UKHL 68, [2004] 2 AC 72, para 7) **[RCLP para 3.60]**.

'failure to act' (s 6(6))—See *Re S (Minors)(Care Order: Implementation of Care Plan), Re W (Minors) (Care Order: Adequacy of Care Plan)* [2002] UKHL 10, [2002] 2 AC 291, [2002] 2 WLR 720, [2002] 2 All ER 192, para 45 **[RCLP para 3.60]**.

7 Proceedings

(1) A person who claims that a public authority has acted (or proposes to act) in a way which is made unlawful by section 6(1) may –

(a)   bring proceedings against the authority under this Act in the appropriate court or tribunal, or

(b)   rely on the Convention right or rights concerned in any legal proceedings,

but only if he is (or would be) a victim of the unlawful act.

(2) In subsection (1)(a) "appropriate court or tribunal" means such court or tribunal as may be determined in accordance with rules; and proceedings against an authority include a counterclaim or similar proceeding.

(3) If the proceedings are brought on an application for judicial review, the applicant is to be taken to have a sufficient interest in relation to the unlawful act only if he is, or would be, a victim of that act.

(4) If the proceedings are made by way of a petition for judicial review in Scotland, the applicant shall be taken to have title and interest to sue in relation to the unlawful act only if he is, or would be, a victim of that act.

(5) Proceedings under subsection (1)(a) must be brought before the end of –

(a)   the period of one year beginning with the date on which the act complained of took place; or

(b)   such longer period as the court or tribunal considers equitable having regard to all the circumstances,

but that is subject to any rule imposing a stricter time limit in relation to the procedure in question.

(6) In subsection (1)(b) "legal proceedings" includes –

(a)   proceedings brought by or at the instigation of a public authority; and

(b)   an appeal against the decision of a court or tribunal.

(7) For the purposes of this section, a person is a victim of an unlawful act only if he would be a victim for the purposes of Article 34 of the Convention if proceedings were brought in the European Court of Human Rights in respect of that act.

(8) Nothing in this Act creates a criminal offence.

(9) In this section "rules" means –

(a)   in relation to proceedings before a court or tribunal outside Scotland, rules made by . . . the Lord Chancellor or the Secretary of State for the purposes of this section or rules of court,

(b)   in relation to proceedings before a court or tribunal in Scotland, rules made by the Secretary of State for those purposes,

(c)   in relation to proceedings before a tribunal in Northern Ireland –

(i)   which deals with transferred matters; and

(ii)   for which no rules made under paragraph (a) are in force,

rules made by a Northern Ireland department for those purposes,

and includes provision made by order under section 1 of the M1Courts and Legal Services Act 1990.

(10) In making rules, regard must be had to section 9.

(11) The Minister who has power to make rules in relation to a particular tribunal may, to the extent he considers it necessary to ensure that the tribunal can provide an appropriate remedy in relation to an act (or proposed act) of a public authority which is (or would be) unlawful as a result of section 6(1), by order add to –

(a) the relief or remedies which the tribunal may grant; or

(b) the grounds on which it may grant any of them.

(12) An order made under subsection (11) may contain such incidental, supplemental, consequential or transitional provision as the Minister making it considers appropriate.

(13) "The Minister" includes the Northern Ireland department concerned.

Amendments—SI 2003/1887; SI 2005/3429.

'proceedings' (s 7(1)(a))—See *Re S (Minors) (Care Order: Implementation of Care Plan); Re W (Minors) (Care Order: Adequacy of Care Plan)* [2002] UKHL 10, [2002] 2 WLR 720, [2002] 1 FLR 815 in which the House of Lords held that 'if a local authority fails to discharge its parental responsibilities properly, and in consequence the rights of the parents under Article 8 are violated, the parents may, as a longstop, bring proceedings against the authority under s 7 ... I say "as a longstop", because other remedies, both of an administrative nature and by way of court proceedings, may also be available in the particular case ... Sometimes court proceedings by way of judicial review of a decision of a local authority may be the appropriate way to proceed. In a suitable case an application for discharge of the care order is available. One would not expect proceedings to be launched under s 7 until any other appropriate remedial routes have first been explored'. These principles will apply equally to children (see *R (Howard League for Penal Reform) v Secretary of State for the Home Department* [2002] EWHC 2497, [2003] 1 FLR 484, paras 65–69). **[RCLP para 6.192].** For the relevant procedure for making a claim see **[RCLP paras 3.80—3.83].** Where it is asserted that there has been a breach of Arts 6 or 8 in public law proceedings under the Children Act 1989 the person alleging the breach must do so, and seek interim relief without delay (*Re P (Adoption: Breach of Care Plan)* [2004] 2 FLR 1109).

8 Judicial remedies

(1) In relation to any act (or proposed act) of a public authority which the court finds is (or would be) unlawful, it may grant such relief or remedy, or make such order, within its powers as it considers just and appropriate.

(2) But damages may be awarded only by a court which has power to award damages, or to order the payment of compensation, in civil proceedings.

(3) No award of damages is to be made unless, taking account of all the circumstances of the case, including –

(a) any other relief or remedy granted, or order made, in relation to the act in question (by that or any other court), and

(b) the consequences of any decision (of that or any other court) in respect of that act,

the court is satisfied that the award is necessary to afford just satisfaction to the person in whose favour it is made.

(4) In determining –

(a) whether to award damages, or

(b) the amount of an award,

the court must take into account the principles applied by the European Court of Human Rights in relation to the award of compensation under Article 41 of the Convention.

(5) A public authority against which damages are awarded is to be treated –

(a) in Scotland, for the purposes of section 3 of the M2Law Reform (Miscellaneous Provisions) (Scotland) Act 1940 as if the award were made in an action of damages in which the authority has been found liable in respect of loss or damage to the person to whom the award is made;

(b)   for the purposes of the M3Civil Liability (Contribution) Act 1978 as liable in respect of damage suffered by the person to whom the award is made.

(6) In this section –

"court" includes a tribunal;
"damages" means damages for an unlawful act of a public authority; and
"unlawful" means unlawful under section 6(1).

9 Judicial acts

(1) Proceedings under section 7(1)(a) in respect of a judicial act may be brought only –

(a)   by exercising a right of appeal;
(b)   on an application (in Scotland a petition) for judicial review; or
(c)   in such other forum as may be prescribed by rules.

(2) That does not affect any rule of law which prevents a court from being the subject of judicial review.

(3) In proceedings under this Act in respect of a judicial act done in good faith, damages may not be awarded otherwise than to compensate a person to the extent required by Article 5(5) of the Convention.

(4) An award of damages permitted by subsection (3) is to be made against the Crown; but no award may be made unless the appropriate person, if not a party to the proceedings, is joined.

(5) In this section –

"appropriate person" means the Minister responsible for the court concerned, or a person or government department nominated by him;
"court" includes a tribunal;
"judge" includes a member of a tribunal, a justice of the peace (or, in Northern Ireland, a lay magistrate) and a clerk or other officer entitled to exercise the jurisdiction of a court;
"judicial act" means a judicial act of a court and includes an act done on the instructions, or on behalf, of a judge; and
"rules" has the same meaning as in section 7(9).

Amendments—Justice (Northern Ireland) Act 2002, s 10(6), Sch 4, para 39.

Remedial action

10 Power to take remedial action

(1) This section applies if –

(a)   a provision of legislation has been declared under section 4 to be incompatible with a Convention right and, if an appeal lies –
    (i)   all persons who may appeal have stated in writing that they do not intend to do so;
    (ii)   the time for bringing an appeal has expired and no appeal has been brought within that time; or
    (iii)   an appeal brought within that time has been determined or abandoned; or
(b)   it appears to a Minister of the Crown or Her Majesty in Council that, having regard to a finding of the European Court of Human Rights made after the

coming into force of this section in proceedings against the United Kingdom, a provision of legislation is incompatible with an obligation of the United Kingdom arising from the Convention.

(2) If a Minister of the Crown considers that there are compelling reasons for proceeding under this section, he may by order make such amendments to the legislation as he considers necessary to remove the incompatibility.

(3) If, in the case of subordinate legislation, a Minister of the Crown considers –

(a) that it is necessary to amend the primary legislation under which the subordinate legislation in question was made, in order to enable the incompatibility to be removed, and

(b) that there are compelling reasons for proceeding under this section,

he may by order make such amendments to the primary legislation as he considers necessary.

(4) This section also applies where the provision in question is in subordinate legislation and has been quashed, or declared invalid, by reason of incompatibility with a Convention right and the Minister proposes to proceed under paragraph 2(b) of Schedule 2.

(5) If the legislation is an Order in Council, the power conferred by subsection (2) or (3) is exercisable by Her Majesty in Council.

(6) In this section "legislation" does not include a Measure of the Church Assembly or of the General Synod of the Church of England.

(7) Schedule 2 makes further provision about remedial orders.

Other rights and proceedings

11 Safeguard for existing human rights

A person's reliance on a Convention right does not restrict –

(a) any other right or freedom conferred on him by or under any law having effect in any part of the United Kingdom; or

(b) his right to make any claim or bring any proceedings which he could make or bring apart from sections 7 to 9.

12 Freedom of expression

(1) This section applies if a court is considering whether to grant any relief which, if granted, might affect the exercise of the Convention right to freedom of expression.

(2) If the person against whom the application for relief is made ("the respondent") is neither present nor represented, no such relief is to be granted unless the court is satisfied –

(a) that the applicant has taken all practicable steps to notify the respondent; or

(b) that there are compelling reasons why the respondent should not be notified.

(3) No such relief is to be granted so as to restrain publication before trial unless the court is satisfied that the applicant is likely to establish that publication should not be allowed.

(4) The court must have particular regard to the importance of the Convention right to freedom of expression and, where the proceedings relate to material which the

respondent claims, or which appears to the court, to be journalistic, literary or artistic material (or to conduct connected with such material), to –

(a)   the extent to which –
        (i)   the material has, or is about to, become available to the public; or
        (ii)   it is, or would be, in the public interest for the material to be published;
(b)   any relevant privacy code.

(5) In this section –

"court" includes a tribunal; and
"relief" includes any remedy or order (other than in criminal proceedings).

'**particular regard**' (s 12(4))—Section 12 requires the domestic courts to pay particular regard to the importance of the right to freedom of expression when considering granting relief which may affect that right (see *Douglas v Hello! Ltd* [2001] QB 967, paras 132–137) **[RCLP paras 9.80 and 11.92]**.

13 Freedom of thought, conscience and religion

(1)If a court's determination of any question arising under this Act might affect the exercise by a religious organisation (itself or its members collectively) of the Convention right to freedom of thought, conscience and religion, it must have particular regard to the importance of that right.

(2) In this section "court" includes a tribunal.

'**particular regard to the importance of that right**' (s 13(1))—For the pre Human Rights Act 1998 position see *R v Secretary of State for the Home Department, ex p Moon* [1996] COD 54, 8 Admin LR 477 and *Redmond-Bate v DPP* (1999) 7 BHRC 375 (DC) **[RCLP para 10.114]**.

Derogations and reservations

14 Derogations

(1) In this Act "designated derogation" means –

any derogation by the United Kingdom from an Article of the Convention, or of any protocol to the Convention, which is designated for the purposes of this Act in an order made by the Secretary of State.

(2) ...

(3) If a designated derogation is amended or replaced it ceases to be a designated derogation.

(4) But subsection (3) does not prevent the Secretary of State from exercising his power under subsection (1) to make a fresh designation order in respect of the Article concerned.

(5)The Secretary of State must by order make such amendments to Schedule 3 as he considers appropriate to reflect –

(a)   any designation order; or
(b)   the effect of subsection (3).

(6) A designation order may be made in anticipation of the making by the United Kingdom of a proposed derogation.

Amendments—SI 2001/1216; SI 2003/1887.

15 Reservations

(1) In this Act "designated reservation" means –

    (a)   the United Kingdom's reservation to Article 2 of the First Protocol to the Convention; and

    (b)   any other reservation by the United Kingdom to an Article of the Convention, or of any protocol to the Convention, which is designated for the purposes of this Act in an order made by the Secretary of State.

(2) The text of the reservation referred to in subsection (1)(a) is set out in Part II of Schedule 3.

(3) If a designated reservation is withdrawn wholly or in part it ceases to be a designated reservation.

(4) But subsection (3) does not prevent the Secretary of State from exercising his power under subsection (1)(b) to make a fresh designation order in respect of the Article concerned.

(5) Secretary of State must by order make such amendments to this Act as he considers appropriate to reflect –

    (a)   any designation order; or

    (b)   the effect of subsection (3).

Amendments—SI 2003/1887.

16 Period for which designated derogations have effect

(1) If it has not already been withdrawn by the United Kingdom, a designated derogation ceases to have effect for the purposes of this Act –

at the end of the period of five years beginning with the date on which the order designating it was made.

(2) At any time before the period –

    (a)   fixed by subsection (1), or

    (b)   extended by an order under this subsection,

comes to an end, the Secretary of State may by order extend it by a further period of five years.

(3) An order under section 14(1) ceases to have effect at the end of the period for consideration, unless a resolution has been passed by each House approving the order.

(4) Subsection (3) does not affect –

    (a)   anything done in reliance on the order; or

    (b)   the power to make a fresh order under section 14(1).

(5) In subsection (3) "period for consideration" means the period of forty days beginning with the day on which the order was made.

(6) In calculating the period for consideration, no account is to be taken of any time during which –

    (a)   Parliament is dissolved or prorogued; or

    (b)   both Houses are adjourned for more than four days.

(7) If a designated derogation is withdrawn by the United Kingdom, the [F28Secretary of State] must by order make such amendments to this Act as he considers are required to reflect that withdrawal.

Amendments—SI 2001/1216; SI 2003/1887.

17 Periodic review of designated reservations

(1) The appropriate Minister must review the designated reservation referred to in section 15(1)(a) –

- (a) before the end of the period of five years beginning with the date on which section 1(2) came into force; and
- (b) if that designation is still in force, before the end of the period of five years beginning with the date on which the last report relating to it was laid under subsection (3).

(2) The appropriate Minister must review each of the other designated reservations (if any) –

- (a) before the end of the period of five years beginning with the date on which the order designating the reservation first came into force; and
- (b) if the designation is still in force, before the end of the period of five years beginning with the date on which the last report relating to it was laid under subsection (3).

(3) The Minister conducting a review under this section must prepare a report on the result of the review and lay a copy of it before each House of Parliament.

Judges of the European Court of Human Rights

18 Appointment to European Court of Human Rights

(1) In this section "judicial office" means the office of –

- (a) Lord Justice of Appeal, Justice of the High Court or Circuit judge, in England and Wales;
- (b) judge of the Court of Session or sheriff, in Scotland;
- (c) Lord Justice of Appeal, judge of the High Court or county court judge, in Northern Ireland.

(2) The holder of a judicial office may become a judge of the European Court of Human Rights ("the Court") without being required to relinquish his office.

(3) But he is not required to perform the duties of his judicial office while he is a judge of the Court.

(4) In respect of any period during which he is a judge of the Court –

- (a) a Lord Justice of Appeal or Justice of the High Court is not to count as a judge of the relevant court for the purposes of section 2(1) or 4(1) of the Senior Courts Act 1981 (maximum number of judges) nor as a judge of the Senior Courts for the purposes of section 12(1) to (6) of that Act (salaries etc.);
- (b) a judge of the Court of Session is not to count as a judge of that court for the purposes of section 1(1) of the M4Court of Session Act 1988 (maximum number of judges) or of section 9(1)(c) of the M5Administration of Justice Act 1973 ("the 1973 Act") (salaries etc.);

(c)   a Lord Justice of Appeal or judge of the High Court in Northern Ireland is not to count as a judge of the relevant court for the purposes of section 2(1) or 3(1) of the Judicature (Northern Ireland) Act 1978 (maximum number of judges) nor as a judge of the Court of Judicature of Northern Ireland for the purposes of section 9(1)(d) of the 1973 Act (salaries etc.);

(d)   a Circuit judge is not to count as such for the purposes of section 18 of the Courts Act 1971 (salaries etc.);

(e)   a sheriff is not to count as such for the purposes of section 14 of the M8Sheriff Courts (Scotland) Act 1907 (salaries etc.);

(f)   a county court judge of Northern Ireland is not to count as such for the purposes of section 106 of the M9County Courts Act Northern Ireland) 1959 (salaries etc.).

(5) If a sheriff principal is appointed a judge of the Court, section 11(1) of the Sheriff Courts (Scotland) Act 1971 (temporary appointment of sheriff principal) applies, while he holds that appointment, as if his office is vacant.

(6) Schedule 4 makes provision about judicial pensions in relation to the holder of a judicial office who serves as a judge of the Court.

(7) The Lord Chancellor or the Secretary of State may by order make such transitional provision (including, in particular, provision for a temporary increase in the maximum number of judges) as he considers appropriate in relation to any holder of a judicial office who has completed his service as a judge of the Court.

(7A) The following paragraphs apply to the making of an order under subsection (7) in relation to any holder of a judicial office listed in subsection (1)(a) –

(a)   before deciding what transitional provision it is appropriate to make, the person making the order must consult the Lord Chief Justice of England and Wales;

(b)   before making the order, that person must consult the Lord Chief Justice of England and Wales.

(7B) The following paragraphs apply to the making of an order under subsection (7) in relation to any holder of a judicial office listed in subsection (1)(c) –

(a)   before deciding what transitional provision it is appropriate to make, the person making the order must consult the Lord Chief Justice of Northern Ireland;

(b)   before making the order, that person must consult the Lord Chief Justice of Northern Ireland.

(7C) The Lord Chief Justice of England and Wales may nominate a judicial office holder (within the meaning of section 109(4) of the Constitutional Reform Act 2005) to exercise his functions under this section.

(7D) The Lord Chief Justice of Northern Ireland may nominate any of the following to exercise his functions under this section –

(a)   the holder of one of the offices listed in Schedule 1 to the Justice (Northern Ireland) Act 2002;

(b)   a Lord Justice of Appeal (as defined in section 88 of that Act).

Amendments—Constitutional Reform Act 2005, ss 15(1), 59(5), Sch 4, Pt 1, para 278, Sch 11, Pts 1–3, paras 1(2), 4(1), (3), 6(1), (3).

Parliamentary procedure

19 Statements of compatibility

(1) A Minister of the Crown in charge of a Bill in either House of Parliament must, before Second Reading of the Bill –

(a)   make a statement to the effect that in his view the provisions of the Bill are compatible with the Convention rights ("a statement of compatibility"); or

(b)   make a statement to the effect that although he is unable to make a statement of compatibility the government nevertheless wishes the House to proceed with the Bill.

(2) The statement must be in writing and be published in such manner as the Minister making it considers appropriate.

Supplemental

20 Orders etc. under this Act

(1) Any power of a Minister of the Crown to make an order under this Act is exercisable by statutory instrument.

(2) The power of the Lord Chancellor or the Secretary of State to make rules (other than rules of court) under section 2(3) or 7(9) is exercisable by statutory instrument.

(3) Any statutory instrument made under section 14, 15 or 16(7) must be laid before Parliament.

(4) No order may be made by the Lord Chancellor or] the Secretary of State under section 1(4), 7(11) or 16(2) unless a draft of the order has been laid before, and approved by, each House of Parliament.

(5) Any statutory instrument made under section 18(7) or Schedule 4, or to which subsection (2) applies, shall be subject to annulment in pursuance of a resolution of either House of Parliament.

(6) The power of a Northern Ireland department to make –

(a)   rules under section 2(3)(c) or 7(9)(c), or
(b)   an order under section 7(11),

is exercisable by statutory rule for the purposes of the Statutory Rules (Northern Ireland) Order 1979.

(7) Any rules made under section 2(3)(c) or 7(9)(c) shall be subject to negative resolution; and section 41(6) of the Interpretation Act Northern Ireland) 1954 (meaning of "subject to negative resolution") shall apply as if the power to make the rules were conferred by an Act of the Northern Ireland Assembly.

(8) No order may be made by a Northern Ireland department under section 7(11) unless a draft of the order has been laid before, and approved by, the Northern Ireland Assembly.

Amendments—SI 2003/1887, SI 2005/3429.

21 Interpretation, etc

(1) In this Act –

"amend" includes repeal and apply (with or without modifications);

"the appropriate Minister" means the Minister of the Crown having charge of the appropriate authorised government department (within the meaning of the Crown Proceedings Act 1947);

"the Commission" means the European Commission of Human Rights;

"the Convention" means the Convention for the Protection of Human Rights and Fundamental Freedoms, agreed by the Council of Europe at Rome on 4th November 1950 as it has effect for the time being in relation to the United Kingdom;

"declaration of incompatibility" means a declaration under section 4;

"Minister of the Crown" has the same meaning as in the Ministers of the Crown Act 1975;

"Northern Ireland Minister" includes the First Minister and the deputy First Minister in Northern Ireland;

"primary legislation" means any –

  (a)   public general Act;
  (b)   local and personal Act;
  (c)   private Act;
  (d)   Measure of the Church Assembly;
  (e)   Measure of the General Synod of the Church of England;
  (f)   Order in Council –
     (i)   made in exercise of Her Majesty's Royal Prerogative;
     (ii)   made under section 38(1)(a) of the Northern Ireland Constitution Act 1973 or the corresponding provision of the Northern Ireland Act 1998; or
     (iii) amending an Act of a kind mentioned in paragraph (a), (b) or (c);

and includes an order or other instrument made under primary legislation (otherwise than by the Welsh Ministers, the First Minister for Wales, the Counsel General to the Welsh Assembly Government, a member of the Scottish Executive, a Northern Ireland Minister or a Northern Ireland department) to the extent to which it operates to bring one or more provisions of that legislation into force or amends any primary legislation;

"the First Protocol" means the protocol to the Convention agreed at Paris on 20th March 1952;

"the Eleventh Protocol" means the protocol to the Convention (restructuring the control machinery established by the Convention) agreed at Strasbourg on 11th May 1994;

"the Thirteenth Protocol" means the protocol to the Convention (concerning the abolition of the death penalty in all circumstances) agreed at Vilnius on 3rd May 2002;

"remedial order" means an order under section 10;

"subordinate legislation" means any –

  (a)   Order in Council other than one –
     (i)   made in exercise of Her Majesty's Royal Prerogative;
     (ii)   made under section 38(1)(a) of the Northern Ireland Constitution Act 1973 or the corresponding provision of the Northern Ireland Act 1998; or
     (iii) amending an Act of a kind mentioned in the definition of primary legislation;
  (b)   Act of the Scottish Parliament;
  (ba) Measure of the National Assembly for Wales;
  (bb) Act of the National Assembly for Wales;
  (c)   Act of the Parliament of Northern Ireland;

(d)   Measure of the Assembly established under section 1 of the Northern Ireland Assembly Act 1973;

(e)   Act of the Northern Ireland Assembly;

(f)   order, rules, regulations, scheme, warrant, byelaw or other instrument made under primary legislation (except to the extent to which it operates to bring one or more provisions of that legislation into force or amends any primary legislation);

(g)   order, rules, regulations, scheme, warrant, byelaw or other instrument made under legislation mentioned in paragraph (b), (c), (d) or (e) or made under an Order in Council applying only to Northern Ireland;

(h)   order, rules, regulations, scheme, warrant, byelaw or other instrument made by a member of the Scottish Executive, Welsh Ministers, the First Minister for Wales, the Counsel General to the Welsh Assembly Government,] a Northern Ireland Minister or a Northern Ireland department in exercise of prerogative or other executive functions of Her Majesty which are exercisable by such a person on behalf of Her Majesty;

"transferred matters" has the same meaning as in the Northern Ireland Act 1998; and

"tribunal" means any tribunal in which legal proceedings may be brought.

(2) The references in paragraphs (b) and (c) of section 2(1) to Articles are to Articles of the Convention as they had effect immediately before the coming into force of the Eleventh Protocol.

(3) The reference in paragraph (d) of section 2(1) to Article 46 includes a reference to Articles 32 and 54 of the Convention as they had effect immediately before the coming into force of the Eleventh Protocol.

(4) The references in section 2(1) to a report or decision of the Commission or a decision of the Committee of Ministers include references to a report or decision made as provided by paragraphs 3, 4 and 6 of Article 5 of the Eleventh Protocol (transitional provisions).

(5) ...

Scope—For the extent of s 21 outside the United Kingdom see s. 22(7).

Amendments—SI 2004/1574; Government of Wales Act 2006, s 160(1), Sch 10, para 56(1)–(4); Armed Forces Act 2006, s 378(2), Sch 17.

22 Short title, commencement, application and extent

(1) This Act may be cited as the Human Rights Act 1998.

(2) Sections 18, 20 and 21(5) and this section come into force on the passing of this Act.

(3) The other provisions of this Act come into force on such day as the Secretary of State may by order appoint; and different days may be appointed for different purposes.

(4) Paragraph (b) of subsection (1) of section 7 applies to proceedings brought by or at the instigation of a public authority whenever the act in question took place; but otherwise that subsection does not apply to an act taking place before the coming into force of that section.

(5) This Act binds the Crown.

(6) This Act extends to Northern Ireland.

(7) ...

Amendments—Armed Forces Act 2006, s 378(2), Sch 17.

SCHEDULES

Schedule 1
The Articles

PART I
THE CONVENTION — RIGHTS AND FREEDOMS

Article 2
Right to life

1 Everyone's right to life shall be protected by law. No one shall be deprived of his life intentionally save in the execution of a sentence of a court following his conviction of a crime for which this penalty is provided by law.

2 Deprivation of life shall not be regarded as inflicted in contravention of this Article when it results from the use of force which is no more than absolutely necessary –

    (a)   in defence of any person from unlawful violence;

    (b)   in order to effect a lawful arrest or to prevent the escape of a person lawfully detained;

    (c)   in action lawfully taken for the purpose of quelling a riot or insurrection.

Article 3
Prohibition of torture

No one shall be subjected to torture or to inhuman or degrading treatment or punishment.

Article 4
Prohibition of slavery and forced labour

1 No one shall be held in slavery or servitude.

2 No one shall be required to perform forced or compulsory labour.

3 For the purpose of this Article the term 'forced or compulsory labour' shall not include –

    (a)   any work required to be done in the ordinary course of detention imposed according to the provisions of Article 5 of this Convention or during conditional release from such detention;

    (b)   any service of a military character or, in case of conscientious objectors in countries where they are recognised, service exacted instead of compulsory military service;

    (c)   any service exacted in case of an emergency or calamity threatening the life or well-being of the community;

    (d)   any work or service which forms part of normal civic obligations.

Article 5
Right to liberty and security

1 Everyone has the right to liberty and security of person. No one shall be deprived of his liberty save in the following cases and in accordance with a procedure prescribed by law –

(a)   the lawful detention of a person after conviction by a competent court;

(b)   the lawful arrest or detention of a person for non-compliance with the lawful order of a court or in order to secure the fulfilment of any obligation prescribed by law;

(c)   the lawful arrest or detention of a person effected for the purpose of bringing him before the competent legal authority on reasonable suspicion of having committed an offence or when it is reasonably considered necessary to prevent his committing an offence or fleeing after having done so;

(d)   the detention of a minor by lawful order for the purpose of educational supervision or his lawful detention for the purpose of bringing him before the competent legal authority;

(e)   the lawful detention of persons for the prevention of the spreading of infectious diseases, of persons of unsound mind, alcoholics or drug addicts or vagrants;

(f)   the lawful arrest or detention of a person to prevent his effecting an unauthorised entry into the country or of a person against whom action is being taken with a view to deportation or extradition.

2 Everyone who is arrested shall be informed promptly, in a language which he understands, of the reasons for his arrest and of any charge against him.

3 Everyone arrested or detained in accordance with the provisions of paragraph 1(c) of this Article shall be brought promptly before a judge or other officer authorised by law to exercise judicial power and shall be entitled to trial within a reasonable time or to release pending trial. Release may be conditioned by guarantees to appear for trial.

4 Everyone who is deprived of his liberty by arrest or detention shall be entitled to take proceedings by which the lawfulness of his detention shall be decided speedily by a court and his release ordered if the detention is not lawful.

5 Everyone who has been the victim of arrest or detention in contravention of the provisions of this Article shall have an enforceable right to compensation.

Article 6
Right to a fair trial

1 In the determination of his civil rights and obligations or of any criminal charge against him, everyone is entitled to a fair and public hearing within a reasonable time by an independent and impartial tribunal established by law. Judgment shall be pronounced publicly but the press and public may be excluded from all or part of the trial in the interest of morals, public order or national security in a democratic society, where the interests of juveniles or the protection of the private life of the parties so require, or to the extent strictly necessary in the opinion of the court in special circumstances where publicity would prejudice the interests of justice.

2 Everyone charged with a criminal offence shall be presumed innocent until proved guilty according to law.

3 Everyone charged with a criminal offence has the following minimum rights –

(a)   to be informed promptly, in a language which he understands and in detail, of the nature and cause of the accusation against him;

(b)   to have adequate time and facilities for the preparation of his defence;

(c)   to defend himself in person or through legal assistance of his own choosing or, if he has not sufficient means to pay for legal assistance, to be given it free when the interests of justice so require;

(d)   to examine or have examined witnesses against him and to obtain the attendance and examination of witnesses on his behalf under the same conditions as witnesses against him;

(e)   to have the free assistance of an interpreter if he cannot understand or speak the language used in court.

Article 7
No punishment without law

1 No one shall be held guilty of any criminal offence on account of any act or omission which did not constitute a criminal offence under national or international law at the time when it was committed. Nor shall a heavier penalty be imposed than the one that was applicable at the time the criminal offence was committed.

2 This Article shall not prejudice the trial and punishment of any person for any act or omission which, at the time when it was committed, was criminal according to the general principles of law recognised by civilised nations.

Article 8
Right to respect for private and family life

1 Everyone has the right to respect for his private and family life, his home and his correspondence.

2 There shall be no interference by a public authority with the exercise of this right except such as is in accordance with the law and is necessary in a democratic society in the interests of national security, public safety or the economic well-being of the country, for the prevention of disorder or crime, for the protection of health or morals, or for the protection of the rights and freedoms of others.

Article 9
Freedom of thought, conscience and religion

1 Everyone has the right to freedom of thought, conscience and religion; this right includes freedom to change his religion or belief and freedom, either alone or in community with others and in public or private, to manifest his religion or belief, in worship, teaching, practice and observance.

2 Freedom to manifest one's religion or beliefs shall be subject only to such limitations as are prescribed by law and are necessary in a democratic society in the interests of public safety, for the protection of public order, health or morals, or for the protection of the rights and freedoms of others.

Article 10
Freedom of expression

1 Everyone has the right to freedom of expression. This right shall include freedom to hold opinions and to receive and impart information and ideas without interference by public authority and regardless of frontiers. This Article shall not prevent States from requiring the licensing of broadcasting, television or cinema enterprises.

2 The exercise of these freedoms, since it carries with it duties and responsibilities, may be subject to such formalities, conditions, restrictions or penalties as are prescribed by law and are necessary in a democratic society, in the interests of national security, territorial integrity or public safety, for the prevention of disorder or crime, for the protection of health or morals, for the protection of the reputation or rights of others, for preventing the disclosure of information received in confidence, or for maintaining the authority and impartiality of the judiciary.

Article 11
Freedom of assembly and association

1 Everyone has the right to freedom of peaceful assembly and to freedom of association with others, including the right to form and to join trade unions for the protection of his interests.

2 No restrictions shall be placed on the exercise of these rights other than such as are prescribed by law and are necessary in a democratic society in the interests of national security or public safety, for the prevention of disorder or crime, for the protection of health or morals or for the protection of the rights and freedoms of others. This Article shall not prevent the imposition of lawful restrictions on the exercise of these rights by members of the armed forces, of the police or of the administration of the State.

Article 12
Right to marry

Men and women of marriageable age have the right to marry and to found a family, according to the national laws governing the exercise of this right.

Article 14
Prohibition of discrimination

The enjoyment of the rights and freedoms set forth in this Convention shall be secured without discrimination on any ground such as sex, race, colour, language, religion, political or other opinion, national or social origin, association with a national minority, property, birth or other status.

Article 16
Restrictions on political activity of aliens

Nothing in Articles 10, 11 and 14 shall be regarded as preventing the High Contracting Parties from imposing restrictions on the political activity of aliens.

Article 17
Prohibition of abuse of rights

Nothing in this Convention may be interpreted as implying for any State, group or person any right to engage in any activity or perform any act aimed at the destruction of any of the rights and freedoms set forth herein or at their limitation to a greater extent than is provided for in the Convention.

Article 18
Limitation on use of restrictions on rights

The restrictions permitted under this Convention to the said rights and freedoms shall not be applied for any purpose other than those for which they have been prescribed.

PART II
THE FIRST PROTOCOL

Article 1
Protection of property

Every natural or legal person is entitled to the peaceful enjoyment of his possessions. No one shall be deprived of his possessions except in the public interest and subject to the conditions provided for by law and by the general principles of international law.

The preceding provisions shall not, however, in any way impair the right of a State to enforce such laws as it deems necessary to control the use of property in accordance with the general interest or to secure the payment of taxes or other contributions or penalties.

Article 2
Right to education

No person shall be denied the right to education. In the exercise of any functions which it assumes in relation to education and to teaching, the State shall respect the right of parents to ensure such education and teaching in conformity with their own religious and philosophical convictions.

Article 3
Right to free elections

The High Contracting Parties undertake to hold free elections at reasonable intervals by secret ballot, under conditions which will ensure the free expression of the opinion of the people in the choice of the legislature.

PART III
ARTICLE 1 OF THE THIRTEENTH PROTOCOL

Article 1
Abolition of the death penalty

The death penalty shall be abolished. No one shall be condemned to such penalty or executed.

Amendments—SI 2004/1574.

Schedule 2
Remedial Orders

1 Orders

(1) A remedial order may –

    (a)   contain such incidental, supplemental, consequential or transitional provision as the person making it considers appropriate;

    (b)   be made so as to have effect from a date earlier than that on which it is made;

(c)   make provision for the delegation of specific functions;
(d)   make different provision for different cases.

(2) The power conferred by sub-paragraph (1)(a) includes –

(a)   power to amend primary legislation (including primary legislation other than that which contains the incompatible provision); and
(b)   power to amend or revoke subordinate legislation (including subordinate legislation other than that which contains the incompatible provision).

(3) A remedial order may be made so as to have the same extent as the legislation which it affects.

(4) No person is to be guilty of an offence solely as a result of the retrospective effect of a remedial order.

2 Procedure

No remedial order may be made unless –

(a)   a draft of the order has been approved by a resolution of each House of Parliament made after the end of the period of 60 days beginning with the day on which the draft was laid; or
(b)   it is declared in the order that it appears to the person making it that, because of the urgency of the matter, it is necessary to make the order without a draft being so approved.

3 Orders laid in draft

(1) No draft may be laid under paragraph 2(a) unless –

(a)   the person proposing to make the order has laid before Parliament a document which contains a draft of the proposed order and the required information; and
(b)   the period of 60 days, beginning with the day on which the document required by this sub-paragraph was laid, has ended.

(2) If representations have been made during that period, the draft laid under paragraph 2(a) must be accompanied by a statement containing –

(a)   a summary of the representations; and
(b)   if, as a result of the representations, the proposed order has been changed, details of the changes.

4 Urgent cases

(1) If a remedial order ('the original order') is made without being approved in draft, the person making it must lay it before Parliament, accompanied by the required information, after it is made.

(2) If representations have been made during the period of 60 days beginning with the day on which the original order was made, the person making it must (after the end of that period) lay before Parliament a statement containing –

(a)   a summary of the representations; and
(b)   if, as a result of the representations, he considers it appropriate to make changes to the original order, details of the changes.

(3) If sub-paragraph (2)(b) applies, the person making the statement must –

(a) make a further remedial order replacing the original order; and
(b) lay the replacement order before Parliament.

(4) If, at the end of the period of 120 days beginning with the day on which the original order was made, a resolution has not been passed by each House approving the original or replacement order, the order ceases to have effect (but without that affecting anything previously done under either order or the power to make a fresh remedial order).

5 Definitions

In this Schedule –

'representations' means representations about a remedial order (or proposed remedial order) made to the person making (or proposing to make) it and includes any relevant Parliamentary report or resolution; and
'required information' means –
(a) an explanation of the incompatibility which the order (or proposed order) seeks to remove, including particulars of the relevant declaration, finding or order; and
(b) a statement of the reasons for proceeding under section 10 and for making an order in those terms.

6 Calculating periods

In calculating any period for the purposes of this Schedule, no account is to be taken of any time during which –

(a) Parliament is dissolved or prorogued; or
(b) both Houses are adjourned for more than four days.

7

(1) This paragraph applies in relation to –

(a) any remedial order made, and any draft of such an order proposed to be made,–
(i) by the Scottish Ministers; or
(ii) within devolved competence (within the meaning of the Scotland Act 1998) by Her Majesty in Council; and
(b) any document or statement to be laid in connection with such an order (or proposed order).

(2) This Schedule has effect in relation to any such order (or proposed order), document or statement subject to the following modifications.

(3) Any reference to Parliament, each House of Parliament or both Houses of Parliament shall be construed as a reference to the Scottish Parliament.

(4) Paragraph 6 does not apply and instead, in calculating any period for the purposes of this Schedule, no account is to be taken of any time during which the Scottish Parliament is dissolved or is in recess for more than four days.

Amendments—SI 2000/2040.

Schedule 3
Derogation and Reservation

...

Amendments—SI 2001/1216, art 4.

CHAPTER 22

EUROPEAN SOCIAL CHARTER (REVISED) STRASBOURG, 3.V.1996

Preamble

The governments signatory hereto, being members of the Council of Europe,

Considering that the aim of the Council of Europe is the achievement of greater unity between its members for the purpose of safeguarding and realising the ideals and principles which are their common heritage and of facilitating their economic and social progress, in particular by the maintenance and further realisation of human rights and fundamental freedoms;

Considering that in the European Convention for the Protection of Human Rights and Fundamental Freedoms signed at Rome on 4 November 1950, and the Protocols thereto, the member States of the Council of Europe agreed to secure to their populations the civil and political rights and freedoms therein specified;

Considering that in the European Social Charter opened for signature in Turin on 18 October 1961 and the Protocols thereto, the member States of the Council of Europe agreed to secure to their populations the social rights specified therein in order to improve their standard of living and their social well-being;

Recalling that the Ministerial Conference on Human Rights held in Rome on 5 November 1990 stressed the need, on the one hand, to preserve the indivisible nature of all human rights, be they civil, political, economic, social or cultural and, on the other hand, to give the European Social Charter fresh impetus;

Resolved, as was decided during the Ministerial Conference held in Turin on 21 and 22 October 1991, to update and adapt the substantive contents of the Charter in order to take account in particular of the fundamental social changes which have occurred since the text was adopted;

Recognising the advantage of embodying in a Revised Charter, designed progressively to take the place of the European Social Charter, the rights guaranteed by the Charter as amended, the rights guaranteed by the Additional Protocol of 1988 and to add new rights,

Have agreed as follows:

Status—The European Social Charter was ratified by the United Kingdom in 1962 and entered into force in 1965. The United Kingdom did not accept Arts 2(1), 4(3), 7(1), (7) and (8), 8(2), (3) and (4) and 12(2), (3) and (4) of the European Social Charter. The revised version of the European Social Charter was produced in 1996. The United Kingdom has signed but not ratified the revised version. An Additional Protocol providing a complaints procedure was added in 1995 (not included in this work). The United Kingdom has accepted none of the provisions of the Additional Protocol. The Additional Protocol has been used to lodge complaints concerning the breach of children's rights (see *Autisme-Europe v France* Complaint No 13/2002) [**RCLP para 2.97**].

PART I

The Parties accept as the aim of their policy, to be pursued by all appropriate means both national and international in character, the attainment of conditions in which the following rights and principles may be effectively realised:

1 Everyone shall have the opportunity to earn his living in an occupation freely entered upon.

2 All workers have the right to just conditions of work.

3 All workers have the right to safe and healthy working conditions.

4 All workers have the right to a fair remuneration sufficient for a decent standard of living for themselves and their families.

5 All workers and employers have the right to freedom of association in national or international organisations for the protection of their economic and social interests.

6 All workers and employers have the right to bargain collectively.

7 Children and young persons have the right to a special protection against the physical and moral hazards to which they are exposed.

8 Employed women, in case of maternity, have the right to a special protection.

9 Everyone has the right to appropriate facilities for vocational guidance with a view to helping him choose an occupation suited to his personal aptitude and interests.

10 Everyone has the right to appropriate facilities for vocational training.

11 Everyone has the right to benefit from any measures enabling him to enjoy the highest possible standard of health attainable.

12 All workers and their dependents have the right to social security.

13 Anyone without adequate resources has the right to social and medical assistance.

14 Everyone has the right to benefit from social welfare services.

15 Disabled persons have the right to independence, social integration and participation in the life of the community.

16 The family as a fundamental unit of society has the right to appropriate social, legal and economic protection to ensure its full development.

17 Children and young persons have the right to appropriate social, legal and economic protection.

8 The nationals of any one of the Parties have the right to engage in any gainful occupation in the territory of any one of the others on a footing of equality with the nationals of the latter, subject to restrictions based on cogent economic or social reasons.

19 Migrant workers who are nationals of a Party and their families have the right to protection and assistance in the territory of any other Party.

20 All workers have the right to equal opportunities and equal treatment in matters of employment and occupation without discrimination on the grounds of sex.

21 Workers have the right to be informed and to be consulted within the undertaking.

22 Workers have the right to take part in the determination and improvement of the working conditions and working environment in the undertaking.

23 Every elderly person has the right to social protection.

24 All workers have the right to protection in cases of termination of employment.

25 All workers have the right to protection of their claims in the event of the insolvency of their employer.

26 All workers have the right to dignity at work.

27 All persons with family responsibilities and who are engaged or wish to engage in employment have a right to do so without being subject to discrimination and as far as possible without conflict between their employment and family responsibilities.

28 Workers' representatives in undertakings have the right to protection against acts prejudicial to them and should be afforded appropriate facilities to carry out their functions.

29 All workers have the right to be informed and consulted in collective redundancy procedures.

30 Everyone has the right to protection against poverty and social exclusion.

31 Everyone has the right to housing.

PART II

The Parties undertake, as provided for in Part III, to consider themselves bound by the obligations laid down in the following articles and paragraphs.

Article 1
The right to work

With a view to ensuring the effective exercise of the right to work, the Parties undertake:

1 to accept as one of their primary aims and responsibilities the achievement and maintenance of as high and stable a level of employment as possible, with a view to the attainment of full employment;

2 to protect effectively the right of the worker to earn his living in an occupation freely entered upon;

3 to establish or maintain free employment services for all workers;

4 to provide or promote appropriate vocational guidance, training and rehabilitation.

Article 2
The right to just conditions of work

With a view to ensuring the effective exercise of the right to just conditions of work, the Parties undertake:

1 to provide for reasonable daily and weekly working hours, the working week to be progressively reduced to the extent that the increase of productivity and other relevant factors permit;

2 to provide for public holidays with pay;

3 to provide for a minimum of four weeks' annual holiday with pay;

4 to eliminate risks in inherently dangerous or unhealthy occupations, and where it has not yet been possible to eliminate or reduce sufficiently these risks, to provide for either a reduction of working hours or additional paid holidays for workers engaged in such occupations;

5 to ensure a weekly rest period which shall, as far as possible, coincide with the day recognised by tradition or custom in the country or region concerned as a day of rest;

6 to ensure that workers are informed in written form, as soon as possible, and in any event not later than two months after the date of commencing their employment, of the essential aspects of the contract or employment relationship;

7 to ensure that workers performing night work benefit from measures which take account of the special nature of the work.

Article 3
The right to safe and healthy working conditions

With a view to ensuring the effective exercise of the right to safe and healthy working conditions, the Parties undertake, in consultation with employers' and workers' organisations:

1 to formulate, implement and periodically review a coherent national policy on occupational safety, occupational health and the working environment. The primary aim of this policy shall be to improve occupational safety and health and to prevent accidents and injury to health arising out of, linked with or occurring in the course of work, particularly by minimising the causes of hazards inherent in the working environment;

2 to issue safety and health regulations;

3 to provide for the enforcement of such regulations by measures of supervision;

4 to promote the progressive development of occupational health services for all workers with essentially preventive and advisory functions.

Article 4
The right to a fair remuneration

With a view to ensuring the effective exercise of the right to a fair remuneration, the Parties undertake:

1 to recognise the right of workers to a remuneration such as will give them and their families a decent standard of living;

2 to recognise the right of workers to an increased rate of remuneration for overtime work, subject to exceptions in particular cases;

3 to recognise the right of men and women workers to equal pay for work of equal value;

4 to recognise the right of all workers to a reasonable period of notice for termination of employment;

5 to permit deductions from wages only under conditions and to the extent prescribed by national laws or regulations or fixed by collective agreements or arbitration awards.

The exercise of these rights shall be achieved by freely concluded collective agreements, by statutory wage-fixing machinery, or by other means appropriate to national conditions.

Article 5
The right to organise

With a view to ensuring or promoting the freedom of workers and employers to form local, national or international organisations for the protection of their economic and social interests and to join those organisations, the Parties undertake that national law shall not be such as to impair, nor shall it be so applied as to impair, this freedom. The extent to which the guarantees provided for in this article shall apply to the police shall be determined by national laws or regulations. The principle governing the application to the members of the armed forces of these guarantees and the extent to which they shall apply to persons in this category shall equally be determined by national laws or regulations.

Article 6
The right to bargain collectively

With a view to ensuring the effective exercise of the right to bargain collectively, the Parties under-take:

1 to promote joint consultation between workers and employers;

2 to promote, where necessary and appropriate, machinery for voluntary negotiations between employers or employers' organisations and workers' organisations, with a view to the regulation of terms and conditions of employment by means of collective agreements;

3 to promote the establishment and use of appropriate machinery for conciliation and voluntary arbitration for the settlement of labour disputes;

and recognise:

4 the right of workers and employers to collective action in cases of conflicts of interest, including the right to strike, subject to obligations that might arise out of collective agreements previously entered into.

Article 7
The right of children and young persons to protection

With a view to ensuring the effective exercise of the right of children and young persons to protection, the Parties undertake:

1 to provide that the minimum age of admission to employment shall be 15 years, subject to exceptions for children employed in prescribed light work without harm to their health, morals or education;

2 to provide that the minimum age of admission to employment shall be 18 years with respect to prescribed occupations regarded as dangerous or unhealthy;

3 to provide that persons who are still subject to compulsory education shall not be employed in such work as would deprive them of the full benefit of their education;

4 to provide that the working hours of persons under 18 years of age shall be limited in accordance with the needs of their development, and particularly with their need for vocational training;

5 to recognise the right of young workers and apprentices to a fair wage or other appropriate allowances;

6 to provide that the time spent by young persons in vocational training during the normal working hours with the consent of the employer shall be treated as forming part of the working day;

7 to provide that employed persons of under 18 years of age shall be entitled to a minimum of four weeks' annual holiday with pay;

8 to provide that persons under 18 years of age shall not be employed in night work with the exception of certain occupations provided for by national laws or regulations;

9 to provide that persons under 18 years of age employed in occupations prescribed by national laws or regulations shall be subject to regular medical control;

10 to ensure special protection against physical and moral dangers to which children and young persons are exposed, and particularly against those resulting directly or indirectly from their work.

'light work' (Art 7(1))—The Committee of Independent Experts has held that the term 'light work' does not automatically exclude domestic and agricultural work (see Conclusions of the Committee of Independent Experts 1, p 42). See also CoE Recommendation 1336 – Combating Child Labour Exploitation as a Matter of Priority [RCLP para 15.179].

Article 8
The right of employed women to protection of maternity

With a view to ensuring the effective exercise of the right of employed women to the protection of maternity, the Parties undertake:

1 to provide either by paid leave, by adequate social security benefits or by benefits from public funds for employed women to take leave before and after childbirth up to a total of at least fourteen weeks;

2 to consider it as unlawful for an employer to give a woman notice of dismissal during the period from the time she notifies her employer that she is pregnant until the end of her maternity leave, or to give her notice of dismissal at such a time that the notice would expire during such a period;

3 to provide that mothers who are nursing their infants shall be entitled to sufficient time off for this purpose;

4 to regulate the employment in night work of pregnant women, women who have recently given birth and women nursing their infants;

5 to prohibit the employment of pregnant women, women who have recently given birth or who are nursing their infants in underground mining and all other work which is unsuitable by reason of its dangerous, unhealthy or arduous nature and to take appropriate measures to protect the employment rights of these women.

Article 9
The right to vocational guidance

With a view to ensuring the effective exercise of the right to vocational guidance, the Parties undertake to provide or promote, as necessary, a service which will assist all persons, including the handicapped, to solve problems related to occupational choice and progress, with due regard to the individual's characteristics and their relation to occupational opportunity: this assistance should be available free of charge, both to young persons, including schoolchildren, and to adults.

Article 10
The right to vocational training

With a view to ensuring the effective exercise of the right to vocational training, the Parties undertake:

1 to provide or promote, as necessary, the technical and vocational training of all persons, including the handicapped, in consultation with employers' and workers' organisations, and to grant facilities for access to higher technical and university education, based solely on individual aptitude;

2 to provide or promote a system of apprenticeship and other systematic arrangements for training young boys and girls in their various employments;

3 to provide or promote, as necessary:

    a   adequate and readily available training facilities for adult workers;
    b   special facilities for the retraining of adult workers needed as a result of technological development or new trends in employment;

4 to provide or promote, as necessary, special measures for the retraining and reintegration of the long-term unemployed;

5 to encourage the full utilisation of the facilities provided by appropriate measures such as:

    a   reducing or abolishing any fees or charges;
    b   granting financial assistance in appropriate cases;
    c   including in the normal working hours time spent on supplementary training taken by the worker, at the request of his employer, during employment;
    d   ensuring, through adequate supervision, in consultation with the employers' and workers' organisations, the efficiency of apprenticeship and other training arrangements for young workers, and the adequate protection of young workers generally.

Article 11
The right to protection of health

With a view to ensuring the effective exercise of the right to protection of health, the Parties undertake, either directly or in co-operation with public or private organisations, to take appropriate measures designed *inter alia*:

1 to remove as far as possible the causes of ill-health;

2 to provide advisory and educational facilities for the promotion of health and the encouragement of individual responsibility in matters of health;

3 to prevent as far as possible epidemic, endemic and other diseases, as well as accidents.

'**effective exercise of the right to protection of health**' (Art 11)—Note that health care must be available to children without discrimination, including children of illegal or undocumented migrants (see *International Federation of Human Rights Leagues (FIDH) v France* Collective Complaint No 14/2002) [**RCLP para 5.91**].

Article 12
The right to social security

With a view to ensuring the effective exercise of the right to social security, the Parties undertake:

1 to establish or maintain a system of social security;

2 to maintain the social security system at a satisfactory level at least equal to that necessary for the ratification of the European Code of Social Security;

3 to endeavour to raise progressively the system of social security to a higher level;

4 to take steps, by the conclusion of appropriate bilateral and multilateral agreements or by other means, and subject to the conditions laid down in such agreements, in order to ensure:

a   equal treatment with their own nationals of the nationals of other Parties in respect of social security rights, including the retention of benefits arising out of social security legislation, whatever movements the persons protected may undertake between the territories of the Parties;

b   the granting, maintenance and resumption of social security rights by such means as the accumulation of insurance or employment periods completed under the legislation of each of the Parties.

Article 13
The right to social and medical assistance

With a view to ensuring the effective exercise of the right to social and medical assistance, the Parties undertake:

1 to ensure that any person who is without adequate resources and who is unable to secure such resources either by his own efforts or from other sources, in particular by benefits under a social security scheme, be granted adequate assistance, and, in case of sickness, the care necessitated by his condition;

2 to ensure that persons receiving such assistance shall not, for that reason, suffer from a diminution of their political or social rights;

3 to provide that everyone may receive by appropriate public or private services such advice and personal help as may be required to prevent, to remove, or to alleviate personal or family want;

4 to apply the provisions referred to in paragraphs 1, 2 and 3 of this article on an equal footing with their nationals to nationals of other Parties lawfully within their territories, in accordance with their obligations under the European Convention on Social and Medical Assistance, signed at Paris on 11 December 1953.

'**on an equal footing**' (Art 13(4))—Note that health care must be available to children without discrimination, including children of illegal or undocumented migrants (see *International Federation of Human Rights Leagues (FIDH) v France* Collective Complaint No 14/2002) [**RCLP para 5.91**].

Article 14
The right to benefit from social welfare services

With a view to ensuring the effective exercise of the right to benefit from social welfare services, the Parties undertake:

1 to promote or provide services which, by using methods of social work, would contribute to the welfare and development of both individuals and groups in the community, and to their adjustment to the social environment;

2 to encourage the participation of individuals and voluntary or other organisations in the establishment and maintenance of such services.

Article 15
The right of persons with disabilities to independence, social integration and participation in the life of the community

With a view to ensuring to persons with disabilities, irrespective of age and the nature and origin of their disabilities, the effective exercise of the right to independence, social integration and participation in the life of the community, the Parties undertake, in particular:

1 to take the necessary measures to provide persons with disabilities with guidance, education and vocational training in the framework of general schemes wherever possible or, where this is not possible, through specialised bodies, public or private;

2 to promote their access to employment through all measures tending to encourage employers to hire and keep in employment persons with disabilities in the ordinary working environment and to adjust the working conditions to the needs of the disabled or, where this is not possible by reason of the disability, by arranging for or creating sheltered employment according to the level of disability. In certain cases, such measures may require recourse to specialised placement and support services;

3 to promote their full social integration and participation in the life of the community in particular through measures, including technical aids, aiming to overcome barriers to communication and mobility and enabling access to transport, housing, cultural activities and leisure.

Article 16
The right of the family to social, legal and economic protection

With a view to ensuring the necessary conditions for the full development of the family, which is a fundamental unit of society, the Parties undertake to promote the economic, legal and social protection of family life by such means as social and family benefits, fiscal arrangements, provision of family housing, benefits for the newly married and other appropriate means.

'social and family benefits' (Art 16)—Benefits may be subject to means testing (see Slovakia Conclusions XVI-2, Romania Conclusions 2002 and Bulgaria Conclusions 2004) [RCLP para 5.187].

'provision of family housing' (Art 16)—See *European Roma Rights Centre (ERRC) v Greece* Collective Complaint No 15/2003 [RCLP para 5.167].

Article 17
The right of children and young persons to social, legal and economic protection

With a view to ensuring the effective exercise of the right of children and young persons to grow up in an environment which encourages the full development of their personality and of their physical and mental capacities, the Parties undertake, either directly or in co-operation with public and private organisations, to take all appropriate and necessary measures designed:

1

    a   to ensure that children and young persons, taking account of the rights and duties of their parents, have the care, the assistance, the education and the training they need, in particular by providing for the establishment or maintenance of institutions and services sufficient and adequate for this purpose;

    b   to protect children and young persons against negligence, violence or exploitation;

c   to provide protection and special aid from the state for children and young persons temporarily or definitively deprived of their family's support;

2 to provide to children and young persons a free primary and secondary education as well as to encourage regular attendance at schools.

Article 18
The right to engage in a gainful occupation in the territory of other Parties

With a view to ensuring the effective exercise of the right to engage in a gainful occupation in the territory of any other Party, the Parties undertake:

1 to apply existing regulations in a spirit of liberality;

2 to simplify existing formalities and to reduce or abolish chancery dues and other charges payable by foreign workers or their employers;

3 to liberalise, individually or collectively, regulations governing the employment of foreign workers;

and recognise:

4 the right of their nationals to leave the country to engage in a gainful occupation in the territories of the other Parties.

Article 19
The right of migrant workers and their families to protection and assistance

With a view to ensuring the effective exercise of the right of migrant workers and their families to protection and assistance in the territory of any other Party, the Parties undertake:

1 to maintain or to satisfy themselves that there are maintained adequate and free services to assist such workers, particularly in obtaining accurate information, and to take all appropriate steps, so far as national laws and regulations permit, against misleading propaganda relating to emigration and immigration;

2 to adopt appropriate measures within their own jurisdiction to facilitate the departure, journey and reception of such workers and their families, and to provide, within their own jurisdiction, appropriate services for health, medical attention and good hygienic conditions during the journey;

3 to promote co-operation, as appropriate, between social services, public and private, in emigration and immigration countries;

4 to secure for such workers lawfully within their territories, insofar as such matters are regulated by law or regulations or are subject to the control of administrative authorities, treatment not less favourable than that of their own nationals in respect of the following matters:

a   remuneration and other employment and working conditions;
b   membership of trade unions and enjoyment of the benefits of collective bargaining;
c   accommodation;

5 to secure for such workers lawfully within their territories treatment not less favourable than that of their own nationals with regard to employment taxes, dues or contributions payable in respect of employed persons;

6 to facilitate as far as possible the reunion of the family of a foreign worker permitted to establish himself in the territory;

7 to secure for such workers lawfully within their territories treatment not less favourable than that of their own nationals in respect of legal proceedings relating to matters referred to in this article;

8 to secure that such workers lawfully residing within their territories are not expelled unless they endanger national security or offend against public interest or morality;

9 to permit, within legal limits, the transfer of such parts of the earnings and savings of such workers as they may desire;

10 to extend the protection and assistance provided for in this article to self-employed migrants insofar as such mea-sures apply;

11 to promote and facilitate the teaching of the national language of the receiving state or, if there are several, one of these languages, to migrant workers and members of their families;

12 to promote and facilitate, as far as practicable, the teaching of the migrant worker's mother tongue to the children of the migrant worker.

Article 20
The right to equal opportunities and equal treatment in matters of employment and occupation without discrimination on the grounds of sex

With a view to ensuring the effective exercise of the right to equal opportunities and equal treatment in matters of employment and occupation without discrimination on the grounds of sex, the Parties undertake to recognise that right and to take appropriate measures to ensure or promote its application in the following fields:

 a access to employment, protection against dismissal and occupational reintegration;
 b vocational guidance, training, retraining and rehabilitation;
 c terms of employment and working conditions, including remuneration;
 d career development, including promotion.

Article 21
The right to information and consultation

With a view to ensuring the effective exercise of the right of workers to be informed and consulted within the undertaking, the Parties undertake to adopt or encourage measures enabling workers or their representatives, in accordance with national legislation and practice:

 a to be informed regularly or at the appropriate time and in a comprehensible way about the economic and financial situation of the undertaking employing them, on the understanding that the disclosure of certain information which could be prejudicial to the undertaking may be refused or subject to confidentiality; and
 b to be consulted in good time on proposed decisions which could substantially affect the interests of workers, particularly on those decisions which could have an important impact on the employment situation in the undertaking.

Article 22
The right to take part in the determination and improvement of the working conditions and working environment

With a view to ensuring the effective exercise of the right of workers to take part in the determination and improvement of the working conditions and working environment in the undertaking, the Parties undertake to adopt or encourage measures enabling workers or their representatives, in accordance with national legislation and practice, to contribute:

a   to the determination and the improvement of the working conditions, work organisation and working environment;
b   to the protection of health and safety within the undertaking;
c   to the organisation of social and socio-cultural services and facilities within the undertaking;
d   to the supervision of the observance of regulations on these matters.

Article 23
The right of elderly persons to social protection

With a view to ensuring the effective exercise of the right of elderly persons to social protection, the Parties undertake to adopt or encourage, either directly or in co-operation with public or private organisations, appropriate measures designed in particular:

–   to enable elderly persons to remain full members of society for as long as possible, by means of:
a   adequate resources enabling them to lead a decent life and play an active part in public, social and cultural life;
b   provision of information about services and facilities available for elderly persons and their opportunities to make use of them;
–   to enable elderly persons to choose their life-style freely and to lead independent lives in their familiar surroundings for as long as they wish and are able, by means of:
a   provision of housing suited to their needs and their state of health or of adequate support for adapting their housing;
b   the health care and the services necessitated by their state;
–   to guarantee elderly persons living in institutions appropriate support, while respecting their privacy, and participation in decisions concerning living conditions in the institution.

Article 24
The right to protection in cases of termination of employment

With a view to ensuring the effective exercise of the right of workers to protection in cases of termination of employment, the Parties undertake to recognise:

a   the right of all workers not to have their employment terminated without valid reasons for such termination connected with their capacity or conduct or based on the operational requirements of the undertaking, establishment or service;
b   the right of workers whose employment is terminated without a valid reason to adequate compensation or other appropriate relief.

To this end the Parties undertake to ensure that a worker who considers that his employment has been terminated without a valid reason shall have the right to appeal to an impartial body.

Article 25
The right of workers to the protection of their claims in the event of the insolvency of their employer

With a view to ensuring the effective exercise of the right of workers to the protection of their claims in the event of the insolvency of their employer, the Parties undertake to provide that workers' claims arising from contracts of employment or employment relationships be guaranteed by a guarantee institution or by any other effective form of protection.

Article 26
The right to dignity at work

With a view to ensuring the effective exercise of the right of all workers to protection of their dignity at work, the Parties undertake, in consultation with employers' and workers' organisations:

1 to promote awareness, information and prevention of sexual harassment in the workplace or in relation to work and to take all appropriate measures to protect workers from such conduct;

2 to promote awareness, information and prevention of recurrent reprehensible or distinctly negative and offensive actions directed against individual workers in the workplace or in relation to work and to take all appropriate measures to protect workers from such conduct.

Article 27
The right of workers with family responsibilities to equal opportunities and equal treatment

With a view to ensuring the exercise of the right to equality of opportunity and treatment for men and women workers with family responsibilities and between such workers and other workers, the Parties undertake:

1 to take appropriate measures:

    a   to enable workers with family responsibilities to enter and remain in employment, as well as to re-enter employment after an absence due to those responsibilities, including measures in the field of vocational guidance and training;
    b   to take account of their needs in terms of conditions of employment and social security;
    c   to develop or promote services, public or private, in particular child daycare services and other childcare arrangements;

2 to provide a possibility for either parent to obtain, during a period after maternity leave, parental leave to take care of a child, the duration and conditions of which should be determined by national legislation, collective agreements or practice;

3 to ensure that family responsibilities shall not, as such, constitute a valid reason for termination of employment.

Article 28
The right of workers' representatives to protection in the undertaking and facilities to be accorded to them

With a view to ensuring the effective exercise of the right of workers' representatives to carry out their functions, the Parties undertake to ensure that in the undertaking:

a   they enjoy effective protection against acts prejudicial to them, including dismissal, based on their status or activities as workers' representatives within the undertaking;

b   they are afforded such facilities as may be appropriate in order to enable them to carry out their functions promptly and efficiently, account being taken of the industrial relations system of the country and the needs, size and capabilities of the undertaking concerned.

Article 29
The right to information and consultation in collective redundancy procedures

With a view to ensuring the effective exercise of the right of workers to be informed and consulted in situations of collective redundancies, the Parties undertake to ensure that employers shall inform and consult workers' representatives, in good time prior to such collective redundancies, on ways and means of avoiding collective redundancies or limiting their occurrence and mitigating their consequences, for example by recourse to accompanying social measures aimed, in particular, at aid for the redeployment or retraining of the workers concerned.

Article 30
The right to protection against poverty and social exclusion

With a view to ensuring the effective exercise of the right to protection against poverty and social exclusion, the Parties undertake:

a   to take measures within the framework of an overall and co-ordinated approach to promote the effective access of persons who live or risk living in a situation of social exclusion or poverty, as well as their families, to, in particular, employment, housing, training, education, culture and social and medical assistance;

b   to review these measures with a view to their adaptation if necessary.

Article 31
The right to housing

With a view to ensuring the effective exercise of the right to housing, the Parties undertake to take measures designed:

1 to promote access to housing of an adequate standard;

2 to prevent and reduce homelessness with a view to its gradual elimination;

3 to make the price of housing accessible to those without adequate resources.

'the right to housing' (Art 31)—See *European Roma Rights Centre (ERRC) v Greece* Collective Complaint No 15/2003 [RCLP para 5.91].

PART III

Article A
Undertakings

1 Subject to the provisions of Article B below, each of the Parties undertakes:

a   to consider Part I of this Charter as a declaration of the aims which it will pursue by all appropriate means, as stated in the introductory paragraph of that part;

b   to consider itself bound by at least six of the following nine articles of Part II of this Charter: Articles 1, 5, 6, 7, 12, 13, 16, 19 and 20;

c   to consider itself bound by an additional number of articles or numbered paragraphs of Part II of the Charter which it may select, provided that the total number of articles or numbered paragraphs by which it is bound is not less than sixteen articles or sixty-three numbered paragraphs.

2 The articles or paragraphs selected in accordance with sub-paragraphs b and c of paragraph 1 of this article shall be notified to the Secretary General of the Council of Europe at the time when the instrument of ratification, acceptance or approval is deposited.

3 Any Party may, at a later date, declare by notification addressed to the Secretary General that it considers itself bound by any articles or any numbered paragraphs of Part II of the Charter which it has not already accepted under the terms of paragraph 1 of this article. Such undertakings subsequently given shall be deemed to be an integral part of the ratification, acceptance or approval and shall have the same effect as from the first day of the month following the expiration of a period of one month after the date of the notification.

4 Each Party shall maintain a system of labour inspection appropriate to national conditions.

Article B
Links with the European Social Charter and the 1988 Additional Protocol

1 No Contracting Party to the European Social Charter or Party to the Additional Protocol of 5 May 1988 may ratify, accept or approve this Charter without considering itself bound by at least the provisions corresponding to the provisions of the European Social Charter and, where appropriate, of the Additional Protocol, to which it was bound.

2 Acceptance of the obligations of any provision of this Charter shall, from the date of entry into force of those obligations for the Party concerned, result in the corresponding provision of the European Social Charter and, where appropriate, of its Additional Protocol of 1988 ceasing to apply to the Party concerned in the event of that Party being bound by the first of those instruments or by both instruments.

PART IV

Article C
Supervision of the implementation of the undertakings contained in this Charter

The implementation of the legal obligations contained in this Charter shall be submitted to the same supervision as the European Social Charter.

Article D
Collective complaints

1 The provisions of the Additional Protocol to the European Social Charter providing for a system of collective complaints shall apply to the undertakings given in this Charter for the States which have ratified the said Protocol.

2 Any State which is not bound by the Additional Protocol to the European Social Charter providing for a system of collective complaints may when depositing its instrument of ratification, acceptance or approval of this Charter or at any time thereafter, declare by notification addressed to the Secretary General of the Council of Europe, that it accepts the supervision of its obligations under this Charter following the procedure provided for in the said Protocol.

PART V

Article E
Non-discrimination

The enjoyment of the rights set forth in this Charter shall be secured without discrimination on any ground such as race, colour, sex, language, religion, political or other opinion, national extraction or social origin, health, association with a national minority, birth or other status.

Article F
Derogations in time of war or public emergency

1 In time of war or other public emergency threatening the life of the nation any Party may take measures derogating from its obligations under this Charter to the extent strictly required by the exigencies of the situation, provided that such measures are not inconsistent with its other obligations under international law.

2 Any Party which has availed itself of this right of derogation shall, within a reasonable lapse of time, keep the Secretary General of the Council of Europe fully informed of the measures taken and of the reasons therefore. It shall likewise inform the Secretary General when such measures have ceased to operate and the provisions of the Charter which it has accepted are again being fully executed.

Article G
Restrictions

1 The rights and principles set forth in Part I when effectively realised, and their effective exercise as provided for in Part II, shall not be subject to any restrictions or limitations not specified in those parts, except such as are prescribed by law and are necessary in a democratic society for the protection of the rights and freedoms of others or for the protection of public interest, national security, public health, or morals.

2 The restrictions permitted under this Charter to the rights and obligations set forth herein shall not be applied for any purpose other than that for which they have been prescribed.

Article H
Relations between the Charter and domestic law or international agreements

The provisions of this Charter shall not prejudice the provisions of domestic law or of any bilateral or multilateral treaties, conventions or agreements which are already in force, or may come into force, under which more favourable treatment would be accorded to the persons protected.

Article I
Implementation of the undertakings given

1 Without prejudice to the methods of implementation foreseen in these articles the relevant provisions of Articles 1 to 31 of Part II of this Charter shall be implemented by:

a   laws or regulations;
b   agreements between employers or employers' organisations and workers' organisations;
c   a combination of those two methods;
d   other appropriate means.

2 Compliance with the undertakings deriving from the provisions of paragraphs 1, 2, 3, 4, 5 and 7 of Article 2, paragraphs 4, 6 and 7 of Article 7, paragraphs 1, 2, 3 and 5 of

Article 10 and Articles 21 and 22 of Part II of this Charter shall be regarded as effective if the provisions are applied, in accordance with paragraph 1 of this article, to the great majority of the workers concerned.

Article J
Amendments

1 Any amendment to Parts I and II of this Charter with the purpose of extending the rights guaranteed in this Charter as well as any amendment to Parts III to VI, proposed by a Party or by the Governmental Committee, shall be communicated to the Secretary General of the Council of Europe and forwarded by the Secretary General to the Parties to this Charter.

2 Any amendment proposed in accordance with the provisions of the preceding paragraph shall be examined by the Governmental Committee which shall submit the text adopted to the Committee of Ministers for approval after consultation with the Parliamentary Assembly. After its approval by the Committee of Ministers this text shall be forwarded to the Parties for acceptance.

3 Any amendment to Part I and to Part II of this Charter shall enter into force, in respect of those Parties which have accepted it, on the first day of the month following the expiration of a period of one month after the date on which three Parties have informed the Secretary General that they have accepted it.

In respect of any Party which subsequently accepts it, the amendment shall enter into force on the first day of the month following the expiration of a period of one month after the date on which that Party has informed the Secretary General of its acceptance.

4 Any amendment to Parts III to VI of this Charter shall enter into force on the first day of the month following the expiration of a period of one month after the date on which all Parties have informed the Secretary General that they have accepted it.

PART VI

Article K
Signature, ratification and entry into force

1 This Charter shall be open for signature by the member States of the Council of Europe. It shall be subject to ratification, acceptance or approval. Instruments of ratification, acceptance or approval shall be deposited with the Secretary General of the Council of Europe.

2 This Charter shall enter into force on the first day of the month following the expiration of a period of one month after the date on which three member States of the Council of Europe have expressed their consent to be bound by this Charter in accordance with the preceding paragraph.

3 In respect of any member State which subsequently expresses its consent to be bound by this Charter, it shall enter into force on the first day of the month following the expiration of a period of one month after the date of the deposit of the instrument of ratification, acceptance or approval.

Article L
Territorial application

1 This Charter shall apply to the metropolitan territory of each Party. Each signatory may, at the time of signature or of the deposit of its instrument of ratification,

acceptance or approval, specify, by declaration addressed to the Secretary General of the Council of Europe, the territory which shall be considered to be its metropolitan territory for this purpose.

2 Any signatory may, at the time of signature or of the deposit of its instrument of ratification, acceptance or approval, or at any time thereafter, declare by notification addressed to the Secretary General of the Council of Europe, that the Charter shall extend in whole or in part to a non-metropolitan territory or territories specified in the said declaration for whose international relations it is responsible or for which it assumes international responsibility. It shall specify in the declaration the articles or paragraphs of Part II of the Charter which it accepts as binding in respect of the territories named in the declaration.

3 The Charter shall extend its application to the territory or territories named in the aforesaid declaration as from the first day of the month following the expiration of a period of one month after the date of receipt of the notification of such declaration by the Secretary General.

4 Any Party may declare at a later date by notification addressed to the Secretary General of the Council of Europe that, in respect of one or more of the territories to which the Charter has been applied in accordance with paragraph 2 of this article, it accepts as binding any articles or any numbered paragraphs which it has not already accepted in respect of that territory or territories. Such undertakings subsequently given shall be deemed to be an integral part of the original declaration in respect of the territory concerned, and shall have the same effect as from the first day of the month following the expiration of a period of one month after the date of receipt of such notification by the Secretary General.

Article M
Denunciation

1 Any Party may denounce this Charter only at the end of a period of five years from the date on which the Charter entered into force for it, or at the end of any subsequent period of two years, and in either case after giving six months' notice to the Secretary General of the Council of Europe who shall inform the other Parties accordingly.

2 Any Party may, in accordance with the provisions set out in the preceding paragraph, denounce any article or paragraph of Part II of the Charter accepted by it provided that the number of articles or paragraphs by which this Party is bound shall never be less than sixteen in the former case and sixty-three in the latter and that this number of articles or paragraphs shall continue to include the articles selected by the Party among those to which special reference is made in Article A, paragraph 1, sub-paragraph b.

3 Any Party may denounce the present Charter or any of the articles or paragraphs of Part II of the Charter under the conditions specified in paragraph 1 of this article in respect of any territory to which the said Charter is applicable, by virtue of a declaration made in accordance with paragraph 2 of Article L.

Article N
Appendix

The appendix to this Charter shall form an integral part of it.

Article O
Notifications

The Secretary General of the Council of Europe shall notify the member States of the Council and the Director General of the International Labour Office of:

a   any signature;

b   the deposit of any instrument of ratification, acceptance or approval;

c   any date of entry into force of this Charter in accordance with Article K;

d   any declaration made in application of Articles A, paragraphs 2 and 3, D, paragraphs 1 and 2, F, paragraph 2, L, paragraphs 1, 2, 3 and 4;

e   any amendment in accordance with Article J;

f   any denunciation in accordance with Article M;

g   any other act, notification or communication relating to this Charter.

In witness whereof, the undersigned, being duly authorised thereto, have signed this revised Charter.

Done at Strasbourg, this 3rd day of May 1996, in English and French, both texts being equally authentic, in a single copy which shall be deposited in the archives of the Council of Europe. The Secretary Gene-ral of the Council of Europe shall transmit certified copies to each member State of the Council of Europe and to the Director General of the International Labour Office.

APPENDIX TO THE REVISED EUROPEAN SOCIAL CHARTER

SCOPE OF THE REVISED EUROPEAN SOCIAL CHARTER IN TERMS OF PERSONS PROTECTED

1 Without prejudice to Article 12, paragraph 4, and Article 13, paragraph 4, the persons covered by Articles 1 to 17 and 20 to 31 include foreigners only in so far as they are nationals of other Parties lawfully resident or working regularly within the territory of the Party concerned, subject to the under-standing that these articles are to be interpreted in the light of the provisions of Articles 18 and 19.

This interpretation would not prejudice the extension of similar facilities to other persons by any of the Parties.

2 Each Party will grant to refugees as defined in the Convention relating to the Status of Refugees, signed in Geneva on 28 July 1951 and in the Protocol of 31 January 1967, and lawfully staying in its territory, treatment as favourable as possible, and in any case not less favourable than under the obligations accepted by the Party under the said convention and under any other existing international instruments applicable to those refugees.

3 Each Party will grant to stateless persons as defined in the Convention on the Status of Stateless Persons done in New York on 28 September 1954 and lawfully staying in its territory, treatment as favourable as possible and in any case not less favourable than under the obligations accepted by the Party under the said instrument and under any other existing international instruments applicable to those stateless persons.

Part I, paragraph 18, and Part II, Article 18, paragraph 1

It is understood that these provisions are not concerned with the question of entry into the territories of the Parties and do not prejudice the provisions of the European Convention on Establishment, signed in Paris on 13 December 1955.

PART II

Article 1, paragraph 2

This provision shall not be interpreted as prohibiting or authorising any union security clause or practice.

Article 2, paragraph 6

Parties may provide that this provision shall not apply:

a　　to workers having a contract or employment relationship with a total duration not exceeding one month and/or with a working week not exceeding eight hours;

b　　where the contract or employment relationship is of a casual and/or specific nature, provided, in these cases, that its non-application is justified by objective considerations.

Article 3, paragraph 4

It is understood that for the purposes of this provision the functions, organisation and conditions of operation of these services shall be determined by national laws or regulations, collective agreements or other means appropriate to national conditions.

Article 4, paragraph 4

This provision shall be so understood as not to prohibit immediate dismissal for any serious offence.

Article 4, paragraph 5

It is understood that a Party may give the undertaking required in this paragraph if the great majority of workers are not permitted to suffer deductions from wages either by law or through collective agreements or arbitration awards, the exceptions being those persons not so covered.

Article 6, paragraph 4

It is understood that each Party may, insofar as it is concerned, regulate the exercise of the right to strike by law, provided that any further restriction that this might place on the right can be justified under the terms of Article G.

Article 7, paragraph 2

This provision does not prevent Parties from providing in their legislation that young persons not having reached the minimum age laid down may perform work in so far as it is absolutely necessary for their vocational training where such work is carried out in accordance with conditions prescribed by the competent authority and measures are taken to protect the health and safety of these young persons.

Article 7, paragraph 8

It is understood that a Party may give the undertaking required in this paragraph if it fulfils the spirit of the undertaking by providing by law that the great majority of persons under eighteen years of age shall not be employed in night work.

Article 8, paragraph 2

This provision shall not be interpreted as laying down an absolute prohibition. Exceptions could be made, for instance, in the following cases:

a　　if an employed woman has been guilty of misconduct which justifies breaking off the employment relationship;

b　　if the undertaking concerned ceases to operate;

c　　if the period prescribed in the employment contract has expired.

Article 12, paragraph 4

The words "and subject to the conditions laid down in such agreements" in the introduction to this paragraph are taken to imply *inter alia* that with regard to benefits which are available independently of any insurance contribution, a Party may require the completion of a prescribed period of residence before granting such benefits to nationals of other Parties.

Article 13, paragraph 4

Governments not Parties to the European Convention on Social and Medical Assistance may ratify the Charter in respect of this paragraph provided that they grant to nationals of other Parties a treatment which is in conformity with the provisions of the said convention.

Article 16

It is understood that the protection afforded in this provision covers single-parent families.

Article 17

It is understood that this provision covers all persons below the age of 18 years, unless under the law applicable to the child majority is attained earlier, without prejudice to the other specific provisions provided by the Charter, particularly Article 7.

This does not imply an obligation to provide compulsory education up to the above-mentioned age.

Article 19, paragraph 6

For the purpose of applying this provision, the term "family of a foreign worker" is understood to mean at least the worker's spouse and unmarried children, as long as the latter are considered to be minors by the receiving State and are dependent on the migrant worker.

Article 20

1 It is understood that social security matters, as well as other provisions relating to unemployment benefit, old age benefit and survivor's benefit, may be excluded from the scope of this article.

2 Provisions concerning the protection of women, particularly as regards pregnancy, confinement and the post-natal period, shall not be deemed to be discrimination as referred to in this article.

3 This article shall not prevent the adoption of specific measures aimed at removing *de facto* inequalities.

4 Occupational activities which, by reason of their nature or the context in which they are carried out, can be entrusted only to persons of a particular sex may be excluded from the scope of this article or some of its provisions. This provision is not to be interpreted as requiring the Parties to embody in laws or regulations a list of occupations which, by reason of their nature or the context in which they are carried out, may be reserved to persons of a particular sex.

Articles 21 and 22

1 For the purpose of the application of these articles, the term "workers' representatives" means persons who are recognised as such under national legislation or practice.

2 The terms "national legislation and practice" embrace as the case may be, in addition to laws and regulations, collective agreements, other agreements between employers and workers' representatives, customs as well as relevant case law.

3 For the purpose of the application of these articles, the term "undertaking" is understood as referring to a set of tangible and intangible components, with or without legal personality, formed to produce goods or provide services for financial gain and with power to determine its own market policy.

4 It is understood that religious communities and their institutions may be excluded from the application of these articles, even if these institutions are "undertakings" within the meaning of paragraph 3. Establishments pursuing activities which are inspired by certain ideals or guided by certain moral concepts, ideals and concepts which are protected by national legislation, may be excluded from the application of these articles to such an extent as is necessary to protect the orientation of the undertaking.

5 It is understood that where in a state the rights set out in these articles are exercised in the various establishments of the undertaking, the Party concerned is to be considered as fulfilling the obligations deriving from these provisions.

6 The Parties may exclude from the field of application of these articles, those undertakings employing less than a certain number of workers, to be determined by national legislation or practice.

Article 22

1 This provision affects neither the powers and obligations of states as regards the adoption of health and safety regulations for workplaces, nor the powers and responsibilities of the bodies in charge of monitoring their application.

2 The terms "social and socio-cultural services and facilities" are understood as referring to the social and/or cultural facilities for workers provided by some undertakings such as welfare assistance, sports fields, rooms for nursing mothers, libraries, children's holiday camps, etc.

Article 23, paragraph 1

For the purpose of the application of this paragraph, the term "for as long as possible" refers to the elderly person's physical, psychological and intellectual capacities.

Article 24

1 It is understood that for the purposes of this article the terms "termination of employment" and "terminated" mean termination of employment at the initiative of the employer.

2 It is understood that this article covers all workers but that a Party may exclude from some or all of its protection the following categories of employed persons:

    a   workers engaged under a contract of employment for a specified period of time or a specified task;

b   workers undergoing a period of probation or a qualifying period of employment, provided that this is determined in advance and is of a reasonable duration;

c   workers engaged on a casual basis for a short period.

3 For the purpose of this article the following, in particular, shall not constitute valid reasons for termination of employment:

a   trade union membership or participation in union activities outside working hours, or, with the consent of the employer, within working hours;

b   seeking office as, acting or having acted in the capacity of a workers' representative;

c   the filing of a complaint or the participation in proceedings against an employer involving alleged violation of laws or regulations or recourse to competent administrative authorities;

d   race, colour, sex, marital status, family responsibilities, pregnancy, religion, political opinion, national extraction or social origin;

e   maternity or parental leave;

f   temporary absence from work due to illness or injury.

4 It is understood that compensation or other appropriate relief in case of termination of employment without valid reasons shall be determined by national laws or regulations, collective agreements or other means appropriate to national conditions.

Article 25

1 It is understood that the competent national authority may, by way of exemption and after consulting organisations of employers and workers, exclude certain categories of workers from the protection provided in this provision by reason of the special nature of their employment relationship.

2 It is understood that the definition of the term "insolvency" must be determined by national law and practice.

3 The workers' claims covered by this provision shall include at least:

a   the workers' claims for wages relating to a prescribed period, which shall not be less than three months under a privilege system and eight weeks under a guarantee system, prior to the insolvency or to the termination of employment;

b   the workers' claims for holiday pay due as a result of work performed during the year in which the insolvency or the termination of employment occurred;

c   the workers' claims for amounts due in respect of other types of paid absence relating to a prescribed period, which shall not be less than three months under a privilege system and eight weeks under a guarantee system, prior to the insolvency or the termination of the employment.

4 National laws or regulations may limit the protection of workers' claims to a prescribed amount, which shall be of a socially acceptable level.

Article 26

It is understood that this article does not require that legislation be enacted by the Parties.

It is understood that paragraph 2 does not cover sexual harassment.

Article 27

It is understood that this article applies to men and women workers with family responsibilities in relation to their dependent children as well as in relation to other members of their immediate family who clearly need their care or support where such responsibilities restrict their possibilities of preparing for, entering, participating in or advancing in economic activity. The terms "dependent children" and "other members of their immediate family who clearly need their care and support" mean persons defined as such by the national legislation of the Party concerned.

Articles 28 and 29

For the purpose of the application of this article, the term "workers' representatives" means persons who are recognised as such under national legislation or practice.

PART III

It is understood that the Charter contains legal obligations of an international character, the application of which is submitted solely to the supervision provided for in Part IV thereof.

Article A, paragraph 1

It is understood that the numbered paragraphs may include articles consisting of only one paragraph.

Article B, paragraph 2

For the purpose of paragraph 2 of Article B, the provisions of the revised Charter correspond to the provisions of the Charter with the same article or paragraph number with the exception of:

a   Article 3, paragraph 2, of the revised Charter which corresponds to Article 3, paragraphs 1 and 3, of the Charter;
b   Article 3, paragraph 3, of the revised Charter which corresponds to Article 3, paragraphs 2 and 3, of the Charter;
c   Article 10, paragraph 5, of the revised Charter which corresponds to Article 10, paragraph 4, of the Charter;
d   Article 17, paragraph 1, of the revised Charter which corresponds to Article 17 of the Charter.

PART V

Article E

A differential treatment based on an objective and reasonable justification shall not be deemed discriminatory.

Article F

The terms "in time of war or other public emergency" shall be so understood as to cover also the *threat* of war.

Article I

It is understood that workers excluded in accordance with the appendix to Articles 21 and 22 are not taken into account in establishing the number of workers concerned.

Article J

The term "amendment" shall be extended so as to cover also the addition of new articles to the Charter.

CHAPTER 23

CHARTER OF FUNDAMENTAL RIGHTS OF THE EUROPEAN UNION (2000/C 364/01)

PREAMBLE

The peoples of Europe, in creating an ever closer union among them, are resolved to share a peaceful future based on common values.

Conscious of its spiritual and moral heritage, the Union is founded on the indivisible, universal values of human dignity, freedom, equality and solidarity; it is based on the principles of democracy and the rule of law. It places the individual at the heart of its activities, by establishing the citizenship of the Union and by creating an area of freedom, security and justice.

The Union contributes to the preservation and to the development of these common values while respecting the diversity of the cultures and traditions of the peoples of Europe as well as the national identities of the Member States and the organisation of their public authorities at national, regional and local levels; it seeks to promote balanced and sustainable development and ensures free movement of persons, goods, services and capital, and the freedom of establishment.

To this end, it is necessary to strengthen the protection of fundamental rights in the light of changes in society, social progress and scientific and technological developments by making those rights more visible in a Charter.

This Charter reaffirms, with due regard for the powers and tasks of the Community and the Union and the principle of subsidiarity, the rights as they result, in particular, from the constitutional traditions and international obligations common to the Member States, the Treaty on European Union, the Community Treaties, the European Convention for the Protection of Human Rights and Fundamental Freedoms, the Social Charters adopted by the Community and by the Council of Europe and the case-law of the Court of Justice of the European Communities and of the European Court of Human Rights.

Enjoyment of these rights entails responsibilities and duties with regard to other persons, to the human community and to future generations.

The Union therefore recognises the rights, freedoms and principles set out hereafter.

Status—The Charter of Fundamental Rights of the European Union came into full legal effect upon the entry into force of the Treaty of Lisbon on 1 December 2009 at which point the Charter became legally binding on EU institutions and national governments of countries within the European Union. It applies to the institutions and bodies of the European Union and national authorities when they are implementing EU law. The United Kingdom negotiated the Protocol on the Application of the Charter of Fundamental Rights of the European Union to Poland and to the United Kingdom (not contained in this work) restricting the interpretation of the Charter in the domestic courts. However, it has been held that the Charter applies to the United Kingdom notwithstanding the terms of the Protocol (*NS v Secretary of State for the Home Department* C-411/10 (2011)). Note that Art 52(3) is key to understanding the status and impact of the Charter and its relationship to the ECHR in that Art 52(3) provides that in so far as the Charter contains rights which correspond to rights guaranteed by the ECHR, the meaning and scope of those rights shall be the same as those laid down by the ECHR. The Charter of Fundamental Rights of the European Union has been cited by the domestic courts (see *R (Howard League for Penal Reform) v Secretary of State for the Home Department* [2002] EWHC 2497, [2003] 1 FLR 484) **[RCLP paras 14.132 and 15.216]**.

Chapter I

Dignity

Article 1
Human dignity

Human dignity is inviolable. It must be respected and protected.

Article 2
Right to life

1. Everyone has the right to life.

2. No one shall be condemned to the death penalty, or executed.

Article 3
Right to the integrity of the person

1. Everyone has the right to respect for his or her physical and mental integrity.

2. In the fields of medicine and biology, the following must be respected in particular:

   — the free and informed consent of the person concerned, according to the procedures laid down by law,
   — the prohibition of eugenic practices, in particular those aiming at the selection of persons,
   — the prohibition on making the human body and its parts as such a source of financial gain,
   — the prohibition of the reproductive cloning of human beings.

'integrity of the person' (Art 3)—See also Directive 2004/23/EC of the European Parliament and Council.

Article 4
Prohibition of torture and inhuman or degrading treatment or punishment

No one shall be subjected to torture or to inhuman or degrading treatment or punishment.

Article 5
Prohibition of slavery and forced labour

1. No one shall be held in slavery or servitude.

2. No one shall be required to perform forced or compulsory labour.

3. Trafficking in human beings is prohibited.

Chapter II
Freedoms

Article 6
Right to liberty and security

Everyone has the right to liberty and security of person.

Article 7
Respect for private and family life

Everyone has the right to respect for his or her private and family life, home and communications.

'**family**' (Art 7)—For the meaning of the word 'family' in the context of European Union law see C249/96 *Grant v Southwest Trains* [1998] ICR 449, para 35 [**RCLP para 8.223**].

Article 8
Protection of personal data

1. Everyone has the right to the protection of personal data concerning him or her.

2. Such data must be processed fairly for specified purposes and on the basis of the consent of the person concerned or some other legitimate basis laid down by law. Everyone has the right of access to data which has been collected concerning him or her, and the right to have it rectified.

3. Compliance with these rules shall be subject to control by an independent authority.

Article 9
Right to marry and right to found a family

The right to marry and the right to found a family shall be guaranteed in accordance with the national laws governing the exercise of these rights.

Article 10
Freedom of thought, conscience and religion

1. Everyone has the right to freedom of thought, conscience and religion. This right includes freedom to change religion or belief and freedom, either alone or in community with others and in public or in private, to manifest religion or belief, in worship, teaching, practice and observance.

2. The right to conscientious objection is recognised, in accordance with the national laws governing the exercise of this right.

Article 11
Freedom of expression and information

1. Everyone has the right to freedom of expression. This right shall include freedom to hold opinions and to receive and impart information and ideas without interference by public authority and regardless of frontiers.

2. The freedom and pluralism of the media shall be respected.

'**freedom and pluralism of the media**' (Art 11(2))—See *Dynamic Medien Vertriebs GmBH v Avides Media AG* (Case C-244/06) [2008] All ER (D) 198 (Feb) on the relationship between the mass media and the welfare of the child [**RCLP para 11.79**].

Article 12
Freedom of assembly and of association

1. Everyone has the right to freedom of peaceful assembly and to freedom of association at all levels, in particular in political, trade union and civic matters, which implies the right of everyone to form and to join trade unions for the protection of his or her interests.

2. Political parties at Union level contribute to expressing the political will of the citizens of the Union.

Article 13
Freedom of the arts and sciences

The arts and scientific research shall be free of constraint. Academic freedom shall be respected.

Article 14
Right to education

1. Everyone has the right to education and to have access to vocational and continuing training.

2. This right includes the possibility to receive free compulsory education.

3. The freedom to found educational establishments with due respect for democratic principles and the right of parents to ensure the education and teaching of their children in conformity with their religious, philosophical and pedagogical convictions shall be respected, in accordance with the national laws governing the exercise of such freedom and right.

Article 15
Freedom to choose an occupation and right to engage in work

1. Everyone has the right to engage in work and to pursue a freely chosen or accepted occupation.

2. Every citizen of the Union has the freedom to seek employment, to work, to exercise the right of establishment and to provide services in any Member State.

3. Nationals of third countries who are authorised to work in the territories of the Member States are entitled to working conditions equivalent to those of citizens of the Union.

Article 16
Freedom to conduct a business

The freedom to conduct a business in accordance with Community law and national laws and practices is recognised.

Article 17
Right to property

1. Everyone has the right to own, use, dispose of and bequeath his or her lawfully acquired possessions. No one may be deprived of his or her possessions, except in the public interest and in the cases and under the conditions provided for by law, subject to fair compensation being paid in good time for their loss. The use of property may be regulated by law in so far as is necessary for the general interest.

2. Intellectual property shall be protected.

Article 18
Right to asylum

The right to asylum shall be guaranteed with due respect for the rules of the Geneva Convention of 28 July 1951 and the Protocol of 31 January 1967 relating to the status of refugees and in accordance with the Treaty establishing the European Community.

Article 19
Protection in the event of removal, expulsion or extradition

1. Collective expulsions are prohibited.

2. No one may be removed, expelled or extradited to a State where there is a serious risk that he or she would be subjected to the death penalty, torture or other inhuman or degrading treatment or punishment.

Chapter III
Equality

Article 20
Equality before the law

Everyone is equal before the law.

Article 21
Non-discrimination

1. Any discrimination based on any ground such as sex, race, colour, ethnic or social origin, genetic features, language, religion or belief, political or any other opinion, membership of a national minority, property, birth, disability, age or sexual orientation shall be prohibited.

2. Within the scope of application of the Treaty establishing the European Community and of the Treaty on European Union, and without prejudice to the special provisions of those Treaties, any discrimination on grounds of nationality shall be prohibited.

Equality (Art 21)—The principle of equality is one of the fundamental principles of EU law (see Case C-152/81: *Ferrario v Commission* [1983] ECR 2357 at 2367; Case C-215/85: *Bundesanstalt für Landwirschaftliche Marktordnung v Raiffeisen Hauptgenossenschaft* [1987] ECR 1279, para 23 and Case C-85/97: *Société Financière D'investissements SPRL (SFI) v Belgian State* [1998] ECR I-7447, para 30). For the application of the non-discrimination principles of the ECHR to EC law see Case C-117/01 *KB v National Health Service Pensions Agency* [2004] ICR 781 and *A v Chief Constable of the West Yorkshire Police* [2004] UKHL 21, [2005] 1 AC 51, para13. For the application of the non discrimination principles of EC law to the ECHR see *DH v Czech Republic* (2008) 47 EHRR 3, para 187. See also Art 13(1) of the Treaty Establishing the European Union [RCLP **paras 4.110–4.114**].

Article 22
Cultural, religious and linguistic diversity

The Union shall respect cultural, religious and linguistic diversity.

Article 23
Equality between men and women

Equality between men and women must be ensured in all areas, including employment, work and pay.

The principle of equality shall not prevent the maintenance or adoption of measures providing for specific advantages in favour of the under-represented sex.

Article 24
The rights of the child

1. Children shall have the right to such protection and care as is necessary for their well-being. They may express their views freely. Such views shall be taken into consideration on matters which concern them in accordance with their age and maturity.

2. In all actions relating to children, whether taken by public authorities or private institutions, the child's best interests must be a primary consideration.

3. Every child shall have the right to maintain on a regular basis a personal relationship and direct contact with both his or her parents, unless that is contrary to his or her interests.

Article 25
The rights of the elderly

The Union recognises and respects the rights of the elderly to lead a life of dignity and independence and to participate in social and cultural life.

Article 26
Integration of persons with disabilities

The Union recognises and respects the right of persons with disabilities to benefit from measures designed to ensure their independence, social and occupational integration and participation in the life of the community.

Chapter IV
Solidarity

Article 27
Workers' right to information and consultation within the undertaking

Workers or their representatives must, at the appropriate levels, be guaranteed information and consultation in good time in the cases and under the conditions provided for by Community law and national laws and practices.

Article 28
Right of collective bargaining and action

Workers and employers, or their respective organisations, have, in accordance with Community law and national laws and practices, the right to negotiate and conclude collective agreements at the appropriate levels and, in cases of conflicts of interest, to take collective action to defend their interests, including strike action.

Article 29
Right of access to placement services

Everyone has the right of access to a free placement service.

Article 30
Protection in the event of unjustified dismissal

Every worker has the right to protection against unjustified dismissal, in accordance with Community law and national laws and practices.

Article 31
Fair and just working conditions

1. Every worker has the right to working conditions which respect his or her health, safety and dignity.

2. Every worker has the right to limitation of maximum working hours, to daily and weekly rest periods and to an annual period of paid leave.

Article 32
Prohibition of child labour and protection of young people at work

The employment of children is prohibited. The minimum age of admission to employment may not be lower than the minimum school-leaving age, without prejudice to such rules as may be more favourable to young people and except for limited derogations.

Young people admitted to work must have working conditions appropriate to their age and be protected against economic exploitation and any work likely to harm their safety, health or physical, mental, moral or social development or to interfere with their education.

Article 33
Family and professional life

1. The family shall enjoy legal, economic and social protection.

2. To reconcile family and professional life, everyone shall have the right to protection from dismissal for a reason connected with maternity and the right to paid maternity leave and to parental leave following the birth or adoption of a child.

'legal, economic and social protection' (Art 33(1))—Article 33(1) is based on Art 16 of the European Social Charter. The second paragraph draws on Council Directive 92/85/EEC on the introduction of measures to encourage improvements in the safety and health at work of pregnant workers and workers who have recently given birth or are breast feeding and Directive 96/34/EC on the framework agreement on parental leave concluded by UNICE, CEEP and the ETUC. See also Council Recommendation 92/241/EEC, of 31 March 1992 on child care; Council Directive 96/34/EEC, of 3 June 1996 on the framework agreement on parental leave concluded by UNICE, CEEP and the ETUC and Council Directive 97/81/EC, of 15 December 1997 concerning the Framework Agreement on part-time work concluded by UNICE, CEEP and the ETUC [**RCLP para 8.48**].

Reconciliation of family and professional life (Art 3(2))—Article 33(2) is based on Art 8 of the Revised European Social Charter and draws on Art 27 (right of workers with family responsibilities to equal opportunities and equal treatment) of the revised Social Charter [**RCLP para 8.48**].

Article 34
Social security and social assistance

1. The Union recognises and respects the entitlement to social security benefits and social services providing protection in cases such as maternity, illness, industrial accidents, dependency or old age, and in the case of loss of employment, in accordance with the rules laid down by Community law and national laws and practices.

2. Everyone residing and moving legally within the European Union is entitled to social security benefits and social advantages in accordance with Community law and national laws and practices.

3. In order to combat social exclusion and poverty, the Union recognises and respects the right to social and housing assistance so as to ensure a decent existence for all those who lack sufficient resources, in accordance with the rules laid down by Community law and national laws and practices.

Article 35
Health care

Everyone has the right of access to preventive health care and the right to benefit from medical treatment under the conditions established by national laws and practices. A high level of human health protection shall be ensured in the definition and implementation of all Union policies and activities.

Article 36
Access to services of general economic interest

The Union recognises and respects access to services of general economic interest as provided for in national laws and practices, in accordance with the Treaty establishing the European Community, in order to promote the social and territorial cohesion of the Union.

Article 37
Environmental protection

A high level of environmental protection and the improvement of the quality of the environment must be integrated into the policies of the Union and ensured in accordance with the principle of sustainable development.

Article 38
Consumer protection

Union policies shall ensure a high level of consumer protection.

Chapter V
Citizens' Rights

Article 39
Right to vote and to stand as a candidate at elections to the European Parliament

1. Every citizen of the Union has the right to vote and to stand as a candidate at elections to the European Parliament in the Member State in which he or she resides, under the same conditions as nationals of that State.

2. Members of the European Parliament shall be elected by direct universal suffrage in a free and secret ballot.

Article 40
Right to vote and to stand as a candidate at municipal elections

Every citizen of the Union has the right to vote and to stand as a candidate at municipal elections in the Member State in which he or she resides under the same conditions as nationals of that State.

Article 41
Right to good administration

1. Every person has the right to have his or her affairs handled impartially, fairly and within a reasonable time by the institutions and bodies of the Union.

2. This right includes:

  — the right of every person to be heard, before any individual measure which would affect him or her adversely is taken;
  — the right of every person to have access to his or her file, while respecting the legitimate interests of confidentiality and of professional and business secrecy;
  — the obligation of the administration to give reasons for its decisions.

3. Every person has the right to have the Community make good any damage caused by its institutions or by its servants in the performance of their duties, in accordance with the general principles common to the laws of the Member States.

4. Every person may write to the institutions of the Union in one of the languages of the Treaties and must have an answer in the same language.

Article 42
Right of access to documents

Any citizen of the Union, and any natural or legal person residing or having its registered office in a Member State, has a right of access to European Parliament, Council and Commission documents.

Article 43
Ombudsman

Any citizen of the Union and any natural or legal person residing or having its registered office in a Member State has the right to refer to the Ombudsman of the Union cases of maladministration in the activities of the Community institutions or bodies, with the exception of the Court of Justice and the Court of First Instance acting in their judicial role.

Article 44
Right to petition

Any citizen of the Union and any natural or legal person residing or having its registered office in a Member State has the right to petition the European Parliament.

Article 45
Freedom of movement and of residence

1. Every citizen of the Union has the right to move and reside freely within the territory of the Member States.

2. Freedom of movement and residence may be granted, in accordance with the Treaty establishing the European Community, to nationals of third countries legally resident in the territory of a Member State.

Article 46
Diplomatic and consular protection

Every citizen of the Union shall, in the territory of a third country in which the Member State of which he or she is a national is not represented, be entitled to protection by the diplomatic or consular authorities of any Member State, on the same conditions as the nationals of that Member State.

Chapter VI
Justice

Article 47
Right to an effective remedy and to a fair trial

Everyone whose rights and freedoms guaranteed by the law of the Union are violated has the right to an effective remedy before a tribunal in compliance with the conditions laid down in this Article.

Everyone is entitled to a fair and public hearing within a reasonable time by an independent and impartial tribunal previously established by law. Everyone shall have the possibility of being advised, defended and represented.

Legal aid shall be made available to those who lack sufficient resources in so far as such aid is necessary to ensure effective access to justice.

Article 48
Presumption of innocence and right of defence

1. Everyone who has been charged shall be presumed innocent until proved guilty according to law.

2. Respect for the rights of the defence of anyone who has been charged shall be guaranteed.

Article 49
Principles of legality and proportionality of criminal offences and penalties

1. No one shall be held guilty of any criminal offence on account of any act or omission which did not constitute a criminal offence under national law or international law at the time when it was committed. Nor shall a heavier penalty be imposed than that which was applicable at the time the criminal offence was committed. If, subsequent to the commission of a criminal offence, the law provides for a lighter penalty, that penalty shall be applicable.

2. This Article shall not prejudice the trial and punishment of any person for any act or omission which, at the time when it was committed, was criminal according to the general principles recognised by the community of nations.

3. The severity of penalties must not be disproportionate to the criminal offence.

Article 50
Right not to be tried or punished twice in criminal proceedings for the same criminal offence

No one shall be liable to be tried or punished again in criminal proceedings for an offence for which he or she has already been finally acquitted or convicted within the Union in accordance with the law.

Chapter VII
General Provisions

Article 51
Scope

1. The provisions of this Charter are addressed to the institutions and bodies of the Union with due regard for the principle of subsidiarity and to the Member States only when they are implementing Union law. They shall therefore respect the rights, observe the principles and promote the application thereof in accordance with their respective powers.

2. This Charter does not establish any new power or task for the Community or the Union, or modify powers and tasks defined by the Treaties.

Article 52
Scope of guaranteed rights

1. Any limitation on the exercise of the rights and freedoms recognised by this Charter must be provided for by law and respect the essence of those rights and freedoms. Subject to the principle of proportionality, limitations may be made only if they are necessary and genuinely meet objectives of general interest recognised by the Union or the need to protect the rights and freedoms of others.

2. Rights recognised by this Charter which are based on the Community Treaties or the Treaty on European Union shall be exercised under the conditions and within the limits defined by those Treaties.

3. In so far as this Charter contains rights which correspond to rights guaranteed by the Convention for the Protection of Human Rights and Fundamental Freedoms, the meaning and scope of those rights shall be the same as those laid down by the said Convention. This provision shall not prevent Union law providing more extensive protection.

Article 53
Level of protection

Nothing in this Charter shall be interpreted as restricting or adversely affecting human rights and fundamental freedoms as recognised, in their respective fields of application, by Union law and international law and by international agreements to which the Union, the Community or all the Member States are party, including the European Convention for the Protection of Human Rights and Fundamental Freedoms, and by the Member States' constitutions.

Article 54
Prohibition of abuse of rights

Nothing in this Charter shall be interpreted as implying any right to engage in any activity or to perform any act aimed at the destruction of any of the rights and freedoms recognised in this Charter or at their limitation to a greater extent than is provided for herein.

CHAPTER 24

UNITED NATIONS GUIDELINES FOR THE PREVENTION OF JUVENILE DELINQUENCY (THE RIYADH GUIDELINES)

The General Assembly,

Bearing in mind the Universal Declaration of Human Rights, the International Covenant on Economic, Social and Cultural Rights and the International Covenant on Civil and Political Rights, as well as other international instruments pertaining to the rights and well-being of young persons, including relevant standards established by the International Labour Organisation,

Bearing in mind also the Declaration of the Rights of the Child, the Convention on the Rights of the Child, and the United Nations Standard Minimum Rules for the Administration of Juvenile Justice (The Beijing Rules),

Recalling General Assembly resolution 40/33 of 29 November 1985, by which the Assembly adopted the Beijing Rules recommended by the Seventh United Nations Congress on the Prevention of Crime and the Treatment of Offenders,

Recalling that the General Assembly, in its resolution 40/35 of 29 November 1985, called for the development of standards for the prevention of juvenile delinquency which would assist Member States in formulating and implementing specialized programmes and policies, emphasizing assistance, care and community involvement, and called upon the Economic and Social Council to report to the Eighth United Nations Congress on the Prevention of Crime and the Treatment of Offenders on the progress achieved with respect to these standards, for review and action,

Recalling also that the Economic and Social Council, in section II of its resolution 1986/10 of 21 May 1986, requested the Eighth Congress to consider the draft standards for the prevention of juvenile delinquency, with a view to their adoption,

Recognizing the need to develop national, regional and international approaches and strategies for the prevention of juvenile delinquency,

Affirming that every child has basic human rights, including, in particular, access to free education,

Mindful of the large number of young persons who may or may not be in conflict with the law but who are abandoned, neglected, abused, exposed to drug abuse, and are in marginal circumstances and in general at social risk,

Taking into account the benefits of progressive policies for the prevention of delinquency and for the welfare of the community,

1. Notes with satisfaction the substantive work accomplished by the Committee on Crime Prevention and Control and the Secretary-General in the formulation of the guidelines for the prevention of juvenile delinquency;

2. Expresses appreciation for the valuable collaboration of the Arab Security Studies and Training Centre at Riyadh, in hosting the International Meeting of Experts on the Development of the United Nations Draft Guidelines for the Prevention of Juvenile Delinquency, held at Riyadh from 28 February to 1 March 1988, in co-operation with the United Nations Office at Vienna;

3. Adopts the United Nations Guidelines for the Prevention of Juvenile Delinquency contained in the annex to the present resolution, to be designated "the Riyadh Guidelines";

4. Calls upon Member States, in their comprehensive crime prevention plans, to apply the Riyadh Guidelines in national law, policy and practice and to bring them to the attention of relevant authorities, including policy makers, juvenile justice personnel, educators, the mass media, practitioners and scholars;

5. Requests the Secretary-General and invites Member States to ensure the widest possible dissemination of the text of the Riyadh Guidelines in all of the official languages of the United Nations;

6. Requests the Secretary-General and invites all relevant United Nations offices and interested institutions, in particular, the United Nations Children's Fund, as well as individual experts, to make a concerted effort to promote the application of the Riyadh Guidelines;

7. Also requests the Secretary-General to intensify research on particular situations of social risk and on the exploitation of children, including the use of children as instruments of criminality, with a view to developing comprehensive countermeasures and to report thereon to the Ninth United Nations Congress on the Prevention of Crime and the Treatment of Offenders;

8. Further requests the Secretary-General to issue a composite manual on juvenile justice standards, containing the United Nations Standard Minimum Rules for the Administration of Juvenile Justice (The Beijing Rules), the United Nations Guidelines on the Prevention of Juvenile Delinquency (The Riyadh Guidelines), and the United Nations Rules for the Protection of Juveniles Deprived of their Liberty, and a set of full commentaries on their provisions;

9. Urges all relevant bodies within the United Nations system to collaborate with the Secretary-General in taking appropriate measures to ensure the implementation of the present resolution;

10. Invites the Sub-Commission on Prevention of Discrimination and Protection of Minorities of the Commission on Human Rights to consider this new international instrument with a view to promoting the application of its provisions;

11. Invites Member States to support strongly the organization of technical and scientific workshops, and pilot and demonstration projects on practical issues and policy matters relating to the application of the provisions of the Riyadh Guidelines and to the establishment of concrete measures for community-based services designed to respond to the special needs, problems and concerns of young persons, and requests the Secretary-General to co-ordinate efforts in this respect;

12. Also invites Member States to inform the Secretary-General on the implementation of the Riyadh Guidelines and to report regularly to the Committee on Crime Prevention and Control on the results achieved;

13. Recommends that the Committee on Crime Prevention and Control request the Ninth Congress to review the progress made in the promotion and application of the Riyadh Guidelines and the recommendations contained in the present resolution, under a separate agenda item on juvenile justice and keep the matter under constant review.

Status – The United Nations Guidelines for the Prevention of Juvenile Delinquency (also known as The Riyadh Guidelines) were adopted by the UN General Assembly on 14 December 1990 (Resolution 45/112) [RCLP para 2.55]. They have at least persuasive authority when interpreting and applying domestic legislation, including Sch 1 of the Human Rights Act 1998 [RCLP para 3.94]. The Guidelines have been cited by the domestic courts (see *R (R) v Durham Constabulary* [2005] UKHL 21, [2005] 2 ALL ER 369, [2005] 1 WLR 1184, para 26) [RCLP paras 3.53 and 16.156]. For the weight to be attached to the Guidelines see *T v United Kingdom* Application No 24724/94 (1999), paras 71–75 and 96 [RCLP para 3.54]. The Committee on the Rights of the Child has endorsed the Guidelines in the context of children who may come into conflict with the law (see Committee on the Rights of the Child General Comment No 10 *Children's Rights in Juvenile Justice* CRC/C/GC/10, p 7, para 18) [RCLP paras 14.8–14.9].

ANNEX
UNITED NATIONS GUIDELINES FOR THE PREVENTION OF JUVENILE DELINQUENCY (THE RIYADH GUIDELINES)

I. Fundamental Principles

1. The prevention of juvenile delinquency is an essential part of crime prevention in society. By engaging in lawful, socially useful activities and adopting a humanistic orientation towards society and outlook on life, young persons can develop non-criminogenic attitudes.

2. The successful prevention of juvenile delinquency requires efforts on the part of the entire society to ensure the harmonious development of adolescents, with respect for and promotion of their personality from early childhood.

3. For the purposes of the interpretation of the present Guidelines, a child-centred orientation should be pursued. Young persons should have an active role and partnership within society and should not be considered as mere objects of socialization or control.

4. In the implementation of the present Guidelines, in accordance with national legal systems, the well-being of young persons from their early childhood should be the focus of any preventive programme.

5. The need for and importance of progressive delinquency prevention policies and the systematic study and the elaboration of measures should be recognized. These should avoid criminalizing and penalizing a child for behaviour that does not cause serious damage to the development of the child or harm to others. Such policies and measures should involve:

(a) The provision of opportunities, in particular educational opportunities, to meet the varying needs of young persons and to serve as a supportive framework for safeguarding the personal development of all young persons, particularly those who are demonstrably endangered or at social risk and are in need of special care and protection;

(b) Specialized philosophies and approaches for delinquency prevention, on the basis of laws, processes, institutions, facilities and a service delivery network aimed at reducing the motivation, need and opportunity for, or conditions giving rise to, the commission of infractions;

(c)   Official intervention to be pursued primarily in the overall interest of the young person and guided by fairness and equity;

(d)   Safeguarding the well-being, development, rights and interests of all young persons;

(e)   Consideration that youthful behaviour or conduct that does not conform to overall social norms and values is often part of the maturation and growth process and tends to disappear spontaneously in most individuals with the transition to adulthood;

(f)   Awareness that, in the predominant opinion of experts, labelling a young person as "deviant", "delinquent" or "pre-delinquent" often contributes to the development of a consistent pattern of undesirable behaviour by young persons.

6. Community-based services and programmes should be developed for the prevention of juvenile delinquency, particularly where no agencies have yet been established. Formal agencies of social control should only be utilized as a means of last resort.

II. Scope of the Guidelines

7. The present Guidelines should be interpreted and implemented within the broad framework of the Universal Declaration of Human Rights, the International Covenant on Economic, Social and Cultural Rights, the International Covenant on Civil and Political Rights, the Declaration of the Rights of the Child and the Convention on the Rights of the Child, and in the context of the United Nations Standard Minimum Rules for the Administration of Juvenile Justice (The Beijing Rules), as well as other instruments and norms relating to the rights, interests and well-being of all children and young persons.

8. The present Guidelines should also be implemented in the context of the economic, social and cultural conditions prevailing in each Member State.

III. General Prevention

9. Comprehensive prevention plans should be instituted at every level of government and include the following:

(a)   In-depth analyses of the problem and inventories of programmes, services, facilities and resources available;

(b)   Well-defined responsibilities for the qualified agencies, institutions and personnel involved in preventive efforts;

(c)   Mechanisms for the appropriate co-ordination of prevention efforts between governmental and non-governmental agencies;

(d)   Policies, programmes and strategies based on prognostic studies to be continuously monitored and carefully evaluated in the course of implementation;

(e)   Methods for effectively reducing the opportunity to commit delinquent acts;

(f)   Community involvement through a wide range of services and programmes;

(g)   Close interdisciplinary co-operation between national, state, provincial and local governments, with the involvement of the private sector, representative citizens of the community to be served, and labour, child-care, health education, social, law enforcement and judicial agencies in taking concerted action to prevent juvenile delinquency and youth crime;

(h)   Youth participation in delinquency prevention policies and processes, including recourse to community resources, youth self-help, and victim compensation and assistance programmes;

(i)   Specialized personnel at all levels.

IV. Socialization Processes

10. Emphasis should be placed on preventive policies facilitating the successful socialization and integration of all children and young persons, in particular through the family, the community, peer groups, schools, vocational training and the world of work, as well as through voluntary organizations. Due respect should be given to the proper personal development of children and young persons, and they should be accepted as full and equal partners in socialization and integration processes.

A. Family

11. Every society should place a high priority on the needs and well-being of the family and of all its members.

12. Since the family is the central unit responsible for the primary socialization of children, governmental and social efforts to preserve the integrity of the family, including the extended family, should be pursued. The society has a responsibility to assist the family in providing care and protection and in ensuring the physical and mental well-being of children. Adequate arrangements including day-care should be provided.

13. Governments should establish policies that are conducive to the bringing up of children in stable and settled family environments. Families in need of assistance in the resolution of conditions of instability or conflict should be provided with requisite services.

14. Where a stable and settled family environment is lacking and when community efforts to assist parents in this regard have failed and the extended family cannot fulfil this role, alternative placements, including foster care and adoption, should be considered. Such placements should replicate, to the extent possible, a stable and settled family environment, while, at the same time, establishing a sense of permanency for children, thus avoiding problems associated with "foster drift".

15. Special attention should be given to children of families affected by problems brought about by rapid and uneven economic, social and cultural change, in particular the children of indigenous, migrant and refugee families. As such changes may disrupt the social capacity of the family to secure the traditional rearing and nurturing of children, often as a result of role and culture conflict, innovative and socially constructive modalities for the socialization of children have to be designed.

16. Measures should be taken and programmes developed to provide families with the opportunity to learn about parental roles and obligations as regards child development and child care, promoting positive parent-child relationships, sensitizing parents to the problems of children and young persons and encouraging their involvement in family and community-based activities.

17. Governments should take measures to promote family cohesion and harmony and to discourage the separation of children from their parents, unless circumstances affecting the welfare and future of the child leave no viable alternative.

18. It is important to emphasize the socialization function of the family and extended family; it is also equally important to recognize the future role, responsibilities, participation and partnership of young persons in society.

19. In ensuring the right of the child to proper socialization, Governments and other agencies should rely on existing social and legal agencies, but, whenever traditional institutions and customs are no longer effective, they should also provide and allow for innovative measures.

B. Education

20. Governments are under an obligation to make public education accessible to all young persons.

21. Education systems should, in addition to their academic and vocational training activities, devote particular attention to the following:

(a)   Teaching of basic values and developing respect for the child's own cultural identity and patterns, for the social values of the country in which the child is living, for civilizations different from the child's own and for human rights and fundamental freedoms;

(b)   Promotion and development of the personality, talents and mental and physical abilities of young people to their fullest potential;

(c)   Involvement of young persons as active and effective participants in, rather than mere objects of, the educational process;

(d)   Undertaking activities that foster a sense of identity with and of belonging to the school and the community;

(e)   Encouragement of young persons to understand and respect diverse views and opinions, as well as cultural and other differences;

(f)   Provision of information and guidance regarding vocational training, employment opportunities and career development;

(g)   Provision of positive emotional support to young persons and the avoidance of psychological maltreatment;

(h)   Avoidance of harsh disciplinary measures, particularly corporal punishment.

22. Educational systems should seek to work together with parents, community organizations and agencies concerned with the activities of young persons.

23. Young persons and their families should be informed about the law and their rights and responsibilities under the law, as well as the universal value system, including United Nations instruments.

24. Educational systems should extend particular care and attention to young persons who are at social risk. Specialized prevention programmes and educational materials, curricula, approaches and tools should be developed and fully utilized.

25. Special attention should be given to comprehensive policies and strategies for the prevention of alcohol, drug and other substance abuse by young persons. Teachers and other professionals should be equipped and trained to prevent and deal with these problems. Information on the use and abuse of drugs, including alcohol, should be made available to the student body.

26. Schools should serve as resource and referral centres for the provision of medical, counselling and other services to young persons, particularly those with special needs and suffering from abuse, neglect, victimization and exploitation.

27. Through a variety of educational programmes, teachers and other adults and the student body should be sensitized to the problems, needs and perceptions of young persons, particularly those belonging to underprivileged, disadvantaged, ethnic or other minority and low-income groups.

28. School systems should attempt to meet and promote the highest professional and educational standards with respect to curricula, teaching and learning methods and approaches, and the recruitment and training of qualified teachers. Regular monitoring and assessment of performance by the appropriate professional organizations and authorities should be ensured.

29. School systems should plan, develop and implement extra-curricular activities of interest to young persons, in co-operation with community groups.

30. Special assistance should be given to children and young persons who find it difficult to comply with attendance codes, and to "drop-outs".

31. Schools should promote policies and rules that are fair and just; students should be represented in bodies formulating school policy, including policy on discipline, and decision-making.

C. *Community*

32. Community-based services and programmes which respond to the special needs, problems, interests and concerns of young persons and which offer appropriate counselling and guidance to young persons and their families should be developed, or strengthened where they exist.

33. Communities should provide, or strengthen where they exist, a wide range of community-based support measures for young persons, including community development centres, recreational facilities and services to respond to the special problems of children who are at social risk. In providing these helping measures, respect for individual rights should be ensured.

34. Special facilities should be set up to provide adequate shelter for young persons who are no longer able to live at home or who do not have homes to live in.

35. A range of services and helping measures should be provided to deal with the difficulties experienced by young persons in the transition to adulthood. Such services should include special programmes for young drug abusers which emphasize care, counselling, assistance and therapy-oriented interventions.

36. Voluntary organizations providing services for young persons should be given financial and other support by Governments and other institutions.

37. Youth organizations should be created or strengthened at the local level and given full participatory status in the management of community affairs. These organizations should encourage youth to organize collective and voluntary projects, particularly projects aimed at helping young persons in need of assistance.

38. Government agencies should take special responsibility and provide necessary services for homeless or street children; information about local facilities, accommodation, employment and other forms and sources of help should be made readily available to young persons.

39. A wide range of recreational facilities and services of particular interest to young persons should be established and made easily accessible to them.

D. *Mass media*

40. The mass media should be encouraged to ensure that young persons have access to information and material from a diversity of national and international sources.

41. The mass media should be encouraged to portray the positive contribution of young persons to society.

42. The mass media should be encouraged to disseminate information on the existence of services, facilities and opportunities for young persons in society.

43. The mass media generally, and the television and film media in particular, should be encouraged to minimize the level of pornography, drugs and violence portrayed and to display violence and exploitation disfavourably, as well as to avoid demeaning and degrading presentations, especially of children, women and interpersonal relations, and to promote egalitarian principles and roles.

44. The mass media should be aware of its extensive social role and responsibility, as well as its influence, in communications relating to youthful drug and alcohol abuse. It should use its power for drug abuse prevention by relaying consistent messages through a balanced approach. Effective drug awareness campaigns at all levels should be promoted.

V. Social Policy

45. Government agencies should give high priority to plans and programmes for young persons and should provide sufficient funds and other resources for the effective delivery of services, facilities and staff for adequate medical and mental health care, nutrition, housing and other relevant services, including drug and alcohol abuse prevention and treatment, ensuring that such resources reach and actually benefit young persons.

46. The institutionalization of young persons should be a measure of last resort and for the minimum necessary period, and the best interests of the young person should be of paramount importance. Criteria authorizing formal intervention of this type should be strictly defined and limited to the following situations: (a) where the child or young person has suffered harm that has been inflicted by the parents or guardians; (b) where the child or young person has been sexually, physically or emotionally abused by the parents or guardians; (c) where the child or young person has been neglected, abandoned or exploited by the parents or guardians; (d) where the child or young person is threatened by physical or moral danger due to the behaviour of the parents or guardians; and (e) where a serious physical or psychological danger to the child or young person has manifested itself in his or her own behaviour and neither the parents, the guardians, the juvenile himself or herself nor non-residential community services can meet the danger by means other than institutionalization.

47. Government agencies should provide young persons with the opportunity of continuing in full-time education, funded by the State where parents or guardians are unable to support the young persons, and of receiving work experience.

48. Programmes to prevent delinquency should be planned and developed on the basis of reliable, scientific research findings, and periodically monitored, evaluated and adjusted accordingly.

49. Scientific information should be disseminated to the professional community and to the public at large about the sort of behaviour or situation which indicates or may result in physical and psychological victimization, harm and abuse, as well as exploitation, of young persons.

50. Generally, participation in plans and programmes should be voluntary. Young persons themselves should be involved in their formulation, development and implementation.

51. Governments should begin or continue to explore, develop and implement policies, measures and strategies within and outside the criminal justice system to prevent domestic violence against and affecting young persons and to ensure fair treatment to these victims of domestic violence.

VI. Legislation and Juvenile Justice Administration

52. Governments should enact and enforce specific laws and procedures to promote and protect the rights and well-being of all young persons.

53. Legislation preventing the victimization, abuse, exploitation and the use for criminal activities of children and young persons should be enacted and enforced.

54. No child or young person should be subjected to harsh or degrading correction or punishment measures at home, in schools or in any other institutions.

55. Legislation and enforcement aimed at restricting and controlling accessibility of weapons of any sort to children and young persons should be pursued.

56. In order to prevent further stigmatization, victimization and criminalization of young persons, legislation should be enacted to ensure that any conduct not considered an offence or not penalized if committed by an adult is not considered an offence and not penalized if committed by a young person.

57. Consideration should be given to the establishment of an office of ombudsman or similar independent organ, which would ensure that the status, rights and interests of young persons are upheld and that proper referral to available services is made. The ombudsman or other organ designated would also supervise the implementation of the Riyadh Guidelines, the Beijing Rules and the Rules for the Protection of Juveniles Deprived of their Liberty. The ombudsman or other organ would, at regular intervals, publish a report on the progress made and on the difficulties encountered in the implementation of the instrument. Child advocacy services should also be established.

58. Law enforcement and other relevant personnel, of both sexes, should be trained to respond to the special needs of young persons and should be familiar with and use, to the maximum extent possible, programmes and referral possibilities for the diversion of young persons from the justice system.

59. Legislation should be enacted and strictly enforced to protect children and young persons from drug abuse and drug traffickers.

VII. Research, Policy Development and Co-ordination

60. Efforts should be made and appropriate mechanisms established to promote, on both a multidisciplinary and an intradisciplinary basis, interaction and co-ordination between economic, social, educational and health agencies and services, the justice system, youth, community and development agencies and other relevant institutions.

61. The exchange of information, experience and expertise gained through projects, programmes, practices and initiatives relating to youth crime, delinquency prevention and juvenile justice should be intensified at the national, regional and international levels.

62. Regional and international co-operation on matters of youth crime, delinquency prevention and juvenile justice involving practitioners, experts and decision makers should be further developed and strengthened.

63. Technical and scientific co-operation on practical and policy-related matters, particularly in training, pilot and demonstration projects, and on specific issues

concerning the prevention of youth crime and juvenile delinquency should be strongly supported by all Governments, the United Nations system and other concerned organizations.

64. Collaboration should be encouraged in undertaking scientific research with respect to effective modalities for youth crime and juvenile delinquency prevention and the findings of such research should be widely disseminated and evaluated.

65. Appropriate United Nations bodies, institutes, agencies and offices should pursue close collaboration and co-ordination on various questions related to children, juvenile justice and youth crime and juvenile delinquency prevention.

66. On the basis of the present Guidelines, the United Nations Secretariat, in co-operation with interested institutions, should play an active role in the conduct of research, scientific collaboration, the formulation of policy options and the review and monitoring of their implementation, and should serve as a source of reliable information on effective modalities for delinquency prevention.

CHAPTER 25

UNITED NATIONS STANDARD MINIMUM RULES FOR THE ADMINISTRATION OF JUVENILE JUSTICE (THE BEIJING RULES)

The General Assembly,

Bearing in mind the Universal Declaration of Human Rights, the International Covenant on Civil and Political Rights and the International Covenant on Economic, Social and Cultural Rights, as well as other international human rights instruments pertaining to the rights of young persons,

Also bearing in mind that 1985 was designated the International Youth Year: Participation, Development, Peace and that the international community has placed importance on the protection and promotion of the rights of the young, as witnessed by the significance attached to the Declaration of the Rights of the Child,

Recalling resolution 4 adopted by the Sixth United Nations Congress on the Prevention of Crime and the Treatment of Offenders, held at Caracas from 25 August to 5 September 1980, which called for the development of standard minimum rules for the administration of juvenile justice and the care of juveniles, which could serve as a model for Member States,

Recalling also Economic and Social Council decision 1984/153 of 25 May 1984, by which the draft rules were forwarded to the Seventh United Nations Congress on the Prevention of Crime and the Treatment of Offenders, through the Interregional Preparatory Meeting, held at Beijing from 14 to 18 May 1984,

Recognizing that the young, owing to their early stage of human development, require particular care and assistance with regard to physical, mental and social development, and require legal protection in conditions of peace, freedom, dignity and security,

Considering that existing national legislation, policies and practices may well require review and amendment in view of the standards contained in the rules,

Considering further that, although such standards may seem difficult to achieve at present in view of existing social, economic, cultural, political and legal conditions, they are nevertheless intended to be attainable as a policy minimum,

1. Notes with appreciation the work carried out by the Committee on Crime Prevention and Control, the Secretary-General, the United Nations Asia and Far East Institute for the Prevention of Crime and the Treatment of Offenders and other United Nations institutes in the development of the Standard Minimum Rules for the Administration of Juvenile Justice;

2. Takes note with appreciation of the report of the Secretary-General on the draft Standard Minimum Rules for the Administration of Juvenile Justice;

3. Commends the Interregional Preparatory Meeting held at Beijing for having finalized the text of the rules submitted to the Seventh United Nations Congress on the Prevention of Crime and the Treatment of Offenders for consideration and final action;

4. Adopts the United Nations Standard Minimum Rules for the Administration of Juvenile Justice recommended by the Seventh Congress, contained in the annex to the present resolution, and approves the recommendation of the Seventh Congress that the Rules should be known as "the Beijing Rules";

5. Invites Member States to adapt, wherever this is necessary, their national legislation, policies and practices, particularly in training juvenile justice personnel, to the Beijing Rules and to bring the Rules to the attention of relevant authorities and the public in general;

6. Calls upon the Committee on Crime Prevention and Control to formulate measures for the effective implementation of the Beijing Rules, with the assistance of the United Nations institutes on the prevention of crime and the treatment of offenders;

7. Invites Member States to inform the Secretary-General on the implementation of the Beijing Rules and to report regularly to the Committee on Crime Prevention and Control on the results achieved;

8. Requests Member States and the Secretary-General to undertake research and to develop a data base with respect to effective policies and practices in the administration of juvenile justice;

9. Requests the Secretary-General and invites Member States to ensure the widest possible dissemination of the text of the Beijing Rules in all of the official languages of the United Nations, including the intensification of information activities in the field of juvenile justice;

10. Requests the Secretary-General to develop pilot projects on the implementation of the Beijing Rules;

11. Requests the Secretary-General and Member States to provide the necessary resources to ensure the successful implementation of the Beijing Rules, in particular in the areas of recruitment, training and exchange of personnel, research and evaluation, and the development of new alternatives to institutionalization;

12. Requests the Eighth United Nations Congress on the Prevention of Crime and the Treatment of Offenders to review the progress made in the implementation of the Beijing Rules and of the recommendations contained in the present resolution, under a separate agenda item on juvenile justice;

13. Urges all relevant organs of the United Nations system, in particular the regional commissions and specialized agencies, the United Nations institutes for the prevention of crime and the treatment of offenders, other intergovernmental organizations and non-governmental organizations to collaborate with the Secretariat and to take the necessary measures to ensure a concerted and sustained effort, within their respective fields of technical competence, to implement the principles contained in the Beijing Rules.

Status—The United Nations Standard Minimum Rules for the Administration of Juvenile Justice (also known as 'The Beijing Rules') were adopted by the UN General Assembly on 29 November 1985 (Resolution 45/112) [**RCLP para 2.52**]. They have at least persuasive authority when interpreting and applying domestic legislation, including Sch 1 of the Human Rights Act 1998 [**RCLP para 3.94**]. Note that the 'Commentary' under each rule forms an integral part of the rule and is not an addition by this author. The rules have been cited by the domestic courts (see *R (R) v Durham Constabulary* [2005] UKHL 21, [2005] 2 ALL ER 369, [2005] 1 WLR 1184, para 26, *A and others v Secretary of State for the Home Department* [2006] 1 All ER 575 at p 596, *Dyer (Procurator Fiscal, Linlithgow) v Watson and another; K v Lord Advocate* [2002] 4 All ER 1, para 23, *R (T) by his mother and litigation friend RT)) v Secretary of State for Justice and another* [2013] EWHC 1119 (Admin) para 24 and *R (HC (a child by his litigation friend CC)) v Secretary of State for the Home Department and another* [2013] EWHC 982 (Admin)) **[RCLP paras 3.34 and 16.156–157]**. For the weight to be attached to the Guidelines see *T v United Kingdom* Application No 24724/94 (1999), paras 71–75 and 96 **[RCLP para 3.54]**. It is important to note that the Beijing Rules are not limited in their scope to criminal proceedings but, by r 3.2, extend to encompass children who are dealt in welfare and care proceedings **[RCLP para 16.60]**. See also Guidelines for Children in the Criminal Justice System (Economic and Social Council Resolution 1997/30 of 21 July 1997).

ANNEX
UNITED NATIONS STANDARD MINIMUM RULES FOR THE ADMINISTRATION OF JUVENILE JUSTICE (BEIJING RULES)

Part one. General principles

1. Fundamental perspectives

1.1 Member States shall seek, in conformity with their respective general interests, to further the well-being of the juvenile and her or his family.

1.2 Member States shall endeavour to develop conditions that will ensure for the juvenile a meaningful life in the community, which, during that period in life when she or he is most susceptible to deviant behaviour, will foster a process of personal development and education that is as free from crime and delinquency as possible.

1.3 Sufficient attention shall be given to positive measures that involve the full mobilization of all possible resources, including the family, volunteers and other community groups, as well as schools and other community institutions, for the purpose of promoting the well-being of the juvenile, with a view to reducing the need for intervention under the law, and of effectively, fairly and humanely dealing with the juvenile in conflict with the law.

1.4 Juvenile justice shall be conceived as an integral part of the national development process of each country, within a comprehensive framework of social justice for all juveniles, thus, at the same time, contributing to the protection of the young and the maintenance of a peaceful order in society.

1.5 These Rules shall be implemented in the context of economic, social and cultural conditions prevailing in each Member State.

1.6 Juvenile justice services shall be systematically developed and co-ordinated with a view to improving and sustaining the competence of personnel involved in the services, including their methods, approaches and attitudes.

Commentary

These broad fundamental perspectives refer to comprehensive social policy in general and aim at promoting juvenile welfare to the greatest possible extent, which will minimize the necessity of intervention by the juvenile justice system, and in turn, will reduce the harm that may be caused by any intervention. Such care measures for the young, before the onset of delinquency, are basic policy requisites designed to obviate the need for the application of the Rules.

Rules 1.1 to 1.3 point to the important role that a constructive social policy for juveniles will play, inter alia, in the prevention of juvenile crime and delinquency. Rule 1.4 defines juvenile justice as an integral part of social justice for juveniles, while rule 1.6 refers to the necessity of constantly improving juvenile justice, without falling behind the development of progressive social policy for juveniles in general and bearing in mind the need for consistent improvement of staff services.

Rule 1.5 seeks to take account of existing conditions in Member States which would cause the manner of implementation of particular rules necessarily to be different from the manner adopted in other States.

'**respective general interests**' (r 1.1)—See also r 17.1(d) ('The well-being of the juvenile shall be the guiding factor in the consideration of her or his case') [**RCLP para 16.9**].

2. Scope of the Rules and definitions used

2.1 The following Standard Minimum Rules shall be applied to juvenile offenders impartially, without distinction of any kind, for example as to race, colour, sex, language, religion, political or other opinions, national or social origin, property, birth or other status.

2.2 For purposes of these Rules, the following definitions shall be applied by Member States in a manner which is compatible with their respective legal systems and concepts:

(a)   A juvenile is a child or young person who, under the respective legal systems, may be dealt with for an offence in a manner which is different from an adult;

(b)   An offence is any behaviour (act or omission) that is punishable by law under the respective legal systems;

(c)   A juvenile offender is a child or young person who is alleged to have committed or who has been found to have committed an offence.

2.3 Efforts shall be made to establish, in each national jurisdiction, a set of laws, rules and provisions specifically applicable to juvenile offenders and institutions and bodies entrusted with the functions of the administration of juvenile justice and designed:

(a)   To meet the varying needs of juvenile offenders, while protecting their basic rights;

(b)   To meet the needs of society;

(c)   To implement the following rules thoroughly and fairly.

Commentary

The Standard Minimum Rules are deliberately formulated so as to be applicable within different legal systems and, at the same time, to set some minimum standards for the handling of juvenile offenders under any definition of a juvenile and under any system of dealing with juvenile offenders. The Rules are always to be applied impartially and without distinction of any kind.

Rule 2.1 therefore stresses the importance of the Rules always being applied impartially and without distinction of any kind. The rule follows the formulation of principle 2 of the Declaration of the Rights of the Child.

Rule 2.2 defines "juvenile" and "offence" as the components of the notion of the "juvenile offender", who is the main subject of these Standard Minimum Rules (see, however, also rules 3 and 4). It should be noted that age limits will depend on, and are explicitly made dependent on, each respective legal system, thus fully respecting the economic, social, political, cultural and legal systems of Member States. This makes for a wide variety of ages coming under the definition of "juvenile", ranging from 7 years to 18 years or above. Such a variety seems inevitable in view of the different national legal systems and does not diminish the impact of these Standard Minimum Rules.

Rule 2.3 is addressed to the necessity of specific national legislation for the optimal implementation of these Standard Minimum Rules, both legally and practically.

3. Extension of the Rules

3.1 The relevant provisions of the Rules shall be applied not only to juvenile offenders but also to juveniles who may be proceeded against for any specific behaviour that would not be punishable if committed by an adult.

3.2 Efforts shall be made to extend the principles embodied in the Rules to all juveniles who are dealt with in welfare and care proceedings.

3.3 Efforts shall also be made to extend the principles embodied in the Rules to young adult offenders.

Commentary

Rule 3 extends the protection afforded by the Standard Minimum Rules for the Administration of Juvenile Justice to cover:

(a)   The so-called "status offences" prescribed in various national legal systems where the range of behaviour considered to be an offence is wider for juveniles than it is for adults (for example, truancy, school and family disobedience, public drunkenness, etc.) (rule 3.1);

(b)   Juvenile welfare and care proceedings (rule 3.2);

(c)   Proceedings dealing with young adult offenders, depending of course on each given age limit (rule 3.3).

The extension of the Rules to cover these three areas seems to be justified. Rule 3.1 provides minimum guarantees in those fields, and rule 3.2 is considered a desirable step in the direction of more fair, equitable and humane justice for all juveniles in conflict with the law.

Extension of rules to welfare and care proceedings (r 3.2)—It is important to note that the Beijing Rules are not limited in their scope to criminal proceedings but, by r 3.2, extend to encompass children who are dealt in welfare and care proceedings [**RCLP para 16.60**]. See also r 14.2 [**RCLP para 9.14**].

4. Age of criminal responsibility

4.1 In those legal systems recognizing the concept of the age of criminal responsibility for juveniles, the beginning of that age shall not be fixed at too low an age level, bearing in mind the facts of emotional, mental and intellectual maturity.

Commentary

The minimum age of criminal responsibility differs widely owing to history and culture. The modern approach would be to consider whether a child can live up to the moral and psychological components of criminal responsibility; that is, whether a child, by virtue of her or his individual discernment and understanding, can be held responsible for essentially anti-social behaviour. If the age of criminal responsibility is fixed too low or if there is no lower age limit at all, the notion of responsibility would become meaningless.

In general, there is a close relationship between the notion of responsibility for delinquent or criminal behaviour and other social rights and responsibilities (such as marital status, civil majority, etc.).

Efforts should therefore be made to agree on a reasonable lowest age limit that is applicable internationally.

'shall not be fixed at too low an age level' (r 4)—See also Committee on the Rights of the Child General Comment No 10 *Children's Rights in Juvenile Justice* CRC/C/GC/10, paras 30–39 [RCLP para 14.16 and 16.63] and V *v United Kingdom* (1999) 30 EHRR 121 [RCLP para 16.124].

5. Aims of juvenile justice

5.1 The juvenile justice system shall emphasize the well-being of the juvenile and shall ensure that any reaction to juvenile offenders shall always be in proportion to the circumstances of both the offenders and the offence.

Commentary

Rule 5 refers to two of the most important objectives of juvenile justice. The first objective is the promotion of the well-being of the juvenile. This is the main focus of those legal systems in which juvenile offenders are dealt with by family courts or administrative authorities, but the well-being of the juvenile should also be emphasized in legal systems that follow the criminal court model, thus contributing to the avoidance of merely punitive sanctions. (See also rule 14.)

The second objective is "the principle of proportionality". This principle is well-known as an instrument for curbing punitive sanctions, mostly expressed in terms of just desert in relation to the gravity of the offence. The response to young offenders should be based on the consideration not only of the gravity of the offence but also of personal circumstances. The individual circumstances of the offender (for example social status, family situation, the harm caused by the offence or other factors affecting personal circumstances) should influence the proportionality of the reaction (for example by having regard to the offender's endeavour to indemnify the victim or to her or his willingness to turn to a wholesome and useful life).

By the same token, reactions aiming to ensure the welfare of the young offender may go beyond necessity and therefore infringe upon the fundamental rights of the young individual, as has been observed in some juvenile justice systems. Here, too, the proportionality of the reaction to the circumstances of both the offender and the offence, including the victim, should be safeguarded.

In essence, rule 5 calls for no less and no more than a fair reaction in any given case of juvenile delinquency and crime. The issues combined in the rule may help to stimulate development in both regards: new and innovative types of reactions are as desirable as precautions against any undue widening of the net of formal social control over juveniles.

6. Scope of discretion

6.1 In view of the varying special needs of juveniles as well as the variety of measures available, appropriate scope for discretion shall be allowed at all stages of proceedings and at the different levels of juvenile justice administration, including investigation, prosecution, adjudication and the follow-up of dispositions.

6.2 Efforts shall be made, however, to ensure sufficient accountability at all stages and levels in the exercise of any such discretion.

6.3 Those who exercise discretion shall be specially qualified or trained to exercise it judiciously and in accordance with their functions and mandates.

Commentary

Rules 6.1, 6.2 and 6.3 combine several important features of effective, fair and humane juvenile justice administration: the need to permit the exercise of discretionary power at all significant levels of processing so that those who make determinations can take the actions deemed to be most appropriate in each individual case; and the need to provide checks and balances in order to curb any abuses of discretionary power and to safeguard the rights of the young offender. Accountability and professionalism are instruments best apt to curb broad discretion. Thus, professional qualifications and expert training are emphasized here as a valuable means of ensuring the judicious exercise of discretion in matters of juvenile offenders. (See also rules 1.6 and 2.2.) The formulation of specific guidelines on the exercise of discretion and the provision of systems of review, appeal and the like in order to permit scrutiny of decisions and accountability are emphasized in this context. Such mechanisms are not specified here, as they do not easily lend themselves to incorporation into international standard minimum rules, which cannot possibly cover all differences in justice systems.

7. Rights of juveniles

7.1 Basic procedural safeguards such as the presumption of innocence, the right to be notified of the charges, the right to remain silent, the right to counsel, the right to the presence of a parent or guardian, the right to confront and cross-examine witnesses and the right to appeal to a higher authority shall be guaranteed at all stages of proceedings.

Commentary

Rule 7.1 emphasizes some important points that represent essential elements for a fair and just trial and that are internationally recognized in existing human rights instruments. (See also rule 14.) The presumption of innocence, for instance, is also to be found in article 11 of the Universal Declaration of Human Rights and in article 14, paragraph 2, of the International Covenant on Civil and Political Rights.

Rules 14 seq. of these Standard Minimum Rules specify issues that are important for proceedings in juvenile cases, in particular, while rule 7.1 affirms the most basic procedural safeguards in a general way.

8. Protection of privacy

8.1 The juvenile's right to privacy shall be respected at all stages in order to avoid harm being caused to her or him by undue publicity or by the process of labelling.

8.2 In principle, no information that may lead to the identification of a juvenile offender shall be published.

Commentary

Rule 8 stresses the importance of the protection of the juvenile's right to privacy. Young persons are particularly susceptible to stigmatization. Criminological research into labelling processes has provided evidence of the detrimental effects (of different kinds) resulting from the permanent identification of young persons as "delinquent" or "criminal".

Rule 8 also stresses the importance of protecting the juvenile from the adverse effects that may result from the publication in the mass media of information about the case (for example the names of young offenders, alleged or convicted). The interest of the individual should be protected and upheld, at least in principle. (The general contents of rule 8 are further specified in rule 21.)

'no information' (r 8.2)—This will include records in respect of juvenile offenders (see also r 21(2) of the 'Beijing Rules') [RCLP paras 9.18 and 16.58].

9. Saving clause

9.1 Nothing in these Rules shall be interpreted as precluding the application of the Standard Minimum Rules for the Treatment of Prisoners adopted by the United Nations and other human rights instruments and standards recognized by the international community that relate to the care and protection of the young.

Commentary

Rule 9 is meant to avoid any misunderstanding in interpreting and implementing the present Rules in conformity with principles contained in relevant existing or emerging international human rights instruments and standards – such as the Universal Declaration of Human Rights; the International Covenant on Economic, Social and Cultural Rights and the International Covenant on Civil and Political Rights; and the Declaration of the Rights of the Child and the draft convention on the rights of the child. It should be understood that the application of the present Rules is without prejudice to any such international instruments which may contain provisions of wider application. (See also rule 27.)

Part two. Investigation and prosecution

10. Initial contact

10.1 Upon the apprehension of a juvenile, her or his parents or guardian shall be immediately notified of such apprehension, and, where such immediate notification is not possible, the parents or guardian shall be notified within the shortest possible time thereafter.

10.2 A judge or other competent official or body shall, without delay, consider the issue of release.

10.3 Contacts between the law enforcement agencies and a juvenile offender shall be managed in such a way as to respect the legal status of the juvenile, promote the well-being of the juvenile and avoid harm to her or him, with due regard to the circumstances of the case.

Commentary

Rule 10.1 is in principle contained in rule 92 of the Standard Minimum Rules for the Treatment of Prisoners.

The question of release (rule 10.2) shall be considered without delay by a judge or other competent official. The latter refers to any person or institution in the broadest sense of the term, including community boards or police authorities having power to release an arrested person. (See also the International Covenant on Civil and Political Rights, article 9, paragraph 3.)

Rule 10.3 deals with some fundamental aspects of the procedures and behaviour on the part of the police and other law enforcement officials in cases of juvenile crime. To "avoid harm" admittedly is flexible wording and covers many features of possible interaction (for example the use of harsh language, physical violence or exposure to the environment). Involvement in juvenile justice processes in itself can be "harmful" to juveniles; the term "avoid harm" should be broadly interpreted, therefore, as doing the least harm possible to the juvenile in the first instance, as well as any additional or undue harm. This is especially important in the initial contact with law enforcement agencies, which might profoundly influence the juvenile's attitude towards the State and society. Moreover, the success of any further intervention is largely dependent on such initial contacts. Compassion and kind firmness are important in these situations.

11. Diversion

11.1 Consideration shall be given, wherever appropriate, to dealing with juvenile offenders without resorting to formal trial by the competent authority, referred to in rule 14.1 below.

11.2 The police, the prosecution or other agencies dealing with juvenile cases shall be empowered to dispose of such cases, at their discretion, without recourse to formal hearings, in accordance with the criteria laid down for that purpose in the respective legal system and also in accordance with the principles contained in these Rules.

11.3 Any diversion involving referral to appropriate community or other services shall require the consent of the juvenile, or her or his parents or guardian, provided that such decision to refer a case shall be subject to review by a competent authority, upon application.

11.4 In order to facilitate the discretionary disposition of juvenile cases, efforts shall be made to provide for community programmes, such as temporary supervision and guidance, restitution, and compensation of victims.

Commentary

Diversion, involving removal from criminal justice processing and, frequently, redirection to community support services, is commonly practised on a formal and informal basis in many legal systems. This practice serves to hinder the negative effects of subsequent proceedings in juvenile justice administration (for example the stigma of conviction and sentence). In many cases, non-intervention would be the best response. Thus, diversion at the outset and without referral to alternative (social) services may be the optimal response. This is especially the case where the offence is of a non-serious nature and where the family, the school or other informal social control institutions have already reacted, or are likely to react, in an appropriate and constructive manner.

As stated in rule 11.2, diversion may be used at any point of decision-making – by the police, the prosecution or other agencies such as the courts, tribunals, boards or councils. It may be exercised by one authority or several or all authorities, according to the rules and policies of the respective systems and in line with the present Rules. It need not necessarily be limited to petty cases, thus rendering diversion an important instrument.

Rule 11.3 stresses the important requirement of securing the consent of the young offender (or the parent or guardian) to the recommended diversionary measure(s). (Diversion to community service without such consent would contradict the Convention concerning the Abolition of Forced Labour.) However, this consent should not be left unchallengeable, since it might sometimes be given out of sheer desperation on the part of the juvenile. The rule underlines that care should be taken to minimize the potential for coercion and intimidation at all levels in the diversion process. Juveniles should not feel pressured (for example in order to avoid court appearance) or be pressured into consenting to diversion programmes. Thus, it is advocated that provision should be made for an objective appraisal of the appropriateness of dispositions involving young offenders by a "competent authority upon application". (The "competent authority" may be different from that referred to in rule 14.)

Rule 11.4 recommends the provision of viable alternatives to juvenile justice processing in the form of community-based diversion. Programmes that involve settlement by victim restitution and those that seek to avoid future conflict with the law through temporary supervision and guidance are especially commended. The merits of individual cases would make diversion appropriate, even when more serious offences have been committed (for example first offence, the act having been committed under peer pressure etc.).

12. Specialization within the police

12.1 In order to best fulfil their functions, police officers who frequently or exclusively deal with juveniles or who are primarily engaged in the prevention of juvenile crime shall be specially instructed and trained. In large cities, special police units should be established for that purpose.

Commentary

Rule 12 draws attention to the need for specialized training for all law enforcement officials who are involved in the administration of juvenile justice. As police are the first point of contact with the juvenile justice system, it is most important that they act in an informed and appropriate manner.

While the relationship between urbanization and crime is clearly complex, an increase in juvenile crime has been associated with the growth of large cities, particularly with rapid and unplanned growth. Specialized police units would therefore be indispensable, not only in the interest of implementing specific principles contained in the present instrument (such as rule 1.6) but more generally for improving the prevention and control of juvenile crime and the handling of juvenile offenders.

13. Detention pending trial

13.1 Detention pending trial shall be used only as a measure of last resort and for the shortest possible period of time.

13.2 Whenever possible, detention pending trial shall be replaced by alternative measures, such as close supervision, intensive care or placement with a family or in an educational setting or home.

13.3 Juveniles under detention pending trial shall be entitled to all rights and guarantees of the Standard Minimum Rules for the Treatment of Prisoners adopted by the United Nations.

13.4 Juveniles under detention pending trial shall be kept separate from adults and shall be detained in a separate institution or in a separate part of an institution also holding adults.

13.5 While in custody, juveniles shall receive care, protection and all necessary individual assistance – social, educational, vocational, psychological, medical and physical – that they may require in view of their age, sex and personality.

Commentary

The danger to juveniles of "criminal contamination" while in detention pending trial must not be underestimated. It is therefore important to stress the need for alternative measures. By doing so, rule 13.1 encourages the devising of new and innovative measures to avoid such detention in the interest of the well-being of the juvenile.

Juveniles under detention pending trial are entitled to all the rights and guarantees of the Standard Minimum Rules for the Treatment of Prisoners as well as the International Covenant on Civil and Political Rights, especially article 9 and article 10, paragraphs 2 (b) and 3.

Rule 13.4 does not prevent States from taking other measures against the negative influences of adult offenders which are at least as effective as the measures mentioned in the rule.

Different forms of assistance that may become necessary have been enumerated to draw attention to the broad range of particular needs of young detainees to be addressed (for example females or males, drug addicts, alcoholics, mentally ill juveniles, young persons suffering from the trauma of arrest for example, etc.).

Varying physical and psychological characteristics of young detainees may warrant classification measures by which some are kept separate while in detention pending trial, thus contributing to the avoidance of victimization and rendering more appropriate assistance.

The Sixth United Nations Congress on the Prevention of Crime and the Treatment of Offenders, in its resolution 4 on juvenile justice standards specified that the Rules, inter alia, should reflect the basic principle that pre-trial detention should be used only as a last resort, that no minors should be held in a facility where they are vulnerable to the negative influences of adult detainees and that account should always be taken of the needs particular to their stage of development.

Part three. Adjudication and disposition

14. Competent authority to adjudicate

14.1 Where the case of a juvenile offender has not been diverted (under rule 11), she or he shall be dealt with by the competent authority (court, tribunal, board, council, etc.) according to the principles of a fair and just trial.

14.2 The proceedings shall be conducive to the best interests of the juvenile and shall be conducted in an atmosphere of understanding, which shall allow the juvenile to participate therein and to express herself or himself freely.

Commentary

It is difficult to formulate a definition of the competent body or person that would universally describe an adjudicating authority. "Competent authority" is meant to include those who preside over courts or tribunals (composed of a single judge or of several members), including professional and lay magistrates as well as administrative boards (for example the Scottish and Scandinavian systems) or other more informal community and conflict resolution agencies of an adjudicatory nature.

The procedure for dealing with juvenile offenders shall in any case follow the minimum standards that are applied almost universally for any criminal defendant under the procedure known as "due process of law". In accordance with due process, a "fair and just trial" includes such basic safeguards as the presumption of innocence, the presentation and examination of witnesses, the common legal defences, the right to remain silent, the right to have the last word in a hearing, the right to appeal, etc. (See also rule 7.1).

15. Legal counsel, parents and guardians

15.1 Throughout the proceedings the juvenile shall have the right to be represented by a legal adviser or to apply for free legal aid where there is provision for such aid in the country.

15.2 The parents or the guardian shall be entitled to participate in the proceedings and may be required by the competent authority to attend them in the interest of the juvenile. They may, however, be denied participation by the competent authority if there are reasons to assume that such exclusion is necessary in the interest of the juvenile.

Commentary

Rule 15.1 uses terminology similar to that found in rule 93 of the Standard Minimum Rules for the Treatment of Prisoners. Whereas legal counsel and free legal aid are needed to assure the juvenile legal assistance, the right of the parents or guardian to participate as stated in rule 15.2 should be viewed as general psychological and emotional assistance to the juvenile – a function extending throughout the procedure.

The competent authority's search for an adequate disposition of the case may profit, in particular, from the co-operation of the legal representatives of the juvenile (or, for that matter, some other personal assistant who the juvenile can and does really trust). Such concern can be thwarted if the presence of parents or guardians at the hearings plays a negative role, for instance, if they display a hostile attitude towards the juvenile; hence, the possibility of their exclusion must be provided for.

16. Social inquiry reports

16.1 In all cases except those involving minor offences, before the competent authority renders a final disposition prior to sentencing, the background and circumstances in which the juvenile is living or the conditions under which the offence has been committed shall be properly investigated so as to facilitate judicious adjudication of the case by the competent authority.

Commentary

Social inquiry reports (social reports or pre-sentence reports) are an indispensable aid in most legal proceedings involving juveniles. The competent authority should be informed of relevant facts about the juvenile, such as social and family background, school career, educational experiences, etc. For this purpose, some jurisdictions use special social services or personnel attached to the court or board. Other personnel, including probation officers, may serve the same function. The rule therefore requires that adequate social services should be available to deliver social inquiry reports of a qualified nature.

17. Guiding principles in adjudication and disposition

17.1 The disposition of the competent authority shall be guided by the following principles:

(a)   The reaction taken shall always be in proportion not only to the circumstances and the gravity of the offence but also to the circumstances and the needs of the juvenile as well as to the needs of the society;

(b)   Restrictions on the personal liberty of the juvenile shall be imposed only after careful consideration and shall be limited to the possible minimum;

(c)   Deprivation of personal liberty shall not be imposed unless the juvenile is adjudicated of a serious act involving violence against another person or of persistence in committing other serious offences and unless there is no other appropriate response;

(d)   The well-being of the juvenile shall be the guiding factor in the consideration of her or his case.

17.2 Capital punishment shall not be imposed for any crime committed by juveniles.

17.3 Juveniles shall not be subject to corporal punishment.

17.4 The competent authority shall have the power to discontinue the proceedings at any time.

Commentary

The main difficulty in formulating guidelines for the adjudication of young persons stems from the fact that there are unresolved conflicts of a philosophical nature, such as the following:

(a)   Rehabilitation versus just desert;

(b)   Assistance versus repression and punishment;

(c)   Reaction according to the singular merits of an individual case versus reaction according to the protection of society in general;

(d)   General deterrence versus individual incapacitation.

The conflict between these approaches is more pronounced in juvenile cases than in adult cases. With the variety of causes and reactions characterizing juvenile cases, these alternatives become intricately interwoven.

It is not the function of Standard Minimum Rules for the Administration of Juvenile Justice to prescribe which approach is to be followed but rather to identify one that is most closely in consonance with internationally accepted principles. Therefore the essential elements as laid down in rule 17.1, in particular in subparagraphs (a) and (c), are mainly to be understood as practical guidelines that should ensure a common starting point; if heeded by the concerned authorities (See also rule 5), they could contribute considerably to ensuring that the fundamental rights of juvenile offenders are protected, especially the fundamental rights of personal development and education.

Rule 17.1 (b) implies that strictly punitive approaches are not appropriate. Whereas in adult cases, and possibly also in cases of severe offences by juveniles, just desert and retributive sanctions might be considered to have some merit, in juvenile cases such considerations should always be outweighed by the interest of safeguarding the well-being and the future of the young person.

In line with resolution 8 of the Sixth United Nations Congress, it encourages the use of alternatives to institutionalization to the maximum extent possible, bearing in mind the need to respond to the specific requirements of the young. Thus, full use should be made of the range of existing alternative sanctions and new alternative sanctions should be developed, bearing the public safety in mind. Probation should be granted to the greatest possible extent via suspended sentences, conditional sentences, board orders and other dispositions.

Rule 17.1 (c) corresponds to one of the guiding principles in resolution 4 of the Sixth Congress which aims at avoiding incarceration in the case of juveniles unless there is no other appropriate response that will protect the public safety.

The provision prohibiting capital punishment in rule 17.2 is in accordance with article 6, paragraph 5, of the International Covenant on Civil and Political Rights.

The provision against corporal punishment is in line with article 7 of the International Covenant on Civil and Political Rights and the Declaration on the Protection of All Persons from Being Subjected to Torture and Other Cruel, Inhuman or Degrading Treatment or Punishment as well as the Convention against Torture and Other Cruel, Inhuman or Degrading Treatment or Punishment and the draft convention on the rights of the child.

The power to discontinue the proceedings at any time (rule 17.4) is a characteristic inherent in the handling of juvenile offenders as opposed to adults. At any time, circumstances may become known to the competent authority which would make a complete cessation of the intervention appear to be the best disposition of the case.

'shall not be subject to corporal punishment' (r 17.3)—See also the UN Rules for the Protection of Children Deprived of Their Liberty rr 66 and 67 and the Committee on the Rights of the Child General Comment No 8 *The Right of the Child to Protection from Corporal Punishment and Other Cruel or Degrading Forms of Punishment* CRC/C/GC/8, para 39.

18. Various disposition measures

18.1 A large variety of disposition measures shall be made available to the competent authority, allowing for flexibility so as to avoid institutionalization to the greatest extent possible. Such measures, some of which may be combined, include:

(a)   Care, guidance and supervision orders;
(b)   Probation;
(c)   Community service orders;
(d)   Financial penalties, compensation and restitution;

(e)   Intermediate treatment and other treatment orders;
(f)   Orders to participate in group counselling and similar activities;
(g)   Orders concerning foster care, living communities or other educational settings;
(h)   Other relevant orders.

18.2 No juvenile shall be removed from parental supervision, whether partly or entirely, unless the circumstances of her or his case make this necessary.

Commentary

Rule 18.1 attempts to enumerate some of the important reactions and sanctions that have been practised and proved successful thus far, in different legal systems. On the whole they represent promising options that deserve replication and further development. The rule does not enumerate staffing requirements because of possible shortages of adequate staff in some regions; in those regions measures requiring less staff may be tried or developed.

The examples given in rule 18.1 have in common, above all, a reliance on and an appeal to the community for the effective implementation of alternative dispositions. Community-based correction is a traditional measure that has taken on many aspects. On that basis, relevant authorities should be encouraged to offer community-based services.

Rule 18.2 points to the importance of the family which, according to article 10, paragraph 1, of the International Covenant on Economic, Social and Cultural Rights, is "the natural and fundamental group unit of society". Within the family, the parents have not only the right but also the responsibility to care for and supervise their children. Rule 18.2, therefore, requires that the separation of children from their parents is a measure of last resort. It may be resorted to only when the facts of the case clearly warrant this grave step (for example child abuse).

19. Least possible use of institutionalization

19.1 The placement of a juvenile in an institution shall always be a disposition of last resort and for the minimum necessary period.

Commentary

Progressive criminology advocates the use of non-institutional over institutional treatment. Little or no difference has been found in terms of the success of institutionalization as compared to non-institutionalization. The many adverse influences on an individual that seem unavoidable within any institutional setting evidently cannot be outbalanced by treatment efforts. This is especially the case for juveniles, who are vulnerable to negative influences. Moreover, the negative effects, not only of loss of liberty but also of separation from the usual social environment, are certainly more acute for juveniles than for adults because of their early stage of development.

Rule 19 aims at restricting institutionalization in two regards: in quantity ("last resort") and in time ("minimum necessary period"). Rule 19 reflects one of the basic guiding principles of resolution 4 of the Sixth United Nations Congress: a juvenile offender should not be incarcerated unless there is no other appropriate response. The rule, therefore, makes the appeal that if a juvenile must be institutionalized, the loss of liberty should be restricted to the least possible degree, with special institutional arrangements for confinement and bearing in mind the differences in kinds of offenders, offences and institutions. In fact, priority should be given to "open" over "closed" institutions. Furthermore, any facility should be of a correctional or educational rather than of a prison type.

20. Avoidance of unnecessary delay

20.1 Each case shall from the outset be handled expeditiously, without any unnecessary delay.

Commentary

The speedy conduct of formal procedures in juvenile cases is a paramount concern. Otherwise whatever good may be achieved by the procedure and the disposition is at risk. As time passes, the juvenile will find it increasingly difficult, if not impossible, to relate the procedure and disposition to the offence, both intellectually and psychologically.

21. Records

21.1 Records of juvenile offenders shall be kept strictly confidential and closed to third parties. Access to such records shall be limited to persons directly concerned with the disposition of the case at hand or other duly authorized persons.

21.2 Records of juvenile offenders shall not be used in adult proceedings in subsequent cases involving the same offender.

Commentary

The rule attempts to achieve a balance between conflicting interests connected with records or files: those of the police, prosecution and other authorities in improving control versus the interests of the juvenile offender. (See also rule 8.) "Other duly authorized persons" would generally include, among others, researchers.

22. Need for professionalism and training

22.1 Professional education, in-service training, refresher courses and other appropriate modes of instruction shall be utilized to establish and maintain the necessary professional competence of all personnel dealing with juvenile cases.

22.2 Juvenile justice personnel shall reflect the diversity of juveniles who come into contact with the juvenile justice system. Efforts shall be made to ensure the fair representation of women and minorities in juvenile justice agencies.

Commentary

The authorities competent for disposition may be persons with very different backgrounds (magistrates in the United Kingdom of Great Britain and Northern Ireland and in regions influenced by the common law system; legally trained judges in countries using Roman law and in regions influenced by them; and elsewhere elected or appointed laymen or jurists, members of community-based boards etc.). For all these authorities, a minimum training in law, sociology, psychology, criminology and behavioural sciences would be required. This is considered as important as the organizational specialization and independence of the competent authority.

For social workers and probation officers, it might not be feasible to require professional specialization as a prerequisite for taking over any function dealing with juvenile offenders. Thus, professional on-the-job instruction would be minimum qualifications.

Professional qualifications are an essential element in ensuring the impartial and effective administration of juvenile justice. Accordingly, it is necessary to improve the recruitment, advancement and professional training of personnel and to provide them with the necessary means to enable them to properly fulfil their functions.

All political, social, sexual, racial, religious, cultural or any other kind of discrimination in the selection, appointment and advancement of juvenile justice personnel should be avoided in order to achieve impartiality in the administration of juvenile justice. This was recommended by the Sixth United Nations Congress. Furthermore, the Sixth Congress called on Member States to ensure the fair and equal treatment of women as criminal justice personnel and recommended that special measures should be taken to recruit, train and facilitate the advancement of female personnel in juvenile justice administration.

Part four. Non-institutional treatment

23. *Effective implementation of disposition*

23.1 Appropriate provisions shall be made for the implementation of orders of the competent authority, as referred to in rule 14.1 above, by that authority itself or by some other authority as circumstances may require.

23.2 Such provisions shall include the power to modify the orders as the competent authority may deem necessary from time to time, provided that such modification shall be determined in accordance with the principles contained in these Rules.

Commentary

Disposition in juvenile cases, more so than in adult cases, tends to influence the offender's life for a long period of time. Thus, it is important that the competent authority or an independent body (parole board, probation office, youth welfare institutions or others) with qualifications equal to those of the competent authority that originally disposed of the case should monitor the implementation of the disposition. In some countries a *juge d'execution des peines* has been installed for this purpose.

The composition, powers and functions of the authority must be flexible; they are described in general terms in rule 23 in order to ensure wide acceptability.

24. *Provision of needed assistance*

24.1 Efforts shall be made to provide juveniles, at all stages of the proceedings, with necessary assistance such as lodging, education or vocational training, employment or any other assistance, helpful and practical, in order to facilitate the rehabilitative process.

Commentary

The promotion of the well-being of the juvenile is of paramount consideration. Thus, rule 24 emphasizes the importance of providing requisite facilities, services and other necessary assistance as may further the best interests of the juvenile throughout the rehabilitative process.

25. Mobilization of volunteers and other community services

25.1 Volunteers, voluntary organizations, local institutions and other community resources shall be called upon to contribute effectively to the rehabilitation of the juvenile in a community setting and, as far as possible, within the family unit.

Commentary

This rule reflects the need for a rehabilitative orientation of all work with juvenile offenders. Co-operation with the community is indispensable if the directives of the competent authority are to be carried out effectively. Volunteers and voluntary services, in particular, have proved to be valuable resources but are at present underutilized. In some instances, the co-operation of ex-offenders (including ex-addicts) can be of considerable assistance.

Rule 25 emanates from the principles laid down in rules 1.1 to 1.6 and follows the relevant provisions of the International Covenant on Civil and Political Rights.

Part five. Institutional treatment

26. Objectives of institutional treatment

26.1 The objective of training and treatment of juveniles placed in institutions is to provide care, protection, education and vocational skills, with a view to assisting them to assume socially constructive and productive roles in society.

26.2 Juveniles in institutions shall receive care, protection and all necessary assistance – social, educational, vocational, psychological, medical and physical – that they may require because of their age, sex and personality and in the interest of their wholesome development.

26.3 Juveniles in institutions shall be kept separate from adults and shall be detained in a separate institution or in a separate part of an institution also holding adults.

26.4 Young female offenders placed in an institution deserve special attention as to their personal needs and problems. They shall by no means receive less care, protection, assistance, treatment and training than young male offenders. Their fair treatment shall be ensured.

26.5 In the interest and well-being of the institutionalized juvenile, the parents or guardians shall have a right of access.

26.6 Inter-ministerial and inter-departmental co-operation shall be fostered for the purpose of providing adequate academic or, as appropriate, vocational training to institutionalized juveniles, with a view to ensuring that they do not leave the institution at an educational disadvantage.

Commentary

The objectives of institutional treatment as stipulated in rules 26.1 and 26.2 would be acceptable to any system and culture. However, they have not yet been attained everywhere, and much more has to be done in this respect.

Medical and psychological assistance, in particular, are extremely important for institutionalized drug addicts, violent and mentally ill young persons.

The avoidance of negative influences through adult offenders and the safeguarding of the well-being of juveniles in an institutional setting, as stipulated in rule 26.3, are in line with one of the basic guiding principles of the Rules, as set out by the Sixth Congress in its resolution 4. The rule does not prevent States from taking other measures against the negative influences of adult offenders, which are at least as effective as the measures mentioned in the rule. (See also rule 13.4.)

Rule 26.4 addresses the fact that female offenders normally receive less attention than their male counterparts, as pointed out by the Sixth Congress. In particular, resolution 9 of the Sixth Congress calls for the fair treatment of female offenders at every stage of criminal justice processes and for special attention to their particular problems and needs while in custody. Moreover, this rule should also be considered in the light of the Caracas Declaration of the Sixth Congress, which, inter alia, calls for equal treatment in criminal justice administration, and against the background of the Declaration on the Elimination of Discrimination against Women and the Convention on the Elimination of All Forms of Discrimination against Women.

The right of access (rule 26.5) follows from the provisions of rules 7.1, 10.1, 15.2 and 18.2. Inter-ministerial and inter-departmental co-operation (rule 26.6) are of particular importance in the interest of generally enhancing the quality of institutional treatment and training.

27. Application of the Standard Minimum Rules for the Treatment of Prisoners adopted by the United Nations

27.1 The Standard Minimum Rules for the Treatment of Prisoners and related recommendations shall be applicable as far as relevant to the treatment of juvenile offenders in institutions, including those in detention pending adjudication.

27.2 Efforts shall be made to implement the relevant principles laid down in the Standard Minimum Rules for the Treatment of Prisoners to the largest possible extent so as to meet the varying needs of juveniles specific to their age, sex and personality.

Commentary

The Standard Minimum Rules for the Treatment of Prisoners were among the first instruments of this kind to be promulgated by the United Nations. It is generally agreed that they have had a world-wide impact. Although there are still countries where implementation is more an aspiration than a fact, those Standard Minimum Rules continue to be an important influence in the humane and equitable administration of correctional institutions.

Some essential protections covering juvenile offenders in institutions are contained in the Standard Minimum Rules for the Treatment of Prisoners (accommodation, architecture, bedding, clothing, complaints and requests, contact with the outside world, food, medical care, religious service, separation of ages, staffing, work, etc.) as are provisions concerning punishment and discipline, and restraint for dangerous offenders. It would not be appropriate to modify those Standard Minimum Rules according to the particular characteristics of institutions for juvenile offenders within the scope of the Standard Minimum Rules for the Administration of Juvenile Justice.

Rule 27 focuses on the necessary requirements for juveniles in institutions (rule 27.1) as well as on the varying needs specific to their age, sex and personality (rule 27.2). Thus, the objectives and content of the rule interrelates to the relevant provisions of the Standard Minimum Rules for the Treatment of Prisoners.

28. Frequent and early recourse to conditional release

28.1 Conditional release from an institution shall be used by the appropriate authority to the greatest possible extent, and shall be granted at the earliest possible time.

28.2 Juveniles released conditionally from an institution shall be assisted and supervised by an appropriate authority and shall receive full support by the community.

Commentary

The power to order conditional release may rest with the competent authority, as mentioned in rule 14.1, or with some other authority. In view of this, it is adequate to refer here to the "appropriate" rather than to the "competent" authority.

Circumstances permitting, conditional release shall be preferred to serving a full sentence. Upon evidence of satisfactory progress towards rehabilitation, even offenders who had been deemed dangerous at the time of their institutionalization can be conditionally released whenever feasible. Like probation, such release may be conditional on the satisfactory fulfilment of the requirements specified by the relevant authorities for a period of time established in the decision, for example relating to "good behaviour" of the offender, attendance in community programmes, residence in half-way houses, etc.

In the case of offenders conditionally released from an institution, assistance and supervision by a probation or other officer (particularly where probation has not yet been adopted) should be provided and community support should be encouraged.

29. Semi-institutional arrangements

29.1 Efforts shall be made to provide semi-institutional arrangements, such as half-way houses, educational homes, day-time training centres and other such appropriate arrangements that may assist juveniles in their proper reintegration into society.

Commentary

The importance of care following a period of institutionalization should not be underestimated. This rule emphasizes the necessity of forming a net of semi-institutional arrangements.

This rule also emphasizes the need for a diverse range of facilities and services designed to meet the different needs of young offenders re-entering the community and to provide guidance and structural support as an important step towards successful reintegration into society.

Part six. Research, planning, policy formulation and evaluation

30. Research as a basis for planning, policy formulation and evaluation

30.1 Efforts shall be made to organize and promote necessary research as a basis for effective planning and policy formulation.

30.2 Efforts shall be made to review and appraise periodically the trends, problems and causes of juvenile delinquency and crime as well as the varying particular needs of juveniles in custody.

30.3 Efforts shall be made to establish a regular evaluative research mechanism built into the system of juvenile justice administration and to collect and analyse relevant data and information for appropriate assessment and future improvement and reform of the administration.

30.4 The delivery of services in juvenile justice administration shall be systematically planned and implemented as an integral part of national development efforts.

Commentary

The utilization of research as a basis for an informed juvenile justice policy is widely acknowledged as an important mechanism for keeping practices abreast of advances in knowledge and the continuing development and improvement of the juvenile justice system. The mutual feedback between research and policy is especially important in juvenile justice. With rapid and often drastic changes in the life-styles of the young and in the forms and dimensions of juvenile crime, the societal and justice responses to juvenile crime and delinquency quickly become outmoded and inadequate.

Rule 30 thus establishes standards for integrating research into the process of policy formulation and application in juvenile justice administration. The rule draws particular attention to the need for regular review and evaluation of existing programmes and measures and for planning within the broader context of overall development objectives.

A constant appraisal of the needs of juveniles, as well as the trends and problems of delinquency, is a prerequisite for improving the methods of formulating appropriate policies and establishing adequate interventions, at both formal and informal levels. In this context, research by independent persons and bodies should be facilitated by responsible agencies, and it may be valuable to obtain and to take into account the views of juveniles themselves, not only those who come into contact with the system.

The process of planning must particularly emphasize a more effective and equitable system for the delivery of necessary services. Towards that end, there should be a comprehensive and regular assessment of the wide-ranging, particular needs and problems of juveniles and an identification of clear-cut priorities. In that connection, there should also be a co-ordination in the use of existing resources, including alternatives and community support that would be suitable in setting up specific procedures designed to implement and monitor established programmes.

CHAPTER 26

UNITED NATIONS RULES FOR THE PROTECTION OF JUVENILES DEPRIVED OF THEIR LIBERTY

The General Assembly,

Bearing in mind the Universal Declaration of Human Rights, the International Covenant on Civil and Political Rights, the Convention against Torture and Other Cruel, Inhuman or Degrading Treatment or Punishment and the Convention on the Rights of the Child, as well as other international instruments relating to the protection of the rights and well-being of young persons,

Bearing in mind also the Standard Minimum Rules for the Treatment of Prisoners adopted by the First United Nations Congress on the Prevention of Crime and the Treatment of Offenders,

Bearing in mind further the Body of Principles for the Protection of All Persons under Any Form of Detention or Imprisonment, approved by the General Assembly by its resolution 43/173 of 9 December 1988 and contained in the annex thereto,

Recalling the United Nations Standard Minimum Rules for the Administration of Juvenile Justice (The Beijing Rules),

Recalling also resolution 21 of the Seventh United Nations Congress on the Prevention of Crime and the Treatment of Offenders, in which the Congress called for the development of rules for the protection of juveniles deprived of their liberty,

Recalling further that the Economic and Social Council, in section II of its resolution 1986/10 of 21 May 1986, requested the Secretary-General to report on progress achieved in the development of the rules to the Committee on Crime Prevention and Control at its tenth session and requested the Eighth United Nations Congress on the Prevention of Crime and the Treatment of Offenders to consider the proposed rules with a view to their adoption,

Alarmed at the conditions and circumstances under which juveniles are being deprived of their liberty world wide,

Aware that juveniles deprived of their liberty are highly vulnerable to abuse, victimization and the violation of their rights,

Concerned that many systems do not differentiate between adults and juveniles at various stages of the administration of justice and that juveniles are therefore being held in gaols and facilities with adults,

1. Affirms that the placement of a juvenile in an institution should always be a disposition of last resort and for the minimum necessary period;

2. Recognizes that, because of their high vulnerability, juveniles deprived of their liberty require special attention and protection and that their rights and well-being should be guaranteed during and after the period when they are deprived of their liberty;

3. Notes with appreciation the valuable work of the Secretariat and the collaboration which has been established between the Secretariat and experts, practitioners, intergovernmental organizations, the non-governmental community, particularly Amnesty International, Defence for Children International and Radda Barnen International (Swedish Save the Children Federation), and scientific institutions concerned with the rights of children and juvenile justice in the development of the United Nations draft Rules for the Protection of Juveniles Deprived of their Liberty;

4. Adopts the United Nations Rules for the Protection of Juveniles Deprived of their Liberty contained in the annex to the present resolution;

5. Calls upon the Committee on Crime Prevention and Control to formulate measures for the effective implementation of the Rules, with the assistance of the United Nations institutes on the prevention of crime and the treatment of offenders;

6. Invites Member States to adapt, wherever necessary, their national legislation, policies and practices, particularly in the training of all categories of juvenile justice personnel, to the spirit of the Rules, and to bring them to the attention of relevant authorities and the public in general;

7. Also invites Member States to inform the Secretary-General of their efforts to apply the Rules in law, policy and practice and to report regularly to the Committee on Crime Prevention and Control on the results achieved in their implementation;

8. Requests the Secretary-General and invites Member States to ensure the widest possible dissemination of the text of the Rules in all of the official languages of the United Nations;

9. Requests the Secretary-General to conduct comparative research, pursue the requisite collaboration and devise strategies to deal with the different categories of serious and persistent young offenders, and to prepare a policy-oriented report thereon for submission to the Ninth United Nations Congress on the Prevention of Crime and the Treatment of Offenders;

10. Also requests the Secretary-General and urges Member States to allocate the necessary resources to ensure the successful application and implementation of the Rules, in particular in the areas of recruitment, training and exchange of all categories of juvenile justice personnel;

11. Urges all relevant bodies of the United Nations system, in particular the United Nations Children's Fund, the regional commissions and specialized agencies, the United Nations institutes for the prevention of crime and the treatment of offenders and all concerned intergovernmental and non-governmental organizations, to collaborate with the Secretary-General and to take the necessary measures to ensure a concerted and sustained effort within their respective fields of technical competence to promote the application of the Rules;

12. Invites the Sub-Commission on Prevention of Discrimination and Protection of Minorities of the Commission on Human Rights to consider this new international instrument, with a view to promoting the application of its provisions;

13. Requests the Ninth Congress to review the progress made on the promotion and application of the Rules and on the recommendations contained in the present resolution, under a separate agenda item on juvenile justice.

Status—The UN Rules for the Protection of Juveniles Deprived of their Liberty were adopted by the UN General Assembly on 14 December 1990 (Resolution 45/133). See also the UN Minimum Standards for Non-Custodial Measures (the 'Tokyo Rules') (Resolution 45/110) also adopted the UN General Assembly on 14 December 1990 (not included in this work) **[RCLP para 2.53]**. The Rules have at least persuasive authority when interpreting and applying domestic legislation, including Sch 1 of the Human Rights Act 1998 **[RCLP para 3.94]**. For the weight to be attached to the Rules see *T v United Kingdom* Application No 24724/94 (1999), paras 71–75 and 96) **[RCLP para 3.54]**. The Rules have been referred to in domestic authorities (see *R (T) by his mother and litigation friend RT)) v Secretary of State for Justice and another* [2013] EWHC 1119 (Admin) para 26).

ANNEX
UNITED NATIONS RULES FOR THE PROTECTION OF JUVENILES DEPRIVED OF THEIR LIBERTY

I. FUNDAMENTAL PERSPECTIVES

1. The juvenile justice system should uphold the rights and safety and promote the physical and mental well-being of juveniles. Imprisonment should be used as a last resort.

2. Juveniles should only be deprived of their liberty in accordance with the principles and procedures set forth in these Rules and in the United Nations Standard Minimum Rules for the Administration of Juvenile Justice (The Beijing Rules). Deprivation of the liberty of a juvenile should be a disposition of last resort and for the minimum necessary period and should be limited to exceptional cases. The length of the sanction should be determined by the judicial authority, without precluding the possibility of his or her early release.

3. The Rules are intended to establish minimum standards accepted by the United Nations for the protection of juveniles deprived of their liberty in all forms, consistent with human rights and fundamental freedoms, with a view to counteracting the detrimental effects of all types of detention and to fostering integration in society.

4. The Rules should be applied impartially, without discrimination of any kind as to race, colour, sex, age, language, religion, nationality, political or other opinion, cultural beliefs or practices, property, birth or family status, ethnic or social origin, and disability. The religious and cultural beliefs, practices and moral concepts of the juvenile should be respected.

5. The Rules are designed to serve as convenient standards of reference and to provide encouragement and guidance to professionals involved in the management of the juvenile justice system.

6. The Rules should be made readily available to juvenile justice personnel in their national languages. Juveniles who are not fluent in the language spoken by the personnel of the detention facility should have the right to the services of an interpreter free of charge whenever necessary, in particular during medical examinations and disciplinary proceedings.

7. Where appropriate, States should incorporate the Rules into their legislation or amend it accordingly and provide effective remedies for their breach, including compensation when injuries are inflicted on juveniles. States should also monitor the application of the Rules.

8. The competent authorities should constantly seek to increase the awareness of the public that the care of detained juveniles and preparation for their return to society is a social service of great importance, and to this end active steps should be taken to foster open contacts between the juveniles and the local community.

9. Nothing in the Rules should be interpreted as precluding the application of the relevant United Nations and human rights instruments and standards, recognized by the international community, that are more conducive to ensuring the rights, care and protection of juveniles, children and all young persons.

10. In the event that the practical application of particular Rules contained in sections II to V, inclusive, presents any conflict with the Rules contained in the present section, compliance with the latter shall be regarded as the predominant requirement.

II. SCOPE AND APPLICATION OF THE RULES

11. For the purposes of the Rules, the following definitions should apply:

    (a)   A juvenile is every person under the age of 18. The age limit below which it should not be permitted to deprive a child of his or her liberty should be determined by law;

    (b)   The deprivation of liberty means any form of detention or imprisonment or the placement of a person in a public or private custodial setting, from which this person is not permitted to leave at will, by order of any judicial, administrative or other public authority.

'juvenile' (r 11(a))—The definition of a 'juvenile' in r 11(a) has been endorsed by the UN Human Rights Committee (see Human Rights Committee General Comment No 21 *Article 10 (Humane Treatment of Persons Deprived of their Liberty)* HRI/GEN/1/Rev 8, p 194, para 13) [RCLP para **16.6**].

12. The deprivation of liberty should be effected in conditions and circumstances which ensure respect for the human rights of juveniles. Juveniles detained in facilities should be guaranteed the benefit of meaningful activities and programmes which would serve to promote and sustain their health and self-respect, to foster their sense of responsibility and encourage those attitudes and skills that will assist them in developing their potential as members of society.

13. Juveniles deprived of their liberty shall not for any reason related to their status be denied the civil, economic, political, social or cultural rights to which they are entitled under national or international law, and which are compatible with the deprivation of liberty.

14. The protection of the individual rights of juveniles with special regard to the legality of the execution of the detention measures shall be ensured by the competent authority, while the objectives of social integration should be secured by regular inspections and other means of control carried out, according to international standards, national laws and regulations, by a duly constituted body authorized to visit the juveniles and not belonging to the detention facility.

15. The Rules apply to all types and forms of detention facilities in which juveniles are deprived of their liberty. Sections I, II, IV and V of the Rules apply to all detention facilities and institutional settings in which juveniles are detained, and section III applies specifically to juveniles under arrest or awaiting trial.

16. The Rules shall be implemented in the context of the economic, social and cultural conditions prevailing in each Member State.

III. JUVENILES UNDER ARREST OR AWAITING TRIAL

17. Juveniles who are detained under arrest or awaiting trial ("untried") are presumed innocent and shall be treated as such. Detention before trial shall be avoided to the extent possible and limited to exceptional circumstances. Therefore, all efforts shall be made to apply alternative measures. When preventive detention is nevertheless used,

juvenile courts and investigative bodies shall give the highest priority to the most expeditious processing of such cases to ensure the shortest possible duration of detention. Untried detainees should be separated from convicted juveniles.

18. The conditions under which an untried juvenile is detained should be consistent with the rules set out below, with additional specific provisions as are necessary and appropriate, given the requirements of the presumption of innocence, the duration of the detention and the legal status and circumstances of the juvenile. These provisions would include, but not necessarily be restricted to, the following:

(a) Juveniles should have the right of legal counsel and be enabled to apply for free legal aid, where such aid is available, and to communicate regularly with their legal advisers. Privacy and confidentiality shall be ensured for such communications;

(b) Juveniles should be provided, where possible, with opportunities to pursue work, with remuneration, and continue education or training, but should not be required to do so. Work, education or training should not cause the continuation of the detention;

(c) Juveniles should receive and retain materials for their leisure and recreation as are compatible with the interests of the administration of justice.

IV. THE MANAGEMENT OF JUVENILE FACILITIES

A. Records

19. All reports, including legal records, medical records and records of disciplinary proceedings, and all other documents relating to the form, content and details of treatment, should be placed in a confidential individual file, which should be kept up to date, accessible only to authorized persons and classified in such a way as to be easily understood. Where possible, every juvenile should have the right to contest any fact or opinion contained in his or her file so as to permit rectification of inaccurate, unfounded or unfair statements. In order to exercise this right, there should be procedures that allow an appropriate third party to have access to and to consult the file on request. Upon release, the records of juveniles shall be sealed, and, at an appropriate time, expunged.

Confidentiality of information (r 19)—See also r 21(2) of the 'Beijing Rules' [**RCLP para 9.18**].

20. No juvenile should be received in any detention facility without a valid commitment order of a judicial, administrative or other public authority. The details of this order should be immediately entered in the register. No juvenile should be detained in any facility where there is no such register.

B. Admission, registration, movement and transfer

21. In every place where juveniles are detained, a complete and secure record of the following information should be kept concerning each juvenile received:

(a) Information on the identity of the juvenile;

(b) The fact of and reasons for commitment and the authority therefor;

(c) The day and hour of admission, transfer and release;

(d) Details of the notifications to parents and guardians on every admission, transfer or release of the juvenile in their care at the time of commitment;

(e) Details of known physical and mental health problems, including drug and alcohol abuse.

22. The information on admission, place, transfer and release should be provided without delay to the parents and guardians or closest relative of the juvenile concerned.

23. As soon as possible after reception, full reports and relevant information on the personal situation and circumstances of each juvenile should be drawn up and submitted to the administration.

24. On admission, all juveniles shall be given a copy of the rules governing the detention facility and a written description of their rights and obligations in a language they can understand, together with the address of the authorities competent to receive complaints, as well as the address of public or private agencies and organizations which provide legal assistance. For those juveniles who are illiterate or who cannot understand the language in the written form, the information should be conveyed in a manner enabling full comprehension.

25. All juveniles should be helped to understand the regulations governing the internal organization of the facility, the goals and methodology of the care provided, the disciplinary requirements and procedures, other authorized methods of seeking information and of making complaints, and all such other matters as are necessary to enable them to understand fully their rights and obligations during detention.

26. The transport of juveniles should be carried out at the expense of the administration in conveyances with adequate ventilation and light, in conditions that should in no way subject them to hardship or indignity. Juveniles should not be transferred from one facility to another arbitrarily.

C. Classification and placement

27. As soon as possible after the moment of admission, each juvenile should be interviewed, and a psychological and social report identifying any factors relevant to the specific type and level of care and programme required by the juvenile should be prepared. This report, together with the report prepared by a medical officer who has examined the juvenile upon admission, should be forwarded to the director for purposes of determining the most appropriate placement for the juvenile within the facility and the specific type and level of care and programme required and to be pursued. When special rehabilitative treatment is required, and the length of stay in the facility permits, trained personnel of the facility should prepare a written, individualized treatment plan specifying treatment objectives and time-frame and the means, stages and delays with which the objectives should be approached.

28. The detention of juveniles should only take place under conditions that take full account of their particular needs, status and special requirements according to their age, personality, sex and type of offence, as well as mental and physical health, and which ensure their protection from harmful influences and risk situations. The principal criterion for the separation of different categories of juveniles deprived of their liberty should be the provision of the type of care best suited to the particular needs of the individuals concerned and the protection of their physical, mental and moral integrity and well-being.

29. In all detention facilities juveniles should be separated from adults, unless they are members of the same family. Under controlled conditions, juveniles may be brought together with carefully selected adults as part of a special programme that has been shown to be beneficial for the juveniles concerned.

30. Open detention facilities for juveniles should be established. Open detention facilities are those with no or minimal security measures. The population in such detention facilities should be as small as possible. The number of juveniles detained in closed facilities should be small enough to enable individualized treatment. Detention facilities for juveniles should be decentralized and of such size as to facilitate access and contact

between the juveniles and their families. Small-scale detention facilities should be established and integrated into the social, economic and cultural environment of the community.

D. Physical environment and accommodation

31. Juveniles deprived of their liberty have the right to facilities and services that meet all the requirements of health and human dignity.

32. The design of detention facilities for juveniles and the physical environment should be in keeping with the rehabilitative aim of residential treatment, with due regard to the need of the juvenile for privacy, sensory stimuli, opportunities for association with peers and participation in sports, physical exercise and leisure-time activities. The design and structure of juvenile detention facilities should be such as to minimize the risk of fire and to ensure safe evacuation from the premises. There should be an effective alarm system in case of fire, as well as formal and drilled procedures to ensure the safety of the juveniles. Detention facilities should not be located in areas where there are known health or other hazards or risks.

33. Sleeping accommodation should normally consist of small group dormitories or individual bedrooms, account being taken of local standards. During sleeping hours there should be regular, unobtrusive supervision of all sleeping areas, including individual rooms and group dormitories, in order to ensure the protection of each juvenile. Every juvenile should, in accordance with local or national standards, be provided with separate and sufficient bedding, which should be clean when issued, kept in good order and changed often enough to ensure cleanliness.

34. Sanitary installations should be so located and of a sufficient standard to enable every juvenile to comply, as required, with their physical needs in privacy and in a clean and decent manner.

35. The possession of personal effects is a basic element of the right to privacy and essential to the psychological well-being of the juvenile. The right of every juvenile to possess personal effects and to have adequate storage facilities for them should be fully recognized and respected. Personal effects that the juvenile does not choose to retain or that are confiscated should be placed in safe custody. An inventory thereof should be signed by the juvenile. Steps should be taken to keep them in good condition. All such articles and money should be returned to the juvenile on release, except in so far as he or she has been authorized to spend money or send such property out of the facility. If a juvenile receives or is found in possession of any medicine, the medical officer should decide what use should be made of it.

36. To the extent possible juveniles should have the right to use their own clothing. Detention facilities should ensure that each juvenile has personal clothing suitable for the climate and adequate to ensure good health, and which should in no manner be degrading or humiliating. Juveniles removed from or leaving a facility for any purpose should be allowed to wear their own clothing.

37. Every detention facility shall ensure that every juvenile receives food that is suitably prepared and presented at normal meal times and of a quality and quantity to satisfy the standards of dietetics, hygiene and health and, as far as possible, religious and cultural requirements. Clean drinking water should be available to every juvenile at any time.

E. Education, vocational training and work

38. Every juvenile of compulsory school age has the right to education suited to his or her needs and abilities and designed to prepare him or her for return to society. Such

education should be provided outside the detention facility in community schools wherever possible and, in any case, by qualified teachers through programmes integrated with the education system of the country so that, after release, juveniles may continue their education without difficulty. Special attention should be given by the administration of the detention facilities to the education of juveniles of foreign origin or with particular cultural or ethnic needs. Juveniles who are illiterate or have cognitive or learning difficulties should have the right to special education.

'Education, vocational training and work' (rr 38–43)—See also Committee on the Rights of the Child General Comment No 10 *Children's Rights in Juvenile Justice* CRC/C/GC/10, p 21, para 89 [RCLP para 13.100].

39. Juveniles above compulsory school age who wish to continue their education should be permitted and encouraged to do so, and every effort should be made to provide them with access to appropriate educational programmes.

40. Diplomas or educational certificates awarded to juveniles while in detention should not indicate in any way that the juvenile has been institutionalized.

41. Every detention facility should provide access to a library that is adequately stocked with both instructional and recreational books and periodicals suitable for the juveniles, who should be encouraged and enabled to make full use of it.

42. Every juvenile should have the right to receive vocational training in occupations likely to prepare him or her for future employment.

43. With due regard to proper vocational selection and to the requirements of institutional administration, juveniles should be able to choose the type of work they wish to perform.

44. All protective national and international standards applicable to child labour and young workers should apply to juveniles deprived of their liberty.

45. Wherever possible, juveniles should be provided with the opportunity to perform remunerated labour, if possible within the local community, as a complement to the vocational training provided in order to enhance the possibility of finding suitable employment when they return to their communities. The type of work should be such as to provide appropriate training that will be of benefit to the juveniles following release. The organization and methods of work offered in detention facilities should resemble as closely as possible those of similar work in the community, so as to prepare juveniles for the conditions of normal occupational life.

46. Every juvenile who performs work should have the right to an equitable remuneration. The interests of the juveniles and of their vocational training should not be subordinated to the purpose of making a profit for the detention facility or a third party. Part of the earnings of a juvenile should normally be set aside to constitute a savings fund to be handed over to the juvenile on release. The juvenile should have the right to use the remainder of those earnings to purchase articles for his or her own use or to indemnify the victim injured by his or her offence or to send it to his or her family or other persons outside the detention facility.

F. Recreation

47. Every juvenile should have the right to a suitable amount of time for daily free exercise, in the open air whenever weather permits, during which time appropriate recreational and physical training should normally be provided. Adequate space, installations and equipment should be provided for these activities. Every juvenile should have additional time for daily leisure activities, part of which should be devoted, if the juvenile so wishes, to arts and crafts skill development. The detention facility should

ensure that each juvenile is physically able to participate in the available programmes of physical education. Remedial physical education and therapy should be offered, under medical supervision, to juveniles needing it.

G. Religion

48. Every juvenile should be allowed to satisfy the needs of his or her religious and spiritual life, in particular by attending the services or meetings provided in the detention facility or by conducting his or her own services and having possession of the necessary books or items of religious observance and instruction of his or her denomination. If a detention facility contains a sufficient number of juveniles of a given religion, one or more qualified representatives of that religion should be appointed or approved and allowed to hold regular services and to pay pastoral visits in private to juveniles at their request. Every juvenile should have the right to receive visits from a qualified representative of any religion of his or her choice, as well as the right not to participate in religious services and freely to decline religious education, counselling or indoctrination.

Religion (r 48)—See also the UN Human Rights Committee General Comment No 22 *Article 18 (Freedom of Thought, Conscience and Religion)* HRI/GEN/1/Rev 8, p 196, para 8 **[RCLP para 10.61]**.

H. Medical care

49. Every juvenile shall receive adequate medical care, both preventive and remedial, including dental, ophthalmological and mental health care, as well as pharmaceutical products and special diets as medically indicated. All such medical care should, where possible, be provided to detained juveniles through the appropriate health facilities and services of the community in which the detention facility is located, in order to prevent stigmatization of the juvenile and promote self-respect and integration into the community.

50. Every juvenile has a right to be examined by a physician immediately upon admission to a detention facility, for the purpose of recording any evidence of prior ill-treatment and identifying any physical or mental condition requiring medical attention.

51. The medical services provided to juveniles should seek to detect and should treat any physical or mental illness, substance abuse or other condition that may hinder the integration of the juvenile into society. Every detention facility for juveniles should have immediate access to adequate medical facilities and equipment appropriate to the number and requirements of its residents and staff trained in preventive health care and the handling of medical emergencies. Every juvenile who is ill, who complains of illness or who demonstrates symptoms of physical or mental difficulties, should be examined promptly by a medical officer.

52. Any medical officer who has reason to believe that the physical or mental health of a juvenile has been or will be injuriously affected by continued detention, a hunger strike or any condition of detention should report this fact immediately to the director of the detention facility in question and to the independent authority responsible for safeguarding the well-being of the juvenile.

53. A juvenile who is suffering from mental illness should be treated in a specialized institution under independent medical management. Steps should be taken, by arrangement with appropriate agencies, to ensure any necessary continuation of mental health care after release.

54. Juvenile detention facilities should adopt specialized drug abuse prevention and rehabilitation programmes administered by qualified personnel. These programmes should be adapted to the age, sex and other requirements of the juveniles concerned, and detoxification facilities and services staffed by trained personnel should be available to drug- or alcohol-dependent juveniles.

55. Medicines should be administered only for necessary treatment on medical grounds and, when possible, after having obtained the informed consent of the juvenile concerned. In particular, they must not be administered with a view to eliciting information or a confession, as a punishment or as a means of restraint. Juveniles shall never be testees in the experimental use of drugs and treatment. The administration of any drug should always be authorized and carried out by qualified medical personnel.

I. Notification of illness, injury and death

56. The family or guardian of a juvenile and any other person designated by the juvenile have the right to be informed of the state of health of the juvenile on request and in the event of any important changes in the health of the juvenile. The director of the detention facility should notify immediately the family or guardian of the juvenile concerned, or other designated person, in case of death, illness requiring transfer of the juvenile to an outside medical facility, or a condition requiring clinical care within the detention facility for more than 48 hours. Notification should also be given to the consular authorities of the State of which a foreign juvenile is a citizen.

57. Upon the death of a juvenile during the period of deprivation of liberty, the nearest relative should have the right to inspect the death certificate, see the body and determine the method of disposal of the body. Upon the death of a juvenile in detention, there should be an independent inquiry into the causes of death, the report of which should be made accessible to the nearest relative. This inquiry should also be made when the death of a juvenile occurs within six months from the date of his or her release from the detention facility and there is reason to believe that the death is related to the period of detention.

58. A juvenile should be informed at the earliest possible time of the death, serious illness or injury of any immediate family member and should be provided with the opportunity to attend the funeral of the deceased or go to the bedside of a critically ill relative.

J. Contacts with the wider community

59. Every means should be provided to ensure that juveniles have adequate communication with the outside world, which is an integral part of the right to fair and humane treatment and is essential to the preparation of juveniles for their return to society. Juveniles should be allowed to communicate with their families, friends and other persons or representatives of reputable outside organizations, to leave detention facilities for a visit to their home and family and to receive special permission to leave the detention facility for educational, vocational or other important reasons. Should the juvenile be serving a sentence, the time spent outside a detention facility should be counted as part of the period of sentence.

60. Every juvenile should have the right to receive regular and frequent visits, in principle once a week and not less than once a month, in circumstances that respect the need of the juvenile for privacy, contact and unrestricted communication with the family and the defence counsel.

61. Every juvenile should have the right to communicate in writing or by telephone at least twice a week with the person of his or her choice, unless legally restricted, and

should be assisted as necessary in order effectively to enjoy this right. Every juvenile should have the right to receive correspondence.

62. Juveniles should have the opportunity to keep themselves informed regularly of the news by reading newspapers, periodicals and other publications, through access to radio and television programmes and motion pictures, and through the visits of the representatives of any lawful club or organization in which the juvenile is interested.

K. Limitations of physical restraint and the use of force

63. Recourse to instruments of restraint and to force for any purpose should be prohibited, except as set forth in rule 64 below.

64. Instruments of restraint and force can only be used in exceptional cases, where all other control methods have been exhausted and failed, and only as explicitly authorized and specified by law and regulation. They should not cause humiliation or degradation, and should be used restrictively and only for the shortest possible period of time. By order of the director of the administration, such instruments might be resorted to in order to prevent the juvenile from inflicting self-injury, injuries to others or serious destruction of property. In such instances, the director should at once consult medical and other relevant personnel and report to the higher administrative authority.

65. The carrying and use of weapons by personnel should be prohibited in any facility where juveniles are detained.

L. Disciplinary procedures

66. Any disciplinary measures and procedures should maintain the interest of safety and an ordered community life and should be consistent with the upholding of the inherent dignity of the juvenile and the fundamental objective of institutional care, namely, instilling a sense of justice, self-respect and respect for the basic rights of every person.

67. All disciplinary measures constituting cruel, inhuman or degrading treatment shall be strictly prohibited, including corporal punishment, placement in a dark cell, closed or solitary confinement or any other punishment that may compromise the physical or mental health of the juvenile concerned. The reduction of diet and the restriction or denial of contact with family members should be prohibited for any purpose. Labour should always be viewed as an educational tool and a means of promoting the self-respect of the juvenile in preparing him or her for return to the community and should not be imposed as a disciplinary sanction. No juvenile should be sanctioned more than once for the same disciplinary infraction. Collective sanctions should be prohibited.

'**corporal punishment**' (r 67)—See also Committee on the Rights of the Child General Comment No 8 *The Right of the Child to Protection from Corporal Punishment and other Cruel and Degrading forms of Punishment* CRC/C/GC/8, para 39 [**RCLP para 15.25**].

68. Legislation or regulations adopted by the competent administrative authority should establish norms concerning the following, taking full account of the fundamental characteristics, needs and rights of juveniles:

    (a)   Conduct constituting a disciplinary offence;
    (b)   Type and duration of disciplinary sanctions that may be inflicted;
    (c)   The authority competent to impose such sanctions;
    (d)   The authority competent to consider appeals.

69. A report of misconduct should be presented promptly to the competent authority, which should decide on it without undue delay. The competent authority should conduct a thorough examination of the case.

70. No juvenile should be disciplinarily sanctioned except in strict accordance with the terms of the law and regulations in force. No juvenile should be sanctioned unless he or she has been informed of the alleged infraction in a manner appropriate to the full understanding of the juvenile, and given a proper opportunity of presenting his or her defence, including the right of appeal to a competent impartial authority. Complete records should be kept of all disciplinary proceedings.

71. No juveniles should be responsible for disciplinary functions except in the supervision of specified social, educational or sports activities or in self-government programmes.

M. Inspection and complaints

72. Qualified inspectors or an equivalent duly constituted authority not belonging to the administration of the facility should be empowered to conduct inspections on a regular basis and to undertake unannounced inspections on their own initiative, and should enjoy full guarantees of independence in the exercise of this function. Inspectors should have unrestricted access to all persons employed by or working in any facility where juveniles are or may be deprived of their liberty, to all juveniles and to all records of such facilities.

73. Qualified medical officers attached to the inspecting authority or the public health service should participate in the inspections, evaluating compliance with the rules concerning the physical environment, hygiene, accommodation, food, exercise and medical services, as well as any other aspect or conditions of institutional life that affect the physical and mental health of juveniles. Every juvenile should have the right to talk in confidence to any inspecting officer.

74. After completing the inspection, the inspector should be required to submit a report on the findings. The report should include an evaluation of the compliance of the detention facilities with the present rules and relevant provisions of national law, and recommendations regarding any steps considered necessary to ensure compliance with them. Any facts discovered by an inspector that appear to indicate that a violation of legal provisions concerning the rights of juveniles or the operation of a juvenile detention facility has occurred should be communicated to the competent authorities for investigation and prosecution.

75. Every juvenile should have the opportunity of making requests or complaints to the director of the detention facility and to his or her authorized representative.

76. Every juvenile should have the right to make a request or complaint, without censorship as to substance, to the central administration, the judicial authority or other proper authorities through approved channels, and to be informed of the response without delay.

77. Efforts should be made to establish an independent office (ombudsman) to receive and investigate complaints made by juveniles deprived of their liberty and to assist in the achievement of equitable settlements.

78. Every juvenile should have the right to request assistance from family members, legal counsellors, humanitarian groups or others where possible, in order to make a complaint. Illiterate juveniles should be provided with assistance should they need to use the services of public or private agencies and organizations which provide legal counsel or which are competent to receive complaints.

N. Return to the community

79. All juveniles should benefit from arrangements designed to assist them in returning to society, family life, education or employment after release. Procedures, including early release, and special courses should be devised to this end.

80. Competent authorities should provide or ensure services to assist juveniles in re-establishing themselves in society and to lessen prejudice against such juveniles. These services should ensure, to the extent possible, that the juvenile is provided with suitable residence, employment, clothing, and sufficient means to maintain himself or herself upon release in order to facilitate successful reintegration. The representatives of agencies providing such services should be consulted and should have access to juveniles while detained, with a view to assisting them in their return to the community.

V. PERSONNEL

81. Personnel should be qualified and include a sufficient number of specialists such as educators, vocational instructors, counsellors, social workers, psychiatrists and psychologists. These and other specialist staff should normally be employed on a permanent basis. This should not preclude part-time or volunteer workers when the level of support and training they can provide is appropriate and beneficial. Detention facilities should make use of all remedial, educational, moral, spiritual, and other resources and forms of assistance that are appropriate and available in the community, according to the individual needs and problems of detained juveniles.

82. The administration should provide for the careful selection and recruitment of every grade and type of personnel, since the proper management of detention facilities depends on their integrity, humanity, ability and professional capacity to deal with juveniles, as well as personal suitability for the work.

83. To secure the foregoing ends, personnel should be appointed as professional officers with adequate remuneration to attract and retain suitable women and men. The personnel of juvenile detention facilities should be continually encouraged to fulfil their duties and obligations in a humane, committed, professional, fair and efficient manner, to conduct themselves at all times in such a way as to deserve and gain the respect of the juveniles, and to provide juveniles with a positive role model and perspective.

84. The administration should introduce forms of organization and management that facilitate communications between different categories of staff in each detention facility so as to enhance co-operation between the various services engaged in the care of juveniles, as well as between staff and the administration, with a view to ensuring that staff directly in contact with juveniles are able to function in conditions favourable to the efficient fulfilment of their duties.

85. The personnel should receive such training as will enable them to carry out their responsibilities effectively, in particular training in child psychology, child welfare and international standards and norms of human rights and the rights of the child, including the present rules. The personnel should maintain and improve their knowledge and professional capacity by attending courses of in-service training, to be organized at suitable intervals throughout their career.

86. The director of a facility should be adequately qualified for his or her task, with administrative ability and suitable training and experience, and should carry out his or her duties on a full-time basis.

87. In the performance of their duties, personnel of detention facilities should respect and protect the human dignity and fundamental human rights of all juveniles, in particular, as follows:

(a)   No member of the detention facility or institutional personnel may inflict, instigate or tolerate any act of torture or any form of harsh, cruel, inhuman or degrading treatment, punishment, correction or discipline under any pretext or circumstance whatsoever;

(b)   All personnel should rigorously oppose and combat any act of corruption, reporting it without delay to the competent authorities;

(c)   All personnel should respect the present Rules. Personnel who have reason to believe that a serious violation of the present Rules has occurred or is about to occur should report the matter to their superior authorities or organs vested with reviewing or remedial power;

(d)   All personnel should ensure the full protection of the physical and mental health of juveniles, including protection from physical, sexual and emotional abuse and exploitation, and should take immediate action to secure medical attention whenever required;

(e)   All personnel should respect the right of the juvenile to privacy, and in particular should safeguard all confidential matters concerning juveniles or their families learned as a result of their professional capacity;

(f)   All personnel should seek to minimize any differences between life inside and outside the detention facility which tend to lessen due respect for the dignity of juveniles as human beings.

CHAPTER 27

UN GUIDELINES FOR THE ALTERNATIVE CARE OF CHILDREN

The Human Rights Council,

Reaffirming the Universal Declaration of Human Rights and the Convention on the Rights of the Child, and celebrating the twentieth anniversary of the Convention in 2009,

Reaffirming also all previous resolutions on the rights of the child of the Council, the Commission on Human Rights and the General Assembly, the most recent being Council resolutions 7/29 of 28 March 2008, 9/13 of 24 September 2008 and 10/8 of 26 March 2009 and Assembly resolution 63/241 of 23 December 2008,

Considering that the Guidelines for the Alternative Care of Children, the text of which is annexed to the present resolution, set out desirable orientations for policy and practice with the intention of enhancing the implementation of the Convention on the Rights of the Child, and of relevant provisions of other international instruments regarding the protection and well-being of children deprived of parental care or who are at risk of being so,

1. *Welcomes* the accomplishment of the Guidelines for the Alternative Care of Children;

2. *Decides* to submit the Guidelines to the General Assembly for adoption on the twentieth anniversary of the Convention on the Rights of the Child.

Status—The United Nations Guidelines for the Alternative Care of Children were adopted by the UN General Assembly on 24 February 2010 (Resolution 64/142) **[RCLP para 8.122]**. They have at least persuasive authority when interpreting and applying domestic legislation, including Sch 1 of the Human Rights Act 1998 **[RCLP para 3.94]**. See also the Declaration of Social and Legal Principles Relating to the Protection of and Welfare of Children with Special Reference to Foster Care Placement and Adoption Nationally and Internationally A/RES/41/85 3 December 1986 (not included in this work).

Scope—Note that the forms of alternative care contemplated by the UN Guidelines do not include (a) children deprived of their liberty by decision of a judicial or administrative authority and who situation is covered by the UN Standard Minimum Rules for the Administration of Juvenile Justice and the UN Rules for the Protection of Juveniles Deprived of their Liberty, (b) care by adoptive parents from the moment the child concerned is effectively placed in their custody pursuant to a final adoption order, the child being considered from that moment to be 'in parental care' (the Guidelines will apply to adoptive placements prior to the final Adoption order) and (c) informal arrangements whereby a child voluntarily stays with relatives or friends for Recreational purposes and reasons not connected with parents inability or unwillingness to provide adequate care (see UN Guidelines for the Alternative Care of Children para 30) **[RCLP para 8.124]**.

ANNEX
GUIDELINES FOR THE ALTERNATIVE CARE OF CHILDREN

I. Purpose

1. The present Guidelines are intended to enhance the implementation of the Convention on the Rights of the Child and of relevant provisions of other international

instruments regarding the protection and well-being of children who are deprived of parental care or who are at risk of being so.

2. Against the background of these international instruments and taking account of the developing body of knowledge and experience in this sphere, the Guidelines set out desirable orientations for policy and practice. They are designed for wide dissemination among all sectors directly or indirectly concerned with issues relating to alternative care, and seek in particular to:

(a) Support efforts to keep children in, or return them to, the care of their family or, failing this, to find another appropriate and permanent solution, including adoption and *kafala* of Islamic law;

(b) Ensure that, while such permanent solutions are being sought, or in cases where they are not possible or are not in the best interests of the child, the most suitable forms of alternative care are identified and provided, under conditions that promote the child's full and harmonious development;

(c) Assist and encourage governments to better implement their responsibilities and obligations in these respects, bearing in mind the economic, social and cultural conditions prevailing in each State; and

(d) Guide policies, decisions and activities of all concerned with social protection and child welfare in both the public and private sectors, including civil society.

II. General Principles and Perspectives

A. The child and the family

3. The family being the fundamental group of society and the natural environment for the growth, well-being and protection of children, efforts should primarily be directed to enabling the child to remain in or return to the care of his/her parents, or when appropriate, other close family members. The State should ensure that families have access to forms of support in the care-giving role.

4. Every child and young person should live in a supportive, protective and caring environment that promotes his/her full potential. Children with inadequate or no parental care are at special risk of being denied such a nurturing environment.

5. Where the child's own family is unable, even with appropriate support, to provide adequate care for the child, or abandons or relinquishes the child, the State is responsible for protecting the rights of the child and ensuring appropriate alternative care, with or through competent local authorities and duly authorized civil society organizations. It is the role of the State, through its competent authorities, to ensure the supervision of the safety, well-being and development of any child placed in alternative care and the regular review of the appropriateness of the care arrangement provided.

6. All decisions, initiatives and approaches falling within the scope of the present Guidelines should be made on a case-by-case basis, with a view notably to ensuring the child's safety and security, and must be grounded in the best interests and rights of the child concerned, in conformity with the principle of non-discrimination and taking due account of the gender perspective. They should respect fully the child's right to be consulted and to have his/her views duly taken into account in accordance with his/her evolving capacities, and on the basis of his/her access to all necessary information. Every effort should be made to enable such consultation and information provision to be carried out in the child's preferred language.

6.bis In applying the present Guidelines, determination of the best interests of the child shall be designed to identify courses of action for children deprived of parental care, or at risk of being so, that are best suited to satisfying their needs and rights, taking into account the full and personal development of their rights in their family, social and cultural environment and their status as subjects of rights, both at the time of the determination and in the longer term. The determination process should take account of, inter alia, the right of the child to be heard and to have his/her views taken into account in accordance with his/her age and maturity.

7. States should develop and implement comprehensive child welfare and protection policies within the framework of their overall social and human development policy, with attention to the improvement of existing alternative care provision, reflecting the principles contained in the present Guidelines.

8. As part of efforts to prevent separation of children from their parents, States should seek to ensure appropriate and culturally sensitive measures:

(a)   To support family care-giving environments whose capacities are limited by factors such as disabilities; drug and alcohol misuse; discrimination against families with indigenous or minority backgrounds; and those living in armed conflict regions or under foreign occupation;

(b)   To provide appropriate care and protection for vulnerable children, such as child victims of abuse and exploitation; abandoned children; children living on the street; children born out of wedlock; unaccompanied and separated children; internally displaced and refugee children; children of migrant workers; children of asylum-seekers; or children living with or affected by HIV/AIDS and other serious illnesses.

9. Special efforts should be made to tackle discrimination on the basis of any status of the child or parents, including poverty, ethnicity, religion, sex, mental and physical disability, HIV/AIDS status or other serious illnesses, whether physical or mental, birth out of wedlock, and socio-economic stigma, and all other statuses and circumstances that can give rise to relinquishment, abandonment and/or removal of a child.

B. Alternative care

10. All decisions concerning alternative care should take full account of the desirability, in principle, of maintaining the child as close as possible to his/her habitual place of residence, in order to facilitate contact and potential reintegration with his/her family and to minimize disruption of his/her educational, cultural and social life.

11. Decisions regarding children in alternative care, including those in informal care, should have due regard for the importance of ensuring children a stable home and of meeting their basic need for safe and continuous attachment to their caregivers, with permanency generally being a key goal.

12. Children must be treated with dignity and respect at all times and must benefit from effective protection from abuse, neglect and all forms of exploitation, whether on the part of care providers, peers or third parties, in whatever care setting they may find themselves.

13. Removal of a child from the care of the family should be seen as a measure of last resort and should be, whenever possible, temporary and for the shortest possible duration. Removal decisions should be regularly reviewed and the child's return to parental care, once the original causes of removal have been resolved or have disappeared, should be in the child's best interests, in keeping with the assessment foreseen in paragraph 48 below.

14. Financial and material poverty, or conditions directly and uniquely imputable to such poverty, should never be the only justification for the removal of a child from

parental care, for receiving a child into alternative care, or for preventing his/her reintegration, but should be seen as a signal for the need to provide appropriate support to the family.

15. Attention must be paid to promoting and safeguarding all other rights of special pertinence to the situation of children without parental care, including, but not limited to, access to education, health and other basic services, the right to identity, freedom of religion or belief, language and protection of property and inheritance rights.

16. Siblings with existing bonds should in principle not be separated by placements in alternative care unless there is a clear risk of abuse or other justification in the best interests of the child. In any case, every effort should be made to enable siblings to maintain contact with each other, unless this is against their wishes or interests.

17. Recognizing that, in most countries, the majority of children without parental care are looked after informally by relatives or others, States should seek to devise appropriate means, consistent with the present Guidelines, to ensure their welfare and protection while in such informal care arrangements, with due respect for cultural, economic, gender and religious differences and practices that do not conflict with the rights and best interests of the child.

18. No child should be without the support and protection of a legal guardian or other recognized responsible adult or competent public body at any time.

19. The provision of alternative care should never be undertaken with a prime purpose of furthering the political, religious or economic goals of the providers.

20. Use of residential care should be limited to cases where such a setting is specifically appropriate, necessary and constructive for the individual child concerned and in his/her best interests.

21. In accordance with the predominant opinion of experts, alternative care for young children, especially those under the age of 3 years, should be provided in family-based settings. Exceptions to this principle may be warranted in order to prevent the separation of siblings and in cases where the placement is of an emergency nature or is for a predetermined and very limited duration, with planned family reintegration or other appropriate long-term care solution as its outcome.

Care outside family based settings to be the exception (para 21)—This principle will apply equally to children with disabilities (see Convention on the Rights of Persons with Disabilities Art 23, the Standard Rules on the Equalisation of Opportunities for Persons with Disabilities r 9(1) and the Committee on the Rights of the Child General Comment No 9 *The Rights of Children with Disabilities* CRC/C/GC/7/ Rev 1, para 36) [RCLP para 8.158].

22. While recognizing that residential care facilities and family-based care complement each other in meeting the needs of children, where large residential care facilities (institutions) remain, alternatives should be developed in the context of an overall deinstitutionalization strategy, with precise goals and objectives, which will allow for their progressive elimination. To this end, States should establish care standards to ensure the quality and conditions that are conducive to the child's development, such as individualized and small-group care, and should evaluate existing facilities against these standards. Decisions regarding the establishment of, or permission to establish, new residential care facilities, whether public or private, should take full account of this deinstitutionalization objective and strategy.

Measures to promote application

23. States should, to the maximum extent of their available resources and, where appropriate, in the framework of development cooperation, allocate human and financial resources to ensure the optimal and progressive implementation of the present Guidelines throughout their respective territories in a timely manner. States should facilitate active cooperation among all relevant authorities and the mainstreaming of child and family welfare issues within all ministries directly or indirectly concerned.

24. States are responsible for determining any need for, and requesting, international cooperation in implementing the present Guidelines. Such requests should be given due consideration and should receive a favourable response wherever possible and appropriate. The enhanced implementation of the present Guidelines should figure in development cooperation programmes. When providing assistance to a State, foreign entities should abstain from any initiative inconsistent with the Guidelines.

25. Nothing in the present Guidelines should be interpreted as encouraging or condoning lower standards than those that may exist in given States, including in their legislation. Similarly, competent authorities, professional organizations and others are encouraged to develop national or professionally-specific guidelines that build upon the letter and spirit of the present Guidelines.

III. Scope of the Guidelines

26. The present Guidelines apply to the appropriate use and conditions of alternative formal care for all persons under the age of 18 years, unless under the law applicable to the child majority is attained earlier. Only where indicated do the Guidelines also apply to informal care settings, having due regard for both the important role played by the extended family and community and the obligations of States for all children not in the care of their parents or legal and customary caregivers, as set out in the Convention on the Rights of the Child.

27. Principles in the present Guidelines are also applicable, as appropriate, to young persons already in alternative care and who need continuing care or support for a transitional period after reaching the age of majority under applicable law.

28. For the purposes of the present Guidelines, and subject notably to the exceptions listed in paragraph 29 below, the following definitions shall apply:

(a) Children without parental care: all children not in the overnight care of at least one of their parents, for whatever reason and under whatever circumstances. Children without parental care who are outside their country of habitual residence or victims of emergency situations may be designated as:
(i) "Unaccompanied" if they are not cared for by another relative or an adult who by law or custom is responsible for doing so; or
(ii) "Separated" if they are separated from a previous legal or customary primary caregiver, but who may nevertheless be accompanied by another relative.

(b) Alternative care may take the form of:
(i) Informal care: any private arrangement provided in a family environment, whereby the child is looked after on an ongoing or indefinite basis by relatives or friends (informal kinship care) or by others in their individual capacity, at the initiative of the child, his/her parents or other person without this arrangement having been ordered by an administrative or judicial authority or a duly accredited body;

(ii)   Formal care: all care provided in a family environment which has been ordered by a competent administrative body or judicial authority, and all care provided in a residential environment, including in private facilities, whether or not as a result of administrative or judicial measures.

(c)   With respect to the environment where it is provided, alternative care may be:

(i)   Kinship care: family-based care within the child's extended family or with close friends of the family known to the child, whether formal or informal in nature;

(ii)   Foster care: situations where children are placed by a competent authority for the purpose of alternative care in the domestic environment of a family other than the children's own family, that has been selected, qualified, approved and supervised for providing such care;

(iii)   Other forms of family-based or family-like care placements;

(iv)   Residential care: care provided in any non-family-based group setting, such as places of safety for emergency care, transit centres in emergency situations, and all other short and long-term residential care facilities including group homes;

(v)   Supervised independent living arrangements for children.

(d)   With respect to those responsible for alternative care:

(i)   Agencies are the public or private bodies and services that organize alternative care for children;

(ii)   Facilities are the individual public or private establishments that provide residential care for children.

29. The scope of alternative care as foreseen in the present Guidelines does not extend, however, to:

(a)   Persons under the age of 18 years who are deprived of their liberty by decision of a judicial or administrative authority as a result of being alleged as, accused of or recognized as having infringed the law, and whose situation is covered by the United Nations Standard Minimum Rules for the Administration of Juvenile Justice and the United Nations Rules for the Protection of Juveniles Deprived of their Liberty;

(b)   Care by adoptive parents from the moment the child concerned is effectively placed in their custody pursuant to a final adoption order, as of which moment, for the purposes of the present Guidelines, the child is considered to be in parental care. The Guidelines are, however, applicable to pre-adoption or probationary placement of a child with the prospective adoptive parents, as far as they are compatible with requirements governing such placements as stipulated in other relevant international instruments;

(c)   Informal arrangements whereby a child voluntarily stays with relatives or friends for recreational purposes and reasons not connected with the parents' general inability or unwillingness to provide adequate care.

30. Competent authorities and others concerned are also encouraged to make use of the present Guidelines, as applicable, at boarding schools, hospitals, centres for children with mental and physical disabilities or other special needs, camps, the workplace and other places which may be responsible for the care of children.

IV. Preventing the Need for Alternative Care

A. Promoting parental care

31. States should pursue policies that ensure support for families in meeting their responsibilities towards the child and promote the right of the child to have a

relationship with both parents. These policies should address the root causes of child abandonment, relinquishment and separation of the child from his/her family by ensuring, inter alia, the right to birth registration, access to adequate housing and to basic health, education and social welfare services, as well as by promoting measures to combat poverty, discrimination, marginalization, stigmatization, violence, child maltreatment and sexual abuse, and substance abuse.

32. States should develop and implement consistent and mutually reinforcing family-oriented policies designed to promote and strengthen parents' ability to care for their children.

33. States should implement effective measures to prevent child abandonment, relinquishment and separation of the child from his/her family. Social policies and programmes should, inter alia, empower families with attitudes, skills, capacities and tools to enable them to provide adequately for the protection, care and development of their children. The complementary capacities of the State and civil society, including non-governmental and community-based organizations, religious leaders and the media should be engaged to this end. These social protection measures should include:

(a)   Family strengthening services, such as parenting courses and sessions, the promotion of positive parent-child relationships, conflict resolution skills, opportunities for employment, income-generation and, where required, social assistance;

(b)   Supportive social services, such as day care, mediation and conciliation services, substance abuse treatment, financial assistance, and services for parents and children with disabilities. Such services, preferably of an integrated and non-intrusive nature, should be directly accessible at community level and should actively involve the participation of families as partners, combining their resources with those of the community and the carer;

(c)   Youth policies aiming at empowering youth to face positively the challenges of everyday life, including when they decide to leave the parental home, and preparing future parents to make informed decisions regarding their sexual and reproductive health and to fulfil their responsibilities in this respect.

34. Various complementary methods and techniques should be used for family support, varying throughout the process of support, such as home visits, group meetings with other families, case conferences and securing commitments by the family concerned. They should be directed towards both facilitating intrafamilial relationships and promoting the family's integration within its community.

35. Special attention should be paid, in accordance with local laws, to the provision and promotion of support and care services for single and adolescent parents and their children, whether or not born out of wedlock. States should ensure that adolescent parents retain all rights inherent to their status both as parents and as children, including access to all appropriate services for their own development, allowances to which parents are entitled, and their inheritance rights. Measures should be adopted to ensure the protection of pregnant adolescents and to guarantee that they do not interrupt their studies. Efforts should also be made to reduce stigma attached to single and adolescent parenthood.

36. Support and services should be available to siblings who have lost their parents or caregivers and choose to remain together in their household, to the extent that the eldest sibling is both willing and deemed capable of acting as the household head. States should ensure, including through the appointment of a legal guardian, a recognized responsible adult or, where appropriate, a public body legally mandated to act as guardian, as

stipulated in paragraph 18 above, that such households benefit from mandatory protection from all forms of exploitation and abuse, and supervision and support on the part of the local community and its competent services, such as social workers, with particular concern for the children's health, housing, education and inheritance rights. Special attention should be given to ensuring the head of such a household retains all rights inherent to his/her child status, including access to education and leisure, in addition to his/her rights as a household head.

37. States should ensure opportunities for day care, including all-day schooling, and respite care which would enable parents better to cope with their overall responsibilities towards the family, including additional responsibilities inherent in caring for children with special needs.

Preventing family separation

38. Proper criteria based on sound professional principles should be developed and consistently applied for assessing the child's and family's situation, including the family's actual and potential capacity to care for the child, in cases where the competent authority or agency has reasonable grounds to believe that the well-being of the child is at risk.

39. Decisions regarding removal or reintegration should be based on this assessment and made by suitably qualified and trained professionals, on behalf of or authorized by a competent authority, in full consultation with all concerned and bearing in mind the need to plan for the child's future.

40. States are encouraged to adopt measures for the integral protection and guarantee of rights during pregnancy, birth and the breastfeeding period, in order to ensure conditions of dignity and equality for the adequate development of the pregnancy and care of the child. Therefore, support programmes should be provided to future mothers and fathers, particularly adolescent parents, who have difficulties in exercising their parental responsibilities. Such programmes should aim at empowering mothers and fathers to exercise their parental responsibilities in conditions of dignity, and at avoiding their being induced to surrender their child because of their vulnerability.

41. When a child is relinquished or abandoned, States should ensure that this may take place in conditions of confidentiality and safety for the child, respecting his/her right to access information on his/her origins where appropriate and possible under the law of the State.

42. States should formulate clear policies to address situations where a child has been abandoned anonymously, which indicate whether and how family tracing should be undertaken and reunification or placement within the extended family pursued. Policies should also allow for timely decision-making on the child's eligibility for permanent family placement and for arranging such placements expeditiously.

43. When a public or private agency or facility is approached by a parent or legal guardian wishing to relinquish a child permanently, the State should ensure that the family receives counselling and social support to encourage and enable them to continue to care for the child. If this fails, a social work or other appropriate professional assessment should be undertaken to determine whether there are other family members who wish to take permanent responsibility for the child, and whether such arrangements would be in the child's best interests. Where such arrangements are not possible or in the child's best interests, efforts should be made to find a permanent family placement within a reasonable period.

44. When a public or private agency or facility is approached by a parent or caregiver wishing to place a child in care for a short or indefinite period, the State should ensure the availability of counselling and social support to encourage and enable them to continue to care for the child. A child should be admitted to alternative care only when such efforts have been exhausted and acceptable and justified reasons for entry into care exist.

45. Specific training should be provided to teachers and others working with children, in order to help them to identify situations of abuse, neglect, exploitation or risk of abandonment and to refer such situations to competent bodies.

46. Any decision to remove a child against the will of his/her parents must be made by competent authorities, in accordance with applicable law and procedures and subject to judicial review, the parents being assured the right of appeal and access to appropriate legal representation.

47. When the child's sole or main carer may be the subject of deprivation of liberty as a result of preventive detention or sentencing decisions, non-custodial remand measures and sentences should be taken in appropriate cases wherever possible, the best interests of the child being given due consideration. States should take into account the best interests of the child when deciding whether to remove children born in prison and children living in prison with a parent. The removal of such children should be treated in the same way as other instances where separation is considered. Best efforts should be made to ensure that children remaining in custody with their parent benefit from adequate care and protection, while guaranteeing their own status as free individuals and access to activities in the community.

B. Promoting family reintegration

48. In order to prepare and support the child and the family for his/her possible return to the family, his/her situation should be assessed by a duly designated individual or team with access to multidisciplinary advice, in consultation with the different actors involved (the child, the family, the alternative caregiver), so as to decide whether the reintegration of the child in the family is possible and in the best interests of the child, which steps this would involve and under whose supervision.

49. The aims of the reintegration and the family's and alternative caregiver's principal tasks in this respect should be set out in writing and agreed on by all concerned.

50. Regular and appropriate contact between the child and his/her family specifically for the purpose of reintegration should be developed, supported and monitored by the competent body.

51. Once decided, reintegration of the child in his/her family should be designed as a gradual and supervised process, accompanied by follow-up and support measures that take account of the child's age, needs and evolving capacities, as well as the cause of the separation.

V. Framework of Care Provision

52. In order to meet the specific psychoemotional, social and other needs of each child without parental care, States should take all necessary measures to ensure that the legislative, policy and financial conditions exist to provide for adequate alternative care options, with priority to familyand community-based solutions.

53. States should ensure the availability of a range of alternative care options, consistent with the general principles of the present Guidelines, for emergency, short-term and long-term care.

54. States should ensure that all entities and individuals engaged in the provision of alternative care for children receive due authorization to do so from a competent authority and be subject to the latter's regular monitoring and review in keeping with the present Guidelines. To this end, these authorities should develop appropriate criteria for assessing the professional and ethical fitness of care providers and for their accreditation, monitoring and supervision.

55. With regard to informal care arrangements for the child, whether within the extended family, with friends or with other parties, States should, where appropriate, encourage such carers to notify the competent authorities accordingly so that they and the child may receive any necessary financial and other support that would promote the child's welfare and protection. Where possible and appropriate, States should encourage and enable informal caregivers, with the consent of the child and parents concerned, to formalize the care arrangement after a suitable lapse of time, to the extent that the arrangement has proved to be in the child's best interests to date and is expected to continue in the foreseeable future.

VI. Determination of the Most Appropriate Form of Care

56. Decision-making on alternative care in the best interests of the child should take place through a judicial, administrative or other adequate and recognized procedure, with legal safeguards, including, where appropriate, legal representation on behalf of children in any legal proceedings. It should be based on rigorous assessment, planning and review, through established structures and mechanisms, and carried out on a case-by-case basis, by suitably qualified professionals in a multidisciplinary team, wherever possible. It should involve full consultation at all stages with the child, according to his/her evolving capacities, and with his/her parents or legal guardians. To this end, all concerned should be provided with the necessary information on which to base their opinion. States should make every effort to provide adequate resources and channels for the training and recognition of the professionals responsible for determining the best form of care so as to facilitate compliance with these provisions.

57. Assessment should be carried out expeditiously, thoroughly and carefully. It should take into account the child's immediate safety and well-being, as well as his/her longer term care and development, and should cover the child's personal and developmental characteristics, ethnic, cultural, linguistic and religious background, family and social environment, medical history and any special needs.

58. The resulting initial and review reports should be used as essential tools for planning decisions from the time of their acceptance by the competent authorities onwards, with a view to, inter alia, avoiding undue disruption and contradictory decisions.

59. Frequent changes in care setting are detrimental to the child's development and ability to form attachments, and should be avoided. Short-term placements should aim at enabling an appropriate permanent solution to be arranged. Permanency for the child should be secured without undue delay through reintegration in his/her nuclear or extended family or, if this is not possible, in an alternative stable family setting or, where paragraph 20 above applies, in stable and appropriate residential care.

60. Planning for care provision and permanency should be carried out from the earliest possible time, ideally before the child enters care, taking into account the immediate and longer term advantages and disadvantages of each option considered, and should comprise short- and long-term propositions.

61. Planning for care provision and permanency should be based on, notably, the nature and quality of the child's attachment to his/her family; the family's capacity to safeguard the child's well-being and harmonious development; the child's need or desire to feel part of a family; the desirability of the child remaining within his/her community and country; his/her cultural, linguistic and religious background; and relationships with siblings, with a view to avoiding their separation.

62. The plan should clearly state, inter alia, the goals of the placement and the measures to achieve them.

63. The child and his/her parents or legal guardians should be fully informed about the alternative care options available, the implications of each option and their rights and obligations in the matter.

64. The preparation, enforcement and evaluation of a protective measure for a child should be carried out, to the greatest extent possible, with the participation of his/her parents or legal guardians and potential foster carers and caregivers, with respect to his/her particular needs, convictions and special wishes. At the request of the child, parents or legal guardians, other important persons in the child's life may also be consulted in any decision-making process, at the discretion of the competent authority.

65. States should ensure that any child who has been placed in alternative care by a properly constituted court, tribunal or administrative or other competent body, as well as his/her parents or others with parental responsibility, are given the opportunity to make representations on the placement decision before a court, are informed of their rights to make such representations and are assisted in doing so.

66. States should ensure the right of any child who has been placed in temporary care to regular and thorough review – preferably at least every three months – of the appropriateness of his/her care and treatment, taking into account notably his/her personal development and any changing needs, developments in his/her family environment, and the adequacy and necessity of the current placement in these lights. The review should be carried out by duly qualified and authorized persons, and fully involve the child and all relevant persons in the child's life.

67. The child should be prepared for all changes of care settings resulting from the planning and review processes.

VII. Provision of Alternative Care

A. Policies

68. It is a responsibility of the State or appropriate level of government to ensure the development and implementation of coordinated policies regarding formal and informal care for all children who are without parental care. Such policies should be based on sound information and statistical data. They should define a process for determining who has responsibility for a child, taking into account the role of the child's parents or principal caregivers in his/her protection, care and development. Presumptive responsibility, unless shown to be otherwise, is with the child's parents or principal caregivers.

69. All State entities involved in the referral of, and assistance to, children without parental care, in cooperation with civil society, should adopt policies and procedures which favour information-sharing and networking between agencies and individuals in order to ensure effective care, aftercare and protection for these children. The location and/or design of the agency responsible for the oversight of alternative care should be established so as to maximize its accessibility to those who require the services provided.

70. Special attention should be paid to the quality of alternative care provision, both in residential and family-based care, in particular with regard to the professional skills, selection, training and supervision of carers. Their role and functions should be clearly defined and clarified with respect to those of the child's parents or legal guardians.

71. In each country, the competent authorities should draw up a document setting out the rights of children in alternative care in keeping with the present Guidelines. Children in alternative care should be enabled to understand fully the rules, regulations and objectives of the care setting and their rights and obligations therein.

72. All alternative care provision should be based on a written statement of the provider's aims and objectives in providing the service and the nature of their responsibilities to the child that reflects the standards set by the Convention on the Rights of the Child, the present Guidelines and applicable law. All providers should be appropriately qualified or approved in accordance with legal requirements to provide alternative care services.

73. A regulatory framework should be established to ensure a standard process for the referral or admission of a child to an alternative care setting.

74. Cultural and religious practices regarding provision of alternative care, including those related to gender perspectives, should be respected and promoted to the extent that they can be shown to be consistent with the children's rights and best interests. The process of considering whether such practices should be promoted should be carried out in a broadly participatory way, involving the cultural and religious leaders concerned, professionals and those caring for children without parental care, parents and other relevant stakeholders, as well as the children themselves.

1. Informal care

75. With a view to ensuring that appropriate conditions of care are met in informal care provided by individuals or families, States should recognize the role played by this type of care and take adequate measures to support its optimal provision on the basis of an assessment of which particular settings may require special assistance or oversight.

76. Competent authorities should, where appropriate, encourage informal carers to notify the care arrangement and should seek to ensure their access to all available services and benefits likely to assist them in discharging their duty to care for and protect the child.

77. The State should recognize the de facto responsibility of informal carers for the child.

78. States should devise special and appropriate measures designed to protect children in informal care from abuse, neglect, child labour and all other forms of exploitation, with particular attention to informal care provided by non-relatives, by relatives previously unknown to the child or far from the child's habitual place of residence.

2. General conditions applying to all forms of formal alternative care arrangements

79. The transfer of a child into alternative care should be carried out with the utmost sensitivity and in a child-friendly manner, in particular involving specially trained and, in principle, non-uniformed personnel.

80. When a child is placed in alternative care, contact with his/her family, as well as with other persons close to him or her, such as friends, neighbours and previous carers, should be encouraged and facilitated, in keeping with the child's protection and best

interests. The child should have access to information on the situation of his/her family members in the absence of contact with them.

81. States should pay special attention to ensuring that children in alternative care because of parental imprisonment or prolonged hospitalization have the opportunity to maintain contact with their parents and receive any necessary counselling and support in that regard.

82. Carers should ensure that children receive adequate amounts of wholesome and nutritious food in accordance with local dietary habits and relevant dietary standards, as well as with the child's religious beliefs. Appropriate nutritional supplementation should also be provided when necessary.

83. Carers should promote the health of the children for whom they are responsible and make arrangements to ensure that medical care, counselling and support are made available as required.

84. Children should have access to formal, non-formal and vocational education in accordance with their rights, to the maximum extent possible in educational facilities in the local community.

85. Carers should ensure that the right of every child, including children with disabilities, living with or affected by HIV/AIDS or having any other special needs, to develop through play and leisure activities is respected and that opportunities for such activities are created within and outside the care setting. Contacts with the children and others in the local community should be encouraged and facilitated.

86. The specific safety, health, nutritional, developmental and other needs of babies and young children, including those with special needs, should be catered for in all care settings, including ensuring their ongoing attachment to a specific carer.

87. Children should be allowed to satisfy the needs of their religious and spiritual life, including by receiving visits from a qualified representative of their religion, and to freely decide to participate or not in religious services, religious education or counselling. The child's own religious background should be respected, and no child should be encouraged or persuaded to change his/her religion or belief during a care placement.

88. All adults responsible for children should respect and promote the right to privacy, including appropriate facilities for hygiene and sanitary needs, respecting gender differences and interaction, and adequate, secure and accessible storage space for personal possessions.

89. Carers should understand the importance of their role in developing positive, safe and nurturing relationships with children, and be able to do so.

90. Accommodation in all alternative care settings should meet the requirements of health and safety.

91. States must ensure through their competent authorities that accommodation provided to children in alternative care, and their supervision in such placements, enable them to be effectively protected against abuse. Particular attention needs to be paid to the age, maturity and degree of vulnerability of each child in determining his/her living arrangements. Measures aimed at protecting children in care should be in conformity with the law and not involve unreasonable constraints on their liberty and conduct in comparison with children of similar age in their community.

92. All alternative care settings should provide adequate protection to children from abduction, trafficking, sale and all other forms of exploitation. Any consequent

constraints on their liberty and conduct should be no more than are strictly necessary to ensure their effective protection from such acts.

93. All carers should promote and encourage children and young people to develop and exercise informed choices, taking account of acceptable risks and the child's age, and according to his/her evolving capacities.

94. States, agencies and facilities, schools and other community services should take appropriate measures to ensure that children in alternative care are not stigmatized during or after their placement. This should include efforts to minimize the identification of the child as being looked after in an alternative care setting.

95. All disciplinary measures and behaviour management constituting torture, cruel, inhuman or degrading treatment, including closed or solitary confinement or any other forms of physical or psychological violence that are likely to compromise the physical or mental health of the child, must be strictly prohibited in conformity with international human rights law. States must take all necessary measures to prevent such practices and ensure that they are punishable by law. Restriction of contact with members of the child's family and other persons of special importance to the child should never be used as a sanction.

96. Use of force and restraints of whatever nature should not be authorized unless strictly necessary for safeguarding the child's or others' physical or psychological integrity, in conformity with the law and in a reasonable and proportionate manner and with respect for the fundamental rights of the child. Restraint by means of drugs and medication should be based on therapeutic needs and should never be employed without evaluation and prescription by a specialist.

97. Children in care should be offered access to a person of trust in whom they may confide in total confidentiality. This person should be designated by the competent authority with the agreement of the child concerned. The child should be informed that legal or ethical standards may require breaching confidentiality under certain circumstances.

98. Children in care should have access to a known, effective and impartial mechanism whereby they can notify complaints or concerns regarding their treatment or conditions of placement. Such mechanisms should include initial consultation, feedback, implementation and further consultation. Young people with previous care experience should be involved in this process, due weight being given to their opinions. This process should be conducted by competent persons trained to work with children and young people.

99. To promote the child's sense of self-identity, a life story book comprising appropriate information, pictures, personal objects and mementoes regarding each step of the child's life should be maintained with the child's participation and made available to the child throughout his/her life.

B. Legal responsibility for the child

100. In situations where the child's parents are absent or are incapable of making day-to-day decisions in the best interests of the child, and the child's placement in alternative care has been ordered or authorized by a competent administrative body or judicial authority, a designated individual or competent entity should be vested with the legal right and responsibility to make such decisions in the place of parents, in full consultation with the child. States should ensure that a mechanism is in place for designating such an individual or entity.

101. Such legal responsibility should be attributed by the competent authorities and be supervised directly by them or through formally accredited entities, including non-governmental organizations. Accountability for the actions of the individual or entity concerned should lie with the designating body.

102. Persons exercising such legal responsibility should be reputable individuals with relevant knowledge of children's issues, an ability to work directly with children, and an understanding of any special and cultural needs of the children to be entrusted to them. They should receive appropriate training and professional support in this regard. They should be in a position to make independent and impartial decisions that are in the best interests of the children concerned and that promote and safeguard each child's welfare.

103. The role and specific responsibilities of the designated person or entity should include:

(a) Ensuring that the rights of the child are protected and that, in particular, the child has appropriate care, accommodation, health-care provision, developmental opportunities, psychosocial support, education and language support;

(b) Ensuring that the child has access to legal and other representation where necessary, consulting with the child so that the child's views are taken into account by decision-making authorities, and advising and keeping the child informed of his/her rights;

(c) Contributing to the identification of a stable solution in the child's best interests;

(d) Providing a link between the child and various organizations that may provide services to the child;

(e) Assisting the child in family tracing;

(f) Ensuring that, if repatriation or family reunification is carried out, it is done in the best interests of the child;

(g) Helping the child to keep in touch with his/her family, when appropriate.

1. Agencies and facilities responsible for formal care

104. Legislation should stipulate that all agencies and facilities must be registered and authorized to operate by social welfare services or another competent authority, and that failure to comply with such legislation constitutes an offence punishable by law. Authorization should be granted and regularly reviewed by the competent authorities on the basis of standard criteria covering, at a minimum, the agency's or facility's objectives, functioning, staff recruitment and qualifications, conditions of care and financial resources and management.

105. All agencies and facilities should have written policy and practice statements consistent with the present Guidelines, setting out clearly their aims, policies, methods and the standards applied for the recruitment, monitoring, supervision and evaluation of qualified and suitable carers to ensure that those aims are met.

106. All agencies and facilities should develop a staff code of conduct, consistent with the present Guidelines, that defines the role of each professional and of the carers in particular and includes clear reporting procedures on allegations of misconduct by any team member.

107. The forms of financing care provision should never be such as to encourage a child's unnecessary placement or prolonged stay in care arrangements organized or provided by an agency or facility.

108. Comprehensive and up-to-date records should be maintained regarding the administration of alternative care services, including detailed files on all children in their care, staff employed and financial transactions.

109. The records on children in care should be complete, up to date, confidential and secure, and include information on their admission and departure and the form, content and details of the care placement of each child, together with any appropriate identity documents and other personal information. Information on the child's family should be included in the child's file as well as in the reports based on regular evaluations. This record should follow the child throughout the alternative care period and be consulted by duly authorized professionals responsible for his/her current care.

110. The above-mentioned records could be made available to the child, as well as to the parents or guardians, within the limits of the child's right to privacy and confidentiality, as appropriate. Appropriate counselling should be provided before, during and after consultation of the record.

111. All alternative care services should have a clear policy on maintaining the confidentiality of information pertaining to each child, which all carers are aware of and adhere to.

112. As a matter of good practice, all agencies and facilities should systematically ensure that, prior to employment, carers and other staff in direct contact with children undergo an appropriate and comprehensive assessment of their suitability to work with children.

113. Conditions of work, including remuneration, for carers employed by agencies and facilities should be such as to maximize motivation, job satisfaction and continuity, and hence their disposition to fulfil their role in the most appropriate and effective manner.

114. Training should be provided to all carers on the rights of children without parental care and on the specific vulnerability of children, in particularly difficult situations, such as emergency placements or placements outside their area of habitual residence. Cultural, social, gender and religious sensitization should also be assured. States should also provide adequate resources and channels for the recognition of these professionals in order to favour the implementation of these provisions.

115. Training in dealing appropriately with challenging behaviour, including conflict resolution techniques and means to prevent acts of harm or self-harm, should be provided to all care staff employed by agencies and facilities.

116. Agencies and facilities should ensure that, wherever appropriate, carers are prepared to respond to children with special needs, notably those living with HIV/AIDS or other chronic physical or mental illnesses, and children with physical or mental disabilities.

2. Foster care

117. The competent authority or agency should devise a system, and should train concerned staff accordingly, to assess and match the needs of the child with the abilities and resources of potential foster carers and to prepare all concerned for the placement.

118. A pool of accredited foster carers should be identified in each locality, who can provide children with care and protection while maintaining ties to family, community and cultural group.

119. Special preparation, support and counselling services for foster carers should be developed and made available to carers at regular intervals, before, during and after the placement.

120. Carers should have, within fostering agencies and other systems involved with children without parental care, the opportunity to make their voice heard and to influence policy.

121. Encouragement should be given to the establishment of associations of foster carers that can provide important mutual support and contribute to practice and policy development.

C. Residential care

122. Facilities providing residential care should be small and organized around the rights and needs of the child, in a setting as close as possible to a family or small group situation. Their objective should generally be to provide temporary care and to contribute actively to the child's family reintegration or, if this is not possible, to secure his/her stable care in an alternative family setting, including through adoption or *kafala* of Islamic law, where appropriate.

123. Measures should be taken so that, where necessary and appropriate, a child solely in need of protection and alternative care may be accommodated separately from children who are subject to the criminal justice system.

124. The competent national or local authority should establish rigorous screening procedures to ensure that only appropriate admissions to such facilities are made.

125. States should ensure that there are sufficient carers in residential care settings to allow individualized attention and to give the child, where appropriate, the opportunity to bond with a specific carer. Carers should also be deployed within the care setting in such a way as to implement effectively its aims and objectives and ensure child protection.

126. Laws, policies and regulations should prohibit the recruitment and solicitation of children for placement in residential care by agencies, facilities or individuals.

D. Inspection and monitoring

127. Agencies, facilities and professionals involved in care provision should be accountable to a specific public authority, which should ensure, inter alia, frequent inspections comprising both scheduled and unannounced visits, involving discussion with and observation of the staff and the children.

128. To the extent possible and appropriate, inspection functions should include a component of training and capacity-building for care providers.

129. States should be encouraged to ensure that an independent monitoring mechanism is in place, with due consideration for the Principles relating to the Status of National Institutions for the Promotion and Protection of Human Rights (Paris Principles). The monitoring mechanism should be easily accessible to children, parents and those responsible for children without parental care. The functions of the monitoring mechanism should include:

(a) Consulting in conditions of privacy with children in all forms of alternative care, visiting the care settings in which they live and undertaking investigations into any alleged situation of violation of children's rights in those settings, on complaint or on its own initiative;

(b)   Recommending relevant policies to appropriate authorities with the aim of improving the treatment of children deprived of parental care and ensuring that it is in keeping with the preponderance of research findings on child protection, health, development and care;

(c)   Submitting proposals and observations concerning draft legislation;

(d)   Contributing independently to the reporting process under the Convention on the Rights of the Child, including to periodic State party reports to the Committee on the Rights of the Child with regard to the implementation of the present Guidelines.

E. Support for aftercare

130. Agencies and facilities should have a clear policy and carry out agreed procedures relating to the planned and unplanned conclusion of their work with children to ensure appropriate aftercare and/or follow-up. Throughout the period of care, they should systematically aim at preparing the child to assume self-reliance and to integrate fully in the community, notably through the acquisition of social and life skills, which are fostered by participation in the life of the local community.

131. The process of transition from care to aftercare should take into consideration the child's gender, age, maturity and particular circumstances and include counselling and support, notably to avoid exploitation. Children leaving care should be encouraged to take part in the planning of aftercare life. Children with special needs, such as disabilities, should benefit from an appropriate support system, ensuring, inter alia, avoidance of unnecessary institutionalization. Both the public and private sectors should be encouraged, including through incentives, to employ children from different care services, particularly children with special needs.

132. Special efforts should be made to allocate to each child, whenever possible, a specialized person who can facilitate his/her independence when leaving care.

133. Aftercare should be prepared as early as possible in the placement and, in any case, well before the child leaves the care setting.

134. Ongoing educational and vocational training opportunities should be imparted as part of life skill education to young people leaving care in order to help them to become financially independent and generate their own income.

135. Access to social, legal and health services, together with appropriate financial support, should also be provided to young people leaving care and during aftercare.

VIII. Care Provision for Children Outside Their Country of Habitual Residence

A. Placement of a child for care abroad

136. The present Guidelines should apply to all public and private entities and all persons involved in arrangements for a child to be sent for care to a country other than his/her country of habitual residence, whether for medical treatment, temporary hosting, respite care or any other reason.

137. States concerned should ensure that a designated body has responsibility for determining specific standards to be met regarding, in particular, the criteria for selecting carers in the host country and the quality of care and follow-up, as well as for supervising and monitoring the operation of such schemes.

138. To ensure appropriate international cooperation and child protection in such situations, States are encouraged to ratify or accede to the Hague Convention of 19

October 1996 on Jurisdiction, Applicable Law, Recognition, Enforcement and Cooperation in Respect of Parental Responsibility and Measures for the Protection of Children.

B. Provision of care for a child already abroad

139. The present Guidelines, as well as other relevant international provisions, should apply to all public and private entities and all persons involved in arrangements for a child needing care while in a country other than his/her country of habitual residence, for whatever reason.

140. Unaccompanied or separated children already abroad should in principle enjoy the same level of protection and care as national children in the country concerned.

141. In determining appropriate care provision, the diversity and disparity of unaccompanied or separated children (such as ethnic and migratory background or cultural and religious diversity) should be taken into consideration on a case-by-case basis.

142. Unaccompanied or separated children, including those who arrive irregularly in a country, should not be, in principle, deprived of their liberty solely for having breached any law governing access to and stay within the territory.

143. Child victims of trafficking should neither be detained in police custody nor subjected to penalties for their involvement under compulsion in unlawful activities.

144. As soon as an unaccompanied child is identified, States are strongly encouraged to appoint a guardian or, where necessary, representation by an organization responsible for his/her care and well-being to accompany the child throughout the status determination and decision-making process.

145. As soon as an unaccompanied or separated child is taken into care, all reasonable efforts should be made to trace his/her family and re-establish family ties, when this is in the best interests of the child and would not endanger those involved.

146. In order to assist in planning the future of an unaccompanied or separated child in a manner that best protects his/her rights, relevant State and social service authorities should make all reasonable efforts to procure documentation and information in order to conduct an assessment of the child's risk and social and family conditions in his/her country of habitual residence.

147. Unaccompanied or separated children must not be returned to their country of habitual residence:

(a)   If, following the risk and security assessment, there are reasons to believe that the child's safety and security are in danger;
(b)   Unless, prior to the return, a suitable caregiver, such as a parent, other relative, other adult caretaker, a Government agency or an authorized agency or facility in the country of origin, has agreed and is able to take responsibility for the child and provide him/her with appropriate care and protection;
(c)   If, for other reasons, it is not in their best interests, according to the assessment of the competent authorities.

148. With the above aims in mind, cooperation among States, regions, local authorities and civil society associations should be promoted, strengthened and enhanced.

149. The effective involvement of consular services or, failing that, legal representatives of the country of origin should be foreseen, when this is in the best interests of the child and would not endanger the child or his/her family.

150. Those responsible for the welfare of an unaccompanied or separated child should facilitate regular communication between the child and his/her family, except where this is against the child's wishes or is demonstrably not in his/her best interests.

151. Placement with a view to adoption or *kafala* of Islamic law should not be considered a suitable initial option for an unaccompanied or separated child. States are encouraged to consider this option only after efforts to determine the location of his/her parents, extended family or habitual carers have been exhausted.

IX. Care in Emergency Situations

A. Application of the Guidelines

152. The present Guidelines should continue to apply in situations of emergency arising from natural and man-made disasters, including international and non-international armed conflicts, as well as foreign occupation. Individuals and organizations wishing to work on behalf of children without parental care in emergency situations are strongly encouraged to operate in accordance with the Guidelines.

153. In such circumstances, the State or de facto authorities in the region concerned, the international community and all local, national, foreign and international agencies providing or intending to provide child-focused services should pay special attention:

(a)   To ensure that all entities and persons involved in responding to unaccompanied or separated children are sufficiently experienced, trained, resourceful and equipped to do so in an appropriate manner;

(b)   To develop, as necessary, temporary and long-term family-based care;

(c)   To use residential care only as a temporary measure until family-based care can be developed;

(d)   To prohibit the establishment of new residential facilities structured to provide simultaneous care to large groups of children on a permanent or long-term basis;

(e)   To prevent the cross-border displacement of children, except under the circumstances described in paragraph 159 below;

(f)   To make cooperation with family tracing and reintegration efforts mandatory.

Preventing separation

154. Organizations and authorities should make every effort to prevent the separation of children from their parents or primary caregivers, unless the best interests of the child so require, and ensure that their actions do not inadvertently encourage family separation by providing services and benefits to children alone rather than to families.

155. Separations initiated by the child's parents or other primary caregivers should be prevented by:

(a)   Ensuring that all households have access to basic food and medical supplies and other services, including education;

(b)   Limiting the development of residential care options and restricting their use to those situations where it is absolutely necessary.

B. Care arrangements

156. Communities should be supported to play an active role in monitoring and responding to care and protection issues facing children in their local context.

157. Care within a child's own community, including fostering, should be encouraged, as it provides continuity in socialization and development.

158. As unaccompanied or separated children may be at heightened risk of abuse and exploitation, monitoring and specific support to carers should be foreseen to ensure their protection.

159. Children in emergency situations should not be moved to a country other than that of their habitual residence for alternative care except temporarily for compelling health, medical or safety reasons. In that case, this should be as close as possible to their home, they should be accompanied by a parent or caregiver known to the child, and a clear return plan should be established.

160. Should family reintegration prove impossible within an appropriate period or be deemed contrary to the child's best interests, stable and definitive solutions, such as *kafala* of Islamic law or adoption, should be envisaged; failing this, other long-term options should be considered, such as foster care or appropriate residential care, including group homes and other supervised living arrangements.

C. Tracing and family reintegration

161. Identifying, registering and documenting unaccompanied or separated children are priorities in any emergency and should be carried out as quickly as possible.

162. Registration activities should be conducted by or under the direct supervision of State authorities and explicitly mandated entities with responsibility for and experience in this task.

163. The confidential nature of the information collected should be respected and systems put in place for safe forwarding and storage of information. Information should only be shared among duly mandated agencies for the purpose of tracing, family reintegration and care.

164. All those engaged in tracing family members or primary legal or customary caregivers should operate within a coordinated system, using standardized forms and mutually compatible procedures, wherever possible. They should ensure that the child and others concerned would not be endangered by their actions.

165. The validity of relationships and the confirmation of the willingness of the child and family members to be reunited must be verified for every child. No action should be taken that may hinder eventual family reintegration, such as adoption, change of name, or movement to places far from the family's likely location, until all tracing efforts have been exhausted.

166. Appropriate records of any placement of a child should be made and kept in a safe and secure manner so that reunification can be facilitated in the future.

CHAPTER 28

GENERAL COMMENTS OF THE COMMITTEE ON THE RIGHTS OF THE CHILD

General Comment No 1 (2001)
Article 29(1): The Aims of Education

Article 29(1), Convention on the Rights of the Child

"1. States Parties agree that the education of the child shall be directed to:

(a) The development of the child's personality, talents and mental and physical abilities to their fullest potential;

(b) The development of respect for human rights and fundamental freedoms, and for the principles enshrined in the Charter of the United Nations;

(c) The development of respect for the child's parents, his or her own cultural identity, language and values, for the national values of the country in which the child is living, the country from which he or she may originate, and for civilizations different from his or her own;

(d) The preparation of the child for responsible life in a free society, in the spirit of understanding, peace, tolerance, equality of sexes, and friendship among all peoples, ethnic, national and religious groups and persons of indigenous origin;

(e) The development of respect for the natural environment."

APPENDIX
GENERAL COMMENT 1 (2001): THE AIMS OF EDUCATION

The significance of article 29 (1)

1. Article 29, paragraph 1, of the Convention on the Rights of the Child is of far-reaching importance. The aims of education that it sets out, which have been agreed to by all States parties, promote, support and protect the core value of the Convention: the human dignity innate in every child and his or her equal and inalienable rights. These aims, set out in the five subparagraphs of article 29 (1) are all linked directly to the realization of the child's human dignity and rights, taking into account the child's special developmental needs and diverse evolving capacities. The aims are: the holistic development of the full potential of the child (29 (1) (a)), including development of respect for human rights (29 (1) (b)), an enhanced sense of identity and affiliation (29 (1) (c)), and his or her socialization and interaction with others (29 (1) (d)) and with the environment (29 (1) (e)).

2. Article 29 (1) not only adds to the right to education recognized in article 28 a qualitative dimension which reflects the rights and inherent dignity of the child; it also insists upon the need for education to be child-centred, child-friendly and empowering, and it highlights the need for educational processes to be based upon the very principles

it enunciates.[1] The education to which every child has a right is one designed to provide the child with life skills, to strengthen the child's capacity to enjoy the full range of human rights and to promote a culture which is infused by appropriate human rights values. The goal is to empower the child by developing his or her skills, learning and other capacities, human dignity, self-esteem and self-confidence. "Education" in this context goes far beyond formal schooling to embrace the broad range of life experiences and learning processes which enable children, individually and collectively, to develop their personalities, talents and abilities and to live a full and satisfying life within society.

3. The child's right to education is not only a matter of access (art. 28) but also of content. An education with its contents firmly rooted in the values of article 29 (1) is for every child an indispensable tool for her or his efforts to achieve in the course of her or his life a balanced, human rights-friendly response to the challenges that accompany a period of fundamental change driven by globalization, new technologies and related phenomena. Such challenges include the tensions between, inter alia, the global and the local; the individual and the collective; tradition and modernity; long- and short-term considerations; competition and equality of opportunity; the expansion of knowledge and the capacity to assimilate it; and the spiritual and the material.[2] And yet, in the national and international programmes and policies on education that really count the elements embodied in article 29 (1) seem all too often to be either largely missing or present only as a cosmetic afterthought.

4. Article 29 (1) states that the States parties agree that education should be directed to a wide range of values. This agreement overcomes the boundaries of religion, nation and culture built across many parts of the world. At first sight, some of the diverse values expressed in article 29 (1) might be thought to be in conflict with one another in certain situations. Thus, efforts to promote understanding, tolerance and friendship among all peoples, to which paragraph (1) (d) refers, might not always be automatically compatible with policies designed, in accordance with paragraph (1) (c), to develop respect for the child's own cultural identity, language and values, for the national values of the country in which the child is living, the country from which he or she may originate, and for civilizations different from his or her own. But in fact, part of the importance of this provision lies precisely in its recognition of the need for a balanced approach to education and one which succeeds in reconciling diverse values through dialogue and respect for difference. Moreover, children are capable of playing a unique role in bridging many of the differences that have historically separated groups of people from one another.

The functions of article 29 (1)

5. Article 29 (1) is much more than an inventory or listing of different objectives which education should seek to achieve. Within the overall context of the Convention it serves to highlight, inter alia, the following dimensions.

6. First, it emphasizes the indispensable interconnected nature of the Convention's provisions. It draws upon, reinforces, integrates and complements a variety of other provisions and cannot be properly understood in isolation from them. In addition to the

---

[1]   In this regard, the Committee takes note of General Comment No. 13 (1999) of the Committee on Economic, Social and Cultural Rights on the right to education, which deals, <u>inter alia</u>, with the aims of education under article 13 (1) of the International Covenant on Economic, Social and Cultural Rights. The Committee also draws attention to the general guidelines regarding the form and contents of periodic reports to be submitted by States parties under article 44, paragraph 1 (b), of the Convention, (CRC/C/58), paras. 112-116.

[2]   United Nations Educational, Scientific and Cultural Organization, *Learning: The Treasure Within*, Report of the International Commission on Education for the 21st Century, 1996, pp. 16-18.

general principles of the Convention - non-discrimination (art. 2), the best interest of the child (art. 3), the right to life, survival and development (art. 6), and the right to express views and have them taken into account (art. 12) – many other provisions may be mentioned, such as but not limited to the rights and responsibilities of parents (arts. 5 and 18), freedom of expression (art. 13), freedom of thought (art. 14), the right to information (art. 17), the rights of children with disabilities (art. 23), the right to education for health (art. 24), the right to education (art. 28), and the linguistic and cultural rights of children belonging to minority groups (art. 30).

7. Children's rights are not detached or isolated values devoid of context, but exist within a broader ethical framework which is partly described in article 29 (1) and in the preamble to the Convention. Many of the criticisms that have been made of the Convention are specifically answered by this provision. Thus, for example, this article underlines the importance of respect for parents, of the need to view rights within their broader ethical, moral, spiritual, cultural or social framework, and of the fact that most children's rights, far from being externally imposed, are embedded within the values of local communities.

8. Second, the article attaches importance to the process by which the right to education is to be promoted. Thus, efforts to promote the enjoyment of other rights must not be undermined, and should be reinforced, by the values imparted in the educational process. This includes not only the content of the curriculum but also the educational processes, the pedagogical methods and the environment within which education takes place, whether it be the home, school, or elsewhere. Children do not lose their human rights by virtue of passing through the school gates. Thus, for example, education must be provided in a way that respects the inherent dignity of the child and enables the child to express his or her views freely in accordance with article 12 (1) and to participate in school life. Education must also be provided in a way that respects the strict limits on discipline reflected in article 28 (2) and promotes non-violence in school. The Committee has repeatedly made clear in its concluding observations that the use of corporal punishment does not respect the inherent dignity of the child nor the strict limits on school discipline. Compliance with the values recognized in article 29 (1) clearly requires that schools be child-friendly in the fullest sense of the term and that they be consistent in all respects with the dignity of the child. The participation of children in school life, the creation of school communities and student councils, peer education and peer counselling, and the involvement of children in school disciplinary proceedings should be promoted as part of the process of learning and experiencing the realization of rights.

9. Third, while article 28 focuses upon the obligations of State parties in relation to the establishment of educational systems and in ensuring access thereto, article 29 (1) underlines the individual and subjective right to a specific quality of education. Consistent with the Convention's emphasis on the importance of acting in the best interests of the child, this article emphasizes the message of child-centred education: that the key goal of education is the development of the individual child's personality, talents and abilities, in recognition of the fact that every child has unique characteristics, interests, abilities, and learning needs.[3] Thus, the curriculum must be of direct relevance to the child's social, cultural, environmental and economic context and to his or her present and future needs and take full account of the child's evolving capacities; teaching methods should be tailored to the different needs of different children. Education must also be aimed at ensuring that essential life skills are learnt by every child and that no

---

[3]   United Nations Educational, Scientific and Cultural Organization, *The Salamanca Statement and Framework for Action on Special Needs Education*, 1994, p. viii.

child leaves school without being equipped to face the challenges that he or she can expect to be confronted with in life. Basic skills include not only literacy and numeracy but also life skills such as the ability to make well-balanced decisions; to resolve conflicts in a non-violent manner; and to develop a healthy lifestyle, good social relationships and responsibility, critical thinking, creative talents, and other abilities which give children the tools needed to pursue their options in life.

10. Discrimination on the basis of any of the grounds listed in article 2 of the Convention, whether it is overt or hidden, offends the human dignity of the child and is capable of undermining or even destroying the capacity of the child to benefit from educational opportunities. While denying a child's access to educational opportunities is primarily a matter which relates to article 28 of the Convention, there are many ways in which failure to comply with the principles contained in article 29 (1) can have a similar effect. To take an extreme example, gender discrimination can be reinforced by practices such as a curriculum which is inconsistent with the principles of gender equality, by arrangements which limit the benefits girls can obtain from the educational opportunities offered, and by unsafe or unfriendly environments which discourage girls' participation. Discrimination against children with disabilities is also pervasive in many formal educational systems and in a great many informal educational settings, including in the home.[4] Children with HIV/AIDS are also heavily discriminated against in both settings.[5] All such discriminatory practices are in direct contradiction with the requirements in article 29 (1) (a) that education be directed to the development of the child's personality, talents and mental and physical abilities to their fullest potential.

11. The Committee also wishes to highlight the links between article 29 (1) and the struggle against racism, racial discrimination, xenophobia and related intolerance. Racism and related phenomena thrive where there is ignorance, unfounded fears of racial, ethnic, religious, cultural and linguistic or other forms of difference, the exploitation of prejudices, or the teaching or dissemination of distorted values. A reliable and enduring antidote to all of these failings is the provision of education which promotes an understanding and appreciation of the values reflected in article 29 (1), including respect for differences, and challenges all aspects of discrimination and prejudice. Education should thus be accorded one of the highest priorities in all campaigns against the evils of racism and related phenomena. Emphasis must also be placed upon the importance of teaching about racism as it has been practised historically, and particularly as it manifests or has manifested itself within particular communities. Racist behaviour is not something engaged in only by "others". It is therefore important to focus on the child's own community when teaching human and children's rights and the principle of non-discrimination. Such teaching can effectively contribute to the prevention and elimination of racism, ethnic discrimination, xenophobia and related intolerance.

12. Fourth, article 29 (1) insists upon a holistic approach to education which ensures that the educational opportunities made available reflect an appropriate balance between promoting the physical, mental, spiritual and emotional aspects of education, the intellectual, social and practical dimensions, and the childhood and lifelong aspects. The overall objective of education is to maximize the child's ability and opportunity to participate fully and responsibly in a free society. It should be emphasized that the type of teaching that is focused primarily on accumulation of knowledge, prompting

---

[4]   See General Comment No. 5 (1994) of the Committee on Economic, Social and Cultural Rights on persons with disabilities.

[5]   See the recommendations adopted by the Committee on the Rights of the Child after its day of general discussion in 1998 on children living in a world with HIV/AIDS (A/55/41, para. 1536).

competition and leading to an excessive burden of work on children, may seriously hamper the harmonious development of the child to the fullest potential of his or her abilities and talents. Education should be child-friendly, inspiring and motivating the individual child. Schools should foster a humane atmosphere and allow children to develop according to their evolving capacities.

13. Fifth, it emphasizes the need for education to be designed and provided in such a way that it promotes and reinforces the range of specific ethical values enshrined in the Convention, including education for peace, tolerance, and respect for the natural environment, in an integrated and holistic manner. This may require a multidisciplinary approach. The promotion and reinforcement of the values of article 29 (1) are not only necessary because of problems elsewhere, but must also focus on problems within the child's own community. Education in this regard should take place within the family, but schools and communities must also play an important role. For example, for the development of respect for the natural environment, education must link issues of environment and sustainable development with socio-economic, sociocultural and demographic issues. Similarly, respect for the natural environment should be learnt by children at home, in school and within the community, encompass both national and international problems, and actively involve children in local, regional or global environmental projects.

14. Sixth, it reflects the vital role of appropriate educational opportunities in the promotion of all other human rights and the understanding of their indivisibility. A child's capacity to participate fully and responsibly in a free society can be impaired or undermined not only by outright denial of access to education but also by a failure to promote an understanding of the values recognized in this article.

Human rights education

15. Article 29 (1) can also be seen as a foundation stone for the various programmes of human rights education called for by the World Conference on Human Rights, held in Vienna in 1993, and promoted by international agencies. Nevertheless, the rights of the child have not always been given the prominence they require in the context of such activities. Human rights education should provide information on the content of human rights treaties. But children should also learn about human rights by seeing human rights standards implemented in practice, whether at home, in school, or within the community. Human rights education should be a comprehensive, life-long process and start with the reflection of human rights values in the daily life and experiences of children.[6]

16. The values embodied in article 29(1) are relevant to children living in zones of peace but they are even more important for those living in situations of conflict or emergency. As the Dakar Framework for Action notes, it is important in the context of education systems affected by conflict, natural calamities and instability that educational programmes be conducted in ways that promote mutual understanding, peace and tolerance, and that help to prevent violence and conflict.[7] Education about international humanitarian law also constitutes an important, but all too often neglected, dimension of efforts to give effect to article 29 (1).

---

[6]   See General Assembly resolution 49/184 of 23 December 1994 proclaiming the United Nations Decade for Human Rights Education.

[7]   Education for All: Meeting our Collective Commitments, adopted at the World Education Forum, Dakar, 26-28 April 2000.

Implementation, monitoring and review

17. The aims and values reflected in this article are stated in quite general terms and their implications are potentially very wide ranging. This seems to have led many States parties to assume that it is unnecessary, or even inappropriate, to ensure that the relevant principles are reflected in legislation or in administrative directives. This assumption is unwarranted. In the absence of any specific formal endorsement in national law or policy, it seems unlikely that the relevant principles are or will be used to genuinely inform educational policies. The Committee therefore calls upon all States parties to take the necessary steps to formally incorporate these principles into their education policies and legislation at all levels.

18. The effective promotion of article 29 (1) requires the fundamental reworking of curricula to include the various aims of education and the systematic revision of textbooks and other teaching materials and technologies, as well as school policies. Approaches which do no more than seek to superimpose the aims and values of the article on the existing system without encouraging any deeper changes are clearly inadequate. The relevant values cannot be effectively integrated into, and thus be rendered consistent with, a broader curriculum unless those who are expected to transmit, promote, teach and, as far as possible, exemplify the values have themselves been convinced of their importance. Pre-service and in-service training schemes which promote the principles reflected in article 29 (1) are thus essential for teachers, educational administrators and others involved in child education. It is also important that the teaching methods used in schools reflect the spirit and educational philosophy of the Convention on the Rights of the Child and the aims of education laid down in article 29 (1).

19. In addition, the school environment itself must thus reflect the freedom and the spirit of understanding, peace, tolerance, equality of sexes, and friendship among all peoples, ethnic, national and religious groups and persons of indigenous origin called for in article 29 (1) (b) and (d). A school which allows bullying or other violent and exclusionary practices to occur is not one which meets the requirements of article 29 (1). The term "human rights education" is too often used in a way which greatly oversimplifies its connotations. What is needed, in addition to formal human rights education, is the promotion of values and policies conducive to human rights not only within schools and universities but also within the broader community.

20. In general terms, the various initiatives that States parties are required to take pursuant to their Convention obligations will be insufficiently grounded in the absence of widespread dissemination of the text of the Convention itself, in accordance with the provisions of article 42. This will also facilitate the role of children as promoters and defenders of children's rights in their daily lives. In order to facilitate broader dissemination, States parties should report on the measures they have taken to achieve this objective and the Office of the High Commissioner for Human Rights should develop a comprehensive database of the language versions of the Convention that have been produced.

21. The media, broadly defined, also have a central role to play, both in promoting the values and aims reflected in article 29 (1) and in ensuring that their activities do not undermine the efforts of others to promote those objectives. Governments are obligated

by the Convention, pursuant to article 17 (a), to take all appropriate steps to "encourage the mass media to disseminate information and material of social and cultural benefit to the child".[8]

22. The Committee calls upon States parties to devote more attention to education as a dynamic process and to devising means by which to measure changes over time in relation to article 29 (1). Every child has the right to receive an education of good quality which in turn requires a focus on the quality of the learning environment, of teaching and learning processes and materials, and of learning outputs. The Committee notes the importance of surveys that may provide an opportunity to assess the progress made, based upon consideration of the views of all actors involved in the process, including children currently in or out of school, teachers and youth leaders, parents, and educational administrators and supervisors. In this respect, the Committee emphasizes the role of national-level monitoring which seeks to ensure that children, parents and teachers can have an input in decisions relevant to education.

23. The Committee calls upon States parties to develop a comprehensive national plan of action to promote and monitor realization of the objectives listed in article 29 (1). If such a plan is drawn up in the larger context of a national action plan for children, a national human rights action plan, or a national human rights education strategy, the Government must ensure that it nonetheless addresses all of the issues dealt with in article 29 (1) and does so from a child-rights perspective. The Committee urges that the United Nations and other international bodies concerned with educational policy and human rights education seek better coordination so as to enhance the effectiveness of the implementation of article 29 (1).

24. The design and implementation of programmes to promote the values reflected in this article should become part of the standard response by Governments to almost all situations in which patterns of human rights violations have occurred. Thus, for example, where major incidents of racism, racial discrimination, xenophobia and related intolerance occur which involve those under 18, it can reasonably be presumed that the Government has not done all that it should to promote the values reflected in the Convention generally, and in article 29 (1) in particular. Appropriate additional measures under article 29 (1) should therefore be adopted which include research on and adoption of whatever educational techniques might have a positive impact in achieving the rights recognized in the Convention.

25. States parties should also consider establishing a review procedure which responds to complaints that existing policies or practices are not consistent with article 29 (1). Such review procedures need not necessarily entail the creation of new legal, administrative, or educational bodies. They might also be entrusted to national human rights institutions or to existing administrative bodies. The Committee requests each State party when reporting on this article to identify the genuine possibilities that exist at the national or local level to obtain a review of existing approaches which are claimed to be incompatible with the Convention. Information should be provided as to how such reviews can be initiated and how many such review procedures have been undertaken within the reporting period.

26. In order to better focus the process of examining States parties' reports dealing with article 29 (1), and in accordance with the requirement in article 44 that reports shall indicate factors and difficulties, the Committee requests each State party to provide a detailed indication in its periodic reports of what it considers to be the most important

---

8   The Committee recalls the recommendations in this respect which emerged from its day of general discussion in 1996 on the child and the media (see A/53/41 para. 1396).

priorities within its jurisdiction which call for a more concerted effort to promote the values reflected in this provision and to outline the programme of activities which it proposes to take over the succeeding five years in order to address the problems identified.

27. The Committee calls upon United Nations bodies and agencies and other competent bodies whose role is underscored in article 45 of the Convention to contribute more actively and systematically to the Committee's work in relation to article 29 (1).

28. Implementation of comprehensive national plans of action to enhance compliance with article 29 (1) will require human and financial resources which should be available to the maximum extent possible, in accordance with article 4. Therefore, the Committee considers that resource constraints cannot provide a justification for a State party's failure to take any, or enough, of the measures that are required. In this context, and in light of the obligations upon States parties to promote and encourage international cooperation both in general terms (arts. 4 and 45 of the Convention) and in relation to education (art. 28 (3)), the Committee urges States parties providing development cooperation to ensure that their programmes are designed so as to take full account of the principles contained in article 29 (1).

General Comment No 2 (2002)
The role of independent national human rights institutions in the promotion and protection of the rights of the child

1.   Article 4 of the Convention on the Rights of the Child obliges States parties to "undertake all appropriate legislative, administrative and other measures for the implementation of the rights recognized in the present Convention". Independent national human rights institutions (NHRIs) are an important mechanism to promote and ensure the implementation of the Convention, and the Committee on the Rights of the Child considers the establishment of such bodies to fall within the commitment made by States parties upon ratification to ensure the implementation of the Convention and advance the universal realization of children's rights. In this regard, the Committee has welcomed the establishment of NHRIs and children's ombudspersons/children's commissioners and similar independent bodies for the promotion and monitoring of the implementation of the Convention in a number of States parties.

2.   The Committee issues this general comment in order to encourage States parties to establish an independent institution for the promotion and monitoring of implementation of the Convention and to support them in this regard by elaborating the essential elements of such institutions and the activities which should be carried out by them. Where such institutions have already been established, the Committee calls upon States to review their status and effectiveness for promoting and protecting children's rights, as enshrined in the Convention on the Rights of the Child and other relevant international instruments.

3.   The World Conference on Human Rights, held in 1993, in the Vienna Declaration and Programme of Action reaffirmed "… the important and constructive role played by national institutions for the promotion and protection of human rights", and encouraged "… the establishment and strengthening of national institutions". The General Assembly and the Commission on Human Rights have repeatedly called for the establishment of national human rights institutions, underlining the important role NHRIs play in promoting and protecting human rights and enhancing public awareness of those rights. In its general guidelines for periodic reports, the Committee requires that States parties furnish information on "any independent body established to promote and protect the rights of the child …",[9] hence, it consistently addresses this issue during its dialogue with States parties.

4.   NHRIs should be established in compliance with the Principles relating to the status of national institutions for the promotion and protection of human rights (The "Paris Principles") adopted by the General Assembly in 1993[10] transmitted by the Commission on Human Rights in 1992.[11] These minimum standards provide guidance for the establishment, competence, responsibilities, composition, including pluralism, independence, methods of operation, and quasi-judicial activities of such national bodies.

5.   While adults and children alike need independent NHRIs to protect their human rights, additional justifications exist for ensuring that children's human rights are given special attention. These include the facts that children's developmental state makes them particularly vulnerable to human rights violations; their opinions are still rarely taken

---

[9]   General guidelines regarding the form and contents of periodic reports to be submitted by States parties under article 44, paragraph 1 (b), of the Convention (CRC/C/58), para. 18.

[10]   Principles relating to the status of national institutions for the promotion and protection of human rights (The "Paris Principles"), General Assembly resolution 48/134 of 20 December 1993, annex.

[11]   Commission on Human Rights resolution 1992/54 of 3 March 1992, annex.

into account; most children have no vote and cannot play a meaningful role in the political process that determines Governments' response to human rights; children encounter significant problems in using the judicial system to protect their rights or to seek remedies for violations of their rights; and children's access to organizations that may protect their rights is generally limited.

6. Specialist independent human rights institutions for children, ombudspersons or commissioners for children's rights have been established in a growing number of States parties. Where resources are limited, consideration must be given to ensuring that the available resources are used most effectively for the promotion and protection of everyone's human rights, including children's, and in this context development of a broad-based NHRI that includes a specific focus on children is likely to constitute the best approach. A broad-based NHRI should include within its structure either an identifiable commissioner specifically responsible for children's rights, or a specific section or division responsible for children's rights.

7. It is the view of the Committee that every State needs an independent human rights institution with responsibility for promoting and protecting children's rights. The Committee's principal concern is that the institution, whatever its form, should be able, independently and effectively, to monitor, promote and protect children's rights. It is essential that promotion and protection of children's rights is "mainstreamed" and that all human rights institutions existing in a country work closely together to this end.

Mandate and powers

8. NHRIs should, if possible, be constitutionally entrenched and must at least be legislatively mandated. It is the view of the Committee that their mandate should include as broad a scope as possible for promoting and protecting human rights, incorporating the Convention on the Rights of the Child, its Optional Protocols and other relevant international human rights instruments – thus effectively covering children's human rights, in particular their civil, political, economic, social and cultural rights. The legislation should include provisions setting out specific functions, powers and duties relating to children linked to the Convention on the Rights of the Child and its Optional Protocols. If the NHRI was established before the existence of the Convention, or without expressly incorporating it, necessary arrangements, including the enactment or amendment of legislation, should be put in place so as to ensure conformity of the institution's mandate with the principles and provisions of the Convention.

9. NHRIs should be accorded such powers as are necessary to enable them to discharge their mandate effectively, including the power to hear any person and obtain any information and document necessary for assessing the situations falling within their competence. These powers should include the promotion and protection of the rights of all children under the jurisdiction of the State party in relation not only to the State but to all relevant public and private entities.

Establishment process

10. The NHRI establishment process should be consultative, inclusive and transparent, initiated and supported at the highest levels of Government and inclusive of all relevant elements of the State, the legislature and civil society. In order to ensure their independence and effective functioning, NHRIs must have adequate infrastructure, funding (including specifically for children's rights, within broad-based institutions), staff, premises, and freedom from forms of financial control that might affect their independence.

Resources

11.   While the Committee acknowledges that this is a very sensitive issue and that State parties function with varying levels of economic resources, the Committee believes that it is the duty of States to make reasonable financial provision for the operation of national human rights institutions in light of article 4 of the Convention. The mandate and powers of national institutions may be meaningless, or the exercise of their powers limited, if the national institution does not have the means to operate effectively to discharge its powers.

Pluralistic representation

12.   NHRIs should ensure that their composition includes pluralistic representation of the various elements of civil society involved in the promotion and protection of human rights. They should seek to involve, among others, the following: human rights, anti-discrimination and children's rights non-governmental organizations (NGOs), including child- and youth-led organizations; trade unions; social and professional organizations (of doctors, lawyers, journalists, scientists, etc.); universities and experts, including children's rights experts. Government departments should be involved in an advisory capacity only. NHRIs should have appropriate and transparent appointment procedures, including an open and competitive selection process.

Providing remedies for breaches of children's rights

13.   NHRIs must have the power to consider individual complaints and petitions and carry out investigations, including those submitted on behalf of or directly by children. In order to be able to effectively carry out such investigations, they must have the powers to compel and question witnesses, access relevant documentary evidence and access places of detention. They also have a duty to seek to ensure that children have effective remedies – independent advice, advocacy and complaints procedures – for any breaches of their rights. Where appropriate, NHRIs should undertake mediation and conciliation of complaints.

14.   NHRIs should have the power to support children taking cases to court, including the power (a) to take cases concerning children's issues in the name of the NHRI and (b) to intervene in court cases to inform the court about the human rights issues involved in the case.

Accessibility and participation

15.   NHRIs should be geographically and physically accessible to all children. In the spirit of article 2 of the Convention, they should proactively reach out to all groups of children, in particular the most vulnerable and disadvantaged, such as (but not limited to) children in care or detention, children from minority and indigenous groups, children with disabilities, children living in poverty, refugee and migrant children, street children and children with special needs in areas such as culture, language, health and education. NHRI legislation should include the right of the institution to have access in conditions of privacy to children in all forms of alternative care and to all institutions that include children.

16.   NHRIs have a key role to play in promoting respect for the views of children in all matters affecting them, as articulated in article 12 of the Convention, by Government and throughout society. This general principle should be applied to the establishment, organization and activities of national human rights institutions. Institutions must ensure that they have direct contact with children and that children are appropriately

involved and consulted. Children's councils, for example, could be created as advisory bodies for NHRIs to facilitate the participation of children in matters of concern to them.

17.   NHRIs should devise specially tailored consultation programmes and imaginative communication strategies to ensure full compliance with article 12 of the Convention. A range of suitable ways in which children can communicate with the institution should be established.

18.   NHRIs must have the right to report directly, independently and separately on the state of children's rights to the public and to parliamentary bodies. In this respect, States parties must ensure that an annual debate is held in Parliament to provide parliamentarians with an opportunity to discuss the work of the NHRI in respect of children's rights and the State's compliance with the Convention.

Recommended activities

19.   The following is an indicative, but not exhaustive, list of the types of activities which NHRIs should carry out in relation to the implementation of children's rights in light of the general principles of the Convention. They should:

(a)   Undertake investigations into any situation of violation of children's rights, on complaint or on their own initiative, within the scope of their mandate;

(b)   Conduct inquiries on matters relating to children's rights;

(c)   Prepare and publicize opinions, recommendations and reports, either at the request of national authorities or on their own initiative, on any matter relating to the promotion and protection of children's rights;

(d)   Keep under review the adequacy and effectiveness of law and practice relating to the protection of children's rights;

(e)   Promote harmonization of national legislation, regulations and practices with the Convention on the Rights of the Child, its Optional Protocols and other international human rights instruments relevant to children's rights and promote their effective implementation, including through the provision of advice to public and private bodies in construing and applying the Convention;

(f)   Ensure that national economic policy makers take children's rights into account in setting and evaluating national economic and development plans;

(g)   Review and report on the Government's implementation and monitoring of the state of children's rights, seeking to ensure that statistics are appropriately disaggregated and other information collected on a regular basis in order to determine what must be done to realize children's rights;

(h)   Encourage ratification of or accession to any relevant international human rights instruments;

(i)   In accordance with article 3 of the Convention requiring that the best interests of children should be a primary consideration in all actions concerning them, ensure that the impact of laws and policies on children is carefully considered from development to implementation and beyond;

(j)   In light of article 12, ensure that the views of children are expressed and heard on matters concerning their human rights and in defining issues relating to their rights;

(k)   Advocate for and facilitate meaningful participation by children's rights NGOs, including organizations comprised of children themselves, in the development of domestic legislation and international instruments on issues affecting children;

(l)   Promote public understanding and awareness of the importance of children's rights and, for this purpose, work closely with the media and undertake or sponsor research and educational activities in the field;

(m)   In accordance with article 42 of the Convention which obligates State parties to "make the principles and provisions of the Convention widely known, by appropriate and active means, to adults and children alike", sensitize the Government, public agencies and the general public to the provisions of the Convention and monitor ways in which the State is meeting its obligations in this regard;

(n)   Assist in the formulation of programmes for the teaching of, research into and integration of children's rights in the curricula of schools and universities and in professional circles;

(o)   Undertake human rights education which specifically focuses on children (in addition to promoting general public understanding about the importance of children's rights);

(p)   Take legal proceedings to vindicate children's rights in the State or provide legal assistance to children;

(q)   Engage in mediation or conciliation processes before taking cases to court, where appropriate;

(r)   Provide expertise in children's rights to the courts, in suitable cases as amicus curiae or intervenor;

(s)   In accordance with article 3 of the Convention which obliges States parties to "ensure that the institutions, services and facilities responsible for the care or protection of children shall conform with the standards established by competent authorities, particularly in the areas of safety, health, in the number and suitability of their staff, as well as competent supervision", undertake visits to juvenile homes (and all places where children are detained for reform or punishment) and care institutions to report on the situation and to make recommendations for improvement;

(t)   Undertake such other activities as are incidental to the above.

Reporting to the Committee on the Rights of the Child and cooperation between NHRIs and United Nations agencies and human rights mechanisms

20.   NHRIs should contribute independently to the reporting process under the Convention and other relevant international instruments and monitor the integrity of government reports to international treaty bodies with respect to children's rights, including through dialogue with the Committee on the Rights of the Child at its pre-sessional working group and with other relevant treaty bodies.

21.   The Committee requests that States parties include detailed information on the legislative basis and mandate and principal relevant activities of NHRIs in their reports to the Committee. It is appropriate for States parties to consult with independent human rights institutions during the preparation of reports to the Committee. However, States parties must respect the independence of these bodies and their independent role in providing information to the Committee. It is not appropriate to delegate to NHRIs the drafting of reports or to include them in the government delegation when reports are examined by the Committee.

22.   NHRIs should also cooperate with the special procedures of the Commission on Human Rights, including country and thematic mechanisms, in particular the Special Rapporteur on the sale of children, child prostitution and child pornography and the Special Representative of the Secretary-General for Children and Armed Conflict.

23. The United Nations has a long-standing programme of assistance for the establishment and strengthening of national human rights institutions. This programme, which is based in the Office of the High Commissioner for Human Rights (OHCHR), provides technical assistance and facilitates regional and global cooperation and exchanges among national human rights institutions. States parties should avail themselves of this assistance where necessary. The United Nations Children's Fund (UNICEF) also offers expertise and technical cooperation in this area.

24. As articulated in article 45 of the Convention, the Committee may also transmit, as it considers appropriate, to any specialized United Nations agency, OHCHR and any other competent body any reports from States parties that contain a request or indicate a need for technical advice or assistance in the establishment of NHRIs.

NHRIs and States parties

25. The State ratifies the Convention on the Rights of the Child and takes on obligations to implement it fully. The role of NHRIs is to monitor independently the State's compliance and progress towards implementation and to do all it can to ensure full respect for children's rights. While this may require the institution to develop projects to enhance the promotion and protection of children's rights, it should not lead to the Government delegating its monitoring obligations to the national institution. It is essential that institutions remain entirely free to set their own agenda and determine their own activities.

NHRIs and NGOs

26. Non-governmental organizations play a vital role in promoting human rights and children's rights. The role of NHRIs, with their legislative base and specific powers, is complementary. It is essential that institutions work closely with NGOs and that Governments respect the independence of both NHRIs and NGOs.

Regional and international cooperation

27. Regional and international processes and mechanisms can strengthen and consolidate NHRIs through shared experience and skills, as NHRIs share common problems in the promotion and protection of human rights in their respective countries.

28. In this respect, NHRIs should consult and cooperate with relevant national, regional and international bodies and institutions on children's rights issues.

29. Children's human rights issues are not constrained by national borders and it has become increasingly necessary to devise appropriate regional and international responses to a variety of child rights issues (including, but not limited to, the trafficking of women and children, child pornography, child soldiers, child labour, child abuse, refugee and migrant children, etc.). International and regional mechanisms and exchanges are encouraged, as they provide NHRIs with an opportunity to learn from each other's experience, collectively strengthen each other's positions and contribute to resolving human rights problems affecting both countries and regions.

General Comment No 3 (2003)
HIV/AIDS and the rights of the child

I. INTRODUCTION[12]

1. The HIV/AIDS epidemic has drastically changed the world in which children live. Millions of children have been infected and have died and many more are gravely affected as HIV spreads through their families and communities. The epidemic impacts on the daily life of younger children, and increases the victimization and marginalization of children, especially those living in particularly difficult circumstances. HIV/AIDS is not a problem of some countries but of the entire world. To truly bring its impact on children under control will require concerted and well-targeted efforts from all countries at all stages of development.

2. Initially children were considered to be only marginally affected by the epidemic. However, the international community has discovered that, unfortunately, children are at the heart of the problem. According to the Joint United Nations Programme on HIV/AIDS (UNAIDS), the most recent trends are alarming: in most parts of the world the majority of new infections are among young people between the ages of 15 and 24, sometimes younger. Women, including young girls, are also increasingly becoming infected. In most regions of the world, the vast majority of infected women do not know that they are infected and may unknowingly infect their children. Consequently, many States have recently registered an increase in their infant and child mortality rates. Adolescents are also vulnerable to HIV/AIDS because their first sexual experience may take place in an environment in which they have no access to proper information and guidance. Children who use drugs are at high risk.

3. Yet, all children can be rendered vulnerable by the particular circumstances of their lives, especially (a) children who are themselves HIV-infected; (b) children who are affected by the epidemic because of the loss of a parental caregiver or teacher and/or because their families or communities are severely strained by its consequences; and (c) children who are most prone to be infected or affected.

II. THE OBJECTIVES OF THE PRESENT GENERAL COMMENT

4. The objectives of the present General Comment are:

    (a)   To identify further and strengthen understanding of all the human rights of children in the context of HIV/AIDS;

---

[12]   At its seventeenth session (1998), the Committee on the Rights of the Child held a day of general discussion on the theme of HIV/AIDS and children's rights, in which it recommended that a number of actions be taken, including facilitating the engagement of States parties on HIV/AIDS issues in relation to the rights of the child. Human rights in relation to HIV/AIDS has also been discussed at the Eighth Meeting of Persons Chairing the Human Rights Treaty Bodies in 1997 and has been taken up by the Committee on Economic, Social and Cultural Rights and the Committee on the Elimination of Discrimination against Women. Similarly, HIV/AIDS has been discussed annually by the Commission on Human Rights for over a decade. UNAIDS and the United Nations Children's Fund (UNICEF) have emphasized the rights of the child in relation to HIV/AIDS in all aspects of their work, and the World AIDS Campaign for 1997 focused on "Children Living in a World with AIDS" and for 1998 on "Force for Change: World AIDS Campaign with Young People". UNAIDS and the Office of the United Nations High Commissioner for Human Rights have also produced *The International Guidelines on HIV/AIDS and Human Rights* (1998) and its *Revised Guideline 6* (2002) to promote and protect human rights in the context of HIV/AIDS. At the international political level, HIV/AIDS-related rights have been recognized in the *Declaration of Commitment on HIV/AIDS*, adopted at the United Nations General Assembly special session, *A World Fit for Children*, adopted at the United Nations General Assembly special session on children, and in other international and regional documents.

(b)   To promote the realization of the human rights of children in the context of HIV/AIDS, as guaranteed under the Convention on the Rights of the Child (hereafter "the Convention");

(c)   To identify measures and good practices to increase the level of implementation by States of the rights related to the prevention of HIV/AIDS and the support, care and protection of children infected with or affected by this pandemic;

(d)   To contribute to the formulation and promotion of child-oriented plans of action, strategies, laws, polices and programmes to combat the spread and mitigate the impact of HIV/AIDS at the national and international levels.

III. THE CONVENTION'S PERSPECTIVES ON HIV/AIDS: THE HOLISTIC CHILD RIGHTS-BASED APPROACH

5. The issue of children and HIV/AIDS is perceived as mainly a medical or health problem, although in reality it involves a much wider range of issues. In this regard, the right to health (article 24 of the Convention) is, however, central. But HIV/AIDS impacts so heavily on the lives of all children that it affects all their rights – civil, political, economic, social and cultural. The rights embodied in the general principles of the Convention – the right to non-discrimination (art. 2), the right of the child to have his/her interest as a primary consideration (art. 3), the right to life, survival and development (art. 6) and the right to have his/her views respected (art. 12) – should therefore be the guiding themes in the consideration of HIV/AIDS at all levels of prevention, treatment, care and support.

6. Adequate measures to address HIV/AIDS can be undertaken only if the rights of children and adolescents are fully respected. The most relevant rights in this regard, in addition to those enumerated in paragraph 5 above, are the following: the right to access information and material aimed at the promotion of their social, spiritual and moral well-being and physical and mental health (art. 17); the right to preventive health care, sex education and family planning education and services (art. 24 (f)); the right to an appropriate standard of living (art. 27); the right to privacy (art. 16); the right not to be separated from parents (art. 9); the right to be protected from violence (art. 19); the right to special protection and assistance by the State (art. 20); the rights of children with disabilities (art. 23); the right to health (art. 24); the right to social security, including social insurance (art. 26); the right to education and leisure (arts. 28 and 31); the right to be protected from economic and sexual exploitation and abuse, and from illicit use of narcotic drugs (arts. 32, 33, 34 and 36); the right to be protected from abduction, sale and trafficking as well as torture or other cruel, inhuman or degrading treatment or punishment (arts. 35 and 37); and the right to physical and psychological recovery and social reintegration (art. 39). Children are confronted with serious challenges to the above-mentioned rights as a result of the epidemic. The Convention, and in particular the four general principles with their comprehensive approach, provide a powerful framework for efforts to reduce the negative impact of the pandemic on the lives of children. The holistic rights-based approach required to implement the Convention is the optimal tool for addressing the broader range of issues that relate to prevention, treatment and care efforts.

A. The right to non-discrimination (art. 2)

7. Discrimination is responsible for heightening the vulnerability of children to HIV and AIDS, as well as seriously impacting the lives of children who are affected by HIV/AIDS, or are themselves HIV infected. Girls and boys of parents living with HIV/AIDS are often victims of stigma and discrimination as they too are often assumed to be infected. As a result of discrimination, children are denied access to information, education (see

the Committee's General Comment No. 1 on the aims of education), health or social care services or community life. At its extreme, discrimination against HIV-infected children has resulted in their abandonment by their family, community and/or society. Discrimination also fuels the epidemic by making children in particular those belonging to certain groups like children living in remote or rural areas where services are less accessible, more vulnerable to infection. These children are thus doubly victimized.

8. Of particular concern is gender-based discrimination combined with taboos or negative or judgemental attitudes to sexual activity of girls, often limiting their access to preventive measures and other services. Of concern also is discrimination based on sexual orientation. In the design of HIV/AIDS-related strategies, and in keeping with their obligations under the Convention, States parties must give careful consideration to prescribed gender norms within their societies with a view to eliminating gender-based discrimination as these norms impact on the vulnerability of both girls and boys to HIV/AIDS. States parties should, in particular, recognize that discrimination in the context of HIV/AIDS often impacts girls more severely than boys.

9. All the above-mentioned discriminatory practices are violations of children's rights under the Convention. Article 2 of the Convention obliges States parties to ensure all the rights set forth in the Convention without discrimination of any kind, "irrespective of the child's or his or her parent's or legal guardian's race, colour, sex, language, religion, political or other opinion, national, ethnic or social origin, property, disability, birth or other status". The Committee interprets "other status" under article 2 of the Convention to include HIV/AIDS status of the child or his/her parent(s). Laws, policies, strategies and practices should address all forms of discrimination that contribute to increasing the impact of the epidemic. Strategies should also promote education and training programmes explicitly designed to change attitudes of discrimination and stigmatization associated with HIV/AIDS.

B. *Best interests of the child (art. 3)*

10. Policies and programmes for the prevention, care and treatment of HIV/AIDS have generally been designed for adults with scarce attention to the principle of the best interests of the child as a primary consideration. Article 3, paragraph 1, of the Convention states "In all actions concerning children, whether undertaken by public or private social welfare institutions, courts of law, administrative authorities or legislative bodies, the best interests of the child shall be a primary consideration". The obligations attached to this right are fundamental to guiding the action of States in relation to HIV/AIDS. The child should be placed at the centre of the response to the pandemic, and strategies should be adapted to children's rights and needs.

C. *The right to life, survival and development (art. 6)*

11. Children have the right not to have their lives arbitrarily taken, as well as to benefit from economic and social policies that will allow them to survive into adulthood and develop in the broadest sense of the word. State obligation to realize the right to life, survival and development also highlights the need to give careful attention to sexuality as well as to the behaviours and lifestyles of children, even if they do not conform with what society determines to be acceptable under prevailing cultural norms for a particular age group. In this regard, the female child is often subject to harmful traditional practices, such as early and/or forced marriage, which violate her rights and make her more vulnerable to HIV infection, including because such practices often interrupt access to education and information. Effective prevention programmes are only those that acknowledge the realities of the lives of adolescents, while addressing sexuality by ensuring equal access to appropriate information, life skills, and to preventive measures.

D. The right to express views and have them taken into account (art. 12)

12. Children are rights holders and have a right to participate, in accordance with their evolving capacities, in raising awareness by speaking out about the impact of HIV/AIDS on their lives and in the development of HIV/AIDS policies and programmes. Interventions have been found to benefit children most when they are actively involved in assessing needs, devising solutions, shaping strategies and carrying them out rather than being seen as objects for whom decisions are made. In this regard, the participation of children as peer educators, both within and outside schools, should be actively promoted. States, international agencies and non-governmental organizations must provide children with a supportive and enabling environment to carry out their own initiatives, and to fully participate at both community and national levels in HIV policy and programme conceptualization, design, implementation, coordination, monitoring and review. A variety of approaches are likely to be necessary to ensure the participation of children from all sectors of society, including mechanisms which encourage children, consistent with their evolving capacities, to express their views, have them heard, and given due weight in accordance with their age and maturity (art. 12, para. 1). Where appropriate, the involvement of children living with HIV/AIDS in raising awareness, by sharing their experiences with their peers and others, is critical both to effective prevention and to reducing stigmatization and discrimination. States parties must ensure that children who participate in these awareness-raising efforts do so voluntarily, after being counselled, and that they receive both the social support and legal protection to allow them to lead normal lives during and after their involvement.

E. Obstacles

13. Experience has shown that many obstacles hinder effective prevention, delivery of care services and support for community initiatives on HIV/AIDS. These are mainly cultural, structural and financial. Denying that a problem exists, cultural practices and attitudes, including taboos and stigmatization, poverty and patronizing attitudes towards children are just some of the obstacles that may block the political and individual commitment needed for effective programmes.

14. With regard to financial, technical and human resources, the Committee is aware that such resources may not be immediately available. However, concerning this obstacle, the Committee wishes to remind States parties of their obligations under article 4. It further notes that resource constraints should not be used by States parties to justify their failure to take any or enough of the technical or financial measures required. Finally, the Committee wishes to emphasize in this regard the essential role of international cooperation.

IV. PREVENTION, CARE, TREATMENT AND SUPPORT

15. The Committee wishes to stress that prevention, care, treatment and support are mutually reinforcing elements and provide a continuum within an effective response to HIV/AIDS.

A. Information on HIV prevention and awareness-raising

16. Consistent with the obligations of States parties in relation to the rights to health and information (arts. 24, 13 and 17), children should have the right to access adequate information related to HIV/AIDS prevention and care, through formal channels (e.g. through educational opportunities and child-targeted media) as well as informal channels (e.g. those targeting street children, institutionalized children or children living in difficult circumstances). States parties are reminded that children require relevant, appropriate and timely information which recognizes the differences in levels of

understanding among them, is tailored appropriately to age level and capacity and enables them to deal positively and responsibly with their sexuality in order to protect themselves from HIV infection. The Committee wishes to emphasize that effective HIV/AIDS prevention requires States to refrain from censoring, withholding or intentionally misrepresenting health-related information, including sexual education and information, and that, consistent with their obligations to ensure the right to life, survival and development of the child (art. 6), States parties must ensure that children have the ability to acquire the knowledge and skills to protect themselves and others as they begin to express their sexuality.

17. Dialogue with community, family and peer counsellors, and the provision of "life skills" education within schools, including skills in communicating on sexuality and healthy living, have been found to be useful approaches to delivering HIV prevention messages to both girls and boys, but different approaches may be necessary to reach different groups of children. States parties must make efforts to address gender differences as they may impact on the access children have to prevention messages, and ensure that children are reached with appropriate prevention messages even if they face constraints due to language, religion, disability or other factors of discrimination. Particular attention must be paid to raising awareness among hard-to-reach populations. In this respect, the role of the mass media and/or oral tradition in ensuring that children have access to information and material, as recognized in article 17 of the Convention, is crucial both to providing appropriate information and to reducing stigmatization and discrimination. States parties should support the regular monitoring and evaluation of HIV/AIDS awareness campaigns to ascertain their effectiveness in providing information, reducing ignorance, stigmatization and discrimination, as well as addressing fear and misperceptions concerning HIV and its transmission among children, including adolescents.

B. The role of education

18. Education plays a critical role in providing children with relevant and appropriate information on HIV/AIDS, which can contribute to increased awareness and better understanding of this pandemic and prevent negative attitudes towards victims of HIV/AIDS (see also the Committee's General Comment No. 1 on the aims of education). Furthermore, education can and should empower children to protect themselves from the risk of HIV infection. In this regard, the Committee wishes to remind States parties of their obligation to ensure that primary education is available to all children, whether infected, orphaned or otherwise affected by HIV/AIDS. In many communities where HIV has spread widely, children from affected families, in particular girls, are facing serious difficulties staying in school and the number of teachers and other school employees lost to AIDS is limiting and threatening to destroy the ability of children to access education. States parties must make adequate provision to ensure that children affected by HIV/AIDS can stay in school and ensure the qualified replacement of sick teachers so that children's regular attendance at schools is not affected, and that the right to education (art. 28) of all children living within these communities is fully protected.

19. States parties must make every effort to ensure that schools are safe places for children, which offer them security and do not contribute to their vulnerability to HIV infection. In accordance with article 34 of the Convention, States parties are under obligation to take all appropriate measures to prevent, inter alia, the inducement or coercion of a child to engage in any unlawful sexual activity.

C. Child and adolescent sensitive health services

20. The Committee is concerned that health services are generally still insufficiently responsive to the needs of children under 18 years of age, in particular adolescents. As the Committee has noted on numerous occasions, children are more likely to use services that are friendly and supportive, provide a wide range of services and information, are geared to their needs, give them the opportunity to participate in decisions affecting their health, are accessible, affordable, confidential and non-judgemental, do not require parental consent and are not discriminatory. In the context of HIV/AIDS and taking into account the evolving capacities of the child, States parties are encouraged to ensure that health services employ trained personnel who fully respect the rights of children to privacy (art. 16) and non-discrimination in offering them access to HIV-related information, voluntary counselling and testing, knowledge of their HIV status, confidential sexual and reproductive health services, and free or low-cost contraceptive, methods and services, as well as HIV-related care and treatment if and when needed, including for the prevention and treatment of health problems related to HIV/AIDS, e.g. tuberculosis and opportunistic infections.

21. In some countries, even when child- and adolescent-friendly HIV-related services are available, they are not sufficiently accessible to children with disabilities, indigenous children, children belonging to minorities, children living in rural areas, children living in extreme poverty or children who are otherwise marginalized within the society. In others, where the health system's overall capacity is already strained, children with HIV have been routinely denied access to basic health care. States parties must ensure that services are provided to the maximum extent possible to all children living within their borders, without discrimination, and that they sufficiently take into account differences in gender, age and the social, economic, cultural and political context in which children live.

D. HIV counselling and testing

22. The accessibility of voluntary, confidential HIV counselling and testing services, with due attention to the evolving capacities of the child, is fundamental to the rights and health of children. Such services are critical to children's ability to reduce the risk of contracting or transmitting HIV, to access HIV-specific care, treatment and support, and to better plan for their futures. Consistent with their obligation under article 24 of the Convention to ensure that no child is deprived of his or her right of access to necessary health services, States parties should ensure access to voluntary, confidential HIV counselling and testing for all children.

23. The Committee wishes to stress that, as the duty of States parties is first and foremost to ensure that the rights of the child are protected, States parties must refrain from imposing mandatory HIV/AIDS testing of children in all circumstances and ensure protection against it. While the evolving capacities of the child will determine whether consent is required from him or her directly or from his or her parent or guardian, in all cases, consistent with the child's right to receive information under articles 13 and 17 of the Convention, States parties must ensure that, prior to any HIV testing, whether by health-care providers in relation to children who are accessing health services for another medical condition or otherwise, the risks and benefits of such testing are sufficiently conveyed so that an informed decision can be made.

24. States parties must protect the confidentiality of HIV test results, consistent with the obligation to protect the right to privacy of children (art. 16), including within health and social welfare settings, and information on the HIV status of children may not be disclosed to third parties, including parents, without the child's consent.

E. Mother-to-child transmission

25. Mother-to-child transmission (MTCT) is responsible for the majority of HIV infections in infants and young children. Infants and young children can be infected with HIV during pregnancy, labour and delivery, and through breastfeeding. States parties are requested to ensure implementation of the strategies recommended by the United Nations agencies to prevent HIV infection in infants and young children. These include: (a) the primary prevention of HIV infection among parents-to-be; (b) the prevention of unintended pregnancies in HIV-infected women, (c) the prevention of HIV transmission from HIV-infected women to their infants; and (d) the provision of care, treatment and support to HIV-infected women, their infants and families.

26. To prevent MTCT of HIV, States parties must take steps, including the provision of essential drugs, e.g. anti-retroviral drugs, appropriate antenatal, delivery and post-partum care, and making HIV voluntary counselling and testing services available to pregnant women and their partners. The Committee recognizes that anti-retroviral drugs administered to a woman during pregnancy and/or labour and, in some regimens, to her infant, have been shown to significantly reduce the risk of transmission from mother to child. However, in addition, States parties should provide support for mothers and children, including counselling on infant feeding options. States parties are reminded that counselling of HIV-positive mothers should include information about the risks and benefits of different infant feeding options, and guidance on selecting the option most likely to be suitable for their situation. Follow-up support is also required in order for women to be able to implement their selected option as safely as possible.

27. Even in populations with high HIV prevalence, the majority of infants are born to women who are not HIV-infected. For the infants of HIV-negative women and women who do not know their HIV status, the Committee wishes to emphasize, consistent with articles 6 and 24 of the Convention, that breastfeeding remains the best feeding choice. For the infants of HIV-positive mothers, available evidence indicates that breastfeeding can add to the risk of HIV transmission by 10-20 per cent, but that lack of breastfeeding can expose children to an increased risk of malnutrition or infectious diseases other than HIV. United Nations agencies have recommended that, where replacement feeding is affordable, feasible, acceptable, sustainable and safe, avoidance of all breastfeeding by HIV-infected mothers is recommended; otherwise, exclusive breastfeeding is recommended during the first months of life and should then be discontinued as soon as it is feasible.

F. Treatment and care

28. The obligations of States parties under the Convention extend to ensuring that children have sustained and equal access to comprehensive treatment and care, including necessary HIV-related drugs, goods and services on a basis of non-discrimination. It is now widely recognized that comprehensive treatment and care includes anti-retroviral and other drugs, diagnostics and related technologies for the care of HIV/AIDS, related opportunistic infections and other conditions, good nutrition, and social, spiritual and psychological support, as well as family, community and home-based care. In this regard, States parties should negotiate with the pharmaceutical industry in order to make the necessary medicines locally available at the lowest costs possible. Furthermore, States parties are requested to affirm, support and facilitate the involvement of communities in the provision of comprehensive HIV/AIDS treatment, care and support, while at the same time complying with their own obligations under the Convention. States parties are called upon to pay special attention to addressing those factors within their societies that hinder equal access to treatment, care and support for all children.

G. Involvement of children in research

29. Consistent with article 24 of the Convention, States parties must ensure that HIV/AIDS research programmes include specific studies that contribute to effective prevention, care, treatment and impact reduction for children. States parties must, nonetheless, ensure that children do not serve as research subjects until an intervention has already been thoroughly tested on adults. Rights and ethical concerns have arisen in relation to HIV/AIDS biomedical research, HIV/ADS operations, and social, cultural and behavioural research. Children have been subjected to unnecessary or inappropriately designed research with little or no voice to either refuse or consent to participation. In line with the child's evolving capacities, consent of the child should be sought and consent may be sought from parents or guardians if necessary, but in all cases consent must be based on full disclosure of the risks and benefits of research to the child. States parties are further reminded to ensure that the privacy rights of children, in line with their obligations under article 16 of the Convention, are not inadvertently violated through the research process and that personal information about children, which is accessed through research, is, under no circumstances, used for purposes other than that for which consent was given. States parties must make every effort to ensure that children and, according to their evolving capacities, their parents and/or their guardians participate in decisions on research priorities and that a supportive environment is created for children who participate in such research.

V. VULNERABILITY AND CHILDREN NEEDING SPECIAL PROTECTION

30. The vulnerability of children to HIV/AIDS resulting from political, economic, social, cultural and other factors determines the likelihood of their being left with insufficient support to cope with the impact of HIV/AIDS on their families and communities, exposed to the risk of infection, subjected to inappropriate research, or deprived of access to treatment, care and support if and when HIV infection sets in. Vulnerability to HIV/AIDS is most acute for children living in refugee and internally displaced persons camps, children in detention, children living in institutions, as well as children living in extreme poverty, children living in situations of armed conflict, child soldiers, economically and sexually exploited children, and disabled, migrant, minority, indigenous, and street children. However, all children can be rendered vulnerable by the particular circumstances of their lives. Even in times of severe resource constraints, the Committee wishes to note that the rights of vulnerable members of society must be protected and that many measures can be pursued with minimum resource implications. Reducing vulnerability to HIV/AIDS requires first and foremost that children, their families and communities be empowered to make informed choices about decisions, practices or policies affecting them in relation to HIV/AIDS.

A. Children affected and orphaned by HIV/AIDS

31. Special attention must be given to children orphaned by AIDS and to children from affected families, including child-headed households, as these impact on vulnerability to HIV infection. For children from families affected by HIV/AIDS, the stigmatization and social isolation they experience may be accentuated by the neglect or violation of their rights, in particular discrimination resulting in a decrease or loss of access to education, health and social services. The Committee wishes to underline the necessity of providing legal, economic and social protection to affected children to ensure their access to education, inheritance, shelter and health and social services, as well as to make them feel secure in disclosing their HIV status and that of their family members when the children deem it appropriate. In this respect, States parties are reminded that these

measures are critical to the realization of the rights of children and to giving them the skills and support necessary to reduce their vulnerability and risk of becoming infected.

32. The Committee wishes to emphasize the critical implications of proof of identity for children affected by HIV/AIDS, as it relates to securing recognition as a person before the law, safeguarding the protection of rights, in particular to inheritance, education, health and other social services, as well as to making children less vulnerable to abuse and exploitation, particularly if separated from their families due to illness or death. In this respect, birth registration is critical to ensuring the rights of the child and is also necessary to minimize the impact of HIV/AIDS on the lives of affected children. States parties are, therefore, reminded of their obligation under article 7 of the Convention to ensure that systems are in place for the registration of every child at or immediately after birth.

33. The trauma HIV/AIDS brings to the lives of orphans often begins with the illness and death of one of their parents, and is frequently compounded by the effects of stigmatization and discrimination. In this respect, States parties are particularly reminded to ensure that both law and practice support the inheritance and property rights of orphans, with particular attention to the underlying gender-based discrimination which may interfere with the fulfilment of these rights. Consistent with their obligations under article 27 of the Convention, States parties must also support and strengthen the capacity of families and communities of children orphaned by AIDS to provide them with a standard of living adequate for their physical, mental, spiritual, moral, economic and social development, including access to psychosocial care, as needed.

34. Orphans are best protected and cared for when efforts are made to enable siblings to remain together, and in the care of relatives or family members. The extended family, with the support of the surrounding community, may be the least traumatic and therefore the best way to care for orphans when there are no other feasible alternatives. Assistance must be provided so that, to the maximum extent possible, children can remain within existing family structures. This option may not be available due to the impact HIV/AIDS has on the extended family. In that case, States parties should provide, as far as possible, for family-type alternative care (e.g. foster care). States parties are encouraged to provide support, financial and otherwise, when necessary, to child-headed households. States parties must ensure that their strategies recognize that communities are at the front line of the response to HIV/AIDS and that these strategies are designed to assist communities in determining how best to provide support to the orphans living there.

35. Although institutionalized care may have detrimental effects on child development, States parties may, nonetheless, determine that it has an interim role to play in caring for children orphaned by HIV/AIDS when family-based care within their own communities is not a possibility. It is the opinion of the Committee that any form of institutionalized care for children should only serve as a measure of last resort, and that measures must be fully in place to protect the rights of the child and guard against all forms of abuse and exploitation. In keeping with the right of children to special protection and assistance when within these environments, and consistent with articles 3, 20 and 25 of the Convention, strict measures are needed to ensure that such institutions meet specific standards of care and comply with legal protection safeguards. States parties are reminded that limits must be placed on the length of time children spend in these institutions, and programmes must be developed to support any children who stay in these institutions, whether infected or affected by HIV/AIDS, to successfully reintegrate them into their communities.

B. Victims of sexual and economic exploitation

36. Girls and boys who are deprived of the means of survival and development, particularly children orphaned by AIDS, may be subjected to sexual and economic exploitation in a variety of ways, including the exchange of sexual services or hazardous work for money to survive, support their sick or dying parents and younger siblings, or to pay for school fees. Children who are infected or directly affected by HIV/AIDS may find themselves at a double disadvantage – experiencing discrimination on the basis of both their social and economic marginalization and their, or their parents', HIV status. Consistent with the right of children under articles 32, 34, 35 and 36 of the Convention, and in order to reduce children's vulnerability to HIV/AIDS, States parties are under obligation to protect children from all forms of economic and sexual exploitation, including ensuring they do not fall prey to prostitution networks, and that they are protected from performing any work likely to be prejudicial to, or to interfere with, their education, health, or physical, mental, spiritual, moral or social development. States parties must take bold action to protect children from sexual and economic exploitation, trafficking and sale and, consistent with the rights under article 39, create opportunities for those who have been subjected to such treatment to benefit from the support and caring services of the State and non-governmental entities engaged in these issues.

C. Victims of violence and abuse

37. Children may be exposed to various forms of violence and abuse which may increase the risk of their becoming HIV-infected, and may also be subjected to violence as a result of their being infected or affected by HIV/AIDS. Violence, including rape and other forms of sexual abuse, can occur in the family or foster setting or may be perpetrated by those with specific responsibilities towards children, including teachers and employees of institutions working with children, such as prisons and institutions concerned with mental health and other disabilities. In keeping with the rights of the child set forth in article 19 of the Convention, States parties have the obligation to protect children from all forms of violence and abuse, whether at home, in school or other institutions, or in the community.

38. Programmes must be specifically adapted to the environment in which children live, to their ability to recognize and report abuses and to their individual capacity and autonomy. The Committee considers that the relationship between HIV/AIDS and the violence or abuse suffered by children in the context of war and armed conflict requires specific attention. Measures to prevent violence and abuse in these situations are critical, and States parties must ensure the incorporation of HIV/AIDS and child rights issues in addressing and supporting children – girls and boys – who were used by military or other uniformed personnel to provide domestic help or sexual services, or who are internally displaced or living in refugee camps. In keeping with States parties' obligations, including under articles 38 and 39 of the Convention, active information campaigns, combined with the counselling of children and mechanisms for the prevention and early detection of violence and abuse, must be put in place within conflict- and disaster-affected regions, and must form part of national and community responses to HIV/AIDS.

Substance abuse

39. The use of substances, including alcohol and drugs, may reduce the ability of children to exert control over their sexual conduct and, as a result, may increase their vulnerability to HIV infection. Injecting practices using unsterilized instruments further increase the risk of HIV transmission. The Committee notes that greater understanding of substance use behaviours among children is needed, including the impact that neglect

and violation of the rights of the child has on these behaviours. In most countries, children have not benefited from pragmatic HIV prevention programmes related to substance use, which even when they do exist have largely targeted adults. The Committee wishes to emphasize that policies and programmes aimed at reducing substance use and HIV transmission must recognize the particular sensitivities and lifestyles of children, including adolescents, in the context of HIV/AIDS prevention. Consistent with the rights of children under articles 33 and 24 of the Convention, States parties are obligated to ensure the implementation of programmes which aim to reduce the factors that expose children to the use of substances, as well as those that provide treatment and support to children who are abusing substances.

VI. RECOMMENDATIONS

40. The Committee hereby reaffirms the recommendations, which emerged at the day of general discussion on children living in a world with HIV/AIDS (CRC/C/80), and calls upon States parties:

(a) To adopt and implement national and local HIV/AIDS-related policies, including effective plans of action, strategies, and programmes that are child-centred, rights-based and incorporate the rights of the child under the Convention, including by taking into account the recommendations made in the previous paragraphs of the present General Comment and those adopted at the United Nations General Assembly special session on children (2002);

(b) To allocate financial, technical and human resources, to the maximum extent possible, to supporting national and community-based action (art. 4), and, where appropriate, within the context of international cooperation (see paragraph 41 below).

(c) To review existing laws or enact new legislation with a view to implementing fully article 2 of the Convention, and in particular to expressly prohibiting discrimination based on real or perceived HIV/AIDS status so as to guarantee equal access for of all children to all relevant services, with particular attention to the child's right to privacy and confidentiality and to other recommendations made by the Committee in the previous paragraphs relevant to legislation;

(d) To include HIV/AIDS plans of action, strategies, policies and programmes in the work of national mechanisms responsible for monitoring and coordinating children's rights and to consider the establishment of a review procedure, which responds specifically to complaints of neglect or violation of the rights of the child in relation to HIV/AIDS, whether this entails the creation of a new legislative or administrative body or is entrusted to an existing national institution;

(e) To reassess their HIV-related data collection and evaluation to ensure that they adequately cover children as defined under the Convention, are disaggregated by age and gender ideally in five-year age groups, and include, as far as possible, children belonging to vulnerable groups and those in need of special protection;

(f) To include, in their reporting process under article 44 of the Convention, information on national HIV/AIDS policies and programmes and, to the extent possible, budgeting and resource allocations at the national, regional and local levels, as well as within these breakdowns the proportions allocated to prevention, care, research and impact reduction. Specific attention must be given to the extent to which these programmes and policies explicitly recognize children (in the light of their evolving capacities) and their rights, and the extent to which HIV-related rights of children are dealt with in laws, policies and practices, with specific attention to discrimination against children on the basis of their HIV status, as well as because they are orphans or the children of parents living with HIV/AIDS. The Committee requests States parties to provide a detailed indication in their reports of what they consider to be the most important priorities within their jurisdiction in relation to children and HIV/AIDS, and to outline the programme of activities they intend to pursue over the coming five years in order to address the problems identified. This would allow activities to be progressively assessed over time.

41. In order to promote international cooperation, the Committee calls upon UNICEF, World Health Organization, United Nations Population Fund, UNAIDS and other relevant international bodies, organizations and agencies to contribute systematically, at the national level, to efforts to ensure the rights of children in the context of HIV/AIDS, and also to continue to work with the Committee to improve the rights of the child in the context of HIV/AIDS. Further, the Committee urges States providing development cooperation to ensure that HIV/AIDS strategies are so designed as to take fully into account the rights of the child.

42. Non-governmental organizations, as well as community-based groups and other civil society actors, such as youth groups, faith-based organizations, women's organizations and traditional leaders, including religious and cultural leaders, all have a vital role to play in the response to the HIV/AIDS pandemic. States parties are called upon to ensure an enabling environment for participation by civil society groups, which includes facilitating collaboration and coordination among the various players, and that these groups are given the support needed to enable them to operate effectively without impediment (in this regard, States parties are specifically encouraged to support the full involvement of people living with HIV/AIDS, with particular attention to the inclusion of children, in the provision of HIV/AIDS prevention, care, treatment and support services).

General comment No 4 (2003)
Adolescent health and development in the context of the Convention on the Rights of the Child

INTRODUCTION

1.   The Convention on the Rights of the Child defines a child as "every human being below the age of 18 years unless, under the law applicable, majority is attained earlier" (art. 1). Consequently, adolescents up to 18 years old are holders of all the rights enshrined in the Convention; they are entitled to special protection measures and, according to their evolving capacities, they can progressively exercise their rights (art. 5).

2.   Adolescence is a period characterized by rapid physical, cognitive and social changes, including sexual and reproductive maturation; the gradual building up of the capacity to assume adult behaviours and roles involving new responsibilities requiring new knowledge and skills. While adolescents are in general a healthy population group, adolescence also poses new challenges to health and development owing to their relative vulnerability and pressure from society, including peers, to adopt risky health behaviour. These challenges include developing an individual identity and dealing with one's sexuality. The dynamic transition period to adulthood is also generally a period of positive changes, prompted by the significant capacity of adolescents to learn rapidly, to experience new and diverse situations, to develop and use critical thinking, to familiarize themselves with freedom, to be creative and to socialize.

3.   The Committee on the Rights of the Child notes with concern that in implementing their obligations under the Convention, States parties have not given sufficient attention to the specific concerns of adolescents as rights holders and to promoting their health and development. This has motivated the Committee to adopt the present general comment in order to raise awareness and provide States parties with guidance and support in their efforts to guarantee the respect for, protection and fulfilment of the rights of adolescents, including through the formulation of specific strategies and policies.

4.   The Committee understands the concepts of "health and development" more broadly than being strictly limited to the provisions defined in articles 6 (right to life, survival and development) and 24 (right to health) of the Convention. One of the aims of this general comment is precisely to identify the main human rights that need to be promoted and protected in order to ensure that adolescents do enjoy the highest attainable standard of health, develop in a well-balanced manner, and are adequately prepared to enter adulthood and assume a constructive role in their communities and in society at large. This general comment should be read in conjunction with the Convention and its two Optional Protocols on the sale of children, child prostitution and child pornography, and on the involvement of children in armed conflict, as well as other relevant international human rights norms and standards.[13]

---

[13]   These include the International Covenant on Civil and Political Rights, the International Covenant on Economic, Social and Cultural Rights, the Convention against Torture and Other Cruel, Inhuman or Degrading Treatment or Punishment, the International Convention on the Elimination of All Forms of Racial Discrimination, the International Convention on the Protection of the Rights of All Migrant Workers and Members of Their Families and the Convention on the Elimination of All Forms of Discrimination Against Women.

I. FUNDAMENTAL PRINCIPLES AND OTHER OBLIGATIONS OF STATES PARTIES

5.   As recognized by the World Conference on Human Rights (1993) and repeatedly stated by the Committee, children's rights too are indivisible and interrelated. In addition to articles 6 and 24, other provisions and principles of the Convention are crucial in guaranteeing that adolescents fully enjoy their right to health and development.

The right to non-discrimination

6.   States parties have the obligation to ensure that all human beings below 18 enjoy all the rights set forth in the Convention without discrimination (art. 2), including with regard to "race, colour, sex, language, religion, political or other opinion, national, ethnic or social origin, property, disability, birth or other status". These grounds also cover adolescents' sexual orientation and health status (including HIV/AIDS and mental health). Adolescents who are subject to discrimination are more vulnerable to abuse, other types of violence and exploitation, and their health and development are put at greater risk. They are therefore entitled to special attention and protection from all segments of society.

Appropriate guidance in the exercise of rights

7.   The Convention acknowledges the responsibilities, rights and duties of parents (or other persons legally responsible for the child) "to provide, in a manner consistent with the evolving capacities of the child, appropriate direction and guidance in the exercise by the child of the rights recognized in the Convention" (art. 5). The Committee believes that parents or other persons legally responsible for the child need to fulfil with care their right and responsibility to provide direction and guidance to their adolescent children in the exercise by the latter of their rights. They have an obligation to take into account the adolescents' views, in accordance with their age and maturity, and to provide a safe and supportive environment in which the adolescent can develop. Adolescents need to be recognized by the members of their family environment as active rights holders who have the capacity to become full and responsible citizens, given the proper guidance and direction.

Respect for the views of the child

8.   The right to express views freely and have them duly taken into account (art. 12) is also fundamental in realizing adolescents' right to health and development. States parties need to ensure that adolescents are given a genuine chance to express their views freely on all matters affecting them, especially within the family, in school, and in their communities. In order for adolescents to be able safely and properly to exercise this right, public authorities, parents and other adults working with or for children need to create an environment based on trust, information-sharing, the capacity to listen and sound guidance that is conducive for adolescents' participating equally including in decision-making processes.

Legal and judicial measures and processes

9.   Under article 4 of the Convention, "States parties shall undertake all appropriate legislative, administrative and other measures for the implementation of the rights recognized" therein. In the context of the rights of adolescents to health and development, States parties need to ensure that specific legal provisions are guaranteed under domestic law, including with regard to setting a minimum age for sexual consent, marriage and the possibility of medical treatment without parental consent. These minimum ages should be the same for boys and girls (article 2 of the Convention) and closely reflect the recognition of the status of human beings under 18 years of age as

rights holders, in accordance with their evolving capacity, age and maturity (arts. 5 and 12 to 17). Further, adolescents need to have easy access to individual complaint systems as well as judicial and appropriate non-judicial redress mechanisms that guarantee fair and due process, with special attention to the right to privacy (art. 16).

Civil rights and freedoms

10.   The Convention defines the civil rights and freedoms of children and adolescents in its articles 13 to 17. These are fundamental in guaranteeing the right to health and development of adolescents. Article 17 states that the child has the right to "access information and material from a diversity of national and international sources, especially those aimed at the promotion of his or her social, spiritual and moral well-being and physical and mental health". The right of adolescents to access appropriate information is crucial if States parties are to promote cost-effective measures, including through laws, policies and programmes, with regard to numerous health-related situations, including those covered in articles 24 and 33 such as family planning, prevention of accidents, protection from harmful traditional practices, including early marriages and female genital mutilation, and the abuse of alcohol, tobacco and other harmful substances.

11.   In order to promote the health and development of adolescents, States parties are also encouraged to respect strictly their right to privacy and confidentiality, including with respect to advice and counselling on health matters (art. 16). Health-care providers have an obligation to keep confidential medical information concerning adolescents, bearing in mind the basic principles of the Convention. Such information may only be disclosed with the consent of the adolescent, or in the same situations applying to the violation of an adult's confidentiality. Adolescents deemed mature enough to receive counselling without the presence of a parent or other person are entitled to privacy and may request confidential services, including treatment.

Protection from all forms of abuse, neglect, violence and exploitation[14]

12.   States parties must take effective measures to ensure that adolescents are protected from all forms of violence, abuse, neglect and exploitation (arts. 19, 32-36 and 38), paying increased attention to the specific forms of abuse, neglect, violence and exploitation that affects this age group. In particular, they should adopt special measures to ensure the physical, sexual and mental integrity of adolescents with disabilities, who are particularly vulnerable to abuse and neglect. States parties should also ensure that adolescents affected by poverty who are socially marginalized are not criminalized. In this regard, financial and human resources need to be allocated to promote research that would inform the adoption of effective local and national laws, policies and programmes. Policies and strategies should be reviewed regularly and revised accordingly. In taking these measures, States parties have to take into account the evolving capacities of adolescents and involve them in an appropriate manner in developing measures, including programmes, designed to protect them. In this context, the Committee emphasizes the positive impact that peer education can have, and the positive influence of proper role models, especially those in the worlds of arts, entertainment and sports.

---

[14]   See also the reports of the Committee's days of general discussion on "Violence against children" held in 2000 and 2001 and the Recommendations adopted in this regard (see CRC/C/100, chap. V and CRC/C/111, chap. V).

Data collection

13.　Systematic data collection is necessary for States parties to be able to monitor the health and development of adolescents. States parties should adopt data-collection mechanisms that allow desegregation by sex, age, origin and socio-economic status so that the situation of different groups can be followed. Data should also be collected to study the situation of specific groups such as ethnic and/or indigenous minorities, migrant or refugee adolescents, adolescents with disabilities, working adolescents, etc. Where appropriate, adolescents should participate in the analysis to ensure that the information is understood and utilized in an adolescent-sensitive way.

II. CREATING A SAFE AND SUPPORTIVE ENVIRONMENT

14.　The health and development of adolescents are strongly determined by the environments in which they live. Creating a safe and supportive environment entails addressing attitudes and actions of both the immediate environment of the adolescent – family, peers, schools and services - as well as the wider environment created by, inter alia, community and religious leaders, the media, national and local policies and legislation. The promotion and enforcement of the provisions and principles of the Convention, especially articles 2-6, 12-17, 24, 28, 29 and 31, are key to guaranteeing adolescents' right to health and development. States parties should take measures to raise awareness and stimulate and/or regulate action through the formulation of policy or the adoption of legislation and the implementation of programmes specifically for adolescents.

15.　The Committee stresses the importance of the family environment, including the members of the extended family and community or other persons legally responsible for the child or adolescent (arts. 5 and 18). While most adolescents grow up in well-functioning family environments, for some the family does not constitute a safe and supportive milieu.

16.　The Committee calls upon States parties to develop and implement, in a manner consistent with adolescents' evolving capacities, legislation, policies and programmes to promote the health and development of adolescents by (a) providing parents (or legal guardians) with appropriate assistance through the development of institutions, facilities and services that adequately support the well-being of adolescents, including, when needed, the provision of material assistance and support with regard to nutrition, clothing and housing (art. 27 (3)); (b) providing adequate information and parental support to facilitate the development of a relationship of trust and confidence in which issues regarding, for example, sexuality and sexual behaviour and risky lifestyles can be openly discussed and acceptable solutions found that respect the adolescent's rights (art. 27 (3)); (c) providing adolescent mothers and fathers with support and guidance for both their own and their children's well-being (art. 24 (f), 27 (2-3)); (d) giving, while respecting the values and norms of ethnic and other minorities, special attention, guidance and support to adolescents and parents (or legal guardians), whose traditions and norms may differ from those in the society where they live; and (e) ensuring that interventions in the family to protect the adolescent and, when necessary, separate her/him from the family, e.g. in case of abuse or neglect, are in accordance with applicable laws and procedures. Such laws and procedures should be reviewed to ensure that they conform to the principles of the Convention.

17.　The school plays an important role in the life of many adolescents, as the venue for learning, development and socialization. Article 29 (1) states that education must be directed to "the development of the child's personality, talents and mental and physical abilities to their fullest potential". In addition, general comment No. 1 on the aims of education states that "Education must also be aimed at ensuring that ... no child leaves school without being equipped to face the challenges that he or she can expect to be confronted with in life. Basic skills should include ... the ability to make well-balanced decisions; to resolve conflicts in a non-violent manner; and to develop a healthy lifestyle [and] good social relationships ...". Considering the importance of appropriate education for the current and future health and development of adolescents, as well as for their children, the Committee urges States parties, in line with articles 28 and 29 of the Convention to (a) ensure that quality primary education is compulsory and available, accessible and free to all and that secondary and higher education are available and accessible to all adolescents; (b) provide well-functioning school and recreational facilities which do not pose health risks to students, including water and sanitation and safe journeys to school; (c) take the necessary actions to prevent and prohibit all forms of violence and abuse, including sexual abuse, corporal punishment and other inhuman, degrading or humiliating treatment or punishment in school, by school personnel as well as among students; (d) initiate and support measures, attitudes and activities that promote healthy behaviour by including relevant topics in school curricula.

18.   During adolescence, an increasing number of young people are leaving school to start working to help support their families or for wages in the formal or informal sector. Participation in work activities in accordance with international standards, as long as it does not jeopardize the enjoyment of any of the other rights of adolescents, including health and education, may be beneficial for the development of the adolescent. The Committee urges States parties to take all necessary measures to abolish all forms of child labour, starting with the worst forms, to continuously review national regulations on minimum ages for employment with a view to making them compatible with international standards, and to regulate the working environment and conditions for adolescents who are working (in accordance with article 32 of the Convention, as well as ILO Conventions Nos. 138 and 182), so as to ensure that they are fully protected and have access to legal redress mechanisms.

19.   The Committee also stresses that in accordance with article 23 (3) of the Convention, the special rights of adolescents with disabilities should be taken into account and assistance provided to ensure that the disabled child/adolescent has effective access to and receives good quality education. States should recognize the principle of equal primary, secondary and tertiary educational opportunities for disabled children/adolescents, where possible in regular schools.

20.   The Committee is concerned that early marriage and pregnancy are significant factors in health problems related to sexual and reproductive health, including HIV/AIDS. Both the legal minimum age and actual age of marriage, particularly for girls, are still very low in several States parties. There are also non-health-related concerns: children who marry, especially girls, are often obliged to leave the education system and are marginalized from social activities. Further, in some States parties married children are legally considered adults, even if they are under 18, depriving them of all the special protection measures they are entitled under the Convention. The Committee strongly recommends that States parties review and, where necessary, reform their legislation and practice to increase the minimum age for marriage with and without parental consent to 18 years, for both girls and boys. The Committee on the Elimination of Discrimination against Women has made a similar recommendation (general comment No. 21 of 1994).

21.   In most countries accidental injuries or injuries due to violence are a leading cause of death or permanent disability among adolescents. In that respect, the Committee is

concerned about the injuries and death resulting from road traffic accidents, which affect adolescents disproportionately. States parties should adopt and enforce legislation and programmes to improve road safety, including driving education for and examination of adolescents and the adoption or strengthening of legislation known to be highly effective such as the obligations to have a valid driver's licence, wear seat belts and crash helmets, and the designation of pedestrian areas.

22. The Committee is also very concerned about the high rate of suicide among this age group. Mental disorders and psychosocial illness are relatively common among adolescents. In many countries symptoms such as depression, eating disorders and self-destructive behaviours, sometimes leading to self-inflicted injuries and suicide, are increasing. They may be related to, inter alia, violence, ill-treatment, abuse and neglect, including sexual abuse, unrealistically high expectations, and/or bullying or hazing in and outside school. States parties should provide these adolescents with all the necessary services.

23. Violence results from a complex interplay of individual, family, community and societal factors. Vulnerable adolescents such as those who are homeless or who are living in institutions, who belong to gangs or who have been recruited as child soldiers are especially exposed to both institutional and interpersonal violence. Under article 19 of the Convention, States parties must take all appropriate measures[15] to prevent and eliminate: (a) institutional violence against adolescents, including through legislation and administrative measures in relation to public and private institutions for adolescents (schools, institutions for disabled adolescents, juvenile reformatories, etc.), and training and monitoring of personnel in charge of institutionalized children or who otherwise have contact with children through their work, including the police; and (b) interpersonal violence among adolescents, including by supporting adequate parenting and opportunities for social and educational development in early childhood, fostering non-violent cultural norms and values (as foreseen in article 29 of the Convention), strictly controlling firearms and restricting access to alcohol and drugs.

24. In light of articles 3, 6, 12, 19 and 24 (3) of the Convention, States parties should take all effective measures to eliminate all acts and activities which threaten the right to life of adolescents, including honour killings. The Committee strongly urges States parties to develop and implement awareness-raising campaigns, education programmes and legislation aimed at changing prevailing attitudes, and address gender roles and stereotypes that contribute to harmful traditional practices. Further, States parties should facilitate the establishment of multidisciplinary information and advice centres regarding the harmful aspects of some traditional practices, including early marriage and female genital mutilation.

25. The Committee is concerned about the influence exerted on adolescent health behaviours by the marketing of unhealthy products and lifestyles. In line with article 17 of the Convention, States parties are urged to protect adolescents from information that is harmful to their health and development, while underscoring their right to information and material from diverse national and international sources. States parties are therefore urged to regulate or prohibit information on and marketing of substances such as alcohol and tobacco, particularly when it targets children and adolescents.[16]

---

[15] Ibid.

[16] As proposed in the Framework Convention on Tobacco Control (2003) of the World Health Organization.

III. INFORMATION, SKILLS DEVELOPMENT, COUNSELLING, AND HEALTH SERVICES

26.   Adolescents have the right to access adequate information essential for their health and development and for their ability to participate meaningfully in society. It is the obligation of States parties to ensure that all adolescent girls and boys, both in and out of school, are provided with, and not denied, accurate and appropriate information on how to protect their health and development and practise healthy behaviours. This should include information on the use and abuse, of tobacco, alcohol and other substances, safe and respectful social and sexual behaviours, diet and physical activity.

27.   In order to act adequately on the information, adolescents need to develop the skills necessary, including self-care skills, such as how to plan and prepare nutritionally balanced meals and proper personal hygiene habits, and skills for dealing with particular social situations such as interpersonal communication, decision-making, and coping with stress and conflict. States parties should stimulate and support opportunities to build such skills through, inter alia, formal and informal education and training programmes, youth organizations and the media.

28.   In light of articles 3, 17 and 24 of the Convention, States parties should provide adolescents with access to sexual and reproductive information, including on family planning and contraceptives, the dangers of early pregnancy, the prevention of HIV/AIDS and the prevention and treatment of sexually transmitted diseases (STDs). In addition, States parties should ensure that they have access to appropriate information, regardless of their marital status and whether their parents or guardians consent. It is essential to find proper means and methods of providing information that is adequate and sensitive to the particularities and specific rights of adolescent girls and boys. To this end, States parties are encouraged to ensure that adolescents are actively involved in the design and dissemination of information through a variety of channels beyond the school, including youth organizations, religious, community and other groups and the media.

29.   Under article 24 of the Convention, States parties are urged to provide adequate treatment and rehabilitation for adolescents with mental disorders, to make the community aware of the early signs and symptoms and the seriousness of these conditions, and to protect adolescents from undue pressures, including psychosocial stress. States parties are also urged to combat discrimination and stigma surrounding mental disorders, in line with their obligations under article 2. Every adolescent with a mental disorder has the right to be treated and cared for, as far as possible, in the community in which he or she lives. Where hospitalization or placement in a psychiatric institution is necessary, this decision should be made in accordance with the principle of the best interests of the child. In the event of hospitalization or institutionalization, the patient should be given the maximum possible opportunity to enjoy all his or her rights as recognized under the Convention, including the rights to education and to have access to recreational activities.[17] Where appropriate, adolescents should be separated from adults. States parties must ensure that adolescents have access to a personal representative other than a family member to represent their interests, when necessary and appropriate.[18] In accordance with article 25 of the Convention, States parties should undertake periodic review of the placement of adolescents in hospitals or psychiatric institutions.

---

[17]   For further guidance on this subject, refer to the Principles for the Protection of Persons with Mental Illness and for the Improvement of Mental Health Care, (General Assembly resolution 46/119 of 17 December 1991, annex).

[18]   Ibid., in particular principles 2, 3 and 7.

30.   Adolescents, both girls and boys, are at risk of being infected with and affected by STDs, including HIV/AIDS.[19] States should ensure that appropriate goods, services and information for the prevention and treatment of STDs, including HIV/AIDS, are available and accessible. To this end, States parties are urged (a) to develop effective prevention programmes, including measures aimed at changing cultural views about adolescents' need for contraception and STD prevention and addressing cultural and other taboos surrounding adolescent sexuality; (b) to adopt legislation to combat practices that either increase adolescents' risk of infection or contribute to the marginalization of adolescents who are already infected with STDs, including HIV; (c) to take measures to remove all barriers hindering the access of adolescents to information, preventive measures such as condoms, and care.

31.   Adolescent girls should have access to information on the harm that early marriage and early pregnancy can cause, and those who become pregnant should have access to health services that are sensitive to their rights and particular needs. States parties should take measures to reduce maternal morbidity and mortality in adolescent girls, particularly caused by early pregnancy and unsafe abortion practices, and to support adolescent parents. Young mothers, especially where support is lacking, may be prone to depression and anxiety, compromising their ability to care for their child. The Committee urges States parties (a) to develop and implement programmes that provide access to sexual and reproductive health services, including family planning, contraception and safe abortion services where abortion is not against the law, adequate and comprehensive obstetric care and counselling; (b) to foster positive and supportive attitudes towards adolescent parenthood for their mothers and fathers; and (c) to develop policies that will allow adolescent mothers to continue their education.

32.   Before parents give their consent, adolescents need to have a chance to express their views freely and their views should be given due weight, in accordance with article 12 of the Convention. However, if the adolescent is of sufficient maturity, informed consent shall be obtained from the adolescent her/himself, while informing the parents if that is in the "best interest of the child" (art. 3).

33.   With regard to privacy and confidentiality, and the related issue of informed consent to treatment, States parties should (a) enact laws or regulations to ensure that confidential advice concerning treatment is provided to adolescents so that they can give their informed consent. Such laws or regulations should stipulate an age for this process, or refer to the evolving capacity of the child; and (b) provide training for health personnel on the rights of adolescents to privacy and confidentiality, to be informed about planned treatment and to give their informed consent to treatment.

IV. VULNERABILITY AND RISK

34.   In ensuring respect for the right of adolescents to health and development, both individual behaviours and environmental factors which increase their vulnerability and risk should be taken into consideration. Environmental factors, such as armed conflict or social exclusion, increase the vulnerability of adolescents to abuse, other forms of violence and exploitation, thereby severely limiting adolescents' abilities to make individual, healthy behaviour choices. For example, the decision to engage in unsafe sex increases adolescents' risk of ill-health.

35.   In accordance with article 23 of the Convention, adolescents with mental and/or physical disabilities have an equal right to the highest attainable standard of physical

---

[19]   For further guidance on this issue, see general comment No. 3 (2003) on HIV/AIDS and the rights of children.

and mental health. States parties have an obligation to provide adolescents with disabilities with the means necessary to realize their rights.[20] States parties should (a) ensure that health facilities, goods and services are available and accessible to all adolescents with disabilities and that these facilities and services promote their self-reliance and their active participation in the community; (b) ensure that the necessary equipment and personal support are available to enable them to move around, participate and communicate; (c) pay specific attention to the special needs relating to the sexuality of adolescents with disabilities; and (d) remove barriers that hinder adolescents with disabilities in realizing their rights.

36.   States parties have to provide special protection to homeless adolescents, including those working in the informal sector. Homeless adolescents are particularly vulnerable to violence, abuse and sexual exploitation from others, self-destructive behaviour, substance abuse and mental disorders. In this regard, States parties are required to (a) develop policies and enact and enforce legislation that protect such adolescents from violence, e.g. by law enforcement officials; (b) develop strategies for the provision of appropriate education and access to health care, and of opportunities for the development of livelihood skills.

37.   Adolescents who are sexually exploited, including in prostitution and pornography, are exposed to significant health risks, including STDs, HIV/AIDS, unwanted pregnancies, unsafe abortions, violence and psychological distress. They have the right to physical and psychological recovery and social reintegration in an environment that fosters health, self-respect and dignity (art. 39). It is the obligation of States parties to enact and enforce laws to prohibit all forms of sexual exploitation and related trafficking; to collaborate with other States parties to eliminate intercountry trafficking; and to provide appropriate health and counselling services to adolescents who have been sexually exploited, making sure that they are treated as victims and not as offenders.

38.   Additionally, adolescents experiencing poverty, armed conflicts, all forms of injustice, family breakdown, political, social and economic instability and all types of migration may be particularly vulnerable. These situations might seriously hamper their health and development. By investing heavily in preventive policies and measures States parties can drastically reduce levels of vulnerability and risk factors; they will also provide cost-effective ways for society to help adolescents develop harmoniously in a free society.

V. NATURE OF STATES' OBLIGATIONS

39.   In exercising their obligations in relation to the health and development of adolescents, States parties shall always take fully into account the four general principles of the Convention. It is the view of the Committee that States parties must take all appropriate legislative, administrative and other measures for the realization and monitoring of the rights of adolescents to health and development as recognized in the Convention. To this end, States parties must notably fulfil the following obligations:

    (a)   To create a safe and supportive environment for adolescents, including within their family, in schools, in all types of institutions in which they may live, within their workplace and/or in the society at large;

    (b)   To ensure that adolescents have access to the information that is essential for their health and development and that they have opportunities to participate in decisions affecting their health (notably through informed consent and the right

---

[20]   United Nations Standard Rules on Equal Opportunities for Persons with Disabilities.

of confidentiality), to acquire life skills, to obtain adequate and age-appropriate information, and to make appropriate health behaviour choices;

(c)   To ensure that health facilities, goods and services, including counselling and health services for mental and sexual and reproductive health, of appropriate quality and sensitive to adolescents' concerns are available to all adolescents;

(d)   To ensure that adolescent girls and boys have the opportunity to participate actively in planning and programming for their own health and development;

(e)   To protect adolescents from all forms of labour which may jeopardize the enjoyment of their rights, notably by abolishing all forms of child labour and by regulating the working environment and conditions in accordance with international standards;

(f)   To protect adolescents from all forms of intentional and unintentional injuries, including those resulting from violence and road traffic accidents;

(g)   To protect adolescents from all harmful traditional practices, such as early marriages, honour killings and female genital mutilation;

(h)   To ensure that adolescents belonging to especially vulnerable groups are fully taken into account in the fulfilment of all aforementioned obligations;

(i)   To implement measures for the prevention of mental disorders and the promotion of mental health of adolescents.

40.   The Committee draws the attention of States parties to the general comment No. 14 on the right to the highest attainable standard of health of the Committee on Economic, Social and Cultural Rights which states that, "States parties should provide a safe and supportive environment for adolescents that ensures the opportunity to participate in decisions affecting their health, to build life skills, to acquire appropriate information, to receive counselling and to negotiate the health-behaviour choices they make. The realization of the right to health of adolescents is dependent on the development of youth-sensitive health care, which respects confidentiality and privacy and includes appropriate sexual and reproductive health services."

41.   In accordance with articles 24, 39 and other related provisions of the Convention, States parties should provide health services that are sensitive to the particular needs and human rights of all adolescents, paying attention to the following characteristics:

(a)   Availability. Primary health care should include services sensitive to the needs of adolescents, with special attention given to sexual and reproductive health and mental health;

(b)   Accessibility. Health facilities, goods and services should be known and easily accessible (economically, physically and socially) to all adolescents, without discrimination. Confidentiality should be guaranteed, when necessary;

(c)   Acceptability. While fully respecting the provisions and principles of the Convention, all health facilities, goods and services should respect cultural values, be gender sensitive, be respectful of medical ethics and be acceptable to both adolescents and the communities in which they live;

(d)   Quality. Health services and goods should be scientifically and medically appropriate, which requires personnel trained to care for adolescents, adequate facilities and scientifically accepted methods.

42.   States parties should, where feasible, adopt a multisectoral approach to the promotion and protection of adolescent health and development by facilitating effective and sustainable linkages and partnerships among all relevant actors. At the national level, such an approach calls for close and systematic collaboration and coordination within Government, so as to ensure the necessary involvement of all relevant government entities. Public health and other services utilized by adolescents should also

be encouraged and assisted in seeking collaboration with, inter alia, private and/or traditional practitioners, professional associations, pharmacies and organizations that provide services to vulnerable groups of adolescents.

43.   A multisectoral approach to the promotion and protection of adolescent health and development will not be effective without international cooperation. Therefore, States parties should, when appropriate, seek such cooperation with United Nations specialized agencies, programmes and bodies, international NGOs and bilateral aid agencies, international professional associations and other non-State actors.

General Comment No 5 (2003)
General measures of implementation of the Convention on the Rights of the Child (arts. 4, 42 and 44, para 6)

FOREWORD

The Committee on the Rights of the Child has drafted this general comment to outline States parties' obligations to develop what it has termed "general measures of implementation". The various elements of the concept are complex and the Committee emphasizes that it is likely to issue more detailed general comments on individual elements in due course, to expand on this outline. Its general comment No. 2 (2002) entitled "The role of independent national human rights institutions in the protection and promotion of the rights of the child" has already expanded on this concept.

Article 4

> "States Parties shall undertake all appropriate legislative, administrative, and other measures for the implementation of the rights recognized in the present Convention. With regard to economic, social and cultural rights, States Parties shall undertake such measures to the maximum extent of their available resources and, where needed, within the framework of international cooperation."

I. INTRODUCTION

1.   When a State ratifies the Convention on the Rights of the Child, it takes on obligations under international law to implement it. Implementation is the process whereby States parties take action to ensure the realization of all rights in the Convention for all children in their jurisdiction.[21] Article 4 requires States parties to take "all appropriate legislative, administrative and other measures" for implementation of the rights contained therein. While it is the State which takes on obligations under the Convention, its task of implementation – of making reality of the human rights of children – needs to engage all sectors of society and, of course, children themselves. Ensuring that all domestic legislation is fully compatible with the Convention and that the Convention's principles and provisions can be directly applied and appropriately enforced is fundamental. In addition, the Committee on the Rights of the Child has identified a wide range of measures that are needed for effective implementation, including the development of special structures and monitoring, training and other activities in Government, parliament and the judiciary at all levels.[22]

2.   In its periodic examination of States parties' reports under the Convention, the Committee pays particular attention to what it has termed "general measures of implementation". In its concluding observations issued following examination, the Committee provides specific recommendations relating to general measures. It expects the State party to describe action taken in response to these recommendations in its subsequent periodic report. The Committee's reporting guidelines arrange the Convention's articles in clusters,[23] the first being on "general measures of

---

[21]   The Committee reminds States parties that, for the purposes of the Convention, a child is defined as "every human being below the age of 18 years unless, under the law applicable to the child, majority is attained earlier" (art. 1).

[22]   In 1999, the Committee on the Rights of the Child held a two-day workshop to commemorate the tenth anniversary of adoption of the Convention on the Rights of the Child by the United Nations General Assembly. The workshop focused on general measures of implementation following which the Committee adopted detailed conclusions and recommendations (see CRC/C/90, para. 291).

[23]   General Guidelines Regarding the Form and Content of Initial Reports to be Submitted by States Parties under Article 44, Paragraph 1 (a) of the Convention, CRC/C/5, 15 October 1991; General Guidelines

implementation" and groups article 4 with article 42 (the obligation to make the content of the Convention widely known to children and adults; see, paragraph 66 below) and article 44, paragraph 6 (the obligation to make reports widely available within the State; see paragraph 71 below).

3.   In addition to these provisions, other general implementation obligations are set out in article 2: "States Parties shall respect and ensure the rights set forth in the present Convention to each child within their jurisdiction without discrimination of any kind ...".

4.   Also under article 3, paragraph 2, "States Parties undertake to ensure the child such protection and care as is necessary for his or her well-being, taking into account the rights and duties of his or her parents, legal guardians, or other individuals legally responsible for him or her, and, to this end, shall take all appropriate legislative and administrative measures."

5.   In international human rights law, there are articles similar to article 4 of the Convention, setting out overall implementation obligations, such as article 2 of the International Covenant on Civil and Political Rights and article 2 of the International Covenant on Economic, Social and Cultural Rights. The Human Rights Committee and the Committee on Economic, Social and Cultural Rights have issued general comments in relation to these provisions which should be seen as complementary to the present general comment and which are referred to below.[24]

6.   Article 4, while reflecting States parties' overall implementation obligation, suggests a distinction between civil and political rights and economic, social and cultural rights in its second sentence: "With regard to economic, social and cultural rights, States Parties shall undertake such measures to the maximum extent of their available resources and, where needed, within the framework of international cooperation." There is no simple or authoritative division of human rights in general or of Convention rights into the two categories. The Committee's reporting guidelines group articles 7, 8, 13-17 and 37 (a) under the heading "Civil rights and freedoms", but indicate by the context that these are not the only civil and political rights in the Convention. Indeed, it is clear that many other articles, including articles 2, 3, 6 and 12 of the Convention, contain elements which constitute civil/political rights, thus reflecting the interdependence and indivisibility of all human rights. Enjoyment of economic, social and cultural rights is inextricably intertwined with enjoyment of civil and political rights. As noted in paragraph 25 below, the Committee believes that economic, social and cultural rights, as well as civil and political rights, should be regarded as justiciable.

7.   The second sentence of article 4 reflects a realistic acceptance that lack of resources – financial and other resources – can hamper the full implementation of economic, social and cultural rights in some States; this introduces the concept of "progressive realization" of such rights: States need to be able to demonstrate that they have implemented "to the maximum extent of their available resources" and, where necessary, have sought international cooperation . When States ratify the Convention,

---

Regarding the Form and Contents of Periodic Reports to be Submitted under Article 44, Paragraph 1 (b) of the Convention on the Rights of the Child, CRC/C/58, 20 November 1996.

[24]   Human Rights Committee, general comment No. 3 (thirteenth session, 1981), *Article 2: Implementation at the national level*; Committee on Economic, Social and Cultural Rights, general comment No. 3 (fifth session, 1990), *The nature of States parties' obligations (article 2, paragraph 1, of the Covenant)*; also general comment No. 9 (nineteenth session, 1998), *The domestic application of the Covenant*, elaborating further on certain elements in general comment No. 3. A compendium of the treaty bodies' general comments and recommendations is published regularly by the Office of the High Commissioner for Human Rights (HRI/GEN/1/Rev.6).

they take upon themselves obligations not only to implement it within their jurisdiction, but also to contribute, through international cooperation, to global implementation (see paragraph 60 below).

8.   The sentence is similar to the wording used in the International Covenant on Economic, Social and Cultural Rights and the Committee entirely concurs with the Committee on Economic, Social and Cultural Rights in asserting that "even where the available resources are demonstrably inadequate, the obligation remains for a State party to strive to ensure the widest possible enjoyment of the relevant rights under the prevailing circumstances ...".[25] Whatever their economic circumstances, States are required to undertake all possible measures towards the realization of the rights of the child, paying special attention to the most disadvantaged groups.

9.   The general measures of implementation identified by the Committee and described in the present general comment are intended to promote the full enjoyment of all rights in the Convention by all children, through legislation, the establishment of coordinating and monitoring bodies – governmental and independent – comprehensive data collection, awareness-raising and training and the development and implementation of appropriate policies, services and programmes. One of the satisfying results of the adoption and almost universal ratification of the Convention has been the development at the national level of a wide variety of new child-focused and child-sensitive bodies, structures and activities – children's rights units at the heart of Government, ministers for children, inter-ministerial committees on children, parliamentary committees, child impact analysis, children's budgets and "state of children's rights" reports, NGO coalitions on children's rights, children's ombudspersons and children's rights commissioners and so on.

10.   While some of these developments may seem largely cosmetic, their emergence at the least indicates a change in the perception of the child's place in society, a willingness to give higher political priority to children and an increasing sensitivity to the impact of governance on children and their human rights.

11.   The Committee emphasizes that, in the context of the Convention, States must see their role as fulfilling clear legal obligations to each and every child. Implementation of the human rights of children must not be seen as a charitable process, bestowing favours on children.

12.   The development of a children's rights perspective throughout Government, parliament and the judiciary is required for effective implementation of the whole Convention and, in particular, in the light of the following articles in the Convention identified by the Committee as general principles:

> Article 2: the obligation of States to respect and ensure the rights set forth in the Convention to each child within their jurisdiction without discrimination of any kind. This non-discrimination obligation requires States actively to identify individual children and groups of children the recognition and realization of whose rights may demand special measures. For example, the Committee highlights, in particular, the need for data collection to be disaggregated to enable discrimination or potential discrimination to be identified. Addressing discrimination may require changes in legislation, administration and resource allocation, as well as educational measures to change attitudes. It should be emphasized that the application of the non-discrimination principle of equal access to rights does not mean

---

[25]   General comment No. 3, HRI/GEN/1/Rev.6, para. 11, p. 16.

identical treatment. A general comment by the Human Rights Committee has underlined the importance of taking special measures in order to diminish or eliminate conditions that cause discrimination.[26]

Article 3 (1): the best interests of the child as a primary consideration in all actions concerning children. The article refers to actions undertaken by "public or private social welfare institutions, courts of law, administrative authorities or legislative bodies". The principle requires active measures throughout Government, parliament and the judiciary. Every legislative, administrative and judicial body or institution is required to apply the best interests principle by systematically considering how children's rights and interests are or will be affected by their decisions and actions – by, for example, a proposed or existing law or policy or administrative action or court decision, including those which are not directly concerned with children, but indirectly affect children.

Article 6: the child's inherent right to life and States parties' obligation to ensure to the maximum extent possible the survival and development of the child. The Committee expects States to interpret "development" in its broadest sense as a holistic concept, embracing the child's physical, mental, spiritual, moral, psychological and social development. Implementation measures should be aimed at achieving the optimal development for all children.

Article 12: the child's right to express his or her views freely in "all matters affecting the child", those views being given due weight. This principle, which highlights the role of the child as an active participant in the promotion, protection and monitoring of his or her rights, applies equally to all measures adopted by States to implement the Convention.

Opening government decision-making processes to children is a positive challenge which the Committee finds States are increasingly responding to. Given that few States as yet have reduced the voting age below 18, there is all the more reason to ensure respect for the views of unenfranchised children in Government and parliament. If consultation is to be meaningful, documents as well as processes need to be made accessible. But appearing to "listen" to children is relatively unchallenging; giving due weight to their views requires real change. Listening to children should not be seen as an end in itself, but rather as a means by which States make their interactions with children and their actions on behalf of children ever more sensitive to the implementation of children's rights.

One-off or regular events like Children's Parliaments can be stimulating and raise general awareness. But article 12 requires consistent and ongoing arrangements. Involvement of and consultation with children must also avoid being tokenistic and aim to ascertain representative views. The emphasis on "matters that affect them" in article 12 (1) implies the ascertainment of the views of particular groups of children on particular issues – for example children who have experience of the juvenile justice system on proposals for law reform in that area, or adopted children and children in adoptive families on adoption law and policy. It is important that Governments develop a direct relationship with children, not simply one mediated through non-governmental organizations (NGOs) or human rights institutions. In the early years of the Convention, NGOs had played a notable role in pioneering participatory approaches with children, but it is in the interests of both Governments and children to have appropriate direct contact.

II. REVIEW OF RESERVATIONS

13. In its reporting guidelines on general measures of implementation, the Committee starts by inviting the State party to indicate whether it considers it necessary to maintain

---

[26]   Human Rights Committee, general comment No. 18 (1989), HRI/GEN/1/Rev.6, pp. 147 et seq.

the reservations it has made, if any, or has the intention of withdrawing them.[27] States parties to the Convention are entitled to make reservations at the time of their ratification of or accession to it (art. 51). The Committee's aim of ensuring full and unqualified respect for the human rights of children can be achieved only if States withdraw their reservations. It consistently recommends during its examination of reports that reservations be reviewed and withdrawn. Where a State, after review, decides to maintain a reservation, the Committee requests that a full explanation be included in the next periodic report. The Committee draws the attention of States parties to the encouragement given by the World Conference on Human Rights to the review and withdrawal of reservations.[28]

14.   Article 2 of the Vienna Convention on the Law of Treaties defines "reservation" as a "unilateral statement, however phrased or named, made by a State, when signing, ratifying, accepting, approving or acceding to a Treaty, whereby it purports to exclude or to modify the legal effect of certain provisions of the Treaty in their application to that State". The Vienna Convention notes that States are entitled, at the time of ratification or accession to a treaty, to make a reservation unless it is "incompatible with the object and purpose of the treaty" (art. 19).

15.   Article 51, paragraph 2, of the Convention on the Rights of the Child reflects this: "A reservation incompatible with the object and purpose of the present Convention shall not be permitted". The Committee is deeply concerned that some States have made reservations which plainly breach article 51 (2) by suggesting, for example, that respect for the Convention is limited by the State's existing Constitution or legislation, including in some cases religious law. Article 27 of the Vienna Convention on the Law of Treaties provides: "A party may not invoke the provisions of its internal law as justification for its failure to perform a treaty".

16.   The Committee notes that, in some cases, States parties have lodged formal objections to such wide-ranging reservations made by other States parties. It commends any action which contributes to ensuring the fullest possible respect for the Convention in all States parties.

III. RATIFICATION OF OTHER KEY INTERNATIONAL HUMAN RIGHTS INSTRUMENTS

17.   As part of its consideration of general measures of implementation, and in the light of the principles of indivisibility and interdependence of human rights, the Committee consistently urges States parties, if they have not already done so, to ratify the two Optional Protocols to the Convention on the Rights of the Child (on the involvement of children in armed conflict and on the sale of children, child prostitution and child pornography) and the six other major international human rights instruments. During its dialogue with States parties the Committee often encourages them to consider ratifying other relevant international instruments. A non-exhaustive list of these instruments is annexed to the present general comment, which the Committee will update from time to time.

---

[27]   General Guidelines Regarding the Form and Contents of Periodic Reports to be Submitted under Article 44, Paragraph 1 (b) of the Convention on the Rights of the Child, CRC/C/58, 20 November 1996, para. 11.
[28]   World Conference on Human Rights, Vienna, 14-25 June 1993, "Vienna Declaration and Programme of Action", A/CONF.157/23.

IV. LEGISLATIVE MEASURES

18.   The Committee believes a comprehensive review of all domestic legislation and related administrative guidance to ensure full compliance with the Convention is an obligation. Its experience in examining not only initial but now second and third periodic reports under the Convention suggests that the review process at the national level has, in most cases, been started, but needs to be more rigorous. The review needs to consider the Convention not only article by article, but also holistically, recognizing the interdependence and indivisibility of human rights. The review needs to be continuous rather than one-off, reviewing proposed as well as existing legislation. And while it is important that this review process should be built into the machinery of all relevant government departments, it is also advantageous to have independent review by, for example, parliamentary committees and hearings, national human rights institutions, NGOs, academics, affected children and young people and others.

19.   States parties need to ensure, by all appropriate means, that the provisions of the Convention are given legal effect within their domestic legal systems. This remains a challenge in many States parties. Of particular importance is the need to clarify the extent of applicability of the Convention in States where the principle of "self-execution" applies and others where it is claimed that the Convention "has constitutional status" or has been incorporated into domestic law.

20.   The Committee welcomes the incorporation of the Convention into domestic law, which is the traditional approach to the implementation of international human rights instruments in some but not all States. Incorporation should mean that the provisions of the Convention can be directly invoked before the courts and applied by national authorities and that the Convention will prevail where there is a conflict with domestic legislation or common practice. Incorporation by itself does not avoid the need to ensure that all relevant domestic law, including any local or customary law, is brought into compliance with the Convention. In case of any conflict in legislation, predominance should always be given to the Convention, in the light of article 27 of the Vienna Convention on the Law of Treaties. Where a State delegates powers to legislate to federated regional or territorial governments, it must also require these subsidiary governments to legislate within the framework of the Convention and to ensure effective implementation (see also paragraphs 40 et seq. below).

21.   Some States have suggested to the Committee that the inclusion in their Constitution of guarantees of rights for "everyone" is adequate to ensure respect for these rights for children. The test must be whether the applicable rights are truly realized for children and can be directly invoked before the courts. The Committee welcomes the inclusion of sections on the rights of the child in national constitutions, reflecting key principles in the Convention, which helps to underline the key message of the Convention – that children alongside adults are holders of human rights. But this inclusion does not automatically ensure respect for the rights of children. In order to promote the full implementation of these rights, including, where appropriate, the exercise of rights by children themselves, additional legislative and other measures may be necessary.

22.   The Committee emphasizes, in particular, the importance of ensuring that domestic law reflects the identified general principles in the Convention (arts. 2, 3, 6 and 12 (see paragraph 12 above)). The Committee welcomes the development of consolidated children's rights statutes, which can highlight and emphasize the Convention's principles. But the Committee emphasizes that it is crucial in addition that all relevant "sectoral" laws (on education, health, justice and so on) reflect consistently the principles and standards of the Convention.

23.   The Committee encourages all States parties to enact and implement within their jurisdiction legal provisions that are more conducive to the realization of the rights of the child than those contained in the Convention, in the light of article 41. The Committee emphasizes that the other international human rights instruments apply to all persons below the age of 18 years.

V. JUSTICIABILITY OF RIGHTS

24.   For rights to have meaning, effective remedies must be available to redress violations. This requirement is implicit in the Convention and consistently referred to in the other six major international human rights treaties. Children's special and dependent status creates real difficulties for them in pursuing remedies for breaches of their rights. So States need to give particular attention to ensuring that there are effective, child-sensitive procedures available to children and their representatives. These should include the provision of child-friendly information, advice, advocacy, including support for self-advocacy, and access to independent complaints procedures and to the courts with necessary legal and other assistance. Where rights are found to have been breached, there should be appropriate reparation, including compensation, and, where needed, measures to promote physical and psychological recovery, rehabilitation and reintegration, as required by article 39.

25.   As noted in paragraph 6 above, the Committee emphasizes that economic, social and cultural rights, as well as civil and political rights, must be regarded as justiciable. It is essential that domestic law sets out entitlements in sufficient detail to enable remedies for non-compliance to be effective.

VI. ADMINISTRATIVE AND OTHER MEASURES

26.   The Committee cannot prescribe in detail the measures which each or every State party will find appropriate to ensure effective implementation of the Convention. But from its first decade's experience of examining States parties' reports and from its ongoing dialogue with Governments and with the United Nations and United Nations-related agencies, NGOs and other competent bodies, it has distilled here some key advice for States.

27.   The Committee believes that effective implementation of the Convention requires visible cross-sectoral coordination to recognize and realize children's rights across Government, between different levels of government and between Government and civil society - including in particular children and young people themselves. Invariably, many different government departments and other governmental or quasi-governmental bodies affect children's lives and children's enjoyment of their rights. Few, if any, government departments have no effect on children's lives, direct or indirect. Rigorous monitoring of implementation is required, which should be built into the process of government at all levels but also independent monitoring by national human rights institutions, NGOs and others.

A. Developing a comprehensive national strategy rooted in the Convention

28.   If Government as a whole and at all levels is to promote and respect the rights of the child, it needs to work on the basis of a unifying, comprehensive and rights-based national strategy, rooted in the Convention.

29.   The Committee commends the development of a comprehensive national strategy or national plan of action for children, built on the framework of the Convention. The Committee expects States parties to take account of the recommendations in its concluding observations on their periodic reports when developing and/or reviewing

their national strategies. If such a strategy is to be effective, it needs to relate to the situation of all children, and to all the rights in the Convention. It will need to be developed through a process of consultation, including with children and young people and those living and working with them. As noted above (para. 12), meaningful consultation with children requires special child-sensitive materials and processes; it is not simply about extending to children access to adult processes.

30.   Particular attention will need to be given to identifying and giving priority to marginalized and disadvantaged groups of children. The non-discrimination principle in the Convention requires that all the rights guaranteed by the Convention should be recognized for all children within the jurisdiction of States. As noted above (para. 12), the non-discrimination principle does not prevent the taking of special measures to diminish discrimination.

31.   To give the strategy authority, it will need to be endorsed at the highest level of government. Also, it needs to be linked to national development planning and included in national budgeting; otherwise, the strategy may remain marginalized outside key decision-making processes.

32.   The strategy must not be simply a list of good intentions; it must include a description of a sustainable process for realizing the rights of children throughout the State; it must go beyond statements of policy and principle, to set real and achievable targets in relation to the full range of economic, social and cultural and civil and political rights for all children. The comprehensive national strategy may be elaborated in sectoral national plans of action – for example for education and health – setting out specific goals, targeted implementation measures and allocation of financial and human resources. The strategy will inevitably set priorities, but it must not neglect or dilute in any way the detailed obligations which States parties have accepted under the Convention. The strategy needs to be adequately resourced, in human and financial terms.

33.   Developing a national strategy is not a one-off task. Once drafted the strategy will need to be widely disseminated throughout Government and to the public, including children (translated into child-friendly versions as well as into appropriate languages and forms). The strategy will need to include arrangements for monitoring and continuous review, for regular updating and for periodic reports to parliament and to the public.

34.   The "national plans of action" which States were encouraged to develop following the first World Summit for Children, held in 1990, were related to the particular commitments set by nations attending the Summit.[29] In 1993, the Vienna Declaration and Programme of Action, adopted by the World Conference on Human Rights, called on States to integrate the Convention on the Rights of the Child into their national human rights action plans.[30]

35.   The outcome document of the United Nations General Assembly special session on children, in 2002, also commits States "to develop or strengthen as a matter of urgency if possible by the end of 2003 national and, where appropriate, regional action plans with a set of specific time-bound and measurable goals and targets based on this plan of

---

[29]   World Summit for Children, "World Declaration on the Survival, Protection and Development of Children and Plan of Action for Implementing the World Declaration on the Survival, Protection and Development of Children in the 1990s", CF/WSC/1990/WS-001, United Nations, New York, 30 September 1990.

[30]   World Conference on Human Rights, Vienna, 14-25 June 1993, "Vienna Declaration and Programme of Action", A/CONF.157/23.

action ...".[31] The Committee welcomes the commitments made by States to achieve the goals and targets set at the special session on children and identified in the outcome document, A World Fit for Children. But the Committee emphasizes that making particular commitments at global meetings does not in any way reduce States parties' legal obligations under the Convention. Similarly, preparing specific plans of action in response to the special session does not reduce the need for a comprehensive implementation strategy for the Convention. States should integrate their response to the 2002 special session and to other relevant global conferences into their overall implementation strategy for the Convention as a whole.

36. The outcome document also encourages States parties to "consider including in their reports to the Committee on the Rights of the Child information on measures taken and results achieved in the implementation of the present Plan of Action".[32] The Committee endorses this proposal; it is committed to monitoring progress towards meeting the commitments made at the special session and will provide further guidance in its revised guidelines for periodic reporting under the Convention.

B. Coordination of implementation of children's rights

37. In examining States parties' reports the Committee has almost invariably found it necessary to encourage further coordination of government to ensure effective implementation: coordination among central government departments, among different provinces and regions, between central and other levels of government and between Government and civil society. The purpose of coordination is to ensure respect for all of the Convention's principles and standards for all children within the State jurisdiction; to ensure that the obligations inherent in ratification of or accession to the Convention are not only recognized by those large departments which have a substantial impact on children - education, health or welfare and so on - but right across Government, including for example departments concerned with finance, planning, employment and defence, and at all levels.

38. The Committee believes that, as a treaty body, it is not advisable for it to attempt to prescribe detailed arrangements appropriate for very different systems of government across States parties. There are many formal and informal ways of achieving effective coordination, including for example inter-ministerial and interdepartmental committees for children. The Committee proposes that States parties, if they have not already done so, should review the machinery of government from the perspective of implementation of the Convention and in particular of the four articles identified as providing general principles (see paragraph 12 above).

39. Many States parties have with advantage developed a specific department or unit close to the heart of Government, in some cases in the President's or Prime Minister's or Cabinet office, with the objective of coordinating implementation and children's policy. As noted above, the actions of virtually all government departments impact on children's lives. It is not practicable to bring responsibility for all children's services together into a single department, and in any case doing so could have the danger of further marginalizing children in Government. But a special unit, if given high-level authority - reporting directly, for example, to the Prime Minister, the President or a Cabinet Committee on children - can contribute both to the overall purpose of making children more visible in Government and to coordination to ensure respect for children's rights across Government and at all levels of Government. Such a unit can be given

[31] *A World Fit for Children*, outcome document of the United Nations General Assembly special session on children, 2002, para. 59.
[32] Ibid., para. 61 (a).

responsibility for developing the comprehensive children's strategy and monitoring its implementation, as well as for coordinating reporting under the Convention.

C. Decentralization, federalization and delegation

40. The Committee has found it necessary to emphasize to many States that decentralization of power, through devolution and delegation of government, does not in any way reduce the direct responsibility of the State party's Government to fulfil its obligations to all children within its jurisdiction, regardless of the State structure.

41. The Committee reiterates that in all circumstances the State which ratified or acceded to the Convention remains responsible for ensuring the full implementation of the Convention throughout the territories under its jurisdiction. In any process of devolution, States parties have to make sure that the devolved authorities do have the necessary financial, human and other resources effectively to discharge responsibilities for the implementation of the Convention. The Governments of States parties must retain powers to require full compliance with the Convention by devolved administrations or local authorities and must establish permanent monitoring mechanisms to ensure that the Convention is respected and applied for all children within its jurisdiction without discrimination. Further, there must be safeguards to ensure that decentralization or devolution does not lead to discrimination in the enjoyment of rights by children in different regions.

D. Privatization

42. The process of privatization of services can have a serious impact on the recognition and realization of children's rights. The Committee devoted its 2002 day of general discussion to the theme "The private sector as service provider and its role in implementing child rights", defining the private sector as including businesses, NGOs and other private associations, both for profit and not-for-profit. Following that day of general discussion, the Committee adopted detailed recommendations to which it draws the attention of States parties.[33]

43. The Committee emphasizes that States parties to the Convention have a legal obligation to respect and ensure the rights of children as stipulated in the Convention, which includes the obligation to ensure that non-State service providers operate in accordance with its provisions, thus creating indirect obligations on such actors.

44. The Committee emphasizes that enabling the private sector to provide services, run institutions and so on does not in any way lessen the State's obligation to ensure for all children within its jurisdiction the full recognition and realization of all rights in the Convention (arts. 2 (1) and 3 (2)). Article 3 (1) establishes that the best interests of the child shall be a primary consideration in all actions concerning children, whether undertaken by public or private bodies. Article 3 (3) requires the establishment of appropriate standards by competent bodies (bodies with the appropriate legal competence), in particular, in the areas of health, and with regard to the number and suitability of staff. This requires rigorous inspection to ensure compliance with the Convention. The Committee proposes that there should be a permanent monitoring mechanism or process aimed at ensuring that all State and non-State service providers respect the Convention.

---

[33] Committee on the Rights of the Child, Report on its thirty-first session, September-October 2002, Day of General Discussion on "The private sector as service provider and its role in implementing child rights", paras. 630-653.

E. Monitoring implementation - the need for child impact assessment and evaluation

45.   Ensuring that the best interests of the child are a primary consideration in all actions concerning children (art. 3 (1)), and that all the provisions of the Convention are respected in legislation and policy development and delivery at all levels of government demands a continuous process of child impact assessment (predicting the impact of any proposed law, policy or budgetary allocation which affects children and the enjoyment of their rights) and child impact evaluation (evaluating the actual impact of implementation). This process needs to be built into government at all levels and as early as possible in the development of policy.

46.   Self-monitoring and evaluation is an obligation for Governments. But the Committee also regards as essential the independent monitoring of progress towards implementation by, for example, parliamentary committees, NGOs, academic institutions, professional associations, youth groups and independent human rights institutions (see paragraph 65 below).

47.   The Committee commends certain States which have adopted legislation requiring the preparation and presentation to parliament and/or the public of formal impact analysis statements. Every State should consider how it can ensure compliance with article 3 (1) and do so in a way which further promotes the visible integration of children in policy-making and sensitivity to their rights.

F. Data collection and analysis and development of indicators

48.   Collection of sufficient and reliable data on children, disaggregated to enable identification of discrimination and/or disparities in the realization of rights, is an essential part of implementation. The Committee reminds States parties that data collection needs to extend over the whole period of childhood, up to the age of 18 years. It also needs to be coordinated throughout the jurisdiction, ensuring nationally applicable indicators. States should collaborate with appropriate research institutes and aim to build up a complete picture of progress towards implementation, with qualitative as well as quantitative studies. The reporting guidelines for periodic reports call for detailed disaggregated statistical and other information covering all areas of the Convention. It is essential not merely to establish effective systems for data collection, but to ensure that the data collected are evaluated and used to assess progress in implementation, to identify problems and to inform all policy development for children. Evaluation requires the development of indicators related to all rights guaranteed by the Convention.

49.   The Committee commends States parties which have introduced annual publication of comprehensive reports on the state of children's rights throughout their jurisdiction. Publication and wide dissemination of and debate on such reports, including in parliament, can provide a focus for broad public engagement in implementation. Translations, including child-friendly versions, are essential for engaging children and minority groups in the process.

50.   The Committee emphasizes that, in many cases, only children themselves are in a position to indicate whether their rights are being fully recognized and realized. Interviewing children and using children as researchers (with appropriate safeguards) is likely to be an important way of finding out, for example, to what extent their civil rights, including the crucial right set out in article 12, to have their views heard and given due consideration, are respected within the family, in schools and so on.

G. Making children visible in budgets

51.　In its reporting guidelines and in the consideration of States parties' reports, the Committee has paid much attention to the identification and analysis of resources for children in national and other budgets.[34] No State can tell whether it is fulfilling children's economic, social and cultural rights "to the maximum extent of ... available resources", as it is required to do under article 4, unless it can identify the proportion of national and other budgets allocated to the social sector and, within that, to children, both directly and indirectly. Some States have claimed it is not possible to analyse national budgets in this way. But others have done it and publish annual "children's budgets". The Committee needs to know what steps are taken at all levels of Government to ensure that economic and social planning and decision-making and budgetary decisions are made with the best interests of children as a primary consideration and that children, including in particular marginalized and disadvantaged groups of children, are protected from the adverse effects of economic policies or financial downturns.

52.　Emphasizing that economic policies are never neutral in their effect on children's rights, the Committee has been deeply concerned by the often negative effects on children of structural adjustment programmes and transition to a market economy. The implementation duties of article 4 and other provisions of the Convention demand rigorous monitoring of the effects of such changes and adjustment of policies to protect children's economic, social and cultural rights.

H. Training and capacity-building

53.　The Committee emphasizes States' obligation to develop training and capacity-building for all those involved in the implementation process – government officials, parliamentarians and members of the judiciary – and for all those working with and for children. These include, for example, community and religious leaders, teachers, social workers and other professionals,including those working with children in institutions and places of detention, the police and armed forces, including peacekeeping forces, those working in the media and many others. Training needs to be systematic and ongoing - initial training and re-training. The purpose of training is to emphasize the status of the child as a holder of human rights, to increase knowledge and understanding of the Convention and to encourage active respect for all its provisions. The Committee expects to see the Convention reflected in professional training curricula, codes of conduct and educational curricula at all levels. Understanding and knowledge of human rights must, of course, be promoted among children themselves, through the school curriculum and in other ways (see also paragraph 69 below and the Committee's General Comment No. 1 (2001) on the aims of education).

54.　The Committee's guidelines for periodic reports mention many aspects of training, including specialist training, which are essential if all children are to enjoy their rights. The Convention highlights the importance of the family in its preamble and in many articles. It is particularly important that the promotion of children's rights should be integrated into preparation for parenthood and parenting education.

55.　There should be periodic evaluation of the effectiveness of training, reviewing not only knowledge of the Convention and its provisions but also the extent to which it has contributed to developing attitudes and practice which actively promote enjoyment by children of their rights.

---

[34]　General Guidelines Regarding the Form and Contents of Periodic Reports to be Submitted under Article 44, Paragraph 1(b), of the Convention on the Rights of the Child, CRC/C/58, 20 November 1996, para. 20.

I. Cooperation with civil society

56.   Implementation is an obligation for States parties, but needs to engage all sectors of society, including children themselves. The Committee recognizes that responsibilities to respect and ensure the rights of children extend in practice beyond the State and State-controlled services and institutions to include children, parents and wider families, other adults, and non-State services and organizations. The Committee concurs, for example, with general comment No. 14 (2000) of the Committee on Economic, Social and Cultural Rights on the right to the highest attainable standard of health, paragraph 42, of which states: "While only States are parties to the Covenant and thus ultimately accountable for compliance with it, all members of society – individuals, including health professionals, families, local communities, intergovernmental and non-governmental organizations, civil society organizations, as well as the private business sector – have responsibilities regarding the realization of the right to health. States parties should therefore provide an environment which facilitates the discharge of these responsibilities."

57.   Article 12 of the Convention, as already emphasized (see paragraph 12 above), requires due weight to be given to children's views in all matters affecting them, which plainly includes implementation of "their" Convention.

58.   The State needs to work closely with NGOs in the widest sense, while respecting their autonomy; these include, for example, human rights NGOs, child- and youth-led organizations and youth groups, parent and family groups, faith groups, academic institutions and professional associations. NGOs played a crucial part in the drafting of the Convention and their involvement in the process of implementation is vital.

59.   The Committee welcomes the development of NGO coalitions and alliances committed to promoting, protecting and monitoring children's human rights and urges Governments to give them non-directive support and to develop positive formal as well as informal relationships with them. The engagement of NGOs in the reporting process under the Convention, coming within the definition of "competent bodies" under article 45 (a), has in many cases given a real impetus to the process of implementation as well as reporting. The NGO Group for the Convention on the Rights of the Child has a very welcome, strong and supportive impact on the reporting process and other aspects of the Committee's work. The Committee underlines in its reporting guidelines that the process of preparing a report "should encourage and facilitate popular participation and public scrutiny of government policies".[35] The media can be valuable partners in the process of implementation (see also paragraph 70).

J. International cooperation

60. Article 4 emphasizes that implementation of the Convention is a cooperative exercise for the States of the world. This article and others in the Convention highlight the need for international cooperation.[36] The Charter of the United Nations (Arts. 55 and 56) identifies the overall purposes of international economic and social cooperation, and members pledge themselves under the Charter "to take joint and separate action in cooperation with the Organization" to achieve these purposes. In the United Nations Millennium Declaration and at other global meetings, including the United Nations General Assembly special session on children, States have pledged themselves, in particular, to international cooperation to eliminate poverty.

---

[35]   Ibid., para. 3.
[36]   The following articles of the Convention relate to international cooperation explicitly: articles 7 (2); 11 (2); 17 (b); 21 (e); 22 (2); 23 (4); 24 (4); 27 (4); 28 (3); 34 and 35.

61. The Committee advises States parties that the Convention should form the framework for international development assistance related directly or indirectly to children and that programmes of donor States should be rights-based. The Committee urges States to meet internationally agreed targets, including the United Nations target for international development assistance of 0.7 per cent of gross domestic product. This goal was reiterated along with other targets in the Monterrey Consensus, arising from the 2002 International Conference on Financing for Development.[37] The Committee encourages States parties that receive international aid and assistance to allocate a substantive part of that aid specifically to children. The Committee expects States parties to be able to identify on a yearly basis the amount and proportion of international support earmarked for the implementation of children's rights.

62. The Committee endorses the aims of the 20/20 initiative, to achieve universal access to basic social services of good quality on a sustainable basis, as a shared responsibility of developing and donor States. The Committee notes that international meetings held to review progress have concluded that many States are going to have difficulty meeting fundamental economic and social rights unless additional resources are allocated and efficiency in resource allocation is increased. The Committee takes note of and encourages efforts being made to reduce poverty in the most heavily indebted countries through the Poverty Reduction Strategy Paper (PRSP). As the central, country-led strategy for achieving the millennium development goals, PRSPs must include a strong focus on children's rights. The Committee urges Governments, donors and civil society to ensure that children are a prominent priority in the development of PRSPs and sectorwide approaches to development (SWAps). Both PRSPs and SWAps should reflect children's rights principles, with a holistic, child-centred approach recognizing children as holders of rights and the incorporation of development goals and objectives which are relevant to children.

63. The Committee encourages States to provide and to use, as appropriate, technical assistance in the process of implementing the Convention. The United Nations Children's Fund (UNICEF), the Office of the High Commissioner for Human Rights (OHCHR) and other United Nations and United Nations-related agencies can provide technical assistance with many aspects of implementation. States parties are encouraged to identify their interest in technical assistance in their reports under the Convention.

64. In their promotion of international cooperation and technical assistance, all United Nations and United Nations-related agencies should be guided by the Convention and should mainstream children's rights throughout their activities. They should seek to ensure within their influence that international cooperation is targeted at supporting States to fulfil their obligations under the Convention. Similarly the World Bank Group, the International Monetary Fund and World Trade Organization should ensure that their activities related to international cooperation and economic development give primary consideration to the best interests of children and promote full implementation of the Convention.

K. Independent human rights institutions

65. In its general comment No. 2 (2002) entitled "The role of independent national human rights institutions in the protection and promotion of the rights of the child", the Committee notes that it "considers the establishment of such bodies to fall within the commitment made by States parties upon ratification to ensure the implementation of the Convention and advance the universal realization of children's rights". Independent

---

[37]   Report of the International Conference on Financing for Development, Monterrey, Mexico, 18-22 March 2002 (A/Conf.198/11).

human rights institutions are complementary to effective government structures for children; the essential element is independence: "The role of national human rights institutions is to monitor independently the State's compliance and progress towards implementation and to do all it can to ensure full respect for children's rights. While this may require the institution to develop projects to enhance the promotion and protection of children's rights, it should not lead to the Government delegating its monitoring obligations to the national institution. It is essential that institutions remain entirely free to set their own agenda and determine their own activities."[38] General comment No. 2 provides detailed guidance on the establishment and operation of independent human rights institutions for children.

Article 42: Making the Convention known to adults and children

> "States Parties undertake to make the principles and provisions of the Convention widely known, by appropriate and active means, to adults and children alike."

66. Individuals need to know what their rights are. Traditionally in most, if not all, societies children have not been regarded as rights holders. So article 42 acquires a particular importance. If the adults around children, their parents and other family members, teachers and carers do not understand the implications of the Convention, and above all its confirmation of the equal status of children as subjects of rights, it is most unlikely that the rights set out in the Convention will be realized for many children.

67. The Committee proposes that States should develop a comprehensive strategy for disseminating knowledge of the Convention throughout society. This should include information on those bodies – governmental and independent – involved in implementation and monitoring and on how to contact them. At the most basic level, the text of the Convention needs to be made widely available in all languages (and the Committee commends the collection of official and unofficial translations of the Convention made by OHCHR. There needs to be a strategy for dissemination of the Convention among illiterate people. UNICEF and NGOs in many States have developed child-friendly versions of the Convention for children of various ages – a process the Committee welcomes and encourages; these should also inform children of sources of help and advice.

68. Children need to acquire knowledge of their rights and the Committee places special emphasis on incorporating learning about the Convention and human rights in general into the school curriculum at all stages. The Committee's general comment No. 1 (2001) entitled "The aims of education" (art. 29, para. 1), should be read in conjunction with this. Article 29, paragraph 1, requires that the education of the child shall be directed to "... the development of respect for human rights and fundamental freedoms ... ". The general comment underlines: "Human rights education should provide information on the content of human rights treaties. But children should also learn about human rights by seeing human rights standards implemented in practice whether at home, in school or within the community. Human rights education should be a comprehensive, lifelong process and start with the reflection of human rights values in the daily life and experiences of children."[39]

69. Similarly, learning about the Convention needs to be integrated into the initial and in-service training of all those working with and for children (see paragraph 53 above). The Committee reminds States parties of the recommendations it made following its meeting on general measures of implementation held to commemorate the tenth anniversary of adoption of the Convention, in which it recalled that "dissemination and

---

38   HRI/GEN/1/Rev. 6, para. 25, p. 295.
39   Ibid., para. 15, p. 286.

awareness-raising about the rights of the child are most effective when conceived as a process of social change, of interaction and dialogue rather than lecturing. Raising awareness should involve all sectors of society, including children and young people. Children, including adolescents, have the right to participate in raising awareness about their rights to the maximum extent of their evolving capacities".[40]

> "The Committee recommends that all efforts to provide training on the rights of the child be practical, systematic and integrated into regular professional training in order to maximize its impact and sustainability. Human rights training should use participatory methods, and equip professionals with skills and attitudes that enable them to interact with children and young people in a manner that respects their rights, dignity and self-respect."[41]

70. The media can play a crucial role in the dissemination of the Convention and knowledge and understanding of it and the Committee encourages their voluntary engagement in the process, which may be stimulated by governments and by NGOs.[42]

Article 44 (6): Making reports under the Convention widely available

> "... States Parties shall make their reports widely available to the public in their own countries."

71. If reporting under the Convention is to play the important part it should in the process of implementation at the national level, it needs to be known about by adults and children throughout the State party. The reporting process provides a unique form of international accountability for how States treat children and their rights. But unless reports are disseminated and constructively debated at the national level, the process is unlikely to have substantial impact on children's lives.

72. The Convention explicitly requires States to make their reports widely available to the public; this should be done when they are submitted to the Committee. Reports should be made genuinely accessible, for example through translation into all languages, into appropriate forms for children and for people with disabilities and so on. The Internet may greatly aid dissemination, and Governments and parliaments are strongly urged to place such reports on their web sites.

73. The Committee urges States to make all the other documentation of the examination of their reports under the Convention widely available to promote constructive debate and inform the process of implementation at all levels. In particular, the Committee's concluding observations should be disseminated to the public including children and should be the subject of detailed debate in parliament. Independent human rights institutions and NGOs can play a crucial role in helping to ensure widespread debate. The summary records of the examination of government representatives by the Committee aid understanding of the process and of the Committee's requirements and should also be made available and discussed.

NOTES
ANNEX I

RATIFICATION OF OTHER KEY INTERNATIONAL HUMAN RIGHTS INSTRUMENTS

As noted in paragraph 17 of the present general comment, the Committee on the Rights of the Child, as part of its consideration of general measures of implementation, and in the light of the principles of indivisibility and interdependence of human rights, consistently urges States parties, if they have not already done so, to ratify the two Optional Protocols to the Convention on the Rights of the Child (on the involvement of children in armed conflict and on the sale of children, child prostitution and child pornography) and the six other major

---

[40] See CRC/C/90, para. 291 (k).
[41] Ibid., para. 291 (l).
[42] The Committee held a day of general discussion on the theme "The child and the media" in 1996, adopting detailed recommendations (see CRC/C/57, paras. 242 et seq.).

international human rights instruments. During its dialogue with States parties the Committee often encourages them to consider ratifying other relevant international instruments. A non-exhaustive list of these instruments is annexed here. The Committee will update this from time to time.

– Optional Protocol to the International Covenant on Civil and Political Rights;

– Second Optional Protocol to the International Covenant on Civil and Political Rights, aiming at the abolition of the death penalty;

– Optional protocol to the Convention on the Elimination of All Forms of Discrimination against Women;

– Optional protocol to the Convention against Torture and Other Cruel, Inhuman or Degrading Treatment or Punishment;

– Convention against Discrimination in Education;

– ILO Forced Labour Convention No. 29, 1930;

– ILO Convention No. 105 on Abolition of Forced Labour, 1957;

– ILO Convention No. 138 Concerning Minimum Age for Admission to Employment, 1973;

– ILO Convention No. 182 on Worst Forms of Child Labour, 1999;

– ILO Convention No. 183 on Maternity Protection, 2000;

– Convention relating to the Status of Refugees of 1951, as amended by the Protocol relating to the Status of Refugees of 1967;

– Convention for the Suppression of the Traffic in Persons and of the Exploitation of the Prostitution of Others (1949);

– Slavery Convention (1926);

– Protocol amending the Slavery Convention (1953);

– The Supplementary Convention on the Abolition of Slavery, the Slave Trade and Institutions and Practices Similar to Slavery (1956);

– Protocol to Prevent, Suppress and Punish Trafficking in Persons, Especially Women and Children, supplementing the United Nations Convention against Transnational Organized Crime of 2000;

– Geneva Convention relative to the Protection of Civilians in Time of War;

– Protocol Additional to the Geneva Conventions of 12 August 1949 and relating to the Protection of Victims of International Armed Conflicts (Protocol I);

– Protocol Additional to the Geneva Conventions of 12 August 1949 and relating to the Protection of Victims of Non-International Armed Conflicts (Protocol II);

– Convention on the Prohibition of the Use, Stockpiling, Production and Transfer of Anti-personnel Mines and of Their Destruction;

– Statute of the International Criminal Court;

– Hague Convention on the Protection of Children and Cooperation in respect of Intercountry Adoption;

– Hague Convention on the Civil Aspects of International Child Abduction;

– Hague Convention on Jurisdiction, Applicable Law, Recognition, Enforcement and Cooperation in respect of Parental Responsibility and Measures for the Protection of Children of 1996.

General Comment No 6 (2005)
Treatment of Unaccompanied and Separated Children Outside Their Country of Origin

I. OBJECTIVES OF THE GENERAL COMMENT

1. The objective of this general comment is to draw attention to the particularly vulnerable situation of unaccompanied and separated children; to outline the multifaceted challenges faced by States and other actors in ensuring that such children are able to access and enjoy their rights; and, to provide guidance on the protection, care and proper treatment of unaccompanied and separated children based on the entire legal framework provided by the Convention on the Rights of the Child (the "Convention"), with particular reference to the principles of non-discrimination, the best interests of the child and the right of the child to express his or her views freely.

2. The issuing of this general comment is motivated by the Committee's observation of an increasing number of children in such situations. There are varied and numerous reasons for a child being unaccompanied or separated, including: persecution of the child or the parents; international conflict and civil war; trafficking in various contexts and forms, including sale by parents; and the search for better economic opportunities.

3. The issuing of the general comment is further motivated by the Committee's identification of a number of protection gaps in the treatment of such children, including the following: unaccompanied and separated children face greater risks of, inter alia, sexual exploitation and abuse, military recruitment, child labour (including for their foster families) and detention. They are often discriminated against and denied access to food, shelter, housing, health services and education. Unaccompanied and separated girls are at particular risk of gender-based violence, including domestic violence. In some situations, such children have no access to proper and appropriate identification, registration, age assessment, documentation, family tracing, guardianship systems or legal advice. In many countries, unaccompanied and separated children are routinely denied entry to or detained by border or immigration officials. In other cases they are admitted but are denied access to asylum procedures or their asylum claims are not handled in an age and gender-sensitive manner. Some countries prohibit separated children who are recognized as refugees from applying for family reunification; others permit reunification but impose conditions so restrictive as to make it virtually impossible to achieve. Many such children are granted only temporary status, which ends when they turn 18, and there are few effective return programmes.

4. Concerns such as these have led the Committee to frequently raise issues related to unaccompanied and separated children in its concluding observations. This general comment will compile and consolidate standards developed, inter alia, through the Committee's monitoring efforts and shall thereby provide clear guidance to States on the obligations deriving from the Convention with regard to this particular vulnerable group of children. In applying these standards, States parties must be cognizant of their evolutionary character and therefore recognize that their obligations may develop beyond the standards articulated herein. These standards shall in no way impair further-reaching rights and benefits offered to unaccompanied and separated children under regional human rights instruments or national systems, international and regional refugee law or international humanitarian law.

II. STRUCTURE AND SCOPE OF THE GENERAL COMMENT

5. This general comment applies to unaccompanied and separated children who find themselves outside their country of nationality (consistent with article 7) or, if stateless, outside their country of habitual residence. The general comment applies to all such children irrespective of their residence status and reasons for being abroad, and whether they are unaccompanied or separated. However, it does not apply to children who have not crossed an international border, even though the Committee acknowledges the many similar challenges related to internally displaced unaccompanied and separated children, recognizes that much of the guidance offered below is also valuable in relation to such children, and strongly encourages States to adopt relevant aspects of this general comment in relation to the protection, care and treatment of unaccompanied and separated children who are displaced within their own country.

6. While the mandate of the Committee is confined to its supervisory function in relation to the Convention, its interpretation efforts must be conducted in the context of the entirety of applicable international human rights norms and, therefore, the general comment adopts a holistic approach to the question of the proper treatment of unaccompanied and separated children. This acknowledges that all human rights, including those contained in the Convention, are indivisible and interdependent. The importance of other international human rights instruments to the protection of the child is also recognized in the preamble to the Convention.

III. DEFINITIONS

7. "Unaccompanied children" (also called unaccompanied minors) are children, as defined in article 1 of the Convention, who have been separated from both parents and other relatives and are not being cared for by an adult who, by law or custom, is responsible for doing so.

8. "Separated children" are children, as defined in article 1 of the Convention, who have been separated from both parents, or from their previous legal or customary primary caregiver, but not necessarily from other relatives. These may, therefore, include children accompanied by other adult family members.

9. A "child as defined in article 1 of the Convention", means "every human being below the age of 18 years unless under the law applicable to the child, majority is attained earlier". This means that any instruments governing children in the territory of the State cannot define a child in any way that deviates from the norms determining the age of majority in that State.

10. If not otherwise specified, the guidelines below apply equally to both unaccompanied and separated children.

11. "Country of origin" is the country of nationality or, in the case of a stateless child, the country of habitual residence.

IV. APPLICABLE PRINCIPLES

(a) Legal obligations of States parties for all unaccompanied or separated children in their territory and measures for their implementation

12. State obligations under the Convention apply to each child within the State's territory and to all children subject to its jurisdiction (art. 2). These State obligations cannot be arbitrarily and unilaterally curtailed either by excluding zones or areas from a State's territory or by defining particular zones or areas as not, or only partly, under the

jurisdiction of the State. Moreover, State obligations under the Convention apply within the borders of a State, including with respect to those children who come under the State's jurisdiction while attempting to enter the country's territory. Therefore, the enjoyment of rights stipulated in the Convention is not limited to children who are citizens of a State party and must therefore, if not explicitly stated otherwise in the Convention, also be available to all children – including asylum-seeking, refugee and migrant children – irrespective of their nationality, immigration status or statelessness.

13. Obligations deriving from the Convention vis-à-vis unaccompanied and separated children apply to all branches of government (executive, legislative and judicial). They include the obligation to establish national legislation; administrative structures; and the necessary research, information, data compilation and comprehensive training activities to support such measures. Such legal obligations are both negative and positive in nature, requiring States not only to refrain from measures infringing on such children's rights, but also to take measures to ensure the enjoyment of these rights without discrimination. Such responsibilities are not only limited to the provision of protection and assistance to children who are already unaccompanied or separated, but include measures to prevent separation (including the implementation of safeguards in case of evacuation). The positive aspect of these protection obligations also extends to requiring States to take all necessary measures to identify children as being unaccompanied or separated at the earliest possible stage, including at the border, to carry out tracing activities and, where possible and if in the child's best interest, to reunify separated and unaccompanied children with their families as soon as possible.

14. As reaffirmed in its general comment No. 5 (2003) (paras. 18-23), States parties to the Convention have to ensure that the provisions and principles of the treaty are fully reflected and given legal effect in relevant domestic legislation. In case of any conflict in legislation, predominance should always be given to the Convention, in light of article 27 of the Vienna Convention on the Law of Treaties.

15. In order to ensure a conducive legal environment and in light of article 41 (b) of the Convention, States parties are also encouraged to ratify other international instruments that address issues relating to unaccompanied and separated children, including the two Optional Protocols to the Convention on the Rights of the Child (on the involvement of children in armed conflict and on the sale of children, child prostitution and child pornography), the Convention against Torture and Other Cruel, Inhuman or Degrading Treatment or Punishment (the "CAT"), the Convention on the Elimination of All Forms of Discrimination against Women, the Convention relating to the Status of Refugees ("the 1951 Refugee Convention") and the Protocol relating to the Status of Refugees, the Convention on the Reduction of Statelessness, the Convention relating to the Status of Stateless Persons, the Hague Convention on Protection of Children and Cooperation in Respect of Inter-Country Adoption, the Hague Convention on Jurisdiction, Applicable Law, Recognition, Enforcement and Cooperation in Respect of Parental Responsibility and Measures for the Protection of Children, the four Geneva Conventions of 12 August 1949, the Protocol Additional to the Geneva Conventions of 12 August 1949 and relating to the Protection of Victims of International Armed Conflicts (Protocol I) of 8 June 1977, the Protocol Additional to the Geneva Conventions of 12 August 1949, and relating to the Protection of Victims of Non-International Armed Conflicts (Protocol II) of 8 June 1997. The Committee also encourages States parties to the Convention and others concerned to take into account

the Office of the United Nations High Commissioner for Refugees (UNHCR)'s Guidelines on Protection and Care (1994) and the Inter-Agency Guiding Principles on Unaccompanied and Separated Children.[43]

16. In view of the absolute nature of obligations deriving from the Convention and their lex specialis character, article 2, paragraph 3, of the International Covenant on Economic, Social and Cultural Rights would not apply with regard to unaccompanied and separated children. In application of article 4 of the Convention, the particular vulnerability of unaccompanied and separated children, explicitly recognized in article 20 of the Convention, must be taken into account and will result in making the assignment of available resources to such children a priority. States are expected to accept and facilitate assistance offered within their respective mandates by the United Nations Children's Fund (UNICEF), UNHCR and other agencies (article 22 (2) of the Convention) in order to meet the needs of unaccompanied and separated children.

17. The Committee believes that reservations made by States parties to the Convention should not in any way limit the rights of unaccompanied and separated children. As is systematically done with States parties during the reporting process, the Committee recommends that, in the light of the Vienna Declaration and Programme of Action adopted at the 1993 World Conference on Human Rights in Vienna,[44] reservations limiting the rights of unaccompanied and separated children be reviewed with the objective of withdrawal.

(b) Non-discrimination (art. 2)

18. The principle of non-discrimination, in all its facets, applies in respect to all dealings with separated and unaccompanied children. In particular, it prohibits any discrimination on the basis of the status of a child as being unaccompanied or separated, or as being a refugee, asylum-seeker or migrant. This principle, when properly understood, does not prevent, but may indeed call for, differentiation on the basis of different protection needs such as those deriving from age and/or gender. Measures should also be taken to address possible misperceptions and stigmatization of unaccompanied or separated children within the society. Policing or other measures concerning unaccompanied or separated children relating to public order are only permissible where such measures are based on the law; entail individual rather than collective assessment; comply with the principle of proportionality; and represent the least intrusive option. In order not to violate the prohibition on non-discrimination, such measures can, therefore, never be applied on a group or collective basis.

(c) Best interests of the child as a primary consideration in the search for short and long-term solutions (art. 3)

19. Article 3 (1) states that "[i]n all actions concerning children, whether undertaken by public or private social welfare institutions, courts of law, administrative authorities or legislative bodies, the best interests of the child shall be a primary consideration". In the case of a displaced child, the principle must be respected during all stages of the displacement cycle. At any of these stages, a best interests determination must be documented in preparation of any decision fundamentally impacting on the unaccompanied or separated child's life.

---

[43] These Guiding Principles are jointly endorsed by the International Committee of the Red Cross, the International Rescue Committee, Save the Children/UK, UNICEF, UNHCR, and World Vision International. They are intended to guide the work of all members of the Inter-Agency Standing Committee with respect to unaccompanied and separated children.

[44] Vienna Declaration and Programme of Action (A/CONF.157/23) adopted by the World Conference on Human Rights, held in Vienna, 14-25 June 1993.

20. A determination of what is in the best interests of the child requires a clear and comprehensive assessment of the child's identity, including her or his nationality, upbringing, ethnic, cultural and linguistic background, particular vulnerabilities and protection needs. Consequently, allowing the child access to the territory is a prerequisite to this initial assessment process. The assessment process should be carried out in a friendly and safe atmosphere by qualified professionals who are trained in age and gender-sensitive interviewing techniques.

21. Subsequent steps, such as the appointment of a competent guardian as expeditiously as possible, serves as a key procedural safeguard to ensure respect for the best interests of an unaccompanied or separated child. Therefore, such a child should only be referred to asylum or other procedures after the appointment of a guardian. In cases where separated or unaccompanied children are referred to asylum procedures or other administrative or judicial proceedings, they should also be provided with a legal representative in addition to a guardian.

22. Respect for best interests also requires that, where competent authorities have placed an unaccompanied or separated child "for the purposes of care, protection or treatment of his or her physical or mental health", the State recognizes the right of that child to a "periodic review" of their treatment and "all other circumstances relevant to his or her placement" (article 25 of the Convention).

(d) The right to life, survival and development (art. 6)

23. The obligation of the State party under article 6 includes protection from violence and exploitation, to the maximum extent possible, which would jeopardize a child's right to life, survival and development. Separated and unaccompanied children are vulnerable to various risks that affect their life, survival and development such as trafficking for purposes of sexual or other exploitation or involvement in criminal activities which could result in harm to the child, or in extreme cases, in death. Accordingly, article 6 necessitates vigilance by States parties in this regard, particularly when organized crime may be involved. While the issue of trafficking of children is beyond the scope of this general comment, the Committee notes that there is often a link between trafficking and the situation of separated and unaccompanied children.

24. The Committee is of the view that practical measures should be taken at all levels to protect children from the risks mentioned above. Such measures could include: priority procedures for child victims of trafficking, the prompt appointment of guardians, the provision of information to children about the risks they may encounter, and establishment of measures to provide follow-up to children particularly at risk. These measures should be regularly evaluated to ensure their effectiveness.

(e) Right of the child to express his or her views freely (art. 12)

25. Pursuant to article 12 of the Convention, in determining the measures to be adopted with regard to unaccompanied or separated children, the child's views and wishes should be elicited and taken into account (art. 12 (1)). To allow for a well-informed expression of such views and wishes, it is imperative that such children are provided with all relevant information concerning, for example, their entitlements, services available including means of communication, the asylum process, family tracing and the situation in their country of origin (arts. 13, 17 and 22 (2)). In guardianship, care and accommodation arrangements, and legal representation, children's views should also be taken into account. Such information must be provided in a manner that is appropriate to the maturity and level of understanding of each child. As participation is dependent on reliable communication, where necessary, interpreters should be made available at all stages of the procedure.

(f) Respect for the principle of non-refoulement

26. In affording proper treatment of unaccompanied or separated children, States must fully respect non-refoulement obligations deriving from international human rights, humanitarian and refugee law and, in particular, must respect obligations codified in article 33 of the 1951 Refugee Convention and in article 3 of CAT.

27. Furthermore, in fulfilling obligations under the Convention, States shall not return a child to a country where there are substantial grounds for believing that there is a real risk of irreparable harm to the child, such as, but by no means limited to, those contemplated under articles 6 and 37 of the Convention, either in the country to which removal is to be effected or in any country to which the child may subsequently be removed. Such non-refoulement obligations apply irrespective of whether serious violations of those rights guaranteed under the Convention originate from non-State actors or whether such violations are directly intended or are the indirect consequence of action or inaction. The assessment of the risk of such serious violations should be conducted in an age and gender-sensitive manner and should, for example, take into account the particularly serious consequences for children of the insufficient provision of food or health services.

28. As underage recruitment and participation in hostilities entails a high risk of irreparable harm involving fundamental human rights, including the right to life, State obligations deriving from article 38 of the Convention, in conjunction with articles 3 and 4 of the Optional Protocol to the Convention on the Rights of the Child on the involvement of children in armed conflict, entail extraterritorial effects and States shall refrain from returning a child in any manner whatsoever to the borders of a State where there is a real risk of underage recruitment, including recruitment not only as a combatant but also to provide sexual services for the military or where there is a real risk of direct or indirect participation in hostilities, either as a combatant or through carrying out other military duties.

(g) Confidentiality

29. States parties must protect the confidentiality of information received in relation to an unaccompanied or separated child, consistent with the obligation to protect the child's rights, including the right to privacy (art. 16). This obligation applies in all settings, including health and social welfare. Care must be taken that information sought and legitimately shared for one purpose is not inappropriately used for that of another.

30. Confidentiality concerns also involve respect for the rights of others. For example, in obtaining, sharing and preserving the information collected in respect of unaccompanied and separated children, particular care must be taken in order not to endanger the well-being of persons still within the child's country of origin, especially the child's family members. Furthermore, information relating to the whereabouts of the child shall only be withheld vis-à-vis the parents where required for the safety of the child or to otherwise secure the "best interests" of the child.

V. RESPONSE TO GENERAL AND SPECIFIC PROTECTION NEEDS

(a) Initial assessment and measures

31. The best interests of the child must also be a guiding principle for determining the priority of protection needs and the chronology of measures to be applied in respect of unaccompanied and separated children. This necessary initial assessment process, in particular, entails the following:

(i) Prioritized identification of a child as separated or unaccompanied immediately upon arrival at ports of entry or as soon as their presence in the country becomes known to the authorities (art. 8). Such identification measures include age assessment and should not only take into account the physical appearance of the individual, but also his or her psychological maturity. Moreover, the assessment must be conducted in a scientific, safe, child and gender-sensitive and fair manner, avoiding any risk of violation of the physical integrity of the child; giving due respect to human dignity; and, in the event of remaining uncertainty, should accord the individual the benefit of the doubt such that if there is a possibility that the individual is a child, she or he should be treated as such;

(ii) Prompt registration by means of an initial interview conducted in an age-appropriate and gender-sensitive manner, in a language the child understands, by professionally qualified persons to collect biodata and social history to ascertain the identity of the child, including, wherever possible, identity of both parents, other siblings, as well as the citizenship of the child, the siblings and the parents;

(iii) In continuation of the registration process, the recording of further information in order to meet the specific needs of the child. This information should include:
   • Reasons for being separated or unaccompanied;
   • Assessment of particular vulnerabilities, including health, physical, psychosocial, material and other protection needs, including those deriving from domestic violence, trafficking or trauma;
   • All available information to determine the potential existence of international protection needs, including those: due to a "well-founded fear of being persecuted for reasons of race, religion, nationality, membership of a particular social group or political opinion" in the child's country of origin (article 1 A (2), 1951 Refugee Convention); deriving from external aggression, occupation, foreign domination or events seriously disturbing public order (article 1 (2), Convention Governing the Specific Aspects of Refugee Problems in Africa); or relating to the indiscriminate effects of generalized violence;

(iv) Unaccompanied and separated children should be provided with their own personal identity documentation as soon as possible;

(v) Tracing of family members to be commenced as early as possible (arts. 22 (2), 9 (3) and 10 (2)).

32. Any further actions relating to the residence and other status of the child in the territory of the State should be based on the findings of an initial protection assessment carried out in accordance with the above procedures. States should refrain from referring unaccompanied and separated children into asylum procedures if their presence in the territory does not raise the question of international refugee protection needs. This is without prejudice to the obligation of States to refer unaccompanied or separated children to relevant procedures serving child protection, such as those foreseen under child welfare legislation.

(b) Appointment of a guardian or adviser and legal representative (arts. 18 (2) and 20 (1))

33. States are required to create the underlying legal framework and to take necessary measures to secure proper representation of an unaccompanied or separated child's best interests. Therefore, States should appoint a guardian or adviser as soon as the unaccompanied or separated child is identified and maintain such guardianship

arrangements until the child has either reached the age of majority or has permanently left the territory and/or jurisdiction of the State, in compliance with the Convention and other international obligations. The guardian should be consulted and informed regarding all actions taken in relation to the child. The guardian should have the authority to be present in all planning and decision-making processes, including immigration and appeal hearings, care arrangements and all efforts to search for a durable solution. The guardian or adviser should have the necessary expertise in the field of childcare, so as to ensure that the interests of the child are safeguarded and that the child's legal, social, health, psychological, material and educational needs are appropriately covered by, inter alia, the guardian acting as a link between the child and existing specialist agencies/individuals who provide the continuum of care required by the child. Agencies or individuals whose interests could potentially be in conflict with those of the child's should not be eligible for guardianship. For example, non-related adults whose primary relationship to the child is that of an employer should be excluded from a guardianship role.

34. In the case of a separated child, guardianship should regularly be assigned to the accompanying adult family member or non-primary family caretaker unless there is an indication that it would not be in the best interests of the child to do so, for example, where the accompanying adult has abused the child. In cases where a child is accompanied by a non-family adult or caretaker, suitability for guardianship must be scrutinized more closely. If such a guardian is able and willing to provide day-to-day care, but unable to adequately represent the child's best interests in all spheres and at all levels of the child's life, supplementary measures (such as the appointment of an adviser or legal representative) must be secured.

35. Review mechanisms shall be introduced and implemented to monitor the quality of the exercise of guardianship in order to ensure the best interests of the child are being represented throughout the decision-making process and, in particular, to prevent abuse.

36. In cases where children are involved in asylum procedures or administrative or judicial proceedings, they should, in addition to the appointment of a guardian, be provided with legal representation.

37. At all times children should be informed of arrangements with respect to guardianship and legal representation and their opinions should be taken into consideration.

38. In large-scale emergencies, where it will be difficult to establish guardianship arrangements on an individual basis, the rights and best interests of separated children should be safeguarded and promoted by States and organizations working on behalf of these children.

(c) Care and accommodation arrangements (arts. 20 and 22)

39. Unaccompanied or separated children are children temporarily or permanently deprived of their family environment and, as such, are beneficiaries of States' obligations under article 20 of the Convention and shall be entitled to special protection and assistance provided by the relevant State.

40. Mechanisms established under national law in order to ensure alternative care for such children in accordance with article 22 of the Convention, shall also cover unaccompanied or separated children outside their country of origin. A wide range of options for care and accommodation arrangements exist and are explicitly acknowledged in article 20 (3) as follows: "... inter alia, foster placement, kafalah of Islamic law, adoption or, if necessary, placement in suitable institutions for the care of

children". When selecting from these options, the particular vulnerabilities of such a child, not only having lost connection with his or her family environment, but further finding him or herself outside of his or her country of origin, as well as the child's age and gender, should be taken into account. In particular, due regard ought to be taken of the desirability of continuity in a child's upbringing and to the ethnic, religious, cultural and linguistic background as assessed in the identification, registration and documentation process. Such care and accommodation arrangements should comply with the following parameters:

- Children should not, as a general rule, be deprived of liberty;
- In order to ensure continuity of care and considering the best interests of the child, changes in residence for unaccompanied and separated children should be limited to instances where such change is in the best interests of the child;
- In accordance with the principle of family unity, siblings should be kept together;
- A child who has adult relatives arriving with him or her or already living in the country of asylum should be allowed to stay with them unless such action would be contrary to the best interests of the child. Given the particular vulnerabilities of the child, regular assessments should be conducted by social welfare personnel;
- Irrespective of the care arrangements made for unaccompanied or separated children, regular supervision and assessment ought to be maintained by qualified persons in order to ensure the child's physical and psychosocial health, protection against domestic violence or exploitation, and access to educational and vocational skills and opportunities;
- States and other organizations must take measures to ensure the effective protection of the rights of separated or unaccompanied children living in child-headed households;
- In large-scale emergencies, interim care must be provided for the shortest time appropriate for unaccompanied children. This interim care provides for their security and physical and emotional care in a setting that encourages their general development;
- Children must be kept informed of the care arrangements being made for them, and their opinions must be taken into consideration.

(d) Full access to education (arts. 28, 29 (1) (c), 30 and 32)

41. States should ensure that access to education is maintained during all phases of the displacement cycle. Every unaccompanied and separated child, irrespective of status, shall have full access to education in the country that they have entered in line with articles 28, 29 (1) (c), 30 and 32 of the Convention and the general principles developed by the Committee. Such access should be granted without discrimination and in particular, separated and unaccompanied girls shall have equal access to formal and informal education, including vocational training at all levels. Access to quality education should also be ensured for children with special needs, in particular children with disabilities.

42. The unaccompanied or separated child should be registered with appropriate school authorities as soon as possible and get assistance in maximizing learning opportunities. All unaccompanied and separated children have the right to maintain their cultural identity and values, including the maintenance and development of their native language. All adolescents should be allowed to enrol in vocational/professional training or education, and early learning programmes should be made available to young children. States should ensure that unaccompanied or separated children are provided

with school certificates or other documentation indicating their level of education, in particular in preparation of relocation, resettlement or return.

43. States shall, in particular where government capacity is limited, accept and facilitate the assistance offered by UNICEF, the United Nations Educational, Scientific and Cultural Organization (UNESCO), UNHCR and other United Nations agencies within their respective mandates, as well as, where appropriate, other competent intergovernmental organizations or non-governmental organizations (art. 22 (2)) in order to meet the educational needs of unaccompanied and separated children.

(e) Right to an adequate standard of living (art. 27)

44. States should ensure that separated and unaccompanied children have a standard of living adequate for their physical, mental, spiritual and moral development. As provided in article 27 (2) of the Convention, States shall provide material assistance and support programmes, particularly with regard to nutrition, clothing and housing.

45. States shall, in particular where government capacity is limited, accept and facilitate the assistance offered by UNICEF, UNESCO, UNHCR and other United Nations agencies within their respective mandates, as well as, where appropriate, other competent intergovernmental organizations or non-governmental organizations (art. 22 (2)) in order to secure an adequate standard of living for unaccompanied and separated children.

(f) Right to enjoy the highest attainable standard of health and facilities for the treatment of illness and rehabilitation of health (arts. 23, 24 and 39)

46. When implementing the right to enjoy the highest attainable standard of health and facilities for the treatment of illness and rehabilitation of health under article 24 of the Convention, States are obligated to ensure that unaccompanied and separated children have the same access to health care as children who are . . . nationals . . . .

47. In ensuring their access, States must assess and address the particular plight and vulnerabilities of such children. They should, in particular, take into account the fact that unaccompanied children have undergone separation from family members and have also, to varying degrees, experienced loss, trauma, disruption and violence. Many such children, in particular those who are refugees, have further experienced pervasive violence and the stress associated with a country afflicted by war. This may have created deep-rooted feelings of helplessness and undermined a child's trust in others. Moreover, girls are particularly susceptible to marginalization, poverty and suffering during armed conflict, and many may have experienced gender-based violence in the context of armed conflict. The profound trauma experienced by many affected children calls for special sensitivity and attention in their care and rehabilitation.

48. The obligation under article 39 of the Convention sets out the duty of States to provide rehabilitation services to children who have been victims of any form of abuse, neglect, exploitation, torture, cruel, inhuman and degrading treatment or armed conflicts. In order to facilitate such recovery and reintegration, culturally appropriate and gender-sensitive mental health care should be developed and qualified psychosocial counselling provided.

49. States shall, in particular where government capacity is limited, accept and facilitate assistance offered by UNICEF, the World Health Organization (WHO), United Nations Joint Programme on HIV/AIDS (UNAIDS), UNHCR and other agencies (art. 22 (2)) within their respective mandates, as well as, where appropriate, other competent intergovernmental organizations or non-governmental organizations in order to meet the health and health-care needs of unaccompanied and separated children.

(g) Prevention of trafficking and of sexual and other forms of exploitation, abuse and violence (arts. 34, 35 and 36)

50. Unaccompanied or separated children in a country outside their country of origin are particularly vulnerable to exploitation and abuse. Girls are at particular risk of being trafficked, including for purposes of sexual exploitation.

51. Articles 34 to 36 of the Convention must be read in conjunction with special protection and assistance obligations to be provided according to article 20 of the Convention, in order to ensure that unaccompanied and separated children are shielded from trafficking, and from sexual and other forms of exploitation, abuse and violence.

52. Trafficking of such a child, or "re-trafficking" in cases where a child was already a victim of trafficking, is one of many dangers faced by unaccompanied or separated children. Trafficking in children is a threat to the fulfilment of their right to life, survival and development (art. 6). In accordance with article 35 of the Convention, States parties should take appropriate measures to prevent such trafficking. Necessary measures include identifying unaccompanied and separated children; regularly inquiring as to their whereabouts; and conducting information campaigns that are age-appropriate, gender-sensitive and in a language and medium that is understandable to the child. Adequate legislation should also be passed and effective mechanisms of enforcement be established with respect to labour regulations and border crossing.

53. Risks are also great for a child who has already been a victim of trafficking, resulting in the status of being unaccompanied or separated. Such children should not be penalized and should receive assistance as victims of a serious human rights violation. Some trafficked children may be eligible for refugee status under the 1951 Convention, and States should ensure that separated and unaccompanied trafficked children who wish to seek asylum or in relation to whom there is otherwise indication that international protection needs exist, have access to asylum procedures. Children who are at risk of being re-trafficked should not be returned to their country of origin unless it is in their best interests and appropriate measures for their protection have been taken. States should consider complementary forms of protection for trafficked children when return is not in their best interests.

(h) Prevention of military recruitment and protection against effects of war (arts. 38 and 39)

Prevention of recruitment

54. State obligations deriving from article 38 of the Convention and from articles 3 and 4 of the Optional Protocol to the Convention on the Rights of the Child on the involvement of children in armed conflict also apply to unaccompanied and separated children. A State must take all necessary measures to prevent recruitment or use of such children by any party to a conflict. This also applies to former child soldiers who have defected from their units and who require protection against re-recruitment.

Care arrangements

55. Care arrangements for unaccompanied and separated children shall be made in a manner which prevents their recruitment, re-recruitment or use by any party to a conflict. Guardianships should not be given to individuals or organizations who are directly or indirectly involved in a conflict.

Former child soldiers

56. Child soldiers should be considered primarily as victims of armed conflict. Former child soldiers, who often find themselves unaccompanied or separated at the cessation of

the conflict or following defection, shall be given all the necessary support services to enable reintegration into normal life, including necessary psychosocial counselling. Such children shall be identified and demobilized on a priority basis during any identification and separation operation. Child soldiers, in particular, those who are unaccompanied or separated, should not normally be interned, but rather, benefit from special protection and assistance measures, in particular as regards their demobilization and rehabilitation. Particular efforts must be made to provide support and facilitate the reintegration of girls who have been associated with the military, either as combatants or in any other capacity.

57. If, under certain circumstances, exceptional internment of a child soldier over the age of 15 years is unavoidable and in compliance with international human rights and humanitarian law, for example, where she or he poses a serious security threat, the conditions of such internment should be in conformity with international standards, including article 37 of the Convention and those pertaining to juvenile justice, and should not preclude any tracing efforts and priority participation in rehabilitation programmes.

Non-refoulement

58. As under-age recruitment and participation in hostilities entails a high risk of irreparable harm involving fundamental human rights, including the right to life, State obligations deriving from article 38 of the Convention, in conjunction with articles 3 and 4 of the Optional Protocol to the Convention on the Rights of the Child on the involvement of children in armed conflict, entail extraterritorial effects and States shall refrain from returning a child in any manner whatsoever to the borders of a State where there is a real risk of under-age recruitment or participation, directly or indirectly, in hostilities.

Child-specific forms and manifestations of persecution[45]

59. Reminding States of the need for age and gender-sensitive asylum procedures and an age and gender-sensitive interpretation of the refugee definition, the Committee highlights that under-age recruitment (including of girls for sexual services or forced marriage with the military) and direct or indirect participation in hostilities constitutes a serious human rights violation and thereby persecution, and should lead to the granting of refugee status where the well-founded fear of such recruitment or participation in hostilities is based on "reasons of race, religion, nationality, membership of a particular social group or political opinion" (article 1A (2), 1951 Refugee Convention).

Rehabilitation and recovery

60. States shall develop, where needed, in cooperation with international agencies and NGOs, a comprehensive age-appropriate and gender-sensitive system of psychological support and assistance for unaccompanied and separated children affected by armed conflict.

(i) Prevention of deprivation of liberty and treatment in cases thereof

61. In application of article 37 of the Convention and the principle of the best interests of the child, unaccompanied or separated children should not, as a general rule, be detained. Detention cannot be justified solely on the basis of the child being unaccompanied or separated, or on their migratory or residence status, or lack thereof. Where detention is exceptionally justified for other reasons, it shall be conducted in

---

[45]   On child-specific forms and manifestations of persecution more generally, see section VI (d) below "Child sensitive assessment of protection needs, taking into account persecution of a child-specific nature".

accordance with article 37 (b) of the Convention that requires detention to conform to the law of the relevant country and only to be used as a measure of last resort and for the shortest appropriate period of time. In consequence, all efforts, including acceleration of relevant processes, should be made to allow for the immediate release of unaccompanied or separated children from detention and their placement in other forms of appropriate accommodation.

62. In addition to national requirements, international obligations constitute part of the law governing detention. With regard to asylum-seeking, unaccompanied and separated children, States must, in particular, respect their obligations deriving from article 31 (1) of the 1951 Refugee Convention. States should further take into account that illegal entry into or stay in a country by an unaccompanied or separated child may also be justified according to general principles of law, where such entry or stay is the only way of preventing a violation of the fundamental human rights of the child. More generally, in developing policies on unaccompanied or separated children, including those who are victims of trafficking and exploitation, States should ensure that such children are not criminalized solely for reasons of illegal entry or presence in the country.

63. In the exceptional case of detention, conditions of detention must be governed by the best interests of the child and pay full respect to article 37 (a) and (c) of the Convention and other international obligations. Special arrangements must be made for living quarters that are suitable for children and that separate them from adults, unless it is considered in the child's best interests not to do so. Indeed, the underlying approach to such a programme should be "care" and not "detention". Facilities should not be located in isolated areas where culturally appropriate community resources and access to legal aid are unavailable. Children should have the opportunity to make regular contact and receive visits from friends, relatives, religious, social and legal counsel and their guardian. They should also be provided with the opportunity to receive all basic necessities as well as appropriate medical treatment and psychological counselling where necessary. During their period in detention, children have the right to education which ought, ideally, to take place outside the detention premises in order to facilitate the continuance of their education upon release. They also have the right to recreation and play as provided for in article 31 of the Convention. In order to effectively secure the rights provided by article 37 (d) of the Convention, unaccompanied or separated children deprived of their liberty shall be provided with prompt and free access to legal and other appropriate assistance, including the assignment of a legal representative.

VI. ACCESS TO THE ASYLUM PROCEDURE, LEGAL SAFEGUARDS AND RIGHTS IN ASYLUM

(a) General

64. The obligation stemming from article 22 of the Convention to take "appropriate measures" to ensure that a child, whether unaccompanied or accompanied, who is seeking refugee status receives appropriate protection entails, inter alia, the responsibility to set up a functioning asylum system and, in particular, to enact legislation addressing the particular treatment of unaccompanied and separated children and to build capacities necessary to realize this treatment in accordance with applicable rights codified in the Convention and in other international human rights, refugee protection or humanitarian instruments to which the State is a party. States facing resource constraints in staging such capacity-building efforts are strongly encouraged to seek international assistance, including that provided by UNHCR.

65. Taking into account the complementary nature of the obligations under article 22 and those deriving from international refugee law, as well as the desirability of

consolidated standards, States should apply international standards relating to refugees as they progressively evolve when implementing article 22 of the Convention.

(b) Access to asylum procedures, regardless of age

66. Asylum-seeking children, including those who are unaccompanied or separated, shall enjoy access to asylum procedures and other complementary mechanisms providing international protection, irrespective of their age. In the case that facts become known during the identification and registration process which indicate that the child may have a well-founded fear or, even if unable to explicitly articulate a concrete fear, the child may objectively be at risk of persecution for reasons of race, religion, nationality, membership of a particular social group or political opinion, or otherwise be in need of international protection, such a child should be referred to the asylum procedure and/or, where relevant, to mechanisms providing complementary protection under international and domestic law.

67. Unaccompanied or separated children for whom there is no indication of being in need of international protection should not automatically, or otherwise, be referred to asylum procedures, but shall be protected pursuant to other relevant child protection mechanisms such as those provided under youth welfare legislation.

(c) Procedural safeguards and support measures (art. 3 (3))

68. Appropriate measures required under article 22 (1) of the Convention must take into account the particular vulnerabilities of unaccompanied and separated children and the national legal framework and conditions. Such measures should be guided by the considerations set out below.

69. An asylum-seeking child should be represented by an adult who is familiar with the child's background and who is competent and able to represent his or her best interests (see section V (b), "Appointment of a guardian or adviser or legal representative"). The unaccompanied or separated child should also, in all cases, be given access, free of charge, to a qualified legal representative, including where the application for refugee status is processed under the normal procedures for adults.

70. Refugee status applications filed by unaccompanied and separated children shall be given priority and every effort should be made to render a decision promptly and fairly.

71. Minimum procedural guarantees should include that the application will be determined by a competent authority fully qualified in asylum and refugee matters. Where the age and maturity of the child permits, the opportunity for a personal interview with a qualified official should be granted before any final decision is made. Wherever the child is unable to communicate directly with the qualified official in a common language, the assistance of a qualified interpreter should be sought. Moreover, the child should be given the "benefit of the doubt", should there be credibility concerns relating to his or her story as well as a possibility to appeal for a formal review of the decision.

72. The interviews should be conducted by representatives of the refugee determination authority who will take into account the special situation of unaccompanied children in order to carry out the refugee status assessment and apply an understanding of the history, culture and background of the child. The assessment process should comprise a case-by-case examination of the unique combination of factors presented by each child, including the child's personal, family and cultural background. The guardian and the legal representative should be present during all interviews.

73. In cases of large-scale refugee movements where individual refugee status determination is not possible, States may grant refugee status to all members of a group. In such circumstances, all unaccompanied or separated children are entitled to be granted the same status as other members of the particular group.

(d) Child-sensitive assessment of protection needs, taking into account persecution of a child-specific nature

74. When assessing refugee claims of unaccompanied or separated children, States shall take into account the development of, and formative relationship between, international human rights and refugee law, including positions developed by UNHCR in exercising its supervisory functions under the 1951 Refugee Convention. In particular, the refugee definition in that Convention must be interpreted in an age and gender-sensitive manner, taking into account the particular motives for, and forms and manifestations of, persecution experienced by children. Persecution of kin; under-age recruitment; trafficking of children for prostitution; and sexual exploitation or subjection to female genital mutilation, are some of the child-specific forms and manifestations of persecution which may justify the granting of refugee status if such acts are related to one of the 1951 Refugee Convention grounds. States should, therefore, give utmost attention to such child-specific forms and manifestations of persecution as well as gender-based violence in national refugee status-determination procedures.

75. Staff involved in status-determination procedures of children, in particular those who are unaccompanied or separated, should receive training on adopting an application of international and national refugee law that is child, cultural, and gender-sensitive. To properly assess asylum claims of children, information on the situation of children, including those belonging to minorities or marginalized groups, should be included in government efforts to collect country-of-origin information.

(e) Full enjoyment of all international refugee and human rights by children granted refugee status (art. 22)

76. Unaccompanied or separated children recognized as refugees and granted asylum do not only enjoy rights under the 1951 Refugee Convention, but are also entitled to the fullest extent to the enjoyment of all human rights granted to children in the territory or subject to the jurisdiction of the State, including those rights which require a lawful stay in the territory.

(f) Children to benefit from complementary forms of protection

77. In the case that the requirements for granting refugee status under the 1951 Refugee Convention are not met, unaccompanied and separated children shall benefit from available forms of complementary protection to the extent determined by their protection needs. The application of such complementary forms of protection does not obviate States' obligations to address the particular protection needs of the unaccompanied and separated child. Therefore, children granted complementary forms of protection are entitled, to the fullest extent, to the enjoyment of all human rights granted to children in the territory or subject to the jurisdiction of the State, including those rights which require a lawful stay in the territory.

78. In line with the generally applicable principles and, in particular, those relating to the responsibilities of States with regard to unaccompanied or separated children finding themselves in their territory, children who are neither granted refugee status nor benefiting from complementary forms of protection, will still enjoy protection under all norms of the Convention as long as they remain de facto within the States' territories and/or subject to its jurisdiction.

VII. FAMILY REUNIFICATION, RETURN AND OTHER FORMS OF DURABLE SOLUTIONS

(a) General

79. The ultimate aim in addressing the fate of unaccompanied or separated children is to identify a durable solution that addresses all their protection needs, takes into account the child's view and, wherever possible, leads to overcoming the situation of a child being unaccompanied or separated. Efforts to find durable solutions for unaccompanied or separated children should be initiated and implemented without undue delay and, wherever possible, immediately upon the assessment of a child being unaccompanied or separated. Following a rights-based approach, the search for a durable solution commences with analysing the possibility of family reunification.

80. Tracing is an essential component of any search for a durable solution and should be prioritized except where the act of tracing, or the way in which tracing is conducted, would be contrary to the best interests of the child or jeopardize fundamental rights of those being traced. In any case, in conducting tracing activities, no reference should be made to the status of the child as an asylum-seeker or refugee. Subject to all of these conditions, such tracing efforts should also be continued during the asylum procedure. For all children who remain in the territory of the host State, whether on the basis of asylum, complementary forms of protection or due to other legal or factual obstacles to removal, a durable solution must be sought.

(b) Family reunification

81. In order to pay full respect to the obligation of States under article 9 of the Convention to ensure that a child shall not be separated from his or her parents against their will, all efforts should be made to return an unaccompanied or separated child to his or her parents except where further separation is necessary for the best interests of the child, taking full account of the right of the child to express his or her views (art. 12) (see also section IV (e), "Right of the child to express his or her views freely"). While the considerations explicitly listed in article 9, paragraph 1, sentence 2, namely, cases involving abuse or neglect of the child by the parents, may prohibit reunification at any location, other best-interests considerations can provide an obstacle to reunification at specific locations only.

82. Family reunification in the country of origin is not in the best interests of the child and should therefore not be pursued where there is a "reasonable risk" that such a return would lead to the violation of fundamental human rights of the child. Such risk is indisputably documented in the granting of refugee status or in a decision of the competent authorities on the applicability of non-refoulement obligations (including those deriving from article 3 of the Convention against Torture and Other Cruel, Inhuman or Degrading Treatment or Punishment and articles 6 and 7 of the International Covenant on Civil and Political Rights). Accordingly, the granting of refugee status constitutes a legally binding obstacle to return to the country of origin and, consequently, to family reunification therein. Where the circumstances in the country of origin contain lower level risks and there is concern, for example, of the child being affected by the indiscriminate effects of generalized violence, such risks must be given full attention and balanced against other rights-based considerations, including the consequences of further separation. In this context, it must be recalled that the survival of the child is of paramount importance and a precondition for the enjoyment of any other rights.

83. Whenever family reunification in the country of origin is not possible, irrespective of whether this is due to legal obstacles to return or whether the best-interests-based

balancing test has decided against return, the obligations under article 9 and 10 of the Convention come into effect and should govern the host country's decisions on family reunification therein. In this context, States parties are particularly reminded that "applications by a child or his or her parents to enter or leave a State party for the purpose of family reunification shall be dealt with by States parties in a positive, humane and expeditious manner" and "shall entail no adverse consequences for the applicants and for the members of their family" (art. 10 (1)). Countries of origin must respect "the right of the child and his or her parents to leave any country, including their own, and to enter their own country" (art. 10 (2)).

(c) Return to the country of origin

84. Return to the country of origin is not an option if it would lead to a "reasonable risk" that such return would result in the violation of fundamental human rights of the child, and in particular, if the principle of non-refoulement applies. Return to the country of origin shall in principle only be arranged if such return is in the best interests of the child. Such a determination shall, inter alia, take into account:

- The safety, security and other conditions, including socio-economic conditions, awaiting the child upon return, including through home study, where appropriate, conducted by social network organizations;
- The availability of care arrangements for that particular child;
- The views of the child expressed in exercise of his or her right to do so under article 12 and those of the caretakers;
- The child's level of integration in the host country and the duration of absence from the home country;
- The child's right "to preserve his or her identity, including nationality, name and family relations" (art. 8);
- The "desirability of continuity in a child's upbringing and to the child's ethnic, religious, cultural and linguistic background" (art. 20).

85. In the absence of the availability of care provided by parents or members of the extended family, return to the country of origin should, in principle, not take place without advance secure and concrete arrangements of care and custodial responsibilities upon return to the country of origin.

86. Exceptionally, a return to the home country may be arranged, after careful balancing of the child's best interests and other considerations, if the latter are rights-based and override best interests of the child. Such may be the case in situations in which the child constitutes a serious risk to the security of the State or to the society. Non-rights-based arguments such as those relating to general migration control, cannot override best interests considerations.

87. In all cases return measures must be conducted in a safe, child-appropriate and gender-sensitive manner.

88. Countries of origin are also reminded in this context of their obligations pursuant to article 10 of the Convention and, in particular, to respect "the right of the child and his or her parents to leave any country, including their own, and to enter their own country".

(d) Local integration

89. Local integration is the primary option if return to the country of origin is impossible on either legal or factual grounds. Local integration must be based on a secure legal status (including residence status) and be governed by the Convention rights that are fully applicable to all children who remain in the country, irrespective of

whether this is due to their recognition as a refugee, other legal obstacles to return, or whether the best-interests-based balancing test has decided against return.

90. Once it has been determined that a separated or unaccompanied child will remain in the community, the relevant authorities should conduct an assessment of the child's situation and then, in consultation with the child and his or her guardian, determine the appropriate long-term arrangements within the local community and other necessary measures to facilitate such integration. The long-term placement should be decided in the best interests of the child and, at this stage, institutional care should, wherever possible, serve only as a last resort. The separated or unaccompanied child should have the same access to rights (including to education, training, employment and health care) as enjoyed by national children. In ensuring that these rights are fully enjoyed by the unaccompanied or separated child, the host country may need to pay special attention to the extra measures required to address the child's vulnerable status, including, for example, through extra language training.

(e) Intercountry adoption (art. 21)

91. States must have full respect for the preconditions provided under article 21 of the Convention as well as other relevant international instruments, including in particular the Hague Convention on Protection of Children and Cooperation in Respect of Inter-Country Adoption and its 1994 Recommendation Concerning the Application to Refugee and other Internationally Displaced Children when considering the adoption of unaccompanied and separated children. States should, in particular, observe the following:

- Adoption of unaccompanied or separated children should only be considered once it has been established that the child is in a position to be adopted. In practice, this means, inter alia, that efforts with regard to tracing and family reunification have failed, or that the parents have consented to the adoption. The consent of parents and the consent of other persons, institutions and authorities that are necessary for adoption must be free and informed. This supposes notably that such consent has not been induced by payment or compensation of any kind and has not been withdrawn;
- Unaccompanied or separated children must not be adopted in haste at the height of an emergency;
- Any adoption must be determined as being in the child's best interests and carried out in keeping with applicable national, international and customary law;
- The views of the child, depending upon his/her age and degree of maturity, should be sought and taken into account in all adoption procedures. This requirement implies that he/she has been counselled and duly informed of the consequences of adoption and of his/her consent to adoption, where such consent is required. Such consent must have been given freely and not induced by payment or compensation of any kind;
- Priority must be given to adoption by relatives in their country of residence. Where this is not an option, preference will be given to adoption within the community from which the child came or at least within his or her own culture;
- Adoption should not be considered:
    - Where there is reasonable hope of successful tracing and family reunification is in the child's best interests;
    - If it is contrary to the expressed wishes of the child or the parents;
    - Unless a reasonable time has passed during which all feasible steps to trace the parents or other surviving family members has been carried out.

> This period of time may vary with circumstances, in particular, those relating to the ability to conduct proper tracing; however, the process of tracing must be completed within a reasonable period of time;

- Adoption in a country of asylum should not be taken up when there is the possibility of voluntary repatriation under conditions of safety and dignity in the near future.

(f) Resettlement in a third country

92. Resettlement to a third country may offer a durable solution for an accompanied or separated child who cannot return to the country of origin and for whom no durable solution can be envisaged in the host country. The decision to resettle an unaccompanied or separated child must be based on an updated, comprehensive and thorough best-interests assessment, taking into account, in particular, ongoing international and other protection needs. Resettlement is particularly called for if such is the only means to effectively and sustainably protect a child against refoulement or against persecution or other serious human rights violations in the country of stay. Resettlement is also in the best interests of the unaccompanied or separated child if it serves family reunification in the resettlement country.

93. The best-interests assessment determination, prior to a decision to resettle, needs also to take into account other factors such as: the envisaged duration of legal or other obstacles to a child's return to his or her home country; the child's right to preserve his or her identity, including nationality and name (art. 8); the child's age, sex, emotional state, educational and family background; continuity/discontinuity of care in the host country; the desirability of continuity in a child's upbringing and to the child's ethnic, religious, cultural and linguistic background (art. 20); the right of the child to preserve his or her family relations (art. 8) and related short, medium and long-term possibilities of family reunion either in the home, host, or resettlement country. Unaccompanied or separated children should never be resettled to a third country if this would undermine or seriously hamper future reunion with their family.

94. States are encouraged to provide resettlement opportunities in order to meet all the resettlement needs related to unaccompanied and separated children.

VIII. TRAINING, DATA AND STATISTICS

(a) Training of personnel dealing with unaccompanied and separated children

95. Particular attention should be paid to the training of officials working with separated and unaccompanied children and dealing with their cases. Specialized training is equally important for legal representatives, guardians, interpreters and others dealing with separated and unaccompanied children.

96. Such training should be specifically tailored to the needs and rights of the groups concerned. Nevertheless, certain key elements should be included in all training programmes, including:

- Principles and provisions of the Convention;
- Knowledge of the country of origin of separated and unaccompanied children;
- Appropriate interview techniques;
- Child development and psychology;
- Cultural sensitivity and intercultural communication.

97. Initial training programmes should also be followed up regularly, including through on-the-job learning and professional networks.

(b) Data and statistics on separated and unaccompanied children

98. It is the experience of the Committee that data and statistics collected with regard to unaccompanied and separated children tends to be limited to the number of arrivals and/or number of requests for asylum. This data is insufficient for a detailed analysis of the implementation of the rights of such children. Furthermore, data and statistics are often collected by a variety of different ministries or agencies, which can impede further analysis and presents potential concerns with regard to confidentiality and a child's right to privacy.

99. Accordingly, the development of a detailed and integrated system of data collection on unaccompanied and separated children is a prerequisite for the development of effective policies for the implementation of the rights of such children.

100. Data collected within such a system should ideally include but not be limited to: basic biographical data on each child (including age, sex, country of origin and nationality, ethnic group); total number of unaccompanied and separated children attempting to enter the country and the number that have been refused entry; number of requests for asylum; number of legal representatives and guardians assigned to such children; legal and immigration status (i.e. asylum-seeker, refugee, temporary resident permit); living arrangements (i.e. in institutions, with families or living independently); enrolment in school or vocational training; family reunifications; and, numbers returned to their country of origin. In addition, States parties should consider collecting qualitative data that would allow them to analyse issues that remain insufficiently addressed, such as for instance, disappearances of unaccompanied and separated children and the impact of trafficking.

General Comment No 7 (2005)
Implementing child rights in early childhood

I. INTRODUCTION

1. This general comment arises out of the Committee's experiences of reviewing States parties' reports. In many cases, very little information has been offered about early childhood, with comments limited mainly to child mortality, birth registration and health care. The Committee felt the need for a discussion on the broader implications of the Convention on the Rights of the Child for young children. Accordingly, in 2004, the Committee devoted its day of general discussion to the theme "Implementing child rights in early childhood". This resulted in a set of recommendations (see CRC/C/143, sect. VII) as well as the decision to prepare a general comment on this important topic. Through this general comment, the Committee wishes to encourage recognition that young children are holders of all rights enshrined in the Convention and that early childhood is a critical period for the realization of these rights. The Committee's working definition of "early childhood" is all young children: at birth and throughout infancy; during the preschool years; as well as during the transition to school (see paragraph 4 below).

II. OBJECTIVES OF THE GENERAL COMMENT

2. The objectives of the general comment are:

(a)   To strengthen understanding of the human rights of all young children and to draw States parties' attention to their obligations towards young children;

(b)   To comment on the specific features of early childhood that impact on the realization of rights;

(c)   To encourage recognition of young children as social actors from the beginning of life, with particular interests, capacities and vulnerabilities, and of requirements for protection, guidance and support in the exercise of their rights;

(d)   To draw attention to diversities within early childhood that need to be taken into account when implementing the Convention, including diversities in young children's circumstances, in the quality of their experiences and in the influences shaping their development;

(e)   To point to variations in cultural expectations and treatment of children, including local customs and practices that should be respected, except where they contravene the rights of the child;

(f)   To emphasize the vulnerability of young children to poverty, discrimination, family breakdown and multiple other adversities that violate their rights and undermine their well-being;

(g)   To contribute to the realization of rights for all young children through formulation and promotion of comprehensive policies, laws, programmes, practices, professional training and research specifically focused on rights in early childhood.

III. HUMAN RIGHTS AND YOUNG CHILDREN

3. **Young children are rights holders.** The Convention on the Rights of the Child defines a child as "every human being below the age of eighteen years unless under the law applicable to the child, majority is attained earlier" (art. 1). Consequently, young children are holders of all the rights enshrined in the Convention. They are entitled to

special protection measures and, in accordance with their evolving capacities, the progressive exercise of their rights. The Committee is concerned that in implementing their obligations under the Convention, States parties have not given sufficient attention to young children as rights holders and to the laws, policies and programmes required to realize their rights during this distinct phase of their childhood. The Committee reaffirms that the Convention on the Rights of the Child is to be applied holistically in early childhood, taking account of the principle of the universality, indivisibility and interdependence of all human rights.

4. **Definition of early childhood.** Definitions of early childhood vary in different countries and regions, according to local traditions and the organization of primary school systems. In some countries, the transition from preschool to school occurs soon after 4 years old. In other countries, this transition takes place at around 7 years old. In its consideration of rights in early childhood, the Committee wishes to include all young children: at birth and throughout infancy; during the preschool years; as well as during the transition to school. Accordingly, the Committee proposes as an appropriate working definition of early childhood the period below the age of 8 years; States parties should review their obligations towards young children in the context of this definition.

5. **A positive agenda for early childhood**. The Committee encourages States parties to construct a positive agenda for rights in early childhood. A shift away from traditional beliefs that regard early childhood mainly as a period for the socialization of the immature human being towards mature adult status is required. The Convention requires that children, including the very youngest children, be respected as persons in their own right. Young children should be recognized as active members of families, communities and societies, with their own concerns, interests and points of view. For the exercise of their rights, young children have particular requirements for physical nurturance, emotional care and sensitive guidance, as well as for time and space for social play, exploration and learning. These requirements can best be planned for within a framework of laws, policies and programmes for early childhood, including a plan for implementation and independent monitoring, for example through the appointment of a children's rights commissioner, and through assessments of the impact of laws and policies on children (see general comment No. 2 (2002) on the role of independent human rights institutions, para. 19).

6. **Features of early childhood.** Early childhood is a critical period for realizing children's rights. During this period:

(a)   Young children experience the most rapid period of growth and change during the human lifespan, in terms of their maturing bodies and nervous systems, increasing mobility, communication skills and intellectual capacities, and rapid shifts in their interests and abilities;

(b)   Young children form strong emotional attachments to their parents or other caregivers, from whom they seek and require nurturance, care, guidance and protection, in ways that are respectful of their individuality and growing capacities;

(c)   Young children establish their own important relationships with children of the same age, as well as with younger and older children. Through these relationships they learn to negotiate and coordinate shared activities, resolve conflicts, keep agreements and accept responsibility for others;

(d)   Young children actively make sense of the physical, social and cultural dimensions of the world they inhabit, learning progressively from their activities and their interactions with others, children as well as adults;

(e)   Young children's earliest years are the foundation for their physical and mental health, emotional security, cultural and personal identity, and developing competencies;

(f)   Young children's experiences of growth and development vary according to their individual nature, as well as their gender, living conditions, family organization, care arrangements and education systems;

(g)   Young children's experiences of growth and development are powerfully shaped by cultural beliefs about their needs and proper treatment, and about their active role in family and community.

7. Respecting the distinctive interests, experiences and challenges facing every young child is the starting point for realizing their rights during this crucial phase of their lives.

8. **Research into early childhood.** The Committee notes the growing body of theory and research which confirms that young children are best understood as social actors whose survival, well-being and development are dependent on and built around close relationships. These relationships are normally with a small number of key people, most often parents, members of the extended family and peers, as well as caregivers and other early childhood professionals. At the same time, research into the social and cultural dimensions of early childhood draws attention to the diverse ways in which early development is understood and enacted, including varying expectations of the young child and arrangements for his or her care and education. A feature of modern societies is that increasing numbers of young children are growing up in multicultural communities and in contexts marked by rapid social change, where beliefs and expectations about young children are also changing, including through greater recognition of their rights. States parties are encouraged to draw on beliefs and knowledge about early childhood in ways that are appropriate to local circumstances and changing practices, and respect traditional values, provided these are not discriminatory, (article 2 of the Convention) nor prejudicial to children's health and well-being (art. 24.3), nor against their best interests (art. 3). Finally, research has highlighted the particular risks to young children from malnutrition, disease, poverty, neglect, social exclusion and a range of other adversities. It shows that proper prevention and intervention strategies during early childhood have the potential to impact positively on young children's current well-being and future prospects. Implementing child rights in early childhood is thus an effective way to help prevent personal, social and educational difficulties during middle childhood and adolescence (see general comment No. 4 (2003) on adolescent health and development).

III. GENERAL PRINCIPLES AND RIGHTS IN EARLY CHILDHOOD

9. The Committee has identified articles 2, 3, 6 and 12 of the Convention as general principles (see general comment No. 5 (2003) on the general measures of implementation of the Convention). Each principle has implications for rights in early childhood.

10. **Right to life, survival and development.** Article 6 refers to the child's inherent right to life and States parties' obligation to ensure, to the maximum extent possible, the survival and development of the child. States parties are urged to take all possible measures to improve perinatal care for mothers and babies, reduce infant and child mortality, and create conditions that promote the well-being of all young children during this critical phase of their lives. Malnutrition and preventable diseases continue to be major obstacles to realizing rights in early childhood. Ensuring survival and physical health are priorities, but States parties are reminded that article 6 encompasses all aspects of development, and that a young child's health and psychosocial well-being are

in many respects interdependent. Both may be put at risk by adverse living conditions, neglect, insensitive or abusive treatment and restricted opportunities for realizing human potential. Young children growing up in especially difficult circumstances require particular attention (see section VI below). The Committee reminds States parties (and others concerned) that the right to survival and development can only be implemented in a holistic manner, through the enforcement of all the other provisions of the Convention, including rights to health, adequate nutrition, social security, an adequate standard of living, a healthy and safe environment, education and play (arts. 24, 27, 28, 29 and 31), as well as through respect for the responsibilities of parents and the provision of assistance and quality services (arts. 5 and 18). From an early age, children should themselves be included in activities promoting good nutrition and a healthy and disease-preventing lifestyle.

11. **Right to non-discrimination.** Article 2 ensures rights to every child, without discrimination of any kind. The Committee urges States parties to identify the implications of this principle for realizing rights in early childhood:

(a) Article 2 means that young children in general must not be discriminated against on any grounds, for example where laws fail to offer equal protection against violence for all children, including young children. Young children are especially at risk of discrimination because they are relatively powerless and depend on others for the realization of their rights;

(b) Article 2 also means that particular groups of young children must not be discriminated against. Discrimination may take the form of reduced levels of nutrition; inadequate care and attention; restricted opportunities for play, learning and education; or inhibition of free expression of feelings and views. Discrimination may also be expressed through harsh treatment and unreasonable expectations, which may be exploitative or abusive. For example:

(i) Discrimination against girl children is a serious violation of rights, affecting their survival and all areas of their young lives as well as restricting their capacity to contribute positively to society. They may be victims of selective abortion, genital mutilation, neglect and infanticide, including through inadequate feeding in infancy. They may be expected to undertake excessive family responsibilities and deprived of opportunities to participate in early childhood and primary education;

(ii) Discrimination against children with disabilities reduces survival prospects and quality of life. These children are entitled to the care, nutrition, nurturance and encouragement offered other children. They may also require additional, special assistance in order to ensure their integration and the realization of their rights;

(iii) Discrimination against children infected with or affected by HIV/AIDS deprives them of the help and support they most require. Discrimination may be found within public policies, in the provision of and access to services, as well as in everyday practices that violate these children's rights (see also paragraph 27);

(iv) Discrimination related to ethnic origin, class/caste, personal circumstances and lifestyle, or political and religious beliefs (of children or their parents) excludes children from full participation in society. It affects parents' capacities to fulfil their responsibilities towards their children. It affects children's opportunities and self-esteem, as well as encouraging resentment and conflict among children and adults;

(v) Young children who suffer multiple discrimination (e.g. related to ethnic origin, social and cultural status, gender and/or disabilities) are especially at risk.

12. Young children may also suffer the consequences of discrimination against their parents, for example if children have been born out of wedlock or in other circumstances that deviate from traditional values, or if their parents are refugees or asylum-seekers. States parties have a responsibility to monitor and combat discrimination in whatever forms it takes and wherever it occurs - within families, communities, schools or other institutions. Potential discrimination in access to quality services for young children is a particular concern, especially where health, education, welfare and other services are not universally available and are provided through a combination of State, private and charitable organizations. As a first step, the Committee encourages States parties to monitor the availability of and access to quality services that contribute to young children's survival and development, including through systematic data collection, disaggregated in terms of major variables related to children's and families' background and circumstances. As a second step, actions may be required that guarantee that all children have an equal opportunity to benefit from available services. More generally, States parties should raise awareness about discrimination against young children in general, and against vulnerable groups in particular.

13. **Best interests of the child.** Article 3 sets out the principle that the best interests of the child are a primary consideration in all actions concerning children. By virtue of their relative immaturity, young children are reliant on responsible authorities to assess and represent their rights and best interests in relation to decisions and actions that affect their well-being, while taking account of their views and evolving capacities. The principle of best interests appears repeatedly within the Convention (including in articles 9, 18, 20 and 21, which are most relevant to early childhood). The principle of best interests applies to all actions concerning children and requires active measures to protect their rights and promote their survival, growth, and well-being, as well as measures to support and assist parents and others who have day-to-day responsibility for realizing children's rights:

(a) *Best interests of individual children.* All decision-making concerning a child's care, health, education, etc. must take account of the best interests principle, including decisions by parents, professionals and others responsible for children. States parties are urged to make provisions for young children to be represented independently in all legal proceedings by someone who acts for the child's interests, and for children to be heard in all cases where they are capable of expressing their opinions or preferences;

(b) *Best interests of young children as a group or constituency.* All law and policy development, administrative and judicial decision-making and service provision that affect children must take account of the best interests principle. This includes actions directly affecting children (e.g. related to health services, care systems, or schools), as well as actions that indirectly impact on young children (e.g. related to the environment, housing or transport).

14. **Respect for the views and feelings of the young child.** Article 12 states that the child has a right to express his or her views freely in all matters affecting the child, and to have them taken into account. This right reinforces the status of the young child as an active participant in the promotion, protection and monitoring of their rights. Respect for the young child's agency - as a participant in family, community and society - is frequently overlooked, or rejected as inappropriate on the grounds of age and immaturity. In many countries and regions, traditional beliefs have emphasized young children's need for

training and socialization. They have been regarded as undeveloped, lacking even basic capacities for understanding, communicating and making choices. They have been powerless within their families, and often voiceless and invisible within society. The Committee wishes to emphasize that article 12 applies both to younger and to older children. As holders of rights, even the youngest children are entitled to express their views, which should be "given due weight in accordance with the age and maturity of the child" (art. 12.1). Young children are acutely sensitive to their surroundings and very rapidly acquire understanding of the people, places and routines in their lives, along with awareness of their own unique identity. They make choices and communicate their feelings, ideas and wishes in numerous ways, long before they are able to communicate through the conventions of spoken or written language. In this regard:

(a)   The Committee encourages States parties to take all appropriate measures to ensure that the concept of the child as rights holder with freedom to express views and the right to be consulted in matters that affect him or her is implemented from the earliest stage in ways appropriate to the child's capacities, best interests, and rights to protection from harmful experiences;

(b)   The right to express views and feelings should be anchored in the child's daily life at home (including, when applicable, the extended family) and in his or her community; within the full range of early childhood health, care and education facilities, as well as in legal proceedings; and in the development of policies and services, including through research and consultations;

(c)   States parties should take all appropriate measures to promote the active involvement of parents, professionals and responsible authorities in the creation of opportunities for young children to progressively exercise their rights within their everyday activities in all relevant settings, including by providing training in the necessary skills. To achieve the right of participation requires adults to adopt a child-centred attitude, listening to young children and respecting their dignity and their individual points of view. It also requires adults to show patience and creativity by adapting their expectations to a young child's interests, levels of understanding and preferred ways of communicating.

IV. PARENTAL RESPONSIBILITIES AND ASSISTANCE FROM STATES PARTIES

15. **A crucial role for parents and other primary caregivers.** Under normal circumstances, a young child's parents play a crucial role in the achievement of their rights, along with other members of family, extended family or community, including legal guardians, as appropriate. This is fully recognized within the Convention (especially article 5), along with the obligation on States parties to provide assistance, including quality childcare services (especially article 18). The preamble to the Convention refers to the family as "the fundamental group of society and the natural environment for the growth and well-being of all its members and particularly children". The Committee recognizes that "family" here refers to a variety of arrangements that can provide for young children's care, nurturance and development, including the nuclear family, the extended family, and other traditional and modern community-based arrangements, provided these are consistent with children's rights and best interests.

16. **Parents/primary caregivers and children's best interests.** The responsibility vested in parents and other primary caregivers is linked to the requirement that they act in children's best interests. Article 5 states that parents' role is to offer appropriate direction and guidance in "the exercise by the child of the rights in the ... Convention". This applies equally to younger as to older children. Babies and infants are entirely dependent on others, but they are not passive recipients of care, direction and guidance.

They are active social agents, who seek protection, nurturance and understanding from parents or other caregivers, which they require for their survival, growth and well-being. Newborn babies are able to recognize their parents (or other caregivers) very soon after birth, and they engage actively in non-verbal communication. Under normal circumstances, young children form strong mutual attachments with their parents or primary caregivers. These relationships offer children physical and emotional security, as well as consistent care and attention. Through these relationships children construct a personal identity and acquire culturally valued skills, knowledge and behaviours. In these ways, parents (and other caregivers) are normally the major conduit through which young children are able to realize their rights.

17. **Evolving capacities as an enabling principle.** Article 5 draws on the concept of "evolving capacities" to refer to processes of maturation and learning whereby children progressively acquire knowledge, competencies and understanding, including acquiring understanding about their rights and about how they can best be realized. Respecting young children's evolving capacities is crucial for the realization of their rights, and especially significant during early childhood, because of the rapid transformations in children's physical, cognitive, social and emotional functioning, from earliest infancy to the beginnings of schooling. Article 5 contains the principle that parents (and others) have the responsibility to continually adjust the levels of support and guidance they offer to a child. These adjustments take account of a child's interests and wishes as well as the child's capacities for autonomous decision-making and comprehension of his or her best interests. While a young child generally requires more guidance than an older child, it is important to take account of individual variations in the capacities of children of the same age and of their ways of reacting to situations. Evolving capacities should be seen as a positive and enabling process, not an excuse for authoritarian practices that restrict children's autonomy and self-expression and which have traditionally been justified by pointing to children's relative immaturity and their need for socialization. Parents (and others) should be encouraged to offer "direction and guidance" in a child-centred way, through dialogue and example, in ways that enhance young children's capacities to exercise their rights, including their right to participation (art. 12) and their right to freedom of thought, conscience and religion (art. 14).[46]

18. **Respecting parental roles.** Article 18 of the Convention reaffirms that parents or legal guardians have the primary responsibility for promoting children's development and well-being, with the child's best interests as their basic concern (arts. 18.1 and 27.2). States parties should respect the primacy of parents, mothers and fathers. This includes the obligation not to separate children from their parents, unless it is in the child's best interests (art. 9). Young children are especially vulnerable to adverse consequences of separations because of their physical dependence on and emotional attachment to their parents/primary caregivers. They are also less able to comprehend the circumstances of any separation. Situations which are most likely to impact negatively on young children include neglect and deprivation of adequate parenting; parenting under acute material or psychological stress or impaired mental health; parenting in isolation; parenting which is inconsistent, involves conflict between parents or is abusive towards children; and situations where children experience disrupted relationships (including enforced separations), or where they are provided with low-quality institutional care. The Committee urges States parties to take all necessary steps to ensure that parents are able to take primary responsibility for their children; to support parents in fulfilling their responsibilities, including by reducing harmful deprivations, disruptions and distortions in children's care; and to take action where young children's well-being may be at risk.

---

[46] See G. Lansdown, *The Evolving Capacities of the Child* (Florence: UNICEF Innocenti Research Centre, 2005).

States parties' overall goals should include reducing the number of young children abandoned or orphaned, as well as minimizing the numbers requiring institutional or other forms of long-term care, except where this is judged to be in a young child's best interests (see also section VI below).

19. **Social trends and the role of the family.** The Convention emphasizes that "both parents have common responsibilities for the upbringing and development of the child", with fathers and mothers recognized as equal caregivers (art. 18.1). The Committee notes that in practice family patterns are variable and changing in many regions, as is the availability of informal networks of support for parents, with an overall trend towards greater diversity in family size, parental roles and arrangements for bringing up children. These trends are especially significant for young children, whose physical, personal and psychological development is best provided for within a small number of consistent, caring relationships. Typically, these relationships are with some combination of mother, father, siblings, grandparents and other members of the extended family, along with professional caregivers specialized in childcare and education. The Committee acknowledges that each of these relationships can make a distinctive contribution to the fulfilment of children's rights under the Convention and that a range of family patterns may be consistent with promoting children's well-being. In some countries and regions, shifting social attitudes towards family, marriage and parenting are impacting on young children's experiences of early childhood, for example following family separations and reformations. Economic pressures also impact on young children, for example, where parents are forced to work far away from their families and their communities. In other countries and regions, the illness and death of one or both parents or other kin due to HIV/AIDS is now a common feature of early childhood. These and many other factors impact on parents' capacities to fulfil their responsibilities towards children. More generally, during periods of rapid social change, traditional practices may no longer be viable or relevant to present parental circumstances and lifestyles, but without sufficient time having elapsed for new practices to be assimilated and new parental competencies understood and valued.

20. **Assistance to parents.** States parties are required to render appropriate assistance to parents, legal guardians and extended families in the performance of their child-rearing responsibilities (arts. 18.2 and 18.3), including assisting parents in providing living conditions necessary for the child's development (art. 27.2) and ensuring that children receive necessary protection and care (art. 3.2). The Committee is concerned that insufficient account is taken of the resources, skills and personal commitment required of parents and others responsible for young children, especially in societies where early marriage and parenthood is still sanctioned as well as in societies with a high incidence of young, single parents. Early childhood is the period of most extensive (and intensive) parental responsibilities related to all aspects of children's well-being covered by the Convention: their survival, health, physical safety and emotional security, standards of living and care, opportunities for play and learning, and freedom of expression. Accordingly, realizing children's rights is in large measure dependent on the well-being and resources available to those with responsibility for their care. Recognizing these interdependencies is a sound starting point for planning assistance and services to parents, legal guardians and other caregivers. For example:

   (a)   An integrated approach would include interventions that impact indirectly on parents' ability to promote the best interests of children (e.g. taxation and benefits, adequate housing, working hours) as well as those that have more immediate consequences (e.g. perinatal health services for mother and baby, parent education, home visitors);

(b)   Providing adequate assistance should take account of the new roles and skills required of parents, as well as the ways that demands and pressures shift during early childhood - for example, as children become more mobile, more verbally communicative, more socially competent, and as they begin to participate in programmes of care and education;

(c)   Assistance to parents will include provision of parenting education, parent counselling and other quality services for mothers, fathers, siblings, grandparents and others who from time to time may be responsible for promoting the child's best interests;

(d)   Assistance also includes offering support to parents and other family members in ways that encourage positive and sensitive relationships with young children and enhance understanding of children's rights and best interests.

21. Appropriate assistance to parents can best be achieved as part of comprehensive policies for early childhood (see section V below), including provision for health, care and education during the early years. States parties should ensure that parents are given appropriate support to enable them to involve young children fully in such programmes, especially the most disadvantaged and vulnerable groups. In particular, article 18.3 acknowledges that many parents are economically active, often in poorly paid occupations which they combine with their parental responsibilities. Article 18.3 requires States parties to take all appropriate measures to ensure that children of working parents have the right to benefit from childcare services, maternity protection and facilities for which they are eligible. In this regard, the Committee recommends that States parties ratify the Maternity Protection Convention, 2000 (No. 183) of the International Labour Organization.

V. COMPREHENSIVE POLICIES AND PROGRAMMES FOR EARLY CHILDHOOD, ESPECIALLY FOR VULNERABLE CHILDREN

22. **Rights-based, multisectoral strategies.** In many countries and regions, early childhood has received low priority in the development of quality services. These services have often been fragmented. They have frequently been the responsibility of several government departments at central and local levels, and their planning has often been piecemeal and uncoordinated. In some cases, they have also been largely provided by the private and voluntary sector, without adequate resources, regulation or quality assurance. States parties are urged to develop rights-based, coordinated, multisectoral strategies in order to ensure that children's best interests are always the starting point for service planning and provision. These should be based around a systematic and integrated approach to law and policy development in relation to all children up to 8 years old. A comprehensive framework for early childhood services, provisions and facilities is required, backed up by information and monitoring systems. Comprehensive services will be coordinated with the assistance provided to parents and will fully respect their responsibilities, as well as their circumstances and requirements (as in articles 5 and 18 of the Convention; see section IV above). Parents should also be consulted and involved in the planning of comprehensive services.

23. **Programme standards and professional training appropriate to the age range.** The Committee emphasizes that a comprehensive strategy for early childhood must also take account of individual children's maturity and individuality, in particular recognizing the changing developmental priorities for specific age groups (for example, babies, toddlers, preschool and early primary school groups), and the implications for programme standards and quality criteria. States parties must ensure that the institutions, services and facilities responsible for early childhood conform to quality standards, particularly in the areas of health and safety, and that staff possess the appropriate psychosocial

qualities and are suitable, sufficiently numerous and well-trained. Provision of services appropriate to the circumstances, age and individuality of young children requires that all staff be trained to work with this age group. Work with young children should be socially valued and properly paid, in order to attract a highly qualified workforce, men as well as women. It is essential that they have sound, up-to-date theoretical and practical understanding about children's rights and development (see also paragraph 41); that they adopt appropriate child-centred care practices, curricula and pedagogies; and that they have access to specialist professional resources and support, including a supervisory and monitoring system for public and private programmes, institutions and services.

24. **Access to services, especially for the most vulnerable.** The Committee calls on States parties to ensure that all young children (and those with primary responsibility for their well-being) are guaranteed access to appropriate and effective services, including programmes of health, care and education specifically designed to promote their well-being. Particular attention should be paid to the most vulnerable groups of young children and to those who are at risk of discrimination (art. 2). This includes girls, children living in poverty, children with disabilities, children belonging to indigenous or minority groups, children from migrant families, children who are orphaned or lack parental care for other reasons, children living in institutions, children living with mothers in prison, refugee and asylum-seeking children, children infected with or affected by HIV/AIDS, and children of alcohol- or drug-addicted parents (see also section VI).

25. **Birth registration.** Comprehensive services for early childhood begin at birth. The Committee notes that provision for registration of all children at birth is still a major challenge for many countries and regions. This can impact negatively on a child's sense of personal identity and children may be denied entitlements to basic health, education and social welfare. As a first step in ensuring the rights to survival, development and access to quality services for all children (art. 6), the Committee recommends that States parties take all necessary measures to ensure that all children are registered at birth. This can be achieved through a universal, well-managed registration system that is accessible to all and free of charge. An effective system must be flexible and responsive to the circumstances of families, for example by providing mobile registration units where appropriate. The Committee notes that children who are sick or disabled are less likely to be registered in some regions and emphasizes that all children should be registered at birth, without discrimination of any kind (art. 2). The Committee also reminds States parties of the importance of facilitating late registration of birth, and ensuring that children who have not been registered have equal access to health care, protection, education and other social services.

26. **Standard of living and social security.** Young children are entitled to a standard of living adequate for their physical, mental, spiritual, moral and social development (art. 27). The Committee notes with concern that even the most basic standard of living is not assured for millions of young children, despite widespread recognition of the adverse consequences of deprivation. Growing up in relative poverty undermines children's well-being, social inclusion and self-esteem and reduces opportunities for learning and development. Growing up in conditions of absolute poverty has even more serious consequences, threatening children's survival and their health, as well as undermining the basic quality of life. States parties are urged to implement systematic strategies to reduce poverty in early childhood as well as combat its negative effects on children's well-being. All possible means should be employed, including "material assistance and support programmes" for children and families (art. 27.3), in order to assure to young

children a basic standard of living consistent with rights. Implementing children's right to benefit from social security, including social insurance, is an important element of any strategy (art. 26).

27. **Health-care provision.** States parties should ensure that all children have access to the highest attainable standard of health care and nutrition during their early years, in order to reduce infant mortality and enable children to enjoy a healthy start in life (art. 24). In particular:

(a)   States parties have a responsibility to ensure access to clean drinking water, adequate sanitation, appropriate immunization, good nutrition and medical services, which are essential for young children's health, as is a stress-free environment. Malnutrition and disease have long-term impacts on children's physical health and development. They affect children's mental state, inhibiting learning and social participation and reducing prospects for realizing their potential. The same applies to obesity and unhealthy lifestyles;

(b)   States parties have a responsibility to implement children's right to health by encouraging education in child health and development, including about the advantages of breastfeeding, nutrition, hygiene and sanitation.[47] Priority should also be given to the provision of appropriate prenatal and post-natal health care for mothers and infants in order to foster healthy family-child relationships, especially between a child and his or her mother (or other primary caregiver) (art. 24.2). Young children are themselves able to contribute to ensuring their personal health and encouraging healthy lifestyles among their peers, for example through participation in appropriate, child-centred health education programmes;

(c)   The Committee wishes to draw States parties' attention to the particular challenges of HIV/AIDS for early childhood. All necessary steps should be taken to: (i) prevent infection of parents and young children, especially by intervening in chains of transmission, especially between father and mother and from mother to baby; (ii) provide accurate diagnoses, effective treatment and other forms of support for both parents and young children who are infected by the virus (including antiretroviral therapies); and (iii) ensure adequate alternative care for children who have lost parents or other primary caregivers due to HIV/AIDS, including healthy and infected orphans. (See also general comment No. 3 (2003) on HIV/AIDS and the rights of the child.)

28. **Early childhood education.** The Convention recognizes the right of the child to education, and primary education should be made compulsory and available free to all (art. 28). The Committee recognizes with appreciation that some States parties are planning to make one year of preschool education available and free of cost for all children. The Committee interprets the right to education during early childhood as beginning at birth and closely linked to young children's right to maximum development (art. 6.2). Linking education to development is elaborated in article 29.1: "States parties agree that the education of the child shall be directed to: (a) the development of the child's personality, talents and mental and physical abilities to their fullest potential". General comment No. 1 on the aims of education explains that the goal is to "empower the child by developing his or her skills, learning and other capacities, human dignity, self-esteem and self-confidence" and that this must be achieved in ways that are child-centred, child-friendly and reflect the rights and inherent dignity of the child (para.

---

[47]   See Global Strategy for Infant and Young Child Feeding, World Health Organization, 2003.

2). States parties are reminded that children's right to education include all children, and that girls should be enabled to participate in education, without discrimination of any kind (art. 2).

29. **Parental and public responsibilities for early childhood education.** The principle that parents (and other primary caregivers) are children's first educators is well established and endorsed within the Convention's emphasis on respect for the responsibilities of parents (sect. IV above). They are expected to provide appropriate direction and guidance to young children in the exercise of their rights, and provide an environment of reliable and affectionate relationships based on respect and understanding (art. 5). The Committee invites States parties to make this principle a starting point for planning early education, in two respects:

  (a) In providing appropriate assistance to parents in the performance of their child-rearing responsibilities (art. 18.2), States parties should take all appropriate measures to enhance parents' understanding of their role in their children's early education, encourage child-rearing practices which are child-centred, encourage respect for the child's dignity and provide opportunities for developing understanding, self-esteem and self-confidence;

  (b) In planning for early childhood, States parties should at all times aim to provide programmes that complement the parents' role and are developed as far as possible in partnership with parents, including through active cooperation between parents, professionals and others in developing "the child's personality, talents and mental and physical abilities to their fullest potential" (art. 29.1 (a)).

30. The Committee calls on States parties to ensure that all young children receive education in the broadest sense (as outlined in paragraph 28 above), which acknowledges a key role for parents, wider family and community, as well as the contribution of organized programmes of early childhood education provided by the State, the community or civil society institutions. Research evidence demonstrates the potential for quality education programmes to have a positive impact on young children's successful transition to primary school, their educational progress and their long-term social adjustment. Many countries and regions now provide comprehensive early education starting at 4 years old, which in some countries is integrated with childcare for working parents. Acknowledging that traditional divisions between "care" and "education" services have not always been in children's best interests, the concept of "Educare" is sometimes used to signal a shift towards integrated services, and reinforces the recognition of the need for a coordinated, holistic, multisectoral approach to early childhood.

31. **Community-based programmes.** The Committee recommends that States parties support early childhood development programmes, including home- and community-based preschool programmes, in which the empowerment and education of parents (and other caregivers) are main features. States parties have a key role to play in providing a legislative framework for the provision of quality, adequately resourced services, and for ensuring that standards are tailored to the circumstances of particular groups and individuals and to the developmental priorities of particular age groups, from infancy through to transition into school. They are encouraged to construct high-quality, developmentally appropriate and culturally relevant programmes and to achieve this by working with local communities rather by imposing a standardized approach to early childhood care and education. The Committee also recommends that States parties pay greater attention to, and actively support, a rights-based approach to early childhood programmes, including initiatives surrounding transition to primary school that ensure

continuity and progression, in order to build children's confidence, communication skills and enthusiasm for learning through their active involvement in, among others, planning activities.

32. **The private sector as service provider.** With reference to its recommendations adopted during its 2002 day of general discussion on "The private sector as service provider and its role in implementing child rights" (see CRC/C/121, paras. 630-653), the Committee recommends that States parties support the activities of the non-governmental sector as a channel for programme implementation. It further calls on all non-State service providers ("for profit" as well as "non-profit" providers) to respect the principles and provisions of the Convention and, in this regard, reminds States parties of their primary obligation to ensure its implementation. Early childhood professionals - in both the State and non-State sectors - should be provided with thorough preparation, ongoing training and adequate remuneration. In this context, States parties are responsible for service provision for early childhood development. The role of civil society should be complementary to - not a substitute for - the role of the State. Where non-State services play a major role, the Committee reminds States parties that they have an obligation to monitor and regulate the quality of provision to ensure that children's rights are protected and their best interests served.

33. **Human rights education in early childhood.** In light of article 29 and the Committee's general comment No. 1 (2001), the Committee also recommends that States parties include human rights education within early childhood education. Such education should be participatory and empowering to children, providing them with practical opportunities to exercise their rights and responsibilities in ways adapted to their interests, concerns and evolving capacities. Human rights education of young children should be anchored in everyday issues at home, in childcare centres, in early education programmes and other community settings with which young children can identify.

34. **Right to rest, leisure and play.** The Committee notes that insufficient attention has been given by States parties and others to the implementation of the provisions of article 31 of the Convention, which guarantees "the right of the child to rest and leisure, to engage in play and recreational activities appropriate to the age of the child and to participate freely in cultural life and the arts". Play is one of the most distinctive features of early childhood. Through play, children both enjoy and challenge their current capacities, whether they are playing alone or with others. The value of creative play and exploratory learning is widely recognized in early childhood education. Yet realizing the right to rest, leisure and play is often hindered by a shortage of opportunities for young children to meet, play and interact in child-centred, secure, supportive, stimulating and stress-free environments. Children's right-to-play space is especially at risk in many urban environments, where the design and density of housing, commercial centres and transport systems combine with noise, pollution and all manner of dangers to create a hazardous environment for young children. Children's right to play can also be frustrated by excessive domestic chores (especially affecting girls) or by competitive schooling. Accordingly, the Committee appeals to States parties, non-governmental organizations and private actors to identify and remove potential obstacles to the enjoyment of these rights by the youngest children, including as part of poverty reduction strategies. Planning for towns, and leisure and play facilities should take account of children's right to express their views (art. 12), through appropriate consultations. In all these respects, States parties are encouraged to pay greater attention and allocate adequate resources (human and financial) to the implementation of the right to rest, leisure and play.

35. **Modern communications technologies and early childhood.** Article 17 recognizes the potential for both traditional print-based media and modern information technology-based mass media to contribute positively to the realization of children's rights. Early childhood is a specialist market for publishers and media producers, who should be encouraged to disseminate material that is appropriate to the capacities and interests of young children, socially and educationally beneficial to their well-being, and which reflects the national and regional diversities of children's circumstances, culture and language. Particular attention should be given to the need of minority groups for access to media that promote their recognition and social inclusion. Article 17 (e) also refers to the role of States parties in ensuring that children are protected from inappropriate and potentially harmful material. Rapid increases in the variety and accessibility of modern technologies, including Internet-based media, are a particular cause for concern. Young children are especially at risk if they are exposed to inappropriate or offensive material. States parties are urged to regulate media production and delivery in ways that protect young children, as well as support parents/caregivers to fulfil their child-rearing responsibilities in this regard (art. 18).

VI. YOUNG CHILDREN IN NEED OF SPECIAL PROTECTION

36. **Young children's vulnerability to risks.** Throughout this general comment the Committee notes that large numbers of young children grow up in difficult circumstances that are frequently in violation of their rights. Young children are especially vulnerable to the harm caused by unreliable, inconsistent relationships with parents and caregivers, or growing up in extreme poverty and deprivation, or being surrounded by conflict and violence or displaced from their homes as refugees, or any number of other adversities prejudicial to their well-being. Young children are less able to comprehend these adversities or resist harmful effects on their health, or physical, mental, spiritual, moral or social development. They are especially at risk where parents or other caregivers are unable to offer adequate protection, whether due to illness, or death, or due to disruption to families or communities. Whatever the difficult circumstances, young children require particular consideration because of the rapid developmental changes they are experiencing; they are more vulnerable to disease, trauma, and distorted or disturbed development, and they are relatively powerless to avoid or resist difficulties and are dependent on others to offer protection and promote their best interests. In the following paragraphs, the Committee draws States parties' attention to major difficult circumstances referred to in the Convention that have clear implications for rights in early childhood. This list is not exhaustive, and children may in any case be subject to multiple risks. In general, the goal of States parties should be to ensure that every child, in every circumstance, receives adequate protection in fulfilment of their rights:

(a) *Abuse and neglect* (art. 19). Young children are frequent victims of neglect, maltreatment and abuse, including physical and mental violence. Abuse very often happens within families, which can be especially destructive. Young children are least able to avoid or resist, least able to comprehend what is happening and least able to seek the protection of others. There is compelling evidence that trauma as a result of neglect and abuse has negative impacts on development, including, for the very youngest children, measurable effects on processes of brain maturation. Bearing in mind the prevalence of abuse and neglect in early childhood and the evidence that it has long-term repercussions, States parties should take all necessary measures to safeguard young children at risk and offer protection to victims of abuse, taking positive steps to support their recovery from trauma while avoiding stigmatization for the violations they have suffered;

(b) *Children without families* (art. 20 and 21). Children's rights to development are at serious risk when they are orphaned, abandoned or deprived of family care or when they suffer long-term disruptions to relationships or separations (e.g. due to natural disasters or other emergencies, epidemics such as HIV/AIDS, parental imprisonment, armed conflicts, wars and forced migration). These adversities will impact on children differently depending on their personal resilience, their age and their circumstances, as well as the availability of wider sources of support and alternative care. Research suggests that low-quality institutional care is unlikely to promote healthy physical and psychological development and can have serious negative consequences for long-term social adjustment, especially for children under 3 but also for children under 5 years old. To the extent that alternative care is required, early placement in family-based or family-like care is more likely to produce positive outcomes for young children. States parties are encouraged to invest in and support forms of alternative care that can ensure security, continuity of care and affection, and the opportunity for young children to form long-term attachments based on mutual trust and respect, for example through fostering, adoption and support for members of extended families. Where adoption is envisaged "the best interests of the child shall be the paramount consideration" (art. 21), not just "a primary consideration" (art. 3), systematically bearing in mind and respecting all relevant rights of the child and obligations of States parties set out elsewhere in the Convention and recalled in the present general comment;

(c) *Refugees* (art. 22). Young children who are refugees are most likely to be disoriented, having lost much that is familiar in their everyday surroundings and relationships. They and their parents are entitled to equal access to health care, education and other services. Children who are unaccompanied or separated from their families are especially at risk. The Committee offers detailed guidance on the care and protection of these children in general comment No. 6 (2005) on the treatment of unaccompanied and separated children outside their country of origin;

(d) *Children with disabilities* (art. 23). Early childhood is the period during which disabilities are usually identified and the impact on children's well-being and development recognized. Young children should never be institutionalized solely on the grounds of disability. It is a priority to ensure that they have equal opportunities to participate fully in education and community life, including by the removal of barriers that impede the realization of their rights. Young disabled children are entitled to appropriate specialist assistance, including support for their parents (or other caregivers). Disabled children should at all times be treated with dignity and in ways that encourage their self-reliance. (See also the recommendations from the Committee's 1997 day of general discussion on "The rights of children with disabilities" contained in document CRC/C/66.);

(e) *Harmful work* (art. 32). In some countries and regions, children are socialized to work from an early age, including in activities that are potentially hazardous, exploitative and damaging to their health, education and long-term prospects. For example, young children may be initiated into domestic work or agricultural labour, or assist parents or siblings engaged in hazardous activities. Even very young babies may be vulnerable to economic exploitation, as when they are used or hired out for begging. Exploitation of young children in the entertainment industry, including television, film, advertising and other modern media, is also a cause for concern. States parties have particular responsibilities in relation to extreme forms of hazardous child labour identified in the Worst Forms of Child Labour Convention, 1999 (No. 182) of the ILO;

(f)   *Substance abuse* (art. 33). While very young children are only rarely likely to be substance abusers, they may require specialist health care if born to alcohol- or drug-addicted mothers, and protection where family members are abusers and they are at risk of exposure to drugs. They may also suffer adverse consequences of alcohol or drug abuse on family living standards and quality of care, as well as being at risk of early initiation into substance abuse;

(g)   *Sexual abuse and exploitation* (art. 34). Young children, especially girls, are vulnerable to early sexual abuse and exploitation within and outside families. Young children in difficult circumstances are at particular risk, for example girl children employed as domestic workers. Young children may also be victims of producers of pornography; this is covered by the Optional Protocol to the Convention on the Rights of the Child on the sale of children, child prostitution and child pornography of 2002;

(h)   *Sale, trafficking and abduction of children* (art. 35). The Committee has frequently expressed concern about evidence of the sale and trafficking of abandoned and separated children for various purposes. As far as the youngest age groups are concerned, these purposes can include adoption, particularly (though not solely) by foreigners. In addition to the Optional Protocol on the sale of children, child prostitution and child pornography, the 1993 Hague Convention on Protection of Children and Cooperation in Respect of Intercountry Adoption provides a framework and mechanism for preventing abuses in this sphere, and the Committee has therefore always consistently and strongly urged all States parties that recognize and/or permit adoption to ratify or accede to this treaty. Universal birth registration, in addition to international cooperation, can help to combat this violation of rights;

(i)   *Deviant behaviour and lawbreaking* (art. 40). Under no circumstances should young children (defined as under 8 years old; see paragraph 4) be included in legal definitions of minimum age of criminal responsibility. Young children who misbehave or violate laws require sympathetic help and understanding, with the goal of increasing their capacities for personal control, social empathy and conflict resolution. States parties should ensure that parents/caregivers are provided adequate support and training to fulfil their responsibilities (art. 18) and that young children have access to quality early childhood education and care, and (where appropriate) specialist guidance/therapies.

37. In each of these circumstances, and in the case of all other forms of exploitation (art. 36), the Committee urges States parties to incorporate the particular situation of young children into all legislation, policies and interventions to promote physical and psychological recovery and social reintegration within an environment that promotes dignity and self-respect (art. 39).

VII. CAPACITY-BUILDING FOR EARLY CHILDHOOD

38. **Resource allocation for early childhood.** In order to ensure that young children's rights are fully realized during this crucial phase of their lives (and bearing in mind the impact of early childhood experiences on their long-term prospects), States parties are urged to adopt comprehensive, strategic and time-bound plans for early childhood within a rights-based framework. This requires an increase in human and financial resource allocations for early childhood services and programmes (art. 4). The Committee acknowledges that States parties implementing child rights in early

childhood do so from very different starting points, in terms of existing infrastructures for early childhood policies, services and professional training, as well as levels of resources potentially available to allocate to early childhood. The Committee also acknowledges that States parties may be faced with competing priorities to implement rights throughout childhood, for example where universal health services and primary education have still not been achieved. It is nonetheless important that there be sufficient public investment in services, infrastructure and overall resources specifically allocated to early childhood, for the many reasons set out in this general comment. In this connection, States parties are encouraged to develop strong and equitable partnerships between the Government, public services, non-governmental organizations, the private sector and families to finance comprehensive services in support of young children's rights. Finally, the Committee emphasizes that where services are decentralized, this should not be to the disadvantage of young children.

39. **Data collection and management.** The Committee reiterates the importance of comprehensive and up-to-date quantitative and qualitative data on all aspects of early childhood for the formulation, monitoring and evaluation of progress achieved, and for assessment of the impact of policies. The Committee is aware that many States parties lack adequate national data collection systems on early childhood for many areas covered by the Convention, and in particular that specific and disaggregated information on children in the early years is not readily available. The Committee urges all States parties to develop a system of data collection and indicators consistent with the Convention and disaggregated by gender, age, family structure, urban and rural residence, and other relevant categories. This system should cover all children up to the age of 18 years, with specific emphasis on early childhood, particularly children belonging to vulnerable groups.

40. **Capacity-building for research in early childhood.** The Committee noted earlier in this general comment that extensive research has been carried out on aspects of children's health, growth, and cognitive, social and cultural development, on the influence of both positive and negative factors on their well-being, and on the potential impact of early childhood care and education programmes. Increasingly, research is also being carried out on early childhood from a human rights perspective, notably on ways that children's participatory rights can be respected, including through their participation in the research process. Theory and evidence from early childhood research has a great deal to offer in the development of policies and practices, as well as in the monitoring and evaluation of initiatives and the education and training of all responsible for the well-being of young children. But the Committee also draws attention to the limitations of current research, through its focus mainly on early childhood in a limited range of contexts and regions of the world. As part of planning for early childhood, the Committee encourages States parties to develop national and local capacities for early childhood research, especially from a rights-based perspective.

41. **Training for rights in early childhood.** Knowledge and expertise about early childhood are not static but change over time. This is due variously to social trends impacting on the lives of young children, their parents and other caregivers, changing policies and priorities for their care and education, innovations in childcare, curricula and pedagogy, as well as the emergence of new research. Implementing child rights in early childhood sets challenges for all those responsible for children, as well as for children themselves as they gain an understanding of their role in their families, schools and communities. States parties are encouraged to undertake systematic child rights training for children and their parents, as well as for all professionals working for and with children, in particular parliamentarians, judges, magistrates, lawyers, law enforcement officials, civil servants, personnel in institutions and places of detention for

children, teachers, health personnel, social workers and local leaders. Furthermore, the Committee urges States parties to conduct awareness-raising campaigns for the public at large.

42. **International assistance.** Acknowledging the resource constraints affecting many States parties seeking to implement the comprehensive provisions outlined in this general comment, the Committee recommends that donor institutions, including the World Bank, other United Nations bodies and bilateral donors support early childhood development programmes financially and technically, and that it be one of their main targets in assisting sustainable development in countries receiving international assistance. Effective international cooperation can also strengthen capacity-building for early childhood, in terms of policy development, programme development, research and professional training.

43. **Looking forward.** The Committee urges all States parties, inter-governmental organizations, non-governmental organizations, academics, professional groups and grass-roots communities to continue advocating for the establishment of independent institutions on children's rights and foster continuous, high-level policy dialogues and research on the crucial importance of quality in early childhood, including dialogues at international, national, regional and local levels.

General Comment No 8 (2006)
The right of the child to protection from corporal punishment and other cruel or degrading forms of punishment (arts. 19; 28, para. 2; and 37, inter alia)

I. OBJECTIVES

1. Following its two days of general discussion on violence against children, held in 2000 and 2001, the Committee on the Rights of the Child resolved to issue a series of general comments concerning eliminating violence against children, of which this is the first. The Committee aims to guide States parties in understanding the provisions of the Convention concerning the protection of children against all forms of violence. This general comment focuses on corporal punishment and other cruel or degrading forms of punishment, which are currently very widely accepted and practised forms of violence against children.

2. The Convention on the Rights of the Child and other international human rights instruments recognize the right of the child to respect for the child's human dignity and physical integrity and equal protection under the law. The Committee is issuing this general comment to highlight the obligation of all States parties to move quickly to prohibit and eliminate all corporal punishment and all other cruel or degrading forms of punishment of children and to outline the legislative and other awareness-raising and educational measures that States must take.

3. Addressing the widespread acceptance or tolerance of corporal punishment of children and eliminating it, in the family, schools and other settings, is not only an obligation of States parties under the Convention. It is also a key strategy for reducing and preventing all forms of violence in societies.

II. BACKGROUND

4. The Committee has, from its earliest sessions, paid special attention to asserting children's right to protection from all forms of violence. In its examination of States parties' reports, and most recently in the context of the United Nations Secretary-General's study on violence against children, it has noted with great concern the widespread legality and persisting social approval of corporal punishment and other cruel or degrading punishment of children.[48] Already in 1993, the Committee noted in the report of its fourth session that it "recognized the importance of the question of corporal punishment in improving the system of promotion and protection of the rights of the child and decided to continue to devote attention to it in the process of examining States parties' reports".[49]

5. Since it began examining States parties' reports the Committee has recommended prohibition of all corporal punishment, in the family and other settings, to more than 130 States in all continents.[50] The Committee is encouraged that a growing number of States are taking appropriate legislative and other measures to assert children's right to respect for their human dignity and physical integrity and to equal protection under the law. The Committee understands that by 2006, more than 100 States had prohibited

---

[48] United Nations Secretary-General's Study on Violence against Children, due to report to United Nations General Assembly, autumn 2006. For details see http://www.violencestudy.org.

[49] Committee on the Rights of the Child, Report on the fourth session, 25 October 1993, CRC/C/20, para. 176.

[50] All the Committee's concluding observations can be viewed at www.ohchr.org.

corporal punishment in their schools and penal systems for children. A growing number have completed prohibition in the home and family and all forms of alternative care.[51]

6. In September 2000, the Committee held the first of two days of general discussion on violence against children. It focused on "State violence against children" and afterwards adopted detailed recommendations, including for the prohibition of all corporal punishment and the launching of public information campaigns "to raise awareness and sensitize the public about the severity of human rights violations in this domain and their harmful impact on children, and to address cultural acceptance of violence against children, promoting instead 'zero-tolerance' of violence".[52]

7. In April 2001, the Committee adopted its first general comment on "The aims of education" and reiterated that corporal punishment is incompatible with the Convention: "... Children do not lose their human rights by virtue of passing through the school gates. Thus, for example, education must be provided in a way that respects the inherent dignity of the child, enables the child to express his or her views freely in accordance with article 12, paragraph 1, and to participate in school life. Education must also be provided in a way that respects the strict limits on discipline reflected in article 28, paragraph 2, and promotes non-violence in school. The Committee has repeatedly made clear in its concluding observations that the use of corporal punishment does not respect the inherent dignity of the child nor the strict limits on school discipline ...".[53]

8. In recommendations adopted following the second day of general discussion, on "Violence against children within the family and in schools", held in September 2001, the Committee called upon States to "enact or repeal, as a matter of urgency, their legislation in order to prohibit all forms of violence, however light, within the family and in schools, including as a form of discipline, as required by the provisions of the Convention . . .".[54]

9. Another outcome of the Committee's 2000 and 2001 days of general discussion was a recommendation that the United Nations Secretary-General should be requested, through the General Assembly, to carry out an in-depth international study on violence against children. The United Nations General Assembly took this forward in 2001.[55] Within the context of the United Nations study, carried out between 2003 and 2006, the need to prohibit all currently legalized violence against children has been highlighted, as has children's own deep concern at the almost universal high prevalence of corporal punishment in the family and also its persisting legality in many States in schools and other institutions, and in penal systems for children in conflict with the law.

---

[51] The Global Initiative to End All Corporal Punishment of Children provides reports on the legal status of corporal punishment at www.endcorporalpunishment.org.

[52] Committee on the Rights of the Child, day of general discussion on State violence against children, Report on the twenty-fifth session, September/October 2000, CRC/C/100, paras. 666-688.

[53] Committee on the Rights of the Child, general comment No. 1, The aims of education, 17 April 2001, CRC/GC/2001/1, para. 8.

[54] Committee on the Rights of the Child, day of general discussion on violence against children within the family and in schools, Report on the twenty-eighth session, September/October 2001, CRC/C/111, paras. 701-745.

[55] General Assembly resolution 56/138.

III. DEFINITIONS

10. "Child" is defined as in the Convention as "every human being below the age of eighteen years unless under the law applicable to the child, majority is attained earlier".[56]

11. The Committee defines "corporal" or "physical" punishment as any punishment in which physical force is used and intended to cause some degree of pain or discomfort, however light. Most involves hitting ("smacking", "slapping", "spanking") children, with the hand or with an implement – a whip, stick, belt, shoe, wooden spoon, etc. But it can also involve, for example, kicking, shaking or throwing children, scratching, pinching, biting, pulling hair or boxing ears, forcing children to stay in uncomfortable positions, burning, scalding or forced ingestion (for example, washing children's mouths out with soap or forcing them to swallow hot spices). In the view of the Committee, corporal punishment is invariably degrading. In addition, there are other non-physical forms of punishment that are also cruel and degrading and thus incompatible with the Convention. These include, for example, punishment which belittles, humiliates, denigrates, scapegoats, threatens, scares or ridicules the child.

12. Corporal punishment and other cruel or degrading forms of punishment of children take place in many settings, including within the home and family, in all forms of alternative care, schools and other educational institutions and justice systems – both as a sentence of the courts and as a punishment within penal and other institutions – in situations of child labour, and in the community.

13. In rejecting any justification of violence and humiliation as forms of punishment for children, the Committee is not in any sense rejecting the positive concept of discipline. The healthy development of children depends on parents and other adults for necessary guidance and direction, in line with children's evolving capacities, to assist their growth towards responsible life in society.

14. The Committee recognizes that parenting and caring for children, especially babies and young children, demand frequent physical actions and interventions to protect them. This is quite distinct from the deliberate and punitive use of force to cause some degree of pain, discomfort or humiliation. As adults, we know for ourselves the difference between a protective physical action and a punitive assault; it is no more difficult to make a distinction in relation to actions involving children. The law in all States, explicitly or implicitly, allows for the use of non-punitive and necessary force to protect people.

15. The Committee recognizes that there are exceptional circumstances in which teachers and others, e.g. those working with children in institutions and with children in conflict with the law, may be confronted by dangerous behaviour which justifies the use of reasonable restraint to control it. Here too there is a clear distinction between the use of force motivated by the need to protect a child or others and the use of force to punish. The principle of the minimum necessary use of force for the shortest necessary period of time must always apply. Detailed guidance and training is also required, both to minimize the necessity to use restraint and to ensure that any methods used are safe and proportionate to the situation and do not involve the deliberate infliction of pain as a form of control.

---

[56] Article 1.

IV. HUMAN RIGHTS STANDARDS AND CORPORAL PUNISHMENT OF CHILDREN

16. Before the adoption of the Convention on the Rights of the Child, the International Bill of Human Rights – the Universal Declaration and the two International Covenants, on Civil and Political Rights and on Economic, Social and Cultural Rights – upheld "everyone's" right to respect for his/her human dignity and physical integrity and to equal protection under the law. In asserting States' obligation to prohibit and eliminate all corporal punishment and all other cruel or degrading forms of punishment, the Committee notes that the Convention on the Rights of the Child builds on this foundation. The dignity of each and every individual is the fundamental guiding principle of international human rights law.

17. The preamble to the Convention on the Rights of the Child affirms, in accordance with the principles in the Charter of the United Nations, repeated in the preamble to the Universal Declaration, that "recognition of the inherent dignity and of the equal and inalienable rights of all members of the human family is the foundation of freedom, justice and peace in the world". The preamble to the Convention also recalls that, in the Universal Declaration, the United Nations "has proclaimed that childhood is entitled to special care and assistance".

18. Article 37 of the Convention requires States to ensure that "no child shall be subjected to torture or other cruel, inhuman or degrading treatment or punishment". This is complemented and extended by article 19, which requires States to "take all appropriate legislative, administrative, social and educational measures to protect the child from all forms of physical or mental violence, injury or abuse, neglect or negligent treatment, maltreatment or exploitation, including sexual abuse, while in the care of parent(s), legal guardian(s) or any other person who has the care of the child". There is no ambiguity: "all forms of physical or mental violence" does not leave room for any level of legalized violence against children. Corporal punishment and other cruel or degrading forms of punishment are forms of violence and States must take all appropriate legislative, administrative, social and educational measures to eliminate them.

19. In addition, article 28, paragraph 2, of the Convention refers to school discipline and requires States parties to "take all appropriate measures to ensure that school discipline is administered in a manner consistent with the child's human dignity and in conformity with the present Convention".

20. Article 19 and article 28, paragraph 2, do not refer explicitly to corporal punishment. The *travaux préparatoires* for the Convention do not record any discussion of corporal punishment during the drafting sessions. But the Convention, like all human rights instruments, must be regarded as a living instrument, whose interpretation develops over time. In the 17 years since the Convention was adopted, the prevalence of corporal punishment of children in their homes, schools and other institutions has become more visible, through the reporting process under the Convention and through research and advocacy by, among others, national human rights institutions and non-governmental organizations (NGOs).

21. Once visible, it is clear that the practice directly conflicts with the equal and inalienable rights of children to respect for their human dignity and physical integrity. The distinct nature of children, their initial dependent and developmental state, their unique human potential as well as their vulnerability, all demand the need for more, rather than less, legal and other protection from all forms of violence.

22. The Committee emphasizes that eliminating violent and humiliating punishment of children, through law reform and other necessary measures, is an immediate and unqualified obligation of States parties. It notes that other treaty bodies, including the Human Rights Committee, the Committee on Economic, Social and Cultural Rights and the Committee against Torture have reflected the same view in their concluding observations on States parties' reports under the relevant instruments, recommending prohibition and other measures against corporal punishment in schools, penal systems and, in some cases, the family. For example, the Committee on Economic, Social and Cultural Rights, in its general comment No. 13 (1999) on "The right to education" stated: "In the Committee's view, corporal punishment is inconsistent with the fundamental guiding principle of international human rights law enshrined in the Preambles to the Universal Declaration and both Covenants: the dignity of the individual. Other aspects of school discipline may also be inconsistent with school discipline, including public humiliation."[57]

23. Corporal punishment has also been condemned by regional human rights mechanisms. The European Court of Human Rights, in a series of judgements, has progressively condemned corporal punishment of children, first in the penal system, then in schools, including private schools, and most recently in the home.[58] The European Committee of Social Rights, monitoring compliance of member States of the Council of Europe with the European Social Charter and Revised Social Charter, has found that compliance with the Charters requires prohibition in legislation against any form of violence against children, whether at school, in other institutions, in their home or elsewhere.[59]

24. An Advisory Opinion of the Inter-American Court of Human Rights, on the *Legal Status and Human Rights of the Child* (2002) holds that the States parties to the American Convention on Human Rights "are under the obligation ... to adopt all positive measures required to ensure protection of children against mistreatment, whether in their relations with public authorities, or in relations among individuals or with non-governmental entities". The Court quotes provisions of the Convention on the Rights of the Child, conclusions of the Committee on the Rights of the Child and also judgements of the European Court of Human Rights relating to States' obligations to protect children from violence, including within the family. The Court concludes that "the State has the duty to adopt positive measures to fully ensure effective exercise of the rights of the child".[60]

25. The African Commission on Human and Peoples' Rights monitors implementation of the African Charter on Human and Peoples' Rights. In a 2003 decision on an individual communication concerning a sentence of "lashes" imposed on students, the

---

[57]   Committee on Economic, Social and Cultural Rights, general comment No. 13, The right to education (art. 13), 1999, para. 41.

[58]   Corporal punishment was condemned in a series of decisions of the European Commission on Human Rights and judgements of the European Court of Human Rights; see in particular *Tyrer v. UK*, 1978; *Campbell and Cosans v. UK*, 1982; *Costello-Roberts v. UK*, 1993; *A v. UK*, 1998. European Court judgements are available at http://www.echr.coe.int/echr.

[59]   European Committee of Social Rights, general observations regarding article 7, paragraph 10, and article 17. *Conclusions XV-2*, Vol. 1, General Introduction, p. 26, 2001; the Committee has since issued conclusions, finding a number of Member States not in compliance because of their failure to prohibit all corporal punishment in the family and in other settings. In 2005 it issued decisions on collective complaints made under the charters, finding three States not in compliance because of their failure to prohibit. For details, see http://www.coe.int/T/E/Human_Rights/Esc/; also *Eliminating corporal punishment: a human rights imperative for Europe's children*, Council of Europe Publishing, 2005.

[60]   Inter-American Court of Human Rights, Advisory Opinion OC-17/2002 of 28 August 2002, paras. 87 and 91.

Commission found that the punishment violated article 5 of the African Charter, which prohibits cruel, inhuman or degrading punishment. It requested the relevant Government to amend the law, abolishing the penalty of lashes, and to take appropriate measures to ensure compensation of the victims. In its decision, the Commission states: "There is no right for individuals, and particularly the Government of a country to apply physical violence to individuals for offences. Such a right would be tantamount to sanctioning State-sponsored torture under the Charter and contrary to the very nature of this human rights treaty."[61] The Committee on the Rights of the Child is pleased to note that constitutional and other high-level courts in many countries have issued decisions condemning corporal punishment of children in some or all settings, and in most cases quoting the Convention on the Rights of the Child.[62]

26. When the Committee on the Rights of the Child has raised eliminating corporal punishment with certain States during the examination of their reports, governmental representatives have sometimes suggested that some level of "reasonable" or "moderate" corporal punishment can be justified as in the "best interests" of the child. The Committee has identified, as an important general principle, the Convention's requirement that the best interests of the child should be a primary consideration in all actions concerning children (art. 3, para. 1). The Convention also asserts, in article 18, that the best interests of the child will be parents' basic concern. But interpretation of a child's best interests must be consistent with the whole Convention, including the obligation to protect children from all forms of violence and the requirement to give due weight to the child's views; it cannot be used to justify practices, including corporal punishment and other forms of cruel or degrading punishment, which conflict with the child's human dignity and right to physical integrity.

27. The preamble to the Convention upholds the family as "the fundamental group of society and the natural environment for the growth and well-being of all its members and particularly children". The Convention requires States to respect and support families. There is no conflict whatsoever with States' obligation to ensure that the human dignity and physical integrity of children within the family receive full protection alongside other family members.

28. Article 5 requires States to respect the responsibilities, rights and duties of parents "to provide, in a manner consistent with the evolving capacities of the child, appropriate direction and guidance in the exercise by the child of the rights recognized in the present

---

61 African Commission on Human and Peoples' Rights, *Curtis Francis Doebbler v. Sudan*, Comm. No. 236/2000 (2003); see para. 42.

62 For example, in 2002 the Fiji Court of Appeal declared corporal punishment in schools and the penal system unconstitutional. The judgement declared: "Children have rights no wit inferior to the rights of adults. Fiji has ratified the Convention on the Rights of the Child. Our Constitution also guarantees fundamental rights to every person. Government is required to adhere to principles respecting the rights of all individuals, communities and groups. By their status as children, children need special protection. Our educational institutions should be sanctuaries of peace and creative enrichment, not places for fear, ill-treatment and tampering with the human dignity of students" (Fiji Court of Appeal, *Naushad Ali v. State*, 2002). In 1996, Italy's highest Court, the Supreme Court of Cassation in Rome, issued a decision that effectively prohibited all parental use of corporal punishment. The judgement states: "... The use of violence for educational purposes can no longer be considered lawful. There are two reasons for this: the first is the overriding importance which the [Italian] legal system attributes to protecting the dignity of the individual. This includes 'minors' who now hold rights and are no longer simply objects to be protected by their parents or, worse still, objects at the disposal of their parents. The second reason is that, as an educational aim, the harmonious development of a child's personality, which ensures that he/she embraces the values of peace, tolerance and co-existence, cannot be achieved by using violent means which contradict these goals" (Cambria, Cass, sez. VI, 18 Marzo 1996 [Supreme Court of Cassation, 6th Penal Section, 18 March 1996], Foro It II 1996, 407 (Italy)). Also see South African Constitutional Court (2000) *Christian Education South Africa v. Minister of Education*, CCT4/00; 2000 (4) SA757 (CC); 2000 (10) BCLR 1051 (CC), 18 August 2000.

Convention". Here again, interpretation of "appropriate" direction and guidance must be consistent with the whole Convention and leaves no room for justification of violent or other cruel or degrading forms of discipline.

29. Some raise faith-based justifications for corporal punishment, suggesting that certain interpretations of religious texts not only justify its use, but provide a duty to use it. Freedom of religious belief is upheld for everyone in the International Covenant on Civil and Political Rights (art. 18), but practice of a religion or belief must be consistent with respect for others' human dignity and physical integrity. Freedom to practise one's religion or belief may be legitimately limited in order to protect the fundamental rights and freedoms of others. In certain States, the Committee has found that children, in some cases from a very young age, in other cases from the time that they are judged to have reached puberty, may be sentenced to punishments of extreme violence, including stoning and amputation, prescribed under certain interpretations of religious law. Such punishments plainly violate the Convention and other international human rights standards, as has been highlighted also by the Human Rights Committee and the Committee against Torture, and must be prohibited.

V. MEASURES AND MECHANISMS REQUIRED TO ELIMINATE CORPORAL PUNISHMENT AND OTHER CRUEL OR DEGRADING FORMS OF PUNISHMENT

1. Legislative measures

30. The wording of article 19 of the Convention builds upon article 4 and makes clear that legislative as well as other measures are required to fulfil States' obligations to protect children from all forms of violence. The Committee has welcomed the fact that, in many States, the Convention or its principles have been incorporated into domestic law. All States have criminal laws to protect citizens from assault. Many have constitutions and/or legislation reflecting international human rights standards and article 37 of the Convention on the Rights of the Child, which uphold "everyone's" right to protection from torture and cruel, inhuman or degrading treatment or punishment. Many also have specific child protection laws that make "ill-treatment" or "abuse" or "cruelty" an offence. But the Committee has learned from its examination of States' reports that such legislative provisions do not generally guarantee the child protection from all corporal punishment and other cruel or degrading forms of punishment, in the family and in other settings.

31. In its examination of reports, the Committee has noted that in many States there are explicit legal provisions in criminal and/or civil (family) codes that provide parents and other carers with a defence or justification for using some degree of violence in "disciplining" children. For example, the defence of "lawful", "reasonable" or "moderate" chastisement or correction has formed part of English common law for centuries, as has a "right of correction" in French law. At one time in many States the same defence was also available to justify the chastisement of wives by their husbands and of slaves, servants and apprentices by their masters. The Committee emphasizes that the Convention requires the removal of any provisions (in statute or common – case law) that allow some degree of violence against children (e.g. "reasonable" or "moderate" chastisement or correction), in their homes/families or in any other setting.

32. In some States, corporal punishment is specifically authorized in schools and other institutions, with regulations setting out how it is to be administered and by whom. And in a minority of States, corporal punishment using canes or whips is still authorized as a sentence of the courts for child offenders. As frequently reiterated by the Committee, the Convention requires the repeal of all such provisions.

33. In some States, the Committee has observed that while there is no explicit defence or justification of corporal punishment in the legislation, nevertheless traditional attitudes to children imply that corporal punishment is permitted. Sometimes these attitudes are reflected in court decisions (in which parents or teachers or other carers have been acquitted of assault or ill-treatment on the grounds that they were exercising a right or freedom to use moderate "correction").

34. In the light of the traditional acceptance of violent and humiliating forms of punishment of children, a growing number of States have recognized that simply repealing authorization of corporal punishment and any existing defences is not enough. In addition, explicit prohibition of corporal punishment and other cruel or degrading forms of punishment, in their civil or criminal legislation, is required in order to make it absolutely clear that it is as unlawful to hit or "smack" or "spank" a child as to do so to an adult, and that the criminal law on assault does apply equally to such violence, regardless of whether it is termed "discipline" or "reasonable correction".

35. Once the criminal law applies fully to assaults on children, the child is protected from corporal punishment wherever he or she is and whoever the perpetrator is. But in the view of the Committee, given the traditional acceptance of corporal punishment, it is essential that the applicable sectoral legislation – e.g. family law, education law, law relating to all forms of alternative care and justice systems, employment law – clearly prohibits its use in the relevant settings. In addition, it is valuable if professional codes of ethics and guidance for teachers, carers and others, and also the rules or charters of institutions, emphasize the illegality of corporal punishment and other cruel or degrading forms of punishment.

36. The Committee is also concerned at reports that corporal punishment and other cruel or degrading punishments are used in situations of child labour, including in the domestic context. The Committee reiterates that the Convention and other applicable human rights instruments protect the child from economic exploitation and from any work that is likely to be hazardous, interferes with the child's education, or is harmful to the child's development, and that they require certain safeguards to ensure the effective enforcement of this protection. The Committee emphasizes that it is essential that the prohibition of corporal punishment and other cruel or degrading forms of punishment must be enforced in any situations in which children are working.

37. Article 39 of the Convention requires States to take all appropriate measures to promote physical and psychological recovery and social reintegration of a child victim of "any form of neglect, exploitation, or abuse; torture or any other form of cruel, inhuman or degrading treatment or punishment". Corporal punishment and other degrading forms of punishment may inflict serious damage to the physical, psychological and social development of children, requiring appropriate health and other care and treatment. This must take place in an environment that fosters the integral health, self-respect and dignity of the child, and be extended as appropriate to the child's family group. There should be an interdisciplinary approach to planning and providing care and treatment, with specialized training of the professionals involved. The child's views should be given due weight concerning all aspects of their treatment and in reviewing it.

2. Implementation of prohibition of corporal punishment and other cruel or degrading forms of punishment

38. The Committee believes that implementation of the prohibition of all corporal punishment requires awareness-raising, guidance and training (see paragraph 45 et seq. below) for all those involved. This must ensure that the law operates in the best interests of the affected children – in particular when parents or other close family members are

the perpetrators. The first purpose of law reform to prohibit corporal punishment of children within the family is prevention: to prevent violence against children by changing attitudes and practice, underlining children's right to equal protection and providing an unambiguous foundation for child protection and for the promotion of positive, non-violent and participatory forms of child-rearing.

39. Achieving a clear and unconditional prohibition of all corporal punishment will require varying legal reforms in different States parties. It may require specific provisions in sectoral laws covering education, juvenile justice and all forms of alternative care. But it should be made explicitly clear that the criminal law provisions on assault also cover all corporal punishment, including in the family. This may require an additional provision in the criminal code of the State party. But it is also possible to include a provision in the civil code or family law, prohibiting the use of all forms of violence, including all corporal punishment. Such a provision emphasizes that parents or other caretakers can no longer use any traditional defence that it is their right ("reasonably" or "moderately") to use corporal punishment if they face prosecution under the criminal code. Family law should also positively emphasize that parental responsibility includes providing appropriate direction and guidance to children without any form of violence.

40. The principle of equal protection of children and adults from assault, including within the family, does not mean that all cases of corporal punishment of children by their parents that come to light should lead to prosecution of parents. The *de minimis* principle – that the law does not concern itself with trivial matters – ensures that minor assaults between adults only come to court in very exceptional circumstances; the same will be true of minor assaults on children. States need to develop effective reporting and referral mechanisms. While all reports of violence against children should be appropriately investigated and their protection from significant harm assured, the aim should be to stop parents from using violent or other cruel or degrading punishments through supportive and educational, not punitive, interventions.

41. Children's dependent status and the unique intimacy of family relations demand that decisions to prosecute parents, or to formally intervene in the family in other ways, should be taken with very great care. Prosecuting parents is in most cases unlikely to be in their children's best interests. It is the Committee's view that prosecution and other formal interventions (for example, to remove the child or remove the perpetrator) should only proceed when they are regarded both as necessary to protect the child from significant harm and as being in the best interests of the affected child. The affected child's views should be given due weight, according to his or her age and maturity.

42. Advice and training for all those involved in child protection systems, including the police, prosecuting authorities and the courts, should underline this approach to enforcement of the law. Guidance should also emphasize that article 9 of the Convention requires that any separation of the child from his or her parents must be deemed necessary in the best interests of the child and be subject to judicial review, in accordance with applicable law and procedures, with all interested parties, including the child, represented. Where separation is deemed to be justified, alternatives to placement of the child outside the family should be considered, including removal of the perpetrator, suspended sentencing, and so on.

43. Where, despite prohibition and positive education and training programmes, cases of corporal punishment come to light outside the family home – in schools, other institutions and forms of alternative care, for example – prosecution may be a reasonable response. The threat to the perpetrator of other disciplinary action or dismissal should also act as a clear deterrent. It is essential that the prohibition of all corporal punishment and other cruel or degrading punishment, and the sanctions that

may be imposed if it is inflicted, should be well disseminated to children and to all those working with or for children in all settings. Monitoring disciplinary systems and the treatment of children must be part of the sustained supervision of all institutions and placements which is required by the Convention. Children and their representatives in all such placements must have immediate and confidential access to child-sensitive advice, advocacy and complaints procedures and ultimately to the courts, with necessary legal and other assistance. In institutions, there should be a requirement to report and to review any violent incidents.

3. Educational and other measures

44. Article 12 of the Convention underlines the importance of giving due consideration to children's views on the development and implementation of educational and other measures to eradicate corporal punishment and other cruel or degrading forms of punishment.

45. Given the widespread traditional acceptance of corporal punishment, prohibition on its own will not achieve the necessary change in attitudes and practice. Comprehensive awareness-raising of children's right to protection and of the laws that reflect this right is required. Under article 42 of the Convention, States undertake to make the principles and provisions of the Convention widely known, by appropriate and active means, to adults and children alike.

46. In addition, States must ensure that positive, non-violent relationships and education are consistently promoted to parents, carers, teachers and all others who work with children and families. The Committee emphasizes that the Convention requires the elimination not only of corporal punishment but of all other cruel or degrading punishment of children. It is not for the Convention to prescribe in detail how parents should relate to or guide their children. But the Convention does provide a framework of principles to guide relationships both within the family, and between teachers, carers and others and children. Children's developmental needs must be respected. Children learn from what adults do, not only from what adults say. When the adults to whom a child most closely relates use violence and humiliation in their relationship with the child, they are demonstrating disrespect for human rights and teaching a potent and dangerous lesson that these are legitimate ways to seek to resolve conflict or change behaviour.

47. The Convention asserts the status of the child as an individual person and holder of human rights. The child is not a possession of parents, nor of the State, nor simply an object of concern. In this spirit, article 5 requires parents (or, where applicable, members of the extended family or community) to provide the child with appropriate direction and guidance, in a manner consistent with his/her evolving capacities, in the exercise by the child of the rights recognized in the Convention. Article 18, which underlines the primary responsibility of parents, or legal guardians, for the upbringing and development of the child, states that "the best interests of the child will be their basic concern". Under article 12, States are required to assure children the right to express their views freely "in all matters affecting the child", with the views of the child being given due weight in accordance with age and maturity. This emphasizes the need for styles of parenting, caring and teaching that respect children's participation rights. In its general comment No. 1 on "The aims of education", the Committee has emphasized the importance of developing education that is "child-centred, child-friendly and empowering".[63]

---

[63] See note 11.

48. The Committee notes that there are now many examples of materials and programmes promoting positive, non-violent forms of parenting and education, addressed to parents, other carers and teachers and developed by Governments, United Nations agencies, NGOs and others.[64] These can be appropriately adapted for use in different States and situations. The media can play a very valuable role in awareness-raising and public education. Challenging traditional dependence on corporal punishment and other cruel or degrading forms of discipline requires sustained action. The promotion of non-violent forms of parenting and education should be built into all the points of contact between the State and parents and children, in health, welfare and educational services, including early childhood institutions, day-care centres and schools. It should also be integrated into the initial and in-service training of teachers and all those working with children in care and justice systems.

49. The Committee proposes that States may wish to seek technical assistance from, among others, UNICEF and UNESCO concerning awareness-raising, public education and training to promote non-violent approaches.

4. Monitoring and evaluation

50. The Committee, in its general comment No. 5 on "General measures of implementation for the Convention on the Rights of the Child (arts. 4, 42 and 44, para. 6) ", emphasizes the need for systematic monitoring by States parties of the realization of children's rights, through the development of appropriate indicators and the collection of sufficient and reliable data.[65]

51. Therefore States parties should monitor their progress towards eliminating corporal punishment and other cruel or degrading forms of punishment and thus realizing children's right to protection. Research using interviews with children, their parents and other carers, in conditions of confidentiality and with appropriate ethical safeguards, is essential in order to accurately assess the prevalence of these forms of violence within the family and attitudes to them. The Committee encourages every State to carry out/commission such research, as far as possible with groups representative of the whole population, to provide baseline information and then at regular intervals to measure progress. The results of this research can also provide valuable guidance for the development of universal and targeted awareness-raising campaigns and training for professionals working with or for children.

52. The Committee also underlines in general comment No. 5 the importance of independent monitoring of implementation by, for example, parliamentary committees, NGOs, academic institutions, professional associations, youth groups and independent human rights institutions (see also the Committee's general comment No. 2 on "The role of independent national human rights institutions in the protection and promotion of the rights of the child").[66] These could all play an important role in monitoring the realization of children's right to protection from all corporal punishment and other cruel or degrading forms of punishment.

---

[64]　The Committee commends, as one example, UNESCO's handbook, *Eliminating corporal punishment: the way forward to constructive child discipline*, UNESCO Publishing, Paris, 2005. This provides a set of principles for constructive discipline, rooted in the Convention. It also includes Internet references to materials and programmes available worldwide.

[65]　Committee on the Rights of the Child, general comment No. 5 (2003), "General measures of implementation for the Convention on the Rights of the Child", para. 2.

[66]　Committee on the Rights of the Child, general comment No. 2 on "The role of independent national human rights institutions in the promotion and protection of the rights of the child", 2002.

VI. REPORTING REQUIREMENTS UNDER THE CONVENTION

53. The Committee expects States to include in their periodic reports under the Convention information on the measures taken to prohibit and prevent all corporal punishment and other cruel or degrading forms of punishment in the family and all other settings, including on related awareness-raising activities and promotion of positive, non-violent relationships and on the State's evaluation of progress towards achieving full respect for children's rights to protection from all forms of violence. The Committee also encourages United Nations agencies, national human rights institutions, NGOs and other competent bodies to provide it with relevant information on the legal status and prevalence of corporal punishment and progress towards its elimination.

General Comment No 9 (2006)
The rights of children with disabilities

I. INTRODUCTION

A. Why a General Comment on children with disabilities?

1. It is estimated that there are 500-650 million persons with disabilities in the world, approximately 10 % of the world population, 150 million of whom are children. More than 80 % live in developing countries with little or no access to services. The majority of children with disabilities in developing countries remain out of school and are completely illiterate. It is recognized that most of the causes of disabilities, such as war, illness and poverty, are preventable which also prevent and/or reduce the secondary impacts of disabilities, often caused by the lack of early/timely intervention. Therefore, more should be done to create the necessary political will and real commitment to investigate and put into practice the most effective actions to prevent disabilities with the participation of all levels of society.

2. The past few decades have witnessed positive focus on persons with disabilities in general and children in particular. The reason for this new focus is explained partly by the fact that the voice of persons with disabilities and of their advocates from national and international non governmental organizations (NGO) is being increasingly heard and partly by the growing attention paid to persons with disabilities within the framework of the human rights treaties and the United Nations human rights treaty bodies. These treaty bodies have considerable potential in advancing the rights of persons with disabilities but they have generally been underused. When adopted in November 1989 the Convention on the Rights of the Child (hereafter "the Convention") was the first human rights treaty that contained a specific reference to disability (article 2 on non-discrimination) and a separate article 23 exclusively dedicated to the rights and needs of children with disabilities. Since the Convention has entered into force (2 September 1990), the Committee on the Rights of the Child (thereafter "the Committee") has paid sustained and particular attention to disability-based discrimination[67] while other human rights treaty bodies have paid attention to disability-based discrimination under "other status" in the context of articles on non-discrimination of their relevant Convention. In 1994 the Committee on Economic, Social and Cultural Rights issued its general comment No. 5 on persons with disabilities and stated in paragraph 15 that "The effects of disability-based discrimination have been particularly severe in the fields of education, employment, housing, transport, cultural life, and access to public places and services." The Special Rapporteur on disability of the United Nations Commission for Social Development was first appointed in 1994 and mandated to monitor of the Standard Rules on the Equalization of Opportunities for Persons with Disabilities, adopted by the General Assembly at its forty-eighth session in 1993 (A/RES/48/96, Annex), and to advance the status of persons with disabilities throughout the world. On 6 October 1997 the Committee devoted its day of general discussion to children with disabilities and adopted a set of recommendations (CRC/C/66, paragraphs 310-339), in which it considered the possibility of drafting a general comment on children with disabilities. The Committee notes with appreciation the work of the Ad-Hoc Committee on a Comprehensive and Integral International Convention on the Protection and Promotion of the Rights and Dignity of Persons with Disabilities, and that it adopted at its eighth session, held in

---

[67] See Wouter Vandenhole, Non-Discrimination and Equality in the View of the UN Human Rights Treaty Bodies, p.170-172, Antwerpen/Oxford, Intersentia 2005.

New York on 25 August 2006, a draft convention on the rights of persons with disabilities to be submitted to the General Assembly at its sixty-first session (A/AC.265/2006/4, Annex II).

3. The Committee, in reviewing State party reports, has accumulated a wealth of information on the status of children with disabilities worldwide and found that in the overwhelming majority of countries some recommendations had to be made specifically to address the situation of children with disabilities. The problems identified and addressed have varied from exclusion from decision-making processes to severe discrimination and actual killing of children with disabilities. Poverty being both a cause and a consequence of disability, the Committee has repeatedly stressed that children with disabilities and their families have the right to an adequate standard of living, including adequate food, clothing and housing, and to the continuous improvement of their living conditions. The question of children with disabilities living in poverty should be addressed by allocating adequate budgetary resources as well as by ensuring that children with disabilities have access to social protection and poverty reduction programmes.

4. The Committee has noted that no reservations or declarations have been entered specifically to article 23 of the Convention by any State party.

5. The Committee also notes that children with disabilities are still experiencing serious difficulties and facing barriers to the full enjoyment of the rights enshrined in the Convention. The Committee emphasizes that the barrier is not the disability itself but rather a combination of social, cultural, attitudinal and physical obstacles which children with disabilities encounter in their daily lives. The strategy for promoting their rights is therefore to take the necessary action to remove those barriers. Acknowledging the importance of articles 2 and 23 of the Convention, the Committee states from the outset that the implementation of the Convention with regards to children with disabilities should not be limited to these articles.

6. The present general comment is meant to provide guidance and assistance to States parties in their efforts to implement the rights of children with disabilities, in a comprehensive manner which covers all the provisions of the Convention. Thus, the Committee will first make some observations related directly to articles 2 and 23, then it will elaborate on the necessity of paying particular attention to and including explicitly children with disabilities within the framework of general measures for the implementation of the Convention. Those observations will be followed by comments on the meaning and the implementation of the various articles of the Convention (clustered in accordance with the Committee's practice) for children with disabilities.

B. Definition

7. According to article 1, paragraph 2, of the draft convention on the rights of persons with disabilities, "Persons with disabilities include those who have long-term physical, mental, intellectual, or sensory impairments which in interaction with various barriers may hinder their full and effective participation in society on an equal basis with others." (A/AC.265/2006/4, Annex II)

II. THE KEY PROVISIONS FOR CHILDREN WITH DISABILITIES (ARTS. 2 AND 23)

A. Article 2

8. Article 2 requires States parties to ensure that all children within their jurisdiction enjoy all the rights enshrined in the Convention without discrimination of any kind. This

obligation requires States parties to take appropriate measures to prevent all forms of discrimination, including on the ground of disability. This explicit mention of disability as a prohibited ground for discrimination in article 2 is unique and can be explained by the fact that children with disabilities belong to one of the most vulnerable groups of children. In many cases forms of multiple discrimination - based on a combination of factors, i.e. indigenous girls with disabilities, children with disabilities living in rural areas and so on - increase the vulnerability of certain groups. It has been therefore felt necessary to mention disability explicitly in the non-discrimination article. Discrimination takes place – often de facto – in various aspects of the life and development of children with disabilities. As an example, social discrimination and stigmatization leads to their marginalization and exclusion, and may even threaten their survival and development if it goes as far as physical or mental violence against children with disabilities. Discrimination in service provision excludes them from education and denies them access to quality health and social services. The lack of appropriate education and vocational training discriminates against them by denying them job opportunities in the future. Social stigma, fears, overprotection, negative attitudes, misbeliefs and prevailing prejudices against children with disabilities remain strong in many communities and lead to the marginalization and alienation of children with disabilities. The Committee shall elaborate on these aspects in the paragraphs below.

9. In general, States parties in their efforts to prevent and eliminate all forms of discrimination against children with disabilities should take the following measures:

(a) Include explicitly disability as a forbidden ground for discrimination in constitutional provisions on non-discrimination and/or include specific prohibition of discrimination on the ground of disability in specific anti-discrimination laws or legal provisions.

(b) Provide for effective remedies in case of violations of the rights of children with disabilities, and ensure that those remedies are easily accessible to children with disabilities and their parents and/or others caring for the child.

(c) Conduct awareness-raising and educational campaigns targeting the public at large and specific groups of professionals with a view to preventing and eliminating de facto discrimination against children with disabilities.

10. Girls with disabilities are often even more vulnerable to discrimination due to gender discrimination. In this context, States parties are requested to pay particular attention to girls with disabilities by taking the necessary measures, and when needed extra measures, in order to ensure that they are well protected, have access to all services and are fully included in society.

B. Article 23

11. Paragraph 1 of article 23 should be considered as the leading principle for the implementation of the Convention with respect to children with disabilities: the enjoyment of a full and decent life in conditions that ensure dignity, promote self reliance and facilitate active participation in the community. The measures taken by States parties regarding the realization of the rights of children with disabilities should be directed towards this goal. The core message of this paragraph is that children with disabilities should be included in the society. Measures taken for the implementation of the rights contained in the Convention regarding children with disabilities, for example in the areas of education and health, should explicitly aim at the maximum inclusion of those children in society.

12. According to paragraph 2 of article 23 States parties to the Convention recognize the right of the child with disability to special care and shall encourage and ensure the

extension of assistance to the eligible child and those responsible for his or her care. The assistance has to be appropriate to the child's condition and the circumstances of the parents or others caring for the child. Paragraph 3 of article 23 gives further rules regarding the costs of specific measures and precisions as to what the assistance should try to achieve.

13.   In order to meet the requirements of article 23 it is necessary that States parties develop and effectively implement a comprehensive policy by means of a plan of action which not only aims at the full enjoyment of the rights enshrined in the Convention without discrimination but which also ensures that a child with disability and her or his parents and/or others caring for the child do receive the special care and assistance they are entitled to under the Convention.

14.   Regarding the specifics of paragraphs 2 and 3 of article 23, the Committee makes the following observations:

(a)   The provision of special care and assistance is subject to available resources and free of charge whenever possible. The Committee urges States parties to make special care and assistance to children with disabilities a matter of high priority and to invest to the maximum extent of available resources in the elimination of discrimination against children with disabilities and towards their maximum inclusion in society.

(b)   Care and assistance shall be designed to ensure that children with disabilities have effective access to and benefit from education, training, health care services, recovery services, preparation for employment and recreation opportunities. The Committee when dealing with specific articles of the Convention will elaborate on the measures necessary to achieve this.

15.   With reference to article 23, paragraph 4, the Committee notes that the international exchange of information between States parties in the areas of prevention and treatment is quite limited. The Committee recommends that States parties take effective, and where appropriate targeted, measures for an active promotion of information as envisaged by article 23, paragraph 4, in order to enable States parties to improve their capabilities and skills in the areas of prevention and treatment of disabilities of children.

16.   It is often not clear how and to which degree the needs of developing countries are taken into account as required by article 23, paragraph 4. The Committee strongly recommends States parties to ensure that, within the framework of bilateral or multilateral development assistance, particular attention be paid to children with disabilities and their survival and development in accordance with the provisions of the Convention, for example, by developing and implementing special programmes aiming at their inclusion in society and allocating earmarked budgets to that effect. States parties are invited to provide information in their reports to the Committee on the activities and results of such international cooperation.

III. GENERAL MEASURES OF IMPLEMENTATION (ARTS. 4, 42 AND 44 (6))[68]

A. Legislation

17.   In addition to the legislative measures recommended with regard to non-discrimination (see paragraph 9 above), the Committee recommends that States

---

[68]   In the present general comment the Committee focuses on the need to pay special attention to children with disabilities in the context of the general measures. For a more elaborated explanation of the content and

parties undertake a comprehensive review of all domestic laws and related regulations in order to ensure that all provisions of the Convention are applicable to all children, including children with disabilities who should be mentioned explicitly, where appropriate. National laws and regulations should contain clear and explicit provisions for the protection and exercise of the specific rights of children with disabilities, in particular those enshrined in article 23 of the Convention.

B. National plans of action and policies

18.   The need for a national plan of action that integrates all the provisions of the Convention is a well-recognized fact and has often been a recommendation made by the Committee to States parties. Plans of action must be comprehensive, including plans and strategies for children with disabilities, and should have measurable outcomes. The draft convention on the rights of persons with disabilities, in its article 4, paragraph 1 c, emphasizes the importance of inclusion of this aspect stating that States parties undertake "to take into account the protection and promotion of the human rights of persons with disabilities in all policies and programmes" (A/AC.265/2006/4, annex II). It is also essential that all programmes be adequately supplied with financial and human resources and equipped with built-in monitoring mechanisms, for example, indicators allowing accurate outcome measurements. Another factor that should not be overlooked is the importance of including all children with disabilities in policies and programmes. Some States parties have initiated excellent programmes, but failed to include all children with disabilities.

C. Data and statistics

19.   In order to fulfil their obligations, it is necessary for States parties to set up and develop mechanisms for collecting data which are accurate, standardized and allow disaggregation, and which reflect the actual situation of children with disabilities. The importance of this issue is often overlooked and not viewed as a priority despite the fact that it has an impact not only on the measures that need to be taken in terms of prevention but also on the distribution of very valuable resources needed to fund programmes. One of the main challenges in obtaining accurate statistics is the lack of a widely accepted clear definition for disabilities. States parties are encouraged to establish an appropriate definition that guarantees the inclusion of all children with disabilities so that children with disabilities may benefit from the special protection and programmes developed for them. Extra efforts are often needed to collect data on children with disabilities because they are often hidden by their parents or others caring for the child.

D. Budget

20.   Allocation of budget: in the light of article 4 "… States parties shall undertake such measures to the maximum extent of their available resources …". Although the Convention does not make a specific recommendation regarding the most appropriate percentage of the State budget that should be dedicated to services and programmes for children, it does insist that children should be a priority. The implementation of this right has been a concern to the Committee since many States parties not only do not allocate sufficient resources but have also reduced the budget allocated to children over the years. This trend has many serious implications especially for children with disabilities who often rank quite low, or even not at all, on priority lists. For example, if a State party is failing to allocate sufficient funds to ensure compulsory and free quality education for all children, it will be unlikely to allocate funds to train teachers for

---

importance of these measures, see the Committee's general comment No. 5 (2003) on general measures of implementation of the Convention on the Rights of the Child.

children with disabilities or to provide for the necessary teaching aids and transportation for children with disabilities. Decentralization and privatization of services are now means of economic reform. However, it should not be forgotten that it is the State Party's ultimate responsibility to oversee that adequate funds are allocated to children with disabilities along with strict guidelines for service delivery. Resources allocated to children with disabilities should be sufficient – and earmarked so that they are not used for other purposes – to cover all their needs, including programmes established for training professionals working with children with disabilities such as teachers, physiotherapists and policymakers; education campaigns; financial support for families; income maintenance; social security; assistive devices; and related services. Furthermore, funding must also be ensured for other programmes aimed at including children with disabilities into mainstream education, inter alia by renovating schools to render them physically accessible to children with disabilities.

E. Coordination body: "Focal point for disabilities"

21.   Services for children with disabilities are often delivered by various governmental and non-governmental institutions, and more often than not, these services are fragmented and not coordinated which result in overlapping of functions and gaps in provisions. Therefore, the setting up of an appropriate coordinating mechanism becomes essential. This body should be multisectoral, including all organizations public or private. It must be empowered and supported from the highest possible levels of Government to allow it to function at its full potential. A coordination body for children with disabilities, as part of a broader coordination system for the rights of the child or a national coordination system for persons with disabilities, would have the advantage of working within an already established system, provided this system is functioning adequately and capable of devoting the adequate financial and human resources necessary. On the other hand, a separate coordination system may help to focus attention on children with disabilities.

F. International cooperation and technical assistance

22.   In order to make information among States parties freely accessible and to cultivate an atmosphere of knowledge-sharing concerning, inter alia, the management and rehabilitation of children with disabilities, States parties should recognize the importance of international cooperation and technical assistance. Particular attention should be paid to developing countries that need assistance in setting up and/or funding programmes that protect and promote the rights of children with disabilities. These countries are experiencing increasing difficulties in mobilizing the adequate resources to meet the pressing needs of persons with disabilities and would urgently need assistance in the prevention of disability, the provision of services and rehabilitation, and in the equalization of opportunities. However, in order to respond to these growing needs, the international community should explore new ways and means of raising funds, including substantial increase of resources, and take the necessary follow-up measures for mobilizing resources. Therefore, voluntary contributions from Governments, increased regional and bilateral assistance as well as contributions from private sources should also be encouraged. UNICEF and the World Health Organization (WHO) have been instrumental in helping developing countries set up and implement specific programmes for children with disabilities. The process of knowledge exchange is also valuable in sharing updated medical knowledge and good practices, such as early identification and community-based approaches to early intervention and support to families, and addressing common challenges.

23.   Countries that have endured, or continue to endure, internal or foreign conflict, during which land mines were laid, face a particular challenge. States parties are often

not privy to plans of the sites where the land mines and unexploded ordnance were planted and the cost of mine clearance is very high. The Committee emphasizes the importance of international cooperation in accordance with the 1997 Convention on the Prohibition of the Use, Stockpiling, Production and Transfer of Anti-Personnel Mines and on their Destruction, in order to prevent injuries and deaths caused by landmines and unexploded ordnance that remain in place. In this regard the Committee recommends that States parties closely cooperate with a view to completely removing all landmines and unexploded ordnance in areas of armed conflict and/or previous armed conflict.

G. Independent monitoring

24.   Both the Convention and the Standard Rules on the Equalization of Opportunities for Persons with Disabilities recognize the importance of the establishment of an appropriate monitoring system.[69] The Committee has very often referred to "the Paris Principles" (A/RES/48/134) as the guidelines which national human rights institutions should follow (see the Committee's general comment No. 2 (2002) on the role of independent national human rights institutions in the promotion and protection of the rights of the child). National human rights institutions can take many shapes or forms such as an Ombudsman or a Commissioner and may be broad-based or specific. Whatever mechanism is chosen, it must be:

(a)   Independent and provided with adequate human and financial resources;

(b)   Well known to children with disabilities and their caregivers;

(c)   Accessible not only in the physical sense but also in a way that allows children with disabilities to send in their complaints or issues easily and confidentially; and

(d)   It must have the appropriate legal authority to receive, investigate and address the complaints of children with disabilities in a manner sensitive to both their childhood and to their disabilities.

H. Civil society

25.   Although caring for children with disabilities is an obligation of the State, NGOs often carry out these responsibilities without the appropriate support, funding or recognition from Governments. States parties are therefore encouraged to support and cooperate with NGOs enabling them to participate in the provision of services for children with disabilities and to ensure that they operate in full compliance with the provisions and principles of the Convention. In this regard the Committee draws the attention of States parties to the recommendations adopted on its day of general discussion on the private sector as a service provider, held on 20 September 2002 (CRC/C/121, paras. 630-653).

I. Dissemination of knowledge and training of professionals

26.   Knowledge of the Convention and its specific provisions devoted to children with disabilities is a necessary and powerful tool to ensure the realization of these rights. States parties are encouraged to disseminate knowledge by, inter alia, conducting systematic awareness-raising campaigns, producing appropriate material, such as a child friendly version of the Convention in print and Braille, and using the mass media to foster positive attitudes towards children with disabilities.

---

[69]   See also the general comment No. 5 (1994) of the Committee on Economic, Social and Cultural Rights regarding persons with disabilities.

27. As for professionals working with and for children with disabilities, training programmes must include targeted and focused education on the rights of children with disabilities as a prerequisite for qualification. These professionals include but are not limited to policymakers, judges, lawyers, law enforcement officers, educators, health workers, social workers and media staff among others.

IV. GENERAL PRINCIPLES

Article 2 - Non-discrimination

28. See paragraphs 8-10 above.

Article 3 - Best interests of the child

29. "In all actions concerning children...the best interests of the child shall be a primary consideration". The broad nature of this article aims at covering all aspects of care and protection for children in all settings. It addresses legislators who are entrusted with setting the legal framework for protecting the rights of children with disabilities as well as the decisions-making processes concerning children with disabilities. Article 3 should be the basis on which programmes and policies are set and it should be duly taken into account in every service provided for children with disabilities and any other action affecting them.

30. The best interests of the child is of particular relevance in institutions and other facilities that provide services for children with disabilities as they are expected to conform to standards and regulations and should have the safety, protection and care of children as their primary consideration, and this consideration should outweigh any other and under all circumstances, for example, when allocating budgets.

Article 6 - Right to life, survival and development

31. The inherent right to life, survival and development is a right that warrants particular attention where children with disabilities are concerned. In many countries of the world children with disabilities are subject to a variety of practices that completely or partially compromise this right. In addition to being more vulnerable to infanticide, some cultures view a child with any form of disability as a bad omen that may "tarnish the family pedigree" and, accordingly, a certain designated individual from the community systematically kills children with disabilities. These crimes often go unpunished or perpetrators receive reduced sentences. States parties are urged to undertake all the necessary measures required to put an end to these practices, including raising public awareness, setting up appropriate legislation and enforcing laws that ensure appropriate punishment to all those who directly or indirectly violate the right to life, survival and development of children with disabilities.

Article 12 - Respect for the views of the child

32. More often than not, adults with and without disabilities make policies and decisions related to children with disabilities while the children themselves are left out of the process. It is essential that children with disabilities be heard in all procedures affecting them and that their views be respected in accordance with their evolving capacities. In order for this principle to be respected, children should be represented in various bodies such as parliament, committees and other forums where they may voice views and participate in the making of decisions that affect them as children in general and as children with disabilities specifically. Engaging children in such a process not only ensures that the policies are targeted to their needs and desires, but also functions as a valuable tool for inclusion since it ensures that the decision-making process is a participatory one. Children should be provided with whatever mode of communication

they need to facilitate expressing their views. Furthermore, States parties should support the training for families and professionals on promoting and respecting the evolving capacities of children to take increasing responsibilities for decision-making in their own lives.

33.   Children with disabilities often require special services in health and education to allow them to achieve their fullest potential and these are further discussed in the relevant paragraphs below. However it should be noted that spiritual, emotional and cultural development and well-being of children with disabilities are very often overlooked. Their participation in events and activities catering to these essential aspects of any child's life is either totally lacking or minimal. Furthermore, when their participation is invited, it is often limited to activities specifically designed for and targeted at children with disabilities. This practice only leads to further marginalization of children with disabilities and increases their feelings of isolation. Programmes and activities designed for the child's cultural development and spiritual well-being should involve and cater to both children with and without disabilities in an integrated and participatory fashion.

V. CIVIL RIGHTS AND FREEDOMS (ARTS. 7, 8, 13-17, AND 37 *A*)

34.   The right to name and nationality, preservation of identity, freedom of expression, freedom of thought, conscience and religion, freedom of association and peaceful assembly, the right to privacy and the right not to be subjected to torture or other cruel inhuman or degrading treatment or punishment and not to be unlawfully deprived of liberty are all universal civil rights and freedoms which must be respected, protected and promoted for all, including children with disabilities. Particular attention should be paid here on areas where the rights of children with disabilities are more likely to be violated or where special programmes are needed for their protection.

A. *Birth registration*

35.   Children with disabilities are disproportionately vulnerable to non-registration at birth. Without birth registration they are not recognized by law and become invisible in government statistics. Non-registration has profound consequences for the enjoyment of their human rights, including the lack of citizenship and access to social and health services and to education. Children with disabilities who are not registered at birth are at greater risk of neglect, institutionalization, and even death.

36.   In the light of article 7 of the Convention, the Committee recommends that States parties adopt all appropriate measures to ensure the registration of children with disabilities at birth. Such measures should include developing and implementing an effective system of birth registration, waiving registration fees, introducing mobile registration offices and, for children who are not yet registered, providing registration units in schools. In this context, States parties should ensure that the provisions of article 7 are fully enforced in conformity with the principles of non-discrimination (art. 2) and of the best interests of the child (art. 3).

B. *Access to appropriate information and mass media*

37.   Access to information and means of communication, including information and communication technologies and systems, enables children with disabilities to live independently and participate fully in all aspects of life. Children with disabilities and their caregivers should have access to information concerning their disabilities so that they can be adequately educated on the disability, including its causes, management and prognosis. This knowledge is extremely valuable as it does not only enable them to adjust and live better with their disabilities, but also allows them to be more involved in

and to make informed decisions about their own care. Children with disabilities should also be provided with the appropriate technology and other services and/or languages, e.g. Braille and sign language, which would enable them to have access to all forms of media, including television, radio and printed material as well as new information and communication technologies and systems, such as the Internet.

38.   On the other hand, States parties are required to protect all children, including children with disabilities from harmful information, especially pornographic material and material that promotes xenophobia or any other form of discrimination and could potentially reinforce prejudices.

C. Accessibility to public transportation and facilities

39.   The physical inaccessibility of public transportation and other facilities, including governmental buildings, shopping areas, recreational facilities among others, is a major factor in the marginalization and exclusion of children with disabilities and markedly compromises their access to services, including health and education. Although this provision may be mostly realized in developed countries, it remains largely un-addressed in the developing world. All States parties are urged to set out appropriate policies and procedures to make public transportation safe, easily accessible to children with disabilities, and free of charge, whenever possible, taking into account the financial resources of the parents or others caring for the child.

40.   All new public buildings should comply with international specifications for access of persons with disabilities and existing public buildings, including schools, health facilities, governmental buildings, shopping areas, undergo necessary alterations that make them as accessible as possible.

VI. FAMILY ENVIRONMENT AND ALTERNATIVE CARE (ARTS. 5, 18 (1-2), 9-11, 19-21, 25, 27 (4), AND 39)

A. Family support and parental responsibilities

41.   Children with disabilities are best cared for and nurtured within their own family environment provided that the family is adequately provided for in all aspects. Such support to families includes education of parent/s and siblings, not only on the disability and its causes but also on each child's unique physical and mental requirements; psychological support that is sensitive to the stress and difficulties imposed on families of children with disabilities; education on the family's common language, for example sign language, so that parents and siblings can communicate with family members with disabilities; material support in the form of special allowances as well as consumable supplies and necessary equipment, such as special furniture and mobility devices that is deemed necessary for the child with a disability to live a dignified, self-reliant lifestyle, and be fully included in the family and community. In this context, support should also be extended to children who are affected by the disabilities of their caregivers. For example, a child living with a parent or other caregiver with disabilities should receive the support that would protect fully his or her rights and allow him or her to continue to live with this parent whenever it is in his or her best interests. Support services should also include different forms of respite care, such as care assistance in the home and day-care facilities directly accessible at community level. Such services enable parents to work, as well as relieve stress and maintain healthy family environments.

B. Violence, abuse and neglect

42.   Children with disabilities are more vulnerable to all forms of abuse be it mental, physical or sexual in all settings, including the family, schools, private and public

institutions, inter alia alternative care, work environment and community at large. It is often quoted that children with disabilities are five times more likely to be victims of abuse. In the home and in institutions, children with disabilities are often subjected to mental and physical violence and sexual abuse, and they are also particularly vulnerable to neglect and negligent treatment since they often present an extra physical and financial burden on the family. In addition, the lack of access to a functional complaint receiving and monitoring mechanism is conducive to systematic and continuing abuse. School bullying is a particular form of violence that children are exposed to and more often than not, this form of abuse targets children with disabilities. Their particular vulnerability may be explained inter alia by the following main reasons:

(a) Their inability to hear, move, and dress, toilet, and bath independently increases their vulnerability to intrusive personal care or abuse;

(b) Living in isolation from parents, siblings, extended family and friends increases the likelihood of abuse;

(c) Should they have communication or intellectual impairments, they may be ignored, disbelieved or misunderstood should they complain about abuse;

(d) Parents or others taking care of the child may be under considerable pressure or stress because of physical, financial and emotional issues in caring for their child. Studies indicate that those under stress may be more likely to commit abuse;

(e) Children with disabilities are often wrongly perceived as being non-sexual and not having an understanding of their own bodies and, therefore, they can be targets of abusive people, particularly those who base abuse on sexuality.

43. In addressing the issue of violence and abuse, States parties are urged to take all necessary measures for the prevention of abuse of and violence against children with disabilities, such as:

(a) Train and educate parents or others caring for the child to understand the risks and detect the signs of abuse of the child;

(b) Ensure that parents are vigilant about choosing caregivers and facilities for their children and improve their ability to detect abuse;

(c) Provide and encourage support groups for parents, siblings and others taking care of the child to assist them in caring for their children and coping with their disabilities;

(d) Ensure that children and caregivers know that the child is entitled as a matter of right to be treated with dignity and respect and they have the right to complain to appropriate authorities if those rights are breached;

(e) Ensure that schools take all measures to combat school bullying and pay particular attention to children with disabilities providing them with the necessary protection while maintaining their inclusion into the mainstream education system;

(f) Ensure that institutions providing care for children with disabilities are staffed with specially trained personnel, subject to appropriate standards, regularly monitored and evaluated, and have accessible and sensitive complaint mechanisms;

(g) Establish an accessible, child-sensitive complaint mechanism and a functioning monitoring system based on the Paris Principles (see paragraph 24 above);

(h) Take all necessary legislative measures required to punish and remove perpetrators from the home ensuring that the child is not deprived of his or her family and continue to live in a safe and healthy environment;

(i) Ensure the treatment and re-integration of victims of abuse and violence with a special focus on their overall recovery programmes.

44.   In this context the Committee would also like to draw States parties' attention to the report of the independent expert for the United Nations study on violence against children (A/61/299) which refers to children with disabilities as a group of children especially vulnerable to violence. The Committee encourages States parties to take all appropriate measures to implement the overarching recommendations and setting-specific recommendations contained in this report.

C. Family-type alternative care

45.   The role of the extended family, which is still a main pillar of childcare in many communities and is considered one of the best alternatives for childcare, should be strengthened and empowered to support the child and his or her parents or others taking care of the child.

46.   Recognizing that the foster family is an accepted and practiced form of alternative care in many States parties, it is nevertheless a fact that many foster families are reluctant to take on the care of a child with disability as children with disabilities often pose a challenge in the extra care they may need and the special requirements in their physical, psychological and mental upbringing. Organizations that are responsible for foster placement of children must, therefore, conduct the necessary training and encouragement of suitable families and provide the support that will allow the foster family to appropriately take care of the child with disability.

D. Institutions

47.   The Committee has often expressed its concern at the high number of children with disabilities placed in institutions and that institutionalization is the preferred placement option in many countries. The quality of care provided, whether educational, medical or rehabilitative, is often much inferior to the standards necessary for the care of children with disabilities either because of lack of identified standards or lack of implementation and monitoring of these standards. Institutions are also a particular setting where children with disabilities are more vulnerable to mental, physical, sexual and other forms of abuse as well as neglect and negligent treatment (see paragraphs 42-44 above). The Committee therefore urges States parties to use the placement in institution only as a measure of last resort, when it is absolutely necessary and in the best interests of the child. It recommends that the States parties prevent the use of placement in institution merely with the goal of limiting the child's liberty or freedom of movement. In addition, attention should be paid to transforming existing institutions, with a focus on small residential care facilities organized around the rights and needs of the child, to developing national standards for care in institutions, and to establishing rigorous screening and monitoring procedures to ensure effective implementation of these standards.

48.   The Committee is concerned at the fact that children with disabilities are not often heard in separation and placement processes. In general, decision-making processes do not attach enough weight to children as partners even though these decisions have a far-reaching impact on the child's life and future. Therefore, the Committee recommends that States parties continue and strengthen their efforts to take into consideration the views of children with disabilities and facilitate their participation in all matters affecting them within the evaluation, separation and placement process in out-of-home care, and during the transition process. The Committee also emphasizes that children should be heard throughout the protection measure process, before making the decision as well as during and after its implementation. In this context, the Committee draws the attention

of the States parties to the Committee's recommendations adopted on its day of general discussion on children without parental care, held on 16 September 2005 (CRC/C/153, paragraphs 636-689).

49. In addressing institutionalization, States parties are therefore urged to set up programmes for de-institutionalization of children with disabilities, re-placing them with their families, extended families or foster care system. Parents and other extended family members should be provided with the necessary and systematic support/training for including their child back into their home environment.

E. Periodic review of placement

50. Whatever form of placement chosen for children with disabilities by the competent authorities, it is essential that a periodic review of the treatment provided to the child, and all other circumstances relevant to his or her placement, is carried out to monitor his or her well being.

VII. BASIC HEALTH AND WELFARE (ARTS. 6, 18 (3), 23, 24, 26, AND 27 (1-3))

A. Right to health

51. Attainment of the highest possible standard of health as well as access and affordability of quality healthcare is an inherent right for all children. Children with disabilities are often left out because of several challenges, including discrimination, inaccessibility due to the lack of information and/or financial resources, transportation, geographic distribution and physical access to health care facilities. Another factor is the absence of targeted health care programmes that address the specific needs of children with disabilities. Health policies should be comprehensive and address early detection of disabilities, early intervention, including psychological and physical treatment, rehabilitation including physical aids, for example limb prosthesis, mobility devices, hearing aids and visual aids.

52. It is important to emphasize that health services should be provided within the same public health system that provides for children with no disabilities, free of charge, whenever possible, and as updated and modernized as possible. The importance of community-based assistance and rehabilitation strategies should be emphasized when providing health services for children with disabilities. States parties must ensure that health professionals working with children with disabilities are trained to the highest possible standard and practice based on a child-centred approach. In this respect, many States parties would greatly benefit from international cooperation with international organizations as well as other States parties.

B. Prevention

53. Causes of disabilities are multiple and, therefore, the quality and level of prevention vary. Inherited diseases that often cause disabilities can be prevented in some societies that practice consanguineous marriages and under such circumstances public awareness and appropriate pre-conception testing would be recommended. Communicable diseases are still the cause of many disabilities around the world and immunization programmes need to be stepped up aiming to achieve universal immunization against all preventable communicable diseases. Poor nutrition has a long-term impact upon children's development and it can lead to disabilities, such as blindness caused by Vitamin A deficiency. The Committee recommends that States parties introduce and strengthen prenatal care for children and ensure adequate quality of the assistance given during the delivery. It also recommends that States parties provide adequate post-natal health-care services and develop campaigns to inform parents and others caring for the

child about basic child healthcare and nutrition. In this regard, the Committee also recommends that the States parties continue to cooperate and seek technical assistance with, among others, WHO and UNICEF.

54.   Domestic and road traffic accidents are a major cause of disability in some countries and policies of prevention need to be established and implemented such as the laws on seat belts and traffic safety. Lifestyle issues, such as alcohol and drug abuse during pregnancy, are also preventable causes of disabilities and in some countries the fetal alcohol syndrome presents a major cause for concern. Public education, identification and support for pregnant mothers who may be abusing such substances are just some of the measures that may be taken to prevent such causes of disability among children. Hazardous environment toxins also contribute to the causes of many disabilities. Toxins, such as lead, mercury, asbestos, etc., are commonly found in most countries. Countries should establish and implement policies to prevent dumping of hazardous materials and other means of polluting the environment. Furthermore, strict guidelines and safeguards should also be established to prevent radiation accidents.

55.   Armed conflicts and their aftermath, including availability and accessibility of small arms and light weapons, are also major causes of disabilities. States parties are obliged to take all necessary measures to protect children from the detrimental effects of war and armed violence and to ensure that children affected by armed conflict have access to adequate health and social services, including psychosocial recovery and social reintegration. In particular, the Committee stresses the importance of educating children, parents and the public at large about the dangers of landmines and unexploded ordnance in order to prevent injury and death. It is crucial that States parties continue to locate landmines and unexploded ordnance, take measures to keep children away from suspected areas, and strengthen their mine clearance activities and, when appropriate, seek the necessary technical and financial support within a framework of international cooperation, including from United Nations agencies. (See also paragraph 23 above on landmines and unexploded ordnance and paragraph 78 below on armed conflicts under special protection measures).

C. Early identification

56.   Very often, disabilities are detected quite late in the child's life, which deprives him or her of effective treatment and rehabilitation. Early identification requires high awareness among health professionals, parents, teachers as well as other professionals working with children. They should be able to identify the earliest signs of disability and make the appropriate referrals for diagnosis and management. Therefore, the Committee recommends that States parties establish systems of early identification and early intervention as part of their health services, together with birth registration and procedures for following the progress of children identified with disabilities at an early age. Services should be both community- and home-based, and easy to access. Furthermore, links should be established between early intervention services, pre-schools and schools to facilitate the smooth transition of the child.

57.   Following identification, the systems in place must be capable of early intervention including treatment and rehabilitation providing all necessary devices that enable children with disabilities to achieve their full functional capacity in terms of mobility, hearing aids, visual aids, and prosthetics among others. It should also be emphasized that these provisions should be offered free of cost, whenever possible, and the process of acquiring such services should be efficient and simple avoiding long waits and bureaucracies.

D. Multidisciplinary care

58. Children with disabilities very often have multiple health issues that need to be addressed in a team approach. Very often, many professionals are involved in the care of the child, such as neurologists, psychologists, psychiatrists, orthopaedic surgeons and physiotherapists among others. Ideally these professionals should collectively identify a plan of management for the child with disability that would ensure the most efficient healthcare is provided.

E. Adolescent health and development

59. The Committee notes that children with disabilities are, particularly during their adolescence, facing multiple challenges and risks in the area of establishing relationships with peers and reproductive health. Therefore, the Committee recommends that States parties provide adolescents with disabilities with adequate, and where appropriate, disability specific information, guidance and counselling and fully take into account the Committee's general comments No. 3 (2003) on HIV/AIDS and the rights of the child and No. 4 (2003) on adolescent health and development in the context of the Convention on the Rights of the Child.

60. The Committee is deeply concerned about the prevailing practice of forced sterilisation of children with disabilities, particularly girls with disabilities. This practice, which still exists, seriously violates the right of the child to her or his physical integrity and results in adverse life-long physical and mental health effects. Therefore, the Committee urges States parties to prohibit by law the forced sterilisation of children on grounds of disability.

F. Research

61. Causes, prevention and management of disabilities do not receive the much needed attention on national and international research agendas. States parties are encouraged to award this issue priority status ensuring funding and monitoring of disability focused research paying particular attention to ethical implications.

VIII. EDUCATION AND LEISURE (ARTS. 28, 29 AND 31)

A. Quality education

62. Children with disabilities have the same right to education as all other children and shall enjoy this right without any discrimination and on the basis of equal opportunity as stipulated in the Convention.[70] For this purpose, effective access of children with disabilities to education has to be ensured to promote "the development of the child's personality, talents and mental and physical abilities to their fullest potential (see articles 28 and 29 of the Convention and the Committee's general comment No. 1 (2001) on the aims of education). The Convention recognizes the need for modification to school practices and for training of regular teachers to prepare them to teach children with diverse abilities and ensure that they achieve positive educational outcomes.

---

[70]   In this context the Committee would like to make a reference to the United Nations Millennium Declaration (A/RES/55/2) and in particular to the Millennium Development Goal No. 2 relating to universal primary education according to which Governments are committed to "ensure that, by 2015, children everywhere, boys and girls alike, will be able to complete a full course of primary schooling and that girls and boys will have equal access to all levels of education". The Committee would also like to refer to other international commitments which endorse the idea of inclusive education, inter alia, the Salamanca Statement and Framework for Action on Special Needs Education adopted by the World Conference on Special Needs Education: Access and Quality, Salamanca, Spain, 7-10 June 1994 (UNESCO and Ministry of Education and Science of Spain) and the Dakar Framework for Action, Education for All: Meeting our Collective Commitments, adopted by the World Education Forum, Dakar, Senegal, 26-28 April 2000.

63.   As children with disabilities are very different from each other, parents, teachers and other specialized professionals have to help each individual child to develop his or her ways and skills of communication, language, interaction, orientation and problem-solving which best fit the potential of this child. Everybody, who furthers the child's skills, abilities and self-development, has to precisely observe the child's progress and carefully listen to the child's verbal and emotional communication in order to support education and development in a well-targeted and most appropriate manner.

B. Self-esteem and self-reliance

64.   It is crucial that the education of a child with disability includes the strengthening of positive self-awareness, making sure that the child feels he or she is respected by others as a human being without any limitation of dignity. The child must be able to observe that others respect him or her and recognize his or her human rights and freedoms. Inclusion of the child with disability in the groups of children of the classroom can show the child that he or she has recognized identity and belongs to the community of learners, peers, and citizens. Peer support enhancing self-esteem of children with disabilities should be more widely recognized and promoted. Education also has to provide the child with empowering experience of control, achievement, and success to the maximum extent possible for the child.

C. Education in the school system

65.   Early childhood education is of particular relevance for children with disabilities as often their disabilities and special needs are first recognized in these institutions. Early intervention is of utmost importance to help children to develop their full potential. If a child is identified as having a disability or developmental delay at an early stage, the child has much better opportunities to benefit from early childhood education which should be designed to respond to her or his individual needs. Early childhood education provided by the State, the community or civil society institutions can provide important assistance to the well-being and development of all children with disabilities (see the Committee's general comment No. 7 (2005) on implementing child rights in early childhood). Primary education, including primary school and, in many States parties, also secondary school, has to be provided for children with disabilities free of costs. All schools should be without communicational barriers as well as physical barriers impeding the access of children with reduced mobility. Also higher education, accessible on the basis of capacities, has to be accessible for qualified adolescents with disabilities. In order to fully exercise their right to education, many children need personal assistance, in particular, teachers trained in methodology and techniques, including appropriate languages, and other forms of communication, for teaching children with a diverse range of abilities capable of using child-centred and individualised teaching strategies, and appropriate and accessible teaching materials, equipment and assistive devices, which States parties should provide to the maximum extent of available resources.

D. Inclusive education

66.   Inclusive education[71] should be the goal of educating children with disabilities. The manner and form of inclusion must be dictated by the individual educational needs of

---

[71]   UNESCO's Guidelines for Inclusion: Ensuring Access to Education for All (UNESCO 2005) provides the following definition "Inclusion is seen as a process of addressing and responding to the diversity of needs of all learners through increasing participation in learning, cultures and communities, and reducing exclusion within and from education. It involves changes and modifications in content, approaches, structures and strategies, with a common vision which covers all children of the appropriate age range and a conviction that

the child, since the education of some children with disabilities requires a kind of support which may not be readily available in the regular school system. The Committee notes the explicit commitment towards the goal of inclusive education contained in the draft convention on the rights of persons with disabilities and the obligation for States to ensure that persons including children with disabilities are not excluded from the general education system on the basis of disability and that they receive the support required, within the general education system, to facilitate their effective education. It encourages States parties which have not yet begun a programme towards inclusion to introduce the necessary measures to achieve this goal. However, the Committee underlines that the extent of inclusion within the general education system may vary. A continuum of services and programme options must be maintained in circumstances where fully inclusive education is not feasible to achieve in the immediate future.

67.   The movement towards inclusive education has received much support in recent years. However, the term inclusive may have different meanings. At its core, inclusive education is a set of values, principles and practices that seeks meaningful, effective, and quality education for all students, that does justice to the diversity of learning conditions and requirements not only of children with disabilities, but for all students. This goal can be achieved by different organizational means which respect the diversity of children. Inclusion may range from full-time placement of all students with disabilities into one regular classroom or placement into the regular class room with varying degree of inclusion, including a certain portion of special education. It is important to understand that inclusion should not be understood nor practiced as simply integrating children with disabilities into the regular system regardless of their challenges and needs. Close cooperation among special educators and regular educators is essential. Schools' curricula must be re-evaluated and developed to meet the needs of children with and without disabilities. Modification in training programmes for teachers and other personnel involved in the educational system must be achieved in order to fully implement the philosophy of inclusive education.

E. Career education and vocational training

68.   Education for career development and transition is for all persons with disabilities regardless of their age. It is imperative to begin preparation at an early age because career development is seen as a process that begins early and continues throughout life. Developing career awareness and vocational skills as early as possible, beginning in the elementary school, enables children to make better choices later in life in terms of employment. Career education in the elementary school does not mean using young children to perform labour that ultimately opens the door for economic exploitation. It begins with students choosing goals according to their evolving capacities in the early years. It should then be followed by a functional secondary school curriculum that offers adequate skills and access to work experience, under systematic coordination and monitoring between the school and the work place.

69.   Career development and vocational skills should be included in the school curriculum. Career awareness and vocational skills should be incorporated into the years of compulsory education. In countries where compulsory education does not go beyond the elementary school years, vocational training beyond elementary school should be mandatory for children with disabilities. Governments must establish policies and allocate sufficient funds for vocational training.

---

it is the responsibility of the regular system to educate all children ... Inclusion is concerned with the identification and removal of barriers ..." (p. 13 and 15).

F. Recreation and cultural activities

70.   The Convention stipulates in article 31 the right of the child to recreation and cultural activities appropriate to the age of the child. This article should be interpreted to include mental, psychological as well as the physical ages and capabilities of the child. Play has been recognized as the best source of learning various skills, including social skills. The attainment of full inclusion of children with disabilities in the society is realized when children are given the opportunity, places, and time to play with each other (children with disabilities and no disabilities). Training for recreation, leisure and play should be included for school-aged children with disabilities.

71.   Children with disabilities should be provided with equal opportunities to participate in various cultural and arts activities as well as sports. These activities must be viewed as both medium of expression and medium of realizing self-satisfying, quality of life.

G. Sports

72.   Competitive and non-competitive sports activities must be designed to include children with disabilities in an inclusive manner, whenever possible. That is to say, a child with a disability who is able to compete with children with no disability should be encouraged and supported to do so. But sports are an area where, because of the physical demands of the sport, children with disabilities will often need to have exclusive games and activities where they can compete fairly and safely. It must be emphasized though that when such exclusive events take place, the media must play its role responsibly by giving the same attention as it does to sports for children with no disabilities.

IX. SPECIAL PROTECTION MEASURES (ARTS. 22, 38, 39, 40, 37 *B-D*, AND 32-36)

A. Juvenile justice system

73.   In the light of article 2 States parties have the obligation to ensure that children with disabilities who are in conflict with the law (as described in article 40, paragraph 1) will be protected not only by the provisions of the Convention which specifically relate to juvenile justice (arts. 40, 37 and 39) but by all other relevant provisions and guarantees contained in the Convention, for example in the area of health care and education. In addition, States parties should take where necessary specific measures to ensure that children with disabilities de facto are protected by and do benefit from the rights mentioned above.

74.   With reference to the rights enshrined in article 23 and given the high level of vulnerability of children with disabilities, the Committee recommends – in addition to the general recommendation made in paragraph 73 above – that the following elements of the treatment of children with disabilities (allegedly) in conflict with the law be taken into account:

(a)   A child with disability who comes in conflict with the law should be interviewed using appropriate languages and otherwise dealt with by professionals such as police officers, attorneys/advocates/social workers, prosecutors and/or judges, who have received proper training in this regard;

(b)   Governments should develop and implement alternative measures with a variety and a flexibility that allow for an adjustment of the measure to the individual capacities and abilities of the child in order to avoid the use of judicial proceedings. Children with disabilities in conflict with the law should be dealt with as much as possible without resorting to formal/legal procedures. Such procedures should only be considered when necessary in the interest of public order. In those cases special efforts have to be made to inform the child about the juvenile justice procedure and his or her rights therein;

(c)   Children with disabilities in conflict with the law should not be placed in a regular juvenile detention centre by way of pre-trial detention nor by way of a punishment. Deprivation of liberty should only be applied if necessary with a view to providing the child with adequate treatment for addressing his or her problems which have resulted in the commission of a crime and the child should be placed in an institution that has the specially trained staff and other facilities to provide this specific treatment. In making such decisions the competent authority should make sure that the human rights and legal safeguards are fully respected.

B. Economic exploitation

75.   Children with disabilities are particularly vulnerable to different forms of economic exploitation, including the worst forms of child labour as well as drug trafficking and begging. In this context, the Committee recommends that States parties which have not yet done so ratify the Convention No. 138 of the International Labour Organization (ILO) concerning the minimum age for admission to employment and ILO Convention No. 182 concerning the prohibition of and immediate action for the elimination of the worst forms of child labour. In the implementation of these conventions States parties should pay special attention to the vulnerability and needs of children with disabilities.

C. Street children

76.   Children with disabilities, specifically physical disabilities, often end up on the streets for a variety of reasons, including economic and social factors. Children with disabilities living and/or working on the streets need to be provided with adequate care, including nutrition, clothing, housing, educational opportunities, life-skills training as well as protection from the different dangers including economic and sexual exploitation. In this regard an individualized approach is necessary which takes full account of the special needs and the capacities of the child. The Committee is particularly concerned that children with disabilities are sometimes exploited for the purpose of begging in the streets or elsewhere; sometimes disabilities are inflicted on children for the purpose of begging. States parties are required to take all necessary actions to prevent this form of exploitation and to explicitly criminalize exploitation in such manner and take effective measures to bring the perpetrators to justice.

D. Sexual exploitation

77.   The Committee has often expressed grave concern at the growing number of child victims of child prostitution and child pornography. Children with disabilities are more likely than others to become victims of these serious crimes. Governments are urged to ratify and implement the Optional Protocol on the sale of children, child prostitution and child pornography (OPSC) and, in fulfilling their obligations to the Optional Protocol, States parties should pay particular attention to the protection of children with disabilities recognizing their particular vulnerability.

E. Children in armed conflict

78.   As previously noted above, armed conflicts are a major cause of disabilities whether children are actually involved in the conflict or are victims of combat. In this context, Governments are urged to ratify and implement the Optional Protocol on the involvement of children in armed conflict (OPAC). Special attention should be paid to

the recovery and social re-integration of children who suffer disabilities as a result of armed conflicts. Furthermore, the Committee recommends that States parties explicitly exclude children with disabilities from recruitment in armed forces and take the necessary legislative and other measures to fully implement that prohibition.

F. Refugee and internally displaced children, children belonging to minorities and indigenous children

79. Certain disabilities result directly from the conditions that have led some individuals to become refugees or internally displaced persons, such as human-caused or natural disasters. For example, landmines and unexploded ordnance kill and injure refugee, internally displaced and resident children long after armed conflicts have ceased. Refugee and internally displaced children with disabilities are vulnerable to multiple forms of discrimination, particularly refugee and internally displaced girls with disabilities, who are more often than boys subject to abuse, including sexual abuse, neglect and exploitation. The Committee strongly emphasizes that refugee and internally displaced children with disabilities should be given high priority for special assistance, including preventative assistance, access to adequate health and social services, including psychosocial recovery and social reintegration. The Office of the United Nations High Commissioner for Refugees (UNHCR) has made children a policy priority and adopted several documents to guide its work in that area, including the Guidelines on Refugee Children in 1988, which are incorporated into UNHCR Policy on Refugee Children. The Committee also recommends that States parties take into account the Committee's general comment No. 6 (2005) on the treatment of unaccompanied and separated children outside of their country of origin.

80. All appropriate and necessary measures undertaken to protect and promote the rights of children with disabilities must include and pay special attention to the particular vulnerability and needs of children belonging to minorities and indigenous children who are more likely to be already marginalized within their communities. Programmes and policies must always be culturally and ethnically sensitive.

General Comment No 10 (2007)
Children's rights in juvenile justice

I. INTRODUCTION

1. In the reports they submit to the Committee on the Rights of the Child (hereafter: the Committee), States parties often pay quite detailed attention to the rights of children alleged as, accused of, or recognized as having infringed the penal law, also referred to as "children in conflict with the law". In line with the Committee's guidelines for periodic reporting, the implementation of articles 37 and 40 of the Convention on the Rights of the Child (hereafter: CRC) is the main focus of the information provided by the States parties. The Committee notes with appreciation the many efforts to establish an administration of juvenile justice in compliance with CRC. However, it is also clear that many States parties still have a long way to go in achieving full compliance with CRC, e.g. in the areas of procedural rights, the development and implementation of measures for dealing with children in conflict with the law without resorting to judicial proceedings, and the use of deprivation of liberty only as a measure of last resort.

2. The Committee is equally concerned about the lack of information on the measures that States parties have taken to prevent children from coming into conflict with the law. This may be the result of a lack of a comprehensive policy for the field of juvenile justice. This may also explain why many States parties are providing only very limited statistical data on the treatment of children in conflict with the law.

3. The experience in reviewing the States parties' performance in the field of juvenile justice is the reason for the present general comment, by which the Committee wants to provide the States parties with more elaborated guidance and recommendations for their efforts to establish an administration of juvenile justice in compliance with CRC. This juvenile justice, which should promote, inter alia, the use of alternative measures such as diversion and restorative justice, will provide States parties with possibilities to respond to children in conflict with the law in an effective manner serving not only the best interests of these children, but also the short- and long-term interest of the society at large.

II. THE OBJECTIVES OF THE PRESENT GENERAL COMMENT

4. At the outset, the Committee wishes to underscore that CRC requires States parties to develop and implement a comprehensive juvenile justice policy. This comprehensive approach should not be limited to the implementation of the specific provisions contained in articles 37 and 40 of CRC, but should also take into account the general principles enshrined in articles 2, 3, 6 and 12, and in all other relevant articles of CRC, such as articles 4 and 39. Therefore, the objectives of this general comment are:

—   To encourage States parties to develop and implement a comprehensive juvenile justice policy to prevent and address juvenile delinquency based on and in compliance with CRC, and to seek in this regard advice and support from the Interagency Panel on Juvenile Justice, with representatives of the Office of the United Nations High Commissioner for Human Rights (OHCHR), the United Nations Children's Fund (UNICEF), the United Nations Office on Drugs and Crime (UNODC) and non-governmental organizations (NGO's), established by ECOSOC resolution 1997/30;

—   To provide States parties with guidance and recommendations for the content of this comprehensive juvenile justice policy, with special attention to prevention of juvenile delinquency, the introduction of alternative measures allowing for responses to juvenile delinquency without resorting to judicial procedures, and for the interpretation and implementation of all other provisions contained in articles 37 and 40 of CRC;

— To promote the integration, in a national and comprehensive juvenile justice policy, of other international standards, in particular, the United Nations Standard Minimum Rules for the Administration of Juvenile Justice (the "Beijing Rules"), the United Nations Rules for the Protection of Juveniles Deprived of their Liberty (the "Havana Rules"), and the United Nations Guidelines for the Prevention of Juvenile Delinquency (the "Riyadh Guidelines").

III. JUVENILE JUSTICE: THE LEADING PRINCIPLES OF A COMPREHENSIVE POLICY

5. Before elaborating on the requirements of CRC in more detail, the Committee will first mention the leading principles of a comprehensive policy for juvenile justice. In the administration of juvenile justice, States parties have to apply systematically the general principles contained in articles 2, 3, 6 and 12 of CRC, as well as the fundamental principles of juvenile justice enshrined in articles 37 and 40.

Non-discrimination (art. 2)

6. States parties have to take all necessary measures to ensure that all children in conflict with the law are treated equally. Particular attention must be paid to de facto discrimination and disparities, which may be the result of a lack of a consistent policy and involve vulnerable groups of children, such as street children, children belonging to racial, ethnic, religious or linguistic minorities, indigenous children, girl children, children with disabilities and children who are repeatedly in conflict with the law (recidivists). In this regard, training of all professionals involved in the administration of juvenile justice is important (see paragraph 97 below), as well as the establishment of rules, regulations or protocols which enhance equal treatment of child offenders and provide redress, remedies and compensation.

7. Many children in conflict with the law are also victims of discrimination, e.g. when they try to get access to education or to the labour market. It is necessary that measures are taken to prevent such discrimination, inter alia, as by providing former child offenders with appropriate support and assistance in their efforts to reintegrate in society, and to conduct public campaigns emphasizing their right to assume a constructive role in society (art. 40 (1)).

8. It is quite common that criminal codes contain provisions criminalizing behavioural problems of children, such as vagrancy, truancy, runaways and other acts, which often are the result of psychological or socio-economic problems. It is particularly a matter of concern that girls and street children are often victims of this criminalization. These acts, also known as Status Offences, are not considered to be such if committed by adults. The Committee recommends that the States parties abolish the provisions on status offences in order to establish an equal treatment under the law for children and adults. In this regard, the Committee also refers to article 56 of the Riyadh Guidelines which reads: "In order to prevent further stigmatization, victimization and criminalization of young persons, legislation should be enacted to ensure that any conduct not considered an offence or not penalized if committed by an adult is not considered an offence and not penalized if committed by a young person."

9. In addition, behaviour such as vagrancy, roaming the streets or runaways should be dealt with through the implementation of child protective measures, including effective support for parents and/or other caregivers and measures which address the root causes of this behaviour.

Best interests of the child (art. 3)

10. In all decisions taken within the context of the administration of juvenile justice, the best interests of the child should be a primary consideration. Children differ from adults in their physical and psychological development, and their emotional and educational needs. Such differences constitute the basis for the lesser culpability of children in conflict with the law. These and other differences are the reasons for a separate juvenile justice system and require a different treatment for children. The protection of the best interests of the child means, for instance, that the traditional objectives of criminal justice, such as repression/retribution, must give way to rehabilitation and restorative justice objectives in dealing with child offenders. This can be done in concert with attention to effective public safety.

The right to life, survival and development (art. 6)

11. This inherent right of every child should guide and inspire States parties in the development of effective national policies and programmes for the prevention of juvenile delinquency, because it goes without saying that delinquency has a very negative impact on the child's development. Furthermore, this basic right should result in a policy of responding to juvenile delinquency in ways that support the child's development. The death penalty and a life sentence without parole are explicitly prohibited under article 37 (a) of CRC (see paragraphs 75-77 below). The use of deprivation of liberty has very negative consequences for the child's harmonious development and seriously hampers his/her reintegration in society. In this regard, article 37 (b) explicitly provides that deprivation of liberty, including arrest, detention and imprisonment, should be used only as a measure of last resort and for the shortest appropriate period of time, so that the child's right to development is fully respected and ensured (see paragraphs 78-88 below).[72]

The right to be heard (art. 12)

12. The right of the child to express his/her views freely in all matters affecting the child should be fully respected and implemented throughout every stage of the process of juvenile justice (see paragraphs 43-45 below). The Committee notes that the voices of children involved in the juvenile justice system are increasingly becoming a powerful force for improvements and reform, and for the fulfilment of their rights.

Dignity (art. 40 (1))

13. CRC provides a set of fundamental principles for the treatment to be accorded to children in conflict with the law:

— Treatment that is consistent with the child's sense of dignity and worth. This principle reflects the fundamental human right enshrined in article 1 of UDHR, which stipulates that all human beings are born free and equal in dignity and rights. This inherent right to dignity and worth, to which the preamble of CRC makes explicit reference, has to be respected and protected throughout the

---

[72] Note that the rights of a child deprived of his/her liberty, as recognized in CRC, apply with respect to children in conflict with the law, and to children placed in institutions for the purposes of care, protection or treatment, including mental health, educational, drug treatment, child protection or immigration institutions.

entire process of dealing with the child, from the first contact with law enforcement agencies and all the way to the implementation of all measures for dealing with the child;

— 	Treatment that reinforces the child's respect for the human rights and freedoms of others. This principle is in line with the consideration in the preamble that a child should be brought up in the spirit of the ideals proclaimed in the Charter of the United Nations. It also means that, within the juvenile justice system, the treatment and education of children shall be directed to the development of respect for human rights and freedoms (art. 29 (1) (b) of CRC and general comment No. 1 on the aims of education). It is obvious that this principle of juvenile justice requires a full respect for and implementation of the guarantees for a fair trial recognized in article 40 (2) (see paragraphs 40-67 below). If the key actors in juvenile justice, such as police officers, prosecutors, judges and probation officers, do not fully respect and protect these guarantees, how can they expect that with such poor examples the child will respect the human rights and fundamental freedom of others?;

— 	Treatment that takes into account the child's age and promotes the child's reintegration and the child's assuming a constructive role in society. This principle must be applied, observed and respected throughout the entire process of dealing with the child, from the first contact with law enforcement agencies all the way to the implementation of all measures for dealing with the child. It requires that all professionals involved in the administration of juvenile justice be knowledgeable about child development, the dynamic and continuing growth of children, what is appropriate to their well-being, and the pervasive forms of violence against children;

— 	Respect for the dignity of the child requires that all forms of violence in the treatment of children in conflict with the law must be prohibited and prevented. Reports received by the Committee show that violence occurs in all phases of the juvenile justice process, from the first contact with the police, during pretrial detention and during the stay in treatment and other facilities for children sentenced to deprivation of liberty. The committee urges the States parties to take effective measures to prevent such violence and to make sure that the perpetrators are brought to justice and to give effective follow-up to the recommendations made in the report on the United Nations Study on Violence Against Children presented to the General Assembly in October 2006 (A/61/299).

14. The Committee acknowledges that the preservation of public safety is a legitimate aim of the justice system. However, it is of the opinion that this aim is best served by a full respect for and implementation of the leading and overarching principles of juvenile justice as enshrined in CRC.

IV. JUVENILE JUSTICE: THE CORE ELEMENTS OF A COMPREHENSIVE POLICY

15. A comprehensive policy for juvenile justice must deal with the following core elements: the prevention of juvenile delinquency; interventions without resorting to judicial proceedings and interventions in the context of judicial proceedings; the minimum age of criminal responsibility and the upper age-limits for juvenile justice; the guarantees for a fair trial; and deprivation of liberty including pretrial detention and post-trial incarceration.

A. Prevention of juvenile delinquency

16. One of the most important goals of the implementation of CRC is to promote the full and harmonious development of the child's personality, talents and mental and physical abilities (preamble, and articles 6 and 29). The child should be prepared to live an individual and responsible life in a free society (preamble, and article 29), in which he/she can assume a constructive role with respect for human rights and fundamental freedoms (arts. 29 and 40). In this regard, parents have the responsibility to provide the child, in a manner consistent with his evolving capacities, with appropriate direction and guidance in the exercise of her/his rights as recognized in the Convention. In the light of these and other provisions of CRC, it is obviously not in the best interests of the child if he/she grows up in circumstances that may cause an increased or serious risk of becoming involved in criminal activities. Various measures should be taken for the full and equal implementation of the rights to an adequate standard of living (art. 27), to the highest attainable standard of health and access to health care (art. 24), to education (arts. 28 and 29), to protection from all forms of physical or mental violence, injury or abuse (art. 19), and from economic or sexual exploitation (arts. 32 and 34), and to other appropriate services for the care or protection of children.

17. As stated above, a juvenile justice policy without a set of measures aimed at preventing juvenile delinquency suffers from serious shortcomings. States parties should fully integrate into their comprehensive national policy for juvenile justice the United Nations Guidelines for the Prevention of Juvenile Delinquency (the Riyadh Guidelines) adopted by the General Assembly in its resolution 45/112 of 14 December 1990.

18. The Committee fully supports the Riyadh Guidelines and agrees that emphasis should be placed on prevention policies that facilitate the successful socialization and integration of all children, in particular through the family, the community, peer groups, schools, vocational training and the world of work, as well as through voluntary organizations. This means, inter alia that prevention programmes should focus on support for particularly vulnerable families, the involvement of schools in teaching basic values (including information about the rights and responsibilities of children and parents under the law), and extending special care and attention to young persons at risk. In this regard, particular attention should also be given to children who drop out of school or otherwise do not complete their education. The use of peer group support and a strong involvement of parents are recommended. The States parties should also develop community-based services and programmes that respond to the special needs, problems, concerns and interests of children, in particular of children repeatedly in conflict with the law, and that provide appropriate counselling and guidance to their families.

19. Articles 18 and 27 of CRC confirm the importance of the responsibility of parents for the upbringing of their children, but at the same time CRC requires States parties to provide the necessary assistance to parents (or other caretakers), in the performance of their parental responsibilities. The measures of assistance should not only focus on the prevention of negative situations, but also and even more on the promotion of the social potential of parents. There is a wealth of information on home- and family-based prevention programmes, such as parent training, programmes to enhance parent-child interaction and home visitation programmes, which can start at a very young age of the child. In addition, early childhood education has shown to be correlated with a lower rate of future violence and crime. At the community level, positive results have been achieved with programmes such as Communities that Care (CTC), a risk-focused prevention strategy.

20. States parties should fully promote and support the involvement of children, in accordance with article 12 of CRC, and of parents, community leaders and other key actors (e.g. representatives of NGOs, probation services and social workers), in the development and implementation of prevention programmes. The quality of this involvement is a key factor in the success of these programmes.

21. The Committee recommends that States parties seek support and advice from the Interagency Panel on Juvenile Justice in their efforts to develop effective prevention programmes.

B. Interventions/diversion (see also section E below)

22. Two kinds of interventions can be used by the State authorities for dealing with children alleged as, accused of, or recognized as having infringed the penal law: measures without resorting to judicial proceedings and measures in the context of judicial proceedings. The Committee reminds States parties that utmost care must be taken to ensure that the child's human rights and legal safeguards are thereby fully respected and protected.

23. Children in conflict with the law, including child recidivists, have the right to be treated in ways that promote their reintegration and the child's assuming a constructive role in society (art. 40 (1) of CRC). The arrest, detention or imprisonment of a child may be used only as a measure of last resort (art. 37 (b)). It is, therefore, necessary – as part of a comprehensive policy for juvenile justice – to develop and implement a wide range of measures to ensure that children are dealt with in a manner appropriate to their well-being, and proportionate to both their circumstances and the offence committed. These should include care, guidance and supervision, counselling, probation, foster care, educational and training programmes, and other alternatives to institutional care (art. 40 (4)).

Interventions without resorting to judicial proceedings

24. According to article 40 (3) of CRC, the States parties shall seek to promote measures for dealing with children alleged as, accused of, or recognized as having infringed the penal law without resorting to judicial proceedings, whenever appropriate and desirable. Given the fact that the majority of child offenders commit only minor offences, a range of measures involving removal from criminal/juvenile justice processing and referral to alternative (social) services (i.e. diversion) should be a well-established practice that can and should be used in most cases.

25. In the opinion of the Committee, the obligation of States parties to promote measures for dealing with children in conflict with the law without resorting to judicial proceedings applies, but is certainly not limited to children who commit minor offences, such as shoplifting or other property offences with limited damage, and first-time child offenders. Statistics in many States parties indicate that a large part, and often the majority, of offences committed by children fall into these categories. It is in line with the principles set out in article 40 (1) of CRC to deal with all such cases without resorting to criminal law procedures in court. In addition to avoiding stigmatization, this approach has good results for children and is in the interests of public safety, and has proven to be more cost-effective.

26. States parties should take measures for dealing with children in conflict with the law without resorting to judicial proceedings as an integral part of their juvenile justice system, and ensure that children's human rights and legal safeguards are thereby fully respected and protected (art. 40 (3) (b)).

27. It is left to the discretion of States parties to decide on the exact nature and content of the measures for dealing with children in conflict with the law without resorting to judicial proceedings, and to take the necessary legislative and other measures for their implementation. Nonetheless, on the basis of the information provided in the reports from some States parties, it is clear that a variety of community-based programmes have been developed, such as community service, supervision and guidance by for example social workers or probation officers, family conferencing and other forms of restorative justice including restitution to and compensation of victims. Other States parties should benefit from these experiences. As far as full respect for human rights and legal safeguards is concerned, the Committee refers to the relevant parts of article 40 of CRC and emphasizes the following:

— Diversion (i.e. measures for dealing with children, alleged as, accused of, or recognized as having infringed the penal law without resorting to judicial proceedings) should be used only when there is compelling evidence that the child committed the alleged offence, that he/she freely and voluntarily admits responsibility, and that no intimidation or pressure has been used to get that admission and, finally, that the admission will not be used against him/her in any subsequent legal proceeding;

— The child must freely and voluntarily give consent in writing to the diversion, a consent that should be based on adequate and specific information on the nature, content and duration of the measure, and on the consequences of a failure to cooperate, carry out and complete the measure. With a view to strengthening parental involvement, States parties may also consider requiring the consent of parents, in particular when the child is below the age of 16 years;

— The law has to contain specific provisions indicating in which cases diversion is possible, and the powers of the police, prosecutors and/or other agencies to make decisions in this regard should be regulated and reviewed, in particular to protect the child from discrimination;

— The child must be given the opportunity to seek legal or other appropriate assistance on the appropriateness and desirability of the diversion offered by the competent authorities, and on the possibility of review of the measure;

— The completion of the diversion by the child should result in a definite and final closure of the case. Although confidential records can be kept of diversion for administrative and review purposes, they should not be viewed as "criminal records" and a child who has been previously diverted must not be seen as having a previous conviction. If any registration takes place of this event, access to that information should be given exclusively and for a limited period of time, e.g. for a maximum of one year, to the competent authorities authorized to deal with children in conflict with the law.

Interventions in the context of judicial proceedings

28. When judicial proceedings are initiated by the competent authority (usually the prosecutor's office), the principles of a fair and just trial must be applied (see section D below). At the same time, the juvenile justice system should provide for ample opportunities to deal with children in conflict with the law by using social and/or educational measures, and to strictly limit the use of deprivation of liberty, and in particular pretrial detention, as a measure of last resort. In the disposition phase of the proceedings, deprivation of liberty must be used only as a measure of last resort and for the shortest appropriate period of time (art. 37 (b)). This means that States parties should have in place a well-trained probation service to allow for the maximum and

effective use of measures such as guidance and supervision orders, probation, community monitoring or day report centres, and the possibility of early release from detention.

29. The Committee reminds States parties that, pursuant to article 40 (1) of CRC, reintegration requires that no action may be taken that can hamper the child's full participation in his/her community, such as stigmatization, social isolation, or negative publicity of the child. For a child in conflict with the law to be dealt with in a way that promotes reintegration requires that all actions should support the child becoming a full, constructive member of his/her society.

C. Age and children in conflict with the law

The minimum age of criminal responsibility

30. The reports submitted by States parties show the existence of a wide range of minimum ages of criminal responsibility. They range from a very low level of age 7 or 8 to the commendable high level of age 14 or 16. Quite a few States parties use two minimum ages of criminal responsibility. Children in conflict with the law who at the time of the commission of the crime are at or above the lower minimum age but below the higher minimum age are assumed to be criminally responsible only if they have the required maturity in that regard. The assessment of this maturity is left to the court/judge, often without the requirement of involving a psychological expert, and results in practice in the use of the lower minimum age in cases of serious crimes. The system of two minimum ages is often not only confusing, but leaves much to the discretion of the court/judge and may result in discriminatory practices. In the light of this wide range of minimum ages for criminal responsibility the Committee feels that there is a need to provide the States parties with clear guidance and recommendations regarding the minimum age of criminal responsibility.

31. Article 40 (3) of CRC requires States parties to seek to promote, inter alia, the establishment of a minimum age below which children shall be presumed not to have the capacity to infringe the penal law, but does not mention a specific minimum age in this regard. The committee understands this provision as an obligation for States parties to set a minimum age of criminal responsibility (MACR). This minimum age means the following:

— Children who commit an offence at an age below that minimum cannot be held responsible in a penal law procedure. Even (very) young children do have the capacity to infringe the penal law but if they commit an offence when below MACR the irrefutable assumption is that they cannot be formally charged and held responsible in a penal law procedure. For these children special protective measures can be taken if necessary in their best interests;

— Children at or above the MACR at the time of the commission of an offence (or: infringement of the penal law) but younger than 18 years (see also paragraphs 35-38 below) can be formally charged and subject to penal law procedures. But these procedures, including the final outcome, must be in full compliance with the principles and provisions of CRC as elaborated in the present general comment.

32. Rule 4 of the Beijing Rules recommends that the beginning of MACR shall not be fixed at too low an age level, bearing in mind the facts of emotional, mental and intellectual maturity. In line with this rule the Committee has recommended States parties not to set a MACR at a too low level and to increase the existing low MACR to an internationally acceptable level. From these recommendations, it can be concluded that a minimum age of criminal responsibility below the age of 12 years is considered by

the Committee not to be internationally acceptable. States parties are encouraged to increase their lower MACR to the age of 12 years as the absolute minimum age and to continue to increase it to a higher age level.

33. At the same time, the Committee urges States parties not to lower their MACR to the age of 12. A higher MACR, for instance 14 or 16 years of age, contributes to a juvenile justice system which, in accordance with article 40 (3) (b) of CRC, deals with children in conflict with the law without resorting to judicial proceedings, providing that the child's human rights and legal safeguards are fully respected. In this regard, States parties should inform the Committee in their reports in specific detail how children below the MACR set in their laws are treated when they are recognized as having infringed the penal law, or are alleged as or accused of having done so, and what kinds of legal safeguards are in place to ensure that their treatment is as fair and just as that of children at or above MACR.

34. The Committee wishes to express its concern about the practice of allowing exceptions to a MACR which permit the use of a lower minimum age of criminal responsibility in cases where the child, for example, is accused of committing a serious offence or where the child is considered mature enough to be held criminally responsible. The Committee strongly recommends that States parties set a MACR that does not allow, by way of exception, the use of a lower age.

35. If there is no proof of age and it cannot be established that the child is at or above the MACR, the child shall not be held criminally responsible (see also paragraph 39 below).

The upper age-limit for juvenile justice

36. The Committee also wishes to draw the attention of States parties to the upper age-limit for the application of the rules of juvenile justice. These special rules – in terms both of special procedural rules and of rules for diversion and special measures – should apply, starting at the MACR set in the country, for all children who, at the time of their alleged commission of an offence (or act punishable under the criminal law), have not yet reached the age of 18 years.

37. The Committee wishes to remind States parties that they have recognized the right of every child alleged as, accused of, or recognized as having infringed the penal law to be treated in accordance with the provisions of article 40 of CRC. This means that every person under the age of 18 years at the time of the alleged commission of an offence must be treated in accordance with the rules of juvenile justice.

38. The Committee, therefore, recommends that those States parties which limit the applicability of their juvenile justice rules to children under the age of 16 (or lower) years, or which allow by way of exception that 16 or 17-year-old children are treated as adult criminals, change their laws with a view to achieving a non-discriminatory full application of their juvenile justice rules to all persons under the age of 18 years. The Committee notes with appreciation that some States parties allow for the application of the rules and regulations of juvenile justice to persons aged 18 and older, usually till the age of 21, either as a general rule or by way of exception.

39. Finally, the Committee wishes to emphasize the fact that it is crucial for the full implementation of article 7 of CRC requiring, inter alia, that every child shall be registered immediately after birth to set age-limits one way or another, which is the case for all States parties. A child without a provable date of birth is extremely vulnerable to all kinds of abuse and injustice regarding the family, work, education and labour, particularly within the juvenile justice system. Every child must be provided with a birth

certificate free of charge whenever he/she needs it to prove his/her age. If there is no proof of age, the child is entitled to a reliable medical or social investigation that may establish his/her age and, in the case of conflict or inconclusive evidence, the child shall have the right to the rule of the benefit of the doubt.

D. The guarantees for a fair trial

40. Article 40 (2) of CRC contains an important list of rights and guarantees that are all meant to ensure that every child alleged as or accused of having infringed the penal law receives fair treatment and trial. Most of these guarantees can also be found in article 14 of the International Covenant on Civil and Political Rights (ICCPR), which the Human Rights Committee elaborated and commented on in its general comment No. 13 (1984) (Administration of justice) which is currently in the process of being reviewed. However, the implementation of these guarantees for children does have some specific aspects which will be presented in this section. Before doing so, the Committee wishes to emphasize that a key condition for a proper and effective implementation of these rights or guarantees is the quality of the persons involved in the administration of juvenile justice. The training of professionals, such as police officers, prosecutors, legal and other representatives of the child, judges, probation officers, social workers and others is crucial and should take place in a systematic and ongoing manner. These professionals should be well informed about the child's, and particularly about the adolescent's physical, psychological, mental and social development, as well as about the special needs of the most vulnerable children, such as children with disabilities, displaced children, street children, refugee and asylum-seeking children, and children belonging to racial, ethnic, religious, linguistic or other minorities (see paragraphs 6-9 above). Since girls in the juvenile justice system may be easily overlooked because they represent only a small group, special attention must be paid to the particular needs of the girl child, e.g. in relation to prior abuse and special health needs. Professionals and staff should act under all circumstances in a manner consistent with the child's dignity and worth, which reinforces the child's respect for the human rights and fundamental freedoms of others, and which promotes the child's reintegration and his/her assuming a constructive role in society (art. 40 (1)). All the guarantees recognized in article 40 (2), which will be dealt with hereafter, are minimum standards, meaning that States parties can and should try to establish and observe higher standards, e.g. in the areas of legal assistance and the involvement of the child and her/his parents in the judicial process.

No retroactive juvenile justice (art. 40 (2) (a))

41. Article 40 (2) (a) of CRC affirms that the rule that no one shall be held guilty of any criminal offence on account of any act or omission which did not constitute a criminal offence, under national or international law, at the time it was committed is also applicable to children (see also article 15 of ICCPR). It means that no child can be charged with or sentenced under the penal law for acts or omissions which at the time they were committed were not prohibited under national or international law. In the light of the fact that many States parties have recently strengthened and/or expanded their criminal law provisions to prevent and combat terrorism, the Committee recommends that States parties ensure that these changes do not result in retroactive or unintended punishment of children. The Committee also wishes to remind States parties that the rule that no heavier penalty shall be imposed than the one that was applicable at the time when the criminal offence was committed, as expressed in article 15 of ICCPR, is in the light of article 41 of CRC, applicable to children in the States parties to ICCPR. No child shall be punished with a heavier penalty than the one applicable at the time of his/her infringement of the penal law. But if a change of law after the act provides for a lighter penalty, the child should benefit from this change.

The presumption of innocence (art. 40 (2) (b) (i))

42. The presumption of innocence is fundamental to the protection of the human rights of children in conflict with the law. It means that the burden of proof of the charge(s) brought against the child is on the prosecution. The child alleged as or accused of having infringed the penal law has the benefit of doubt and is only guilty as charged if these charges have been proven beyond reasonable doubt. The child has the right to be treated in accordance with this presumption and it is the duty of all public authorities or others involved to refrain from prejudging the outcome of the trial. States parties should provide information about child development to ensure that this presumption of innocence is respected in practice. Due to the lack of understanding of the process, immaturity, fear or other reasons, the child may behave in a suspicious manner, but the authorities must not assume that the child is guilty without proof of guilt beyond any reasonable doubt.

The right to be heard (art. 12)

43. Article 12 (2) of CRC requires that a child be provided with the opportunity to be heard in any judicial or administrative proceedings affecting the child, either directly or through a representative or an appropriate body in a manner consistent with the procedural rules of national law.

44. It is obvious that for a child alleged as, accused of, or recognized as having infringed the penal law, the right to be heard is fundamental for a fair trial. It is equally obvious that the child has the right to be heard directly and not only through a representative or an appropriate body if it is in her/his best interests. This right must be fully observed at all stages of the process, starting with pretrial stage when the child has the right to remain silent, as well as the right to be heard by the police, the prosecutor and the investigating judge. But it also applies to the stages of adjudication and of implementation of the imposed measures. In other words, the child must be given the opportunity to express his/her views freely, and those views should be given due weight in accordance with the age and maturity of the child (art. 12 (1)), throughout the juvenile justice process. This means that the child, in order to effectively participate in the proceedings, must be informed not only of the charges (see paragraphs 47-48 below), but also of the juvenile justice process as such and of the possible measures.

45. The child should be given the opportunity to express his/her views concerning the (alternative) measures that may be imposed, and the specific wishes or preferences he/she may have in this regard should be given due weight. Alleging that the child is criminally responsible implies that he/she should be competent and able to effectively participate in the decisions regarding the most appropriate response to allegations of his/her infringement of the penal law (see paragraph 46 below). It goes without saying that the judges involved are responsible for taking the decisions. But to treat the child as a passive object does not recognize his/her rights nor does it contribute to an effective response to his/her behaviour. This also applies to the implementation of the measure(s) imposed. Research shows that an active engagement of the child in this implementation will, in most cases, contribute to a positive result.

The right to effective participation in the proceedings (art 40 (2) (b) (iv))

46. A fair trial requires that the child alleged as or accused of having infringed the penal law be able to effectively participate in the trial, and therefore needs to comprehend the charges, and possible consequences and penalties, in order to direct the legal representative, to challenge witnesses, to provide an account of events, and to make appropriate decisions about evidence, testimony and the measure(s) to be imposed. Article 14 of the Beijing Rules provides that the proceedings should be conducted in an

atmosphere of understanding to allow the child to participate and to express himself/herself freely. Taking into account the child's age and maturity may also require modified courtroom procedures and practices.

Prompt and direct information of the charge(s) (art. 40 (2) (b) (ii))

47. Every child alleged as or accused of having infringed the penal law has the right to be informed promptly and directly of the charges brought against him/her. Prompt and direct means as soon as possible, and that is when the prosecutor or the judge initially takes procedural steps against the child. But also when the authorities decide to deal with the case without resorting to judicial proceedings, the child must be informed of the charge(s) that may justify this approach. This is part of the requirement of article 40 (3) (b) of CRC that legal safeguards should be fully respected. The child should be informed in a language he/she understands. This may require a presentation of the information in a foreign language but also a "translation" of the formal legal jargon often used in criminal/juvenile charges into a language that the child can understand.

48. Providing the child with an official document is not enough and an oral explanation may often be necessary. The authorities should not leave this to the parents or legal guardians or the child's legal or other assistance. It is the responsibility of the authorities (e.g. police, prosecutor, judge) to make sure that the child understands each charge brought against him/her. The Committee is of the opinion that the provision of this information to the parents or legal guardians should not be an alternative to communicating this information to the child. It is most appropriate if both the child and the parents or legal guardians receive the information in such a way that they can understand the charge(s) and the possible consequences.

Legal or other appropriate assistance (art. 40 (2) (b) (ii))

49. The child must be guaranteed legal or other appropriate assistance in the preparation and presentation of his/her defence. CRC does require that the child be provided with assistance, which is not necessarily under all circumstances legal but it must be appropriate. It is left to the discretion of States parties to determine how this assistance is provided but it should be free of charge. The Committee recommends the State parties provide as much as possible for adequate trained legal assistance, such as expert lawyers or paralegal professionals. Other appropriate assistance is possible (e.g. social worker), but that person must have sufficient knowledge and understanding of the various legal aspects of the process of juvenile justice and must be trained to work with children in conflict with the law.

50. As required by article 14 (3) (b) of ICCPR, the child and his/her assistant must have adequate time and facilities for the preparation of his/her defence. Communications between the child and his/her assistance, either in writing or orally, should take place under such conditions that the confidentiality of such communications is fully respected in accordance with the guarantee provided for in article 40 (2) (b) (vii) of CRC, and the right of the child to be protected against interference with his/her privacy and correspondence (art. 16 of CRC). A number of States parties have made reservations regarding this guarantee (art. 40 (2) (b) (ii) of CRC), apparently assuming that it requires exclusively the provision of legal assistance and therefore by a lawyer. That is not the case and such reservations can and should be withdrawn.

Decisions without delay and with involvement of parents (art. 40 (2) (b) (iii))

51. Internationally there is a consensus that for children in conflict with the law the time between the commission of the offence and the final response to this act should be as short as possible. The longer this period, the more likely it is that the response loses its

desired positive, pedagogical impact, and the more the child will be stigmatized. In this regard, the Committee also refers to article 37 (d) of CRC, where the child deprived of liberty has the right to a prompt decision on his/her action to challenge the legality of the deprivation of his/her liberty. The term "prompt" is even stronger – and justifiably so given the seriousness of deprivation of liberty – than the term "without delay" (art. 40 (2) (b) (iii) of CRC), which is stronger than the term "without undue delay" of article 14 (3) (c) of ICCPR.

52. The Committee recommends that the States parties set and implement time limits for the period between the commission of the offence and the completion of the police investigation, the decision of the prosecutor (or other competent body) to bring charges against the child, and the final adjudication and decision by the court or other competent judicial body. These time limits should be much shorter than those set for adults. But at the same time, decisions without delay should be the result of a process in which the human rights of the child and legal safeguards are fully respected. In this decision-making process without delay, the legal or other appropriate assistance must be present. This presence should not be limited to the trial before the court or other judicial body, but also applies to all other stages of the process, beginning with the interviewing (interrogation) of the child by the police.

53. Parents or legal guardians should also be present at the proceedings because they can provide general psychological and emotional assistance to the child. The presence of parents does not mean that parents can act in defence of the child or be involved in the decision-making process. However, the judge or competent authority may decide, at the request of the child or of his/her legal or other appropriate assistance or because it is not in the best interests of the child (art. 3 of CRC), to limit, restrict or exclude the presence of the parents from the proceedings.

54. The Committee recommends that States parties explicitly provide by law for the maximum possible involvement of parents or legal guardians in the proceedings against the child. This involvement shall in general contribute to an effective response to the child's infringement of the penal law. To promote parental involvement, parents must be notified of the apprehension of their child as soon as possible.

55. At the same time, the Committee regrets the trend in some countries to introduce the punishment of parents for the offences committed by their children. Civil liability for the damage caused by the child's act can, in some limited cases, be appropriate, in particular for the younger children (e.g. below 16 years of age). But criminalizing parents of children in conflict with the law will most likely not contribute to their becoming active partners in the social reintegration of their child.

Freedom from compulsory self-incrimination (art. 40 (2) (b) (iii))

56. In line with article 14 (3) (g) of ICCPR, CRC requires that a child be not compelled to give testimony or to confess or acknowledge guilt. This means in the first place – and self-evidently – that torture, cruel, inhuman or degrading treatment in order to extract an admission or a confession constitutes a grave violation of the rights of the child (art. 37 (a) of CRC) and is wholly unacceptable. No such admission or confession can be admissible as evidence (article 15 of the Convention against Torture and Other Cruel, Inhuman or Degrading Treatment or Punishment).

57. There are many other less violent ways to coerce or to lead the child to a confession or a self-incriminatory testimony. The term "compelled" should be interpreted in a broad manner and not be limited to physical force or other clear violations of human rights. The age of the child, the child's development, the length of the interrogation, the child's lack of understanding, the fear of unknown consequences or of a suggested

possibility of imprisonment may lead him/her to a confession that is not true. That may become even more likely if rewards are promised such as: "You can go home as soon as you have given us the true story", or lighter sanctions or release are promised.

58. The child being questioned must have access to a legal or other appropriate representative, and must be able to request the presence of his/her parent(s) during questioning. There must be independent scrutiny of the methods of interrogation to ensure that the evidence is voluntary and not coerced, given the totality of the circumstances, and is reliable. The court or other judicial body, when considering the voluntary nature and reliability of an admission or confession by a child, must take into account the age of the child, the length of custody and interrogation, and the presence of legal or other counsel, parent(s), or independent representatives of the child. Police officers and other investigating authorities should be well trained to avoid interrogation techniques and practices that result in coerced or unreliable confessions or testimonies.

Presence and examination of witnesses (art. 40 (2) (b) (iv))

59. The guarantee in article 40 (2) (b) (iv) of CRC underscores that the principle of equality of arms (i.e. under conditions of equality or parity between defence and prosecution) should be observed in the administration of juvenile justice. The term "to examine or to have examined" refers to the fact that there are distinctions in the legal systems, particularly between the accusatorial and inquisitorial trials. In the latter, the defendant is often allowed to examine witnesses although he/she rarely uses this right, leaving examination of the witnesses to the lawyer or, in the case of children, to another appropriate body. However, it remains important that the lawyer or other representative informs the child of the possibility to examine witnesses and to allow him/her to express his/her views in that regard, views which should be given due weight in accordance with the age and maturity of the child (art. 12).

The right to appeal (art. 40 (2) (b) (v))

60. The child has the right to appeal against the decision by which he is found guilty of the charge(s) brought against him/her and against the measures imposed as a consequence of this guilty verdict. This appeal should be decided by a higher, competent, independent and impartial authority or judicial body, in other words, a body that meets the same standards and requirements as the one that dealt with the case in the first instance. This guarantee is similar to the one expressed in article 14 (5) of ICCPR. This right of appeal is not limited to the most serious offences.

61. This seems to be the reason why quite a few States parties have made reservations regarding this provision in order to limit this right of appeal by the child to the more serious offences and/or imprisonment sentences. The Committee reminds States parties to the ICCPR that a similar provision is made in article 14 (5) of the Covenant. In the light of article 41 of CRC, it means that this article should provide every adjudicated child with the right to appeal. The Committee recommends that the States parties withdraw their reservations to the provision in article 40 (2) (b) (v).

Free assistance of an interpreter (art. 40 (2) (vi))

62. If a child cannot understand or speak the language used by the juvenile justice system, he/she has the right to get free assistance of an interpreter. This assistance should not be limited to the court trial but should also be available at all stages of the juvenile justice process. It is also important that the interpreter has been trained to work with children, because the use and understanding of their mother tongue might be different from that of adults. Lack of knowledge and/or experience in that regard may impede the child's full understanding of the questions raised, and interfere with the right to a fair

trial and to effective participation. The condition starting with "if", "if the child cannot understand or speak the language used", means that a child of a foreign or ethnic origin for example, who – besides his/her mother tongue – understands and speaks the official language, does not have to be provided with the free assistance of an interpreter.

63. The Committee also wishes to draw the attention of States parties to children with speech impairment or other disabilities. In line with the spirit of article 40 (2) (vi), and in accordance with the special protection measures provided to children with disabilities in article 23, the Committee recommends that States parties ensure that children with speech impairment or other disabilities are provided with adequate and effective assistance by well-trained professionals, e.g. in sign language, in case they are subject to the juvenile justice process (see also in this regard general comment No. 9 (The rights of children with disabilities) of the Committee on the Rights of the Child.

Full respect of privacy (arts. 16 and 40 (2) (b) (vii))

64. The right of a child to have his/her privacy fully respected during all stages of the proceedings reflects the right to protection of privacy enshrined in article 16 of CRC. "All stages of the proceedings" includes from the initial contact with law enforcement (e.g. a request for information and identification) up until the final decision by a competent authority, or release from supervision, custody or deprivation of liberty. In this particular context, it is meant to avoid harm caused by undue publicity or by the process of labelling. No information shall be published that may lead to the identification of a child offender because of its effect of stigmatization, and possible impact on his/her ability to have access to education, work, housing or to be safe. It means that a public authority should be very reluctant with press releases related to offences allegedly committed by children and limit them to very exceptional cases. They must take measures to guarantee that children are not identifiable via these press releases. Journalists who violate the right to privacy of a child in conflict with the law should be sanctioned with disciplinary and when necessary (e.g. in case of recidivism) with penal law sanctions.

65. In order to protect the privacy of the child, most States parties have as a rule – sometimes with the possibility of exceptions – that the court or other hearings of a child accused of an infringement of the penal law should take place behind closed doors. This rule allows for the presence of experts or other professionals with a special permission of the court. Public hearings in juvenile justice should only be possible in well-defined cases and at the written decision of the court. Such a decision should be open for appeal by the child.

66. The Committee recommends that all States parties introduce the rule that court and other hearings of a child in conflict with the law be conducted behind closed doors. Exceptions to this rule should be very limited and clearly stated in the law. The verdict/sentence should be pronounced in public at a court session in such a way that the identity of the child is not revealed. The right to privacy (art. 16) requires all professionals involved in the implementation of the measures taken by the court or another competent authority to keep all information that may result in the identification of the child confidential in all their external contacts. Furthermore, the right to privacy also means that the records of child offenders should be kept strictly confidential and closed to third parties except for those directly involved in the investigation and adjudication of, and the ruling on, the case. With a view to avoiding stigmatization and/or prejudgements, records of child offenders should not be used in adult proceedings in subsequent cases involving the same offender (see the Beijing Rules, rules 21.1 and 21.2), or to enhance such future sentencing.

67. The Committee also recommends that the States parties introduce rules which would allow for an automatic removal from the criminal records of the name of the child who committed an offence upon reaching the age of 18, or for certain limited, serious offences where removal is possible at the request of the child, if necessary under certain conditions (e.g. not having committed an offence within two years after the last conviction).

E. Measures (see also chapter IV, section B, above)

Pretrial alternatives

68. The decision to initiate a formal criminal law procedure does not necessarily mean that this procedure must be completed with a formal court sentence for a child. In line with the observations made above in section B, the Committee wishes to emphasize that the competent authorities – in most States the office of the public prosecutor – should continuously explore the possibilities of alternatives to a court conviction. In other words, efforts to achieve an appropriate conclusion of the case by offering measures like the ones mentioned above in section B should continue. The nature and duration of these measures offered by the prosecution may be more demanding, and legal or other appropriate assistance for the child is then necessary. The performance of such a measure should be presented to the child as a way to suspend the formal criminal/juvenile law procedure, which will be terminated if the measure has been carried out in a satisfactory manner.

69. In this process of offering alternatives to a court conviction at the level of the prosecutor, the child's human rights and legal safeguards should be fully respected. In this regard, the Committee refers to the recommendations set out in paragraph 27 above, which equally apply here.

Dispositions by the juvenile court/judge

70. After a fair and just trial in full compliance with article 40 of CRC (see chapter IV, section D, above), a decision is made regarding the measures which should be imposed on the child found guilty of the alleged offence(s). The laws must provide the court/judge, or other competent, independent and impartial authority or judicial body, with a wide variety of possible alternatives to institutional care and deprivation of liberty, which are listed in a non-exhaustive manner in article 40 (4) of CRC, to assure that deprivation of liberty be used only as a measure of last resort and for the shortest possible period of time (art. 37 (b) of CRC).

71. The Committee wishes to emphasize that the reaction to an offence should always be in proportion not only to the circumstances and the gravity of the offence, but also to the age, lesser culpability, circumstances and needs of the child, as well as to the various and particularly long-term needs of the society. A strictly punitive approach is not in accordance with the leading principles for juvenile justice spelled out in article 40 (1) of CRC (see paragraphs 5-14 above). The Committee reiterates that corporal punishment as a sanction is a violation of these principles as well as of article 37 which prohibits all forms of cruel, inhuman and degrading treatment or punishment (see also the Committee's general comment No. 8 (2006) (The right of the child to protection from corporal punishment and other cruel or degrading forms of punishment)). In cases of severe offences by children, measures proportionate to the circumstances of the offender and to the gravity of the offence may be considered, including considerations of the need of public safety and sanctions. In the case of children, such considerations must always be outweighed by the need to safeguard the well-being and the best interests of the child and to promote his/her reintegration.

72. The Committee notes that if a penal disposition is linked to the age of a child, and there is conflicting, inconclusive or uncertain evidence of the child's age, he/she shall have the right to the rule of the benefit of the doubt (see also paragraphs 35 and 39 above).

73. As far as alternatives to deprivation of liberty/institutional care are concerned, there is a wide range of experience with the use and implementation of such measures. States parties should benefit from this experience, and develop and implement these alternatives by adjusting them to their own culture and tradition. It goes without saying that measures amounting to forced labour or to torture or inhuman and degrading treatment must be explicitly prohibited, and those responsible for such illegal practices should be brought to justice.

74. After these general remarks, the Committee wishes to draw attention to the measures prohibited under article 37 (a) of CRC, and to deprivation of liberty.

Prohibition of the death penalty

75. Article 37 (a) of CRC reaffirms the internationally accepted standard (see for example article 6 (5) of ICCPR) that the death penalty cannot be imposed for a crime committed by a person who at that time was under 18 years of age. Although the text is clear, there are States parties that assume that the rule only prohibits the execution of persons below the age of 18 years. However, under this rule the explicit and decisive criteria is the age at the time of the commission of the offence. It means that a death penalty may not be imposed for a crime committed by a person under 18 regardless of his/her age at the time of the trial or sentencing or of the execution of the sanction.

76. The Committee recommends the few States parties that have not done so yet to abolish the death penalty for all offences committed by persons below the age of 18 years and to suspend the execution of all death sentences for those persons till the necessary legislative measures abolishing the death penalty for children have been fully enacted. The imposed death penalty should be changed to a sanction that is in full conformity with CRC.

No life imprisonment without parole

77. No child who was under the age of 18 at the time he or she committed an offence should be sentenced to life without the possibility of release or parole. For all sentences imposed upon children the possibility of release should be realistic and regularly considered. In this regard, the Committee refers to article 25 of CRC providing the right to periodic review for all children placed for the purpose of care, protection or treatment. The Committee reminds the States parties which do sentence children to life imprisonment with the possibility of release or parole that this sanction must fully comply with and strive for the realization of the aims of juvenile justice enshrined in article 40 (1) of CRC. This means inter alia that the child sentenced to this imprisonment should receive education, treatment, and care aiming at his/her release, reintegration and ability to assume a constructive role in society. This also requires a regular review of the child's development and progress in order to decide on his/her possible release. Given the likelihood that a life imprisonment of a child will make it very difficult, if not impossible, to achieve the aims of juvenile justice despite the possibility of release, the Committee strongly recommends the States parties to abolish all forms of life imprisonment for offences committed by persons under the age of 18.

F. Deprivation of liberty, including pretrial detention and post-trial incarceration

78. Article 37 of CRC contains the leading principles for the use of deprivation of liberty, the procedural rights of every child deprived of liberty, and provisions concerning the treatment of and conditions for children deprived of their liberty.

Basic principles

79. The leading principles for the use of deprivation of liberty are: (a) the arrest, detention or imprisonment of a child shall be in conformity with the law and shall be used only as a measure of last resort and for the shortest appropriate period of time; and (b) no child shall be deprived of his/her liberty unlawfully or arbitrarily.

80. The Committee notes with concern that, in many countries, children languish in pretrial detention for months or even years, which constitutes a grave violation of article 37 (b) of CRC. An effective package of alternatives must be available (see chapter IV, section B, above), for the States parties to realize their obligation under article 37 (b) of CRC to use deprivation of liberty only as a measure of last resort. The use of these alternatives must be carefully structured to reduce the use of pretrial detention as well, rather than "widening the net" of sanctioned children. In addition, the States parties should take adequate legislative and other measures to reduce the use of pretrial detention. Use of pretrial detention as a punishment violates the presumption of innocence. The law should clearly state the conditions that are required to determine whether to place or keep a child in pretrial detention, in particular to ensure his/her appearance at the court proceedings, and whether he/she is an immediate danger to himself/herself or others. The duration of pretrial detention should be limited by law and be subject to regular review.

81. The Committee recommends that the State parties ensure that a child can be released from pretrial detention as soon as possible, and if necessary under certain conditions. Decisions regarding pretrial detention, including its duration, should be made by a competent, independent and impartial authority or a judicial body, and the child should be provided with legal or other appropriate assistance.

Procedural rights (art. 37 (d))

82. Every child deprived of his/her liberty has the right to prompt access to legal and other appropriate assistance, as well as the right to challenge the legality of the deprivation of his/her liberty before a court or other competent, independent and impartial authority, and to a prompt decision on any such action.

83. Every child arrested and deprived of his/her liberty should be brought before a competent authority to examine the legality of (the continuation of) this deprivation of liberty within 24 hours. The Committee also recommends that the States parties ensure by strict legal provisions that the legality of a pretrial detention is reviewed regularly, preferably every two weeks. In case a conditional release of the child, e.g. by applying alternative measures, is not possible, the child should be formally charged with the alleged offences and be brought before a court or other competent, independent and impartial authority or judicial body, not later than 30 days after his/her pretrial detention takes effect. The Committee, conscious of the practice of adjourning court hearings, often more than once, urges the States parties to introduce the legal provisions necessary to ensure that the court/juvenile judge or other competent body makes a final decision on the charges not later than six months after they have been presented.

84. The right to challenge the legality of the deprivation of liberty includes not only the right to appeal, but also the right to access the court, or other competent, independent and impartial authority or judicial body, in cases where the deprivation of liberty is an

administrative decision (e.g. the police, the prosecutor and other competent authority). The right to a prompt decision means that a decision must be rendered as soon as possible, e.g. within or not later than two weeks after the challenge is made.

Treatment and conditions (art. 37 (c))

85. Every child deprived of liberty shall be separated from adults. A child deprived of his/her liberty shall not be placed in an adult prison or other facility for adults. There is abundant evidence that the placement of children in adult prisons or jails compromises their basic safety, well-being, and their future ability to remain free of crime and to reintegrate. The permitted exception to the separation of children from adults stated in article 37 (c) of CRC, "unless it is considered in the child's best interests not to do so", should be interpreted narrowly; the child's best interests does not mean for the convenience of the States parties. States parties should establish separate facilities for children deprived of their liberty, which include distinct, child-centred staff, personnel, policies and practices.

86. This rule does not mean that a child placed in a facility for children has to be moved to a facility for adults immediately after he/she turns 18. Continuation of his/her stay in the facility for children should be possible if that is in his/her best interest and not contrary to the best interests of the younger children in the facility.

87. Every child deprived of liberty has the right to maintain contact with his/her family through correspondence and visits. In order to facilitate visits, the child should be placed in a facility that is as close as possible to the place of residence of his/her family. Exceptional circumstances that may limit this contact should be clearly described in the law and not be left to the discretion of the competent authorities.

88. The Committee draws the attention of States parties to the United Nations Rules for the Protection of Juveniles Deprived of their Liberty, adopted by the General Assembly in its resolution 45/113 of 14 December 1990. The Committee urges the States parties to fully implement these rules, while also taking into account as far as relevant the Standard Minimum Rules for the Treatment of Prisoners (see also rule 9 of the Beijing Rules). In this regard, the Committee recommends that the States parties incorporate these rules into their national laws and regulations, and make them available, in the national or regional language, to all professionals, NGOs and volunteers involved in the administration of juvenile justice.

89. The Committee wishes to emphasize that, inter alia, the following principles and rules need to be observed in all cases of deprivation of liberty:

— Children should be provided with a physical environment and accommodations which are in keeping with the rehabilitative aims of residential placement, and due regard must be given to their needs for privacy, sensory stimuli, opportunities to associate with their peers, and to participate in sports, physical exercise, in arts, and leisure time activities;

— Every child of compulsory school age has the right to education suited to his/her needs and abilities, and designed to prepare him/her for return to society; in addition, every child should, when appropriate, receive vocational training in occupations likely to prepare him/her for future employment;

— Every child has the right to be examined by a physician upon admission to the detention/correctional facility and shall receive adequate medical care throughout his/her stay in the facility, which should be provided, where possible, by health facilities and services of the community;

— The staff of the facility should promote and facilitate frequent contacts of the child with the wider community, including communications with his/her family, friends and other persons or representatives of reputable outside organizations, and the opportunity to visit his/her home and family;

— Restraint or force can be used only when the child poses an imminent threat of injury to him or herself or others, and only when all other means of control have been exhausted. The use of restraint or force, including physical, mechanical and medical restraints, should be under close and direct control of a medical and/or psychological professional. It must never be used as a means of punishment. Staff of the facility should receive training on the applicable standards and members of the staff who use restraint or force in violation of the rules and standards should be punished appropriately;

— Any disciplinary measure must be consistent with upholding the inherent dignity of the juvenile and the fundamental objectives of institutional care; disciplinary measures in violation of article 37 of CRC must be strictly forbidden, including corporal punishment, placement in a dark cell, closed or solitary confinement, or any other punishment that may compromise the physical or mental health or well-being of the child concerned;

— Every child should have the right to make requests or complaints, without censorship as to the substance, to the central administration, the judicial authority or other proper independent authority, and to be informed of the response without delay; children need to know about and have easy access to these mechanisms;

— Independent and qualified inspectors should be empowered to conduct inspections on a regular basis and to undertake unannounced inspections on their own initiative; they should place special emphasis on holding conversations with children in the facilities, in a confidential setting.

V. THE ORGANIZATION OF JUVENILE JUSTICE

90. In order to ensure the full implementation of the principles and rights elaborated in the previous paragraphs, it is necessary to establish an effective organization for the administration of juvenile justice, and a comprehensive juvenile justice system. As stated in article 40 (3) of CRC, States parties shall seek to promote the establishment of laws, procedures, authorities and institutions specifically applicable to children in conflict with the penal law.

91. What the basic provisions of these laws and procedures are required to be, has been presented in the present general comment. More and other provisions are left to the discretion of States parties. This also applies to the form of these laws and procedures. They can be laid down in special chapters of the general criminal and procedural law, or be brought together in a separate act or law on juvenile justice.

92. A comprehensive juvenile justice system further requires the establishment of specialized units within the police, the judiciary, the court system, the prosecutor's office, as well as specialized defenders or other representatives who provide legal or other appropriate assistance to the child.

93. The Committee recommends that the States parties establish juvenile courts either as separate units or as part of existing regional/district courts. Where that is not immediately feasible for practical reasons, the States parties should ensure the appointment of specialized judges or magistrates for dealing with cases of juvenile justice.

94. In addition, specialized services such as probation, counselling or supervision should be established together with specialized facilities including for example day treatment centres and, where necessary, facilities for residential care and treatment of child

offenders. In this juvenile justice system, an effective coordination of the activities of all these specialized units, services and facilities should be promoted in an ongoing manner.

95. It is clear from many States parties' reports that non-governmental organizations can and do play an important role not only in the prevention of juvenile delinquency as such, but also in the administration of juvenile justice. The Committee therefore recommends that States parties seek the active involvement of these organizations in the development and implementation of their comprehensive juvenile justice policy and provide them with the necessary resources for this involvement.

VI. AWARENESS-RAISING AND TRAINING

96. Children who commit offences are often subject to negative publicity in the media, which contributes to a discriminatory and negative stereotyping of these children and often of children in general. This negative presentation or criminalization of child offenders is often based on misrepresentation and/or misunderstanding of the causes of juvenile delinquency, and results regularly in a call for a tougher approach (e.g. zero-tolerance, three strikes and you are out, mandatory sentences, trial in adult courts and other primarily punitive measures). To create a positive environment for a better understanding of the root causes of juvenile delinquency and a rights-based approach to this social problem, the States parties should conduct, promote and/or support educational and other campaigns to raise awareness of the need and the obligation to deal with children alleged of violating the penal law in accordance with the spirit and the letter of CRC. In this regard, the States parties should seek the active and positive involvement of members of parliament, NGOs and the media, and support their efforts in the improvement of the understanding of a rights-based approach to children who have been or are in conflict with the penal law. It is crucial for children, in particular those who have experience with the juvenile justice system, to be involved in these awareness-raising efforts.

97. It is essential for the quality of the administration of juvenile justice that all the professionals involved, inter alia, in law enforcement and the judiciary receive appropriate training on the content and meaning of the provisions of CRC in general, particularly those directly relevant to their daily practice. This training should be organized in a systematic and ongoing manner and should not be limited to information on the relevant national and international legal provisions. It should include information on, inter alia, the social and other causes of juvenile delinquency, psychological and other aspects of the development of children, with special attention to girls and children belonging to minorities or indigenous peoples, the culture and the trends in the world of young people, the dynamics of group activities, and the available measures dealing with children in conflict with the penal law, in particular measures without resorting to judicial proceedings (see chapter IV, section B, above).

VII. DATA COLLECTION, EVALUATION AND RESEARCH

98. The Committee is deeply concerned about the lack of even basic and disaggregated data on, inter alia, the number and nature of offences committed by children, the use and the average duration of pretrial detention, the number of children dealt with by resorting to measures other than judicial proceedings (diversion), the number of convicted children and the nature of the sanctions imposed on them. The Committee urges the States parties to systematically collect disaggregated data relevant to the information on the practice of the administration of juvenile justice, and necessary for

the development, implementation and evaluation of policies and programmes aiming at the prevention and effective responses to juvenile delinquency in full accordance with the principles and provisions of CRC.

99. The Committee recommends that States parties conduct regular evaluations of their practice of juvenile justice, in particular of the effectiveness of the measures taken, including those concerning discrimination, reintegration and recidivism, preferably carried out by independent academic institutions. Research, as for example on the disparities in the administration of juvenile justice which may amount to discrimination, and developments in the field of juvenile delinquency, such as effective diversion programmes or newly emerging juvenile delinquency activities, will indicate critical points of success and concern. It is important that children are involved in this evaluation and research, in particular those who have been in contact with parts of the juvenile justice system. The privacy of these children and the confidentiality of their cooperation should be fully respected and protected. In this regard, the Committee refers the States parties to the existing international guidelines on the involvement of children in research.

General Comment No 11 (2009)
Indigenous children and their rights under the Convention

INTRODUCTION

1. In the preamble of the Convention on the Rights of the Child, States parties take "*due account of the importance and cultural values of each people for the protection and harmonious development of the child*". While all the rights contained in the Convention apply to all children, whether indigenous or not, the Convention on the Rights of the Child was the first core human rights treaty to include specific references to indigenous children in a number of provisions.

2. Article 30 of the Convention states that "*In those States in which ethnic, religious, or linguistic minorities or persons of indigenous origin exist, a child belonging to such a minority or who is indigenous shall not be denied the right, in community with other members of his or her group, to enjoy his or her own culture, to profess and practise his or her own religion or to use his or her own language.*"

3. Furthermore, article 29 of the Convention provides that "education of the child shall be directed to the preparation of the child for responsible life in a free society, in the spirit of understanding, peace, tolerance, equality of sexes, and friendship among all peoples, ethnic, national and religious groups and persons of indigenous origin".

4. Article 17 of the Convention also makes specific mention as States parties shall "encourage the mass media to have particular regard for the linguistic needs of the child who belongs to a minority group or who is indigenous".

5. The specific references to indigenous children in the Convention are indicative of the recognition that they require special measures in order to fully enjoy their rights. The Committee on the Rights of the Child has consistently taken into account the situation of indigenous children in its reviews of periodic reports of States parties to the Convention. The Committee has observed that indigenous children face significant challenges in exercising their rights and has issued specific recommendations to this effect in its concluding observations. Indigenous children continue to experience serious discrimination contrary to article 2 of the Convention in a range of areas, including in their access to health care and education, which has prompted the need to adopt this general comment.

6. In addition to the Convention on the Rights of the Child, various human rights treaties, have played an important role in addressing the situation of indigenous children and their right not to be discriminated, namely, the International Convention on the Elimination of All Forms of Racial Discrimination, 1965, the International Covenant on Civil and Political Rights, 1966, and the International Covenant on Economic, Social and Cultural Rights, 1966.

7. The International Labour Organization Convention No. 169 concerning Indigenous and Tribal Peoples in Independent Countries, 1989 contains provisions which advance the rights of indigenous peoples and specifically highlights the rights of indigenous children in the area of education.

8. In 2001, the United Nations Commission on Human Rights appointed a Special Rapporteur on the situation of human rights and fundamental freedoms of indigenous peoples, subsequently confirmed by the Human Rights Council in 2007. The Council has requested the Special Rapporteur to pay particular attention to the situation of

indigenous children and several recommendations included in his annual and mission reports have focused on their specific situation.

9. In 2003, the United Nations Permanent Forum on Indigenous Issues held its second session on the theme indigenous children and youth and the same year the Committee on the Rights of the Child held its annual Day of General Discussion on the rights of indigenous children and adopted specific recommendations aimed primarily at States parties but also United Nations entities, human rights mechanisms, civil society, donors, the World Bank and regional development banks.

10. In 2007, the United Nations General Assembly adopted the Declaration on the Rights of Indigenous Peoples which provides important guidance on the rights of indigenous peoples, including specific reference to the rights of indigenous children in a number of areas.

OBJECTIVES AND STRUCTURE

11. This general comment on the rights of indigenous children as provided for by the Convention on the Rights of the Child draws on the legal developments and initiatives outlined above.

12. The primary objective of this general comment is to provide States with guidance on how to implement their obligations under the Convention with respect to indigenous children. The Committee bases this general comment on its experience in interpreting the provisions of the Convention in relation to indigenous children. Furthermore, the general comment is based upon the recommendations adopted following the Day of General Discussion on indigenous children in 2003 and reflects a consultative process with relevant stakeholders, including indigenous children themselves.

13. The general comment aims to explore the specific challenges which impede indigenous children from being able to fully enjoy their rights and highlight special measures required to be undertaken by States in order to guarantee the effective exercise of indigenous children's rights. Furthermore, the general comment seeks to encourage good practices and highlight positive approaches in the practical implementation of rights for indigenous children.

14. Article 30 of the Convention and the right to the enjoyment of culture, religion and language are key elements in this general comment; however the aim is to explore the various provisions which require particular attention in their implementation in relation to indigenous children. Particular emphasis is placed on the interrelationship between relevant provisions, notably with the general principles of the Convention as identified by the Committee, namely, non-discrimination, the best interests of the child, the right to life, survival and development and the right to be heard.

15. The Committee notes that the Convention contains references to both minority and indigenous children. Certain references in this general comment may be relevant for children of minority groups and the Committee may decide in the future to prepare a general comment specifically on the rights of children belonging to minority groups.

ARTICLE 30 AND GENERAL OBLIGATIONS OF STATES

16. The Committee recalls the close linkage between article 30 of the Convention on the Rights of the Child and article 27 of the International Covenant on Civil and Political Rights. Both articles specifically provide for the right, in community with other members of his or her group, to enjoy his or her own culture, to profess and practise his or her own religion or to use his or her own language. The right established is conceived as

being both individual and collective and is an important recognition of the collective traditions and values in indigenous cultures. The Committee notes that the right to exercise cultural rights among indigenous peoples may be closely associated with the use of traditional territory and the use of its resources.[73]

17. Although article 30 is expressed in negative terms, it nevertheless recognizes the existence of a "right" and requires that it "shall not be denied". Consequently, a State party is under an obligation to ensure that the existence and the exercise of this right are protected against their denial or violation. The Committee concurs with the Human Rights Committee that positive measures of protection are required, not only against the acts of the State party itself, whether through its legislative, judicial or administrative authorities, but also against the acts of other persons within the State party.[74]

18. In this context, the Committee also supports the Committee on the Elimination of Racial Discrimination in its call upon States parties *to recognize and respect indigenous distinct cultures, history, language and way of life as an enrichment of the State's cultural identity and to promote its preservation.*[75]

19. The presence of indigenous peoples is established by self-identification as the fundamental criterion for determining their existence.[76] There is no requirement for States parties to officially recognize indigenous peoples in order for them to exercise their rights.

20. Based on its reviews of States parties reports, the Committee on the Rights of the Child has observed that in implementing their obligations under the Convention many States parties give insufficient attention to the rights of indigenous children and to promotion of their development. The Committee considers that special measures through legislation and policies for the protection of indigenous children should be undertaken in consultation with the communities concerned[77] and with the participation of children in the consultation process, as provided for by article 12 of the Convention. The Committee considers that consultations should be actively carried out by authorities or other entities of States parties in a manner that is culturally appropriate, guarantees availability of information to all parties and ensures interactive communication and dialogue.

21. The Committee urges States parties to ensure that adequate attention is given to article 30 in the implementation of the Convention. States parties should provide detailed information in their periodic reports under the Convention on the special measures undertaken in order to guarantee that indigenous children can enjoy the rights provided in article 30.

22. The Committee underlines that cultural practices provided by article 30 of the Convention must be exercised in accordance with other provisions of the Convention and under no circumstances may be justified if deemed prejudicial to the child's dignity, health and development.[78] Should harmful practices be present, inter alia early marriages and female genital mutilation, the State party should work together with indigenous communities to ensure their eradication. The Committee strongly urges

---

[73] Human Rights Committee, general comment No. 23 on article 27, CCPR/C/Rev.1/Add.5, 1994, paras. 3.2, 7. Recommendations of CRC Day of General Discussion on the Rights of Indigenous Children, 2003, para. 4.

[74] Human Rights Committee, general comment No. 23 on article 27, CCPR/C/Rev.1/Add.5, 1994, para. 6.1.

[75] Committee on the Elimination of Racial Discrimination, general recommendation No. 23 on Indigenous Peoples, 1997, contained in A/52/18, Annex V.

[76] ILO Convention concerning Indigenous and Tribal Peoples in Independent Countries No. 169, article 1 (2).

[77] ILO Convention No. 169, articles 2, 6, 27.

[78] UNICEF Innocenti Digest No. 11, Ensuring the Rights of Indigenous Children, 2004, p. 7.

States parties to develop and implement awareness-raising campaigns, education programmes and legislation aimed at changing attitudes and address gender roles and stereotypes that contribute to harmful practices.[79]

GENERAL PRINCIPLES (ARTS. 2, 3, 6 AND 12 OF THE CONVENTION)

Non-discrimination

23. Article 2 sets out the obligation of States parties to ensure the rights of each child within its jurisdiction without discrimination of any kind. Non-discrimination has been identified by the Committee as a general principle of fundamental importance for the implementation of all the rights enshrined in the Convention. Indigenous children have the inalienable right to be free from discrimination. In order to effectively protect children from discrimination, it is a State party obligation to ensure that the principle of non-discrimination is reflected in all domestic legislation and can be directly applied and appropriately monitored and enforced through judicial and administrative bodies. Effective remedies should be timely and accessible. The Committee highlights that the obligations of the State party extend not only to the public but also to the private sector.

24. As previously stated in the Committee's general comment No. 5 on general measures of implementation, the non-discrimination obligation requires States actively to identify individual children and groups of children the recognition and realization of whose rights may demand special measures. For example, the Committee highlights, in particular, the need for data collection to be disaggregated to enable discrimination or potential discrimination to be identified. Addressing discrimination may furthermore require changes in legislation, administration and resource allocation, as well as educational measures to change attitudes.[80]

25. The Committee, through its extensive review of State party reports, notes that indigenous children are among those children who require positive measures in order to eliminate conditions that cause discrimination and to ensure their enjoyment of the rights of the Convention on equal level with other children. In particular, States parties are urged to consider the application of special measures in order to ensure that indigenous children have access to culturally appropriate services in the areas of health, nutrition, education, recreation and sports, social services, housing, sanitation and juvenile justice.[81]

26. Among the positive measures required to be undertaken by States parties is disaggregated data collection and the development of indicators for the purposes of identifying existing and potential areas of discrimination of indigenous children. The identification of gaps and barriers to the enjoyment of the rights of indigenous children is essential in order to implement appropriate positive measures through legislation, resource allocation, policies and programmes.[82]

27. States parties should ensure that public information and educational measures are taken to address the discrimination of indigenous children. The obligation under article 2 in conjunction with articles 17, 29.1 (d) and 30 of the Convention requires States to develop public campaigns, dissemination material and educational curricula, both in schools and for professionals, focused on the rights of indigenous children and the elimination of discriminatory attitudes and practices, including racism. Furthermore,

---

[79] CRC, general comment No. 4 on Adolescent Health, 2003, para. 24.
[80] CRC, general comment No. 5 on General Measures of Implementation, 2003, para. 12.
[81] Recommendations of CRC Day of General Discussion on the Rights of Indigenous Children, 2003, para. 9.
[82] Ibid., para. 6.

States parties should provide meaningful opportunities for indigenous and non-indigenous children to understand and respect different cultures, religions, and languages.

28. In their periodic reports to the Committee, States parties should identify measures and programmes undertaken to address discrimination of indigenous children in relation to the Declaration and Programme of Action adopted at the 2001 World Conference against Racism, Discrimination, Xenophobia and Related Intolerance.[83]

29. In the design of special measures, States parties should consider the needs of indigenous children who may face multiple facets of discrimination and also take into account the different situation of indigenous children in rural and urban situations. Particular attention should be given to girls in order to ensure that they enjoy their rights on an equal basis as boys. States parties should furthermore ensure that special measures address the rights of indigenous children with disabilities.[84]

Best interests of the child

30. The application of the principle of the best interests of the child to indigenous children requires particular attention. The Committee notes that the best interests of the child is conceived both as a collective and individual right, and that the application of this right to indigenous children as a group requires consideration of how the right relates to collective cultural rights. Indigenous children have not always received the distinct consideration they deserve. In some cases, their particular situation has been obscured by other issues of broader concern to indigenous peoples, (including land rights and political representation).[85] In the case of children, the best interests of the child cannot be neglected or violated in preference for the best interests of the group.

31. When State authorities including legislative bodies seek to assess the best interests of an indigenous child, they should consider the cultural rights of the indigenous child and his or her need to exercise such rights collectively with members of their group. As regards legislation, policies and programmes that affect indigenous children in general, the indigenous community should be consulted and given an opportunity to participate in the process on how the best interests of indigenous children in general can be decided in a culturally sensitive way. Such consultations should, to the extent possible, include meaningful participation of indigenous children.

32. The Committee considers there may be a distinction between the best interests of the individual child, and the best interests of children as a group. In decisions regarding one individual child, typically a court decision or an administrative decision, it is the best interests of the specific child that is the primary concern. However, considering the collective cultural rights of the child is part of determining the child's best interests.

33. The principle of the best interests of the child requires States to undertake active measures throughout their legislative, administrative and judicial systems that would systematically apply the principle by considering the implication of their decisions and actions on children's rights and interests.[86] In order to effectively guarantee the rights of indigenous children such measures would include training and awareness-raising among relevant professional categories of the importance of considering collective cultural rights in conjunction with the determination of the best interests of the child.

---

[83]   Recommendations of CRC Day of General Discussion on the Rights of Indigenous Children, 2003, para. 12.
[84]   Convention on the Rights of Persons with Disabilities, preamble. United Nations Declaration on the Rights of Indigenous Peoples, A/RES/61/295, articles 21, 22.
[85]   UNICEF Innocenti Digest No. 11, Ensuring the Rights of Indigenous Children, 2004, p. 1.
[86]   CRC, general comment No. 5 on General Measures of Implementation, 2003, para. 12.

The right to life, survival and development

34. The Committee notes with concern that disproportionately high numbers of indigenous children live in extreme poverty, a condition which has a negative impact on their survival and development. The Committee is furthermore concerned over the high infant and child mortality rates as well as malnutrition and diseases among indigenous children. Article 4 obliges States parties to address economic, social and cultural rights to the maximum extent of their available resources and where needed with international cooperation. Articles 6 and 27 provide the right of children to survival and development as well as an adequate standard of living. States should assist parents and others responsible for the indigenous child to implement this right by providing culturally appropriate material assistance and support programmes, particularly with regard to nutrition, clothing and housing. The Committee stresses the need for States parties to take special measures to ensure that indigenous children enjoy the right to an adequate standard of living and that these, together with progress indicators, be developed in partnership with indigenous peoples, including children.

35. The Committee reiterates its understanding of development of the child as set out in its general comment No. 5, as a "holistic concept embracing the child's physical, mental, spiritual, moral, psychological and social development".[87] The Preamble of the Convention stresses the importance of the traditions and cultural values of each person, particularly with reference to the protection and harmonious development of the child. In the case of indigenous children whose communities retain a traditional lifestyle, the use of traditional land is of significant importance to their development and enjoyment of culture.[88] States parties should closely consider the cultural significance of traditional land and the quality of the natural environment while ensuring the children's right to life, survival and development to the maximum extent possible.

36. The Committee reaffirms the importance of the Millennium Development Goals (MDGs) and calls on States to engage with indigenous peoples, including children, to ensure the full realization of the MDGs with respect to indigenous children.

Respect for the views of the child

37. The Committee considers that, in relation to article 12, there is a distinction between the right of the child as an individual to express his or her opinion and the right to be heard collectively, which allows children as a group to be involved in consultations on matters involving them.

38. With regard to the individual indigenous child, the State party has the obligation to respect the child's right to express his or her view in all matters affecting him or her, directly or through a representative, and give due weight to this opinion in accordance with the age and maturity of the child. The obligation is to be respected in any judicial or administrative proceeding. Taking into account the obstacles which prevent indigenous children from exercising this right, the State party should provide an environment that encourages the free opinion of the child. The right to be heard includes the right to representation, culturally appropriate interpretation and also the right not to express one's opinion.

39. When the right is applied to indigenous children as a group, the State party plays an important role in promoting their participation and should ensure that they are consulted on all matters affecting them. The State party should design special strategies to guarantee that their participation is effective. The State party should ensure that this

---

[87]   Ibid.
[88]   UNICEF Innocenti Digest No. 11, Ensuring the Rights of Indigenous Children, 2004, p. 8.

right is applied in particular in the school environment, alternative care settings and in the community in general. The Committee recommends States parties to work closely with indigenous children and their communities to develop, implement and evaluate programmes, policies and strategies for implementation of the Convention.

CIVIL RIGHTS AND FREEDOMS (ARTS. 7, 8, 13-17 AND 37 (A) OF THE CONVENTION)

Access to information

40. The Committee underlines the importance that the media have particular regard for the linguistic needs of indigenous children, in accordance with articles 17 (d) and 30 of the Convention. The Committee encourages States parties to support indigenous children to have access to media in their own languages. The Committee underlines the right of indigenous children to access information, including in their own languages, in order for them to effectively exercise their right to be heard.

Birth registration, nationality and identity

41. States parties are obliged to ensure that all children are registered immediately after birth and that they acquire a nationality. Birth registration should be free and universally accessible. The Committee is concerned that indigenous children, to a greater extent than non-indigenous children, remain without birth registration and at a higher risk of being stateless.

42. Therefore, States parties should take special measures in order to ensure that indigenous children, including those living in remote areas, are duly registered. Such special measures, to be agreed following consultation with the communities concerned, may include mobile units, periodic birth registration campaigns or the designation of birth registration offices within indigenous communities to ensure accessibility.

43. States parties should ensure that indigenous communities are informed about the importance of birth registration and of the negative implications of its absence on the enjoyment of other rights for non-registered children. States parties should ensure that information to this effect is available to indigenous communities in their own languages and that public awareness campaigns are undertaken in consultation with the communities concerned.[89]

44. Furthermore, taking into account articles 8 and 30 of the Convention, States parties should ensure that indigenous children may receive indigenous names of their parents' choice in accordance with their cultural traditions and the right to preserve his or her identity. States parties should put in place national legislation that provides indigenous parents with the possibility of selecting the name of their preference for their children.

45. The Committee draws the attention of States to article 8 (2) of the Convention which affirms that a child who has been illegally deprived of some or all of the elements of his or her identity shall be provided with appropriate assistance and protection in order to re-establish speedily his or her identity. The Committee encourages States parties to bear in mind article 8 of the United Nations Declaration on the Rights of Indigenous Peoples which sets out that effective mechanisms should be provided for prevention of, and redress for, any action which deprives indigenous peoples, including children, of their ethnic identities.

---

[89] UNICEF Innocenti Digest No. 11, Ensuring the Rights of Indigenous Children, 2004, p. 9.

FAMILY ENVIRONMENT AND ALTERNATIVE CARE (ARTS. 5, 18 (PARAS. 1-2), 9-11, 19-21, 25, 27 (PARA. 4) AND 39 OF THE CONVENTION)

46. Article 5 of the Convention requires States parties to respect the rights, responsibilities and duties of parents or where applicable, the members of the extended family or community to provide, in a manner consistent with the evolving capacities of all children, appropriate direction and guidance in the exercise by the child of the rights recognized in the Convention. States parties should ensure effective measures are implemented to safeguard the integrity of indigenous families and communities by assisting them in their child-rearing responsibilities in accordance with articles 3, 5, 18, 25 and 27 (3) of the Convention.[90]

47. States parties should, in cooperation with indigenous families and communities, collect data on the family situation of indigenous children, including children in foster care and adoption processes. Such information should be used to design policies relating to the family environment and alternative care of indigenous children in a culturally sensitive way. Maintaining the best interests of the child and the integrity of indigenous families and communities should be primary considerations in development, social services, health and education programmes affecting indigenous children.[91]

48. Furthermore, States should always ensure that the principle of the best interests of the child is the paramount consideration in any alternative care placement of indigenous children and in accordance with article 20 (3) of the Convention pay due regard to the desirability of continuity in the child's upbringing and to the child's ethnic, religious, cultural and linguistic background. In States parties where indigenous children are overrepresented among children separated from their family environment, specially targeted policy measures should be developed in consultation with indigenous communities in order to reduce the number of indigenous children in alternative care and prevent the loss of their cultural identity. Specifically, if an indigenous child is placed in care outside their community, the State party should take special measures to ensure that the child can maintain his or her cultural identity.

BASIC HEALTH AND WELFARE (ARTS. 6, 18 (PARA. 3), 23, 24, 26, 27 (PARAS. 1-3) OF THE CONVENTION)

49. States parties shall ensure that all children enjoy the highest attainable standard of health and have access to health-care service. Indigenous children frequently suffer poorer health than non-indigenous children due to inter alia inferior or inaccessible health services. The Committee notes with concern, on the basis of its reviews of States parties' reports, that this applies both to developing and developed countries.

50. The Committee urges States parties to take special measures to ensure that indigenous children are not discriminated against enjoying the highest attainable standard of health. The Committee is concerned over the high rates of mortality among indigenous children and notes that States parties have a positive duty to ensure that indigenous children have equal access to health services and to combat malnutrition as well as infant, child and maternal mortality.

51. States parties should take the necessary steps to ensure ease of access to health-care services for indigenous children. Health services should to the extent possible be community based and planned and administered in cooperation with the peoples

---

[90]   Recommendations of CRC Day of General Discussion on the Rights of Indigenous Children, 2003, para. 17.
[91]   Ibid.

concerned.[92] Special consideration should be given to ensure that health-care services are culturally sensitive and that information about these is available in indigenous languages. Particular attention should be given to ensuring access to health care for indigenous peoples who reside in rural and remote areas or in areas of armed conflict or who are migrant workers, refugees or displaced. States parties should furthermore pay special attention to the needs of indigenous children with disabilities and ensure that relevant programmes and policies are culturally sensitive.[93]

52. Health-care workers and medical staff from indigenous communities play an important role by serving as a bridge between traditional medicine and conventional medical services and preference should be given to employment of local indigenous community workers.[94] States parties should encourage the role of these workers by providing them with the necessary means and training in order to enable that conventional medicine be used by indigenous communities in a way that is mindful of their culture and traditions. In this context, the Committee recalls article 25 (2) of the ILO Convention No. 169 and articles 24 and 31 of the United Nations Declaration on the Rights of Indigenous Peoples on the right of indigenous peoples to their traditional medicines.[95]

53. States should take all reasonable measures to ensure that indigenous children, families and their communities receive information and education on issues relating to health and preventive care such as nutrition, breastfeeding, pre-and postnatal care, child and adolescent health, vaccinations, communicable diseases (in particular HIV/AIDS and tuberculosis), hygiene, environmental sanitation and the dangers of pesticides and herbicides.

54. Regarding adolescent health, States parties should consider specific strategies in order to provide indigenous adolescents with access to sexual and reproductive information and services, including on family planning and contraceptives, the dangers of early pregnancy, the prevention of HIV/AIDS and the prevention and treatment of sexually transmitted infections (STIs). The Committee recommends States parties to take into account its general comments No. 3 on HIV/AIDS and the rights of the child (2003) and No. 4 on adolescent health (2003) for this purpose.[96]

55. In certain States parties suicide rates for indigenous children are significantly higher than for non-indigenous children. Under such circumstances, States parties should design and implement a policy for preventive measures and ensure that additional financial and human resources are allocated to mental health care for indigenous children in a culturally appropriate manner, following consultation with the affected community. In order to analyse and combat the root causes, the State party should establish and maintain a dialogue with the indigenous community.

EDUCATION (ARTS. 28, 29 AND 31 OF THE CONVENTION)

56. Article 29 of the Convention sets out that the aims of education for all children should be directed to, among other objectives, the development of respect for the child's cultural identity, language and values and for civilizations different from his or her own. Further objectives include the preparation of the child for responsible life in a free society, in the spirit of understanding peace, tolerance, equality of sexes and friendship

---

[92] ILO Convention No. 169, article 25 (1, 2).
[93] CRC, general comment No. 9 on The Rights of Children with Disabilities, 2006.
[94] ILO Convention No. 169, article 25 (3).
[95] United Nations Declaration on the Rights of Indigenous Peoples, A/RES/61/295, articles 24, 31.
[96] CRC, general comment No. 3 on HIV/AIDS and the Rights of the Child, 2003 and general comment No. 4 on Adolescent Health, 2003.

among all peoples, ethnic, national and religious groups and persons of indigenous origin. The aims of education apply to education for all children and States should ensure these are adequately reflected in the curricula, content of materials, teaching methods and policies. States are encouraged to refer to the Committee's general comment No. 1 on the aims of education for further guidance.[97]

57. The education of indigenous children contributes both to their individual and community development as well as to their participation in the wider society. Quality education enables indigenous children to exercise and enjoy economic, social and cultural rights for their personal benefit as well as for the benefit of their community. Furthermore, it strengthens children's ability to exercise their civil rights in order to influence political policy processes for improved protection of human rights. Thus, the implementation of the right to education of indigenous children is an essential means of achieving individual empowerment and self-determination of indigenous peoples.

58. In order to ensure that the aims of education are in line with the Convention, States parties are responsible for protecting children from all forms of discrimination as set out in article 2 of the Convention and for actively combating racism. This duty is particularly pertinent in relation to indigenous children. In order to effectively implement this obligation, States parties should ensure that the curricula, educational materials and history textbooks provide a fair, accurate and informative portrayal of the societies and cultures of indigenous peoples.[98] Discriminatory practices, such as restrictions on the use of cultural and traditional dress, should be avoided in the school setting.

59. Article 28 of the Convention sets out that States parties shall ensure that primary education is compulsory and available to all children on the basis of equal opportunity. States parties are encouraged to make secondary and vocational education available and accessible to every child. However, in practice, indigenous children are less likely to be enrolled in school and continue to have higher drop out and illiteracy rates than non-indigenous children. Most indigenous children have reduced access to education due to a variety of factors including insufficient educational facilities and teachers, direct or indirect costs for education as well as a lack of culturally adjusted and bilingual curricula in accordance with article 30. Furthermore, indigenous children are frequently confronted with discrimination and racism in the school setting.

60. In order for indigenous children to enjoy their right to education on equal footing with non-indigenous children, States parties should ensure a range of special measures to this effect. States parties should allocate targeted financial, material and human resources in order to implement policies and programmes which specifically seek to improve the access to education for indigenous children. As established by article 27 of the ILO Convention No. 169, education programmes and services should be developed and implemented in cooperation with the peoples concerned to address their specific needs. Furthermore, governments should recognize the right of indigenous peoples to establish their own educational institutions and facilities, provided that such institutions meet minimum standards established by the competent authority in consultation with these peoples.[99] States should undertake all reasonable efforts to ensure that indigenous communities are aware of the value and importance of education and of the significance of community support for school enrolment.

---

[97] CRC, general comment No. 1 on the Aims of Education, 2001.
[98] ILO Convention No. 169, article 31, United Nations Declaration on the Rights of Indigenous Peoples, A/RES/61/295, article 15.
[99] ILO Convention No. 169, article 27.

61. States parties should ensure that school facilities are easily accessible where indigenous children live. If required, States parties should support the use of media, such as radio broadcasts and long distance education programmes (internet-based) for educational purposes and establish mobile schools for indigenous peoples who practice nomadic traditions. The school cycle should take into account and seek to adjust to cultural practices as well as agricultural seasons and ceremonial periods. States parties should only establish boarding schools away from indigenous communities when necessary as this may be a disincentive for the enrolment of indigenous children, especially girls. Boarding schools should comply with culturally sensitive standards and be monitored on a regular basis. Attempts should also be made to ensure that indigenous children living outside their communities have access to education in a manner which respects their culture, languages and traditions.

62. Article 30 of the Convention establishes the right of the indigenous child to use his or her own language. In order to implement this right, education in the child's own language is essential. Article 28 of ILO Convention No. 169 affirms that indigenous children shall be taught to read and write in their own language besides being accorded the opportunity to attain fluency in the official languages of the country.[100] Bilingual and intercultural curricula are important criteria for the education of indigenous children. Teachers of indigenous children should to the extent possible be recruited from within indigenous communities and given adequate support and training.

63. With reference to article 31 of the Convention, the Committee notes the many positive benefits of participation in sports, traditional games, physical education, and recreational activities and calls on States parties to ensure that indigenous children enjoy the effective exercise of these rights.

SPECIAL PROTECTION MEASURES (ARTS. 22, 30, 38, 39, 40, 37 (B)-(D), 32-36 OF THE CONVENTION)

Children in armed conflict and refugee children

64. Through its periodic reviews of States parties' reports, the Committee has concluded that indigenous children are particularly vulnerable in situations of armed conflict or in situations of internal unrest. Indigenous communities often reside in areas which are coveted for their natural resources or that, because of remoteness, serve as a base for non-State armed groups. In other situations, indigenous communities reside in the vicinity of borders or frontiers which are disputed by States.[101]

65. Indigenous children in such circumstances have been, and continue to face risks of being, victims of attacks against their communities, resulting in death, rape and torture, displacement, enforced disappearances, the witnessing of atrocities and the separation from parents and community. Targeting of schools by armed forces and groups has denied indigenous children access to education. Furthermore, indigenous children have been recruited by armed forces and groups and forced to commit atrocities, sometimes even against their own communities.

66. Article 38 of the Convention obliges States parties to ensure respect for the rules of humanitarian law, to protect the civilian population and to take care of children who are affected by armed conflict. States parties should pay particular attention to the risks indigenous children face in hostilities and take maximum preventive measures in consultation with the communities concerned. Military activities on indigenous

---

[100] ILO Convention No. 169, article 28.
[101] UNICEF Innocenti Digest No. 11, Ensuring the Rights of Indigenous Children, 2004, p. 13.

territories should be avoided to the extent possible, the Committee recalls article 30 of the United Nations Declaration on the Rights of Indigenous Peoples in this regard.[102] States parties should not require military conscription of indigenous children under the age of 18 years. States parties are encouraged to ratify and implement the Optional Protocol on the Involvement of Children in Armed Conflict.

67. Indigenous children who have been victims of recruitment in armed conflict should be provided with the necessary support services for reintegration into their families and communities. Consistent with article 39 of the Convention, States parties shall take all appropriate measures to promote physical and psychological recovery and social reintegration of a child victim of any form of exploitation, abuse, torture or any other form of cruel, inhuman or degrading treatment or punishment or armed conflicts. In the case of indigenous children, this should be done giving due consideration to the child's cultural and linguistic background.

68. Indigenous children who have been displaced or become refugees should be given special attention and humanitarian assistance in a culturally sensitive manner. Safe return and restitution of collective and individual property should be promoted.

Economic exploitation

69. Article 32 of the Convention provides that all children should be protected from economic exploitation and from performing any work that is likely to be hazardous or to interfere with the child's education, or to be harmful to the child's health or physical, mental, spiritual, moral or social development. In addition, ILO Convention No. 138 (Minimum Age Convention) and Convention No. 182 (Worst Forms of Child Labour Convention) set parameters for distinguishing child labour that needs abolition, on the one hand, and acceptable work done by children, including such activities that allow indigenous children to acquire livelihood skills, identity and culture, on the other. Child labour is work that deprives children of their childhood, their potential and dignity and that is harmful to their physical and mental development.[103]

70. Provisions in the Convention on the Rights of the Child refer to the use of children in illicit production and trafficking of drugs (art. 33), sexual exploitation (art. 34), trafficking in children (art. 35), children in armed conflicts (art. 38). These provisions are closely related to the definition of the worst forms of child labour under ILO Convention No. 182. The Committee notes with grave concern that indigenous children are disproportionately affected by poverty and at particular risk of being used in child labour, especially its worst forms, such as slavery, bonded labour, child trafficking, including for domestic work, use in armed conflict, prostitution and hazardous work.

71. The prevention of exploitative child labour among indigenous children (as in the case of all other children) requires a rights-based approach to child labour and is closely linked to the promotion of education. For the effective elimination of exploitative child labour among indigenous communities, States parties must identify the existing barriers to education and the specific rights and needs of indigenous children with respect to school education and vocational training. This requires that special efforts be taken to maintain a dialogue with indigenous communities and parents regarding the importance and benefits of education. Measures to combat exploitative child labour furthermore require analysis of the structural root causes of child exploitation, data collection and

---

[102] United Nations Declaration on the Rights of Indigenous Peoples, A/RES/61/295, article 30.
[103] ILO, Handbook on Combating Child Labour among Indigenous and Tribal Peoples, 2006, p. 9.

the design and implementation of prevention programmes, with adequate allocation of financial and human resources by the State party, to be carried out in consultation with indigenous communities and children.

Sexual exploitation and trafficking

72. Articles 34 and 35 of the Convention with consideration to the provisions of article 20, call on States to ensure that children are protected against sexual exploitation and abuse as well as the abduction, sale or traffic of children for any purposes. The Committee is concerned that indigenous children whose communities are affected by poverty and urban migration are at a high risk of becoming victims of sexual exploitation and trafficking. Young girls, particularly those not registered at birth, are especially vulnerable. In order to improve the protection of all children, including indigenous, States parties are encouraged to ratify and implement the Optional Protocol on the sale of children, child prostitution and child pornography.

73. States should, in consultation with indigenous communities, including children, design preventive measures and allocate targeted financial and human resources for their implementation. States should base preventive measures on studies which include documentation of the patterns of violations and analysis of root causes.

Juvenile justice

74. Articles 37 and 40 of the Convention ensure the rights of children within, and in interaction with, State judicial systems. The Committee notes with concern that incarceration of indigenous children is often disproportionately high and in some instances may be attributed to systemic discrimination from within the justice system and/or society.[104] To address these high rates of incarceration, the Committee draws the attention of States parties to article 40 (3) of the Convention requiring States to undertake measures to deal with children alleged as, accused of, or recognized as having infringed the penal law without resorting to judicial proceedings, whenever appropriate. The Committee, in its general comment No. 10 on children's rights in juvenile justice (2007) and in its concluding observations, has consistently affirmed that the arrest, detention or imprisonment of a child may be used only as a measure of last resort.[105]

75. States parties are encouraged to take all appropriate measures to support indigenous peoples to design and implement traditional restorative justice systems as long as those programmes are in accordance with the rights set out in the Convention, notably with the best interests of the child.[106] The Committee draws the attention of States parties to the United Nations Guidelines for the Prevention of Juvenile Delinquency, which encourage the development of community programmes for the prevention of juvenile delinquency.[107] States parties should seek to support, in consultation with indigenous peoples, the development of community-based policies, programmes and services which consider the needs and culture of indigenous children, their families and communities. States should provide adequate resources to juvenile justice systems, including those developed and implemented by indigenous peoples.

76. States parties are reminded that pursuant to article 12 of the Convention, all children should have an opportunity to be heard in any judicial or criminal proceedings affecting them, either directly or through a representative. In the case of indigenous children,

---

[104] CRC, general comment No. 1 on Children's Rights in Juvenile Justice, 2007, para. 6.
[105] Ibid. para. 23.
[106] Recommendations of Day of General Discussion on the Rights of Indigenous Children, 2003, para. 13.
[107] United Nations Guidelines for the Prevention of Juvenile Delinquency, "the Riyadh Guidelines", 1990.

States parties should adopt measures to ensure that an interpreter is provided free of charge if required and that the child is guaranteed legal assistance, in a culturally sensitive manner.

77. Professionals involved in law enforcement and the judiciary should receive appropriate training on the content and meaning of the provisions of the Convention and its Optional Protocols, including the need to adopt special protection measures for indigenous children and other specific groups.[108]

States parties' obligations and monitoring of the implementation of the Convention

78. The Committee reminds States parties that ratification of the Convention on the Rights of the Child obliges States parties to take action to ensure the realization of all rights in the Convention for all children within their jurisdiction. The duty to respect and protect requires each State party to ensure that the exercise of the rights of indigenous children is fully protected against any acts of the State party by its legislative, judicial or administrative authorities or by any other entity or person within the State party.

79. Article 3 of the Convention requires States parties to ensure that in all actions concerning children, the best interests of the child shall be a primary consideration. Article 4 of the Convention requires States parties to undertake measures to implement the Convention to the maximum extent of their available resources. Article 42 sets out that States parties are further required to ensure that children and adults are provided information on the principles and provisions of the Convention.

80. In order to effectively implement the rights of the Convention for indigenous children, States parties need to adopt appropriate legislation in accordance with the Convention. Adequate resources should be allocated and special measures adopted in a range of areas in order to effectively ensure that indigenous children enjoy their rights on an equal level with non-indigenous children. Further efforts should be taken to collect and disaggregate data and develop indicators to evaluate the degree of implementation of the rights of indigenous children. In order to develop policy and programming efforts in a culturally sensitive manner, States parties should consult with indigenous communities and directly with indigenous children. Professionals working with indigenous children should be trained on how consideration should be given to cultural aspects of children's rights.

81. The Committee calls for States parties to, when applicable, better integrate information in their periodic reports to the Committee on the implementation of indigenous children's rights and on the adoption of special measures in this regard. Furthermore, the Committee requests States parties to strengthen efforts to translate and disseminate information about the Convention and its Optional Protocols and the reporting process among indigenous communities and children, in order for them to actively participate in the monitoring process. Furthermore, indigenous communities are encouraged to utilize the Convention as an opportunity to assess the implementation of the rights of their children.

82. Finally, the Committee urges States parties to adopt a rights-based approach to indigenous children based on the Convention and other relevant international standards, such as ILO Convention No. 169 and the United Nations Declaration on the Rights of Indigenous Peoples. In order to guarantee effective monitoring of the implementation of the rights of indigenous children, States parties are urged to strengthen direct cooperation with indigenous communities and, if required, seek technical cooperation

---

[108] CRC, general comment No. 1 on Children's Rights in Juvenile Justice, 2007, para. 97.

from international agencies, including United Nations entities. Empowerment of indigenous children and the effective exercise of their rights to culture, religion and language provide an essential foundation of a culturally diverse State in harmony and compliance with its human rights obligations.

General Comment No 12 (2009)
The right of the child to be heard

The right of the child to be heard

Article 12 of the Convention on the Rights of the Child provides:

> "1. States Parties shall assure to the child who is capable of forming his or her own views the right to express those views freely in all matters affecting the child, the views of the child being given due weight in accordance with the age and maturity of the child.
>
> 2. For this purpose the child shall in particular be provided the opportunity to be heard in any judicial and administrative proceedings affecting the child, either directly, or through a representative or an appropriate body, in a manner consistent with the procedural rules of national law."

I. INTRODUCTION

1. Article 12 of the Convention on the Rights of the Child (the Convention) is a unique provision in a human rights treaty; it addresses the legal and social status of children, who, on the one hand lack the full autonomy of adults but, on the other, are subjects of rights. Paragraph 1 assures, to every child capable of forming his or her own views, the right to express those views freely in all matters affecting the child, the views of the child being given due weight in accordance with age and maturity. Paragraph 2 states, in particular, that the child shall be afforded the right to be heard in any judicial or administrative proceedings affecting him or her.

2. The right of all children to be heard and taken seriously constitutes one of the fundamental values of the Convention. The Committee on the Rights of the Child (the Committee) has identified article 12 as one of the four general principles of the Convention, the others being the right to non-discrimination, the right to life and development, and the primary consideration of the child's best interests, which highlights the fact that this article establishes not only a right in itself, but should also be considered in the interpretation and implementation of all other rights.

3. Since the adoption of the Convention in 1989, considerable progress has been achieved at the local, national, regional and global levels in the development of legislation, policies and methodologies to promote the implementation of article 12. A widespread practice has emerged in recent years, which has been broadly conceptualized as "participation", although this term itself does not appear in the text of article 12. This term has evolved and is now widely used to describe ongoing processes, which include information-sharing and dialogue between children and adults based on mutual respect, and in which children can learn how their views and those of adults are taken into account and shape the outcome of such processes.

4. States parties reaffirmed their commitment to the realization of article 12 at the twenty-seventh special session of the General Assembly on children in 2002.[109] However, the Committee notes that, in most societies around the world, implementation of the child's right to express her or his view on the wide range of issues that affect her or him, and to have those views duly taken into account, continues to be impeded by many long-standing practices and attitudes, as well as political and economic barriers. While difficulties are experienced by many children, the Committee particularly recognizes that certain groups of children, including younger boys and girls, as well as children belonging to marginalized and disadvantaged groups, face particular barriers in

---

[109]   Resolution S-27/2 "A world fit for children", adopted by the General Assembly in 2002.

the realization of this right. The Committee also remains concerned about the quality of many of the practices that do exist. There is a need for a better understanding of what article 12 entails and how to fully implement it for every child.

5. In 2006, the Committee held a day of general discussion on the right of the child to be heard in order to explore the meaning and significance of article 12, its linkages to other articles, and the gaps, good practices and priority issues that need to be addressed in order to further the enjoyment of this right.[110] The present general comment arises from the exchange of information which took place on that day, including with children, the accumulated experience of the Committee in reviewing States parties' reports, and the very significant expertise and experience of translating the right embodied in article 12 into practice by governments, non-governmental organizations (NGOs), community organizations, development agencies, and children themselves.

6. The present general comment will first present a legal analysis of the two paragraphs of article 12 and will then explain the requirements to fully realize this right, including in judicial and administrative proceedings in particular (sect. A). In section B, the connection of article 12 with the three other general principles of the Convention, as well as its relation to other articles, will be discussed. The requirements and the impact of the child's right to be heard in different situations and settings are outlined in section C. Section D sets out the basic requirements for the implementation of this right, and the conclusions are presented in section E.

7. The Committee recommends that States parties widely disseminate the present general comment within government and administrative structures as well as to children and civil society. This will necessitate translating it into the relevant languages, making child-friendly versions available, holding workshops and seminars to discuss its implications and how best to implement it, and incorporating it into the training of all professionals working for and with children.

II. OBJECTIVES

8. The overall objective of the general comment is to support States parties in the effective implementation of article 12. In so doing it seeks to:

- Strengthen understanding of the meaning of article 12 and its implications for governments, stakeholders, NGOs and society at large
- Elaborate the scope of legislation, policy and practice necessary to achieve full implementation of article 12
- Highlight the positive approaches in implementing article 12, benefitting from the monitoring experience of the Committee
- Propose basic requirements for appropriate ways to give due weight to children's views in all matters that affect them

III. THE RIGHT TO BE HEARD: A RIGHT OF THE INDIVIDUAL CHILD AND A RIGHT OF GROUPS OF CHILDREN

9. The general comment is structured according to the distinction made by the Committee between the right to be heard of an individual child and the right to be heard as applied to a group of children (e.g. a class of schoolchildren, the children in a neighbourhood, the children of a country, children with disabilities, or girls). This is a

---

[110] See the recommendations of the day of general discussion in 2006 on the right of the child to be heard, available at: http://www2.ohchr.org/english/bodies/crc/docs/discussion/Final_Recommendations_after_DGD.doc.

relevant distinction because the Convention stipulates that States parties must assure the right of the child to be heard according to the age and maturity of the child (see the following legal analysis of paragraphs 1 and 2 of article 12).

10. The conditions of age and maturity can be assessed when an individual child is heard and also when a group of children chooses to express its views. The task of assessing a child's age and maturity is facilitated when the group in question is a component of an enduring structure, such as a family, a class of schoolchildren or the residents of a particular neighbourhood, but is made more difficult when children express themselves collectively. Even when confronting difficulties in assessing age and maturity, States parties should consider children as a group to be heard, and the Committee strongly recommends that States parties exert all efforts to listen to or seek the views of those children speaking collectively.

11. States parties should encourage the child to form a free view and should provide an environment that enables the child to exercise her or his right to be heard.

12. The views expressed by children may add relevant perspectives and experience and should be considered in decision-making, policymaking and preparation of laws and/or measures as well as their evaluation.

13. These processes are usually called participation. The exercise of the child's or children's right to be heard is a crucial element of such processes. The concept of participation emphasizes that including children should not only be a momentary act, but the starting point for an intense exchange between children and adults on the development of policies, programmes and measures in all relevant contexts of children's lives.

14. In section A (Legal analysis) of the general comment, the Committee deals with the right to be heard of the individual child. In section C (The implementation of the right to be heard in different settings and situations), the Committee considers the right to be heard of both the individual child and children as a group.

A. Legal analysis

15. Article 12 of the Convention establishes the right of every child to freely express her or his views, in all matters affecting her or him, and the subsequent right for those views to be given due weight, according to the child's age and maturity. This right imposes a clear legal obligation on States parties to recognize this right and ensure its implementation by listening to the views of the child and according them due weight. This obligation requires that States parties, with respect to their particular judicial system, either directly guarantee this right, or adopt or revise laws so that this right can be fully enjoyed by the child.

16. The child, however, has the right not to exercise this right. Expressing views is a choice for the child, not an obligation. States parties have to ensure that the child receives all necessary information and advice to make a decision in favour of her or his best interests.

17. Article 12 as a general principle provides that States parties should strive to ensure that the interpretation and implementation of all other rights incorporated in the Convention are guided by it.[111]

---

[111] See the Committee's general comment No. 5 (2003) on general measures of implementation for the Convention on the Rights of the Child (CRC/GC/2003/5).

18. Article 12 manifests that the child holds rights which have an influence on her or his life, and not only rights derived from her or his vulnerability (protection) or dependency on adults (provision).[112] The Convention recognizes the child as a subject of rights, and the nearly universal ratification of this international instrument by States parties emphasizes this status of the child, which is clearly expressed in article 12.

1. Literal analysis of article 12

(a) Paragraph 1 of article 12

(i) "Shall assure"

19. Article 12, paragraph 1, provides that States parties "shall assure" the right of the child to freely express her or his views. "Shall assure" is a legal term of special strength, which leaves no leeway for State parties' discretion. Accordingly, States parties are under strict obligation to undertake appropriate measures to fully implement this right for all children. This obligation contains two elements in order to ensure that mechanisms are in place to solicit the views of the child in all matters affecting her or him and to give due weight to those views.

(ii) "Capable of forming his or her own views"

20. States parties shall assure the right to be heard to every child "capable of forming his or her own views". This phrase should not be seen as a limitation, but rather as an obligation for States parties to assess the capacity of the child to form an autonomous opinion to the greatest extent possible. This means that States parties cannot begin with the assumption that a child is incapable of expressing her or his own views. On the contrary, States parties should presume that a child has the capacity to form her or his own views and recognize that she or he has the right to express them; it is not up to the child to first prove her or his capacity.

21. The Committee emphasizes that article 12 imposes no age limit on the right of the child to express her or his views, and discourages States parties from introducing age limits either in law or in practice which would restrict the child's right to be heard in all matters affecting her or him. In this respect, the Committee underlines the following:

- First, in its recommendations following the day of general discussion on implementing child rights in early childhood in 2004, the Committee underlined that the concept of the child as rights holder is " . . . anchored in the child's daily life from the earliest stage".[113] Research shows that the child is able to form views from the youngest age, even when she or he may be unable to express them verbally.[114] Consequently, full implementation of article 12 requires recognition of, and respect for, non-verbal forms of communication including play, body language, facial expressions, and drawing and painting, through which very young children demonstrate understanding, choices and preferences.
- Second, it is not necessary that the child has comprehensive knowledge of all aspects of the matter affecting her or him, but that she or he has sufficient understanding to be capable of appropriately forming her or his own views on the matter.
- Third, States parties are also under the obligation to ensure the implementation of this right for children experiencing difficulties in making their views heard.

---

[112] The Convention is commonly referred to by the three "ps": provision, protection and participation.
[113] CRC/C/GC/7/Rev.1, para. 14.
[114] Cf. Lansdown G., "The evolving capacities of the child", Innocenti Research Centre, UNICEF/Save the Children, Florence (2005).

For instance, children with disabilities should be equipped with, and enabled to use, any mode of communication necessary to facilitate the expression of their views. Efforts must also be made to recognize the right to expression of views for minority, indigenous and migrant children and other children who do not speak the majority language.

- Lastly, States parties must be aware of the potential negative consequences of an inconsiderate practice of this right, particularly in cases involving very young children, or in instances where the child has been a victim of a criminal offence, sexual abuse, violence, or other forms of mistreatment. States parties must undertake all necessary measures to ensure that the right to be heard is exercised ensuring full protection of the child.

(iii) "The right to express those views freely"

22. The child has the right "to express those views freely". "Freely" means that the child can express her or his views without pressure and can choose whether or not she or he wants to exercise her or his right to be heard. "Freely" also means that the child must not be manipulated or subjected to undue influence or pressure. "Freely" is further intrinsically related to the child's "own" perspective: the child has the right to express her or his own views and not the views of others.

23. States parties must ensure conditions for expressing views that account for the child's individual and social situation and an environment in which the child feels respected and secure when freely expressing her or his opinions.

24. The Committee emphasizes that a child should not be interviewed more often than necessary, in particular when harmful events are explored. The "hearing" of a child is a difficult process that can have a traumatic impact on the child.

25. The realization of the right of the child to express her or his views requires that the child be informed about the matters, options and possible decisions to be taken and their consequences by those who are responsible for hearing the child, and by the child's parents or guardian. The child must also be informed about the conditions under which she or he will be asked to express her or his views. This right to information is essential, because it is the precondition of the child's clarified decisions.

(iv) "In all matters affecting the child"

26. States parties must assure that the child is able to express her or his views "in all matters affecting" her or him. This represents a second qualification of this right: the child must be heard if the matter under discussion affects the child. This basic condition has to be respected and understood broadly.

27. The Open-ended Working Group established by the Commission on Human Rights, which drafted the text of the Convention, rejected a proposal to define these matters by a list limiting the consideration of a child's or children's views. Instead, it was decided that the right of the child to be heard should refer to "all matters affecting the child". The Committee is concerned that children are often denied the right to be heard, even though it is obvious that the matter under consideration is affecting them and they are capable of expressing their own views with regard to this matter. While the Committee supports a broad definition of "matters", which also covers issues not explicitly mentioned in the Convention, it recognizes the clause "affecting the child", which was added in order to clarify that no general political mandate was intended. The practice, however, including the World Summit for Children, demonstrates that a wide interpretation of matters affecting the child and children helps to include children in the

social processes of their community and society. Thus, States parties should carefully listen to children's views wherever their perspective can enhance the quality of solutions.

(v) "Being given due weight in accordance with the age and maturity of the child"

28. The views of the child must be "given due weight in accordance with the age and maturity of the child". This clause refers to the capacity of the child, which has to be assessed in order to give due weight to her or his views, or to communicate to the child the way in which those views have influenced the outcome of the process. Article 12 stipulates that simply listening to the child is insufficient; the views of the child have to be seriously considered when the child is capable of forming her or his own views.

29. By requiring that due weight be given in accordance with age and maturity, article 12 makes it clear that age alone cannot determine the significance of a child's views. Children's levels of understanding are not uniformly linked to their biological age. Research has shown that information, experience, environment, social and cultural expectations, and levels of support all contribute to the development of a child's capacities to form a view. For this reason, the views of the child have to be assessed on a case-by-case examination.

30. Maturity refers to the ability to understand and assess the implications of a particular matter, and must therefore be considered when determining the individual capacity of a child. Maturity is difficult to define; in the context of article 12, it is the capacity of a child to express her or his views on issues in a reasonable and independent manner. The impact of the matter on the child must also be taken into consideration. The greater the impact of the outcome on the life of the child, the more relevant the appropriate assessment of the maturity of that child.

31. Consideration needs to be given to the notion of the evolving capacities of the child, and direction and guidance from parents (see para. 84 and sect. C below).

(b) Paragraph 2 of article 12

(i) The right "to be heard in any judicial and administrative proceedings affecting the child"

32. Article 12, paragraph 2, specifies that opportunities to be heard have to be provided in particular "in any judicial and administrative proceedings affecting the child". The Committee emphasizes that this provision applies to all relevant judicial proceedings affecting the child, without limitation, including, for example, separation of parents, custody, care and adoption, children in conflict with the law, child victims of physical or psychological violence, sexual abuse or other crimes, health care, social security, unaccompanied children, asylum-seeking and refugee children, and victims of armed conflict and other emergencies. Typical administrative proceedings include, for example, decisions about children's education, health, environment, living conditions, or protection. Both kinds of proceedings may involve alternative dispute mechanisms such as mediation and arbitration.

33. The right to be heard applies both to proceedings which are initiated by the child, such as complaints against ill-treatment and appeals against school exclusion, as well as to those initiated by others which affect the child, such as parental separation or adoption. States parties are encouraged to introduce legislative measures requiring decision makers in judicial or administrative proceedings to explain the extent of the consideration given to the views of the child and the consequences for the child.

34. A child cannot be heard effectively where the environment is intimidating, hostile, insensitive or inappropriate for her or his age. Proceedings must be both accessible and

child-appropriate. Particular attention needs to be paid to the provision and delivery of child-friendly information, adequate support for self-advocacy, appropriately trained staff, design of court rooms, clothing of judges and lawyers, sight screens, and separate waiting rooms.

(ii) "Either directly, or through a representative or an appropriate body"

35. After the child has decided to be heard, he or she will have to decide how to be heard: "either directly, or through a representative or appropriate body". The Committee recommends that, wherever possible, the child must be given the opportunity to be directly heard in any proceedings.

36. The representative can be the parent(s), a lawyer, or another person (inter alia, a social worker). However, it must be stressed that in many cases (civil, penal or administrative), there are risks of a conflict of interest between the child and their most obvious representative (parent(s)). If the hearing of the child is undertaken through a representative, it is of utmost importance that the child's views are transmitted correctly to the decision maker by the representative. The method chosen should be determined by the child (or by the appropriate authority as necessary) according to her or his particular situation. Representatives must have sufficient knowledge and understanding of the various aspects of the decision-making process and experience in working with children.

37. The representative must be aware that she or he represents exclusively the interests of the child and not the interests of other persons (parent(s)), institutions or bodies (e.g. residential home, administration or society). Codes of conduct should be developed for representatives who are appointed to represent the child's views.

(iii) "In a manner consistent with the procedural rules of national law"

38. The opportunity for representation must be "in a manner consistent with the procedural rules of national law". This clause should not be interpreted as permitting the use of procedural legislation which restricts or prevents enjoyment of this fundamental right. On the contrary, States parties are encouraged to comply with the basic rules of fair proceedings, such as the right to a defence and the right to access one's own files.

39. When rules of procedure are not adhered to, the decision of the court or the administrative authority can be challenged and may be overturned, substituted, or referred back for further juridical consideration.

2. Steps for the implementation of the child's right to be heard

40. Implementation of the two paragraphs of article 12 requires five steps to be taken in order to effectively realize the right of the child to be heard whenever a matter affects a child or when the child is invited to give her or his views in a formal proceeding as well as in other settings. These requirements have to be applied in a way which is appropriate for the given context.

(a) Preparation

41. Those responsible for hearing the child have to ensure that the child is informed about her or his right to express her or his opinion in all matters affecting the child and, in particular, in any judicial and administrative decision-making processes, and about the impact that his or her expressed views will have on the outcome. The child must, furthermore, receive information about the option of either communicating directly or through a representative. She or he must be aware of the possible consequences of this choice. The decision maker must adequately prepare the child before the hearing,

providing explanations as to how, when and where the hearing will take place and who the participants will be, and has to take account of the views of the child in this regard.

(b) The hearing

42. The context in which a child exercises her or his right to be heard has to be enabling and encouraging, so that the child can be sure that the adult who is responsible for the hearing is willing to listen and seriously consider what the child has decided to communicate. The person who will hear the views of the child can be an adult involved in the matters affecting the child (e.g. a teacher, social worker or caregiver), a decision maker in an institution (e.g. a director, administrator or judge), or a specialist (e.g. a psychologist or physician).

43. Experience indicates that the situation should have the format of a talk rather than a one-sided examination. Preferably, a child should not be heard in open court, but under conditions of confidentiality.

(c) Assessment of the capacity of the child

44. The child's views must be given due weight, when a case-by-case analysis indicates that the child is capable of forming her or his own views. If the child is capable of forming her or his own views in a reasonable and independent manner, the decision maker must consider the views of the child as a significant factor in the settlement of the issue. Good practice for assessing the capacity of the child has to be developed.

(d) Information about the weight given to the views of the child (feedback)

45. Since the child enjoys the right that her or his views are given due weight, the decision maker has to inform the child of the outcome of the process and explain how her or his views were considered. The feedback is a guarantee that the views of the child are not only heard as a formality, but are taken seriously. The information may prompt the child to insist, agree or make another proposal or, in the case of a judicial or administrative procedure, file an appeal or a complaint.

(e) Complaints, remedies and redress

46. Legislation is needed to provide children with complaint procedures and remedies when their right to be heard and for their views to be given due weight is disregarded and violated.[115] Children should have the possibility of addressing an ombudsman or a person of a comparable role in all children's institutions, inter alia, in schools and day-care centres, in order to voice their complaints. Children should know who these persons are and how to access them. In the case of family conflicts about consideration of children's views, a child should be able to turn to a person in the youth services of the community.

47. If the right of the child to be heard is breached with regard to judicial and administrative proceedings (art. 12, para. 2), the child must have access to appeals and complaints procedures which provide remedies for rights violations. Complaints procedures must provide reliable mechanisms to ensure that children are confident that using them will not expose them to risk of violence or punishment.

---

[115] See the Committee's general comment No. 5 (2003) on general measures of implementation of the Convention on the Rights of the Child, para. 24.

3. Obligations of States parties

(a) Core obligations of States parties

48. The child's right to be heard imposes the obligation on States parties to review or amend their legislation in order to introduce mechanisms providing children with access to appropriate information, adequate support, if necessary, feedback on the weight given to their views, and procedures for complaints, remedies or redress.

49. In order to fulfil these obligations, States parties should adopt the following strategies:

- Review and withdraw restrictive declarations and reservations to article 12
- Establish independent human rights institutions, such as children's ombudsmen or commissioners with a broad children's rights mandate[116]
- Provide training on article 12, and its application in practice, for all professionals working with, and for, children, including lawyers, judges, police, social workers, community workers, psychologists, caregivers, residential and prison officers, teachers at all levels of the educational system, medical doctors, nurses and other health professionals, civil servants and public officials, asylum officers and traditional leaders
- Ensure appropriate conditions for supporting and encouraging children to express their views, and make sure that these views are given due weight, by regulations and arrangements which are firmly anchored in laws and institutional codes and are regularly evaluated with regard to their effectiveness
- Combat negative attitudes, which impede the full realization of the child's right to be heard, through public campaigns, including opinion leaders and the media, to change widespread customary conceptions of the child

(b) Specific obligations with regard to judicial and administrative proceedings

(i) The child's right to be heard in civil judicial proceedings

50. The main issues which require that the child be heard are detailed below:

Divorce and separation

51. In cases of separation and divorce, the children of the relationship are unequivocally affected by decisions of the courts. Issues of maintenance for the child as well as custody and access are determined by the judge either at trial or through court-directed mediation. Many jurisdictions have included in their laws, with respect to the dissolution of a relationship, a provision that the judge must give paramount consideration to the "best interests of the child".

52. For this reason, all legislation on separation and divorce has to include the right of the child to be heard by decision makers and in mediation processes. Some jurisdictions, either as a matter of policy or legislation, prefer to state an age at which the child is regarded as capable of expressing her or his own views. The Convention, however, anticipates that this matter be determined on a case-by-case basis, since it refers to age and maturity, and for this reason requires an individual assessment of the capacity of the child.

Separation from parents and alternative care

53. Whenever a decision is made to remove a child from her or his family because the child is a victim of abuse or neglect within his or her home, the view of the child must be

---

[116] See the Committee's general comment No. 2 (2002) on the role of independent human rights institutions.

taken into account in order to determine the best interests of the child. The intervention may be initiated by a complaint from a child, another family member or a member of the community alleging abuse or neglect in the family.

54. The Committee's experience is that the child's right to be heard is not always taken into account by States parties. The Committee recommends that States parties ensure, through legislation, regulation and policy directives, that the child's views are solicited and considered, including decisions regarding placement in foster care or homes, development of care plans and their review, and visits with parents and family.

Adoption and kafalah of Islamic law

55. When a child is to be placed for adoption or *kafalah* of Islamic law and finally will be adopted or placed in *kafalah*, it is vitally important that the child is heard. Such a process is also necessary when step-parents or foster families adopt a child, although the child and the adopting parents may have already been living together for some time.

56. Article 21 of the Convention states that the best interests of the child shall be the paramount consideration. In decisions on adoption, *kafalah* or other placement, the "best interests" of the child cannot be defined without consideration of the child's views. The Committee urges all States parties to inform the child, if possible, about the effects of adoption, *kafalah* or other placement, and to ensure by legislation that the views of the child are heard.

(ii) The child's right to be heard in penal judicial proceedings

57. In penal proceedings, the right of child to express her or his views freely in all matters affecting the child has to be fully respected and implemented throughout every stage of the process of juvenile justice.[117]

The child offender

58. Article 12, paragraph 2, of the Convention requires that a child alleged to have, accused of, or recognized as having, infringed the penal law, has the right to be heard. This right has to be fully observed during all stages of the judicial process, from the pre-trial stage when the child has the right to remain silent, to the right to be heard by the police, the prosecutor and the investigating judge. It also applies through the stages of adjudication and disposition, as well as implementation of the imposed measures.

59. In case of diversion, including mediation, a child must have the opportunity to give free and voluntary consent and must be given the opportunity to obtain legal and other advice and assistance in determining the appropriateness and desirability of the diversion proposed.

60. In order to effectively participate in the proceedings, every child must be informed promptly and directly about the charges against her or him in a language she or he understands, and also about the juvenile justice process and possible measures taken by the court. The proceedings should be conducted in an atmosphere enabling the child to participate and to express her/himself freely.

61. The court and other hearings of a child in conflict with the law should be conducted behind closed doors. Exceptions to this rule should be very limited, clearly outlined in national legislation and guided by the best interests of the child.

---

[117] See the Committee's general comment No. 10 (2007) on children's rights in juvenile justice (CRC/C/GC/10).

The child victim and child witness

62. The child victim and child witness of a crime must be given an opportunity to fully exercise her or his right to freely express her or his view in accordance with United Nations Economic and Social Council resolution 2005/20, "Guidelines on Justice in Matters involving Child Victims and Witnesses of Crime".[118]

63. In particular, this means that every effort has to be made to ensure that a child victim or/and witness is consulted on the relevant matters with regard to involvement in the case under scrutiny, and enabled to express freely, and in her or his own manner, views and concerns regarding her or his involvement in the judicial process.

64. The right of the child victim and witness is also linked to the right to be informed about issues such as availability of health, psychological and social services, the role of a child victim and/or witness, the ways in which "questioning" is conducted, existing support mechanisms in place for the child when submitting a complaint and participating in investigations and court proceedings, the specific places and times of hearings, the availability of protective measures, the possibilities of receiving reparation, and the provisions for appeal.

(iii) The child's right to be heard in administrative proceedings

65. All States parties should develop administrative procedures in legislation which reflect the requirements of article 12 and ensure the child's right to be heard along with other procedural rights, including the rights to disclosure of pertinent records, notice of hearing, and representation by parents or others.

66. Children are more likely to be involved with administrative proceedings than court proceedings, because administrative proceedings are less formal, more flexible and relatively easy to establish through law and regulation. The proceedings have to be child-friendly and accessible.

67. Specific examples of administrative proceedings relevant for children include mechanisms to address discipline issues in schools (e.g. suspensions and expulsions), refusals to grant school certificates and performance-related issues, disciplinary measures and refusals to grant privileges in juvenile detention centres, asylum requests from unaccompanied children, and applications for driver's licences. In these matters a child should have the right to be heard and enjoy the other rights "consistent with the procedural rules of national law".

B. The right to be heard and the links with other provisions of the Convention

68. Article 12, as a general principle, is linked to the other general principles of the Convention, such as article 2 (the right to non-discrimination), article 6 (the right to life, survival and development) and, in particular, is interdependent with article 3 (primary consideration of the best interests of the child). The article is also closely linked with the articles related to civil rights and freedoms, particularly article 13 (the right to freedom of expression) and article 17 (the right to information). Furthermore, article 12 is connected to all other articles of the Convention, which cannot be fully implemented if the child is not respected as a subject with her or his own views on the rights enshrined in the respective articles and their implementation.

69. The connection of article 12 to article 5 (evolving capacities of the child and appropriate direction and guidance from parents, see para. 84 of the present general

---

[118]   United Nations Economic and Social Council resolution 2005/20, in particular arts. 8, 19 and 20. Available at: www.un.org/ecosoc/docs/2005/Resolution%202005-20.pdf.

comment) is of special relevance, since it is crucial that the guidance given by parents takes account of the evolving capacities of the child.

1. Articles 12 and 3

70. The purpose of article 3 is to ensure that in all actions undertaken concerning children, by a public or private welfare institution, courts, administrative authorities or legislative bodies, the best interests of the child are a primary consideration. It means that every action taken on behalf of the child has to respect the best interests of the child. The best interests of the child is similar to a procedural right that obliges States parties to introduce steps into the action process to ensure that the best interests of the child are taken into consideration. The Convention obliges States parties to assure that those responsible for these actions hear the child as stipulated in article 12. This step is mandatory.

71. The best interests of the child, established in consultation with the child, is not the only factor to be considered in the actions of institutions, authorities and administration. It is, however, of crucial importance, as are the views of the child.

72. Article 3 is devoted to individual cases, but, explicitly, also requires that the best interests of children as a group are considered in all actions concerning children. States parties are consequently under an obligation to consider not only the individual situation of each child when identifying their best interests, but also the interests of children as a group. Moreover, States parties must examine the actions of private and public institutions, authorities, as well as legislative bodies. The extension of the obligation to "legislative bodies" clearly indicates that every law, regulation or rule that affects children must be guided by the "best interests" criterion.

73. There is no doubt that the best interests of children as a defined group have to be established in the same way as when weighing individual interests. If the best interests of large numbers of children are at stake, heads of institutions, authorities, or governmental bodies should also provide opportunities to hear the concerned children from such undefined groups and to give their views due weight when they plan actions, including legislative decisions, which directly or indirectly affect children.

74. There is no tension between articles 3 and 12, only a complementary role of the two general principles: one establishes the objective of achieving the best interests of the child and the other provides the methodology for reaching the goal of hearing either the child or the children. In fact, there can be no correct application of article 3 if the components of article 12 are not respected. Likewise, article 3 reinforces the functionality of article 12, facilitating the essential role of children in all decisions affecting their lives.

2. Articles 12, 2 and 6

75. The right to non-discrimination is an inherent right guaranteed by all human rights instruments including the Convention on the Rights of the Child. According to article 2 of the Convention, every child has the right not to be discriminated against in the exercise of his or her rights including those provided under article 12. The Committee stresses that States parties shall take adequate measures to assure to every child the right to freely express his or her views and to have those views duly taken into account without discrimination on grounds of race, colour, sex, language, religion, political or other opinion, national, ethnic or social origin, property, disability, birth or other status. States parties shall address discrimination, including against vulnerable or marginalized groups of children, to ensure that children are assured their right to be heard and are enabled to participate in all matters affecting them on an equal basis with all other children.

76. In particular, the Committee notes with concern that, in some societies, customary attitudes and practices undermine and place severe limitations on the enjoyment of this right. States parties shall take adequate measures to raise awareness and educate the society about the negative impact of such attitudes and practices and to encourage attitudinal changes in order to achieve full implementation of the rights of every child under the Convention.

77. The Committee urges States parties to pay special attention to the right of the girl child to be heard, to receive support, if needed, to voice her view and her view be given due weight, as gender stereotypes and patriarchal values undermine and place severe limitations on girls in the enjoyment of the right set forth in article 12.

78. The Committee welcomes the obligation of States parties in article 7 of the Convention on the Rights of Persons with Disabilities to ensure that children with disabilities are provided with the necessary assistance and equipment to enable them to freely express their views and for those views to be given due weight.

79. Article 6 of the Convention on the Rights of the Child acknowledges that every child has an inherent right to life and that States parties shall ensure, to the maximum extent possible, the survival and development of the child. The Committee notes the importance of promoting opportunities for the child's right to be heard, as child participation is a tool to stimulate the full development of the personality and the evolving capacities of the child consistent with article 6 and with the aims of education embodied in article 29.

3. Articles 12, 13 and 17

80. Article 13, on the right to freedom of expression, and article 17, on access to information, are crucial prerequisites for the effective exercise of the right to be heard. These articles establish that children are subjects of rights and, together with article 12, they assert that the child is entitled to exercise those rights on his or her own behalf, in accordance with her or his evolving capacities.

81. The right to freedom of expression embodied in article 13 is often confused with article 12. However, while both articles are strongly linked, they do elaborate different rights. Freedom of expression relates to the right to hold and express opinions, and to seek and receive information through any media. It asserts the right of the child not to be restricted by the State party in the opinions she or he holds or expresses. As such, the obligation it imposes on States parties is to refrain from interference in the expression of those views, or in access to information, while protecting the right of access to means of communication and public dialogue. Article 12, however, relates to the right of expression of views specifically about matters which affect the child, and the right to be involved in actions and decisions that impact on her or his life. Article 12 imposes an obligation on States parties to introduce the legal framework and mechanisms necessary to facilitate active involvement of the child in all actions affecting the child and in decision-making, and to fulfil the obligation to give due weight to those views once expressed. Freedom of expression in article 13 requires no such engagement or response from States parties. However, creating an environment of respect for children to express their views, consistent with article 12, also contributes towards building children's capacities to exercise their right to freedom of expression.

82. Fulfilment of the child's right to information, consistent with article 17 is, to a large degree, a prerequisite for the effective realization of the right to express views. Children need access to information in formats appropriate to their age and capacities on all issues of concern to them. This applies to information, for example, relating to their rights, any proceedings affecting them, national legislation, regulations and policies,

local services, and appeals and complaints procedures. Consistent with articles 17 and 42, States parties should include children's rights in the school curricula.

83. The Committee also reminds States parties that the media are an important means both of promoting awareness of the right of children to express their views, and of providing opportunities for the public expression of such views. It urges various forms of the media to dedicate further resources to the inclusion of children in the development of programmes and the creation of opportunities for children to develop and lead media initiatives on their rights.[119]

4. Articles 12 and 5

84. Article 5 of the Convention states that States parties shall respect the responsibilities, rights and duties of parents, legal guardians, or members of the extended family or community as provided for by local custom, to give direction and guidance to the child in her or his exercise of the rights recognized in the Convention. Consequently, the child has a right to direction and guidance, which have to compensate for the lack of knowledge, experience and understanding of the child and are restricted by his or her evolving capacities, as stated in this article. The more the child himself or herself knows, has experienced and understands, the more the parent, legal guardian or other persons legally responsible for the child have to transform direction and guidance into reminders and advice and later to an exchange on an equal footing. This transformation will not take place at a fixed point in a child's development, but will steadily increase as the child is encouraged to contribute her or his views.

85. This requirement is stimulated by article 12 of the Convention, which stipulates that the child's views must be given due weight, whenever the child is capable of forming her or his own views. In other words, as children acquire capacities, so they are entitled to an increasing level of responsibility for the regulation of matters affecting them.[120]

5. Article 12 and the implementation of child rights in general

86. In addition to the articles discussed in the preceding paragraphs, most other articles of the Convention require and promote children's involvement in matters affecting them. For these manifold involvements, the concept of participation is ubiquitously used. Unquestionably, the lynchpin of these involvements is article 12, but the requirement of planning, working and developing in consultation with children is present throughout the Convention.

87. The practice of implementation deals with a broad range problems, such as health, the economy, education or the environment, which are of interest not only to the child as an individual, but to groups of children and children in general. Consequently, the Committee has always interpreted participation broadly in order to establish procedures not only for individual children and clearly defined groups of children, but also for groups of children, such as indigenous children, children with disabilities, or children in general, who are affected directly or indirectly by social, economic or cultural conditions of living in their society.

88. This broad understanding of children's participation is reflected in the outcome document adopted by the twenty-seventh special session of the General Assembly entitled "A world fit for children". States parties have promised "to develop and implement programmes to promote meaningful participation by children, including

---

[119] Day of general discussion on the child and the media (1996): www.unhchr.ch/html/menu2/6/ crc/doc/days/media.pdf.

[120] General comment No. 5 (2003) on general measures of implementation for the Convention on the Rights of the Child.

adolescents, in decision-making processes, including in families and schools and at the local and national levels" (para. 32, subpara. 1). The Committee has stated in its general comment No. 5 on general measures of implementation for the Convention on the Rights of the Child: "It is important that Governments develop a direct relationship with children, not simply one mediated through non-governmental organizations (NGOs) or human rights institutions."[121]

C. The implementation of the right to be heard in different settings and situations

89. The right of the child to be heard has to be implemented in the diverse settings and situations in which children grow up, develop and learn. In these settings and situations, different concepts of the child and her or his role exist, which may invite or restrict children's involvement in everyday matters and crucial decisions. Various ways of influencing the implementation of the child's right to be heard are available, which States parties may use to foster children's participation.

1. In the family

90. A family where children can freely express views and be taken seriously from the earliest ages provides an important model, and is a preparation for the child to exercise the right to be heard in the wider society.[14] Such an approach to parenting serves to promote individual development, enhance family relations and support children's socialization and plays a preventive role against all forms of violence in the home and family.

91. The Convention recognizes the rights and responsibilities of parents, or other legal guardians, to provide appropriate direction and guidance to their children (see para. 84 above), but underlines that this is to enable the child to exercise his or her rights and requires that direction and guidance are undertaken in a manner consistent with the evolving capacities of the child.

92. States parties should encourage, through legislation and policy, parents, guardians and childminders to listen to children and give due weight to their views in matters that concern them. Parents should also be advised to support children in realizing the right to express their views freely and to have children's views duly taken into account at all levels of society.

93. In order to support the development of parenting styles respecting the child's right to be heard, the Committee recommends that States parties promote parent education programmes, which build on existing positive behaviours and attitudes and disseminate information on the rights of children and parents enshrined in the Convention.

94. Such programmes need to address:

- The relationship of mutual respect between parents and children
- The involvement of children in decision-making
- The implication of giving due weight to the views of every family member
- The understanding, promotion and respect for children's evolving capacities
- Ways of dealing with conflicting views within the family

95. These programmes have to reinforce the principle that girls and boys have equal rights to express their views.

96. The media should play a strong role in communicating to parents that their children's participation is of high value for the children themselves, their families and society.

---

[121] Ibid., para. 12.

2. In alternative care

97. Mechanisms must be introduced to ensure that children in all forms of alternative care, including in institutions, are able to express their views and that those views be given due weight in matters of their placement, the regulations of care in foster families or homes and their daily lives. These should include:

- Legislation providing the child with the right to information about any placement, care and/or treatment plan and meaningful opportunities to express her or his views and for those views to be given due weight throughout the decision-making process.
- Legislation ensuring the right of the child to be heard, and that her or his views be given due weight in the development and establishment of child-friendly care services.
- Establishment of a competent monitoring institution, such as a children's ombudsperson, commissioner or inspectorate, to monitor compliance with the rules and regulations governing the provision of care, protection or treatment of children in accordance with the obligations under article 3. The monitoring body should be mandated to have unimpeded access to residential facilities (including those for children in conflict with the law), to hear the views and concerns of the child directly, and to monitor the extent to which his or her views are listened to and given due weight by the institution itself.
- Establishment of effective mechanisms, for example, a representative council of the children, both girls and boys, in the residential care facility, with the mandate to participate in the development and implementation of the policy and any rules of the institution.

3. In health care

98. The realization of the provisions of the Convention requires respect for the child's right to express his or her views and to participate in promoting the healthy development and well-being of children. This applies to individual health-care decisions, as well as to children's involvement in the development of health policy and services.

99. The Committee identifies several distinct but linked issues that need consideration in respect of the child's involvement in practices and decisions relating to her or his own health care.

100. Children, including young children, should be included in decision-making processes, in a manner consistent with their evolving capacities. They should be provided with information about proposed treatments and their effects and outcomes, including in formats appropriate and accessible to children with disabilities.

101. States parties need to introduce legislation or regulations to ensure that children have access to confidential medical counselling and advice without parental consent, irrespective of the child's age, where this is needed for the child's safety or well-being. Children may need such access, for example, where they are experiencing violence or abuse at home, or in need of reproductive health education or services, or in case of conflicts between parents and the child over access to health services. The right to counselling and advice is distinct from the right to give medical consent and should not be subject to any age limit.

102. The Committee welcomes the introduction in some countries of a fixed age at which the right to consent transfers to the child, and encourages States parties to give consideration to the introduction of such legislation. Thus, children above that age have an entitlement to give consent without the requirement for any individual professional

assessment of capacity after consultation with an independent and competent expert. However, the Committee strongly recommends that States parties ensure that, where a younger child can demonstrate capacity to express an informed view on her or his treatment, this view is given due weight.

103. Physicians and health-care facilities should provide clear and accessible information to children on their rights concerning their participation in paediatric research and clinical trials. They have to be informed about the research, so that their informed consent can be obtained in addition to other procedural safeguards.

104. States parties should also introduce measures enabling children to contribute their views and experiences to the planning and programming of services for their health and development. Their views should be sought on all aspects of health provision, including what services are needed, how and where they are best provided, discriminatory barriers to accessing services, quality and attitudes of health professionals, and how to promote children's capacities to take increasing levels of responsibility for their own health and development. This information can be obtained through, inter alia, feedback systems for children using services or involved in research and consultative processes, and can be transmitted to local or national children's councils or parliaments to develop standards and indicators of health services that respect the rights of the child.[122]

4. In education and school

105. Respect for right of the child to be heard within education is fundamental to the realization of the right to education. The Committee notes with concern continuing authoritarianism, discrimination, disrespect and violence which characterize the reality of many schools and classrooms. Such environments are not conducive to the expression of children's views and the due weight to be given these views.

106. The Committee recommends that States parties take action to build opportunities for children to express their views and for those views to be given due weight with regard to the following issues.

107. In all educational environments, including educational programmes in the early years, the active role of children in a participatory learning environment should be promoted.[123] Teaching and learning must take into account life conditions and prospects of the children. For this reason, education authorities have to include children's and their parents' views in the planning of curricula and school programmes.

108. Human rights education can shape the motivations and behaviours of children only when human rights are practised in the institutions in which the child learns, plays and lives together with other children and adults.[124] In particular, the child's right to be heard is under critical scrutiny by children in these institutions, where children can observe, whether in fact due weight is given to their views as declared in the Convention.

109. Children's participation is indispensable for the creation of a social climate in the classroom, which stimulates cooperation and mutual support needed for child-centred interactive learning. Giving children's views weight is particularly important in the elimination of discrimination, prevention of bullying and disciplinary measures. The Committee welcomes the expansion of peer education and peer counselling.

---

[122] The Committee also draws attention to its general comment No. 3 (2003) on HIV/Aids and the rights of the child, paras. 11 and 12, and its general comment No. 4 (2003) on adolescent health, para. 6.

[123] "A human rights-based approach to Education for All: A framework for the realization of children's right to education and rights within education", UNICEF/UNESCO (2007).

[124] Committee on the Rights of the Child, general comment No. 1 (2001) on the aims of education (art. 29, para. 1 of the Convention), (CRC/GC/2001/1).

110. Steady participation of children in decision-making processes should be achieved through, inter alia, class councils, student councils and student representation on school boards and committees, where they can freely express their views on the development and implementation of school policies and codes of behaviour. These rights need to be enshrined in legislation, rather than relying on the goodwill of authorities, schools and head teachers to implement them.

111. Beyond the school, States parties should consult children at the local and national levels on all aspects of education policy, including, inter alia, the strengthening of the child-friendly character of the educational system, informal and non-formal facilities of learning, which give children a "second chance", school curricula, teaching methods, school structures, standards, budgeting and child-protection systems.

112. The Committee encourages States parties to support the development of independent student organizations, which can assist children in competently performing their participatory roles in the education system.

113. In decisions about the transition to the next level of schools or choice of tracks or streams, the right of the child to be heard has to be assured as these decisions deeply affect the child's best interests. Such decisions must be subject to administrative or judicial review. Additionally, in disciplinary matters, the right of the child to be heard has to be fully respected.[125] In particular, in the case of exclusion of a child from instruction or school, this decision must be subject to judicial review as it contradicts the child's right to education.

114. The Committee welcomes the introduction of child-friendly school programmes in many countries, which seek to provide interactive, caring, protective and participatory environments that prepare children and adolescents for active roles in society and responsible citizenship within their communities.

5. In play, recreation, sports and cultural activities

115. Children require play, recreation, physical and cultural activities for their development and socialization. These should be designed taking into account children's preferences and capacities. Children who are able to express their views should be consulted regarding the accessibility and appropriateness of play and recreation facilities. Very young children and some children with disabilities, who are unable to participate in formal consultative processes, should be provided with particular opportunities to express their wishes.

6. In the workplace

116. Children working at younger ages than permitted by laws and International Labour Organization Conventions Nos. 138 (1973) and 182 (1999) have to be heard in child-sensitive settings in order to understand their views of the situation and their best interests. They should be included in the search for a solution, which respects the economic and socio-structural constraints as well as the cultural context under which these children work. Children should also be heard when policies are developed to eliminate the root causes of child labour, in particular regarding education.

117. Working children have a right to be protected by law against exploitation and should be heard when worksites and conditions of work are examined by inspectors investigating the implementation of labour laws. Children and, if existing,

---

[125] States parties should refer to the Committee's general comment No. 8 (2006) on the right of the child to protection from corporal punishment and other cruel or degrading forms of punishment, which explains participatory strategies to eliminate corporal punishment (CRC/C/GC/8).

representatives of working children's associations should also be heard when labour laws are drafted or when the enforcement of laws is considered and evaluated.

7. In situations of violence

118. The Convention establishes the right of the child to be protected from all forms of violence and the responsibility of States parties to ensure this right for every child without any discrimination. The Committee encourages States parties to consult with children in the development and implementation of legislative, policy, educational and other measures to address all forms of violence. Particular attention needs to be paid to ensuring that marginalized and disadvantaged children, such as exploited children, street children or refugee children, are not excluded from consultative processes designed to elicit views on relevant legislation and policy processes.

119. In this regard, the Committee welcomes the findings of the Secretary-General's Study on Violence against Children, and urges States Parties to implement fully its recommendations, including the recommendation to provide the space for children to freely express their views and give these views due weight in all aspects of prevention, reporting and monitoring violence against them.[126]

120. Much of the violence perpetrated against children goes unchallenged both because certain forms of abusive behaviour are understood by children as accepted practices, and due to the lack of child-friendly reporting mechanisms. For example, they have no one to whom they can report in confidence and safety about experienced maltreatment, such as corporal punishment, genital mutilation or early marriage, and no channel to communicate their general observations to those accountable for implementation of their rights. Thus, effective inclusion of children in protective measures requires that children be informed about their right to be heard and to grow up free from all forms of physical and psychological violence. States parties should oblige all children's institutions to establish easy access to individuals or organizations to which they can report in confidence and safety, including through telephone helplines, and to provide places where children can contribute their experience and views on combating violence against children.

121. The Committee also draws the attention of States parties to the recommendation in the Secretary-General's Study on Violence against Children to support and encourage children's organizations and child-led initiatives to address violence and to include these organizations in the elaboration, establishment and evaluation of anti-violence programmes and measures, so that children can play a key role in their own protection.

8. In the development of prevention strategies

122. The Committee notes that the voices of children have increasingly become a powerful force in the prevention of child rights violations. Good practice examples are available, inter alia, in the fields of violence prevention in schools, combating child exploitation through hazardous and extensive labour, providing health services and education to street children, and in the juvenile justice system. Children should be consulted in the formulation of legislation and policy related to these and other problem areas and involved in the drafting, development and implementation of related plans and programmes.

9. In immigration and asylum proceedings

123. Children who come to a country following their parents in search of work or as refugees are in a particularly vulnerable situation. For this reason it is urgent to fully

---

[126] Report of the independent expert for the United Nations Study on Violence against Children (A/61/299).

implement their right to express their views on all aspects of the immigration and asylum proceedings. In the case of migration, the child has to be heard on his or her educational expectations and health conditions in order to integrate him or her into school and health services. In the case of an asylum claim, the child must additionally have the opportunity to present her or his reasons leading to the asylum claim.

124. The Committee emphasizes that these children have to be provided with all relevant information, in their own language, on their entitlements, the services available, including means of communication, and the immigration and asylum process, in order to make their voice heard and to be given due weight in the proceedings. A guardian or adviser should be appointed, free of charge. Asylum-seeking children may also need effective family tracing and relevant information about the situation in their country of origin to determine their best interests. Particular assistance may be needed for children formerly involved in armed conflict to allow them to pronounce their needs. Furthermore, attention is needed to ensure that stateless children are included in decision-making processes within the territories where they reside.[127]

10. In emergency situations

125. The Committee underlines that the right embodied in article 12 does not cease in situations of crisis or in their aftermath. There is a growing body of evidence of the significant contribution that children are able to make in conflict situations, post-conflict resolution and reconstruction processes following emergencies.[128] Thus, the Committee emphasized in its recommendation after the day of general discussion in 2008 that children affected by emergencies should be encouraged and enabled to participate in analysing their situation and future prospects. Children's participation helps them to regain control over their lives, contributes to rehabilitation, develops organizational skills and strengthens a sense of identity. However, care needs to be taken to protect children from exposure to situations that are likely to be traumatic or harmful.

126. Accordingly, the Committee encourages States parties to support mechanisms which enable children, in particular adolescents, to play an active role in both post-emergency reconstruction and post-conflict resolution processes. Their views should be elicited in the assessment, design, implementation, monitoring and evaluation of programmes. For example, children in refugee camps can be encouraged to contribute to their own safety and well-being through the establishment of children's forums. Support needs to be given to enable children to establish such forums, while ensuring that their operation is consistent with children's best interests and their right to protection from harmful experiences.

11. In national and international settings

127. Much of the opportunity for children's participation takes place at the community level. The Committee welcomes the growing number of local youth parliaments, municipal children's councils and ad hoc consultations where children can voice their views in decision-making processes. However, these structures for formal representative participation in local government should be just one of many approaches to the implementation of article 12 at the local level, as they only allow for a relatively small number of children to engage in their local communities. Consulting hours of politicians and officials, open house and visits in schools and kindergartens create additional opportunities for communication.

---

[127] Cf. the Committee's general comment No. 6 (2005) on the treatment of unaccompanied and separated children outside their country of origin (CRC/GC/2005/6).

[128] "The participation of children and young people in emergencies: a guide for relief agencies", UNICEF, Bangkok (2007).

128. Children should be supported and encouraged to form their own child-led organizations and initiatives, which will create space for meaningful participation and representation. In addition, children can contribute their perspectives, for example, on the design of schools, playgrounds, parks, leisure and cultural facilities, public libraries, health facilities and local transport systems in order to ensure more appropriate services. In community development plans that call for public consultation, children's views should be explicitly included.

129. Such participation opportunities are, meanwhile, established in many countries also on the district, regional, federal state and national levels, where youth parliaments, councils and conferences provide forums for children to present their views and make them known to relevant audiences. NGOs and civil society organizations have developed practices to support children, which safeguard the transparency of representation and counter the risks of manipulation or tokenism.

130. The Committee welcomes the significant contributions by UNICEF and NGOs in promoting awareness-raising on children's right to be heard and their participation in all domains of their lives, and encourages them to further promote child participation in all matters affecting them, including at the grass-roots, community, and national or international levels, and to facilitate exchanges of best practices. Networking among child-led organizations should be actively encouraged to increase opportunities for shared learning and platforms for collective advocacy.

131. At the international level, children's participation at the World Summits for Children convened by the General Assembly in 1990 and 2002, and the involvement of children in the reporting process to the Committee on the Rights of the Child have particular relevance. The Committee welcomes written reports and additional oral information submitted by child organizations and children's representatives in the monitoring process of child rights implementation by States parties, and encourages States parties and NGOs to support children to present their views to the Committee.

D. Basic requirements for the implementation of the right of the child to be heard

132. The Committee urges States parties to avoid tokenistic approaches, which limit children's expression of views, or which allow children to be heard, but fail to give their views due weight. It emphasizes that adult manipulation of children, placing children in situations where they are told what they can say, or exposing children to risk of harm through participation are not ethical practices and cannot be understood as implementing article 12.

133. If participation is to be effective and meaningful, it needs to be understood as a process, not as an individual one-off event. Experience since the Convention on the Rights of the Child was adopted in 1989 has led to a broad consensus on the basic requirements which have to be reached for effective, ethical and meaningful implementation of article 12. The Committee recommends that States parties integrate these requirements into all legislative and other measures for the implementation of article 12.

134. All processes in which a child or children are heard and participate, must be:

(a) Transparent and informative – children must be provided with full, accessible, diversity-sensitive and age-appropriate information about their right to express their views freely and their views to be given due weight, and how this participation will take place, its scope, purpose and potential impact;

(b)   Voluntary – children should never be coerced into expressing views against their wishes and they should be informed that they can cease involvement at any stage;

(c)   Respectful – children's views have to be treated with respect and they should be provided with opportunities to initiate ideas and activities. Adults working with children should acknowledge, respect and build on good examples of children's participation, for instance, in their contributions to the family, school, culture and the work environment. They also need an understanding of the socio-economic, environmental and cultural context of children's lives. Persons and organizations working for and with children should also respect children's views with regard to participation in public events;

(d)   Relevant – the issues on which children have the right to express their views must be of real relevance to their lives and enable them to draw on their knowledge, skills and abilities. In addition, space needs to be created to enable children to highlight and address the issues they themselves identify as relevant and important;

(e)   Child-friendly – environments and working methods should be adapted to children's capacities. Adequate time and resources should be made available to ensure that children are adequately prepared and have the confidence and opportunity to contribute their views. Consideration needs to be given to the fact that children will need differing levels of support and forms of involvement according to their age and evolving capacities;

(f)   Inclusive – participation must be inclusive, avoid existing patterns of discrimination, and encourage opportunities for marginalized children, including both girls and boys, to be involved (see also para. 88 above). Children are not a homogenous group and participation needs to provide for equality of opportunity for all, without discrimination on any grounds. Programmes also need to ensure that they are culturally sensitive to children from all communities;

(g)   Supported by training – adults need preparation, skills and support to facilitate children's participation effectively, to provide them, for example, with skills in listening, working jointly with children and engaging children effectively in accordance with their evolving capacities. Children themselves can be involved as trainers and facilitators on how to promote effective participation; they require capacity-building to strengthen their skills in, for example, effective participation awareness of their rights, and training in organizing meetings, raising funds, dealing with the media, public speaking and advocacy;

(h)   Safe and sensitive to risk – in certain situations, expression of views may involve risks. Adults have a responsibility towards the children with whom they work and must take every precaution to minimize the risk to children of violence, exploitation or any other negative consequence of their participation. Action necessary to provide appropriate protection will include the development of a clear child-protection strategy which recognizes the particular risks faced by some groups of children, and the extra barriers they face in obtaining help. Children must be aware of their right to be protected from harm and know where to go for help if needed. Investment in working with families and communities is important in order to build understanding of the value and implications of participation, and to minimize the risks to which children may otherwise be exposed;

(i)   Accountable – a commitment to follow-up and evaluation is essential. For example, in any research or consultative process, children must be informed as to how their views have been interpreted and used and, where necessary, provided with the opportunity to challenge and influence the analysis of the findings. Children are also entitled to be provided with clear feedback on how their participation has influenced any outcomes. Wherever appropriate, children should be given the opportunity to participate in follow-up processes or activities. Monitoring and evaluation of children's participation needs to be undertaken, where possible, with children themselves.

E. Conclusions

135. Investment in the realization of the child's right to be heard in all matters of concern to her or him and for her or his views to be given due consideration, is a clear and immediate legal obligation of States parties under the Convention. It is the right of every child without any discrimination. Achieving meaningful opportunities for the implementation of article 12 will necessitate dismantling the legal, political, economic, social and cultural barriers that currently impede children's opportunity to be heard and their access to participation in all matters affecting them. It requires a preparedness to challenge assumptions about children's capacities, and to encourage the development of environments in which children can build and demonstrate capacities. It also requires a commitment to resources and training.

134. Fulfilling these obligations will present a challenge for States parties. But it is an attainable goal if the strategies outlined in this general comment are systematically implemented and a culture of respect for children and their views is built.

General comment No 13 (2011)
The right of the child to freedom from all forms of violence

I. INTRODUCTION

1. Article 19 states the following:

> "1. States Parties shall take all appropriate legislative, administrative, social and educational measures to protect the child from all forms of physical or mental violence, injury or abuse, neglect or negligent treatment, maltreatment or exploitation, including sexual abuse, while in the care of parent(s), legal guardian(s) or any other person who has the care of the child.

> "2. Such protective measures should, as appropriate, include effective procedures for the establishment of social programmes to provide necessary support for the child and for those who have the care of the child, as well as for other forms of prevention and for identification, reporting, referral, investigation, treatment and follow-up of instances of child maltreatment described heretofore, and, as appropriate, for judicial involvement."

2. **Rationale for the present general comment.** The Committee on the Rights of the Child (hereinafter: the Committee) issues the present general comment on article 19 of the Convention on the Rights of the Child (hereinafter: the Convention), since the extent and intensity of violence exerted on children is alarming. Measures to end violence must be massively strengthened and expanded in order to effectively put an end to these practices which jeopardize children's development and societies' potential non-violent solutions for conflict resolution.

3. **Overview.** The general comment is based on the following fundamental assumptions and observations:

(a) "No violence against children is justifiable; all violence against children is preventable";[129]

(b) A child rights-based approach to child caregiving and protection requires a paradigm shift towards respecting and promoting the human dignity and the physical and psychological integrity of children as rights-bearing individuals rather than perceiving them primarily as "victims";

(c) The concept of dignity requires that every child is recognized, respected and protected as a rights holder and as a unique and valuable human being with an individual personality, distinct needs, interests and privacy;

(d) The principle of the rule of law should apply fully to children as it does to adults;

(e) Children's rights to be heard and to have their views given due weight must be respected systematically in all decision-making processes, and their empowerment and participation should be central to child caregiving and protection strategies and programmes;

(f) The right of children to have their best interests be a primary consideration in all matters involving or affecting them must be respected, especially when they are victims of violence, as well as in all measures of prevention;

(g) Primary prevention, through public health, education, social services and other approaches, of all forms of violence is of paramount importance;

(h) The Committee recognizes the primary position of families, including extended families, in child caregiving and protection and in the prevention of violence. Nevertheless, the Committee also recognizes that the majority of violence takes

---

[129] Report of the independent expert for the United Nations study on violence against children (A/61/299), para. 1.

place in the context of families and that intervention and support are therefore required when children become the victims of hardship and distress imposed on, or generated in, families;

(i)   The Committee is also aware of widespread and intense violence applied against children in State institutions and by State actors including in schools, care centres, residential homes, police custody and justice institutions which may amount to torture and killing of children, as well as violence against children frequently used by armed groups and State military forces.

4. Definition of violence. For the purposes of the present general comment, "violence" is understood to mean "all forms of physical or mental violence, injury or abuse, neglect or negligent treatment, maltreatment or exploitation, including sexual abuse" as listed in article 19, paragraph 1, of the Convention. The term violence has been chosen here to represent all forms of harm to children as listed in article 19, paragraph 1, in conformity with the terminology used in the 2006 United Nations study on violence against children, although the other terms used to describe types of harm (injury, abuse, neglect or negligent treatment, maltreatment and exploitation) carry equal weight.[130] In common parlance the term violence is often understood to mean only physical harm and/or intentional harm. However, the Committee emphasizes most strongly that the choice of the term violence in the present general comment must not be interpreted in any way to minimize the impact of, and need to address, non-physical and/or non-intentional forms of harm (such as, inter alia, neglect and psychological maltreatment).

5. States' obligations and the responsibilities of family and other actors. References to "States parties" relate to the obligations of States parties to assume their responsibilities towards children not only at the national level, but also at the provincial and municipal levels. These special obligations are due diligence and the obligation to prevent violence or violations of human rights, the obligation to protect child victims and witnesses from human rights violations, the obligation to investigate and to punish those responsible, and the obligation to provide access to redress human rights violations. Regardless of whether violence takes place, States parties have a positive and active obligation to support and assist parents and other caregivers to secure, within their abilities and financial capacities and with respect for the evolving capacities of the child, the living conditions necessary for the child's optimal development (arts. 18 and 27). States parties, furthermore, shall ensure that all persons who, within the context of their work, are responsible for the prevention of, protection from, and reaction to violence and in the justice systems are addressing the needs and respecting the rights of children.

6. Evolution of general comment No. 13. The present general comment builds on the existing guidance provided by the Committee in its review of States parties' reports and the respective concluding observations, the recommendations of two days of general discussion on violence against children, held in 2000 and 2001, general comment No. 8 (2006) on the right of the child to protection from corporal punishment and other cruel or degrading forms of punishment, and references in other general comments to the topic of violence. The present general comment draws attention to the recommendations of the 2006 report of the independent expert for the United Nations study on violence against children (A/61/299) and calls on States parties to implement those recommendations without delay. It calls attention to the detailed guidance available in the Guidelines for the Alternative Care of Children.[131] It also draws on the expertise and

---

[130]   Translations of the Convention into other languages do not necessarily include exact equivalents of the English term "violence".

[131]   General Assembly resolution 64/142, annex.

experience of United Nations agencies, Governments, non-governmental organizations (NGOs), community organizations, development agencies, and children themselves in seeking to implement article 19 in practice.[132]

7. Article 19 in context. The Committee recognizes that:

(a) Article 19 is one of many provisions in the Convention directly relating to violence. The Committee also recognizes the direct relevance to article 19 of the Optional Protocol on the sale of children, child prostitution and child pornography and the Optional Protocol on the involvement of children in armed conflict. However, the Committee holds that article 19 forms the core provision for discussions and strategies to address and eliminate all forms of violence in the context of the Convention more broadly;

(b) Article 19 is strongly linked to a broad range of provisions in the Convention beyond those relating directly to violence. In addition to the articles containing the rights identified as principles of the Convention (see section V of the present general comment), implementation of article 19 must be situated in the context of articles 5, 9, 18 and 27;

(c) Children's rights to respect for their human dignity, physical and psychological integrity and to equal protection under the law are also recognized in other international and regional human rights instruments;

(d) Implementation of article 19 requires cooperation within and between national, regional and international human rights bodies, mechanisms and United Nations agencies;

(e) Cooperation is needed in particular with the Special Representative of the Secretary-General on Violence against Children, who has the mandate to promote the implementation of the recommendations of the United Nations study on violence against children in close collaboration with Member States and a wide range of partners, including United Nations agencies and organizations, civil society organizations and children, in order to safeguard the child's right to freedom from all forms of violence.

8. Dissemination. The Committee recommends that States parties widely disseminate the present general comment within government and administrative structures, to parents, other caregivers, children, professional organizations, communities and civil society at large. All channels of dissemination, including print media, the Internet and children's own communication means, should be used. This will necessitate translating it into relevant languages, including sign languages, Braille and easy-to-read formats for children with disabilities. It also requires making culturally appropriate and child-friendly versions available, holding workshops and seminars, implementing age- and disability-specific support to discuss its implications and how best to implement it, and incorporating it into the training of all professionals working for and with children.

9. Reporting requirements under the Convention. The Committee refers States parties to the reporting requirements outlined in the treaty-specific reporting guidelines (CRC/C/58/Rev.2 and Corr.1), in general comment No. 8 (para. 53), and in the concluding observations of the Committee adopted following the dialogues with representatives of States parties. The current general comment consolidates and specifies the measures on which States parties are expected to give information in the reports to be submitted under article 44 of the Convention. The Committee also recommends that States parties include information on progress made towards implementing the recommendations of the United Nations study on violence against children (A/61/299,

---

[132] See the Guidelines on Justice in Matters involving Child Victims and Witnesses of Crime (Economic and Social Council resolution 2005/20, annex).

para. 116). Reporting should comprise laws and other regulations taken to prohibit violence and to intervene appropriately when violence occurs and also measures for the prevention of violence, awareness-raising activities and the promotion of positive, non-violent relationships. In the reports it should be furthermore specified who has responsibility for the child and family at each stage of intervention (including prevention), what those responsibilities are, at what stage and under what circumstances professionals can intervene, and how different sectors work together.

10. **Additional sources of information.** The Committee also encourages United Nations agencies, national human rights institutions, NGOs and other competent bodies to provide it with relevant information on the legal status and prevalence of all forms of violence and progress towards their elimination.

II. OBJECTIVES

11. The present general comment seeks:

(a)   To guide States parties in understanding their obligations under article 19 of the Convention to prohibit, prevent and respond to all forms of physical or mental violence, injury or abuse, neglect or negligent treatment, maltreatment or exploitation of children, including sexual abuse, while in the care of parent(s), legal guardian(s) or any other person who has the care of the child, including State actors;

(b)   To outline the legislative, judicial, administrative, social and educational measures that States parties must take;

(c)   To overcome isolated, fragmented and reactive initiatives to address child caregiving and protection which have had limited impact on the prevention and elimination of all forms of violence;

(d)   To promote a holistic approach to implementing article 19 based on the Convention's overall perspective on securing children's rights to survival, dignity, well-being, health, development, participation and non-discrimination – the fulfilment of which are threatened by violence;

(e)   To provide States parties and other stakeholders with a basis on which to develop a coordinating framework for eliminating violence through comprehensive child rights-based caregiving and protection measures;

(f)   To highlight the need for all States parties to move quickly to fulfil their obligations under article 19.

III. VIOLENCE IN CHILDREN'S LIVES

12. **Challenges.** The Committee acknowledges and welcomes the numerous initiatives developed by Governments and others to prevent and respond to violence against children. In spite of these efforts, existing initiatives are in general insufficient. Legal frameworks in a majority of States still fail to prohibit all forms of violence against children, and where laws are in place, their enforcement is often inadequate. Widespread social and cultural attitudes and practices condone violence. The impact of measures taken is limited by lack of knowledge, data and understanding of violence against children and its root causes, by reactive efforts focusing on symptoms and consequences rather than causes, and by strategies which are fragmented rather than integrated. Resources allocated to address the problem are inadequate.

13. **The human rights imperative.** Addressing and eliminating the widespread prevalence and incidence of violence against children is an obligation of States parties under the Convention. Securing and promoting children's fundamental rights to respect for their human dignity and physical and psychological integrity, through the prevention of all

forms of violence, is essential for promoting the full set of child rights in the Convention. All other arguments presented here reinforce but do not replace this human rights imperative. Strategies and systems to prevent and respond to violence must therefore adopt a child rights rather than a welfare approach. (See para. 53 for more details).

14. **Societal development and children's contribution.** A respectful, supportive child-rearing environment free from violence supports the realization of children's individual personalities and fosters the development of social, responsible and actively contributing citizens in the local community and larger society. Research shows that children who have not experienced violence and who develop in a healthy manner are less likely to act violently, both in childhood and when they become adults. Preventing violence in one generation reduces its likelihood in the next. Implementation of article 19 is therefore a key strategy for reducing and preventing all forms of violence in societies and for promoting "social progress and better standards of life" and "freedom, justice and peace in the world" for the "human family" in which children have a place and a value equal to that of adults (Convention preamble).

15. **Survival and development – the devastating impact of violence against children.** Children's survival and their "physical, mental, spiritual, moral and social development" (art. 27, para. 1) are severely negatively impacted by violence, as described below:

(a) The short- and long-term health consequences of violence against children and child maltreatment are widely recognized. They include: fatal injury; non-fatal injury (possibly leading to disability); physical health problems (including failure to thrive, later lung, heart and liver disease and sexually transmitted infections); cognitive impairment (including impaired school and work performance); psychological and emotional consequences (such as feelings of rejection and abandonment, impaired attachment, trauma, fear, anxiety, insecurity and shattered self-esteem); mental health problems (such as anxiety and depressive disorders, hallucinations, memory disturbances and suicide attempts); and health-risk behaviours (such as substance abuse and early initiation of sexual behaviour);

(b) Developmental and behavioural consequences (such as school non-attendance and aggressive, antisocial, self-destructive and interpersonal destructive behaviours) can lead, inter alia, to deterioration of relationships, exclusion from school and coming into conflict with the law). There is evidence that exposure to violence increases a child's risk of further victimization and an accumulation of violent experiences, including later intimate partner violence.[133]

(c) The impact on children, in particular adolescents, of high-handed or "zero tolerance" State policies in response to child violence is highly destructive as it is a punitive approach victimizing children by reacting to violence with more violence. Such policies are often shaped by public concerns over citizens' security and by the high profile given to these issues by mass media. State policies on public security must carefully consider the root causes of children's offences in order to provide a way out of a vicious circle of retaliating violence with violence.

16. **The cost of violence against children.** The human, social and economic costs of denying children's rights to protection are enormous and unacceptable. Direct costs may include medical care, legal and social welfare services and alternative care. Indirect costs may include possible lasting injury or disability, psychological costs or other impacts on

---

[133] See Paulo Sérgio Pinheiro, independent expert for the United Nations Secretary-General's study on violence against children, *World Report on Violence against Children* (Geneva, 2006), pp. 63-66.

a victim's quality of life, disruption or discontinuation of education, and productivity losses in the future life of the child. They also include costs associated with the criminal justice system as a result of crimes committed by children who have experienced violence. The social costs arising from a demographic imbalance due to the discriminatory elimination of girls before birth are high and have potential implications for increased violence against girls including abduction, early and forced marriage, trafficking for sexual purposes and sexual violence.

IV. LEGAL ANALYSIS OF ARTICLE 19

A. Article 19, paragraph 1

1. "... all forms of ..."

17. No exceptions. The Committee has consistently maintained the position that all forms of violence against children, however light, are unacceptable. "All forms of physical or mental violence" does not leave room for any level of legalized violence against children. Frequency, severity of harm and intent to harm are not prerequisites for the definitions of violence. States parties may refer to such factors in intervention strategies in order to allow proportional responses in the best interests of the child, but definitions must in no way erode the child's absolute right to human dignity and physical and psychological integrity by describing some forms of violence as legally and/or socially acceptable.

18. The need for child rights-based definitions. States parties need to establish national standards for child well-being, health and development as securing these conditions is the ultimate goal of child caregiving and protection. Clear operational legal definitions are required of the different forms of violence outlined in article 19 in order to ban all forms of violence in all settings. These definitions must take into account the guidance provided in the present general comment, must be sufficiently clear to be usable and should be applicable in different societies and cultures. Efforts to standardize definitions internationally (in order to facilitate data collection and cross-country exchange of experiences) should be encouraged.

19. Forms of violence – overview. The following non-exhaustive lists outlining forms of violence apply to all children in all settings and in transit between settings. Children can experience violence at the hands of adults, and violence may also occur among children. Furthermore, some children harm themselves. The Committee recognizes that forms of violence often co-occur and that they can span the categories used here for convenience. Both girls and boys are at risk of all forms of violence, but violence often has a gender component. For example, girls may experience more sexual violence at home than boys whereas boys may be more likely to encounter – and experience violence within – the criminal justice system. (See also para. 72 (b) on the gender dimensions of violence).

20. Neglect or negligent treatment. Neglect means the failure to meet children's physical and psychological needs, protect them from danger, or obtain medical, birth registration or other services when those responsible for children's care have the means, knowledge and access to services to do so. It includes:

(a)   Physical neglect: failure to protect a child from harm,[134] including through lack of supervision, or failure to provide the child with basic necessities including adequate food, shelter, clothing and basic medical care;

(b)   Psychological or emotional neglect: including lack of any emotional support and love, chronic inattention to the child, caregivers being "psychologically

---

[134] States parties are also obliged to support caregivers to prevent accidents (art. 19 and art. 24, para. 2 (e)).

unavailable" by overlooking young children's cues and signals, and exposure to intimate partner violence, drug or alcohol abuse;

(c)   Neglect of children's physical or mental health: withholding essential medical care;

(d)   Educational neglect: failure to comply with laws requiring caregivers to secure their children's education through attendance at school or otherwise; and

(e)   Abandonment: a practice which is of great concern and which can disproportionately affect, inter alia, children out of wedlock and children with disabilities in some societies.[135]

21. Mental violence. "Mental violence", as referred to in the Convention, is often described as psychological maltreatment, mental abuse, verbal abuse and emotional abuse or neglect and this can include:

(a)   All forms of persistent harmful interactions with the child, for example, conveying to children that they are worthless, unloved, unwanted, endangered or only of value in meeting another's needs;

(b)   Scaring, terrorizing and threatening; exploiting and corrupting; spurning and rejecting; isolating, ignoring and favouritism;

(c)   Denying emotional responsiveness; neglecting mental health, medical and educational needs;

(d)   Insults, name-calling, humiliation, belittling, ridiculing and hurting a child's feelings;

(e)   Exposure to domestic violence;

(f)   Placement in solitary confinement, isolation or humiliating or degrading conditions of detention; and

(g)   Psychological bullying and hazing[136] by adults or other children, including via information and communication technologies (ICTs) such as mobile phones and the Internet (known as "cyberbullying").

22. Physical violence. This includes fatal and non-fatal physical violence. The Committee is of the opinion that physical violence includes:

(a)   All corporal punishment and all other forms of torture, cruel, inhuman or degrading treatment or punishment; and

(b)   Physical bullying and hazing by adults and by other children.

23. Children with disabilities may be subject to particular forms of physical violence such as:

(a)   Forced sterilization, particularly girls;

(b)   Violence in the guise of treatment (for example electroconvulsive treatment (ECT) and electric shocks used as "aversion treatment" to control children's behaviour); and

(c)   Deliberate infliction of disabilities on children for the purpose of exploiting them for begging in the streets or elsewhere.

24. Corporal punishment. In general comment No. 8 (para. 11), the Committee defined "corporal" or "physical" punishment as any punishment in which physical force is used

---

[135] In many countries children are abandoned because parents and caregivers living in poverty do not have the means to support them. According to the definition, neglect is a failure of care when parents have the means to meet their children's needs. The Committee has often urged States parties to "render appropriate assistance to parents and legal guardians in the performance of their child-rearing responsibilities" (art. 18, para. 2 of the Convention).

[136] "Hazing" refers to rituals and other activities involving harassment, violence or humiliation which are used as a way of initiating a person into a group.

and intended to cause some degree of pain or discomfort, however light. Most involves hitting ("smacking", "slapping", "spanking") children, with the hand or with an implement - a whip, stick, belt, shoe, wooden spoon, etc. But it can also involve, for example, kicking, shaking or throwing children, scratching, pinching, biting, pulling hair or boxing ears, caning, forcing children to stay in uncomfortable positions, burning, scalding, or forced ingestion. In the view of the Committee, corporal punishment is invariably degrading. Other specific forms of corporal punishment are listed in the report of the independent expert for the United Nations study on violence against children (A/61/299, paras. 56, 60 and 62).

25. Sexual abuse and exploitation. Sexual abuse and exploitation includes:

(a)   The inducement or coercion of a child to engage in any unlawful or psychologically harmful sexual activity;[137]

(b)   The use of children in commercial sexual exploitation; and

(c)   The use of children in audio or visual images of child sexual abuse;

(d)   Child prostitution, sexual slavery, sexual exploitation in travel and tourism, trafficking (within and between countries) and sale of children for sexual purposes and forced marriage. Many children experience sexual victimization which is not accompanied by physical force or restraint but which is nonetheless psychologically intrusive, exploitive and traumatic.

26. Torture and inhuman or degrading treatment or punishment. This includes violence in all its forms against children in order to extract a confession, to extrajudicially punish children for unlawful or unwanted behaviours, or to force children to engage in activities against their will, typically applied by police and law-enforcement officers, staff of residential and other institutions and persons who have power over children, including non-State armed actors. Victims are often children who are marginalized, disadvantaged and discriminated against and who lack the protection of adults responsible for defending their rights and best interests. This includes children in conflict with the law, children in street situations, minorities and indigenous children, and unaccompanied children. The brutality of such acts often results in life-long physical and psychological harm and social stress.

27. Violence among children. This includes physical, psychological and sexual violence, often by bullying, exerted by children against other children, frequently by groups of children, which not only harms a child's physical and psychological integrity and well-being in the immediate term, but often has severe impact on his or her development, education and social integration in the medium and long term. Also, violence by youth gangs takes a severe toll on children, whether as victims or as participants. Although children are the actors, the role of adults responsible for these children is crucial in all attempts to appropriately react and prevent such violence, ensuring that measures do not exacerbate violence by taking a punitive approach and using violence against violence.

28. Self-harm. This includes eating disorders, substance use and abuse, self-inflicted injuries, suicidal thoughts, suicide attempts and actual suicide. Suicide among adolescents is of particular concern to the Committee.

29. Harmful practices. These include, but are not limited to:

---

[137] Sexual abuse comprises any sexual activities imposed by an adult on a child, against which the child is entitled to protection by criminal law. Sexual activities are also considered as abuse when committed against a child by another child, if the child offender is significantly older than the child victim or uses power, threat or other means of pressure. Sexual activities between children are not considered as sexual abuse if the children are older than the age limit defined by the State party for consensual sexual activities.

(a) Corporal punishment and other cruel or degrading forms of punishment;
(b) Female genital mutilation;
(c) Amputations, binding, scarring, burning and branding;
(d) Violent and degrading initiation rites; force-feeding of girls; fattening; virginity testing (inspecting girls' genitalia);
(e) Forced marriage and early marriage;
(f) "Honour" crimes; "retribution" acts of violence (where disputes between different groups are taken out on children of the parties involved); dowry-related death and violence;
(g) Accusations of "witchcraft" and related harmful practices such as "exorcism";
(h) Uvulectomy and teeth extraction.

30. Violence in the mass media. Mass media, especially tabloids and the yellow press, tend to highlight shocking occurrences and as a result create a biased and stereotyped image of children, in particular of disadvantaged children or adolescents, who are often portrayed as violent or delinquent just because they may behave or dress in a different way. Such stirred-up stereotypes pave the way for State policies based on a punitive approach, which may include violence as a reaction to assumed or factual misdemeanours of children and young persons.

31. Violence through information and communications technologies.[138] Child protection risks in relation to ICT comprise the following overlapping areas:

(a) Sexual abuse of children to produce both visual and audio child abuse images facilitated by the Internet and other ICT;
(b) The process of taking, making, permitting to take, distributing, showing, possessing or advertising indecent photographs or pseudophotographs ("morphing") and videos of children and those making a mockery of an individual child or categories of children;
(c) Children as users of ICT:
   (i) As recipients of information, children may be exposed to actually or potentially harmful advertisements, spam, sponsorship, personal information and content which is aggressive, violent, hateful, biased, racist, pornographic,[139] unwelcome and/or misleading;
   (ii) As children in contact with others through ICT, children may be bullied, harassed or stalked (child "luring") and/or coerced, tricked or persuaded into meeting strangers off-line, being "groomed" for involvement in sexual activities and/or providing personal information;
   (iii) As actors, children may become involved in bullying or harassing others, playing games that negatively influence their psychological development, creating and uploading inappropriate sexual material, providing misleading information or advice, and/or illegal downloading, hacking, gambling, financial scams and/or terrorism.[140]

---

[138] Information technologies such as the Internet and mobile phones have great potential as positive tools to help keep children safe and as a way to report suspected or actual violence or maltreatment. A protective environment needs to be created through regulation and monitoring of information technologies including empowering children to safely use these technologies.

[139] Exposure to pornography can lead to an increase in child-on-child sexual abuse as children exposed to pornography "try out" what they have seen in practice with younger children or those to whom they have easy access and over whom they have control.

[140] Adapted from a table developed by the EUKids Online project, cited in *AUPs in Context: Establishing Safe and Responsible Online Behaviours* (Becta, 2009), p. 6. See also the Rio de Janeiro Declaration and Call for Action to Prevent and Stop Sexual Exploitation of Children and Adolescents. Available from http://iiicongressomundial.net/congresso/arquivos/Rio%20Declaration%20and%20Call%20for%20 Action%20-%20FINAL%20Version.pdf.

32. Institutional and system violations of child rights. Authorities at all levels of the State responsible for the protection of children from all forms of violence may directly and indirectly cause harm by lacking effective means of implementation of obligations under the Convention. Such omissions include the failure to adopt or revise legislation and other provisions, inadequate implementation of laws and other regulations and insufficient provision of material, technical and human resources and capacities to identify, prevent and react to violence against children. It is also an omission when measures and programmes are not equipped with sufficient means to assess, monitor and evaluate progress or shortcomings of the activities to end violence against children. Also, in the commission of certain acts, professionals may abuse children's right to freedom from violence, for example, when they execute their responsibilities in a way that disregards the best interests, the views and the developmental objectives of the child.

2. *"while in the care of..."*

33. Definition of "caregivers". The Committee considers that, while respecting the evolving capacities and progressive autonomy of the child, all human beings below the age of 18 years are nonetheless "in the care of" someone, or should be. There are only three conditions for children: emancipated,[141] in the care of primary or proxy caregivers, or in the de facto care of the State. The definition of "caregivers", referred to in article 19, paragraph 1, as "parent(s), legal guardian(s) or any other person who has the care of the child", covers those with clear, recognized legal, professional-ethical and/or cultural responsibility for the safety, health, development and well-being of the child, primarily: parents, foster parents, adoptive parents, caregivers in *kafalah* of Islamic law, guardians, extended family and community members; education, school and early childhood personnel; child caregivers employed by parents; recreational and sports coaches – including youth group supervisors; workplace employers or supervisors; and institutional personnel (governmental or non-governmental) in the position of caregivers – for example responsible adults in health-care, juvenile-justice and drop-in and residential-care settings. In the case of unaccompanied children, the State is the de facto caregiver.

34. Definition of care settings. Care settings are places where children spend time under the supervision of their "permanent" primary caregiver (such as a parent or guardian) or a proxy or "temporary" caregiver (such as a teacher or youth group leader) for periods of time which are short-term, long-term, repeated or once only. Children will often pass between caregiving settings with great frequency and flexibility but their safety in transit between these settings is still the responsibility of the primary caregiver – either directly, or via coordination and cooperation with a proxy caregiver (for example to and from school or when fetching water, fuel, food or fodder for animals). Children are also considered to be "in the care of" a primary or proxy caregiver while they are physically unsupervised within a care setting, for example while playing out of sight or surfing the Internet unsupervised. Usual care settings include family homes, schools and other educational institutions, early childhood care settings, after-school care centres, leisure, sports, cultural and recreational facilities, religious institutions and places of worship. In medical, rehabilitative and care facilities, at the workplace and in justice settings children are in the custody of professionals or State actors, who must observe the best interests of the child and ensure his or her rights to protection, well-being and

---

[141] In line with the Committee's previous recommendation to States parties to increase the age for marriage to 18 years for both girls and boys (general comment No. 4 (2003) on adolescent health and development in the context of the Convention of the Rights of the Child, para. 20), and given their specific vulnerability to maltreatment, the Committee considers that article 19 applies also to children under the age of 18 who have attained majority or emancipation through early marriage and/or forced marriage.

development. A third type of setting in which children's protection, well-being and development also must be secured, are neighbourhoods, communities and camps or settlements for refugees and people displaced by conflict and/or natural disasters.[142]

35. Children without obvious primary or proxy caregivers. Article 19 also applies to children without a primary or proxy caregiver or another person who is entrusted with the protection and well-being of the child such as, for instance, children in child-headed households, children in street situations, children of migrating parents or unaccompanied children outside their country of origin.[143] The State party is obliged to take responsibility as the de facto caregiver or the one "who has the care of the child", even if these children are not within the context of physical care settings such as foster homes, group homes or NGO facilities. The State party is under the obligation "to ensure the child such protection and care as is necessary for his or her well-being" (art. 3, para. 2) and to "ensure alternative care" to "a child temporarily or permanently deprived of his or her family environment" (art. 20). There are different ways to guarantee the rights of these children, preferably in family-like care arrangements, which must be carefully examined with respect to the risk of these children being exposed to violence.

36. Perpetrators of violence. Children may be subjected to violence by primary or proxy caregivers and/or by others against whom their caregiver does provide protection (for example neighbours, peers and strangers). Furthermore, children are at risk of being exposed to violence in many settings where professionals and State actors have often misused their power over children, such as schools, residential homes, police stations or justice institutions. All of these conditions fall under the scope of article 19, which is not limited to violence perpetrated solely by caregivers in a personal context.

3. "shall take …"

37. "Shall take" is a term which leaves no leeway for the discretion of States parties. Accordingly, States parties are under strict obligation to undertake "all appropriate measures" to fully implement this right for all children.

4. "all appropriate legislative, administrative, social and educational measures"

38. General measures of implementation and monitoring. The Committee draws the attention of States parties to general comment No. 5 (2003) on general measures of implementation of the Convention on the Rights of the Child.[144] The Committee also refers States parties to its general comment No. 2 (2002) on the role of independent national human rights institutions in the promotion and protection of the rights of the child. These measures of implementation and monitoring are essential to bring article 19 into reality.

39. "*All appropriate. . .* measures". The term "appropriate" refers to the broad range of measures cutting across all sectors of Government, which must be used and be effective in order to prevent and respond to all forms of violence. "Appropriate" cannot be interpreted to mean acceptance of some forms of violence. An integrated, cohesive, interdisciplinary and coordinated system is required, which incorporates the full range of measures identified in article 19, paragraph 1, across the full range of interventions listed in paragraph 2. Isolated programmes and activities which are not integrated into

---

[142] The United Nations study on violence against children describes settings in which violence against children occurs; see also the detailed guidance available in the Guidelines for the Alternative Care of Children.

[143] As defined in the Committee's general comment No. 6 (2005), para. 7.

[144] See in particular paras. 9 (range of measures required), 13 and 15 (regarding withdrawal and eligibility of reservations), and 66 and 67 (dissemination of the Convention).

sustainable and coordinated government policy and infrastructures will have limited effects. Child participation is essential in the development, monitoring and evaluation of the measures outlined here.

40. Legislative measures refer to both legislation, including the budget, and the implementing and enforcing measures. They comprise national, provincial and municipal laws and all relevant regulations, which define frameworks, systems, mechanisms and the roles and responsibilities of concerned agencies and competent officers.

41. State parties that have not yet done so must:

(a)　Ratify the two Optional Protocols to the Convention, and other international and regional human rights instruments that provide protection for children, including the Convention on the Rights of Persons with Disabilities and its Optional Protocol and the Convention against Torture and Other Cruel, Inhuman or Degrading Treatment or Punishment;

(b)　Review and withdraw declarations and reservations contrary to the object and purpose of the Convention or otherwise contrary to international law;

(c)　Strengthen cooperation with treaty bodies and other human rights mechanisms;

(d)　Review and amend domestic legislation in line with article 19 and its implementation within the holistic framework of the Convention, establishing a comprehensive policy on child rights and ensuring absolute prohibition of all forms of violence against children in all settings and effective and appropriate sanctions against perpetrators;[145]

(e)　Provide adequate budget allocations for the implementation of legislation and all other measures adopted to end violence against children;

(f)　Ensure the protection of child victims and witnesses and effective access to redress and reparation;

(g)　Ensure that relevant legislation provides adequate protection of children in relation to media and ICT;

(h)　Establish and implement social programmes to promote optimal positive child-rearing by providing, through integrated services, necessary support for the child and for those who have the care of the child;

(i)　Enforce law and judicial procedures in a child-friendly way, including remedies available to children when rights are violated;

(j)　Establish and support an independent national institution of children's rights.

42. Administrative measures should reflect governmental obligations to establish policies, programmes, monitoring and oversight systems required to protect the child from all forms of violence. These include:

(a)　*At the national and sub-national government levels*:

　(i)　Establishing a government focal point to coordinate child protection strategies and services;

　(ii)　Defining the roles, responsibilities and relationships between stakeholders on inter-agency steering committees with a view to their effectively managing, monitoring and holding accountable the implementing bodies at national and subnational levels;

　(iii)　Ensuring that the process of decentralizing services safeguards their quality, accountability and equitable distribution;

---

[145]　In the context of "sanctions", the term "perpetrators" excludes children who harm themselves. The treatment of children who harm other children must be educational and therapeutic.

    (iv)   Implementing systematic and transparent budgeting processes in order to make the best use of allocated resources for child protection, including prevention;

    (v)   Establishing a comprehensive and reliable national data collection system in order to ensure systematic monitoring and evaluation of systems (impact analyses), services, programmes and outcomes based on indicators aligned with universal standards, and adjusted for and guided by locally established goals and objectives;

    (vi)   Providing independent national human rights institutions with support and promoting the establishment of specific child rights mandates such as child rights ombudsmen where these do not yet exist.[146]

(b)   *At the levels of governmental, professional and civil society institutions*:

    (i)   Developing and implementing (through participatory processes which encourage ownership and sustainability):

       a.   Intra- and inter-agency child protection policies;

       b.   Professional ethics codes, protocols, memoranda of understanding and standards of care for all childcare services and settings (including daycare centres, schools, hospitals, sport clubs and residential institutions etc.);

    (ii)   Involving academic teaching and training institutions with regard to child protection initiatives;

    (iii)   Promoting good research programmes.

43. Social measures should reflect governmental commitment to fulfilling child protection rights and provide for basic and targeted services. They can be initiated and implemented by both State and civil society actors under the responsibility of the State. Such measures include:

(a)   *Social policy measures to reduce risk and prevent violence against children, for example*:

    (i)   Integration of child caregiving and protection measures into mainstream systems of social policy;

    (ii)   Identification and prevention of factors and circumstances which hinder vulnerable groups' access to services and full enjoyment of their rights (including indigenous and minority children and children with disabilities, among others);

    (iii)   Poverty reduction strategies, including financial and social support to families at risk;

    (iv)   Public health and safety, housing, employment and education policies;

    (v)   Improved access to health, social welfare and justice services;

    (vi)   "Child-friendly cities" planning;

    (vii)   Reduced demand for and access to alcohol, illegal drugs and weapons;

    (viii) Collaboration with the mass media and the ICT industry to devise, promote and enforce global standards for child caregiving and protection;

    (ix)   Development of guidelines for protecting children from information and material produced by mass media disrespecting the human dignity and integrity of the child, abolishing stigmatizing language, refraining from the dissemination of re-victimizing reports on events in family or

---

[146] See general comment No. 2, in particular paras. 1, 2, 4 and 19.

elsewhere affecting a child and promoting professional methods of investigation based on the use of diverse sources which can be examined by all parties involved;

(x) Opportunities for children to express their view and expectations in the media and be not only engaged in children's programmes, but also involved in the production and transmission of all kinds of information, including as reporters, analysts and commentators in order to support an adequate image of children and childhood in the public.

(b) *Social programmes to support the child individually and to support the child's family and other caregivers to provide optimal positive child-rearing, for example*:

(i) For children: childcare, early child development and after-school care programmes; child and youth groups and clubs; counselling support to children experiencing difficulties (including self-harm); 24-hour toll-free child helplines with trained personnel; foster family services which are subject to periodic review;

(ii) For families and other caregivers: community-based mutual-help groups to address psychosocial and economic challenges (for example parenting and micro-credit groups); welfare programmes to support families' standard of living, including direct allowances to children at a certain age; counselling support to caregivers having difficulties with employment, housing and/or child-rearing; therapeutic programmes (including mutual help groups) to assist caregivers with challenges related to domestic violence, addictions to alcohol or drugs or with other mental health needs.

44. Educational measures should address attitudes, traditions, customs and behavioural practices which condone and promote violence against children. They should encourage open discussion about violence, including the engagement of media and civil society. They should support children's life skills, knowledge and participation and enhance the capacities of caregivers and professionals in contact with children. They can be initiated and implemented by both State and civil society actors under the responsibility of the State. Specific examples include, but are not limited to:

(a) *For all stakeholders*: public information programmes, including awareness campaigns, via opinion leaders and the media, to promote positive child-rearing and to combat negative societal attitudes and practices which condone or encourage violence; dissemination of the Convention, the present general comment and State party reports in child friendly and accessible formats; supporting measures to educate and advise on protection in the context of ICTs;

(b) *For children*: provision of accurate, accessible and age-appropriate information and empowerment on life skills, self-protection and specific risks, including those relating to ICTs and how to develop positive peer relationships and combat bullying; empowerment regarding child rights in general - and in particular on the right to be heard and to have their views taken seriously - through the school curriculum and in other ways;

(c) *For families and communities*: education on positive child-rearing for parents and caregivers; provision of accurate and accessible information on specific risks and how to listen to children and take their views seriously;

(d) *For professionals and institutions (government and civil society)*:

(i) Providing initial and in-service general and role-specific training (including inter-sectoral where necessary) on a child rights approach to article 19 and its application in practice, for all professionals and non-professionals working with, and for, children (including teachers at all levels of the educational system, social workers, medical doctors, nurses and other health professionals, psychologists, lawyers, judges, police, probation and prison officers, journalists, community workers, residential caregivers, civil servants and public officials, asylum officers and traditional and religious leaders);

(ii) Developing officially recognized certification schemes in association with educational and training institutions and professional societies in order to regulate and acknowledge such training;

(iii) Ensuring that the Convention is part of the educational curriculum of all professionals expected to work with and for children;

(iv) Supporting "child-friendly schools" and other initiatives which include, inter alia, respect for children's participation;

(v)   Promoting research on child caregiving and protection.

B. Article 19, paragraph 2

"such protective measures should, as appropriate, include…"

45. Range of interventions. A holistic child protection system requires the provision of comprehensive and integrated measures across the full range of stages identified in article 19, paragraph 2, taking account of the socio-cultural traditions and legal system of the respective State party.[147]

46. Prevention. The Committee emphasizes in the strongest terms that child protection must begin with proactive prevention of all forms of violence as well as explicitly prohibit all forms of violence. States have the obligation to adopt all measures necessary to ensure that adults responsible for the care, guidance and upbringing of children will respect and protect children's rights. Prevention includes public health and other measures to positively promote respectful child-rearing, free from violence, for all children, and to target the root causes of violence at the levels of the child, family, perpetrator, community, institution and society. Emphasis on general (primary) and targeted (secondary) prevention must remain paramount at all times in the development and implementation of child protection systems. Preventive measures offer the greatest return in the long term. However, commitment to prevention does not lessen States' obligations to respond effectively to violence when it occurs.

47. Prevention measures include, but are not limited to:

(a) *For all stakeholders*:
(i)   Challenging attitudes which perpetuate the tolerance and condoning of violence in all its forms, including gender, race, colour, religion, ethnic or social origin, disability and other power imbalances;

(ii) Disseminating information regarding the Convention's holistic and positive approach to child protection through creative public campaigns, schools and peer education, family, community and institutional educational initiatives, professionals and professional groups, NGOs and civil society;

(iii) Developing partnerships with all sectors of society, including children themselves, NGOs and the media;

(b) *For children*:

---

[147] The detailed guidance available in the Guidelines for the Alternative Care of Children should also be taken into account at each stage.

> (i)   Registering all children to facilitate their access to services and redress procedures;
>
> (ii)   Supporting children to protect themselves and their peers through awareness of their rights and development of social skills as well as age-appropriate empowerment strategies;
>
> (iii)   Implementing "mentoring" programmes that engage responsible and trusted adults in the lives of children identified as needing extra support beyond that provided by their caregivers;

(c)   *For families and communities*:

> (i)   Supporting parents and caregivers to understand, embrace and implement good child-rearing, based on knowledge of child rights, child development and techniques for positive discipline in order to support families' capacity to provide children with care in a safe environment;
>
> (ii)   Providing pre- and post-natal services, home visitation programmes, quality early-childhood development programmes, and income-generation programmes for disadvantaged groups;
>
> (iii)   Strengthening the links between mental health services, substance abuse treatment and child protection services;
>
> (iv)   Providing respite programmes and family support centres for families facing especially difficult circumstances;
>
> (v)   Providing shelters and crisis centres for parents (mostly women) who have experienced violence at home and their children;
>
> (vi)   Providing assistance to the family by adopting measures that promote family unity and ensure for children the full exercise and enjoyment of their rights in private settings, abstaining from unduly interfering in children's private and family relations, depending on circumstances.[148]

(d)   *For professionals and institutions (Government and civil society)*:

> (i)   Identifying prevention opportunities and informing policy and practice on the basis of research studies and data collection;
>
> (ii)   Implementing, through a participatory process, rights-based child protection policies and procedures and professional ethics codes and standards of care;
>
> (iii)   Preventing violence in care and justice settings by, inter alia, developing and implementing community-based services in order to make use of institutionalization and detention only as a last resort and only if in the best interest of the child.

48. Identification.[149] This includes identifying risk factors for particular individuals or groups of children and caregivers (in order to trigger targeted prevention initiatives) and identifying signs of actual maltreatment (in order to trigger appropriate intervention as early as possible). This requires that all who come in contact with children are aware of risk factors and indicators of all forms of violence, have received guidance on how to interpret such indicators, and have the necessary knowledge, willingness and ability to take appropriate action (including the provision of emergency protection). Children must be provided with as many opportunities as possible to signal emerging problems before they reach a state of crisis, and for adults to recognize and act on such problems even if the child does not explicitly ask for help. Particular vigilance is needed when it comes to marginalized groups of children who are rendered particularly vulnerable due

---

[148]   Human Rights Committee, general comment No. 17 (1989) on the rights of the child; European Court of Human Rights, *Olsson vs. Sweden* (No. 1), Judgement of 24 March 1988, Series A No. 130, para. 81; Inter-American Court of Human Rights, *Velásquez Rodríguez vs. Honduras*, Judgement on the Merits, 10 January 1989, Series C, No. 3, para. 172.

[149]   Paragraphs 48 ff can also be applied to processes in informal and customary systems of justice.

to their alternative methods of communicating, their immobility and/or the perceived view that they are incompetent, such as children with disabilities. Reasonable accomodation should be provided to ensure that they are able to communicate and signal problems on an equal basis with others.

49. Reporting.[150] The Committee strongly recommends that all States parties develop safe, well-publicized, confidential and accessible support mechanisms for children, their representatives and others to report violence against children, including through the use of 24-hour toll-free hotlines and other ICTs. The establishment of reporting mechanisms includes: (a) providing appropriate information to facilitate the making of complaints; (b) participation in investigations and court proceedings; (c) developing protocols which are appropriate for different circumstances and made widely known to children and the general public; (d) establishing related support services for children and families; and (e) training and providing ongoing support for personnel to receive and advance the information received through reporting systems. Reporting mechanisms must be coupled with, and should present themselves as help-oriented services offering public health and social support, rather than as triggering responses which are primarily punitive. Children's right to be heard and to have their views taken seriously must be respected. In every country, the reporting of instances, suspicion or risk of violence should, at a minimum, be required by professionals working directly with children. When reports are made in good faith, processes must be in place to ensure the protection of the professional making the report.

50.Referral. The person receiving the report should have clear guidance and training on when and how to refer the issue to whichever agency is responsible for coordinating the response. Following this, intersectoral referrals may be made by trained professionals and administrators when children are found to be in need of protection (immediate or longer-term) and specialized support services. Professionals working within the child protection system need to be trained in inter-agency cooperation and protocols for collaboration. The process will involve: (a) a participatory, multi-disciplinary assessment of the short- and long-term needs of the child, caregivers and family, which invites and gives due weight to the child's views as well as those of the caregivers and family; (b) sharing of the assessment results with the child, caregivers and family; (c) referral of the child and family to a range of services to meet those needs; and (d) follow-up and evaluation of the adequateness of the intervention.

51. Investigation. Investigation of instances of violence, whether reported by the child, a representative or an external party, must be undertaken by qualified professionals who have received role-specific and comprehensive training, and require a child rights-based and child-sensitive approach. Rigorous but child-sensitive investigation procedures will help to ensure that violence is correctly identified and help provide evidence for administrative, civil, child-protection and criminal proceedings. Extreme care must be taken to avoid subjecting the child to further harm through the process of the investigation. Towards this end, all parties are obliged to invite and give due weight to the child's views.

52. Treatment. "Treatment" is one of the many services needed to "promote physical and psychological recovery and social reintegration" for children who have experienced violence, and must take place "in an environment which fosters the health, self-respect and dignity of the child" (art. 39). In this respect attention must be given to: (a) inviting and giving due weight to the child's views; (b) the safety of the child; (c) the possible need for her or his immediate safe placement; and (d) the predictable influences of

---

[150] See also the Guidelines on Justice in Matters involving Child Victims and Witnesses of Crime.

potential interventions on the child's long-term well-being, health and development. Medical, mental health, social and legal services and support may be required for children upon identification of abuse, as well as longer-term follow-up services. A full range of services, including family group conferencing and other similar practices, should be made available. Services and treatment for perpetrators of violence, especially child perpetrators, are also needed. Children who are aggressive towards other children have often been deprived of a caring family and community environment. They must be regarded as victims of their child-rearing conditions, which imbue them with frustration, hatred and aggression. Educational measures must have priority and be directed to improve their pro-social attitudes, competencies and behaviours. Simultaneously, the life conditions of these children must be examined in order to promote their care and support and that of other children in the family and neighbourhood. In terms of children who harm themselves, it is recognized that this is a result of severe psychological distress and may be a result of violence by others. Self-harm should not be criminalized. Interventions must be supportive and not in any way punitive.

53. Follow-up. The following must always be clear: (a) who has responsibility for the child and family from reporting and referral all the way through to follow-up; (b) the aims of any course of action taken – which must be fully discussed with the child and other relevant stakeholders; (c) the details, deadlines for implementation and proposed duration of any interventions; and (d) mechanisms and dates for the review, monitoring and evaluation of actions. Continuity between stages of intervention is essential and this may best be achieved through a case management process. Effective help requires that actions, once decided through a participatory process, must not be subject to undue delay. The follow-up must be understood in the context of article 39 (recovery and reintegration), article 25 (periodic review of treatment and placements), article 6, paragraph 2 (right to development) and article 29 (aims of education which present intentions and aspirations for development). Contact of the child with both parents should be ensured in accordance with article 9, paragraph 3, unless this is contrary to the best interests of the child.

54. Judicial involvement.[151] At all times and in all cases, due process must be respected. In particular, the protection and the further development of the child and his or her best interests (and the best interests of other children where there is a risk of a perpetrator reoffending) must form the primary purpose of decision-making, with regard given to the least intrusive intervention as warranted by the circumstances. Furthermore, the Committee recommends the respect of the following guarantees:

(a)   Children and their parents should be promptly and adequately informed by the justice system or other competent authorities (such as the police, immigration, or educational, social or health-care services);

(b)   Child victims of violence should be treated in a child-friendly and sensitive manner throughout the justice process, taking into account their personal situation, needs, age, gender, disability and level of maturity and fully respecting their physical, mental and moral integrity;

(c)   Judicial involvement should be preventive where possible, proactively encouraging positive behaviour as well as prohibiting negative behaviour. Judicial involvement should be an element of a coordinated and integrated approach across sectors, supporting and facilitating other professionals to

---

[151]   See also: Guidelines of the Committee of Ministers of the Council of Europe on child friendly justice, adopted on 17 November 2010; Guidelines on Justice in Matters involving Child Victims and Witnesses of Crime; and General Assembly resolution 65/213.

work with children, caregivers, families and communities, and facilitating access to the full range of child caregiving and protection services available;

(d) In all proceedings involving children victims of violence, the celerity principle must be applied, while respecting the rule of law.

55. Judicial involvement may consist of the following:

(a) Differentiated and mediated responses such as family group conferencing, alternative dispute-resolution mechanisms, restorative justice and kith and kin agreements (where processes are human-rights respecting, accountable and managed by trained facilitators);

(b) Juvenile or family court intervention leading to a specific measure of child protection;

(c) Criminal law procedures, which must be strictly applied in order to abolish the widespread practice of de jure or de facto impunity, in particular of State actors;

(d) Disciplinary or administrative proceedings against professionals for neglectful or inappropriate behaviour in dealing with suspected cases of child maltreatment (either internal proceedings in the context of professional bodies for breaches of codes of ethics or standards of care, or external proceedings);

(e) Judicial orders to ensure compensation and rehabilitation for children who have suffered from violence in its various forms.

56. When appropriate, juvenile or family specialized courts and criminal procedures should be established for child victims of violence. This could include the establishment of specialized units within the police, the judiciary and the prosecutor's office with the possibility of providing accomodations in the judicial process to ensure equal and fair participation of children with disabilities. All professionals working with and for children and involved in such cases should receive specific interdisciplinary training on the rights and needs of children of different age groups, as well as on proceedings that are adapted to them. While implementing a multidisciplinary approach, professional rules on confidentiality should be respected. The decision to separate a child from his or her parent(s) or family environment must be made only when it is in the child's best interests (art. 9 and art. 20, para. 1). However, in cases of violence where perpetrators are primary caregivers, within the child rights safeguards listed above, and depending on the severity and other factors, intervention measures focusing on social and educational treatment and a restaurative approach are often preferable to a purely punitive judicial involvement. Effective remedies should be available, including compensation to victims and access to redress mechanisms and appeal or independent complaint mechanisms.

57. Effective procedures. Such protective measures as mentioned in article 19, paragraphs 1 and 2, and as integrated into a systems-building approach (see para.71), require "effective procedures" to ensure their enforcement, quality, relevance, accessibility, impact and efficiency. Such procedures should include:

(a) Inter-sectoral coordination, mandated by protocols and memorandums of understanding as necessary;

(b) The development and implementation of systematic and ongoing data collection and analysis;

(c) The development and implementation of a research agenda; and

(d) The development of measurable objectives and indicators in relation to policies, processes and outcomes for children and families.

58. Outcome indicators should focus on the child's positive development and well-being as a rights-bearing person, beyond a purely narrow focus on incidence, prevalence and

types or extent of violence. Child death reviews, critical injury reviews, inquests and systemic reviews must also be taken into account when identifying the underlying causes of violence and in recommending corrective courses of actions. Research must build on the existing body of international and national child protection knowledge and benefit from interdisciplinary and international collaboration in order to maximize complementarity. (See also para. 72(j) on accountability in relation to national coordinating frameworks).

V. INTERPRETATION OF ARTICLE 19 IN THE BROADER CONTEXT OF THE CONVENTION

59. Definition of a child rights approach. Respect for the dignity, life, survival, well-being, health, development, participation and non-discrimination of the child as a rights-bearing person should be established and championed as the pre-eminent goal of States parties' policies concerning children. This is best realized by respecting, protecting and fulfilling all of the rights in the Convention (and its Optional Protocols). It requires a paradigm shift away from child protection approaches in which children are perceived and treated as "objects" in need of assistance rather than as rights holders entitled to non-negotiable rights to protection. A child rights approach is one which furthers the realization of the rights of all children as set out in the Convention by developing the capacity of duty bearers to meet their obligations to respect, protect and fulfil rights (art. 4) and the capacity of rights holders to claim their rights, guided at all times by the rights to non-discrimination (art. 2), consideration of the best interests of the child (art. 3, para. 1), life, survival and development (art. 6), and respect for the views of the child (art. 12). Children also have the right to be directed and guided in the exercise of their rights by caregivers, parents and community members, in line with children's evolving capacities (art. 5). This child rights approach is holistic and places emphasis on supporting the strengths and resources of the child him/herself and all social systems of which the child is a part: family, school, community, institutions, religious and cultural systems.

60. Article 2 (non-discrimination). The Committee stresses that States parties shall take adequate measures to assure to every child the right to protection from all forms of violence "without discrimination of any kind, irrespective of the child's or his or her parent's or legal guardian's race, colour, sex, language, religion, political or other opinion, national, ethnic or social origin, property, disability, birth or other status". This includes discrimination based on prejudices towards commercially sexually exploited children, children in street situations or children in conflict with the law or based on children's clothing and behaviour. States parties must address discrimination against vulnerable or marginalized groups of children, such as outlined in paragraph 72 (g) of the present general comment, and make proactive efforts to ensure that such children are assured their right to protection on an equal basis with all other children.

61. Article 3 (best interests of the child). The Committee emphasizes that the interpretation of a child's best interests must be consistent with the whole Convention, including the obligation to protect children from all forms of violence. It cannot be used to justify practices, including corporal punishment and other forms of cruel or degrading punishment, which conflict with the child's human dignity and right to physical integrity. An adult's judgment of a child's best interests cannot override the obligation to respect all the child's rights under the Convention. In particular, the Committee maintains that the best interests of the child are best served through:

(a)   Prevention of all forms of violence and the promotion of positive child-rearing, emphasizing the need for a focus on primary prevention in national coordinating frameworks;

(b)   Adequate investment in human, financial and technical resources dedicated to the implementation of a child rights-based and integrated child protection and support system.

62. Article 6 (life, survival and development). Protection from all forms of violence must be considered not only in terms of the child's right to "life" and "survival", but also in terms of their right to "development", which must be interpreted in line with the overall goal of child protection. Thus, the obligation of the State party includes comprehensive protection from violence and exploitation which would jeopardize a child's right to life, survival and development. The Committee expects States to interpret "development" in its broadest sense as a holistic concept, embracing the child's physical, mental, spiritual, moral, psychological and social development. Implementation measures should be aimed at achieving the optimal development for all children.

63. Article 12 (right to be heard). The Committee is of the opinion that child participation promotes protection and child protection is key to participation. The child's right to be heard commences already with very young children who are particularly vulnerable to violence. Children's views must be invited and given due weight as a mandatory step at every point in a child protection process. The child's right to be heard has particular relevance in situations of violence (see the Committee's general comment No. 12 (2009), paras. 118 ff). With regard to family and child-rearing, the Committee expressed that this right plays a preventive role against all forms of violence in the home and family. The Committee furthermore underlines the importance of children's participation in the development of prevention strategies in general and in school, in particular in the elimination and prevention of bullying, and other forms of violence in school. Initiatives and programmes that are aimed at strengthening children's own capacities to eliminate violence should be supported. As the experience of violence is inherently disempowering, sensitive measures are needed to ensure that child protection interventions do not further disempower children but rather contribute positively to their recovery and reintegration via carefully facilitated participation. The Committee notes that barriers to participation are faced by particularly marginalized and/or discriminated groups. Addressing these barriers is especially relevant for child protection, as such children are often among those most affected by violence.

64. The following two articles of the Convention also have all-embracing relevance which gives them particular significance for the implementation of article 19.

65. Article 4 (appropriate measures). Article 4 obliges States parties to undertake all appropriate measures to implement all the rights in the Convention, including article 19. In applying article 4 of the Convention, it must be noted that the right to protection from all forms of violence outlined in article 19 is a civil right and freedom. Implementation of article 19 is therefore an immediate and unqualified obligation of States parties. In the light of article 4, whatever their economic circumstances, States are required to undertake all possible measures towards the realization of the rights of the child, paying special attention to the most disadvantaged groups (see the Committee's general comment No. 5, para. 8). The article stresses that available resources must be utilized to the maximum extent.

66. Article 5 (direction and guidance consistent with evolving capacities). Implementation of article 19 requires recognition of, and support for, the primary importance of parents, extended families, legal guardians and community members in the caregiving and protection of children and the prevention of violence. This approach

is consistent with article 5, which promotes respect for the responsibilities, rights and duties of caregivers to provide, in a manner consistent with the evolving capacities of the child, appropriate direction and guidance in the exercise by the child of the rights recognized in the Convention (including in article 19). (See also para. 72 (d) on the primacy of familes in the context of national coordinating frameworks and other articles relevant to families).

67. Other relevant articles. The Convention contains numerous articles which relate explicitly or implicitly to violence and child protection. Article 19 should be read in conjunction with these articles. These comprehensive references demonstrate the need to take account of the pervasive threat to the implementation of child rights by violence in all its forms and to ensure the protection of children in all situations of life and development.

VI. NATIONAL COORDINATING FRAMEWORK ON VIOLENCE AGAINST CHILDREN

68. Beyond national plans of action. The Committee recognizes that many national plans of action adopted by States parties to implement the rights of the child include measures to prohibit, prevent and eliminate all forms of violence against children. Such plans of action, while contributing to more enjoyment by children of their rights, have nevertheless faced many challenges in their implementation, monitoring, evaluation and follow-up. For example, they have often lacked links with the overall development policy, programmes, budget and coordinating mechanisms. In order to establish a more feasible and flexible instrument, the Committee is proposing a "coordinating framework on violence against children" for all child rights-based measures to protect children from violence in all its forms and to support a protective environment.[152] Such a coordinating framework can be used in place of national plans of action where these do not yet exist or where they are proving unwieldy. Where national plans of action are being effectively implemented already, the coordinating framework can nonetheless complement those efforts, stimulate discussion and generate new ideas and resources to improve their functioning.

69. National coordinating framework on violence against children. This coordinating framework can provide a common frame of reference and a mechanism for communication among Government ministries and also for State and civil society actors at all levels with regard to needed measures, across the range of measures and at each stage of intervention identified in article 19. It can promote flexibility and creativity and allow for the development and implementation of initiatives led simultaneously by both Government and community, but which are nonetheless contained within an overall cohesive and coordinated framework. In previous reccommendations and general comments, including its general comment No. 5 on general measures of implementation, the Committee has already urged States parties to develop plans and strategies for specific aspects of the Convention (for example juvenile justice or early childhood). It is in this context that the Committee recommends the development of a national coordinating framework on protection against all forms of violence, including comprehensive prevention measures.

70. Different starting points. The Committee acknowledges that protecting children from all forms of violence is highly challenging in most countries and that States parties

---

[152] See also the overarching recommendations of the independent expert for the United Nations study on violence against children (A/61/299), para. 96.

are designing and implementing measures from very different starting points, in terms of existing legal, institutional and service infrastructures, cultural customs and professional competencies, as well as levels of resources.

71. The process of developing a national coordinating framework. There is no single model for such coordinating frameworks for freedom from all forms of violence. Some countries have invested in a discrete system of protecting children whereas others prefer to integrate protection issues into mainstream systems of implementing the rights of children. Experience shows that the process of developing a system is essential to its successful implementation. Skilful facilitation is required to ensure the participation of and ownership by senior representatives of all stakeholder groups, possibly through a multidisciplinary working group which has appropriate decision-making power, which meets regularly and which is prepared to be ambitious. A system of prevention and protection against all forms of violence should build on the strengths in existing formal and informal structures, services and organizations. Gaps should be identified and filled, based on the obligations outlined in article 19 and the Convention more broadly, and in other international and regional human rights instruments, and supported by the guidance provided in the United Nations study on violence against children, the present general comment and additional implementation supports. National planning should be a transparent and inclusive process, with full disclosure to the general public and assurance of the involvement of Government, NGOs, research and professional practice experts, parents and children. It should be accessible and understandable to both children and adults. The national coordinating framework should be fully costed and financed, including human and technical resources, and presented, if possible, within the national child budget.

72. Elements to be mainstreamed into national coordinating frameworks. The following elements need to be mainstreamed across the measures (legislative, administrative, social and educational) and stages of intervention (from prevention through to recovery and reintegration):

    (a)   *Child rights approach.* This approach is based on the declaration of the child as a rights holder and not a beneficiary of benevolent activities of adults. It includes respecting and encouraging consultation and cooperation with, and the agency of, children in the design, implementation, monitoring and evaluation of the coordinating framework and specific measures therein, taking account of the age and evolving capacities of the child or children;

    (b)   *The gender dimensions of violence against children.* States parties should ensure that policies and measures take into account the different risks facing girls and boys in respect of various forms of violence in various settings. States should address all forms of gender discrimination as part of a comprehensive violence-prevention strategy. This includes addressing gender-based stereotypes, power imbalances, inequalities and discrimination which support and perpetuate the use of violence and coercion in the home, in school and educational settings, in communities, in the workplace, in institutions and in society more broadly. Men and boys must be actively encouraged as strategic partners and allies, and along with women and girls, must be provided with opportunities to increase their respect for one another and their understanding of how to stop gender discrimination and its violent manifestations;

    (c)   *Primary (general) prevention.* See paragraph 42 of the present general comment for details;

(d)　*The primary position of families in child caregiving and protection strategies.*[153] Families (including extended families and other forms of family-type care arrangements) have the greatest potential to protect children and to prevent violence. Families can also support and empower children to protect themselves. The need to strengthen family life, support families and work with families with challenges must therefore be a priority child protection activity at every stage of intervention, particularly prevention (through establishing good child caregiving) and in early intervention. However, the Committee also recognizes that much of the violence experienced by children, including sexual abuse, takes place within a family context and stresses the necessity of intervening in families if children are exposed to violence by family members;

(e)　*Resilience and protective factors.* It is of critical importance to understand resilience and protective factors, i.e. internal and external strengths and supports which promote personal security and reduce abuse and neglect and their negative impact. Protective factors include stable families; nurturing child-rearing by adults who meet the child's physical and psychosocial needs; positive non-violent discipline; secure attachment of the child to at least one adult; supportive relationships with peers and others (including teachers); a social environment that fosters pro-social, non-violent and non-discriminatory attitudes and behaviours; high levels of community social cohesion; and thriving social networks and neighbourhood connections;

(f)　*Risk factors.* Proactive, tailored measures need to be taken to reduce the risk factors to which individual children or groups of children may be exposed in general or in particular contexts. This includes parental risk factors such as substance abuse, mental health problems and social isolation as well as family risk factors such as poverty, unemployment, discrimination and marginalization. At a universal level all children aged 0-18 years are considered vulnerable until the completion of their neural, psychological, social and physical growth and development. Babies and young children are at higher risk due to the immaturity of their developing brain and their complete dependency on adults. Both girls and boys are at risk, but violence often has a gender component;

(g)　*Children in potentially vulnerable situations.* Groups of children which are likely to be exposed to violence include, but are not limited to, children: not living with their biological parents, but in various forms of alternative care; not registered at birth; in street situations; in actual or perceived conflict with the law; with physical disabilities, sensory disabilities, learning disabilities, psychosocial disabilities and congenital, acquired and/or chronic illnesses or serious behavioural problems; who are indigenous[154] and from other ethnic minorities; from minority religious or linguistic groups; who are lesbian, gay, transgender or transsexual; at risk of harmful traditional practices; in early marriage (especially girls, and especially but not exclusively forced marriage); in hazardous child labour, including the worst forms; who are on the move as migrants or refugees, or who are displaced and/or trafficked; who have already experienced violence; who experience and witness violence in the home and in

---

[153]　See also the Guidelines for the Alternative Care of Children.

[154]　In some societies, in contrast to non-indigenous families, "neglect" as distinct from "abuse" is the primary reason leading to the removal of indigenous children from their families. Non-punitive family support services and interventions directly addressing causes (such as poverty, housing and historical circumstances) are often more appropriate. Specific efforts are required to address discrimination in the provision of services and the range of intervention options available to indigenous and other minority communities.

communities; in low socio-economic urban environments, where guns, weapons, drugs and alcohol may be easily available; living in accident- or disaster-prone areas or in toxic environments; affected by HIV/AIDS or who are themselves HIV infected; who are malnourished; looked after by other children; who are themselves carers and heads of households; born to parents who are themselves still under 18; who are unwanted, born prematurely or part of a multiple birth; hospitalized with inadequate supervision or contact with caregivers; or exposed to ICTs without adequate safeguards, supervision or empowerment to protect themselves. Children in emergencies are extremely vulnerable to violence when, as a consequence of social and armed conflicts, natural disasters and other complex and chronic emergencies, social systems collapse, children become separated from their caregivers and caregiving and safe environments are damaged or even destroyed;

(h) *Resource allocation.* Human, financial and technical resources needed across different sectors must be allocated to the maximum extent of available resources. Robust monitoring mechanisms must be developed and implemented to ensure accountability regarding allocation of budgets and their efficient utilization;

(i) *Coordination mechanisms.* Mechanisms must be explicitly outlined to ensure effective coordination at central, regional and local levels, between different sectors and with civil society, including the empirical research community. These mechanisms must be supported by the administrative measures outlined above;

(j) *Accountability.* It must be ensured that States parties, national and local agencies and organizations, and relevant civil society stakeholders proactively and cooperatively establish and apply standards, indicators, tools, and systems of monitoring, measurement and evaluation to fulfil their obligations and commitments to protect children from violence. The Committee has consistently expressed its support for systems of accountability, including in particular through data collection and analysis, indicator construction, monitoring and evaluation as well as support for independent human rights institutions. The Committee recommends that States parties publish an annual report on progress made with regard to the prohibition, prevention and elimination of violence, submit it to parliament for consideration and discussion, and invite all relevant stakeholders to respond to the information contained therein.

VII. RESOURCES FOR IMPLEMENTATION AND THE NEED FOR INTERNATIONAL COOPERATION

73. States parties' obligations. In the light of States parties' obligations under articles 4 and 19, inter alia, the Committee considers that resource constraints cannot provide a justification for a State party's failure to take any, or enough, of the measures that are required for child protection. States parties are therefore urged to adopt comprehensive, strategic and time-bound coordinating frameworks for child caregiving and protection. In particular the Committee highlights the necessity to consult with children in the development of these strategies, frameworks and measures.

74. Sources of support. Within the context of different starting points highlighted in paragraph 70 and on the understanding that budgets at national and decentralized levels should be the primary source of funds for child caregiving and protection strategies, the Committee draws the attention of States parties to the avenues of international cooperation and assistance outlined in articles 4 and 45 of the Convention. The

Committee calls upon the following partners to support, both financially and technically, child protection programmes, including training, which take full account of the requirements stipulated in article 19 and the Convention more broadly:[155] States parties providing development cooperation; donor institutions (including the World Bank, private sources and foundations); United Nations agencies and organizations; and other international and regional bodies and organizations. This financial and technical support should be provided systematically through strong and equitable partnerships, at the national and international levels. Child rights-based protection programmes should be one of the main components in assisting sustainable development in countries receiving international assistance. The Committee also encourages such bodies to continue to work with the Committee, the Special Representative of the Secretary-General on Violence against Children and other international and regional human rights mechanisms to advance this goal.

75. Resources needed at the international level. Investment is also needed in the following areas at the international level to assist States parties to fulfil their obligations in relation to article 19:

(a)   Human resources: improved communication, cooperation and individual exchange within and between professional associations (for example medical, mental health, social work, legal, education, child maltreatment, academic/research, child rights and training organizations/institutions); improved communication and cooperation within and between civil society groups (for example research communities, NGOs, child-led organizations, faith-based organizations, organizations of persons with disabilities, community and youth groups, and individual experts involved in the development and exchange of knowledge and practice);

(b)   Financial resources: improved coordination, monitoring and evaluation of donor aid; further development of financial and human capital analyses in order for economists, researchers and States parties to fully measure the costs of implementing holistic child protection systems (with an emphasis on primary prevention) versus the costs of managing the direct and indirect (including intergenerational) impact of violence at the individual, community, national and even international levels; and reviews by international financial institutions of "their policies and activities to take account of the impact they may have on children";[156]

(c)   Technical resources: evidence-based indicators, systems, models (including model legislation), tools, guidelines, protocols and practice standards for use by communities and professionals, with guidance on their adaptation to different contexts; a platform for systematic sharing and accessing of information (knowledge and practice); universally established clarity and transparency in budgeting for child rights and child protection, as well as in outcome monitoring of child protection during up and down cycles of economies and challenging circumstances (technical assistance should be established over time, through information, models and related training).

76. Regional and international cross-border cooperation. In addition to development assistance, cooperation is also needed to address child protection issues which cut across

---

[155]   See general comment No. 5 (paras. 61, 62 and 64) on: the need for the mainstreaming of children's rights into international cooperation and technical assistance; the need for such cooperation and assistance to be guided by, and to fully promote implementation of, the Convention; the allocation of a substantive part of international aid and assistance specifically to children; and the need for Poverty Reduction Strategy Papers and sector-wide approaches to development to include a strong focus on children's rights.

[156]   A/61/299, para. 117.

national borders such as: cross-border movement of children – either unaccompanied or with their families – either voluntarily or under duress (for example due to conflict, famine, natural disasters or epidemics) which can put children at risk of harm; cross-border trafficking of children for labour, sexual exploitation, adoption, removal of body parts or other purposes; conflict which cuts across borders and which may compromise a child's safety and access to protection systems, even if the child remains in the country of origin; and disasters that impact several countries simultaneously. Specific legislation, policies, programmes and partnerships may be required to protect children affected by cross-border child protection issues (for example cybercrime and extraterritorial prosecution of those who sexually abuse children through travel and tourism and traffickers of families and children), whether these children are in traditional caregiving situations or where the State is the de facto caregiver, as in the case of unaccompanied children.

General comment No 14 (2013) on the right of the child to have his or her best interests taken as a primary consideration (art. 3, para 1)

Adopted by the Committee at its sixty-second session (14 January – 1 February 2013)

"In all actions concerning children, whether undertaken by public or private social welfare institutions, courts of law, administrative authorities or legislative bodies, the best interests of the child shall be a primary consideration."

Convention on the Rights of the Child (art 3, para. 1)

I. INTRODUCTION

A. The best interests of the child: a right, a principle and a rule of procedure

1. Article 3, paragraph 1, of the Convention on the Rights of the Child gives the child the right to have his or her best interests assessed and taken into account as a primary consideration in all actions or decisions that concern him or her, both in the public and private sphere. Moreover, it expresses one of the fundamental values of the Convention. The Committee on the Rights of the Child (the Committee) has identified article 3, paragraph 1, as one of the four general principles of the Convention for interpreting and implementing all the rights of the child,[157] and applies it is a dynamic concept that requires an assessment appropriate to the specific context.

2. The concept of the "child's best interests" is not new. Indeed, it pre-dates the Convention and was already enshrined in the 1959 Declaration of the Rights of the Child (para. 2), the Convention on the Elimination of All Forms of Discrimination against Women (arts. 5 (b) and 16, para. 1 (d)), as well as in regional instruments and many national and international laws.

3. The Convention also explicitly refers to the child's best interests in other articles: article 9: separation from parents; article 10: family reunification; article 18: parental responsibilities; article 20: deprivation of family environment and alternative care; article 21: adoption; article 37(c): separation from adults in detention; article 40, paragraph 2 (b) (iii): procedural guarantees, including presence of parents at court hearings for penal matters involving children in conflict with the law. Reference is also made to the child's best interests in the Optional Protocol to the Convention on the sale of children, child prostitution and child pornography (preamble and art. 8) and in the Optional Protocol to the Convention on a communications procedure (preamble and arts. 2 and 3).

4. The concept of the child's best interests is aimed at ensuring both the full and effective enjoyment of all the rights recognized in the Convention and the holistic development of the child.[158] The Committee has already pointed out[159] that "an adult's judgment of a child's best interests cannot override the obligation to respect all the child's rights under the Convention." It recalls that there is no hierarchy of rights in the Convention; all the rights provided for therein are in the "child's best interests" and no right could be compromised by a negative interpretation of the child's best interests.

---

[157] The Committee's general comment No. 5 (2003) on the general measures of implementation of the Convention on the Rights of the Child, para. 12; and No. 12 (2009) on the right of the child to be heard, para. 2.

[158] The Committee expects States to interpret development as a "holistic concept, embracing the child's physical, mental, spiritual, moral, psychological and social development" (general comment No. 5, para. 12).

[159] General comment No. 13 (2011) on the right to protection from all forms of violence, para. 61.

5. The full application of the concept of the child's best interests requires the development of a rights-based approach, engaging all actors, to secure the holistic physical, psychological, moral and spiritual integrity of the child and promote his or her human dignity.

6. The Committee underlines that the child's best interests is a threefold concept:

(a)   A substantive right: The right of the child to have his or her best interests assessed and taken as a primary consideration when different interests are being considered in order to reach a decision on the issue at stake, and the guarantee that this right will be implemented whenever a decision is to be made concerning a child, a group of identified or unidentified children or children in general. Article 3, paragraph 1, creates an intrinsic obligation for States, is directly applicable (self-executing) and can be invoked before a court.

(b)   A fundamental, interpretative legal principle: If a legal provision is open to more than one interpretation, the interpretation which most effectively serves the child's best interests should be chosen. The rights enshrined in the Convention and its Optional Protocols provide the framework for interpretation.

(c)   A rule of procedure: Whenever a decision is to be made that will affect a specific child, an identified group of children or children in general, the decision-making process must include an evaluation of the possible impact (positive or negative) of the decision on the child or children concerned. Assessing and determining the best interests of the child require procedural guarantees. Furthermore, the justification of a decision must show that the right has been explicitly taken into account. In this regard, States parties shall explain how the right has been respected in the decision, that is, what has been considered to be in the child's best interests; what criteria it is based on; and how the child's interests have been weighed against other considerations, be they broad issues of policy or individual cases.

7. In the present general comment, the expression "the child's best interests" or "the best interests of the child" covers the three dimensions developed above.

B. Structure

8. The scope of the present general comment is limited to article 3, paragraph 1, of the Convention and does not cover article 3, paragraph 2, which pertains to the well-being of the child, nor article 3, paragraph 3, which concerns the obligation of States parties to ensure that institutions, services and facilities for children comply with the established standards, and that mechanisms are in place to ensure that the standards are respected.

9. The Committee states the objectives (chapter II) of the present general comment and presents the nature and scope of the obligation of States parties (chapter III). It also provides a legal analysis of article 3, paragraph 1 (chapter IV), showing the links to other general principles of the Convention. Chapter V is dedicated to the implementation, in practice, of the principle of best interests of the child, while chapter VI provides guidelines on disseminating the general comment.

II. OBJECTIVES

10. The present general comment seeks to ensure the application of and respect for the best interests of the child by the States parties to the Convention. It defines the requirements for due consideration, especially in judicial and administrative decisions as well as in other actions concerning the child as an individual, and at all stages of the adoption of laws, policies, strategies, programmes, plans, budgets, legislative and

budgetary initiatives and guidelines – that is, all implementation measures – concerning children in general or as a specific group. The Committee expects that this general comment will guide decisions by all those concerned with children, including parents and caregivers.

11. The best interests of the child is a dynamic concept that encompasses various issues which are continuously evolving. The present general comment provides a framework for assessing and determining the child's best interests; it does not attempt to prescribe what is best for the child in any given situation at any point in time.

12. The main objective of this general comment is to strengthen the understanding and application of the right of children to have their best interests assessed and taken as a primary consideration or, in some cases, the paramount consideration (see paragraph 38 below). Its overall objective is to promote a real change in attitudes leading to the full respect of children as rights holders. More specifically, this has implications for:

(a) The elaboration of all implementation measures taken by governments;
(b) Individual decisions made by judicial or administrative authorities or public entities through their agents that concern one or more identified children;
(c) Decisions made by civil society entities and the private sector, including profit and non-profit organizations, which provide services concerning or impacting on children;
(d) Guidelines for actions undertaken by persons working with and for children, including parents and caregivers.

III. NATURE AND SCOPE OF THE OBLIGATIONS OF STATES PARTIES

13. Each State party must respect and implement the right of the child to have his or her best interests assessed and taken as a primary consideration, and is under the obligation to take all necessary, deliberate and concrete measures for the full implementation of this right.

14. Article 3, paragraph 1, establishes a framework with three different types of obligations for States parties:

(a) The obligation to ensure that the child's best interests are *appropriately integrated and consistently applied* in every action taken by a public institution, especially in all implementation measures, administrative and judicial proceedings which directly or indirectly impact on children;
(b) The obligation to ensure that all judicial and administrative decisions as well as policies and legislation concerning children demonstrate that the child's best interests have been a primary consideration. This includes describing how the best interests have been examined and assessed, and what weight has been ascribed to them in the decision.
(c) The obligation to ensure that the interests of the child have been assessed and taken as a primary consideration in decisions and actions taken by the private sector, including those providing services, or any other private entity or institution making decisions that concern or impact on a child.

15. To ensure compliance, States parties should undertake a number of implementation measures in accordance with articles 4, 42 and 44, paragraph 6, of the Convention, and ensure that the best interests of the child are a primary consideration in all actions, including:

(a) Reviewing and, where necessary, amending domestic legislation and other sources of law so as to incorporate article 3, paragraph 1, and ensure that the requirement to consider the child's best interests is reflected and implemented in all national laws and regulations, provincial or territorial legislation, rules governing the operation of private or public institutions providing services or impacting on children, and judicial and administrative proceedings at any level, both as a substantive right and as a rule of procedure;

(b) Upholding the child's best interests in the coordination and implementation of policies at the national, regional and local levels;

(c) Establishing mechanisms and procedures for complaints, remedy or redress in order to fully realize the right of the child to have his or her best interests appropriately integrated and consistently applied in all implementation measures, administrative and judicial proceedings relevant to and with an impact on him or her;

(d) Upholding the child's best interests in the allocation of national resources for programmes and measures aimed at implementing children's rights, and in activities receiving international assistance or development aid;

(e) When establishing, monitoring and evaluating data collection, ensure that the child's best interests are explicitly spelled out and, where required, support research on children's rights issues;

(f) Providing information and training on article 3, paragraph 1, and its application in practice to all those making decisions that directly or indirectly impact on children, including professionals and other people working for and with children;

(g) Providing appropriate information to children in a language they can understand, and to their families and caregivers, so that they understand the scope of the right protected under article 3, paragraph 1, as well as creating the necessary conditions for children to express their point of view and ensuring that their opinions are given due weight;

(h) Combating all negative attitudes and perceptions which impede the full realization of the right of the child to have his or her best interests assessed and taken as a primary consideration, through communication programmes involving mass media and social networks as well as children, in order to have children recognized as rights holders.

16. In giving full effect to the child's best interests, the following parameters should be borne in mind:

(a) The universal, indivisible, interdependent and interrelated nature of children's rights;

(b) Recognition of children as right holders;

(c) The global nature and reach of the Convention;

(d) The obligation of States parties to respect, protect and fulfill all the rights in the Convention;

(e) Short-, medium- and long-term effects of actions related to the development of the child over time.

IV. LEGAL ANALYSIS AND LINKS WITH THE GENERAL PRINCIPLES OF THE CONVENTION

A. Legal analysis of article 3, paragraph 1

1. "In all actions concerning children"

(a) "in all actions"

17. Article 3, paragraph 1 seeks to ensure that the right is guaranteed in all decisions and actions concerning children. This means that every action relating to a child or children has to take into account their best interests as a primary consideration. The word "action" does not only include decisions, but also all acts, conduct, proposals, services, procedures and other measures.

18. In action or failure to take action and omissions are also "actions", for example, when social welfare authorities fail to take action to protect children from neglect or abuse.

(b) "concerning"

19. The legal duty applies to all decisions and actions that directly or indirectly affect children. Thus, the term "concerning" refers first of all, to measures and decisions directly concerning a child, children as a group or children in general, and secondly, to other measures that have an effect on an individual child, children as a group or children in general, even if they are not the direct targets of the measure. As stated in the Committee's general comment No. 7 (2005), such actions include those aimed at children (e.g. related to health, care or education), as well as actions which include children and other population groups (e.g. related to the environment, housing or transport) (para. 13 (b)). Therefore, "concerning" must be understood in a very broad sense.

20. Indeed, all actions taken by a State affect children in one way or another. This does not mean that every action taken by the State needs to incorporate a full and formal process of assessing and determining the best interests o the child. However, where a decision will have a major impact on a child or children, a greater level of protection and detailed procedures to consider their best interests is appropriate.

Thus, in relation to measures that are not directly aimed at the child or children, the term "concerning" would need to be clarified in the light of the circumstances of each case in order to be able to appreciate the impact of the action on the child or children.

(c) "children"

21. The term "children" refers to all persons under the age of 18 within the jurisdiction of a State party, without discrimination of any kind, in line with articles 1 and 2 of the Convention.

22. Article 3, paragraph 1, applies to children as individuals and places an obligation on States parties to assess and take the child's best interests as a primary consideration in individual decisions.

23. However, the term "children" implies that the right to have their best interests duly considered applies to children not only as individuals, but also in general or as a group. Accordingly, States have the obligation to assess and take as a primary consideration the best interests of children as a group or in general in all actions concerning them. This is

particularly evident for all implementation measures. The Committee[160] underlines that the child's best interests is conceived both as a collective and individual right, and that the application of this right to indigenous children as a group requires consideration of how the right relates to collective cultural rights.

24 That is not to say that in a decision concerning an individual child, his or her interests must be understood as being the same as those of children in general. Rather, article 3, paragraph 1, implies that the best interests of a child must be assessed individually. Procedures for establishing the best interests of children individually and as a group can be found in chapter V below.

2. "By public or private social welfare institutions, courts of law, administrative authorities or legislative bodies"

25. The obligation of the States to duly consider the child's best interests is a comprehensive obligation encompassing all public and private social welfare institutions, courts of law, administrative authorities and legislative bodies involving or concerning children. Although parents are not explicitly mentioned in article 3, paragraph 1, the best interests of the child "will be their basic concern" (art. 18, para. 1).

(a) "public or private social welfare institutions"

26. These terms should not be narrowly construed or limited to social institutions *stricto sensu*, but should be understood to mean all institutions whose work and decisions impact on children and the realization of their rights. Such institutions include not only those related to economic, social and cultural rights (e.g. care, health, environment, education, business, leisure and play, etc.), but also institutions dealing with civil rights and freedoms (e.g. birth registration, protection against violence in all settings, etc.). Private social welfare institutions include private sector organizations – either for-profit or non-profit – which play a role in the provision of services that are critical to children's enjoyment of their rights, and which act on behalf of or alongside Government services as an alternative.

(b) "courts of law"

27. The Committee underlines that "courts" refer to all judicial proceedings, in all instances – whether staffed by professional judges or lay persons – and all relevant procedures concerning children, without restriction. This includes conciliation, mediation and arbitration processes.

28. In criminal cases, the best interests principle applies to children in conflict (i.e. alleged, accused or recognized as having infringed) or in contact (as victims or witnesses) with the law, as well as children affected by the situation of their parents in conflict with the law. The Committee[161] underlines that protecting the child's best interests means that the traditional objectives of criminal justice, such as repression or retribution, must give way to rehabilitation and restorative justice objectives, when dealing with child offenders.

29. In civil cases, the child may be defending his or her interests directly or through a representative, in the case of paternity, child abuse or neglect, family reunification, accommodation, etc. The child may be affected by the trial, for example in procedures concerning adoption or divorce, decisions regarding custody, residence, contact or other issues which have an important impact on the life and development of the child, as well

---

[160] General comment No.11 (2009) on indigenous children and their rights under the Convention, para. 30.
[161] General comment No. 10 (2007) on children's rights in juvenile justice, para. 10.

as child abuse or neglect proceedings. The courts must provide for the best interests of the child to be considered in all such situations and decisions, whether of a procedural or substantive nature, and must demonstrate that they have effectively done so.

(c) "administrative authorities"

30. The Committee emphasizes that the scope of decisions made by administrative authorities at all levels is very broad, covering decisions concerning education, care, health, the environment, living conditions, protection, asylum, immigration, access to nationality, among others. Individual decisions taken by administrative authorities in these areas must be assessed and guided by the best interests of the child, as for all implementation measures.

(d) "legislative bodies"

31. The extension of States parties' obligation to their "legislative bodies" shows clearly that article 3, paragraph 1, relates to children in general, not only to children as individuals. The adoption of any law or regulation as well as collective agreements – such as bilateral or multilateral trade or peace treaties which affect children – should be governed by the best interests of the child. The right of the child to have his or her best interests assessed and taken as a primary consideration should be explicitly included in all relevant legislation, not only in laws that specifically concern children. This obligation extends also to the approval of budgets, the preparation and development of which require the adoption of a best-interests-of-the-child perspective for it to be child-rights sensitive.

3. "The best interests of the child"

32. The concept of the child's best interests is complex and its content must be determined on a case-by-case basis. It is through the interpretation and implementation of article 3, paragraph 1, in line with the other provisions of the Convention, that the legislator, judge, administrative, social or educational authority will be able to clarify the concept and make concrete use thereof. Accordingly, the concept of the child's best interests is flexible and adaptable. It should be adjusted and defined on an individual basis, according to the specific situation of the child or children concerned, taking into consideration their personal context, situation and needs. For individual decisions, the child's best interests must be assessed and determined in light of the specific circumstances of the particular child. For collective decisions – such as by the legislator –, the best interests of children in general must be assessed and determined in light of the circumstances of the particular group and/or children in general. In both cases, assessment and determination should be carried out with full respect for the rights contained in the Convention and its Optional Protocols.

33. The child's best interests shall be applied to all matters concerning the child or children, and taken into account to resolve any possible conflicts among the rights enshrined in the Convention or other human rights treaties. Attention must be placed on identifying possible solutions which are in the child's best interests. This implies that States are under the obligation to clarify the best interests of all children, including those in vulnerable situations, when adopting implementation measures.

34. The flexibility of the concept of the child's best interests allows it to be responsive to the situation of individual children and to evolve knowledge about child development. However, it may also leave room for manipulation; the concept of the child's best interests has been abused by Governments and other State authorities to justify racist

policies, for example; by parents to defend their own interests in custody disputes; by professionals who could not be bothered, and who dismiss the assessment of the child's best interests as irrelevant or unimportant.

35. With regard to implementation measures, ensuring that the best interests of the child are a primary consideration in legislation and policy development and delivery at all levels of Government demands a continuous process of child rights impact assessment (CRIA) to predict the impact of any proposed law, policy or budgetary allocation on children and the enjoyment of their rights, and child rights impact evaluation to evaluate the actual impact of implementation.[162]

4. "Shall be a primary consideration"

36. The best interests of a child shall be a primary consideration in the adoption of all measures of implementation. The words "shall be" place a strong legal obligation on States and mean that States may not exercise discretion as to whether children's best interests are to be assessed and ascribed the proper weight as a primary consideration in any action undertaken.

37. The expression "primary consideration" means that the child's best interests may not be considered on the same level as all other considerations. This strong position is justified by the special situation of the child: dependency, maturity, legal status and, often, voicelessness. Children have less possibility than adults to make a strong case for their own interests and those involved in decisions affecting them must be explicitly aware of their interests. If the interests of children are not highlighted, they tend to be overlooked.

38. In respect of adoption (art. 21), the right of best interests is further strengthened; it is not simply to be "**a primary** consideration" but "**the paramount** consideration". Indeed, the best interests of the child are to be the determining factor when taking a decision on adoption, but also on other issues.

39. However, since article 3, paragraph 1, covers a wide range of situations, the Committee recognizes the need for a degree of flexibility in its application. The best interests of the child – once assessed and determined – might conflict with other interests or rights (e.g. of other children, the public, parents, etc.). Potential conflicts between the best interests of a child, considered individually, and those of a group of children or children in general have to be resolved on a case-by-case basis, carefully balancing the interests of all parties and finding a suitable compromise. The same must be done if the rights of other persons are in conflict with the child's best interests. If harmonization is not possible, authorities and decision-makers will have to analyse and weigh the rights of all those concerned, bearing in mind that the right of the child to have his or her best interests taken as a primary consideration means that the child's interests have high priority and not just one of several considerations. Therefore, a larger weight must be attached to what serves the child best.

40. Viewing the best interests of the child as "primary" requires a consciousness about the place that children's interests must occupy in all actions and a willingness to give priority to those interests in all circumstances, but especially when an action has an undeniable impact on the children concerned.

---

[162] General comment No. 5 (2003) on general measures of implementation of the Convention on the Rights of the Child, para. 45.

B. The best interests of the child and links with other general principles of the Convention

1. The child's best interests and the right to non-discrimination (art. 2)

41. The right to non-discrimination is not a passive obligation, prohibiting all forms of discrimination in the enjoyment of rights under the Convention, but also requires appropriate proactive measures taken by the State to ensure effective equal opportunities for all children to enjoy the rights under the Convention. This may require positive measures aimed at redressing a situation of real inequality.

2. The child's best interests and the right to life, survival and development (art. 6)

42. States must create an environment that respects human dignity and ensures the holistic development of every child. In the assessment and determination of the child's best interests, the State must ensure full respect for his or her inherent right to life, survival and development.

3. The child's best interests and the right to be heard (art. 12)

43. Assessment of a child's best interests must include respect for the child's right to express his or her views freely and due weight given to said views in all matters affecting the child. This is clearly set out in the Committee's general comment No. 12 which also highlights the inextricable links between articles 3, paragraph 1, and 12. The two articles have complementary roles: the first aims to realize the child's best interests, and the second provides the methodology for hearing the views of the child or children and their inclusion in all matters affecting the child, including the assessment of his or her best interests. Article 3, paragraph 1, cannot be correctly applied if the requirements of article 12 are not met. Similarly, article 3, paragraph 1, reinforces the functionality of article 12, by facilitating the essential role of children in all decisions affecting their lives.[163]

44. The evolving capacities of the child (art. 5) must be taken into consideration when the child's best interests and right to be heard are at stake. The Committee has already established that the more the child knows, has experienced and understands, the more the parent, legal guardian or other persons legally responsible for him or her have to transform direction and guidance into reminders and advice, and later to an exchange on an equal footing.[164] Similarly, as the child matures, his or her views shall have increasing weight in the assessment of his or her best interests. Babies and very young children have the same rights as all children to have their best interests assessed, even if they cannot express their views or represent themselves in the same way as older children. States must ensure appropriate arrangements, including representation, when appropriate, for the assessment of their best interests; the same applies for children who are not able or willing to express a view.

45. The Committee recalls that article 12, paragraph 2, of the Convention provides for the right of the child to be heard, either directly or through a representative, in any judicial or administrative proceeding affecting him or her (see further chapter V.B below).

---

[163] General comment No. 12, paras. 70-74.
[164] Ibid., para. 84.

V. IMPLEMENTATION: ASSESSING AND DETERMINING THE CHILD'S BEST INTERESTS

46. As stated earlier, the "best interests of the child" is a right, a principle and a rule of procedure based on an assessment of all elements of a child's or children's interests in a specific situation. When assessing and determining the best interests of the child in order to make a decision on a specific measure, the following steps should be followed:

(a)   First, within the specific factual context of the case, find out what are the relevant elements in a best-interests assessment, give them concrete content, and assign a weight to each in relation to one another;

(b)   Secondly, to do so, follow a procedure that ensures legal guarantees and proper application of the right.

47. Assessment and determination of the child's best interests are two steps to be followed when required to make a decision. The "best-interests assessment" consists in evaluating and balancing all the elements necessary to make a decision in a specific situation for a specific individual child or group of children. It is carried out by the decision-maker and his or her staff – if possible a multidisciplinary team – and requires the participation of the child. The "best-interests determination" describes the formal process with strict procedural safeguards designed to determine the child's best interests on the basis of the best-interests assessment.

A. Best interests assessment and determination

48. Assessing the child's best interests is a unique activity that should be undertaken in each individual case, in the light of the specific circumstances of each child or group of children or children in general. These circumstances relate to the individual characteristics of the child or children concerned, such as, inter alia, age, sex, level of maturity, experience, belonging to a minority group, having a physical, sensory or intellectual disability, as well as the social and cultural context in which the child or children find themselves, such as the presence or absence of parents, whether the child lives with them, quality of the relationships between the child and his or her family or caregivers, the environment in relation to safety, the existence of quality alternative means available to the family, extended family or caregivers, etc.

49. Determining what is in the best interests of the child should start with an assessment of the specific circumstances that make the child unique. This implies that some elements will be used and others will not, and also influences how they will be weighted against each other. For children in general, assessing best interests involves the same elements.

50. The Committee considers it useful to draw up a non-exhaustive and non-hierarchical list of elements that could be included in a best-interests assessment by any decision-maker having to determine a child's best interests. The non-exhaustive nature of the elements in the list implies that it is possible to go beyond those and consider other factors relevant in the specific circumstances of the individual child or group of children. All the elements of the list must be taken into consideration and balanced in light of each situation. The list should provide concrete guidance, yet flexibility.

51. Drawing up such a list of elements would provide guidance for the State or decision-maker in regulating specific areas affecting children, such as family, adoption and juvenile justice laws, and if necessary, other elements deemed appropriate in accordance with its legal tradition may be added. The Committee would like to point out that, when adding elements to the list, the ultimate purpose of the child's best interests should be to ensure the full and effective enjoyment of the rights recognized in the Convention and the holistic development of the child. Consequently, elements that

are contrary to the rights enshrined in the Convention or that would have an effect contrary to the rights under the Convention cannot be considered as valid in assessing what is best for a child or children.

1. Elements to be taken into account when assessing the child's best interests

52. Based on these preliminary considerations, the Committee considers that the elements to be taken into account when assessing and determining the child's best interests, as relevant to the situation in question, are as follows:

(a) The child's views

53. Article 12 of the Convention provides for the right of children to express their views in every decision that affects them. Any decision that does not take into account the child's views or does not give their views due weight according to their age and maturity, does not respect the possibility for the child or children to influence the determination of their best interests.

54. The fact that the child is very young or in a vulnerable situation (e.g. has a disability, belongs to a minority group, is a migrant, etc.) does not deprive him or her of the right to express his or her views, nor reduces the weight given to the child's views in determining his or her best interests. The adoption of specific measures to guarantee the exercise of equal rights for children in such situations must be subject to an individual assessment which assures a role to the children themselves in the decision-making process, and the provision of reasonable accommodation[165] and support, where necessary, to ensure their full participation in the assessment of their best interests.

(b) The child's identity

55. Children are not a homogeneous group and therefore diversity must be taken into account when assessing their best interests. The identity of the child includes characteristics such as sex, sexual orientation, national origin, religion and beliefs, cultural identity, personality. Although children and young people share basic universal needs, the expression of those needs depends on a wide range of personal, physical, social and cultural aspects, including their evolving capacities. The right of the child to preserve his or her identity is guaranteed by the Convention (art. 8) and must be respected and taken into consideration in the assessment of the child's best interests.

56. Regarding religious and cultural identity, for example, when considering a foster home or placement for a child, due regard shall be paid to the desirability of continuity in a child's upbringing and to the child's ethnic, religious, cultural and linguistic background (art. 20, para. 3), and the decision-maker must take into consideration this specific context when assessing and determining the child's best interests. The same applies in cases of adoption, separation from or divorce of parents. Due consideration of the child's best interests implies that children have access to the culture (and language, if possible) of their country and family of origin, and the opportunity to access information about their biological family, in accordance with the legal and professional regulations of the given country (see art. 9, para. 4).

57. Although preservation of religious and cultural values and traditions as part of the identity of the child must be taken into consideration, practices that are inconsistent or incompatible with the rights established in the Convention are not in the child's best

---

[165] See Convention on the Rights of Persons with Disabilities, art. 2: "Reasonable accommodation" means necessary and appropriate modification and adjustments not imposing a disproportionate or undue burden, where needed in a particular case, to ensure [...] the enjoyment or exercise on an equal basis with others of all human rights and fundamental freedoms.

interests. Cultural identity cannot excuse or justify the perpetuation by decision-makers and authorities of traditions and cultural values that deny the child or children the rights guaranteed by the Convention.

(c) Preservation of the family environment and maintaining relations

58. The Committee recalls that it is indispensable to carry out the assessment and determination of the child's best interests in the context of potential separation of a child from his or her parents (arts. 9, 18 and 20). It also underscores that the elements mentioned above are concrete rights and not only elements in the determination of the best interests of the child.

59. The family is the fundamental unit of society and the natural environment for the growth and well-being of its members, particularly children (preamble of the Convention). The right of the child to family life is protected under the Convention (art. 16). The term "family" must be interpreted in a broad sense to include biological, adoptive or foster parents or, where applicable, the members of the extended family or community as provided for by local custom (art. 5).

60. Preventing family separation and preserving family unity are important components of the child protection system, and are based on the right provided for in article 9, paragraph 1, which requires "that a child shall not be separated from his or her parents against their will, except when [...] such separation is necessary for the best interests of the child". Furthermore, the child who is separated from one or both parents is entitled "to maintain personal relations and direct contact with both parents on a regular basis, except if it is contrary to the child's best interests" (art. 9, para. 3). This also extends to any person holding custody rights, legal or customary primary caregivers, foster parents and persons with whom the child has a strong personal relationship.

61. Given the gravity of the impact on the child of separation from his or her parents, such separation should only occur as a last resort measure, as when the child is in danger of experiencing imminent harm or when otherwise necessary; separation should not take place if less intrusive measures could protect the child. Before resorting to separation, the State should provide support to the parents in assuming their parental responsibilities, and restore or enhance the family's capacity to take care of the child, unless separation is necessary to protect the child. Economic reasons cannot be a justification for separating a child from his or her parents.

62. The Guidelines for the Alternative Care of Children[166] aims to ensure that children are not placed in alternative care unnecessarily; and that where alternative care is provided, it is delivered under appropriate conditions responding to the rights and best interests of the child. In particular, "financial and material poverty, or conditions directly and uniquely imputable to such poverty, should never be the only justification for the removal of a child from parental care [. . .] but should be seen as a signal for the need to provide appropriate support to the family" (para. 15).

63. Likewise, a child may not be separated from his or her parents on the grounds of a disability of either the child or his or her parents.[167] Separation may be considered only in cases where the necessary assistance to the family to preserve the family unit is not effective enough to avoid a risk of neglect or abandonment of the child or a risk to the child's safety.

---

[166] General Assembly resolution 64/142, annex.
[167] Convention on the Rights of Persons with Disabilities, art. 23, para. 4.

64. In case of separation, the State must guarantee that the situation of the child and his or her family has been assessed, where possible, by a multidisciplinary team of well-trained professionals with appropriate judicial involvement, in conformity with article 9 of the Convention, ensuring that no other option can fulfil the child's best interests.

65. When separation becomes necessary, the decision-makers shall ensure that the child maintains the linkages and relations with his or her parents and family (siblings, relatives and persons with whom the child has had strong personal relationships) unless this is contrary to the child's best interests. The quality of the relationships and the need to retain them must be taken into consideration in decisions on the frequency and length of visits and other contact when a child is placed outside the family.

66. When the child's relations with his or her parents are interrupted by migration (of the parents without the child, or of the child without his or her parents), preservation of the family unit should be taken into account when assessing the best interests of the child in decisions on family reunification.

67. The Committee is of the view that shared parental responsibilities are generally in the child's best interests. However, in decisions regarding parental responsibilities, the only criterion shall be what is in the best interests of the particular child. It is contrary to those interests if the law automatically gives parental responsibilities to either or both parents. In assessing the child's best interests, the judge must take into consideration the right of the child to preserve his or her relationship with both parents, together with the other elements relevant to the case.

68. The Committee encourages the ratification and implementation of the conventions of the Hague Conference on Private International Law,[168] which facilitate the application of the child's best interests and provide guarantees for its implementation in the event that the parents live in different countries.

69. In cases where the parents or other primary caregivers commit an offence, alternatives to detention should be made available and applied on a case-by-case basis, with full consideration of the likely impacts of different sentences on the best interests of the affected child or children.[169]

70. Preservation of the family environment encompasses the preservation of the ties of the child in a wider sense. These ties apply to the extended family, such as grandparents, uncles/aunts as well friends, school and the wider environment and are particularly relevant in cases where parents are separated and live in different places.

(d) Care, protection and safety of the child

71. When assessing and determining the best interests of a child or children in general, the obligation of the State to ensure the child such protection and care as is necessary for his or her well-being (art. 3, para. 2) should be taken into consideration. The terms "protection and care" must also be read in a broad sense, since their objective is not stated in limited or negative terms (such as "to protect the child from harm"), but rather in relation to the comprehensive ideal of ensuring the child's "well-being" and development. Children's well-being, in a broad sense includes their basic material, physical, educational, and emotional needs, as well as needs for affection and safety.

---

[168] These include No. 28 on the Civil Aspects of International Child Abduction, 1980; No. 33 on Protection of Children and Co-operation in Respect of Intercountry Adoption, 1993; No. 23 on the Recognition and Enforcement of Decisions Relating to Maintenance Obligations, 1973; No. 24 on the Law Applicable to Maintenance Obligations, 1973.

[169] See recommendations of the Day of general discussion on children of incarcerated parents (2011).

72. Emotional care is a basic need of children; if parents or other primary caregivers do not fulfil the child's emotional needs, action must be taken so that the child develops a secure attachment. Children need to form an attachment to a caregiver at a very early age, and such attachment, if adequate, must be sustained over time in order to provide the child with a stable environment.

73. Assessment of the child's best interests must also include consideration of the child's safety, that is, the right of the child to protection against all forms of physical or mental violence, injury or abuse (art. 19), sexual harassment, peer pressure, bullying, degrading treatment, etc.,[170] as well as protection against sexual, economic and other exploitation, drugs, labour, armed conflict, etc.(arts. 32-39).

74. Applying a best-interests approach to decision-making means assessing the safety and integrity of the child at the current time; however, the precautionary principle also requires assessing the possibility of future risk and harm and other consequences of the decision for the child's safety.

(e) Situation of vulnerability

75. An important element to consider is the child's situation of vulnerability, such as disability, belonging to a minority group, being a refugee or asylum seeker, victim of abuse, living in a street situation, etc. The purpose of determining the best interests of a child or children in a vulnerable situation should not only be in relation to the full enjoyment of all the rights provided for in the Convention, but also with regard to other human rights norms related to these specific situations, such as those covered in the Convention on the Rights of Persons with Disabilities, the Convention relating to the Status of Refugees, among others.

76. The best interests of a child in a specific situation of vulnerability will not be the same as those of all the children in the same vulnerable situation. Authorities and decision-makers need to take into account the different kinds and degrees of vulnerability of each child, as each child is unique and each situation must be assessed according to the child's uniqueness. An individualized assessment of each child's history from birth should be carried out, with regular reviews by a multidisciplinary team and recommended reasonable accommodation throughout the child's development process.

(f) The child's right to health

77. The child's right to health (art. 24) and his or her health condition are central in assessing the child's best interest. However, if there is more than one possible treatment for a health condition or if the outcome of a treatment is uncertain, the advantages of all possible treatments must be weighed against all possible risks and side effects, and the views of the child must also be given due weight based on his or her age and maturity. In this respect, children should be provided with adequate and appropriate information in order to understand the situation and all the relevant aspects in relation to their interests, and be allowed, when possible, to give their consent in an informed manner.[171]

78. For example, as regards adolescent health, the Committee[172] has stated that States parties have the obligation to ensure that all adolescents, both in and out of school, have access to adequate information that is essential for their health and development in order to make appropriate health behaviour choices. This should include information on

---

[170]   General comment No. 13 (2011) on the right of the child to freedom from all forms of violence.

[171]   General comment No. 15 (2013) on the right of the child to the enjoyment of the highest attainable standard of health (art. 24), para. 31.

[172]   General comment No. 4 (2003) on adolescent health and development in the context of the Convention on the Rights of the Child.

use and abuse of tobacco, alcohol and other substances, diet, appropriate sexual and reproductive information, dangers of early pregnancy, prevention of HIV/AIDS and of sexually transmitted diseases. Adolescents with a psychosocial disorder have the right to be treated and cared for in the community in which he or she lives, to the extent possible. Where hospitalization or placement in a residential institution is necessary, the best interests of the child must be assessed prior to taking a decision and with respect for the child's views; the same considerations are valid for younger children. The health of the child and possibilities for treatment may also be part of a best-interests assessment and determination with regard to other types of significant decisions (e.g. granting a residence permit on humanitarian grounds).

(g) The child's right to education

79. It is in the best interests of the child to have access to quality education, including early childhood education, non-formal or informal education and related activities, free of charge. All decisions on measures and actions concerning a specific child or a group of children must respect the best interests of the child or children, with regard to education. In order to promote education, or better quality education, for more children, States parties need to have well-trained teachers and other professionals working in different education-related settings, as well as a child-friendly environment and appropriate teaching and learning methods, taking into consideration that education is not only an investment in the future, but also an opportunity for joyful activities, respect, participation and fulfilment of ambitions. Responding to this requirement and enhancing children's responsibilities to overcome the limitations of their vulnerability of any kind, will be in their best interests.

2. Balancing the elements in the best-interests assessment

80. It should be emphasized that the basic best-interests assessment is a general assessment of all relevant elements of the child's best interests, the weight of each element depending on the others. Not all the elements will be relevant to every case, and different elements can be used in different ways in different cases. The content of each element will necessarily vary from child to child and from case to case, depending on the type of decision and the concrete circumstances, as will the importance of each element in the overall assessment.

81. The elements in the best-interests assessment may be in conflict when considering a specific case and its circumstances. For example, preservation of the family environment may conflict with the need to protect the child from the risk of violence or abuse by parents. In such situations, the elements will have to be weighted against each other in order to find the solution that is in the best interests of the child or children.

82. In weighing the various elements, one needs to bear in mind that the purpose of assessing and determining the best interests of the child is to ensure the full and effective enjoyment of the rights recognized in the Convention and its Optional Protocols, and the holistic development of the child.

83. There might be situations where "protection" factors affecting a child (e.g. which may imply limitation or restriction of rights) need to be assessed in relation to measures of "empowerment" (which implies full exercise of rights without restriction). In such situations, the age and maturity of the child should guide the balancing of the elements. The physical, emotional, cognitive and social development of the child should be taken into account to assess the level of maturity of the child.

84. In the best-interests assessment, one has to consider that the capacities of the child will evolve. Decision-makers should therefore consider measures that can be revised or

adjusted accordingly, instead of making definitive and irreversible decisions. To do this, they should not only assess the physical, emotional, educational and other needs at the specific moment of the decision, but should also consider the possible scenarios of the child's development, and analyse them in the short and long term. In this context, decisions should assess continuity and stability of the child's present and future situation.

B. Procedural safeguards to guarantee the implementation of the child's best interests

85. To ensure the correct implementation of the child's right to have his or her best interests taken as a primary consideration, some child-friendly procedural safeguards must be put in place and followed. As such, the concept of the child's best interests is a rule of procedure (see para. 6 (b) above).

86. While public authorities and organizations making decisions that concern children must act in conformity with the obligation to assess and determine the child's best interests, people who make decisions concerning children on a daily basis (e.g. parents, guardians, teachers, etc.) are not expected to follow strictly this two-step procedure, even though decisions made in everyday life must also respect and reflect the child's best interests.

87. States must put in place formal processes, with strict procedural safeguards, designed to assess and determine the child's best interests for decisions affecting the child, including mechanisms for evaluating the results. States must develop transparent and objective processes for all decisions made by legislators, judges or administrative authorities, especially in areas which directly affect the child or children.

88. The Committee invites States and all persons who are in a position to assess and determine the child's best interests to pay special attention to the following safeguards and guarantees:

(a) Right of the child to express his or her own views

89. A vital element of the process is communicating with children to facilitate meaningful child participation and identify their best interests. Such communication should include informing children about the process and possible sustainable solutions and services, as well as collecting information from children and seeking their views.

90. Where the child wishes to express his or her views and where this right is fulfilled through a representative, the latter's obligation is to communicate accurately the views of the child. In situations where the child's views are in conflict with those of his or her representative, a procedure should be established to allow the child to approach an authority to establish a separate representation for the child (e.g. a guardian ad litem), if necessary.

91. The procedure for assessing and determining the best interests of children as a group is, to some extent, different from that regarding an individual child. When the interests of a large number of children are at stake, Government institutions must find ways to hear the views of a representative sample of children and give due consideration to their opinions when planning measures or making legislative decisions which directly or indirectly concern the group, in order to ensure that all categories of children are covered. There are many examples of how to do this, including children's hearings, children's parliaments, children-led organizations, children's unions or other representative bodies, discussions at school, social networking websites, etc.

(b) Establishment of facts

92. Facts and information relevant to a particular case must be obtained by well-trained professionals in order to draw up all the elements necessary for the best-interests assessment. This could involve interviewing persons close to the child, other people who are in contact with the child on a daily basis, witnesses to certain incidents, among others. Information and data gathered must be verified and analysed prior to being used in the child's or children's best-interests assessment.

(c) Time perception

93. The passing of time is not perceived in the same way by children and adults. Delays in or prolonged decision-making have particularly adverse effects on children as they evolve. It is therefore advisable that procedures or processes regarding or impacting children be prioritized and completed in the shortest time possible. The timing of the decision should, as far as possible, correspond to the child's perception of how it can benefit him or her, and the decisions taken should be reviewed at reasonable intervals as the child develops and his or her capacity to express his or her views evolves. All decisions on care, treatment, placement and other measures concerning the child must be reviewed periodically in terms of his or her perception of time, and his or her evolving capacities and development (art. 25).

(d) Qualified professionals

94. Children are a diverse group, with each having his or her own characteristics and needs that can only be adequately assessed by professionals who have expertise in matters related to child and adolescent development. This is why the formal assessment process should be carried out in a friendly and safe atmosphere by professionals trained in, inter alia, child psychology, child development and other relevant human and social development fields, who have experience working with children and who will consider the information received in an objective manner. As far as possible, a multidisciplinary team of professionals should be involved in assessing the child's best interests.

95. The assessment of the consequences of alternative solutions must be based on general knowledge (i.e. in the areas of law, sociology, education, social work, psychology, health, etc.) of the likely consequences of each possible solution for the child, given his or her individual characteristics and past experience.

(e) Legal representation

96. The child will need appropriate legal representation when his or her best interests are to be formally assessed and determined by courts and equivalent bodies. In particular, in cases where a child is referred to an administrative or judicial procedure involving the determination of his or her best interests, he or she should be provided with a legal representative, in addition to a guardian or representative of his or her views, when there is a potential conflict between the parties in the decision.

(f) Legal reasoning

97. In order to demonstrate that the right of the child to have his or her best interests assessed and taken as a primary consideration has been respected, any decision concerning the child or children must be motivated, justified and explained. The motivation should state explicitly all the factual circumstances regarding the child, what elements have been found relevant in the best-interests assessment, the content of the elements in the individual case, and how they have been weighted to determine the child's best interests. If the decision differs from the views of the child, the reason for that should be clearly stated. If, exceptionally, the solution chosen is not in the best

interests of the child, the grounds for this must be set out in order to show that the child's best interests were a primary consideration despite the result. It is not sufficient to state in general terms that other considerations override the best interests of the child; all considerations must be explicitly specified in relation to the case at hand, and the reason why they carry greater weight in the particular case must be explained. The reasoning must also demonstrate, in a credible way, why the best interests of the child were not strong enough to be outweigh the other considerations. Account must be taken of those circumstances in which the best interests of the child must be the paramount consideration (see paragraph 38 above).

(g) Mechanisms to review or revise decisions

98. States should establish mechanisms within their legal systems to appeal or revise decisions concerning children when a decision seems not to be in accordance with the appropriate procedure of assessing and determining the child's or children's best interests. There should always be the possibility to request a review or to appeal such a decision at the national level. Mechanisms should be made known to the child and be accessible by him or her directly or by his or her legal representative, if it is considered that the procedural safeguards had not been respected, the facts are wrong, the best-interests assessment had not been adequately carried out or that competing considerations had been given too much weight. The reviewing body must look into all these aspects.

(h) Child-rights impact assessment (CRIA)

99. As mentioned above, the adoption of all measures of implementation should also follow a procedure that ensures that the child's best interests are a primary consideration. The child-rights impact assessment (CRIA) can predict the impact of any proposed policy, legislation, regulation, budget or other administrative decision which affect children and the enjoyment of their rights and should complement ongoing monitoring and evaluation of the impact of measures on children's rights.[173] CRIA needs to be built into Government processes at all levels and as early as possible in the development of policy and other general measures in order to ensure good governance for children's rights. Different methodologies and practices may be developed when undertaking CRIA. At a minimum, they must use the Convention and its Optional Protocols as a framework, in particular ensuring that the assessments are underpinned by the general principles and have special regard for the differentiated impact of the measure(s) under consideration on children. The impact assessment itself could be based on input from children, civil society and experts, as well as from relevant Government departments, academic research and experiences documented in the country or elsewhere. The analysis should result in recommendations for amendments, alternatives and improvements and be made publicly available.[174]

VI. DISSEMINATION

100. The Committee recommends that States widely disseminate the present general comment to parliaments, governments and the judiciary, nationally and locally. It should also be made known to children – including those in situations of exclusion –, all professionals working for and with children (including judges, lawyers, teachers, guardians, social workers, staff of public or private welfare institutions, health staff,

---

[173] General comment No. 16 (2013) on State obligations regarding the impact of the business sector on children's rights, paras. 78-81.

[174] States may draw guidance from the Report of the Special Rapporteur on the right to food on Guiding principles on human rights impact assessments of trade and investment agreements (A/HRC/19/59/Add.5).

teachers, etc.) and civil society at large. To do this, the general comment should be translated into relevant languages, child-friendly/appropriate versions should be made available, conferences, seminars, workshops and other events should be held to share best practices on how best to implement it. It should also be incorporated into the formal pre- and in-service training of all concerned professionals and technical staff.

101. States should include information in their periodic reporting to the Committee on the challenges they face and the measures they have taken to apply and respect the child's best interests in all judicial and administrative decisions and other actions concerning the child as an individual, as well as at all stages of the adoption of implementation measures concerning children in general or as a specific group.

General comment No 15 (2013) on the right of the child to the enjoyment of the highest attainable standard of health (art. 24)

Adopted by the Committee at its sixty-second session (14 January – 1 February 2013)

I. INTRODUCTION

1. The present general comment is based on the importance of approaching children's health from a child-rights perspective that all children have the right to opportunities to survive, grow and develop, within the context of physical, emotional and social well-being, to each child's full potential. Throughout this general comment, "child" refers to an individual below the age of 18 years, in accordance with article 1 of the Convention on the Rights of the Child (hereinafter "the Convention"). Despite the remarkable achievements in fulfilling children's rights to health in recent years since the adoption of the Convention, significant challenges remain. The Committee on the Rights of the Child (hereinafter "the Committee") recognizes that most mortality, morbidity and disabilities among children could be prevented if there were political commitment and sufficient allocation of resources directed towards the application of available knowledge and technologies for prevention, treatment and care. The present general comment was prepared with the aim of providing guidance and support to States parties and other duty bearers to support them in respecting, protecting and fulfilling children's right to the enjoyment of the highest attainable standard of health (hereinafter "children's right to health").

2. The Committee interprets children's right to health as defined in article 24 as an inclusive right, extending not only to timely and appropriate prevention, health promotion, curative, rehabilitative and palliative services, but also to a right to grow and develop to their full potential and live in conditions that enable them to attain the highest standard of health through the implementation of programmes that address the underlying determinants of health. A holistic approach to health places the realization of children's right to health within the broader framework of international human rights obligations.

3. The Committee addresses this general comment to a range of stakeholders working in the fields of children's rights and public health, including policymakers, programme implementers and activists, as well as parents and children themselves. It is explicitly generic in order to ensure its relevance to a wide range of children's health problems, health systems and the varied contexts that exist in different countries and regions. It focuses primarily on article 24, paragraphs 1 and 2, and also addresses article 24, paragraph 4.[175] Implementation of article 24 must take into account all human rights principles, especially the guiding principles of the Convention, and must be shaped by evidence-based public health standards and best practices.

4. In the Constitution of the World Health Organization, States have agreed to regard health as a state of complete physical, mental and social well-being and not merely the absence of disease or infirmity.[176] This positive understanding of health provides the public health foundation for the present general comment. Article 24 explicitly mentions primary health care, an approach to which was defined in the Declaration of

---

[175] Article 24, paragraph 3, is not covered because a general comment on harmful practices is currently being developed.

[176] Preamble to the Constitution of the World Health Organization (WHO) as adopted by the International Health Conference, New York, 22 July 1946

Alma-Ata[177] and reinforced by the World Health Assembly.[178] This approach emphasizes the need to eliminate exclusion and reduce social disparities in health; organize health services around people's needs and expectations; integrate health into related sectors; pursue collaborative models of policy dialogue; and increase stakeholder participation, including the demand for and appropriate use of services.

5. Children's health is affected by a variety of factors, many of which have changed during the past 20 years and are likely to continue to evolve in the future. This includes the attention given to new health problems and changing health priorities, such as: HIV/AIDS, pandemic influenza, non-communicable diseases, importance of mental health care, care of the new born, and neonatal and adolescent mortality; increased understanding of the factors that contribute to death, disease and disability in children, including structural determinants, such as the global economic and financial situation, poverty, unemployment, migration and population displacements, war and civil unrest, discrimination and marginalization. There is also a growing understanding of the impact of climate change and rapid urbanization on children's health; the development of new technologies, such as vaccines and pharmaceuticals; a stronger evidence base for effective biomedical, behavioural and structural interventions, as well as some cultural practices that relate to child-rearing and have proved to have a positive impact on children.

6. Advances in information and communication technologies have created new opportunities and challenges to achieve children's right to health. Despite the additional resources and technologies that have now become available to the health sector, many countries still fail to provide universal access to basic children's health promotion, prevention and treatment services. A wide range of different duty bearers need to be involved if children's right to health is to be fully realized and the central role played by parents and other caregivers needs to be better recognized. Relevant stakeholders will need to be engaged, working at national, regional, district and community levels, including governmental and non-governmental partners, private sector and funding organizations. States have an obligation to ensure that all duty bearers have sufficient awareness, knowledge and capacity to fulfil their obligations and responsibilities, and that children's capacity is sufficiently developed to enable them to claim their right to health.

II. PRINCIPLES AND PREMISES FOR REALIZING CHILDREN'S RIGHT TO HEALTH

A. *The indivisibility and interdependence of children's rights*

7. The Convention recognizes the interdependence and equal importance of all rights (civil, political, economic, social and cultural) that enable all children to develop their mental and physical abilities, personalities and talents to the fullest extent possible. Not only is children's right to health important in and of itself, but also the realization of the right to health is indispensable for the enjoyment of all the other rights in the Convention. Moreover, achieving children's right to health is dependent on the realization of many other rights outlined in the Convention.

B. *Right to non-discrimination*

8. In order to fully realize the right to health for all children, States parties have an obligation to ensure that children's health is not undermined as a result of

---

[177] Declaration of Alma-Ata, International Conference on Primary Health Care, Alma-Ata, 6–12 September 1978.

[178] World Health Assembly, Primary health care including health systems strengthening, document A62/8.

discrimination, which is a significant factor contributing to vulnerability. A number of grounds on which discrimination is proscribed are outlined in article 2 of the Convention, including the child's, parent's or legal guardian's race, colour, sex, language, religion, political or other opinion, national, ethnic or social origin, property, disability, birth or other status. These also include sexual orientation, gender identity and health status, for example HIV status and mental health.[179] Attention should also be given to any other forms of discrimination that might undermine children's health, and the implications of multiple forms of discrimination should also be addressed.

9. Gender-based discrimination is particularly pervasive, affecting a wide range of outcomes, from female infanticide/foeticide to discriminatory infant and young child feeding practices, gender stereotyping and access to services. Attention should be given to the differing needs of girls and boys, and the impact of gender-related social norms and values on the health and development of boys and girls. Attention also needs to be given to harmful gender-based practices and norms of behaviour that are ingrained in traditions and customs and undermine the right to health of girls and boys.

10. All policies and programmes affecting children's health should be grounded in a broad approach to gender equality that ensures young women's full political participation; social and economic empowerment; recognition of equal rights related to sexual and reproductive health; and equal access to information, education, justice and security, including the elimination of all forms of sexual and gender-based violence.

11. Children in disadvantaged situations and under-served areas should be a focus of efforts to fulfil children's right to health. States should identify factors at national and subnational levels that create vulnerabilities for children or that disadvantage certain groups of children. These factors should be addressed when developing laws, regulations, policies, programmes and services for children's health, and work towards ensuring equity.

C. *The best interests of the child*

12. Article 3, paragraph 1, of the Convention places an obligation on public and private social welfare institutions, courts of law, administrative authorities and legislative bodies to ensure that the best interests of the child are assessed and taken as a primary consideration in all actions affecting children. This principle must be observed in all health-related decisions concerning individual children or children as a group. Individual children's best interests should be based on their physical, emotional, social and educational needs, age, sex, relationship with parents and caregivers, and their family and social background, and after having heard their views according to article 12 of the Convention.

13. The Committee urges States to place children's best interests at the centre of all decisions affecting their health and development, including the allocation of resources, and the development and implementation of policies and interventions that affect the underlying determinants of their health. For example, the best interests of the child should:

   (a)   Guide treatment options, superseding economic considerations where feasible;
   (b)   Aid the resolution of conflict of interest between parents and health workers; and

---

[179]   General comment No. 4 (2003) on adolescent health and development in the context of the Convention on the Rights of the Child, *Official Records of the General Assembly, Fifty-ninth Session, Supplement No. 41* (A/59/41), annex X, para. 6.

(c)   Influence the development of policies to regulate actions that impede the physical and social environments in which children live, grow and develop.

14. The Committee underscores the importance of the best interests of the child as a basis for all decision-making with regard to providing, withholding or terminating treatment for all children. States should develop procedures and criteria to provide guidance to health workers for assessing the best interests of the child in the area of health, in addition to other formal, binding processes that are in place for determining the child's best interests. The Committee in its general comment No. 3[180] has underlined that adequate measures to address HIV/AIDS can be undertaken only if the rights of children and adolescents are fully respected. The child's best interests should therefore guide the consideration of HIV/AIDS at all levels of prevention, treatment, care and support.

15. In its general comment No. 4, the Committee underlined the best interests of the child to have access to appropriate information on health issues.[181] Special attention must be given to certain categories of children, including children and adolescents with psychosocial disabilities. Where hospitalization or placement in an institution is being considered, this decision should be made in accordance with the principle of the best interests of the child, with the primary understanding that it is in the best interests of all children with disabilities to be cared for, as far as possible, in the community in a family setting and preferably within their own family with the necessary supports made available to the family and the child.

D. Right to life, survival and development and the determinants of children's health

16. Article 6 highlights the States parties' obligation to ensure the survival, growth and development of the child, including the physical, mental, moral, spiritual and social dimensions of their development. The many risks and protective factors that underlie the life, survival, growth and development of the child need to be systematically identified in order to design and implement evidence-informed interventions that address a wide range of determinants during the life course.

17. The Committee recognizes that a number of determinants need to be considered for the realization of children's right to health, including individual factors such as age, sex, educational attainment, socioeconomic status and domicile; determinants at work in the immediate environment of families, peers, teachers and service providers, notably the violence that threatens the life and survival of children as part of their immediate environment; and structural determinants, including policies, administrative structures and systems, social and cultural values and norms.[182]

18. Among the key determinants of children's health, nutrition and development are the realization of the mother's right to health[183] and the role of parents and other caregivers. A significant number of infant deaths occur during the neonatal period, related to the poor health of the mother prior to, and during, the pregnancy and the immediate

---

[180] General comment No. 3 (2003) on HIV/AIDS and the rights of the child, *Official Records of the General Assembly, Fifty-ninth Session, Supplement No. 41* (A/59/41), annex IX.

[181] General comment No. 4 (2003) on adolescent health and development in the context of the Convention, *Official Records of the General Assembly, Fifty-ninth Session, Supplement No. 41* (A/59/41), annex X, para. 10.

[182] See general comment No. 13 (2011) on the right of the child to be free from all forms of violence, *Official Records of the General Assembly, Sixty-seventh Session, Supplement No. 41* (A/67/41), annex V.

[183] See Committee on the Elimination of Discrimination against Women, general recommendation No. 24 (1999) on women and health, *Official Records of the General Assembly, Fifty-fourth Session, Supplement No. 38* (A/54/38/Rev.1), chap. I, sect. A.

post-partum period, and to suboptimal breastfeeding practices. The health and health-related behaviours of parents and other significant adults have a major impact on children's health.

E. Right of the child to be heard

19. Article 12 highlights the importance of children's participation, providing for children to express their views and to have such views seriously taken into account, according to age and maturity.[184] This includes their views on all aspects of health provisions, including, for example, what services are needed, how and where they are best provided, barriers to accessing or using services, the quality of the services and the attitudes of health professionals, how to strengthen children's capacities to take increasing levels of responsibility for their own health and development, and how to involve them more effectively in the provision of services, as peer educators. States are encouraged to conduct regular participatory consultations, which are adapted to the age and maturity of the child, and research with children, and to do this separately with their parents, in order to learn about their health challenges, developmental needs and expectations as a contribution to the design of effective interventions and health programmes.

F. Evolving capacities and the life course of the child

20. Childhood is a period of continuous growth from birth to infancy, through the preschool age to adolescence. Each phase is significant as important developmental changes occur in terms of physical, psychological, emotional and social development, expectations and norms. The stages of the child's development are cumulative and each stage has an impact on subsequent phases, influencing the children's health, potential, risks and opportunities. Understanding the life course is essential in order to appreciate how health problems in childhood affect public health in general.

21. The Committee recognizes that children's evolving capacities have a bearing on their independent decision-making on their health issues. It also notes that there are often serious discrepancies regarding such autonomous decision-making, with children who are particularly vulnerable to discrimination often less able to exercise this autonomy. It is therefore essential that supportive policies are in place and that children, parents and health workers have adequate rights-based guidance on consent, assent and confidentiality.

22. To respond and understand children's evolving capacities and the different health priorities along the life cycle, data and information that are collected and analysed should be disaggregated by age, sex, disability, socioeconomic status and sociocultural aspects and geographic location, in accordance with international standards. This makes it possible to plan, develop, implement and monitor appropriate policies and interventions that take into consideration the changing capacities and needs of children over time, and that help to provide relevant health services for all children.

---

[184] See general comment No. 12 (2009) on the right of the child to be heard, *Official Records of the General Assembly, Sixty-fifth Session, Supplement No. 41* (A/65/41), annex IV.

III. NORMATIVE CONTENT OF ARTICLE 24

A. Article 24, paragraph 1

"States parties recognize the right of the child to the enjoyment of the highest attainable standard of health"

23. The notion of "the highest attainable standard of health" takes into account both the child's biological, social, cultural and economic preconditions and the State's available resources, supplemented by resources made available by other sources, including non-governmental organizations, the international community and the private sector.

24. Children's right to health contains a set of freedoms and entitlements. The freedoms, which are of increasing importance in accordance with growing capacity and maturity, include the right to control one's health and body, including sexual and reproductive freedom to make responsible choices. The entitlements include access to a range of facilities, goods, services and conditions that provide equality of opportunity for every child to enjoy the highest attainable standard of health.

"and to facilities for the treatment of illness and rehabilitation of health"

25. Children are entitled to quality health services, including prevention, promotion, treatment, rehabilitation and palliative care services. At the primary level, these services must be available in sufficient quantity and quality, functional, within the physical and financial reach of all sections of the child population, and acceptable to all. The health-care system should not only provide health-care support but also report the information to relevant authorities for cases of rights violations and injustice. Secondary and tertiary level care should also be made available, to the extent possible, with functional referral systems linking communities and families at all levels of the health system.

26. Comprehensive primary health-care programmes should be delivered alongside proven community-based efforts, including preventive care, treatment of specific diseases and nutritional interventions. Interventions at the community level should include the provision of information, services and commodities as well as prevention of illness and injury through, e.g., investment in safe public spaces, road safety and education on injury, accident and violence prevention.

27. States should ensure an appropriately trained workforce of sufficient size to support health services for all children. Adequate regulation, supervision, remuneration and conditions of service are also required, including for community health workers. Capacity development activities should ensure that service providers work in a child-sensitive manner and do not deny children any services to which they are entitled by law. Accountability mechanisms should be incorporated to ensure that quality assurance standards are maintained.

"States parties shall strive to ensure that no child is deprived of his or her right of access to such health care services"

28. Article 24, paragraph 1, imposes a strong duty of action by States parties to ensure that health and other relevant services are available and accessible to all children, with special attention to under-served areas and populations. It requires a comprehensive primary health-care system, an adequate legal framework and sustained attention to the underlying determinants of children's health.

29. Barriers to children's access to health services, including financial, institutional and cultural barriers, should be identified and eliminated. Universal free birth registration is

a prerequisite and social protection interventions, including social security such as child grants or subsidies, cash transfers and paid parental leave, should be implemented and seen as complementary investments.

30. Health-seeking behaviour is shaped by the environment in which it takes place, including, inter alia, the availability of services, levels of health knowledge, life skills and values. States should seek to ensure an enabling environment to encourage appropriate health-seeking behaviour by parents and children.

31. In accordance with their evolving capacities, children should have access to confidential counselling and advice without parental or legal guardian consent, where this is assessed by the professionals working with the child to be in the child's best interests. States should clarify the legislative procedures for the designation of appropriate caregivers for children without parents or legal guardians, who can consent on the child's behalf or assist the child in consenting, depending on the child's age and maturity. States should review and consider allowing children to consent to certain medical treatments and interventions without the permission of a parent, caregiver, or guardian, such as HIV testing and sexual and reproductive health services, including education and guidance on sexual health, contraception and safe abortion.

B. Article 24, paragraph 2

32. In accordance with article 24, paragraph 2, States should put in place a process for identifying and addressing other issues relevant to children's right to health. This requires, inter alia, an in-depth analysis of the current situation in terms of priority health problems and responses, and the identification and implementation of evidence-informed interventions and policies that respond to key determinants and health problems, in consultation with children when appropriate.

Article 24, paragraph 2 (a). "To diminish infant and child mortality"

33. States have an obligation to reduce child mortality. The Committee urges particular attention to neonatal mortality, which constitutes an increasing proportion of under-5 mortality. Additionally, States parties should also address adolescent morbidity and mortality, which is generally under-prioritized.

34. Interventions should include attention to still births, pre-term birth complications, birth asphyxia, low birth weight, mother-to-child transmission of HIV and other sexually transmitted infections, neonatal infections, pneumonia, diarrhoea, measles, under- and malnutrition, malaria, accidents, violence, suicide and adolescent maternal morbidity and mortality. Strengthening health systems to provide such interventions to all children in the context of the continuum of care for reproductive, maternal, newborn and children's health, including screening for birth defects, safe delivery services and care for the newborn are recommended. Maternal and perinatal mortality audits should be conducted regularly for the purposes of prevention and accountability.

35. States should put particular emphasis on scaling up simple, safe and inexpensive interventions that have proven to be effective, such as community-based treatments for pneumonia, diarrhoeal disease and malaria, and pay particular attention to ensuring full protection and promotion of breastfeeding practices.

Article 24, paragraph 2 (b). "To ensure the provision of necessary medical assistance and health care to all children with emphasis on the development of primary health care"

36. States should prioritize universal access for children to primary health-care services provided as close as possible to where children and their families live, particularly in

community settings. While the exact configuration and content of services will vary from country to country, in all cases effective health systems will be required, including: a robust financing mechanism; a well-trained and adequately paid workforce; reliable information on which to base decisions and policies; well-maintained facilities and logistics systems to deliver quality medicines and technologies; and strong leadership and governance. Health-service provision within schools provides an important opportunity for health promotion, to screen for illness, and increases the accessibility of health services for in-school children.

37. Recommended packages of services should be used, for example the Essential Interventions, Commodities and Guidelines for Reproductive, Maternal, Newborn and Child Health.[185] States have an obligation to make all essential medicines on the World Health Organization Model Lists of Essential Medicines, including the list for children (in paediatric formulations where possible) available, accessible and affordable.

38. The Committee is concerned by the increase in mental ill-health among adolescents, including developmental and behavioural disorders; depression; eating disorders; anxiety; psychological trauma resulting from abuse, neglect, violence or exploitation; alcohol, tobacco and drug use; obsessive behaviour, such as excessive use of and addiction to the Internet and other technologies; and self-harm and suicide. There is growing recognition of the need for increased attention for behavioural and social issues that undermine children's mental health, psychosocial wellbeing and emotional development. The Committee cautions against over-medicalization and institutionaliza-tion, and urges States to undertake an approach based on public health and psychosocial support to address mental ill-health among children and adolescents and to invest in primary care approaches that facilitate the early detection and treatment of children's psychosocial, emotional and mental problems.

39. States have the obligation to provide adequate treatment and rehabilitation for children with mental health and psychosocial disorders while abstaining from unnecessary medication. The 2012 resolution of the World Health Assembly on the global burden of mental health disorders and the need for a comprehensive coordinated response from health and social sectors at the country level[186] notes that there is increasing evidence of the effectiveness and cost-effectiveness of interventions to promote mental health and prevent mental disorders, particularly in children. The Committee strongly encourages States to scale up these interventions by mainstreaming them through a range of sectoral policies and programmes, including health, education and protection (criminal justice), with the involvement of families and communities. Children at risk because of their family and social environments require special attention in order to enhance their coping and life skills and promote protective and supportive environments.

40. There is a need to recognize the particular challenges to children's health for children affected by humanitarian emergencies, including those resulting in large-scale displacements due to natural or man-made disasters. All possible measures should be taken to ensure that children have uninterrupted access to health services, to (re)unite them with their families and to protect them not only with physical support, such as food and clean water, but also to encourage special parental or other psychosocial care to prevent or address fear and traumas.

---

[185] The Partnership for Maternal, Newborn and Child Health, *A Global Review of the Key Interventions Related to Reproductive, Maternal, Newborn and Child Health* (Geneva, 2011).

[186] Resolution WHA65.4, adopted at the Sixty-fifth World Health Assembly on 25 May 2012.

Article 24, paragraph 2 (c). "To combat disease and malnutrition, including within the framework of primary health care, through, inter alia, the application of readily available technology and through the provision of adequate nutritious foods and clean drinking-water, taking into consideration the dangers and risks of environmental pollution"

(a) The application of readily available technology

41. As new, proven technologies in children's health, including drugs, equipment and interventions, become available, States should introduce them into policies and services. Mobile arrangements and community-based efforts can substantially reduce some risks and should be made universally available and these include: immunization against the common childhood diseases; growth and developmental monitoring, especially in early childhood; vaccination against human papillomavirus for girls; tetanus toxoid injections for pregnant women; access to oral rehydration therapy and zinc supplementation for diarrhoea treatment; essential antibiotics and antiviral drugs; micronutrient supplements, such as vitamins A and D, iodized salt and iron supplements; and condoms. Health workers should advise parents how they can access and administer these simple technologies as required.

42. The private sector, which includes business enterprises and not-for-profit organizations that impact on health, is taking an increasingly important role in the development and refinement of technology, drugs, equipment, interventions and processes that can contribute to significant advances in children's health. States should ensure that benefits reach all children who need them. States can also encourage public-private partnerships and sustainability initiatives that can increase access and affordability of health technology.

(b) The provision of adequate nutritious foods

43. Measures for fulfilling States' obligations to ensure access to nutritionally adequate, culturally appropriate and safe food[187] and to combat malnutrition will need to be adopted according to the specific context. Effective direct nutrition interventions for pregnant women include addressing anaemia and folic acid and iodine deficiency and providing calcium supplementation. Prevention and management of pre-eclampsia and eclampsia, should be ensured for all women of reproductive age to benefit their health and ensure healthy foetal and infant development.

44. Exclusive breastfeeding for infants up to 6 months of age should be protected and promoted and breastfeeding should continue alongside appropriate complementary foods preferably until two years of age, where feasible. States' obligations in this area are defined in the "protect, promote and support" framework, adopted unanimously by the World Health Assembly.[188] States are required to introduce into domestic law, implement and enforce internationally agreed standards concerning children's right to health, including the International Code on Marketing of Breast-milk Substitutes and the relevant subsequent World Health Assembly resolutions, as well as the World Health Organization Framework Convention on Tobacco Control. Special measures should be taken to promote community and workplace support for mothers in relation to pregnancy and breastfeeding and feasible and affordable childcare services; and

---

[187] See International Covenant on Economic, Social and Cultural Rights, art. 11, and Committee on Economic, Social and Cultural Rights, general comment No. 12 (1999) on the right to adequate food, *Official Records of the Economic and Social Council, 2011, Supplement No. 2* (E/2000/22), annex V.

[188] See WHO and United Nations Children's Fund (UNICEF), *Global Strategy for Infant and Young Child Feeding* (Geneva, 2003).

compliance with the International Labour Organization Convention No. 183 (2000) concerning the revision of the Maternity Protection Convention (Revised), 1952.

45. Adequate nutrition and growth monitoring in early childhood are particularly important. Where necessary, integrated management of severe acute malnutrition should be expanded through facility and community-based interventions, as well as treatment of moderate acute malnutrition, including therapeutic feeding interventions.

46. School feeding is desirable to ensure all pupils have access to a full meal every day, which can also enhance children's attention for learning and increase school enrolment. The Committee recommends that this be combined with nutrition and health education, including setting up school gardens and training teachers to improve children's nutrition and healthy eating habits.

47. States should also address obesity in children, as it is associated with hypertension, early markers of cardiovascular disease, insulin resistance, psychological effects, a higher likelihood of adult obesity, and premature death. Children's exposure to "fast foods" that are high in fat, sugar or salt, energy-dense and micronutrient-poor, and drinks containing high levels of caffeine or other potentially harmful substances should be limited. The marketing of these substances – especially when such marketing is focused on children – should be regulated and their availability in schools and other places controlled.

(c) The provision of clean drinking water

48. Safe and clean drinking water and sanitation are essential for the full enjoyment of life and all other human rights.[189] Government departments and local authorities responsible for water and sanitation should recognize their obligation to help realize children's right to health, and actively consider child indicators on malnutrition, diarrhoea and other water-related diseases and household size when planning and carrying out infrastructure expansion and the maintenance of water services, and when making decisions on amounts for free minimum allocation and service disconnections. States are not exempted from their obligations, even when they have privatized water and sanitation.

(d) Environmental pollution

49. States should take measures to address the dangers and risks that local environmental pollution poses to children's health in all settings. Adequate housing that includes non-dangerous cooking facilities, a smoke-free environment, appropriate ventilation, effective management of waste and the disposal of litter from living quarters and the immediate surroundings, the absence of mould and other toxic substances, and family hygiene are core requirements to a healthy upbringing and development. States should regulate and monitor the environmental impact of business activities that may compromise children's right to health, food security and access to safe drinking water and to sanitation.

50. The Committee draws attention to the relevance of the environment, beyond environmental pollution, to children's health. Environmental interventions should, inter alia, address climate change, as this is one of the biggest threats to children's health and exacerbates health disparities. States should, therefore, put children's health concerns at the centre of their climate change adaptation and mitigation strategies.

---

[189] General Assembly resolution 64/292 on the human right to water and sanitation.

Article 24, paragraph 2 (d). "To ensure appropriate pre-natal and post-natal health care for mothers"

51. The Committee notes that preventable maternal mortality and morbidity constitute grave violations of the human rights of women and girls and pose serious threats to their own and their children's right to health. Pregnancy and child birth are natural processes, with known health risks that are susceptible to both prevention and therapeutic responses, if identified early. Risk situations can occur during pregnancy, delivery and the ante- and postnatal periods and have both short- and long-term impact on the health and well-being of both mother and child.

52. The Committee encourages States to adopt child-sensitive health approaches throughout different periods of childhood such as (a) the baby-friendly hospital initiative[190] which protects, promotes and supports rooming-in and breastfeeding; (b) child-friendly health policies focused on training health workers to provide quality services in a way that minimizes the fear, anxiety and suffering of children and their families; and (c) adolescent-friendly health services which require health practitioners and facilities to be welcoming and sensitive to adolescents, to respect confidentiality and to deliver services that are acceptable to adolescents.

53. The care that women receive before, during and after their pregnancy has profound implications for the health and development of their children. Fulfilling the obligation to ensure universal access to a comprehensive package of sexual and reproductive health interventions should be based on the concept of a continuum of care from pre-pregnancy, through pregnancy, childbirth and throughout the post-partum period. Timely and good-quality care throughout these periods provides important opportunities to prevent the intergenerational transmission of ill-health and has a high impact on the health of the child throughout the life course.

54. The interventions that should be made available across this continuum include, but are not limited to: essential health prevention and promotion, and curative care, including the prevention of neonatal tetanus, malaria in pregnancy and congenital syphilis; nutritional care; access to sexual and reproductive health education, information and services; health behaviour education (e.g. relating to smoking and substance use); birth preparedness; early recognition and management of complications; safe abortion services and post-abortion care; essential care at childbirth; and prevention of mother-to-child HIV transmission, and care and treatment of HIV-infected women and infants. Maternal and newborn care following delivery should ensure no unnecessary separation of the mother from her child.

55. The Committee recommends that social protection interventions include ensuring universal coverage or financial access to care, paid parental leave and other social security benefits, and legislation to restrict the inappropriate marketing and promotion of breast-milk substitutes.

56. Given the high rates of pregnancy among adolescents globally and the additional risks of associated morbidity and mortality, States should ensure that health systems and services are able to meet the specific sexual and reproductive health needs of adolescents, including family planning and safe abortion services. States should work to ensure that girls can make autonomous and informed decisions on their reproductive health. Discrimination based on adolescent pregnancy, such as expulsion from schools, should be prohibited, and opportunities for continuous education should be ensured.

---

[190] UNICEF/WHO, Baby-Friendly Hospital Initiative (1991).

57. Taking into account that boys and men are crucial to planning and ensuring healthy pregnancies and deliveries, States should integrate education, awareness and dialogue opportunities for boys and men into their policies and plans for sexual, reproductive and children's health services.

Article 24, paragraph 2 (e). "To ensure that all segments of society, in particular parents and children, are informed, have access to education and are supported in the use of basic knowledge of children's health and nutrition, the advantages of breastfeeding, hygiene and environmental sanitation and the prevention of accidents"

58. The obligations under this provision include providing health-related information and support in the use of this information. Health-related information should be physically accessible, understandable and appropriate to children's age and educational level.

59. Children require information and education on all aspects of health to enable them to make informed choices in relation to their lifestyle and access to health services. Information and life skills education should address a broad range of health issues, including: healthy eating and the promotion of physical activity, sports and recreation; accident and injury prevention; sanitation, hand washing and other personal hygiene practices; and the dangers of alcohol, tobacco and psychoactive substance use. Information and education should encompass appropriate information about children's right to health, the obligations of Governments, and how and where to access health information and services, and should be provided as a core part of the school curriculum, as well as through health services and in other settings for children who are not in school. Materials providing information about health should be designed in collaboration with children and disseminated in a wide range of public settings.

60. Sexual and reproductive health education should include self-awareness and knowledge about the body, including anatomical, physiological and emotional aspects, and should be accessible to all children, girls and boys. It should include content related to sexual health and well-being, such as information about body changes and maturation processes, and designed in a manner through which children are able to gain knowledge regarding reproductive health and the prevention of gender-based violence, and adopt responsible sexual behaviour.

61. Information about children's health should be provided to all parents individually or in groups, the extended family and other caregivers through different methods, including health clinics, parenting classes, public information leaflets, professional bodies, community organizations and the media.

Article 24, paragraph 2 (f). "To develop preventive health care, guidance for parents and family planning education and services"

(a) Preventive health care

62. Prevention and health promotion should address the main health challenges facing children within the community and the country as a whole. These challenges include diseases and other health challenges, such as accidents, violence, substance abuse and psychosocial and mental health problems. Preventive health care should address communicable and non-communicable diseases and incorporate a combination of biomedical, behavioural and structural interventions. Preventing non-communicable diseases should start early in life through the promotion and support of healthy and non-violent lifestyles for pregnant women, their spouses/partners and young children.

63. Reducing the burden of child injuries requires strategies and measures to reduce the incidence of drowning, burns and other accidents. Such strategies and measures should

include legislation and enforcement; product and environmental modification; supportive home visits and promotion of safety features; education, skills development and behaviour change; community-based projects; and pre-hospital and acute care, as well as rehabilitation. Efforts to reduce road traffic accidents should include legislating for the use of seatbelts and other safety devices, ensuring access to safe transport for children and according them due consideration in road planning and traffic control. The support of the related industry and the media is essential in this respect.

64. Recognizing violence as a significant cause of mortality and morbidity in children, particularly adolescents, the Committee emphasizes the need to create an environment that protects children from violence and encourages their participation in attitudinal and behavioural changes at home, in schools and in public spaces; to support parents and caregivers in healthy child-rearing; and to challenge attitudes which perpetuate the tolerance and condoning of violence in all forms, including by regulating the depiction of violence by mass media.

65. States should protect children from solvents, alcohol, tobacco and illicit substances, increase the collection of relevant evidence and take appropriate measures to reduce the use of such substances among children. Regulation of the advertising and sale of substances harmful to children's health and of the promotion of such items in places where children congregate, as well as in media channels and publications that are accessed by children are recommended.

66. The Committee encourages States parties that have not yet done so to ratify the international drug control conventions[191] and the World Health Organization Framework Convention on Tobacco Control. The Committee underscores the importance of adopting a rights-based approach to substance use and recommends that, where appropriate, harm reduction strategies should be employed to minimize the negative health impacts of substance abuse.

(b) Guidance for parents

67. Parents are the most important source of early diagnosis and primary care for small children, and the most important protective factor against high-risk behaviours in adolescents, such as substance use and unsafe sex. Parents also play a central role in promoting healthy child development, protecting children from harm due to accidents, injuries and violence and mitigating the negative effects of risk behaviours. Children's socialization processes, which are crucial for understanding and adjusting to the world in which they grow up, are strongly influenced by their parents, extended family and other caregivers. States should adopt evidence-based interventions to support good parenting, including parenting skills education, support groups and family counselling, in particular for families experiencing children's health and other social challenges.

68. In the light of the impact of corporal punishment on children's health, including fatal and non-fatal injury and the psychological and emotional consequences, the Committee reminds States of their obligation to take all appropriate legislative, administrative, social and educational measures to eliminate corporal punishment and other cruel or degrading forms of punishment in all settings, including the home.[192]

---

[191] Single Convention on Narcotic Drugs, 1961; Convention on Psychotropic Substances, 1971; United Nations Convention against Illicit Traffic in Narcotic Drugs and Psychotropic Substances, 1988.

[192] General comment No. 8 (2006) on the right of the child to protection from corporal punishment and other cruel or degrading forms of punishment, *Official Records of the General Assembly, Sixty-third Session, Supplement No. 41* (A/63/41), annex II.

(c) Family planning

69. Family planning services should be situated within comprehensive sexual and reproductive health services and should encompass sexuality education, including counselling. They can be considered part of the continuum of services described in article 24, paragraph 2 (d), and should be designed to enable all couples and individuals to make sexual and reproductive decisions freely and responsibly, including the number, spacing and timing of their children, and to give them the information and means to do so. Attention should be given to ensuring confidential, universal access to goods and services for both married and unmarried female and male adolescents. States should ensure that adolescents are not deprived of any sexual and reproductive health information or services due to providers' conscientious objections.

70. Short-term contraceptive methods such as condoms, hormonal methods and emergency contraception should be made easily and readily available to sexually active adolescents. Long-term and permanent contraceptive methods should also be provided. The Committee recommends that States ensure access to safe abortion and post-abortion care services, irrespective of whether abortion itself is legal.

IV. OBLIGATIONS AND RESPONSIBILITIES

A. State parties' obligations to respect, protect and fulfil

71. States have three types of obligations relating to human rights, including children's right to health: to respect freedoms and entitlements, to protect both freedoms and entitlements from third parties or from social or environmental threats, and to fulfil the entitlements through facilitation or direct provision. In accordance with article 4 of the Convention, States parties shall fulfil the entitlements contained in children's right to health to the maximum extent of their available resources and, where needed, within the framework of international cooperation.

72. All States, regardless of their level of development, are required to take immediate action to implement these obligations as a matter of priority and without discrimination of any kind. Where the available resources are demonstrably inadequate, States are still required to undertake targeted measures to move as expeditiously and effectively as possible towards the full realization of children's right to health. Irrespective of resources, States have the obligation not to take any retrogressive steps that could hamper the enjoyment of children's right to health.

73. The core obligations, under children's right to health, include:

(a)   Reviewing the national and subnational legal and policy environment and, where necessary, amending laws and policies;
(b)   Ensuring universal coverage of quality primary health services, including prevention, health promotion, care and treatment services, and essential drugs;
(c)   Providing an adequate response to the underlying determinants of children's health; and
(d)   Developing, implementing, monitoring and evaluating policies and budgeted plans of actions that constitute a human rights-based approach to fulfilling children's right to health.

74. States should demonstrate their commitment to progressive fulfilment of all obligations under article 24, prioritizing this even in the context of political or economic crisis or emergency situations. This requires that children's health and related policies, programmes and services be planned, designed, financed and implemented in a sustainable manner.

B. Responsibilities of non-State actors

75. The State is responsible for realizing children's right to health regardless of whether or not it delegates the provision of services to non-State actors. In addition to the State, a wide range of non-State actors who provide information and services related to children's health and its underlying determinants have specific responsibilities and impact in this regard.

76. States' obligations include a duty to promote awareness of non-State actors' responsibilities and to ensure that all non-State actors recognize, respect and fulfil their responsibilities to the child, applying due diligence procedures where necessary.

77. The Committee calls on all non-State actors engaged in health promotion and services, especially the private sector, including the pharmaceutical and health-technology industry as well as the mass media and health service providers, to act in compliance with the provisions of the Convention and to ensure compliance by any partners who deliver services on their behalf. Such partners include international organizations, banks, regional financial institutions, global partnerships, the private sector (private foundations and funds), donors and any other entities providing services or financial support to children's health, particularly in humanitarian emergencies or politically unstable situations.

1. Responsibilities of parents and other caregivers

78. The responsibilities of parents and other caregivers are expressly referred to in several provisions of the Convention. Parents should fulfil their responsibilities while always acting in the best interests of the child, if necessary with the support of the State. Taking the child's evolving capacity into account, parents and caregivers should nurture, protect and support children to grow and develop in a healthy manner. Although not explicit in article 24, paragraph 2 (f), the Committee understands any reference to parents to also include other caregivers.

2. Non-State service providers and other non-State actors

(a) Non-State service providers

79. All health service providers, including non-State actors, must incorporate and apply to the design, implementation and evaluation of their programmes and services all relevant provisions of the Convention, as well as the criteria of availability, accessibility, acceptability and quality, as described in chapter VI, section E, of the present general comment.

(b) Private sector

80. All business enterprises have an obligation of due diligence with respect to human rights, which include all rights enshrined under the Convention. States should require businesses to undertake children's rights due diligence. This will ensure that business enterprises identify, prevent and mitigate their negative impact on children's right to health including across their business relationships and within any global operations. Large business enterprises should be encouraged and, where appropriate, required to make public their efforts to address their impact on children's rights.

81. Among other responsibilities and in all contexts, private companies should: refrain from engaging children in hazardous labour while ensuring they comply with the minimum age for child labour; comply with the International Code of Marketing of Breast-milk Substitutes and the relevant subsequent World Health Assembly resolutions; limit advertisement of energy-dense, micronutrient-poor foods, and drinks containing

high levels of caffeine or other substances potentially harmful to children; and refrain from the advertisement, marketing and sale to children of tobacco, alcohol and other toxic substances or the use of child images.

82. The Committee acknowledges the profound impact of the pharmaceutical sector on the health of children and calls on pharmaceutical companies to adopt measures towards enhancing access to medicines for children, paying particular attention to the Human Rights Guidelines for Pharmaceutical Companies in relation to Access to Medicines.[193] At the same time, States should ensure that pharmaceutical companies monitor the use, and refrain from promoting excessive prescription and use of, drugs and medicines on children. Intellectual property rights should not be applied in ways that cause necessary medicines or goods to be unaffordable for the poor.

83. Private health insurance companies should ensure that they do not discriminate against pregnant women, children or mothers on any prohibited grounds and that they promote equality through partnerships with State health insurance schemes based on the principle of solidarity and ensuring that inability to pay does not restrict access to services.

(c) Mass and social media

84. Article 17 of the Convention delineates the responsibilities of mass media organizations. In the context of health, these can be further expanded to include promoting health and healthy lifestyles among children; providing free advertising space for health promotion; ensuring the privacy and confidentiality of children and adolescents; promoting access to information; not producing communication programmes and material that are harmful to child and general health; and not perpetuating health-related stigma.

(d) Researchers

85. The Committee underscores the responsibility of entities, including academics, private companies and others, undertaking research involving children to respect the principles and provisions of the Convention and the International Ethical Guidelines for Biomedical Research Involving Human Subjects.[194] The Committee reminds researchers that the best interests of the child shall always prevail over the interest of general society or scientific advancement.

V. INTERNATIONAL COOPERATION

86. States parties to the Convention have obligations not only to implement children's right to health within their own jurisdiction, but also to contribute to global implementation through international cooperation. Article 24, paragraph 4, requires States and inter-State agencies to pay particular attention to the children's health priorities among the poorest parts of the population and in developing States.

87. The Convention should guide all international activities and programmes of donor and recipient States related directly or indirectly to children's health. It requires partner States to identify the major health problems affecting children, pregnant women and mothers in recipient countries and to address them in accordance with the priorities and principles established by article 24. International cooperation should support State-led health systems and national health plans.

---

[193] See also Human Rights Council resolution 15/22 on the right of everyone to the enjoyment of the highest attainable standard of physical and mental health.

[194] Council for International Organizations of Medical Sciences/WHO, Geneva, 1993.

88. States have individual and joint responsibility, including through United Nations mechanisms, to cooperate in providing disaster relief and humanitarian assistance in times of emergency. In these cases, States should consider prioritizing efforts to realize children's right to health, including through appropriate international medical aid; distribution and management of resources, such as safe and potable water, food and medical supplies; and financial aid to the most vulnerable or marginalized children.

89. The Committee reminds States to meet the United Nations target of allocating 0.7 per cent of gross national income to international development assistance, as financial resources have important implications for the realization of children's right to health in resource-limited States. In order to ensure the highest impact, States and inter-State agencies are encouraged to apply the Paris Principles on Aid Effectiveness and the principles of the Accra Agenda for Action.

VI. FRAMEWORK FOR IMPLEMENTATION AND ACCOUNTABILITY

90. Accountability is at the core of the enjoyment of children's right to health. The Committee reminds the State party of their obligations to ensure that relevant government authorities and service providers are held accountable for maintaining the highest possible standards of children's health and health care until they reach 18 years of age.

91. States should provide an environment that facilitates the discharge of all duty bearers' obligations and responsibilities with respect to children's right to health and a regulatory framework within which all actors should operate and can be monitored, including by mobilizing political and financial support for children's health-related issues and building the capacity of duty bearers to fulfil their obligations and children to claim their right to health.

92. With the active engagement of the Government, parliament, communities, civil society and children, national accountability mechanisms must be effective and transparent and aim to hold all actors responsible for their actions. They should, inter alia, devote attention to the structural factors affecting children's health including laws, policies and budgets. Participatory tracking of financial resources and their impact on children's health is essential for State accountability mechanisms.

A. Promoting knowledge of children's right to health (art. 42)

93. The Committee encourages States to adopt and implement a comprehensive strategy to educate children, their caregivers, policymakers, politicians and professionals working with children about children's right to health, and the contributions they can make to its realization.

B. Legislative measures

94. The Convention requires States parties to adopt all appropriate legislative, administrative and other measures for the implementation of children's right to health without discrimination. National laws should place a statutory obligation on the State to provide the services, programmes, human resources and infrastructure needed to realize children's right to health and provide a statutory entitlement to essential, child sensitive, quality health and related services for pregnant women and children irrespective of their ability to pay. Laws should be reviewed to assess any potential discriminatory effect or impediment to realizing children's right to health and repealed where required. Where necessary, international agencies and donors should provide development aid and technical assistance for such legal reforms.

95. Legislation should fulfil a number of additional functions in the realization of children's right to health by defining the scope of the right and recognizing children as rights-holders; clarifying the roles and responsibilities of all duty bearers; clarifying what services children, pregnant women and mothers are entitled to claim; and regulating services and medications to ensure that they are of good quality and cause no harm. States must ensure that adequate legislative and other safeguards exist to protect and promote the work of human rights defenders working on children's right to health.

C. Governance and coordination

96. States are encouraged to ratify and implement international and regional human rights instruments relevant to children's health and to report on all aspects of children's health accordingly.

97. Sustainability in children's health policy and practice requires a long-term national plan that is supported and entrenched as a national priority. The Committee recommends that States establish and make use of a comprehensive and cohesive national coordinating framework on children's health, built upon the principles of the Convention, to facilitate cooperation between government ministries and different levels of government as well as interaction with civil society stakeholders, including children. Given the high number of government agencies, legislative branches and ministries working on children's health-related policies and services at different levels, the Committee recommends that the roles and responsibilities of each be clarified in the legal and regulatory framework.

98. Particular attention must be given to identifying and prioritizing marginalized and disadvantaged groups of children, as well as children who are at risk of any form of violence and discrimination. All activities should be fully costed, financed and made visible within the national budget.

99. A "child health in all policies" strategy should be used, highlighting the links between children's health and its underlying determinants. Every effort should be made to remove bottlenecks that obstruct transparency, coordination, partnership and accountability in the provision of services affecting children's health.

100. While decentralization is required to meet the particular needs of localities and sectors, this does not reduce the direct responsibility of the central or national Government to fulfil its obligations to all children within its jurisdiction. Decisions about allocations to the various levels of services and geographical areas should reflect the core elements of the approach to primary health care.

101. States should engage all sectors of society, including children, in implementation of children's right to health. The Committee recommends that such engagement include: the creation of conditions conducive to the continual growth, development and sustainability of civil society organizations, including grass-roots and community-level groups; active facilitation of their involvement in the development, implementation and evaluation of children's health policy and services; and provision of appropriate financial support or assistance in obtaining financial support.

1. The role of parliaments in national accountability

102. In children's health-related issues, parliaments have the responsibility to legislate, ensuring transparency and inclusiveness, and encourage continued public debate and a culture of accountability. They should create a public platform for reporting and debating performance and promoting public participation in independent review mechanisms. They should also hold the executive accountable for implementing the

recommendations emerging from independent reviews and ensure that the results of the reviews inform subsequent national plans, laws, policies, budgets and further accountability measures.

2. The role of national human rights institutions in national accountability

103. National human rights institutions have an important role to play in reviewing and promoting accountability, providing children with relief for violations of their right to health and advocating systemic change for the realization of that right. The Committee recalls its general comment No. 2, and reminds States that the mandate of children's commissioners or children's ombudsmen should include ensuring the right to health, and the mandate holders should be well-resourced and independent from the Government.[195]

D. Investing in children's health

104. In their decisions about budget allocation and spending, States should strive to ensure availability, accessibility, acceptability and quality of essential children's health services for all, without discrimination.

105. States should continually assess the impact of macroeconomic policy decisions on children's right to health, particularly children in vulnerable situations, prevent any decisions that may compromise children's rights, and apply the "best interests" principle when making such decisions. States should also consider obligations under article 24 in all aspects of their negotiations with international financial institutions and other donors, to ensure that children's right to health is given adequate consideration in international cooperation.

106. The Committee recommends that States parties:

(a)   Legislate for a specific proportion of public expenditure to be allocated to children's health and create an accompanying mechanism that allows for systematic independent evaluation of this expenditure;

(b)   Meet World Health Organization-recommended minimum health expenditure per capita and prioritize children's health in budgetary allocations;

(c)   Make investment in children visible in the State budget through detailed compilation of resources allocated to them and expended; and

(d)   Implement rights-based budget monitoring and analysis, as well as child impact assessments on how investments, particularly in the health sector, may serve the best interests of the child.

107. The Committee underlines the importance of assessment tools in the use of resources and recognizes the need to develop measurable indicators to assist States parties in monitoring and evaluating progress in the implementation of children's right to health.

E. The action cycle

108. States parties' fulfilment of their obligations under article 24 requires engagement in a cyclical process of planning, implementation, monitoring and evaluation to then inform further planning, modified implementation and renewed monitoring and evaluation efforts. States should ensure the meaningful participation of children and incorporate feedback mechanisms to facilitate necessary adjustments throughout the cycle.

---

[195]   See general comment No. 2 (2002) on the role of independent national human rights institutions in the promotion and protection of the rights of the child, *Official Records of the General Assembly, Fifty-ninth Session, Supplement No. 41* (A/59/41), annex VIII.

109. At the heart of the development, implementation and monitoring of policies, programmes and services that aim to realize children's right to health is the availability of relevant and reliable data. This should include: appropriately disaggregated data across the life course of the child, with due attention to vulnerable groups; data on priority health problems, including new and neglected causes of mortality and morbidity; and data on the key determinants of children's health. Strategic information requires data collected through routine health information systems, special surveys and research, and should include both quantitative and qualitative data. These data should be collected, analysed, disseminated and used to inform national and subnational policies and programmes.

1. Planning

110. The Committee notes that, in order to inform the implementation, monitoring and evaluation of activities to fulfil obligations under article 24, States should carry out situation analyses of existing problems, issues and infrastructure for delivery of services. The analysis should assess the institutional capacity and the availability of human, financial, and technical resources. Based on the outcome of the analysis, a strategy should be developed involving all stakeholders, both State and non-State actors and children.

111. The situation analysis will provide a clear idea of national and subnational priorities and strategies for their achievement. Benchmarks and targets, budgeted action plans and operational strategies should be established along with a framework for monitoring and evaluating policies, programmes and services and promoting accountability for children's health. This will highlight how to build and strengthen existing structures and systems to be consonant with the Convention.

2. Criteria for performance and implementation

112. States should ensure that all children's health services and programmes comply with the criteria of availability, accessibility, acceptability and quality.

(a) Availability

113. States should ensure that there are functioning children's health facilities, goods, services and programmes in sufficient quantity. States need to ensure that they have sufficient hospitals, clinics, health practitioners, mobile teams and facilities, community health workers, equipment and essential drugs to provide health care to all children, pregnant women and mothers within the State. Sufficiency should be measured according to need with particular attention given to under-served and hard to reach populations.

(b) Accessibility

114. The element of accessibility has four dimensions:

   (a)   *Non-discrimination*: Health and related services as well as equipment and supplies must be accessible to all children, pregnant women and mothers, in law and in practice, without discrimination of any kind;
   (b)   *Physical accessibility*: Health facilities must be within accessible distance for all children, pregnant women and mothers. Physical accessibility may require additional attention to the needs of children and women with disabilities. The Committee encourages States to prioritize the establishment of facilities and services in under-served areas and to invest in mobile outreach approaches, innovative technologies, and well-trained and supported community health workers, as ways of reaching especially vulnerable groups of children;

(c) *Economic accessibility/affordability*: Lack of ability to pay for services, supplies or medicines should not result in the denial of access. The Committee calls on States to abolish user fees and implement health-financing systems that do not discriminate against women and children on the basis of their inability to pay. Risk-pooling mechanisms such as tax and insurance should be implemented on the basis of equitable, means-based contributions;

(d) *Information accessibility*: Information on health promotion, health status and treatment options should be provided to children and their caregivers in a language and format that is accessible and clearly understandable to them.

(c) Acceptability

115. In the context of children's right to health, the Committee defines acceptability as the obligation to design and implement all health-related facilities, goods and services in a way that takes full account of and is respectful of medical ethics as well as children's needs, expectations, cultures, views and languages, paying special attention to certain groups, where necessary.

(d) Quality

116. Health-related facilities, goods and services should be scientifically and medically appropriate and of good quality. Ensuring quality requires, inter alia, that (a) treatments, interventions and medicines are based on the best available evidence; (b) medical personnel are skilled and provided with adequate training on maternal and children's health, and the principles and provisions of the Convention; (c) hospital equipment is scientifically approved and appropriate for children; (d) drugs are scientifically approved, have not expired, are child-specific (when necessary) and are monitored for adverse reactions; and (e) regular quality of care assessments of health institutions are conducted.

3. Monitoring and evaluation

117. A well-structured and appropriately disaggregated set of indicators should be established for monitoring and evaluation to meet the requirements under the performance criteria above. The data should be used to redesign and improve policies, programmes and services in support of fulfilment of children's right to health. Health information systems should ensure that data should be reliable, transparent, and consistent, while protecting the right to privacy for individuals. States should regularly review their health information system, including vital registration and disease surveillance, with a view to its improvement.

118. National accountability mechanisms should monitor, review and act on their findings. Monitoring means providing data on the health status of children, regularly reviewing the quality of children's health services and how much is spent thereon and where, on what and on whom it is spent. This should include both routine monitoring and periodic, in-depth evaluations. Reviewing means analysing the data and consulting children, families, other caregivers and civil society to determine whether children's health has improved and whether Governments and other actors have fulfilled their commitments. Acting means using evidence emerging from these processes to repeat and expand what is working and to remedy and reform what is not.

F. Remedies for violations of the right to health

119. The Committee strongly encourages States to put in place functional and accessible complaints mechanisms for children that are community-based and render it possible for children to seek and obtain reparations when their right to health is violated or at risk. States should also provide for broad rights of legal standing, including class actions.

120. States should ensure and facilitate access to courts for individual children and their caregivers and take steps to remove any barriers to access remedies for violations of children's right to health. National human rights institutions, children's ombudspersons, health-related professional associations and consumers' associations can play an important role in this regard.

VII. DISSEMINATION

121. The Committee recommends that States widely disseminate the present general comment with parliament and across Government, including within ministries, departments and municipal and local-level bodies working on children's health issues.

General comment No 16 (2013) on State obligations regarding the impact of the business sector on children's rights

Adopted by the Committee at its sixty-second session (14 January – 1 February 2013)

I. INTRODUCTION AND OBJECTIVES

1. The Committee on the Rights of the Child recognizes that the business sector's impact on children's rights has grown in past decades because of factors such as the globalized nature of economies and of business operations and the ongoing trends of decentralization, and outsourcing and privatizing of State functions that affect the enjoyment of human rights. Business can be an essential driver for societies and economies to advance in ways that strengthen the realization of children's rights through, for example, technological advances, investment and the generation of decent work. However, the realization of children's rights is not an automatic consequence of economic growth and business enterprises can also negatively impact children's rights.

2. States have obligations regarding the impact of business activities and operations on children's rights arising from the Convention on the Rights of the Child, the Optional Protocol on the sale of children, child prostitution and child pornography and the Optional Protocol on the involvement of children in armed conflict. These obligations cover a variety of issues, reflecting the fact that children are both rights-holders and stakeholders in business as consumers, legally engaged employees, future employees and business leaders and members of communities and environments in which business operates. The present general comment aims to clarify these obligations and outline the measures that should be undertaken by States to meet them.

3. For the purposes of the present general comment, the business sector is defined as including all business enterprises, both national and transnational, regardless of size, sector, location, ownership and structure. The general comment also addresses obligations regarding not-for-profit organizations that play a role in the provision of services that are critical to the enjoyment of children's rights.

4. It is necessary for States to have adequate legal and institutional frameworks to respect, protect and fulfil children's rights, and to provide remedies in case of violations in the context of business activities and operations. In this regard, States should take into account that:

   (a) Childhood is a unique period of physical, mental, emotional and spiritual development and violations of children's rights, such as exposure to violence, child labour or unsafe products or environmental hazards may have lifelong, irreversible and even transgenerational consequences;
   (b) Children are often politically voiceless and lack access to relevant information. They are reliant on governance systems, over which they have little influence, to have their rights realized. This makes it hard for them to have a say in decisions regarding laws and policies that impact their rights. In the process of decision-making, States may not adequately consider the impact on children of business-related laws and policies, while, conversely, the business sector often exerts a powerful influence on decisions without reference to children's rights;
   (c) It is generally challenging for children to obtain remedy – whether in the courts or through other mechanisms – when their rights are infringed upon, even more so by business enterprises. Children often lack legal standing, knowledge of remedy mechanisms, financial resources and adequate legal representation.

Furthermore, there are particular difficulties for children in obtaining remedy for abuses that occur in the context of businesses' global operations.

5. Given the broad range of children's rights that can be affected by business activities and operations, the present general comment does not examine every pertinent article of the Convention and its protocols. Instead it seeks to provide States with a framework for implementing the Convention as a whole with regard to the business sector whilst focusing on specific contexts where the impact of business activities on children's rights can be most significant. The present general comment aims to provide States with guidance on how they should:

(a) Ensure that the activities and operations of business enterprises do not adversely impact on children's rights;

(b) Create an enabling and supportive environment for business enterprises to respect children's rights, including across any business relationships linked to their operations, products or services and across their global operations; and

(c) Ensure access to effective remedy for children whose rights have been infringed by a business enterprise acting as a private party or as a State agent.

6. The present general comment draws from the experience of the Committee in reviewing State parties' reports and its day of general discussion on the private sector as service provider in 2002.[196] It is also informed by regional and international consultations with numerous stakeholders, including children, as well as by public consultations that have taken place since 2011.

7. The Committee is mindful of the relevance to the general comment of existing and evolving national and international norms, standards and policy guidance on business and human rights. The general comment is consistent with international conventions, including the International Labour Organization (ILO) Conventions No. 182 (1999) concerning the Prohibition and Immediate Action for the Elimination of the Worst Forms of Child Labour and No. 138 (1973) concerning Minimum Age for Admission to Employment. The Committee recognizes the relevance of the United Nations "Protect, Respect and Remedy" Framework and the Guiding Principles on Business and Human Rights adopted by the Human Rights Council, and of the ILO Tripartite Declaration of Principles concerning Multinationals and Social Policy. Other documents, such as the Organisation for Economic Co-operation and Development (OECD) Guidelines for Multinational Enterprises, the Global Compact, the United Nations Study on Violence against Children and the Children's Rights and Business Principles have been useful references for the Committee.

II. SCOPE AND APPLICATION

8. The present general comment principally addresses States' obligations under the Convention and the Optional Protocols thereto. At this juncture, there is no international legally binding instrument on the business sector's responsibilities vis-à-vis human rights. However, the Committee recognizes that duties and responsibilities to respect the rights of children extend in practice beyond the State and State-controlled services and institutions and apply to private actors and business enterprises. Therefore, all businesses must meet their responsibilities regarding children's rights and States must ensure they do so. In addition, business enterprises should not undermine the States' ability to meet their obligations towards children under the Convention and the Optional Protocols thereto.

---

[196] Committee on the Rights of the Child, report on its thirty-first session, CRC/C/121, annex II.

9. The Committee acknowledges that voluntary actions of corporate responsibility by business enterprises, such as social investments, advocacy and public policy engagement, voluntary codes of conduct, philanthropy and other collective actions, can advance children's rights. States should encourage such voluntary actions and initiatives as a means to create a business culture which respects and supports children's rights. However, it should be emphasized that such voluntary actions and initiatives are not a substitute for State action and regulation of businesses in line with obligations under the Convention and its protocols or for businesses to comply with their responsibilities to respect children's rights.

10. It is important to recall that the Convention and the Optional Protocols thereto engage the State as a whole, regardless of its internal structures, branches or organization. Furthermore, decentralization of power, through devolution and delegation, does not reduce the direct responsibility of the State to meet its obligations to all children within its jurisdiction.

11. The present general comment first considers the relationship between State obligations regarding business activities and the general principles of the Convention. It then defines the general nature and scope of State obligations with regards to children's rights and the business sector. An examination follows of the scope of obligations in contexts where the impact of business activities and operations on children's rights is most significant, including when business enterprises are service providers, children are affected in the informal economy, States engage with international organizations and businesses operate abroad in areas where there is insufficient State protection for children's rights. The present general comment concludes by outlining a framework for implementation and dissemination.

III. GENERAL PRINCIPLES OF THE CONVENTION AS THEY RELATE TO BUSINESS ACTIVITIES

12. Children's rights are universal, indivisible, interdependent and interrelated. The Committee has established four general principles within the Convention as the basis for all State decisions and actions relating to business activities and operations in conformity with a child rights approach.[197]

A. *The right to non-discrimination (art. 2)*

13. Article 2 of the Convention calls on States to respect and ensure rights to each child in their jurisdiction "without discrimination of any kind, irrespective of a child's or his or her parent's or legal guardian's race, colour, sex, language, religion, political or other opinion, national, ethnic or social origin, property, disability, birth or other status". States must ensure that all legislation, policies and programmes that deal with business issues are not intentionally or unintentionally discriminatory towards children in their content or implementation; for instance, those that address access to employment for parents or caregivers, or access to goods and services for children with disabilities.

14. States are required to prevent discrimination in the private sphere in general and provide remedy if it occurs. States should collect statistical data that is appropriately disaggregated and other information to identify discrimination against children in the context of business activities and operations and mechanisms should be established to monitor and investigate discriminatory practices within the business sector. States should also take steps to create a supportive environment for business to respect the right to

---

[197] See Committee on the Rights of the Child, general comment No. 13 (2011) on the right of the child to be free from all forms of violence, *Official Records of the General Assembly, Sixty-seventh Session, Supplement No. 41* (A/67/41), annex V, para. 59.

protection from discrimination by promoting knowledge and understanding of the right within the business sector, including within the media, marketing and advertising sectors. Awareness-raising and sensitization among business enterprises should be aimed at challenging and eradicating discriminatory attitudes towards all children, especially those in vulnerable situations.

B. The best interests of the child (art. 3, para. 1)

15. Article 3, paragraph 1, of the Convention provides that the best interests of the child shall be a primary consideration for States in all actions concerning children. States are obliged to integrate and apply this principle in all legislative, administrative and judicial proceedings concerning business activities and operations that directly or indirectly impact on children. For example, States must ensure that the best interests of the child are central to the development of legislation and policies that shape business activities and operations, such as those relating to employment, taxation, corruption, privatization, transport and other general economic, trade or financial issues.

16. Article 3, paragraph 1, is also directly applicable to business enterprises that function as private or public social welfare bodies by providing any form of direct services for children, including care, foster care, health, education and the administration of detention facilities.

17. The Convention and the Optional Protocols thereto provide the framework for assessing and determining the best interests of the child. The obligation to make the best interests of the child a primary consideration becomes crucial when States are engaged in weighing competing priorities, such as short-term economic considerations and longer-term development decisions. States should be in a position to explain how the right to have the best interests of the child considered has been respected in decision-making, including how it has been weighed against other considerations.[198]

C. The right to life, survival and development (art. 6)

18. Article 6 of the Convention acknowledges that every child has an inherent right to life and that States shall ensure the survival and development of the child. The Committee states its understanding of development of the child in general comment No. 5 (2003) on general measures of implementation of the Convention, as a "holistic concept, embracing the child's physical, mental, spiritual, moral, psychological and social development".[199]

19. The activities and operations of business enterprises can impact on the realization of article 6 in different ways. For example, environmental degradation and contamination arising from business activities can compromise children's rights to health, food security and access to safe drinking water and sanitation. Selling or leasing land to investors can deprive local populations of access to natural resources linked to their subsistence and cultural heritage; the rights of indigenous children may be particularly at risk in this context.[200] The marketing to children of products such as cigarettes and alcohol as well as foods and drinks high in saturated fats, trans-fatty acids, sugar, salt or additives can

---

[198] See General Comment No. 14 (2013) on the right of the child to have his/her best interests taken as a primary consideration: article 3, paragraph 1, of the Convention on the Rights of the Child, forthcoming, para. 6.

[199] See *Official Records of the General Assembly, Fifty-ninth Session, Supplement No. 41* (A/59/41), annex XI, para. 12.

[200] General comment No. 11 (2009) on indigenous children and their rights under the convention, *Official Records of the General Assembly, Sixty-fifth Session, Supplement No. 41* (A/65/41), annex III, para. 35.

have a long-term impact on their health.[201] When business employment practices require adults to work long hours, older children, particularly girls, may take on their parent's domestic and childcare obligations, which can negatively impact their right to education and to play; additionally, leaving children alone or in the care of older siblings can have implications for the quality of care and the health of younger children.

20. Measures for implementing article 6 with regard to the business sector will need to be adapted according to context and include preventive measures such as effective regulation and monitoring of advertising and marketing industries and the environmental impact of business. In the context of care of children, particularly young children, other measures will be needed for creating an enabling environment for business to respect article 6 through, for example, the introduction of family-friendly workplace policies. Such policies must take account of the impact of working hours of adults on the survival and development of the child at all stages of development and must include adequately remunerated parental leave.[202]

D. The right of the child to be heard (art. 12)

21. Article 12 of the Convention establishes the right of every child to freely express her or his views, in all matters affecting her or him, and the subsequent right for those views to be given due weight, according to the child's age and maturity. States should hear children's views regularly – in line with general comment No. 12[203] – when developing national and local-level business-related laws and policies that may affect them. In particular, States should consult with children who face difficulties in making themselves heard, such as the children of minority and indigenous groups, children with disabilities as stated in articles 4, paragraph 3, and 7 of the Convention on the Rights of Persons with Disabilities,[204] and children in similar situations of vulnerability. Governmental bodies, such as education and labour inspectorates, concerned with regulating and monitoring the activities and operations of business enterprises should ensure that they take into account the views of affected children. States should also hear children when child-rights impact assessments of proposed business-related policy, legislation, regulations, budget or other administrative decisions are undertaken.

22. Children have a specific right "to be heard in any judicial and administrative proceedings affecting the child" (art. 12, para. 3, of the Convention). This includes judicial proceedings and mechanisms of conciliation and arbitration that concern abuses of children's rights caused or contributed to by business enterprises. As set out in general comment No. 12, children should be allowed to voluntarily participate in such proceedings and be provided the opportunity to be heard directly or indirectly through the assistance of a representative or appropriate body that has sufficient knowledge and understanding of the various aspects of the decision-making process as well as experience in working with children.

23. There may be instances when business consults communities that may be affected by a potential business project. In such circumstances, it can be critical for business to seek the views of children and consider them in decisions that affect them. States should provide businesses with specific guidance emphasizing that such processes must be

---

[201] See general comment No. 15 (2013) on the right of the child to the highest attainable standard of health, forthcoming, para. 47.

[202] See passim general comment No. 7 (2005) on implementing child rights in early childhood, *Official Records of the General Assembly, Sixty-first Session, Supplement No. 41* (A/61/41), annex III.

[203] General comment No. 12 (2009) on the right of the child to be heard, *Official Records of the General Assembly, Sixty-fifth Session, Supplement No. 41* (A/65/41), annex IV.

[204] General comment No. 9 (2006) on the rights of children with disabilities, *Official Records of the General Assembly, Sixty-third Session, Supplement No. 41* (A/63/41), annex III, passim.

accessible, inclusive and meaningful to children and take into account the evolving capacities of children and their best interests at all times. Participation should be voluntary and occur in a child-friendly environment that challenges and does not reinforce patterns of discrimination against children. Where possible, civil society organizations that are competent in facilitating child participation should be involved.

IV. NATURE AND SCOPE OF STATE OBLIGATIONS

A. General obligations

24. The Convention provides for a set of rights for children that impose a particular level of obligations on the State in view of the special status of children; there is a particular gravity to violations of children's rights because they often have severe and long-lasting impact on child development. Article 4 sets out the obligation for States to undertake all appropriate legislative, administrative and other measures for the implementation of the rights in the Convention and devote the maximum amount of available resources to the realization of economic, social and cultural rights of the child.

25. Under international human rights law there are three types of obligation on States: to respect, to protect and to fulfil human rights.[205] They encompass obligations of result and obligations of conduct. States are not relieved of their obligations under the Convention and the Optional Protocols thereto when their functions are delegated or outsourced to a private business or non-profit organization. A State will thereby be in breach of its obligations under the Convention where it fails to respect, protect and fulfil children's rights in relation to business activities and operations that impact on children. The scope of these duties is explored further below, whilst the required framework for implementation is discussed in chapter VI.

B. The obligation to respect, protect and fulfil

1. The obligation to respect

26. The obligation to respect means that States should not directly or indirectly facilitate, aid and abet any infringement of children's rights. Furthermore, States have the obligation to ensure that all actors respect children's rights, including in the context of business activities and operations. To achieve this, all business-related policy, legislation or administrative acts and decision-making should be transparent, informed and include full and continuous consideration of the impact on the rights of the child.

27. The obligation to respect also implies that a State should not engage in, support or condone abuses of children's rights when it has a business role itself or conducts business with private enterprises. For example, States must take steps to ensure that public procurement contracts are awarded to bidders that are committed to respecting children's rights. State agencies and institutions, including security forces, should not collaborate with or condone the infringement of the rights of the child by third parties. Furthermore, States should not invest public finances and other resources in business activities that violate children's rights.

2. The obligation to protect

28. States have an obligation to protect against infringements of rights guaranteed under the Convention and the Optional Protocols thereto by third parties. This duty is of primary importance when considering States' obligations with regards to the business

---

[205] See Committee on Economic, Social and Cultural Rights, general comment No. 13 (1999) on the right to education, *Official Records of the Economic and Social Council, 2000, Supplement No. 2* (E/2000/22), annex VI, para. 46.

sector. It means that States must take all necessary, appropriate and reasonable measures to prevent business enterprises from causing or contributing to abuses of children's rights. Such measures can encompass the passing of law and regulation, their monitoring and enforcement, and policy adoption that frame how business enterprises can impact on children's rights. States must investigate, adjudicate and redress violations of children's rights caused or contributed to by a business enterprise. A State is therefore responsible for infringements of children's rights caused or contributed to by business enterprises where it has failed to undertake necessary, appropriate and reasonable measures to prevent and remedy such infringements or otherwise collaborated with or tolerated the infringements.

3. The obligation to fulfil

29. The obligation to fulfil requires States to take positive action to facilitate, promote and provide for the enjoyment of children's rights. This means that States must implement legislative, administrative, budgetary, judicial, promotional and other measures in conformity with article 4 relating to business activities that impact on children's rights. Such measures should ensure the best environment for full realization of the Convention and the Optional Protocols thereto. To meet this obligation, States should provide stable and predictable legal and regulatory environments which enable business enterprises to respect children's rights. This includes clear and well-enforced law and standards on labour, employment, health and safety, environment, anti-corruption, land use and taxation that comply with the Convention and the Optional Protocols thereto. It also includes law and policies designed to create equality of opportunity and treatment in employment; measures to promote vocational training and decent work, and to raise living standards; and policies conducive to the promotion of small and medium enterprises. States should put in place measures to promote knowledge and understanding of the Convention and the Optional Protocols thereto within government departments, agencies and other State-based institutions that shape business practices, and foster a culture in business that is respectful of children's rights.

4. Remedies and reparations

30. States have an obligation to provide effective remedies and reparations for violations of the rights of the child, including by third parties such as business enterprises. The Committee states in its general comment No. 5 that for rights to have meaning, effective remedies must be available to redress violations.[206] Several provisions in the Convention call for penalties, compensation, judicial action and measures to promote recovery after harm caused or contributed to by third parties.[207] Meeting this obligation entails having in place child-sensitive mechanisms – criminal, civil or administrative – that are known by children and their representatives, that are prompt, genuinely available and accessible and that provide adequate reparation for harm suffered. Agencies with oversight powers relevant to children's rights, including labour, education and health and safety inspectorates, environmental tribunals, taxation authorities, national human rights institutions and bodies focusing on equality in the business sector can also play a role in the provision of remedies. These agencies can proactively investigate and monitor abuses and may also have regulatory powers allowing them to impose administrative sanctions

---

[206] General comment No. 5 (2003), para. 24. States should also take into account the Basic Principles and Guidelines on the Right to a Remedy and Reparation for Victims of Gross Violations of International Human Rights Law and Serious Violations of International Humanitarian Law adopted by General Assembly resolution 60/147 of 2005.

[207] For example, see Convention on the Rights of the Child, arts. 32, para. 2; 19; and 39.

on businesses which infringe on children's rights. In all cases, children should have recourse to independent and impartial justice, or judicial review of administrative proceedings.

31. When determining the level or form of reparation, mechanisms should take into account that children can be more vulnerable to the effects of abuse of their rights than adults and that the effects can be irreversible and result in lifelong damage. They should also take into account the evolving nature of children's development and capacities and reparation should be timely to limit ongoing and future damage to the child or children affected; for example, if children are identified as victims of environmental pollution, immediate steps should be taken by all relevant parties to prevent further damage to the health and development of children and repair any damage done. States should provide medical and psychological assistance, legal support and measures of rehabilitation to children who are victims of abuse and violence caused or contributed to by business actors. They should also guarantee non-recurrence of abuse through, for example, reform of relevant law and policy and their application, including prosecution and sanction of the business actors concerned.

V. STATE OBLIGATIONS IN SPECIFIC CONTEXTS

32. Business activities and operations can impact on a broad range of children's rights. However, the Committee has identified the following non-exhaustive, specific contexts where the impact of business enterprises can be significant and where States' legal and institutional frameworks are often insufficient, ineffective or under pressure.

A. Provision of services for the enjoyment of children's rights

33. Business enterprises and non-profit organizations can play a role in the provision and management of services such as clean water, sanitation, education, transport, health, alternative care, energy, security and detention facilities that are critical to the enjoyment of children's rights. The Committee does not prescribe the form of delivery of such services but it is important to emphasize that States are not exempted from their obligations under the Convention when they outsource or privatize services that impact on the fulfilment of children's rights.

34. States must adopt specific measures that take account of the involvement of the private sector in service delivery to ensure the rights enumerated in the Convention are not compromised.[208] They have an obligation to set standards in conformity with the Convention and closely monitor them. Inadequate oversight, inspection and monitoring of these bodies can result in serious violations of children's rights such as violence, exploitation and neglect. They must ensure that such provision does not threaten children's access to services on the basis of discriminatory criteria, especially under the principle of protection from discrimination, and that, for all service sectors, children have access to an independent monitoring body, complaints mechanisms and, where relevant, to judicial recourse that can provide them with effective remedies in case of violations. The Committee recommends that there should be a permanent monitoring mechanism or process aimed at ensuring that all non-State service providers have in place and apply policies, programmes and procedures which are in compliance with the Convention.[209]

---

[208] See Committee on the Rights of the Child, report on its thirty-first session, CRC/C/121, annex II.
[209] See general comment No. 5, para. 44.

B. The informal economy

35. The informal economy engages an important part of the economically active population in many countries and contributes significantly to gross national product. However, children's rights can be particularly at risk from business activities that take place outside of the legal and institutional frameworks that regulate and protect rights. For example, products that are manufactured or handled in this context, such as toys, garments or foodstuffs, can be unhealthy and/or unsafe for children. Also, a concentrated number of children are often found in hidden areas of informal work, such as small family enterprises, agricultural and hospitality sectors. Such work frequently involves precarious employment status, low, irregular or no remuneration, health risks, a lack of social security, limited freedom of association and inadequate protection from discrimination and violence or exploitation. It can prevent children from attending school, doing schoolwork and having adequate rest and play, potentially infringing articles 28, 29 and 31 of the Convention. Moreover, parents or caregivers working in the informal economy often have to work long hours to obtain subsistence-level earnings, thus seriously limiting their opportunities to exercise parental responsibilities or care for children in their charge.

36. States should put in place measures to ensure that business activities take place within appropriate legal and institutional frameworks in all circumstances regardless of size or sector of the economy so that children's rights can be clearly recognized and protected. Such measures can include: awareness-raising, conducting research and gathering data on the impact of the informal economy upon children's rights, supporting the creation of decent jobs that provide adequate pay to working parents or caregivers; implementing clear and predictable land-use laws; improving the provision of social protection to low-income families; and supporting informal sector enterprises by providing skills training, registration facilities, effective and flexible credit and banking services, appropriate tax arrangements and access to markets, inter alia.

37. States must regulate working conditions and ensure safeguards to protect children from economic exploitation and work that is hazardous or interferes with their education or harms their health or physical, mental, spiritual, moral or social development. Such work is often found, albeit not exclusively, within the informal and family economies. Therefore, States are required to design and implement programmes aimed at reaching businesses in these contexts, including by enforcing international standards regarding legal minimum age for work and appropriate conditions of work, investing in education and vocational training and providing support for the satisfactory transition of children to the world of work. States should ensure that social and child protection policies reach all, especially families in the informal economy.

C. Children's rights and global operations of business

38. Business enterprises increasingly operate on a global scale through complex networks of subsidiaries, contractors, suppliers and joint ventures. Their impact on children's rights, whether positive or negative, is rarely the result of the action or omission of a single business unit, whether it is the parent company, subsidiary, contractor, supplier or others. Instead, it may involve a link or participation between businesses units located in different jurisdictions. For example, suppliers may be involved in the use of child labour, subsidiaries may be engaged in land dispossession and contractors or licensees may be involved in the marketing of goods and services that are harmful to children. There are particular difficulties for States in discharging their obligations to respect, protect and fulfil the rights of the child in this context owing, among other reasons, to the fact that business enterprises are often legally separate entities located in different jurisdictions even when they operate as an economic unit

which has its centre of activity, registration and/or domicile in one country (the home State) and is operational in another (the host State).

39. Under the Convention, States have the obligation to respect and ensure children's rights within their jurisdiction. The Convention does not limit a State's jurisdiction to "territory". In accordance with international law, the Committee has previously urged States to protect the rights of children who may be beyond their territorial borders. It has also emphasized that State obligations under the Convention and the Optional Protocols thereto apply to each child within a State's territory and to all children subject to a State's jurisdiction.[210]

40. Extraterritorial obligations are also explicitly referred to in the Optional Protocol on the sale of children, child prostitution and child pornography. Article 3, paragraph 1, provides that each State shall ensure that, as a minimum, offences under it are fully covered by its criminal or penal law, whether such offences are committed domestically or transnationally. Under article 3, paragraph 4, of Optional Protocol on the sale of children, child prostitution and child pornography, liability for these offences, whether criminal, civil or administrative, should be established for legal persons, including business enterprises. This approach is consistent with other human rights treaties and instruments that impose obligations on States to establish criminal jurisdiction over nationals in relation to areas such as complicity in torture, enforced disappearance and apartheid, no matter where the abuse and the act constituting complicity is committed.

41. States have obligations to engage in international cooperation for the realization of children's rights beyond their territorial boundaries. The preamble and the provisions of the Convention consistently refer to the "importance of international cooperation for improving the living conditions of children in every country, in particular in the developing countries".[211] General comment No. 5 emphasizes that "implementation of the Convention is a cooperative exercise for the States of the world".[212] As such, the full realization of children's rights under the Convention is in part a function of how States interact. Furthermore, the Committee highlights that the Convention has been nearly universally ratified; thus realization of its provisions should be of major and equal concern to both host and home States of business enterprises.

42. Host States have the primary responsibility to respect, protect and fulfil children's rights in their jurisdiction. They must ensure that all business enterprises, including transnational corporations operating within their borders, are adequately regulated within a legal and institutional framework that ensures that they do not adversely impact on the rights of the child and/or aid and abet violations in foreign jurisdictions.

43. Home States also have obligations, arising under the Convention and the Optional Protocols thereto, to respect, protect and fulfil children's rights in the context of businesses' extraterritorial activities and operations, provided that there is a reasonable link between the State and the conduct concerned. A reasonable link exists when a business enterprise has its centre of activity, is registered or domiciled or has its main place of business or substantial business activities in the State concerned.[213] When

---

[210] General comment No. 6 (2005) on treatment of unaccompanied and separated children outside their country of origin, *Official Records of the General Assembly, Sixty-first Session, Supplement No. 41* (A/61/41), annex II, para. 12.

[211] See Convention on the Rights of the Child, arts. 4; 24, para. 4; 28, para. 3; 17 and 22, para. 2; as well as Optional Protocol on the sale of children, child prostitution and child pornography, art. 10, and Optional Protocol on the involvement of children in armed conflict, art. 10.

[212] General comment No. 5, para. 60.

[213] See Maastricht Principles on Extraterritorial Obligations of States in the area of Economic, Social and Cultural Rights, principle 25 (2012).

adopting measures to meet this obligation, States must not violate the Charter of the United Nations and general international law nor diminish the obligations of the host State under the Convention.

44. States should enable access to effective judicial and non-judicial mechanisms to provide remedy for children and their families whose rights have been violated by business enterprises extraterritorially when there is a reasonable link between the State and the conduct concerned. Furthermore, States should provide international assistance and cooperation with investigations and enforcement of proceedings in other States.

45. Measures to prevent the infringement of children's rights by business enterprises when they are operating abroad include:

(a) Making access to public finance and other forms of public support, such as insurance, conditional on a business carrying out a process to identify, prevent or mitigate any negative impacts on children's rights in their overseas operations;

(b) Taking into account the prior record of business enterprises on children's rights when deciding on the provision of public finance and other forms of official support;

(c) Ensuring that State agencies with a significant role regarding business, such as export credit agencies, take steps to identify, prevent and mitigate any adverse impacts the projects they support might have on children's rights before offering support to businesses operating abroad and stipulate that such agencies will not support activities that are likely to cause or contribute to children's rights abuses.

46. Both home and host States should establish institutional and legal frameworks that enable businesses to respect children's rights across their global operations. Home States should ensure that there are effective mechanisms in place so that the government agencies and institutions with responsibility for implementation of the Convention and the Optional Protocols thereto coordinate effectively with those responsible for trade and investment abroad. They should also build capacity so that development assistance agencies and overseas missions that are responsible for promoting trade can integrate business issues into bilateral human rights dialogues, including children's rights, with foreign Governments. States that adhere to the OECD Guidelines for Multinational Enterprises should support their national contact points in providing mediation and conciliation for matters that arise extraterritorially by ensuring that they are adequately resourced, independent and mandated to work to ensure respect for children's rights in the context of business issues. Recommendations issued by bodies such as the OECD national contact points should be given adequate effect.

D. International organizations

47. All States are called upon, under article 4 of the Convention, to cooperate directly in the realization of the rights in the Convention through international cooperation and through their membership in international organizations. In the context of business activities, these international organizations include international development, finance and trade institutions, such as the World Bank Group, the International Monetary Fund and the World Trade Organization, and others of a regional scope, in which States act collectively. States must comply with their obligations under the Convention and the Optional Protocols thereto when acting as members of such organizations and they should not accept loans from international organizations, or agree to conditions set forth by such organizations, if these loans or policies are likely to result in violations of the rights of children. States also retain their obligations in the field of development

cooperation and should ensure that cooperation policies and programmes are designed and implemented in compliance with the Convention and the Optional Protocols thereto.

48. A State engaged with international development, finance and trade organizations must take all reasonable actions and measures to ensure that such organizations act in accordance with the Convention and the Optional Protocols thereto in their decision-making and operations, as well as when entering into agreements or establishing guidelines relevant to the business sector. Such actions and measures should go beyond the eradication of child labour and include the full realization of all children's rights. International organizations should have standards and procedures to assess the risk of harm to children in conjunction with new projects and to take measures to mitigate risks of such harm. These organizations should put in place procedures and mechanisms to identify, address and remedy violations of children's rights in accordance with existing international standards, including when they are committed by or result from activities of businesses linked to or funded by them.

E. Emergencies and conflict situations

49. There are particular challenges for both host and home States in meeting their obligations to respect, protect and fulfil the rights of the child when businesses are operating in situations where protection institutions do not work properly because of conflict, disaster or the breakdown of social or legal order. It is important to emphasize that the Convention and the Optional Protocols thereto apply at all times and that there are no provisions allowing for derogation of their provisions during emergencies.

50. In such contexts, there may be a greater risk of child labour being used by business enterprises -(including within supply chains and subsidiaries), of child soldiers being used or of corruption and tax evasion occurring. Given the heightened risks, home States should require business enterprises operating in situations of emergency and conflict to undertake stringent child-rights due diligence tailored to their size and activities. Home States should also develop and implement laws and regulations that address specific foreseeable risks to children's rights from business enterprises that are operating transnationally. This can include a requirement to publish actions taken to ensure that companies' operations do not contribute to serious violations of children's rights, and a prohibition on the sale or transfer of arms and other forms of military assistance when the final destination is a country in which children are known to be, or may potentially be, recruited or used in hostilities.

51. A home State should provide businesses with current, accurate and comprehensive information of the local children's rights context when they are operating or planning to operate in areas affected by conflict or emergency. Such guidance should emphasize that companies have identical responsibilities to respect children's rights in such settings as they do elsewhere. Children can be affected by violence, including sexual abuse or exploitation, child trafficking and gender-based violence in conflict zones and this must be recognized by States when providing guidance to businesses.

52. The obligations of host and home States under the relevant provisions of the Convention should be emphasized when business is operating in areas affected by conflict: Article 38 requires respect for the rules of international humanitarian law, article 39 obliges States to provide appropriate psychological recovery and social reintegration and the Optional Protocol on the involvement of children in armed conflict contains provisions regarding recruitment of children into armed forces under 18 years of age. When operating in areas affected by conflict, business enterprises may employ private security companies and may risk being involved in violations such as

exploitation and/or use of violence against children in the course of protecting facilities or other operations. To prevent this, both home and host States should introduce and implement national legislation that includes a specific prohibition on such companies recruiting children or using them in hostilities; requirements for effective measures to protect children from violence and exploitation; and mechanisms for holding personnel accountable for abuses of children's rights.

VI. FRAMEWORK FOR IMPLEMENTATION

A. *Legislative, regulatory and enforcement measures*

1. Legislation and regulation

53. Legislation and regulation are essential instruments for ensuring that the activities and operations of business enterprises do not adversely impact on or violate the rights of the child. States should enact legislation that gives effect to the rights of the child by third parties and provides a clear and predictable legal and regulatory environment which enables business enterprises to respect children's rights. To meet their obligation to adopt appropriate and reasonable legislative and regulatory measures to ensure that business enterprises do not infringe on children's rights, States will need to gather data, evidence and research for identifying specific business sectors of concern.

54. In conformity with article 18, paragraph 3, of the Convention, States should create employment conditions within business enterprises which assist working parents and caregivers in fulfilling their responsibilities to children in their care such as: the introduction of family-friendly workplace policies, including parental leave; support and facilitate breastfeeding; access to quality childcare services; payment of wages sufficient for an adequate standard of living; protection from discrimination and violence in the workplace; and, security and safety in the workplace.

55. Ineffective taxation systems, corruption and mismanagement of government revenues from, among others, State-owned businesses and corporate taxation, can limit the resources available for the fulfilment of children's rights in accordance with article 4 of the Convention. In addition to any existing obligations under anti-bribery and anti-corruption instruments,[214] States should develop and implement effective laws and regulations to obtain and manage revenue flows from all sources, ensuring transparency, accountability and equity.

56. States should implement article 32 of the Convention to ensure the prohibition of economic exploitation and hazardous work for children. Some children are above the minimum working age, in line with international standards, and therefore can be legitimately working as employees, while still needing to be protected, for instance, from work that is hazardous to their health, safety or moral development and ensuring that their rights to education, development and recreation are promoted and protected.[215] States must set a minimum age for employment; appropriately regulate working hours and conditions; and establish penalties to effectively enforce article 32. They must have functioning labour inspection and enforcement systems and capacities in place. States should also ratify and enact into domestic law both of the fundamental ILO conventions relating to child labour.[216] Under article 39, States must take all appropriate measures to

---

[214] Such as the OECD Convention on Combating Bribery of Foreign Public Officials in International Business Transactions and/or the United Nations Convention Against Corruption.

[215] See general comment No. 17 (2013) on the right of the child to rest, leisure, play, recreational activities, cultural life and the arts (art. 31), forthcoming.

[216] ILO Conventions Nos. 182 (1999) concerning the Prohibition and Immediate Action for the Elimination of the Worst Forms of Child Labour and 138 (1973) concerning Minimum Age for Admission to Employment.

promote the physical and psychological recovery and social reintegration of a child who has experienced any form of violence, neglect, exploitation, or abuse, including economic exploitation.

57. States are also required to implement and enforce internationally agreed standards concerning children's rights, health and business, including the World Health Organization Framework Convention on Tobacco Control, and the International Code of Marketing of Breast-milk Substitutes and relevant subsequent World Health Assembly resolutions. The Committee is aware that the activities and operations of the pharmaceutical sector can have a profound impact on the health of children. Pharmaceutical companies should be encouraged to improve the access, availability, acceptability and quality of medicines for children taking into consideration existing guidance.[217] Furthermore, intellectual property rights should be applied in ways that promote the affordability of medicines.[218]

58. The mass media industry, including advertising and marketing industries, can have positive as well as negative impacts on children's rights. Under article 17 of the Convention, States have obligations to encourage the mass media, including private media, to disseminate information and materials of social and cultural benefit to the child, for example regarding healthy lifestyles. The media must be regulated appropriately to protect children from harmful information, especially pornographic materials and materials that portray or reinforce violence, discrimination and sexualized images of children, while recognizing children's right to information and freedom of expression. States should encourage the mass media to develop guidelines to ensure full respect for the rights of the child, including their protection from violence and from portrayals that perpetuate discrimination, in all media coverage. States should establish copyright exceptions which permit the reproduction of books and other printed publications in formats that are accessible for children with visual or other impairments.

59. Children may regard marketing and advertisements that are transmitted through the media as truthful and unbiased and consequently can consume and use products that are harmful. Advertising and marketing can also have a powerful influence over children's self-esteem, for example when portraying unrealistic body images. States should ensure that marketing and advertising do not have adverse impacts on children's rights by adopting appropriate regulation and encouraging business enterprises to adhere to codes of conduct and use clear and accurate product labelling and information that allow parents and children to make informed consumer decisions.

60. Digital media is of particular concern, as many children can be users of the Internet but also become victims of violence such as cyber-bullying, cyber-grooming, trafficking or sexual abuse and exploitation through the Internet. Although companies may not be directly involved in such criminal acts, they can be complicit in these violations through their actions; for example, child sex tourism can be facilitated by travel agencies operating on the Internet, as they enable the exchange of information and the planning of sex tourism activities. Child pornography can be indirectly facilitated by Internet businesses and credit-card providers. As well as meeting their obligations under the Optional Protocol on the sale of children, child prostitution and child pornography, States should provide children with age-appropriate information regarding web-related safety so they can manage the risks and know where to go for help. They should

---

[217] Human Rights Guidelines for Pharmaceutical Companies in relation to Access to Medicines; Human Rights Council resolution 15/22.

[218] See general comment No. 15, para. 82; World Trade Organization, Declaration on the TRIPS Agreement and Public Health, WT/MIN(01)/DEC/2.

coordinate with the information and communication technology industry so that it develops and puts in place adequate measures to protect children from violent and inappropriate material.

2. Enforcement measures

61. Generally, it is the lack of implementation or the poor enforcement of laws regulating business that pose the most critical problems for children. There are a number of measures States should employ to ensure effective implementation and enforcement, including:

(a) Strengthening regulatory agencies responsible for the oversight of standards relevant to children's rights such as health and safety, consumer rights, education, environment, labour and advertising and marketing so that they have sufficient powers and resources to monitor and to investigate complaints and to provide and enforce remedies for abuses of children's rights;

(b) Disseminating laws and regulations regarding children's rights and business to stakeholders, including children and business enterprises;

(c) Training judges and other administrative officials as well as lawyers and legal aid providers to ensure the correct application of the Convention and its protocols on business and children's rights, international human rights standards and relevant national legislation and to promote the development of national jurisprudence; and

(d) Providing effective remedy through judicial or non-judicial mechanisms and effective access to justice.

3. Children's rights and due diligence by business enterprises

62. To meet their obligation to adopt measures to ensure that business enterprises respect children's rights, States should require businesses to undertake child-rights due diligence. This will ensure that business enterprises identify, prevent and mitigate their impact on children's rights including across their business relationships and within global operations.[219] Where there is a high risk of business enterprises being involved in violations of children's rights because of the nature of their operations or their operating contexts, States should require a stricter process of due diligence and an effective monitoring system.

63. Where child-rights due diligence is subsumed within a more general process of human-rights due diligence, it is imperative that the provisions of the Convention and the Optional Protocols thereto influence decisions. Any plan of action and measures to prevent and/or remedy human rights abuses must have special consideration for the differentiated impact on children.

64. States should lead by example, requiring all State-owned enterprises to undertake child-rights due diligence and to publicly communicate their reports on their impact on children's rights, including regular reporting. States should make public support and services, such as those provided by an export credit agency, development finance and investment insurance conditional on businesses carrying out child-rights due diligence.

65. As part of child-rights due diligence, large business enterprises should be encouraged and, where appropriate, required to make public their efforts to address child-rights impacts. Such communication should be available, efficient and comparable across enterprises and address measures taken by business to mitigate potential and actual adverse impacts for children caused by their activities. Business enterprises should be

---

[219] See UNICEF, Save the Children and Global Compact, Children's Rights and Business Principles (2011).

required to publish the actions taken to ensure that the goods and services they produce or commercialize do not involve serious violations of children's rights, such as slavery or forced labour. Where reporting is mandatory, States should put in place verification and enforcement mechanisms to ensure compliance. States may support reporting by creating instruments to benchmark and recognize good performance with regard to children's rights.

B. Remedial measures

66. Children often find it difficult to access the justice system to seek effective remedies for abuse or violations of their rights when business enterprises are involved. Children may lack legal standing, which prevents them from pursuing a claim; children and their families often lack knowledge about their rights and the mechanisms and procedures available to them to seek redress or may lack confidence in the justice system. States may not always investigate breaches of criminal, civil or administrative laws committed by business enterprises. There are vast power imbalances between children and business and, often, prohibitive costs involved in litigation against companies as well as difficulties in securing legal representation. Cases involving business are frequently settled out of court and in the absence of a body of developed case law; children and their families in jurisdictions where judicial precedent is persuasive may be more likely to abandon undertaking litigation given uncertainty surrounding the outcome.

67. There are particular difficulties in obtaining remedy for abuses that occur in the context of businesses' global operations. Subsidiaries or others may lack insurance or have limited liability; the way in which transnational corporations are structured in separate entities can make identification and attribution of legal responsibility to each unit challenging; access to information and evidence located in different countries can be problematic when building and defending a claim; legal aid may be difficult to obtain in foreign jurisdictions and various legal and procedural hurdles can be used to defeat extraterritorial claims.

68. States should focus their attention on removing social, economic and juridical barriers so that children can in practice have access to effective judicial mechanisms without discrimination of any kind. Children and their representatives should be provided with information about remedies through, for example, the school curriculum, youth centres or community-based programmes. They should be allowed to initiate proceedings in their own right and have access to legal aid and the support of lawyers and legal aid providers in bringing cases against business enterprises to ensure equality of arms. States that do not already have provision for collective complaints, such as class actions and public interest litigation, should introduce these as a means of increasing accessibility to the courts for large numbers of children similarly affected by business actions. States may have to provide special assistance to children who face obstacles to accessing justice, for example, because of language or disability or because they are very young.

69. Age should not be a barrier to a child's right to participate fully in the justice process. Likewise, special arrangements should be developed for child victims and witnesses in both civil and criminal proceedings, in line with the Committee's general comment No. 12. Furthermore, States should implement the Guidelines on Justice in Matters involving Child Victims and Witnesses of Crime.[220] Confidentiality and privacy must be respected and children should be kept informed of progress at all stages of the process, giving due weight to the child's maturity and any speech, language or communication difficulties they might have.

---

[220] Adopted by the Economic and Social Council in its resolution 2005/20.

70. The Optional Protocol on the sale of children, child prostitution and child pornography requires that States enact criminal legislation that also applies to legal entities, including business enterprises. States should consider the adoption of criminal legal liability – or another form of legal liability of equal deterrent effect – for legal entities, including business enterprises, in cases concerning serious violations of the rights of the child, such as forced labour. National tribunals should have jurisdiction over these serious violations, in accordance with accepted rules of jurisdiction.

71. Non-judicial mechanisms, such as mediation, conciliation and arbitration, can be useful alternatives for resolving disputes concerning children and enterprises. They must be available without prejudice to the right to judicial remedy. Such mechanisms can play an important role alongside judicial processes, provided they are in conformity with the Convention and the Optional Protocols thereto and with international principles and standards of effectiveness, promptness and due process and fairness. Grievance mechanisms established by business enterprises can provide flexible and timely solutions and at times it may be in a child's best interests for concerns raised about a company's conduct to be resolved through them. These mechanisms should follow criteria that include: accessibility, legitimacy, predictability, equitability, rights compatibility, transparency, continuous learning and dialogue.[221] In all cases, access to courts or judicial review of administrative remedies and other procedures should be available.

72. States should make every effort to facilitate access to international and regional human rights mechanisms, including the Optional Protocol to the Convention on the Rights of the Child on a communications procedure, so that an individual child or a group of children, or others acting on his/her/their behalf, are able to obtain remedy for State failure to adequately respect, protect and fulfil children's rights in relation to business activities and operations.

C. Policy measures

73. States should encourage a business culture that understands and fully respects children's rights. To this end, States should include the issue of children's rights and business in the overall context of the national policy framework for implementation of the Convention. They should develop guidance that explicitly sets out government expectations for business enterprises to respect children's rights in the context of its own business activities, as well as within business relationships linked to operations, products or services and activities abroad when they operate transnationally. This should include the implementation of zero-tolerance policies for violence in all business activities and operations. As required, States should signpost and encourage adherence to relevant corporate responsibility initiatives.

74. In many contexts, small and medium-sized enterprises represent a large part of the economy and it is particularly important that States provide them with readily available tailored guidance and support on how to respect children's rights and comply with national legislation while avoiding unnecessary administrative burdens. States should also encourage larger companies to use their influence over small and medium-sized enterprises to strengthen children's rights throughout their value chains.

---

[221] Report of the Special Representative of the Secretary-General on the issue of human rights and transnational corporations and other business enterprises, John Ruggie, Guiding Principles on Business and Human Rights: Implementing the United Nations "Protect, Respect and Remedy" Framework, A/HRC/17/31, guiding principle 31.

D. Coordination and monitoring measures

1. Coordination

75. Full implementation of the Convention and the Optional Protocols thereto requires effective cross-sectoral coordination, among government agencies and departments and across different levels of government, from local to regional and central.[222] Typically, the departments and agencies directly involved with business policies and practices work separately from departments and agencies with direct responsibility for children's rights. States must ensure that governmental bodies, as well as parliamentarians, that shape business law and practices are aware of the State's obligations with regard to children's rights. They may require relevant information, training and support so that they are equipped to ensure full compliance with the Convention when developing law and policy and entering into economic, trade and investment agreements. National human rights institutions can play an important role as catalysts for linking different governmental departments concerned with children's rights and with business.

2. Monitoring

76. States have an obligation to monitor violations of the Convention and the Optional Protocols thereto committed or contributed to by business enterprises, including in their global operations. This can be achieved, for instance, through: gathering data that can be used to identify problems and inform policy; investigating abuses; collaborating with civil society and national human rights institutions; and making business accountable publicly by using business reporting on their impact on children's rights to assess their performance. In particular, national human rights institutions can be involved, for example in receiving, investigating and mediating complaints of violations; conducting public inquiries into large-scale abuses, mediating in conflict situations and undertaking legislative reviews to ensure compliance with the Convention. Where necessary, States should broaden the legislative mandate of national human rights institutions to accommodate children's rights and business.

77. When States develop national strategies and plans of action for implementation of the Convention and the Optional Protocols thereto, they should include explicit reference to the measures required to respect, protect and fulfil children's rights in the actions and operations of business enterprises. States should also ensure that they monitor progress in implementation of the Convention in the activities and operations of business. This can be achieved both internally through the use of child rights impact assessments and evaluations, as well as through collaboration with other bodies such as parliamentary committees, civil society organizations, professional associations and national human rights institutions. Monitoring should include asking children directly for their views on the impact of business on their rights. Different mechanisms for consultation can be used, such as youth councils and parliaments, social media, school councils and associations of children.

3. Child-rights impact assessments

78. Ensuring that the best interests of the child are a primary consideration in business-related legislation and policy development and delivery at all levels of government demands continuous child-rights impact assessments. These can predict the impact of any proposed business-related policy, legislation, regulations, budget or other

---

[222] General comment No. 5, para. 37.

administrative decisions which affect children and the enjoyment of their rights[223] and should complement ongoing monitoring and evaluation of the impact of laws, policies and programmes on children's rights.

79. Different methodologies and practices may be developed when undertaking child-rights impact assessments. At a minimum they must use the framework of the Convention and the Optional Protocols thereto, as well as relevant concluding observations and general comments issued by the Committee. When States conduct broader impact assessments of business-related policy, legislation or administrative practices, they should ensure that these assessments are underpinned by the general principles of the Convention and the Optional Protocols thereto and have special regard for the differentiated impact on children of the measures under consideration.[224]

80. Child-rights impact assessments can be used to consider the impact on all children affected by the activities of a particular business or sector but can also include assessment of the differential impact of measures on certain categories of children. The assessment of the impact itself may be based upon input from children, civil society and experts, as well as from relevant government departments, academic research and experiences documented in the country or elsewhere. The analysis should result in recommendations for amendments, alternatives and improvements and be publicly available.[225]

81. To ensure an impartial and independent process, the State may consider appointing an external actor to lead the assessment process. This can have significant advantages, but the State, as the party ultimately responsible for the result, must ensure that the actor undertaking the assessment is competent, honest and impartial.

E. Collaborative and awareness-raising measures

82. While it is the State that takes on obligations under the Convention, the task of implementation needs to engage all sectors of society, including business, civil society and children themselves. The Committee recommends that States adopt and implement a comprehensive strategy to inform and educate all children, parents and caregivers that business has a responsibility to respect children's rights wherever they operate, including through child-friendly and age-appropriate communications, for example through the provision of education about financial awareness. Education, training and awareness-raising about the Convention should also be targeted at business enterprises to emphasize the status of the child as a holder of human rights, encourage active respect for all of the Convention's provisions and challenge and eradicate discriminatory attitudes towards all children and especially those in vulnerable and disadvantaged situations. In this context, the media should be encouraged to provide children with information about their rights in relation to business and raise awareness among businesses of their responsibility to respect children's rights.

83. The Committee highlights that national human rights institutions can be involved in raising awareness of the Convention's provisions amongst business enterprises, for instance by developing good practice guidance and policies for businesses and disseminating them.

84. Civil society has a critical role in the independent promotion and protection of children's rights in the context of business operations. This includes monitoring and holding business accountable; supporting children to have access to justice and remedies;

---

[223] General comment No. 5, para. 45.
[224] General comment No. 14, para. 99.
[225] Ibid.

contributing to child-rights impact assessments; and raising awareness amongst businesses of their responsibility to respect children's rights. States should ensure conditions for an active and vigilant civil society, including effective collaboration with and support to independent civil society organizations, child and youth-led organizations, academia, chambers of commerce and industry, trade unions, consumer associations and professional institutions. States should refrain from interfering with these and other independent organizations and facilitate their involvement in public policy and programmes relating to children's rights and business.

VII. DISSEMINATION

85. The Committee recommends that States widely disseminate the present general comment with parliament and across government, including within ministries, departments and municipal/local-level bodies working on business issues and those responsible for trade and investment abroad, such as development assistance agencies and overseas missions. The present general comment should be distributed to business enterprises, including those operating transnationally, as well as to small and medium-sized enterprises and actors in the informal sector. It should also be distributed and made known to professionals working for and with children, including judges, lawyers and legal aid providers, teachers, guardians, social workers, officials of public or private welfare institutions, as well as to all children and civil society. This will require translating it into relevant languages, making accessible and child-friendly versions available, holding workshops and seminars to discuss its implications and how best to implement it, and incorporating it into the training of all relevant professionals.

86. States should include information in their periodic reporting to the Committee on the challenges they face and the measures they have taken to respect, protect and fulfil children's rights in the context of the activities and operations of business enterprises both domestically and, where appropriate, transnationally.

General comment No 17 (2013) on the right of the child to rest, leisure, play, recreational activities, cultural life and the arts (art. 31)

Adopted by the Committee at its sixty-second session (14 January – 1 February 2013)

I. INTRODUCTION

1. The importance of play and recreation in the life of every child has long been acknowledged by the international community, as evidenced by the proclamation in the 1959 Declaration of the Rights of the Child: "The child shall have full opportunity for play and recreation [...]; society and the public authorities shall endeavour to promote the enjoyment of this right" (art. 7). This proclamation was further strengthened in the Convention on the Rights of the Child (the Convention) of 1989 which explicitly states in article 31 that "States Parties recognize the right of the child to rest and leisure, to engage in play and recreational activities appropriate to the age of the child and and to participate freely in cultural life and the arts."

2. However, based on its reviews of the implementation of the rights of the child under the Convention, the Committee is concerned by the poor recognition given by States to the rights contained in article 31. Poor recognition of their significance in the lives of children results in lack of investment in appropriate provisions, weak or non-existent protective legislation and the invisibility of children in national and local-level planning. In general, where investment is made, it is in the provision of structured and organized activities, but equally important is the need to create time and space for children to engage in spontaneous play, recreation and creativity, and to promote societal attitudes that support and encourage such activity.

3. The Committee is particularly concerned about the difficulties faced by particular categories of children in relation to enjoyment and conditions of equality of the rights defined in article 31, especially girls, poor children, children with disabilities, indigenous children, children belonging to minorities, among others.

4. Furthermore, profound changes in the world are having a major impact on children's opportunities to enjoy the rights provided for in article 31. The urban population, especially in developing countries, is increasing significantly, as is violence worldwide in all its forms – at home, in schools, in mass media, in the streets. The implications, along with the commercialization of play provisions, are influencing the ways children engage in recreation, as well as in cultural and artistic activities. For many children in both rich and poor countries, child labour, domestic work or increasing educational demands serve to reduce the time available for the enjoyment of these rights.

5. This general comment has been developed to address these concerns, raise the profile, awareness and understanding among States of the centrality of the rights in article 31 in the life and development of every child, and urge them to elaborate measures to ensure their implementation. The rights in article 31 have universal application in the diversity of communities and societies in the world and respect the value of all cultural traditions and forms. Every child should be able to enjoy these rights regardless of where he or she lives, his or her cultural background or his or her parental status.

6. This general comment only touches tangentially on the issue of sport, as it is a major issue in its own right. In respect of cultural life, the general comment focuses primarily on aspects related to creative or artistic activities, rather than the broader definition embraced in article 30 on the right of the child to enjoy his or her own culture.

II. OBJECTIVES

7. The present general comment seeks to enhance the understanding of the importance of article 31 for children's well-being and development; to ensure respect for and strengthen the application of the rights under article 31, as well as other rights in the Convention, and to highlight the implications for the determination of:

(a) Consequent obligations of States in the elaboration of all implementation measures, strategies and programmes aimed at the realization and full implementation of the rights defined in article 31;

(b) The role and responsibilities of the private sector, including companies working in the areas of recreation, cultural and artistic activities, as well as civil society organizations providing such services for children;

(c) Guidelines for all individuals working with children, including parents, on all actions undertaken in the area of play and recreation.

III. SIGNIFICANCE OF ARTICLE 31 IN CHILDREN'S LIVES

8. Article 31 must be understood holistically, both in terms of its constituent parts and also in its relationship with the Convention in its entirety. Each element of article 31is mutually linked and reinforcing, and when realized, serves to enrich the lives of children. Together, they describe conditions necessary to protect the unique and evolving nature of childhood. Their realization is fundamental to the quality of childhood, to children's entitlement to optimum development, to the promotion of resilience and to the realization of other rights. Indeed, environments in which play and recreational opportunities are available to all children provide the conditions for creativity; opportunities to exercise competence through self-initiated play enhances motivation, physical activity and skills development; immersion in cultural life enriches playful interactions; rest ensures that children have the necessary energy and motivation to participate in play and creative engagement.

9. Play and recreation are essential to the health and well-being of children and promote the development of creativity, imagination, self-confidence, self-efficacy, as well as physical, social, cognitive and emotional strength and skills. They contribute to all aspects of learning;[226] they are a form of participation in everyday life and are of intrinsic value to the child, purely in terms of the enjoyment and pleasure they afford. Research evidence highlights that playing is also central to children's spontaneous drive for development, and that it performs a significant role in the development of the brain, particularly in the early years. Play and recreation facilitate children's capacities to negotiate, regain emotional balance, resolve conflicts and make decisions. Through their involvement in play and recreation, children learn by doing; they explore and experience the world around them; experiment with new ideas, roles and experiences and in so doing, learn to understand and construct their social position within the world.

10. Both play and recreation can take place when children are on their own, together with their peers or with supportive adults. Children's development can be supported by loving and caring adults as they relate to children through play. Participation with children in play provides adults with unique insights and understanding into the child's perspectives. It builds respect between generations, contributes to effective understanding and communication between children and adults and affords opportunities to provide guidance and stimulus. Children benefit from recreational activities involving adults, including voluntary participation in organized sports, games and other recreational activities. However, the benefits are diminished, particularly in

---

[226] UNESCO, _Education for the twenty-first century: issues and prospects_ (Paris, 1998).

the development of creativity, leadership and team spirit if control by adults is so pervasive that it undermines the child's own efforts to organize and conduct his or her play activities.

11. Involvement in a community's cultural life is an important element of children's sense of belonging. Children inherit and experience the cultural and artistic life of their family, community and society, and through that process, they discover and forge their own sense of identity and, in turn, contribute to the stimulation and sustainability of cultural life and traditional arts.

12. In addition, children reproduce, transform, create and transmit culture through their own imaginative play, songs, dance, animation, stories, painting, games, street theatre, puppetry, festivals, and so on. As they gain understanding of the cultural and artistic life around them from adult and peer relationships, they translate and adapt its meaning through their own generational experience. Through engagement with their peers, children create and transmit their own language, games, secret worlds, fantasies and other cultural knowledge. Children's play generates a "culture of childhood," from games in school and in the playground to urban activities such as playing marbles, free running, street art and so on. Children are also at the forefront in using digital platforms and virtual worlds to establish new means of communication and social networks, through which different cultural environments and artistic forms are being forged. Participation in cultural and artistic activities are necessary for building children's understanding, not only of their own culture, but other cultures, as it provides opportunities to broaden their horizons and learn from other cultural and artistic traditions, thus contributing towards mutual understanding and appreciation of diversity.

13. Finally, rest and leisure are as important to children's development as the basics of nutrition, housing, health care and education. Without sufficient rest, children will lack the energy, motivation and physical and mental capacity for meaningful participation or learning. Denial of rest can have an irreversible physical and psychological impact on the development, health and well-being of children. Children also need leisure, defined as time and space without obligations, entertainment or stimulus, which they can choose to fill as actively or inactively as they wish.

IV. LEGAL ANALYSIS OF ARTICLE 31

A. Article 31, paragraph 1

14. States parties recognize the right of the child to:

(a) **Rest:** The right to rest requires that children are afforded sufficient respite from work, education or exertion of any kind, to ensure their optimum health and well-being. It also requires that they are provided with the opportunity for adequate sleep. In fulfilling the right to both respite from activity and adequate sleep, regard must be afforded to children's evolving capacities and their developmental needs.

(b) **Leisure:** Leisure refers to time in which play or recreation can take place. It is defined as free or unobligated time that does not involve formal education, work, home responsibilities, performance of other life-sustaining functions or engaging in activity directed from outside the individual. In other words it is largely discretionary time to be used as the child chooses.

(c) **Play:** Children's play is any behaviour, activity or process initiated, controlled and structured by children themselves; it takes place whenever and wherever opportunities arise. Caregivers may contribute to the creation of environments in which play takes place, but play itself is non-compulsory, driven by intrinsic motivation and undertaken for its own sake, rather than as a means to an end. Play involves the exercise of autonomy, physical, mental or emotional activity, and has the potential to take infinite forms, either in groups or alone. These forms will change and be adapted throughout the course of childhood. The key characteristics of play are fun, uncertainty, challenge, flexibility and non-productivity. Together, these factors contribute to the enjoyment it produces and the consequent incentive to continue to play. While play is often considered non-essential, the Committee reaffirms that it is a fundamental and vital dimension of the pleasure of childhood, as well as an essential component of physical, social, cognitive, emotional and spiritual development.

(d)   **Recreational activities:** Recreation is an umbrella term used to describe a very broad range of activities, including, inter alia, participation in music, art, crafts, community engagement, clubs, sports, games, hiking and camping, pursuing hobbies. It consists of activities or experiences, chosen voluntarily by the child, either because of the immediate satisfaction provided or because he or she perceives that some personal or social value will be gained by accomplishing them. Recreation often takes place in spaces specifically designed for it. While many recreational activities may be organized and managed by adults, recreation should be a voluntary activity. Compulsory or enforced games and sports or compulsory involvement in a youth organization, for example, do not constitute recreation.

(e)   **Appropriate to the age of the child:** Article 31emphasizes the importance of activities appropriate to the age of the child. In respect of play and recreation, the age of the child must be taken into account in determining the amount of time afforded; the nature of spaces and environments available; forms of stimulation and diversity; the degree of necessary adult oversight and engagement to ensure safety and security. As children grow older, their needs and wants evolve from settings that afford play opportunities to places offering opportunities to socialize, be with peers or be alone. They will also explore progressively more opportunities involving risk-taking and challenge. These experiences are developmentally necessary for adolescents, and contribute to their discovery of identity and belonging.

(f)   **Cultural life and the arts:** The Committee endorses the view that it is through cultural life and the arts that children and their communities express their specific identity and the meaning they give to their existence, and build their world view representing their encounter with external forces affecting their lives.[227] Cultural and artistic expression is articulated and enjoyed in the home, school, streets and public spaces, as well as through dance, festivals, crafts, ceremonies, rituals, theatre, literature, music, cinema, exhibitions, film, digital platforms and video. Culture derives from the community as a whole; no child should be denied access either to its creation or to its benefits. Cultural life emerges from within the culture and community, rather than imposed from above, with the role of States being to serve as facilitators not suppliers.[228]

(g)   **Participate freely:** The right of children to participate freely in cultural life and the arts requires that States parties respect and abstain from interfering in the child's access to, choice of and engagement in such activities, subject to the obligation to ensure the protection of the child and the promotion of the child's

---

[227] Committee on Economic, Social and Cultural Rights, general comment No. 21 (2009) on the right of everyone to take part in cultural life, para. 13.

[228] See UNESCO, "Mexico City Declaration on Cultural Policies," World Conference on Cultural Policies, Mexico City, 26 July – 6 August 1982.

best interests. States parties must also ensure that others do not restrict that right. The child's decision to exercise or not exercise this right is his or her choice and, as such, should be recognized, respected and protected.

B. Article 31, paragraph 2

15. States Parties shall respect and promote the right of the child:

(a) **Participate fully in cultural and artistic life:** The right to participate fully has three inter-related and mutually reinforcing dimensions:
(i) **Access** necessitates that children are provided the opportunities to experience cultural and artistic life and to learn about a wide range of different forms of expression;
(ii) **Participation** requires that concrete opportunities are guaranteed for children, individually or as a group, to express themselves freely, to communicate, act and engage in creative activities, with a view to the full development of their personalities;
(iii) **Contribution to cultural life** encompasses the right of children to contribute to the spiritual, material, intellectual and emotional expressions of culture and the arts, thereby furthering the development and transformation of the society to which he or she belongs.

(b) **Encourage the provision of appropriate opportunities:** Although the requirement to encourage the provision of appropriate opportunities specifies cultural, artistic, recreational and leisure activity, the Committee interprets it as including play also, further to article 4 of the Convention. States parties must therefore ensure the necessary and appropriate preconditions for participation to facilitate and promote opportunities for the realization of the rights under article 31. Children can only realize their rights if the necessary legislative, policy, budgetary, environmental and service frameworks are in place.

(c) **Provision of equal opportunities:** Every child must be afforded equal opportunities to enjoy his or her rights under article 31.

V. ARTICLE 31 IN THE BROADER CONTEXT OF THE CONVENTION

A. Links with the general principles of the Convention

16. **Article 2 (non-discrimination):** The Committee emphasizes that States parties shall take all appropriate measures to ensure that all children have the opportunity to realize their rights under article 31 without discrimination of any kind, irrespective of the child's or his or her parent's or legal guardian's race, colour, sex, language, religion, political or other opinion, national, ethnic or social origin, property, disability, birth or other status. Particular attention should be given to addressing the rights of certain groups of children, including, inter alia, girls, children with disabilities, children living in poor or hazardous environments, children living in poverty, children in penal, health-care or residential institutions, children in situations of conflict or humanitarian disaster, children in rural communities, asylum-seeking and refugee children, children in street situations, nomadic groups, migrant or internally displaced children, children of indigenous origin and from minority groups, working children, children without parents and children subjected to significant pressure for academic attainment.

17. **Article 3 (best interests of the child):** The Committee emphasizes that the realization of the rights under article 31is, by definition, in the child's best interests. The obligation to consider the child's best interests applies to children as individuals and as a group or constituency. All legislative, policy and budgetary measures, as well as measures relating to environmental or service provision, which are likely to impact on the rights provided

for in article 31 must take into consideration the best interests of children. This would apply, for example, to regulations relating to health and safety, solid waste disposal and collection, residential and transportation planning, design and accessibility of the urban landscape, provision of parks and other green spaces, determination of school hours, child labour and education legislation, planning applications or legislation governing privacy on the Internet, among others.

18. Article 6 (life, survival and development): State parties must ensure, to the maximum extent possible, the life, survival and development of the child. In this regard, the Committee draws attention to the need to recognize the positive value of each dimension of article 31 in promoting the development and evolving capacities of children. This also requires that the measures introduced to implement article 31 are in accordance with the developmental needs of children at all ages. States parties should promote awareness and understanding of the centrality of play for children's development among parents, caregivers, government officials and all professionals working with and for children.

19. Article 12 (right to be heard): Children, as individuals and as a group, have the right to express their views on all matters of concern to them, which should be given due weight, in accordance with their age and maturity, and they should receive adequate support to express their views, where necessary. Children are entitled to exercise choice and autonomy in their play and recreational activities, as well as in their participation in cultural and artistic activities. The Committee underlines the importance of providing opportunities for children to contribute to the development of legislation, policies, strategies and design of services to ensure the implementation of the rights under article 31. Such contribution could include their involvement, for example, in consultations on policies related to play and recreation, on legislation affecting educational rights and school organization and curriculum or protective legislation relating to child labour, on the development of parks and other local facilities, on urban planning and design for child-friendly communities and environments, and their feedback could be sought on opportunities for play or recreation and cultural activities within the school and the wider community.[229]

B. Links with other relevant rights

20. Article 13: The right to freedom of expression is fundamental to the right to participate freely in cultural and artistic activity. Children have the right to express themselves in whatever way they choose, subject only to restrictions as defined by law and when necessary to ensure respect for the rights and reputations of others, and for the protection of national security, public order and public health or morals.

21. Article 15: Children have the right to exercise choice in their friendships, as well as membership of social, cultural, sporting and other forms of organization. Freedom of association represents an integral dimension of their rights under article 31, as children together create forms of imaginative play that are rarely achieved in adult-child relations. Children need to engage with peers of both sexes, as well as with people of different abilities, classes, cultures and ages, in order to learn cooperation, tolerance, sharing and resourcefulness. Play and recreation create the opportunities for the formation of friendships and can play a key role in strengthening civil society, contributing towards the social, moral and emotional development of the child, shaping culture and building communities. State parties must facilitate opportunities to enable children to meet freely with their peers at the community level. They must also respect

---

[229] See the Committee's general comment No.12 (2009) on the right of the child to be heard.

and support the right of children to establish, join and leave associations, and the right to peaceful assembly. However, children should never be compelled to participate or join organizations.

22. **Article 17:** Children are entitled to information and materials which are of social and cultural benefit and which derive from a diversity of community, national and international sources. Access to such information and materials is essential for their realization of the right to participate fully in cultural and artistic activity. States parties are encouraged to ensure that children are provided with the widest possible access, through different media, to information and materials related to their own culture and to other cultures, in a language that they understand, including sign language and Braille, and by permitting exceptions to copyright laws in order to ensure the availability of printed materials in alternative formats. In so doing, care must be taken to protect and preserve cultural diversity and to avoid cultural stereotypes.

23. **Article 22:** Refugee and asylum-seeking children face profound challenges in realizing their rights under article 31 as they often experience both dislocation from their own traditions and culture and exclusion from the culture of the host country. Efforts must be made to ensure that refugee and asylum-seeking children have equal opportunities with children from the host country to enjoy the rights provided for in article 31. Recognition must also be afforded to the right of refugee children to preserve and practice their own recreational, cultural and artistic traditions.

24. **Article 23:** Accessible and inclusive environments and facilities must be made available[230] to children with disabilities to enable them to enjoy their rights under article 31. Families, caregivers and professionals must recognize the value of inclusive play, both as a right and as a means of achieving optimum development, for children with disabilities. States parties should promote opportunities for children with disabilities, as equal and active participants in play, recreation and cultural and artistic life, by awareness-raising among adults and peers, and by providing age-appropriate support or assistance.

25. **Article 24:** Not only does the realization of the rights provided for in article 31 contribute to the health, well-being and development of children, but also appropriate provision for children to enjoy the rights under article 31 when they are ill and/or hospitalized will play an important role in facilitating their recovery.

26. **Article 27:** Inadequate standard of living, insecure or overcrowded conditions, unsafe and unsanitary environments, inadequate food, enforced harmful or exploitative work can all serve to limit or deny children the opportunity to enjoy their rights under article 31. States parties are encouraged to take into account the implications for children's rights under article 31 when developing policies relating to social protection, employment, housing and access to public spaces for children, especially those living without opportunities for play and recreation in their own homes.

27. **Articles 28 and 29:** Education must be directed to the development of the child's personality, talents and mental and physical abilities to the fullest potential. Implementation of the rights under article 31 is essential to achieving compliance with the right provided for in article 29. For children to optimize their potential, they require opportunities for cultural and artistic development as well as participation in sports and games. The Committee also emphasizes that the rights under article 31 are of positive benefit to children's educational development; inclusive education and inclusive play are mutually reinforcing and should be facilitated during the course of every day throughout

---

[230] See Convention on the Rights of Persons with Disabilities, arts. 7, 9 and 30.

early childhood education and care (preschool) as well as primary and secondary school. While relevant and necessary for children of all ages, play is particularly significant in the early years of schooling. Research has shown that play is an important means through which children learn.

28. Article 30: Children from ethnic, religious or linguistic minorities should be encouraged to enjoy and participate in their own cultures. States should respect the cultural specificities of children from minority communities as well as children of indigenous origin, and ensure that they are afforded equal rights with children from majority communities to participate in cultural and artistic activities reflecting their own language, religion and culture.

29. Article 32: The Committee notes that in many countries, children are engaged in arduous work which denies them their rights under article 31. Furthermore, millions of children are working as domestic workers or in non-hazardous occupations with their families without adequate rest or education, throughout most of their childhood. States need to take all necessary measures to protect all child workers from conditions that violate their rights under article 31.

30. Articles 19, 34, 37 and 38: Violence, sexual exploitation, deprivation of liberty by unlawful or arbitrary means and forced service in armed conflicts impose conditions that seriously impede or even eliminate children's abilities to enjoy play, recreation and participation in cultural life and the arts. Bullying by other children can also be a major impediment to the enjoyment of the rights under article 31. Those rights can only be realized if States parties take all necessary measures to protect children from such acts.

31. Article 39: States parties should ensure that children who have experienced neglect, exploitation, abuse or other forms of violence are provided with support for recovery and reintegration. Children's experiences, including those which are painful and damaging, can be communicated through play or artistic expression. Opportunities to realize the rights under article 31 can provide a valuable means through which children can externalize traumatic or difficult life experiences in order to make sense of their past and better cope with their future. Play and artistic expression would enable them to communicate, better understand their own feelings and thoughts, prevent or resolve psychosocial challenges and learn to manage relationships and conflicts through a natural, self-guided, self-healing process.

VI. CREATING THE CONTEXT FOR THE REALIZATION OF ARTICLE 31

A. Factors for an optimum environment

32. Children have a spontaneous urge to play and participate in recreational activities and will seek out opportunities to do so in the most unfavourable environments. However, certain conditions need to be assured, in accordance with children's evolving capacities, if they are to realize their rights under article 31 to the optimum extent. As such, children should have:

(i)   Freedom from stress;
(ii)   Freedom from social exclusion, prejudice or discrimination;
(iii)   An environment secure from social harm or violence;
(iv)   An environment sufficiently free from waste, pollution, traffic and other physical hazards to allow them to circulate freely and safely within their local neighbourhood;
(v)   Availability of rest appropriate to their age and development;
(vi)   Availability of leisure time, free from other demands;
(vii)   Accessible space and time for play, free from adult control and management;

(viii) Space and opportunities to play outdoors unaccompanied in a diverse and challenging physical environment, with easy access to supportive adults, when necessary;

(ix) Opportunities to experience, interact with and play in natural environments and the animal world;

(x) Opportunities to invest in their own space and time so as to create and transform their world, using their imagination and languages;

(xi) Opportunities to explore and understand the cultural and artistic heritage of their community, participate in, create and shape it;

(xii) Opportunities to participate with other children in games, sports and other recreational activities, supported, where necessary, by trained facilitators or coaches;

(xiii) Recognition by parents, teachers and society as a whole of the value and legitimacy of the rights provided for in article 31.

B. Challenges to be addressed in the realization of article 31

33. Lack of recognition of the importance of play and recreation: In many parts of the world, play is perceived as "deficit" time spent in frivolous or unproductive activity of no intrinsic worth. Parents, caregivers and public administrators commonly place a higher priority on studying or economic work than on play, which is often considered noisy, dirty, disruptive and intrusive. Moreover, adults often lack the confidence, skill or understanding to support children's play and to interact with them in a playful way. Both the right of children to engage in play and recreation and their fundamental importance of those activities for children's well-being, health and development are poorly understood and undervalued. When play is recognized, it is usually physically active play and competitive games(sport) that are valued above fantasy or social drama, for example. The Committee emphasizes that greater recognition of the forms and locations of play and recreation preferred by older children is particularly necessary. Adolescents often seek places to meet with their peers and explore their emerging independence and transition to adulthood. This is an important dimension for the development of their sense of identity and belonging.

34. Unsafe and hazardous environments: Features in the environment which impact on the rights provided for in article 31 can either serve as protective or risk factors for children's health, development and safety. In respect of younger children, spaces which provide opportunities for exploration and creativity should enable parents and caregivers to maintain oversight, including by means of eye and voice contact. Children need access to inclusive spaces that are free from inappropriate hazards and close to their own homes, as well as with measures to promote safe, independent mobility as their capacities evolve.

35. The majority of the world's poorest children face physical hazards such as polluted water; open sewer systems; overcrowded cities; uncontrolled traffic; poor street lighting and congested streets; inadequate public transport; lack of safe local play areas, green spaces and cultural facilities; informal urban "slum" settlements in hazardous, violent or toxic environments. In post-conflict environments, children can also be harmed by landmines and unexploded ordnance. Indeed, children are at particular risk both because their natural curiosity and exploratory play increases the likelihood of exposure and because the impact of an explosion is greater on a child.

36. Human factors can also combine to place children at risk in the public environment: high levels of crime and violence; community unrest and civil strife; drug and gang-related violence; risk of kidnapping and child trafficking; open spaces dominated by hostile youth or adults; aggression and sexual violence towards girls. Even where

parks, playgrounds, sports facilities and other provisions exist, they may often be in locations where children are at risk, unsupervised and exposed to hazards. The dangers posed by all these factors severely restrict children's opportunities for safe play and recreation. The increasing erosion of many spaces traditionally available to children creates a need for greater Government intervention to protect the rights under article 31.

37. **Resistance to children's use of public spaces:** Children's use of public space for play, recreation and their own cultural activities is also impeded by the increasing commercialization of public areas, from which children are excluded. Furthermore, in many parts of the world, there is decreasing tolerance of children in public spaces. The introduction, for example, of curfews on children; gated communities or parks; reduced noise-level tolerance; playgrounds with strict rules for "acceptable" play behaviour; restrictions on access to shopping malls builds a perception of children as "problems" and/or delinquents. Adolescents, in particular, are widely perceived as a threat by widespread negative media coverage and representation, and discouraged from using public spaces.

38. The exclusion of children has significant implications for their development as citizens. Shared experience of inclusive public spaces by different age groups serves to promote and strengthen civil society and encourage children to recognize themselves as citizens with rights. States are encouraged to promote dialogue between older and younger generations to encourage greater recognition of children as rights holders, and of the importance of networks of diverse community spaces in local areas or municipalities which can accommodate the play and recreational needs of all children.

39. **Balancing risk and safety:** Fears over the physical and human risks to which children are exposed within their local environments are leading, in some parts of the world, to increasing levels of monitoring and surveillance, with consequent constraints on their freedom to play and opportunities for recreation. In addition, children themselves can pose a threat to other children in their play and recreational activities – for example, bullying, abuse of younger children by older children and group pressure to engage in high risk-taking. While children must not be exposed to harm in the realization of their rights under article 31, some degree of risk and challenge is integral to play and recreational activities and is a necessary component of the benefits of these activities. A balance is needed between, on the one hand, taking action to reduce unacceptable hazards in children's environment, such as closing local streets to traffic, improving street lighting or creating safe boundaries for school playgrounds, and on the other hand, informing, equipping and empowering children to take the necessary precautions to enhance their own safety. The best interests of the child and listening to children's experiences and concerns should be mediating principles for determining the level of risk to which children can be exposed.

40. **Lack of access to nature:** Children come to understand, appreciate and care for the natural world through exposure, self-directed play and exploration with adults who communicate its wonder and significance. Memories of childhood play and leisure in nature strengthen resources with which to cope with stress, inspire a sense of spiritual wonder and encourage stewardship for the earth. Play in natural settings also contributes towards agility, balance, creativity, social cooperation and concentration. Connection to nature through gardening, harvesting, ceremonies and peaceful contemplation is an important dimension of the arts and heritage of many cultures. In an increasingly urbanized and privatized world, children's access to parks, gardens, forests, beaches and other natural areas is being erodedm, and children in low-income urban areas are most likely to lack adequate access to green spaces.

41. Pressure for educational achievement: Many children in many parts of the world are being denied their rights under article 31 as a consequence of an emphasis on formal academic success. For example:

(i)   Early childhood education is increasingly focused on academic targets and formal learning at the expense of participation in play and attainment of broader development outcomes;

(ii)   Extracurricular tuition and homework are intruding on children's time for freely chosen activities;

(iii) The curriculum and daily schedule often lack recognition of the necessity of or provision for play, recreation and rest;

(iv)   The use of formal or didactic educational methods in the classroom do not take advantage of opportunities for active playful learning;

(v)   Contact with nature is decreasing in many schools with children having to spend more time indoors;

(vi)   Opportunities for cultural and artistic activities and the provision of specialist arts educators in school are, in some countries, being eroded in favour of more academic subjects.

(vii) Restrictions on the type of play in which children can engage in school serve to inhibit their opportunities for creativity, exploration and social development.

42. Overly structured and programmed schedules: For many children, the ability to realize the rights provided for in article 31 is restricted by the imposition of adult-decided activities, including, for example, compulsory sports, rehabilitative activities for children with disabilities or domestic chores, particularly for girls, which allow little or no time for self-directed activities. Where Government investment exists, it tends to focus on organized competitive recreation, or sometimes children are required or pressured to participate in youth organizations not of their own choosing. Children are entitled to time that is not determined or controlled by adults, as well as time in which they are free of any demands – basically to do "nothing", if they so desire. Indeed, the absence of activity can serve as a stimulus to creativity. Narrowly focusing all of a child's leisure time into programmed or competitive activities can be damaging to his or her physical, emotional, cognitive and social well-being.[231]

43. Neglect of article 31 in development programmes: Early childhood care and development work in many countries focuses exclusively on issues of child survival with no attention paid to the conditions that enable children to thrive. Programmes often only deal with nutrition, immunization and preschool education with little or no emphasis on play, recreation, culture and the arts. The personnel running the programmes are not appropriately trained to support these aspects of the child's development needs.

44. Lack of investment in cultural and artistic opportunities for children: Children's access to cultural and artistic activities are often restricted by a range of factors, including lack of parental support; cost of access; lack of transport; the adult-centred focus of many exhibitions, plays and events; failure to engage children in the content, design, location and forms of provision. Greater emphasis is needed in the creation of spaces to stimulate creativity. Operators of arts and cultural venues should look beyond their physical spaces to consider how their programmes reflect and respond to the cultural lives of the community they represent. Children's participation in the arts requires a more child-centred approach which commissions and displays children's

---

[231] Marta Santos Pais, "The Convention on the Rights of the Child," in OHCHR, *Manual on Human Rights Reporting* (Geneva, 1997), pp. 393 to 505.

creations and also engages them in the structure and programmes offered. Such engagement during childhood can serve to stimulate cultural interests for life.

45. Growing role of electronic media: Children in all regions of the world are spending increasing periods of time engaged in play, recreational, cultural and artistic activities, both as consumers and creators, via various digital platforms and media, including watching television, messaging, social networking, gaming, texting, listening to and creating music, watching and making videos and films, creating new art forms, posting images. Information and communication technologies are emerging as a central dimension of children's daily reality. Today, children move seamlessly between offline and online environments. These platforms offer huge benefits – educationally, socially and culturally – and States are encouraged to take all necessary measures to ensure equality of opportunity for all children to experience those benefits. Access to the Internet and social media is central to the realization of article 31 rights in the globalized environment.

46. However, the Committee is concerned at the growing body of evidence indicating the extent to which these environments, as well as the amounts of time children spend interacting with them, can also contribute to significant potential risk and harm to children.[232] For example:

(i)   Access to the Internet and social media is exposing children to cyberbullying, pornography and cybergrooming. Many children attend Internet cafes, computer clubs and game halls with no adequate restrictions to access or effective monitoring systems;

(ii)   The increasing levels of participation, particularly among boys, in violent video games appears to be linked to aggressive behaviour as the games are highly engaging and interactive and reward violent behaviour. As they tend to be played repeatedly, negative learning is strengthened and can contribute to reduced sensitivity to the pain and suffering of others as well as aggressive or harmful behaviour toward others. The growing opportunities for online gaming, where children may be exposed to a global network of users without filters or protections, are also a cause for concern.

(iii)   Much of the media, particularly mainstream television, fail to reflect the language, cultural values and creativity of the diversity of cultures that exist across society. Not only does such monocultural viewing limit opportunities for all children to benefit from the potential breadth of cultural activity available, but it can also serve to affirm a lower value on non-mainstream cultures. Television is also contributing to the loss of many childhood games, songs, rhymes traditionally transmitted from generation to generation on the street and in the playground;

(iv)   Growing dependence on screen-related activities is thought to be associated with reduced levels of physical activity among children, poor sleep patterns, growing levels of obesity and other related illnesses.

47. Marketing and commercialization of play: The Committee is concerned that many children and their families are exposed to increasing levels of unregulated commercialization and marketing by toy and game manufacturers. Parents are pressured to purchase a growing number of products which may be harmful to their children's development or are antithetical to creative play, such as products that promote television programmes with established characters and storylines which impede imaginative exploration; toys with microchips which render the child as a passive observer; kits with

---

[232] UNICEF, *Child Safety Online: Global Challenges and Strategies. Technical report* (Florence, Innocenti Research Centre, 2012).

a pre-determined pattern of activity; toys that promote traditional gender stereotypes or early sexualization of girls; toys containing dangerous parts or chemicals; realistic war toys and games. Global marketing can also serve to weaken children's participation in the traditional cultural and artistic life of their community.

VII. CHILDREN REQUIRING PARTICULAR ATTENTION TO REALIZE THEIR RIGHTS UNDER ARTICLE 31

48. Girls: A combination of significant burdens of domestic responsibilities and sibling and family care, protective concerns on the part of parents, lack of appropriate facilities and cultural assumptions imposing limitations on the expectations and behaviour of girls can serve to diminish their opportunities to enjoy the rights provided for in article 31, particularly in the adolescent years. In addition, gender differentiation in what is considered girls' and boys' play and which is widely reinforced by parents, caregivers, the media and producers/manufacturers of games and toys serve to maintain traditional gender-role divisions in society. Evidence indicates that whereas boys' games prepare them for successful performance in a wide range of professional and other settings in modern society, girls' games, in contrast, tend to direct them towards the private sphere of the home and future roles as wives and mothers. Adolescent boys and girls are often discouraged from engaging in joint recreational activities. Furthermore, girls generally have lower participation rates in physical activities and organized games as a consequence of either external cultural or self-imposed exclusion or lack of appropriate provision. This pattern is of concern in the light of the proven physical, psychological, social and intellectual benefits associated with participation in sports activities.[233] Given these widespread and pervasive barriers impeding girls' realization of their rights under article 31, the Committee urges States parties to take action to challenge gender stereotypes which serve to compound and reinforce patterns of discrimination and inequality of opportunity.

49. Children living in poverty: Lack of access to facilities, inability to afford the costs of participation, dangerous and neglected neighbourhoods, the necessity to work and a sense of powerlessness and marginalization all serve to exclude the poorest children from realizing the rights provided for in article 31. For many, the risks to their health and safety outside the home are compounded by home environments which provide no or little space or scope for play or recreation. Children without parents are particularly vulnerable to loss of their rights under article 31; children in street situations are not afforded play provisions, and are commonly actively excluded from city parks and playgrounds, although they use their own creativity to utilize the informal setting of the streets for play opportunities. Municipal authorities must recognize the importance of parks and playgrounds for the realization of the rights provided for under article 31 by children living in poverty and engage in dialogue with them in respect of policing, planning and development initiatives. States need to take action to ensure both access to and opportunities for cultural and artistic activities for all children, as well as equal opportunities for play and recreation.

50. Children with disabilities: Multiple barriers impede access by children with disabilities to the rights provided for in article 31, including exclusion from school; informal and social arenas where friendships are formed and where play and recreation take place; isolation at the home; cultural attitudes and negative stereotypes which are hostile to and rejecting of children with disabilities; physical inaccessibility of, inter alia, public spaces, parks, playgrounds and equipment, cinemas, theatres, concert halls, sports facilities and arenas; policies that exclude them from sporting or cultural venues on the

---

[233] UNESCO, International Charter of Physical Education and Sport, 1978.

grounds of safety; communication barriers and failure to provide interpretation and adaptive technology; lack of accessible transport. Children with disabilities can also be hindered in the enjoyment of their rights if investment is not made to render radio, television, computers and tablets accessible, including through the use of assistive technologies. In this regard, the Committee welcomes article 30 of the Convention on the Rights of Persons with Disabilities which emphasizes the obligations of States parties to ensure that children with disabilities have equal access with other children to participation in play, recreation, sporting and leisure activities, including in the mainstream school system. Pro-active measures are needed to remove barriers and promote accessibility to and availability of inclusive opportunities for children with disabilities to participate in all these activities.[234]

51. Children in institutions: Many children spend all or part of their childhood in institutions, including, inter alia, residential homes and schools, hospitals, detention centres, remand homes and refugee centres, where opportunities for play, recreation and participation in cultural and artistic life may be limited or denied. The Committee stresses the need for States to work towards the de-institutionalization of children; but until that goal is reached, States should adopt measures to ensure that all such institutions guarantee both spaces and opportunities for children to associate with their peers in the community, to play and to participate in games, physical exercise, cultural and artistic life. Such measures should not be restricted to compulsory or organized activities; safe and stimulating environments are needed for children to engage in free play and recreation. Wherever possible, children should be afforded these opportunities within local communities. Children living in institutions for significant periods of time also require appropriate literature, periodicals and access to the Internet, as well as support to enable them to make use of such resources. Availability of time, appropriate space, adequate resources and equipment, trained and motivated staff and provision of dedicated budgets are needed to create the necessary environments to ensure that every child living in an institution can realize his or her rights under article 31.

52. Children from indigenous and minority communities: Ethnic, religious, racial or caste discrimination can serve to exclude children from realizing their rights under article 31. Hostility, assimilation policies, rejection, violence and discrimination may result in barriers to enjoyment by indigenous and minority children of their own cultural practices, rituals and celebrations, as well as to their participation in sports, games, cultural activities, play and recreation alongside other children. States have an obligation to recognize, protect and respect the right of minority groups to take part in the cultural and recreational life of the society in which they live, as well as to conserve, promote and develop their own culture.[235] However, children from indigenous communities also have the right to experience and explore cultures beyond the boundaries of their own family traditions. Cultural and artistic programmes must be based on inclusion, participation and non-discrimination.

53. Children in situations of conflict, humanitarian and natural disasters: The rights provided for in article 31 are often given lower priority in situations of conflict or disaster than the provision of food, shelter and medicines. However, in these situations, opportunities for play, recreation and cultural activity can play a significant therapeutic and rehabilitative role in helping children recover a sense of normality and joy after their experience of loss, dislocation and trauma. Play, music, poetry or drama can help refugee children and children who have experienced bereavement, violence, abuse or

---

[234] General comment No. 9 (2006) on the rights of children with disabilities.
[235] United Nations Declaration on the Rights of Indigenous Peoples (General Assembly resolution 61/295, annex).

exploitation, for example, to overcome emotional pain and regain control over their lives. Such activities can restore a sense of identity, help them make meaning of what has happened to them, and enable them experience fun and enjoyment. Participation in cultural or artistic activities, as well as in play and recreation, offers children an opportunity to engage in a shared experience, to re-build a sense of personal value and self-worth, to explore their own creativity and to achieve a sense of connectedness and belonging. Settings for play also provide opportunities for monitors to identify children suffering from the harmful impact of conflict.

VIII. STATES PARTIES' OBLIGATIONS

54. Article 31 imposes three obligations on States parties to guarantee that the rights it covers are realized by every child without discrimination:

(a) The obligation **to respect** requires States parties to refrain from interfering, directly or indirectly, in the enjoyment of the rights provided for in article 31;

(b) The obligation **to protect** requires States parties to take steps to prevent third parties from interfering in the rights under article 31;

(c) The obligation **to fulfil** requires States parties to introduce the necessary legislative, administrative, judicial, budgetary, promotional and other measures aimed at facilitating the full enjoyment of the rights provided for in article 31 by undertaking action to make available all necessary services, provision and opportunities.

55. While the International Covenant on Economic, Social and Cultural Rights provides for the progressive realization of economic, social and cultural rights and recognizes the problems arising from limited resources, it imposes on States parties the specific and continuing obligation, even where resources are inadequate, to "strive to ensure the widest possible enjoyment of the relevant rights under the prevailing circumstances".[236] As such, no regressive measures in relation to the rights under article 31 are permitted. Should any such deliberate measure be taken, the State would have to prove that it has carefully considered all the alternatives, including giving due weight to children's expressed views on the issue, and that the decision was justified, bearing in mind all other rights provided for in the Convention.

56. The obligation to respect includes the adoption of specific measures aimed at achieving respect for the right of every child, individually or in association with others, to realise his or her rights under article 31, including:

(a) **Support for caregivers:** Guidance, support and facilitation with regard to the rights under article 31should be provided to parents and caregivers in line with article 18, paragraph 2, of the Convention. Such support could be in the form of practical guidance, for example, on how to listen to children while playing; create environments that facilitate children's play; allow children to play freely and play with children. It could also address the importance of encouraging creativity and dexterity; balancing safety and discovery; the developmental value of play and guided exposure to cultural, artistic and recreational activities.

(b) **Awareness raising:** States should invest in measures to challenge widespread cultural attitudes which attach low value to the rights provided for in article 31, including:

---

[236] Committee on Economic, Social and Cultural Rights, general comment No. 3 (1990) on the nature of States parties obligations, para. 11.

(i)   Public awareness of both the right to and the significance of play, recreation, rest, leisure and participation in cultural and artistic activities for both boys and girls of all ages in contributing to the enjoyment of childhood, promoting the optimum development of the child and building positive learning environments;

(ii)   Measures to challenge the pervasive negative attitudes, particularly towards adolescents, which lead to restrictions on the opportunities for the enjoyment of their rights under article 31. In particular, opportunities should be created for children to represent themselves in the media.

57. The obligation to protect requires that States parties take action to prevent third parties from interfering in or restricting the rights provided for in article 31. Accordingly, States are obliged to ensure:

(a)   **Non-discrimination:** Legislation is required to guarantee access for every child, without discrimination on any ground, to all recreational, cultural and artistic environments, including public and private spaces, natural spaces, parks, playgrounds, sporting venues, museums, cinemas, libraries, theatres, as well as to cultural activities, services and events;

(b)   **Regulation of non-State actors:** Legislation, regulations and guidelines should be introduced, together with the necessary budgetary allocation and effective mechanisms for monitoring and enforcement, to ensure that all members of civil society, including the corporate sector, comply with the provisions of article 31, including, inter alia:

(i)   Employment protection for all children to guarantee appropriate limitations on the nature, hours and days of work, rest periods and facilities for recreation and rest, consistent with their evolving capacities. States are also encouraged to ratify and implement ILO conventions Nos. 79, 90, 138 and 182;[237]

(ii)   Establishment of safety and accessibility standards for all play and recreational facilities, toys and games equipment;

(iii)   Obligations to incorporate provision and opportunity for the realization of the rights under article 31 in urban and rural development proposals;

(iv)   Protection from cultural, artistic or recreational material which might be injurious to children's well-being, including protection and classification systems governing media broadcasting and film, taking into account the provisions of both article 13 on freedom of expression and article 18 on the responsibilities of parents;

(v)   Introduction of regulations prohibiting the production of realistic war games and toys for children;

(c)   **Protection of children from harm:** Child protection policies, procedures, professional ethics, codes and standards for all professionals working with children in the field of play, recreation, sports, culture and the arts must be introduced and enforced. Recognition must also be given to the need to protect children from potential harm that may be imposed by other children in the exercise of their rights under article 31;[238]

(d)   **Online safety:** Measures should be introduced to promote online access and accessibility, as well as safety for children. These should include action to empower and inform children to enable them to act safely online, to become

---

[237] ILO conventions No. 79 – Night Work of Young Persons (Non-Industrial Occupations); No. 90 – Night Work of Young Persons (Industry); No. 138 – Minimum Age Convention; No. 182 – Worst Forms of Child Labour Convention.

[238] General comment No. 13 (2011) on the right of the child to freedom from all forms of violence.

confident and responsible citizens of digital environments and to report abuse or inappropriate activity when it is encountered. Measures are also needed to reduce impunity of abusive adults through legislation and international collaboration; limit access to harmful or adult-rated material and gaming networks; improve information for parents, teachers and policymakers to raise awareness of the potential harm associated with violent games and develop strategies for promoting safer and attractive options for children;

(e)   **Post-conflict safety:** Active measures should be taken to restore and protect the righhts under article 31in post-conflict and disaster situations, including, inter alia:

- Encouraging play and creative expression to promote resilience and psychological healing;
- Creating or restoring safe spaces, including schools, where children can participate in play and recreation as part of the normalization of their lives;
- In areas where landmines pose a threat to the safety of children, investment must be made to ensure the complete clearing of landmines and cluster-bombs from all affected areas;[239]

(f)   **Marketing and media:** Action should be initiated to:

- Review policies concerning the commercialization of toys and games to children, including through children's television programmes and directly related advertisements, with particular regard to those promoting violence, girls or boys in a sexual way and reinforcing gender and disability stereotypes;
- Limit exposure to advertising during peak viewing hours for children;

(g)   **Complaint mechanisms:** Independent, effective, safe and accessible mechanisms must be in place for children to make complaints and seek redress if their rights under article 31 are violated.[240] Children need to know who they can complain to and how (what procedure) to do so. State are encouraged to sign and ratify the Optional Protocol to the Convention on the Rights of the Child on a communications procedure (OPIC), which will allow individual children to submit complaints of violations.

58. The obligation to fulfil requires that States parties adopt a wide range of measures to ensure the fulfilment of all the rights provided for under article 31. In accordance with article 12 of the Convention, all such measures, both at the national and local levels, and including planning, design, development, implementation and monitoring should be developed in collaboration with children themselves, as well as NGOs and community-based organizations, through, for example, children's clubs and associations, community arts and sports groups, representative organizations of children and adults with disabilities, representatives from minority communities and play organisations.[241] In particular, consideration should be given to the following:

(a)   **Legislation and planning:** The Committee strongly encourages States to consider introducing legislation to ensure the rights under article 31 for every child, together with a timetable for implementation. Such legislation should address the principle of sufficiency – all children should be given sufficient time and space to exercise these rights. Consideration should also be given to the development of a dedicated plan, policy or framework for article 31 or to its

---

[239]   Protocol on Explosive Remnants of War (Protocol V to the Convention on Certain Conventional Weapons).
[240]   General comment No. 2 (2002) on the role of independent national human rights institutions in the promotion and protection of the rights of the child.
[241]   General comment No. 12 (2009) on the right of the child to be heard.

incorporation into an overall national plan of action for the implementation of the Convention. Such a plan should address the implications of article 31 for boys and girls of all age groups, as well as children in marginalized groups and communities; it should also recognize that creating time and space for children's self-directed activity is as important as the provision of facilities and opportunities for organized activities;

(b) **Data collection and research:** Indicators for compliance, as well as mechanisms for monitoring and evaluating implementation need to be developed in order to ensure accountability to children in the fulfilment of obligations under article 31. States need to collect population-based data, disaggregated by age, sex, ethnicity and disability, to gain an understanding of the extent and nature of children's engagement in play, recreation and cultural and artistic life. Such information should inform planning processes, and provide the basis for measuring progress in implementation. Research is also needed into the daily lives of children and their caregivers and the impact of housing and neighbourhood conditions in order to understand how they use local environments; the barriers they encounter in enjoying the rights under article 31; the approaches they adopt to surmount those barriers and the action needed to achieve greater realization of those rights. Such research must actively involve children themselves, including children from the most marginalized communities;

(c) **Cross departmental collaboration in national and municipal government:** Planning for play, recreation and cultural and artistic activities requires a broad and comprehensive approach involving cross-departmental collaboration and accountability between national, regional and municipal authorities. Relevant departments include not only those dealing directly with children, such as health, education, social services, child protection, culture, recreation and sports, but also those concerned with water and sanitation, housing, parks, transport, environment and city planning, all of which impact significantly on the creation of environments in which children can realize their rights under article 31;

(d) **Budgets:** Budgets should be reviewed to ensure that the allocation for children, in respect of cultural, artistic, sports, recreational and play activities, is inclusive and consistent with their representation as a proportion of the population as a whole, and distributed across the provision for children of all ages, for example: budgetary support for the production and dissemination of children's books, magazines and papers; various formal and non-formal artistic expressions for children; accessible equipment and buildings and public spaces; resources for facilities such as sports clubs or youth centres. Consideration should be given to the cost of measures required to ensure access for the most marginalized children, including the obligation to provide reasonable accommodation to ensure equality of access for children with disabilities;

(e) **Universal design:**[242] Investment in universal design is necessary with regard to play, recreational, cultural, arts and sports facilities, buildings, equipment and services, consistent with the obligations to promote inclusion and protect children with disabilities from discrimination. States should engage with non-State actors to ensure the implementation of universal design in the planning and production of all materials and venues, for example, accessible

---

[242] The term "universal design" was coined by Ronald Mace to describe the concept of designing all products and the built environment to be aesthetic and usable to the greatest extent possible by everyone, regardless of their age, ability or status in life; see also art. 4, para. 1 (f) of the Convention on the Rights of Persons with Disabilities.

entrances to be used by wheelchair users and inclusive design for play environments, including those in schools;

(f) **Municipal planning:** Local municipalities should assess provision of play and recreation facilities to guarantee equality of access by all groups of children, including through child-impact assessments. Consistent with the obligations under article 31, public planning must place a priority on the creation of environments which promote the well-being of the child. In order to achieve the necessary child-friendly urban and rural environments, consideration should be given to, inter alia:

- Availability of inclusive parks, community centres, sports and playgrounds that are safe and accessible to all children;
- Creation of a safe living environment for free play, including design of zones in which players, pedestrians and bikers have priority;
- Public safety measures to protect areas for play and recreation from individuals or groups who threaten children's safety;
- Provision of access to landscaped green areas, large open spaces and nature for play and recreation, with safe, affordable and accessible transport;
- Road traffic measures, including speed limits, levels of pollution, school crossings, traffic lights, and calming measures to ensure the rights of children to play safely within their local communities;
- Provision of clubs, sports facilities, organized games and activities for both girls and boys of all ages and from all communities;
- Dedicated and affordable cultural activities for children of all ages and from all communities, including theatre, dance, music, art exhibitions, libraries and cinema. Such provision should comprise opportunities for children to produce and create their own cultural forms as well as exposure to activities produced by adults for children;
- Review of all cultural policies, programmes and institutions to ensure their accessibility and relevance for all children and to ensure that they take into account the needs and aspirations of children and support their emerging cultural practices;

(g) **Schools:** Educational environments should play a major role in fulfilling the obligations under article 31, including:

- **Physical environment of settings:** States parties should aim to ensure the provision of adequate indoor and outdoor space to facilitate play, sports, games and drama, during and around school hours; active promotion of equal opportunities for both girls and boys to play; adequate sanitation facilities for boys and girls; playgrounds, play landscapes and equipment that are safe and properly and regularly inspected; playgrounds with appropriate boundaries; equipment and spaces designed to enable all children, including children with disabilities, to participate equally; play areas which afford opportunities for all forms of play; location and design of play areas with adequate protection and with the involvement of children in the design and development;
- **Structure of the day:** Statutory provision, including homework, should guarantee appropriate time during the day to ensure that children have sufficient opportunity for rest and play, in accordance with their age and developmental needs;
- **School curriculum:** Consistent with obligations under article 29 concerning the aims of education, appropriate time and expertise must be allocated within the school curriculum for children to learn,

participate in and generate cultural and artistic activities, including music, drama, literature, poetry and art, as well as sports and games;[243]

- **Educational pedagogy:** Learning environments should be active and participatory and offer, especially in the early years, playful activities and forms of engagement;

(h) **Training and capacity-building:** All professionals working with or for children, or whose work impacts on children (Government officials, educators, health professionals, social workers, early years and care workers, planners and architects, etc.), should receive systematic and ongoing training on the human rights of children, including the rights embodied in article 31. Such training should include guidance on how to create and sustain environments in which the rights under article 31 can be most effectively realized by all children.

59. International cooperation: The Committee encourages international cooperation in the realization of the rights provided for in article 31 through the active engagement of United Nations agencies including UNICEF, UNESCO, UNHCR, UN Habitat, UNOSDP, UNDP, UNEP and WHO, as well as international, national and local NGOs.

IX. DISSEMINATION

60. The Committee recommends that States parties disseminate this general comment widely within Government and administrative structures, to parents, other caregivers, children, professional organizations, communities and civil society at large. All channels of dissemination, including print media, the Internet and children's own communication means should be used. This will necessitate translation into relevant languages, including sign languages, Braille and easy-to-read formats for children with disabilities. It also requires making culturally appropriate and child-friendly versions available.

States parties are also encouraged to report fully to the Committee on the Rights of the Child on the measures they have adopted to encourage the full implementation of article 31 for all children.

---

[243] General comment No. 1 (2001) on the aims of education.

INDEX

References are to page numbers.